Organizational Behavior

ORGANIZATIONAL BEHAVIOR

Foundations, Theories, and Analyses

John B. Miner

UNIVERSITY PRESS

2002

OXFORD
UNIVERSITY PRESS

Oxford   New York
Auckland   Bangkok   Buenos Aires   Cape Town   Chennai
Dar es Salaam   Delhi   Hong Kong   Istanbul   Karachi   Kolkata
Kuala Lumpur   Madrid   Melbourne   Mexico City   Mumbai   Nairobi
São Paulo   Shanghai   Singapore   Taipei   Tokyo   Toronto

and an associated company in Berlin

Published by Oxford University Press, Inc.
198 Madison Avenue, New York, New York 10016

www.oup.com

Oxford is a registered trademark of Oxford University Press

Library of Congress Cataloging-in-Publication Data
Miner, John B.
Organizational behavior: foundations, theories, and analyses / by John B. Miner
p. cm.
Includes bibliographical references and index.
ISBN 0-19-512214-3
1. Organizational behavior: foundations, theories, and analyses.   I. Title
HD58.7 .M5457   2002
658′.001 — dc21   2001021710

9 8 7 6 5 4 3 2 1
Printed in the United States of America
on acid-free paper

To Jennifer and Heather Miner —
our contribution to the future

Preface

Its title largely defines what this book is about: it presents a host of organizational behavior theories, evaluates each, including research bearing on it, and places the theories in a historical context that consists of the circumstances and values of the emerging field of organizational behavior. There is a good deal that would pass as biography as well, and at the end an agenda for organizational behavior's future, but the essence of the volume is its coverage of the theories themselves.

Since books of this type are rather unusual, it may prove helpful to outline what the reader might gain from a perusal of these pages. First and foremost is a gain in knowledge of the field. Few people are able to devote the time to broad study of the literature that retirement has made possible for me. I believe that even the most serious scholars of organizational behavior will find some new theories and certain provocative ideas here. In this vein the book should prove useful to those who are searching for subjects to investigate, hypotheses to test, and research designs to use. Several

books present many of these theories without moving on to evaluation; others consider a circumscribed set of theories and do evaluate them. What I have attempted is to provide a broad overview of organizational behavior's theories, along with an assessment of the validity and usefulness of each.

In addition to unearthing research opportunities, the book may also prove a useful source for those who aspire to write theory. It can provide examples of good theories (which have advanced knowledge substantially) and also of not-so-good theories (which have led us up blind alleys). Theorists, like others, need role models; most of the theorists considered here have had such models, and building a strong science for the future will require theorists who do the same. Furthermore, a reading of what is said here can serve to aid in establishing the frontiers of existing knowledge — thus to stave off reinventing what we already know, and to establish a starting point for true creative contribution. Penciling in boundaries in this manner at various points in time is essential for any advancing field.

Finally, there is the historical perspective. For many, the coverage of organizational behavior's history will be of value in its own right. Some people do not care much for history, while others consider it a major area of interest. For these latter, this book provides probably as close to a comprehensive history of organizational behavior as exists at the present time. Surely more definitive and extensive such chronicles will appear in years to come, but for the present at least this is a potentially very useful source of information on the early years of our still emerging field.

This said, what are the various audiences for the book? Certainly anyone who is considering studying organizational behavior, or who is engaged in such study, or who has studied in the field previously (especially where a major in organizational behavior is involved); this would be true whether the study is at the undergraduate level, the master's, or the doctorate. Managers and administrators in any type of organization constitute a potential audience (given what we know about their concerns, this should be particularly true of those at the higher levels). Many professionals and scholars within organizational behavior or in related disciplines will find the book relevant. This would include people in industrial/organizational psychology, organizational sociology, economics, political science, cultural anthropology, human resources and industrial relations, educational administration, and public administration; it would also encompass contingent disciplines in the business schools, such as strategic management, entrepreneurship, and production management, as well as those areas that interact with organizational behavior there, such as accounting and marketing, including business school deans. Finally, those with a specialty in business or management history, and perhaps associated areas of philosophy as well, will find much of interest here. But, whoever the reader may be, be advised that the going may not always be easy. Just as the theories are on occasion complex and difficult to understand at first exposure, their interpretation and evaluation may well take on these same qualities.

It may prove helpful at this point to indicate what this book is and is not. The emphasis is on theories and the context in which they have emerged. This means that the content is driven by the existence of established theories, not some overall framework for the organizational behavior field as a whole, as is often true of basic textbooks. Certain areas that one might anticipate finding treated here may be underrepresented or even totally lacking; the reason is that theory in these areas has not developed to a significant degree. This is a problem. No attempt is made to deal with this problem now, but it does provide potential subject matter for future publications.

Because organizational behavior grew out of multiple disciplinary origins, as is documented in part I, there is considerable overlap at times into psychology, sociology, political science, and anthropology. I have tried to keep this overlap to a minimum, however, and to focus on theories that are indigenous to organizational behavior. Economic theory is not included for this same reason, and also because of the historical fact that organizational behavior emerged in the business schools with the specific objective of supplementing economics, not merging with it. In recent years the policy/strategy field has taken on a distinct status, and many of us in organizational behavior have contributed to that development. But policy/strategy, with its close ties to economics, has become a separate discipline now; theories of this type are not treated in this book for this reason. There has to be some delimitation on the subject matter to be covered, and this appears to be an important exclusion that must be made. Perhaps we are approaching a time when a book entitled "Strategic Management: Foundations, Theories and Analyses" should be written.

Consonant with the development of the policy/strategy field, a greater merging of the micro and macro components of organizational behavior has occurred. Although there remain those who identify, often strongly, with one or the other of these segments, enough theories now exist that bridge these two domains so that it is meaningless to separate them. Thus this book is dedicated to treating both the micro and macro segments of the field, and in equal detail, as well as to combining the two.

Roughly 20 years ago I wrote two separate books, *Theories of Organizational Behavior* (1980) and *Theories of Organizational Structure and Process* (1982), both published by Dryden Press, and both long out of print. It would not be representative of the field to dichotomize the subject matter in this way today. I have, however, incorporated considerable material from these sources here as appropriate to the task at hand. Approximately half of the theories considered in this volume were discussed 20 years ago as well, although in the interim many have changed significantly, as have their research bases. Many of the theories added are of more recent vintage, as is evident in parts VII through X, but changing perspectives and theoretical thrusts have made it appropriate to add certain theories that had their genesis in an earlier period, too.

This volume differs from my previous efforts as well in that a great deal of new research is considered. The coverage with regard to all theories is intended to be up to date through the third quarter of 2000, and in a few cases somewhat after that. The literature reviewed is extensive, amounting to over 2,300 chapter-end references. Well over 1,300 of these are from the period since 1980 when *Theories of Organizational Behavior* was published—this despite the fact that much of the material covered is historical in nature.

Certain other features have been instituted as well. Several reviewers of the original proposal called for the addition of more context to the theories themselves. As a consequence the historical background in part I was developed and the treatment of scientific considerations was expanded. Biographical material was introduced throughout, and I added considerable discussion of theoretical trends and the role that values (particularly humanism) have played in organizational behavior theorizing. Part XI contains an analysis of the current state of the organizational behavior field and some suggestions for future directions.

The framework used to present the theories is both historical and content based. The historical aspect is reflected in the treatment of theoretical stances that antedated but influenced organizational behavior theory in part I, the presentation of first-generation theory in parts II through VI, and the discussions of the newer second-generation theories in parts VII through X. Part XI then looks to the future. This historical organization is clearly apparent as one moves through the various chapters in order.

It is also possible to take up each content area as a distinct whole, however, by reshuffling the chapters that follow those of part I. Thus new combinations can be formed as follows:

Part II with Part VII (Motivation and Perception)

Part III with Part VIII (Leadership)

Parts IV and V with Part IX (Concepts of Organization)

Part VI with Part X (Organizational Decision Making)

The chapters have been written so that such a reordering along subject matter lines is entirely feasible.

A third way of approaching the book also deserves mention, and in fact may be the most appropriate for a number of readers. That is to use the volume for purposes of reference, engaging in spot reading here and there, as the need arises. To facilitate such use, a rather detailed table of contents is provided at the beginning. Furthermore, comprehensive indexes at the end of the book contain references to the text by author name and by subject matter. Some users may wish to leaf directly to the reference sections at the end of each chapter, which on the average contain about 80 literature listings per chapter.

A question arises as to how the theories were chosen. For the most part, theories discussed in the two previous books were included; in turn, the selection of these was guided by a brief survey of knowledgeable scholars of the time, who nominated theories for inclusion. To this list I have added a large number of theories, many of them more recent, which also met the criteria (1) that the author(s) has produced substantial theoretical work, (2) that this theoretical work is identified with the field of organizational behavior, and (3) that the theory is recognized as significant within organizational behavior. This third point was addressed by drawing on other published sources, most specifically the following:

Arthur Bedeian's *Management Laureates: A Collection of Autobiographical Essays*—Volumes 1–5 (JAI Press, 1992–1998)

Derek Pugh and David Hickson's *Great Writers on Organizations: The Omnibus Edition* (Dartmouth, 1993)

Harold Pollard's *Trends in Management Thinking: 1960–1970* (Gulf, 1978); as well as his *Developments in Management Thought* (Crane, Russak, 1974)

Daniel Wren and Ronald Greenwood's *Management Innovators* (Oxford University Press, 1998)

Henry Tosi's *Theories of Organization* (Wiley, 1984)

Navin Mathur's *Life and Works of Management Thinkers* (Sahitya Bhawan, 1990)

Lex Donaldson's *American Anti-Management Theories of Organization* (Cambridge University Press, 1995)

This is not to say that my choices have been devoid of individual discretion, but they have been influenced substantially by others who are knowledgeable within the field. There is also some developing evidence that supports these choices. At this writing a survey dealing with the many theories contained in this volume has been completed (although not fully analyzed) with some 95 responses (42 percent of the mailing) received. The questionnaire asks for additional nominations of theories not noted, and roughly half of the respondents did so. Yet no new organizational behavior theory appears to have had the support of more than a handful of those who returned the survey. The implication is that my choices do cover the field rather well, although I suspect that some might quarrel with the breadth of my coverage. On the assumption that it is better to err in favor of too many theories rather than too few, I take the survey results to indicate considerable substantiation of the contents of this book.

What I have said regarding these theories, however, reflects only my position based on quite intensive study. I have read what others have had to say regarding these theories, but in the end it is my own judgment that is reflected here. My goal has been to be as objective in rendering that judgment as a scientist can be. Given the increasing specialization within our field, it is becoming harder to identify people with the broad perspective required to describe and evaluate theories across the whole spectrum of organizational behavior. Perhaps that very fact makes the need for a book such as this the greater.

Acknowledgments

I am indebted to a great many people who contributed in one way or another to the writing of this volume. These contributions have come in several forms, and I want to acknowledge them here.

First are the reviewers who have provided very useful feedback to me on various versions, components, proposals, and finally in a few instances on the book as a whole. These are Theresa Lant (New York University), Jerry Wofford (University of Texas), Dennis Middlemist (Colorado State University), Andrew Ward (Emory University), Jone Pearce (University of California at Irvine), Terri Scandura (University of Miami), Milton Blood (American Assembly of Collegiate Schools of Business), and now recently as the whole project has come together, Robert Liden (University of Illinois at Chicago) and Edwin Locke (University of Maryland). Benjamin Schneider (University of Maryland) also helped set me on the right track in the very early period as my ideas for the book were forming. I thank all of these people for their efforts and contributions. It has not always been possible to

follow their suggestions in totality, but I am sure that they will all find certain of their ideas in the pages that follow.

A second group of contributors provided publications and information that I needed. Derek Pugh (Open University in the U.K.) was extremely helpful in the beginning. Arthur Bedeian (Louisiana State University) has furnished many publications of a historical nature and provided much other useful information as my ideas developed; he has been a major contributor on a continuing basis. Francis Yammarino (State University of New York at Binghamton) provided many back copies of *Leadership Quarterly* that I lacked and assisted in numerous other ways.

Then there are the editors. It is a travesty of the current business situation that editors do not stay in one place very long. However, I have benefited tremendously from the input to this volume that three editors have furnished. William Hicks (formerly at Jossey-Bass and now of Stanford University Press) has been a source of many helpful ideas at various points as the book developed. Kenneth MacLeod (a former editor of mine at Macmillan, and throughout most of this project at Oxford University Press) has been a continuing contributor in many ways from the original signing, to providing much needed publications, to offering the wisdom that comes from many years of successful experience as an editor; he has been everything that an editor should be and I appreciate his efforts very much. Finally, and more recently, Martha Cooley has taken over the reins at Oxford University Press and guided the book into production. We have not worked together long, but over that period she has been most helpful.

Barbara Miner, my wife, has made it possible to operate a publishing activity in my retirement that would otherwise have been out of the question. She has done everything that needed to be done to prepare this volume for publication except actually write the manuscript, and believe me there was a great deal that "needed to be done." Our collaboration has been a continuing pleasure, and I thank her for that and her many contributions. Our little "mom and pop" entrepreneurial venture has been a real joy, because of her.

Eugene, Oregon   J.B.M.
February 2001

Contents

Part VIII   Second-Generation Theories: Leadership

Part IX   Second-Generation Theories: Concepts of Organization

Part X   Second-Generation Theories: Organizational Decision Making

Part XI   From Generation to Generation

Part I

Foundations and Origins

Chapter 1

Theory, Research, and Knowledge of Organizational Behavior

What is *organizational behavior?* It is a social science discipline—much like cultural anthropology, economics, political science, psychology, and sociology. That means that it uses the scientific method to establish truth and to validate its theories. It is a discipline that historically has had its intellectual home in business schools. And it is a new discipline relative to the other social sciences, having its origins in the middle of the twentieth century. The key points are that it is a science and that it has a history which, though short, has been quite turbulent.

Although the exact boundaries of the discipline are somewhat fuzzy (see Blood, 1994), the focus is clearly on the world of organizations. The concern is, first, with the behavior and nature of the people within organizations and, second, with the behavior and nature of organizations within their environments. By the time the discipline approached 25 years of age, organizational behavior clearly had stretched beyond the first domain and incorporated the second (see Miles, 1980; Pfeffer, 1982). This is historically consistent in that both the study of the behavior and nature of people and the study of the behavior and nature of organizations emerged in business schools in the same places at the same times, even though the term *organizational behavior* was applied to the latter only somewhat later.

In line with its professional school origins, organizational behavior is an applied discipline, concerned with matters of practice and application. Despite this orientation, however, it has relatively few members who actually devote their primary professional efforts to the practice of organizational behavior in business and other organizational settings; rather, most are concentrated in academia teaching, writing, and conducting research. In my opinion this is unfortunate; the field would be better off if it expanded its practitioner efforts rather than reduce its academic efforts. We will return to this theme often throughout the book.

Although several other terms have become intertwined with organizational behavior over the years, none of them has achieved quite the same level of acceptance. One is *organization(al) theory*, which has come to refer almost exclusively to the study of the behavior and nature of organizations in their environments. A second is *organization(al) science*, which appears to cover essentially the same ground as organizational behavior, and which in many respects I prefer as a designation for our field (see Miner, 1984, 1990). However, right now *organizational behavior* has won the day. Finally, there is the term *organization(al) studies*, which also has a broad connotation and extends, at least in the recent period, beyond the science of organizations to incorporate several different philosophical positions (see Clegg, Hardy, & Nord, 1996).

Having explained what organizational behavior is, I need to say something about what it is not. It is not *strategic management*, a field that has recently emerged and achieved some stature (see Schendel & Hofer, 1979) and which has differentiated itself at the border that previously existed between organizational behavior and economics, borrowing from and overlapping with each. Also, organizational behavior is not *economics*, although in recent years there has been some confounding of the two fields and some even foresee a possible future takeover of organizational behavior by economics (see, for example, Pfeffer, 1995). However, economics was well established in business schools long before organizational behavior arrived, and organizational behavior was spawned — in large part at the behest of economists — as a separate

and distinct discipline. Historically the two are clearly different entities with very different origins.

Finally, organizational behavior is not *philosophy*. That, however, is a rather complex story. As a science our field is closely tied to, though separate from, the philosophy of science. In this respect it is like all other sciences, and the relationship can be expected to continue as long as organizational behavior defines itself as a social science. But, from the very beginning, philosophy has been threaded into organizational behavior in other respects as well — and not always to the benefit of either field. Sometimes, in certain respects organizational behavior and philosophy have become almost indistinguishable from one another. Understanding what is involved here requires a background in the nature of science, scientific theory, scientific research, and the history of science — in short, in the scientific foundations of the field. It also requires a background in the ways in which philosophy has become threaded into organizational behavior at various points in time. These matters are considered in these introductory chapters of part I.

SCIENCE AND ITS THEORY

The primary focus of this book, however, is on the major theories that have evolved within the broad field of organizational behavior, and on the theorists who created them. The goal is to provide an understanding of these theories and thus to determine what they can tell us that might prove useful to people who participate in organizations.

In point of fact, we all participate in various organizations — such as schools, companies, and hospitals — throughout our lives, and we devote a large percentage of our time to such participation. Most people would like to function more effectively in organizations and to contribute to more effective functioning of the organizations themselves. It seems logical that the more we know about organizations and the way they operate, the better should be our chances of coping with them adequately and of achieving our own goals within them and for them. This process of creating knowledge is what theories of organizational behavior attempt to do.

To create a foundation for understanding organizational behavior theories, it is important to know what scientific theory is and what it is not, as well as how theory relates to research and how research either supports or fails to support theory. These are the concerns of this chapter. The intent is to provide a basic understanding that can be drawn on as specific theories are discussed in the remainder of the book.

The remaining chapters of part I take up the origins of the organizational behavior field and its theories. The objective is to establish the *Zeitgeist* within which the theories were discovered and gained acceptance. An idea too outlandish to be even considered at one point in time in one cultural context may win wide acclaim later when times have changed (Boring, 1950). Thus, an understanding of the backgrounds from which theories came to the fore, and of the values that nurtured and thwarted them, is crucial to any real appreciation. In much of part I the context that spawned the organizational behavior field, including certain ideas and even theories that were already on the scene under other disciplinary names, is the focus of the discussion. I will refer to this discussion often as we consider specific theories later in the book.

Theory and Practice

Theory is the cornerstone of any science. It provides the ideas that fuel research and practice. Theories of organizational behavior are potentially as useful when they are applied to organizations as are theories of physics and chemistry when they are used in developing new manufacturing technologies and consumer products, or as are theories of biology when they are used to advance medical practice. However, the relationship between theory and practice (or application, or usefulness) in organizational behavior is often misunderstood. For many people the term *theory* evokes images of a speculative, ivory-towered world, far removed from reality. Theories do not sound helpful in understanding the practical facts of organizational life. Yet one hears such statements as that of the eminent psychologist Kurt Lewin (1945), who said that "nothing is so practical as a good theory." And this dictum continues to receive widespread acceptance today (see, for example, Van de Ven, 1989).

In fact, confusion on this score is widespread; the subject requires consideration here at the outset because a particular reader's preconceptions regarding the theory-practice relationship (or the lack thereof) can color that person's thinking about the entire field. The idea that theory is somehow "ivory tower" while practice is "real world" — and that the two are distinct and separate — permeates much current discussion of business school education and of the role of the discipline of organizational behavior (Raelin, 1993; Wren, Buckley, & Michaelsen, 1994; Marsden & Townley, 1996). Even attempts to clarify this situation seem to lead to only a deepening confusion (Brief & Dukerich, 1991).

In this context let me return to Lewin's (1945) dictum. What Lewin meant by a "good" theory is one that is validated by adequate research. To be truly useful, a theory must be intimately intertwined with research (Snizek & Furhman, 1980), and, to the extent that it is, it has the potential for moving beyond philosophical speculation to become a sound basis for action. Good theory is thus practical because it advances knowledge in a field, guides research to important questions, and enlightens practice in some manner (Van de Ven, 1989).

Some theories are obviously more concerned with application than others. Some, at the time of inception, may fail to meet the test of usefulness, only to find their way to a juncture with practice later on. Some theories are never tested or fail the test of research, and so they are not very good theories, at least as far as anyone can tell. In any event, a good theory of organizational behavior has the potential for valid applications and thus can prove useful if it is applied correctly. A theory in an applied field, such as organizational behavior, that is so divorced from application (so ivory tower?) that it has no potential for speaking to practice is very unlikely to be a *good* theory. This is the viewpoint that guides the analyses and interpretations presented throughout this book. Research indicates also that such theories are not patently obvious to practitioners; good theories take managers in directions that they would not otherwise have gone (Priem & Rosenstein, 2000).

Science Defined

Science is an enterprise by which a particular kind of ordered knowledge is obtained about natural phenomena by means of controlled observations and theoretical interpretations. Ideally, this science, of which organizational behavior is a part, lives up to the following:

1. The definitions are precise.
2. The data collecting is objective.
3. The findings are replicable.
4. The approach is systematic and cumulative.

5. The purposes are understanding and prediction, plus, in the applied arena, control.
(Berelson & Steiner, 1964)

The usually accepted goals of scientific effort are
to increase understanding and to facilitate prediction
(Dubin, 1978). At its best, science will achieve both
of these goals. However, there are many instances in
which prediction has been accomplished with considerable precision, even though true understanding of
the underlying phenomena is minimal; this is characteristic of much of the forecasting that companies do
as a basis for strategic planning, for example. Similarly,
understanding can be far advanced, even though prediction lags behind. For instance, we know a great
deal about the various factors that influence the level
of people's work performance, but we do not know
enough about the interaction of these factors in specific instances to predict with high accuracy exactly
how well an individual will do in a particular job.

In an applied field, such as organizational behavior, the objectives of understanding and prediction
are joined by a third objective — to influence or manage the future, and thus to achieve control. An economic science that explained business cycles fully
and predicted fluctuations precisely would represent
a long step toward holding unemployment at a desired
level. Similarly, knowledge of the dynamics of organizations and the capacity to predict the occurrence of
particular structures and processes would seem to offer
the possibility of engineering a situation to maximize
organizational effectiveness. To the extent that limited
unemployment or increased organizational effectiveness is desired, science then becomes a means to these
goals. In fact, much scientific work is undertaken to
influence the world around us. To the extent that
applied science meets such objectives, it achieves a
major goal.

Role of Theory in Science

Scientific method evolves in ascending levels of abstractions (Brown & Ghiselli, 1955). At the most basic
level it portrays and retains experience in symbols.
Although the symbols may be mathematical, to date
in organizational behavior they have been primarily
linguistic. Once abstractions are converted to symbols,
experience may be mentally manipulated, and relationships may be established. There are two ways to
do that:

- *Description* uses symbols to classify, order, and
  correlate events. It remains at a low level of
  abstraction and is closely tied to observation and
  sensory experience. In essence it is a matter of
  ordering symbols to make them adequately portray events. The objective is to answer "what"
  questions.
- *Explanation* moves to a higher level of abstraction in that it attempts to establish meanings
  behind events. It attempts to identify causal, or at
  least concomitant, relationships so that observed
  phenomena make some logical sense.

Theory Defined

At its maximal point, explanation creates *theory*. Scientific theory is a patterning of logical constructs, or
interrelated symbolic concepts, into which the known
facts regarding a phenomenon, or theoretical domain,
may be fitted. A theory is a generalization, applicable
within stated boundaries, that specifies the relationships between factors. Thus it is an attempt to make
sense out of observations that in and of themselves do
not contain any inherent and obvious logic (Dubin,
1976). The objective is to answer "how," "when," and
"why" questions.

Since theory is so central to science, a certain
amount of repetition related to this topic may be for-
given. John Campbell (1990) defines theory as a collection of assertions, both verbal and symbolic, which
identifies what variables are important for what reasons, specifies how they are interrelated and why, and
describes the conditions under which they should be
or not be related. Robert Sutton and Barry Staw (1995)
place their emphasis somewhat differently, but with
much the same result. For them theory is about the
connections among phenomena — a story about why
acts, events, structure, and thoughts occur. It emphasizes the nature of causal relationships and identifies
what comes first, as well as the timing of events. It is
laced with a set of logically interconnected arguments.
It can have implications that we have not previously
seen and that run counter to our common sense.

How Theory Works

Figure 1.1 provides a picture of the components of a
theory. A theory is thus a system of constructs and
variables with the constructs related to one another
by propositions and the variables by hypotheses. The

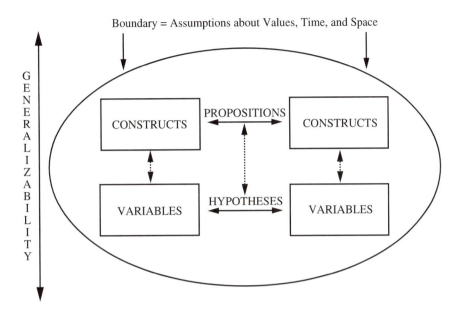

FIGURE 1.1 The components of theories and the way they function. From Samuel B. Bacharach (1989), Organizational Theories: Some Criteria for Evaluation, *Academy of Management Review*, 14, 499. Copyright 1989 by Academy of Management. Reproduced with permission.

whole is bounded by the assumptions, both implicit and explicit, that the theorist holds with regard to the theory (Bacharach, 1989).

Constructs are "terms which, though not observational either directly or indirectly, may be applied or even defined on the basis of the observables" (Kaplan, 1964, p. 55). They are abstractions created to facilitate understanding. Variables are observable, they have multiple values, and they derive from constructs. In essence they are operationalizations of constructs and were created to permit testing of hypotheses. In contrast to the abstract constructs, variables are concrete. Propositions are statements of relationships among constructs. Hypotheses are similar statements involving variables. Research attempts to refute or confirm hypotheses, not propositions per se.

All theories occupy a domain within which they should prove effective and outside of which they should not. These domain-defining, bounding assumptions (see figure 1.1) are in part a product of the implicit values held by the theorist relative to the theoretical content. These values typically go unstated, and, if that is the case, they cannot be measured. Spatial boundaries restrict the effective use of the theory to specific units, such as types of organizations or kinds of people. Temporal boundaries restrict the effective use of the theory to specific time periods. To the extent they are explicitly stated, spatial and temporal boundaries can be measured and thus made operational. Taken together they place some limitation on the generalizability of a theory.

Organizational behavior has often been criticized for using highly ambiguous theoretical constructs—and it is not at all clear what they mean (see, for example, Sandelands & Drazin, 1989). This same ambiguity extends to boundary definitions and domain statements. In a rather cynical vein Graham Astley and Raymond Zammuto (1992) even argue that this ambiguity is functional for a theorist in that it increases the conceptual appeal of a theory. Conflicting positions do not become readily apparent, and the domain of application may appear much greater than the empirical reality. Such purposeful creation of ambiguity can cause the constructs and ideas of a theory to be extended into the world of practice to an extent that is not empirically warranted. Not surprisingly, these views immediately met substantial opposition (Beyer, 1992; Donaldson, 1992). The important point, however, is that science does not condone this type of theoretical ambiguity. Precise definitions are needed to make science effective, and a theory that resorts to ambiguity is to that extent a poor theory.

Assumptions of Science

Science must make certain assumptions about the world around us. These assumptions might not be factually true, and to the extent they are not, science will have limited value. However, to the extent science operates on these assumptions and produces a degree of valid understanding, prediction, and influence, it appears more worthwhile to adopt the assumptions.

First, science assumes that certain natural groupings of phenomena exist, so that classification can occur and generalization within a category is meaningful. For some years, for instance, the field then called business policy, operating from its origins in the case method, assumed that each company is essentially unique. This assumption effectively blocked the development of scientific theory and research in the field. Increasingly, however, the assumption of uniqueness has been disappearing, and generalizations applicable to classes of organizations have emerged (see, for instance, Steiner & Miner, 1986). As a result, scientific theory and research in the field of strategic management are burgeoning.

Second, science assumes some degree of constancy, or stability, or permanence in the world. Science cannot operate in a context of complete random variation; the goal of valid prediction is totally unattainable under such circumstances. Thus objects and events must retain some degree of similarity from one time to another. In a sense this is an extension of the first assumption, but now over time rather than across units (see McKelvey, 1997, for a discussion of these premises). For instance, if organizational structures, once introduced, did not retain some stability, any scientific prediction of their effect on organizational performance would be impossible. Fortunately, they do have some constancy, but not always as much as might be desired.

Third, science assumes that events are determined and that causes exist. This is the essence of explanation and theorizing. It may not be possible to prove a specific causation with absolute certainty, but evidence can be adduced to support certain causal expla-nations and reject others. In any event, if one does not assume some kind of causation, there is little point in scientific investigation; the assumption of determinism is what sparks scientific effort. If, for instance, one assumes that organizational role prescriptions do not influence individual performance, then the whole area of organizational design moves outside the realm of scientific inquiry. Organizational behavior must assume some kind of causal impact of the organization on its members. It then becomes the task of science to determine the nature of this impact.

Fourth and finally, because science is firmly rooted in observation and experience, it is necessary to assume some degree of trustworthiness for the human processes of perceiving, remembering, and reasoning. This trustworthiness is always relative, but it must exist to some degree. The rules under which science operates are intended to increase the degree of reliability with which scientific observation and recording operate. The purpose is to achieve an objective, rational, replicable result, which will be convincing to those who are knowledgeable in the area of study.

Rules of Scientific Inquiry

If the findings of research are to be replicated and the generalizations from research are to be valid, concepts must be clearly defined in terms of the procedures used to measure them. This has been a major problem in the field of organizational behavior. Often theoretical concepts are stated in such an ambiguous manner and the conditions for their measurement are left so uncertain that the researcher is hard put to devise an adequate test of the theory.

Moreover, scientific observation must be controlled so that causation may be attributed correctly. The objective is to be certain that an outcome is in fact produced by what is believed to produce it and not by something else. Control of this kind is achieved through the use of various experimental designs, or through measurement and statistical adjustment. In the complex world of organizational functioning, establishing controls sufficient to pin down causation often has proved to be difficult.

Then, because science is concerned with generalization to contexts that extend far beyond a given experiment, it is essential that research use samples that are adequate in both size and conditions of their selection. One must have confidence that the results obtained are generalizable and can be put to use outside the research situation. The field of statistics becomes important for organizational behavior because of its potential for determining how much confidence can be placed in a particular research outcome.

Finally, and this bears repeating, science requires that its propositions, hypotheses, and theories be stated in terms that can be tested empirically. This is where philosophy and science part company. Unfortunately, organizational behavior has not always clearly separated scientific from philosophical statements. The result has been considerable confusion, and on occasion effort has been wasted on attempts to test theories that are not really testable as stated. Samuel Bacharach (1989) provides a good discussion of this "falsifiability" requirement.

These rules of scientific inquiry are elaborated as they apply to research design in a later section of this chapter. Bill McKelvey (1997) labels the rules as indicative of an "organizational realist" approach to organizational behavior.

Theory Building

A distinction is often made between deductive and inductive theory. In building a theory by deduction, one first establishes a set of premises. Then certain logical consequences of these premises are deduced and subsidiary concepts are established. The starting point is rational thought, and logical consistency is a major concern in development of the theory. Often such theories are stated in mathematical terms.

In contrast, inductive theory builds up from observation, often from research, rather than down from a set of premises. Essentially, one puts together a theory that best seems to explain what is known in a given area at the present time. Then new tests of this theory, or of hypotheses derived from it, are carried out just as they would be if the theory were developed deductively.

Linda Gottfredson (1983) points to three ways in which inductive theory may be developed from research findings. First, one may immerse oneself in the data generated by past research, but with a healthy skepticism regarding any interpretations by others found with these data. Second, one may pick one or more specific patterns of results to explain, thus narrowing the theory-building task to a more limited domain than general theory. Third, one may try to resolve inconsistencies, anomalies, puzzling results, and incompatible points of view in the literature and in the data reported there.

A major pitfall in the use of the inductive approach in theory building is that the research from which the theory is induced may tend to become confused with an adequate test of the theory. Thus the same research is used twice for two different purposes, and a self-fulfilling prophecy results. In the case of truly deductive theories, this is not possible. When theories are developed inductively, it is crucial that they be tested on a new sample in a manner that is entirely independent of the pre-theory research. If one goes back to the prior sample or to data used in developing the theory, anything unique and ungeneralizable (attributable to chance fluctuation) in that particular situation is very likely to be confirmed. As a result, a theory that is erroneous insofar as generalization and practical usefulness are concerned may well be accepted.

It is actually more useful to think of theories as falling at points along a deductive to inductive continuum than as falling into distinct categories. Probably no theory is completely devoid of some inductive input. Still, there are instances of theories arising from entirely inductive processes. Such instances are often referred to as *dust-bowl empiricism*, implying that no theory is involved at all. However, the result may look very much like a theory.

An example of dust-bowl empiricism would be a study in which a great many measures, say several hundred, are obtained on a sample of organizations. These data are then put into a computer, and closely related measures are identified through the use of correlation techniques, factor analysis, or some similar procedure. What emerges is a set of hypothesized relationships among variables—a set of statements very much like an inductively derived theory. This "theory" is then tested on a new sample of organizations, using the appropriate measures to make sure that it does not incorporate relationships that represent mere chance fluctuations associated with the particular sample from which the theory was induced.

Any theory, irrespective of the method of construction and the extent of research confirmation, should always be treated as provisional in nature. Theories are constructed to be modified or replaced as new knowledge is developed; this is the way science advances. Furthermore, modification on the basis of research tends to be inductive rather than deductive. Findings emerge that do not quite fit the existing theory. Accordingly, the theory is changed so that these new data can be explained, and a test is then made of the revised theory. As a result of this kind of theoretical tinkering, even predominantly deductive theories may take on a strong inductive element over time; if they do not, they may well be replaced.

Defining a Good (or Strong) Theory

In order to evaluate theories, science needs some criteria for deciding whether a theory is good or not so good. It is evident from what has been said already that some explanatory statements may not meet the requirements of scientific theory at all, and that what was good theory at one time may be not-so-good theory some years later.

First, theories should contribute to the goals of science. They should aid understanding, permit prediction, and facilitate influence. The more they do these things, the better they are. A theory that is comprehensive in its coverage of the phenomena that it explains is preferable to one that is limited in scope. However, broad scope alone is not enough. Many so-called grand theories attempt too much and fail simply because they do not really explain the wide range of phenomena they attempt to consider (Pinder & Moore, 1980).

Second, there should be a clear delineation of the domain of the theory. The boundaries of application should be specified so that the theory is not used in situations for which it was never intended. Definition of the coverage of a theory often has been neglected in the social sciences generally (Dubin, 1978), and the field of organizational behavior is no exception.

Third, theory should direct research efforts to important matters. The number of research studies that could be done in the world is almost infinite. Yet most of these studies, even if the time and effort to carry them out were available, would not yield significant results in a statistical sense, and many of those that did would be trivial in terms of their usefulness. Good theory helps us focus research efforts on salient variables, identify important relationships, and come up with truly *significant* findings in every sense of the word. Basically, then, good theory protects the researcher from wasting time.

Fourth, at their best, theories yield a kind of added value to research efforts. If several hypotheses derived from a theory are confirmed by research, then the whole body of the theory becomes available for use. Thus theory-based research has the potential for yielding not just a few isolated facts, but powerful explanation and prediction across the whole domain of the theory. This aspect of good theory is one of its most practical consequences. Unfortunately, many theories do not have this cumulative character.

Fifth, theories should be readily testable. It should be clear exactly what must be done to either confirm or disconfirm them. On occasion, experimenters will carry out studies that they believe to be adequate tests of a theory, only to have the theorist say, "That is not what I meant." When theory is well formulated, this situation should rarely arise. Ideally, the theorist will identify the variables of the theory in operational terms.

Sixth, good theory is not only confirmed by research derived from it, but is also logically consistent within itself and with other known facts. In the case of complex theories, it is entirely possible to develop propositions that would predict diametrically opposed outcomes in the same situation. This is particularly likely to happen when the theorist comes at the same subject matter from different directions, using different concepts and assumptions. Such internal, logical inconsistencies must be ironed out if the theory is to be of much use. Furthermore, theories do not exist in a vacuum; they are part of the total body of scientific knowledge. At any given time it may not be entirely clear how a particular theory fits into the larger scientific configuration, but a theory that from the outset quite obviously does not fit at all is to that degree deficient. Theories should build on what is known and fit consistently into the entire network of existing knowledge (Hartman, 1988).

Seventh, the best theory is the one that is simplest in statement. If a given set of phenomena can be explained parsimoniously with a few variables, that theory should be preferred over one that achieves the same level of explanation with a much more complex set of variables and relationships. Science does not value complexity in its own right; there is enough of that all around us in nature. Highly complex and involved theories are often very difficult to put into practice. Thus the ultimate objective must be to replace them with simpler explanations. Unfortunately, the process of inductive theory modification often demands that new constructs and variables be added continually as unanticipated findings emerge and need to be explained. Under such circumstances a theory may fall of its own weight, for it is just too cumbersome to be useful.

Theories that consistently fail to attain these criteria (and thus ultimately emerge as bad) can have negative consequences for science (Webster & Starbuck, 1988). They can well sustain themselves for a considerable period of time and lead science in wrong directions. They can also produce confusion and conflict, which block scientific progress. All this argues for immediate testing of new theories so that their status can be established quickly. Without this, the risk of impediment to scientific advance is substantial.

At a very high level of abstraction, the ultimate goal of science, and its theory as well, is to discover truth. This involves a firm belief that there is a reality out there external to the observer within which this truth exists. Knowing this truth, based in reality, is plagued with uncertainty. Science seeks truth with the full recognition that it never can be known with absolute certainty—only approximations to certainty are possible. This view has been categorized as "scientific realism" or "organizational realism" (Hunt, 1990, 1992; McKinley, 1995; McKelvey, 1997). Such a view reflects the predominant position in organizational behavior at the present time.

However, a minority position does exist, and it emphasizes the socially constructed nature of organizational phenomena and espouses a subjectivity that seems to deny the existence of outside reality altogether (see Weiss, 2000, for an extended discussion of this view). Accordingly, truth takes a back seat to novelty, provocativeness, and uniqueness. In this view, the goal of theory construction and the basis for theory evaluation is not truth, but uniqueness (Mone & McKinley, 1993). These are not the values of science, but they do reflect a current philosophical position. We will return to "contra" views of this kind later, but for now it is sufficient to indicate that those approaches that are not intended to achieve the goals of science (such as truth) cannot be evaluated as good theories in a scientific sense.

Kinds of Theories

Theories can be good or bad, or more frequently somewhere in-between; they can seek truth or have some other goal. Many additional ways to classify theo-

ries exist as well. Although the labels that result often are self-evident, several approaches require more discussion.

Micro, Macro, and Meso

Micro theory in organizational behavior deals with the behaviors and nature of individuals and small groups in organizations. It has been strongly influenced by psychology, and many theorists of this kind were originally trained in that field. A good understanding of the micro approach can be had from a reading of Staw (1991).

Macro theory focuses on the behavior and nature of organizations, not of individuals and groups. Parts of the organization may be of concern as well, and so may the environment surrounding the organization. Sociology has played a role in the development of macro theory very similar to that played by psychology in micro theory. In a companion piece to the Staw (1991) article, Jeffrey Pfeffer (1991) offers a good example of how macro theorizing works.

This distinction between micro and macro levels has been part of the organizational behavior field since its early years. A more recent arrival, at least in terms of terminology, is meso theory. Robert House, Denise Rousseau, and Melissa Thomas-Hunt (1995) define the meso approach as concerning the simultaneous study of at least two levels, where one level deals with individual or group processes or variables, one level deals with organizational processes or variables, and bridging or linking propositions are set forth to relate the two levels. An example of meso theorizing is presented in a book by Henry Tosi (1992).

Tosi's (1992) book contains a number of theoretical propositions that may be used to illustrate the macro-micro-meso distinctions:

The relevant environment of an organization is defined as external organizations or institutions that have direct effects on decisions and processes in the focal organization (p. 29)—*macro*.

The degree of volatility of the environmental sectors affects the structure of subsystem relationships in organizations (p. 34)—*macro*.

When individual personality manifests itself, it usually does so with respect to interactions with others or toward the organization, not in terms of work patterns or levels of performance (p. 82)—*micro*.

A particular leader's action is interpreted and attributions are made in the situational context. Different situations may result in different attributions about the same acts. It is the nature of the attribution, not the behavior itself that is related to effectiveness (p. 196) — *micro*.

The dominant form of conflict in organic organizations is rivalry. The bases for the rivalry will be

1. competition for resources for projects in process and/or
2. status-based competition between specialists from different disciplines.

There will be moderate to low levels of vertical conflict in organic organizations (p. 110) — *meso*.

Power striving predispositions will lead to power striving and political behavior when organizations are loosely coupled (p. 128) — *meso*.

Typologies as Theory

A number of theories set forth various categories of organizations, environments, people, or groups, usually in the range of two to five. These formulations may deal with ideal types — that is, sets of intellectual, hypothetical constructs that are created purely to study variety and change and which are not necessarily found in their complete form in the real world at all (Lammers, 1988). At the other extreme are formulations that use only empirically derived clusters, based on real world data, which are created using the techniques of dust-bowl empiricism (Ketchen & Shook, 1996). There are variants between these two as well.

The terms *typology* and *taxonomy* may be applied to these formulations, but they have not been used in a consistent manner, and there is no universal agreement on either definitions or appropriate approaches for them (Rich, 1992). Some people even decry the use of such classification systems entirely, viewing them as inherently unsound (Donaldson, 1996). Given this situation, a working approach to theories of this kind is needed. I believe the following discussion is consistent with the dominant position in the field of organizational behavior at the present time. If not, the position is at least a widely accepted one (Sanchez, 1993; Doty & Glick, 1994; Miller, 1996).

The term *typology* is used to refer to a set of types developed on an a priori conceptual basis to operate as and serve the purposes of a theory. These constructs may be of an ideal nature or they may to varying degrees be intended to reflect the actual nature of the real world. These conceptual typologies are viewed as theories, and they may be good or not so good, just like any other theory. Taxonomies, in contrast, are empirically derived clusterings that were developed through multivariate analysis of existing data. As such, they are data, not theories; description, not explanation. However, theoretical formulations may be developed inductively starting from taxonomies, thus folding a taxonomy into a more comprehensive theoretical system. Thus, a taxonomy alone does not constitute a theory, but each instance needs to be considered separately. (For a more extended treatment of these matters, see Miner, 1997.)

Grounded Theory

Grounded theory focuses on qualitative data for the purpose of developing systematic, limited domain theories about observed phenomena. It derives its data from participant observation, direct observation, semi-structured or even unstructured interviews, and case studies in essentially the same manner that an anthropologist might use in studying a culture. Facets of these research data are sorted out of the mass of available qualitative information by means of consciously adopted strategies. These emerging concepts, grounded in the data, become the foundation of a growing theoretical understanding of the phenomena studied (Glaser & Strauss, 1967; Turner, 1983).

Such a theoretical approach is inductive, and the results are theoretical accounts of relatively small segments of reality. This approach attempts to distill out the essence of these segments, and in doing so creates a theory that is rich in terms of the depth of its content, but not very broad. These grounded theory accounts may be used to develop more formal theory, however; they can focus on a specific domain of more general interest. Within organizational behavior one will find little by way of grounded theorizing in the original sense, but more formal theories (which have their origins in such grounded theorizing) are in evidence. In any event, it is important to keep in mind that the proper role of grounded theory is to generate theories, not to test them (Parry, 1998).

MEASUREMENT OF VARIABLES AND DESIGN OF RESEARCH

To a substantial degree, the value of a theory is inherent in the research it sparks and in the extent to which the theory is confirmed by this research. Research is only possible, however, to the extent that measures of the variables of the theory are developed — that is, to the extent that the constructs are made operational. These twin topics of measurement and research concern us in this section. The objective here is not to provide a detailed treatment. However, in later chapters, we will be asking questions such as "Does this measure really effectively represent the constructs of the theory?" and "Does this research provide an appropriate test of the theory?" The answers to these questions will draw on some knowledge of both measurement procedures and research design, and the ensuing discussion is intended to provide a basis for understanding in these areas.

Measuring Variables

Measures used in organizational research have often fallen short of what might be desired (Price & Mueller, 1986). Many of organizational behavior's theories use constructs that are far removed from those that were previously measured in the social sciences. Thus it has been necessary in many cases to develop reliable and valid measures to represent new constructs, which is a time-consuming process. Many organizational measures are still at a primitive stage of development, and this situation can seriously hamper the interpretation of research results. For a number of years, for instance, expectancy theory (Vroom, 1964) was thought to have limited value because the new measures used to test it were deficient. Only later, with greater attention to measurement problems, did the full value of the theory become apparent.

Reliability

A major concern in research is the reliability of measurement. Measures that are sufficiently stable and unambiguous will not produce sizable differences in score values when they are applied to the same phenomenon on separate occasions. The reliability of a measure is usually established by a correlation coefficient. Different approaches are used to determine this reliability coefficient, but all approaches approximate the ideal procedure, which uses parallel forms of the same measure. Parallel forms exist when two indices of the same construct contain the same number of items of each type, concentrate equally on the various aspects of the construct, and produce the same average scores and distributions of scores through the range

of possible values. Once such parallel measures have been developed, reliability is determined by administering both measures in the same sample and correlating the scores on the two measures.

The value of a reliability coefficient fluctuates to some extent, depending on whether the parallel form or some other approach is used. However, if one wishes to use a measure in an individual situation — to measure the work motivation of a *particular* person, for instance, or to compute the average span of control in a *certain* company — reliability coefficients above .90 are required. In contrast, if one is dealing with group data such as mean work motivation scores in two units of a company or average span of control in relation to profitability in a number of companies, values down to about .70, and sometimes less, typically are acceptable. These standards represent what amount to "rules of thumb" or working conventions. Like many such conventions in science, they are enforced by gatekeepers such as journal editors and thesis or dissertation chairpersons.

The matter of reliability of measurement is important in research because it is impossible to interpret outcomes when unreliable measures are used and results are not statistically significant. The failure to obtain evidence of a relationship between two variables could be due to the fact that there is no relationship. But if one or both measures of the two variables are unreliable, a relationship may well exist that has not been discovered because of inadequate measures. The only satisfactory way to resolve this uncertainty is to develop and use measures of high reliability. Then if relationships are not found, they are very unlikely to exist in the world of reality.

Validity

The variables of a theory need to be made operational in the form of specific measures. Accordingly, the measures must truly reflect the underlying constructs; they must provide valid data regarding the phenomena that they are supposed to represent. If, in fact, they measure constructs other than the ones they are intended to measure, the theory may well be assumed to be disconfirmed when it is actually correct. Worse still, a theory may be accepted when its variables have actually been incorrectly stated (Stone-Romero, 1994).

I once developed an index intended to measure conformity to organizational norms (Miner, 1962, 1965). Subsequent research revealed that the index was almost completely unrelated to any other measure of conformity that could be identified in the literature. However, moderate relationships were found with measures of intelligence. Apparently, if the measure did tap some tendency to conform, it was not the same construct that other researchers had in mind when they used the term *conformity*. A much more likely interpretation was that we had developed a measure whose most pronounced component was intelligence, not conformity. Faced with what now appeared to be a dead end insofar as our conformity research was concerned, we abandoned that particular line of study.

This example demonstrates how one goes about determining the validity of a measure. If the measure is what it purports to be, there are certain phenomena to which it should be related and certain other phenomena to which it should not be related. In the case of conformity, there were other indices of the construct available. Often, when a new and highly innovative theory is under test, other measures are not available. Nevertheless, it should be possible to identify certain relationships that would be expected to appear with a high degree of likelihood. In this process, however, it is important not to rely on *face validity* alone. The measure that looks to be appropriate as an index of a given variable on further investigation may or may not prove to tap that construct.

As we shall see later, establishing the validity of a particular construct measure is not easy. To some degree the answer is always inferential. Yet there are organizational measures in which one can have considerable faith, while there are others that, even after long years of use, leave considerable doubt as to their construct validity. Certain statistical procedures have been developed to aid in construct validation (Bagozzi, Yi, & Phillips, 1991), and these can be quite useful under appropriate circumstances. However, they do not circumvent the need for close reasoning and careful research design.

Research Design

Research conducted to test theories characteristically investigates hypothesized relationships between variables. Such research is first concerned with whether a relationship exists at all and then with the causal nature of that relationship. Research focused on the existence of a relationship is relatively easy to conduct; however, research into the causal problem is clearly much less tractable.

The study of causation typically requires the collection of data over time, on the premise that the cause must be shown to precede the effect. There are now techniques, however, known collectively as causal modeling approaches, that under appropriate circumstances can be used with data collected at one time, as well as longitudinally. These techniques have expanded in number, in complexity, and in explanatory power over the past 20 years. Their use is increasing rapidly, and they appear to offer considerable promise in evaluating causal hypotheses (Medsker, Williams, & Holahan, 1994; Williams & James, 1994).

Another factor that makes identification of causal relationships difficult is the need for establishing adequate controls. Control may be accomplished statistically through the use of procedures that measure unwanted variables and then remove their effects from the relationship under study. However, these statistical techniques require that the data satisfy certain assumptions, and in many cases it is not at all clear that these assumptions can be met. The alternative is to control variables through the original design of the study. That is not always easy.

Laboratory Experiments

Much of the research on causal relationships has been done in the laboratory. An extreme instance of this laboratory research is computer simulation in which no real subjects are involved. More frequently, the experiment is of the small group or group dynamics type; experimental variables are introduced among subjects, often college sophomores, and the results are measured under highly controlled conditions. Because the study is conducted outside the real world of ongoing organizations, it is easier to use longitudinal measures and to control unwanted variables. Yet even here major difficulties in maintaining controls exist. Furthermore, the results are very much a function of the variables considered (this is particularly true of computer simulations). If the real world, or at least the key elements of that world, is not effectively modeled in the laboratory, the results of laboratory experiments will not transfer.

This said, it appears that in many areas such transfers do occur (Locke, 1986). Laboratory studies often appear to be well conducted, or conceivably field research is deficient in important areas, with the result that similar results are obtained. In any event, the evidence to date is that laboratory research, with its greater control, is much more valid than was previously anticipated. There may be conditions under which this is not true. A degree of field research on laboratory findings still seems warranted. But, assuming initial confirmation, the need for extensive reiteration of these initial results does not seem as great as previously thought.

Field Experiments

The ideal situation is to take the techniques of sample selection, repetitive measurement, and variable control that are associated with laboratory research into the real world and to conduct the same kind of research with ongoing organizations. In such a context, the myriad variables that may be important do in fact operate, and any results obtained there can be expected to characterize the actual organizations to which any meaningful theory is addressed. The problem is that all the difficulties of designing and conducting good experiments that were so easily handled in the laboratory now become overwhelming. Real organizations have innumerable ways of resisting and undermining objective scientific research—not out of contrariness, but because the goals of the real world and the laboratory are different.

The difficulties of conducting causal research in organizations may be illustrated by a study by James Belasco and Harrison Trice (1969) on the effects of a particular management development program. The study used 119 managers divided into four groups. Managers were assigned to each group on a random basis within sex, type of work supervised, and division groupings. In this manner, as many factors as possible were held constant across the four groups to control for spurious factors that might contaminate the findings and make causal attribution difficult.

One group of managers was pretested, trained, and posttested on knowledge, attitudes, and behavior. The objective was to see if a change occurred on any of these factors. A second group took the pretest, received no training, and then took the posttest. If this group changed as much as the first, then clearly the training was not the cause of change. If this group did not change as much as the first, then the training remained a strong contender as a cause. A third group underwent no pretest, received training, and took the posttest. By comparing the posttest result for the third group with that for the first group, it was possible to identify any apparent change due to a sensitizing effect of the pretest (the groups were similar in all other respects). The problem addressed here is control for any effects the pretest may have had in alerting the managers to what they were supposed to learn later in training. The fourth group received no pretest, no training, and only the posttest. This group, in comparison with the others, yields a measure of the effects of the passage of time only, and therefore isolates time from either repeated measurement or training as factors.

Clearly this kind of research requires a large number of subjects, the opportunity to assign them into groups as desired for research purposes, and extensive collaboration from the sponsoring organization throughout the study. And, as elaborate as the research plan is, it could be argued that a fifth group, created to undergo some training of a relatively neutral nature, should have been included to create a placebo situation and cancel out any so-called Hawthorne effect produced by receiving special attention (see chapter 2 for more detail on this phenomenon). Thus even this very complex experiment cannot be said to have achieved the ideal in terms of control. Such studies are very difficult to conduct, yet they continue to appear in the literature (see, for example, Holdnak, Clemons, & Bushardt, 1990).

Quasi-Experimental Designs

Realistically, elegant research designs with all possible controls are unlikely to be implemented in many organizations, and if an organization does decide to go this route, it may well be an atypical organization. Accordingly, certain variants have been proposed (Cook, Campbell, & Peracchio, 1990). These designs represent major advances over the noncausal, correlational analyses, but no one such study answers all questions. Basically, these studies use as many components of the ideal experimental design as possible, while recognizing that it is better to conduct some kind of research related to causes than to do nothing. Hopefully, the larger number of research investigations carried out will compensate for the relative relaxation of control requirements. Accordingly, several interlocking investigations should develop the same level of knowledge as one very elegant study. Nevertheless, it is easy to relax scientific standards to the point where replication is not possible and thus not obtain any scientific knowledge that can be substantiated. Some trends in qualitative research on organizations show this tendency. It is important to maintain a clear distinction between scientific research and personal narrative in testing organizational behavior theories (Schaubroeck & Kuehn, 1992).

Requirements for Conducting Experimental Research

Blackburn (1987) has set forth a list of what he labels the 10 commandments for conducting experimental research. These can serve as a guide in assessing research used to test theories in the organizational behavior field.

1. Thou shalt assess the extent to which the change actually took effect.
2. Whenever possible, thou shalt use multiple measures.
3. Whenever possible, thou shalt use unobtrusive measures.
4. Thou shalt seek to avoid changes in measurement procedures.
5. Thou shalt endeavor to use a randomized experimental design whenever possible.
6. In the absence of random assignment, thou shalt not select experimental or control groups on the basis of some characteristic that the group may possess to some unusual degree.
7. Thou shalt use appropriate statistical analyses to examine the differences between the experimental and control groups.
8. Whenever possible, thou shalt collect time-series data.
9. To the greatest extent possible, thou shalt protect the employee, the organization, and the experiment—in that order.
10. Thou shalt report fully and honestly the procedures and results of the research.

Many of these points are illustrated in a book edited by Peter Frost and Ralph Stablein (1992), which provides detailed descriptions of what actually happened in connection with seven research studies. This book is also a good source of information regarding ways in which qualitative research may be employed for purposes of inductive theory development.

THEORETICAL KNOWLEDGE OF ORGANIZATIONAL BEHAVIOR

The high visibility of certain formulations that are clearly closer to philosophy than to scientific theory has led some to question whether organizational behavior truly possesses any theories at all (Tosi, 1984). This negative position has received additional support from some individuals, a number of them scientists who place very little stock in theory building in any event and prefer the slow but solid pace of unswerving empiricism. Yet there do appear to be a number of real scientific theories that deal with organizations—or at least explanations so advanced that not to call them theories is something of a quibble. This is not to say that these theories are necessarily and entirely valid; some of them have not been fully tested. But overall they have contributed substantially to our knowledge of organizations.

Alternatively, there is a rather sizable body of literature that raises serious objections to the scientific concepts we have been considering. If one follows these views, a quite different picture of our theoretical knowledge of organizational behavior emerges.

Objections to Scientific Dictates

A common method of dealing with antithetical positions is to simply ignore them and thus avoid the need to cite them or to consider the views at all (Martin & Frost, 1996). I clearly could do this here. Yet the concept of science that is set forth in the preceding pages is what underlies the whole field of organizational behavior, and to simply ignore objections to it does not appear to be either intellectually honest or to truly reflect the reality of the times.

Frontal Attacks

One "contra" position is that science as a whole, and certainly the organizational behavior part of it, has not proven convincing as a superior form of knowledge, that new narratives and new epistemologies are needed to supersede science, and that basically science has had its day and now has run out of steam (Burrell, 1996). This is an across-the-board dismissal, and it applies to all aspects of science. In my opinion, this line of assault requires an equally direct response. Given the realities of the world around us, such arguments for the demise of science make no sense and are best lumped with similar "end of the world" scenarios.

In addition to such blanket attacks, a number of more specific objections have been raised, and they typically focus on some individual aspect of scientific theory or research. One such approach is to challenge the various assumptions of science (Kilduff & Mehra, 1997). For instance, the argument may be that natural groupings of organizations, groups, and individuals do not occur — that uniqueness is everywhere — and thus generalization from samples is not warranted. Another such argument is that things change so fast that the stability and constancy science requires is nonexistent; science gives way to journalism — the recording and explaining of fleeting phenomena. Yet another challenge asserts either that events are not determined, and thus cause and effect relationships do not exist, or that social science, as distinct from natural science is concerned with meanings and significance, not causes. Finally, the trustworthiness of human processes of perception, memory, or reasoning may be questioned, thus introducing challenges to the observation and experience on which science is based. Advocates of these positions tend to give more credence to qualitative research than to quantitative. Qualitative research is accordingly moved from its role as an adjunct to inductive theory building to a central role in theory testing.

Other objections are concerned with the objectivity and relevance of scientific research (Behling, 1980). These views emphasize the fact that people as the subjects of research react differently when they become aware of the researchers' hypotheses or when they experience a feeling of being controlled in the experimental situation; thus the research process itself poses a threat to generalization. Alternatively, research studies, especially laboratory studies, may be viewed as lacking the realism required for generalization. Objections of these kinds seem to assert that all organizational behavior research is bad research and that researchers cannot overcome these threats to their findings through creative methodologies. Data such as those summarized in Edwin Locke (1986) on the close proximity of laboratory and field research findings are totally ignored.

Postmodernism and Siblings

Some of the strongest attacks on social science, and inherently on organizational behavior, stem from a group of philosophies called critical theory, poststructuralism, and postmodernism (Agger, 1991). These philosophies all had their origins outside the United States, and it is there that they originally had the greatest effect. In certain respects they have been in-

fluenced by Marxist ideology. The three differ in a number of their aspects, but the opposition to social science is pervasive. Science is portrayed as a source of authority and a perpetuator of the status quo. As such, it must be replaced. Objective analysis and a reliance on mathematics are rejected.

The preferred approach to gaining knowledge in these philosophies is one that focuses on obtaining detailed understandings of specific situations at a particular point in time. This approach has much in common with that of grounded theory, although references to that specific procedure by name appear to be rare since David Silverman (1971). Studies in this vein collect a great deal of information and often present much of the raw data to the reader in undigested form in lieu of statistical analyses. Typically the studies are used to both create theory and confirm it at one and the same time. Literary methods and storytelling may be used to present the results of data collection (Jermier, 1985). Indeed, the analysis of language and its usage has become pervasive within postmodernism (Alvesson & Kärreman, 2000).

When grounded theory is used to create more formal theories, it parts company with postmodernism and its siblings to join company with science. This distinction is important. The qualitative approaches involved may serve to generate scientific theory, *or* they may yield the self-fulfilling prophesies of postmodernism.

Threats from Within

Although critical theory, poststructuralism, and postmodernism have been slow to take root in the United States, there have been manifestations of similar ways of thinking here for some time. This has been most characteristic of those in the organizational behavior field who espouse humanistic values with a substantial amount of passion (see Lawler, Mohrman, Mohrman, Ledford, & Cummings, 1985; Tannenbaum, Margulies, & Massarik, 1985). Chris Argyris has attacked scientific research methodology on numerous occasions and proposes an anthropological approach, devoid of statistical analysis, to replace it (see, for instance, Argyris, 1980).

These attacks from within are described by Lex Donaldson (1992), an Australian, as an outgrowth primarily of certain trends in organizational behavior in the United States. He summarizes this complex of ideas as follows:

1. It stresses the empirical world as subjectively perceived and enacted rather than as brute fact.
2. It asserts the superiority of qualitative over quantitative methods.
3. It reveres paradox in both the content of theory and the formal expression of theory.
4. It holds that scientific creativity is primarily linguistic inventiveness.
5. It sees itself as championing creativity.
6. It is counter cultural in the sense of being ever-ready to cock a snook at the establishment and established ideas.
7. It would also claim that practicing managers would be better aided not by plodding positivism but by taking a mind-trip. (Donaldson, 1992, p. 462)

This description is presented in connection with a rebuttal to an article by Astley and Zammuto (1992), to place that article in context.

Many rebuttals to the various objections to scientific dictates are scattered throughout this chapter. In addition to those by Donaldson (1992, 1996), more rebuttals may be found in Orlando Behling (1980) and John Campbell (1990). Not infrequently, the objections create a description of science that, although incorrect, makes it easy to mount an attack. In this process, science may very well be redefined as art, with all the freedom to embody values and eliminate burdensome rules that art permits. Many of those who object to the standards and strictures of good theory and good research seem to be trying to remove what they perceive to be barriers that keep them from using the garb of science to advocate their values. This is a tactic that goes back at least to Elton Mayo (1933), as we will see in chapter 2. Good science — whether in the form of theory construction or exemplary research — is very hard work. The rules of the game are onerous, and they make good science difficult. But that is as it should be; they are there for a reason.

Furthermore, as Bernice Pescosolido and Beth Rubin (2000) note, "the fault of postmodernism is that even in its radical insistence on diversity, it insists that its practitioners 'line up'" (p. 71). There is no freedom from rules of some kind, even in postmodernism.

Values and Knowledge

Values are conceptions of good and bad that tend to carry with them a great deal of emotion. They at-

tach to certain ideas and patterns of behavior, and they provoke behavior consistent with the values as well.

Values in Organizational Behavior

Organizational behavior appears to have been influenced by two primary value dimensions throughout much of its history. One dimension extends from humanistic to scientific values, and these values will be invoked in some detail in connection with the discussion in chapter 5. In recent years the humanistic pole increasingly has been joined by the often similar values of postmodernism and its siblings. The other dimension is essentially disciplinary in origin. At one end is psychology, while the other end is anchored primarily in sociology, joined on occasion by anthropology, political science, and economics. Basically, these are values related to micro and macro levels of analysis.

This latter disciplinary dimension has undergone some transformation over the years. In an earlier period, the dimension ranged from behavioral science (dominated in large part by psychology) to classical management theory. As classical theory has faded from the scene (see Miner, 1995), the value differentiation involved has been replaced by one within the behavioral science designation itself. At present, it appears to be particularly concerned with variations in the value placed on the study of individuals in organizations (see House, Shane, & Herold, 1996; Nord & Fox, 1996).

Values of these kinds can play a useful role in theory construction, in part by focusing attention on specific areas of endeavor, and in part by motivating concerted efforts to construct theories that end by fostering understanding and prediction. However, values other than those that foster objectivity, have no place in the conduct of research and thus in testing theory. To the extent they might intervene at this stage, replications of initial studies should serve to identify them. Finally, values can reappear in the evaluation segment of the overall theory process, the part that involves reaching a consensus among knowledgeable scholars regarding the goodness of a theory, and thus the contribution to knowledge involved (Miner, 1990). The result is that people with different values may evaluate through different lenses; as a consequence, consensus may be hard to obtain.

Dispositions versus Situations — A Value-Laden Controversy

An example of how values may produce different views and impede consensus is provided by the dispute over the study of individuals in organizations that was previously noted. This dispute simmered over a period of 10 years or more (Alderfer, 1977; Salancik & Pfeffer, 1977, 1978; ; Salancik, 1984; Stone, 1984; Stone & Gueutal, 1984) before bursting into flame (Davis-Blake & Pfeffer, 1989).

The last article contained an attack on the dispositional approach that underlies the concept of individual differences and the application of personality theory in organizational behavior. Dispositions are defined as unobservable mental states (constructs) such as needs, values, attitudes, and personalities that are relatively stable over time and that, to varying degrees, serve as determinants of attitudes and behavior in organizations. The argument is that dispositions are a mirage and therefore the only significant determinants of individual organizational behavior are situational in nature. Thus an antithesis is created, pitting psychological constructs against sociological.

More recently, Walter Nord and Suzy Fox (1996) have authored an essay with the thesis that the individual (and individual personality) has disappeared from organizational behavior, being replaced by a contextual dimension consisting of attributes of the physical and social systems in which people exist (situations). The intent is to document the view that theories and research dealing with individual personality and dispositions have lost status, to the point where organizational behavior is no longer interested in individual differences (and by implication *should* not be). There is reason to believe that this second attack from the sociological perspective may leave something to be desired in its coverage of the personality-related literature, but as an attack by fait accompli, it clearly reveals the values of the authors.

These position statements from the situationalist perspective have not gone unanswered. In defense of the dispositional view, Jennifer George (1992) has offered a detailed consideration of much of the theory and research supporting an important role for personality in organizational behavior. House et al. (1996) also make a strong case for the retention of personality-based perspectives. The following quotation appears to present a more balanced view of the issues and leaves the door open to both types of theory and research. It provides an instance of how extreme values may be reconciled and consensus thereby achieved.

> Personality is important for understanding at least certain classes of organizational phenomena. Obviously, this does not imply that situational factors are unimportant. Rather, it suggests that organizations do not stamp out all individual differences; being a member of an organization does not neutralize or negate one's own enduring predispositions to think, feel, and act in certain ways. An extreme situationalist perspective denies organizational participants their individuality and exaggerates organizations' abilities to manipulate and control their members. Likewise, an extreme dispositional position credits too much power to the individual and ignores important situational influences on feelings, thoughts, and behaviors. Hence, personality and situational factors are needed to understand much of organizational life. (George, 1992, pp. 205–206)

Role of Consensus

Threats to a unified science of organizational behavior take two major forms — those that relate specifically to science, including its theory and method, and those that impair unity by jeopardizing the creation of a stable and widely recognized body of knowledge that might be presented to practitioners as a basis for their actions. The latter is the concern of this discussion.

The Consensus Problem

A lack of consensus appears to exist in the field of organizational behavior, and as a result the field's limited amount of hard knowledge is often bemoaned. The evidence is there, but the consensus of knowledgeable scholars that makes it knowledge often is out of reach because conflicting values block the way. Testimony to this effect is not hard to find.

In the introduction to his volume dealing with organizational behavior's conceptual base, Edwin Hartman (1988) discusses this fragmentation using terms such as "disarray," "no consensus," "conflict," "disunity," and "disagreements." The authors of a more recent handbook of the field (Clegg et al., 1996) use their introduction to paint a picture that presents organizational behavior as infused with controversy and partisan politics; this latter volume appears in its own way to contribute to the fragmentation as well, even to extol it.

A well-argued treatment of the consensus problem is by Pfeffer (1993), and it subsequently has sparked a great deal of debate pro and con. The thesis of this essay is that when sciences have developed shared theoretical structures and methodological approaches about which there is substantial consensus, these sciences and their members have experienced a number of positive consequences, including increased allocations of monetary and other resources. Organizational behavior, being fragmented as it is, holds a position low in the pecking order when rewards and resources are distributed among the sciences. In short, we are not viewed as doing a very good job, and this is true because of our lack of consensus. Pfeffer argues that consensus can be attained through the efforts of an elite network of individuals who use political positions and processes to impose a uniformity of view on a discipline. He seems to say that this should happen in organizational behavior. This appeal for consensus is reiterated in a later report (Pfeffer, 1995), but it is apparent that he prefers consensus around certain theoretical positions over others.

Not surprisingly, a number of organizational behaviorists jumped up to dispute Pfeffer on a variety of grounds (Cannella & Paetzold, 1994; Perrow, 1994; Van Maanen, 1995a, 1995b). In general, the thrust of these views is that consensus is not really a desirable goal after all and that enforced consensus is particularly undesirable. Tolerance for diverse approaches, theories, and methods should not be suppressed, and in any event there is no one best way that clearly deserves a dominant position. On occasion, this rebuttal is mixed with a substantial dose of anti-science rhetoric (Van Maanen, 1995b).

All this having been said, it remains true that science relies on some degree of consensus among knowledgeable scholars and that science has proved over and over again that its methods can advance understanding, prediction, and control to the benefit of human society. Certainly, some degree of "disconsensus" can be absorbed and innovative, creative contributions should not just be tolerated but be supported. The questions are how much consensus is needed and in what areas; these are empirical questions, as Pfeffer (1995) notes. It is amazing, once the emotions that values arouse are activated, how difficult it is to see the balanced, middle ground. For a bal-

anced discussion of these issues from a perspective tempered by the passage of time, see Frances Fabian (2000).

Inability to Compare Competing Theories

One outgrowth of the consensus problem is the view that one cannot decide objectively between competing theories that use different languages, hold different assumptions, and have different constructs, thus reflecting totally disparate value systems. Under these circumstances comparisons are impossible in the same sense that "comparing apples and oranges" is impossible. Science is said to be at a loss in such instances, and among the theory pluralism that we face at present, science becomes essentially useless (Scherer & Dowling, 1995). Note that this argument requires a large number of very different theories coming together from different directions to offer contradictory solutions to common problems. This must be so if science is to be effectively neutralized. Thus, "create as many new and unique theories as you possibly can" becomes the rallying cry of proponents of this view; they are out to sink consensus. Practitioners in particular are left helpless to make decisions in the face of this barrage of competing theories and may be expected to eschew organizational behavior altogether.

The response to this line of reasoning is that it creates a pseudo-problem, a mirage, that is readily soluble in that science serves to test theories through research which is just as applicable to competing theories as to any others (McKinley, 1995). Although valid, this position needs some amplification, however.

First, the theory pluralism that exists at present is not made up exclusively of scientific theories. There are a number of philosophical statements in existence that do not generate testable hypotheses and thus are not falsifiable. Subtracting this philosophical content reduces the degree of theory pluralism substantially. For example, many of the phenomena that exist in this world have multiple religious explanations, and scientific explanations (confirmed by research) as well. To include the religious "theories," which are untestable, as part of the total count of scientific theories is unwarranted.

Second, a close study of existing organizational behavior theories reveals that the most frequent situation is one where the theories occupy different, nonoverlapping domains (Miner, 1980, 1982). There are instances of overlap and even some cases of competing positions, but this is not the norm by any means. Those who argue that an inability to compare competing theories is a major barrier to attaining consensus are simply wrong, at least insofar as organizational behavior is concerned; there are not that many competing theories.

Third, competing theories can be compared by using appropriate research designs. Differential experimentation, which serves to determine the relative effectiveness of various approaches or hypotheses, is commonly conducted. Any good theory contains clear specifications for operationalizing its variables, and these may be used in comparative research. For a good example of how research to deal with competing theoretical positions may be conducted, see Gary Latham, Miriam Erez, and Edwin Locke (1988) and the more extended treatment of this research contained in Frost and Stablein (1992). What is clearly evident here is that with sufficient creative input into the research process, science can handle competing theoretical positions (see also McKinley, 1995, on this point). Thus a basis for achieving consensus, where it might otherwise appear to be lacking, does exist within science. Toward this same end, various other approaches have also been proposed but they do not rely on research to bring the parties together (Scherer & Steinmann, 1999).

Fourth, a consensus of knowledgeable scholars can develop in the absence of agreement among protagonists. The motivation-hygiene theory (Herzberg, Mausner, & Snyderman, 1959) is generally assumed to be deficient in a number of respects, based on extensive research conducted to test aspects of the theory. Yet to my knowledge, Herzberg never repudiated his theory and continued to hold out against the growing consensus until his death. This is not unusual and it does not matter. A few voices in opposition do not vitiate consensus.

Fifth, it is not correct to say consensus is totally lacking in organizational behavior, as the Herzberg example illustrates. It may well be more frequently negative than positive in its conclusions, but even agreement among knowledgeable scholars in support of a theory occurs quite often. But the qualifier *among knowledgeable scholars* is important here. Organizational behavior has developed a breadth and a depth of information that defies comprehension by a single person. There are specialties and subspecialties, and it is these that furnish the knowledgeable scholars

whose judgment is at issue. To add in the many who know little or nothing about a particular theory and its research is bound to create an appearance of disconsensus as competing values become involved against an ambiguous (uncertain) background, but that is not the kind of consensus science seeks.

Sixth, practitioners (such as managers) do not require a consensus on the part of organizational behavior to adopt the tools, technology, and theories of that discipline. It would certainly be helpful if such a consensus existed, but managers in a particular area of a business, say human resources, are not necessarily uninformed consumers; they can make judgments as to the validity and usefulness of what comes to them from organizational behavior, and they do so all the time. Many of these inputs from organizational behavior prove useful and help solve important practical problems. As a former practitioner of organizational behavior in the personnel research unit of a large corporation and a consultant in that area throughout my professional career, I can attest to the practical value of these inputs. In actuality, the freedom from political wars that the practitioner has may compensate for any lack of knowledge. Certainly errors are made, but low levels of consensus do not prevent practitioners from making choices among the potpourri of organizational behavior tools, technologies, and theories. And again, as Donaldson (1992) contends, the degree of consensus available to practitioners is probably greater than the critics have maintained.

Road to Consensus

It becomes apparent from the preceding discussion that it would be very useful to have an operational measure of consensus on various matters, within organizational behavior. With hard data on what knowledgeable scholars think, it would be possible to avoid much of the ambiguity that surrounds this treatment.

Actually, during the 1980s a certain amount of data on the extent of consensus around first-generation organizational behavior theories that had achieved considerable visibility did become available (Miner, 1990). The correlations among data from different sources ranking these theories as to their validity ranged from .74 to .94. This is indicative of a considerable amount of consensus. I suspect, however, that other less well known theories of that time and more recent, second-generation theories, both of which would have less research on them available, would not elicit this same high level of consensus. In any event, it is evident that organizational behavior can elicit consensus regarding its theories, and the discipline has done so with regard to a limited set. More empirical research of this kind is needed, however.

One might think that consensus could be obtained by noting the most frequently cited publications in the field, and then building a picture of organizational behavior's knowledge base from the content of these publications. Unfortunately, however, evidence indicates that those publications that do particularly well in citation counts do so not because of the perceived quality of the publication or its usefulness to practitioners, but because of the usefulness to scholars of the field in carrying out their professional tasks (Shadish, 1989). This is not the stuff out of which a picture of our knowledge base can be created.

Yet there are some signs that point to improving consensus as organizational behavior matures. One such sign is the increasing degree to which citations to other disciplines are appearing in the journals (Blackburn, 1990). Discourse across disciplines is on the upswing; talking only with those people within the field who represent a reflection of one's own image is decreasing. When communication opens up in this way, at least the potential for consensus opens up as well.

Another encouraging sign is the relatively recent emergence not of meso theories per se, since such theories have in fact been in existence for some time, but of an explicit concern with the identification and creation of such theories, which bridge a major value gap in the field. To the extent they prove valid, meso theories can represent a major integrating force within organizational behavior.

In writing meso theory one is forced to deal both with psychological and sociological variables, as well as with the literature that surrounds those variables. The result should be an integrated theory that not only ties together the two levels of analysis but also commits the author to some type of synthesis of the two value positions. Accordingly, a strong commitment to a meso approach to theorizing could go a long way toward fostering consensus and firming up a stable, knowledgeable base for organizational behavior. This could involve the development of theories that bring together elements drawn from existing micro and macro theories, or from any such more-limited theories that are developed in the future.

Another sign that we may be on the road to integration that is more personal in nature involves the two books on theory that I wrote in the early 1980s (Miner, 1980, 1982). At that time the available theories clearly fell into micro and macro groupings, and thus the content of the two books was easily determined. Recently, in returning to this agenda, with the objective of expanding and updating the prior work, it has become increasingly apparent that the content split (micro and macro) that so easily produced two separate volumes before is no longer feasible. Organizational behavior has become so intertwined that two separate books of this kind can no longer represent the realities of the field. This is why the present volume is being published as a single entity (and why it is quite large as well).

In short, although it does seem that consensus is at a rather low level overall within organizational behavior, there are subfields and sectors where this is not the case. Thus a body of accepted knowledge does exist within the field and is available to practitioners—a smaller body than many would desire, but still something. Furthermore, there are certain trends in evidence that seem to argue for improved consensus in the future. Unfortunately, other trends, specifically the expanding "contra" presence and the associated efforts to obstruct consensus, lead to the opposite conclusion.

CONCLUSIONS

The philosophy of science as set forth here places considerable emphasis on the role of theory. The reason is that although quantum leaps in science are very rare in any event, they are only possible if theory provides the opportunity. Organizational behavior has had its share of theories, and enough of these have proven useful to move the field forward quite rapidly. However, it is important to understand that further progress requires more good theories, and these will only be created if the field fully recognizes what theory is and how it operates. Theory, however, only becomes useful if it is validated by research. Managers are unlikely to accept theories and apply them to their work unless there is reason to believe that the theories are empirically valid (Donaldson, 1992). At the same time, research results are the agents that determine whether theories are true or false.

This chapter has delved into the characteristics of

research that can be used to test scientific theories. In all of this it should be understood that organizational behavior research may serve additional functions beyond merely testing theory. Hypotheses derived from practice may be evaluated through research to determine whether what has been assumed to be true is really true. Areas that present particular problems may be studied to obtain a clearer picture of the landscape. The point is that scientific research in organizational behavior is not simply a matter of theory testing. Yet theory testing is probably the most important function of organizational behavior research, because a well-validated theory can establish a wide range of knowledge.

In the preceding discussion, certain terms that are found in the references, and which are often used in the literature, have been deliberately avoided. This is in part because these terms have taken on a variety of value-laden excess meanings that tend to stereotype the user. In some instances the terms are too ambiguous for most scientific purposes as well. Thomas Kuhn (1970) in introducing the term *paradigm* intentionally used it with a wide range of meanings (Astley & Zammuto, 1992), and it continues to possess this same ambiguity today. In addition to paradigm, I have avoided such terms as *normal science, positivist theory,* and *incommensurability* for the same reasons. I join McKelvey (1997) in urging that we purge our literature of words that we truly do not understand.

This is not to say that most of the concepts that appear to be covered by these terms are not treated here—to the contrary, they are treated in detail, but using other words. Nor am I trying to avoid labeling my own position. The discussion to this point in part I clearly identifies my commitment to science and spells out at considerable length the concept of science I have in mind. Terms such as *paradigm, normal science, positivist theory,* and *incommensurability* come to organizational behavior from philosophy, however. As a result, there is no commitment to make them precise and specific, in the mode of science. At the same time, there is no necessary commitment on the part of organizational behavior to make them part of our vocabulary—and we should not.

References

Agger, Ben (1991). Critical Theory, Poststructuralism, Postmodernism: Their Sociological Relevance. *Annual Review of Sociology,* 17, 105–131.

Alderfer, Clayton P. (1977). A Critique of Salancik and Pfeffer's Examination of Need Satisfaction Theories. *Administrative Science Quarterly,* 22, 658–669.

Alvesson, Mats, & Kärreman, Dan (2000). Taking the Linguistic Turn in Organizational Research—Challenges, Responses, Consequences. *Journal of Applied Behavioral Science,* 36, 136–158.

Argyris, Chris (1980). *Inner Contradictions of Rigorous Research.* New York: Academic Press.

Astley, W. Graham, & Zammuto, Raymond F. (1992). Organization Science, Managers, and Language Games. *Organization Science,* 3, 443–460.

Bacharach, Samuel B. (1989). Organizational Theories: Some Criteria for Evaluation. *Academy of Management Review,* 14, 496–515.

Bagozzi, Richard P.; Yi, Youjae; & Phillips, Lynn W. (1991). Assessing Construct Validity in Organizational Research. *Administrative Science Quarterly,* 36, 421–458.

Behling, Orlando (1980). The Case for the Natural Science Model for Research in Organizational Behavior and Organization Theory. *Academy of Management Review,* 5, 483–490.

Belasco, James A., & Trice, Harrison M. (1969). *The Assessment of Change in Training and Therapy.* New York: McGraw-Hill.

Berelson, Bernard, & Steiner, Gary (1964). *Human Behavior: An Inventory of Scientific Findings.* New York: Harcourt, Brace & World.

Beyer, Janice M. (1992). Metaphors, Misunderstandings, and Mischief: A Commentary. *Organization Science,* 3, 467–474.

Blackburn, Richard S. (1987). Experimental Design in Organizational Settings. In Jay W. Lorsch (Ed.), *Handbook of Organizational Behavior* (pp. 126–139). Englewood Cliffs, NJ: Prentice Hall.

Blackburn, Richard S. (1990). Organizational Behavior: Whom Do We Talk to and Who Talks to Us? *Journal of Management,* 16, 279–305.

Blood, Milton R. (1994). The Role of Organizational Behavior in the Business School Curriculum. In Jerald Greenberg (Ed.), *Organizational Behavior: The State of the Science* (pp. 207–220). Hillsdale, NJ: Erlbaum.

Boring, Edwin G. (1950). *A History of Experimental Psychology.* New York: Appleton-Century-Crofts.

Brief, Arthur P., & Dukerich, Janet M. (1991). Theory in Organizational Behavior: Can It Be Useful? *Research in Organizational Behavior,* 13, 327–352.

Brown, Clarence W., & Ghiselli, Edwin E. (1955). *Scientific Method in Psychology.* New York: McGraw-Hill.

Burrell, Gibson (1996). Normal Science, Paradigms, Metaphors, Discourses, and Genealogies of Analysis. In Stewart R. Clegg, Cynthia Hardy, & Walter R. Nord (Eds.), *Handbook of Organization Studies* (pp. 642–658). London: Sage.

Campbell, John P. (1990). The Role of Theory in Industrial and Organizational Psychology. In Marvin D. Dunnette & Leaetta M. Hough (Eds.), *Handbook of Industrial and Organizational Psychology* (Vol. 1, pp. 39–73). Palo Alto, CA: Consulting Psychologists Press.

Cannella, Albert A., & Paetzold, Ramona L. (1994). Pfeffer's Barriers to the Advance of Organizational Science: A Rejoinder. *Academy of Management Review*, 19, 331–341.

Clegg, Stewart R.; Hardy, Cynthia; & Nord, Walter R. (1996). *Handbook of Organization Studies*. London: Sage.

Cook, Thomas D.; Campbell, Donald T.; & Peracchio, Laura (1990). Quasi Experimentation. In Marvin D. Dunnette & Leaetta M. Hough (Eds.), *Handbook of Industrial and Organizational Psychology* (Vol. 1, pp. 491–576). Palo Alto, CA: Consulting Psychologists Press.

Davis-Blake, Alison, & Pfeffer, Jeffrey (1989). Just a Mirage: The Search for Dispositional Effects in Organizational Research. *Academy of Management Review*, 14, 385–400.

Donaldson, Lex (1992). The Weick Stuff: Managing beyond Games. *Organization Science*, 3, 461–466.

Donaldson, Lex (1996). *For Positivist Organization Theory*. London: Sage.

Doty, D. Harold, & Glick, William H. (1994). Typologies as a Unique Form of Theory Building: Toward Improving Understanding and Modeling. *Academy of Management Review*, 19, 230–251.

Dubin, Robert (1976). Theory Building in Applied Areas. In Marvin D. Dunnette (Ed.), *Handbook of Industrial and Organizational Psychology* (pp. 17–39). Chicago: Rand McNally.

Dubin, Robert (1978). *Theory Building*. New York: Free Press.

Fabian, Frances H. (2000). Keeping the Tension: Pressures to Keep the Controversy in the Management Discipline. *Academy of Management Review*, 25, 350–371.

Frost, Peter J., & Stablein, Ralph E. (1992). *Doing Exemplary Research*. Newbury Park, CA: Sage.

George, Jennifer M. (1992). The Role of Personality in Organizational Life: Issues and Evidence. *Journal of Management*, 18, 185–213.

Glaser, Barney G., & Strauss, Anselm L. (1967). *The Discovery of Grounded Theory*. Chicago: Aldine.

Gottfredson, Linda S. (1983). Creating and Criticizing Theory. *Journal of Vocational Behavior*, 23, 203–212.

Hartman, Edwin (1988). *Conceptual Foundations of Organization Theory*. Cambridge, MA: Ballinger.

Herzberg, Frederick; Mausner, Bernard; & Snyderman, Barbara S. (1959). *The Motivation to Work*. New York: Wiley.

Holdnak, B. J.; Clemons, Tanya C.; & Bushardt, Stephen C. (1990). Evaluation of Organization Training by the Solomon Four Group Design: A Field Study in Self-Esteem Training. *Journal of Managerial Psychology*, 5(5), 25–31.

House, Robert J.; Rousseau, Denise M.; & Thomas-Hunt, Melissa (1995). The Meso Paradigm: A Framework for the Integration of Micro and Macro Organizational Behavior. *Research in Organizational Behavior*, 17, 71–114.

House, Robert J.; Shane, Scott A.; & Herold, David M. (1996). Rumors of the Death of Dispositional Research Are Vastly Exaggerated. *Academy of Management Review*, 21, 203–224.

Hunt, Shelby D. (1990). Truth in Marketing Theory and Research. *Journal of Marketing*, 54(July), 1–15.

Hunt, Shelby D. (1992). For Reason and Realism in Marketing. *Journal of Marketing*, 56(April), 89–102.

Jermier, John M. (1985). "When the Sleeper Walks": A Short Story Extending Themes in Radical Organization Theory. *Journal of Management*, 11(2), 67–80.

Kaplan, Abraham (1964). *The Conduct of Inquiry*. San Francisco: Chandler.

Ketchen, David J., & Shook, Christopher, L. (1996). The Application of Cluster Analysis in Strategic Management Research: An Analysis and Critique. *Strategic Management Journal*, 17, 441–458.

Kilduff, Martin, & Mehra, Ajay (1997). Postmodernism and Organizational Research. *Academy of Management Review*, 22, 453–481.

Kuhn, Thomas (1970). *The Structure of Scientific Revolutions*. Chicago: University of Chicago Press.

Lammers, Cornelis (1988). Transience and Persistence of Ideal Types in Organizational Theory. *Research in the Sociology of Organizations*, 6, 203–224.

Latham, Gary P.; Erez, Miriam; & Locke, Edwin A. (1988). Resolving Scientific Disputes by the Joint Design of Crucial Experiments by the Antagonists: Application to the Erez-Latham Dispute Regarding Participating in Goal Setting. *Journal of Applied Psychology*, 73, 753–772.

Lawler, Edward E.; Mohrman, Alan M.; Mohrman, Susan A.; Ledford, Gerald E.; & Cummings, Thomas G. (1985). *Doing Research That Is Useful for Theory and Practice*. San Francisco: Jossey-Bass.

Lewin, Kurt (1945). The Research Center for Group Dynamics at Massachusetts Institute of Technology. *Sociometry*, 8, 126–135.

Locke, Edwin A. (1986). *Generalizing from Laboratory to Field Settings*. Lexington, MA: Lexington Books.

Marsden, Richard, & Townley, Barbara (1996). The Owl of Minerva: Reflections on Theory in Practice. In Stewart R. Clegg, Cynthia Hardy, & Walter R. Nord (Eds.), *Handbook of Organization Studies* (pp. 659–675). London: Sage.

Martin, Joanne, & Frost, Peter (1996). The Organizational Culture War Games: A Struggle for Intellectual Dominance. In Stewart R. Clegg, Cynthia Hardy, & Walter R. Nord (Eds.), *Handbook of Organization Studies* (pp. 599–621). London: Sage.

Mayo, Elton (1933). *The Human Problems of an Industrial Civilization*. New York: Macmillan.

McKelvey, Bill (1997). Quasi-natural Organization Science. *Organization Science*, 8, 352–380.

McKinley, William (1995). Commentary on Scherer and Dowling. *Advances in Strategic Management*, 12A, 249–260.

Medsker, Gina J.; Williams, Larry J.; & Holahan, Patricia J. (1994). A Review of Current Practices for Evaluating Causal Models in Organizational Behavior and Human Resource Management Research. *Journal of Management*, 20, 439–464.

Miles, Robert H. (1980). *Resource Book in Macro Organizational Behavior*. Santa Monica, CA: Goodyear.

Miller, Danny (1996). Configurations Revisited. *Strategic Management Journal*, 17, 505–512.

Miner, John B. (1962). Conformity among University Professors and Business Executives. *Administrative Science Quarterly*, 7, 96–109.

Miner, John B. (1965). A Statistical Model for the Study of Conformity. In Fred Massarik & Philburn Ratoosh (Eds.), *Mathematical Explorations in Behavioral Science* (pp. 95–111). Homewood, IL: Irwin.

Miner, John B. (1980). *Theories of Organizational Behavior*. Hinsdale, IL: Dryden.

Miner, John B. (1982). *Theories of Organizational Structure and Process*. Hinsdale, IL: Dryden.

Miner, John B. (1984). The Validity and Usefulness of Theories in an Emerging Organizational Science. *Academy of Management Review*, 9, 297–306.

Miner, John B. (1990). The Role of Values in Defining the 'Goodness' of Theories in Organizational Science. *Organization Studies*, 11, 161–178.

Miner, John B. (1995). *Administrative and Management Theory*. Aldershot, UK: Dartmouth.

Miner, John B. (1997). *A Psychological Typology of Successful Entrepreneurs*. Westport, CT: Quorum.

Mone, M. A., & McKinley, William (1993). The Uniqueness Value and Its Consequences for Organization Studies. *Journal of Management Inquiry*, 2, 284–296.

Nord, Walter R., & Fox, Suzy (1996). The Individual in Organizational Studies: The Great Disappearing Act? In Stuart R. Clegg, Cynthia Hardy, & Walter R. Nord (Eds.), *Handbook of Organization Studies* (pp. 148–174). London: Sage.

Parry, Ken W. (1998). Grounded Theory and Social Process: A New Direction for Leadership Research. *Leadership Quarterly*, 9, 85–105.

Perrow, Charles (1994). Pfeffer Slips! *Academy of Management Review*, 19, 191–194.

Pescosolido, Bernice A., & Rubin, Beth A. (2000). The Web of Group Affiliations Revisited: Social Life, Postmodernism, and Sociology. *American Sociological Review*, 65, 52–76.

Pfeffer, Jeffrey (1982). *Organizations and Organization Theory*. Marshfield, MA: Pitman.

Pfeffer, Jeffrey (1991). Organization Theory and Structural Perspectives on Management. *Journal of Management*, 17, 789–803.

Pfeffer, Jeffrey (1993). Barriers to the Advance of Organizational Science: Paradigm Development as a Dependent Variable. *Academy of Management Review*, 18, 599–620.

Pfeffer, Jeffrey (1995). Mortality, Reproducibility, and the Persistence of Styles of Theory. *Organization Science*, 6, 681–686.

Pinder, Craig C., & Moore, Larry F. (1980). *Middle Range Theory and the Study of Organizations*. Boston: Martinus Nijhoff.

Price, James L., & Mueller, Charles W. (1986). *Handbook of Organizational Measurement*. Marshfield, MA: Pitman.

Priem, Richard L., & Rosenstein, Joseph (2000). Is Organization Theory Obvious to Practitioners? A Test of One Established Theory. *Organization Science*, 11, 509–524.

Raelin, Joseph A. (1993). Theory and Practice: Their Roles, Relationship, and Limitations in Advanced Management Education. *Business Horizons*, 36(3), 85–89.

Rich, Philip (1992). The Organizational Taxonomy: Definition and Design. *Academy of Management Review*, 17, 758–781.

Salancik, Gerald R. (1984). On Priming, Consistency, and Order Effects in Job Attitude Assessment: With a Note on Current Research. *Journal of Management*, 10, 250–254.

Salancik, Gerald R., & Pfeffer, Jeffrey (1977). An Examination of Need-Satisfaction Models of Job Attitudes. *Administrative Science Quarterly*, 22, 427–456.

Salancik, Gerald R., & Pfeffer, Jeffrey (1978). A Social Information Processing Approach to Job Attitudes and Task Design. *Administrative Science Quarterly*, 23, 224–253.

Sanchez, Julio C. (1993). The Long and Thorny Way to an Organizational Taxonomy. *Organization Studies*, 14, 73–92.

Sandelands, Lloyd, & Drazin, Robert (1989). On the Language of Organization Theory. *Organization Studies*, 10, 457–478.

Schaubroeck, John, & Kuehn, Kermit (1992). Research Designs in Industrial and Organizational Psychology. *International Review of Industrial and Organizational Psychology*, 7, 99–121.

Schendel, Dan E., & Hofer, Charles W. (1979). *Strategic Management: A New View of Business Policy and Planning*. Boston: Little, Brown.

Scherer, Andreas G., & Dowling, Michael J. (1995). Towards a Reconciliation of the Theory-Pluralism in Strategic Management: Incommensurability and the Constructivist Approach of the Erlangen School. *Advances in Strategic Management*, 12A, 195–247.

Scherer, Andreas G., & Steinmann, Horst (1999). Some Remarks on the Problem of Incommensurability in Organization Studies. *Organization Studies*, 20, 519–544.

Shadish, William R. (1989). The Perception and Evaluation of Quality in Science. In Barry Gholson, William R. Shadish, Robert A. Neimeyer, & Arthur C. Houts (Eds.), *Psychology of Science: Contributions to Metascience* (pp. 383–426). Cambridge: Cambridge University Press.

Silverman, David (1971). *The Theory of Organizations*. New York: Basic Books.

Snizek, William E., & Furhman, Ellsworth R. (1980). Theoretical Observations on Applied Behavioral Science. *Journal of Applied Behavioral Science*, 16, 93–103.

Staw, Barry M. (1991). Dressing Up Like an Organization: When Psychological Theories Can Explain Organizational Action. *Journal of Management*, 17, 805–819.

Steiner, George A., & Miner, John B. (1986). *Management Policy and Strategy*. New York: Macmillan.

Stone, Eugene F. (1984). Misperceiving and/or Misrepresenting the Facts: A Reply to Salancik. *Journal of Management*, 10, 255–258.

Stone, Eugene F., & Gueutal, Hal G. (1984). On the Premature Death of Need-Satisfaction Models: An Investigation of Salancik and Pfeffer's View on Priming and Consistency Artifacts. *Journal of Management*, 10, 237–249.

Stone-Romero, Eugene F. (1994). Construct Validity Issues in Organizational Behavior Research. In Jerald Greenberg (Ed.), *Organizational Behavior: The State of the Science* (pp. 155–179). Hillsdale, NJ: Erlbaum.

Sutton, Robert I., & Staw, Barry M. (1995). What Theory Is Not. *Administrative Science Quarterly*, 40, 371–384.

Tannenbaum, Robert; Margulies, Newton; & Massarik, Fred (1985). *Human Systems Development*. San Francisco: Jossey-Bass.

Tosi, Henry L. (1984). *Theories of Organization*. New York: Wiley.

Tosi, Henry L. (1992). *The Environment/Organization/Person Contingency Model: A Meso Approach to the Study of Organizations*. Greenwich, CT: JAI Press.

Turner, Barry A. (1983). The Use of Grounded Theory for the Qualitative Analysis of Organizational Behavior. *Journal of Management Studies*, 20, 333–348.

Van de Ven, Andrew H. (1989). Nothing Is Quite So Practical as a Good Theory. *Academy of Management Review*, 14, 486–489.

Van Maanen, John (1995a). Fear and Loathing in Organization Studies. *Organization Science*, 6, 687–692

Van Maanen, John (1995b). Style as Theory. *Organization Science*, 6, 133–143.

Vroom, Victor H. (1964). *Work and Motivation*. New York: Wiley.

Webster, Jane, & Starbuck, William H. (1988). Theory Building in Industrial and Organizational Psychology. *International Review of Industrial and Organizational Psychology*, 3, 93–138.

Weiss, Richard M. (2000). Taking Science out of Organization Science: How Would Postmodernism Reconstruct the Analysis of Organizations? *Organization Science*, 11, 709–731.

Williams, Larry J., & James, Lawrence R. (1994). Causal Models in Organizational Behavior Research: From Path Analysis to LISREL and Beyond. In Jerald Greenberg (Ed.), *Organizational Behavior: The State of the Science* (pp. 181–205). Hillsdale, NJ: Erlbaum.

Wren, Daniel A.; Buckley, M. Ronald; & Michaelsen, Larry K. (1994). The Theory/Applications Balance in Management Pedagogy: Where Do We Stand? *Journal of Management*, 20, 141–157.

Chapter 2

Multidisciplinary Origins of Organizational Behavior

Elton Mayo, Chester Barnard, and Kurt Lewin

We have considered the scientific foundations of organizational behavior and how the field has progressed as a science. We have looked into the uneasy relationship with philosophy that continues to yield both positive consequences in fostering theory and negative consequences in diluting the commitment to science. Now we focus on the subject of historical origins, a topic that is of concern in both chapters 2 and 3. Understanding these historical origins is no less important than understanding the scientific foundations, if one is to truly comprehend organizational behavior theory in the present (Bedeian, 1998).

In chapters 2 and 3 the discussion deals with those origins that have influenced the course organizational behavior has taken, but which were not at the time part of the field (because it did not exist). These origins span a roughly 50-year period during the first half of the twentieth century. The key names are Elton Mayo, Chester Barnard, Kurt Lewin, Mary Parker Follett, and Max Weber, plus Henri Fayol and Frederick Taylor, whose influence was of a very different type than the preceding five. As will become evident, the disciplinary basis of these individuals is extremely diverse.

A word is in order regarding the way in which these key influential persons were identified. The starting point was to establish my own list, working from a background of experience in writing an earlier book (Miner, 1971). The result was the seven individuals noted above. This list was then checked against inclusion in various books that consider the contributions of key individuals to organizational thinking, and which go back to a period before the emergence of organizational behavior and include both intellectual contributors and practitioners. These validation sources were *Developments in Management Thought* (Pollard, 1974), *Great Writers on Organizations: The Omnibus Edition* (Pugh & Hickson, 1993), and *Management Innovators: The People and Ideas That Have Shaped Modern Business* (Wren & Greenwood, 1998).

Four of the seven individuals are spotlighted in all three books, thus clearly supporting their inclusion here; these are Mayo, Barnard, Follett, and Taylor, Fayol is considered twice, but not in Daniel Wren and Ronald Greenwood (1998). The latter volume gives particular attention to U.S. contributors, although others are considered as well, and includes many practitioners who are not known for their writings; this one omission of Fayol does not seem to invalidate his being profiled here. Weber is presented only in Derek Pugh and David Hickson (1993), which is a curious situation that seems to reflect the fact that the other books are less concerned with contributions to sociological thinking and macro level theorizing. Since I want to give full coverage to the origins of organizational behavior in this particular regard, not including Weber would seem to be an act of neglect.

Finally, there is Kurt Lewin, who is on my list but is not even mentioned in the indexes of any of the three sources used to validate my selections. In spite of this situation, I believe a good case can be made for the inclusion of Lewin among the early contributors to the development of organizational behavior, and I attempt to make that case in this chapter. However, note that in this single instance the field really has not supported my judgment.

DATING THE ORIGIN OF ORGANIZATIONAL BEHAVIOR

In chapters 2 and 3 we are concerned only with the predecessors and roots of organizational behavior, not with the theorists and researchers who came on the scene as the field moved into high gear. Thus it is important here to identify a point at which organizational behavior became established as a distinct discipline. There is a certain arbitrariness in doing this because the emergence was actually quite gradual, and the consensus that ultimately established the fact of existence developed gradually as well. The problem of pinpointing a date is further confounded by the fact that during the 1940s and 1950s a number of often competing designations existed—human relations, human organization, administrative science, behavioral science, organization theory, as well as organizational behavior toward the end of this period. Nevertheless, I believe the founding can be narrowed down to a specific time period.

Some level of concern with organizational issues existed within psychology from the point that industrial psychology came on the scene in the first decade of the 1900s (Gilmer, 1981). However, the term *organizational* was not added to the name of the division of the American Psychological Association involved until 1970, long after organizational behavior clearly had come into existence. There was something variously referred to as *organizational psychology* or *managerial psychology* (Leavitt, 1958) present well before 1970, but it existed as part of psychology not as a separate discipline.

Somewhat the same situation occurred within sociology and anthropology. William Whyte (1983) dates the beginnings of "our field" back to the initiation of the Hawthorne research in the 1920s. However, that field carried the title *human relations* and it was defined narrowly. Paul Lawrence (1987), pointing largely to developments at the Harvard Business School, argues for a beginning in the early 1940s. Larry Greiner (1979) puts the origins of the field in the latter part of that decade. All three of these individuals had ties to Harvard and to sociology/anthropology. In the 1940s *human relations* was the prevailing term (Gardner & Moore, 1945). Over time, the subject matter broadened somewhat, but there remained a close association with sociology; human relations continued to be the term applied well into the 1950s, and even to some degree into the 1960s (Davis, 1992).

Within anthropology, the Society for Applied Anthropology used the title *Human Organization* for its journal from the late 1940s on (Adams & Preiss, 1960). However, again, this was a development *within* anthropology, not separate from it. The human relations movement came the closest to breaking away from the basic disciplines, but its ties to science were shaky and its influence peaked during the 1940s and early 1950s (Porter & Bigley, 1995); its focus and content covered only part of what became organizational behavior.

The term *management* was used in the business schools for many years and is reflected in the founding of the Academy of Management in 1936. Yet at its beginning this was not a scientific discipline, and it has come to possess a breadth that extends well beyond organizational behavior—to strategic management and production management, for instance.

Given all this, the time frame for the creation of organizational behavior seems to come down to sometime in the 1950s. Karlene Roberts et al. (1990) say the early 1950s, based on their interviews with early contributors to the field. Milton Blood (1994) takes the position that organizational behavior really began with the pronounced movement of social scientists into the business schools starting around 1955. Paul Goodman and David Whetten (1998) attribute the beginning of the field to this same phenomenon. Elsewhere I have ascribed the birth to the latter 1950s (Miner, 1997). The *Administrative Science Quarterly* and the *Journal of the Academy of Management*, both major publications that have come to stress the scientific foundations of organizational behavior, were founded in the business schools in 1956 and 1958, respectively.

On balance, 1955 appears to be at least adequate as a designated startup date, with the recognition that 5 years either way from this median would not represent a real distortion. Insofar as theory is concerned, the first generation of contributions that arose out of the initiation of organizational behavior appears to have extended over a period of roughly 20 years (1955–1974).

MAYO AND HAWTHORNE

The Hawthorne research was carried out at a large manufacturing plant operated by Western Electric, a subsidiary of AT&T, on the outskirts of Chicago. This Hawthorne Works was the site of various studies that extended from November 1924 to February 1933; a related endeavor focused on employee counseling was initiated in February 1936 and terminated for all practical purposes in early 1956.

This research through much of its history was a joint effort among Western Electric personnel, Har-

vard Business School professors, and MIT professors. However, the task of describing and interpreting the studies and results fell to the Harvard contingent primarily. Mayo was the dominant force within that contingent, and his ideas are the ones that have lived on to influence organizational behavior the most.

The major sources for these ideas are two books by Mayo (1933, 1945). Two additional books provided not only reflections of Mayo's ideas but also more detail on the research at Hawthorne: F. J. Roethlisberger and William J. Dickson (1939) and Dickson and Roethlisberger (1966). A volume containing papers produced at a symposium convened to honor the fiftieth anniversary of the initiation of the Hawthorne studies provides both a testimonial to the significance of the research and a picture of its influence (Cass & Zimmer, 1975). In the following treatment I rely not only on these sources but also on the excellent historical discussion provided by Richard Gillespie (1991).

Cast of Characters

Elton Mayo was born and educated in Australia. In the family tradition he began a medical career there, but failed his second-year exams. Additional courses in medicine in Edinburgh and London moved him no closer to an M.D. degree. Subsequently, he returned to Australia and completed a degree in philosophy and psychology. He then taught philosophy for a number of years at the just established University of Queensland. By 1922 he had decided to leave Australia for the United States.

In this country he ultimately established contact with a number of influential financial and psychological leaders and through them obtained a research position at the University of Pennsylvania (Trahair, 1984). This position and almost all of Mayo's subsequent work was funded by the Rockefeller family and later the Rockefeller Foundation. Yet the research conducted with these funds in various Philadelphia textile mills had limited success, largely due to the overriding constraints that were imposed by practical business considerations. As a result Mayo, with the help of his foundation friends, moved to the Harvard Business School in 1926 and became involved in the Hawthorne research in 1928. He remained at Harvard, and involved primarily with Hawthorne matters, until his retirement in 1947. He then assumed a position as adviser on industrial relations to the British government, but two years later, in 1949, he died.

As this brief biographical sketch indicates, Mayo achieved little success in life before his Harvard appointment at the age of 46. An effective speaker and proficient in cultivating influential friends and mentors, he nevertheless had little by way of academic credentials and practically no training in the conduct of scientific research. In actual fact he was much more of a social philosopher than the psychologist or psychiatrist he would have preferred to be.

Fritz Jules Roethlisberger was a protégé of Mayo's, 18 years his junior, who was introduced into the ongoing Hawthorne research in 1930. He had an undergraduate degree in engineering from MIT and dabbled with a doctorate in philosophy at Harvard, but without ever completing the degree requirements. (He did receive an M.A.) Mayo obtained funding for him from the Rockefeller Foundation, and the two worked together for many years at Hawthorne and Harvard. Ultimately, Roethlisberger rose to full professor at the Harvard Business School and had a distinguished career as a writer and teacher in the areas of communications, training, and counseling. Like Mayo, he was not schooled in the conduct of scientific research. He died in 1974 at the age of 76.

William Dickson came to the Hawthorne research in 1929 in a summer job intended to support his work on a Ph.D. in economics at the University of Chicago, which he had begun the previous year. He never returned to school, rising to various positions in personnel research at Hawthorne and retiring in 1969 as assistant superintendent for personnel research at New York headquarters. In late 1932 Dickson went to Harvard to help write up the research conducted to that point. He remained at Harvard until February 1936

writing *Management and the Worker*; then he returned to Hawthorne.

Dickson was one of many Western Electric personnel managers who were involved in the research, but he was the only one who assumed a major and continuing role in presenting it to the public. Note that Dickson, like Mayo and Roethlisberger, was not well trained in the conduct of scientific research. This is important, as we shall see shortly. Yet the Rockefeller philanthropies spent over $1.5 million in support of Mayo and his colleagues in the 20-year span from 1923 to 1943.

Research at Hawthorne

Table 2.1 presents a chronology of the various studies. Note that Mayo was not involved at all in the illumination experiments and only entered into the relay assembly test room a year after it had been designed by Hawthorne personnel. At no point did he actually remain in Chicago to conduct any research project for an extended period; his visits were in and out, and frequently there were long periods in between. Among the Harvard people, Roethlisberger was present the most, but he did not enter onto the scene at Hawthorne until the relay assembly test room work was more than half completed. Clair Turner, professor of biology and public health at MIT, worked entirely independently of the Harvard contingent and focused on the relay assembly test room. He did not contribute to the interpretation of the research, and one gets the impression that his input overall was marginal at best.

The illumination experiments were part of a broad research program under the direction of the National

TABLE 2.1 Chronology of the Hawthorne research

Event	Date
Illumination experiments	
First series:	November 1924 to April 1925
Second series:	February to April 1926
Third series:	September 1926 to April 1927
Relay assembly test room	May 1927 to February 1933 — 24 experimental periods
Mayo (Harvard) and Turner (MIT) come aboard	April/May 1928
Second relay assembly group	August 1928 to March 1929
Interviewing program (plantwide)	September 1928 to January 1931
Mica splitting test room	October 1928 to March 1931
Bank wiring observation room	November 1931 to May 1932
Counseling program (plantwide)	February 1936 to early 1956

Research Council. The impetus behind this program came from the electrical industry, which wished to foster the installation of artificial lighting throughout manufacturing industry. The underlying hypothesis was that artificial lighting would raise production levels substantially. The lead researchers for the Hawthorne segment of the research program were from MIT. The experiments appear to have been well conducted, using both experimental and control groups, and they looked into payment schemes and variations in supervision, as well as lighting. The studies were unable to establish any consistent difference between experimental and control conditions, and thus the hypothesis of an increase in production with better lighting was not confirmed. No final report was ever prepared on this research; the National Research Council withdrew its support in early 1927 (see Wren & Greenwood, 1998).

Relay Assembly Test Room

Believing that the key to productivity increases resided more in the workers than in the environment, the Western Electric people set up a small group of six female assemblers in a separate room to continue the research. The design called for the group to serve as its own control; there were no control groups per se, although some comparison data were obtained from regular operations. Changes in experimental conditions were introduced in each of the 24 periods and were based primarily on the hypotheses of the observer who shared the room with the assemblers. No overall program for experimental changes existed at the beginning. Experimental variables tested at one time or another, and often in conjunction with one another, were pay system variations, rest pauses, morning tea, early stopping times, changed positions, days off, and variations in weekly hours.

Productivity was measured in terms of assembled units produced per hour. The average output per employee per hour over the full course of the study was as follows:

Period	Time (No. Weeks)	Productivity (Assembled Units/Hour)
Periods 1–4	20 weeks	50.6
Periods 5–8	26 weeks	57.1
Periods 9–12	37 weeks	61.9
Periods 13–16	75 weeks	68.1
Periods 17–20	80 weeks	69.1
Periods 21–24	32 weeks	70.5

From period 17 on, the hours worked per week were reduced, largely as a result of decreased product demand as occasioned by the onset of the depression. Note that at this point, production leveled off considerably, rather than rising sharply as it had previously.

As a set of experiments, the relay assembly test room research left much to be desired. In particular, using the subjects as their own controls, rather than introducing control groups, made attributing causation almost impossible, especially given the changing economic circumstances in the United States over the period of the research and the increase in labor union activity. The experiments violated many of the requirements for conducting experimental research (see chapter 1). For example, many appropriate statistical analyses were not carried out at the time of the research, and two low-producing subjects were removed from the experiment entirely during period 7 and replaced with much more productive assemblers.

Research Innovations in 1928

Close to the 1-year point of the relay assembly room experiments, it became evident to the Hawthorne people that the research was not yielding definitive information. Accordingly, a number of innovations were introduced. First, the Harvard and the MIT consultants were brought in. This produced some new hypotheses to investigate, but no clear interpretations of the existing data. Second, several new studies were introduced to get at specific hypotheses. These utilized typists, mica splitters, armature straighteners, and a second group of relay assemblers as subjects.

Some of these studies appear to have disappeared into oblivion over time, with no record of the results. Full reporting of all the studies at Hawthorne did not occur. One suspects that the researchers simply lost interest in research that did not appear to be going anywhere.

The second relay assembly group was instituted to study the effects of a group payment system, but with other conditions held constant; thus the subjects remained under regular supervision and in normal working conditions. These results provided considerable support for the influence of payment systems on output, and went at least part way toward explaining the first relay assembly findings. The study was short-lived, however, because of conflict between the experimental group and the regular department.

The mica splitting test room was established to study the effects of various experimental conditions when workers were paid an individual piece rate. Again there was a rise in productivity, although some drop-off occurred later, apparently under the pressure of depression-related factors. All in all, this research, too, seemed to indicate that earnings levels were important in any rise in output.

The final innovation introduced in 1928 was what ultimately became a plantwide interviewing program. Interviewing had been employed with workers who were under study as early as 1925, but now it was applied everywhere. The result was something like a large-scale attitude survey. The results were used to improve working conditions and to design supervisory training programs. Extensive analyses, including statistical analyses, were made of the interview data. However, no effort was made to compare the subsequent productivity of groups that did and did not undergo the interviews. Thus, the overall contribution to unraveling the relay assembly results was minimal.

Bank Wiring Observation Room

The bank wiring observation room was a separate room, but otherwise standard working conditions were maintained. No experimental interventions were introduced. There was an observer in the room, but supervision was handled in the regular manner. Output proved to be steady, but somewhat below management expectations: it was restricted by the workers apparently out of a fear that management would take advantage of them if they performed to capacity. This, however, was not a new finding; evidence of similar phenomena when piece-rate systems of payment are used had existed for many years. Two cliques clearly developed among the 14 male workers, and each of them exhibited very different group norms.

This was intended as an observational study of group dynamics. It was essentially anthropological in nature and was strongly influenced by the noted anthropologist W. Lloyd Warner, then on the faculty at Harvard. Warner, however, did not publish any findings. The observations clearly indicated that management's control over the workers was of a limited nature. There was little here to help explain the earlier results.

Counseling Program

Counseling was introduced at Hawthorne some 3 years after the prior studies had ceased; thus nothing happened during the depth of the depression. From 1936 to 1941 the program grew steadily at Hawthorne, but during much of the period it was small in scope. From 1942 to 1948 counseling became an established personnel activity and spread to other Western Electric facilities. By 1948 some 55 counselors were employed at Hawthorne, and they served two-thirds of the workforce. The period from 1949 to 1955 was one in which the program became increasingly an object of critical evaluation and the number of counselors declined steadily. By early 1956 no counselors were on the rolls, although the program structure existed on paper for another 5 years.

In what sense was this counseling activity part of the Hawthorne research, rather than simply a transient personnel procedure? Initially, the goals of science and research were an inherent part of the program, and it was viewed as a human relations effort that was directly linked to the prior inquiries, especially the interviewing. However, other than some studies of the manifest content of employee concerns, little research was conducted. Research that might provide useful input to management decision making was minimal at best. No evaluative studies comparing counseling with no counseling, or one type of counseling approach with another, were undertaken. The counselors were not researchers, and ultimately the research function disappeared from the program completely.

Why did the counseling program cease? Dickson and Roethlisberger (1966) decline to deal with this issue, but Gillespie (1991) offers five reasons:

1. The costs of the program were high and clearly evident, while the benefits were difficult to demonstrate, especially given the lack of evaluative research.
2. The program became bureaucratized and lacked a clear goal; once the research function disappeared, the major objective was survival.
3. The decentralized structure introduced into Western Electric made for many more small plants and sharply reduced the distance between management and the worker, thus obviating the need for counseling.
4. As unions came to represent more Western Electric employees and become more powerful,

the need for the often-parallel counseling structure decreased; some no doubt went so far as to argue that the growth of union representation reflected the failure of the counseling program.

5. As supervisors were increasingly trained in human relations approaches, they came to replace the counselors to a substantial degree; there never was a meaningful integration of the human relations training and counseling functions.

Put more succinctly, the reason for the demise could well have been that "it simply may not have worked" (Highhouse, 1999).

Interpretations

As we move from the conduct of the research and personnel programs at Hawthorne to the dissemination of interpretations of research results and program evaluations to the public, an important division of labor should be noted. At Hawthorne, management controlled the various activities, but the interpretation process was carried out primarily at Harvard by Mayo, Roethlisberger, and Dickson, supported by Rockefeller Foundation money. As a consequence, these writers had a great deal more discretion than would have been the case had personnel researchers at Hawthorne done the writing. This is not to say that the two groups were necessarily at odds, only that Mayo and those who worked with him on preparing the interpretations were far removed from the research scene and in a position to introduce their own views. None of these people had full knowledge of what had happened at Hawthorne.

Mayo

In Mayo's view, the conduct of the Hawthorne research had revealed many inadequacies in existing scientific approaches and had accordingly forced major changes in scientific method on the investigators. Thus, at the outset, there was an attempt to avoid the constraints of good science and to gain acceptance for approaches that otherwise might be questioned. Furthermore, Mayo took the position that the research was undertaken not to find ways of increasing productivity, but to promote scientific understanding—the development of more precise and biological knowledge of the human situation in industry, and of the

conditions that affect human capacity for work. The significance of the Hawthorne studies extended far beyond a single company's desire to increase output.

Mayo discounted the charge that industrial work was by its nature monotonous and fatiguing. What the researchers did in the relay assembly test room was strengthen the inner equilibrium of the workers so that they were able to achieve a mental steady state, which, in turn, made them resistant to a wide range of external conditions. Worker complaints should be viewed as more indicative of the person's situation and internal state than of workplace conditions; complaints about supervision were particularly prejudiced and irrational.

Drawing on the psychiatric literature, Mayo argued that workers could be jolted into obsessive thinking and mild neuroses by events that disturbed their equilibrium. Output would decline accordingly. Restriction of output was thus an exasperated response to a poor work situation, not a rational means of collective action. In turn, this poor work situation was a reflection of the general social disorganization of an industrial society, where traditional social norms and values had broken down under the stress of rapid social change. Thus, the relay assembly and bank wiring rooms were placed at opposite poles of social organization, with the latter the more characteristic in industrial society.

Mayo used the relay assembly room to illustrate the need for teamwork and cooperation. Feelings of security and certainty derive from membership in a group. Managers need to foster the organization of work teams and the participation of these teams in the purposes of the organization. Consultation with the workers, and preferably self-determination by the workers themselves, should be encouraged. Workers should be provided an opportunity to talk about their problems, and supervisors should be trained to cope with these human situations. The objective in all of this is to create a kind of spontaneous cooperation throughout the company of the kind that characterizes well-organized social structures. Thus the three persistent problems of management are:

1. The application of science and technical skill to some material or product to meet the economic needs of society.
2. The systematic ordering of operations.
3. The organization of teamwork, and thus of sustained cooperation, to meet the social needs of society.

The problem of the administrative elite was that it was technically and economically oriented and lacked understanding of human and social needs. The future of society depended on a managerial class that could restore opportunities for human collaboration and fully recognize the need for social solidarity. Revolution occurred when the ruling class failed to administer society effectively, and that required a class, trained by the universities, to use methods of promoting human collaboration effectively (human relations training).

Roethlisberger and Dickson

Roethlisberger and Dickson (1939) generally followed Mayo philosophically, but they wrote from a stance that was much closer to Hawthorne and that dealt much less with societal problems. They noted the tendency of complaining workers to project their troubles on others and thus to overthink the situation. Meanings are colored too much by personal experiences outside the work situation. Complaints cannot be taken seriously as criticisms of company policies or conditions. This obsessive thinking is widespread and has much in common with the preoccupations found in psychoneurosis. To hide industrial problems under general terms such as fatigue, monotony, and supervision may well fail to differentiate among the various types of interferences involved, and thus among the different kinds of disequilibrium that may be operating.

Industry is faced with two major sets of problems — problems of external balance (economic) and problems of internal equilibrium. The latter are concerned with maintaining a social organization in which individuals and groups can work together to satisfy their personal and collective desires. In this context, informal organization, although capable of restricting output, is not bad; in fact, it is a necessary prerequisite for effective collaboration. The parts of a plant social system are interdependent: changes in one part create changes in other parts. If a small change is introduced, equilibrium will be disturbed, and a reaction to restore equilibrium will be activated. The technical organization can change more rapidly than the social; the formal organization more rapidly than the informal. In these disparities exists the potential for imbalance, which can breed distrust and resistance to change.

Returning to the research itself, the authors deny that fatigue caused any problems in the relay assembly room. Rest pauses produced increased output, not because they reduced fatigue, but because of their social function; it was their meaning that was important. Similarly, neither the physical conditions of the work nor the repetitive nature or monotony of the work was related to output rate. Monotony can be reduced by social interaction, but if this is restricted or proscribed, morbid preoccupations and daydreams may surface, to the detriment of output. Such obsessive thinking can breed complaints and grievances, as well.

Wage incentives and wage incentive systems were a continuing concern of the Hawthorne research. Yet the interpreters consistently felt that none of the results gave the slightest substantiation to the view that the workers were primarily motivated by economic interest. In fact, the interpreters contended that the efficacy of a wage incentive is so dependent on its tie to other factors that separating it out as an independent cause is impossible.

Mayo, as well as Roethlisberger, emphasized the importance of social needs and sentiments, in addition to economic needs, in work and productivity. They both stressed the role of informal groups and organizations and the need for equilibrium between these and the technical and formal organizations. Roethlisberger, in particular, was concerned with problems of communication, especially interpersonal communication (as between supervisor and worker). He stressed that communication and listening skills were crucial to effective managing (Roethlisberger, 1953).

Complications

Mayo, Roethlisberger, and Dickson said that the social factor had been badly overlooked, and that a full understanding of factory work required going beyond the considerations emphasized by scientific management to matters such as employee attitudes, social motives, and group processes (especially informal processes). Thus the human relations movement was born, and a major part of the foundation for the organizational behavior discipline was put in place. A number of larger companies soon instituted human relations training programs for supervisors, as well as attitude surveys (the Hawthorne interviewing program was one such approach) and counseling programs designed to improve employee attitudes. All these represented major influences on practice, and to a degree on theory as well.

The idea that industrialization had disrupted traditional social relationships was important in this thinking. Workers were frustrated in a social sense; informal groups, restriction of output, and the like represented their attempts to deal with social frustration. A new social code had to be reestablished to facilitate collaboration in industrial organizations. Without it, workers would continue to experience social deprivation and a kind of social pathology; productivity would suffer as a result. Here the interpretations became more tenuous; it is not clear that the Hawthorne research said this.

Skepticism on this score has accelerated over the years to the point where it is now widely accepted that Mayo, Roethlisberger, and Dickson went well beyond the Hawthorne data in setting forth their interpretations. This view is reflected in writings from a variety of political and disciplinary perspectives (Bramel & Friend, 1981; Yorks & Whitsett, 1985; Wren, 1987). One could argue that the Hawthorne data provided an inductive source from which the authors' theory was derived. There are two problems with this:

1. That is not what the authors said; they claimed that their interpretations reflected the actual results of the Hawthorne studies and that those studies validated their theories.
2. The authors' interpretations are a mixture of social philosophy and theory, and they are so generally stated that direct tests would be difficult. In particular, much of Mayo's writing is clearly social philosophy masquerading as science. In short, the interpretations are not really theories at all.

Many people have interpreted the Hawthorne research in ways that differ from the Harvard group's interpretations. In fact, interpreting the studies has become something of an intellectual game among scholars of the field, a game with few rules and many outcomes. I believe this has happened because the research was so poorly designed and conducted that its only product was ambiguity. Remember that the social factors the Harvard authors invoke were never measured in the experimental research at all. We simply do not know what happened at Hawthorne, why production rose in the relay assembly test room, and so on. We never will. The research was so out of control that it cannot yield answers.

One hope is that after-the-fact statistical analyses might salvage something. Mayo and Roethlisberger were not trained in statistics and offer little other than examples of raw data. Turner did carry out some early statistical analyses on the relay assembly test room data, but no evidence of important conclusions exists. Thomas North Whitehead (1938), an economist in the Harvard group, subjected the data to extensive analyses, repeating Turner's work and extending it in many directions. Yet there were few significant findings. No significant correlations could be established between the various independent variables and the dependent variable of output. Because there were no measures of the social factors considered in the interpretations, their impact could not be assessed in any meaningful manner, although Whitehead tried to do so using the output data.

Much later Richard Franke and James Kaul (1978) carried out extensive statistical analyses on the original data, using techniques not available at the time of the studies themselves. These analyses played up the significance of such factors as the replacement of subjects, the pay system, and the depression, but again the lack of measures of social factors confound the interpretations. The major conclusion from all of the statistical efforts has to be that one cannot compensate for basic deficiencies in research design and measurement in this manner.

Impact and Influence

The people whose names have come to be associated with the Hawthorne studies have backgrounds — although not very extensive ones — in medicine, philosophy, psychology, and economics. None held a doctorate, and none had been trained in research. Yet these people concentrated on the study of behavior in organizations at a point in time when few had such interests. Furthermore, they trained others in human relations and, in fact, established a school of thought around that viewpoint. Many people today tend to associate these views with sociology, and the followers of the Hawthorne researchers tend to identify with that field. Yet the reality is that Hawthorne attracted a multidisciplinary hodgepodge.

Some idea of the influence on organizational behavior exerted from Hawthorne may be obtained by looking into the fiftieth anniversary volume (Cass & Zimmer, 1975). Although the research itself was severely flawed, the ideas that grew up around it have had a significant effect on the field of organizational behavior. Of the 16 professional papers in the anniversary book, 9 are authored by major organizational behavior theorists of that time. All nine either recognize the importance of Hawthorne for their own work or for related developments in the field. The names of these theorists are Paul Lawrence, Robert Kahn, Edgar Schein, Richard Hackman, Edward Lawler, Harry Levinson, Fred Fiedler, Victor Vroom, and Jay Lorsch. Of these, the direct lineage from Hawthorne is most in evidence for Lawrence and Lorsch who received their doctorates from the Harvard Business School and remained there. Yet the truly significant conclusion is that this diverse array of theorists, from a wide range of backgrounds and orientations, identify Hawthorne as a major intellectual building block of organizational behavior.

An interesting point, however, involves the citations the anniversary volume's authors make to Hawthorne's cast of characters. Roethlisberger and Dickson are cited frequently; yet Mayo appears but once — in Robert Kahn's (1975) paper on the "Hawthorne effect," which interprets that effect as primarily a matter of participation in decision making. The inescapable conclusion is that Mayo's direct effect on the field seems to have paled over the years. There can be no doubt that during the 1930s and 1940s Mayo was at the height of his influence. I do not know why this influence has declined, but I believe it has. It may be that his message was especially attuned to the problems of his time and lost impact as new ideas thrust their way to the fore (see O'Connor, 1999).

BARNARD'S VIEWS
ON MANAGEMENT

Now we consider the views of Chester Barnard, a product of a very different background, who was associated in his scholarly period with the same group at Harvard. As is the case in this chapter, the Barnard scenario extends across both business practice and the academic world. He has exerted influence on a number of aspects of organizational behavior, but particularly on work related to managerial decision making (Simon, 1991).

Barnard's career overlapped with those of the Hawthorne researchers, both temporally and geographically. His speeches and writings span four decades — from the 1920s to the 1950s. However, his most important contribution was the widely acclaimed book *The Functions of the Executive* (Barnard, 1938). This book and another containing his addresses and papers, *Organization and Management* (Barnard, 1948) provide the basis for this discussion. In addition, I have drawn heavily on the treatments of Barnard's life and writings by William Wolf (1974) and William Scott (1992).

To place Barnard's ideas in context, it is important to know that he spent his entire career either becoming, or serving as, a top-level executive. Thus, essentially, his writings represented an avocation. He wrote from his experience, his reading of the work of others, and his personal contacts, primarily with scholars on the Harvard faculty. He was not a researcher; he viewed himself as a theorist, and in many respects he was, but his writings contain a goodly amount of untestable philosophy as well. Thus I refer to his "views" on management in the title of this section.

Background

Barnard grew up in a poor, but highly intellectual family. At an early age he showed a preference for elite organizational affiliations, the first example of which was attending Mount Hermon, one of the better-known New England prep schools. Subsequently, he went on to Harvard, where he majored in economics. Based on this fact and other considerations as well, some economists have claimed Barnard as one of their own (see, for example, Williamson, 1990). However, he himself had serious misgivings about the value of economics for understanding organizations, and it is clear that his thinking was influenced more by people outside that field than from those within it.

In 1909, just short of his degree, Barnard terminated his studies at Harvard. Clearly, his limited means were a major factor that contributed to this decision. He obtained a job in the Statistical Department at AT&T and rapidly emerged as an expert on telephone rates. He remained in a corporate staff capacity for over 10 years, moving then to a position as vice president with Pennsylvania Bell. He became president of the newly formed New Jersey Bell Telephone Company at the age of 41, and he held this position for over 20 years.

In 1948 Barnard left New Jersey Bell to become president of the Rockefeller Foundation. He remained in this position until he reached the mandatory retirement age of 65. Subsequently, he served for a number of years on the board of the federal government's National Science Foundation. Although it was a part-time position, this work demanded a great deal of his time, particularly during his four years as chairman. He retired from this position in 1956 and died 5 years later, at the age of 74.

The Pareto Circle

The Pareto Circle was an informal group of scholars centered in the Harvard Business School. The membership changed somewhat during the 1930s and early 1940s when the circle existed, but all were men of considerable academic stature. Among them were Elton Mayo and Fritz Roethlisberger, sociologists George Homans and Talcott Parsons, anthropologist Clyde Kluckhohn, psychologist Henry Murray, and economist Joseph Schumpeter. The leader and driving force behind the group was Lawrence Henderson, a noted biochemist with an M.D. degree who was housed in the business school and taught sociology there. Barnard was not a full-fledged member of the circle, having more of an adjunct status, since his major employer was New Jersey Bell. However, he was frequently at Harvard serving on committees, giving lectures, and talking with faculty members. He was influenced considerably by the Pareto Circle, and, in turn, he influenced the thinking of several of its members, including his friend Henderson. Actually Barnard's initial entrée to his Harvard relationships came through his efforts to raise money to endow professorships there. This led to his being appointed to an advisory committee and ultimately to his Pareto Circle ties (Wren & Greenwood, 1998).

As a group, the members were politically conservative, and a major force in drawing them together was a desire to refute the rising influence of Karl Marx at a point during the depression when his views had widespread acceptance among the Harvard faculty. The focal point for their discussions and writings was a book by the Italian sociologist Vilfredo Pareto (1935). Pareto emphasized concepts such as social systems, social equilibrium, cooperation rather than the class conflict of Marx, and elite leadership. We have already seen many of these ideas in Mayo's interpretations of the Hawthorne research. Pareto's book seemed to provide an ideological defense against the rising tide of Marxism (Keller, 1984). Barnard's own conservatism, as well as his desires for the stimulus of academic association and an elite reference group, drew him to this circle. His views, like those of Mayo, were strongly influenced by Pareto's writings and the circle's interpretation of them.

Scholar-Manager Combination

Barnard was almost unique among scholars of his time in that his primary career was that of manager, not academician. This brought him knowledge and a perspective that others could not emulate; the unusual combination involved made for a great many creative ideas, ideas that have had an immeasurable impact on organizational behavior. But was Barnard as effective as a manager as he turned out to be as a scholar?

The answer is that, although he had many strengths, he probably was not as effective. A number of those who worked for him at New Jersey Bell appear to have been lukewarm about his skill as a manager, viewing him as a better staff man (which he was for many years) than a line executive. Also, in spite of being on a fast track destined for promotion to the highest levels of corporate management, with the president of the company his mentor, he ended his AT&T career with one of the operating companies, not corporate headquarters. New Jersey Bell itself failed to produce a profit picture that equaled several other operating companies during his tenure. Return on invested capital was in the 7% range in the early years, but it declined to 1% as he left for the Rockefeller Foundation.

One possible reason for Barnard's lackluster performance as a company manager is that he did not devote his full energies to managing. Throughout his business career he was frequently involved in outside activities—serving on and for a variety of associations, boards, committees, councils, commissions, and administrations. He held several governmental appointments and was president of the United Service Organizations (USO) during World War II. All this required many absences, often of considerable duration, and much delegating to those who covered for him at New Jersey Bell. Furthermore, Barnard did a great deal of reading related to his scholarly pursuits and wrote extensively, although more frequently in the form of speeches and for private distribution than for publication (Wolf, 1974, lists 108 articles, lectures, and manuscripts). With the time spent at Harvard, these outside activities would seem to have stretched the man rather thin insofar as his New Jersey Bell work was concerned. It looks very much as if he enjoyed being a scholar and working in outside roles that challenged his intellect more than managing his company. He does not appear to fit the picture of the man of action that characterized the most successful managers of the period (Locke, 2000).

Theory and Philosophy

Barnard's views are expressed not as a single formulation with a rich network of relationships between variables, but for the most part as a set of independent topic discussions, consistent with the fact that the initial mode of their presentation was a lecture series. The primary such treatments are considered below.

Open Systems Concepts and Cooperation

If there is an overarching concept, this is it: Formal organization is a type of cooperation that at its best is conscious, deliberate, and purposeful. To achieve this cooperation, changes must be made in the motives of organization members, changes that without such efforts would not occur. When favorable to the cooperative system, these motive changes become resources to the system. Cooperative systems must somehow create a surplus of member satisfactions. If the member gets back from the cooperative system only what is put in, no incentive or net satisfaction exists and cooperation is unlikely.

An organizational system is composed of the activities of human beings. These activities become a system by virtue of the fact that they are coordinated. The activities are not confined to the behavior of members or employees of the organization. They include anything that represents a contribution or receipt of energy by the system—a customer making a purchase, a supplier delivering supplies, an investor providing capital. Organizational systems of this kind have the characteristics of any system. Thus, they are entities that must be treated as a whole because each part is related to every other; the components are accordingly interdependent variables.

Formal and Informal Organization

A formal organization is defined as a system of consciously coordinated activities or forces of two or more people. The survival of this organization requires maintaining equilibrium, both internally and in rela-

tion to the external situation. In fact, the services, behavior, and influences of people are what constitute the organization, and, consequently, there must be a willingness on the part of people to contribute effort to the cooperative system. This willingness cannot develop without an objective for cooperation—what is believed by the organization's contributors to be its purpose. Communication is the means by which the common purpose is established.

The communication system is a system of objective authority and operates on certain principles:

1. Channels of communication should be clearly established and known.
2. A definite formal channel of communication to every organizational member should exist.
3. The line of communication should be as direct or short as possible.
4. The complete line of communication should be used so that no points on the line are bypassed.
5. People such as officers and supervisors, who serve as communication centers, should be competent.
6. The line of communication should be kept constantly open when the organization is functioning.
7. Every communication should be authenticated so that the communicator is actually known to occupy a position of authority.

Complex organizations are built out of basic units overlaid with units of executive structure. The size of units is determined by the limitations of effective leadership. In turn, these limitations depend on the complexity of both purpose and technology, the difficulty of communication, the extent to which communication is needed, and the complexity of existing interpersonal relations. Thus spans of control are established.

The defining characteristic of informal organization is that it occurs and continues without a conscious joint purpose. However, common or joint results may well occur. This type of organization establishes various attitudes, understandings, customs, and the like; it also creates conditions that may give rise to formal organization. Within the context of formal organizations informal groupings have the functions of fostering communication, maintaining cohesiveness, and providing for feelings of personal integrity and independent choice. Informal organization may occur at the executive level, as well as among workers, where it serves to ensure compatibility of personnel and a degree of fit within the executive ranks. It represents the political aspects of personal relationships within formal organizations, and it serves a useful purpose in communicating opinions and suspicions that cannot pass through formal channels. A fully developed informal executive organization appears indispensable to the effective functioning of the formal organization.

Incentives and Authority

One way an organization may secure contributions is through providing inducements. Inducements may be in the form of material things, such as money; personal nonmaterial opportunities, such as prestige or power; desirable physical conditions of work; ideal benefactions, such as pride of workmanship and a sense of loyalty; associational attractiveness in the sense of social compatibility at work; adaptation of conditions to established habits and attitudes of members; the opportunity for enlarged participation in significant events; or the condition of communion, whereby people feel a sense of social integration and mutual support. In general, material rewards, particularly money, are ineffective beyond a minimal subsistence level.

If an organization is not in a position to provide incentives of these kinds sufficient to obtain the required contributions, the alternative is to resort to persuasion. Under the category of persuasion, Barnard notes the following: coercion by force; the rationalization of opportunity through various types of propaganda and appeals to existing motives; and inculcation of motives, via education and cultural indoctrination.

Organizations are effective primarily because they can achieve *cooperative* efforts from a number of individuals who, as a total, integrated system, represent more than the sum of the individual efforts. Individuals are induced to contribute to such a cooperative system through the use of various incentives, including pay. One of the things they give is a willingness to follow authority. Thus Barnard's view of authority is bottom up and by the consent of the governed. Individuals decide what range of authority they will let the organization exercise over them and thus accept; within this range they will do whatever they are told — this is termed the *zone of indifference*. The size of this zone is influenced by the inducements offered: the more the organization gives, the wider the range of personal discretion the individual is willing to give up.

How this *acceptance theory* of authority and the zone of indifference work may be illustrated from the consulting field. A consultant working for a large firm expects to be away from home overnight during the regular workweek, and it is a matter of indifference whether this involves being sent to Seattle, St. Louis, or San Antonio. However, spending weekends away from home is another matter; such a requirement would meet with considerable resistance. But a change in inducements — perhaps the offer of a partnership in the firm — could shift the balance in this regard so that contributing weekends away from home, when requested by the managing partner, might well be accepted with no questions at all.

Communications have the presumption of authority when they originate in a communications center and are within the scope of that center, as well as relevant to the situations recipients face. This is the *authority of position*. However, there are some individuals who, because of superior ability, are able to exercise authority regardless of position. This type of reliance on personal respect to obtain contributions is the *authority of leadership*. When these two are combined, people generally will grant considerable authority, accepting orders that extend far beyond the zone of indifference.

Decision Making

Free will is limited in part because the power of choice disappears if the number of equal opportunities is large. Thus, in many areas the processes of decision are essentially means of narrowing choices to the point where humans can deal with them. The capacity of most people to make decisions is quite narrow.

Acts of decision involving logical processes are characteristic of organizational behavior more than of individual behavior. Within organizations, the decision process deals with, first, the choice of whether to contribute effort. Second, there are decisions of a nonpersonal nature that relate to organizational effects and purposes. The latter may be delegated, while the former may not. In this connection Barnard endorses the position that executives should not decide questions that are not immediately pertinent, should not make decisions prematurely, should not make decisions that cannot be implemented, and should not decide matters that others should decide.

The analysis required for an organizational decision is in essence a search for strategic factors. These are the factors whose control will establish new systems or sets of conditions that meet the needs of the purpose at hand. The discrimination of strategic factors is largely a technological matter that depends on the procurement of methods of magnifying details. Among these methods are chemical analysis, mechanical analysis, telescopes, statistical processes, and, above all in the business world, balance sheets.

Although he recognizes and extols logical reasoning for a number of purposes, Barnard also has many good things to say of nonlogical processes and intuition. In numerous cases we make decisions in a nonrational manner and then impute rational processes to the outcomes. This type of *rationalization* leads to a general deprecation of nonlogical process and an exaggeration of the degree of rationality that exists in the world. Here Barnard seems to be closely allied with Mayo, and both clearly take their lead from Pareto.

Executive Functions

Executive functions serve to maintain the system of cooperative effort. As Barnard presents them, they differ substantially from the management functions proposed by many other writers. The first function involves providing a system of communication. Inherent in this function are two tasks — to create positions as communication centers, and to select people to fill these positions who will communicate effectively. Either may be changed on occasion to perfect the total communication process by adjusting one to the other. The second function is to promote the securing of essential efforts (personal services) from individuals. This involves bringing people into a cooperative relationship with the organization through recruiting; then eliciting the necessary services, after people have been brought into the relationship, by arranging for appropriate inducements and incentives. Finally, the third function is to formulate and define purpose. This requires the assignment of responsibility and the delegation of authority. The organization established to define purpose is an organization that specifies the work to be done.

This three-pronged executive process is devoted to the integration of the whole: to finding the effective balance or equilibrium between local and broad factors, between general and specific requirements.

Status Systems and Leadership

By 1938 Barnard had not tackled the question of status systems, but later he did turn his attention to the subject. There are two types of these systems. The first type of status system is *functional*. It is lateral or horizontal in nature, and here status depends on the particular function performed or, better, the potential for performing a function. Those with functional status are viewed as experts, able to give advice in a particular field; they are seen as specialists or professionals who have expert knowledge by virtue of their education and particular experience. The second type of status system is *scalar*. Here the system is vertical in nature, and status is determined by superiority or subordination in a chain of command (formal authority), as well as by the nature and extent of assigned jurisdiction.

Status is established and maintained by various ceremonies, insignia, titles, perquisites, and restrictions of office. Status considerations are a constant matter of concern for executives, particularly with regard to the system of organizational communication and the system of incentives, along with being a means of fixing responsibility. Status systems have their origins in differences in the acquired characteristics of people, in the varying difficulties of particular activities, and in the social evaluation of these activities.

As distinct from authority, Barnard had relatively little to say about leadership by 1938, but his comments later are interesting. He notes that the democratic process adds greatly to the complexities of leadership. The leader must not only deal with the technical situation external to the organization and the internal operative organizational situation, but now with the democratically produced majority opinion and often with various minority positions as well. These political factors can produce so many complications that it is common practice (especially in business) to exclude much of what is done from the democratic process. There are many instances where the introduction of democracy is clearly superior, but in many other situations (such as those involving crisis or danger) democracy is an inferior approach and cannot be practiced effectively. This should be recognized.

Responsibility and Morality

Responsibility is the power of a private code of morals to control the behavior of an individual in the face of strong contrary desires. Responsibility is thus that aspect of an individual through which whatever morality is present becomes effective in behavior. The private code of morals that derives from a formal organization is an aspect of the organization personality and also of the zone of indifference. An important feature of executive work is that it imposes the need to create moral codes for others, above and beyond one's own moral code. In this connection, it is widely recognized that executives are expected to create (secure, inspire) morale in an organization.

Toward the end of his life Barnard (1958) returned to these ethical issues. Because they are social systems, organizations give expression to (reflect) the mores, culture patterns, assumptions, convictions, unconscious beliefs, and the like that make these organizations largely autonomous moral institutions on which instrumental political, economic, religious, or other functions are then superimposed. In the case of various specialized functions, such as those of the executive, it is very difficult to convey to outsiders the nature of the moral problems that exist. Public misunderstanding of organizations is due primarily to a lack of appreciation of the moral elements that are involved in various specialized activities and to the great difficulty of explaining what these moral elements are. One gets the impression that Barnard feels that only fellow executives can understand and deal with the moral conflicts inherent in executive work; outsiders simply do not understand.

Impact and Influence

Barnard's views and writings have had a tremendous impact. He brought a new view to the scholarship of organizations—a special combination of sociology, psychology, economics, and practical managerial experience. Many of the first-generation theories of organizational behavior have been enhanced by the thinking of this man.

Nevertheless, it is well to recognize that there are those who find his unreconstructed managerialism excessive. Scott's comments in this regard are to the point:

> I am ambivalent about Barnard. On the one hand, I am suspicious of the concentrated organizational power that he advocated, and I detest an elitism based on it. I find the subordination of an individual's moral character to the imperatives of con-

trived organizational collectives, which he also recommended, a repugnant idea. On the other hand, his intellect, his vast accomplishments in the affairs of business, government, philanthropy, and public service, his prodigious writings, and his profound personal integrity impress me beyond telling. (1992, p. xii)

I do not find in Barnard's published writings the elitism that Scott notes, but elitism of this kind was clearly in evidence within the Pareto Circle at Harvard. To the degree that Barnard's influence has been less than it might have been, his identification with and championing of a managerial class appear to be responsible.

I have noted that Barnard had a strong influence on Herbert Simon and his formulations regarding decision-making processes. Simon repeatedly acknowledges this influence in his *Administrative Behavior* (1947). In fact, Barnard critically reviewed the original manuscript for that book and wrote a foreword for the first edition. Simon's views on the decision to participate in an organization and on organizational authority derive from Barnard. In many respects, Simon took the abstract philosophizing of Barnard and converted it into testable propositions that could be subjected to scientific research.

Barnard's acceptance theory of authority has had wide appeal among those who developed theories that support participative management—what has more recently come to be called *empowerment*—in organizations. This includes the theorists led by Rensis Likert who worked together at the University of Michigan, as well as a number of advocates of organization development. These people were clearly strongly influenced by Kurt Lewin to whom we will turn next, and he is their major intellectual parent, but Barnard is widely cited by them as well. He also had considerable impact on systems theorists of all persuasions (see Katz & Kahn, 1978; Thompson, 1967).

Barnard's unique contribution was that he was able to combine a first-hand, personal knowledge of managing in a large corporation with not only scholarly knowledge but also a particular type of scholarship that is attuned to the values and viewpoints of the times. His ties to Harvard, the Pareto Circle, and the Hawthorne researchers provided a perspective that made his writings much more broadly acceptable than would likely have been the case otherwise for a practicing manager. When two streams of ideas that have not previously been placed in close proximity are combined like this, the result is usually a creative flaring. Certainly it was in Barnard's case.

LEWIN: PERSONALITY THEORY AND SOCIAL PSYCHOLOGY ARRIVE

Kurt Lewin, the subject of this section, exhibits some of the effects of a similar combining of disparate perspectives. However, the disparate factors involved in his contributions were quite different in nature.

Lewin was trained as a psychologist; he was a researcher, as well as a theorist. His contributions to psychology were eclectic in terms of area, and it was only toward the end of his life that he concentrated on the social psychological studies and ideas that make him particularly relevant for organizational behavior. Barnard apparently read Lewin and was influenced by his views on field theory, which closely approximated those of Barnard and the Pareto Circle regarding open systems theory (Wolf, 1973).

Early in his career Lewin's major contributions were in the area of personality theory. He wrote several books on that subject during this period and established himself as a major theorist (Hall & Lindzey, 1957). However, his interest in personality theory gradually gave way to social psychology, in particular to group dynamics and action research. He was a man of broad humanist sympathies and democratic values, differing in his political perspective rather sharply from Mayo and Barnard. In the late 1930s and 1940s, when his writings of most relevance for organizational behavior appeared, Lewin wrote primarily in the form of journal articles and papers in edited volumes.

Background

Lewin's life was split into two distinct phases. In the early period, spread over 43 years (1890 to 1933), Lewin was based in Germany. In the later period, from 1933 to 1947, when he died in an automobile accident, Lewin lived and worked in the United States. Lewin was Jewish, and he moved to this country because he foresaw the persecution that was to come under Hitler and the Nazis.

In Germany

Lewin was born in Prussia and attended the Universities of Freiberg and Munich before receiving his doctorate from the University of Berlin in 1914. He served for 4 years in the German army during World War I and then returned to Berlin, where he rose to a professorship in 1926. He was strongly influenced during the German years by the Gestalt psychologists with whom he worked, including Max Wertheimer and Wolfgang Köhler. Over time he developed a group around himself at the Psychological Institute of the University of Berlin, consisting of a number of like-minded scholars.

During this German period Lewin published some articles that presaged his later social psychology (Papanek, 1973). One paper dealt with job design in farm work, while another focused on humanizing the activities of factory workers employed under Taylor's scientific management. There was a theme of job enrichment in these papers and also in several additional studies of the field of forces that operated on individual textile workers. These early papers illustrated Lewin's use of field theoretic concepts, linked laboratory experiments to applied problems (action research), and focused on individuals not groups.

Early in the 1930s Lewin was invited to Stanford University by Lewis Terman, originator of the Stanford-Binet tests. He returned to Germany, but apparently this visit set in motion a process that shortly resulted in a permanent move to the United States.

In the United States

Presumably as a consequence of his association with Terman and of some research he had conducted in the area, Lewin came to the United States perceived as a specialist in child development. He first joined the School of Home Economics at Cornell University as a child psychologist, and after 2 years he moved to the Child Welfare Research Station at the University of Iowa. Both of these positions were generously funded by the Rockefeller Foundation. At Iowa Lewin began to concentrate more on groups rather than on individuals, and again, as in Berlin, he surrounded himself with a group of scholars, many of whom joined him in his research (Ash, 1992).

At Iowa Lewin moved increasingly toward a kind of industrial social psychology that was focused on groups and action research. To further this objective, he ultimately moved to the Massachusetts Institute of Technology in Cambridge where he became director of the Research Center for Group Dynamics, whose funding was arranged primarily by Lewin himself.

Again he created a group of young scholars interested in the topics that he found interesting. After Lewin's death the center moved briefly to Syracuse University and then on to the University of Michigan where it became part of Rensis Likert's Institute for Social Research (Cannell & Kahn, 1984). Over the years the center served to foster Lewin's early work on sensitivity training and T-groups through the development of the National Training Laboratories (NTL) and also established a long informal exchange with the Tavistock Institute of Human Relations in England. An outgrowth of this relationship was joint publication of the journal *Human Relations*. Thus Lewin's influence was extended in many directions.

Contributions Relevant for Organizational Behavior

Lewin typically formulated many of his field-theoretic ideas in terms of mathematical symbols and spatial diagrams. The most widely cited of his mathematical formulations is $B = f(P,E)$ — that is, behavior is a functional interaction of person and environment. However, many such formulas are sprinkled throughout his works, as are life-space diagrams and forcefield pictures (see, for example, Lewin, 1943).

How important these accoutrements really are to his theorizing is a serious question. They appear to represent a personal language that serves to describe what is already known much more than to predict experimental results. Although they may foster understanding, and many who have struggled with them may have major doubts even on that score, these after-the-fact formulas and diagrams in and of themselves clearly are not predictive theoretical statements or hypotheses. Lewin's field theory is not a mathematical theory in spite of the symbolic nomenclature used to present it (Hall & Lindzey, 1957). Thus, in the following I will utilize only the verbal language.

Leadership Climates

Conclusions on the effects of varying leadership climates were derived from experimental research conducted at the University of Iowa (Lewin, Lippitt, & White, 1939; Lippitt & White, 1958). This research served to establish Lewin's reputation in the United States. In it the effects of authoritarian (German) and democratic (American) leadership climates were contrasted. The research reflects in a microcosm the pattern of Lewin's own life and is a direct outgrowth of the juxtaposition of the two cultures. In addition, the study, apparently as a result of a misunderstanding among the researchers (Wren, 1994), came to include a laissez-faire condition or climate as well.

The ways in which these three climates were put into operation are set forth in table 2.2. In the major study, the four groups experienced all three climates in succession; thus comparisons could be made across groups and also within groups (using a group as its own control). The subjects were 11-year-old boys grouped into 5-member clubs that met after school to participate in various activities — mask-making, mural painting, soap carving, model airplane construction, and the like — over an experimental period of 5 months.

Clubs were matched on patterns of interpersonal relationships; intellectual, physical, and socioeconomic status; and personality characteristics to control for these factors. The four adult leaders were systematically assigned across climate conditions and clubs. The behaviors and conversations of both leaders and club members were recorded in detail by four observers. These were then categorized for purposes of quantitative analysis. The interrater agreement of the observers was .84. Observations of leader behaviors, and reports obtained from the boys, indicated that the experimental conditions did in fact "take."

The findings with regard to aggression in the authoritarian groups were mixed — in some clubs manifestations of aggression were very frequent and in other clubs they were very infrequent (apathy). Democracy seemed to produce a mid-range frequency of aggressive expression and laissez-faire a rather high level (presumably because there was no control on emotional expression from either the leader or the group). The democratic climate was much liked, the authoritarian much disliked, and on-balance the laissez-faire context was more liked than disliked.

Achievement levels were much higher under the authoritarian and democratic climates than under laissez-faire. The lack of accomplishment in the latter instance was clearly evident to the boys and a source of dissatisfaction. They talked about doing better, but could not coordinate their efforts to do so. The major difference between authoritarian and democratic groups was that in the first instance productivity dropped off sharply when the leader left the room; in the democratic clubs it did not. As a whole, the results seemed to offer strong confirmation of the hypothesis

TABLE 2.2 Methods used to create leadership climates

Functions	Authoritarian climate	Democratic climate	Laissez-faire climate
Policy determination	By the leader	By group discussion and decision, assisted by the leader	Freedom for group or individual decision without leader participation
Task activities	Techniques and steps dictated by the leader one at a time	Perspective gained during first discussion; steps to goal sketched by group; technical advice provided by the leader in the form of multiple alternatives from which group made choices	Materials supplied by leader; leader indicated he would supply information if asked; leader not involved in work discussions
Division of labor and companions	Dictated by the leader	Members chose own work companions and group decided division of labor	No participation by the leader
Praise and criticism by leader	Personal by leader; aloof from group participation; friendly or impersonal, not hostile	Objective or fact-minded; a regular group member, but without doing a lot of the actual work	Very infrequent; only when questioned; no participation in course of the work

that democratic leadership climates are to be preferred.

Change Processes

Working from these findings on the value of group decision and democratic process, Lewin (1947, 1958) developed a theoretical structure to deal with change processes and carried out a program of research on change. The result was a good theory that has indeed turned out to be very practical (see chapter 1). It has served for many years as a guide for organizational development practitioners (Goldstein, 1993; Marshak, 1993). Recent work suggests that Lewin's force-field analysis applies within a limited domain and that there are situations beyond the boundaries of that domain in which Lewin's views are less applicable. Nevertheless, this is a theory that has moved application a long way.

The research on change was initially conducted to foster changes in eating habits necessitated by World War II shortages. Housewives were identified as the gatekeepers whose decisions would have to be altered if broader change were to occur. The research design involved exposing groups of housewives to attractive lectures that linked nutrition to the war effort and attempted to persuade them to change the eating habits of their families. Another set of groups was given the same information, but the leader rapidly moved to a group discussion of how "housewives like ourselves" might react to the prospect of change. A group decision was reached in the sense that there was a show of hands as to who would commit to initiating the change.

This experimental approach was used to increase the use of beef hearts, sweetbreads, and kidneys; to expand home consumption of fresh and evaporated milk; and to foster giving cod liver oil and orange juice to their babies by new mothers. Other studies used similar designs to study changes in the productivity levels of factory sewing-machine operators and the decision to eat whole wheat rather than white bread by members of a students' eating cooperative. In all of these instances, the evidence provided strong support for the use of group decision techniques in bringing about change.

The underlying theory states that before change the force field is in equilibrium between forces favorable to change and those resisting it; or, as Lewin preferred to say, a quasi-stationary social equilibrium exists. For change to occur, this equilibrium must be disturbed, either by adding forces favoring the desired change or by diminishing opposing forces. Ultimately, a new equilibrium is established, but in the former case at a high tension level and in the latter case at a low tension level. Since high tension has the potential for aggressiveness, emotionality, and a lack of constructiveness, diminishing resistance to change is usually the preferred approach to change. Group decision appears to be such an approach. Figure 2.1 provides a picture of Lewin's force-field analysis.

Social habits represent inner resistances to change. The inner resistance must be unfrozen, usually by the action of some party external to the group, which is called an environmental force. Groups hold to standards that can represent forces against change. If an individual varies widely from such a standard, that person will be ridiculed, punished, and ultimately rejected from group membership. Assuming a desire for group membership in good standing, members can be expected to hold closely to the standards of the group. However, if the group standards can be modified in some way, then the individual would be expected to change as well so as to stay close to them. This is what group decision is about—modifying group-based habits that serve to resist change.

This whole process may be conceptualized as one of, first, *unfreezing* the existing level; second, *moving* to a new level; and, third, *freezing* group life on the new level so that a permanent and stable equilibrium that resists further change is established. Unfreezing is often difficult and may require different approaches under varying conditions. Accordingly, merely applying the group decision approach—to increase factory production standards, for instance—without a thorough study of the circumstances, is unlikely to prove effective.

Lewin and Paul Grabbe (1945) note that one way to change an aspect of an individual is for that person to accept membership in a new group, a new culture, with different standards and values. New perceptions result from new identifications and memberships. How-

ever, for these changes to occur, the new group and culture cannot be forced on the person; that only creates hostility. Belongingness to the new group must be experienced as an "in-group" feeling. To achieve this, the group must be voluntarily chosen. It has been noted that people who at one point in their lives identify with the far left end of the political spectrum (socialism, communism) may at another point come to identify with arch-conservative causes at the opposite pole. Lewin attributes these types of changes to shifting group identifications and memberships. New values are accepted as the individual comes to experience belongingness in a new in-group.

Expansion of Agenda

As his ideas regarding group decision making, democratic leadership, and change developed, Lewin expanded his activities into the national arena (Marrow, 1969, 1972). He was instrumental in organizing the Society for the Psychological Study of Social Issues, which united various liberal groupings within the American Psychological Association and promoted action research beyond the universities. During World War II he did morale research for the military, then community research for the American Jewish Committee. All this eventuated in his move to MIT and the Center for Group Dynamics. In this period he established a relationship with Alfred Marrow, a psychologist who also headed the family firm known as Harwood Manufacturing Company. Harwood, a textile firm, became the site for a number of well-known studies that were carried out by researchers from the Center for Group Dynamics, but it was Lewin who first developed the contact in order to extend his research into the industrial arena.

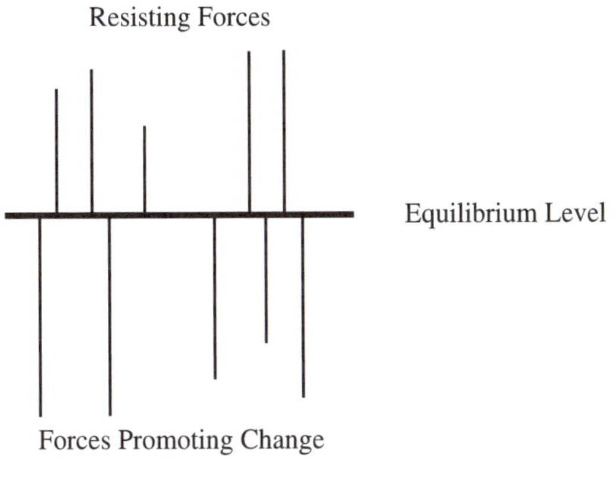

FIGURE 2.1 Kurt Lewin's force field analysis of the change process

Another manifestation of action research was the development of sensitivity training and T-groups. This innovation is usually traced to a workshop conducted at Connecticut State Teachers College in New Britain in 1946 by Lewin and others from the Center for Group Dynamics (Bradford, Gibb, & Benne, 1964). However, it is apparent that Lewin was doing something very similar several years before at Iowa (Papanek, 1973). T-groups are often very useful as a method of unfreezing resistances in a group. The lack of structure and ambiguity create a fertile ground for new learning and new values. Clearly, in the latter years of his life Lewin moved from theory and university-based research to action research that was intended to produce changes in the world around him. He often advocated engaging the subjects of research in the design and conduct of the studies in which they participated in order to foster a sense of "ownership" of the results and thus to facilitate change.

Level of Aspiration

Lewin's statements regarding level of aspiration are important as they relate to subsequent theory and research in the area of goal setting. They are thus somewhat separate from the work on leadership climates and change processes, although field theory continues to be employed. Lewin himself was primarily a theorist in this area, and based his formulations on the research of others (Lewin, 1936; Lewin, Dembo, Festinger, & Sears, 1944).

Levels within a person's goal structure may include a dream goal, a somewhat more realistic wish goal, the goal sought when an effort to be objective is involved, and a minimal goal should bad luck be operating. Somewhere on this scale is what the person really tries for at the time in a given situation — the action goal. Also some ideal goals will be established above this. Knowledge of one's standing relative to a group will have an influence here, as will individual differences with respect to seeking success and avoiding failure.

Three variables appear to play a primary role in setting goals — the seeking of success, the avoiding of failure, and a cognitive factor representing a probability judgment. These factors operate in a context involving a choice of future objective. The strength (valence) of the success and failure variables and the value of the subjective probability estimate depend on numerous factors in the life space, particularly the way past experience with the task is viewed, the standards introduced by group and cultural comparisons, and the individual's personality.

An example of how these factors may operate in practice is given by Marrow (1972), who describes a situation at Harwood on which Lewin offered his advice. The company had moved its operations from New England to Virginia and, as a consequence, had to train a large number of new machine operators. The standard for acceptable production under the piece rate system was 60 units, brought with the company from New England. However, a number of apprentices were having difficulty reaching this standard during training, and turnover was unusually high. Lewin suggested that the company look into the circumstances under which people who quit experienced success and failure.

There was ample evidence that desire for success was consistently high, but fear of failure seemed to accelerate over the training period. Over time, doubts seemed to arise as to whether the 60-unit goal was possible; progress slowed noticeably as that goal came into sight. The problem was not money, since the standard wage was guaranteed irrespective of production level. The closer they got to the goal, the less the apprentices expected to reach it. They saw how hard it was, and their cognitive probabilities of goal attainment shifted accordingly. A check on turnover rates indicated that for those who reached 30 units the figure was 20 percent; at 45 units it was up to 60 percent; at 55 units it was an unusually high 96 percent; over the goal of 60 units turnover dropped to 11 percent. As tension and frustrations spiraled upward, more and more apprentices left the field and became turnover casualties.

The solution was to eliminate the 60-unit goal and replace it with a series of short-range goals that rose slowly to the 60-unit figure, thus permitting a continuing feeling of success. When this change was made, turnover decreased by more than half, and the escalating tension so apparent previously was no longer in evidence. Fear of failure had declined, and probability judgments regarding goal attainment were higher. There was no longer a reason to leave the field.

Impact and Influence

As Wolf has noted:

[Lewin] has had a significant impact upon modern management. His concepts are widely used and his students are among the dominant contributors to human relations, personnel, and industrial psychology. Yet many students of management are completely unaware of Lewin and his contributions. His name is seldom mentioned in texts dealing with management or personnel relations. The failure to recognize Lewin's role in the evolving field of management is a serious neglect, for his philosophy of science, research methodology and approach provide a potential for advancing the discipline of management. Kurt Lewin was an innovative researcher whose ingenuity in experimental design provides a scientific basis for many of our current concepts. (1973, p. 322)

Within organizational behavior Lewin has had a major impact on organization development (Bennis, Benne, & Chin, 1961), on the various theories that serve to foster participative management (see, for instance, Emery & Trist, 1973), on work in the field of group dynamics (Cartwright & Zander, 1968), and on theorizing related to goal setting (Locke & Latham, 1990). However, among those noted here as contributors to the origins of organizational behavior, Lewin is the only one who was trained in the conduct of science and was able to carry out significant research himself. Perhaps his greatest contribution was in bringing science to our field.

Lewin brought science to the study of organizations, but he also brought humanistic and democratic values as well. In many respects, his research supported his values. He was not guilty of using science to provide cachet for his personal philosophy, as Mayo and even some of Lewin's followers appear to have been.

Given what we know now, it is worthwhile to return to a question raised previously: Is Kurt Lewin a legitimate influential worthy of a keynote role in the annals of organizational behavior with the likes of Mayo, Barnard, and the others? I submit that he is, and that the evidence contained in this chapter provides sufficient justification. But then, why is it that his contribution has not been widely recognized? Why do those who chronicle the historical origins of the field fail to include his name?

One possibility is that Lewin's values served to limit his place in organizational behavior's history. He is, for instance, given chapter level treatment in several books that chronicle the history of ideas in various psychological subject areas — personality (Hall & Lindzey, 1957), learning (Hilgard, 1948), and ex-

perimental (Murphy, 1949). Perhaps his liberal values are more acceptable to psychology than to organizational behavior. Of the seven contributors considered in chapters 2 and 3, Lewin indeed would appear to be the farthest to the left politically. Yet organizational behavior historically has been anything but a bulwark of the right wing, and ideas such as Lewin's have been readily accepted in the field. The same can be said for his unique status among the seven as a psychologist and a research scientist. Psychology and research have permeated organizational behavior from its beginning; there seems little here to explain the rejection. The thought occurs that his being a Jew may have been a factor. However, the professions, of which organizational behavior is one, have provided a source of opportunity for Jews, not a place where discrimination operates to limit recognition (Korman, 1988).

Other hypotheses might be run up against the data in the same manner, and in all likelihood would fail to meet the test, just as those already considered have. My guess is that there really is no one factor that provides an explanation. Rather, I suspect that the key is that Kurt Lewin was so different from the others on so many grounds (other than being male). To date, at least, this is not the kind of person who fits whatever stereotypes we may have of the key influentials in organizational behavior's history.

CONCLUSIONS

The individuals of concern in this chapter brought a sprinkling of philosophy, management, sociology, and psychology to the study of organizational behavior. In large part each has influenced a different group of theories within the field so that this disciplinary segmentation was maintained into the next generation.

Mayo, Barnard, and Lewin made their major contributions in a period extending from the latter 1920s to the early 1950s. Thus they provide what amount to proximate contributions to the emergence of organizational behavior as a separate field. Their work was followed very closely by that emergence, and a number of their students and contemporaries were in the vanguard as organizational behavior came on the scene. In the next chapter we consider a group of contributors who are farther back in the temporal pipeline. Yet they are equally significant for the origins of organizational behavior.

References

Adams, Richard N., & Preiss, Jack J. (1960). *Human Organization Research: Field Relations and Techniques.* Homewood, IL: Dorsey.

Ash, Mitchell G. (1992). Cultural Contexts and Scientific Change in Psychology. *American Psychologist, 47,* 198–207.

Barnard, Chester I. (1938). *The Functions of the Executive.* Cambridge, MA: Harvard University Press.

Barnard, Chester I. (1948). *Organization and Management.* Cambridge, MA: Harvard University Press.

Barnard, Chester I. (1958). Elementary Conditions of Business Morals. *California Management Review, 1,* 1–13.

Bedeian, Arthur G. (1998). Exploring the Past. *Journal of Management History, 4*(1), 4–15.

Bennis, Warren G.; Benne, Kenneth D.; & Chin, Robert (1961). *The Planning of Change.* New York: Holt, Rinehart & Winston.

Blood, Milton R. (1994). The Role of Organizational Behavior in the Business School Curriculum. In J. Greenberg (Ed.), *Organizational Behavior: The State of the Science* (pp. 207–220). Hillsdale, NJ: Erlbaum..

Bradford, Leland P.; Gibb, Jack R.; & Benne, Ken D. (1964). *T-Group Theory and Laboratory Method.* New York: Wiley.

Bramel, Dana, & Friend, Ronald (1981). Hawthorne, the Myth of the Docile Worker, and Class Bias in Psychology. *American Psychologist, 36,* 867–878.

Cannell, Charles F., & Kahn, Robert L. (1984). Some Factors in the Origins and Development of the Institute for Social Research, the University of Michigan. *American Psychologist, 39,* 1256–1266.

Cartwright, Dorwin, & Zander, Alvin (1968). *Group Dynamics: Research and Theory.* New York: Harper & Row.

Cass, Eugene L., & Zimmer, Frederick G. (1975). *Man and Work in Society.* New York: Van Nostrand Reinhold.

Davis, Keith (1992). A Journey through Management in Transition. In Arthur G. Bedeian (Ed.), *Management Laureates: A Collection of Autobiographical Essays* (Vol. 1, pp. 269–400). Greenwich, CT: JAI Press.

Dickson, William J., & Roethlisberger, F. J. (1966). *Counseling in an Organization: A Sequel to the Hawthorne Researches.* Boston: Harvard University, Graduate School of Business Administration.

Emery, Fred E., & Trist, Eric L. (1973). *Towards a Social Ecology.* London: Plenum.

Franke, Richard H., & Kaul, James D. (1978). The Hawthorne Experiments: First Statistical Interpretations. *American Sociological Review, 43,* 623–643.

Gardner, Burleigh B., & Moore, David G. (1945). *Human Relations in Industry.* Homewood, IL: Irwin.

Gillespie, Richard (1991). *Manufacturing Knowledge: A History of the Hawthorne Experiments.* Cambridge: Cambridge University Press.

Gilmer, B. von Haller (1981). The Early Development of Industrial-Organizational Psychology. In Joseph A. Sgro (Ed.), *Virginia Tech Symposium on Applied Behavioral Science* (Vol. 1, pp. 3–16). Lexington, MA: D.C. Heath.

Goldstein, Jeffrey (1993). Beyond Lewin's Force Field: A New Model for Organizational Change Interventions. *Advances in Organization Development, 2,* 72–88.

Goodman, Paul S., & Whetten, David A. (1998). Fifty Years of Organizational Behavior from Multiple Perspectives. In Maurice F. Neufeld & Jean T. McKelvey (Eds.), *Industrial Relations at the Dawn of the New Millenium* (pp. 33–53). Ithaca: New York State School of Industrial and Labor Relations, Cornell University.

Greiner, Larry E. (1979). A Recent History of Organizational Behavior. In Steven Kerr (Ed.), *Organizational Behavior* (pp. 3–14). Columbus, OH: Grid.

Hall, Calvin S., & Lindzey, Gardner (1957). *Theories of Personality.* New York: Wiley.

Highhouse, Scott (1999). The Brief History of Personnel Counseling in Industrial-Organizational Psychology. *Journal of Vocational Behavior, 55,* 318–336.

Hilgard, Ernest R. (1948). *Theories of Learning.* New York: Appleton-Century-Crofts.

Kahn, Robert L. (1975). In Search of the Hawthorne Effect. In Eugene L. Cass & Frederick G. Zimmer (Eds.), *Man and Work in Society* (pp. 49–63). New York: Van Nostrand Reinhold.

Katz, Daniel, & Kahn, Robert L. (1978). *The Social Psychology of Organizations.* New York: Wiley.

Keller, Robert T. (1984). The Harvard "Pareto Circle" and the Historical Development of Organization Theory. *Journal of Management, 10,* 193–203.

Korman, Abraham K. (1988). *The Outsiders: Jews and Corporate America.* Lexington, MA: D.C. Heath.

Lawrence, Paul R. (1987). Historical Development of Organizational Behavior. In Jay W. Lorsch (Ed.), *Handbook of Organizational Behavior* (pp. 1–9). Englewood Cliffs, NJ: Prentice Hall.

Leavitt, Harold J. (1958). *Managerial Psychology: An Introduction to Individuals, Pairs, and Groups in Organizations.* Chicago: University of Chicago Press.

Lewin, Kurt (1936). Psychology of Success and Failure. *Occupations, 14,* 926–930.

Lewin, Kurt (1943). Defining the "Field at a Given Time." *Psychological Review, 50,* 292–310.

Lewin, Kurt (1947). Frontiers in Group Dynamics: Concept, Method and Reality in Social Science; Social Equilibria and Social Change. *Human Relations*, 1, 5–41.

Lewin, Kurt (1958). Group Decision and Social Change. In Eleanor E. Maccoby, Theodore M. Newcomb, & Eugene L. Hartley (Eds.), *Readings in Social Psychology* (pp. 197–211). New York: Henry Holt.

Lewin, Kurt; Dembo, Tamara; Festinger, Leon; & Sears, Pauline S. (1944). Level of Aspiration. In J. McVicker Hunt (Ed.), *Personality and the Behavior Disorders*, (pp. 333–378). New York: Ronald.

Lewin, Kurt, & Grabbe, Paul (1945). Conduct, Knowledge, and Acceptance of New Values. *Journal of Social Issues*, 1(3), 56–64.

Lewin, Kurt; Lippitt, Ronald; & White, Ralph K. (1939). Patterns of Aggressive Behavior in Experimentally Created "Social Climates." *Journal of Social Psychology*, 10, 271–299.

Lippitt, Ronald, & White, Ralph K. (1958). An Experimental Study of Leadership and Group Life. In Eleanor E. Maccoby, Theodore M. Newcomb, & Eugene L. Hartley (Eds.), *Readings in Social Psychology* (pp. 496–511). New York: Henry Holt.

Locke, Edwin A. (2000). *The Prime Movers—Traits of the Great Wealth Creators*. New York: AMACOM.

Locke, Edwin A., & Latham, Gary P. (1990). *A Theory of Goal Setting and Task Performance*. Englewood Cliffs, NJ: Prentice Hall.

Marrow, Alfred J. (1969). *The Practical Theorist: The Life and Work of Kurt Lewin*. New York: Basic Books.

Marrow, Alfred J. (1972). *The Failure of Success*. New York: AMACOM.

Marshak, Robert J. (1993). Lewin Meets Confucius: A Re-view of the OD Model of Change. *Journal of Applied Behavioral Science*, 29, 393–415.

Mayo, Elton (1933). *The Human Problems of an Industrial Civilization*. New York: Macmillan.

Mayo, Elton (1945). *The Social Problems of an Industrial Civilization*. Boston: Harvard University, Graduate School of Business Administration.

Miner, John B. (1971). *Management Theory*. New York: Macmillan.

Miner, John B. (1997). Participating in Profound Change. *Academy of Management Journal*, 40, 1421–1429.

Murphy, Gardner (1949). *Historical Introduction to Modern Psychology*. New York: Harcourt, Brace.

O'Connor, Ellen S. (1999). The Politics of Management Thought: A Case Study of the Harvard Business School and the Human Relations School. *Academy of Management Review*, 24, 117–131.

Papanek, Miriam Lewin (1973). Kurt Lewin and His Contributions to Modern Management Theory. *Academy of Management Proceedings*, 33, 317–322.

Pareto, Vilfredo (1935). *The Mind and Society*. New York: Harcourt, Brace (English translation).

Pollard, Harold R. (1974). *Developments in Management Thought*. New York: Crane, Russak.

Porter, Lyman W., & Bigley, Gregory A. (1995). *Human Relations: Theory and Developments*. Aldershot, UK: Dartmouth.

Pugh, Derek S., & Hickson, David J. (1993). *Great Writers on Organizations: The Omnibus Edition*. Aldershot, UK: Dartmouth.

Roberts, Karlene H.; Weissenberg, Peter; Whetten, David; Pearce, Jone; Glick, William; Bedeian, Arthur; Miller, Howard; & Klimoski, Richard (1990). Reflections on the field of Organizational Behavior. *Journal of Management Systems*, 2(1), 25–38.

Roethlisberger, F. J. (1953). The Administrator's Skill: Communication. *Harvard Business Review*, 31(6), 55–62.

Roethlisberger, F. J., & Dickson, William J. (1939). *Management and the Worker: An Account of a Research Program Conducted by the Western Electric Company: Hawthorne Works, Chicago*. Cambridge, MA: Harvard University Press.

Scott, William G. (1992). *Chester I. Barnard and the Guardians of the Managerial State*. Lawrence: University of Kansas Press.

Simon, Herbert A. (1947). *Administrative Behavior: A Study of Decision-Making Processes in Administrative Organization*. New York: Free Press.

Simon, Herbert A. (1991). *Models of My Life*. New York: Basic Books.

Thompson, James D. (1967). *Organizations in Action*. New York: McGraw-Hill.

Trahair, Richard S. C. (1984). *The Humanist Temper: The Life and Work of Elton Mayo*. New Brunswick, NJ: Transaction Books.

Whitehead, Thomas N. (1938). *The Industrial Worker: A Statistical Study of Human Relations in a Group of Manual Workers*. Cambridge, MA: Harvard University Press.

Whyte, William F. (1983). Worker Participation: International and Historical Perspectives. *Journal of Applied Behavioral Science*, 19, 395–407.

Williamson, Oliver E. (1990). *Organization Theory: From Chester Barnard to the Present and Beyond*. New York: Oxford University Press.

Wolf, William B. (1973). The Impact of Kurt Lewin on Management Thought. *Academy of Management Proceedings*, 33, 322–325.

Wolf, William B. (1974). *The Basic Barnard: An Introduction to Chester I. Barnard and His Theories of Organization and Management*. Ithaca: New York State School of Industrial and Labor Relations, Cornell University.

Wren, Daniel A. (1987). Management History: Issues and Ideas for Teaching and Research. *Journal of Management*, 13, 339–350.

Wren, Daniel A. (1994). *The Evolution of Management Thought*. New York: Wiley.

Wren, Daniel A., & Greenwood, Ronald G. (1998). *Management Innovators: The People and Ideas That Have Shaped Modern Business*. New York: Oxford University Press.

Yorks, Lyle, & Whitsett, David A. (1985). Hawthorne, Topeka, and the Issue of Science versus Advocacy in Organizational Behavior. *Academy of Management Review*, 10, 21–30.

Chapter 3

Multidisciplinary Origins of Organizational Behavior

Mary Parker Follett, Max Weber, Henri Fayol, and Frederick Taylor

The writers to which we now turn were not social science researchers in the manner of Kurt Lewin.

In many respects they are more similar to Chester Barnard. They had ideas that, in the context of their times—and, many would argue, even in the context of the present—were innovative and prophetic. They were thinkers and philosophers, and sometimes practitioners, who dealt with organizational problems. Their work consistently antedates the major contributions of the individuals considered in the previous chapter, but it has been no less influential for organizational behavior.

FOLLETT: SOCIAL PHILOSOPHER AND PROPHET OF MANAGEMENT

Mary Follett was born in 1868 and died in 1933; her influence on organizational behavior was exerted only a few years earlier than the people considered in the preceding chapter. She was a political and social philosopher, and her occupation was social worker. Her early writing was in the field of political science, and it was only in her later years that she began to focus on business organizations specifically.

After writing several books concerned primarily with political science and democratic process, which earned her substantial acclaim in that field (Sethi, 1962), Follett's first book that deals directly with organizational behavior issues was *Creative Experience* (Follett, 1924). Her subsequent writings were prepared initially as lectures, which she gave frequently as her ideas became better known; sources for these lecture papers are Henry C. Metcalf and Lyndall F. Urwick (1940), Elliot M. Fox and Urwick (1973), and Urwick (1949). I have relied on these books, as well as on Pauline Graham's (1995) very comprehensive treatment of Follett's life and work.

Background

Follett grew up outside Boston in a well-to-do family from which she ultimately received an inheritance that made her financially independent. She attended Thayer Academy in the Boston area and entered what was shortly to become Radcliffe College. At the age of 30, after a year at Cambridge University in England and considerable time spent preparing her first book on the workings of the legislative process, Follett received her degree from Radcliffe. Her major areas of study were government, philosophy, and economics. Subsequently, she did postgraduate work in Paris, but she did not receive a degree. She returned to Boston in 1900. There she remained until the latter years of her life. Her circle of friends and acquaintances included a distinguished group of writers, philosophers, lawyers, politicians, and aristocrats; she drew upon them extensively for her lectures and writing.

As a social worker, Follett developed programs to provide social, recreational, and vocational guidance opportunities to young people. During her 25 years in this occupation she managed various activities, initiated ideas, and implemented them. She served on a series of boards and committees dealing with such matters as placement bureaus, community centers, and minimum wage administration. She was particularly influential in getting placement centers established in the Boston public schools.

During the 1920s Follett became increasingly interested in business organizations and their functioning. She was never a management consultant in the usual sense of that term, but she did advise business managers frequently, and she lectured widely on business topics. These lectures were given to various conferences, university groups, and professional associations in both the United States and England. From 1929 until her death Follett lived in England and studied industrial conditions in that country. Her final lectures in early 1933 were given at the London School of Economics.

To what extent discrimination in some form has contributed to the degree that Follett has or has not received the recognition that is her just due is a matter of some debate. The pros and cons of this issue are considered in the preface (by Rosabeth Kanter) and the introduction (by Peter Drucker) to Pauline Graham's (1995) book. Certainly gender per se did produce certain problems at the time that would not have stood in the way of an equally situated male. Yet Follett had the advantages of inherited money and entrée to important people, too. Without doubt, she is unique among her peers in the success she achieved and in the early influence she exerted on organizational behavior. Among those who exerted similar influence, she is the only woman; that in itself is testimonial to the importance of her views. For those who may wish to pursue the more recent experiences of women in organizational behavior, I would recommend the book edited by Dianne Cyr and Blaize Reich (1996).

Views on Business Management

Although she was not trained in psychology, Follett read widely in that field, and this influence shows at many points in her writings. In particular, she was attracted by the concepts of *gestalt* psychology, which serve to emphasize the total situation surrounding any event.

Furthermore, at this early point she recognized what various organizational behavior theorists have stressed since then: that people often act first, and only after the fact develop reasons for what they do. Follett thus refers to the inevitable tendency to make an ideal of what is already fact. In this and many other respects she represents a prophet for views and concepts that were to reemerge many years later.

Some sense of her approach is inherent in the following:

1. Behavior is both internally and externally conditioned.

2. Behavior is a function of the interweaving between activity of the organism and activity in the environment.
3. By this interlocking activity of individual and situation each is creating itself anew.
4. Thus, relating each anew.
5. Thus, producing the evolving situation.

Conflict

Conflict is neither good nor bad; it is simply a matter of difference. Three ways of dealing with conflict exist: domination, compromise, and integration. Domination is immediately effective, but not always successful in the long run. Compromise requires that each side give up something so that the activity interrupted by the conflict may continue. Yet the need to back down to some extent makes compromise unattractive to all. Integration is thus the preferred way of dealing with conflict. Here a solution is found that permits both sides to achieve their goals; neither must sacrifice anything. This approach by its nature leads to invention of new approaches to a situation — to finding new ways that are mutually attractive. Unfortunately, however, not all conflicts are amenable to solution via integration.

The first rule is that for integration to occur, all parties must bring the whole situation out in the open, uncover the issues. If issues are evaded or suppressed, it usually means that someone is really seeking domination, not integration. When the field of desires is clearly evident, the situation may be evaluated, and then revaluation can occur so that ways in which interests may fit with one another may be identified. The most dramatic features of a conflict situation need not be the most significant for resolution; identifying the real issues may require some search. The second rule is that the demands of both sides must be broken down into their constituent elements. This breaking up of wholes is crucial. In the process there must be a careful scrutiny of the language used in order to establish what is really meant; what do the symbols say?

In all of this it is important to anticipate demands, differences, and sources of conflict. One must prepare for response, must carry out the inventive process in one's mind, so that its products may be considered in advance to see if they might be worthy. This is difficult because one is always dealing with an evolving situation, a moving target created by the interactions involved in real time.

The obstacles to integration are the following. First, integration requires substantial talent—sometimes a capacity for brilliant inventiveness. Not all people have this talent. Second, many people enjoy domination, often to the point that they cannot give it up. Third, the conflict may become the subject of theorizing, of intellectualization, rather than being taken as a matter for specific action. As a consequence, getting down to some definite activity may be inordinately delayed. Fourth, the language used may in some respect raise a red flag. Conflict resolution requires careful attention to language. Fifth, there is the matter of the undue influence of leaders (the manipulation of the unscrupulous and the suggestibility of the crowd). This can be a major barrier to integration. Sixth and finally, because we are typically trained more in the process of domination than in the art of cooperation, many people have not learned how to integrate.

Perhaps some understanding of the prophetic nature of these views may be gained from the fact that 40 years later Richard Walton and Robert McKersie (1965) gave integration a central position in their typology of labor negotiation approaches. They reference Follett frequently on the subject.

Power

Follett provides what she says is an interim definition of *power*. It is the ability to make things happen, to serve as a causal agent, to initiate change. In contrast, *control* is power exercised as the means to a specific end, and *authority* is control vested in a position.

Power usually implies power-over, the object being some person or group. Within business organizations, this type of independent power is not desirable. Rather, joint power is preferable, a concept of power-with, which is co-active rather than coercive. Although Follett discusses power-over at length, she provides much less detail on power-with, except to say that the distinction has status in law—one has rights over a slave, but rights with a servant. The impression one gets is that power-with implies the pursuit of a common purpose.

One method of reducing power-over is through the use of integration. Integration of a party's desires makes it unnecessary to gain power over others to satisfy those desires. In the process of developing an integrative solution, a back-and-forth interactive influence is put into play that makes for a build-up of power-with. Taking known facts into consideration tends to reduce power-over, while withholding of facts serves as a means to increase power-over.

Power-over can be reduced through (1) integration; (2) recognizing the need to submit to the law of the situation, where facts are known and the logic of these facts is compelling for all; and (3) making the business a functional unity, where each component has its function, corresponding as far as possible with available capacity, and it has the authority and responsibility that go with the function.

Follett did not believe that power could be delegated, because power does not become genuine until it is matched by an equal capacity to exercise it. Thus delegating power to workers can well be fruitless. A manager cannot share power with anyone who is in a subordinate position, but opportunities for others to develop their own power can be provided. In this view, approaches that are predicated on a balance of power, equal power, and even collective bargaining to the extent that it relies on a forced equilibrium are dedicated to power-over and thus rejected. Equal power sets the stage for a fight; power-with is unifying and thus makes fighting unnecessary. Follett was an advocate of employee associations that can bring about a greater functional unity within an organization, but not of international unions that seek only to increase their own power.

How can these negative consequences be avoided? One way is by depersonalizing orders. Orders should arise out of the demands of the situation, not of a person. Yet fear of exercising authority, with a consequent laissez-faire leadership, should not govern, either. The demands of the situation do need communication and explanation. Furthermore, arbitrary order-giving can be reduced by virtue of the fact that the manager serves as trainer. Valuable training in new methods, to explain more fully what has previously been misunderstood, as well as to get an employee started on a job, are essential to work performance. Another rule is to explain the reasons for an order to the extent that is feasible and needed. Finally, everyone in an organization should have a full understanding of the organization's purpose and thus of the underlying reasons behind a directive.

Managers need to be trained in giving orders. This training should consider ways of preparing the way for orders by creating attitudes that will foster carrying them out; it should deal with the provision of stimuli and incentives to follow the methods suggested; and it should emphasize the creation of opportunities to convert these methods into habits. Orders do not obtain their validity from the consent of those who receive them. They achieve validity from a long process to which both order-giver and receiver have contributed for some time.

Giving Orders

Orders should not come down from on high, but rather should arise out of the work to be done; thus many subordinates may contribute. People should not "obey orders" but instead should follow standard practice. Such standard practice is based on research, which may include input from anyone in the organization. Managers serve as a source of information regarding standard practice, once it is developed; there is no call for arbitrariness in this picture.

Arbitrary approaches have several disadvantages, one of which is that useful input from the person doing the job is lost when cooperation from that source is not invited. Second, arbitrariness promotes friction and antagonism. Third, pride in the work tends to be sacrificed, and thus interest in the final result is lost. Fourth and finally, a sense of responsibility in the subordinate is decreased; if blind obedience is required, the subordinate cannot be held responsible for the outcome.

Authority

Research and scientific study must determine function, and people should have authority exactly equal to their function or job. The job itself, rather than position in a hierarchy, is the main source of authority. Thus authority comes with knowledge, with experience, and with the skill that permits applying that knowledge and experience.

A management decision is only a moment in a lengthy process. The growth of a decision, and thus the gradual accumulation of authority, not the last step, is what needs to be studied. Focusing on the last step only, on the highest level manager involved, creates the illusion of authority (Follett, 1926). Before decisions are made, almost everything in that decision has already been considered and added to it. Given the conclusions and judgments made at lower levels and then passed up to the chief executive, there are few instances where the decision can actually be changed dramatically at the top. Interacting influences escalate to a point at which we tend to believe the decision occurs, but this is only the illusion of final authority, and it blinds us to the true nature of the decision process. This is not to say that final authority is totally nonexistent, only that it is often overemphasized.

Genuine authority does not stem from separating people into classes specifying those who command and those who obey. It stems from one person's work fitting into the work of another, and then through this intermingling of forces a power being created, which, in turn, serves to control the forces that generated it.

Leadership

Leadership is not primarily a matter of personality, and particularly not a matter of a dominant personality. The requisites of leadership are, first, a full knowledge of one's job; second, the ability to grasp a total situation in all its aspects and to find the unifying thread; third, the ability to organize the experience of a group so as to obtain the full power of that group and direct it to the common purpose; fourth, the ability to anticipate the evolving situation, to see possible new paths and to try them, as well as to measure results with a view to determining how functional the various paths are.

Also important is the role of the follower in leadership. That role is less to follow than to keep the leader in control of the situation. Both leader and follower are following a common purpose. Followers should help leaders do this, just as leaders should help followers.

Follett comes down strongly in favor of leadership that derives from function, as opposed to leadership based on either position or personality. She does not deny the existence of the latter two, however. In fact, she provides a long list of leadership qualities — sincerity, steadfastness, control of temper, ability to develop others, willingness to serve as an example, and many others. But she believes, consistent with her views regarding management as a profession, that leadership based on function and capacity to perform the function is crucial. Accordingly, leadership is not something one is born with; it can at least in part be learned.

Coordination and Control

Follett has much to say on the topics of coordination and control. For amplification of her treatment, see the paper by L. D. Parker (1984) and the chapter by Robert Daiute in his series of essays (1964). Here are her main points.

The essence of business organizations is that they somehow combine their multiple responsibilities, their scattered authorities, and their varied types of leadership into a single unity. Three principles of unity may be identified. One is that a system of cross-functioning between units should be established so that frequent communication occurs both horizontally and vertically. This may be informal, but it should be expected. There may be a system of committees created to serve the cross-functioning purpose. Second is that, although differences may be settled by domination, compromise, or integration, the last should be paramount. Integration is particularly useful in resolving differences between managers and experts. Arbitration, because it involves domination, is not as effective. Third is the development of a sense of collective responsibility. Joint responsibility for the enterprise as a whole is a major contributory factor to enterprise success. Out of these three principles comes unity, but unity must be maintained on a continuing basis by a host of on-going processes. It is always threatening to disappear.

With regard to control, Follett notes two points. Control is much more a matter of controlling facts than of controlling people. With cost accounting and unit budgeting, control has become more impersonal, and this is as it should be. Arbitrary orders thus give way to the study of data and analyses. Second, central control is not a matter of radiation from a central source of authority, and thus superimposed, but a gathering up of controls that exist at various points throughout the enterprise. Commands from the top are replaced by the correlation of many controls.

Follett equates organization with control, in the sense that the object of organization is control. But she also tends at times to view control and coordination as involving the same processes. Thus her four fundamental principles of organization are stated as principles of control and coordination as well:

1. Coordination should involve the reciprocal relating of all the factors in a situation. This reciprocal relating requires the interpenetrating of every part of the organization by every other part and then once again by every other part as it has been permeated by all. This is the goal of all coordination efforts. It does not involve any loss of individuality for the sake of the whole, however.

2. Coordination should be by direct contact of the responsible individuals.
3. Coordination should occur in the early stages. If people are confronted with policies that have already been formulated, and are merely asked to endorse them, not only is their input lost but also antagonism seems inevitable. This principle applies as well to managers and workers. Managers and workers should share in joint control, but only as the parties are competent to have a valid opinion. And joint control means being brought in at the early stages.
4. Coordination should be a continuing process that goes on all the time. In this way, the circle from planning to activity and then from activity back to further planning remains unbroken.

Management as a Profession

Follett sincerely believed that management should seek to achieve the stature of a profession and that it was indeed in the process of becoming one. In discussing this aspect of her work I draw on two articles (Follett, 1927, 1955).

Follett treats at some length the various criteria for becoming a profession. She notes first a foundation of science and a motive of service. Business is one of the necessary functions of society, and, as such, like the professions, it is much more than a method for private gain. In addition, the professions tend to elicit love of the work and a sense of satisfaction when that work is done well. Professions establish group codes of conduct so that the errors of the personal equation may be corrected. Professional associations are formed, which serve to establish, maintain, and improve standards; to keep members up to standards; to educate the public so that these standards can be appreciated; to protect the public from those professionals whose behavior has failed to reach the standards or who deliberately flaunt them; and to protect individual professionals from each other. In essence, the objectives of a professional association become a corporate responsibility.

Business can well learn from the professions when it comes to maintaining standards. It also needs to do much more by way of educating the public to its standards, and, in fact, to develop these standards fully. Management has in place some of the basic essentials of a profession, but there is a need to do more on this score.

Scientific method is increasingly being applied to management as reflected in the scientific management of Frederick Taylor and his followers, in the increasing specialization or functionalization of management, and in the decline in arbitrary authority (replaced by scientific knowledge). What is needed now is to apply science to the whole of business — to human relations problems, as well as to the technical ones. Another requirement is to analyze managerial work in a manner comparable to what the Taylor system has done with workers' jobs.

Management also needs to do much more to organize the body of knowledge on which it is to rest. With more systematic comparison of experiences and experimentation, standards can be developed more fully. Also a body of knowledge to be used in the "professional" training of managers can be established. This training is an essential condition for management to become a profession. Remember that when Follett wrote, there were only a few business schools in existence, and these few had only a short history. Her only mention of these schools is to praise the use of the case method at the Harvard Business School as a means of organizing the experiential knowledge of business.

Impact and Influence

Follett wrote with a charming style. Her approach is to serve as a reporter on cutting edge developments in the business world, to describe what the most progressive companies are doing, and to show why these developments are the road to the future. All the while, she is in fact propounding a normative philosophy of what the business world should be. Her reports are not merely reports but examples for her advocacy. They may well be somewhat selective, but then she is not engaged in journalism but in setting forth her philosophy. In any event, part of the appeal of Follett's writing is that it provides a picture of her culture — partly Boston Brahmin and partly British. The examples are taken from personal experience, the issues of the times, and the business world as she knows it, but they all serve to paint the picture. It is very hard to disagree with what she has to say. On top of everything else, she is against fighting; does not like domineering, bossy people; and believes strongly in the value of knowledge.

Much has been made of Follett's probably unintended capacity for prophecy. Her ideas frequently have been picked up by others, typically many years later, and either expanded or in some cases used entirely in the manner in which she stated them. I have noted some instances of this, but my presentation does not do her justice in this regard. Detailed discussions of her prophetic contributions are scattered through the commentaries in Graham's (1995) book — in particular, those written by Rosabeth Kanter, John Child, Nitin Nohria, Warren Bennis, Henry Mintzberg, and Paul Lawrence.

These commentaries also raise a question regarding the extent to which Follett has been adequately credited when her ideas are used by and incorporated into the writings of others. The upshot of this discussion appears to be that not infrequently well-known theorists of the first generation do draw upon Follett without citing her. Sometimes the omissions seem to be unintentional; the ideas were in the air at the time, readily available for the picking. Yet in other cases Follett's concepts appear to have been quite consciously misappropriated. It serves no purpose to name names on this score, but certainly Follett's influence extended well beyond what a mere citation count would seem to indicate.

Yet many theorists do credit Follett for making important contributions to their thinking. Thus, Rensis Likert, in developing the theory of System 4 and 4T, notes the importance of integrative solutions, of the law of the situation, and of the authority of facts (Likert & Likert, 1976). Paul Lawrence and Jay Lorsch (1967), in elaborating their contingency theory of organization, draw on Follett to describe methods of achieving integration and to explain alternatives to formal, authoritarian organizational structures. Various organization development advocates make use of such ideas as integrative solutions to conflicts (Bennis, Benne, & Chin, 1969) and the law of the situation (McGregor, 1967). Karl Weick (1995), in discussing the process of enactment in his book on sense making in organizations, draws heavily on Follett's view that behavior is both internally and externally conditioned.

The very frequency with which Follett's ideas have influenced later thinking suggests that many people often consider them valid. I am one of those people. However, there are instances in which some degree of skepticism seems warranted. It is easy to lose one's critical sense while reading her prose. Take for instance her advocacy of management as a profession. Many of the steps to this end that she advances have been taken, many additional advocates have come on the scene. Yet management is still not a profession; you can get into it from many directions,

not just via an M.B.A. from an American Assembly of Collegiate Schools of Business (AACSB) school. This prophecy has been slow to come to fruition.

The problem as I see it is that Follett's experience dealt entirely with medium-sized and large corporations. She had little knowledge of entrepreneurship, and she did not consider it in her writings. Yet entrepreneurs with very little formal education of any kind, and few other accoutrements of a profession either, can make tremendous contributions to society in the form of employment, products, services, capital creation, and so on. And they do this as managers. It would not be in the interest of society to exclude them from a managerial profession as unqualified. Therein lies the problem for management as a profession.

Although the issues she deals with are only partially overlapping, Follett writes from a position that is similar to Barnard. She has a certain practical proclivity, and she clearly understands and sympathizes with management. Yet there are aspects of her writing and of the stand she takes on some issues that tend to endear her to those of a more humanist bent. In fact, she has been adopted by many within organizational behavior who identify with her behavioral humanist approach, and it is often these people who ascribe to her the greatest skills as a prophet (see, for instance, the commentaries by Bennis and Lawrence in Graham, 1995). Furthermore, her ideas have recently been applied in support of various organization development approaches (Boje & Rosile, 2001).

WEBER AND HIS THEORY OF BUREAUCRACY

Max Weber has been adopted by the field of sociology in part at least because, although he wrote in German, much of his work was translated into English by sociologists. His life covered essentially the same period as Follett's; however, he died younger, at the age of 56 in 1920. Accordingly, his major work was completed well before Follett began to write on organizational matters. His writings were known in this country, and, indeed, Chester Barnard read them in the German, but only to a very limited audience, for many years.

Weber's views were formally introduced in the United States through a variety of translations and compilations. The most comprehensive, though still incomplete, early statements of his theory of bureaucracy appeared in the translations by Hans Gerth and

C. Wright Mills (Weber, 1946) and by Talcott Parsons and A. M. Henderson (Weber, 1947). The following discussion draws primarily on the comprehensive, three-volume *Economy and Society* translated by Guenther Roth and Claus Wittich (Weber, 1968), especially on the first and third volumes. Parsons, a member of the Pareto Circle at Harvard, was particularly instrumental in bringing Weber's theories to this country and to the English-speaking world in general. Note, however, that this did not happen, insofar as his theory of bureaucracy is concerned, until a quarter century after Weber's death.

Background

Weber was originally educated in Germany as a lawyer. Much of his early writing dealt with legal history. In addition to law and history, Weber produced major contributions in the fields of economics, religion, and political science. However, he became best known in sociology, the field in which his theory of bureaucracy had the greatest influence. Though associated with several German and Austrian universities, Weber stayed longest at the University of Heidelberg. Due to a substantial inheritance and intermittent periods of debilitating depression, he did not teach regularly and, in fact, spent a number of years as a private scholar (Marianne Weber, 1975).

Although not of major concern here, Weber was more widely known initially for his thesis that one consequence of the rise of Protestantism in previously Catholic Europe was the development of capitalism (Weber, 1930). In this view, the Protestant ethic said that God intended profitability and blessed it as well; that waste, and thus not devoting time to profitable labor, was contrary to God's will; that division of labor was to be desired, since it contributed to the quality and quantity of production; and that hard work was in the nature of a duty to God, which contributed to the accumulation of wealth that, in turn, should be put back into capitalistic endeavors. These views reflect the scope of Weber's intellect. In many ways he was rewriting history. There is some evidence of this tendency in his writings related to bureaucracy as well.

Weber on Bureaucracy

Weber's approach to theory construction is scholarly, and his statements often are documented from a historical perspective. Though some people, particularly those of a human relations bent, typically view classical management theory and bureaucratic theory as comparable, even to the point of not differentiating between them, a reading of the two indicates major differences. Weber is primarily interested in the role of bureaucracy in the historical development of society and its organizational forms. Classical theory focuses on problems of managerial practice. Both fail to operationalize variables and conduct relevant research, but Weber is much more concerned with clarity of definition.

There has been considerable controversy regarding certain aspects of the translation of Weber (Weiss, 1983). In order to make as clear as possible the interpretation I place on his writings, the following discussion uses direct quotations more frequently than has been the case in the treatments of other scholars. These quotations are consistently from the more comprehensive Roth and Wittich (Weber, 1968) translation.

Nature of Organization

Weber sees an organization as a particular type of social relationship that is either closed to outsiders or limits their admission and has its regulations enforced by a chief, usually with the assistance of an administrative staff. The key factor is some hierarchy of authority that serves to ensure that members will carry out the order governing the organization. This order may be self-enacted or imposed by an outside agency. Organizational structure refers to the specific manner in which the authority is distributed.

The concept of rules plays an important role in Weber's theory, especially rationally established rules. A *formal organization* is one with a continuously and rationally operating staff. Such a staff possesses power—a probability that its commands will be obeyed. It utilizes discipline—a probability that, as a result of habit, commands will result in immediate and automatic obedience.

This staff, which is comparable to the managerial component of today's organizations, is a special group that can be trusted to execute existing policy and carry out commands. It may be tied to the chief in a number of ways, including custom, emotion, and material interest. A key factor in the continued domination of the organization by those at the top is the law of the small number:

The ruling minority can quickly reach understanding among its members; it is thus able at any time quickly to initiate that rationally organized action which is necessary to preserve its position of power. Consequently it can easily squelch any action of the masses threatening its power. . . . Another benefit of the small number is the ease of secrecy as to the intentions and resolutions of the rulers and the state of their information. (Weber, 1968, p. 952)

Pure Types of Authority: Rational-Legal

Weber's theory gives considerable attention to concepts such as authority, domination, command, power, and discipline; this focus appears to have alienated theorists of a human relations orientation. Yet these are important concepts for organizational theory.

Authority is said to be legitimized or validated by appeal to one or more of three possible grounds — rational-legal rules, personal authority invested with the force of tradition, and charisma. These are pure types that rarely occur alone in nature. In practice, systems of authority typically are mixtures or modifications of the three.

Rational-legal authority provides a basis for the organizational structure termed bureaucracy:

[It involves] a system of consciously made *rational* rules (which may be agreed upon or imposed from above), which meet with obedience as generally binding norms whenever such obedience is claimed by him whom the rule designates. In that case every single bearer of powers of command is legitimated by the system of rational norms, and his power is legitimate insofar as it corresponds with the norm. Obedience is thus given to the norms rather than to the person. (Weber, 1968, p. 954)

Norms are established because of expediency and/or value-rationality; they apply to the members of the organization, but may extend beyond that to the sphere of power of the organization. There is a consistent system of rules — stated in the abstract, but applied to particular cases. Even those in authority are thus subject to an impersonal order. An individual obeys only as an organization member and in response to the law or an impersonal order, not to an individual. Thus obedience is required only within a legitimate, rationally established jurisdiction.

The categories of rational-legal authority are described as follows:

1. A continuous rule-bound conduct of official business.

2. A specified sphere of competence (jurisdiction). This involves:
   a. A sphere of obligations to perform functions which have been marked off as part of a systematic division of labor.
   b. The provision of the incumbent with the necessary powers.
   c. That the necessary means of compulsion are clearly defined and their use is subject to definite conditions. . . .
3. The organization of offices follows the principle of hierarchy; that is each lower office is under the control and supervision of a higher one. . . .
4. The rules which regulate the conduct of an office may be technical rules or norms.
5. . . . It is a matter of principle that the members of the administrative staff should be completely separated from ownership of the means of production. . . . There exists, furthermore, in principle complete separation of the organization's property (respectively capital), and the personal property (household) of the official.
6. . . . There is also a complete absence of appropriation of his official position by the incumbent. . . . .
7. Administrative acts, decisions, and rules are formulated and recorded in writing.
8. Legal authority can be exercised in a wide variety of different forms. (Weber, 1968, pp. 218–219)

Traditional and Charismatic Authority

Traditional authority derives from the personal loyalty that is associated with a common upbringing. It is based on the sanctity of long-standing rules and powers, on tradition, and on custom. To some extent, these traditions specify the exact content of command, but they may also provide a wide range for individual discretion. Thus traditional authority attaches to the person, not to an impersonal position. It tends to be present where positions of power are filled on the basis of family membership, as in kingdoms and family-owned firms. Here, as in the traditional family, obedience is to the person.

Like traditional authority, charismatic authority is also personal. The leader's personality interacts with followers so that they attribute supernatural, superhuman, or at least exceptional powers to the leader. Charismatic authority rests on recognition by others and results in complete devotion to the leader. The hierarchical powers on which charisma is based must be frequently demonstrated and serve to benefit the followers, or authority will disappear. Typically, a charismatic community emerges over which the leader often exercises arbitrary control. Irrationality and emotional ties are characteristic. Economic considerations are downplayed. Free of ties to rules, whether rationally or traditionally derived, this kind of authority can be a major force for change and revolution.

Combined Authority

Authority and willingness to obey are based on beliefs. These beliefs, which bestow prestige, are typically complex, and, accordingly, few organizations operate from a single authority base. Rational-legal authority tends to become infused with tradition over time. Bureaucratic organizations tend to be headed at the very top by charismatic leaders, not bureaucratic officials, and they function more effectively if this is so.

Historically, many organizations develop from charismatic, to rational-legal, to traditional, and then as traditional authority fails, organizations return to the revolutionary charismatic form. Charismatic authority alone is highly unstable. The charismatic community that maintains itself over time must become rationalized or traditionalized to some degree. This routinization of charisma is particularly important to succession.

Weber views the emergence of an administrative staff as essential to stable organization. Continued obedience requires an effort to enforce the existing order, and this, in turn, is a consequence of a solidarity of interests, a consistent value system that extends beyond the chief and the staff. At some points, Weber appears to equate the very existence of an organization with some degree of rationalized bureaucracy, but he is not consistent in this regard.

Though a generally authoritarian orientation is often attributed to bureaucratic theory, Weber is clearly positively disposed toward certain democratic and collegial forms. In establishing patterns of succession and routinizing charismatic systems, elections and other democratic procedures may emerge. Such procedures can be a major antiauthoritarian force and a force for rationality. As organizations become large, full collegiality is no longer possible, but other forms of democracy involving representation are still viable. In fact, Weber tends to associate the democratization of society with the growth of bureaucratic organizations. Under such conditions, bureaucracy contributes to the leveling of social and economic differences. At the same time, democracy may come into conflict with bureaucratic tendencies under certain conditions; for instance, a bureaucratic emphasis on career service may conflict with democratic endorsements of election for short terms and the possibility of recall from office.

Aspects of Bureaucracy

Many aspects of bureaucracy have been considered as a natural outgrowth of the discussion of different types of legitimate authority—especially the rational-legal type—but other factors are involved. Furthermore, Weber viewed bureaucracy as a modern organizational form, superior to other forms in a number of respects. He tended to associate it not only with societal, if not organizational, democracy, but also with the growth of a capitalistic, economic system and with a certain disesteem for "irrational" religion.

Bureaucracy involves sets of jurisdictional areas ordered by rules. Needed activities are assigned to jurisdictions as duties, authority to elicit behavior to carry out these duties is strictly defined and delimited, and the filling of positions is based on preestablished qualifications. There is a clearly established hierarchy of subordination and appeal. Management positions presuppose thorough training in a specialized area. In addition, a comprehensive knowledge of the organization's rules is required. In a fully developed bureaucracy, the needs for the various kinds of knowledge and expertise and for their application are sufficient to produce a full-time position.

Entry into bureaucratic management is based on a set course of training and usually on performance on prescribed examinations. Appointment tends to be by superior authority (election represents a departure from true bureaucracy). After appointment, the individual enters into a career in the organization and can expect to progress up the hierarchy. Compensation is a salary plus a pension in old age. Certain rights go with appointment to the office and protect an incumbent against arbitrary, personal action.

Bureaucratic systems dominate through knowledge, and this fact gives them their rationality. The result is a climate of formal impersonality, without hatred or passion and hence without affection or enthusiasm. Movement toward such an organizational form is fostered by sheer growth of an organization and, consequently, of the administrative task. Bureaucracy is also fostered by the qualitative expansion of administrative tasks — the knowledge explosion and the taking on of added activities by the organization.

Normative Statements

Weber described bureaucracy at considerable length and placed it in historical perspective, but he also hypothesized that the kind of organization he described would be more effective than alternative forms on a number of counts:

> The purely bureaucratic type of administrative organization — that is, the monocratic variety of bureaucracy — is, from a purely technical point of view, capable of attaining the highest degree of efficiency and is in this sense formally the most rational known means of exercising authority over human beings. It is superior to any other form in precision, in stability, in the stringency of its discipline, and in its reliability. It thus makes possible a particularly high degree of calculability of results for the heads of the organization and for those acting in relation to it. It is finally superior both in intensive efficiency and in the scope of its operations, and is formally capable of application to all kinds of administrative tasks. (Weber, 1968, p. 223)

And again:

> The fully developed bureaucratic apparatus compares with other organizations exactly as does the machine with the non-mechanical modes of production. Precision, speed, unambiguity, knowledge of the files, continuity, discretion, unity, strict subordination, reduction of friction and of material and personal costs — these are raised to the optimum point in the strictly bureaucratic administration. . . . As far as complicated tasks are concerned, paid bureaucratic work is not only more precise but, in the last analysis, it is often cheaper than even formally unremunerated honorific service. (pp. 973–974)

Nowhere does Weber contend that the members of such organizations will be happier or more satisfied, but he does contend that bureaucracy works, and to some degree it works for individual members also by freeing them from the inequities of arbitrary authority. Ultimately, bureaucracy works so well that it is practi-

cally indestructible. Once such a system is set in motion it is almost impossible to stop, except from the very top; the sum of the parts is an effective organization, but no one part, no single official, is powerful enough to disrupt the whole.

Contrasts with Other Forms

Weber contrasts bureaucracy with other types of organizations that rely more heavily on traditional and charismatic authority, what he calls prebureaucratic forms. Traditional authority is particularly manifest in patrimonial organizations, which lack the bureaucratic separation of private and official spheres. Under traditional conditions, decisions tend to be ad hoc rather than predetermined by rules, and loyalty is not to the duties of an impersonal office, but to a ruler as a person. Ineffectiveness becomes a matter of arousing the ruler's disfavor rather than failing to perform the duties of the position. Feudalism involves much that is patrimonial, but relationships are more fixed than in many other such forms. Elements of routinized charisma are in evidence as well.

In a sense, charismatic authority is antithetical to the idea of organization. Yet a personal staff of disciples characteristically arises to form a charismatic aristocracy. The basic system tends to be communal, with the leader issuing dispensations according to his personal desires. Under such conditions the leader can introduce changes rapidly — there are no rules or traditions to block them. Bureaucracy can produce change as well, but it does so by first changing the material and social order along rational lines, and then the individuals.

Discipline in a modern factory is much the same as in the military or on a plantation, but it is more rational:

> With the help of suitable methods of measurement, the optimum profitability of the individual worker is calculated like that of any material means of production. On this basis like the American system of scientific management it triumphantly proceeds with its rational conditioning and training of work performances, thus drawing the ultimate conclusions from the mechanization and discipline of the plant. . . . This whole process of rationalization, in the factory as elsewhere, and especially in the bureaucratic state machine, parallels the centralization of the material implements of organization in the hands of the master. Thus,

discipline inexorably takes over ever larger areas as the satisfaction of political and economic needs is increasingly rationalized. This universal phenomenon more and more restricts the importance of charisma and of individually differentiated conduct. (Weber, 1968, p. 1156)

Weber does not say he likes all this; in fact, his writing is quite objective and neutral. But he certainly respects it, and he appears to be to some degree afraid of it as well.

Impact and Influence

One reason for the extensive discussion of Weber's ideas that has occurred over the years is the uncertainty as to what he really said. These differences are based only in part on difficulties of translation. Weber often returned to the same subjects, approaching them from different angles and providing fuel for numerous interpretive debates (Turner, 1983). Thus, Weber's statements are on occasion conflicting or ambiguous on the role of collegiality vis-à-vis bureaucracy; the extent to which bureaucracy may be defined as a self-contained and self-perpetuating entity as opposed to a tool of the user; the relationship of centralization to bureaucracy; the power of bureaucracy; the degree of voluntary versus imperative control that is inherent in rational-legal authority; and the distinction between the concept of organization as a whole and its bureaucratic subtype. Weber strove for clarity of definition but conveyed a message of considerable fuzziness on certain issues (Abrahamsson, 1977). Scientifically, the theory is logically inconsistent to a degree.

Weber was not totally unaware that there are dysfunctions and unanticipated consequences of bureaucracy. Such matters were considered, though they were not his major concern. Thus, the existence and activities of the informal organization represent departures from the ideal type. That Weber did not deal with such matters at length reflects the nature of his domain choice. He wanted to establish how and why bureaucracy works under ideal conditions. This in itself is a massive undertaking, and one cannot legitimately fault Weber for not extending his theory with the same detail into new domains. Yet, others have done so since.

Much the same argument applies to the contention that Weber failed to consider interactions between the organization and the environment and produced an overly limited, closed-system theory. As Howard Aldrich and Jeffrey Pfeffer (1976) point out, Weber's historical and comparative analyses dealt at length with the impact of social structure on bureaucracy. And Kenneth McNeil (1978) has drawn on Weber's views as a frame of reference for describing how organizations gain power over their environments. Certainly, Weber's formulations regarding external forces are incomplete, relative to his theory of internal factors. Nevertheless, significant theory construction almost inevitably requires focusing on some one domain at the expense of others.

In general, research on this theory of internal factors, to the extent it has been conducted with appropriate samples and measures, has supported the descriptive theory, though more as a composite of variables than as a single type. Formalization, standardization, and specialization tend to be highly correlated, and thus to vary together, as the theory would predict.

A considerable body of research relates large size in both composite units and total organizations to the bureaucratic nexus. There are studies that find only a weak relationship here, and there is reason to question whether size is necessarily a cause of the structure, but size typically has something to do with bureaucracy. Though small bureaucracies are possible, small organizations are more likely to take some other form. Furthermore, bureaucratization seems unlikely to continue unabated beyond some level of growth. Nevertheless, bureaucracy appears to be the preferred method of structuring large organizations of any type. Thus, the overall data support Weber on this point.

The centralization-decentralization variable and results related to it have been the subject of major controversy. Some view Weber's bureaucracy as incorporating centralization, while others think just the opposite. There is considerable confusion regarding how centralization should be operationalized and what the limits of the construct are. This is only part — but a very important part — of the construct validity problem that plagues the theory as a whole.

For present purposes it seems appropriate to view formalization and standardization as methods of indirect control that are separate and distinct from centralization of decision making. Though strategic decisions with regard to financial resources and product market position may not follow the same pattern, movement to greater bureaucratization and growth can, and frequently do, call forth greater decentralization of other types of decisions. This has not been a universal find-ing, but it has been a frequent finding in studies limited to bureaucratic organizations of some size and a relatively narrow definition of the centralization-decentralization variable. Such a conceptualization is supported by strategy and structure theory (Chandler, 1962). Clearly, inverse relationships between bureaucratization and centralization occur frequently enough to consider Weber's theory inadequate in this area.

With regard to the role of rationality and knowledge in bureaucracy Weber appears to have been both right and wrong. Knowledge related to strategic decision making and policy implementation for the specific organization does concentrate at the top of the hierarchy, and greater rationality tends to accrue with it. However, knowledge that is less organization-specific does not relate to the bureaucratic hierarchy in the manner Weber proposed. This latter, professional knowledge is a source of power, and in a general sense Weber was correct in equating authority and knowledge. But he did not differentiate rational-legal authority from the value-rational type that underlies professional systems (Satow, 1975). Not only does Weber's theory fail to comprehend professional organizations, which appear to fall outside its domain, but it also fails to deal with professional systems, knowledge, and authority lying predominantly within bureaucratic organizations. To this latter extent, it is deficient within its own domain. Such professional components within bureaucratic organizations do not appear to be mere deviant cases but, rather, separate, distinct systems with their own characteristics and sources of authority.

We know little about Weber's normative theory of bureaucratic superiority. Whether a bureaucratic system at its best is superior to a professional system at its best, for instance, is a completely unanswered question. Furthermore, the significance and role of charismatic leaders at the top of bureaucratic organizations remains highly uncertain. Still, there is evidence that increases in various bureaucratic characteristics, as organizations approach the ideal type, are associated with more positive organizational outcomes. What causes what has not been definitely established, but there is no reason to doubt that, within bureaucratic systems, increasing bureaucratization yields the results Weber anticipated. This may not be true for all components of bureaucracy, but it does appear to hold for a basic core.

A whole set of theories arose out of Weber's formulations regarding bureaucracy, many of which attempt to move well beyond what has been considered here. Without question, Weber's insights have exerted substantial influence on subsequent research and theory, although there has been considerable fluctuation in the extent of that impact at different times over the past half century. Overall, however, our understanding of organizations took a quantum leap when Weber's theory of organizations finally became widely known. Those who desire more comprehensive knowledge of the consequences of that leap should consult Jay Conger (1993) on charismatic leadership and Stewart Clegg (1995) on the influence of Weber's macro theory.

Milestones in the move from Weber's formulations to modern-day leadership theory are Robert House (1977) and Bernard Bass (1985, 1998). Macro organizational behavior contributions that owe a primary debt to Weber include Philip Selznick's (1949) analysis of the Tennessee Valley Authority and Alvin Gouldner's (1954) study of a gypsum plant. Other sociologists who have drawn heavily on Weber to develop their theories include Peter Blau (1974) and James Thompson (1967). In the present day, Weber's influence is particularly apparent in the new institutionalism of sociologists such as Walter Powell and Paul DiMaggio (1991) and W. Richard Scott (1995). Although sociology has perpetuated the Weberian tradition most, political science has been a contributor as well (see, for instance, Victor Thompson, 1961, 1976).

For many, the classical management thinkers, Fayol and Taylor, are one and the same with Weber. This is a total misconception. There are major differences in the content of the formulations involved, and in the role these formulations played for organizational behavior as well.

CLASSICAL MANAGEMENT THEORISTS: THE ANTIHEROES — FAYOL AND TAYLOR

The classical management theorists considered in this section played a very different role in the genesis of organizational behavior than the individuals we have been considering. Their work and ideas are important because they served as objects of attack by various organizational behavior theorists, not because their thinking served to positively influence later organizational behavior theory. It is important to understand these classical theories to appreciate the nature of and reasons for the attacks. The writers who attempted to turn Fayol and Taylor and their followers into anti-heroes were primarily associated with the human relations component of organizational behavior, but there were attacks from other directions as well. For these and other reasons, the classical theories no longer provide an active theoretical thrust within organizational behavior, and they have not for some time (Miner, 1995). There are remaining influences on practice, however.

Given certain perceived similarities between Weber and the classical theorists, it comes as no surprise that certain of the attacks extended to Weber as well. However, Weber has had numerous advocates, primarily among the macro theorists who have clarified and extended his views and put them to research test. A major reason Weber remains something of a hero within organizational behavior, while the classical theorists have been ignored or labeled with an antihero designation, is that Weber has received considerable support from research, and the classical theorists have had relatively little such support.

Backgrounds

Henri Fayol was born in 1841 and graduated in 1860 in mining engineering from the School of Mines at St. Etienne in France. He immediately joined the company with which he spent his entire career; this company became Commentry-Fourchamboult et Décazeville, and he subsequently became its chief executive officer. Fayol's rise within this firm was rapid. He became an expert on underground fires and spontaneous combustion, on geological structures in France, and on mine safety. He conducted research in these areas and published it (Breeze, 1985). His writings on management came late in his career. The major theoretical publication appeared in 1916 when Fayol was 75 years old and still active as an executive. He continued to write on the subject of management until his death in 1925 (Breeze & Bedeian, 1988).

Although the 1916 book had some impact in France and was first translated into English in a limited edition in 1929, it was not until 20 years later under the title *General and Industrial Management* (Fayol, 1949) that it received wide recognition. Thus both Fayol and Weber reached the United States at roughly the same time; they do not appear to have influenced one another.

Fayol's work spawned a number of elaborations and extensions, especially in the years immediately following its major translation into English; among the best known are those of Lyndall Urwick (1952), Ralph Davis (1951), and Harold Koontz and Cyril O'Donnell (1955). Subsequent statements in the classical tradition have appeared largely in management textbooks, again with considerable variation around the central themes (Miner, 1971). Early formulations in a similar vein are presented in books by James Mooney and Alan Reiley (1931) and Luther Gulick and Urwick (1937), for example. Neither Fayol nor any of these individuals who espoused comparable views in the classical management tradition conducted any research to actually test the theory in any form.

Frederick W. Taylor (1856–1915), without the need for translation that Weber's and Fayol's works faced, became widely known in this country considerably earlier. Indeed, his theories were known throughout the world, and to Follett, Weber, and Fayol. His major writings were *Shop Management* (1903) and *The Principles of Scientific Management* (1911), both of which were widely read shortly after publication.

Taylor, like Follett and Weber — but not Fayol — came from a wealthy family. He grew up and spent most of his life in the Philadelphia area. He attended Exeter Academy in New Hampshire and was destined for Harvard. However, instead of attending college, he undertook a 4-year apprenticeship as a pattern-maker and machinist at Enterprise Hydraulic Works in Philadelphia. From there he moved to Midvale Steel and rose rapidly, to chief engineer, in 6 years. While at Midvale he enrolled in a home study program in mechanical engineering given by Stevens Institute of Technology, from which he graduated with an undergraduate degree in 1883, apparently after very little classroom attendance. During this period he invented a wide range of mechanical devices, conducted numerous experiments on metal cutting, began his work on the timing and desired performance of production tasks, and introduced piece-rate incentive systems to the company.

After 12 years at Midvale, Taylor moved on to various positions at a number of manufacturing firms, most of which were held in the role of consultant. There was a considerable stint at Bethlehem Steel. He lectured frequently, including teaching at the Harvard Business School every winter from 1909 to 1914. Largely at the suggestion of Louis Brandeis, a lawyer, the term *scientific management* was applied to Taylor's system. Over time, the unions became increasingly vocal in their opposition to this approach (Hoxie, 1915). Taylor died at age 59.

Largely in connection with his consulting activities, Taylor came to surround himself with a number of people who served both to promote scientific management and in some cases to modify it. Several of these — including Carl Barth, Henry Gantt, Frank and Lillian Gilbreth, Harrington Emerson, and Morris Cooke (Wren, 1994) — became quite famous in their own right. Selections written by other individuals in the scientific management circle and published in the *Bulletin of the Taylor Society* are contained in a book by Donald Del Mar and Rodger Collons (1976). For a number of reasons — including Taylor's controversial nature, his important ideas, and the availability of biographical material — the man and his work have been the subject of a spate of biographical books. Sudhir Kakar (1970) provides a psychoanalytic interpretation. Daniel Nelson (1980) places Taylor in the context of the industrialization of America. Charles Wrege and Ronald Greenwood (1991) focus on Taylor as an individual and the influence of those around him. Robert Kanigel's (1997) treatment is characterized by more balance than the others.

Fayol's Statements

Fayol's (1949) major work in the field of management consisted of two parts — "Necessity and Possibility of Teaching Management" and "Principles and Elements of Management." Two additional parts, "Personal Observations and Experience" and "Lessons of the War," were projected but never published. These latter parts were to deal with applications, some of which are discussed in Fayol's later writings and speeches (see Brodie, 1967).

At the time Fayol wrote, theory was distinctly lacking in the management field. Fayol felt that there was a great need for management education to supplement technical education such as the training he himself had received in engineering, and he believed that the existence of a body of theory was a necessary precondition for such education. This was the underlying rationale for his theorizing.

Definition of Management

Fayol specified the essential activities or functions of industrial organizations to be the following:

1. Technical — production, manufacture, adaptation
2. Commercial — buying, selling, exchange
3. Financial — search for and optimum use of capital
4. Security — protection of property and persons
5. Accounting — stocktaking, balance sheets, costs, statistics
6. Managerial — planning, organization, command, coordination, control

Management is spread like all other activities, between the head and members of the body corporate, but it is concentrated particularly within top management. The distinct increase in hypothesized need for managerial ability, as compared with the decrease or stability of other abilities that comes with an increase in occupational level, is indicated in table 3.1. At the lower levels it is technical ability that matters most; at higher levels it is managerial ability. The definition of technical ability varies, of course, within commercial, financial, and other functions. The head of a very small firm will need considerable technical ability, but this need, like that for commercial ability, will decrease with increasing size; in contrast, managerial ability requirements will increase with size.

Principles of Management

The principles are defined as flexible and capable of adaptation, rather than rigid and absolute. Using them is an art. Fayol set forth 14 such principles of management. Behavior in accord with them will contribute to a more effective organization. The list is not exhaustive, but they apply widely. Regarding them, Fayol said: "This code is indispensable. Be it a case of commerce, industry, politics, religion, war, or philanthropy, in every concern there is a management function to be performed and for its performance there must be principles, that is to say acknowledged truths regarded as proven on which to rely" (1949, pp. 41–42).

1. *Division of work.* Division of labor or specialization at the worker and managerial levels reduces the number of objects to which attention must be given and therefore yields increased quality and quantity of

TABLE 3.1 Fayol's hypothesized ability requirements at various occupational levels

Occupational level	Distribution of required abilities (%)					
	Technical	Commercial	Financial	Security	Accounting	Managerial
Production worker	85	—	—	5	5	5
Foreman	60	5	—	10	10	15
Superintendent	45	5	—	10	15	25
Section head	30	5	5	10	20	30
Department head	30	10	5	10	10	35
Plant manager	15	15	10	10	10	40
General manager	10	10	10	10	10	50

SOURCE: Adapted from Henri Fayol (1949), *General and Industrial Management* (London: Pitman), 8

output for the same amount of overall effort. There are limits beyond which division of work should not be carried out, however. How these limits may be determined is not clearly specified.

2. *Authority and responsibility.* Managers should exercise authority, both as it derives from the office held and as it derives from the intelligence, experience, and other personal qualities of the manager. At the same time, responsibility must be commensurate with authority in that rewards and penalties accrue, depending on how effectively authority is used. Determining and measuring the authority of a given manager as it relates to a particular outcome and establishing appropriate sanctions are viewed as major difficulties. Fayol recognized the underlying measurement problems here; he also recognized a natural tendency to seek authority and avoid responsibility. In neither case does he present a solution, other than to call for integrity and moral character.

3. *Discipline.* Discipline is a condition for effective operation of a business. It consists of obedience, application, energy, behavior, and outward marks of respect, all given on the basis of some formal or informal employment contract between the individual and the firm. To function as it should, discipline requires good managers, clear and equitable agreements, and the judicious application of sanctions such as warnings, fines, suspensions, and other, similar disciplinary actions.

4. *Unity of command.* An individual should receive orders with regard to a particular action from one source only. Dual command is to be avoided. Examples of situations where dual command may arise are superiors bypassing subordinate managers to direct that manager's subordinates, two friends or

family members both heading up a firm, unclear boundaries between two departments at the same level, and conditions of role ambiguity in general.

5. *Unity of direction.* Unity of direction applies to coordination of effort and is a principle of organizations. A group of activities having the same objective should be placed under a single head and a single plan. Fayol does not discuss the bases for differentiating objectives that might be applied here.

6. *Subordination of individual interests to general interest.* For effective functioning, the interests of the organization as a whole must take precedence over those of individuals or groups. Subordination of interests is one basis for reconciling conflicting interests. In some instances, interests of a different order appear to have equal claims. Such conflicts must be reconciled rather than being permitted to continue. Possible means to this end are the firmness and good example of managers, fair agreements, and constant supervision.

7. *Remuneration of personnel.* Insofar as possible, payments should be fair and equitable, should reward well-directed effort, and should not exceed reasonable limits. Various methods of achieving these goals are discussed, but without any clear resolution. One index of effective remuneration is that the pay agreement afford satisfaction to employer and employee alike, but it is recognized that this may not be possible. There is a need for precise definitions and operationalizations of concepts such as fairness, reasonable limits, and the like.

8. *Centralization.* The amount of centralization, as opposed to decentralization, should be optimal for the particular concern. Contingency variables are firm size, personal character of the manager, manager's

moral worth, reliability of subordinates, and condition of the business. The degree of centralization may vary considerably, depending on the relative potential effectiveness of the manager or subordinate. Fayol's formulations in this area are not specific, but he does recognize a number of relevant contingency factors.

9. *Scalar chain.* In the simplest case, communication should occur up and down the scalar chain of authority—in figure 3.1 from E_1 up to A, and if necessary, back down to E_2. But vertical communication through this many steps may consume too much time. Where speed is essential, firms should resort to what has been called Fayol's gangplank—horizontal communication authorized by managers at the next higher level. This, too, is indicated in figure 3.1. In general, Fayol seems to think that horizontal communication should be used more widely than it is. Surprisingly, he did not include the scalar chain principle in all versions of his theory (Brodie, 1967).

10. *Order.* To avoid loss of material, there should be a place for everything and everything in its place. In addition, the prescribed place should be one that facilitates the carrying out of necessary activities. However, the principle of order applies not only to material things, but also to people. Thus there should be an appointed place for each employee, and each employee should be in that place. Again, the appointed place should be appropriate to the task to be performed. This principle means good organization and selection, and it implies the existence of an organization chart.

11. *Equity.* Employees should be treated with kindness and justice, which together equal equity. The object is to elicit devotion and loyalty in return. Ideally, a sense of equity will permeate the whole scalar chain.

12. *Stability of tenure of personnel.* Employees and managers alike need time to settle into their jobs before they can achieve maximum performance. They should be given this opportunity, and thus considerable stability of personnel should prevail. A lack of stability is both a cause and effect of poor management. At the same time, there can be too much stability. In common with all the other principles, stability of tenure of personnel is also a question of proportion. No specific guidelines for establishing when the correct proportion exists are given, however.

13. *Initiative.* Initiative is thinking out a plan and executing it, as well as having the freedom to do these things. Initiative of this kind should be encouraged; it is particularly valuable to an organization in difficult times. The manager who facilitates the initiative of subordinates is far superior to the manager who does not, because initiative can serve as a source of both satisfaction and motivation.

14. *Esprit de corps.* Essentially this is a principle of unity. Harmony should be fostered and conflict minimized. Unity of command is one means to this end. Fayol comes out strongly against the application of such ideas as "divide and conquer" in the organization. Creating dissension among one's subordinates thwarts coordination and teamwork. Verbal communication should be used whenever possible because, being two-way, it permits rapid resolution of conflicts. Written communication often fosters conflict.

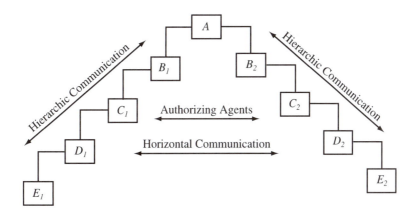

FIGURE 3.1 Fayol's scalar chain and the gangplank

Elements of Management

Fayol specified five elements of management.

1. *Planning.* Planning involves foresight—assessing the future and making provisions for it. It requires the development of a plan of action based on contributions from throughout the business. Fayol comes out strongly in favor of planning that is characterized by unity, continuity, flexibility, and precision. One would expect more effective organizations to be characterized by a greater use of planning and forecasting.

2. *Organizing.* Though a distinction is made between the material organization and the human, only the latter is considered. The human organization is established to carry out managerial functions and implement the principles of management. The basic structure is pyramidal in that each group of 10, 20, or 30 workers brings in a foreman; two, three, or four foremen make necessary a superintendent, two or three superintendents give rise to a department manager, and the number of links of the scalar chain continues to increase in this way up to the ultimate superior; each new superior has usually no more than four or five immediate subordinates.

Fayol considers staffing the existing structure part of the organizing function. In addition to the line positions that extend from operatives to the board of directors, it is necessary to fill certain staff positions attached to the general manager's office that serve to complement the general manager's capabilities. This is the general staff concept, and there are no levels of authority within this component. Such staff members may be consultants, and they may devote only part of their time to the staff position. To the extent it violates unity of command, Fayol rejects direct supervision of one person by several functional specialists.

Evaluation, especially of managerial personnel, is also part of the organizing function. Among the factors to be considered are health and physical fitness, intelligence, moral qualities, general education, management knowledge, knowledge of the other functions (technical, commercial, etc.), and specialized ability characteristic of the concern. Only the last requirement varies from one business to another; thus managerial capabilities are highly transferable.

3. *Command.* Command activates the organization structure. It involves knowing the personnel thoroughly and eliminating incompetents; being knowledgeable about employer-employee agreements; setting a good example; conducting periodic organization audits; setting up conferences among one's chief assistants to establish unity of direction; avoiding an excess of detail; and generally fostering unity, energy, initiative, and loyalty. Being knowledgeable about subordinates, and command in general, is facilitated by a limited span of control. Effective performance of the command function is partly a matter of personal skill and partly a result of having a good grasp of the management principles.

4. *Coordination.* The various activities of an organization must be harmonized into a single whole, and that is the function of coordination. Basically, it is a matter of establishing rightful proportions for the parts, ensuring that these proportions are maintained, and adapting means to ends. Under such conditions, the various departments work in harmony with each other, communicating as needed, rather than operating in isolation as ends in themselves. The component units know their role in the total effort and what interdependencies exist with other units. Departmental scheduling is constantly fine-tuned to external circumstances, rather than carried out without reference to organizational goals, loyalties, and needs for initiative.

The prime method of achieving coordination is a periodic conference of department heads. Where this is physically not possible, an alternative is to use the liaison officers attached to the staff to coordinate departments. In either case, the need to facilitate horizontal communication is clearly evident.

5. *Control.* Control is the process of checking the realities of operations against plans and taking steps to correct deviations. It assumes the existence of up-to-date plans and the use of sanctions to achieve compatibility with them in a timely manner. Fayol notes that, if they are not devised correctly and monitored effectively, control systems may create duality of management. To the extent inspection is inherent in the control system, it should be impartial and objective.

Statements after 1916

Fayol continued to write on the subject of management during the 9 years between the publication of *General and Industrial Management* in 1916 and his death. Much of this material is not generally available. There have been a few translations into English (Fayol, 1937, 1970), and several summarizations of other works have been published (Brodie, 1967; Breeze & Bedeian, 1988).

Little modification occurred after publication of the primary theory. Many of the later papers deal with applications, and there are numerous restatements of parts of the theory. Fayol did come to view his own formulations and the scientific management ideas of Taylor as more complementary than conflicting (de Freminville, 1927).

Taylor's Statements

Taylor was concerned primarily with factory management, and within that context his emphasis was mostly on the management of production workers. In this respect, his frame of reference differs sharply from that of Fayol, who developed his ideas from a perspective of top management. It is not surprising that the two men, the engineer and the corporation president, created principles of management that differed sharply from each other. Fayol wrote from a macro perspective; Taylor from a micro viewpoint.

Principles of Management

Although he is often credited with only four principles of management, Taylor's writings abound with prescriptive statements, often stated in moralistic terms, indicating what a manager should do to improve effectiveness (Filipetti, 1953). The basic four, however, are these:

1. Develop a science for the work of each person. This involves determining how the work can best be performed by experimenting with it, conducting motion and time studies, and often applying mathematical formulas.
2. Scientifically select the best individual for the job, train that person to be able to perform the job better and better, and finally pay higher wages than ever before to reward the increased productivity.
3. Cooperate with the workers to ensure that the work is in fact done in the prescribed manner; make the knowledge of the job (principle 1) and the worker selected (principle 2) come together. This should include, but not be limited to, providing for increased earnings for those who follow the prescribed methods most closely.
4. Divide the work so that activities such as planning, organizing, and controlling are the responsibility of management; the worker, in contrast, has the responsibility for doing. This division is predicated on the assumption that

most workers do not have the capability to create the science of their work.

Conditions for Change

Scientific management based on these principles cannot exist without a complete mental revolution, which takes considerable time to achieve and affects both managers and workers. The workers must learn and accept a new set of duties to management. Restriction of output (Taylor called it soldiering) must be abandoned in favor of greater output and making more money. At the same time, management must undergo a mental revolution and assume duties toward employees, including not changing standards when employee earnings increase sharply under piece-rate systems.

In accordance with the principles, Taylor advocated that the planning process be separated from the work and carried out by a centralized planning group; he also advocated that specialized or functional foremanship be introduced. According to this concept, a production worker would report to different foremen, depending on which aspect of the work was involved. Thus, an individual might have many bosses, but each would operate within a narrow, strictly delimited zone of influence and expertise. This concept is illustrated in figure 3.2.

The Exception Principle

Taylor placed strong emphasis on the *exception principle*. Output standards and routine procedures were to be established through the use of precise measurement; management should then give its attention only to those cases where standards were not met or exceeded to a marked degree, and where established procedures were not or could not be followed. As the exception principle implies, Taylor generally advocated dealing with one individual at a time, but he was not unaware of the ways in which group influences might operate to produce a restriction of output. The discovery of these restrictive practices is widely attributed to the human relations researchers who followed him by some 15 or 20 years. Yet Taylor's writings are sprinkled with references to group pressures and their impact on production (Boddewyn, 1961).

While the exception principle was intended to focus primarily on ineffective performers and to deal with them, it also singled out outstanding performers, who may have developed an approach to their work

Activities Planners

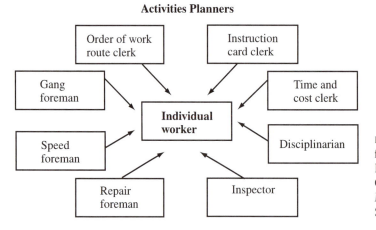

FIGURE 3.2 Taylor's functional foreman concept. Adapted from Frank B. Gilbreth & Lillian M. Gilbreth (1917), *Applied Motion Study* (New York: Sturgis and Walton).

that was even better than the one scientific study had identified. Thus the "one best way" established by job study was not etched in concrete; it could be improved upon, and Taylor had a procedure for flagging possible innovations to improve it.

It should be emphasized that the use of the adjective *scientific* to describe Taylor's views is by no means a misnomer. He was an advocate of research and experimentation in management, and he conducted studies to determine how various jobs might best be performed. He developed a number of techniques for controlled observation and the measurement of behavior.

Impact of the Classical Theorists

Many organizational behavior theorists of other orientations have used the classical theories as foils against which to pit their own formulations (see, for example, Argyris 1957; Bennis, 1966; Likert, 1967). These attacks contend that classical theory is inadequate because it fails to predict and explain a large number of phenomena. Under a variety of conditions of organizational membership, technology, environmental context, and the like the theories do not work. Also, they have been attacked as failing to meet the requirements of good scientific theory, as reflected in a pervasive ambiguity of statement and a lack of logical consistency (Simon, 1947/1976). These criticisms appear justified. Both Fayol and Taylor have also been attacked as espousing views that are inherently inhumane. Whether this is true appears to depend on what passages are quoted and one's definition of inhumane. In any event, this issue is beyond the purview of a

book such as this, which is primarily concerned with science, not philosophy.

Research

A rather large body of research has been marshaled on occasion in support of the formulations of classical theory. However, much of this research was conducted for reasons that have no direct relationship to the testing of classical theory. Its relevance is not at all clear. Fayol and Taylor and their followers did not operationalize their variables; in fact, they described them in very ambiguous terms. They did not do research on their theories, and because they were in the best position to know what they really were talking about, the opportunity to test the theories has now been lost.

This is not to say that both Fayol and Taylor did not conduct research; both did. However, their research was in the field of engineering, and in Taylor's case human factors. Neither knew much about the kind of research that came to underlie the field of organizational behavior. That approach was in its early infancy at the time. But the followers extended into a period when much more was known. That, for whatever reason, they did not resort to research on the theories they espoused accounts in large part for the present-day failure of those theories.

There have been attempts, even in the 1990s, to tie the classical theories to phenomena of recent vintage. Richard Hodgetts (1995) has done this with Taylor's principles and Wren (1990) with Fayol's elements of management. The problem with all such efforts is in the interpretation of Taylor and Fayol. Were they really saying the same things that are now being said some 75 years later? Given the ambiguity of the early statements, it seems possible to make them fit almost any context. But do they really fit?

Applications

Because both Fayol and Taylor were practicing managers, the appeal of their theories for practitioners is not surprising. Managers use the terminology of the theories widely, and consultants still call on their precepts to substantiate their recommendations—and perhaps to develop them, too. Textbooks have characteristically been modeled around the elements of management for a number of years. Yet studies designed to measure the effects of applications directly are practically nonexistent. There are cross-sectional studies and endless anecdotal testimonials. What is lacking are instances in which classical precepts are implemented, potential consequences are measured before and after, and the results are compared with similar results obtained under controlled conditions.

Fayol was involved in three applications, or potential applications, of his ideas. One was a study within the company he headed, Commentry-Fourchambault et Décazeville (Fayol, 1970); the second was a consulting engagement with the French government in the Department of Posts, Telegraphs, and Telephones (Fayol, 1937; Brodie, 1967); and the third was a similar engagement with the tobacco monopoly in France (Brodie, 1967).

Of the three, only the company application can make any claim to success:

> [The firm] was declining and on the road to bankruptcy, when a change occurred in 1888, in the way in which the administrative function was carried out; and, without modification of anything else, without improvement in any of the adverse factors, the business began to prosper and has not stopped growing since. With the same mines and factories, with the same financial resources, the same markets, the same board of directors and the same personnel, solely because of a new method of administration the company experienced a rise comparable to its earlier fall. (Fayol, 1970, p. 148)

Success is attributed specifically to a strategic action program that was based on annual and 10-year forecasts, the existence of an organization chart, observation of the necessary principles with regard to command, meetings of department and division heads, and universal control based on accounting data.

In the case of the Department of Posts, Telegraphs, and Telephones, Fayol (1937) points out many departures from his theoretical prescriptions and recommends appropriate corrections; span of control is a major concern. He recommended plans of action, regular meetings, organization charts, horizontal communication, and time study, among other changes. Yet the results were disappointing. The recommendations and results in the case of the tobacco monopoly were much the same. It could be argued that his theory was specific to his own company, where it was developed.

Taylor describes many applications of his ideas and provides glowing testimonials to their success. There seems little doubt that studying jobs and finding out how best to do them can make a difference. But there is nothing to indicate the value added by his management principles and the mental revolution. Job study and industrial engineering certainly have survived and prospered, but the rest of scientific management has not fared as well. Functional foremanship failed, largely because it created role conflict (and thus violated unity of command). The division of labor involved appears to have been excessive. Nevertheless, the exception principle clearly did contribute to practice and continues to do so today.

A quote from Wren and Greenwood provides an idea of how Taylor has come to influence practice at the present time:

> Many of his notions provided foundations for current practice. Examples include setting standards for evaluating performance and for product quality, and an "exception principle," under which managers look for both good and bad exceptions to standards so corrective action, such as quality control, can be taken. What is today called Japanese-style management is an outgrowth of Taylor's ideas, which were introduced into Japan in the early 1910s. The Japanese like Taylor's emphasis on mutual interests, cooperation, and harmony. (1998, p. 138)

A final point involves Fayol's five elements of management. In some form, these elements have been widely used in training managers. They continue to be applied in the structuring of management textbooks. However, the variations in the lists of functions employed by different authors is huge. There is no firm reliance on Fayol's elements, and, indeed, several of his functions may well be omitted from any given list. The tie to Fayol has become tenuous over time. Furthermore, this structuring is a characteristic of management, not organizational behavior, textbooks. One simply would not construct a book on organizational behavior in this manner, thus adding to the distancing that has occurred between the field and classical management theory.

Nevertheless, if the objective is to understand the nature of managerial work, a very good case can be made that Fayol's elements, in some version or mix, do provide a useful framework (Carroll & Gillen, 1987). Furthermore, experience and skill in these kinds of activities make for greater managerial success. Thus, classical theory is not totally devoid of research support in all areas.

CONCLUSIONS

In the preceding chapter, the disciplinary origins of organizational behavior were traced to roots in philosophy, management, sociology, and psychology. To this list we can now add political science, social work, law, history, and engineering. Truly, the field came together from a very wide range of disciplinary origins. As we will see in the next chapter, this has represented both a source of strength and stimulation and a barrier to integration and unobstructed communication.

Yet there is another sense in which organizational behavior's origins exhibit an amazing degree of similarity—the frequent geographical ties to the Boston area. Elton Mayo came from Australia and touched down at several outlying stations, but he did his major work at Harvard. Chester Barnard grew up nearby and attended Harvard, and in his scholarly years the ties to Harvard were strong and prolonged. Kurt Lewin came from Germany via Iowa; however, he ended up at MIT, and that is where his contributions to the beginnings of organizational behavior became most apparent.

Mary Follett attended the women's college of Harvard and spent almost her whole life in the Boston area. Max Weber lived and worked in Germany. Yet his theories were introduced to this country primarily through the efforts of Talcott Parsons of Harvard. Not surprisingly, the imputed antiheroes, Fayol and Taylor, never lived in the Boston area. Certainly Fayol was far away in France, but Taylor did in fact lecture at Harvard a few months a year for 5 years.

Whether anything in particular should be made of this geographical concentration would require a control group of eminent early contributors to other disciplines before an answer to the hypothesis could be established. I am not in a position to conduct such a comparison study. Yet on the face of it, the affinity for the Boston area, and for Harvard, seems unusual.

References

Abrahamsson, Bengt (1977). *Bureaucracy or Participation: The Logic of Organization.* Beverly Hills, CA: Sage.

Aldrich, Howard E., & Pfeffer, Jeffrey (1976). Environments of Organizations. *Annual Review of Sociology,* 2, 79–105.

Argyris, Chris (1957). *Personality and Organization.* New York: Harper & Row.

Bass, Bernard M. (1985) *Leadership and Performance beyond Expectations.* New York: Free Press.

Bass, Bernard M. (1998). *Transformational Leadership: Industrial, Military, and Educational Impact.* Mahwah, NJ: Erlbaum.

Bennis, Warren G. (1966). *Changing Organizations.* New York: McGraw-Hill.

Bennis, Warren G.; Benne, Kenneth D.; & Chin, Robert (1969). *The Planning of Change.* New York: Holt, Rinehart & Winston.

Blau, Peter M. (1974). *On the Nature of Organizations.* New York: Wiley.

Boddewyn, Jean J. (1961). Frederick Winslow Taylor Revisited. *Academy of Management Journal,* 4, 100–107.

Boje, D. M., & Rosile, Grace A. (2001). Where's the Power in Empowerment? Answers from Follett and Clegg. *Journal of Applied Behavioral Science,* 37, 90–117.

Breeze, John D. (1985). Harvest from the Archives: The Search for Fayol and Carlioz. *Journal of Management,* 11, 43–54.

Breeze, John D., & Bedeian, Arthur G. (1988). *The Administrative Writings of Henri Fayol: A Bibliographic Investigation.* Monticello, IL: Vance Bibliographies.

Brodie, M. B. (1967). *Fayol on Administration.* London: Lyon, Grant & Green.

Carroll, Stephen J., & Gillen, Dennis J. (1987). Are the Classical Management Functions Useful in Describing Managerial Work? *Academy of Management Review,* 12, 38–51.

Chandler, Alfred D. (1962) *Strategy and Structure: Chapters in the History of the American Industrial Enterprise.* Cambridge, MA: MIT Press.

Clegg, Stewart R. (1995). Of Values and Occasional Irony: Max Weber in the Context of the Sociology of Organizations. *Research in the Sociology of Organizations*, 13, 1–46.

Conger, Jay A. (1993). Max Weber's Conceptualization of Charismatic Authority: Its Influence on Organizational Research. *Leadership Quarterly*, 4, 277–288.

Cyr, Dianne, & Reich, Blaize H. (1996). *Scaling the Ivory Tower: Stories from Women in Business School Faculties*. Westport, CT: Praeger.

Daiute, Robert J. (1964). Mary Parker Follett: Integration. In Robert J. Daiute (Ed.), *Scientific Management and Human Relations* (pp. 30–36). New York: Holt, Rinehart, & Winston.

Davis, Ralph C. (1951). *The Fundamentals of Top Management*. New York: Harper & Row.

de Freminville, Charles (1927). Henri Fayol: A Great Engineer, a Great Scientist and a Great Management Leader. *Bulletin of the Taylor Society*, February.

Del Mar, Donald, & Collons, Rodger D. (1976). *Classics in Scientific Management: A Book of Readings*. University: University of Alabama Press.

Fayol, Henri (1937). The Administrative Theory in the State. In Luther Gulick & Lyndall F. Urwick (Eds.), *Papers on the Science of Administration* (pp. 99–114). New York: Institute of Public Administration.

Fayol, Henri (1949). *General and Industrial Management* (Constance Storrs, trans.). London: Pitman.

Fayol, Henri (1970). The Importance of the Administrative Factor. In Ernest Dale (Ed.), *Readings in Management: Landmarks and New Frontiers* (pp. 148–149). New York: McGraw-Hill.

Filipetti, George. (1953). *Industrial Management in Transition*. Homewood, IL: Irwin.

Follett, Mary P. (1924). *Creative Experience*. New York: Longmans, Green.

Follett, Mary P. (1926). The Illusion of Final Authority. *Bulletin of the Taylor Society*, 2(5).

Follett, Mary P. (1927). Management as a Profession. In Henry C. Metcalf (Ed.), *Business Management as a Profession* (pp. 73–87). Chicago: A. W. Shaw.

Follett, Mary P. (1955). When Business Management Becomes a Profession. *Advanced Management Journal*, July, 22–26.

Fox, Elliot M., & Urwick, Lyndall F. (1973). *Dynamic Administration: The Collected Papers of Mary Parker Follett*. London: Pitman.

Gilbreth, Frank B., & Gilbreth, Lillian M. (1917). *Applied Motion Study*. New York: Sturgis and Walton.

Gouldner, Alvin (1954). *Patterns of Industrial Bureaucracy*. New York: Free Press.

Graham, Pauline (1995). *Mary Parker Follett—Prophet of Management*. Boston: Harvard Business School Press.

Gulick, Luther, & Urwick, Lyndall F. (1937). *Papers on the Science of Administration*. New York: Institute of Public Administration.

Hodgetts, Richard M. (1995). Frederick Taylor: Alive and Well and Ready for the 21st Century. *Academy of Management Proceedings*, 55, 218–222.

House, Robert J. (1977). A 1976 Theory of Charismatic Leadership. In James G. Hunt & Lars L. Larson (Eds.), *Leadership: The Cutting Edge* (pp. 194–205). Carbondale: Southern Illinois University Press.

Hoxie, R. F. (1915). *Scientific Management and Labor*. New York: Appleton-Century-Crofts.

Kakar, Sudhir (1970). *Frederick Taylor: A Study in Personality and Innovation*. Cambridge, MA: MIT Press.

Kanigel, Robert (1997). *The One Best Way: Frederick Winslow Taylor and the Enigma of Efficiency*. New York: Viking.

Koontz, Harold, & O'Donnell, Cyril (1955). *Principles of Management: An Analysis of Managerial Functions*. New York: McGraw-Hill.

Lawrence, Paul R., & Lorsch, Jay W. (1967). *Organization and Environment: Managing Differentiation and Integration*. Boston: Graduate School of Business Administration, Harvard University.

Likert, Rensis (1967). *The Human Organization: Its Management and Value*. New York: McGraw-Hill.

Likert, Rensis, & Likert, Jane G. (1976). *New Ways of Managing Conflict*. New York: McGraw-Hill.

McGregor, Douglas (1967). *The Professional Manager* (edited posthumously by Caroline McGregor & Warren G. Bennis). New York: McGraw-Hill.

McNeil, Kenneth (1978). Understanding Organizational Power: Building on the Weberian Legacy. *Administrative Science Quarterly*, 23, 65–90.

Metcalf, Henry C., & Urwick, Lyndall F. (1940). *Dynamic Administration: The Collected Papers of Mary Parker Follett*. New York: Harper.

Miner, John B. (1971). *Management Theory*. New York: Macmillan.

Miner, John B. (1995). *Administrative and Management Theory*. Aldershot, UK: Dartmouth.

Mooney, James D., & Reiley, Alan C. (1931). *Onward Industry! The Principles of Organization and Their Significance to Modern Industry*. New York: Harper & Row.

Nelson, Daniel (1980). *Frederick W. Taylor and the Rise of Scientific Management*. Madison: University of Wisconsin Press.

Parker, L. D. (1984). Control in Organizational Life: The Contribution of Mary Parker Follett. *Academy of Management Review*, 9, 736–745.

Powell, Walter W., & DiMaggio, Paul J. (1991). *The New Institutionalism in Organizational Analysis*. Chicago: University of Chicago Press.

Satow, Roberta L. (1975). Value-Rational Authority and Professional Organizations: Weber's Missing Type. *Administrative Science Quarterly*, 20, 526–531.

Scott, W. Richard (1995). *Institutions and Organizations*. Thousand Oaks, CA: Sage.

Selznick, Philip (1949). *TVA and the Grass Roots*. Berkeley: University of California Press.

Sethi, Narendra K. (1962). Mary Parker Follett: Pioneer in Management Theory. *Journal of the Academy of Management*, 5, 214–221.

Simon, Herbert A. (1947/1976). *Administrative Behavior: A Study of Decision-Making Processes in Administrative Organization*. New York: Free Press.

Taylor, Frederick W. (1903). *Shop Management*. New York: Harper & Row.

Taylor, Frederick W. (1911). *The Principles of Scientific Management*. New York: Harper & Row.

Thompson, James D. (1967). *Organizations in Action*. New York: McGraw-Hill.

Thompson, Victor A. (1961). *Modern Organization*. New York: Knopf.

Thompson, Victor A. (1976). *Bureaucracy and the Modern World*. Morristown, NJ: General Learning Press.

Turner, Stephen P. (1983). Weber on Action. *American Sociological Review*, 48, 506–519.

Urwick, Lyndall F. (1949). *Freedom and Coordination — Lectures in Business Organization by Mary Parker Follett.*. London: Management Publications Trust.

Urwick, Lyndall F. (1952). *Notes on the Theory of Organization*. New York: American Management Association.

Walton, Richard E., & McKersie, Robert B. (1965). *A Behavioral Theory of Labor Negotiations: An Analysis of a Social Interaction System*. New York: McGraw-Hill.

Weber, Marianne (1975). *Max Weber: A Biography* (Harry Zohn, trans. & ed.). New York: Wiley.

Weber, Max (1930). *The Protestant Ethic and the Spirit of Capitalism* (Talcott Parsons, trans.). London: Allen & Unwin.

Weber, Max (1946). *From Max Weber: Essays in Sociology* (Hans H. Gerth & C. Wright Mills, trans. & eds.). New York: Oxford University Press.

Weber, Max (1947). *The Theory of Social and Economic Organization* (Talcott Parsons & A. M. Henderson, trans. & eds.). New York: Free Press.

Weber, Max (1968). *Economy and Society*, 3 vols. (Guenther Roth & Claus Wittich, trans. & eds.). New York: Bedminster.

Weick, Karl E. (1995). *Sensemaking in Organizations*. Thousand Oaks, CA: Sage.

Weiss, Richard M. (1983). Weber on Bureaucracy: Management Consultant or Political Theorist? *Academy of Management Review*, 8, 242–248.

Wrege, Charles D., & Greenwood, Ronald G. (1991). *Frederick W. Taylor, Father of Scientific Management: Myth and Reality*. Homewood, IL: Business One Irwin.

Wren, Daniel A. (1990). Was Henri Fayol a Real Manager? *Academy of Management Proceedings*, 50, 138–142.

Wren, Daniel A. (1994). *The Evolution of Management Thought*. New York: Wiley.

Wren, Daniel A., & Greenwood, Ronald G. (1998). *Management Innovators: The People and Ideas That Have Shaped Modern Business*. New York: Oxford University Press.

Chapter 4

Establishing the Ground against Which Organizational Behavior Became Figure

In the area of perception, within the larger context of experimental psychology, Gestalt psychologists have long given special attention to figure-ground relationships (Ellis, 1950). Figures tend to vary widely in the way they are perceived, depending on the nature of the ground against which they are superimposed. In the same manner, information is interpreted relative to the context that surrounds it (Erez, 1996).

In this chapter I explore the ground that existed for organizational behavior and its theories over the period of approximately 25 years, which extended from the late 1940s to the early 1970s. Much of this ground stems from the nature and characteristics of the business schools of that time. By exploring this ground, we will gain a much better understanding of the meaning that attaches to certain activities within organizational behavior itself (as figure). This is the period during which organizational behavior actually emerged and strengthened its position. Knowing how that happened, and against what context, is important to understanding what the field has become today.

The flow from chapter 3 to chapter 4 is continuous. Chapters 2 and 3 established the ideas that were available and described the people who created them. The scene was set intellectually for the new discipline to appear. However, some catalyst was needed to make the potential a reality, to move across the threshold to identity, to establish the benchmarks that indicate that a new discipline was formed. Beyond this, however, in the early years certain sources of support were needed to give the fledgling discipline strength and an opportunity to grow. With this infusion from outside, capabilities could develop within, eventuating in a set of theories, a body of knowledge, that grew from the discipline itself, thus creating intellectual and scientific legitimacy for organizational behavior.

All this has been a hard-won victory. Many people have contributed to it, and I will note a large number of them in what follows. Perhaps in the process the treatment will provide a better understanding of why those who helped to create and develop the field often react as strongly as they do in opposition to threats to the field's integrity. In any event, this emergence and growth of organizational behavior against the context or ground that existed inside and around the business schools is the subject matter of this chapter. This is the direct history that has shaped the present (see Barley & Kunda, 1992, and Bedeian, 1998, for various views on this point).

FOUNDATIONS, THEIR REPORTS, AND THE AFTERMATH

Two foundations played a very active role in what happened in the business schools during the 1950s and 1960s. These are the Ford and Carnegie Foundations, each of which independently surveyed the current state of the schools and issued now widely cited reports. A great deal can be learned about the origins of organizational behavior from a perusal of the processes inherent in this foundation activism.

Ford Foundation (1954–1964)

Of the two foundations, Ford was by far the most active. Its program for business schools was initiated in 1954 and extended across a period of more than 10 years. In the process, over $35 million was spent (Porter & McKibbin, 1988).

Conferences and Conference Volumes

One of the most visible components of the Ford Foundation's program was the sponsorship of a variety of conferences, usually operated by a particular business school to which money was appropriated for this purpose. These conferences, and the books resulting, provided high visibility for a brand of scholarship that focused on the application of mathematical and social science skills to organizational problems. Some examples are the following:

- A conference convened at Cambria Pines, California, in 1961 by UCLA with a wide range of participants, including people from both within and outside business schools. These scholars included psychologists, philosophers, statisticians, psychiatrists, sociologists, political scientists, and economists. The publication was entitled *Mathematical Explorations in Behavioral Science* (Massarik & Ratoosh, 1965).
- A conference held at UCLA in 1962, involving management theorists, business school administrators, and management practitioners. The management theorists included a range of social scientists. The conference volume, *Toward a Unified Theory of Management*, was edited by Harold Koontz (1964).
- A conference sponsored by the University of Pittsburgh in that city in 1962. The participants were psychologists, sociologists, management scholars, political scientists, applied anthropologists, and economists. Small grants were made to members of the conference to set up cross-disciplinary seminars, to reward outstanding graduate student research, and to fund exploratory research on organizational problems. The conference volume was called *The Social Science of Organizations* (Leavitt, 1963). This conference was repeated in 1963, and a second conference volume resulted—*Approaches to Organizational Design* (Thompson, 1966).

In addition, several variants on this theme were applied. The University of Wisconsin was funded to bring visiting scholars to Madison for periods of time to lecture and advise on research. These scholars included a sociologist, an industrial psychologist, a social anthropologist, an anthropologist, a mathematical psychologist, and a social psychologist. The papers they prepared were published under the title *Social Science Approaches to Business Behavior* (Strother, 1962). At the University of Oregon professors from various areas across the campus were brought together to focus on the conduct of an experimental graduate-level course in administrative organization. Papers were prepared by several political scientists, an education professor, and an accountant; they were published in *The Study of Administration* (Wengert, Harwood, Marquis, & Goldhammer, 1961). Subsequently, the course involved was taught on a multidisciplinary basis in the business school for a number of years.

The link between these efforts (and there were a number of others like them) and the objective of promoting a multidisciplinary approach to the study of organizations within the business schools is clearly evident.

Retraining and Research Support

Substantial money was applied to the process of retraining existing business administration faculty members. This took a number of different forms. Faculty members were sent to summer workshops, which were conducted most notably at Carnegie Tech and Chicago. The goal was to teach faculty how to upgrade their courses and research through the use of advanced analytical techniques and approaches. Fellowships were provided for faculty members to study psychology and sociology, mathematics, and statistics. A year-long program was conducted at Harvard to create quantitative upgrading. Efforts such as the one at Wisconsin to bring in visiting professors were often aimed at retraining existing faculty.

Often large grants were made to specific universities for purposes of retraining, research support, and attracting personnel. This was the case at Carnegie Tech, Chicago, Harvard, MIT, and Stanford among others (Sheehan, 1964). From 1953 to 1961 the Ford Foundation gave $2 million to the Harvard Business School, including $100,000 for Roethlisberger to prepare human relations practitioners to work in industry (Gillespie, 1991). Doctoral research was supported, and a program to award prizes for outstanding dissertations was introduced. This approach is described by Thomas Carroll, Ford Foundation vice president, in the foreword to Victor Vroom's published dissertation:

The competition is intended to generalize standards of excellence in research on business by graduate students. It should give widespread professional recognition to persons recently awarded doctorates in business whose dissertation research is especially distinguished by its analytical content and strong roots in underlying disciplines. It is also intended to give recognition to a select number of persons outside business schools who in their doctoral dissertations pursued with distinction interests relevant to business. (1960, p. v)

The Graduate School of Industrial Administration at Carnegie Tech had behavioral scientists and mathematicians on its faculty from its inception in 1949. The major role that they played in retraining and research is described in Herbert Simon's (1991) autobiography.

State of the Business Schools

Why did the Ford Foundation invest its money in these ways? The answer is contained in the report prepared by Robert Gordon and James Howell (1959), entitled *Higher Education for Business*. This report appeared well after the program of aid to business schools was initiated, as that program was escalating. Gordon, the senior author, was chairman of the department of economics at the University of California at Berkeley. He helped prepare the report while he was on leave at the Ford Foundation, beginning in 1956. Howell was a faculty member in economics at the Stanford Graduate School of Business.

The business schools are described as being in a state of flux and uncertainty. They were searching for academic respectability. Much of business education was at a low level and was narrowly vocational in nature. Dissatisfaction with the quality of what was taught was widespread. Personal career counseling of students was nonexistent, and screening of applicants on personal qualities needed for competent performance in business was lacking. Courses were overly descriptive in nature and far too narrow in content. Standards for mathematical competence were low, and coursework in organization and management was in a state of total confusion. The students attracted were certainly numerous but, on balance, quite untalented.

Most business school faculties appeared to be seriously wanting; there was a creeping intellectual obsolescence. The quality of both teaching and research was not high. Faculty members were ill prepared for both, and, in fact, little research in the true meaning of the term was being produced. Gordon and Howell

(1959) noted that this was the case even though doctoral degrees in economics outnumbered those in business administration among business schools faculty by almost 20 percent. Doctorates in other fields were infrequent (psychology was in the 1 to 3 percent range). Yet only 40 percent of all faculty members held a doctorate. Doctoral training itself in the business schools tended to be of inadequate quality, and the numbers produced were low relative to need. Porter and McKibbin (1988) interpreted the competence levels of business school faculties overall at that time as deserving a grade of D at best, and perhaps less charitably as a clear F, based on the data reported. This situation was reflected in the very low level of esteem accorded the business schools in the university pecking order.

Recommendations Relevant
for Organizational Behavior

What did Gordon and Howell (1959) recommend, given this situation? Most relevant for organizational behavior is the push for substantially increased input from the disciplines of psychology, sociology, and cultural anthropology, with an assist from geography, political science, and history. Yet there was a curious ambivalence regarding the role of industrial psychology. Some of the work on the measurement and use of personality factors in the selection of potential managers was discussed in a very critical manner, with only the most lukewarm endorsement overall. In addition, the relevance of industrial psychology research for the resuscitation of the academic field of personnel management was completely ignored.

This ambivalence is also evident with regard to bringing the targeted social scientists onto business school faculties permanently, and in substantial numbers. The authors noted that retreading existing business school faculty into half-baked social scientists was unlikely to work. They also said that drawing on the talents of faculty permanently housed in the social sciences did not seem promising, either. Yet they did not commit to having needed courses offered entirely within the business schools. The social scientists did not need to settle down to teaching business courses but should only contribute their research findings and enrich business teaching. The influx of some such faculty members was noted as an experiment to be watched. There was little likelihood that the addition

to the total supply of business faculty members from this source would be substantial.

Yet the question was posed: What should the business schools teach in order to develop an understanding of organizational behavior and some modicum of organizational skills? (Yes, the term "organizational behavior" was used here.) First, the inchoate nature of the field was noted. Second, four different aspects of the field should be distinguished:

- *Management analysis* — a rational approach to resource allocation within the firm that draws on production management beginning with Taylor and extends to operations analysis; it is often highly quantitative
- *Organization theory* — an approach concerned with the scientific study of human behavior in organizations or the internal organizational environment; it draws heavily on the social sciences
- *Principles of management* — an approach derived from management practice that seeks to describe and distill a set of generalizations called principles; it has its origins in Fayol and his followers
- *Human relations* — an approach that emphasizes the development of rules that can be applied to situations managers are likely to encounter; it is focused on practical considerations and situations

These four aspects, which later came to be labeled "schools," are frequently overlapping in content, but they tend to have different sets of proponents. All four should be represented in the business curriculum somewhere. Organization theory and principles of management, in some unspecified mix, should be incorporated into the core curriculum. Perhaps some human relations should be included. The authors appear to have had difficulty formulating specific recommendations, given the confusion that characterizes the field.

Carnegie Foundation (1959)

The Carnegie Foundation report was prepared independently of the Ford Foundation's effort, although there was some exchange of information. The principal findings and recommendations were reached separately. The Carnegie approach rested almost exclusively on the report itself, following a precedent established by the similar report prepared on medical education many years before (Flexner, 1910). That report proved to be extremely influential in reforming medical education in this country.

The report itself was authored by Frank Pierson, professor of economics at Swarthmore College, a liberal arts college that does not have a business school. Its title is *The Education of American Businessmen: A Study of University-College Programs in Business Administration* (Pierson, 1959). Of the book's 24 chapters, only 11 were prepared by Pierson, but these chapters constitute the body of the report itself. The remaining chapters were prepared by 13 separate contributors and deal with specific aspects of curriculum or other specialized topics. Of those 13 contributors, 8 had long-term ties to some business school; the remaining 5 had no such ties.

State of the Business Schools

Pierson (1959) had the following to say on the state of business education. Work in such fields as accounting, business law, marketing, and production was the subject of widespread attack, suggesting no difference from trade schools. Developments in management and human relations were the butt of criticism and even ridicule. Students were considered to be of inferior quality. These criticisms all appear justified. Students were often of low capability, and the better students among them found little challenge in their business courses. Most business schools appeared to have cut themselves off from other branches of learning, thus removing any serious intellectual content. Academic work of a scientific nature appeared to have been avoided, and admission standards were set at a low level. The subject matter taught was ill defined and lacked a sharp analytical focus. Interest in developing programs of first-rate academic quality appeared to be lacking.

Business school faculties overall were in need of major improvements. Given that doctoral programs in business were often ill defined, the tendency was to hire people who had doctorates in economics. However, the more promising graduates in economics tended to shy away from business school positions. Opportunities for persons holding doctorates outside business and economics in business schools were very limited. A review of faculty requirements, teaching conditions, and teaching methods gave cause for serious concern. Doctoral dissertations in business often

involved descriptions of business practice and required little use of sophisticated analytical methods. The same was true of business school research generally, but the real problem was the dearth of research of any kind.

Recommendations Revelant for Organizational Behavior

The primary recommendation was for substantial upgrading in every respect. In particular, there was a need for upgrading in the areas of mathematics, psychology, and sociology. Although at the graduate level this might be accomplished through courses offered within the business schools, undergraduate coursework offered for business students in these areas should be left in the hands of the liberal arts departments involved. This placed a burden on these departments to meet the needs of business students, however. Social psychology and industrial sociology were mentioned as requiring particular attention. Although coursework in management should be incorporated into the core curriculum, the field was so inchoate that offering a major in it did not seem appropriate.

With regard to bringing psychologists and sociologists into the business schools, there was again uncertainty. Finding faculty members who were competent in both an applied business field and the underlying social science discipline would be difficult. One or two such individuals might be added to work in management, business policy, marketing, and personnel management. Anyone added in this manner needed to be prepared to make the study of business a permanent intellectual interest and at the same time to maintain close ties to the basic discipline. Whether this could be accomplished on a wide scale seemed doubtful. Retraining of existing business faculty in social psychology and industrial sociology, however, was recommended.

View from Carnegie Tech

Within the Carnegie Foundation report, George Bach (1959), dean of the Graduate School of Industrial Administration at Carnegie Tech, has a chapter on managerial decision making as an organizing concept for the business school curriculum. He recommended a foundation stem (or concentration) in administrative process and organizational behavior to go along with stems in economic analysis and quantitative methods. This organizational behavior stem should consider the firm as a going organization and also the behavior of individuals and groups within organizations. The content covered should be descriptive of business firms, but, more important, it should deal with analytical concepts and theory. The needed knowledge for this purpose was rapidly emerging.

Such an effort would require a considerable number of teachers with new expertise. Borrowing faculty temporarily from outside the business school would not work; nor would having an outsider teach an occasional course. Retooling existing business school faculty to teach organizational behavior was only a partial solution at best. Such people were unlikely to add new knowledge to the field through research and development, simply because their primary training was not in the social science disciplines. They were almost certain to be rapidly outdistanced by new doctoral students coming from the business schools. The only solution was to import faculty trained in the social science disciplines, people who would become thoroughly engrossed in business teaching and research. The business schools badly needed this kind of importation.

Harold Leavitt (1960), a psychologist and an import at Carnegie Tech in Bach's school, endorsed this position strongly. He felt that social scientists can learn about business more easily than business faculty can retrain as social scientists. He also felt that business school psychology and sociology are quite different from the versions of these subjects to be found in the liberal arts departments.

At least from Carnegie Tech, which had at least as much experience with these matters as any of the business schools, the call to bring social scientists onto business faculties permanently was loudly and unambiguously expressed.

Impact of the Foundation Activities

The points made and the recommendations of the two reports are not identical, but they are similar. The picture painted of the ground for organizational behavior is disturbing, yet in some respects it is also encouraging. Both reports recommended bringing social science subject matter and research skills into the business schools. However, contrary to what is often assumed, neither report came out unequivocally in favor of adding a substantial cohort of social scientists

directly into existing faculties. A little reading between the lines suggests that the reports' authors may well have been concerned that any large-scale importation of this kind might create major controversy and conflict in a situation that was already characterized by considerable flux. Thus other changes might be jeopardized. It remained for Carnegie Tech, a greenfield site (a startup situation) that had already incorporated social scientists from the beginning, to speak out strongly on this issue.

A second point, not always widely recognized, is that economists were already well established in the business schools in the mid-1950s. In fact, this was a major problem for the authors of the reports. Even with the extensive participation of economists, the schools had performed poorly and were held in low regard by the rest of the university community. Many business school deans and administrators were economists by training. A major incentive for them to carry out the reports' recommendations was that, by doing so, the stature of the whole business area might be raised. It is safe to assume that opinion leaders from within the economics discipline served in a very important way to bring the field of organizational behavior into existence in this early period.

Finally, organizational behavior at the time of the reports was in a state of chaos. It hardly had a name that members of the field would recognize, let alone a domain and a mandate. We will return to this matter of uncertainty later.

American Assembly of Collegiate Schools of Business (1988)

The American Assembly of Collegiate Schools of Business (AACSB) is a professional body that was created to represent and accredit business schools. Its active participants are the deans of these schools. In the early 1980s, in the context of its planning activities, this body began to grapple with various issues related to the future of business education (American Assembly of Collegiate Schools of Business & European Foundation for Management Development, 1982). As this effort evolved, a decision emerged to redo the kind of survey that initially had been carried out for the Ford and Carnegie Foundations. The idea was to undertake a 25-year follow-up. This study extended over a 3-year period, and a report ultimately was published (Porter & McKibbin, 1988).

The study makes possible a good picture of the state of the business schools in the mid-1980s; much survey data were collected through interviews and questionnaires that were intended to pinpoint the views of a wide range of stakeholders. Comparing these results with those obtained in the 1950s provides a view of the aftermath of the earlier foundation activities. Several aspects of this comparison need to be kept in mind, however. First, this report was internally generated *from* the business schools, not externally generated *about* them. Second, financial support for the study was solicited and obtained from about 30 large corporations. As a result of this sponsorship arrangement, the likelihood of the report's being highly critical of the business schools was diminished, and the ties between these schools and corporate America (not small firms) were accentuated.

Lyman Porter is a psychologist, with a doctorate in that subject from Yale, who came into the business schools on the wave of the foundation activities in the mid-1960s. He had prepared a background report that was used in connection with the Gordon and Howell (1959) volume. His entire professional career has been spent at the University of California—first in the psychology department at Berkeley, and then in administration (including a stint as dean) in the School of Management at Irvine. Lawrence McKibbin has degrees in business from Stanford and has had substantial business experience in the financial area. He helped develop business schools in various countries, served as dean at Wichita State University and the University of Oklahoma, and was president of AACSB as the follow-up study got under way.

State of the Business Schools 25 Years Later

The business schools grew—the number of master's degrees awarded went from 4,500 to 60,000, for example. The typical curriculum has become far more academically solid and thus more respectable. The aptitudes of business students, especially those at the M.B.A. and doctoral levels, have risen dramatically. This improvement is recognized in the university community and in the corporate world. The quality of faculty is at least the equal of what one finds elsewhere on campus, and in some quarters it is said to be higher. The previous derision has disappeared, and the intellectual climate within the schools is much better. Respectability has been attained on campus,

and in the business community as well. As a result, relations with business and industry are much improved. Pay levels for business school faculty are well above those in many other segments of the university, something that was not the case in the 1950s.

Porter and McKibbin's comments on current perceptions of intercampus relations stand in sharp contrast in a number of respects to what existed in the 1950s:

- Business schools feel rather good about themselves; deans perceive their schools to have reasonably high status on campus.
- For many academic institutions, there is a constant battle for resources; the typical business school regards itself as overburdened—too many students—and underfunded.
- While there are exceptions, the typical school sees itself as pretty much a "stand alone" operation; there is little interaction—or perceived need for interaction—with other academic units on campus.
- Provosts think highly of their business schools; they believe business faculties are academically competent; but they decry the isolationism of the business school; they do not see campus-wide academic leadership coming from the business school. (1988, p. 187)

Although Porter and McKibbin do not discuss this, values seem to play an important role in the relative isolation of business school faculties. These faculties tend to be more conservative, especially with regard to the role of business in society, than the dominant liberal arts faculties. Surrounded by a predominantly liberal sea, most business faculties have chosen isolationism as the best way of coping with the potential for conflict involved, especially in the aftermath of the activism of the late 1960s and 1970s (Miner, 1974; Levine, 1980).

State of Organizational Behavior

As Porter and McKibbin (1988) noted, business schools have hired people who hold doctorates and have training in disciplines other than the functional areas of business in relatively large numbers. Included are individuals from the social sciences, mathematics, and statistics. The result has been increased status on campus in these areas.

The original push from the foundations was to increase the emphasis on social science and quantitative knowledge. Thus, looking at these two together is appropriate. Table 4.1 provides useful data. Let us focus on the first two groups (business school deans and faculty) initially. Here the most pronounced trend is for the faculty to advocate a more quantitative emphasis. In both groups, organizational behavior is considered worthy of more emphasis, but only by a small margin.

These results are reinforced by data on the specific subject areas that are thought to need more emphasis; there are four: business communications, entrepreneurship, international business and management, and management information systems. Organizational behavior is not on this list—neither for deans nor for faculty. Furthermore, the faculty listed organizational behavior as one of the areas that should be deemphasized, albeit with only a small number expressing this opinion.

If now we look at the rest of table 4.1, and contrast the results with the relatively lukewarm support for organizational behavior within the business schools, the disparities are striking. Stakeholders of all descriptions who are out in the business world want more organizational behavior in the curriculum, and in most cases they want less quantitative material. At least from this perspective, the consensus is that the gains achieved as organizational behavior became a discipline and established itself in the business schools are not enough; much more is needed.

Undernourished Emphases

Porter and McKibbin (1988, pp. 316–325) discuss six areas that they conclude need more emphasis, and in the process they reflect some of the concerns expressed in table 4.1 from the corporate direction. They say that "the incorporation of concepts from mathematics and the social/behavioral sciences along with an emphasis on the analytical and rigorous, as opposed to the descriptive and superficial, has demonstrably improved the quality of business school curricula significantly over the span of the last two and a half decades" (p. 316). However, in the "more is needed" category they note the following concerns:

1. Breadth—business students are more narrowly educated than they should be.
2. The external organizational environment—there needs to be an increase in attention to the external environment: governmental relations, societal trends, legal climate, international developments.

TABLE 4.1 Views concerning the appropriateness of current emphasis in the business schools' curriculum on quantitative and organizational behavior subject matter

Respondent groups	Appropriateness of emphasis (% answering)		
	Too much	About right	Too little
Business school deans			
Quantitative analysis	16	70	15
Organizational behavior	11	68	21
Business school faculty			
Quantitative analysis	14	59	27
Organizational behavior	17	60	23
Recent M.B.A. alumni			
Quantitative analysis	14	73	13
Organizational behavior	8	62	30
Corporate chief executive officers			
Quantitative analysis	35	57	8
Organizational behavior	9	24	67
Vice presidents and directors of human resources			
Quantitative analysis	42	54	4
Organizational behavior	7	21	72

SOURCE: Adapted from Lyman W. Porter & Lawrence E. McKibbin (1988), *Management Education and Development: Drift or Thrust into the 21st Century* (New York: McGraw-Hill), 69

3. The international dimension — business schools have a long way to go before it can be said that the international dimension has truly become an integral part of their programs.
4. The information/service society — how can an information orientation be effectively incorporated into business courses and research?
5. Cross-functional integration — there is a need to provide sufficient attention to an integrated approach to problems that cut across specific functional areas, problems like those found in entrepreneurship and strategic management.
6. "Soft" (people) skills — current trends in business have the effect of increasing the need for effective skills in dealing with other people, and with oneself.

Obviously the last of these points — the need for more people skills — has the most relevance for organizational behavior, but all six problem areas offer opportunities for the field. Interestingly, just as in the 1950s, it appears most likely that these opportunities will be fully realized and major changes will be invoked as a result of pressures brought to bear from the outside — in this case from the business community, not as formerly, from the major foundations.

Effect of the AACSB Report

One reaction to the Porter and McKibbin study is that it is well done and thorough, but its impact on business school activities is likely to be minimal for internal political reasons (Cummings, 1990a, 1990b). This view is consistent with the findings within the academic community favoring a generally status quo position insofar as any further growth of organizational behavior's contribution and influence is concerned (see table 4.1). This argument says that the behavioral revolution has occurred, it is over, and little further change is likely. Such evidence as there is tends to support this position (Shipper, 1999). For instance, there has been little if any improvement in the managerial (people) skills possessed by M.B.A. graduates since the AACSB report was published — this despite the demonstration that skills of this kind are valid predictors of managerial performance levels and that they are teachable.

Another view is more negative regarding the Porter and McKibbin effort itself, portraying it as essentially a "power grab" by the AACSB (Calás & Smircich, 1990). This interpretation reflects the antiauthority

attitudes that have been identified with postmodernism and endorses much more radical changes than those espoused by the authors of the report. It could be written off as yet another attack on business school deans in their positions of authority. Yet this view does strike a nerve. Should we not have an evaluation of the consequences of the 1950s activism, either by the same foundations involved originally or by representatives of our consumers in the business world? This is not what Calás and Smircich (1990) want, but their arguments certainly suggest it. In any event, I strongly suspect that if there is to be further expansion of the role of organizational behavior in business schools, building on the base of substantial success achieved to date, it will come as a result of a further augmented voice from our stakeholders in the business world.

One such voice has emerged and is, in fact, becoming accentuated. Although to date this voice has not had specific relevance for organizational behavior, it does have the potential for such application, and it certainly has relevance for business schools as a whole. This is the evaluation and rating process now joined (or shortly to be joined) by *Business Week, U.S. News & World Report, The Financial Times,* and *Forbes.* These published evaluations have raised their share of defensiveness (see Elsbach & Kramer, 1996). They have also produced some "inflationary" statistics and resulted in several deans' losing their jobs. But in the long run such reports could focus on the deficiencies and strengths of various schools, including those in the organizational behavior area. This would serve a very useful purpose.

Fifty Years of Organizational Behavior

The relatively rosy picture of the period since organizational behavior was born can almost certainly be attributed in large part to the impact of the Ford and Carnegie reports and the foundation activism that surrounded them. This is not to say, however, that the business schools as currently constituted and organizational behavior are not without their critics. (A review of some criticisms and a proposal for major change are included in Ackoff, 1994.) Such continuing skepticism is certainly healthy if it does not expand out of proportion and if it seeks solutions, not anarchy. Business schools had a very long way to go back in 1950, and they have in fact come a very long way since, largely as a result of the advent of the field of organizational behavior. The AACSB report documents this, but it also points up the need, and potential, for further change.

The behavioral revolution was in many respects an organizational behavior phenomenon. It was fomented to a substantial degree by the Ford and Carnegie Foundations, but behind that was the influence of a number of economists who not only wrote the foundation reports but also implemented their recommendations, and they may well have been responsible for getting the foundations involved in the first place. Business schools were in serious trouble on a number of counts, and they were in danger of being overwhelmed by a burgeoning student population, but at the same time their academic status on campus had sunk to a new low and many economists were caught up in this state of affairs. Economists in business schools and in liberal arts departments sparked the rescue attempt. Neither mainstream psychology nor sociology had any inclination to do this, and the business school disciplines alone lacked the clout to generate such a change. Yet as the revolution escalated, many individuals and groups joined the bandwagon. It became a real success.

MANAGEMENT LAUREATES

In many respects, the success of business schools resulted from the efforts of certain opinion leaders, many of them theorists, who came to populate the business schools in the early period. Here we look more closely at these people and how they came to the business schools.

Starting in 1992 Arthur Bedeian began to edit a series of volumes of autobiography entitled *Management Laureates* (Bedeian, 1992, 1993, 1993, 1996, 1998). At this writing there are five such volumes containing 49 autobiographical essays by outstanding contributors to the management field as a whole. Bedeian does not say how these laureates were selected, but it can be assumed that although the decision was the editor's, he was heavily influenced by his knowledge of management history—a field in which he has specialized for many years. In any event, there can be no doubt that these people are influentials. There certainly are others who are similarly influential, and indeed a few such people were nominated for inclusion in the volumes who did not contribute autobiographies. Three of these were included in our analyses.

The particular value of these autobiographies for current purposes is that they provide insight into the careers of people who were influenced by the activism of the foundations in the 1950s and 1960s. What happened to these individuals and who became influentials or opinion leaders during this period of change? And in particular what happened to those who were, or have become, identified with the field of organizational behavior?

Career Transitions

Table 4.2 contains the results of an analysis of these autobiographical essays and, in the case of the three who declined the nomination, of other biographical source materials. Note, first, that almost three-quarters (73 percent) of the laureates have come to identify themselves and are identified with organizational behavior. This is a very impressive showing for organizational behavior in a period when at its beginning the field did not even exist. The next most frequent

TABLE 4.2 Origins of 52 scholars nominated for inclusion in the Laureates Series, Volumes 1–5 (Bedeian, 1992, 1993, 1993, 1996, 1998)

Categories for analysis	N	%
Total laureates		
Organizational behavior	38	73
Other (strategy, production, systems, IR)	14	27
Organizational behavior group		
Major theorists	24	63
Other (researchers, writers)	14	37
Year of entry into business school		
1954 or earlier	5	13
1955–59	5	13
1960–64	9	24
1965–69	10	26
1970–73	6	16
Never entered	3	8
Source of entry into business schools		
Graduate business studies	9	24
Immediately after doctoral studies	5	13
From non-business school employment	21	55
Never entered	3	8
Discipline prior to organizational behavior		
Psychology	18	47
Management	8	21
Political science	3	8
Sociology	3	8
Industrial relations	3	8
Other (journalism, engineering, math)	3	8

disciplinary identification is strategic management, with 13 percent. Furthermore, of the organizational behavior scholars, the majority have made major theoretical contributions to the field. Some 46 percent of the management laureates (24 of the 52) are organizational behavior theorists of note and 63 percent of the laureates in organizational behavior are major theorists. At the very least it can be said that developing organizational behavior theory is not a career route detrimental to success. In fact, theory building seems to be a primary means to recognition. Major theoretic contributions are defined by virtue of selection for inclusion at a later point in this book.

Business School Entry

The organizational behavior laureates entered a business school, if they did, in the 25-year period that extends from 1973. Up through the 1950s the rate of entry was relatively slow, and the only source of multiple entries was Carnegie Tech. The real surge came during the 1960s when the foundations appear to have had their greatest impact. The hesitancy and pessimism the foundations exhibited regarding direct entry into business schools did not carry the day; the more frontal approach advocated from Carnegie Tech prevailed. The apparent fall-off in the 1970s appears to be entirely a consequence of the shorter time span involved and the need for a number of years to achieve laureate status. The last autobiographee first entered a business school in 1973. The three who never moved to a business school include a successful entrepreneur who went from a psychology department to the business world and two sociologists who, despite close brushes with business schools, never actually made the move.

Although the modal pattern is one of entry from employment in a liberal arts department, there are several instances of movement from the business world as well. Among those who made the move during graduate studies and prior to obtaining the doctorate (and thus who held business terminal degrees), there is a heavy concentration in volumes 4 and 5, the most recent of the laureates volumes. The pattern of direct employment in a business school subsequent to a social science doctorate is relatively infrequent. Apparently in the generation involved, moving to a business school occurred, most typically, after building up some employment experience elsewhere, or the individual entered a business school early to obtain a degree. The latter approach has accelerated recently; it appears to be the method of choice today.

Disciplinary Sources

As table 4.2 shows, a large proportion of the transitions occurred among psychologists; this is the discipline that fed into business schools the most. The largest number of these people have a background in industrial psychology, which was achieved either through initial training or career employment. Given the tendency of the foundation reports to ignore this particular group, or even to criticize its work, this result is in certain respects surprising. Not only do a substantial number of people come from this source, but they achieve laureate status as well. Yet one might also expect this, in view of the positive disposition toward business, something industrial psychologists have in common with many economists.

The only other discipline with any numbers is management. Included here are primarily those who received traditional management degrees, which included very little input from either the social sciences or statistics. They have become successful in the field of organizational behavior in large part because they were able to re-teach themselves subsequent to receiving their terminal degree. They noted where the field was going and then took the matter of getting there into their own hands.

The data from the laureates volumes suggest a great deal of diversity in this group of people who helped lead organizational behavior to its present position. Obviously, the group is not representative of the larger number who decided to try their hand at becoming business professors. Yet the findings from this analysis are informative simply because such a large number of opinion leaders are involved (Katz & Lazarsfeld, 1955).

Perceptions of Business Schools

The essays contain a certain amount of commentary regarding the internal environments of business schools, although this commentary is uneven in that some of the autobiographies contain much more of it than others. Accordingly, any quantitative analysis seems unwarranted, but the qualitative information does provide a useful addition to our picture of the ground that existed and against which organizational behavior as it emerged became figure.

Remember, however, that we are talking about a very successful group of people. What happened to them may be far from typical. There is also a problem in that the data offer no method of discriminating what is unique to the emerging organizational behavior field from "academe in general." We have no control group. In a few instances, the laureates provide information that links their experiences to the rise of organizational behavior, but this is the exception, not the rule. More frequently, readers will have to rely on their own sources to fill in the blanks.

Positive Themes

One of the most pervasive themes is the emphasis on the value of being able to follow problems wherever they might lead. Business schools are viewed as providing greater freedom in this regard. In contrast, liberal arts departments often create artificial, discipline-based boundaries on intellectual endeavor. I remember, while teaching in a psychology department on leave from my regular business school position, being strongly pressed not to use a book by Amitai Etzioni, a sociologist, in one of my classes, even though it was clearly the best suited to my purpose and had served well in my business school teaching. The following quotations may help give a better feel for how this problem orientation operated:

It is here where I believe that professional schools provide a more user-friendly environment. As I look at professional schools, they are developing their own identity. They are increasingly unconflicted about the importance of scholarship that is problem-centered. They are increasingly proud of teaching about a world of practice. They are increasingly providing the conditions where the best and the brightest who seek to be problem-centered can flourish. (Argyris, 1992, p. 54)

My big career shift occurred in 1962 when I moved from the Department of Psychology at Berkeley where I was visiting into the Graduate School of Management at the University of Pittsburgh. I felt I shared more interests in common with problem-oriented management faculties than with the discipline-oriented psychology faculties. (Bass, 1992, p. 76)

I've kept looking for important problems where research might contribute to a solution as well as contribute to theory. . . . I've been lucky to have been based at the Harvard Business School (HBS) all these years. There's a strong problem-solving orientation at HBS and I've been given support and encouragement all along the way. (Lawrence & Lawrence, 1993, p. 113)

This problem focus carried with it in many instances an opportunity to deal with practical issues and the applications of organizational behavior. At the same time, it seemed to be part of a broader freedom to teach and research whatever seemed to be appropriate. This freedom, although not universal, was widespread; many laureates experienced it in one form or another:

I asked McGregor (Bavelas was away) for guidance. Doug said quite bluntly that it did not make any difference, that what was needed was my approach, and that I should figure out for myself what and how to teach. This message correlated with what Dean Edward Pennell Brooks had told me about the Sloan School. He didn't care what we did so long as it was a new approach, and so long as it was clearly different from the "school up the river." Innovation was the watchword of the day. . . . I fell back on basic psychology and was quite academic in my approach. . . . The Sloan School's message on research was very similar to the message on teaching—"You figure it out." (Schein, 1993, pp. 42–43)

Had I been offered a position in a psychology department my research would not look at all like it does today. I like to take a much broader brush to a problem than is characteristic of most research done in psychology departments. For that I am grateful to my business school setting. (Roberts, 1998, p. 219)

Closely related to this greater freedom is the exposure to new approaches that a number of laureates reported. For example:

The Ford Foundation, through its prestige and resources, successfully encouraged a rather radical change in the educational practices of American business schools during the 1960s. The Ford Foundation encouraged many schools to recruit to their faculties social scientists, mathematicians and statisticians. . . . Thus the attainment of my Ph.D. in

1960 was a photo finish with my obsolescence. . . . In the mid-1960s, the editorial review boards of the journals reflected the new wave of rigor that was becoming pervasive in U.S. business schools. . . . I either had to retrain or resign myself to being a second-class academic from the outset. . . . I chose to retrain. (House, 1993, pp. 51–52)

The organizational behavior group at Yale in many respects was very cohesive. We met regularly to talk about research and debate issues. For all of us it was a stimulating, growth producing experience. It opened my eyes to a set of organizational issues that I had not been exposed to at Berkeley. (Lawler, 1993, p. 86)

Inherent in the intellectual freedom and openness to new ideas was an overall climate of intellectual stimulation. This seemed to be part of the culture in many schools, and it permeated faculties and doctoral students alike. On occasion, the increased concern with practice and application was a force in creating this intellectual stimulation also. There are a number of comments around this theme:

This is as good a place as any to talk about the remarkable string of doctoral students that I have been privileged to be associated with as a major advisor during my years in GSA (GSM) at Irvine. . . . My energy and efforts at UC-Irvine has been invested — with abundance of pleasurable returns — in working with doctoral students. (Porter, 1993, pp. 18–20)

I learned what was going on in leading business schools and the interests of their faculties. It was a stimulating year! Influences upon my research efforts will be noted later. . . . At Harvard I became familiar through my fellow students with the curricula and research programs of leading business schools and gained respect for them. (Mahoney, 1998, pp. 144–145)

The autobiographies contained many references to the supportive environments found in the business schools. Some of these references were specific and personal, some more general:

My chairman was John F. Mee, and he was a truly remarkable, supportive person. He undoubtedly helped me more than any other person in my career. He gave me a very good start with supervi-

sion of doctoral dissertations, guided me through my first major consulting job, and supported me with the faculty. He gave me my start in the Academy of Management and helped me arrange to coauthor my first book. (Davis, 1992, pp. 275–276)

My acquaintances who took jobs at MIT and Stanford never fulfilled the promise they had shown as students, whereas almost all my colleagues at Purdue went on to exceptional success. I attribute this outcome to our supportive environment. Purdue's deans rewarded professors who did research with kind words and summer support; and they let us create a separate department of behavioral scientists. (Starbuck, 1993, p. 77)

Perhaps other positive themes could be teased from the autobiographies, but the preceding are clearly the most important. There is, however, one other theme that is not so widely mentioned, but which may be of more significance than the written statements imply. The laureates are successful people in the field. You would think that being rewarded for their performance — in terms of money and status — would be important to them. Little is said on this score, but what is said is worth noting:

I rose quickly through the ranks in the Academy of Management, serving in various capacities, including chairman of the Organizational Behavior Division, editor of the *Academy of Management Journal*, and eventually President. Wisconsin provided an ideal environment for that type of professional development. I was affirmed and rewarded for those kinds of contributions. (Cummings, 1992, p. 245)

One of the reasons I have remained at Maryland was because I was treated very well by business school Dean Rudy Lamone. Rudy was strongly merit-oriented and always rewarded people for their performance, keeping political issues to a minimum. (Locke, 1993, p. 228)

Negative Themes

These generally positive features are counterbalanced by a certain amount of discipline-based conflict. Those who had occupied the territory first were not always willing to give up the ground they already held. In some respects organizational behavior served to expand the size of the total domain, but this was not always true. Conflicts over ownership of courses, budgets, positions, respectability of academic endeavors, and the like are reported. Most frequently these controversies involved professors with a principles of management persuasion or economists, simply because these were the largest groups likely to have overlapping turfs with organizational behavior. To a certain extent the fears of the foundation report authors appear to have been realized, even at Carnegie Tech, which started out so well.

Where conflict did occur, and this was far from universal, it often simmered below the threshold, influencing events but not becoming overt. When the battle really heated up, however, the usual outcome was that organizational behavior lost, at least temporarily. Sometimes this meant moving to another department within the business school or outside. Sometimes the move was temporary, sometimes permanent. Not infrequently, the leader of the organizational behavior component left the university involved. Yet the meaning of this is hard to evaluate. These people were much in demand, opportunities were all around them, and making a move usually resulted in a substantial compensation increase. There certainly was some push from within in these cases, but once that happened, the pull from without often came to dominate.

As we turn to the perceptions of various laureates regarding this conflict, it is important to recognize that a business school that is conducive to the development of organizational behavior at one point in time may be anything but at another point. Swings of major amplitude can occur almost overnight; a prominent factor is some change in the administrative component of the school. With this in mind, let us look at what the autobiographees say:

The promotion process . . . did not proceed smoothly. . . . [There] was opposition to my promotion by a group of economists who felt my work was too based on the study of attitudinal data. In their research paradigm attitude data were soft data, and did not warrant scientific research. . . . My promotion was put off [Note: Lawler left Yale shortly afterward]. (Lawler, 1993, p. 88)

Conflict . . . developed between a colleague and myself at Oregon. . . . The colleague was made head of the newly formed Personnel and Industrial Management Department. . . . He seemed to view the department as the bottom link of a hierarchic

chain of command; he was in charge. My view was more like a community of scholars with a senior scholar representing the group. . . . Things got so bad at one point that my courses, and myself with them, were all transferred to the Accounting and Business Statistics Department. . . . That move was countermanded by a dean returning from sabbatical [Note: Miner left the University of Oregon shortly afterward]. (Miner, 1993, p. 300)

Too often we take for granted the institutional settings in which scholarship takes place. Nurturing of collegiality is a function which is either overlooked or relegated to deans or department chairs. My experience at both Yale and Carnegie Mellon taught me the fragility of these settings—of how quickly a tradition of collaboration could erode or be destroyed altogether. (Vroom, 1993, p. 277)

Such conflict was not limited to interdisciplinary confrontations. There were schisms occasioned by other factors as well. The following quotations provide examples:

By the mid-1970s OB was split. On the one hand were the scientists, on the other the humanists . . . who carried the normative optimism of the early 1960s to the extreme. For them, there was a very simple one best way: it involved sensitivity training, encounter groups, OD and the like. . . . The differences were dramatically illustrated in a meeting which David Bradford, Hal Leavitt, Ray Miles, and I [George Strauss] organized in Berkeley around 1973 of a group that later became the Organizational Behavior Teaching Society. At one point we divided into subgroups to discuss what OB should teach. One group, with Bob Tannenbaum as its guru, sat on the floor. The other, which included Larry Cummings as spokesperson, sat around a table. The reports of the groups were predictable. (Strauss, 1993, p. 176)

Georgia Southern College was a nightmare. The culture within the School of Business Administration was rife with backbiting and politics. Much of this emanated from the management style of the School's dean. . . . The dean's antics had resulted in the formation of two principal coalitions whose members literally would not speak to one another. . . . To make matters worse, my success in publishing was a threat to all sides. By "speeding up the race" I had inadvertently discredited the self-serving belief that by being at a small school with limited resources and a heavy teaching load, one couldn't be expected to do much more than meet classes. (Bedeian, 1998a, p. 14).

The matter of discrimination was also among the negative themes. By discrimination, I do not necessarily mean the legal type; that needs to be defined by the courts, and none of the instances reported involved legal action. However, feelings and perceptions of discrimination were present. Most instances involved gender issues, and the examples concentrate on these; age discrimination appears to have been present also on occasion:

At Michigan State . . . during my doctoral program the overall situation was somewhat difficult because, initially, I was somewhat ignored by the doctoral students. . . . I am sure that I sometimes got upset when I shouldn't have and let things go by that I should have confronted. . . . Many of the problems seemed to stem from people's prior expectations. . . . During most of my doctoral program, I was unaware of how rare females in management doctoral programs really were. Thus, I did not initially fully recognize how far on the cutting edge of change the Michigan State University Management Department had moved in accepting me. (Bartol, 1996, pp. 14–16)

I am the lowest paid full professor in the OB area at Berkeley, and by quite a substantial amount. . . . I make eighty-one cents for every dollar the man who was promoted to the same rank at the same time I was makes. And this is before consulting, summer monies, endowed chairs, etc., which have all advantaged the men in our department, and others across the country. (Roberts, 1998, pp. 229–230)

There are other instances of low pay reported in the autobiographees, although that has not been the norm in the group. Typically, this type of situation is corrected by a move to a higher paying position at another university, an option that was not readily available to Roberts. A more frequent problem appears to have been the heavy teaching loads present in some situations, as well as other teaching-related difficulties:

The teaching norm was survival. Teaching two business policy and one principles of management course six days a week was a hardship. Classes were large and student/faculty interaction was minimal. (Slocum, 1996, p. 285)

I found efforts to teach faculty in the [Harvard] Business School psychoanalytic theory not particularly successful. . . . I was disappointed in the absence of critical intellectual discussion in the Business School. . . . Tenured professors saw no need to learn more, and their juniors depended on them for their promotions. (Levinson, 1993, p. 195)

Several laureates noted that Harvard Business School's unswerving commitment to case collecting and case teaching, although strongly practice oriented, is somewhat intellectually constraining.

The only other negative theme of any significance involved intellectual isolation and a lack of colleagues with which to work. This problem was most typical in small business schools and small programs. Some examples:

My first exposure to the Cornell culture was Urie Bronfenbrenner's somewhat blunt version of what life there was like. He said in essence, you wouldn't be here unless you were really good; now all you have to do is more of what got you here and let the rest of us do what got us here. . . . That sounded a lot more anomic than what I had been used to. . . . The place didn't prove to be quite that harsh. But the amount of interaction with colleagues did go down somewhat, partly because there simply were fewer of them. (Weick, 1993, p. 303)

I was growing increasingly restive in Buffalo. I felt out of touch with the main currents in the field, especially the macro side of the field. My department was increasingly micro in focus and the Dean told me flatly that he saw no possibility of hiring anyone else in the macro side of the field. (Beyer, 1996, p. 71)

At UCLA I was professor of Organizational Behavior and Social Ecology. . . . I had been asked to go there by the Behavioral Science people, but I found that I wasn't in their group. I was put in a group called Management Theory, with people I'd never heard of. I was in a new country, in a new department, and I didn't know the politics. (Trist, 1993, p. 208)

On balance, the business schools produced a very mixed reaction from the laureates. In spite of their success in this context, the laureates also experienced some highly traumatic situations. Their salvation seems to have been their mobility; ultimately, most found what they were looking for, simply because they were in demand and lots of opportunities were available. Yet there is a factor inherent in the following quotation that should be considered, and which is probably understated in the autobiographies:

On moving to a business school in 1960, I received a handwritten note from a political science savant who minced no words: "You, sir, are a TRAITOR," a reaction motivated by the difficult times then being experienced by Political Science. (Golembiewski, 1992, p. 378)

Promotion and Tenure

One possibility, given all the conflict, is that promotions and tenure would be hard to achieve. We have seen at least one instance where this was in fact the case. Certainly during the early 1960s, among young assistant and associate professors, there was much discussion of the inherent problems involved. Yet, with all the mobility and with people coming into the business schools from the outside all the time, neither promotion nor tenure presented much of a problem; typically, these matters were negotiated before a move. At least, that was often the case for those in the laureates' shoes:

I had earned my doctoral degree in a little more than two years, earned tenure at Berkeley while in my twenties, and came to Stanford as a full professor in my early thirties. (Pfeffer, 1996, p. 223)

Despite this type of evidence that barriers to promotion were not operative, instances where barriers did exist are cited as well. We have already noted the problems Lawler had at Yale.

Alan Meyer . . . came up for promotion to tenure. The tenured professors' discussion of this case dramatized the ideological split. An economist who had not published since he received tenure observed that there were already enough high-quality professors in organizational science. Karl Weick had written a letter saying Meyer's article was the best ASQ had published. . . . A statistician conjectured that Weick was only trying to make it appear ASQ published good articles; because of its lack of statistical rigor, the research did not meet minimum scientific standards. (Starbuck, 1993, p. 101)

The evidence provided by an analysis of the management laureates' data indicates that the business schools did change, as the foundation reports anticipated, but once social movements of any kind are set in motion, the exact nature of the change is hard to predict—and to control. Certainly this was true of the changes in the business schools. The influx of full-time faculty was apparently much greater than expected, and the disciplinary mix was different as well. Yet these results stem only from the laureates, a key group, but only a fraction of the total. We need information that obtains from a more comprehensive sample, not only regarding the transition process but also about perceptions of the business schools—their climates and cultures—as well.

PSYCHOLOGISTS IN BUSINESS SCHOOLS

In the early 1960s a group of psychologists newly relocated into business schools organized themselves informally for purposes of networking and collecting information on the psychology–business school interface. The data amassed by this group serve to supplement those from the laureates, and they do so by using somewhat more representative samples.

Psychologists Associated with Schools of Business and Industrial Administration

The group that came to call itself Psychologists Associated with Schools of Business and Industrial Administration (PAWSBIA) started operation in 1962 and met at the American Psychological Association annual meetings. There was some talk of attempting to establish a formal identity within APA, but support for this was lukewarm and it never did happen. The major tangible thing the organization accomplished was to conduct surveys and report on the results. It did, however, provide a certain amount of social support to its members at a time when stress levels were likely to be rather high.

There was a steering committee and at times a chairman of that committee. That is almost all the structure the group ever possessed. In the early years, Bernard Bass (then at the University of Pittsburgh), Raymond Katzell (at New York University), Donald Marquis (at MIT), and I (then at the University of

Oregon) were on the steering committee. Later it came to include Renato Tagiuri (at Harvard University), Lyman Porter (at the Berkeley and then Irvine campuses of the University of California), Frederick Massarik (at UCLA) and Victor Vroom (then at Carnegie Tech).

PAWSBIA remained reasonably active until 1966. After that, it became largely dormant but technically survived until mid-1969 when it was officially terminated. Only a year later, the organizational behavior division of the Academy of Management was founded, with several of the key players being prior members of the PAWSBIA steering committee. In many respects, the organizational behavior division was an outgrowth of the previously purely psychological activity. At least for many, the two served essentially the same functions.

The two surveys conducted by PAWSBIA provided input to three publications (Miner, 1963a, 1963b, 1966). In addition, presentations of the results were made to the American Psychological Association, Academy of Management, and American Marketing Association.

1962 Survey

The first survey used a mailing list that had been obtained by collecting addresses from those who attended the annual meeting. With some supplementing, and based on an 80 percent return, information of some kind was obtained from 25 schools. Reasonably complete questionnaires were provided by 20 of these. Individual replies numbered 45, and 55 faculty members who taught business administration students were identified. However, the number of psychologists who answered individual questions often varied downward from the base 45. The universities represented are the larger ones.

Findings

The great majority of the psychologists held professional school appointments only. Only 10 had joint appointments in psychology, and only two of the universities utilized the joint appointment exclusively. It is safe to say that at that time psychologists who taught business courses could not assume they would receive an appointment in liberal arts as well; the psychology departments appeared to be quite restrictive on that score.

Table 4.3 contains data for 7 of the 20 questions included in the survey. The listing is selective because a number of questions turned out to be poor. In these cases the results were ambiguous, and it proved impossible to establish what they meant. Adequate pretesting of the questionnaire would have prevented this, but the fact is we did an inadequate job of instrument development. Indeed, that as many questions proved usable as did, is a rather lucky circumstance.

First, the behavioral revolution is by no means a psychological phenomenon. We know that now, but it was true even then. Well over half the schools had other social scientists in the fold—primarily sociologists, but anthropologists and political scientists to a degree as well. Among the psychologists, the industrial area (it only later became industrial/organizational, largely due to the influence of its business school component) is by far the most heavily represented. Again, one cannot help wondering why the foundation reports did not recognize this pattern. Social psychology is the only other major contributor. Many of these social psychologists consider themselves sociologists as well, and, indeed, a number may have been educated in joint programs. The legacy from Kurt Lewin is clearly evident in the proportionate emphasis on social psychology. Adding up the multispecialists who count a business school area, in addition to psychology, as a discipline in which they are proficient yields a total of 36 percent. This then, in addition to sociology, is a major supplementary skill. If industrial relations is added, it equals sociology.

Second, there are certain distinguishing characteristics of these psychologists. One such characteristic is that their extensive involvement in research extends to formal recognition. Only a third do not have some release time for research; another third have 50 percent or more of their workload allocated to research. Consistent with this emphasis, two-thirds are involved in doctoral education. Note that Ph.D. and D.B.A. schools seem to be clearly separated, and the latter were abundant at the time. The schools surveyed were larger and were heavily involved in doctoral education. Not unexpectedly, the psychologists who came aboard gravitated rapidly to the doctoral component of their schools and appear to be exerting substantial influence in this area. The foundations should have been pleased with this outcome.

Third, questions dealing with the relationship between the psychology department and the business

TABLE 4.3 Responses to selected questions, 1962 survey

Question/choices	Response (%)	Question/choices	Response (%)
Do behavioral scientists other than psychologists or economists offer courses in your department or school?		Which would best characterize the situation at your school between the regular psychology department and the school of business?	
Yes	63 (of schools)		
No	37 (of schools)	Integrated efforts in teaching and/or research	14 (of schools)
If Yes, what major field?		Cooperative, mutually helpful but independent efforts	43 (of schools)
Sociologist	48		
Anthropologist	19	Occasional cooperation in teaching and/or research	33 (of schools)
Political scientist	14		
Social scientist	9	Not on speaking terms; no cooperative effort	10 (of schools)
What fields within psychology do you identify with most strongly?		On your campus, suppose a psychologist—(A) was in the regular department of psychology or (B) was in a school of business. Assuming they were of equal rank, competence, stature, etc., indicate whether A or B or (N) neither would be more favored on each of the following:	
Industrial	76		
Social	58		
General — experimental	9		
Clinical/counseling	9	Research facilities (A) Psychology	32
Measurement/statistics	6	(B) Business	11
Educational	3	(N) Neither	57
In what disciplines other than psychology do you consider yourself proficient?		Access to graduate students in	
Sociology	41	psychology (A) Psychology	79
Anthropology	12	(B) Business	0
Business management	12	(N) Neither	21
Personnel management	8	Prestige (A) Psychology	43
Business organization	8	(B) Business	18
Marketing	8	(N) Neither	39
Industrial relations	4	Teaching load (A) Psychology	23
Political science	4	(B) Business	33
Is any portion of your work load officially allocated to research? If so, what percentage?		(N) Neither	44
		Assistance (A) Psychology	17
None	33	(B) Business	29
<20	13	(N) Neither	54
20 to 39	13	Travel funds (A) Psychology	8
40 to 49	7	(B) Business	32
50	30	(N) Neither	60
100	4	Intellectual stimulation (A) Psychology	34
Are you a major professor for the doctorate? If so, what degree?		(B) Business	17
		(N) Neither	49
Not major professor	32	Salary, promotion (A) Psychology	12
Ph.D.	38	(B) Business	38
D.B.A.	30	(N) Neither	50
		Freedom (A) Psychology	23
		(B) Business	23
		(N) Neither	54

NOTE: This survey was conducted by the Psychologists Associated with Schools of Business and Industrial Administration in 1962 among its member schools.

school were asked. On balance, this relationship tends to be somewhat at a distance, but cooperative; rarely is it strained. The question on which unit provides the more favorable working circumstances indicates that, in most respects, the two do not differ. This is consistently the modal response, except in two instances, with psychology providing better access to students in that field and somewhat more prestige. Comparing the two units, where differences do exist, psychology comes out on top in four areas and business in another four, with one evenly split. Yet, the business schools appear to weigh in most heavily with regard to extrinsic satisfactions—travel funds, pay, promotion, and so on—while the intrinsic rewards of prestige and intellectual stimulation are associated more with the psychology department. Remember that this survey was conducted only 3 years after the foundation reports were published.

Courses Taught

Table 4.4 lists 15 courses taught by psychologists—3 at the doctoral level, 7 at the master's level, 4 undergraduate, and 1 in a nondegree program for upper-level executives. Before considering these courses in any detail, this discussion should be prefaced with some treatment of what psychologists teach. We found that of the 117 separate courses noted, somewhat over 50 percent are in the field of management broadly defined. Another 25 percent are in personnel management. After that, the courses are widely dispersed—marketing (consumer behavior) and research methods primarily; some pure psychology, labor relations, statistics, and production.

Overall, and this is true of the management area as well, roughly three-quarters of the courses are clearly influenced to a substantial degree by social science content. However, the remaining courses sound quite typical of what existed before the social scientists arrived, and psychologists are teaching them. Such is the situation with principles of management and primarily case courses in industrial administration. It may be that when taught by psychologists these courses take a different form than the catalog copy would suggest, but this is by no means certain.

Of the courses taught by psychologists, 28 percent are exclusively for undergraduates and another 15 percent are upper-division courses to which graduate students may be admitted. Thus, in this sample, graduate teaching predominates, even though only three of the schools are exclusively graduate schools. Cases appear to be just as popular among psychologists as among other business school professors, but they may be different types of cases. Business games, role playing, and sensitivity training are less frequent in terms of the number of universities involved. However, if a school introduces sensitivity training, it tends to do so in several courses.

In table 4.4 the three doctoral courses—Comparative Organization Theories, Seminar in Research Methods, and Advanced Topics in Organizational Behavior—are all quite sophisticated and new to the business school scene. These are certainly the kinds of courses to which business school teachers-to-be should be exposed. The master's level courses are more of a mixed bag. Some are a clear reflection of new trends and social science innovations—Organizational Conflict and Change, Consultative Methods, Organizations, Organization and Staffing. Group and Individual Behavior is a sensitivity training course, and questions have been raised about the intellectual content of such efforts, but the input from the social sciences is certainly there. The remaining two courses—Administration: Theory and Action and, in particular, General Management Problems—have more of a traditional management flavor. Yet it is difficult to establish how a psychologist might teach them.

Below the graduate level, the diversity becomes more acute. Leadership Principles and Practice uses a sensitivity training laboratory, Principles of Business Organization is a classical management theory course, Psychological Foundations of Administration definitely draws on psychological sources while adding a focus that is as much consumer behavior as organizational, and Social Organization of Enterprise is a course in the human relations tradition going back to Mayo and Roethlisberger. One suspects that the executive development course, Administrative Practices, has a similar orientation.

All in all, table 4.4 reflects the tremendous variation in approach at the various schools. There is no one best way to teach this kind of subject matter. In fact, there are more like 15 best ways. To this should be added that with the exception of books on management principles, there were few if any basic textbooks available and there was little agreement as to content in any event. Without question, the advent of organizational behavior texts later on represented a force for more uniformity.

Supplemental Data from Directory Search

In addition to the survey findings themselves, some data on the 55 psychologists identified through the survey could be established by resort to the *1963 American Psychological Association Directory*. At that time these directories contained very detailed biographical data. With regard to division membership, Industrial Psychology was highest with 22 members, Personality and Social was second with 16, the Society for the

TABLE 4.4 Courses taught in the organizational behavior area, 1962 survey

Course title, description	University, degree
Comparative Organization Theories Criteria for a theory. Analysis of theories of small groups, and formal and informal organization. Integration of theories. Each student outlines and abstracts a major theory. It is discussed in class to determine the extent to which it meets the criterion of a theory. Research designs are suggested by class members for testing the major hypotheses contained in the theory.	Ohio State University, Doctoral
Organizational Conflict and Change Factors contributing to internal conflict and to changed patterns of behavior within organizations, from the viewpoint of business management; managerial decision making and conflict; implications of cultural values for the administration of scientific research groups; labor management conflict; coercion and manipulation; planned change.	University of Oregon, Master's
Consultative Methods Methods of developing a consulting relationship with individuals, groups, organizations, and communities. Diagnostic and procedural frameworks for consulting practice, with special emphasis on the mediation role. The use of role playing, organization laboratories, action research, and other approaches in improving various aspects of social systems, e.g., decision making and problem solving, adaptive capacity, and integration of system objectives.	Case Institute of Technology, Master's
Group and Individual Behavior By examining relationships developing within their own unstructured group, members explore such interpersonal and group phenomena as membership and participation, power and control, interpersonal trust. Emphasis is placed on the development of each member's ability to understand and respond effectively to ongoing events in a group.	Yale University, Master's
Seminar in Research Methods Logic, measurement, and inference in social science. Operationism, explanation, measurement and observation, scaling, sampling, analysis of data, styles of research, research relationships. Classic social-science works are analyzed as to method, and each student presents a research design at the end of the first term. In the second term selected substantive areas are further explored, and students carry out a research project involving the collection of data, either individually or in small groups.	Cornell University, Doctoral
Leadership Principles and Practice Knowledge and skills leading to effectiveness in interpersonal relations. Understanding of oneself as a leader, and others as individuals and as members of working groups. Understanding of group process, including group leadership. Lectures and sensitivity training laboratory.	University of California at Los Angeles, Undergraduate
Principles of Business Organization The present pattern of business management, development of a theory of management, functions of a manager, authority and responsibility, leadership, the span of management, basic departmentalization, line and staff relationships, service departments, centralization of authority, committees, the board of directors, staffing, direction, planning and control.	University of Wisconsin, Undergraduate
Administration: Theory and Action Organization and executive behavior is viewed primarily from the standpoint of the effects of internal structure and processes. Concepts in the analysis of organization and administrative behavior, analytic techniques in the understanding of interacting systems of action, models of administrative action, models of organization, values, value determination, value reconciliation, and human consequences of administrative action and organizational models at both the executive and employee levels.	Michigan State University, Master's
Psychological Foundations of Administration A study of the psychological principles that underlie the relationships of a business firm with (1) customers, (2) investors, (3) the general public, (4) other business groups of suppliers, distributors, dealers, and local merchants. The course aims to provide the student with a knowledge of the research tools of psychology, as well as with the practical administrative consequences of this science in the areas of public relations, communication, motivation in advertising and sales promotion, corporate image, plant and community relations, and management appraisal.	Boston College, Undergraduate

(continued)

TABLE 4.4 (continued)

Course title, description	University, degree
Administrative Practices The course is concerned with individual, interpersonal, group, and social processes relevant to administrative practice. Methods used vary, depending on the topic and phase of the course.	Harvard University, High-level executives
General Management Problems Principles of management applied to selected case histories, relating to problems in the areas of production, marketing, personnel, finance, sales, public relations, etc. Stress placed on administrative problem solving and decision making at the levels of top and middle management through case studies and business games.	Wayne State University, Master's
Social Organization of Enterprise The course deals with human relations in business. Topics such as motivation, communication, and executive development are included. Primarily lecture and discussion, with special projects.	University of Notre Dame, Undergraduate
Organizations An integration of scientific studies from many disciplines that relate to problems of organization structure and process, leadership, communication, content, and decision making.	University of Denver, Master's
Advanced Topics in Organizational Behavior Intensive examination of selected current issues and developments in theory, research, and practice related to human behavior in industrial and other formal organizations. A seminar course, addressed to advanced problems of both a substantive nature (e.g., new research areas) and a professional nature (e.g., ethical issues).	New York University, Doctoral
Organization and Staffing Translation of organization goals and objectives to specific manpower goals and objectives, as well as staffing to meet the organization's manpower needs. Techniques for recruitment, selection, and assignment of manpower resources for optimal utilization.	University of Minnesota, Master's

NOTE: These are courses selected for their diversity, identified through the survey conducted by the Psychologists Associated with Schools of Business and Industrial Administration organization in 1962.

Psychological Study of Social Issues (which Lewin helped found) was third with 11, Consulting was fourth with 8, and Evaluation and Measurement had 6. No other division had as many as 5 members. Experimental Psychology had 2, Clinical Psychology had 3, and Engineering Psychology only 1. Of course, some of these psychologists held multiple division memberships. These data from a new source add a certain degree of construct validity to the survey findings, and to the evidence from the laureates as well.

Given the concentration of specialization, some concentration of doctoral degree–granting institution might be expected as well. Not so. Only Ohio State University (with 7) and New York University (with 6) stand out, and both grant a large number of doctorates generally. Harvard University and the University of Michigan have 4 each; MIT, Columbia University, University of Chicago, and UCLA have 3 each. All in all, 24 universities are represented. Of the 55 psychologists, 78 percent received the doctorate from a university other than the one where currently employed. Inbreeding is not very pronounced.

We looked at the matter of prior business experience, because it seemed feasible to expect the business world might be a major source of business school psychologists. Again our hypothesis was not confirmed. Of the 55, 39 had had no full-time business experience. A number, however, had done extensive consulting on the side. There were indeed 5 individuals who had worked for a consulting firm on a full-time basis, usually in a high-level capacity and often for a number of years. Among these people personal knowledge of business was extensive. Another 6 people had worked, also after obtaining the Ph.D., in corporations of various kinds. However, their positions were not at a high level within management, and many did not remain long in business firms. The remaining 5 worked in business positions before obtaining the Ph.D., either as graduate students or in positions of a nonpsychological nature.

The typical pattern is one of psychological education, followed immediately by academic employment, leading eventually to employment in a business school. We do not know whether this same pattern is characteristic of nonpsychologist business school professors, but it probably is, with the exception that entry into the business school is earlier (either before or immediately after the doctorate). In any event, organizational behavior some 40 years ago did not involve any more hands-on business experience than it does today.

1964 Survey

During 1963 the PAWSBIA steering committee attempted to obtain funding for a much more extensive survey of psychologists in business schools. We had a pilot study (the 1962 effort) and had gradually accumulated a much larger listing of target individuals and universities. We thought we were ripe for foundation funding to conduct a study that would establish what impact the foundation activism had had some 5 years after the reports appeared. We could not have been more wrong. The Ford Foundation was rapidly scaling back its investment in business education, and the Carnegie Foundation never had made a major investment beyond the report. These were policy decisions at the board level; funding for a survey was out of the question.

As a consequence, PAWSBIA settled for a relatively simple survey of a kind that would permit the development of a member directory, containing information on areas of teaching and research specialization. The idea was to distribute such a listing with the purpose of stimulating informal communication and networking. That was done, with a directory of 174 names and addresses, to most of which were appended statements of areas of specialization. The response rate was 88 percent and 145 completed questionnaires were obtained. The results are given in table 4.5.

By this time, the term *organizational behavior* was well established, and 78 percent of the respondents identify with it. Management was endorsed by 47 percent, but in most instances these are people who also check organizational behavior. On only 6 percent of the questionnaires is this not the case. Adding this 6 percent to the 78 gives 84 percent of the respondents who appear to be specializing in the micro or macro study of organizations. This is sufficient critical mass — over 120 people — to say that by the mid-1960s

the push to get psychologists with an interest in studying organizations into some relationship with business schools had had considerable success.

The only other field with a substantial representation among psychologists is personnel management. Only 19 individuals had a marketing/advertising specialization; all who indicated advertising checked marketing as well. Also it appears that teaching specialization serves to define specialization in general much more than research/writing specialization does.

To get some indication of the degree of concentration of the psychologists within universities, a tally was made using the total address list of 174. There were some universities with 5 or more people — Yale, the City University of New York, New York University, UCLA, Harvard, Stanford, MIT, Michigan, Cornell, Carnegie Tech, and Southern California. But only one had over 10. A total of 40 universities had just one person; another 14 had two or three. Understand, however, that by no means all of these psychologists are full-time in a business school. Many are in psychology departments or elsewhere on campus, but with some relationship to the business school. Probably they are best defined in most cases as the kind of people who would have joined the organizational behavior division of the Academy of Management had such a division existed at that time.

The conclusion that emerges from this analysis is that, with a few exceptions, the association of psychologists with business schools was a very unstable phenomenon in those days. Remove one or two people, and there is nothing there at all. Even some of the schools with relatively large representations have experienced major downward fluctuations over the years.

Survey Interpretations

It may be of some historical interest to consider the interpretations placed on these findings at the time they were written up. One approach was to consider what psychologists might be doing in business schools, but rarely were (Miner, 1963b). There was little evidence of activity in the production area, in spite of major increases in employment in the human engineering field at the time. One might have thought that in view of the apparent shortage of professors qualified to teach production, experimental psychologists with applied interests would have been recruited to fill the void. There is no evidence that this happened.

TABLE 4.5 Areas of specialization, 1964 survey (N = 145)

Areas of specialization	Answering (%)		
	Overall (general) specialization	Teaching specialization	Research/writing specialization
Organizational behavior	78	70	58
Management	47	44	30
Personnel management	46	45	23
Experimental design	21	19	6
Labor relations	14	10	7
Marketing	13	11	10
Statistics	12	11	3
Advertising	5	4	3
Human engineering	4	2	3
Operations research	3	2	2

NOTE: This survey was conducted by the Psychologists Associated with Schools of Business and Industrial Administration in 1964 among target psychologists.

Students taught: Undergraduate, n = 55; Graduate, n = 81; managers and administrators, n = 39.

Many psychologists with backgrounds in psychometrics, research design, and experimental psychology should be qualified to teach statistics. There were lots of statistics sections to teach. Yet activity on this front appears minimal. The surveys identify very few people doing this.

The marketing and advertising area is another where psychologists could bring skills in market research and consumer behavior to bear, but few are doing so. The difficulty here appears to be a shortage of qualified psychologists. Skills of this kind are typically honed in the business world and, once gained, the people who have them are likely to stay where the rewards are greatest.

Finally there was an almost complete lack of courses that deal specifically with personality theory and what might be called the clinical psychology of industry. Some such material is embedded in organizational behavior courses. However, little evidence was found that clinical psychologists were bringing the subject matter of that field to the business schools as a separate entity. Mayo clearly would have bemoaned the lack of activity on this front.

Approximately half of the business schools surveyed indicated an intent to add behavioral scientists in the near future, but the demand was in organizational behavior to include a number of opportunities for sociologists, and in research design. Production, statistics, marketing, and clinical applications were not where the need was considered greatest.

A point also emphasized is reflected in the following:

Psychologists as a group appear to need a much greater commitment to our existing economic system and an increased understanding of the practical realities of the business world. There is a widespread mistrust of business management as it is currently structured, which on occasion seems to border on outright distaste. In the writer's opinion these feelings must inevitably obstruct and distort the psychologist's influence on collegiate management education, and his contribution to knowledge of human functioning within the context of modern business organizations. (Miner, 1963a, p. 66)

This is the value clash problem. There is no question that it reflects my having recently moved from a business position to academe. Unfortunately, the surveys provide little evidence on this issue. In all likelihood, this is less of a concern for industrial psychologists, and that may help explain why so many from that group were attracted to the business schools. That experimental and clinical psychologists were not attracted may simply reflect the disparity of their values. It is unfortunate that empirical data on value orientations were not obtained in connection with the surveys. However, we are not much better informed in this regard today. What we think we know regarding this key factor is much more inferential than empirical.

CONCLUSIONS

In this chapter I have taken up the evidence from systematic attempts to assess the state of the business schools in the 1950s and early 1960s. What we find is considerable confirmation of the same conclusions, derived from data collected in a number of different ways. As the changes began to appear, a number of theories emerged with them, born of the multidisciplinary milieu that was created. But before beginning to take up those theories, the high level of uncertainty, instability, and ambiguity that characterized the business school scene and spawned the theories needs to be elaborated in much more detail. We need to understand both the stress created and the creative spark as well. That is the task of the next chapter.

References

Ackoff, Russell L. (1994). *The Democratic Corporation: A Radical Prescription for Recreating Corporate America and Rediscovering Success.* New York: Oxford University Press.

American Assembly of Collegiate Schools of Business & European Foundation for Management Development (1982). *Management for the XXI Century: Education and Development.* Boston: Kluwer-Nijhoff.

Argyris, Chris (1992). Looking Backward and Inward in Order to Contribute to the Future. In Arthur G. Bedeian (Ed.), *Management Laureates* (Vol. 1, pp. 41–64). Greenwich, CT: JAI Press.

Bach, George L. (1959). Managerial Decision Making as an Organizing Concept. In Frank C. Pierson (Ed.), *The Education of American Businessmen* (pp. 319–354). New York: McGraw-Hill.

Barley, Stephen R., & Kunda, Gideon (1992). Design and Devotion: Surges of Rational and Normative Ideologies of Control in Managerial Discourse. *Administrative Science Quarterly*, 37, 363–399.

Bartol, Kathryn M. (1996). Challenged on the Cutting Edge. In Arthur G. Bedeian (Ed.), *Management Laureates* (Vol. 4, pp. 1–37). Greenwich, CT: JAI Press.

Bass, Bernard M. (1992). A Transformational Journey. In Arthur G. Bedeian (Ed.), *Management Laureates* (Vol. 1, pp. 65–105). Greenwich, CT: JAI Press.

Bedeian, Arthur G. (1992, 1993, 1993, 1996, 1998). *Management Laureates: A Collection of Autobiographical Essays.* 5 vols. Greenwich, CT: JAI Press.

Bedeian, Arthur G. (1998a). And Fate Walked In. In Arthur G. Bedeian (Ed.), *Management Laureates* (Vol. 5, pp. 1–40). Greenwich, CT: JAI Press.

Bedeian, Arthur G. (1998b). Exploring the Past. *Journal of Management History*, 4(1), 4–15.

Beyer, Janice M. (1996). Performing, Achieving, and Belonging. In Arthur G. Bedeian (Ed.), *Management Laureates* (Vol. 4, pp. 39–84). Greenwich, CT: JAI Press.

Calás, Marta B., & Smircich, Linda (1990). Thrusting Toward More of the Same with the Porter-McKibbin Report. *Academy of Management Review*, 15, 698–705.

Cummings, Larry L. (1990a). Management Education Drifts into the 21st Century. *Academy of Management Executive*, 4(3), 66–67.

Cummings, Larry L. (1990b). Reflections on *Management Education and Development: Drift or Thrust Into the 21st Century? Academy of Management Review*, 15, 694–696.

Cummings, Larry L. (1992). Calling, Disciplines, and Attempts at Listening. In Arthur G. Bedeian (Ed.), *Management Laureates* (Vol. 1, pp. 237–266). Greenwich, CT: JAI Press.

Davis, Keith (1992). A Journey through Management in Transition. In Arthur G. Bedeian (Ed.), *Management Laureates* (Vol. 1, pp. 267–300). Greenwich, CT: JAI Press.

Ellis, Willis D. (1950). *A Source Book of Gestalt Psychology.* New York: Humanities Press.

Elsbach, Kimberly D., & Kramer, Roderick M. (1996). Members' Responses to Organizational Identity Threats: Encountering and Countering the *Business Week* Rankings. *Administrative Science Quarterly*, 41, 442–476.

Erez, Miriam (1996). Rhythms of an Academic's Life: Crossing Cultural Borders. In Peter J. Frost & M. Susan Taylor (Eds.), *Rhythms of Academic Life: Personal Accounts of Careers in Academia* (pp. 19–29). Thousand Oaks, CA: Sage.

Flexner, Abraham (1910). *Medical Education in the United States and Canada.* New York: Carnegie Foundation for the Advancement of Teaching.

Gillespie, Richard (1991). *Manufacturing Knowledge: A History of the Hawthorne Experiments.* Cambridge: Cambridge University Press.

Golembiewski, Robert T. (1992). Mid-Career Perspectives. In Arthur G. Bedeian (Ed.), *Management Laureates* (Vol. 1, pp. 371–416). Greenwich, CT: JAI Press.

Gordon, Robert A., & Howell, James E. (1959). *Higher Education for Business.* New York: Columbia University Press.

House, Robert J. (1993). Slow Learner and Late Bloomer. In Arthur G. Bedeian (Ed.), *Management Laureates* (Vol. 2, pp. 39–78). Greenwich, CT: JAI Press.

Katz, Elihu, & Lazarsfeld, Paul F. (1955). *Personal Influence: The Part Played by People in the Flow of Mass Communications.* New York: Free Press.

Koontz, Harold (1964). *Toward a Unified Theory of Management.* New York: McGraw-Hill.

Lawler, Edward E. (1993). Understanding Work Motivation and Organizational Effectiveness: A Career-Long Journey. In Arthur G. Bedeian (Ed.), *Management Laureates* (Vol. 2, pp. 79–109). Greenwich, CT: JAI Press.

Lawrence, Paul R., & Lawrence, Anne T. (1993). Doing Problem-Oriented Research: A Daughter's Interview. In Arthur G. Bedeian (Ed.), *Management Laureates* (Vol. 2, pp. 111–147). Greenwich, CT: JAI Press.

Leavitt, Harold J. (1960). Behavioral Science in the Business School. In Maurice W. Lee, Fred C. Foy, Richard M. Paget, Howard G. Bowen, Fred C. Cole, William B. Aycock, Samuel Goldberg, & Harold J. Leavitt (Eds.), *Views on Business Education* (pp. 75–85). Chapel Hill: School of Business Administration, University of North Carolina.

Leavitt, Harold J. (1963). *The Social Science of Organizations.* Englewood Cliffs, NJ: Prentice Hall.

Levine, Arthur (1980). *When Dreams and Heroes Died: A Portrait of Today's College Student.* San Francisco: Jossey-Bass.

Levinson, Harry (1993). Teacher as Leader. In Arthur G. Bedeian (Ed.), *Management Laureates* (Vol. 2, pp. 177–214). Greenwich, CT: JAI Press.

Locke, Edwin A. (1993). Principled Ambition. In Arthur G. Bedeian (Ed.), *Management Laureates* (Vol. 2, pp. 215–248). Greenwich, CT: JAI Press.

Mahoney, Thomas A. (1998). The Life and Times of a Perennial Student. In Arthur G. Bedeian (Ed.), *Management Laureates* (Vol. 5, pp. 129–170). Greenwich, CT.: JAI Press.

Massarik, Fred, & Ratoosh, Philburn (1965). *Mathematical Explorations in Behavioral Science.* Homewood, IL: Irwin.

Miner, John B. (1963a). The Psychologist's Impact upon Collegiate Management Education. *Academy of Management Proceedings*, 23, 62–68.

Miner, John B. (1963b). Psychology and the School of Business Curriculum. *Journal of the Academy of Management*, 6, 284–289.

Miner, John B. (1966). Psychologists in Marketing Education. *Journal of Marketing*, 30(1), 7–9,

Miner, John B. (1974). *The Human Constraint: The Coming Shortage of Managerial Talent.* Washington, DC: BNA Books.

Miner, John B. (1993). Pursuing Diversity in an Increasingly Specialized Organizational Science. In Arthur G. Bedeian (Ed.), *Management Laureates* (Vol. 2, pp. 283–319). Greenwich, CT: JAI Press.

Pfeffer, Jeffrey (1996). Taking the Road Less Traveled: Serendipity and the Influence of Others in a Career. In Arthur G. Bedeian (Ed.), *Management Laureates* (Vol. 4, pp. 201–233). Greenwich, CT: JAI Press.

Pierson, Frank C. (1959). *The Education of American Businessmen: A Study of University-College Programs in Business Administration.* New York: McGraw-Hill.

Porter, Lyman W. (1993). An Unmanaged Pursuit of Management. In Arthur G. Bedeian (Ed.), *Management Laureates* (Vol. 3, pp. 1–29). Greenwich, CT: JAI Press.

Porter, Lyman W., & McKibbin, Lawrence E. (1988). *Management Education and Development: Drift or Thrust into the 21st Century?* New York: McGraw-Hill.

Roberts, Karlene H. (1998). Having the Bubble. In Arthur G. Bedeian (Ed.), *Management Laureates* (Vol. 5, pp. 207–242). Greenwich, CT: JAI Press.

Schein, Edgar H. (1993). The Academic As Artist: Personal and Professional Roots. In Arthur G. Bedeian (Ed.), *Management Laureates* (Vol. 3, pp. 31–62). Greenwich, CT: JAI Press.

Sheehan, Robert (1964). New Report Card on the Business Schools. *Fortune*, 70(6), 1–12.

Shipper, Frank (1999). A Comparison of Managerial Skills of Middle Managers with MBAs, with Masters' and Undergraduate Degrees Ten Years after the Porter and McKibbin Report. *Journal of Managerial Psychology*, 14, 150–163.

Simon, Herbert A. (1991). *Models of My Life.* New York: Basic Books.

Slocum, John W. (1996). Never Say Never! In Arthur G. Bedeian (Ed.), *Management Laureates* (Vol. 4, pp. 277–311). Greenwich, CT: JAI Press.

Starbuck, William H. (1993). "Watch Where You Step!" Or Indiana Starbuck amid the Perils of Academe (Rated PG). In Arthur G. Bedeian (Ed.), *Management Laureates* (Vol. 3, pp. 63–110). Greenwich, CT: JAI Press.

Strauss, George (1993). Present at the Beginning: Some Personal Notes on OB's Early Days and Later. In Arthur G. Bedeian (Ed.), *Management Laureates* (Vol. 3, pp. 145–190). Greenwich, CT: JAI Press.

Strother, George B. (1962). *Social Science Approaches to Business Behavior.* Homewood, IL: Irwin.

Thompson, James D. (1966). *Approaches to Organizational Design.* Pittsburgh, PA: University of Pittsburgh Press.

Trist, Eric L. (1993). Guilty of Enthusiasm. In Arthur G. Bedeian (Ed.), *Management Laureates* (Vol. 3, pp. 191–221). Greenwich, CT: JAI Press.

Vroom, Victor H. (1960). *Some Personality Determinants of the Effects of Participation*. Englewood Cliffs, NJ: Prentice Hall.

Vroom, Victor H. (1993). Improvising and Muddling Through. In Arthur G. Bedeian (Ed.), *Management Laureates* (Vol. 3, pp. 257–284). Greenwich, CT: JAI Press.

Weick, Karl E. (1993). Turning Context into Text. In Arthur G. Bedeian (Ed.), *Management Laureates* (Vol. 3, pp. 285–323). Greenwich, CT: JAI Press.

Wengert, Egbert S.; Harwood, Dale S.; Marquis, Lucian; & Goldhammer, Keith (1961). *The Study of Administration*. Eugene: University of Oregon Press.

Chapter 5

Uncertainty and
the Genesis of Theory

In the initial section of this chapter the discussion focuses, first, on the situation within business schools, including the interface with the broader university, and, second, on the external environment, especially those aspects of that environment that create uncertainty and instability. From there we move to the intellectual environment for organizational behavior in the early period, with particular emphasis on the "schools" phenomenon (including the four aspects discussed in the preceding chapter). Finally, I describe some of my own personal experiences over the time from the middle 1950s on to the present as these experiences relate to the development of my theoretical positions.

UNCERTAINTY FACTOR

The initial impact of the foundation activism and the activities of a number of influential economists was to stir up the business schools, creating high uncertainty levels and considerable disruption of the status quo. The situation was not unlike the unfreezing phase of social change described by Kurt Lewin (1947, 1958). The change process was initiated from the outside primarily, and it created sufficient disequilibrium so that movement to a new level was possible. However, stabilization at that new level did not occur for a long time, and in the interim there was continuing uncertainty as to (1) what the outcome might be and (2) insofar as individuals were concerned, whether that outcome would include their participation.

Uncertainty within the University

We start with several descriptions of the internal business school environments that existed at the time in particular universities. Chapter 4, in considering the management laureate autobiographies, contains much material of this kind, but a more in-depth treatment is desirable.

Washington University

This description is provided by Walter Nord (1996), who entered the business school at Washington University as the first social scientist in 1967. He had just completed a doctorate in social psychology, which included considerable work in sociology, at the same university. Washington University is a private school, and its business component at the time was quite small. Nord describes himself as a Marxist in political belief, but indicates that he has kept these values out of the classroom except in doctoral seminars.

Never having had any business coursework himself, and without a role model of any kind, Nord faced a situation in his teaching that provided considerable latitude and few guidelines. He could experiment as he saw fit and introduce subjects that interested him. Initially he drew heavily on his earlier training, including many ideas from B. F. Skinner's brand of behaviorism. He used the latter's *Walden Two* (1948) in his first-year M.B.A. class. In general, other faculty members and administrators were supportive. The small size of the business school, and departments outside it as well, encouraged a great deal of interdisciplinary interaction.

At first, the strong practical orientation of the students created some problems. Nord was not used to this from his background, and it put him on the defen-

sive. Ultimately, however, it proved to be a stimulus for learning. Both Victor Vroom (1993) and Edgar Schein (1993) describe similar experiences. Also, the lack of appropriate teaching materials — including textbooks that covered the new material — created difficulties. There was little available that dealt with the specific subject matter Nord wanted to teach. However, an opportunity to self-design was fostered by the fact that he was teaching courses that had never been taught at the university before. With no set agenda, he was free to teach things that he wanted to learn about, and he did. His final resolution to the teaching materials problem was to prepare a collection of readings (Nord, 1972). He overcame the initial anxiety he felt with regard to using cases in teaching by spending time at the Harvard Business School and observing the approach used there.

Nord contrasts his experiences at that time with the current scene. The use of the standardized course evaluations that exist today would definitely have discouraged his innovative tendencies. Then, quality was valued without any narrow definition of the boundaries of the subject matter, whereas today that is not true. That he was able to thrive in this situation Nord attributes to the combination of his somewhat anarchistic, iconoclastic personality and a social environment that surrounded him with supportive people who valued quality and continuous learning, while creating a low level of established routine. He continued to thrive, or at least survive, at the Washington University business school for over 20 years. Unfortunately, he does not provide us with information on the ways in which his Marxist values may have created problems in this context.

The following quotations provide a certain degree of authenticity for some of the points made here, while documenting the ambiguity and uncertainty that prevailed:

> Because there were few people like me in the business school, and no one, including me, knew exactly what an organizational psychologist should do, I had a great deal of latitude. As a result, I was in a situation where I had room to experiment and introduce things that I was interested in. (Nord, 1996, p. 85)

> I did not fit into the established routines and was surrounded by developmentally oriented people. I was always allowed and encouraged to introduce and/or keep open to a variety of perspectives. . . .

I had the opportunity to be a self-designing system. . . . The opportunity I had to self-design was promoted by the fact that I was frequently teaching courses that had never been taught locally before. Thus there was no particular set agenda and I was free to bring in things that I wanted. (Nord, 1996, p. 86)

Carnegie Institute of Technology

The next scenario derives from a very different context and deals primarily with topics other than teaching. It is provided in the autobiography of Herbert Simon (1991), who died in 2001 (see Anderson, 2001). Simon came to Carnegie from the political science department of another technological university at a time when the Graduate School of Industrial Administration was being founded (1949). He remained there throughout his career, although his base of operations gradually shifted to the psychology department. It is testimony to his multidisciplinary capabilities that he also received the Nobel Prize in economics.

The starting assumption of the new school appears to have been that the business education of the era was a wasteland of vocationalism and strongly in need of transformation to science-based professionalism. The model for the new school emphasized a diverse array of behavioral scientists to include a heavy emphasis on economics. There were no classical management theorists already in residence, and so this did not represent a problem. However, Simon reports an early conflict between those with a more applied bent and the neoclassical economists who were intent on retaining their professional purity. There were also some clear conflicts between Simon's own theorizing about managerial decision making and the theories espoused by the same economists. These problems seem to have been exacerbated by a university culture that supported the use of certain controls on both teaching and research (which was heavily funded). Which group was to exert the control?

By the early 1960s it became evident that the neoclassical economists were to have control. At Carnegie, organizational behavior's dominance ended in the period when it was just beginning to pick up steam elsewhere. The emphasis shifted to sophisticated mathematical techniques in operations research and neoclassical economic theory. A number of people with other interests left for attractive opportunities elsewhere. Simon, who had been developing a re-

search program in cognitive processes and computer modeling, began to withdraw to the psychology department and finally moved his office there around 1970.

What is evident here is an escalating conflict between organizational behavior and economics that existed in spite of the fact that, at Carnegie as elsewhere, economists played an important role in fostering the development of organizational behavior in the first place. Simon also indicates a degree of conflict between the industrial administration segment of the university and the liberal arts segment, especially the humanities. He speaks of the latter's demeaning attitude toward what they considered vocationalism, of their espousal of uselessness, of their portrayal of skill as a dirty word. It is apparent that here as elsewhere the business school was subjected to a degree of one-upmanship and that the dialogue involved often became heated. It was not just business versus the humanities, but science versus the humanities as well.

The situation as it ultimately evolved at Carnegie has been described as follows by a participant:

Carnegie was not the source of interdisciplinary work that it had been in the early sixties. While there were still no departments within the school, the creation of a strong group of economists who were committed to theoretical issues within economics foreshadowed similar coalitions within operations research and in organizational behavior. Furthermore, Leavitt and March had moved on to other universities; Cyert was about to become president of the university; and Simon had left the field of organizational behavior more than a decade earlier. (Vroom, 1993, p. 270)

Variability across Universities

Although the subject matter of the descriptions differs, the wide disparity between the Washington University and Carnegie experiences is still striking. Paul Lawrence (1987), speaking from his long tenure at the Harvard Business School, has something to say on this score. He notes, first, that the decade starting in 1958 was an unusually productive time; as organizational behavior grew in this period, it produced many innovative theories, and Harvard was a participant in that process. Second, and this also is based on the Harvard situation, the business schools and organizational behavior were subjected to considerable discipline-based stereotyping and even denigration. Among other things, the field's members were criticized for being merely servants of power. The echoing voices within the halls of academe became strident here, often loud enough to be heard outside.

Lawrence gives substantial attention to the multidisciplinary nature of organizational behavior. As direct recruitment of psychologists and sociologists increased in the 1960s, the immigrants threatened to overwhelm the natives, with all the tension the foundation reports anticipated. He also notes that organizational behavior exhibited great flexibility in responding to the value issues of the period. Although some may criticize this as fadism, it has the appeal of permitting involvement in social issues at the time they are happening. Lawrence finds this flexibility to follow current problems appealing; certainly, the Harvard Business School has been at the forefront in this regard.

Another source of information is a chapter by Milton Blood (1994) written from the author's perspective as a long-time administrator with the American Assembly of Collegiate Schools of Business, and before that as a faculty member in the school of business at Georgia Tech (1974–1983). Blood is a psychologist, but he feels that the multidisciplinary roots of organizational behavior are hurting the field now and create a fuzzy identity with unclear boundaries.

Although he was not present at the birth of organizational behavior, Blood is close enough to these origins and knowledgeable enough regarding them to have useful insights. He says:

> The field of management was based on anecdotal and experientially derived knowledge; the new OB faculty came from empirically based social science disciplines. Industrial psychologists brought in their penchant for individual differences research, their correlational approaches to knowledge creation, and their disdain for knowledge that is not empirically authenticated. The clash of epistemologies must have created as many agreements-to-disagree as it created opportunities to pool perspectives. At any rate, in some schools OB supplemented an existing management department. In others, OB supplanted management. In still others, OB grew up as a separate, parallel field that competed for the same topic areas under different names and approaches. (Blood, 1994, p. 211)

A personal example may help make clearer the tensions and different epistemologies that Blood describes. The following memo was written by my department head at the University of Oregon, a scholar in the management principles tradition, during 1964:

> In has become increasingly apparent that you are not adhering to proper organization channels in your attempts to foster your self-interest. After a discussion with Dean Lindholm yesterday I came to the conclusion that you should be notified in formal fashion that you are transgressing the fundamental precepts of sound organization. Specifically, I refer to your chronic bypassing of your department head, myself in this instance and Dr. Mark Greene during the previous three years. I suggest that in the future all business matters pertinent to your position in the School of Business Administration be routed through my office, at least as a matter of courtesy, before you approach Dean Lindholm. Bypassing the department head as you have been doing for the past four years is a serious breach of both etiquette and organization structure.

It is evident that the differences were not merely confined to the intellectual treatment of distant business conditions; they applied to the here-and-now university setting as well.

Such conflicts did not occur everywhere, as the Washington University scenario indicates. Furthermore, overlapping jurisdictions with other social science departments outside the business school were much less likely to be a source of tension than overlaps within. The following letter written to me in 1962 by Robert Dubin, research professor of sociology at the University of Oregon, illustrates how potential problems could be and often were handled:

> This letter will serve to confirm the conclusions reached in our conference last Friday. The University course committee had recommended that there be consultation between representatives of the School of Business Administration and the Department of Sociology to establish mutual understandings regarding course offerings in the two areas. We acted as the respective representatives and came to the following agreements.
>
> 1. That the possibilities of overlap occurred principally in the area dealing with formal organization, variously characterized in sociology as the study of bureaucracy and industrial sociology, and in the School of Business Administration as the study of management and supervision.

2. That the subject matter of such courses in sociology is analytically oriented while the subject matter of such courses in the School of Business Administration is professionally oriented. This difference in orientation is significant as the major criterion for separating courses into the two academic realms.

3. That the respective sociology courses usually are taught at the advanced undergraduate level, with possibilities of graduate credit, while the complementary courses in business administration are usually taught at the graduate level as part of intensive professional training.

4. That we find no conflicts among the present course offerings or those now proposed by either division of the University. Furthermore, we expect that if the major criterion as set forth in #2 above is followed in the future, such conflicts need never arise.

5. That the Sociology Department would be pleased to send its students undertaking graduate preparation for professional management positions (e.g. supervision of research organizations) into the relevant School of Business Administration courses for training. We view such courses as pertinent to the development of professional management skills, thereby serving the entire University.

6. That the School of Business Administration will continue to make use of the pertinent courses in the Sociology Department that contribute to the training of students in the general management area, and such professionally specialized areas as personnel administration and marketing.

I believe these six points cover the substance of our discussions and agreements. Please be sure that the Department of Sociology welcomed this opportunity to examine an area of instruction that is of common concern to our respective departments. We stand ready to continue the cooperation that has characterized our relations in the past.

Where conflict did arise, it inevitably created an environment of uncertainty and stress. There was always the possibility that some group would win and some other would lose. Simon's exodus to the psychology department at Carnegie is a case in point. At Oregon by about 2 years after the time the memo quoted above was written, the existing organizational behavior contingent had disappeared from the university.

Uncertainty in the Outside World

The considerations I mention in this section differ from those noted previously in that they refer to organizations and events that had their origins outside any particular university. They spread across all, or almost all, business schools and in some cases had much wider implications than that. Yet they were unsettling and accordingly added to the stress and uncertainty; probably, they accentuated the unfreezing as well.

Professional Associations

In the early years, there was no professional association for those in the field of organizational behavior. The largest segment was made up of psychologists, and members of Division 14 of the American Psychological Association represented the largest contingent. The problem was that not all of the imports by any means were psychologists, and not all the psychologists were of the industrial variety. We saw this in the last chapter. Furthermore, Division 14 was strongly oriented to psychology department faculty and their students who had embarked on a career in the business world. There was curiosity and interest regarding those members who had wandered off into the business schools, but initially at least some skepticism. There was enough ambivalence all around then so that a true joining of the parties was unlikely. It was not until 1970 that Division 14 assumed the title of Industrial/Organizational Psychology, which reflected formal recognition of the tie to organizational behavior.

The Academy of Management was another matter. Initially its concerns were not those of organizational behavior. However, around 1960, with a stagnant membership, attention began to focus on methods of achieving growth (Wrege, 1986), and ultimately this led to a much more open stance toward previously unrepresented groups generally. The problem in the early period, however, was that the interests of the Academy and organizational behavior were unaligned. Information on the content of the *Journal of the Academy of Management* in the late 1950s indicates that two areas dominated—management education and development (pedagogy) and organization and management theory (principles) (Adams & Davis, 1986; Mowday, 1997). There was little of an empirical nature. The meetings were characterized by these same emphases.

As Paul Gordon (1997) reports, by the mid-1960s the situation at the *Journal* began to change. There was a shift away from more exclusive identification with general management principles and processes, personnel administration, and the production management of the day to a wider range of concerns. By the 1968–1969 period organizational behavior had become the dominant topic area, and that pattern continued for another 20 years with the peak in 1978–1979. By 1973–1975 this pattern of change produced the first editor of the *Journal* who had been trained as a psychologist (Miner, 1997a). Clearly the Academy of Management had by that time become the professional association for organizational behavior. However, before that happened there was considerable shifting back and forth; this instability did little to ameliorate the uncertainty and lack of a clear professional identity that characterized organizational behavior at the time.

Yet there are still vestiges of these early problems. As the Academy grew, it quite naturally became segmented into divisions. As Larry Cummings (1978) wrote, five of these divisions — organizational behavior, organization and management theory, personnel and human resources, organizational development, and organizational communication — are concerned with organizational analysis or science. He hoped that these divisions could somehow be tied together, and he thought he saw signs of this happening. Those signs are still present, but a single professional entity for organizational behavior or organizational science remains a dream for the future. Without it, a degree of instability is perpetuated.

Computers

An article published by Harold Leavitt and Thomas Whisler (1958) sets the scene for this discussion. It describes the state of affairs existing at that time as they were occasioned by the rapid ascent of a new technology. This new technology was made up of (1) high-speed computers that could process information rapidly, (2) statistical and mathematical methods for decision making, and (3) computer programs to simulate higher order thought processes (which were only on the horizon). These developments, all of which involved computers in one way or another, had introduced a great deal of uncertainty. It was hard to tell what their eventual impact would be.

The question of how computers would influence management, organization structures, employment levels, and the like yielded a rapid response in the form of research on organizations that had introduced computers on a major scale. By the late 1960s the answers began to come in (see Myers, 1967; Reif, 1968; Whisler, 1970). In this respect there was uncertainty in the business schools, and elsewhere, for some time, but research ultimately served to reduce the problem. Other computer-related sources of uncertainty were less tractable.

One had to do with the use of computers to simulate cognitive processes. Where would this lead? How successful would it be? What would be the effect on social science generally, and on organizational behavior? Few had any idea, although Simon and those who worked with him were convinced that important advances were in store (Simon, 1991). There was the feeling that major breakthroughs could well reorient the whole study of decision making, but would that occur?

Moreover, computers threatened to replace the calculators that had been the mainstay of statistical analyses for years. Research could be simplified enormously, but the technology was slow to develop and programs often did not work. Computer games were the next advance in teaching technology, but few knew how to use them and even fewer how to develop them. Computer technology appeared to be redesigning the jobs of people in organizational behavior and in many other fields. Yet this was not happening smoothly, and what its limits were was hard to establish.

Student Activism

One other source of uncertainty came to permeate the external, and ultimately the internal, environments of business schools during the 1960s. These matters relate to student activism and protest and the New Left ideology that characterized the student movement at that time. The events of this period were widely studied, and considerable information is available regarding them and the students who participated (see Lipset & Schaflander, 1971; Kerpelman, 1972; Miner, 1974).

Starting in 1962 with peace demonstrations in Washington, D.C., and the formation of Students for a Democratic Society, the pace of student activism and militancy began to accelerate. By the fall of 1964 the Berkeley campus of the University of California was faced with large-scale demonstrations, which then spread to most of the larger campuses in the country. The turmoil that ensued continued to the end of the 1960s and beyond.

Business schools and the discipline of organizational behavior faced an interesting situation during this period. A major target was the business community and the economic system, which was consistent with New Left ideology. As contributors to the creation of corporate bureaucracies and representatives of the free enterprise system, business schools were objects of attack. Yet, in general, business students and faculty exhibited neither activist attitudes nor behavior to any significant degree (Peterson, 1968). Student activism was at its peak among the social science disciplines, and faculty support was greatest there, too—particularly in sociology, but also in psychology and political science, and to a somewhat lesser extent in economics. These statistics posed a problem for organizational behavior because among the relatively conservative business faculties, those who had close ties to the social sciences were sometimes viewed as suspect.

The turmoil was great enough everywhere, and it did extend to the business schools to a degree. Whether rightly or not, however, and we know little on this score, organizational behavior was caught up in the controversy more than most disciplines. Its position is best viewed as precarious—from one side it represented the enemy; from the other side it was considered a sympathizer with the enemy. This is the essence of a lose-lose situation, and it made for a few sleepless nights.

Uncertainty and the Individual

As we have seen, the ground that existed during the early history of organizational behavior bordered on the chaotic. This was a period of unfreezing and gradual movement to a new ground. However, the unfreezing did not stop when the movement began; nor when the movement continued either. This continuing ferment occurred within the business schools, but it was fed as well from the outside, on occasion by factors that had little if any relation to the movement of the social sciences into the business school context. I have chosen to discuss the three such factors that seem most salient to me. This is not to argue that other

sources of uncertainty did not operate in that period as well.

The treatment in this chapter has concentrated on portraying the ambiguity and lack of structure that characterized the times when organizational behavior came into being. We have considered certain sources of uncertainty, and we have noted that stress sometimes resulted for participants. Some people did not function well under these circumstances; they needed more structure to be at their best. There were defections from the ranks of organizational behavior in the early years—people who returned to the basic departments outside the business schools or moved to business employment of various kinds.

Yet others responded well to the uncertainty; in fact, they appear to have thrived under these circumstances. These were often the people who created the theories that emerged so frequently during the 1950s, 1960s, and early 1970s, the theoretical binge that accompanied the early growth of organizational behavior.

CONTEXT OF THEORY AS ORGANIZATIONAL BEHAVIOR EMERGED

We turn now to the positive consequences of uncertainty and to the process of theory building in the period.

Given the uncertainties on other fronts, it is appropriate to ask about the intellectual context that existed as organizational behavior developed. Remember that we are talking about a field which at the time had very fuzzy boundaries, a condition that remains true today, although I believe to a lesser extent. Nevertheless, we need to understand where this discipline with its fuzzy boundaries stood in the late 1950s and 1960s in terms of its intellectual development. For that, we must turn to some history of science to get the positioning right.

Some History of Science

In its early days, organizational behavior went through a transitional process—gradually moving from the realm of philosophy to that of science. An understanding of this transitional phase, and what typically happens in it, is essential to any discussion of the intellectual environment that existed at the time.

Role of Philosophy

Philosophy may be viewed as an effort to discover the ultimate nature of things through a process of systematic reflection. The term is also used to refer to a set of speculative beliefs or convictions. In either sense, philosophy departs from science in that it does not emphasize controlled research; its output of ideas is not subject to confirmation and rejection based on research evidence.

Within the milieu of organizational behavior, philosophy initially took the form of attempts to discover the essential elements of managing and operating organizations through systematic reflection.

Similar efforts characterized the early work in the physical and biological sciences. Mankind had many conceptions regarding the nature of the universe and the world around him before physics, chemistry, astronomy, and biology assumed major roles in this regard. In each instance, the desire for something more definite, for more valid understanding and prediction, led to the gradual development of a science where only an aspect of philosophy had been before.

In the natural sciences (Roberts, Hulin, & Rousseau, 1978), and in the social sciences as well (Wadia, 1968), it has been typical for the interval between development within philosophy and emergence as a science divorced from philosophical origins to be marked by a great deal of conflict between various schools of thought. This is a time when true theory begins to emerge, but research evidence to discriminate among theories is lacking. Because the needed research has not yet been completed, or on occasion cannot be completed since the theories are untestable, diatribe and invective often replace it. This is a phase; it tends to dissipate when theories and hypotheses are adequately tested — when there is enough research evidence so that sophisticated rationalization is no longer of any avail.

Psychology As an Example

Among the social sciences, psychology provides a good example of this historical process. Psychology traces its philosophical origins to the writings of such men as Descartes, Leibnitz, Locke, Berkeley, Hume, Hartley, the Mills (father and son), Bain, Kant, and Herbart (Boring, 1950). These men dealt with topics that later became the subject of psychological theory and research. It was not until the 1870s that psychology as a science showed clear signs of emergence.

In the ensuing decades, a variety of schools of thought began to appear. By 1933, Edna Heidbreder was able to describe *Seven Psychologies*; her chapter titles are also descriptive:

> Titchener and Structuralism
>
> The Psychology of William James
>
> Functionalism and the University of Chicago
>
> Behaviorism
>
> Dynamic Psychology and Columbia University
>
> Gestalt Psychology
>
> Freud and the Psychoanalytic Movement

Robert Woodworth and Mary Sheehan (1964), in a book that appeared in its first edition in 1931, describe the following:

> Functional psychology
>
> Structural psychology
>
> Associationism
>
> Psychoanalysis
>
> Personalistic and organismic psychologies
>
> Purposivism or hormic psychology
>
> Behaviorism
>
> Gestalt psychology

All of these schools had been initially established by 1912.

Schools of thought tend to be identified with specific individuals or universities, or both. With the deaths of founding fathers and changes in university faculties, the schools of psychological thought have gradually faded. It is not that they have disappeared; nor have they been replaced by other schools. Each has contributed in important ways to present knowledge. Yet no grand superschool, or synthesis of conflicting views, has appeared. It is simply that the outpouring of psychological research since World War II has caught up with the schools. As a result, we know considerably more about which of the pronouncements within each school are correct, which are wrong, and which are unimportant.

Currently, there is considerable development of theory in psychology, although many scholars would argue for more. However, a theory does not now typically accelerate into a school with polemics and counterpolemics. Rather, new theories are subjected to the criterion of scientific research by which they stand or fall. This is not to argue that conflict has disappeared from psychology. That is probably too much to ask of any field. But much of the conflict follows the lines of specialties and subspecialties, rather than theories. Theories generate conflict primarily when they remain untested, and that is mostly when they are new. New theories, by definition, do not have the time to generate large followings and solidify these followings into various schools, however.

I should emphasize that the concept of *schools* as a transitional state set forth here is not the only way in which the term is used in the organizational behavior literature. There are alternative definitions (see, for example, McKinley, Mone, & Moon, 1999), and it is important to be aware of the differences.

Schools and Organizational Behavior

During the 1960s organizational behavior was at the height of its schools phase. Many lists of these schools of thought were proposed, often to showcase a particular school that the author advocated. This was the intellectual environment of the period, and for that reason we need to consider some of these lists. One such list, which we have already touched on, was incorporated in the Robert Gordon and James Howell (1959) report that was prepared for the Ford Foundation (see chapter 4):

Management analysis—the quantitative approach extending from Taylor to operations analysis (see chapter 3)

Organization theory—the social science approach to the study of organizational phenomena

Principles of management—the views of Fayol and his followers (see chapter 3)

Human relations—the approach to supervision that emerged from the Hawthorne studies (see chapter 2)

In some instances these schools dealt with quite different subject matters; then the controversy was likely to be over method, not theoretical content. However, there were problem-focused conflicts as well,

where theories appeared to clash. With all the (perhaps intentional) ambiguity regarding domains and concepts, however, it was often difficult to say whether or not real antitheses existed.

Harold Koontz and His Jungle

Probably the most widely recognized listings of schools were those proposed by Harold Koontz. There were two of them, published almost 20 years apart. These listings are given in table 5.1. Koontz himself identifies with the management process, or operational, school. In his discussions he is a strong advocate for that school and an equally strong critic of many of the other schools.

Over the interval between the two listings, what Koontz calls the "jungle" of schools appears to have become much more dense. By 1980 the original 6 schools have increased to 10, and 1 of them has split into 2 as well. There has been considerable renaming and some additions of key individuals. Much of what is added stems from new developments, but there is some rethinking of prior views also. In any event, Koontz's formulations make it evident that there was a great deal of conflict and uncertainty involving different groups and that even identifying these groups with certainty presented major problems.

Views of William Scott

William Scott also proposed two sets of schools at different times. The first (Scott, 1961) notes three influential theories rooted in three separate schools:

1. The classical doctrine—deals with the anatomy of formal organization (Taylor, Mooney, Reiley, Brech, Allen)
2. Neoclassical theory of organization—is identified with the human relations movement and was inspired by the Hawthorne studies (Gardner, Moore, K. Davis)
3. Modern organization theory—possesses distinctive qualities in its conceptual-analytic base, its reliance on empirical research, and its integrative nature; the only meaningful way to study organization is as a system (March, Simon, Haire)

Here Scott identifies with the third alternative, but in a later publication this preference is less clear (Scott, 1968). Table 5.2 sets forth this new position. Scott

TABLE 5.1 Koontz's schools in the management theory jungle at two points in time

Koontz (1961, 1962)	Koontz (1980)
1. Management process (Fayol, Taylor, Mooney, Brown, Urwick, Koontz)	Operational: emphasizes concepts, principles, theory, and techniques underpinning practice
2. Empirical (Dale)	Empirical or case: emphasizes the study of managerial successes and failures in individual cases (Harvard Business School)
3. Human behavior (Tannenbaum, Weschler, Massarik, Dubin)	a. Interpersonal behavior: emphasizes individuals and their motivations; psychology (Maslow, Herzberg, Litwin) b. Group behavior: emphasizes behavior of people in groups; sociology and cultural anthropology (Argyris)
4. Social systems (March, Simon, Barnard)	Cooperative social systems: emphasizes human relationships within cooperative social systems (Pareto)
5. Decision theory (Luce, Raiffa)	Decision theory: emphasizes the central role of decision making
6. Mathematical (Miller, Starr, Churchman)	Mathematical or management science: emphasizes mathematical processes, concepts, symbols, and models
	7. Sociotechnical systems: emphasizes harmonizing social and technical systems (Trist)
	8. Systems: emphasizes the systems view of organizations as an assemblage of interconnected or interdependent parts forming a complex unity (Johnson, Kast, Rosenzweig)
	9. Contingency or situational: emphasizes the idea that what managers do depends on a given set of circumstances (Lorsch)
	10. Managerial roles: emphasizes roles developed from observation (Mintzberg)

talks about creeds and other options in describing these five alternatives. The first three — scientific management, human relations, and industrial humanism — are stated as creeds, but implicit in them are distinct schools of thought. Yet they were not the same schools as in 1961. The remaining two alternatives — constitutionalism and management science — reflect a new wave of literature that was both growing and impressive, but as yet was undigested by scholars of the field. By implication, these are projected schools of the future. Scott seemed to believe that the management science approach would win out ultimately. For the present, however, we are left with a picture of conflicting and changing ideologies, creeds, theories, and schools.

Charles Perrow's History of Organizational Theory

Charles Perrow (1973) presents what amounts to a running commentary in which one school superseded another over time. Yet vestiges of prior schools remained so that into the early 1970s some version of all the schools still existed. These schools are as follows:

1. Scientific management or classical (Taylor)
2. Human relations (Barnard, Roethlisberger, Dickson; later: Bennis, Likert, McGregor, Blake)
3. Bureaucratic (Weber, the numbers men)
4. Political science — power, conflict, and decisions (Simon, March)

TABLE 5.2 William Scott's (1968) implicit schools

Schools	Starting points	Assumptions about the nature of man	Attitude toward power	Justification for the use of power	Means of handling conflict
Scientific management	Management	Weak, corrupt, and invariable	Keep power submerged as far as possible beneath the surface of interpersonal relations	Necessary for maintaining order and getting people to act contrary to their nature	Mutuality of interests through productivity
Human relations	Management	Good, mildly plastic, capable of wide differences among individuals		Necessary to preserve order and induce organizational solidarity	Integration of interests through manipulation of needs
Industrial humanism	Man	Good, plastic, and capable of infinite perfectability	→	Necessary to hasten the progress of individual perfection and organizational harmony	Leveling confrontation, personal awareness, interpersonal competence, and intergroup problem solving leading to consensus and democratization
Constitutionalism	Processes that produce formal and informal pacts	Predisposed to act in a framework of negotiated laws and rules—political	Power determines who gets what; a fact of organizational life; should not be submerged	Does not need justification	Rule by mutual expectation, which reduces ambiguity and conflict
Management science	Technology	Materialistic, pleasure-seeking, comfort-loving, motivated to produce and consume	Power should be manifest & vested in a technical elite because they have the expertise to use it	Rationality	Equitable and generous distribution of rewards based on technical ingenuity and efficiency

SOURCE: Adapted from William G. Scott (1968), Technology and Organizational Government: A Speculative Inquiry into the Functionality of Management Creeds, *Academy of Management Journal*, 11, 303, 307

5. Technology (Woodward, Thompson, Lawrence, Lorsch, Perrow)
6. Institutional—goals, environments, and systems (Selznick, Katz, Kahn)

This approach repackages some of the ideas and people considered previously. It places more emphasis on sociology-based schools, which is not surprising since Perrow is a sociologist. The account is entertaining but at times somewhat confusing. There is reference to a Buck Rogers school best represented by Warren Bennis, but Bennis is also a member of the human relations school. What does come through strongly is that, amidst the controversy, schools rose to power and sank almost to oblivion very rapidly, and with little or no reference to scientific research.

Schools and More Schools

A number of other lists from the 1960s exerted a degree of influence at the time, usually in favor of one school or another. Among these are those in Bennis (1966), Etzioni (1964), Gordon (1963), Krupp (1961), Pugh (1966), and Woolf (1965). These classification systems often use new names and introduce new insights, but basically they are all concerned with some combination drawn from the lists of schools already considered. As a group, however, they demonstrate exactly how great the preoccupation with conflicting schools was at the time. This preoccupation extended to myself (Miner, 1971). My version ran as follows: classical (Fayol, Urwick), human relations (Mayo, Roethlisberger), structuralist (Weber), behavioral humanist (Likert, McGregor), and decision making (Simon, Barnard).

A particularly interesting portrayal is set forth in figure 5.1. Fred Luthans (1973) positions his seven schools in a sequence over time with all coalescing into the contingency school shortly after 1980. Note, however, that this sequence was proposed at a point in time just beyond the mid-point of the diagram. Things have not turned out exactly as projected, and, in fact, a problem exists because the contingency school can be traced back to the 1960s. Nevertheless, the idea of a sequence of schools, with some being superseded by others, matches Perrow's approach— and both were proposed in 1973. Contrary to what Koontz proposed, these views depict a jungle of reducing density.

It is hard to find agreement in the schools literature.

Intellectual Context in Related Arenas

A question arises as to the intellectual environment elsewhere in the world, outside the United States and particularly in Europe where organizational behavior had a good foothold. Information in this regard is provided by Geert Hofstede and M. Sami Kassem (1976). Things appear to have been very different there. One factor was that few business schools existed outside the United States in the early period. Thus the process of importing social scientists, and creating a field of organizational behavior within business schools, had not occurred.

What was to become organizational behavior in Europe focused on macro structural issues and was dominated by sociologists housed in sociology departments or in independent research units. The predominant methodology was comparative case analysis. The ideology was focused on conflict, consistent with a Marxian orientation. In general, the ties to practice were limited, and theorizing was accordingly more abstract than practical. Although Europe fed into the mélange of schools that existed in the United States at various points—and had held a dominant position at one time prior to World War II with Fayol, Weber, Lewin, Pareto, and the like—there was less schools-type controversy during the 1950s and 1960s in Europe.

A second arena relates to practice, especially in the United States. Did the schools phenomenon carry over into management and produce the same set of disparate approaches there? The results of a comprehensive survey conducted by the National Industrial Conference Board (Rush, 1969) is revealing on that score. First, the survey indicates that the ideas of six social scientists had particularly captured the attention of managers; these six were McGregor, Maslow, Herzberg, Likert, Argyris, and Blake. All fit into what I have called the behavioral humanist school. Organizational behavior outside this school was hardly recognized. Second, and consistent with the first, industrial applications of organizational behavior were best described as follows:

It is an applied science, which is normative and value centered.

Although oriented toward economic objectives, it is humanistic and optimistic.

It is concerned with the total climate or milieu and with the organization as a total system.

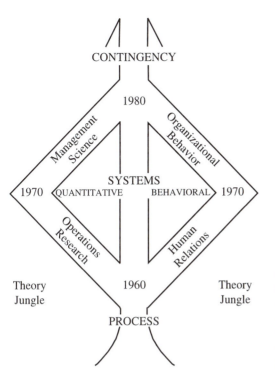

FIGURE 5.1 Sequence of schools proposed by Luthans (1973). From Fred Luthans (1973), The Contingency Theory of Management: A Path out of the Jungle, *Business Horizons*, 16(3), 69. Copyright 1973 by the Board of Trustees at Indiana University, Kelley School of Business. Reprinted with permission from *Business Horizons*.

The major concern is with the use of groups, particularly with the aim of promoting participation.

The development of interpersonal competence is a primary goal.

It is an ongoing process to manage change.

The data indicate that, although conflict was the order of the day in academe, this was not the case in the business world; the battle had been won there almost before it started. Yet this was true only for those who had an opinion. If asked what views they held relative to organizational behavior, a number of business people of that time would certainly have answered "none" or "don't know."

Finally, a question arises regarding the spillover effect from organizational behavior to personnel management. Consistent with the times, controversy appears to have prevailed in personnel as well (Dunnette & Bass, 1963; Patten, 1964). Much of this controversy was related to schools of thought.

From Schools to Scientific Theory

Over the years, and certainly since the early 1980s, the schools controversy has diminished steadily. Many of the schools of thought seem to have disappeared. Some have left the field, some have faded into nonexistence, some have engaged in a process of co-optation to the point where they are hardly recognizable. With the support of research, a few have become established as major theories or theoretical positions. With all of their divisiveness, these schools are now of primarily historical significance; they are no longer a dominant feature on the organizational behavior scene. This is what would be expected, given the history of other sciences. But there surely was an extended period of high controversy and uncertainty in the theoretical world of organizational behavior before the schools began to disappear.

Some, no doubt, would contend that this schools phase disappeared only to be replaced by a new schools phase that is even more controversial and interlaced with ideas from philosophy. I do not believe this is fully true, although in certain respects it is. It is apparent, for instance, that the macro component of organizational behavior is infused with what look to be schools—population ecology, neoinstitutional theory, resource dependence theory, structural contingency theory, and perhaps others. However, on closer scrutiny it becomes evident that these "schools" are surrounded by a body of research — research that takes them out of the realm of philosophy and into science. They are testable and they have been tested; perhaps not to the degree they should be and certainly not to an extent that would produce consensus, but sufficiently to remove them from philosophy. Thus, these are not schools in the same sense that classical management and human relations were.

The same cannot be said for postmodernism and its siblings. They are very much in the realm of philosophy, and they have entered organizational behavior primarily through the medium of theory, and to some extent research as well, as they seek to redefine research to a particular type of qualitative standard. They have had considerable appeal in some quarters based on a largely countercultural emphasis. They seem to eulogize divisiveness and conflict to a point that appears anarchist in nature. They are philosophical positions with nontestable propositions, they have not generated a body of scientific research, and they arouse considerable emotionality. This looks very much like a school or a set of quite similar schools. Why we are now experiencing this throwback to an earlier period is not entirely clear. It may be that the activism of the 1960s and early 1970s produced a group of people in organizational behavior who now are of an age to exert considerable influence and who are predisposed to accept "contra" positions that are anti-science because science represents control and authority.

Another point arises out of the fact that both the first and second generations in organizational behavior have created and experienced substantial conflict. Which had more? I do not think we know, and presumably we never will. However, the potential negative consequences of the first-generation conflicts were greater, simply because the field was more fragile and had a very small body of research to point to to bolster its scientific status.

The intellectual environment of the early period was characterized by organizational behavior's status somewhere between philosophy and science. The schools phase was in control — or perhaps out of control is a better description. The solution to this source of confusion has clearly been scientific research, lots of research. Over time, slowly and very hesitantly, with slips backward in many individual cases, the discipline of organizational behavior has been able to establish itself and move to a scientific footing. That status is currently under attack, but it remains strong.

As Lawrence (1987) noted, the period from the late 1950s on was a very productive one for theory construction. This appears to be because the unfreezing process that was associated with social scientists who were entering the business schools forced a number of people and lives out of established patterns, with the result that ideas that had never been juxtaposed before suddenly were. New combinations were everywhere, available for the picking. And as people did the picking, new theories were created. Certainly, the harvest at that time was strongly influenced by prevailing values. Certain combinations of ideas that were ripe for picking were allowed to wither because the values of the times did not give them visibility. Yet a great many new combinations were found. Thus, all the controversy appears to have had its share of positive consequences, as well as negative ones.

A PERSONAL AND THEORETICAL ODYSSEY

The preceding discussion has provided an extended panorama of the ground against which organizational behavior became figure. However, it remains to show just how the theories and research developed or adopted by organizational behavior fit into and were influenced by their settings. Obviously, different theories achieved their positions on the ground in different ways, and in most instances we can gain only a partial understanding of this process because not all the facts are available. One solution to this dilemma is to solicit stories from individuals, describing their experiences as their theories and research developed. This approach has the disadvantage that it is dependent on the vagaries of post hoc constructions; memory does not always serve us well in these personally relevant situations. Nevertheless, there is the advantage that the person has actually experienced the development involved.

This said, I propose to present my own role motivation theories, and how they came to be, in the hope that this story will prove useful in interpreting others' contributions. My approach is in the same vein as that taken in several edited volumes that have appeared recently (Frost & Stablein, 1992; Cyr & Reich, 1996; Frost & Taylor, 1996).

Background

My education was all in psychology, in both clinical psychology and personality theory. My graduate work was done at Clark University and at Princeton University, which granted the doctorate in 1955. None of the universities I attended had a business school at the time; in fact, none even offered coursework in industrial psychology. My dissertation involved studying manpower utilization from the perspective of intellectual talent supplies—a combination of administering an intelligence test to a national sample and analyzing the data to determine how well society was using this resource.

Somehow this educational background got converted into rather brief employment stints teaching industrial psychology in the psychology departments at Georgia Tech and Brooklyn College. Next, in 1956, came an offer from Eli Ginzberg, an economist and manpower specialist of considerable international repute, to join the research staff of the Conservation of Human Resources project in the Graduate School of Business at Columbia University. This was my first brush with a business school, and although it did not last very long it taught me a great deal that was entirely new. Also at this time, a personal psychoanalysis that had been in process since my graduate student days was completed. By late 1957 my odyssey had taken me to a position as a psychologist in the corporate personnel research unit of the Atlantic Refining Company in Philadelphia.

While employed at Atlantic, I began work on an M.B.A. in industrial relations at the Wharton School of the University of Pennsylvania, thus entering a business school for the second time. Within a year, however, my status shifted from student to adjunct faculty member at Wharton. During this period, George Taylor, economist and distinguished labor arbitrator, became my mentor. He convinced me to move to a business school permanently. With his help, and that of the chief economist at Atlantic who was leaving to join the business faculty at the University of Chicago, a number of job opportunities came my way.

The upshot was that in 1960 we moved west to the University of Oregon, hired by Richard Lindholm, another economist and dean of the business school there. This third brush with a business school proved enduring. There have been moves—from Oregon to Maryland to Georgia State, and ultimately to the State University of New York at Buffalo—but with the exception of a year each on leave with the psychology department at Berkeley and the New York office of McKinsey and Company, my career has been spent in business schools ever since joining the University

of Oregon faculty. However, consulting to various business firms has been a major activity throughout, contributing both to my knowledge of business practice and to my research database.

This background discussion has been a somewhat hurried trip, touching down only on those points that are particularly relevant for the ensuing material. A more leisurely voyage is available in Miner (1993a).

Theory behind Managerial Role Motivation Training

One of my activities with the research unit at Columbia was to help prepare a book to describe the factors that caused World War II soldiers to be discharged prematurely. We had Army personnel records, Veterans Administration records, military unit histories, and follow-up questionnaires on these men. From these we developed a schema of the strategic factors that caused failure, as well as case histories to illustrate our points. The schema that finally emerged looked as follows (Ginzberg, Miner, Anderson, Ginsburg, & Herma, 1959):

Personality (physical condition, intelligence, emotional stability, motivation)

Family (separation, breakup)

Immediate Group (cohesion, leadership)

Military Organization (investment, planning and improvisation, discipline and overpermissiveness, assignment)

Conflict of Cultural Values (equity, religious and moral values)

Situational Stress (location, combat)

This work on the determinants of emotional disorders and performance failure drew on my background in clinical psychology, and it was from that perspective that we prepared several articles during my stay at Columbia (Miner & Anderson, 1958a, 1958b). However, what proved to be much more important in the long run was the insight this work gave me into the dynamics of ineffective performance and the human resource management issues involved. Here I was on completely new ground.

Role Motivation Training at Atlantic Refining

Shortly after my arrival at Atlantic, the training director asked me to teach a course for managers in the

R&D department with the objective of arousing their interest in managing. Many had been promoted into management based on their scientific accomplishments and continued to give more attention to the professional aspects of their work than to the managerial. Could I stimulate them to become better managers?

While I was at Columbia, it had occurred to me that the schema we had created might be converted to a diagnostic framework that managers could use to determine what factors were contributing to the ineffective performance of their subordinates. Once these operating factors were identified, a determination could be made as to which could be changed, and a plan for corrective action to restore effective performance could be established. Basically, this involved transferring the diagnosis and treatment model of clinical psychology (and medicine) to my newly found world of human resource management.

Faced with the challenge presented by the training director, the possibility of teaching this diagnostic approach to supervision to the R&D people began to form in my mind. The problem-solving approach involved might appeal to them as scientists. Furthermore, they would be cast in the role of manager, responsible for those assigned to them and for getting the work accomplished as well. My thought was that we could construct a role model for them, make that role model attractive, and give them the tools to perform in accordance with what the model prescribed. In the terminology of psychoanalysis, this meant helping the managers develop a particular type of ego ideal. This was my approach to dealing with the upside of the problem. On the downside was the possibility that some managers had avoided managing because it created anxiety. By extending the model of ineffective performance and its causes to them personally, it might be possible to get them involved in diagnosing and correcting their own performance failures. In particular, it seemed that attention should focus on sources of phobic reactions to the managerial situation. By providing the managers with what amounted to psychoanalytic interpretations of their unconscious motives, and how these might yield anxiety on the job, perhaps some diminution in negative affect could be achieved.

This was the very rudimentary theory that drove the creation of a course administered to 72 R&D managers at Atlantic. Evaluations conducted on this course indicated that managerial motivation was in fact increased, and thus support for the theory was obtained (Miner, 1960a). This was also the first research involving managerial role motivation theory, and we will consider how that theory entered in shortly. Note that, as initially developed, the theory underlying the training in managerial role motivation was strongly influenced by my psychoanalytic background. However, it was both more than and less than a full psychoanalytic statement.

Formulations Related to Ineffective Performance

The schema of strategic determinants of ineffective performance first developed at Columbia has gone through several iterations. The Atlantic course, with variations, has been taught many times. The course was initially written up in book form in Miner (1963), and the version of the schema presented there has held up reasonably well. Table 5.3 presents the most recent statement. Some of the questions that training of this kind elicits are discussed in Miner (1986).

To a large extent, these formulations regarding the schema have been more a product of my psychological training than of my business school experience, at least since Columbia. However, there is one aspect of this work where input from the business schools has been crucial. After auditing a course in accounting shortly after joining the faculty of the University of Oregon, I became quite interested in the concept of control. This led me into the literature on the subject and particularly to a book by William Jerome (1961). Gradually, my writing, and teaching, began to incorporate aspects of the control model into discussions of the nature of ineffective performance and methods of dealing with it. The approach that finally emerged is depicted in figure 5.2.

Managerial (Hierarchic) Role Motivation Theory

The training director at Atlantic brought home to me the importance of managerial motivation, later called motivation to manage and designated by others using terms such as the will, the desire, and the need to manage. A search of the literature of the time (1957) yielded little on the topic. Accordingly, there seemed to be no alternative but to try to develop a measure myself, validate it, and apply it to evaluate role motiva-

TABLE 5.3 Schema of strategic factors that may contribute to ineffective performance

Problems	Factors involved
Intelligence and job knowledge problems	Insufficient verbal ability Insufficient special ability Insufficient job knowledge Defect of judgment or memory
Emotional problems	Frequent disruptive emotion: anxiety, depression, anger, excitement, shame, guilt, jealousy Neurosis: with anxiety, depression, anger predominating Psychosis: with anxiety, depression, anger predominating Alcohol and drug problems
Motivational problems	Strong motives frustrated at work: pleasure in success, fear of failure, avoidance motives, dominance, desire to be popular, social motivation, need for attention Unintegrated means used to satisfy strong motives Low personal work standards Generalized low work motivation
Physical problems	Physical illness or handicap, including brain disorders Physical disorders of emotional origin Inappropriate physical characteristics Insufficient muscular or sensory ability or skill
Family-related problems	Family crises: divorce, death, severe illness Separation from the family and isolation Predominance of family considerations over job demands
Work-group problems	Negative consequences of group cohesion Ineffective management Inappropriate managerial standards or criteria
Organizational problems	Insufficient organizational action Placement error Organizational overpermissiveness Excessive spans of control Inappropriate organizational standards and criteria
Society-related problems	Application of legal sanctions Other enforcement of societal values, including the use of inappropriate value-based criteria Conflict between job demands and cultural values: equity, freedom, moral and religious values
Problems related to the work situation	Negative consequences of economic forces Negative consequences of geographic location Detrimental conditions in the work setting Excessive danger Problems inherent in the work itself

SOURCE: John B. Miner (1985), *People Problems: The Executive Answers Book* (New York: Random House), 312–314. Reprinted with permission.

tion training to see if the training raised levels of managerial motivation.

Original Organization-Specific Theory

Initially we tried to develop a measure labeled Supervisory Interest from the Kuder Preference Record, in part because we had considerable data on that instrument. The research using this home-grown measure yielded significant validities, but the correlations were low (Miner, 1960b). Ultimately, the conclusion was that we should continue our search in the hope of finding a better measure. Subsequent research indicates that this was a wise decision (see chapter 12 of Miner, 1977).

The next step was to develop a sentence-completion instrument using item stems (beginnings of sentences) and a scoring system that adhered closely to

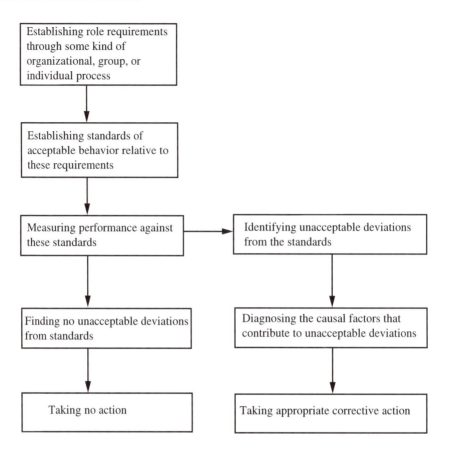

FIGURE 5.2 Steps in the control process as applied to instances of ineffective performance. Adapted from John B. Miner (1988), *Organizational Behavior: Performance and Productivity* (New York: Random House), 20.

the local definition of "the good manager" as held at the Atlantic Refining Company, particularly at corporate headquarters. My source of information was partly participant observation and partly a very close reading of a large number of management appraisal documents. The theory that resulted was in the grounded theory tradition, although this was not apparent to me at the time.

The theory development process involved writing possible items for the test, paring these down through a "quick and dirty" item analysis, and then abstracting the implicit theory behind this measure after the fact. Thus, theory construction was a highly inductive process. Clearly, the items were all intended to relate to managerial motivation at Atlantic from the beginning, but the components of that motivation emerged from a conceptual grouping of these items after we learned how people responded to them. When these components had been teased out of the data, it also became evident that, in formulating the items in the first place, I had been influenced to some degree by certain sources in the psychological literature — Pelz (1952), Kahn and Katz (1953), and Fleishman, Harris, and Burtt (1955), among others.

Furthermore, the idea behind the components was that managers were evaluated relative to informal role prescriptions inherent in the Atlantic situation, prescriptions that managers either met (behaved in accordance with) and thus were highly valued (judged effective) or did not meet and thus were judged ineffective. This was a purely psychological approach to role behavior predicated on individual differences. The more sociological view — that roles mandate individual behavior — did not come to my attention until several years later (Faris, 1962). (For a discussion of the current status of role theory in organizational behavior see Ashforth, 2001.)

Components of Managerial Motivation

The components of managerial motivation that were identified in the items were the following:

Favorable attitudes to superiors

Desire to compete

Desire to exercise power

Desire to perform in the masculine role, and thus to assert oneself

Desire to be distinct and different

Desire to perform routine duties responsibly

To the extent scores on the items in each grouping were consistently positive, the person was assumed to possess the motive (or motive constellation) involved. However, many people gave negative responses, often a number of them. This was not merely indicative of a lack of the particular type of motivation; it reflected a desire not to do these things, to avoid such behavior. My theory was that, following psychoanalytic theory, this occurred because the type of motivation aroused by the role requirement had become associated with anxiety and guilt. Consequently, the motives were driven to the level of the unconscious in order to avoid recognizing them. Yet this attempt may be only partially successful, and the negative emotion persists:

Thus, favorable attitudes to superiors can mean unnatural behavior, perhaps involving sexual activity with a parental figure.

Competitiveness can mean out-of-control aggression and violence, even murder.

Power motivation can mean acting superior, authoritarianism, and dictatorial behavior.

Masculinity can mean questioning one's sexual identity for women, and macho sexual arousal for men.

Being distinct and different can mean showing off, phoniness, and even exhibitionism.

Performing routine duties can carry implications of dishonesty, vindictiveness, and jealousy.

The underlying dynamics involved here are described in more detail in Miner (1975). The point is that informal role requirements involved in managerial work of the kind performed at Atlantic can elicit phobic reactions to the managerial situation. My theorizing in this respect derived primarily from counseling managers whose performance had proven unsatisfactory.

When this theory, as operationalized in what came to be called the Miner Sentence Completion Scale (Form H), was put to test at Atlantic, it proved to have considerable validity (Miner, 1965). Correlations with success criteria as high as the low .40s were obtained, and a majority of the components of managerial motivation were supported. Also, when the test was used in a pretest-posttest design with experimental and control groups to evaluate managerial role motivation training, it proved capable of identifying the hypothesized changes.

Theory Applied to Bureaucracy

For some time, my impression was that the theory we had developed, and supported, was simply applicable to Atlantic, or perhaps the oil industry. After all, it had been created to model the Atlantic situation and all of the testing had been done there, too. Then, after moving to a business school, I began to be exposed to the sociological literature on organizations, not just the psychological, and ultimately to read Weber and those who followed him. It quickly became apparent to me that this was what I had been talking about all along. Atlantic was not just Atlantic; it was a bureaucracy. This seems simple now, but it was not for me then. It was a revelation.

The result was a long series of studies to test out the theories in new contexts. The very first of these are described in Miner (1965); many more are compiled in Miner (1977). Initially most of the research was my own, but gradually it spread to joint authorships, studies by doctoral students, and completely independent investigations. The theory was expanded to state that managerial motivation would explain and predict the success of managers in bureaucratic organizations with multiple levels of hierarchy, but it would not work with nonmanagers, and it would not work in structures other than the bureaucratic.

Gradually it came to my attention that people in the business world and in the business schools were using the managerial motivation construct as an explanatory tool in their writings. Some of these views are included in Miner (1975): the writings of Marvin Bower (from McKinsey and Company), Sterling Livingston (from the Harvard Business School), Henry Mintzberg (from the business school at McGill University), and Thomas Patten (from the labor school at Michigan State). Again, as with the finding of bureaucracy, the result of these writings was to encourage my faith in the widespread applicability of the theories from Atlantic. Without my move into a business school environment, it seems very unlikely that the program of research that emerged would ever have existed.

Figure 5.3 sets forth the hierarchic role motivation theory as formulated during the early 1970s, although this particular picture was not created until much later.

Professional, Task, and Group Role Motivation Theories

Sometime in the mid-1970s the limitations of the hierarchic theory began to bother me. It was restricted to the domain of bureaucratic organizations, and there were other organizational forms to which it did not apply. My attempts to wrestle with this problem settled first on a concept of control hypothesized to operate broadly through various organizational systems (see chapter 28 of Miner, 1977). Later the idea of inducement systems was substituted (Miner, 1980a), and specific role prescriptions and their motivational bases were identified. Finally, research hypotheses were stated:

Hypothesis 1. In hierarchic systems, managerial motivation should be at a high level in top manage-

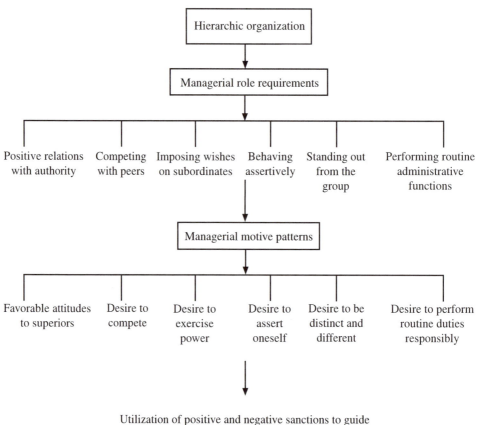

FIGURE 5.3 Outline of managerial (hierarchic) role motivation theory. Adapted from John B. Miner (1993), *Role Motivation Theories* (London: Routledge), 11.

ment and it should be positively correlated with other managerial success indexes; managerial motivation should not differentiate in these ways within other types of systems.

Hypothesis 2. In professional systems, professional motivation should be at a high level among senior professionals, and it should be positively correlated with other professional success indexes; professional motivation should not differentiate in these ways within other types of systems.

Hypothesis 3. In group systems, group motivation should be at a high level among emergent leaders, and it should be positively correlated with other group-determined success indexes; group motivation should not differentiate in these ways within other types of systems.

Hypothesis 4. In task systems, task (achievement) motivation should be at a high level among task performers (entrepreneurs, for example), and it should be positively correlated with task success indexes; task motivation should not differentiate in these ways within other types of systems. (Miner, 1982, p. 298)

Professional Theory

The professional system did not arise out of test items as the hierarchic theory did. Specific role prescriptions were developed, and motivational patterns that fit them were then stated. The source of these formulations was in part my own professional experience as a psychologist and university professor. However, substantial input came for the existing literature, primarily of a sociological nature (Etzioni, 1964; Vollmer & Mills, 1966; Sorensen & Sorensen, 1974; Satow, 1975; and others). Again, exposure to this literature came only from being in a professional school. Had my experience been limited to the disciplinary confines of psychology, the existence of this literature almost certainly would have remained forever hidden.

The components of professional motivation thus identified were as follows:

Desire to learn and acquire knowledge

Desire to exhibit independence

Desire to acquire status

Desire to help others

Value-based identification with the profession

The way in which these patterns fit into the theory is indicated in figure 5.4. A measure of the motives involved was constructed in much the same manner as for the hierarchic theory, except that the five motive patterns were known at the outset, and this fact guided the selection of items. The resulting instrument, the Miner Sentence Completion Scale (Form P), was used in a subsequent validation study among members of the Academy of Management. Correlations with professional success criteria were consistently high; in contrast, Form H correlations with these same criteria were rarely significant. The theory appeared to have considerable support in this sample, which consisted almost entirely of business school professors (Miner, 1980b). It has been supported in other studies as well.

Task Theory

Task theory is basically an adaptation of David McCelland's (1961) work on achievement motivation, work that I have been following since my graduate student days. Thus the theory itself is essentially psychological. However, the research we have done in the entrepreneurship area to test the theory has been strongly influenced by Norman Smith, a marketing professor at the University of Oregon. We have been collaborating together on research since the latter 1960s, and Smith's intimate knowledge of entrepreneurship has been a major factor in whatever success our studies have achieved; he has taught me a great deal. (This is another plus for business schools.)

Initially we set out to test the hypothesis that entrepreneurs found companies to have something to manage, and thus managerial motivation should be the major source of entrepreneurship accomplishment. This hypothesis had only limited success at best (Smith & Miner, 1983). From there, we turned to task theory using McClelland (1961) as a guide and influenced by the marked success achievement motivation has shown over the years as a predictor of entrepreneurial accomplishment. Bradley Johnson (1990) reports on 23 studies conducted since 1960, 20 of which demonstrate some relation to entrepreneurial activity.

The components of our theory were as follows:

Desire to achieve through one's own efforts

Desire to avoid risk

Desire for feedback on performance

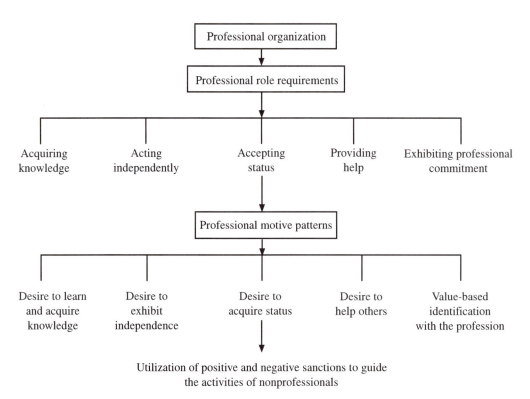

FIGURE 5.4 Outline of professional role motivation theory. Adapted from John B. Miner (1993), *Role Motivation Theories* (London: Routledge), 15.

Desire to introduce innovative solutions

Desire to plan and establish goals

Of these, only the second (risk) departs to some degree from McClelland (1961). The theory as a whole is outlined in figure 5.5. A measure was constructed using the sentence completion format—the Miner Sentence Completion Scales (Form T). In turn, this measure was employed in a major study of high-tech entrepreneurs. Support was obtained for the theory as a whole, and for all five of its components (Miner, Smith, & Bracker, 1989). Subsequent work has continued to indicate the validity of the theory in the entrepreneurial domain.

A related program of theory and research further serves to emphasize the extent to which being in a business school setting has facilitated my work. In this instance, data were derived from an entrepreneurship development program and from an M.B.A. course in entrepreneurship—both of which are unique to the business school context. The theory sets forth a typology of entrepreneurs that consists of personal achievers, real managers, expert idea generators, and empathic super salespeople (Miner, 1997b). Although the Miner Sentence Completion Scales are used in this research, the overall theory itself is not a role motivation theory, and thus extended treatment is not appropriate here.

Group Theory

Group role motivation theory exists as a theory, but the motives involved have not been operationalized, and the theory tested, as of this writing. The theory is almost completely a consequence of the literature on autonomous work groups, sensitivity training, and organization development. My own experience with organizational systems of this type is limited, in contrast to hierarchic, professional, and entrepreneurial organizations where my experience has been substantial. Thus, input from personal exposure is less of a factor here. The literature that exerted the most influence is in the tradition of Kurt Lewin—from MIT, the University of Michigan, and the Tavistock organization in England. It is basically a behavioral humanist literature, and there have been a great many contributors.

The components of the theory derived from this literature are as follows:

Desire to interact socially and affiliate with others

Desire for continuing belongingness in a group

Favorable attitudes toward peers

Desire to have cooperative/collaborative relationships

Desire to participate in democratic processes

The way in which these components fit into the group organizational form is shown in figure 5.6.

Organizational Types

The previous discussion, and the research described, have focused at the level of individual motivation and primarily use the various Miner Sentence Completion Scales. But the theories are meso theories that deal as much with organizational forms, and the informal role requirements they posit, as with intrinsic motive patterns. In the early years we made certain assumptions about the type of organizations we were dealing with and thus the types of motive patterns that should and should not prove appropriate. We appear to have been correct in these assumptions most of the time.

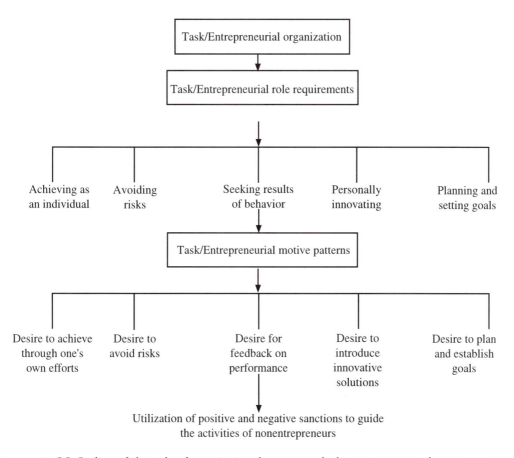

FIGURE 5.5 Outline of the task role motivation theory as applied to entrepreneurial organization. Adapted from John B. Miner (1993), *Role Motivation Theories* (London: Routledge), 18.

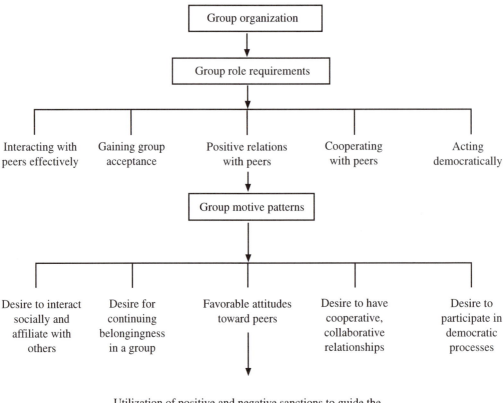

FIGURE 5.6 Outline of the group role motivation theory. Adapted from John B. Miner (1993), *Role Motivation Theories* (London: Routledge), 22.

Otherwise the predictor-criterion relationships found would not have been in evidence.

If the theories predict particular types of person-organization fit (Kristof, 1996) and if role behavior and role requirements are to mesh, there is a clear need for a measure of the four organization types. This became evident in the late 1970s as the three organizational forms beyond the hierarchic were developed. As a result, John Oliver (1982) created an instrument, the Oliver Organization Description Questionnaire, to differentiate the four organizational forms. In this instance the measurement expertise needed was psychological in nature, and, in fact, we called on a psychometrician in the psychology department to help us in this regard. But writing the items also required a broad knowledge of organizational types and their characteristics. This is not an instrument

that would have been generated entirely within a psychological context.

We have used Oliver's questionnaire extensively in research conducted in recent years (see Wilderom & Miner, 1991; Miner, Crane, & Vandenberg, 1994). It has proven very helpful in identifying organization-wide and unit structures, and thus the theoretical domain involved.

Evaluation and Impact

The role motivation theories are very much a creature of social science in the business schools and the development of organizational behavior. Theory, research, and the milieu of the time are all intricately intertwined. Certainly, for all its conflict and inherent uncertainty, the business school environment served as a catalyst in this instance for whatever creative contribution was achieved. There is every reason to believe that the same stimulus to intellectual output operated in the case of many other theories as well.

The various role motivation theories have received much favorable attention. This is particularly true of the hierarchic theory (see, for instance, the literature reviews of Cornelius, 1983; Adler & Weiss, 1988; and Latham, 1988, as well as the meta-analyses of Nathan & Alexander, 1985; and Carson & Gilliard, 1993). The other three theories are newer, and there has been less time to evaluate them. The group theory is really nothing more than speculation at the moment, because of the lack of measures and research tests, although some research has appeared recently that seems to bear on the theory's hypotheses in a favorable manner (Taggar, Hackett, & Saha, 1999; Shaw, Duffy, & Stark, 2000). The task theory is so closely allied to achievement motivation theory that it can hardly be said to exist as a separate entity. The professional theory appears to be quite powerful, but the research to date is still limited.

What criticism there has been, and it is certainly not negligible, has been directed at the hierarchic formulations. However, the culprit has been much more the measure used than the theory itself. In addition, there have been concerns regarding the decline in managerial motivation scores that occurred during the 1960s and early 1970s. This phenomenon was not predicted by the theory itself but, rather, was a happenstance finding that proved so intriguing that we devoted a great deal of research attention to it (Miner, 1974).

In general, I will not deal in any detail with these criticisms here because that has already been done in Miner (1993b) and because the focus of the criticisms is on measurement, not theory. To take up these criticisms would add little to our story except to demonstrate what we already know—that the history of organizational behavior has been rife with conflict and controversy.

There is one consideration that bears mention, however. The tendency has been to view managerial motivation, or motivation to manage, as ranging along a continuum from autocracy and authoritarianism on one end to participation and democracy at the other. This has tended to put the theory squarely in the middle of the behavioral humanism debate; valuewise it has been viewed by some as a "bad" theory, espousing a politically incorrect position. People have

even contacted me to help them use the Miner Sentence Completion Scale (Form H) to select managers who obtain very low scores, in the mistaken belief that these managers would be more participative.

The fact of the matter is that high motivation-to-manage people are not necessarily authoritarian, and those with low scores are not particularly democratic. The dimension involved runs from a desire to do the things good bureaucratic managers do to a desire not to do these things—and thus to the basically laissez-faire style that Lewin and his coworkers found produced low achievement. It has nothing to do with the debate about the superiority of participative management. Yet, it is not surprising, given the history of the times (the schools and all the controversy around them), that hierarchic role motivation theory became caught up in this environment.

Finally, note should be made of the most recent tally of the results of research on role motivation theories (see Miner, 1993b). Overall there are 57 studies to draw on and these describe 92 criterion relationships. In 92 percent of the latter, the results are significant and consistent with theoretical predictions. When the analysis is conducted outside the appropriate domain (with 28 studies and 59 criterion relationships), 100 percent of the results prove to be nonsignificant, or (in six cases) significant in a negative direction. The lowest number of criterion relationships involved in this tally for any of the three theories is 13 (for the professional theory). To these results should be added recent findings from China on female managers that consistently support the hierarchic theory (Chen, Yu, & Miner, 1997).

Very recently we have undertaken a comprehensive test of the hierarchic, professional, and task role motivation theories using a sample of members of my class at Princeton. These are people who now have had long, and in certain cases quite distinguished, careers in the three areas—as managers, as professionals, and as entrepreneurs. The theoretical hypotheses predict that in each instance those with a career in a given organizational domain should score high on the motives that fit that domain and, just as importantly, they should score relatively low on the motives that fit the other two domains. The results strongly support these differential hypotheses—all three of them. Role motivation theory, which in its totality is very much a product of organizational behavior's history, performs well in this first overall test of three of its four components. This sample has also been combined with reanalyses of older data to test the hypothesis that leadership roles take different forms in different organizational contexts and require different types of people to perform in these roles effectively—people whose motives are strongly congruent with the particular organizational type involved. Across some six separate analyses, this hypothesis is confirmed with a median correlation of .72 (Miner, 2002).

CONCLUSIONS

There is repeated evidence that organizational behavior was born in a context of high uncertainty and instability. Predicting the future was difficult, if not impossible. The long period of unfreezing created a conglomeration of disciplines and ideas, many of which had never been in close proximity to one another before. For many people, exposure to this environment was very stressful; the number who escaped to alternative careers was not insignificant.

Yet others found the opportunities, the swirl of ideas, and the rewards attractive. Not only that, but a substantial creative outpouring occurred from these people. In presenting my own experience, I hope to have contributed a better understanding of what happened during this period as organizational behavior came into being.

References

Adams, Sheila A., & Davis, Keith (1986). *Academy of Management Journal*: The First Decade. In Daniel A. Wren & John A. Pearce (Eds.), *Papers Dedicated to the Development of Modern Management* (pp. 89–94). Academy of Management.

Adler, Seymour, & Weiss, Howard M. (1988). Recent Developments in the Study of Personality and Organizational Behavior. *International Review of Industrial and Organizational Psychology*, 3, 307–330.

Anderson, John R. (2001). Herbert A. Simon (1916–2001). *American Psychologist*, 56, 516–518.

Ashforth, Blake E. (2001). *Role Transitions in Organizational Life: An Identity-Based Perspective.* Mahwah, NJ: Erlbaum.

Bennis, Warren G. (1966). *Changing Organizations: Essays on the Development and Evolution of Human Organization.* New York: McGraw-Hill.

Blood, Milton R. (1994). The Role of Organizational Behavior in the Business School Curriculum. In J. Greenberg (Ed.), *Organizational Behavior: The State of the Science* (pp. 207–220). Hillsdale, NJ: Erlbaum.

Boring, Edwin G. (1950). *A History of Experimental Psychology.* New York: Appleton-Century-Crofts.

Carson, Kenneth P., & Gilliard, Debora J. (1993). Construct Validity of the Miner Sentence Completion Scale. *Journal of Occupational and Organizational Psychology*, 66, 171–175.

Chen, Chao C.; Yu, K. C.; & Miner, John B. (1997). Motivation to Manage: A Study of Women in Chinese State-Owned Enterprises. *Journal of Applied Behavioral Science*, 160–173.

Cornelius, Edwin T. (1983). The Use of Projective Techniques in Personnel Selection. *Research in Personnel and Human Resources Management*, 1, 127–168.

Cummings, Larry L. (1978). Toward Organizational Behavior. *Academy of Management Review*, 3, 90–98.

Cyr, Dianne, & Reich, Blaize H. (1996). *Scaling the Ivory Tower: Stories from Women in Business School Faculties.* Westport, CT: Praeger.

Dunnette, Marvin D., & Bass, Bernard M. (1963). Behavioral Scientists and Personnel Management. *Industrial Relations*, 2, 115–130.

Etzioni, Amitai (1964). *Modern Organizations.* Englewood Cliffs, NJ: Prentice Hall.

Faris, Robert E. L. (1962). Interaction Levels and Intergroup Relations. In Muzafer Sherif (Ed.), *Intergroup Relations and Leadership* (pp. 24–45). New York: Wiley.

Fleishman, Edwin A.; Harris, Edwin F.; & Burtt, Harold E. (1955). *Leadership and Supervision in Industry.* Columbus: Bureau of Educational Research, Ohio State University.

Frost, Peter J., & Stablein, Ralph E. (1992). *Doing Exemplary Research.* Newbury Park, CA: Sage.

Frost, Peter J., & Taylor, M. Susan (1996). *Rhythms of Academic Life: Personal Accounts of Careers in Academia.* Thousand Oaks, CA: Sage.

Ginzberg, Eli; Miner, John B.; Anderson, James K.; Ginsburg, Sol W.; & Herma, John L. (1959). *Breakdown and Recovery.* New York: Columbia University Press.

Gordon, Paul J. (1963). Transcend the Current Debate on Administrative Theory. *Academy of Management Journal*, 6, 290–302.

Gordon, Paul J. (1997). Recollections of a Publishing Enthusiast. *Academy of Management Journal*, 40, 1414–1417.

Gordon, Robert A., & Howell, James E. (1959). *Higher Education for Business.* New York: Columbia University Press.

Heidbreder, Edna (1933). *Seven Psychologies.* New York: Appleton-Century-Crofts.

Hofstede, Geert, & Kassem, M. Sami (1976). *European Contributions to Organization Theory*. Amsterdam: Van Gorcum.

Jerome, William T. (1961). *Executive Control: The Catalyst*. New York: Wiley.

Johnson, Bradley R. (1990). Toward a Multidimensional Model of Entrepreneurship: The Case of Achievement Motivation and the Entrepreneur. *Entrepreneurship Theory and Practice*, 14(3), 39–54.

Kahn, Robert L., & Katz, Daniel (1953). Leadership Practices in Relation to Productivity and Morale. In Dorwin Cartwright & Alvin Zander (Eds.), *Group Dynamics: Research and Theory* (pp. 554–570). Evanston, IL: Row, Peterson.

Kerpelman, Larry C. (1972). *Activists and Nonactivists: A Psychological Study of American College Students*. New York: Behavioral Publications.

Koontz, Harold (1961). The Management Theory Jungle. *Journal of the Academy of Management*, 4, 174–188.

Koontz, Harold (1962). Making Sense of Management Theory. *Harvard Business Review*, 40(4), 24–48.

Koontz, Harold (1980). The Management Theory Jungle Revisited. *Academy of Management Review*, 5, 175–187.

Kristof, Amy L. (1996). Person-Organization Fit: An Integrative Review of its Conceptualizations, Measurement, and Implications. *Personnel Psychology*, 49, 1–49.

Krupp, Sherman (1961). *Patterns in Organization Analysis: A Critical Examination*. Philadelphia: Chilton.

Latham, Gary P. (1988). Human Resource Training and Development. *Annual Review of Psychology*, 39, 545–582.

Lawrence, Paul R. (1987). Historical Development of Organizational Behavior. In Jay W. Lorsch (Ed.), *Handbook of Organizational Behavior* (pp. 1–9). Englewood Cliffs, NJ: Prentice Hall.

Leavitt, Harold J., & Whisler, Thomas L. (1958). Management in the 1980s. *Harvard Business Review*, 36(6), 41–48.

Lewin, Kurt (1947). Frontiers in Group Dynamics: Concept, Method and Reality in Social Science; Social Equilibria and Social Change. *Human Relations*, 1, 5–41.

Lewin, Kurt (1958). Group Decision and Social Change. In Eleanor E. Maccoby, Theodore M. Newcomb, & Eugene L. Hartley (Eds.), *Readings in Social Psychology* (pp. 197–211). New York: Henry Holt.

Lipset, Seymour M., & Schaflander, Gerald M. (1971). *Passion and Politics: Student Activism in America*. Boston: Little, Brown.

Luthans, Fred (1973). The Contingency Theory of Management: A Path Out of the Jungle. *Business Horizons*, 16(3), 67–72.

McClelland, David C. (1961). *The Achieving Society*. Princeton, NJ: VanNostrand.

McKinley, William; Mone, Mark A.; & Moon, Gyewan (1999). Determinants and Development of Schools in Organization Theory. *Academy of Management Review*, 24, 634–648.

Miner, John B. (1960a). The Effect of a Course in Psychology on the Attitudes of Research and Development Supervisors. *Journal of Applied Psychology*, 44, 224–232.

Miner, John B. (1960b). The Kuder Preference Record in Management Appraisal. *Personnel Psychology*, 13, 187–196.

Miner, John B. (1963). *The Management of Ineffective Performance*. New York: McGraw-Hill.

Miner, John B. (1965). *Studies in Management Education*. New York: Springer.

Miner, John B. (1971). *Management Theory*. New York: Macmillan.

Miner, John B. (1974). *The Human Constraint: The Coming Shortage of Managerial Talent*. Washington, DC: BNA Books.

Miner, John B. (1975). *The Challenge of Managing*. Philadelphia: W. B. Saunders.

Miner, John B. (1977). *Motivation to Manage: A Ten Year Update on the "Studies in Management Education" Research*. Eugene, OR: Organizational Measurement Systems Press.

Miner, John B. (1980a). Limited Domain Theories of Organizational Energy. In Craig C. Pinder & Larry F. Moore (Eds.), *Middle Range Theory and the Study of Organizations* (pp. 273–286). Boston: Martinus Nijhoff.

Miner, John B. (1980b). The Role of Managerial and Professional Motivation in the Career Success of Management Professors. *Academy of Management Journal*, 23, 487–508.

Miner, John B. (1982). The Uncertain Future of the Leadership Concept: Revisions and Clarifications. *Journal of Applied Behavioral Science*, 18, 293–307.

Miner, John B. (1985). *People Problems: The Executive Answer Book*. New York: Random House.

Miner, John B. (1986). Managerial Role Motivation Training. *Journal of Managerial Psychology*, 1(1), 25–30.

Miner, John B. (1993a). Pursuing Diversity in an Increasingly Specialized Organizational Science. In Arthur G. Bedeian (Ed.), *Management Laureates: A Collection of Autobiographical Essays* (Vol. 2, pp. 283–319). Greenwich, CT: JAI Press .

Miner, John B. (1993b). *Role Motivation Theories*. London: Routledge.

Miner, John B. (1997a). Participating in Profound Change. *Academy of Management Journal*, 40, 1420–1428.

Miner, John B. (1997b). *A Psychological Typology of Successful Entrepreneurs*. Westport, CT: Quorum.

Miner, John B. (2002). The Role Motivation Theories of Organizational Leadership. In Francis J. Yammarino & Bruce J. Avolio (Eds.), *Transformational and Charismatic Leadership: The Road Ahead*. New York: Elsevier.

Miner, John B., & Anderson, James K. (1958a). Intelligence and Emotional Disturbance: Evidence from Army and Veterans Administration Records. *Journal of Abnormal and Social Psychology*, 56, 75–81.

Miner, John B., & Anderson, James K. (1958b). The Postwar Occupational Adjustment of Emotionally Disturbed Soldiers. *Journal of Applied Psychology*, 42, 317–322.

Miner, John B.; Crane, Donald P.; & Vandenberg, Robert J. (1994). Congruence and Fit in Professional Role Motivation Theory. *Organization Science*, 5, 86–97.

Miner, John B.; Smith, Norman R.; and Bracker, Jeffrey S. (1989). Role of Entrepreneurial Task Motivation in the Growth of Technologically Innovative Firms. *Journal of Applied Psychology*, 74, 554–560.

Mowday, Richard T. (1997). Celebrating 40 Years of the *Academy of Management Journal*. *Academy of Management Journal*, 40, 1400–1413.

Myers, Charles A. (1967). *The Impact of Computers on Management*. Cambridge, MA: MIT Press.

Nathan, Barry R., & Alexander, Ralph A. (1985). An Application of Meta-Anaysis to Theory Building and Construct Validation. *Academy of Management Proceedings*, 45, 224–228.

Nord, Walter R. (1972). *Concepts and Controversy in Organizational Behavior*. Pacific Palisades, CA: Goodyear.

Nord, Walter R. (1996). Research/Teaching Boundaries. In Peter J. Frost & M. Susan Taylor (Eds.), *Rhythms of Academic Life: Personal Accounts of Careers in Academia* (pp. 83–89) . Thousand Oaks, CA: Sage.

Oliver, John E. (1982). An Instrument for Classifying Organizations. *Academy of Management Journal*, 25, 855–866.

Patten, Thomas H. (1964). Criticism and Comment: Behavioral Scientists and Personnel Management. *Industrial Relations*, 3, 109–114.

Pelz, Donald C. (1952). Influence: A Key to Effective Leadership in the First-Line Supervisor. *Personnel*, 29, 209–217.

Perrow, Charles (1973). The Short and Glorious History of Organizational Theory. *Organizational Dynamics*, 2(1), 2–15.

Peterson, Richard E. (1968). *The Scope of Organized Student Protests in 1967–1968*. Princeton, NJ: Educational Testing Service.

Pugh, Derek S. (1966). Modern Organization Theory: A Psychological and Sociological Study. *Psychological Bulletin*, 66, 235–251.

Reif, William E. (1968). *Computer Technology and Management Organization*. Iowa City: College of Business Administration, University of Iowa.

Roberts, Karlene H.; Hulin, Charles L.; & Rousseau, Denise M. (1978). *Developing an Interdisciplinary Science of Organizations*. San Francisco: Jossey-Bass.

Rush, Harold M. F. (1969). *Behavioral Science: Concepts and Management Application*. New York: National Industrial Conference Board.

Satow, Roberta L. (1975). Value Rational Authority and Professional Organizations: Weber's Missing Type. *Administrative Science Quarterly*, 20, 526–531.

Schein, Edgar H. (1993). The Academic As Artist: Personal and Professional Roots. In Arthur G. Bedeian (Ed.), *Management Laureates: A Collection of Autobiographical Essays* (Vol. 3, pp. 31–62). Greenwich, CT: JAI Press.

Scott, William G. (1961). Organization Theory: An Overview and an Appraisal. *Journal of the Academy of Management*, 4, 7–26.

Scott, William G. (1968). Technology and Organization Government: A Speculative Inquiry into the Functionality of Management Creeds. *Academy of Management Journal*, 11, 301–313.

Shaw, Jason D.; Duffy, Michelle K.; & Stark, Eric M. (2000). Interdependence and Preference for Group Work: Main and Congruence Effects on the Satisfaction and Performance of Group Members. *Journal of Management*, 26, 259–279.

Simon, Herbert A. (1991). *Models of My Life*. New York: Basic Books.

Skinner, B. F. (1948). *Walden Two*. New York: Macmillan.

Smith, Norman R., & Miner, John B. (1983). Type of Entrepreneur, Type of Firm, and Managerial Motivation: Implications for Organizational Life Cycle Theory. *Strategic Management Journal*, 4, 325–340.

Sorensen, James E., & Sorensen, Thomas L. (1974). The Conflict of Professionals in Bureaucratic Organizations. *Administrative Science Quarterly*, 19, 98–105.

Taggar, Simon; Hackett, Rick; & Saha, Sudhir (1999). Leadership Emergence in Autonomous Work Teams: Antecedents and Outcomes. *Personnel Psychology*, 52, 899–926.

Vollmer, Howard M., & Mills, Donald L. (1966). *Professionalization*. Englewood Cliffs, NJ: Prentice Hall.

Vroom, Victor H. (1993). Improvising and Muddling Through. In Arthur G. Bedeian (Ed.), *Management Laureates: A Collection of Autobiographical Essays* (Vol. 3, pp. 257–284). Greenwich, Ct: JAI Press.

Wadia, Maneck S. (1968). *Management and the Behavioral Sciences*. Boston: Allyn & Bacon.

Whisler, Thomas L. (1970). *The Impact of Computers on Organizations*. New York: Praeger.

Wilderom, Celeste P. M., & Miner, John B. (1991). Defining Voluntary Groups and Agencies within Organization Science. *Organization Science*, 2, 366–378.

Woodworth, Robert S., & Sheehan, Mary R. (1964). *Contemporary Schools of Psychology*. New York: Ronald.

Woolf, Donald A. (1965). The Management Theory Jungle Revisited. *Advanced Management Journal*, 30(4), 6–15.

Wrege, Charles D. (1986). The Inception, Early Struggles, and Growth of the Academy of Management. In Daniel A. Wren & John A. Pearce (Eds.), *Papers Dedicated to the Development of Modern Management* (pp. 78–88). Briarcliff Manor, NY: Academy of Management.

Part II

First-Generation Theories: Motivation

Chapter 6

Theories of Motivation Rooted in Personality Theory

The organizational behavior theories to be considered in this chapter derive on the psychological side from the writings on psychoanalysis by Sigmund Freud and those on personology by Henry Murray. Neither Freud nor Murray made any direct contributions to organizational behavior or management, and for that reason they were not discussed previously. However, both are in the line of intellectual descent of the major theorists to be considered here—Abraham Maslow, David McClelland, and Harry Levinson.

Freud developed the theory and technique of psychoanalysis over a lengthy period that started in the decade before the turn of the century and extended until his death in 1939 (Jones, 1953, 1955, 1957). His theories of the unconscious and of the psychopathology of everyday life (Freud, 1938) have probably influenced organizational behavior the most. An example of how these ideas have found their way into the field is contained in the discussion of hierarchic role motivation theory in the previous chapter.

Murray, like Freud, was educated as a physician and came to personality theory after an early career devoted to medicine (Triplet, 1992). His life spanned the years from 1893 to 1988, but his book describing research conducted at the Harvard Psychological

Clinic (Murray, 1938) has had the greatest influence on organizational behavior. In this volume, Murray presents his theory of psychological needs, which he classifies or categorizes in various ways. Among the 27 needs, those for achievement, affiliation, autonomy, dominance, harm avoidance, and understanding are particularly relevant for organizational behavior. These needs are used in analyzing stories given to the pictures of his Thematic Apperception Test.

NEED HIERARCHY THEORY

The major figure associated with need hierarchy theory is the psychologist Abraham Maslow. A derivative theory, which we will also consider, is the existence, relatedness, and growth formulation of Clayton Alderfer, a psychologist as well.

Background

Maslow was born in 1908 and grew up in New York City. His psychology training was obtained at the University of Wisconsin, where he worked in the field of comparative psychology and was particularly involved in research on primate behavior. After a postdoctoral research position at Columbia University, he moved across town to Brooklyn College, where he spent 14 years teaching and doing research. His early publications were in comparative psychology and came increasingly to deal with dominance behavior in primates. During the latter 1930s, he transferred this interest in dominance to the human level and extended it to human sexuality. Before long, he had shifted to personality theory almost entirely, using his research to legitimize his new role. He became interested in psychoanalysis during this period and established a clinical practice (Maslow, 1987).

In 1951 Maslow moved to the Boston area to chair the psychology department at the newly established Brandeis University. He remained there until shortly before his death at the age of 62 in 1970. Over time, he became increasingly involved in humanistic causes, helping to found the Association for Humanistic Psychology and exerting a major influence on the development of the human potential movement. He served as president of the American Psychological Association in 1967.

Need hierarchy theory itself spans over 25 years of Maslow's life. Thus, the theory as set forth here is distinctly emergent. It was originally presented in the psychological literature as a general theory of motivation with little thought of specific applications to management and organizations. In fact, much of Maslow's writing on motivation took him into areas far removed from organizational behavior. The implications of the theory for organizations were first grasped by others, and it was not until the later years of his life that Maslow himself became interested in this type of theoretical application (see Hoffman, 1999). Nevertheless, the focus here is exclusively on the theory as it applies to organizational matters.

Maslow did not move into a business school at any point in his career. He was 50 years old by the time organizational behavior began to emerge as a discipline, and his first exposure to the world of business in any professional sense occurred only eight years before he died. Yet his views have been adopted by organizational behavior, as have his humanistic values by a major segment of the field. Much of this occurred during the schools phase (see chapter 5).

Statement of the Theory

Maslow's first brief statement of need hierarchy theory occurred in a footnote appended to an article published in 1943 (Maslow, 1943a). Later that same year a more comprehensive presentation appeared (Maslow, 1943b).

Basic Needs

The key variables of the theory are certain motives or needs that are posited as existing within an individual and that combine with biological, cultural, and situational factors to determine behavior. The motive state of a worker is not expected to equate with his or her performance, but it should be a major determinant of performance.

The needs of the theory are viewed as biological or instinctive in nature in that they characterize human beings in general and have a genetic base (Maslow, 1969). They often influence behavior unconsciously; the individual is usually totally unaware of the motivational origins of his behavior. In Maslow's view, the number of needs that human beings are said to possess is largely a function of the level of abstraction used in describing them. Maslow prefers to use a relatively high level of abstraction and, in reality, presents a set of categories of human needs (Maslow, 1954, 1970,

1987), thus following the approach taken by Murray (1938). Maslow's categories are physiological, safety, love, esteem, self-actualization, cognitive, and aesthetic.

In the *physiological* category Maslow places the chemical needs of the body— sexual desire, hunger, sleepiness, activity needs, desired sensory satisfactions, and the like. Many but not all of these needs have a localized somatic base; such a base exists for hunger, thirst, and sex, but not for sleepiness. When these physiological needs are not satisfied, the individual becomes totally preoccupied with the object involved. Thus, a very hungry person thinks of practically nothing except food.

The need to be free from danger— the *safety* category— can have the same pervasive quality as the physiological needs. People are motivated to avoid wild animals, extremes of temperature, assault, disease, and the like— things that might represent a threat to their safety. However, in adults in our society the expression of this type of motivation tends to be inhibited so that people try to show that they are not afraid for their safety; thus, the existence of such needs may not be evident on the surface. As a clinician Maslow devotes particular attention to the sense of insecurity and the consequent anxiety experienced by many emotionally ill individuals. He likens their need states to those of young children who have strong needs for protection against a threatening world.

Maslow uses the category *love* in a very comprehensive sense to include affiliation and general belongingness. He has in mind the need for friends, spouses, children, parents, group membership, and the like. The love needs involve both giving and receiving. They should be clearly distinguished from sexual desire, which may be studied as a purely physiological need.

The *esteem* category needs fall into two broad groupings. In the first—a type that is essentially internal in orientation—there are desires for such feelings as strength, achievement, adequacy, confidence, independence, and freedom. In the second, esteem may derive from external sources, such as reputation, prestige, recognition, attention, importance, and appreciation. In either case, satisfaction of these needs results in self-confidence and a sense of adequacy; thwarting them produces feelings of inferiority and helplessness.

The *self-actualization* category is both the most significant and the least clearly understood of Maslow's need groupings. It refers to the desire to realize or actualize one's full potential; in Maslow's words, "to become more and more what one is, to become everything that one is capable of becoming" (1943b, p. 382). Since Maslow recognizes sizable individual differences, this means that self-actualizing in one person can be quite different from that in another. In people with any creative potential, self-actualization means the manifestation of this potential. However, creative behavior may reflect needs other than self-actualization; noncreative people can also self-actualize. Since Maslow devoted considerable attention over the years to developing his concept of the need for self-actualization, we will return to this construct in later sections.

Maslow is somewhat more tentative in his statements regarding the category of *cognitive* needs, and he does not always mention them in discussing his theory. However, when he does consider them, he clearly distinguishes two components. Both appear to represent a motivational aspect of intelligence. There is first the desire to know; this involves being aware of reality, getting the facts, and satisfying curiosity. Distinct from this is another set of needs that relates to understanding and explanation. Included in this category are desires to systematize, organize, analyze, and seek out relationships and meanings. Although Maslow does not say so, what he describes is closely allied to the goals of science.

Maslow is not always clear in his discussion of the category of *aesthetic* needs about whether or not they characterize all people. It is apparent that he has seen individuals in his clinical practice in whom these needs are strong, and he expands his theory in order to handle these cases. What he has in mind is a craving for beauty in one's surroundings and, when ugliness prevails, a real sense of deprivation, even sickness. Aesthetic needs may well overlap with cognitive needs. Overall, Maslow gives relatively little attention to aesthetic needs and does not define them or their role with great precision.

In accordance with his view that need categories are a function of the level of abstraction employed, Maslow invokes a higher level of abstraction to separate the basic human needs into two groups— deficiency and growth. Generally, the growth designation is reserved for self-actualization, and all other basic needs are treated as deficiency needs. However, Maslow is not entirely consistent in this usage. On occasion he notes specific needs (such as self-respect) that are not associated with self-actualization but do not qualify for the deficiency designation (Maslow, 1962, 1968). In any event, deficiency need deprivation is related to illness, either physical or psychological; thus, by satisfying these needs an individual avoids pathological states. Growth needs, in contrast, are on a different continuum; their satisfaction produces positive health. Although admitting the difficulty of dealing with the deficiency-growth distinction in the research context, Maslow introduces it to deal with certain qualitative differences in people in his clinical practice.

Relationships among the Needs

Maslow arranges the physiological, safety, love, esteem, and self-actualization needs in what he calls a "hierarchy of prepotency." Because physiological needs are the most prepotent, they are lowest on the scale. If a person were totally deprived of need satisfactions, physiological desires would dominate his motivational life. Once physiological needs are reasonably well satisfied, safety needs take center stage, and so on. Thus, when a need is satisfied, it disappears for all practical purposes as a motivating force and is replaced by needs at a higher level; the individual continues to be motivated, but the nature of that motivation changes. Should the more prepotent need subsequently be deprived again, it will shift back as the current need.

Various writers have interpreted Maslow's need hierarchy relationships in mutually exclusive terms. Exclusivity certainly makes the conduct of research testing the theory much easier, but it is not what the theory says, as indicated by the following statement:

> Most members of our society who are normal are partially satisfied in all their basic needs and partially unsatisfied in all their basic needs at the same time. A realistic description of the hierarchy would be in terms of decreasing percentages of satisfaction as we go up the hierarchy of prepotency. For instance, if I may assign arbitrary figures for the sake of illustration, it is as if the average citizen is satisfied perhaps 85 per cent in his physiological needs, 70 per cent in his love needs, 40 per cent in his self-esteem needs, and 10 per cent in his self-actualization needs. (Maslow, 1943b, pp. 388–389)

Furthermore, Maslow describes the emergence of higher level needs as a gradual process that extends over a considerable, unspecified time period. Thus,

as a more prepotent need is increasingly satisfied, needs at the next higher level will attain a proportionately greater influence over behavior.

Unfortunately for those who desire simplicity in their theories, Maslow's clinical experience leads him to the conclusion that the specified prepotency relationships among the five need categories, although to be expected on the average, do not hold for all individuals (Maslow, 1954, 1970, 1987). In some people, such as the chronically unemployed, higher level needs may become permanently deadened. Thus, these needs do not emerge with the satisfaction of more prepotent needs, and the individual continues to be quite satisfied with what others would consider to be very little.

Another exception occurs among certain people whose lower level needs have long been satisfied and who have lived for many years at the top of the hierarchy. Such people may assume a martyr role in accordance with their values and hold to these values in spite of considerable and extended lower level need deprivation. India's Mahatma Gandhi would be an example.

Maslow also discusses several reversals where, for instance, esteem appears to be prepotent over love, but the theory is not very specific at this point, and it is not clear whether the reversals are real or only apparent. Throughout his writings Maslow often appears to be caught between theoretical orthodoxy and his clinical insights. The result is a much richer presentation at the expense of theoretical precision.

Role of Cognitive and Aesthetic Needs

The cognitive and aesthetic needs have typically been ignored by writers and researchers who have concerned themselves with the Maslow theory; in fact, Maslow himself gave these needs relatively little attention. The result has been some confusion. One writer treats these needs as part of the prepotency hierarchy, inserting them after the esteem needs and before self-actualization in an order that extends up from the desire to know, through understanding, to the aesthetic needs (Roe, 1956). This appears to be a misinterpretation.

Maslow views the cognitive needs to know and to understand as constituting a separate hierarchy, with knowledge prepotent over understanding. The relationship of this hierarchy and of the aesthetic needs to the other is simply not specified, except that all three types of needs are placed in the deficiency rather than the growth category.

Elaboration of the Self-Actualization Construct

Of all his theoretical formulations, the self-actualization or growth needs appear to have intrigued Maslow most. Over the years he elaborated this part of his theory most extensively. Yet he did not achieve the degree of scientific certainty that the extent of his writing would suggest. This is because he often moved outside the realm of science in discussing self-actualization into the philosophical domains of phenomenology and existentialism (Huizinga, 1970). At times Maslow comes very close to equating self-actualization with a type of religious conversion.

Although various people experience a degree of self-actualization at widely spaced points in their lives, this type of motivation typically becomes paramount as a lifestyle (in those relatively few in whom it is truly possible) only as a person nears the age of 50. In the healthy person, physiological needs are predominantly satisfied in infancy, safety needs in childhood, love needs in adolescence, and self-esteem needs during adulthood.

Thus, self-actualization is something that typically occurs late in life (Thornton, Privette, & Bundrick,

1999). When it does occur it is self-reinforcing; the more self-actualization is experienced, the stronger it becomes as a need. Thus, self-actualization is totally unlike the other needs; it is never fully satisfied and can only continue to grow. It is intrinsic growth of what is already in the organism, or, more accurately, of what *is* the organism. Yet it takes a high degree of satisfaction of lower order needs before self-actualization emerges. It is very fragile in its prepotency, and only a limited number of people fully experience it.

In his later formulations Maslow did not consider self-actualization as a necessary consequence of satisfying lower level needs (Maslow, 1967). The move to a self-actualizing level can occur when a person is free of illness, gratified to a sufficient degree in lower level needs, positively using his or her capacities, *and* committed to a particular set of values. At this point, one's work becomes a calling or mission and is indistinguishable from play. Such a move to self-actualization and its values may be totally suppressed in a particular culture or even an organization, however; it is a potential, not an inevitable reality. The values involved are set forth in table 6.1, along with some examples of their deprivation. It is indicative of Maslow's own uncertainty that some of these self-actualizing (growth) values overlap with the cognitive and aesthetic (deficiency) needs. Because he approaches his subject matter from different directions, Maslow

TABLE 6.1 Values espoused by self-actualizing people and examples of their deprivation

Value	Deprivation
1. Truth	Dishonesty, disbelief, mistrust
2. Goodness	Evil, utter selfishness
3. Beauty	Ugliness, vulgarity
4. Unity, wholeness	Chaos, atomism, disintegration
5. Transcendence of dichotomies	Black and white dichotomies, polarization, low synergy
6. Aliveness, process	Deadness, emptiness, robotizing
7. Uniqueness	Sameness, uniformity
8. Perfection	Sloppiness, poor workmanship
9. Necessity	Accident, unpredictability
10. Completion, finality	Incompleteness, cessation of striving
11. Justice	Injustice, lawlessness
12. Order	Chaos, breakdown of authority
13. Simplicity	Overcomplexity, confusion
14. Richness, totality, comprehensiveness	Poverty, loss of interest
15. Effortlessness	Fatigue, strain, gracelessness
16. Playfulness	Grimness, depression, cheerlessness
17. Self-sufficiency	Dependence, contingency
18. Meaningfulness	Meaninglessness, despair

SOURCE: Adapted from Abraham Maslow (1967), A Theory of Metamotivation: The Biological Rooting of the Value Life, *Journal of Humanistic Psychology*, 7, 108–109

does indeed reach different conclusions, and the inconsistencies are never resolved.

Finally, as further evidence of the convergence of the theory with religion, there is his concept of eupsychia — "the culture that would be generated by 1000 self-actualizing people on some sheltered island where they would not be interfered with" (Maslow, 1965). The parallel with various utopias and the kingdom of God is compelling. In this and other respects Maslow has a tendency to carry his concept of self-actualization into the domain of mysticism, and it is very difficult to decipher exactly what he means.

Implications of Need Hierarchy Theory for Organizations

Why is this kind of theory important for the study of organizations? One answer is that it has been widely adopted by managers and used by them to guide their decisions about employees. There is little question that Maslow's original article (1943b) has been one of the most influential in the field of organizational behavior.

However, the more basic consideration that makes need hierarchy theory important for organizations is that if the theory is valid, it tells us some significant things about how organizations should be managed. Figure 6.1 presents one view of the relationships among company policies and leadership styles, the degree of activation and satisfaction of needs at various levels in the hierarchy, and productivity and turnover/absenteeism. In this figure it is assumed that physiological needs are satisfied. The term *membership* is substituted for Maslow's *love*, and self-esteem is broken into its internal and external components. The implication is that to the extent management can control conditions in the work group's environment, it can induce certain motivational patterns and obtain the resulting benefits of increased productive output and reduced turnover and absenteeism. Once one moves beyond the safety needs, it appears to be highly desirable to create conditions that activate the highest possible need level (Clark, 1960).

Other implications of the theory may be noted. When job conditions are poor in terms of pay and security, the theory predicts that employees will focus on aspects of the work itself, and significant motivational consequences can be obtained only by making changes in this regard. As conditions improve, the behavior of supervisors takes on increased signifi-

cance. Finally, with a much improved environment, the role of the supervisor diminishes, and the nature of the work itself reemerges as motivationally salient, but now in relation to self-actualization and not to satisfaction of physiological and safety needs.

The theory also predicts that as people move up in the managerial hierarchy they will be motivated by higher and higher need levels; thus, managers at various levels should be treated differently. Furthermore, employees can be expected always to want more, no matter what the organization does, but the specific things desired will change. The organization cannot give enough by way of growth and development; it is the nature of the self-actualization need that once activated and satisfied, it becomes a stimulus to an even greater desire for satisfaction. Thus, it is a continuing source of motivation.

In his own writing in the field of organizations, Maslow is very clear that his theory indicates that companies should do all they can to provide the highest level of need satisfaction possible (Maslow, 1965). The self-actualizing manager is the best manager. Authoritarian leadership is rejected because it thwarts the esteem needs of subordinates. Yet Maslow is realistic: "Treating people well spoils them for being treated badly. That is, they become less contented and willing to accept lower life conditions" (p. 261). Once one takes the higher level need route in management, it will be difficult to go back.

Need hierarchy theory is attractive as a basis for managerial decision making for a number of reasons, but one of the most important is that it is primarily an "on the average" theory. Except in the case of self-actualization, it neither stresses individual differences nor requires the measurement of each individual motivational pattern before action but, rather, considers groups of individuals as defined in part by external circumstances. In this regard it is particularly suited to the use of broad managerial policies (which also operate on the average) in dealing with human resource matters. Management by policy is the prevailing mode in organizations other than the very smallest.

Evaluation and Impact

Given the widespread acceptance of Maslow's theory by managers, and its attractiveness as a basis for formulating human resource policies, it becomes very important to assess Maslow's formulations in terms of

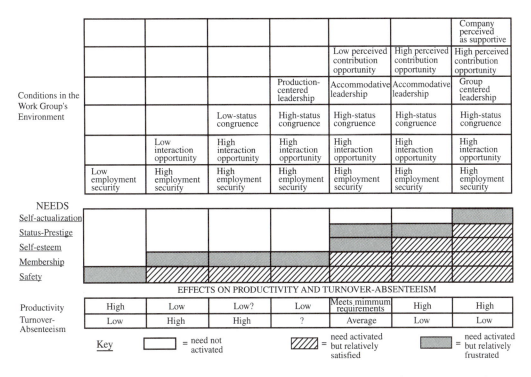

FIGURE 6.1 Relations between conditions in the work group's environment and motivation, satisfaction, productivity, and turnover/absenteeism assuming need hierarchy theory. From James V. Clark (1960), Motivation in Work Groups: A Tentative View, *Human Organization*, 13, 202. Copyright 1960 by *Human Organization* (Society for Applied Anthropology). Reprinted with permission.

their internal consistency, testability, and degree of research support.

Philosophical and Logical Considerations

Maslow's formulations often border on the philosophical, especially in the treatment of self-actualization. They do have strong religious and moral overtones, and they are humanistic. Thus, a legitimate question is whether Maslow was writing in the realm of science or the realm of philosophy. On this point Maslow is quite specific:

This book, like my previous one, is full of affirmations which are based on pilot researches, bits of evidence, on personal observation, on theoretical deduction and on sheer hunch. These are generally phrased so that they can be proven true or false. That is they are hypotheses, i.e., presented for testing rather than for final belief. They are

also obviously relevant and pertinent, i.e., their possible correctness or incorrectness is important to other branches of psychology. They matter. They should therefore generate research and I expect they will. For these reasons I consider this book to be in the realm of science or pre-science, rather than of exhortation, or of personal philosophy, or literary expression. (Maslow, 1962, pp. v–vi)

Thus, Maslow himself clearly opts for science. Yet he did only one research study bearing on his theory and did very little to establish operational measures of his major variables. There certainly are some logical inconsistencies in the theory, especially in relation to the deficiency-growth formulations. Furthermore, Maslow's treatment of self-actualization does move into a mystical-religious arena where empirical tests of his propositions are almost impossible. There is a question whether the theory has been put forth in a manner that permits scientific confirmation or rejection.

A number of logical criticisms have been raised regarding need hierarchy theory (Locke & Henne, 1986). For example, the inherent nature and logical consistency of the various need groupings have been questioned. Above the physiological level little evidence exists for the basic nature of Maslow's needs, and in some areas he appears to be putting together "apples and oranges." The concept of self-actualization is never intelligibly defined. It is almost impossible to know when this motive is operating, because the real person must be established in advance, and this can vary individually. Furthermore, the theory continually confuses needs (what is good for a person) and values (what the person views as good), as in the case of aesthetic needs and beauty as a value.

There is little question that as a theoretical statement what Maslow has written leaves much to be desired. Yet one cannot read him without recognizing a genuine desire to grapple intellectually with extremely important topics and to consider anything that appears to offer contradictory evidence. His writings offer a stimulating portrayal of an outstanding mind in action and perhaps a self-actualizing person as well, although Maslow denies it. Even if parts of the theory are untestable, and even if unintelligible and major logical inconsistencies exist, there still remains a sizable body of theory that does not suffer from these deficiencies. Thus, the ultimate test must be empirical: Does the theory or a major part of it achieve the support of scientific research?

Maslow Study of Self-Actualization

The only research that Maslow carried out on his theory, other than efforts aimed strictly at measurement, involved the self-actualization construct. What Maslow set out to do was to identify a group of self-actualizing people and then study them clinically to try to get a clearer picture of what self-actualization is (Maslow, 1987). He may have had in mind as an ultimate goal the development of a measure similar to his tests of self-esteem and psychological security. However, this was not accomplished.

Initially, 3,000 college students were screened, but only one was found to be truly self-actualizing. From this, Maslow (1987, p. 126) concluded that "self-actualization of the sort I have found in my older subjects was not possible in our society for young, developing people." In the end, the sample was developed from among acquaintances and public or histori-

cal figures. There were 13 individuals who were considered certain self-actualizers, including Lincoln and Jefferson; 12 who fell short but were sufficiently close to provide some insights; and 26 who showed signs of developing toward self-actualization.

These people were studied by whatever methods were available, and a list of qualities of self-actualizing people was developed. There was much room for personal bias in both the selection of subjects and the identification of characteristics, and Maslow admitted the lack of adequate experimental controls. Nevertheless, as a pilot or exploratory effort, the findings are of interest. The characteristics of self-actualizing people as reported by Maslow are as follows:

More efficient perceptions of reality and more comfortable relations with it

Acceptance of themselves, of others, and of the realities of life

Spontaneity and naturalness

A focusing on real problems outside themselves

The quality of detachment and a need for privacy

Autonomy and relative independence of the physical and social environment

Continued freshness of appreciation

Frequent mystic experiences

Feelings of identification, sympathy, and affection for mankind

Deeper and more profound interpersonal relationships

A democratic character structure

Strong commitment to ethical and moral standards

A philosophical, unhostile sense of humor

Creativeness

A certain resistance to or inner detachment from the prevailing culture

The capacity to resolve dichotomies

Measuring the Variables

The greatest obstacle to research on Maslow's formulations has proved to be measurement. With a few possible exceptions Maslow did not provide operational definitions of his variables. It was almost 20 years after the first publication of the theory before measuring instruments began to be developed. Accordingly, the theory went untested for a considerable period, during which it won increasing acceptance simply on its inherent appeal.

The few measures that Maslow did develop are important not so much for themselves as for the approach he used in constructing them. One is a measure of self-esteem that was designed specifically for use with women (Maslow, 1942). The other is a measure of psychological security-insecurity that is intended to tap certain safety needs (Maslow, 1951). As a pure measure of a theoretical variable, however, this latter test suffers from a confounding of the safety need construct with the need for love (Huizinga, 1970).

Maslow's approach in developing these instruments was to identify a high and a low group of subjects (on the variable under study) that were initially based on clinical investigation. These extreme groups were then studied intensively, and a tentative measuring instrument was developed. Then the groups were purged of doubtful cases using the measuring instrument as a guide, and the measure was modified to better differentiate the groups. Through this iterative process, extreme groups of subjects (who, for example, were all either very secure or very insecure) were finally established; items were included in the final test only if these two groups responded to them differently. This is a time-consuming process but is clearly the one Maslow recommended for developing measures of his theoretical variables. Because none of the measures developed since are based on such a process, it is entirely possible that many of the difficulties that have occurred with measures could have been avoided had Maslow's recommendations been followed. In any event, measures were developed and research was conducted using them.

Reliability has been a problem, but reliable measures have been developed. For some time it appeared that factors matching Maslow's needs could not be established, but that difficulty, too, was overcome. However, the factor-analytic studies do not in any sense prove the basic or instinctive nature of these needs. What emerges from a factor analysis is largely a function of the items put in. Thus, all that has been demonstrated is that if appropriate items are selected the needs can be measured as factor-pure entities.

None of the existing measures achieves the degree of sophistication Maslow envisaged. It is clear from his discussion of the iterative approach that he had in mind the creation of lengthy, separate measures for each need category, and possibly even for groupings

within categories. Furthermore, he viewed motivation as largely an unconscious process. Yet, the self-report measures that have been used rely on conscious processes. The method of choice in measuring unconscious motivation is some kind of projective technique. We will consider this whole matter in detail later. It is sufficient to indicate now that no need hierarchy study has effectively used measures that tap unconscious motivation.

One of the most obvious measurement problems exists in the area of self-actualization, which is a very imprecise concept. Ideally, measures would utilize information on a person's capabilities and potential to construct a very individualized instrument. The alternative has been to use items at a high level of abstraction to obtain indices of the desire for "growth," "development," and so forth. Such measures produce a rather large number of self-actualizers even in younger groups. But Maslow contends that self-actualization is a rare phenomenon and almost unheard of in the early years. Existing measures are not tapping the construct Maslow had in mind, although it is not certain if that construct was defined precisely enough to permit adequate operational use. Maslow's own research indicates that he may have tried to create a measure and failed. One possible approach would be to use the values set forth in table 6.1 to construct an appropriate measure of self-actualization.

Research on Prepotency

In distinguishing between deficiency and growth needs, Maslow established a high-level cutting point between esteem and self-actualization. Yet the research seems to support a low-level cut (see, for instance, Betz, 1982). It does seem useful to think of at least some among the physiological and safety needs as dominating. When these needs are not satisfied, they tend to dominate the personality in an all-pervasive manner, so that other types of strivings are shut out. Although it might be argued that these types of needs are almost universally satisfied in our society, there is ample evidence that this is not true. One example might be a low-pay, low-seniority, low-skill family breadwinner in an industry that is characterized by major cyclical swings, working in an area with sizable unemployment from which she cannot move because of family commitments. Other examples would be alcoholic and drug-using employees, as well as neurotics who suffer from severe phobias that are activated by the work situation. There also are jobs that must be performed under conditions of real, continuing danger.

For those individuals whose physiological and safety needs are reasonably satisfied on a continuing basis, other needs do become important in determining behavior. In this instance only, there does appear to be some kind of prepotency. But what needs can be expected to emerge in what degree of dominance over behavior appears to depend on individual development experiences and to vary widely from person to person. Given the nature of the research evidence, it appears best not to assume any certain need hierarchy above the most basic level. Individuals seem to have their own hierarchies (Landy & Becker, 1987).

Beyond this two-step differentiation — and the recognition that needs such as those for social relationships, self-esteem and dignity, autonomy, and creative challenge can be important in human behavior — need hierarchy theory has not yet contributed in a major way to either scientific knowledge or organizational practice. Available research does not support the Maslow theory to any significant degree. This does not imply that the theory is wrong, merely that it has not been supported. Other studies using other approaches might yield different conclusions, but for the moment the evidence is nonconfirming, and the longer this condition holds, the more scientific interest is likely to wane. In actual fact, there has been little activity on this front since the early 1980s. As we will see, however, need hierarchy theory has had an impact in that certain aspects of the theory have found their way into other formulations.

Existence, Relatedness, and Growth (ERG) Theory

ERG theory was formulated by Clayton Alderfer (1972) to deal with certain of the shortcomings that have been noted in the original need hierarchy formulations. It is an attempt to revise Maslow's theory to make it agree more with the research findings.

Alderfer was educated as an industrial psychologist and received his doctorate from Yale in 1966. Much of his career was spent in the School of Organization and Management at Yale, and ERG theory was developed during this period. Much of the early research on Maslow's theory came out of Yale in the late 1960s and early 1970s, and Alderfer was influenced primarily by his colleagues there, rather than by any direct working relationship with Maslow.

Statement of the Theory

Alderfer's modifications involved a telescoping of the Maslow need categories, a change in the prepotency relationships, and certain additions to the theory. The correspondence between the two theories is as follows:

Alderfer	*Maslow*
Existence needs	Physiological needs
	Safety needs of a material type
Relatedness needs	Safety needs of an interpersonal type
	Love or belongingness needs
	Esteem needs of an interpersonal type
Growth needs	Esteem needs that are self-confirmed
	Self-actualization

In its original form, ERG theory set forth seven basic propositions regarding need relationships:

1. The less existence needs are satisfied, the more they will be desired (follows Maslow).
2. The less relatedness needs are satisfied, the more existence needs will be desired (reverse of Maslow).
3. The more existence needs are satisfied, the more relatedness needs will be desired (same orientation as Maslow).
4. The less relatedness needs are satisfied, the more they will be desired (follows Maslow).
5. The less growth needs are satisfied, the more relatedness needs will be desired (reverse of Maslow).
6. The more relatedness needs are satisfied, the more growth needs will be desired (same orientation as Maslow).
7. The more growth needs are satisfied, the more they will be desired (follows Maslow).

Going beyond the issues that were of concern to Maslow, Alderfer set forth a number of propositions that deal with the effect of desires on satisfactions:

8a. When existence materials are scarce, then the higher chronic existence desires are and the less existence satisfaction.
8b. When existence materials are not scarce, then there will be no differential existence satisfaction as a function of chronic existence desire.
9a. In highly satisfying relationships there is no

differential relatedness satisfaction as a function of chronic relatedness desires.

9b. In normal relationships, persons very high and very low on chronic relatedness desires tend to obtain lower satisfaction than do persons with moderate desires.

9c. In highly dissatisfying relationships, then the higher chronic relatedness desires are, the more relatedness satisfaction there is.

10a. In challenging discretionary settings, then the higher chronic growth desires are, the more growth satisfaction there is.

10b. In nonchallenging, nondiscretionary settings, there will be no differential growth satisfaction as a function of chronic growth desires.

Alderfer's Early Research and Theoretical Revisions

Whereas Maslow did not make his theoretical variables operational in terms of specific measures (to any but a very limited degree), Alderfer constructed a specific measure of both desire and satisfaction for all three of his need categories. These scales generally contain items that can be grouped together in a factor analysis, are quite reliable, and are valid measures of the constructs involved.

A number of studies were conducted using these instruments in different settings to test the propositions. A given proposition typically was tested in several different samples. The samples included managers, nonmanagerial employees, students, and professionals.

The results of this program of research are given in table 6.2. Propositions 3 (satisfying existence needs activates relatedness needs) and 5 (depriving growth needs activates relatedness needs) clearly did not receive much research support. The other propositions that were tested generally received sufficient support to maintain their viability. However, in several cases the support was quite mixed.

In a number of instances when the research data did not consistently support ERG propositions, Alderfer felt he could identify certain factors that might account for obtaining support in one setting and not in another. Accordingly, he proposed several inductive revisions of his seven original theoretical statements. These are (numbered as in the original list) as follows:

2. When both existence and relatedness needs are relatively dissatisfied, then the less relatedness needs are satisfied, the more existence needs will be desired.

4. When relatedness needs are relatively dissatisfied, then the less relatedness needs are satisfied, the more they will be desired; when relatedness needs are relatively satisfied, then the more relatedness needs are satisfied, the more they will be desired.

6. When both relatedness and growth needs are relatively satisfied, then the more relatedness needs are satisfied, the more growth needs will be desired.

7. When growth needs are relatively dissatisfied, then the less growth needs are satisfied, the

TABLE 6.2 Summary of research testing the ERG Theory (Alderfer, 1972)

Proposition number	Number of samples	Nature of results
1	6	Consistent support* in all samples
2	6	Supported* in 5 samples
3	6	Not supported* at all
4	8	Supported* in 6 samples
5	6	Supported* in 1 sample
6	8	Supported* in 3 samples
7	8	Supported* in 3 samples
8a	Not tested	
8b	Not tested	
9a	2	Supported* in 1 sample
9b	3	Supported* in 1 sample
9c	2	Supported* in 1 sample
10a	2	Consistent support* in both samples
10b	Not tested	

*$p < .05$.

more they will be desired; when growth needs are relatively satisfied, then the more growth needs are satisfied, the more they will be desired.

In presenting the propositions in curvilinear form, Alderfer has no doubt put them in closer alliance with his research data. Nevertheless, the propositions grew out of the data and must be subjected to subsequent independent tests. Furthermore, the revisions tend to upset the internal logical integrity of the original formulations. Thus, the revised theory is at a lower level of abstraction and tends to approach a set of empirical generalizations. Accordingly, it becomes more cumbersome to use ERG theory.

Subsequent Research

Research on Alderfer's formulations continued through the 1970s but dropped off sharply in the early 1980s, following the same pattern as with Maslow's theory. Alderfer, Robert Kaplan, and Ken Smith (1974) provided confirmatory evidence for the revised proposition 4 in a carefully controlled laboratory study using practicing managers as subjects. The predicted curvilinear relationship between relatedness satisfaction and desire was obtained. Later, John Wanous and Abram Zwany (1977) obtained some evidence of curvilinear relationships in a study of telephone company employees. This study is of additional significance because it used measures of ERG needs that differed from those developed by Alderfer, and it still obtained a factor structure that closely approximates the ERG classification. A later report by Alderfer and Richard Guzzo (1979) describes the development of new scales and provides some tangential research support for the theory.

However, John Rauschenberger, Neal Schmitt, and John Hunter (1980) report on an extensive study carried out over time using high school graduates, which failed to support either ERG theory or Maslow's original formulations. The conflict between these findings and Alderfer's has not been reconciled, and we are left with much the same conclusion as previously. Research has not supported the need hierarchy line of theorizing to a significant extent, and interest in following this approach further has clearly waned. It would take a major theoretical, or research, breakthrough to revive it.

ACHIEVEMENT MOTIVATION THEORY

Achievement motivation theory is the creation of David McClelland, whose debt to Murray (1938) is similar to Maslow's. At least two other theories that deal with achievement present related views. John Atkinson (1977, 1982; see also Atkinson & Feather, 1966; Atkinson & Raynor, 1974) casts his formulations in expectancy theory terms that differ from McClelland's, even though the two collaborated on research in the early years. Bernard Weiner (1972, 1982) obtained his doctorate with Atkinson and concentrates on developing a viewpoint based in attribution theory. The theories of Atkinson and Weiner are interesting and important. However, they were developed outside the business schools, and they never have been absorbed significantly by organizational behavior. For that reason it seems appropriate to concentrate on McClelland's formulations, which have had a major impact and are closer to the central concerns of this book.

Background

Born in 1917, McClelland attended Wesleyan University and obtained a doctorate in experimental psychology from Yale in 1941. Not long afterward he returned to Wesleyan to chair the psychology department and begin the collaboration with Atkinson and others that led to achievement motivation theory. In 1956 he moved to Harvard and, like Maslow, by that time had converted from experimental psychology to personality theory, a field in which he has remained throughout his career. After his retirement from Harvard in 1987, he joined the faculty of the psychology department at Boston University as a research professor of psychology, and he remained there until his death (Winter, 2000). McClelland died in March 1998.

McClelland was not a member of a business school faculty at any time (McClelland, 1984). However, his business interests are reflected in his founding of McBer & Company, a consulting and contract research firm, where he served as chairman of the board for many years. His theoretical ideas have been clearly relevant for organizational behavior since the publication of *The Achieving Society* in 1961. In addition he has written frequently for business school publications (see, for example, McClelland, 1962, 1965a; McClelland & Burnham, 1976, 1995; Miron & McClelland,

1979). Thus, he is not a psychologist whose views found their way to organizational behavior through the efforts of others; he has been an active participant in the literature of the field from the early 1960s on. At that time, however, he was in his mid-40s and well into his career. Most social scientists who made the move into business schools did so at a considerably younger age.

Emergence of a Theory

Achievement motivation theory receives its name from the motive that has been the dominant focus of concern since 1948. In a sense, the designation is a misnomer at present. The theory has been developmental, undergoing considerable branching and, on occasion, revision. The achievement motivation construct has been stretched to include not only hope of success but also fear of failure and even fear of success. In addition, at least two other motives — those for power and for affiliation — must now be considered part of the theory.

Scope and Early Development

The domain of achievement motivation theory is much more limited than that of Maslow's theory. It focuses on three motives (often broadly stated) and relates them to organizational behavior or behavior that appears to have relevance for organizations. The theory follows the three motives well beyond the organizational context into a great variety of aspects of daily life; however, our concern will be only with achievement motivation theory as related to organizations.

The two major motives of the theory, achievement and power, would seem to fall within Maslow's esteem category, although achievement motivation has some aspects in common with self-actualization. Affiliation motivation would clearly fall in the social category. However, despite these overlaps and the origins of both theories in clinical psychology and personality theory, need hierarchy theory and achievement motivation theory represent distinctly different concepts of the motivational process.

The theory originated in an investigation into the relationship between hunger needs and the degree to which food imagery dominates thought processes (Atkinson & McClelland, 1948). It was found that the longer the subjects had gone without food, the more certain food-related words appeared in stories they wrote in response to various pictures. Subsequently, this arousal-based approach to studying motives was extended to affiliation, power, aggression, sex, fear, and achievement. However, in the early years achievement motivation saw the greatest theoretical development (McClelland, Atkinson, Clark, & Lowell, 1953).

In McClelland's view, all motives are learned, becoming arranged in a hierarchy of potential for influencing behavior that varies from individual to individual; thus Maslow-like fixed hierarchies of an instinctoid (Maslow's term) nature are rejected. As people develop, they learn to associate positive and negative feelings with certain things that happen to and around them. Thus, achievement situations such as a challenging task may elicit feelings of pleasure, and ultimately a person may be characterized by strong achievement motivation. For such a person, achievement is directed toward the top of the motive hierarchy; it takes only minimal achievement cues to activate the expectation of pleasure and thus increase the likelihood of achievement striving. Under such circumstances weaker motives are likely to give way to the achievement motive and assume a distinct secondary role in influencing behavior. Thus, if one asks such people to tell stories about a picture that contains potential achievement cues, their achievement motivations will be aroused, just as hunger was in the subjects deprived of food, and their stories will reflect what is on their minds — achievement.

Achievement Situations

McClelland (1961, 1962) specifies certain characteristics of the situations that are preferred by, and tend to elicit achievement striving from, people with a strong need for achievement.

First, these situations permit people to attain success through their own efforts and abilities rather than through chance. Thus these are situations in which it is possible to take personal responsibility and get personal credit for the outcome. The credit need not come from others. To such individuals, achieving through their own efforts is intrinsically satisfying.

Second, achievement situations are characterized by intermediate levels of difficulty and risk. Were the task to be too difficult, the chance of succeeding would be minimal and the probability of motive satisfaction low. Easy tasks represent things that anyone can do, thus there is little satisfaction in accomplishing them. Achievement- motivated people tend to calculate the risks involved in situations and pick those situations where they anticipate feeling slightly overextended by the challenges, but not too overextended.

Third, the situation must be one in which there is clear and unambiguous feedback on the success of one's efforts. There is little opportunity for achievement satisfaction when a person cannot tell success from failure; thus, the situation must provide for knowledge of results within a reasonable time.

In addition to these three major features, McClelland posits two other aspects of achievement situations: they permit innovation and novel solutions, thus allowing a greater sense of satisfaction when solutions are attained, and they also require a distinct future orientation, thinking ahead and planning, what McClelland calls "anticipation of future possibilities."

Quite apparently these various situational characteristics are epitomized in the entrepreneurial role, and, indeed, McClelland did have this role in mind as he developed his theory. In his view it is the prospect of achievement satisfaction, not money, that drives the successful entrepreneur; money is important only as a source of feedback on how one is doing. To some extent, then, the theory represents a deduction from a model of entrepreneurship, but also it is derived inductively from a wide range of research studies (McClelland, 1961). If all this sounds very similar to task role motivation theory as discussed in the previous chapter, of course it is.

Economic Development

The theory as stated to this point is important for organizational behavior because it tells about the motivation of the key individual in the founding and development of business organizations — the successful entrepreneur. However, McClelland goes on to relate achievement motivation to the economic growth and decline of whole societies, thus considerably extending the applicable scope of the theory.

The starting point for this set of propositions is Max Weber's theory that modern capitalism arose out of the Protestant Reformation in Europe. It was Weber's view that Protestantism, in contrast with the existing Catholicism, fostered self-reliance and working hard to make the most of what one had, as well as the rationalization of life through attempting to improve

oneself in every way. Weber formulated his theory in broad social terms:

Protestantism and $\longrightarrow$ Economic development
the cultural values
it produced

McClelland accepts this formulation but adds a level of psychological explanation:

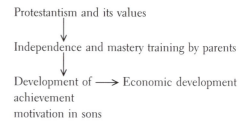

As stated, this is a theory applicable to male children only. It assumes a generational lag (roughly 50 years) between the emergence of values that foster self-reliance and economic growth. Economic decline occurs with affluence, again with a generational lag. As parents become affluent, they turn over child rearing to others, such as slaves, and the conditions for developing strong achievement motivation are lost. Lacking the driving force of the achievement need and its associated entrepreneurship, the society goes into economic eclipse.

In his formulations of the early 1960s McClelland does not clearly distinguish the domain of his theory, and he is not yet certain about the role of power motivation in the business world, although he does view it as important. These problems are related. At some points McClelland appears to equate entrepreneurship and the management of business organizations generally, making his theory of achievement motivation an overall theory of business development and management. Thus, little room is left for power motivation to play a significant role. At other times he sees some managerial jobs, such as those in marketing and sales, as more entrepreneurial than others, thus leaving a place for the power construct. In the end the matter is left open: "Whether n Power is an essential ingredient in managerial success, as we have argued n Achievement is, or an accidental feature of the private enterprise system, cannot be settled" (McClelland, 1961, p. 290). More recently, the theory has been filled out in this regard (McClelland, 1975).

Role of Power Motivation

By the mid-1970s McClelland had moved to the position that achievement motivation was of organizational significance primarily within the limited domain of entrepreneurship and that other constructs were needed to explain managerial effectiveness in large corporations. Thus, "a high need to achieve does not equip a man to deal effectively with managing human relationships. For instance, a salesman with high n Achievement does not necessarily make a good sales manager" (McClelland, 1975). And again, "the good manager in a large company does not have a high need for achievement" (McClelland & Burnham, 1976).

McClelland (1975) views power motivation as the essential ingredient for understanding and predicting managerial success, although such power needs must be couched in an appropriate motivational context to yield the desired result.

The revised theory states that power motivation may be manifested in behavior in a variety of ways and that different individuals develop different characteristic modes of expression, one of which is managing. In part at least, the mode of expression is a function of the stage to which the power motive has developed in the individual; there is a hierarchy of growth or development, and people must experience one stage to reach the next. Adults may be at any one of the four stages at a point in time, and many never rise above the first level.

At *stage I* power motivation involves seeking to derive strength from others. Such people tend to attach themselves to strong people and obtain a sense of strength and power from that relationship. At *stage II* the source of strength shifts to the self, and a feeling of power is derived from being oneself and "doing one's own thing" (shades of self-actualization); at this stage power satisfaction does not involve influencing others at all. In contrast, *stage III* power motivation does involve having an effect on other people, including dominating them and winning out over them in competitive endeavor. Also included at this stage is the satisfaction of power needs through helping behavior, which clearly establishes the weaker status of the person helped. At *stage IV* the self moves into the background, and a feeling of power is derived from influencing others for the sake of some greater good, such as corporate success.

McClelland then distinguishes between what he calls *personalized power* and *socialized power*. Personalized power is characterized by dominance-submission and win-lose. Satisfaction comes from conquering others. In an extensive series of studies, McClelland and his colleagues have shown that this kind of power motivation can be related to heavy drinking and that people with strong personalized power motivation experience considerable satisfaction from fantasies of power elicited under alcohol (McClelland, Davis, Kalin, & Wanner, 1972). In contrast, socialized power involves a subtle mix of power motivation and inhibition, such that there is a "concern for group goals, for finding those goals that will move men, for helping the group to formulate them, for taking initiative in providing means of achieving them, and for giving group members the feeling of competence they need to work hard for them" (McClelland, 1975, p. 265). Power motivation is mixed with a degree of altruism and of pragmatism; it is satisfied in many ways that will work and get results, not just aggrandize the self.

Adding in Affiliation Motivation

The theoretical relationships between the various types of power motivation and managerial performance are set forth in table 6.3. The effective organizational manager begins to emerge in late stage III with the advent of socialized power motivation (thus the addition of inhibitory tendencies). However, individuals at lower developmental stages may function effectively in some managerial roles.

It is important to note that affiliation motivation, which in earlier formulations had received relatively little attention insofar as theoretical statements involving the field of organizational behavior were concerned, now assumes a significant role. If affiliative needs are too strong, the consequences for managerial effectiveness are said to be negative. McClelland and Burnham (1976, p. 103) explain this proposition as follows: "For a bureaucracy to function effectively, those who manage it must be universalistic in applying rules. That is, if they make exceptions for the particular needs of individuals, the whole system will break down. The manager with a high need for being liked is precisely the one who wants to stay on good terms with everybody, and, therefore, is the one most likely to make exceptions in terms of particular needs." In other words, strong affiliation motivation interferes with and subverts effective managerial performance.

TABLE 6.3 Development of the power motive and managerial performance

Maturity stage	Motivational pattern	Effect on management
I	Desire to influence others is low; in this sense power motivation is low	Generally not assertive enough to manage well
II	Power motivation expressed in ways having little to do with others	Not related to managing
III (early)	High power motivation coupled with low inhibition and low affiliation motivation	The conquistador pattern or the feudal lord
III (late)	High power motivation coupled with high inhibition and low affiliation motivation	The imperial pattern: personalized power shades into socialized power
IV	High power motivation of an altruistic type coupled with high inhibition and low affiliation motivation	Selfless leadership and efficient organizational management

SOURCE: Adapted from David C. McClelland (1975), *Power: The Inner Experience* (New York: Irvington), 264

It may have similar effects on the relationship between achievement motivation and entrepreneurial success.

On the other hand, McClelland (1975) does accept a formulation originally put forth and documented by George Litwin and Adrienne Siebrecht (1967) that for managers who perform in an integrator role, such as project and product managers, a more balanced motivational pattern is desirable, perhaps even with affiliative needs stronger than power needs. Such individuals have little position power and need to work through personal relationships.

Varying Concepts of Power

Not all theorists associated with the achievement motivation viewpoint have advocated stances identical to that of McClelland regarding the nature of power motivation. The positions taken by Joseph Veroff and Joanne Veroff (1972) and Winter (1973) vary at several points, even though both are generally aligned with the McClelland approach to motivation and its study.

The Veroffs take the position that power motivation is primarily a negative process that involves avoiding feelings of weakness. Although McClelland would agree that such motivation exists, especially in the early stages of motivational development, it is certainly not his prevailing view of power needs in the organizational context. Winter posits hope of power and fear of power as two distinct motivational processes, which appear to have much in common with the personalized and socialized categories but are not the same. Hope of power, for instance, is viewed as a source of excessive drinking *and* of organizational effectiveness.

Fear of power is not entirely allied with altruistic power striving; it accounts for various kinds of emotional pathology as well. Thus, regarding the McClelland socialized/personalized differentiation, Winter says, "I do not think that power can be so neatly divided into 'good' and 'bad' . . . both aspects of the power motive are mixed" (1973, p. 163).

Motivational Change and Development

One aspect of the McClelland theory relates to the acquisition of motives. Motives that are important for business development and effective continued operation, such as achievement needs and the socialized power motive, are said to be subject to the effects of appropriate educational processes (McClelland, 1965b; McClelland & Winter, 1969). What is proposed is that these motives can be moved to a more dominant position in the individual motive hierarchy, and thus they will exert a more pervasive influence on behavior.

Educational efforts of this kind are considered most likely to "work" under certain circumstances:

1. When the person has numerous reasons to believe that he can, will, or should develop the motive.
2. When developing the motive appears to be rational in the light of career and life situation considerations.
3. When the individual understands the meaning and various aspects of the motive.
4. When this understanding of the motive is linked to actions and behavior.

5. When the understanding is closely tied to everyday events.
6. When the motive is viewed positively as contributing to an improved self-image.
7. When the motive is viewed as consistent with prevailing cultural values.
8. When the individual commits himself to achieving concrete goals that are related to the motive.
9. When the individual maintains progress toward attaining these goals.
10. When the environment in which change occurs is one in which the person feels supported and respected as an individual who can guide his own future.
11. When the environment dramatizes the importance of self-study and makes it an important value of the group involved in the change effort.
12. When the motive is viewed as an indication of membership in a new reference group.

More Recent Contributions

Since the preceding formulations were advanced, McClelland has devoted his energies to integrating the views of Atkinson, Weiner, and others into a more general theory of human motivation and behavior (see, for example, McClelland, 1985). Although they are potentially useful for organizational behavior, these ideas have not yet been cast in such a way as to focus on the issues of the field.

Another thrust has been concerned with the study of human competence at work (see McClelland, 1973, 1994, 1998; Spencer & Spencer, 1993). This approach folds the theory of achievement, power, and affiliation motives into a more comprehensive framework to determine what makes for higher levels of competence in various positions. It is not so much a theory of human competence or performance as a procedure for studying such factors as motives, traits, self-concepts, knowledge, and skills as they interact to produce superior as opposed to average performance. This competency framework has spawned a great many derivatives over the years, and a substantial consulting industry as well (Athey & Orth, 1999; Briscoe & Hall, 1999). We will consider some of the results of this approach in the next section.

Evaluation and Impact

Achievement motivation theory had its origins in research that measured the effects of motive-arousing

stimuli through the analysis of stories told by the subjects after they saw appropriate pictures. Thus, measures of major variables were present from the beginning, and the research-retarding effects of a lack of theory-based measures that plagued need hierarchy theory have not occurred.

Measurement Procedures

The method of choice in measuring the various motives of achievement motivation theory has been to use derivatives of the Thematic Apperception Test (TAT) that was originally developed by Murray, relying on content scoring procedures that had their origins in clinical practice (see Tomkins, 1947; Stein, 1948). Typically, from four to six pictures, selected to focus on the motive of greatest concern, are used. Each picture is exposed briefly, from 10 to 20 seconds, and the subject is then asked to write a story about it within a specified time interval, usually 5 minutes. The story is to contain answers to the following questions:

1. What is happening? Who are the people?
2. What has led up to this situation? That is, what has happened in the past?
3. What is being thought? What is wanted? By whom?
4. What will happen? What will be done?

This procedure is much more structured than the traditional one used in clinical practice. There the pictures tend to be more ambiguous, there are no set time intervals for viewing the pictures and providing stories, the stories usually are given orally and recorded, and the instructions are not fully repeated for each picture. In addition, the original TAT contained 20 pictures. The achievement motivation theory TATs have the advantages of permitting group administration and greater manageability, but they lose something in the richness of fantasy content. Nevertheless, they remain projective in nature and thus do permit the measurement of unconscious motives.

Over the years, a number of self-report measures that use a multiple-choice format have been developed as substitutes for the TAT. Because they are less cumbersome to administer and score, these approaches are attractive. Considerable tension has become manifest between advocates of the projective TAT and of the more objective self-report procedures. Only recently have answers emerged as to the relative merits of the two, and they are discussed next.

Projective measurement places heavy demands on the scorer. A coding system must be developed, learned, and applied consistently. In developing a coding system for a particular motive, the preferred approach among achievement motivation theorists has been to compare stories produced in neutral and motive arousal situations and to generate a scoring system from the differences. One alternative that is occasionally used is to compare groups of known high and low characteristic motivational levels. In either case, the coding systems are typically very detailed, and numerous examples are provided. When sufficient time is spent learning these coding systems, quite high levels of agreement can be achieved among different scorers. A number of studies have dealt with this kind of scorer reliability. Heinz Heckhausen (1967) reports correlations ranging from .80 to .90 or better as typical. Atkinson (1977) reviews a number of studies in which the median correlation was in the upper .80s.

Self-report procedures do not face this problem of scorer reliability. However, the items and the multiple-choice alternatives must be developed based on a considerable understanding of what is to be measured and how to go about doing so. With regard to achievement motivation, at least, that understanding often has not been present. The result is that many self-report scales do not measure the totality of the achievement motivation construct (Kanfer & Heggestad, 1997).

A major argument against the TAT approach has been that even with adequate scorer reliability, test reliability is inadequate. There are many problems inherent in determining the reliability of projective techniques and, consequently, the correlations reported may have underestimated the reliability of the TAT measures (Cornelius, 1983). There is now good reason to believe this is the case (McClelland, 1985). Accordingly, knowledgeable scholars have increasingly come to the conclusion that projective measures work at least as well as those of a self-report nature (Hogan, 1991).

To test this conclusion, William Spangler (1992) has carried out meta-analyses that use a large number of studies. His results support McClelland's contentions regarding the TAT. In fact, TAT-based correlations with outcome criteria were significantly higher than were self-report correlations. Under the conditions specified by the theory, the TAT validities are substantial. Furthermore, a low but significant correlation was found between the two approaches to achievement motivation. This would appear to explain why both have on occasion proven useful in predicting performance indices. An approach that uses the sentence-completion method (also projective in nature) has produced very promising results (Miner, 1993), but was not included in the Spangler (1992) analysis. The particular sentence-completion scale involved measures the components of task role motivation theory—components that are very similar to those of McClelland's achievement situation.

Achievement Motivation and Entrepreneurship

In the previous chapter data were presented that indicate support for task role motivation theory, and for McClelland's views on achievement motivation, as both relate to entrepreneurial accomplishment. By now there is indeed substantial evidence to the effect that individuals who start their own businesses and make them succeed tend to have high levels of achievement motivation. Furthermore, the growth and success of such entrepreneurial enterprises also are closely related to the achievement needs of the founder. Thus, the prototype achievement situation (personal responsibility and credit, minimal risk taking, feedback, opportunity for innovation, and future orientation) does turn out to provide fertile ground for the efforts of the highly achievement-motivated person.

Research support of this kind carries up to the present. A study conducted in Ecuador, Malawi, and India, using the competency approach, consistently found that stronger achievement motivation differentiated superior entrepreneurs from those whose success was at the average level (Spencer & Spencer, 1993). Robert Baum, Edwin Locke, and Shelley Kirkpatrick (1998) indicate that vision attributes and content, involving planning and establishing goals, operate to cause growth of entrepreneurial firms. This reflects the operation of at least one component of achievement motivation. It appears to indicate a degree of convergence among achievement motivation theory, the task version of role motivation theory, and goal-setting theory.

Achievement Motivation and Economic Development

The primary source of data on economic development is McClelland's (1961) book *The Achieving Society*. This work contains a mass of data focused on the relationship between achievement motivation and economic development.

Because TAT protocols on past societies were not available, various substitutes were used and scored in a manner as analogous to the TAT scoring procedure as possible. The objective was to use cultural products that represented distillations of the values and valued motives of the society, especially those related to transmitting the culture to future generations. Thus, indices of achievement motivation were derived from folk tales, school readers for children, cultural artifacts, characteristic literature, and other sources. This research indicated many relationships between achievement imagery and economic growth, often established in terms of electric power output. However, there is a lag of many years between cause and effect.

Data on the United States from 1800 to 1950 have been developed using fourth-grade readers to generate achievement motivation scores and the rate of recorded patents as an index of economic activity (de-Charms & Moeller, 1962). The data show a steady rise in achievement imagery until 1890, and then a steady decline, which by 1950 had reached the same level as in 1850. A similar curve was found for the patent data, but the familiar lag between the two indices was much less in evidence, perhaps because patents must precede actual production by a number of years.

Although the support for an achievement motivation theory of economic development is strong, there is reason to believe that other factors, and even other motives, may also be involved. For instance, low levels of affiliation motivation have consistently been found to be precursors of economic growth. Power motivation appears to be an important factor in the larger countries, particularly those already more industrialized. The role of affiliation motivation is also in evidence in the study of the United States (deCharms & Moeller, 1962), with lower levels of motivation characterizing the period of greatest growth. McClelland himself (1966) has shown that educational level operates independently of achievement motivation, yet contributes sizably to economic growth.

The net effect of findings such as these has been a decline in research along the lines that McClelland originally advocated. A quotation from a review of the subject provides insight into what has happened:

Confronted by evidence that psychology probably accounts for a very small proportion of the variance in macroeconomic wellbeing, by warnings that the encouragement of entrepreneurship in settings where the opportunity structure is deficient may produce frustration and domestic or international turmoil, and by evidence that in some societies achievement is defined explicitly in terms of group norms rather than individual accomplishment, interest in studying achievement motivation cross-culturally waned. (Segall, 1986, p. 543)

There is also a problem in that the time span between rises in motivation and measured economic growth is quite variable in different studies. Which factors cause this lag need much more investigation. In general, the theory appears to apply primarily to lesser developed countries than to growth in that sector of the world that is dominated by large multinational corporations. The concepts related to the Protestant ethic and independence training of sons receive only mixed support as well. For instance, it appears that the most important factor in the development of achievement motivation is not independence training but exposure to a parental role model of an entrepreneurial nature.

Power Motivation and Management

The theory as it relates to power motivation has been the subject of considerable confirmatory research in recent years. Particularly impressive is a long-term predictive study that was conducted at AT&T. The results given in table 6.4 indicate that socialized power—with a combination of high power, low affiliation, and high inhibition (see table 6.3)—leads to more promotions (McClelland & Boyatzis, 1982). This does not hold for technical managers, however, where specialized skills other than the managerial may play a significant role in the work. Winter (1991) carried out an analysis of this same data set using TAT measures of power and responsibility (rather than power, affiliation, and inhibition) and obtained essentially the same results. Note that in both instances power motivation played a key role in the predictive process.

In another major study, Robert House, William Spangler, and James Woycke (1991) used this same predictive pattern involving power motivation to analyze the inaugural addresses of U.S. presidents. These data were then compared with various historical indices of presidential performance. The power motiva-

TABLE 6.4 Relationships between socialized power (as reflected in high power motivation, low affiliation motivation, and high inhibition) and promotion among non-technical managers

	Promoted (%)	
	Managers not having predictive pattern	Managers having predictive pattern
Level of management achieved after 8 years		
Lower management	64	34
Middle management	36	66
Level of management achieved after 16 years		
Lower management	43	21
Middle management	57	79

NOTE: Predictive pattern = high power, low affiliation, high inhibition.

SOURCE: Adapted from David C. McClelland & Richard E. Boyatzis (1982), Leadership Motive Pattern and Long-Term Success in Management, *Journal of Applied Psychology, 67,* 739

tion pattern was quite effective as a predictor of performance.

Enough is known now to make it clear that power motivation is a strong predictor of management success. Yet as McClelland (1975) notes, there are situations where achievement motivation emerges as a better predictor for managers. After reviewing the relevant literature, House and Ram Aditya (1997) conclude that a need to specify the boundary conditions under which the theory holds remains a problem. Given the apparent convergence with the hierarchic role motivation theory, which incorporates several measures of power motivation, as well as of potential inhibitors, it may be that the best way to delimit the theoretical domain would be in terms of bureaucratic theory (Miner, 1993).

Research Using Female Subjects

As noted, achievement motivation theory is intended more for males than for females, partly because of the independence training aspect and partly because the scoring system that operationalizes the theory was developed using male subjects. The result has been that when females have been studied the results often have not been the same as those found with males; in fact, there frequently have been no results at all, where results might have been expected. It has also been found that fear of success is much more prevalent among females, thus lowering their achievement motivation scores.

Yet reason exists to question these findings as they apply to today's world (Spence, 1983). Fear of success seems to differentiate males and females less now. Achievement motivation has been found to play a significant role in the personality dynamics of many female entrepreneurs (Langan-Fox & Roth, 1995). The sharp differences that separated males and females on achievement-related variables in the past appear to be disappearing, as employment patterns and cultural values have changed.

Research on Motivational Development

The hypothesis that motives can be moved up the individual hierarchy, and thus made to exert more extensive influence on behavior through exposure to appropriate training, has been generally confirmed. Although most of the research has been conducted with achievement motivation training, there are some data on the development of power motivation.

The major thrusts of achievement motivation training have been in the development of capitalism among black people in the United States, in stimulating economic growth in lesser developed countries, and in stimulating better performance from schoolchildren, especially disadvantaged children. A typical course lasts roughly a week and includes games and simulations, goal setting and planning, lectures, TAT analysis, case discussions, films, action team discussions, and contests in achievement thinking. The objective is to induce the 12 conditions hypothesized to be conducive to motivational change.

There is considerable evidence now that such achievement motivation training does increase the target motive and that, given appropriate external circumstances, this increased motivation will yield expanded entrepreneurial behavior (McClelland & Winter, 1969; Miron & McClelland, 1979; Spencer & Spencer, 1993). However, the training should not be used indiscriminately. Developing achievement motivation in an individual whose environment does not permit satisfaction of the motive can be self-defeating. In the past when this has been done, the people involved have either left the environment (quit to take more gratifying jobs) or attempted to change the existing environment through pressure tactics and other conflict-generating efforts.

On theoretical grounds, power motivation training should be equally effective, and there is some evidence to this effect even though data for courses that use the McClelland format are not extensive. Nevertheless, managerial role motivation training, which has been studied much more, does yield motivational change consistently, and, more significant, these changes occur most frequently in the area of power motivation (Miner, 1993). Thus, it is apparent that development can occur with regard to power, as well as achievement.

With respect to development, and in numerous other respects, achievement motivation theory continues to be highly viable, and useful.

PSYCHOANALYTIC THEORY APPLIED TO ORGANIZATIONS

Harry Levinson has been cited for his unique skill in taking psychological theory and knowledge and showing how it applies to the everyday functioning of organizations (Levinson, 1993a). However, it is specifically psychoanalytic theory in the Freudian tradition that he has utilized, and his contribution goes beyond merely applying a theory to a new context; he has made new theory in the process.

Background

Levinson was born in 1922 and obtained a doctorate in clinical psychology from the University of Kansas

30 years later. He received extensive clinical training with the Veterans Administration and the Menninger Foundation, and he worked at the Topeka State Hospital. He completed a personal psychoanalysis.

For 14 years he headed up a program in industrial mental health at the Menninger Foundation, offering seminars to managers and industrial physicians that dealt with the psychoanalytic aspects of leadership and the management of change (Levinson, 1993b). In 1962 he spent a year at the Sloan School of Management at MIT, and in 1967 he spent another year at the University of Kansas School of Business. In 1968 Levinson moved to the Harvard Business School and established a separate institute to conduct the seminars he had originated in Topeka. Over time, the Harvard Business School appointment tapered off, but there were also teaching stints at Boston University and Pace University in the business area. The one stable factor over the years has been the Levinson Institute, with various locations in the Boston area, and its programs. Toward the latter part of his career, Levinson was employed at the Harvard Medical School; he is now emeritus from there.

Beginning in the latter half of the 1950s Levinson began to publish extensively — books for a managerial audience, articles for that same audience, and, most notably, a stream of articles in the *Harvard Business Review* that extend into the 1990s. Of these, "On Being a Middle Manager" (Levinson, 1969), "What Killed Bob Lyons" (Levinson, 1963, 1981), and "When Executives Burn Out" (Levinson, 1981b, 1996) have proven particularly noteworthy. A number of his books represent compilations of articles that were originally published elsewhere.

Major Contributions

In Levinson (1993b) the author sets forth a list of what he considers to be his major contributions. These eight provide a framework for this presentation:

1. Recasting psychoanalytic theory, as it was evolving, into forms that could be used by lay people and professionals in working with organizations
2. Conceptualizing the ego ideal / self-image relationship
3. Evolving a diagnostic process to provide a systematic way of studying organizations
4. Developing a model for teaching consultation

5. Integrating the concepts of motivation in management under a psychoanalytic umbrella
6. Developing the concept of executive as teacher
7. Advancing the concepts of ministration, maturation, and mastery as three stages in development
8. Giving meaning to the psychological contract in its unconscious form

These contributions vary in their degree of attention to theoretical concerns, but we will touch on all of them to some extent.

Recasting Psychoanalytic Theory

Levinson has published relatively little in the scholarly literature, and what there is has been almost entirely in the form of book reviews or articles in medical journals. His major interest was in interpreting various organizational phenomena in psychoanalytic terms and in explaining psychoanalytic theory to lay people, mostly managers. His intended audience determined his communication mediums—his seminars and the more popular publication sources.

Good examples of the recasting or popularizing of psychoanalytic theory are Levinson (1964) and Levinson (1987); both of these are authentic presentations. Levinson (1992) contains a recasting aimed at helping people make career decisions. Also noteworthy are Levinson (1970), which deals with executive stress, and the two editions (although titled differently)—*The Exceptional Executive* (Levinson, 1968) and *Executive* (Levinson, 1981a), both of which contain considerable new theory, as well as some recasting of psychoanalytic theory in general.

The Ego Ideal / Self-Image Relationship

The ego ideal is a component of the superego, which is comparable to our conscience except that unconscious factors may be involved. This ego ideal—a critical element in motivation—is the internal image of oneself at one's future best toward which a person is always striving (Levinson, 1974, 1992). People also have a self-image, a view of themselves at a given time, which is usually some distance from the ego ideal. The larger the gap between ego ideal and self-image, the lower the self-esteem and the greater the feeling of self-criticism, internally directed anger, and inadequacy. This process may be depicted as follows:

$$\text{Self-Esteem} = \frac{1}{\text{Ego Ideal} - \text{Self-Image}}$$

When the gap here is large, people experience very unpleasant depression, and they are motivated to close the gap in some way. Money, supervision, time, and types of work have significance for people only as they relate to the ego ideal. The stress that comes from low self-esteem can drive achievement (to match the ego ideal), but it can also lead to self-destruction. Drastic changes at work can threaten self-esteem, yielding helplessness and depression. When people are angry with themselves because the gap is too large, they are likely to spill their aggression over into their work. Changes and crises produce this.

Finally, the ego ideal of the leader becomes an important social anchor for the followers. Adults identify with a leader just as, when children, they did with their parents. Leaders are thus transference figures; they are reacted to as if they were parents. Accordingly, their ego ideals, as exhibited in their behavior, have a strong influence on those who work for them (Levinson, 1981a).

A Diagnostic Process for Organizations

Levinson (1972) presents a framework for organizational diagnosis that grew out of a multiyear case study of the Kansas Power and Light Company early in his career. This study used clinical and anthropological methods. The recommended steps in organizational diagnosis are as follows:

1. Obtain a detailed organizational history that considers the forces acting on the organization over time, as well as its characteristic adaptive patterns and modes for coping with crises.
2. Produce a description of the organization, including its structure, physical facilities, people, finances, practices, procedures, policies, values, technologies, and the context in which the organization operates.
3. Develop an interpretation of observations, interviews, questionnaires, and other data about the organization's characteristic ways of receiving, processing, and acting upon information, as well as about the personality characteristics of the dominant organizational figures and organizational personality style.
4. Summarize and interpret all these findings with a diagnostic formulation.

5. Write and present a feedback report to the organization to establish a basis for organizational action aimed at solving existing problems; this report should be presented at the top first and then at lower levels.

Levinson (1973) clearly distinguishes this approach from organizational development, about which he has serious misgivings. He feels that any such change procedure requires a comprehensive theory of personality (psychoanalysis) and a range of interventions from which choices, based on a comprehensive diagnosis, can be made. Neither of these features characterized the organizational development of the time, which was strongly committed to sensitivity training and encounter techniques.

Teaching Consultation

The preceding says a good deal about Levinson's approach to consultation. Teaching consulting skills is not a basic theoretical matter, and, accordingly, this particular contribution will receive relatively little attention. However, a good example is provided in an article that deals with consulting to a family business faced with succession problems (Levinson, 1983). The article emphasizes the deep complexities of the family business, the multiple rivalries, the difficulty of family secrets, and the displacement of hostilities from generation to generation. The ideal is for the consultant to establish trust in the process of carrying out individual diagnostic interviews with the cast of characters, and then to bring the family together, as in a family therapy model. Yet Levinson is not optimistic about the chances for success in these situations; issues of intense rivalry over years can easily splinter the family group and defeat problem-solving efforts.

Integrating Concepts of Motivation

The problem with the carrot and stick formulations that have dominated motivation theorizing is that they unconsciously assume that people are jackasses to be manipulated and controlled (Levinson, 1973). Thus the reward-punishment model provokes an automatic resistance to management's messages. People tend to avoid, evade, escape, deny, and reject both the jackass assumption and the military style hierarchy that is its instrument.

Starting from this position Levinson dichotomizes theories of motivation into outside or environmental types of theory (e.g., Watson and Skinner), where behavior is shaped by forces outside the self, and inside types (e.g., Freud and Piaget), where people unfold and develop from biologically based givens. These positions and their consequences are noted in table 6.5. In the column headed "major work role," the alternatives are self-explanatory, except for "involvement," which means that people are engaged in joint problem solving. In the column headed "organization structures," note that organizations that are designed to render services or solve problems require more coordination and mutual interaction, as in project and matrix structures. In the column headed "ethos," "economic man" implies rationality and being motivated by money, "social man" adds in a role for social relationships, and "self-actualizing man" emphasizes actualization of potential and reduced power differentials, but all are based on reward-punishment concepts of motivation. In discussing the latter type of theory Levinson mentions McGregor, Argyris, Likert, Blake and Mouton, Herzberg, and Maslow. Although he recognizes some value in these views, he chides them for failing to understand individual differences and to adopt a systematic theory of personality.

"Psychological man," in contrast, is based on a comprehensive psychoanalytic view. People pass through stages of development and interact with their environment. An ego ideal evolves, toward which an individual strives; this is the most powerful motivating force. To attain the ego ideal, a person must manage drives of sex and aggression and the feelings and wishes derived from them — love, hate, dependency, and mastery of their environment. Organizations tend to recapitulate the family structure, and members evolve conscious and unconscious contracts with them to maintain their psychological equilibria. Leadership and power are a reality. Bureaucracy per se is neither good nor bad. Leaders serve in a father figure role. Much of this analysis flies in the face of behavioral humanism, which flourished in the same period. Yet Levinson sees his conception of psychological man as an integration of all the foregoing types of theories — economic man, social man, and self-actualizing man.

Executive as Teacher

Throughout his career Levinson (1964, 1981, 1989, 1992) has given substantial attention to the teaching role of managers and the learning role of those who

TABLE 6.5 Schematic of approaches to understanding people at work

Theory of motivation	Major work role	Organization structure	Ethos	Advocates
Outside	Laborer, artisan	Families, kinship systems	Economic man	Managers, economists, industrial engineers
	Machine tender	Bureaucratic	Social man	Mayo; human relations school
Inside	Service	Project, matrix	Self-actualizing man	Neo-Lewinians, humanistic psychologists, organizational sociologists
Inside-outside	Involvement	Multiform	Psychological man	Psychoanalytically trained psychologists and psychiatrists

SOURCE: Harry Levinson (1973), *The Great Jackass Fallacy* (Boston: Graduate School of Business Administration, Harvard University), 32. Copyright 1976. Reprinted with permission.

work for them. This means an emphasis on coaching, counseling, teaching, supporting, providing an opportunity to talk about feelings of rivalry and disappointment, and to ventilate anger and jealousy. Basically this is a normative concept—managers should teach—and as parent figures they should provide an identification source and an ego ideal to be emulated. This is how leaders develop, thus meeting the needs of organizations and society. Positive transference from the parent-child relationship to the boss-subordinate one facilitates learning and development.

Part of a manager's teaching role is to deal with ineffective performance in a subordinate, as discussed in chapter 5 in connection with the presentation of role motivation theory. Managers also need to protect against the possibility that they might serve as a cause of ineffective performance. In many cases it will be necessary to shape the behavior of a subordinate, in a sense following the inherent grain of the person and helping the person attain a refinement that would otherwise not be possible; this means finding real strengths and encouraging them. Mentoring serves a similar purpose in providing a particular kind of role model.

Ministration, Maturation, and Mastery

Content needs and motives of various kinds are given considerable attention in the theories of this chapter. Levinson is no exception. His 1981 treatment of his views on this score is comprehensive, but there are other treatments elsewhere in his writings as well.

Ministration needs call for someone else to do something for a person and are in many respects related to dependency. They are often at the core of a member's relationship to an organization. Included are the more specific needs for gratification, closeness, support, protection, and guidance. These needs start in infancy but extend through adult life. Leaders, supervisors, and managers need to take steps to fulfill needs of this kind for subordinates. Among others, Rensis Likert (1961) has given particular attention to the need for support.

Maturation needs imply that a person has the potential for development and expansion. Given the right circumstances—a congenial climate, adequate nourishment, and protection against inhibiting external factors—they will evolve naturally. They serve to prevent intellectual and competitive scrawniness. People have a natural tendency toward growth, learning, and problem solving. Stimulating people to these activities requires conditions that foster creativity or fruitful spontaneity. Creative acts involve a combination of primary process (the primitive and nonlogical, which occurs in dreams and fantasies) and secondary process (the logical, orderly, and analytical thinking that emanates from the ego). The task for management is to prevent the "dampening down" process that inhibits such a fruitful combination. This is an active leadership process; it is not necessarily fostered by democratic management, and certainly not by the kind that views a leader with any strength as anathema.

When both ministration and maturation needs have been adequately met at each step of development, the conditions are established for the gratification of mastery needs. Each person must master enough of his or her world to survive in it. Ego development of this kind is beneficial to both individual and organization. The greater the sense of mastery people have in an organization, the more flexible they are, the more uninhibited and innovative they become, and the less they are threatened by change. Mastery needs include the need for ambitious striving, for realistic achievement, for rivalry with affection, and for consolidation. Consolidation means integration of the personality. The problem with contemporary personality theories (and organizational behavior, too) is that they consider only bits and pieces of a person. It is a strength of psychoanalysis that it permits a more comprehensive treatment and emphasizes integration and consolidation.

Psychological Contract

Levinson's views on the psychological contract between organizations and their members stem from the early studies at Kansas Power and Light Company (Levinson, Price, Munden, Mandl, & Solley, 1962; Price & Levinson, 1964). People unconsciously choose organizations to meet their psychological needs and to support their psychological defenses. These differ from person to person. Similarly, organizations have various, often unspecified, needs. The implicit contract that results is subject to frequent renegotiation, which, in turn, is the basis for effective superior-subordinate relationships. Levinson has developed a questionnaire to measure the degree to which this contract is being fulfilled.

This psychological contract is strongly influenced by the ego ideal. It specifies the kinds of needs and expectancies people bring to an organization and unconsciously expect it to fulfill. Thus some people will expect rigid and authoritarian supervisors if that is the type of family structure they have experienced; others will expect the opposite. Expectations of this kind relate to the way the organization handles dependency needs and provides job security, the extent to which psychological distance is maintained (involving affection, privacy, and control), and the way in which concerns about change are met. When the psychological contract is fulfilled, and reciprocation operates, good mental health tends to be present. When this is not the case, outright hostility, sabotage, accidents, turnover, and physical symptoms are likely.

Psychological Factors in Corporate Failure

Subsequent to his 1993 listing of his major contributions Levinson (1994) added one more. This relates to the failure of American corporations to adapt to changing world economic circumstances in recent years. Some companies have merged, some have downsized, some have disappeared, but overall there has been a massive managerial debacle. Within role motivation theory, this phenomenon is traced to a decline in motivation to manage, which has permeated management at all levels (Miner, Ebrahimi, & Wachtel, 1995). Levinson, however, places greater emphasis on managerial failures at the very top level. His argument is not for less leadership, more participation, and perhaps a degree of laissez-faire. Rather, he has consistently emphasized the importance of strong leadership at the top, especially in organizations that must undergo significant change (Levinson & Rosenthal, 1984). Levinson starts with several psychological verities:

1. All organizations recapitulate the family structure.
2. Human beings differentiate themselves into in-groups and out-groups, and they develop an in-group narcissism.
3. All organizations have developmental histories and evolve adaptive patterns to deal with complexity.
4. Humans experience continuous change and experience change as loss; loss must be mourned if the depressive feelings that result are not to retard adaptation.
5. All groups follow a leader, and often the founding leader's policies, practices, and structures endure.

He then notes that the troubled companies have been significantly family companies, tended to promote from within, became significantly narcissistic, lacked a chief executive who can cope with increasingly complex information, and had chief executives who were unable to take psychological factors seriously into account. The organizations-as-family often did things to maximize dependency. Chief executives viewed themselves as brothers to a set of siblings in the executive suite and so could not take hostile action against them out of guilt and an unconscious inhibition against fratricide. Having encouraged dependency, chief executives could not elicit competitive postures from these dependent people. Changes from what a predecessor had established were viewed as an indictment of the predecessor and thus were approached with reluctance. Overvaluing themselves and deluded by self-satisfied thinking, chief executives developed condescending contempt for competitors and critics; denial is the handmaiden of narcissism. Narcissism of this kind can become inflated to the point where it is destructive. The change that does occur creates feelings of loss and depression, both of which become an anchor that drags on organizational innovation. Many chief executives are simply not able conceptually to meet the challenges they face.

It is out of these kinds of phenomena that Levinson builds his case for the failure of many top executives and their firms. It is an impressive case. A further discussion of the requirements of executive leadership, which in many respects extends this analysis of corporate failure, is contained in Levinson (1998).

Evaluation and Impact

The scientific status of Levinson's formulations presents some major problems. Reviews of scientific research on Freudian psychoanalysis go back a long way (see Sears, 1942, 1944). Even then there clearly was a body of research to review. There have been many studies and reviews since. Although not overly sympathetic to controlled research of this kind, Levinson does cite several publications that he views as giving support to psychoanalytic theory (Silverman, 1976; Leak & Christopher, 1982). The conclusion has to be that different components of psychoanalytic theory have been supported to varying degrees. We are not dealing with an all or none situation. For a good, up-to-date review of the evidence in this regard, see Drew Westen (1998). Yet even if the support were universal, that would not necessarily validate Levinson's version of the theory as applied to organizations. That theory contains new formulations and extensions.

Levinson has not conducted research beyond a few investigations of a theory-forming, anthropological nature. However, he has carried out a number of case analyses, and he has created measures that could be used in research. For reasons that are not entirely clear, his ideas have not stimulated others to conduct research on them; perhaps this is because the procedures that would be involved are more germane to clinical psychology than to organizational behavior.

In his writings Levinson appears to appeal more to personal experience than to scientific research. In this respect, certain of his views come closer to philosophy than to science. Yet in building on the framework of long-standing psychoanalytic theorizing, he uses such concepts as unconscious motivation, the superego, and ego development, all of which appear to have considerable scientific justification. For many people his concepts are appealing, his ideas are logically convincing (once the premises of psychoanalytic theory are accepted), and his hypotheses provide a wealth of material for further investigation. Many of us who have a familiarity with personality theory and psychoanalysis find here a great deal that makes inherent sense.

Yet that next step — the move to scientific research — has not been taken. We do not know what it would reveal. And that remains a major problem. One cannot help but wonder, now, if it ever will be taken. Levinson's most recent writing deals with retirement and the problems of adapting to it, but characteristically research on the subject is not included (Levinson & Wofford, 2000). This lack of concern with research tends to be generally characteristic of psychoanalytic writings on organizations by those other than Levinson (see Gabriel, 1999).

CONCLUSIONS

The theories considered in this chapter deal with content motives, classified in various ways. Overall, the conclusion appears to be that individual differences in the motives possessed are more characteristic than static patterns. Maslow would have argued otherwise, but his approach did not prevail. What we have, then, is a wide range of specific motives that may prove important in organizational behavior; these motives extend from self-actualization to achievement motivation to the pull of the ego ideal, and to many other motives in between. We also have a number of views as to how these motives operate and how organizations should deal with them. Although some of this theorizing ends by supporting a type of behavioral humanism, this approach is by no means universal. Need hierarchy theory does, but role motivation and achievement motivation theory are essentially neutral on this score (although they recognize bureaucracy), and psychoanalytic theory applied to organizations is on occasion quite negative.

In chapter 7 we will consider several theories that appear to more closely approximate need hierarchy theory in this regard. They, too, are rooted in personality theory, but they focus on job enrichment, a procedure that is intended to give employees a greater role in their work. Thus, we continue the discussion of personality-oriented approaches to motivation into the next chapter. At that point we will be in a better position to summarize the personality-based approach to motivation in organizational behavior.

References

Alderfer, Clayton P. (1972). *Existence, Relatedness, and Growth: Human Needs in Organizational Settings.* New York: Free Press.

Alderfer, Clayton P., & Guzzo, Richard A. (1979). Life Experiences and Adults' Enduring Strength of Desires in Organizations. *Administrative Science Quarterly, 24,* 347–361.

Alderfer, Clayton P.; Kaplan, Robert E.; & Smith, Ken K. (1974). The Effect of Variations in Relatedness Need Satisfaction on Relatedness Desires. *Administrative Science Quarterly, 19,* 507–532.

Athey, Timothy R., & Orth, Michael S. (1999). Emerging Competency Methods for the Future. *Human Resource Management, 38,* 215–226.

Atkinson, John W. (1977). Motivation for Achievement. In T. Blass (Ed.), *Personality Variables in Social Behavior* (pp. 25–108). Hillsdale, NJ: Erlbaum.

Atkinson, John W. (1982). Old and New Conceptions of How Expected Consequences Influence Actions. In Norman T. Feather (Ed.), *Expectations and Actions: Expectancy-Value Models in Psychology* (pp. 17–52). Hillsdale, NJ: Erlbaum.

Atkinson, John W., & Feather, Norman T. (1966). *A Theory of Achievement Motivation.* New York: Wiley.

Atkinson, John W., & McClelland, David C. (1948). The Projective Expression of Needs: II. The Effect of Different Intensities of the Hunger Drive on Thematic Apperception. *Journal of Experimental Psychology, 38,* 643–658.

Atkinson, John W., & Raynor, Joel O. (1974). *Motivation and Achievement.* New York: Wiley.

Baum, J. Robert; Locke, Edwin A.; & Kirkpatrick, Shelley A. (1998). A Longitudinal Study of the Relation of Vision and Vision Communication to Venture Growth in Entrepreneurial Firms. *Journal of Applied Psychology, 83,* 43–54.

Betz, Ellen L. (1982). Need Fulfillment in the Career Development of Women. *Journal of Vocational Behavior, 20,* 53–66.

Briscoe, Jon P., & Hall, Douglas T. (1999). Grooming and Picking Leaders Using Competency Frameworks: Do They Work? An Alternative Approach and New Guidelines for Practice. *Organizational Dynamics, 28*(2), 37–52.

Clark, James V. (1960). Motivation in Work Groups: A Tentative View. *Human Organization, 13,* 199–208.

Cornelius, Edwin T. (1983). The Use of Projective Techniques in Personnel Selection. *Research in Personnel and Human Resources Management, 1,* 127–168.

deCharms, Richard, & Moeller, Gerald H. (1962). Values Expressed in American Children's Readers: 1800–1950. *Journal of Abnormal and Social Psychology, 64,* 136–142.

Freud, Sigmund (1938). *The Basic Writings of Sigmund Freud* (transl. and ed. A. A. Brill). New York: Random House.

Gabriel, Yiannis (1999). *Organizations in Depth: The Psychoanalysis of Organizations.* Thousand Oaks, CA: Sage.

Heckhausen, Heinz (1967). *The Anatomy of Achievement Motivation.* New York: Academic Press.

Hoffman, Edward (1999). *The Right to Be Human: A Biography of Abraham Maslow.* New York: McGraw-Hill.

Hogan, Robert T. (1991). Personality and Personality Measurement. In Marvin D. Dunnette & Leaetta M. Hough (Eds.), *Handbook of Industrial and Organizational Psychology* (Vol. 2, pp. 873–919). Palo Alto, CA: Consulting Psychologists Press.

House, Robert J., & Aditya, Ram N. (1997). The Social Scientific Study of Leadership: Quo Vadis? *Journal of Management, 23,* 409–473.

House, Robert J.; Spangler, William D.; & Woycke, James (1991). Personality and Charisma in the U.S. Presidency: A Psychological Theory of Leader Effectiveness. *Administrative Science Quarterly, 36,* 364–396.

Huizinga, Gerard (1970). *Maslow's Need Hierarchy in the Work Situation.* Groningen, the Netherlands: Wolters, Noordhoff.

Jones, Ernest (1953, 1955, 1957). *The Life and Work of Sigmund Freud,* Vol. 1–3. New York: Basic Books.

Kanfer, Ruth, & Heggestad, Eric D. (1997). Motivational Traits and Skills: A Person-Centered Approach to Work Motivation. *Research in Organizational Behavior, 19,* 1–56.

Landy, Frank J., & Becker, Wendy S. (1987). Motivation Theory Reconsidered. *Research in Organizational Behavior, 9,* 1–38.

Langan-Fox, Janice, & Roth, Susanna (1995). Achievement Motivation and Female Entrepreneurs. *Jour-*

nal of Occupational and Organizational Psychology, 68, 209–218.

Leak, Gary K., & Christopher, Steven B. (1982). Freudian Psychoanalysis and Sociobiology. American Psychologist, 37, 313–322.

Levinson, Harry (1963, 1981). What Killed Bob Lyons. Harvard Business Review, 59(2), 144–162.

Levinson, Harry (1964). Emotional Health in the World of Work. New York: Harper & Row.

Levinson, Harry (1968). The Exceptional Executive: A Psychological Conception. Cambridge, MA: Harvard University Press.

Levinson, Harry (1969). On Being a Middle Manager. Harvard Business Review, 47(4), 51–60.

Levinson, Harry (1970). Executive Stress. New York: Harper & Row.

Levinson, Harry (1972). Organizational Diagnosis. Cambridge, MA: Harvard University Press.

Levinson, Harry (1973). The Great Jackass Fallacy. Boston: Graduate School of Business Administration, Harvard University.

Levinson, Harry (1974). On the Motivation of Individuals. In Joseph W. McGuire (Ed.), Contemporary Management: Issues and Viewpoints (pp. 570–574). Englewood Cliffs, NJ: Prentice Hall.

Levinson, Harry (1981a). Executive. Cambridge, MA: Harvard University Press.

Levinson, Harry (1981b, 1996). When Executives Burn Out. Harvard Business Review, 74(4), 153–163.

Levinson, Harry (1983). Consulting with Family Businesses: What to Look For, What to Look Out For. Organizational Dynamics, 12(1), 71–80.

Levinson, Harry (1987). Psychoanalytic Theory in Organizational Behavior. In Jay W. Lorsch (Ed.), Handbook of Organizational Behavior (pp. 51–61). Englewood Cliffs, NJ: Prentice Hall.

Levinson, Harry (1989). Designing and Managing Your Career. Boston: Harvard Business School Press.

Levinson, Harry (1992). Career Mastery. San Francisco: Berrett-Koehler.

Levinson, Harry (1993a). Award for Distinguished Professional Contribution. American Psychologist, 48, 355–356.

Levinson, Harry (1993b). Teacher as Leader. In Arthur G. Bedeian (Ed.), Management Laureates: A Collection of Autobiographic Essays (Vol. 2, pp. 179–214). Greenwich, CT: JAI Press.

Levinson, Harry (1994). Why the Behemoths Fell: Psychological Roots of Corporate Failure. American Psychologist, 49, 428–436.

Levinson, Harry (1998). A Clinical Approach to Executive Selection. In Richard Jeanneret & Rob Silzer (Eds.), Individual Psychological Assessment: Predicting Behavior in Organizational Settings (pp. 228–242). San Francisco: Jossey-Bass.

Levinson, Harry; Price, Charlton R.; Munden, Kenneth J.; Mandl, Harold J.; & Solley, Charles M. (1962). Men, Management, and Mental Health. Cambridge, MA: Harvard University Press.

Levinson, Harry, & Rosenthal, Stuart (1984). CEO: Corporate Leadership in Action. New York: Basic Books.

Levinson, Harry, & Wofford, Jerry C. (2000). Approaching Retirement as the Flexibility Phase. Academy of Management Executive, 14(2), 84–95.

Likert, Rensis (1961). New Patterns of Management. New York: McGraw-Hill.

Litwin, George H., & Siebrecht, Adrienne (1967). Integrators and Entrepreneurs: Their Motivation and Effect on Management. Hospital Progress, 48(9), 67–71.

Locke, Edwin A., & Henne, Douglas (1986). Work Motivation Theories. International Review of Industrial and Organizational Psychology, 1, 1–35.

Maslow, Abraham H. (1942). The Social Personality Inventory: A Test of Self-esteem in Women. Palo Alto, CA: Consulting Psychologists Press.

Maslow, Abraham H. (1943a). Preface to Motivation Theory. Psychosomatic Medicine, 5, 85–92.

Maslow, Abraham H. (1943b). A Theory of Human Motivation. Psychological Review, 50, 370–396.

Maslow, Abraham H. (1951). The S-I Test. Palo Alto, CA: Consulting Psychologists Press.

Maslow, Abraham H. (1954, 1970). Motivation and Personality. New York: Harper & Row.

Maslow, Abraham H. (1962, 1968). Toward a Psychology of Being. Princeton, NJ: Van Nostrand.

Maslow, Abraham H. (1965). Eupsychian Management. Homewood, IL: Irwin.

Maslow, Abraham H. (1967). A Theory of Metamotivation: The Biological Rooting of the Value Life. Journal of Humanistic Psychology, 7, 93–127.

Maslow, Abraham H. (1969). Toward a Humanistic Biology. American Psychologist, 24, 724–735.

Maslow, Abraham H. (1987). Motivation and Personality (ed. Robert Frager, James Fadiman, Cynthia McReynolds, & Ruth Cox). New York: Harper & Row.

McClelland, David C. (1961). The Achieving Society. Princeton, NJ: Van Nostrand.

McClelland, David C. (1962). Business Drive and National Achievement. Harvard Business Review, 40(4), 99–112.

McClelland, David C. (1965a). Achievement Motivation Can Be Developed. Harvard Business Review, 43(6), 3–20.

McClelland, David C. (1965b). Toward a Theory of Motive Acquisition. *American Psychologist*, 20, 321–333.

McClelland, David C. (1966). Does Education Accelerate Economic Growth? *Economic Development and Cultural Change*, 14, 257–278.

McClelland, David C. (1973). Testing for Competency Rather than Intelligence. *American Psychologist*, 28, 1–14.

McClelland, David C. (1975). *Power: The Inner Experience*. New York: Irvington.

McClelland, David C. (1984). *Motives, Personality, and Society: Selected Papers*. New York: Praeger.

McClelland, David C. (1985). How Motives, Skills, and Values Determine What People Do. *American Psychologist*, 40, 812–825.

McClelland, David C. (1994). The Knowledge-Testing-Educational Complex Strikes Back. *American Psychologist*, 49, 66–69.

McClelland, David C. (1998). Identifying Competence with Behavioral-Event Interviews. *Psychological Science*, 9, 331–339.

McClelland, David C.; Atkinson, John W.; Clark, Russell A.; & Lowell, Edgar L. (1953). *The Achievement Motive*. New York: Appleton-Century-Crofts.

McClelland, David C., & Boyatzis, Richard E. (1982). Leadership Motive Pattern and Long-Term Success in Management. *Journal of Applied Psychology*, 67, 737–743.

McClelland, David C., & Burnham, David H. (1976, 1995). Power Is the Great Motivator. *Harvard Business Review*, 73(1), 126–139.

McClelland, David C.; Davis, William N.; Kalin, Rudolph; & Wanner, Eric (1972). *The Drinking Man: Alcohol and Human Motivation*. New York: Free Press.

McClelland, David C., & Winter, David G. (1969). *Motivating Economic Achievement*. New York: Free Press.

Miner, John B. (1993). *Role Motivation Theories*. London: Routledge.

Miner, John B.; Ebrahimi, Bahman; & Wachtel, Jeffrey M. (1995). How Deficiencies in Motivation to Manage Contribute to the United States' Competitiveness Problem (and What Can Be Done about It). *Human Resource Management*, 34, 363–387.

Miron, David, & McClelland, David C. (1979). The Impact of Achievement Motivation Training on Small Business. *California Management Review*, 21(4), 13–28.

Murray, Henry A. (1938). *Explorations in Personality: A Clinical and Experimental Study of Fifty Men of College Age*. New York: Oxford University Press.

Price, Charlton R., & Levinson, Harry (1964). Work and Mental Health. In Arthur B. Shostak & William

Gomberg (Eds.), *Blue Collar World: Studies of the American Worker* (pp. 397–405). Englewood Cliffs, NJ: Prentice Hall.

Rauschenberger, John; Schmitt, Neal; & Hunter, John E. (1980). A Test of the Need Hierarchy Concept by a Markov Model of Change in Need Strength. *Administrative Science Quarterly*, 25, 654–670.

Roe, Anne (1956). *The Psychology of Occupations*. New York: Wiley.

Sears, Robert R. (1942). *Survey of Objective Studies of Psychoanalytic Concepts*. New York: Social Science Research Council.

Sears, Robert R. (1944). Experimental Analysis of Psychoanalytic Phenomena. In J. McVicker Hunt (Ed.), *Personality and the Behavior Disorders* (pp. 306–332). New York: Ronald.

Segall, Marshall H. (1986). Culture and Behavior: Psychology in Global Perspective. *Annual Review of Psychology*, 37, 523–564.

Silverman, Lloyd H. (1976). Psychoanalytic Theory: The Reports of My Death Are Greatly Exaggerated. *American Psychologist*, 31, 621–637.

Spangler, William D. (1992). Validity of Questionnaire and TAT Measures of Need for Achievement: Two Meta-Analyses. *Psychological Bulletin*, 112, 140–154.

Spence, Janet T. (1983). *Achievement and Achievement Motives: Psychological and Sociological Approaches*. San Francisco: W. H. Freeman.

Spencer, Lyle M., & Spencer, Signe M. (1993). *Competence at Work: Models for Superior Performance*. New York: Wiley.

Stein, Morris I. (1948). *The Thematic Apperception Test: An Introductory Manual for Its Clinical Use with Adult Males*. Cambridge, MA: Addison-Wesley.

Thornton, Frances; Privette, Gayle; & Bundrick, Charles M. (1999). Peak Performance of Business Leaders: An Experience Parallel to Self-Actualization Theory. *Journal of Business and Psychology*, 14, 253–264.

Tomkins, Silvan S. (1947). *The Thematic Apperception Test: The Theory and Technique of Interpretation*. New York: Grune & Stratton.

Triplet, Rodney G. (1992). Henry A. Murray — The Making of a Psychologist? *American Psychologist*, 47, 299–307.

Veroff, Joseph, & Veroff, Joanne B. (1972). Reconsideration of a Measure of Power Motivation. *Psychological Bulletin*, 78, 279–291.

Wanous, John P.. & Zwany, Abram (1977). A Cross-Sectional Test of Need Hierarchy Theory. *Organizational Behavior and Human Performance*, 18, 78–97.

Weiner, Bernard (1972). *Theories of Motivation: From Mechanism to Cognition*. Chicago: Markham.

Weiner, Bernard (1982). An Attributionally Based Theory

of Motivation and Emotion: Focus, Range, and Issues. In Norman T. Feather (Ed.), *Expectations and Actions: Expectancy-Value Models in Psychology* (pp. 163–204). Hillsdale, NJ: Erlbaum.

Westen, Drew (1998). The Scientific Legacy of Sigmund Freud: Toward a Psychodynamically Informed Psychological Science. *Psychological Bulletin*, 124, 333–371.

Winter, David G. (1973). *The Power Motive*. New York: Free Press.

Winter, David G. (1991). A Motivational Model of Leadership: Predicting Long-Term Management Success from TAT Measures of Power Motivation and Responsibility. *Leadership Quarterly*, 2, 67–80.

Winter, David G. (2000). David C. McClelland (1917–1998). *American Psychologist*, 55, 540–541.

Chapter 7

Motivation Theories That Relate to Job Enrichment

Job enrichment as such appears to have begun with a project initiated at IBM in the mid-1940s (Walker, 1962). At that time the approach was called job enlargement, and it included both adding tasks to a job horizontally (strictly speaking, job enlargement) and adding requirements for greater skill and judgment, thus enriching the job vertically. The intent even at this early point was to introduce more interest, variety, and significance into the work.

This approach spread within IBM and eventually to other companies. It arose out of practical concerns and initially was devoid of theory. Scientific management had produced a simplification of many manufacturing jobs, with the result that both the content and the skills required shrunk. It was only natural that the cycle would swing back the other way eventually. Yet theorists and advocates with strong humanist values flocked to job enrichment quickly. They saw their work in this field as reversing what they regarded as the dysfunctional application of Taylorism (Yorks & Whitsett, 1989). During the 1960s this groundswell built to the point where demonstration projects seemed to be everywhere, and significant theories to guide the new practices emerged (Hackman, 1975). By the early 1970s job enrichment was being endorsed as a solution to the country's productivity problems by the U.S. Department of Health, Education and Welfare (1972).

This chapter deals with the two major theoretical positions that emerged to support and refine the originally atheoretical practice of job enrichment. Both these theories had ties to need hierarchy theory, and strong roots in personality theory. They are motivation-hygiene theory, which came on the scene first primarily through the efforts of Frederick Herzberg, and job characteristics theory, which was developed in its ultimate form by Richard Hackman and Greg Oldham at a somewhat later date.

MOTIVATION-HYGIENE THEORY

The theory to which we now turn often is referred to as *two-factor theory*, a designation that has its rationale in the dual nature of its approach to the sources of job satisfaction and, ultimately, to job motivation. The prime generator of the theory, Herzberg, prefers the term *motivation-hygiene*; therefore, this designation is used here.

The initial source of the theory appears to be a comprehensive review of the literature on job attitudes and satisfaction that was undertaken by Herzberg and his associates at Psychological Service of Pittsburgh (Herzberg, Mausner, Peterson, & Capwell, 1957). This review revealed often-conflicting results, although with some slight overall tendency for job satisfaction to be positively correlated with job performance levels. To this finding Herzberg added an insight that was derived from his background in the field of mental health—the idea that mental health is not just the obverse of mental illness but, rather, a totally separate process. He developed the hypothesis that a similar discontinuity exists in the field of job satisfaction (Herzberg, 1976). Subsequent research produced a list of factors that contribute to satisfaction at work (motivation factors) and another separate list of factors that contribute to dissatisfaction (hygiene factors). Thus, the theory is an amalgam of deductive and inductive components so closely intertwined with the early research that the two cannot be separated effectively (Herzberg, Mausner, & Snyderman, 1959).

Background

Herzberg grew up in New York City and enrolled in the City University of New York (CUNY). After service during World War II, in Europe, he completed his undergraduate degree in psychology and moved on to graduate work in the field at the University of Pittsburgh. There he obtained a Ph.D. in clinical psychology, after an internship at Mayview State Hospital and also received a Master of Public Health degree (Herzberg, 1991, 1993). It was at the age of 27, in 1950, that he was awarded the doctorate. In the early 1950s his publications were primarily in the clinical area (the Rorschach test, electroshock therapy, etc.), but during that decade he gradually came to write and work in industrial psychology.

For a while he was employed by John Flanagan, who developed the critical incident technique for job study and performance appraisal, at the American Institutes for Research; later he joined Psychological Service of Pittsburgh. In 1960 he accepted a joint appointment in psychology and in the medical school with Case Western Reserve University in Cleveland. There he wrote on his theory, published several related articles in the *Harvard Business Review*, became heavily involved in consulting and speaking on job enrichment, and headed a graduate program in industrial mental health. Clearly, Herzberg had been very close to the business school boundary for some time, but it was not until 1972 that he crossed it, becoming a professor of management at the University of Utah. He has remained there throughout his career since that time.

Evolution of the Theory

Herzberg is a self-confessed humanist in the tradition of Abraham Maslow. He considers what he calls *motivator needs* to be comparable to the latter's self-actualization. However, he does not accept the prepotency concept, and in this respect he breaks with Maslow (Herzberg, 1993).

Motivation-hygiene theory is presented in three volumes (Herzberg et al., 1959; Herzberg, 1966, 1976). The most recent of these is primarily a compendium of articles that had been published previously, the majority of them in the early 1970s. Although the basics of the theory that were established in 1959 have remained firm, Herzberg has elaborated considerably on them since then.

Motivation to Work

The first volume promulgating the theory also contains a detailed report of the initial research. This research sought to explore two hypotheses:

1. The factors that cause positive job attitudes and those that cause negative attitudes are different.
2. The factors and the performance or personal consequences associated with the sequences of job events that extend over long time periods differ from those associated with sequences of events of short duration.

Based on certain outcomes of this research, the factors leading to job satisfaction and to job dissatisfaction were specified and thus became part of the theory.

Job satisfaction is viewed as an outgrowth of achievement, recognition (verbal), the work itself (challenging), responsibility, and advancement (promotion). These five factors are considered to be closely related, both conceptually and empirically. When they are present in a job, the individual's basic needs will be satisfied, and positive feelings and improved performance will result. The basic needs specified are those related to personal growth and self-actualization, and these are said to be satisfied by the five intrinsic aspects of the work itself.

In contrast, job dissatisfaction results from a different set of factors, all of which characterize the context in which the work is performed. These are company policy and administrative practices, supervision (technical quality), interpersonal relations (especially with supervision), physical working conditions, job security, benefits, and salary. These dissatisfiers, or hygiene factors, when appropriately provided can serve to remove dissatisfaction and improve performance up to a point, but they cannot be relied on to generate really positive job feelings or the high levels of performance that are potentially possible. To accomplish these outcomes, management must shift gears and move into motivation.

This means that although good hygiene should be provided, it will yield benefits only up to a certain point. Beyond that, the focus needs to be on the intrinsic aspects of the work itself, not on its context: "Jobs must be restructured to increase to the maximum the ability of workers to achieve goals meaningfully related to the doing of the job. . . . The individual should have some measure of control over the way in which the job is done in order to realize a sense of achievement and of personal growth" (Herzberg et al., 1959, p. 132).

Just as the Hawthorne studies had shifted concern away from the physical environment and toward the social environment, this view continued to move the field away from interest in the physical environment and toward an emphasis on the effects of the intrinsic nature of the work (Oldham, Cummings, & Zhou, 1995).

Work and the Nature of Man

With the second book, Herzberg (1966) began to add philosophical embellishments to what had been an eminently scientific and testable theory. Thus, the fringe benefits and other hygiene factors provided by large corporations were equated with the welfare state, and the motivation-hygiene distinction was extended beyond the work context through the use of extensive biblical analogies. More specifically, mankind was described as possessing two sets of basic needs — animal needs relating to environmental survival and human needs relating to "the tasks with which he is uniquely involved." The former needs are allied with the notion of mankind as sinful and perpetually condemned to suffer and avoid suffering, as epitomized by Adam's fall. In addition, mankind may be characterized, like Abraham, as a capable being who possesses innate potential and who was created in the image of God.

Herzberg summarizes his expanded position regarding human motivation:

> The human animal has two categories of needs. One set stems from his animal disposition, that side of him previously referred to as the Adam view of man; it is centered on the avoidance of loss of life, hunger, pain, sexual deprivation and in other primary drives, in addition to the infinite varieties of learned fears that become attached to these basic drives. The other segment of man's nature, according to the Abraham concept of the human being, is man's compelling urge to realize his own potentiality by continuous psychological growth. . . . These two characteristics must be constantly viewed as having separate biological, psychological and existential origins. (1966, p. 56)

Although most people are best characterized in terms of both sets of needs, Herzberg also described individuals who are dominated by one set or the other. Thus, there are high growth-oriented people who actually experience what they interpret as unhappiness when they are deprived of motivators, and there are people who are completely fixated on seeking hygiene, such as the mentally ill.

Hygiene seekers are generally considered to be poor risks for a company, because they tend to be motivated over short time periods and require constant doses of external reward; they cannot be relied on in crisis. Furthermore, a lack of motivators in a job tends to sensitize people to any lack of hygiene factors, with the result that more and more hygiene must be provided to obtain the same level of performance. Herzberg emphasizes strongly the need for companies to build motivators into their jobs.

To facilitate this he recommends that industrial relations departments be organized into two formal divisions, one to deal with hygiene matters and the other to deal with motivators. Assuming that most current departments are focused largely on hygiene, he devotes primary attention to what would be added with the division concerned with motivator needs. Among the tasks recommended are reeducation of organization members to a motivator orientation (from the current welfare orientation); job enlargement; and remedial work in the areas of technological obsolescence, poor employee performance, and administrative failure.

Managerial Choice

The third volume that presents motivation-hygiene theory (Herzberg, 1976) places much greater emphasis on job enrichment applications. However, it also extends the theory in several respects.

One such extension uses the two-factor concept to develop typologies of workers. The normal types are described as follows:

1. The person who has both hygiene and motivator fulfillment, who is not unhappy and is also very happy.
2. The person who is on both need systems but has little fulfillment in the hygiene area, even though motivator satisfaction is good. Such a "starving artist" is both unhappy and happy.
3. The person who is also on both need systems but whose satisfactions are reversed — hygienes are good but motivators are poor; such people are not unhappy but neither are they happy.
4. The down and out person who is lacking in fulfillment generally and is both unhappy and lacking in happiness.

To these four, Herzberg adds certain abnormal profiles that characterize people who are not actually on the motivator dimension at all and who attempt to substitute increased hygiene for this motivator deficiency.

Such people may also resort to psychological mechanisms, such as denial of their hygiene needs and fantasied motivator satisfaction, which further compound their hygiene problems. In these pathological instances, an inversion occurs in that fulfillment of hygiene needs may be viewed as satisfying, not merely as an avoidance of dissatisfaction.

A distinction is also made within the motivator factors. Achievement and recognition are described as preparatory in nature and as having, in common with hygiene factors, relatively short-term effects. The work itself, responsibility, and growth and advancement are generators that truly motivate people. In job redesign, these latter factors should be emphasized.

Throughout his writings Herzberg has wrestled with the role of salary. The most frequently stated position is that it is a hygiene factor. Yet there are contradictory statements in the 1976 book, which contains articles published at different times. A 1971 article clearly states, "Money is a hygiene factor" (Herzberg, 1976, p. 305). But in 1974, the following statement appears: "Because of its ubiquitous nature, salary commonly shows up as a motivator as well as hygiene. Although primarily a hygiene factor, it also often takes on some of the properties of a motivator, with dynamics similar to those of recognition for achievement" (Herzberg, 1976, p. 71). It appears that the motivation-hygiene problem created by compensation is very similar to the problem created by power motivation in the development of achievement motivation theory (see chapter 6).

A final point that needs to be made is that Herzberg has gradually become increasingly critical of his fellow social scientists and of alternative theories. His justification is that he was attacked first. Others may well view what he considers attacks as merely the presentation of objective scientific evidence. In any event, Herzberg has resorted to statements such as the following:

> Engrossed with their artificial measures and rarified statistics, social scientists have too long neglected the language and experience of people at work. . . . Their error is attempting to manipulate their instruments to produce a relationship that simply does not reflect the psychological and organizational realities in many companies. (1976, pp. 54–55)

Are such statements attempts to play to the stereotypes of management practitioners, as some have charged, or do they represent valid, scientific criticism? Certainly they reflect the existence of considerable controversy. The answers, though, must be found in an objective evaluation of the research evidence.

Applications to Job Enrichment

From the beginning, Herzberg has advocated restructuring jobs to place greater reliance on motivators. The techniques of this kind that evolved over the years are now designated by the term *orthodox job enrichment*, to differentiate them from similar approaches that do not have their origins in motivation-hygiene theory. Although Herzberg has been a major influence in the development of procedures for job redesign, a great deal has happened in this area that is not attributable either to him or to his theory. Furthermore, his self-designation as the "father of job enrichment" may be only partially correct, since efforts of this kind can be traced back many years, as noted earlier in this chapter.

Process of Orthodox Job Enrichment

Herzberg (1976) makes a strong point that what he is *not* talking about is participative management, socio-technical systems, industrial democracy, or organizational development. Yet there is a marked tendency for a great variety of activities to creep into and become part of a job enrichment effort. By definition, orthodox job enrichment involves the introduction of motivators, not hygienes, into a job. Yet, pay raises and various interpersonal factors have accompanied such efforts on occasion. Accordingly, it is important to understand clearly what is implied by the term.

Herzberg (1976) has identified a number of factors that, although not limited to orthodox job enrichment alone, are primary to the approach:

1. Direct feedback of performance results to the employee in a nonevaluative manner and usually not through a superior. An example would be targets on a rifle range that fall down when hit.
2. The existence of a customer or client, either within or outside the organization, for whom work is performed. The unit assemblers who depend on the outcome of various prior manufacturing operations fit this designation; so do a salesperson's external customers.

3. The opportunity for individuals to feel that they are growing psychologically through new learning that is meaningful. For instance, a laboratory technician may be given a chance to learn many of the skills needed by a research scientist.
4. Being able to schedule one's own work, with requirements set by realistic deadlines. Thus, work breaks might be taken when scheduled by the individual, not by management.
5. Doing the job in one's own unique manner and using time accordingly. For example, individuals who finish their tasks ahead of time can be allowed to use the remaining work periods as they see fit.
6. Providing employees with minibudgets that make them directly responsible for costs. In this way cost and profit centers are pushed down to the lowest possible level, where employees may be authorized to approve expenditures within realistic limits.
7. Communication with the individuals needed to get the job done, regardless of any possible hierarchic constraints. Accordingly, an employee whose work requires discussion with a supervisor in another department would be permitted to do so directly.
8. Maintaining individual accountability for results. For instance, responsibility for quality control may be taken away from a supervisor or external unit and built back into the job.

An indication of what these changes may involve is provided by a job enrichment program that was carried out within a certain sales unit:

1. Reports on each customer call were eliminated. Salespeople were to use their own discretion in passing on information to or making requests of management.
2. Salespeople determined their own calling frequencies and kept records only as might be needed for purposes such as staff reviews.
3. The technical service department agreed to provide service as needed by the individual salesperson. Communication between salesperson and technician was direct, with any needed paperwork cleared after the event.
4. If customers complained about product performance, salespeople could make settlements of up to $250 if they considered it appropriate.
5. When faulty material was delivered or customers proved to have overstocked goods, salespeople could deal with these issues directly, with no limit on sales value of material returned.

6. Salespeople were given a discretionary range of about 10 percent on quoted prices for most items, although quotations other than list prices did have to be reported to management. (Herzberg, 1976)

Results at AT&T

One of the first applications of job enrichment in which Herzberg was directly involved occurred at AT&T (Ford, 1969, 1973). The initial study was conducted in the treasury department among clerical personnel who answer inquiries from AT&T shareholders. Job changes were introduced for certain employees, with the objective of providing greater opportunities for achievement, recognition, responsibility, advancement, and psychological growth. The jobs of other employees remained unchanged. The results are described as follows:

The achieving or experimental group clearly exceeded the control and uncommitted groups on a variety of criteria, such as turnover, the quality of customer service, productivity, lowered costs, lower absence rates, and source of managerial upgrading. . . . Only the experimental group members felt significantly better about the task at which they work. The upward change in this group is most striking. (Ford, 1969, p. 39)

Because of this result, the program was expanded into a variety of departments—commercial, comptroller, plant, traffic, and engineering. In most cases the practice of comparing experimental (enriched job) and control (job not enriched) groups was continued. The overall results were very favorable, although there were instances when job enrichment did not have much effect. Some supervisors clearly resisted it, and 10 to 15 percent of the employees did not want the added responsibility. Blue-collar jobs proved most resistant to enrichment.

Results in the U.S. Air Force

Another program of job enrichment was initiated at Hill Air Force Base in Utah after Herzberg arrived in the state, and then it spread to a number of other installations (Herzberg, 1976, 1977; Herzberg & Zautra, 1976). The enriched jobs varied from aircraft maintenance to routine clerical, and from contract document preparation to foreign military sales. Results obtained with the initial 11 jobs that were changed indicated savings of over $250,000 in a 10-month period. The largest part of this saving occurred in two aircraft maintenance activities; several projects ran into considerable difficulty and did not yield tangible benefits. When tangible benefits were obtained, the return included reduced costs for materials, fuel, and personnel, and increased units of production. When the program was subsequently expanded:

The results were dramatic: a $1.75 million saving in 2 years on 29 projects that had matured to the point where careful auditing of savings was possible. The dollar benefits accrued from reduced sick leave, a lower rate of personnel turnover, less overtime and rework, a reduction in man-hours, and material savings. (Herzberg, 1977, p. 25)

Table 7.1 contains data on reported increases in job satisfaction experienced over 12 months before job enrichment and again during the months of job change. It is apparent that job satisfaction did increase and that all motivators studied, except recognition, also showed an increase. Data on hygiene factors were not obtained.

Evaluation and Impact

It is to Herzberg's credit that he proposed measures of his theoretical variables when the theory was first

TABLE 7.1 Before and after measures of job satisfaction for job enrichment projects

	Reported increase (%)	
Measure	Before enrichment	During enrichment
Overall satisfaction factors	33	76
Recognition for achievement	15	20
Achievement	28	67
Work itself	10	70
Responsibility	15	80
Advancement	23	62
Growth	30	72

SOURCE: Adapted from Frederick Herzberg & Alex Zautra (1976), Orthodox Job Enrichment: Measuring True Quality in Job Satisfaction, *Personnel*, 53(5), 66

presented and that he has conducted research on the theory from the beginning. As might be expected, these circumstances have served to stimulate considerable research by others. The result has been that both Herzberg's measures and his interpretation of his findings have been seriously challenged. To understand what has happened, it is necessary to start with the original research that spawned motivation-hygiene theory (Herzberg et al., 1959).

Original Study

The measurement procedure developed by Herzberg and his associates was a derivative of the critical incident technique that had been used previously by John Flanagan (1954), primarily in the evaluation of job performance. However, while Flanagan asked his subjects to focus on good and bad performance, Herzberg asked for incidents describing "a time when you felt exceptionally good or a time when you felt exceptionally bad about your job, either a long-range sequence of events or a short-range incident." Subjects were requested to provide several such incidents. In each instance a series of probing questions was asked regarding the incident to determine what factors were related to the job attitude expressed; these factors might be either antecedent objective occurrences (first level) or attributed internal reasons for the feelings (second level). Also, the perceived consequences or effects of the attitudes were explored with regard to such matters as job performance, tenure on the job, emotional adjustment, interpersonal relationships, and the like.

The outcome is a set of stories from each subject that specify a sequence of factors to attitudes to effects. These stories are somewhat similar to those elicited using the Thematic Apperception Test (TAT). However, there is no standardized external stimulus such as that provided by the TAT pictures, and a story here is about the subject rather than about someone else. Both of these considerations reduce the psychological distance of the stories and thus increase the degree to which defensiveness may be manifested in them.

In the major study, this procedure was applied to a large sample of accountants and engineers. The content of the stories was analyzed using 39 scoring categories. Agreement between coders was at the 95 percent level. The data indicate that recognition, achievement, responsibility, the work itself, and their related feelings are more commonly associated with job satisfaction than with dissatisfaction. Advancement operates in a similar manner as a first-level factor, but not at the second level. The remaining differences all occur on factors that cannot be measured at both levels. Within this context, group feeling is a satisfier, whereas interpersonal relations with supervisors and peers, technical supervision, company policy and administration, working conditions, and factors in personal life are dissatisfiers. The data for second-level factors also indicate that a feeling of fairness or unfairness is a dissatisfier.

The findings obtained are certainly consistent with the original hypotheses, and they largely fit the theory as it ultimately evolved based on interpretations of this study. Nevertheless, the data yield several factors that emerge equally as satisfiers and dissatisfiers, among them the possibility of growth, salary, and status, as well as feelings of pride and shame. Furthermore, although dissatisfiers rarely yield meaningful frequencies as satisfiers, the reverse is not true. At one level or another, recognition, achievement, advancement, and the work itself all operate as dissatisfiers as well as satisfiers more than 10 percent of the time.

Data on the factors that are associated with long- and short-term event sequences are not presented. The original hypothesis dealing with the differential causes and effects of sequences of job events that extend over long and short time periods appears to have been dropped from the theory; it does not appear in later formulations.

The data on effects stemming from feelings of satisfaction and dissatisfaction are introduced with appropriate qualifications, because of the lack of objective confirmation. Nevertheless, later they are given considerable credence. Reports of satisfaction were associated with reports of positive effects, including improved performance, continued employment, improved attitude toward the company, improved mental health, better interpersonal relationships, and improved morale. In contrast, reports of dissatisfaction were associated with the reverse trends, although the overall results were less pronounced. These results "may be attributed to the unwillingness of some interviewees to admit to doing their jobs less well than usual" (Herzberg et al., 1959, p. 87).

Whatever the merits of this original study and of the interpretation the authors place on it, it is best viewed as an inductive source from which the theory was, if not totally generated, at least specifically delineated in terms of its operative variables. Given this situation, it is best to look to subsequent research for adequate empirical tests.

Closely Allied Research

A number of studies that used the methods of the original research, or minor variants, were conducted in the years immediately following the original work and are summarized by Herzberg (1966) as providing support for his theory. Most of these studies did not consider effects, and a number did not deal with second-level factors. Sequence duration was given practically no attention.

There is no question that when significant results are obtained in these studies they are much more likely to support the theory than refute it. It is also evident that certain of the first-level factors are much more likely to receive support from the data than others. Among the motivators, achievement and recognition are strongly supported, but possibility of growth is not supported at all. Among the hygienes, company policy and administration and also technical supervision are supported, but not salary, status, or job security. The data also indicate that motivators often operate as dissatisfiers instead.

As research has continued using the techniques of the original study, the theory appears to continue to be supported on balance, but certain problems remain. The tendency for motivators to appear frequently as dissatisfiers, as well as satisfiers, represents a continuing difficulty. This tendency to appear in the wrong context is less characteristic of the hygienes, unless (and this clearly does occur) a true reversal is in evidence. Such reversals (or inversions) can apparently appear for salary and the various interpersonal relations factors, and there they can be sizable; they also may appear for status.

In view of Herzberg's own expressed concerns about the findings of the original study dealing with performance and personal effects, and the clear implications of these findings for the motivational as opposed to merely attitudinal hypotheses of the theory, it is surprising that so little research has focused on this area. A study conducted by Donald Schwab, H. William DeVitt, and Larry Cummings (1971), using essentially the same methods as the original research and dealing only with effects in the area of job performance, does serve to amplify the Herzberg findings.

Favorable performance effects were reported often as an outgrowth of satisfying job experiences; to a lesser extent, unfavorable performance effects were associated with dissatisfying experiences. This pattern is consistent with the one originally reported.

One might assume from this result that the introduction of motivators is the key to improving employee performance. However, hygiene factors were occasionally reported as sources of satisfaction, and it was possible to determine in these instances that improved performance effects were reported to as great a degree as those for the motivators. Thus, it would appear that when hygiene factors operate as satisfiers — in this case, primarily interpersonal relations with a supervisor — they may be perceived as a source of performance stimulation just as much as motivators are. Furthermore, when there is dissatisfaction, motivators can have just as negative an effect as hygienes. It is the level of job satisfaction-dissatisfaction that yields the reported performance effect, not the presence of motivators or hygienes.

A study carried out by Herzberg, J. Mathapo, Yoash Wiener, and L. Wiesen (1974) centers on the hypothesis that when hygienes are reported as sources of satisfaction, the inversions are characteristic of the mentally ill. Using the same method as in the previous research, hospitalized mental patients were found to attribute job satisfaction to hygiene factors 36 percent of the time, as contrasted with an average of 19 percent of the time for employed people. Furthermore, the evidence indicates that the frequency of inversions increases with the severity of the disorder. A second study of inversion percentages by the same investigators compared outpatients with varying degrees of diagnosed mental illness who were currently employed. Those with relatively minimal disturbances had an inversion percentage of 15; the more severely disturbed had 27.

The results of these studies are certainly consistent with motivation-hygiene theory, and the research was indeed stimulated by the theory. The research design does not rule out other interpretations of the data, such as the possibility that the mentally ill might easily tolerate and express certain kinds of logical inconsistencies.

Using Alternative Methods

In a number of its aspects, motivation-hygiene theory has received support from research that uses the methods of the original study. Almost from the beginning, however, questions have been raised as to whether these methods might not somehow operate in and of themselves to determine the results; thus, the findings could be a direct consequence of the method per se, not the underlying attitudinal and motivational facts, and therefore they might not be replicable when other methods are used.

Many of the early findings obtained when alternative methods were used were indeed negative for the theory. However, there were problems with these methods as well. As research progressed, many of these problems were overcome. Yet the failure to support motivation-hygiene theory continued. For instance, it appears that satisfaction tends to be more characteristic than dissatisfaction and that both are equally likely to be occasioned by motivators and hygienes. Also, defensiveness appears to be a major factor contributing to the results that were originally obtained with the critical incidents. Robert Kahn (1961) suggested at an early point that these results were contaminated by the fact that respondents supplied information on job attitudes, the factors that occasioned them, *and* their behavioral consequences; the components of the sequence could easily be coordinated to make the person look good. From research that measures defensiveness, as well as from studies that introduce more psychological distance into the measurement process, it now appears that Kahn was right; common method variance does operate.

Current State of the Theory

Motivation-hygiene theory has probably created as much controversy as any theory we will consider. There are several reasons for this, many having little relationship to either the scientific or the managerial usefulness of the theory. This controversy does make objective evaluation more difficult. It has been almost impossible not to be assigned an adversary position if one makes any kind of statement regarding the theory. Yet rational objective evaluation is crucial for both scientific advance and management practice.

The theory has been steadily losing components in subsequent tests and reformulations. Its focus has shifted, and even in the original study, data were collected without the results being reported. Concepts such as long- and short-term sequences, second-level factors, and behavioral outcome effects have virtually disappeared from consideration. Ratings of the strength

of feelings (importance) were included in the original data collection, but only frequency data were reported. By no means can all of this phenomenon of lost concepts be attributed to the major theorist. Yet, somehow, a great deal of the original theory has disappeared; it is no longer tested or even much mentioned. One gets the impression that this is by mutual consent.

This same phenomenon applies to the testing of the theory. The following statement is indicative:

> In an ideal world we would not only have been able to ask people about the times when they felt exceptionally good or bad about their jobs, but also to go out and find people who felt exceptionally good or bad about their job and watch them over long periods. . . . Such observation, especially when carried out by more than one observer to obtain measures of reliability, would be of great value. (Herzberg et al., 1959, p. 19)

Similarly, Kahn (1961) asked for independent measures of environmental factors, job attitudes, and performance criteria. Yet neither Herzberg, nor his advocates, nor his critics have conducted research of the kind these statements imply. Thus, we have to rely on less than ideal data.

The incident technique as used in the original study must be considered most predisposed toward the theory. But even this technique yields certain findings that are inconsistent with that theory. At this level, the problem appears to be not in the overall trend of the data but in the findings for specific factors. Abstractions such as content and context, motivators and hygienes, and the like simply do not hold when one gets closer to specifics. Opportunity for growth, which should be the essence of a self-actualizing motivator, is no more a source of satisfaction than dissatisfaction. Salary, interpersonal relations, status, and security are not just sources of dissatisfaction; they are often equally likely to be sources of satisfaction, and in certain groups some of them may well be predominant sources of satisfaction. Ray Hackman's (1969) reanalysis of the original study data clearly supports these conclusions. Achievement and the work itself also are repeatedly found to be sources of both dissatisfaction and satisfaction.

There is little question that motivation-hygiene theory is most vulnerable on the grounds that its support derives almost entirely from the critical incident method and that this method is subject to influence by defense mechanisms. Short of observational studies and entirely independent measures of variables, the weight of the evidence now clearly favors the interpretation involving defense mechanisms insofar as the hygiene-dissatisfaction part of the theory is concerned. On theoretical grounds, given the very limited projective element in the incident measures and the reduction of psychological distance thus occasioned, one would expect defensiveness to manifest itself, as Kahn (1961) noted; the data from a number of studies that use quite varied research designs support this conclusion.

The self-report data on effects are particularly suspect on such logical grounds. And indeed the limited research that has been focused specifically on this matter raises serious questions as to whether the motivators do produce positive behavioral outcomes and the hygienes negative outcomes. Although the results of research on job enrichment have been invoked in support of the theory's hypotheses regarding performance effects (Herzberg, 1976), it is clear that these results could well be occasioned by other factors and that they apply only to certain of the motivator variables. In a number of areas the theory has great difficulty in dealing with hygiene-dissatisfaction relationships.

It seems that motivation-hygiene theory lacks the support needed to confirm it, in spite of an extended period of testing and a great deal of research. Rather surprisingly, the type of study recognized from the beginning as required to provide a definitive test has not been conducted. Therefore a new thrust in the research might yield different conclusions.

The problem now is that researchers have lost interest in the theory, apparently assuming it is unlikely to yield valid predictions. In recent years the number of related studies has dropped off sharply, and the level of scientific concern is now low. Thus, more elegantly designed tests may simply never be conducted. One could have hoped that the author of the theory would conduct these studies, but he became more concerned with applications in the area of job enrichment. It is as if the process of losing components has come to its ultimate conclusion: now the applications may well have lost the entire theory.

Current State of Practice

The tremendous appeal that motivation-hygiene theory has had for practitioners cannot be doubted. It appears simple, although Herzberg (1976, p. 323)

admits to only partially understanding it himself. Its religious, ethical, and moral overtones may well fill a strong managerial need. Furthermore, the idea that investments in salary, fringe benefits, working conditions, and the like yield benefits only up to a point (and thus can be restricted on rational grounds) is bound to appeal to the cost-conscious manager. These appeals are probably reinforced for some by the anti-academic, anti-intellectual thrust of much of Herzberg's writing.

Yet it is well to avoid uncritical acceptance. Salary is not just a dissatisfier; it clearly operates as a source of satisfaction in many cases, as do status, security, and interpersonal relationships. To believe otherwise may well lead one far astray. Whether these factors yield satisfactions or not depends very much on the individual; in some cases those who derive satisfactions from such factors may be mentally ill, but one should not apply such a blanket designation to all.

The suggestion that industrial relations departments be divided into motivator and hygiene units is interesting, but its validity rests on that of the underlying theory. That such an approach has not been widely adopted may be a result of misgivings on the latter score. It would appear that many human resource functions such as selection, training, compensation, and appraisal are so concerned with all aspects of motivation that an artificial separation could only be self-defeating.

But these matters are not of crucial significance. The major applied outgrowth of motivation-hygiene theory has been the rejuvenation, if not the creation, of job enrichment. This is an important accomplishment, and it justifies the emergence of the theory, no matter what its deficiencies. Job enrichment as a motivational technique can work—with some people, under certain circumstances, for some period of time—and Herzberg has been saying so for a long time.

Yet when one attempts to tie job enrichment back into motivation-hygiene theory, one encounters all kinds of difficulties. For example, job enrichment has nothing to do with hygienes at all; it involves adding only motivators to the job and thus relates at best to half of the theory. Furthermore, the motivators emphasized are those called *generators*—the work itself, responsibility, opportunity for growth, and advancement; achievement and recognition are downplayed. However, achievement and recognition are by far the most strongly supported motivators when the incident method is used to test the theory.

The research indicates that, even in the most appropriate context, 10 to 15 percent of those exposed to job enrichment do not respond and in other contexts the total effect may be nil. Yet the theory provides no basis for predicting these failures and gives short shrift to the troublesome idea of individual differences.

Finally, one does not need motivation-hygiene theory to understand the results from job enrichment. This will become increasingly clear as we address job characteristics theory.

JOB CHARACTERISTICS THEORY

Job enrichment has had an intense appeal for organizational behavior, and it has attracted both theorists and researchers in substantial numbers. The approach to which we now turn, job characteristics theory, emerged originally out of the collaboration of Edward Lawler and Richard Hackman. Hackman has remained a steady contributor over the years, and he is the one who adopted the name *job characteristics theory*. Lawler, however, became increasingly interested in other issues and disappeared from the theory as it developed. He was replaced by Greg Oldham.

Both sociotechnical systems theory and organization development theory (in certain of its variations) also deal with job enrichment; both make job enrichment an important aspect of their applications in practice. However, these theories are directly concerned with many factors other than the motivating effects of jobs on incumbents. In both practice and in the range of their primary variables they extend far beyond the immediate job or even the work group context in which the job is performed. Thus, they are best treated separately from theories of job enrichment per se.

Background

Job characteristics theory arose out of a context in the School of Industrial Administration at Yale University that was strongly disposed toward theory and research dealing with personality variables. From the late 1960s on, and well into the 1970s, a group of people within this school made major contributions in this area. There were numerous tests of the Maslow formulations that eventually resulted in Alderfer's ERG theory. Job characteristics theory arose out of this same orientation.

Lawler brought to this effort a strong predilection for, and research background in, expectancy theory (see chapter 8) coming from his doctoral studies in psychology at Berkeley (Lawler, 1969). Hackman had done research and written on the ways in which different types of tasks and task characteristics influence behavioral outcomes (Hackman, 1968, 1969a, 1969b). Later, in his writing on job enrichment that was done independent from Lawler, Hackman has given expectancy theory formulations a less central role, although he did not completely reject them.

Hackman was born in 1940 and received a Ph.D. in social psychology from the University of Illinois in 1966. From Illinois he went directly to Yale, where Lawler had already been on the faculty since 1964. Oldham, who was born in 1947, came to Yale also in this period and received his Ph.D. from the School of Industrial Administration in 1974. He left Yale a year earlier, however, to join the business school at the University of Illinois. Lawler left Yale in 1972 to move to the University of Michigan. Hackman remained at Yale until 1986 when he returned to a psychology department, at Harvard, where he has remained since. Oldham has continued at the University of Illinois in business. Thus, this group was together at Yale only very briefly, in part due to the financial pressures the university was experiencing at that time and in part due to negative pressures on the organizational behavior group that were emanating from the economics component of the school (Lawler, 1993).

Development of the Theory

Like many theories, job characteristics theory has undergone considerable expansion since its first statement. In general, this expansion has been devoted to achieving increased precision of predictions and to extending the boundaries within which the theory can operate. To place the theory in context, it first appeared at a point between Herzberg's second and third books when job enrichment was in its heyday.

The Original Hackman-Lawler Theory

As originally stated, the theory rested on five propositions drawn from both need hierarchy theory and expectancy theory. These serve as a basis for the more specific hypotheses to follow:

1. To the extent that individuals believe they can obtain an outcome they value by engaging in some particular behavior or class of behaviors, the likelihood that they will actually engage in that behavior is enhanced.
2. Outcomes are valued by individuals to the extent that they satisfy the physiological or psychological needs of the individual, or to the extent that they lead to other outcomes which satisfy such needs or are expected by the individual to do so.
3. Thus, to the extent conditions at work can be arranged so that employees can satisfy their own needs best by working effectively toward organizational goals, employees will in fact tend to work hard toward the achievement of these goals.
4. Most lower level needs (e.g., physical well-being, security) can be (and often are) reasonably well satisfied for individuals in contemporary society on a continuing basis and, therefore, will not serve as motivational incentives except under unusual circumstances. This is not the case, however, for certain higher order needs (e.g., needs for personal growth and development or feelings of worthwhile accomplishment).
5. Individuals who are capable of higher order need satisfaction will in fact experience such satisfaction when they learn that they have, as a result of their own efforts, accomplished something that they personally believe is worthwhile or meaningful. Specifically, individuals who desire higher order need satisfactions should be most likely to obtain them when they work effectively on meaningful jobs which provide feedback on the adequacy of their personal work activities. (Hackman & Lawler, 1971, p. 262)

In this early version of the theory four characteristics were proposed as essential to jobs constructed to engage higher-order needs. Essentially what was hypothesized is that these four elements must be introduced into a job to enrich it and thus make it motivating for individuals with strong higher-order needs. These four characteristics or task attributes are taken from earlier work by Arthur Turner and Paul Lawrence (1965).

The first is *autonomy*, defined as an indication of the degree to which individuals feel personally responsible for their work and thus that they own their work outcomes. The authors consider autonomy as a necessary but not sufficient condition for experiencing personal responsibility for work or for attributing performance to one's own efforts.

Second, there must be a high degree of *task identity*, which is defined as including a distinct sense of a beginning and an ending, as well as high visibility of the intervening transformation process itself, the manifestation of the transformation process in the final product, and a transformation process of considerable magnitude. As a subcomponent of this characteristic, the opportunity to use skills and abilities that are personally valued (and use them effectively) is noted.

Third, there must be sufficient *variety*, another factor contributing to the meaningfulness of the work, but only truly challenging variety, variety that taps a number of different skills of importance to the worker.

Fourth and finally, the job must provide *feedback* on the level of accomplishment. Such feedback may be built into the task itself, or it may stem from external sources (e.g., supervisors and coworkers). In any case, what makes the difference is the perception of feedback, just as it is the perception of autonomy, task identity, and variety.

The theory anticipates that satisfaction, performance, and attendance should be higher when the four core characteristics are present in a job. The theory specifies that all four must be present for these consequences to accrue. Furthermore, these relationships are moderated by the level of higher-order need strength (motivation) in the individual. When higher-order need strength is pronounced, the four core job dimensions should yield particularly high satisfaction, performance, and attendance levels. The implication is that many jobs in many organizations lack the core dimensions and should be redesigned (enriched) to provide them. Essentially this is the version of the theory to which Lawler remained committed (Lawler, 1973).

The Later Hackman-Oldham Theory

Job characteristics theory as such was explicated initially by Hackman and Oldham (1976), and then in what has become its complete form in a 1980 book (see also Oldham, 1996). This complete model is set forth in figure 7.1. The number of core job characteristics is now extended to five, with the inclusion of *task significance* as a third contributor to the meaningfulness of work. This latter characteristic, which was in fact part of the early 1940s IBM formulations, is de-

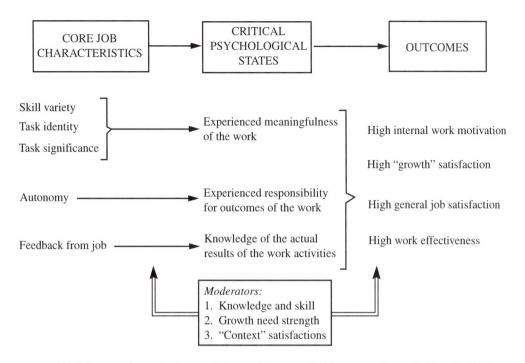

FIGURE 7.1 The complete job characteristics model. From J. Richard Hackman & Greg G. Oldham (1980), *Work Redesign* (Reading, MA: Addison-Wesley), 90. Copyright 1980. Reprinted by permission of Pearson Education, Inc.

fined as involving the degree to which the job has a substantial impact on the lives or work of other people, either in the immediate organization or in the environment external to it.

The critical psychological states noted in figure 7.1 are defined as follows:

1. Experienced meaningfulness of the work — the degree to which an individual experiences the job as one that is generally meaningful, valuable, and worthwhile
2. Experienced responsibility for outcomes of the work — the degree to which an individual feels personally accountable for the results of the work done
3. Knowledge of the actual results of the work activities — the degree to which an individual knows and understands, on a continuing basis, how effectively he or she is performing the job

The model is explicitly employed to develop a formula to compute the motivating potential score (MPS) for a given job:

$$MPS = \frac{\text{Skill Variety} + \text{Task Identity} + \text{Task Significance}}{3}$$

$$\times \text{Autonomy} \times \text{Feedback from job}$$

It should be noted that this formula departs from the Hackman and Lawler (1971) view. There, all core characteristics had to be high; here, autonomy and feedback, as well as one or more of the three contributors to meaningfulness, must be high, but a zero on one of the latter three does not now have the potential for producing an overall zero MPS score.

The original higher-order need strength moderator has been respecified as *growth need strength* (i.e., a strong need for personal growth), following the lead established by Alderfer's ERG theory. The moderator process is also extended to include the knowledge and skill required to do the work well. Otherwise, as inadequate work causes negative consequences, there will be disillusionment with the enriched job and, ultimately, a tendency to avoid it. Finally, for enrichment to work, there must be a degree of overall satisfaction with the job context. If a person worries about job security, feels unfairly compensated, and encounters problems with coworkers and the boss, that person cannot give much attention to the challenge of job enrichment.

These moderator relationships have been summarized as follows:

> The worst possible circumstance for a job that is high in motivating potential would be when the job incumbent is only marginally competent to perform the work *and* has low needs for personal growth at work *and* is highly dissatisfied with one or more aspects of the work context. The job clearly would be too much for that individual, and negative personal and work outcomes would be predicted. It would be better, for the person as well as for the organization, for the individual to perform relatively more simple and routine work. On the other hand, if an individual is fully competent to carry out the work required by a complex, challenging task *and* has strong needs for personal growth *and* is well satisfied with the work context, then we would expect both high personal satisfaction and high work motivation and performance. (Hackman & Oldham, 1980, p. 88)

At one point an additional moderator was espoused by both Lawler (1973) and Hackman (1977). This is the degree to which the organizational climate is of a mechanistic or organic type, following Tom Burns and G. M. Stalker (1961). In general, an organic climate was considered favorable for job enrichment. This moderator has disappeared from the theory more recently. As in this instance, the matter of the precise nature of the moderator process has created many problems for the authors over the years. In characterizing the theory as involving person-environment fit, for instance, Carol Kulik, Oldham, and Hackman (1987) say that job characteristics theory is a means of analyzing the fit between job characteristics (environment) and the abilities and needs (person) of jobholders. Although context satisfactions might be viewed as an aspect of the person, this moderator receives relatively little attention when the theory is reformulated in terms of fit.

Another area that has presented difficulties is that of outcomes. It follows from the theory that job enrichment that "takes" (is known to actually occur) should result in outcomes such as high internal work motivation, high growth satisfaction, and high general job satisfaction (not to include satisfaction with specific

aspects of the job context such as security, pay, supervision, etc.). High work effectiveness is another matter, however; it includes the quality of output for certain, and it may include the quantity as well (but not always). It does not include low absenteeism and low turnover, although both have been considered likely outcomes of job enrichment in the past (but no longer are). The outcomes specified in figure 7.1 represent the findings from research, much more than the theory's inherent logic. Many are simply empirical generalizations.

Action Principles

A set of guidelines for enriching jobs, derived from the five core job characteristics of the theory, has been developed. These so-called action principles represent specific hypotheses regarding how enriched jobs may be achieved, as follows:

> If enriched jobs and increased motivating potential are to be achieved, then—
>
> 1. Natural work units should be formed, in order to increase *task identity* and *task significance*.
> 2. Tasks should be combined, in order to increase *skill variety* and *task identity*.
> 3. Client relationships with the ultimate user should be established, in order to increase *skill variety, autonomy,* and *feedback*.
> 4. The job should be vertically loaded with responsibilities and controls formerly reserved for management, in order to increase *autonomy*.
> 5. Feedback channels should be opened, especially channels flowing directly from the job itself, in order to increase *feedback*.

These guidelines have much in common with those set forth for orthodox job enrichment. At the level of actual practice the two approaches have a good deal in common; at the level of theoretical origins they are considerably more diverse. What is different about the job characteristics approach is that it says job enrichment should not be attempted everywhere, with everyone. It is simply not appropriate in some work contexts and for some types of people. Thus, individual and organizational diagnosis should precede any attempt to enrich jobs.

The five action principles are diagrammed in figure 7.2. There is no doubt that Hackman and Oldham have serious questions regarding the utility of these

IMPLEMENTING PRINCIPLES   CORE JOB CHARACTERISTICS

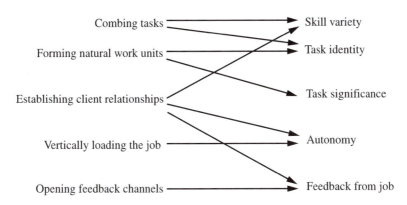

FIGURE 7.2 Links between the implementing principles and the core job characteristics. From J. Richard Hackman & Greg G. Oldham (1980), *Work Redesign* (Reading, MA: Addison-Wesley), 135. Copyright 1980. Reprinted by permission of Pearson Education, Inc.

principles in many applications; their claims are quite conservative. They note that changes may be so small as to exert very little impact, and that even when substantial changes are obtained they may vanish quickly (Oldham & Hackman, 1980). They attribute both of these sources of failure to negative properties that are built into certain organizations as social systems—properties that create resistances that simply cannot be overcome.

Group Tasks

Given Hackman's long-term interest in group processes, it is not surprising that job characteristics theory soon came to consider the design of group, as opposed to individual, tasks (Hackman & Morris, 1975; Hackman, 1978). The theorizing in this area is not as precise as that discussed to this point, but it does expand the boundaries of theoretical applications considerably.

Work group effectiveness is viewed as a consequence of the level of effort group members bring to the task, the amount of knowledge and skill relevant to task work the members have, and the appropriateness of the task performance strategies of the group. Thus group outcomes are considered to be a function of task factors. These so-called *interim criteria*, in turn, are hypothesized to result from group design factors such as the design of the group task, the composition of the group, and group norms about performance

processes (Hackman & Oldham, 1980; Hackman, 1987).

In essence, what is proposed is that the five core characteristics be applied at the work group level rather than at the individual level. This means that there must be two additional job characteristics: (1) task-required interdependence, in that the task itself requires members to work together and rely on each other, and (2) opportunities for social interaction, in that members are in social proximity and conditions foster communication about the work. Group task performance, like individual task performance, assumes sufficient appropriate knowledge and skills to complete the task successfully.

The effects of the group's effort, knowledge, and strategies are potentially constrained by the *technology*—a paced assembly line, for instance. They are also potentially constrained by imperfections in the *interpersonal processes* within the group, such as might be created by intense personal animosities, for instance. Thus, these two factors, technology and interpersonal processes, moderate the final effect of the efforts, knowledge, and strategies that emanate from the group on outcomes, including the overall quality of task performance.

Designing tasks on a group basis is recommended under the following conditions:

1. When the group can assume responsibility for a total product or service, but the nature of the

work is such that individuals cannot; thus, when the meaningful work potential of even the best possible individual job is low.

2. When the work is of such a nature that high interdependence among individual workers is essential.

3. When the workers involved have high social need strength, with the result that enrichment of individual jobs risks breaking up satisfying group relationships.

4. When the motivating potential of the job would be expected to be much higher if arranged as a group task rather than as a set of individual tasks.

In contrast, individual (as opposed to group) task design is recommended:

1. When the individuals have high needs for personal growth but weak needs for social relationships at work.

2. When the prospect of dysfunctional conflict within a group is high.

3. When there is no inherent interdependence in the work of the individuals.

4. When the expertise needed to design group tasks, an inherently difficult process, is lacking.

In many cases technological or interpersonal factors will make group task design infeasible. In any event, group task enrichment is a much more complex and less well understood process than individual job enrichment. It assumes the existence of self-managed, or autonomous, work groups whose work is enriched by taking over their own supervision (Hackman & Oldham, 1980). There has, in fact, been little research dealing with this group task component of the theory.

Rural-Urban Moderator

A full appreciation of job characteristics theory requires some understanding of a parallel theoretical thread that operated in the same time period, spawned its own research, and exerted a certain amount of influence as the Hackman-Oldham theory developed. Initially, this approach involved a rural-urban moderator and was developed on an ad hoc basis to explain certain findings as they emerged from the Turner and Lawrence (1965) research. Since these findings were obtained only after an extensive search of the data, they may well have represented chance phenomena

and thus had to be considered hypotheses for further testing.

In the primary analyses, it was found that blue-collar workers in more enriched jobs were generally absent less, but no clear relationships with job satisfaction were apparent. However, the secondary analyses revealed that the relationship with absenteeism characterized "town" workers only and that these same workers also exhibited the expected association between enriched jobs and satisfaction. For "city" workers, mostly from the Catholic religion, there was a negative relationship between enrichment and satisfaction.

Various possible explanations of these results were explored, although the Turner and Lawrence data do not permit reaching firm conclusions. Among the alternatives considered were the possibilities (1) that the town workers had stronger higher-order needs in accord with need hierarchy theory, (2) that they had strong achievement needs (and the city workers stronger affiliation motivation) in accord with achievement motivation theory, and (3) that the city workers were characterized by anomie (or normlessness) while the town workers were not, in accord with various sociological conceptions.

A number of studies that relate to this rural-urban factor subsequently emanated from the University of Illinois and Charles Hulin (1971). Among the alternative Turner and Lawrence formulations regarding the moderator process, this research has come closest to emphasizing anomie and thus the third alternative. However, Hulin prefers to think in terms of alienation from middle-class norms. Urban workers are said to be so alienated; rural workers are not and, in fact, espouse these norms strongly. According to Hulin, the fact that writers and researchers in this area also come from middle-class backgrounds accounts for the historical tendency to generalize that what is true of rural workers applies to all workers and thus to prescribe job enrichment as a panacea for everyone.

The early evidence amassed by Hulin relating to the rural-urban, alienation hypothesis is generally favorable, as are the results of Hulin's own studies. However, even in 1971, there were several conflicting findings. The data appear to support the idea of a moderator process, with job enrichment working for some people but not others. Hulin, like Turner and Lawrence before him, remains somewhat uncertain as to the exact nature of this process.

As research continued, the idea that some type of

value or norm differential moderates the relationship between job characteristics and outcome received increasing support. Subjects with strong intrinsic work values were more satisfied and showed more performance improvement when they worked on an enriched task than did those with strong extrinsic work values. There was evidence for a similar kind of moderating effect when using a measure of commitment to Protestant ethic values. In these studies, however the relationships, although typically statistically significant, were not strong. One has the feeling that the moderators used are somehow hitting only the edges of the target and not the bull's eye.

Furthermore, as research continued, support for the type of gross rural-urban differential noted by Turner and Lawrence (1965) became more and more tenuous. A review by Jon Pierce and Randall Dunham (1976) questioned the value of the sociological explanations except as they served to point the way for more precise formulations such as those of job characteristics theory. Given the trend of the findings and known changes in population characteristics, it seems likely that, although the rural-urban moderator concept may have possessed some validity at an earlier point in time, it no longer holds true. The increasing mobility of the population and changes in cultural values appear to have eliminated its explanatory power.

As these alternative formulations appeared, and then stumbled, job characteristics theory took on new strength, simply by virtue of its survival and its more compelling logic.

Evaluation and Impact

One of the major strengths of job characteristics theory is that its variables are amenable to relatively easy operationalization. As a consequence, the measurement problem was tackled at an early date and considerable progress was made. Among other considerations, this has meant that direct tests of the theory could be carried out; also it has facilitated research directed at determining the conditions under which job enrichment efforts actually "take" and thus serve to expand job scope.

Measurement and Operationalization

The first major effort at measurement of job enrichment was conducted by Turner and Lawrence (1965). The indices thus created had a considerable impact on the Hackman and Lawler (1971) measures, which, in turn, formed the basis for the current Job Diagnostic Survey (Hackman & Oldham, 1980). Turner and Lawrence developed a number of scales to be used in rating jobs by those who had knowledge of them. Several of these scales were combined into a single overall measure called the Requisite Task Attribute Index. Included were items that deal with variety, autonomy, required interaction, optional interaction, knowledge and skill, and responsibility. An additional measure of task identity subsequently proved of considerable value, although it was not used in the composite index. All of these variables were intercorrelated at approximately the .50 level.

Hackman and Lawler (1971) drew items from the Turner and Lawrence measures to obtain their indices of variety, autonomy, task identity, and feedback. They also developed measures of dealing with others (required interaction) and friendship opportunities (optional interaction) from the same source. The four measures of job characteristics had reliabilities averaging .77, but the two social measures proved to be of unacceptable reliability. A measure of higher-order need strength based on an employee rating of how much the individual would like to have an opportunity for growth, variety, a feeling of worthwhile accomplishment, and the like had a reliability of .89.

The Job Diagnostic Survey represents a considerable refinement of these preliminary measures. It contains the following measures:

- Job dimensions — the five core characteristics, plus the factor called "dealing with others," and an index of feedback from external agents, not the job itself
- Critical psychological states — the three specified by the theory
- Affective reactions to the job — general satisfaction; internal work motivation; and specific satisfactions with regard to security, pay, coworkers, supervision, and growth opportunity
- Growth need strength — both the index of what the individual would like from a job and one in which choices are made between alternative jobs

With the exception of certain moderators and the variables introduced when the theory is extended to group tasks, the Job Diagnostic Survey provides a comprehensive coverage of the variables of the theory. The reported reliabilities for individual scales range from .56 to .88, with a median of .72. There is good evidence that the instrument does discriminate among different jobs.

Some question has been raised as to the psychometric soundness of the Job Diagnostic Survey on the grounds that factor-analytic studies yield varied dimensionality under different circumstances and that the emerging factor structure may not match the five core theoretical variables. Yet overall measures, such as the motivating potential score, can be useful in spite of these findings. Furthermore, since the validity of the various measures has been established, the lack of a consistently supportive factor structure does not necessarily indicate defects in either the measures or the theory (Kulik, Oldham, & Langner, 1988).

Assessments of the psychometric properties of the Job Diagnostic Survey based on a considerable body of research certainly give it passing marks—probably even much better ones (Taber & Taylor, 1990; Fried, 1991). Furthermore, other measures of theoretical variables have been developed, freeing research from the need to rely on a single measure. Certainly these measures have facilitated the rapid emergence of research to test various aspects of job characteristics theory.

In addition, in various places the theorists have set forth a series of diagnostic steps to undertake, along with a list of guidelines for implementing job enrichment. These normative statements underline the practical value of the Job Diagnostic Survey:

Step 1. Check scores in the areas of motivation and satisfaction to see if problems exist in these areas. If they do, and job outcomes are deficient, then job enrichment may well be called for.

Step 2. Check the motivating potential scores of the jobs to see if they are low. If they are not, job enrichment is not likely to be the answer.

Step 3. Check scores for the five core dimensions to see what the basic strengths and weaknesses of the present job are. In this way it is possible to identify specific areas for change.

Step 4. Check to see what the growth need strength levels of job incumbents are. One can proceed with more confidence in enriching the jobs of employees with high growth needs since they are ready for the change.

Step 5. Check the scores for various aspects of job satisfaction and other information sources for roadblocks that might obstruct change or for special opportunities that might facilitate it.

The prescriptive guidelines for implementation are as follows:

Guide 1. Diagnose the work system in terms of some theory of work redesign before introducing any change to see what is possible and what kinds of changes are most likely to work.

Guide 2. Keep the focus of the change effort on the work itself, rather than the other aspects of the work context, so that real job enrichment does occur.

Guide 3. Prepare in advance for any possible problems and side effects, especially among employees whose jobs are not directly affected by the change; develop appropriate contingency plans.

Guide 4. Evaluate the project on a continuing basis to see if anticipated changes actually are occurring and using as many and as objective measures as possible.

Guide 5. Confront difficult problems as early in the project as possible.

Guide 6. Design change processes in such a way as to fit the objectives of the job enrichment. Thus if autonomy in work is to be an objective, autonomy should be respected in designing the new jobs in the first place; in other words, be consistent with the theory in guiding the change effort throughout.

Research by the Theory's Authors

In the early period, much of the research related to job characteristics theory came from the theory's authors. This research tested the theory at points, but it also contributed inductive generalizations that changed the theory. The research contributions in this period included Hackman and Lawler (1971); Lawler, Hackman, and Stanley Kaufman (1973); Linda Frank and Hackman (1975); Hackman and Oldham (1976); Oldham, Hackman, and Jone Pearce (1976); and Oldham (1976). Certainly these studies contributed support for the theory more often than not, but they cannot be said to be definitive on that score. There were instances where nothing seems to have happened, simply because the job enrichment interventions did not take and thus job enrichment did not occur. An important contribution of this research was that it was possible to show that common method variance of the kind that plagued the Herzberg studies could not be invoked to explain away the findings of job characteristics theory. Also, there was some quite consistent support for certain of the moderator hypotheses (see table 7.2). Note that although only 6 of the differences between high and low correlations are significant, 19 of 21 differences are in the predicated direction.

Since the early 1980s, research of this kind by the theory's authors has largely dried up, with the occasional exception of a study involving Oldham. Noteworthy, however, are two studies: one by Oldham and Hackman (1981), which introduced certain macro and structural factors into the theory, and another by Oldham et al. (1982), which dealt with the referents employees use in evaluating and reacting to the complexity of their jobs. Although seemingly important, neither extension of the basic theory has elicited further investigation.

State of the Theory by the Mid-1980s

Shortly after the middle of the 1980s, sufficient research had accumulated, from the theory's authors and from others, so that a major stocktaking occurred. This most frequently took the form of a quantitative meta-analysis (Loher, Noe, Moeller, & Fitzgerald, 1985; Spector, 1985; Fried & Ferris, 1987). Overall, these analyses provided considerable support for the theory. Because of the somewhat varied research that was included, the results were not always the same. In particular, the predicted outcomes tended to vary, yet all analyses indicate prediction of some outcomes. The core job characteristics and the critical psychological states are important features of the model. Among

TABLE 7.2 Correlation between motivating potential score and outcome variables, as moderated by growth need strength and context satisfactions

	Outcome variable		
Strength or satisfaction	Related performance	Salary	Intrinsic motivation
All subjects	.16	.22	.36
Growth need strength			
High	.25	(.44)	.36
Low	.00	(.03)	.21
Pay satisfaction			
High	.21	.20	(.47)
Low	.10	.24	(.25)
Security satisfaction			
High	.25	.23	.32
Low	.08	.20	.33
Coworker satisfaction			
High	(.33)	(.31)	.33
Low	(.02)	(.05)	.26
Supervisory satisfaction			
High	.29	.29	.34
Low	.08	.17	.26
Combined satisfaction			
High	.26	.30	.36
Low	.13	.13	.25
Growth need strength plus combined satisfaction			
High	(.32)	(.50)	.24
Low	(−.19)	(−.06)	.15

NOTE: Parentheses indicate that the differences between high and low correlations are statistically significant ($p < .05$).

SOURCE: Adapted from Greg R. Oldham, J. Richard Hackman, & Jone L. Pearce (1976), Conditions under Which Employees Respond Positively to Enriched Work, *Journal of Applied Psychology*, 6, 398–401

the moderators only growth need strength had been studied enough to warrant a conclusion, but evidence for its effect was obtained. A comparison of the results of laboratory and field studies indicates that, where sufficient research is available to reach a conclusion, the findings are favorable for the theory, independent of which approach is used (Stone, 1986).

In this body of research from the 1970s and early 1980s it is evident that any given study may fail to support either some core characteristic, or the way a given psychological state operates, or the effect on a particular outcome. Such failures to obtain statistical significance may reflect sample fluctuations or the realities of specific situations. As long as certain positive results are obtained, assuming that some type of job enrichment is present (takes), there is no need for a study to support every tenet of the theory.

Recent Findings

In spite of the limited activity by its authors on the job characteristics theory front, research has continued up to the present. Several studies have now been conducted which consider job enrichment effects over extended periods of time. These multiyear investigations have shown both positive effects on performance (Griffin, 1991) and on absenteeism (Rentsch & Steel, 1998). Although job enrichment studies may appropriately use either experimental interventions or existing variations in the degree of enrichment across a range of jobs, longitudinal analyses of the impacts of interventions are more elegant. One such study showed an effect of enrichment in a field setting on actual observed performance (Luthans, Kemmerer, Paul, & Taylor, 1987). Another demonstrated the role of the growth need strength moderator in predicting the quantity and quality of measured performance output (Graen, Scandura, & Graen, 1986).

The important role of the critical psychological states in the model (see figure 7.1) has been supported, although they may not operate in exactly the same manner vis-à-vis core characteristics and outcomes as originally hypothesized (Renn & Vandenberg, 1995). Also it appears that calculating the motivating potential score by using any multiplicative relationship between core characteristics yields less than optimal results (see, for example, Hinton & Biderman, 1995). Simply adding the five scores works best.

Not all of the more recent findings are positive for the theory, although the positive results far outweigh the negative. A study by Gary Johns, Jia Lin Xie, and Yongqing Fang (1992), for instance, is generally supportive of the theory but provides only minimal evidence of growth need moderator effects and no evidence for the operation of other moderators. Robert Tiegs, Lois Tetrick, and Yitzhak Fried (1992) also failed to support the various moderator hypotheses.

These studies, however, raise certain questions that future research needs to address. The original idea of job enrichment was to overcome the demotivating effects of job fragmentation that was brought about by scientific management, in low-level positions; job enrichment was to take from higher-level jobs, particularly those of managers, and add this component to make routine, highly specialized jobs more stimulating. Yet, increasingly, one finds managerial and professional jobs used to study job enrichment. Are we talking about the same thing? Also it is now evident that some outcomes may be predicted in a given study, but not others (and that absenteeism and turnover are legitimate outcomes for the theory). Should not any test of the theory, then, consider all potential outcomes before reaching negative conclusions regarding the theory's tenability?

Critique from the Social Information Processing Perspective

As part of a more general attack on need-based views of motivation, which would appear to encompass all of the theories considered in this and the preceding chapters, Gerald Salancik and Jeffrey Pfeffer (1977, 1978) proposed an alternative interpretation of the findings of research on the job characteristics theory. Their critique is entirely conceptual, in that they do not back it up with any of their own research on job enrichment. Yet, at least for a period of time, this critique had substantial impact, and it may well still make a contribution to the development of an expanded theory.

The critique operates from the position that, as adaptive organisms, individuals adapt their attitudes, behavior, and beliefs to their social context and to the realities of their past and present behaviors and situations. This is the essence of the social information processing perspective. Characteristics of a job, for instance, are not given but are constructed out of an individual's perceptions. The behavior of a person can serve as information out of which that person constructs attitudes; other features of the social context can produce similar effects.

From this line of argument, Salancik and Pfeffer developed a number of reinterpretations of job characteristics research:

1. The distribution of a questionnaire can focus attention on particular aspects of a job, thus priming the respondent to pay attention to certain information and to a large degree predetermining the response. This is what has elsewhere been labeled *pretest sensitization.*
2. Individuals are aware of their own responses to questions and, in an effort to be consistent in the pattern of their responses, may generate many of the results found in job enrichment research. This is what elsewhere has been called *common method variance*; it is the problem discussed with regard to the Herzberg data.
3. Cooptation of job dimensions and criteria constructed by the organization and its managers may cause employees to define their work situations in certain predetermined ways. This may include *coopting* the values and consequences of a job design program in which they have agreed to participate.

Processes of a social information type clearly can operate in the context of job enrichment research. This has been demonstrated on numerous occasions, and with reference to the introduction of a variety of artifacts such as priming, consistency, and cooptation (see for example Adler, Skov, & Salvemini, 1985; O'Reilly & Caldwell, 1985; Glick, Jenkins, & Gupta, 1986). The difficulty for the Salancik and Pfeffer hypotheses, however, is that there is also ample evidence that social information processing factors cannot be used to explain away the results of job characteristics theory research. The theory simply has not been refuted by this line of attack (Ilgen & Hollenbeck, 1991; Griffin & McMahan 1994), although it did undergo a few growing pains. Thus, at present, job characteristics theory remains a viable approach, which, in spite of the loss of its authors and some diminution of the rate of related research, continues to offer considerable promise.

Idea of Optimal Job Scope

In many cases the desires of a company's work force for enriched work can be met simply through the traditional practices of upgrading and promotion, par-

ticularly if the company is growing and has a limited number of employees for whom enrichment is appropriate. However, there are many circumstances where work force composition and promotional opportunities make this an insufficient solution. On the one hand, with the downsizing of U.S. corporations, promotions have become fewer and job enrichment via this route is less available. On the other hand, downsizing may compel the combining of previously existing jobs to create a type of forced job enlargement and enrichment. This raises the very real possibility that the scope of certain jobs might be pushed upward to a point where their positive potential is exhausted.

There has been discussion in the literature for a number of years regarding the idea that individuals at a particular time have what amounts to an optimal task scope that is ideal for their particular capabilities and personality makeup (Miner & Dachler, 1973; Schwab & Cummings, 1976; Champoux, 1980; Xie & Johns, 1995). In this view individual differences are pronounced and important. Jobs can be too enriched for a particular person, just as people can be promoted "over their head" and fail because of an inability to cope emotionally or intellectually. Similarly, jobs can be insufficiently enriched, and it is in such cases that job characteristics theory or some modification of it becomes valuable as a guide.

Research is beginning to demonstrate some type of curvilinear relation between job scope and positive outcomes. The results on growth need strength suggest that this curve may vary from one person to another. Applications such as this may well represent the future of job characteristics theory, expanding its domain considerably.

CONCLUSIONS

It is a fact of life that those who dabble in personality-based theories and research will eventually find themselves under attack. That is clearly evident with regard to the theories considered in chapters 5 through 7. This is not a phenomenon that is limited to the scholarly world; it extends to the popular literature and to the legislative halls as well. Attacking has a long history. Within organizational behavior, the tendency has been to establish an antithesis between the individual and the external situation, with the attacks often coming from those who espouse a situational view of the causation of human experience and behavior. More recently this has involved scholars with a sociological perspective (see, for example, Salancik & Pfeffer, 1977, 1978), but this has not necessarily been the case in the past.

For those who have a strong commitment to the importance of individual differences it would be appealing if this pattern of attacks could be written off as a product of some propensity to react against the study of human personality (probing into the private soul). It is not that easy. Certainly something of this kind is involved in some instances. But the attacks are not all bias; many have been appropriate, have contributed useful ideas, and have identified problems in research design and measurement. We have seen this in a number of the preceding discussions of theory in this volume. The problem is to separate the wheat from the chaff.

Dispositional Effects as Mirage

It is important first to distinguish generalized attacks from criticisms focused on specific theories. The Salancik and Pfeffer papers took job characteristics theory as their primary target, but the arguments were extended to include need theories in general. The first of these, the 1977 article, elicited a reasoned response from Alderfer (1977), who presented counterarguments to a number of the Salancik and Pfeffer statements about need theories. The latter were apparently aware of the Alderfer arguments at the time they wrote their 1978 paper, since they cite his critique. Yet the 1978 paper includes no reasoned response to Alderfer at all, only several brief comments that appear to be in the nature of asides.

This same tendency to shun direct debate occurs again in the context of a study by Eugene Stone and Hal Gueutal (1984), which appeared to show that the priming and consistency artifacts proposed by Salancik and Pfeffer were not an important consideration in need satisfaction research. Salancik (1984) replied, attacking the research and defending his original position. Yet when Stone (1984) vigorously, and apparently effectively, took issue with Salancik and presented arguments for the validity of his research, Salancik declined to reply even when given an opportunity to do so by the journal's editor.

Five years later Alison Davis-Blake and Jeffrey Pfeffer (1989) published a paper, still without research data of its own, that contained a major attack not on job characteristics theory per se, or need theories overall, but on what they call the *dispositional approach*. This controversy is discussed briefly in chapter 1 here. Dispositions are defined as unobservable mental states (needs, values, attitudes, or personalities) that are relatively stable over time and that to some extent act as determinants of attitudes and behavior in organizations. The argument is that dispositions so defined are a mirage and that the truly important determinants of organizational behavior are situational in nature. Thus, the arena is extended to include all theories of motivation that are rooted in personality theory. There is no mention in this article of either Alderfer (1977) or Stone (1984). Subsequently, Pfeffer (1991) wrote a well-reasoned argument for the study of situational influences in organizations, now specified in terms of the constraints and opportunities for social interaction and comparison that derive from existing structural realities. Here the tone is much more balanced in nature; negative attacks on dispositions are downplayed, and in fact there is no mention of the 1989 essay at all.

Another publication in much the same vein as Davis-Blake and Pfeffer (1989) was authored by Walter Nord, whom we met in chapter 5 (Nord & Fox, 1996). Nord, as noted previously, has a background in social psychology and sociology. The thesis of the article is that the individual has disappeared from the field of organizational behavior, having been replaced by the contextual dimension that consists of attributes of the physical and social systems in which individuals exist. The authors attempt to document that theories and research dealing with individual personality and dispositions have lost status to a more situational concern, to the point where organizational behavior is no longer interested in individual differences.

In connection with this documentation, Nord and Fox (1996) give considerable attention to the papers variously authored by Salancik, Pfeffer, and Davis-Blake. Yet their attention to the major theories of the field, and the research that surrounds them, is minimal to nonexistent. There is no citation at all of Levinson, Herzberg, Lawler, Hackman, Oldham, or Miner. Only Alderfer's 1977 reply is noted, not ERG theory per se. Maslow is noted in passing (with one citation), and McClelland is described as a leadership theorist (again with one citation). These omissions inevitably raise questions regarding the objectivity of this attack by fait accompli.

Dispositional Effects as Reality

As might be expected, these attacks on the role and significance of personality factors have not gone unanswered. In addition to the Alderfer (1977) and Stone (1984) replies, there is a detailed presentation by Jennifer George (1992) which considers much of the theory and research that supports an important role for personality in understanding, predicting, and influencing human experience and behavior in organizations.

Another line of argument to the same effect began with an article by Robert House (1988). These ideas were developed further into a detailed critique of Davis-Blake and Pfeffer (1989) some years later (House, Shane, & Herold, 1996). Taken together, these various replies seem to make a strong case for the retention of personality-based perspectives in organizational behavior and for the position that theory and research of this kind remain vibrant within the field, even though under attack. The quotation from George (1992) given in chapter 1 of this volume provides a good summing-up of the current state of affairs. It calls for a live and let live approach in the future and suggests that the pseudo-dichotomy between personality and situation be left to die a natural death. Both personality and situational constructs are important components of theory.

References

Adler, Seymour; Skov, Richard B.; & Salvemini, Nat J. (1985). Job Characteristics and Job Satisfaction: When Cause Becomes Consequence. *Organizational Behavior and Human Decision Processes*, 35, 266–278.

Alderfer, Clayton P. (1977). A Critique of Salancik and Pfeffer's Examination of Need Satisfaction Theories. *Administrative Science Quarterly*, 22, 658–669.

Burns, Tom, & Stalker, G. M. (1961). *The Management of Innovation*. New York: Oxford University Press.

Champoux, Joseph E. (1980). A Three-Sample Test of Some Extensions to the Job Characteristics Model of Work Motivation. *Academy of Management Journal*, 23, 466–478.

Davis-Blake, Alison, & Pfeffer, Jeffrey (1989). Just a Mirage: The Search for Dispositional Effects in Organizational Research. *Academy of Management Review*, 14, 385–400.

Flanagan, John (1954). The Critical Incident Technique. *Psychological Bulletin*, 51, 327–358.

Ford, Robert N. (1969). *Motivation through the Work Itself*. New York: American Management Association.

Ford, Robert N. (1973). Job Enrichment Lessons from AT&T. *Harvard Business Review*, 51(1), 96–106.

Frank, Linda L., & Hackman, J. Richard (1975). A Failure of Job Enrichment: The Case of the Change That Wasn't. *Journal of Applied Behavioral Science*, 11, 413–436.

Fried, Yitzhak (1991). Meta-Analytic Comparison of the Job Diagnostic Survey and Job Characteristics Inventory as Correlates of Work Satisfaction and Performance. *Journal of Applied Psychology*, 76, 690–697.

Fried, Yitzhak, & Ferris, Gerald R. (1987). The Validity of the Job Characteristics Model: A Review and Meta-Analysis. *Personnel Psychology*, 40, 287–322.

George, Jennifer M. (1992). The Role of Personality in Organizational Life: Issues and Evidence. *Journal of Management*, 18, 185–213.

Glick, William H.; Jenkins, G. Douglas; & Gupta, Nina (1986). Method versus Substance: How Strong Are Underlying Relationships between Job Characteristics and Attitudinal Outcomes? *Academy of Management Journal*, 29, 441–464.

Graen, George B.; Scandura, Terri A.; & Graen, Michael R. (1986). A Field Experimental Test of the Moderating Effects of Growth Need Strength on Productivity. *Journal of Applied Psychology*, 71, 484–491.

Griffin, Ricky W. (1991). Effects of Work Redesign on Employee Perceptions, Attitudes, and Behaviors: A Long-Term Investigation. *Academy of Management Journal*, 34, 425–435.

Griffin, Ricky W., & McMahan, Gary C. (1994). Motivation through Job Design. In Jerald Greenberg (Ed.), *Organizational Behavior: The State of the Science* (pp. 23–43). Hillsdale, NJ: Erlbaum.

Hackman, J. Richard (1968). Effects of Task Characteristics on Group Products. *Journal of Experimental Social Psychology*, 4, 162–187.

Hackman, J. Richard (1969a). Nature of the Task as a Determiner of Job Behavior. *Personnel Psychology*, 22, 435–444.

Hackman, J. Richard (1969b). Toward Understanding the Role of Tasks in Behavioral Research. *Acta Psychologica*, 31, 97–128.

Hackman, J. Richard (1975). On the Coming Demise of Job Enrichment. In Eugene L. Cass & Frederick G. Zimmer (Eds.), *Man and Work in Society* (pp. 97–115). New York: Van Nostrand Reinhold.

Hackman, J. Richard (1977). Work Design. In J. Richard

Hackman & J. Lloyd Suttle (Eds.), *Improving Life at Work: Behavioral Science Approaches to Organizational Change* (pp. 96–162). Santa Monica, CA: Goodyear.

Hackman, J. Richard (1978). The Design of Self-Managing Work Groups. In Bert T. King, Siegfried S. Streufert, & Fred E. Fiedler (Eds.), *Managerial Control and Organizational Democracy* (pp. 61–91). Washington, DC: Winston.

Hackman, J. Richard (1987). The Design of Work Teams. In Jay W. Lorsch (Ed.), *Handbook of Organizational Behavior* (pp. 315–342). Englewood Cliffs, NJ: Prentice Hall.

Hackman, J. Richard, & Lawler, Edward E. (1971). Employee Reactions to Job Characteristics. *Journal of Applied Psychology*, 55, 259–286.

Hackman, J. Richard, & Morris, Charles G. (1975). Group Tasks, Group Interaction Processes, and Group Performance Effectiveness: A Review and Proposed Integration. In Leonard Berkowitz (Ed.), *Advances in Experimental Psychology* (Vol. 8). New York: Academic Press.

Hackman, J. Richard, & Oldham, Greg R. (1976). Motivation through the Design of Work: Test of a Theory. *Organizational Behavior and Human Performance*, 16, 250–279.

Hackman, J. Richard, & Oldham, Greg R. (1980). *Work Redesign*. Reading, MA: Addison-Wesley.

Hackman, Ray C. (1969). *The Motivated Working Adult*. New York: American Management Association.

Herzberg, Frederick (1966). *Work and the Nature of Man*. Cleveland, OH: World.

Herzberg, Frederick (1976). *The Managerial Choice: To Be Efficient and to Be Human*. Homewood, IL: Dow-Jones-Irwin.

Herzberg, Frederick (1977). Orthodox Job Enrichment: A Common Sense Approach to People at Work. *Defense Management Journal*, April, 21–27.

Herzberg, Frederick (1991). A Visit with Fred Herzberg. *Houghton Mifflin Company Management Newsletter*, 4(3), 2–6.

Herzberg, Frederick (1993). Happiness and Unhappiness: A Brief Autobiography. In Arthur G. Bedeian (Ed.), *Management Laureates: A Collection of Autobiographical Essays* (Vol. 2, pp. 1–37). Greenwich, CT: JAI Press.

Herzberg, Frederick; Mathapo, J.; Wiener, Yoash; & Wiesen, L. (1974). Motivation-Hygiene Correlates of Mental Health: An Examination of Motivational Inversion in a Clinical Population. *Journal of Consulting and Clinical Psychology*, 42, 411–419.

Herzberg, Frederick; Mausner, Bernard; Peterson, R. O.; & Capwell, Dora F. (1957). *Job Attitudes: Review of Research and Opinion*. Pittsburgh, PA: Psychological Service of Pittsburgh.

Herzberg, Frederick; Mausner, Bernard; & Snyderman, Barbara S. (1959). *The Motivation to Work*. New York: Wiley.

Herzberg, Frederick, & Zautra, Alex (1976). Orthodox Job Enrichment: Measuring True Quality in Job Satisfaction. *Personnel*, 53(5), 54–68.

Hinton, Michelle, & Biderman, Michael (1995). Empirically Derived Job Characteristics Measures and the Motivating Potential Score. *Journal of Business and Psychology*, 9, 355–364.

House, Robert J. (1988). Power and Personality in Complex Organizations. *Research in Organizational Behavior*, 10, 305–357.

House, Robert J.; Shane, Scott A.; & Herold, David M. (1996). Rumors of the Death of Dispositional Research Are Vastly Exaggerated. *Academy of Management Review*, 21, 203–224.

Hulin, Charles L. (1971). Individual Differences and Job Enrichment—The Case against General Treatments. In John R. Maher (Ed.), *New Perspectives in Job Enrichment* (pp. 159–191). New York: Van Nostrand Reinhold.

Ilgen, Daniel R., & Hollenbeck, John R. (1991). The Structure of Work: Job Design and Roles. In Marvin D. Dunnette & Leaetta M. Hough (Eds.), *Handbook of Industrial and Organizational Psychology* (Vol. 2, pp. 165–207). Palo Alto, CA: Consulting Psychologists Press.

Johns, Gary; Xie, Jia Lin; & Fang, Yongqing (1992). Mediating and Moderating Effects in Job Design. *Journal of Management*, 18, 657–676.

Kahn, Robert L. (1961). Review of *The Motivation to Work*. *Contemporary Psychology*, 6, 9–10.

Kulik, Carol T.; Oldham, Greg R.; & Hackman, J. Richard (1987). Work Design as an Approach to Person-Environment Fit. *Journal of Vocational Behavior*, 31, 278–296.

Kulik, Carol T.; Oldham, Greg R.; & Langner, Paul H. (1988). Measurement of Job Characteristics: Comparison of the Original and the Revised Job Diagnostic Survey. *Journal of Applied Psychology*, 73, 462–466.

Lawler, Edward E. (1969). Job Design and Employee Motivation. *Personnel Psychology*, 22, 426–435.

Lawler, Edward E. (1973). *Motivation in Work Organizations*. Monterey, CA: Brooks/Cole.

Lawler, Edward E. (1993). Understanding Work Motivation and Organizational Effectiveness: A Career-Long Journey. In Arthur G. Bedeian (Ed.), *Management Laureates: A Collection of Autobiographical Essays* (Vol. 2, pp. 81–109). Greenwich, CT: JAI Press.

Lawler, Edward E.; Hackman, J. Richard; & Kaufman,

Stanley (1973). Effects of Job Redesign: A Field Experiment. *Journal of Applied Social Psychology*, 3, 49–62.

Loher, Brian T.; Noe, Raymond A.; Moeller, Nancy L.; & Fitzgerald, Michael P. (1985). A Meta-Analysis of the Relation of Job Characteristics to Job Satisfaction. *Journal of Applied Psychology*, 70, 280–289.

Luthans, Fred; Kemmerer, Barbara; Paul, Robert; & Taylor, Lew (1987). Impact of a Job Redesign Intervention on Salesperson's Observed Performance Behaviors. *Group and Organization Studies*, 12, 55–72.

Miner, John B., & Dachler, H. Peter (1973). Personnel Attitudes and Motivation. *Annual Review of Psychology*, 24, 379–402.

Nord, Walter R., & Fox, Suzy (1996). The Individual in Organizational Studies: The Great Disappearing Act? In Stuart R. Clegg, Cynthia Hardy, & Walter R. Nord (Eds.), *Handbook of Organization Studies* (pp. 148–174). London: Sage.

Oldham, Greg R. (1976). Job Characteristics and Internal Motivation: The Moderating Effect of Interpersonal and Individual Variables. *Human Relations*, 29, 559–569.

Oldham, Greg R. (1996). Job Design. *International Review of Industrial and Organizational Psychology*, 11, 33–60.

Oldham, Greg R.; Cummings, Anne; & Zhou, Jing (1995). The Spatial Configuration of Organizations: A Review of the Literature and Some New Research Directions. *Research in Personnel and Human Resources Management*, 13, 1–37.

Oldham, Greg R., & Hackman, J. Richard (1980). Work Design in the Organizational Context. *Research in Organizational Behavior*, 2, 247–278.

Oldham, Greg R., & Hackman, J. Richard (1981). Relationships between Organizational Structure and Employee Reactions: Comparing Alternative Frameworks. *Administrative Science Quarterly*, 26, 66–83.

Oldham, Greg R.; Hackman, J. Richard; & Pearce, Jone L. (1976). Conditions under Which Employees Respond Positively to Enriched Work. *Journal of Applied Psychology*, 61, 395–403.

Oldham, Greg R.; Nottenburg, Gail; Kassner, Marcia W.; Ferris, Gerald; Fedor, Donald; & Masters, Marick (1982). The Selection and Consequences of Job Comparisons. *Organizational Behavior and Human Performance*, 29, 84–111.

O'Reilly, Charles A., & Caldwell, David F. (1985). The Impact of Normative Social Influence and Cohesiveness on Task Perceptions and Attitudes: A Social Information Processing Approach. *Journal of Occupational Psychology*, 58, 193–206.

Pfeffer, Jeffrey (1991). Organization Theory and Structural Perspectives on Management. *Journal of Management*, 17, 789–803.

Pierce, Jon L., & Dunham, Randall B. (1976). Task Design: A Literature Review. *Academy of Management Review*, 1, 83–97.

Renn, Robert W., & Vandenberg, Robert J. (1995). The Critical Psychological States: An Underrepresented Component in Job Characteristics Research. *Journal of Management*, 21, 279–303.

Rentsch, Joan R., & Steel, Robert P. (1998). Testing the Durability of Job Characteristics as Predictors of Absenteeism over a Six-Year Period. *Personnel Psychology*, 51, 165–190.

Salancik, Gerald R. (1984). On Priming, Consistency, and Order Effects in Job Attitude Assessment: With a Note on Current Research. *Journal of Management*, 10, 250–254.

Salancik, Gerald R., & Pfeffer, Jeffrey (1977). An Examination of Need-Satisfaction Models of Job Attitudes. *Administrative Science Quarterly*, 22, 427–456.

Salancik, Gerald R., & Pfeffer, Jeffrey (1978). A Social Information Processing Approach to Job Attitudes and Task Design. *Administrative Science Quarterly*, 23, 224–253.

Schwab, Donald P., & Cummings, Larry L. (1976). A Theoretical Analysis of the Impact of Task Scope on Employee Performance. *Academy of Management Review*, 1, 23–35.

Schwab, Donald P.; DeVitt, H. William; & Cummings, Larry L. (1971). A Test of the Adequacy of the Two-Factor Theory as a Predictor of Self-Report Performance Effects. *Personnel Psychology*, 24, 293–303.

Spector, Paul E. (1985). Higher-Order Need Strength as a Moderator of the Job Scope–Employee Outcome Relationship: A Meta-Analysis. *Journal of Occupational Psychology*, 58, 119–127.

Stone, Eugene F. (1984). Misperceiving and/or Misrepresenting the Facts: A Reply to Salancik. *Journal of Management*, 10, 255–258.

Stone, Eugene F. (1986). Job Scope–Job Satisfaction and Job Scope–Job Performance Relationships. In Edwin A. Locke (Ed.), *Generalizing from Laboratory to Field Settings* (pp. 189–206). Lexington, MA: Lexington Books.

Stone, Eugene F., & Gueutal, Hal G. (1984). On the Premature Death of Need-Satisfaction Models: An Investigation of Salancik and Pfeffer's Views on Priming and Consistency Artifacts. *Journal of Management*, 10, 237–249.

Taber, Tom D., & Taylor, Elisabeth (1990). A Review and Evaluation of the Psychometric Properties of the Job Diagnostic Survey. *Personnel Psychology*, 43, 467–500.

Tiegs, Robert B.; Tetrick, Lois E.; & Fried, Yitzhak (1992). Growth Need Strength and Context Satisfactions as Moderators of the Relations of the Job

Characteristics Model. *Journal of Management*, 18, 575–593.

Turner, Arthur N., & Lawrence, Paul R. (1965). *Industrial Jobs and the Worker: An Investigation of Response to Task Attributes*. Boston: Harvard Graduate School of Business Administration.

U.S. Department of Health, Education and Welfare. (1972). *Work in America*. Cambridge, MA: MIT Press.

Walker, Charles R. (1962). *Modern Technology and Civilization: An Introduction to Human Problems in the Machine Age*. New York: McGraw-Hill.

Xie, Jia Lin, & Johns, Gary (1995). Job Scope and Stress: Can Job Scope Be Too High? *Academy of Management Journal*, 38, 1288–1309.

Yorks, Lyle, & Whitsett, David A. (1989). *Scenarios of Change: Advocacy and the Diffusion of Job Redesign in Organizations*. New York: Praeger.

Chapter 8

Theories of Motivation Rooted in Learning Theory

Just as personality theory contributed to the development of certain organizational behavior theories of motivation, learning theory has contributed in a similar manner. For learning to occur it must be energized in some manner, and that is where motivation comes in. Thus learning theory and motivation have long been intertwined.

The two theories considered in this chapter have had multiple contributors, many of whom have worked independently of one another. Thus, the development in both theoretical areas has been somewhat sporadic and disjointed. Yet there have been major theories whose statements stand out from the others. In this regard the formulations of Victor Vroom and of Lyman Porter and Edward Lawler (setting forth their concepts of expectancy theory) and the formulations of Fred Luthans (setting forth his organizational behavior modification theory) appear to predominate.

Behind these major theorists, back in the lineage of learning theory, lie certain early theorists whose influences were important even though they made no direct contribution to organizational behavior. These people are Edward Tolman, whose theories on learning sparked expectancy theory, and B. F. Skinner, whose theories were the major source of organizational behavior modification. In addition, certain contributions to learning theory from Kurt Lewin need to be considered with regard to expectancy theory.

Tolman was born in 1886 and obtained his doctorate in psychology from Harvard University in 1915. After 3 years at Northwestern University, he moved to the University of California at Berkeley, where he remained throughout his career. There, Tolman Hall, which houses the psychology department, is named for him. Much of his research was with animals, and out of this he developed his sign-gestalt theory of learning. His major contributions insofar as providing underpinnings for expectancy theory were Tolman 1932 and 1959; Tolman died in the latter year.

Lewin's views on motivation were in many respects similar to Tolman's, and their publications occurred in the same time period (Lewin, 1938, 1951). As we saw in chapter 2, Lewin was eclectic in his work, touching on many areas within psychology. Although not a learning theorist per se, his topological and vector psychology was relevant for learning theory (Hilgard, 1948), and it is this aspect of his work that influenced expectancy theory.

Skinner was born in 1904 and died in 1990. His contributions to psychology span a 60-year period, and his descriptive behaviorism has had a deep impact on psychological thinking (Lattal, 1992). He obtained his doctorate in psychology from Harvard University in 1931 and subsequently served on the psychology faculties of the Universities of Minnesota and Indiana before returning to Harvard in 1948. In the early years Skinner's research focused on animals, and he gave little attention to practical applications of his ideas in any form. Gradually, however, his horizons expanded. Skinner 1953, 1971, and 1974 are the three books that provide the most comprehensive statements regarding matters that have relevance for the study of organizations, although none touches directly on the field of organizational behavior.

EXPECTANCY THEORIES

During the 1960s a number of variants on expectancy theory were proposed, and a sizable body of research began to develop. Actually, the first such research within organizational behavior was conducted by Basil Georgopoulos, Gerald Mahoney, and Nyle Jones (1957) as part of a research program of the Survey Research Center at the University of Michigan. However, no formal theory of motivation was formulated in connection with that research. That task remained for Vroom (1964), who was at Michigan at the time

the early research was done. Several years later Porter and Lawler (1968), collaborating initially at the University of California at Berkeley, not long after Tolman's death, expanded and extended these statements. These two versions of expectancy theory have stood the test of time and historical scrutiny, and are generally recognized as representing the major contributions (Steers, Porter, & Bigley, 1996).

Background

Vroom grew up in Montreal and received both his undergraduate degree in psychology and his master's degree in industrial psychology from McGill University, the latter in 1955 at the age of 23. From there he moved to the United States, where he received a Ph.D. in industrial psychology from the University of Michigan. His doctoral dissertation (Vroom, 1960) was a 1959 award winner in the Ford Foundation Doctoral Dissertation Series. In 1960 he joined the psychology faculty at the University of Pennsylvania, and it was during his 3 years there that much of the writing on *Work and Motivation* (Vroom, 1964), presenting his version of expectancy theory, was done. His entry into the business school world came with an appointment to the Graduate School of Industrial Administration at Carnegie just as the conflict between the economists and organizational behavior (see chapter 5) was at its peak. In 1972 Vroom moved to the Yale School of Industrial Administration at a time when, as it turned out, that school was immersed in many of the same problems that had existed at Carnegie (Vroom, 1993). Yet he has remained at Yale over the many years since.

Porter was born in 1930 and grew up in Indiana. His undergraduate work was in psychology at Northwestern University. From there he went to Yale University in experimental psychology, but in his final year he shifted informally to industrial psychology. Upon receiving his doctorate in 1956 he took a position in industrial psychology at Berkeley. Although he had several publications related to aspects of learning, consistent with his background in experimental psychology, Porter did not publish in the industrial area until after his arrival in California.

In 1960 Lawler came to Berkeley as a graduate student in psychology, and shortly afterward the Porter-Lawler collaboration that eventuated in the second version of expectancy theory began. This effort was highly influenced by the publication of Vroom's 1964 book. Later in that same year Lawler completed his degree and joined the School of Industrial Administration at Yale. Porter also left Berkeley shortly—in 1967 (after a visiting year working with Lawler at Yale) to join the University of California at Irvine's Graduate School of Administration. There he subsequently served as dean of the school for a number of years and has remained ever since (Porter, 1993).

Lawler was born in 1938 and came to Berkeley via an undergraduate major in psychology at Brown University. From Berkeley he went to a business school, at Yale, and then back to a psychology department at Michigan (see chapter 7). His major appointment at Michigan, however, was in the Institute for Social Research. Subsequently he moved to the business school at the University of Southern California, where he became involved in conducting large-scale research projects not unlike those in which he had been involved at Michigan (Lawler, 1993), but now with primarily corporate funding. He has remained at USC for some 20 years to date.

These are the primary authors of expectancy theory, but there were others who made theoretical and research contributions in the 1960s. Among these, Jay Galbraith and Larry Cummings (1967) and George Graen (1969) deserve special mention. Graen's formulations are particularly noteworthy because they led into his vertical dyad linkage theory of leadership; we will consider this theory in chapter 12.

Variants on the Expectancy Theory Theme

All versions of expectancy theory have been proposed by authors who conducted research on the subject as well. As has been the practice previously, consideration will be given to theoretical statements first and then to the authors' research.

The Georgopoulos, Mahoney, and Jones (1957) Hypotheses

This study aimed at identifying the factors that are associated with high and low levels of productivity. The Survey Research Center program, of which the study was a part, was focused primarily on the role of supervisory practices but this particular study dealt only with the motivation-productivity relationship. The theoretical hypotheses were formulated as derivations from prior work in the field of psychology and

guided the conduct of the research. They were intended to deal only with the conscious, rational aspects of employee motivation.

The major variables considered are:

1. Individual needs as reflected in the goals sought. Examples of these goals would be making more money or getting along well in the work group.
2. Individual perceptions of the relative usefulness of productivity behavior (high or low) as a means of attaining desired goals (in theoretical terms, the instrumentality of various productivity levels or the extent to which they are seen as providing a path to a goal).
3. The amount of freedom from restraining factors the individual has in following the desired path. Examples of constraining factors might be supervisory and work group pressures or limitations of ability and knowledge.

The basic hypothesis is as follows:

If a worker sees high productivity as a path leading to the attainment of one or more of his personal goals, he will tend to be a high producer. Conversely, if he sees low productivity as a path to the achievement of his goals he will tend to be a low producer. (Georgopoulos et al., 1957, p. 346)

This relationship between motivation and performance is moderated by the amount of freedom to act. When freedom is high, motivation will readily appear in productivity levels. When barriers operate, the hypothesized relationships will be disrupted and the correlation of motivation to performance will be reduced. Path-goal perceptions are conceived as expectancies or estimated probabilities that there will be a given amount of payoff as a consequence of certain types of job behavior. Accordingly, high productivity may be viewed as likely to produce a desired goal (thus having a positive valence) or to impede goal attainment (thus having a negative valence).

Vroom's Theory of Work and Motivation

The initial preliminary statements of Vroom's expectancy theory appear in the published version of his doctoral dissertation (Vroom, 1960). These statements have much in common with the views of his University of Michigan colleagues (Georgopoulos et al.) and in the early statements of Atkinson's theory. Subsequently, Vroom expanded his ideas into a more formally stated expectancy theory of work and motivation (Vroom, 1964). Thus, all of the original thinking regarding applications of expectancy theory to employee motivation emanated from the University of Michigan.

Vroom's theory starts with the idea that people tend to prefer certain goals, or outcomes, over others. They thus anticipate experiencing feelings of satisfaction should such a preferred outcome be achieved. The term *valence* is applied to this feeling about specific outcomes. If there is positive valence, having the outcome is preferred to not having it. If negative valence exists, not having the outcome is preferred. Outcomes may acquire valence either in their own right or because they are expected to lead to other outcomes that are anticipated sources of satisfaction or dissatisfaction. Thus the accumulation of earnings per se might be viewed as inherently satisfying to one person, but to another it is important as a means to the end of buying a sports car.

As a basis for establishing the valence of a specific outcome, Vroom sets forth the following proposition:

> The valence of an outcome to a person is a monotonically increasing function of the algebraic sum of the products of the valences of all other outcomes and his conceptions of its instrumentality for the attainment of these other outcomes. (Vroom, 1964, p. 17)

Thus the size of the valence of an outcome depends on the extent to which it is viewed as a means to various other outcomes and the valence of the other outcomes. Since the proposition calls for the multiplication of the perceived instrumentality by the valence of each other outcome, any such outcome that has no valence for a person or that has no instrumental relationship to the outcome whose valence is being computed takes on a zero value, adding nothing to the final sum. An outcome with a large valence would tend to be one that is linked to many other outcomes, one that is considered highly instrumental to the attainment of a large number of these other outcomes, and one that is linked to other outcomes having large valences. Vroom specifically applies this first proposition to the topics of occupational choice (calculation of the valence of an occupation), job satisfaction (calculation of the valence of a job held), and job perfor-

mance (calculation of the valence of effective performance in a job held). The last was the single concern of Georgopoulos and his associates.

An additional and central variable in the theory is *expectancy*. People develop varying conceptions of the probability or degree of certainty that the choice of a particular alternative action will indeed lead to a desired outcome. In contrast to instrumentality, which is an outcome-outcome link, expectancy involves an action-outcome linkage. Expectancies combine with total valence to yield a person's aroused motivation or potential for a given course of action. Vroom (1964) uses the term *force* to describe this combination and offers the following proposition:

> The force on a person to perform an act is a monotonically increasing function of the algebraic sum of the products of all the valences of all outcomes and the strength of his expectancies that the act will be followed by the attainment of these outcomes. (p. 18)

The total force for an action is uninfluenced by outcomes that have no valence and also by outcomes that are viewed as totally unlikely to result from the actions, since, again, a multiplicative relationship between the two variables is posited. People are expected to choose among action alternatives in a rational manner to maximize force (in a positive direction). When an action is linked to many very positively valent outcomes by strong expectations that it will yield these outcomes, the force can be sizable. The theory makes specific statements with regard to the implications of the second proposition for occupational choice (calculation of the force on a person to enter an occupation), job satisfaction (calculation of the force on a person to remain in a job held), and job performance (calculation of the force on a person to exert a given amount of effort in the performance of a job held). Since the last of these statements has been the subject of considerable further theorizing and research, it is given in full:

> The force on a person to exert a given amount of effort in performance of his job is a monotonically increasing function of the algebraic sum of the products of the valences of different levels of performance and his expectancies that this amount of effort will be followed by their attainment. (Vroom, 1964, p. 284)

The Porter-Lawler Model

Porter and Lawler (1968) present a model that draws heavily on Vroom but goes beyond the limited concept of motivational force to performance as a whole. Vroom (1964) himself moves in this direction by stating that ability and motivation relate to performance in a multiplicative manner:

$$Performance = f(Ability \times Motivation)$$

The variables of the Porter-Lawler theory are as follows:

1. Value of reward—how attractive or desirable an outcome is (valence)
2. Effort-reward probability—a perception of whether differential rewards are based on differential effort; this breaks down into effort-performance (expectancy) and performance-reward (instrumentality) components
3. Effort—the energy expended to perform a task (force)
4. Abilities and traits—the long-term characteristics of a person
5. Role perceptions—the types of effort a person considers necessary to effective job performance
6. Performance—a person's accomplishment on tasks that comprise the job
7. Rewards—desirable states of affairs received from either one's own thinking or the actions of others (intrinsic and extrinsic outcomes)
8. Perceived equitable rewards—the amount of rewards a person considers fair
9. Satisfaction—the extent to which rewards received meet or exceed the perceived equitable level (dissatisfaction results from underreward inequity only)

In line with prior formulations, the first two variables (value of reward and effort-reward probability), when multiplied together, are said to produce the third variable (effort). Following Vroom, abilities and traits also have a multiplicative relationship to effort in determining performance. A similar relationship to effort (in establishing performance level) holds for role perceptions. Because of the intervention of such factors between effort and performance, effort and performance cannot be expected to be perfectly related.

Porter and Lawler also posit certain feedback loops that make their theory more dynamic over time than Vroom's. First, to the extent that performance does result in reward, the perceived effort-reward probability is increased. Second, when satisfaction is experienced after receiving a reward, it tends to influence the future value (valence) of that reward. The nature of this effect varies with the particular reward (outcome).

Figure 8.1 sets forth these interrelationships as they were originally conceived. Since this initial statement, Porter has moved on to other endeavors and has made no significant contributions to the development of expectancy theory. However, one gets the impression that were he to return to this subject, he would focus his efforts on integrating macro variables into the model (Luthans, 1990; Porter, 1996).

Lawler's Subsequent Statements

We have seen (chapter 7) that Lawler introduced expectancy thinking into the initial version of job characteristics theory. He has also modified the theory in several respects, although the overall change is not marked. He has elaborated certain factors that may influence effort-reward probabilities and thus has continued the tendency to make the model dynamic over time, in contrast to Vroom's static approach (Lawler, 1971, 1973). The most important change is an additional feedback loop from performance, to effort-reward expectancy, to the effect that within normal limits heightened performance will yield greater self-esteem and thus subsequently higher expectancy. In addition, a much clearer distinction is made between intrinsic and extrinsic rewards.

Figure 8.2 depicts the central motivational chain of expectancy theory, devoid of feedback loops and ancillary forces. This is the basic model as set forth by Lawler (1981), and it is the model that he continues to endorse (Lawler, 1994). In this model *effort-to-performance expectancy* refers to the expectation (assessed probability) that if effort is exerted, the result will be successful performance (though successful performance may *not* result because the job is too difficult, the evaluation process is deficient, or the individual lacks the needed skills). *Performance-to-outcome expectancy* refers to the expectation (assessed probability) that should effort be successfully exerted, something that is desired will result, such as a financial reward. An incentive system may be in effect that specifies a certain pay level for so many units produced. The person believes this and expects to be paid

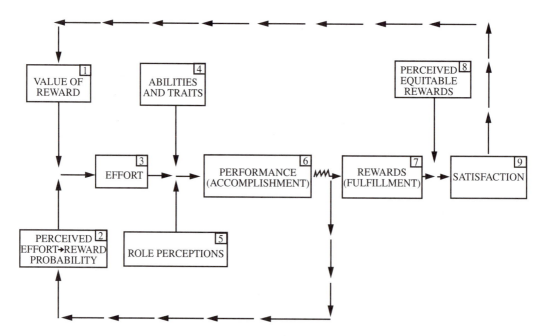

FIGURE 8.1 The original Porter-Lawler model. From Lyman W. Porter & Edward E. Lawler (1968), *Managerial Attitudes and Performance* (Homewood, IL: Irwin), 17. Copyright 1968. Reproduced with permission of The McGraw-Hill Companies.

the designated amount upon completing the specified number of units. This is a performance-to-outcome expectancy. But it makes a difference only if the outcome, such as pay, has *valence* — that is, value or attractiveness. If the person has just inherited a fortune and does not care about the relatively small amount of pay involved, then additional pay as an outcome will not work as well in the motivational calculus as, say, an improvement in working conditions.

The distinction between first- and second-level outcomes goes back to Vroom (1964) who used the terms *focal* and *other*; Galbraith and Cummings (1967) were explicit in using the terminology of figure 8.2 to apply to this distinction. The concepts involved are important. A person may value pay in its own right — for instance, an entrepreneur who views the business's earnings and his own as feedback on how well he has achieved through his own efforts — as an index of

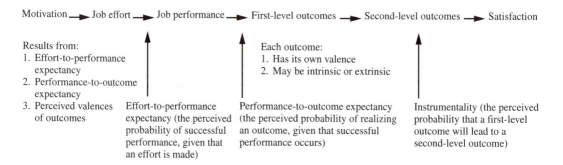

FIGURE 8.2 Lawler's (1981) portrayal of the basic expectancy theory model. Adapted from pages 21, 231, and 234, Edward E. Lawler (1981), *Pay and Organization Development* (Reading, MA: Addison-Wesley).

performance. But pay may also be a means to second-level outcomes. A person may want the money in order to achieve an affluent lifestyle and impress others who are viewed as important. Then pay must be considered in terms of its *instrumentality* for gaining the second-level outcome of a more affluent lifestyle. If the pay involved is not enough to gain what is desired, then it lacks instrumentality—and motivational impact. *Intrinsic outcomes* are those that come from within a person: feelings of accomplishment, of doing important work, of freedom. *Extrinsic outcomes* are provided or mediated by external forces: a superior, the organization, other work-group members. This too is an important distinction.

The level of motivation in a given job situation is expressed in expectancy theory terms by a formula. Questionnaires are used to measure the components of this formula, and the scores obtained are inserted in it. The formula is as follows:

Motivation = Effort-to-performance expectancy
× the sum of all operating factors
(performance-to-outcome expectancies
× their valences)

Inherent in this formula are the following ideas:

1. A person's motivation to perform is determined by the performance-to-outcome expectancy multiplied by the valence of the outcome. The valence of the first-level outcome subsumes the instrumentalities and valences of the related second-level outcomes. The relationship is multiplicative; no motivation exists when either performance-to-outcome expectancy or valence is 0.
2. Since a level of performance has multiple outcomes associated with it, the products of all performance-to-outcome expectancies × valence combinations are added together for all the outcomes seen as relevant to the specific performance.
3. The summed performance-to-outcome expectancies × valences is then multiplied by the effort-to-performance expectancy. Again, the multiplicative relationship indicates that if either effort-to-performance expectancy or the summed performance-to-outcome expectancies times their valences is 0, motivation is 0.
4. Summarizing, the strength of a person's motivation to perform effectively is influenced by:
   • the person's belief that effort can be converted into performance and

• the net attractiveness of the events that are perceived to stem from good performance. (Lawler, 1981, pp. 232–233)

Evaluation and Impact

Most versions of expectancy theory were introduced preliminary to a research study that tested the theoretical formulation. These seminal studies are important not only because they bear directly on matters of theoretical validity but also because they have tended to set the scene (particularly in experimental design and measurement) for almost all of the research that has followed.

The Georgopoulos, Mahoney, and Jones (1957) Research on Productivity

As noted, the hypotheses of this study were formulated as part of a study of motivation-performance relationships. The sample consisted of production workers for a household appliances company. The measures used were all derived from a questionnaire and thus constitute entirely conscious self-reports of the variables.

The goals studied were the 3 ranked as most important by all the subjects out of a list of 10. These same rankings were used to determine whether each of the 3 was important to an individual subject. The three goals were:

1. Making more money in the long run.
2. Getting along well with the work group.
3. Promotion to a higher base rate of pay.

The instrumentality of either high or low productivity for attaining these goals was established through a rating scale that extended from "helping," through a neutral value, to "hurting." For instance, high productivity might be rated as helping a great deal to make more money and low productivity as hurting a little in achieving the same goal.

Productivity was reported in terms of the percentage of the standard usually achieved, on the basis of the standard hour incentive system in effect in the company. Freedom from restraining factors was established according to both reported freedom and amount of job experience.

As indicated in table 8.1, the data tend to confirm the basic instrumentality hypothesis in that those who view performance levels as instrumentally related to

TABLE 8.1 Percentage of those with various instrumental perceptions who are high performers when various goals are involved

	Instrumental perceptions			
Goal involved	High productivity helps achieve the goal	High productivity hurts achieving the goal	Low productivity hurts achieving the goal	Low productivity helps achieve the goal
Making more money in the long run	(38	21)*	(30	22)
Getting along well with the work group	32	23	33	28
Being promoted to a higher base rate	26	23	(32	12)

*Differences within parentheses are significant ($p < .05$).

SOURCE: Adapted from Basil S. Georgopoulos, Gerald M. Mahoney, & Nyle W. Jones (1957), A Path-Goal Approach to Productivity, *Journal of Applied Psychology*, 41, 349

goals in a positive sense are more likely to be high producers. However, the differences are not pronounced, and only three of the six differences attain accepted levels of statistical significance. Other data indicate that the presence of a stronger need to achieve a goal tends to be associated with an increase in relationship between instrumentality and productivity; freedom from restraining factors also tends to have the same facilitating effect. Again, the differences are often small, and consistent statistical significance occurs only for the goal of making more money in the long run. Overall, the results do support expectancy theory, but not strongly.

Vroom's Research on Organizational Choice

Although Vroom does not present research of his own on expectancy theory in his 1964 volume, he did publish an article 2 years later that bears on the subject (Vroom, 1966). This research is related only to the first of his basic propositions, since it does not concern itself with expectancies and deals only with the occupational choice question, not with job satisfaction or job performance.

The subjects were business students about to obtain master's degrees from Carnegie-Mellon University. The objective was to predict the attractiveness of various potential employing organizations (and ultimately the choice itself) from a knowledge of what goals were important to the individual and how instrumental membership in each organization was perceived to be as a means of achieving each goal. Questionnaire ratings on a number of variables were obtained prior to choice. Job goals or outcomes such as

a chance to benefit society, freedom from supervision, high salary, and the like were rated in terms of their importance to the person. The three organizations in which the subject was most interested were then evaluated to establish the degree to which the student thought each might provide an opportunity to satisfy each type of goal. Combining these two variables, an instrumentality-goal index was calculated for each organization and related both to the attractiveness rating given the organization and to the subsequent choice.

The results indicate clearly that organizations viewed as providing a means to achieving important goals were considered more attractive. Eliminating organizations that ultimately did not make an offer, 76 percent of the students subsequently chose the organization with the highest instrumentality-goal score. Although providing only a partial test of the theory, Vroom's research results are entirely consistent with it. Similar support of the theory was obtained in a follow-up study conducted several years after actual employment (Vroom and Deci, 1971).

The Porter-Lawler Studies

The most extensive investigation by Porter and Lawler and the one that is presented immediately after the major elaboration of their theory was conducted among the managers of seven different organizations — three state government departments (employment, conservation, retail liquor) and four private firms (a large processor of canned goods, a large chemical firm, an aerospace company, and a utility). In all, some 563 managers below the officer level were included (Porter & Lawler, 1968).

The study focuses primarily on pay as an outcome. Questionnaire measures of a number of theoretical variables were obtained from the managers, including measures of value of reward, effort-reward probability, effort, role perceptions, performance, rewards, perceived equitable rewards, and satisfaction. Ratings of effort and performance also were obtained from the managers' immediate supervisors.

Insofar as pay is concerned, the data do support the hypothesis that value of reward and perceived effort-reward probability combine to influence effort. Those who view pay as important and who consider pay to be tied to their efforts put more effort into their work, and this is true whether self or superior perceptions of effort are used. The same relationship also holds for performance but to a somewhat lesser degree. This, too, is what the theory predicts, since additional factors intervene between effort and performance in the model. Among these are role perceptions; data are presented indicating that certain kinds of role perceptions (when combined with the effort measures) do increase the precision with which performance level is predicted.

In another study of 154 managers in five organizations, the authors collected and analyzed data using several outcomes in addition to pay, such as promotion, friendship, and opportunity to use skills and abilities (Lawler & Porter, 1967). There were 7 outcomes in all. Basically, the approach was the same as that used in the preceding research except that data for more outcomes were combined in the predictors. As indicated in table 8.2, including value of reward (valence) in the prediction formula did make a difference; the correlations are consistently higher than without it. Job effort was consistently predicted more accurately than the further removed job performance. Yet the overall level of the coefficients is quite low for multiple correlation analyses. Only the four values of .30 or above are statistically significant. Considering that three of these four significant correlations involve self-ratings whose independence of the measures can be questioned, the overall results do not offer strong support of the theory.

In a later study Lawler (1968) used some of the same managers and obtained his measures twice, with a 1-year interval between measurements. This time the multiple correlations were higher, and statistical significance was much more frequently attained. The data over time are consistent with the hypothesis that preexisting perceived probabilities and valences of outcomes tend to exert a causal influence on subsequent performance.

A final early study related to the Porter-Lawler version of expectancy theory was conducted by Richard Hackman and Porter (1968), with telephone company service representatives as subjects. A variety of

TABLE 8.2 Multiple correlations for seven outcomes of effort-reward probabilities alone and in combination with value of reward (valence) as predictors of job effort and performance

Rating	Effort-reward probability alone	Effort-reward probability multiplied by value of reward
By the manager's superior		
Job effort	.22	.27
Job performance	.17	.18
By the manager's peers		
Job effort	.25	.30*
Job performance	.21	.21
By the manager himself		
Job effort	.32*	.44*
Job performance	.25	.38*

*Correlations are significant at $p < .05$.

SOURCE: Adapted from Edward E. Lawler and Lyman W. Porter (1967), Antecedent Attitudes of Effective Managerial Performance, *Organizational Behavior and Human Performance*, 2, 136

performance criteria were predicted using effort-reward probability multiplied by value of reward as the predictor. In this instance, the rewards (or outcomes) considered were generated directly by the service representatives themselves in interviews; thus, they were the rewards the subjects perceived to be actually present. Although the correlations with performance criteria are significant in almost all instances, the median value is only .27.

Overall, these various studies by Porter and Lawler do provide considerable support for the expectancy theories. Yet, given that this theoretical approach has identified an important way of looking at motivation at work, even Porter and Lawler appear puzzled by the low correlations found in many of the investigations.

Philosophical and Logical Questions

Certain questions were raised regarding the philosophical underpinnings and basic assumptions of expectancy theory at an early point (see, for example, Locke, 1975), especially as they relate to decision theory. One such question is whether the concept of hedonism, as incorporated in the expected satisfaction definition of the valence variable, is tenable. The essence of the argument here is that much human behavior is self-punitive. The difficulty of dealing with behavior of this kind, and with reactions to guilt, casts doubt on the strictly hedonistic formulations. Furthermore, there is reason to believe that many people do not attempt to maximize even when they do strive for satisfaction but, rather, accept some lesser level of effort. Issues like this have not really been faced by expectancy theorists. At the very least, they suggest that there are behaviors, and perhaps people, to whom the theory may apply in a very limited way.

Questions may also be raised as to whether people can engage in the cognitive processes implied by the theory, such as (1) weighting all possible outcomes as they contribute to other outcomes, and then others, to the point of infinite regress, or (2) multiplying valences and instrumentalities in a manner that, according to the theory, assumes very complex internalized measurement processes. The theory assumes common tendencies to project one's thoughts into a future time span and to search for alternatives for all human beings, since it is silent on individual differences in these respects. Yet, it is apparent that people do differ in both time perspective and the proclivity for search. Finally, on occasion individuals do act out

of unconscious motives and in ways that cannot be based on the calculative, highly rational processes that expectancy theory specifies: impulsive behavior, the repetition compulsions of neurotic individuals, and the like are examples.

These questions do not void expectancy theories as useful methods of predicting and understanding work behavior. They do suggest that the theories may deal with only part of organizational behavior and that their propositions may well represent only approximations of human motivational processes (perhaps overly complex in certain respects and overly simplistic in others). Under these circumstances the theories could still work quite well in the theoretical domains to which they apply.

Another line of questioning has to do with the extent to which expectancy theories must meet the various rationality assumptions that have been developed for formal decision theory. Vroom (1964) notes certain similarities between his formulations and those of subjective, expected utility theory. Others have drawn out these parallels more fully, even to the point of considering expectancy theories of motivation as special cases within the broader context of decision theory.

Attempts to relate expectancy theories to rationality assumptions or postulates taken from decision theory have not always come to identical conclusions. However, if such assumptions are to be considered part of the theory or implicit in its basic propositions, then the range of empirical support that is required to validate these propositions is greatly expanded. Furthermore, those who have compared expectancy theories to criteria that have been derived from decision theory clearly imply that expectancy theories are wanting in these respects.

However, strong arguments have been advanced that expectancy theories need not meet all of the tests derived from decision theory. For instance, it has been contended that the theory presupposes a lack of correlation (independence) between expectancy and valence and that such independence probably does not exist in reality. Regardless of the empirical facts, there is reason to conclude that independence is not necessary for the propositions of expectancy theory to prove valid.

Another assumption, transitivity, is generally conceded to be necessary for expectancy theories. Accordingly, if an outcome A is preferred to another outcome B, and B in turn is preferred to C, then A must be preferred to C. If this is not the case and C has greater valence than A, then intransitivity exists. To the extent that people actually think in intransitive terms, expectancy theory, with its strong reliance on rationality, is in trouble. Luckily for the theory, the evidence currently available suggests that intransitivity is a relatively uncommon phenomenon.

It seems appropriate to conclude that a number of rationality assumptions that have been derived from decision theory do not represent necessary conditions for expectancy theories. If the theory works in the prediction of performance, effort expenditure, job satisfaction, occupational choice, and the like, then it is not necessary to give major attention to these considerations. To the extent that it fails to predict such factors, they become likely causes that require exploration.

Applications

Most of the literature on expectancy theory gives only fleeting attention, if any, to practical applications. The major exception to this generally nonpractice-oriented approach is a series of statements about the administration of compensation and other reward systems initiated in the Porter and Lawler (1968) volume and continuing through a number of subsequent publications by Lawler.

Four recommendations for practice grew out of the original Porter and Lawler research, although the fourth is not a direct derivative of the theory per se:

1. Companies should collect systematic information as to what employees want from their jobs (value of rewards or valence) and their perceived probabilities of obtaining rewards relative to the effort they put out. This information could then be used in designing reward systems.
2. Companies should make sure that employees understand the role prescriptions for their jobs so that efforts are not misdirected and thus wasted.
3. Companies should take steps to tie rewards to performance in the minds of employees (to establish perceived contingencies). This argues against giving pay increases across the board, cost of living raises, and incentive raises that are kept secret, thus preventing any relative evaluation of their value. It argues for:
   a. tailoring rewards to what the individual wants
   b. giving more extrinsic rewards and more opportunities to obtain intrinsic rewards to superior performers than to inferior performers
   c. permitting employees to see and believe that high performance results in high reward; thus, for example, secrecy about pay should be removed so that contingencies can be observed, and the best and most credible source of information should be used to evaluate performance, even to the point of obtaining peer- and self-ratings
4. Continuously measure and monitor employee attitudes.

In his subsequent writings Lawler has placed particular emphasis on procedures that create performance-outcome contingencies and on individualized approaches that, among other things, adjust rewards to valent outcomes. His most unique contributions in these respects have been the emphasis on eliminating pay secrecy and a call for the use of "cafeteria" compensation systems, which permit employees to structure their own compensation (pay and benefits) packages to place the greatest relative emphasis on what they desire the most. In recent years the term *line-of-sight* has been applied to the expectancy theory view that, in order to be motivators, rewards must be seen as important and obtainable by the individual involved (Lawler, 1994).

In certain respects, the highly rationalized organization that expectancy theory demands seems comparable to the ideal bureaucracy of organizational theory. Yet some people have allied expectancy theory with participative management. Either form can probably be compatible with expectancy theory, provided decisions are made in some manner, and those decisions emphasize performance-reward contingencies. It would appear that such decisions might be somewhat easier to obtain in the hierarchic context of a bureaucracy but that if such contingencies do emerge from participative processes, the latter will facilitate the kind of information exchange that causes the contingencies to be widely recognized.

In any event, the theory argues for selecting employees who are likely to have high scores on the various expectancy theory measures and who thus will bring a maximal amount of effort or force to the work context. Such individuals should be most responsive to a situation within the domain of expectancy theory and least susceptible to any detrimental side effects.

A rather sizable body of research indicates that the people who bring the most motivational energy to their work (as that energy is determined from expectancy theory) are those generally referred to as *internals*. These people believe that events in their lives are largely subject to their own influence; in contrast, *externals* see themselves as largely at the mercy of fate, luck, and more powerful individuals. Given the rational, hedonistic emphasis of expectancy theory, it is not surprising that internals tend to emerge as strongly motivated in these terms. The research consistently yields this result (Mitchell, 1982). Furthermore, the idea of selecting people to fit an expectancy theory context has received research support as well (Miller & Grush, 1988).

Research Evidence

Research tests have yielded sufficient theoretical support so that it seems safe to conclude that expectancy theories are on the right track. They certainly do not explain all motivated behavior in all types of work organizations, but they do explain enough to be worth pursuing. The early research was far from conclusive in that the theory often emerged as invalid in a specific context, and, even when validity was established, the correlations tended to be low. Now, enough is known so that studies can be designed that will yield not only significant results but also correlations well above those that plagued the early research.

As Graen (1969) has indicated, expectancy theory works best when contingencies can be established in a concrete manner between effective job performance and attaining favorable role outcomes. In other words, people have to see that putting out effort to do what the job requires will give them what they want. When rewards are not so structured or existing performance-reward relationships are so ambiguous that they are not readily perceived, the theory appears to predict very little.

In addition to observing this boundary condition for the theory, a test also must utilize measures that are not only reliable but valid operationalizations of the theoretical variables. In the past these measurement requirements have not always been met, but it is now apparent that they can be met if sufficient attention is given to the selection or initial development of the measures (Ilgen, Nebeker, & Pritchard, 1981).

Most of the early studies used lists of outcomes that were developed by those who conducted the research. However, it has become evident that expectancy theory predictions that are derived from a limited set of

outcomes as specified by each subject outperform the predictions made from a longer, entirely researcher established, standard list. These and other findings in the studies argue for the use of an individualized approach to outcome generation. However, one may wish to focus research attention on specific types of motivation, as Porter and Lawler (1968) did with pay as an outcome. In such cases, researcher designation of outcomes is entirely appropriate.

Vroom states that "people choose from among alternative acts, the one corresponding to the strongest positive (or weakest negative) force" (1964, p. 19). The implication is that force values for various alternative acts should be computed for each subject; the highest would then be predicted to result in behavior. Yet the approach used in all of the early research was to develop only one force prediction per subject and then run correlations with criterion measures across a number of subjects. In contrast to this typical across-subjects approach, the within-subjects procedure yields separate correlations between predicted force and criterion values for each subject. These correlations may then be averaged to get a composite measure. Using this latter approach does in fact yield a higher level of theoretical confirmation.

It is apparent also that correlations can often be raised by including measures of variables that are extraneous to the basic expectancy theory formulations—for instance, the family and peer pressure indices from certain of the occupational choice studies. To do this certainly contributes to our overall understanding of human motivation; however, extending the research in this manner contributes little to our understanding of expectancy theory and of how and why its component variables work. There is a real risk that the expectancy concepts may become lost in a mélange of other constructs so that true understanding of the basic theory is impaired.

Without question, research on expectancy theory has come a long way, and predictions have improved accordingly as problems in the early studies have been unearthed, dealt with, and solved. Yet, there are remaining issues. One involves the use of multiplicative composites such as expectancy × valence in correlational analyses. There are inherent problems in doing this, and these problems are present in expectancy theory research (Evans, 1991). Interestingly, however, research indicates that many people do not employ multiplicative information processing, as the expectancy model implies, but rather prefer additive processes (Harrell & Stahl, 1986). This situation is similar to that noted in chapter 7 for job characteristics theory. Thus, ideally, multiplicative and additive information processors would be identified in advance and appropriate procedures would be applied in analyzing data from each. Individual differences continue to force their way into a theory that originally gave little attention to them.

A recent meta-analytic review of the research (Van Eerde & Thierry, 1996) confirms certain earlier conclusions and identifies some new ones. Within-subject, as opposed to between-subject, analyses continue to produce higher validity coefficients. When the total expectancy theory model (see figure 8.2) is used in the analysis, results are consistently supportive of the theory, but similar results are often reported for components of the theory. Thus expectancy × valence and valence × instrumentality seemed to work just as well as the full valence-instrumentality-expectancy model (although a number of the studies used a multiplicative approach incorrectly). The highest correlations were obtained with preference (the attractiveness of preference ratings of jobs, occupations, or organizations), intention (either to apply for a job or to turnover in a job), and effort (including measures of effort expenditure on a task such as time spent, effort ratings by supervisors, self-reports of effort spent on a task or applying for a job, and intended effort). Performance (including measures of productivity, gain in performance, task performance, grades, performance ratings by supervisors, and self-ratings) and choice (the actual voluntary turnover, job choice, and organizational choice) produced lower validities.

The results suggest that common method variance may have inflated some of the findings. However, it is also true that roughly one-third of the studies were conducted in the 1960s and early 1970s when methodological problems were frequent, thus depressing correlations overall. Other evidence indicates that expectancy theory is particularly suited to occupation/organizational choice situations (Wanous, Keon, & Latack, 1983). In this context validity coefficients in the .70s are not uncommon. Extensions to the job-seeking efforts of the unemployed would seem to be a fruitful application (Feather, 1992; Lynd-Stevenson, 1999).

Intrinsic and Extrinsic Motivation

In general, expectancy theory formulations have distinguished between extrinsic and intrinsic motivation, but they have viewed the two as additive, so that the distinction is of no special importance. There is, however, a line of reasoning and research that challenges this additive assumption. Statements of this position (see Deci & Ryan, 1985) pose a clear threat to expectancy theory in this regard.

Intrinsic motivation is defined as based on the desire for competence and self-determination. Among those who challenge expectancy theory, intrinsic motivation is measured almost exclusively by observing the amount of time spent on a task during a period when the subjects have a free choice as to what to do with their time. Intrinsic motivation is said to be facilitated by enhancing the subject's sense of self-determination—by, for instance, providing a choice of what to work on or what order to work on tasks—and by enhancing a sense of competence through the use of positive feedback. Extrinsic rewards, among which money is the most often cited, have a controlling aspect and an informational aspect. If the controlling aspect is salient, intrinsic motivation is decreased. If the informational or feedback aspect is salient and positive, intrinsic motivation is increased.

Many organizational behavior scholars have found it difficult to accept the view that extrinsic motivation often operates to reduce intrinsic motivation. The results of research testing expectancy theory do not seem to be consistent with such an interpretation. Furthermore, incentive pay systems repeatedly have been found to increase performance levels. It is hard to believe they should be abandoned because they control intrinsic motivation and thus reduce it. It seems unlikely that the phenomenon described by Edward Deci and Richard Ryan (1985) has practical relevance. Many jobs, such as those of a managerial, professional, and entrepreneurial nature, frequently appear to engage such high levels of intrinsic motivation that performance is impervious to any possible negative extrinsic impact. Also, some kind of explicit or implicit inducement-contribution contract that involves extrinsic inducements, including pay, is the prevailing norm in the world of work, and under such circumstances the phenomenon described by Deci on the current evidence does not appear to operate.

As a result of these and other considerations, reviewers have generally come to reject the idea that a subtractive relationship exists, as is implied by what has been called cognitive evaluation theory (Locke & Henne, 1986; Thierry, 1990; Bartol & Locke, 2000), or they have concluded that more study is required before accepting the theory is warranted. There is some evidence that intrinsic motivation should be conceptualized as episodic and temporally bounded, and this too has lead to reviewer concerns (Kanfer, 1992). Particularly significant are the results of a meta-analysis that used the nature of the research design employed as a contingency variable. These results are described as follows:

> Multiple measures are necessary to determine the convergent validity of a construct to avoid methodological weaknesses inherent in a particular measure. Free-time and performance measures, two different operationalizations of intrinsic motivation, do not converge, i.e. react similarly under similar experimental treatments. The lack of convergence suggests that different constructs, may be being measured and that the two measures should not be used interchangeably as operationalizations of intrinsic motivation. Subsequent research should specify the domain of observables for the construct of intrinsic motivation more clearly. (Wiersma, 1992, p. 112)

This lack of construct validity is inherent in the fact that 88 percent of the free time study results operate in a manner that is consistent with predictions from cognitive evaluation theory, but only 15 percent of the results produced from studies using performance results support that theory. Combining the two sets of findings, which to be entirely proper one should not do, gives a value of −.136, in the direction posited by cognitive evaluation theory, but far from significantly different from 0. Clearly there is something going on here that needs explaining, but Deci's theory does not provide a full explanation.

More recent analyses unfortunately have not resolved this puzzle. At last count there were something like eight meta-analyses of the literature that in one way or another considered the issue at hand. Furthermore, unlike what has been the case in most other literatures, the results obtained do not always coincide; in fact a substantial controversy now exists as to what the literature really says, and whose approach to aggregating it is most valid (or least flawed). It is quite possible now to find a meta-analysis that supports almost any position one wishes to espouse.

Out of all this have come several conclusions that, although they do not solve the problems, may point the way in the right direction:

- An undermining effect can be demonstrated with considerable consistency, and the free-time condition is particularly likely to elicit this effect (Deci, Koestner, & Ryan, 1999a).
- There are conditions where rewards such as money do not necessarily undermine intrinsic motivation; undermining is less pronounced in the case of performance-contingent rewards than otherwise (Deci, Koestner, & Ryan, 1999a).
- Meta-analysis may well not be the method of choice for combining literatures that are procedurally diverse, theoretically derived, and empirically complex — like the cognitive evaluation theory literature (Lepper, Henderlong, & Gingras, 1999).
- When one focuses only on more applied studies, the results indicate a positive or null (not negative) relationship between reward and intrinsic motivation (Eisenberger, Pierce, & Cameron, 1999).
- The undermining effect is particularly pronounced among children (Deci, Koestner, & Ryan, 1999b).

The hope is that these conclusions might point to findings that undermining does not operate with adults, in employing organizations, where performance-contingent rewards are used. Perhaps there are more areas of exclusion as well. However, the research breakthroughs to provide definitive answers in this regard are still off in the future.

Current Emphases

In the 1990s expectancy theory was not well represented in the literature emanating from the United States, although publications coming from other parts of the world do not show this diminution. The decline here appears to be due to the fact that (1) much of the excitement occurred some years ago, (2) utilizing these ideas directly in practice is difficult, and (3) expectancy theory frequently has been integrated into or tied to other theories (Mitchell, 1997).

We have considered the first and second of these explanations. The third does not necessarily represent so much a decline in interest in expectancy theory as a reorientation of interest. Nevertheless, there clearly has been an increasing tendency to look at expectancy theory in conjunction with other theories (Kanfer, 1992). We will consider these matters in the remainder of this chapter, in chapter 9, and at points elsewhere in this book, as we take up these other theories. In particular, goal-setting theory and research have come to take on the concepts and terminology of expectancy theory.

Overall, the expectancy theory framework taken in a general sense seems at the present time to have achieved a position where it is widely supported by a diverse array of reviewers (Pinder, 1998; Ambrose & Kulik, 1999; Bartol & Locke, 2000). We do not know as much as might be desired about how it works in a cognitive sense, but we do believe it works.

ORGANIZATIONAL BEHAVIOR MODIFICATION AND OPERANT LEARNING

We turn now to the legacy that B. F. Skinner left to organizational behavior. Skinner himself, however, wrote little and conducted no research that dealt directly with organizational topics; his concerns were either with individual behavior or with the broad spectrum of culture and societal functioning. Thus, it has fallen to others to extrapolate Skinner's ideas into the organizational setting and to conduct research related to those extrapolations. Skinner indicates his own relationship to the field of organizational study in the following quotation from one of the interviews that represent his only specific published contributions to the field:

> I'm not a specialist in industrial psychology. I have only a casual acquaintance with the kinds of things done by Douglas McGregor and Abe Maslow. They do not strike me as being particularly effective. You can classify motives and still neglect contingencies of reinforcement, and the contingencies are the important thing. Behavior modification is beginning to get into industry, and that may mean a change. Up to now it's been most effective in psychotherapy, in handling disturbed and retarded children, in the design of classroom management, and in programmed instruction. It is possible that we're going to see an entirely different kind of psychology in industry. Unfortunately there are not yet many people who understand the principle. It is not something that can be taken over by the nonprofessional to use as a rule of thumb. In the not-too-distant future, however, a new breed of industrial manager may be able to apply the principles of operant conditioning effectively. (Skinner & Dowling, 1973, p. 40)

Background

A number of different individuals published extensions of Skinner's ideas to the organizational domain during the late 1960s and early 1970s. The industrial *Zeitgeist* appears to have been ripe for this kind of approach, since an earlier effort (Aldis, 1961) had almost no impact. Some of these extrapolations are presented as direct restatements of Skinner's previously published views; others do not even acknowledge a debt to Skinner. But all are directly concerned with the process of influencing employee behavior to desired ends by using techniques of behavior modification.

The initial statement in this period appears to be that of Walter Nord (1969). This was soon followed by articles by Fred Luthans and Donald White (1971), Melvin Sorcher (1971), and Everett Adam and William Scott (1971). Among these early contributors, Luthans stands out on a number of grounds. His theoretical treatment is more comprehensive, deals with a wider range of topics, and attempts a greater depth of explanation. He has written about a number of research applications and has continued to write on the subject over a period of many years; the other early writers, however, have since turned to other endeavors. Beginning in 1971 Luthans has conducted his research and set forth his theory in conjunction with a number of doctoral students and former students, but throughout he has remained the central figure in what he termed at an early point organizational behavior modification, or simply O. B. Mod. (Luthans, 1973).

Luthans did his undergraduate work at the University of Iowa in engineering and mathematics. He entered the business school there in 1961, and after completing his M.B.A. continued on in the Ph.D. program. He received his doctorate from Iowa in 1965 at the young age of 25. From there he entered the military and taught at West Point for several years, before he accepted a faculty position at the University of Nebraska, where he has remained throughout his career.

Luthans became interested in Skinner's ideas while doing training work with the Nebraska State Mental Health System during the late 1960s. There he learned about the successes being achieved with these ideas, applying them to the treatment side of mental health. He set out to determine whether similar successes might be achieved by applying operant-based learning approaches and techniques in human resource management (Luthans, 1996). He has been studying the subject ever since.

As an introduction to organizational behavior modification I start with certain formulations set forth by Clay Hamner during the early to mid-1970s. These formulations provide a particularly useful bridge between Skinner and O. B. Mod. Hamner received his doctorate in organizational behavior from Indiana University and has taught there, at Michigan State University, at Northwestern University, and at Duke University—all in their business schools. During the 1980s he began moving out of the field of organizational behavior and ultimately took up other endeavors.

Hamner's Formulations of Reinforcement Theory

The basic concept of the theory is *learning*, which is defined as "a relatively permanent change in behavior potentiality that results from reinforced practice or experience" (Hamner, 1974a, p. 87). Performance is the translation of what is learned into practice. Through reinforcement, certain behaviors are strengthened and intensified and thus occur more frequently.

Behavior may occur in a reflex manner in response to changes in the environment. This type of behavior is of little concern for the theory. What is important is *operant* behavior—that is, behavior emitted by a person that influences or has an effect on the individual's outside world. Operant behaviors are learned as consequences accrue in the form of rewards and punishments that are applied contingent upon whether certain behaviors do or do not occur. Thus, the role of the supervisor becomes one of orchestrating reinforcements to produce desired behaviors at a high frequency; this is how performance can be improved.

Operant learning involves a process whereby reinforcers are applied to initially randomly emitted behaviors. Accordingly, to understand a person's behavior one must know the situation in which the behavior occurs, the nature of the behavior, and the reinforcing consequences. To influence a person's behavior in a desired direction one must know how to arrange correctly the contingencies of reinforcement. The major hypotheses of the theory relate to the relative effectiveness of manipulating the contingencies of reinforcement in different ways.

Type of Contingencies

Four different types of arrangements of contingencies are specified. Two serve to strengthen desired behavior (positive reinforcement and avoidance learning), and two serve to weaken undesired behavior (extinction and punishment). "A *positive reinforcer* is a stimulus which, when added to a situation, strengthens the probability of an operant response" (Skinner, 1953, p. 73). Certain reinforcers such as food, water, and sex are innate and thus operate independent of past experiences. In the work context, however, the important reinforcers are learned, such as advancement, praise, recognition, and money. What is a reinforcer for one person may not be for another; it depends on the individual's past reinforcement history.

Hamner (1974a) describes three steps in the successful application of reinforcement theory in the work environment:

1. Select reinforcers that are powerful and durable for the individual
2. Design contingencies so as to make the occurrence of reinforcing events contingent on desired behavior
3. Design contingencies so that a reliable procedure for eliciting the desired behavior is established

The third point is important because if one cannot ever find the desired behavior to reward, learning cannot occur. Training thus becomes a method of *shaping* behavior so that it can be controlled by reinforcement procedures. Separate aspects and approximations of the total desired behavior are reinforced until finally the behavior as a whole is shaped; learning to drive a car might be an example.

Avoidance learning operates in a manner similar to positive reinforcement except that the desired behavior serves to prevent the onset of a noxious stimulus, or, in a variant, terminates such a stimulus that already exists. In the workplace, supervisory criticism is often such a noxious stimulus. Although avoidance learning is effective under certain circumstances, many behavior modification advocates, including Skinner, much prefer positive reinforcement.

Extinction occurs when a previously utilized positive reinforcer is withheld. Under such circumstances the behavior involved may continue for some time, but as the reward continually fails to appear, the behavior diminishes and ultimately is extinguished entirely. This approach is appropriate when an individual brings undesired behaviors to the job or when an undesired behavior has inadvertently been reinforced in the past.

Many behavior modification advocates prefer extinction to *punishment* as a method of influencing behavior, on the grounds that punishment may have certain negative side effects. Skinner himself does not favor the use of punishment. There are, however, many behavior modification approaches in use that draw heavily on the reinforcement effects of punishment. There is no unanimity on this matter.

Hamner (1974a) and Hamner and Hamner (1976) present several rules for using operant conditioning techniques, which might best be considered as hypotheses with regard to how desired behaviors may be obtained:

1. Do not give the same level of reward to all; differentiate based on some performance standard.
2. Failure to respond to behavior has reinforcing consequences; these consequences should be recognized, and nonactions as well as actions should be adjusted to the desired ends.
3. Tell a person what behavior gets reinforced.
4. Tell a person what he or she is doing wrong.
5. Do not punish in front of others; there may be undesirable side effects not only for the person punished but for the others as well.
6. Make the consequences equal to the behavior.

Schedules of Reinforcement

Although a variety of different reinforcement schedules are possible, certain ones are of particular theoretical and practical relevance. *Continuous reinforcement* occurs when every instance of the desired behavior is followed by the reinforcer. This approach often is not practical in a complex work environment in which managers supervise many employees. Although continuous reinforcement fosters rapid learning, it also produces behavior that is subject to rapid extinction, should the reinforcer be removed for any reason.

Overall, some kind of *partial reinforcement* schedule is recommended. Partial reinforcement, when reinforcement does not occur after every emergence of an operant, is relatively slow but has the advantage of

considerable permanence. Four such schedules require discussion:

Fixed interval — reinforcement occurs when the desired behavior manifests itself after a set period of time has passed since the previous reinforcement

Variable interval — reinforcement occurs at some variable interval of time around an average

Fixed ratio — reinforcement occurs after a fixed number of desired behaviors are produced

Variable ratio — reinforcement occurs after a number of desired responses, with this number changing from one reinforcement to the next, varying around an average

These schedules are presented in order of anticipated increasing effectiveness. Fixed interval procedures tend to yield cyclical fluctuations with desired behaviors maximized just prior to reinforcement. In general, the variable approaches produce slower extinction and more stable performance levels. The variable ratio schedule is considered to be particularly attractive, although it may not be as easy to implement. In all instances it is important that the reinforcer follow the desired behavior as closely as possible.

Stages in Developing a Positive Reinforcement Program

Hamner (1974b) and Hamner and Hamner (1976) have set forth certain steps or stages that should be followed when introducing a positive reinforcement program into a company. In essence, this is an applied theory of performance maximization. Underlying these statements is the view that positive reinforcement should be maximized and punishment should be minimized. Furthermore, worker attitudes as a cause of behavior are ignored on the grounds that behavior can be fully explained in terms of the work situation and the contingencies of reinforcement.

The first stage is to define performance in strictly behavioral terms and to conduct a performance audit with the objective of establishing a baseline for measuring future performance. This procedure makes it possible to determine what the current performance situation is, in as objective a manner as possible.

The second stage involves setting specific and reasonable performance goals for each worker, expressed in measurable terms. These goals, however they may be established, are external to the individual; there is no invoking of experiential concepts such as intentions, expectations, and the like.

The third stage is to have the employee maintain a continuing record of work, a schedule of reinforcements. This way it is possible for the individual to picture how current work contrasts with that of the performance audit stage and with the goals established in stage two. The objective is to create a situation in which behavior that will warrant positive reinforcement occurs. One way of doing this is to shorten the time intervals of measurement as much as possible.

The fourth stage is described as follows:

> The supervisor looks at the self-feedback report of the employee and/or other indications of performance (e.g. sales records) and then praises the positive aspects of the employee's performance (as determined by the performance audit and goals set). This extrinsic reinforcement should strengthen the desired performance, while the withholding of praise for the performance which falls below the goal should give the employee incentive to improve that level of performance. Since the worker already knows the areas of his or her deficiencies, there is no reason for the supervisor to criticize. . . . Use of positive reinforcement leads to a greater feeling of self-control, while the avoidance of negative reinforcement keeps the individual from feeling controlled or coerced. (Hamner, 1974b, p. 285)

Although the preceding discussion focuses on reinforcement by praise, other approaches may be used as appropriate to the individual's reinforcement history, including money, freedom to choose one's activities, opportunity to see oneself achieving, higher status on some dimension, and power over others.

Organizational Behavior Modification Theory

Organizational behavior modification is set forth in two books and several articles. There is a 1970s version most fully presented in the book *Organizational Behavior Modification* (Luthans & Kreitner, 1975) and then a 1980s version, which is different in important respects, presented in *Organizational Behavior Modification and Beyond* (Luthans & Kreitner, 1985). We will start with the 1970s approach.

Rejection of Internal States as Causes

Luthans and Kreitner (1975) are explicit in following Skinner with regard to the rejection of internal states (attitudes, motives, feelings, and the like) as causes of behavior. Behavior is said to be strictly a function of its consequences, not of internal motives; thus the theory is really one of learning, not motivation, although the ultimate outcome remains performance, as in the preceding theories. Unobservable internal states are irrelevant to understanding behavior and generally are mere concomitants of the behaviors themselves. Inner-state constructs such as achievement motivation, expectancy, intentions and goals, self-actualization, feelings of equity, and so on have no place in the theory. At least they are said not to. In this sense it represents a radical departure from previous theories (Luthans & Otteman, 1973).

This 1970s theory, in contrast to others that generally espouse behaviorist principles but include internal variables in their formulations as well, fully accepts the following position:

> What we feel are conditions of our bodies, most of them closely associated with behavior and with the circumstances in which we behave. We both strike *and* feel angry for a common reason, and that reason lies in the environment. In short, the bodily conditions we feel are *collateral products* of our genetic and environmental histories. They have no explanatory force; they are simply additional facts to be taken into account. (Skinner, 1975, p. 43)

Stages of the 1970s Behavioral Contingency Management Model

Luthans and Kreitner (1975) present an approach to identifying and managing the critical performance-related behaviors of employees in organizations. They call this approach the behavioral contingency management model for organizational behavior modification. This model presents a series of stages not unlike those suggested by Hamner:

1. Identify performance-related behaviors using the following questions as guidelines:
   a. Can the behavior be reduced to *observable* behavioral events?

b. Can one *count* how often each behavior occurs?

c. *Exactly* what must the person do before a behavior is recorded?

d. Is a key *performance-related* behavior involved?

2. Measure to establish frequencies of behaviors using such procedures as tally sheets and time sampling.

3. Identify existing contingencies of reinforcement to determine where the behavior takes place and what its consequences are by:

a. Analyzing histories of reinforcement.

b. Using self-report measures.

c. Resorting to systematic trial and error to identify reinforcers.

4. Carry out the intervention process as follows:

a. Develop an intervention strategy considering such environmental variables as structures, processes, technologies, groups, and tasks.

b. Apply the appropriate strategy using suitable types of contingencies.

c. Measure to establish the frequencies of behaviors after intervention.

d. Maintain desired behaviors through the use of appropriate schedules of reinforcement.

5. Evaluate the overall performance impacts.

Obviously there are differences in this approach as opposed to Hamner, such as with regard to establishing goals and the techniques of measurement used. But overall the similarities are greater than the differences. The two together provide a reasonably good picture of how behavior modification theory can reduce to practice.

Shaping, Modeling, and Self-Control in the 1970s

Shaping, which is considered only relatively briefly by Hamner, is described in a step-by-step manner in table 8.3. The following quotation serves to amplify that statement:

Closer approximations to the target response are emitted and contingently reinforced. The less desirable approximations, including those reinforced earlier in the shaping process, are put on extinction. In this manner, behavior may actually be shaped into what is desired. Shaping solves the problem of waiting for the opportunity to reinforce a desired response. It is a particularly important technique in behavior modification if a desired response is not currently in a person's behavior repertoire. (Luthans & Kreitner, 1975, p. 55)

Table 8.3 also sets forth the steps in modeling, a type of learning that has a somewhat uncertain status in behavior modification. Note that phrases such as attention, participation, and demonstration of positive consequences come into the discussion—implying internal causal states that a true behaviorist would consider irrelevant to theory construction. It is difficult to deal with modeling or imitation without resort to such constructs; yet complex behaviors do become learned rather quickly, obviously too quickly to be a result of shaping. Luthans and Kreitner (1975) follow Albert Bandura (1971) in making this kind of learning part of their theory even though it is almost impossible to handle it without resort to internal constructs such as imagination, memory, and the like. At this point a certain amount of logical inconsistency is introduced into their theory.

This same problem plagues the discussion of self-control as well, another concept of somewhat uncertain status in behavior modification theory. In the strict behavioral sense, self-control involves the manipulation of environmental consequences by the individual to determine his or her own behavior. However, most people who try to put the idea in the employment context, including Luthans and Kreitner (1975), find it impossible not to invoke internal constructs.

Status of Punishment

Hamner notes that punishment as a type of contingency can have certain negative side effects that make it relatively unattractive. In contrast, Luthans is more accepting of the use of punishment, while recognizing its limitations. Four such side effects are noted:

1. Punishment serves to suppress behavior temporarily rather than to change it permanently, with the result that a method of continued punitive reinforcement must be devised; often this requires a manager's continued presence.

2. Punishment generates emotional behavior, often against the punisher.

3. Punishment may serve not to suppress behavior temporarily, but to stifle it permanently under any and all circumstances, thus producing a degree of behavioral inflexibility.

TABLE 8.3 Strategies for shaping and modeling

Shaping	Modeling
Define the performance-related target behavior	Identify the target behavior desired.
If the target behavior is a complex chain, reduce it to a discrete, observable, and measurable sequence of steps.	Select the appropriate model and its medium, such as in-person demonstration, training film.
Be sure the individual is able to meet the skill and ability requirements of each step.	Be sure the individual is capable of meeting the skill requirements of the target behavior.
Select appropriate positive reinforcers based on the individual's history of reinforcement.	Structure a favorable learning context with regard to attention, participation, and the target behavior.
Structure the contingent environment so that antecedent conditions will foster desired behavior.	Model the target behavior and support it by activities such as role playing; demonstrate the positive consequences of the modeled behavior.
Make all positive reinforcements contingent on increasingly close approximations to the target behavior so that the behavioral chain is built gradually.	Reinforce all progress of the modeled behavior.
Once the target behavior is achieved, reinforce it at first continuously and then on a variable basis.	Once the target behavior is achieved, reinforce it at first continuously and then on a variable basis.

SOURCE: Adapted from Fred Luthans & Robert Kreitner (1975), *Organizational Behavior Modification* (Glenview, IL: Scott, Foresman), 132–133, 140–141

4. A frequently punishing individual may assume the role of a conditioned aversive stimulus, with the result that he or she disrupts self-control efforts and cannot effectively administer positive reinforcers.

These considerations generally are consistent with those discussed by Nord (1969), who also indicates that punishment does not necessarily produce the desired behavior, only the cessation of the punished behavior. Another undesired behavior may be next in the response hierarchy, replacing the one punished. Yet, given all these arguments, punishment is still widely used in managing organizations and in behavior modification (Luthans & Kreitner, 1973).

Organizational Behavior Modification in the 1980s

By the early 1980s two versions of the theory were clearly in evidence. There was the antecedent (environmental context) → behavior → consequences of behavior (A-B-C) model that characterized the 1970s (see, for example, Thompson & Luthans, 1983). There was also a model labeled S-O-B-C: situation (the stimulus and the broader antecedent environment, overt or covert) ← → organism (the cognitive processes that play a mediating role; the person) ← → behavior (the response or pattern of behavior, overt or covert)

← → consequences (the contingent consequence which can be reinforcing or punishing, overt or covert) (see, for example, Davis & Luthans, 1980). The S-O-B-C model adds *social learning*, whereby people learn by observing other people, to the earlier view. This is manifest in the "organism" component and in the use of the term *covert* to imply a process within the person. By the middle of the 1980s these two models, or theoretical versions, had been combined so that social learning now had been made explicit and internal states as causes were no longer rejected (Kreitner & Luthans, 1984; Luthans & Kreitner, 1985). Thus the logical inconsistency previously noted is cleared up.

Luthans draws heavily on the social learning theory of Bandura (1977) for this new version of his theory. The processes inherent in social learning are depicted in figure 8.3. Here people influence their environment, which, in turn, influences their thoughts and behavior. Social learning extends the operant, A-B-C model of learning, with its entirely external emphasis, by explaining how individuals process environmental stimuli. Accordingly it becomes much easier to explain why similar people in similar situations often behave in very different ways.

Figure 8.4 presents the revised and integrated model, the S-O-B-C approach. Under *situation*, cues do not actually cause subsequent behavior, but they

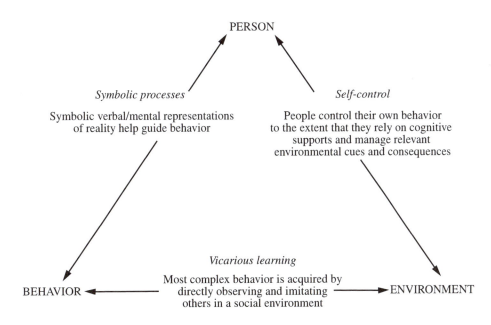

FIGURE 8.3 A model of the social learning process. From Robert Kreitner & Fred Luthans (1984), A Social Learning Approach to Behavioral Management: Radical Behaviorists "Mellowing Out," *Organizational Dynamics*, 13(2), 55. Copyright 1984. Reprinted with permission from Elsevier Science.

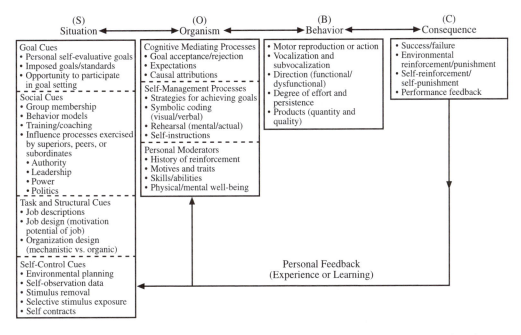

FIGURE 8.4 The 1980s expanded model of organizational behavior modification. From Fred Luthans & Robert Kreitner (1985), *Organizational Behavior Modification and Beyond: An Operant and Social Learning Approach* (Glenview, IL: Scott, Foresman), 220. Copyright 1985. Reprinted by permission of Pearson Education, Inc.

do set the occasion for the behavior to be emitted in an operant manner. Under *organism*, the role that cognitive mediating and self-control processes play, as influenced by personal characteristics, is depicted. Note that *expectations* are explicitly included, bringing the revised theory much closer to expectancy theory. Under *behavior*, a number of dimensions are introduced, including subvocalization (thought). Under *consequences*, self-reinforcement (self-control) is noted and a feedback loop is introduced, indicating that consequences (1) influence mediating cognitions, self-management processes, and personal moderators and (2) give power to situational cues.

Consonant with the introduction of social learning, the theory now says that much learning occurs through modeling one's behavior on the actions of others. People select, organize, and change stimuli around them as they learn new behaviors; they also anticipate consequences of their acts—rewards and punishments, for instance—and their behaviors are motivated accordingly. In contrast to radical behaviorists, social learning theorists believe that cognitive processes play an important role in learning.

With the incorporation of social learning concepts, organizational behavior modification can deal with approaches such as *self-management*, whereby people regulate their own actions. Self-management requires the deliberate manipulation of stimuli, internal processes, and responses to achieve personally identified behavioral outcomes. In figure 8.4 note the frequent reference to internal thought processes—planning, personal goals, self-contracts, mental rehearsal, expectations, and the like—and the important causal role given these processes in the creation of self-controlled behavior.

Self-management is much more important in organizations than has generally been recognized, although it is not sufficient in and of itself to produce a coordinated organizational effort. Self-management has the advantage that it reduces the chance of criticism on grounds of unethical manipulation of others for one's own benefit, as when a manager "uses" a subordinate. Self-management has the quality of self-determination and self-control, as opposed to being controlled by others.

Luthans (1996) is not entirely comfortable with the S-O-B-C model; he really prefers the radical A-B-C version with its much greater parsimony, and he considers the empirical support to be greater there

as well. Yet he views the extension as necessary to handling a wider range of phenomena.

Reaching out to Other Theories

Since the mid-1980s Luthans on several occasions has proposed further extensions of organizational behavior modification theory beyond the integration with social learning theory. The objective in each instance appears to be to expand the theoretical domain covered and to widen the number of phenomena that are explained. Examples are ties to goal-setting theory, attribution theory, and macro-oriented organizational perspectives (Luthans & Martinko, 1987). More recently, ties have been proposed with social cognitive theory and with the self-efficiency construct (Stajkovic & Luthans, 1998). This latter approach again brings Luthans together with Bandura (1997; Wood & Bandura, 1989).

These extensions have not been worked out in the same degree of theoretical detail as with the social learning theory integration, and, accordingly, at present they cannot be considered components in full standing of organizational behavior modification theory. It appears that Luthans is attempting to draft a comprehensive general theory of human motivation and behavior in organizational contexts, but the theoretical links necessary to achieve this objective have not been established as yet.

Evaluation and Impact

Starting in the late 1960s and continuing to the present, a number of organizations have undertaken sizable, continuing applications of behavior modification with the objective of reducing absenteeism, increasing output, achieving cost savings, and the like. These applications typically involve specific, relatively large components within the organization. In most instances they do not represent controlled experiments as much as demonstrations of the feasibility of behavior modification. Frequently, hard data on successes and failures are lacking, and one must rely on testimonials. Yet there have been a sizable number of well-controlled studies as well. We will focus on the latter because it is there that any meaningful evaluation of organizational behavior modification must obtain its data. The research in which Luthans has been involved is particularly relevant.

Research Involving Luthans

Although Luthans—in collaboration with various students and former students—has published considerable research testing his theory, certain studies stand out. A test using salespeople in a department store, for instance, is described by Luthans (1996) as his strongest methodologically and as the most comprehensive study on the impact of O. B. Mod. The design used experimental and control groups constituted from the membership of randomly selected departments (Luthans, Paul, & Baker, 1981). There was also a feature whereby subjects served as their own controls using a baseline period, intervention, and then a return to baseline conditions. Criterion data were derived from periodic observations of behavior, which yielded from 93 to 98 percent agreement, depending on the reliability measure used. The intervention made available contingent rewards, consisting of time off with pay, equivalent cash, and eligibility for a company-paid vacation for performance above standard. Engaging in selling and other performance-related behavior was very similar during the first baseline period for both experimental and control groups. These behaviors increased dramatically in the experimental (but not control) group during the intervention. This pattern of increase carried over into the return to baseline period, although the difference between experimentals and controls was less pronounced. When nonwork behavior was used as a criterion, these results were repeated except that, of course, the measure dropped with the intervention. That the measures after intervention did not return to baseline levels is not totally unexpected, but it does invoke post hoc explanation.

A later study conducted in a manufacturing context using an ABAB design, but without a control group, yielded a more typical result (Luthans, Maciag, & Rosenkrantz, 1983). In such a study the steps are as follows:

A. *The baseline period.* Establish a baseline measure of behavior prior to learning.
B. *The period of intervention.* Introduce the learning intervention while continuing to measure.
A. *The period of no intervention.* When the behavior has stabilized at a new level, withdraw the learning intervention and reestablish baseline conditions. This reversal should cause the behavior to revert to the baseline level.

B. *The period when intervention was reintroduced.* When the behavior has stabilized back at the baseline level, reintroduce the same learning intervention and see if the behavior frequency changes once again.

If withdrawing the intervention (the second A step) does not cause the behavior to shift back toward the baseline level (as it does in figure 8.5), it is possible that some external factor, such as a pay raise, produced the initial results.

Another research effort that occasions special mention from Luthans (1996) was carried out in a Russian factory (Welsh, Luthans, & Sommer, 1993). A within-subject experimental design similar to that used in the department store was employed, but without control groups. Three different experimental interventions were compared: (1) provision of extrinsic rewards consisting of American goods rarely available in Russia contingent upon performance improvement, (2) provision of social rewards (praise and recognition) by supervisors trained to contingently administer these rewards, and (3) initiation of participative decision making whereby the workers come up with suggestions for job enrichment and were empowered to carry them out. There is no specific evidence as to whether job enrichment per se actually "took" as an intervention. The first intervention increased production levels, and then there was a partial reversion to baseline levels subsequent to the withdrawal of the intervention. The second intervention produced a similar effect, except that the decline after withdrawal was significant. The third intervention actually produced a decline in production levels. This last result is attributed to culturally based mistrust of participative procedures.

Taken as a whole these studies demonstrate considerable validity for organizational behavior modification, using both varied experimental designs and varied research contexts and types of subjects.

Meta-Analysis of O. B. Mod. Studies

A meta-analysis conducted by Stajkovic and Luthans (1997) draws on a much larger research base, but it also reaches a very favorable conclusion for organizational behavior modification. The inclusion requirements for the meta-analysis were established in such a way that over 60 percent of the studies used involved

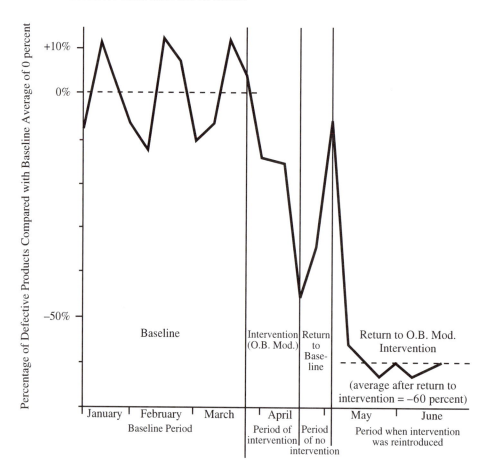

FIGURE 8.5 Reversal analysis of the effects of O. B. Mod. intervention on the number of defective products produced. From Fred Luthans, Walter S. Maciag, & Stuart A. Rosenkrantz (1983), O.B. Mod.: Meeting the Productivity Challenge with Human Resources Management, *Personnel*, 60(2), 35. Copyright 1983. Used with permission ACC Communications, Inc.

Luthans as a coauthor, and most of the remaining studies were authored by a person with ties to the University of Nebraska. Thus, this essentially is a test of the theory proposed by Luthans. Although Luthans has endorsed single-subject studies (Luthans & Davis, 1982), such studies were excluded from the analysis on the grounds that generalization is not warranted. However, the average effect size is based on only 25 subjects, which is a typical situation in behavior modification research.

Across the 19 studies and 115 effect sizes there was a significant increase in performance, which amounted to a 17 percent improvement, with the introduction of an organizational behavior modification intervention. This increase existed for both manufacturing and service organizations, but it was greater in the manufacturing context. Financial, nonfinancial, and social reinforcers all demonstrated significant effects on outcomes.

Does Behavior Modification Work?

There is considerable evidence that a theory that ignores cognitive variables does not work very well in explaining behavior when it moves into the realm of complex organizations. Extrapolators have consistently felt compelled to repudiate the radical behaviorism of Skinner and to introduce internal, cognitive factors. One reason for this is that under Skinnerian assumptions the only true way to understand and predict behavior, taking into account individual differences, is to comprehend the person's full reinforcement history. But this is a practical impossibility for mature working adults. Cognitively based theories typically view present thoughts, feelings, attitudes, and the like as providing an adequate representation of past experience and learning; accordingly, they offer a feasible method of dealing with factors that radical behaviorism cannot deal with practically.

Behaviorists argue that their theoretical approach has the advantage of parsimony. But in science, parsimony is a positive value only, "all else being equal." In this case all is not equal; cognitive theories add something above and beyond the strict behaviorist approach in the areas of understanding, prediction, and managing the future. That is why when behavior modification moves into organizations, cognitive variables tend to emerge even when the theorists do their best to avoid them. This appears to be particularly true in dealing with such clearly important phenomena as modeling or imitation and self-control. But the question then becomes whether behavior modification and operant learning theory are needed at all. As a number of writers have indicated, expectancy theory and goal-setting theory, perhaps even equity theory, may be more suitable (see, for instance, Locke, 1980).

The question thus becomes this: How well does behavior modification work, if at all? We have already seen from the Stajkovic and Luthans (1997) meta-analysis that one version of it works quite well. A review reported by Judith Komaki, Timothy Coombs, and Stephen Schepman (1996), which covered a much larger number of studies (51), found that 92 percent of these resulted in substantial improvements in performance. These positive results extended across a variety of target behaviors, a variety of different consequences, and a range of subjects and settings, and in some cases they have been shown to operate over periods of many years. Many examples of the diversity of successful research applications may be found in Richard O'Brien, Alyce Dickinson, and Michael Rosow (1982). A review that updated their prior analysis, and as a result substantially increased the number of studies, reported a similar 93 percent success rate (Komaki, Coombs, Redding, & Schepman, 2000).

A key aspect of the theory—noted by Hamner, Luthans, and many others—relates to the use of various schedules of reinforcement. In general, the research strongly supports the application of contingent reinforcement, but beyond this things become more cloudy. Continuous reinforcement appears to be much more effective, in contrast to partial reinforcement schedules, than theory predicts. There is some evidence that the predicted superiority of variable ratio schedules can be anticipated among very experienced workers. However, there are numerous circumstances under which it is not superior. At present it is not at all clear which reinforcement schedule or how much reinforcement is best (Mitchell, 1997). There appear to be major variations with the particular people involved.

Organizational behavior modification in some variant has been used widely and apparently successfully in practice. The unique practical contribution that this theory provides in contrast to other theories is captured in the following quotation:

> Where then lies the distinctiveness of the OB Mod approach? Its major characteristic may be the mental set with which the manager approaches a situation. OB Mod requires the manager to observe quantifiable behaviors, to establish base rates in order to determine the extent of the problem, to determine what reinforcers are supporting the undesirable behaviors, to estimate what stimulus will reinforce the desired behavior, and to chart the frequency of the desired behavior after the reinforcement intervention. It is this critical look at behaviors and contingencies that promises to provide a refreshing addition to the organizational behavior literature. (Korman, Greenhaus, & Badin, 1977, p. 189)

Given that a manager has developed the mental set implied by organizational behavior modification, where is the approach likely to work best? One requirement is that precise behavioral measures of the central performance variables in the work be possible. This is much more feasible for manual work than for managerial and professional positions. In any job there is always the risk that one will measure and reinforce behavior that is easily measured but contributes little if anything to actual performance.

Another requirement is that it be possible to control the contingencies of reinforcement. Much of the success of behavior modification has been achieved with children, often in schools; with hospitalized mental patients; with prisoners; and, of course, originally with animals. In these cases control is relatively easy. In many jobs it is not so easy—for instance, when reinforcements administered by coworkers have long been a primary influence on individual performance. This need for control capability is closely related to a need for simplicity and independence. Developing an appropriate reinforcement approach becomes increasingly difficult as jobs become more complex, involving interacting performance dimensions, and relate to other jobs as subsystems of a larger whole. Behavior modification risks producing sufficient behavior rigidity so that the individual follows one particular course at the expense of other important goals. In interactive situations that call for coordinated effort, it can well yield something less than an optimal overall result.

Does Behavior Modeling Work?

Other than in the area of self-management, organizational behavior modification has been used primarily in dealing with nonmanagers in hierarchical organizations. Below the managerial level, it is much easier to prevent unintended environmental factors from intervening and disrupting the learning process. In contrast, *behavior modeling*, which like self-management is closely allied to social learning theory, has been used much more frequently at the managerial level. The approach is outlined in table 8.3. It received its initial impetus from a book on the subject by Arnold Goldstein and Melvin Sorcher (1974).

There is good evidence that modeling on the behaviors of superiors perceived as effective is an important method by which managers develop their own leadership styles. Thus the underlying premise of the approach is upheld. In addition, the studies that have been undertaken to evaluate the approach in terms of its impact on performance are generally favorable (Mayer & Russell, 1987). A problem arises, however, because in actual practice wide variations in the techniques employed exist, and little knowledge is available as to which of these techniques is the most effective. Furthermore, like most organizational behavior modification programs, behavior modeling can prove to be expensive. Accordingly, training in this area needs to be evaluated on a cost-benefit basis to determine how it stacks up against alternative management development procedures. In this connection it should be noted that behavior modeling seems to have relatively little impact on long-term values and attitudes, with the result that training effects may dissipate if they are not reinforced in the actual continuing work situation.

Practical experience indicates that teaching managers to use behavior modification techniques effec-

tively is not easy. At a minimum it requires a sizable investment in management development procedures. Although behavior modeling appears to have considerable promise, it is not clear that, as used in the role play component of the training it is a necessary condition for behavioral change. Considerable evidence of the type noted in chapter 6 in connection with the discussion of achievement motivation training, indicates that mental modeling in a person's mind alone can achieve similar results. Thinking one's way into a role initially, based on lectures, discussions, examples, and the like, may be less threatening and thus even more effective. Such an approach is inconsistent with the basic tenets of radical behaviorism and thus is less likely to be used by advocates of behavior modification.

Does Self-Control Work?

A second offshoot of behavior modification that has received increased attention in recent years, and which like behavior modeling has an uncertain status among radical behaviorists because of its reliance on internal constructs, is self-control. I use the term *self-control* to include concepts such as self-regulation, self-management, and self-leadership, all of which have appeared to designate variations in technique of the same type as found in behavior modeling (Williams, 1997).

Self-control in some form has an extended history in clinical psychology where it has a great deal of support. Labeled as *self-management*, there is no outside role model, and a person is taught to control and manipulate aspects of the environment so as to reward and punish behaviors that do and do not lead to intended results. The process may·be described as follows:

> Self-management is an effort by an individual to control his or her behavior. Self-management involves goal setting, establishing a contract, monitoring the ways in which the environment is hindering the attainment of the goals, and administering reinforcement or punishment based on self-evaluation. The first step in effective self-management is for the individual to set and commit to specific goals. Otherwise, self-monitoring—a precondition for self-evaluation—has no effect on behavior. Written contracts increase commitment by spelling out the reinforcing conditions for accepting the goal. (Frayne, 1991, p. 3)

Training that teaches people how to train themselves in this manner has been found very effective in reducing absenteeism (Latham & Frayne, 1989; Frayne, 1991; Frayne & Geringer, 2000). Other applications have proven successful as well (Kanfer, 1992). Clearly this is a very promising extension of organizational behavior modification. To the extent it incorporates goal-setting theory, it provides another instance of reaching out to other theories.

As previously noted, self-control procedures of any kind tend to relieve behavior modification of some of the ethical pressure it has been under, and this is another major plus for self-control. The reasoning here needs some explanation.

One of the reasons that organizational advocates of behavior modification often do not mention Skinner and attempt to disassociate themselves from his views is that certain of Skinner's writings — such as *Beyond Freedom and Dignity* (1971) — have elicited strong negative reactions on strictly ethical grounds. There has been a distinct tendency to avoid this "bad press" by using terms other than *behaviorism* and *operant conditioning*. Yet it is important to understand and evaluate these ethical considerations wherever they may be involved. Court decisions related to the use of behavior modifications procedures in the treatment of the emotionally ill have appeared with some frequency.

The primary ethical issue has been manipulation (Luthans & Kreitner, 1985). The argument is that behavior modification techniques put too much power in the hands of management, create debilitating dependencies on superiors, are essentially totalitarian rather than democratic in concept, and ignore both the rights of the individual and the principle of individual consent. Behavior modification thus becomes a method of using others for one's own purposes at their expense. It is particularly unethical when techniques of punishment and avoidance learning are employed, because individual suffering is added to the manipulation.

The purpose here is not to debate these issues but to provide an awareness of reactions that may follow the introduction of an organizational behavior modification effort. Militant union officials, social activists, and dedicated liberals often have been at the forefront of the opposition. However, it is important to recognize that any valid theory of the kind discussed in this book could well elicit the same reactions. The reason that the other theories typically have not, and behavior modification has, is that the latter creates an explicit image of mindless obedience to the will of others, devoid of any voluntary component. The cognitive theories imply a greater degree of control over one's own behavior. In practice, however, when some people understand the theory fully and others are totally unaware of it, this difference may be misleading. Thus, as our knowledge of organizational behavior advances, the potential for misuse and manipulation for personal gain can become a basic social issue with regard to any theory.

CONCLUSIONS

Expectancy theory and organizational behavior modification have a great deal in common, and there are major differences as well. As to the similarities: both derive from learning theory, both place strong reliance on contingent reinforcement, and both have demonstrated considerable validity in predicting a wide range of outcomes. No doubt the two account for much common variance in these outcomes. The differences are in the terminology, the focus on internal as opposed to external factors, and the extent to which useful applications have been developed.

One might think that combining the two theories would produce a much more powerful composite, giving expectancy theory a set of applications to practice and organizational behavior modification a set of processes to go in the black box that has been the organism or person. This would still leave unconscious motivation outside the composite theory, but it would go a long way toward handling individual motivational differences. Indeed, the way in which Luthans has been reaching out to other theories appears to be consistent with this scenario, although his focus appears to be more on theories that are closest to behavior modification, such as social learning theory and social cognitive theory.

One major barrier to integration of the two theoretical approaches is that two completely different sets of terminologies are involved. Yet theories, almost by definition, inevitably develop their own terminologies. In all likelihood a composite of expectancy and behavior modification theories would have to develop its own new terminology as well. Perhaps a greater barrier is that expectancy theory is not the only claimant to filling in the black box that radical behaviorism leaves. Two other claimants are equity theory and goal-setting theory. These theories require further explanation before their relation to behavior modification theory can be made clear; they concern us in the next chapter.

References

Adam, Everett E., & Scott, William E. (1971). The Application of Behavioral Conditioning Procedures to the Problems of Quality Control. *Academy of Management Journal*, 14, 175–193.

Aldis, Owen (1961). Of Pigeons and Men. *Harvard Business Review*, 39(4), 59–63.

Ambrose, Maureen L., & Kulik, Carol T. (1999). Old Friends, New Faces: Motivation Research in the 1990s. *Journal of Management*, 25, 231–292.

Bandura, Albert (1971). *Psychological Modeling: Conflicting Theories*. Chicago: Aldine-Atherton.

Bandura, Albert (1977). *Social Learning Theory*. Englewood Cliffs, NJ: Prentice Hall.

Bandura, Albert (1997). *Self-Efficacy: The Exercise of Control*. New York: W. H. Freeman.

Bartol, Kathryn M., & Locke, Edwin A. (2000). Incentives and Motivation. In Sara L. Rynes & Barry Gerhart (Eds.), *Compensation in Organizations: Current Research and Practice* (pp. 104–147). San Francisco: Jossey-Bass.

Davis, Tim R. V., & Luthans, Fred (1980). A Social Learning Approach to Organizational Behavior. *Academy of Management Review*, 5, 281–290.

Deci, Edward L.; Koestner, Richard; & Ryan, Richard M. (1999a). A Meta-Analytic Review of Experiments Examining the Effects of Extrinsic Rewards on Intrinsic Motivation. *Psychological Bulletin*, 125, 627–668.

Deci, Edward L.; Koestner, Richard; & Ryan, Richard M. (1999b). The Undermining Effect Is a Reality after All—Extrinsic Rewards, Task Interest, and Self-Determination: Reply to Eisenberger, Pierce, and Cameron (1999) and Lepper, Henderlong, and Gingras (1999). *Psychological Bulletin*, 125, 692–700.

Deci, Edward L., & Ryan, Richard M. (1985). *Intrinsic Motivation and Self-Determination in Human Behavior*. New York: Plenum.

Eisenberger, Robert; Pierce, W. David; & Cameron, Judy (1999). Effects of Reward on Intrinsic Motivation—Negative, Neutral, and Positive: Comment on Deci, Koestner, and Ryan (1999). *Psychological Bulletin*, 125, 677–691.

Evans, Martin G. (1991). The Problem of Analyzing Multiplicative Composites. *American Psychologist*, 46, 6–15.

Feather, Norman T. (1992). Expectancy-Value Theory and Unemployment Effects. *Journal of Occupational and Organizational Psychology*, 65, 315–330.

Frayne, Colette A. (1991). *Reducing Absenteeism through Self-Management Training: A Research-Based Analysis and Guide*. Westport, CT: Quorum.

Frayne, Colette A., & Geringer, J. Michael (2000). Self-Management Training for Improving Job Performance: A Field Experiment Involving Salespeople. *Journal of Applied Psychology*, 85, 361–372.

Galbraith, Jay, & Cummings, Larry L. (1967). An Empirical Investigation of the Motivational Determinants of Task Performance: Interactive Effects between Instrumentality-Valence and Motivation-Ability. *Organizational Behavior and Human Performance*, 2, 237–257.

Georgopoulos, Basil S.; Mahoney, Gerald M.; & Jones, Nyle W. (1957). A Path-Goal Approach to Productivity. *Journal of Applied Psychology*, 41, 345–353.

Goldstein, Arnold P., & Sorcher, Melvin (1974). *Changing Supervisor Behavior*. New York: Pergamon.

Graen, George (1969). Instrumentality Theory of Work Motivation: Some Experimental Results and Suggested Modifications. *Journal of Applied Psychology Monograph*, 53(2).

Hackman, L. Richard, & Porter, Lyman W. (1968). Expectancy Theory Predictions of Work Effectiveness. *Organizational Behavior and Human Performance*, 3, 417–426.

Hamner, W. Clay (1974a). Reinforcement Theory and Contingency Management in Organizational Settings. In Henry L. Tosi & W. Clay Hamner (Eds.), *Organizational Behavior and Management: A Contingency Approach* (pp. 86–112). Chicago: St. Clair Press.

Hamner, W. Clay (1974b). Worker Motivation Programs: Importance of Climate, Structure, and Performance Consequences. In W. Clay Hamner & Frank L. Schmidt (Eds.), *Contemporary Problems in Personnel: Readings for the Seventies* pp. 280–308). Chicago: St. Clair Press.

Hamner, W. Clay, & Hamner, Ellen P. (1976). Behavior Modification on the Bottom Line. *Organizational Dynamics*, 4(4), 3–21.

Harrell, Adrian, & Stahl, Michael (1986). Additive Information Processing and the Relationship between Expectancy of Success and Motivational Force. *Academy of Management Journal*, 29, 424–433.

Hilgard, Ernest R. (1948). *Theories of Learning*. New York: Appleton-Century-Crofts.

Ilgen, Daniel R.; Nebeker, Delbert M.; & Pritchard, Robert D. (1981). Expectancy Theory Measures: An Empirical Comparison in an Experimental Simulation. *Organizational Behavior and Human Performance*, 28, 189–223.

Kanfer, Ruth (1992). Work Motivation: New Directions in Theory and Research. *International Review of Industrial and Organizational Psychology*, 7, 1–53.

Komaki, Judith L.; Coombs, Timothy; Redding, Thomas P.; & Schepman, Stephen (2000). A Rich and Rigorous Examination of Applied Behavior Analysis Research in the World of Work. *International Review of Industrial and Organizational Psychology*, 15, 265–367.

Komaki, Judith L.; Coombs, Timothy; & Schepman, Stephen (1996). Motivational Implications of Reinforcement Theory. In Richard M. Steers, Lyman W. Porter, & Gregory A. Bigley (Eds.), *Motivation and Leadership at Work* (pp. 34–52). New York: McGraw-Hill.

Korman, Abraham K.; Greenhaus, Jeffrey H.; & Badin, Irwin J. (1977). Personnel Attitudes and Motivation. *Annual Review of Psychology*, 28, 175–196.

Kreitner, Robert, & Luthans, Fred (1984). A Social Learning Approach to Behavioral Management: Radical Behaviorists "Mellowing Out." *Organizational Dynamics*, 13(2), 47–65.

Latham, Gary P., & Frayne, Colette A. (1989). Self-Management Training for Increasing Job Attendance: A Follow-up and a Replication. *Journal of Applied Psychology*, 74, 411–416.

Lattal, Kennon A. (1992). B. F. Skinner and Psychology. *American Psychologist*, 47, 1269–1272.

Lawler, Edward E. (1968). A Correlational-Causal Analysis of the Relationship between Expectancy Attitudes and Job Performance. *Journal of Applied Psychology*, 52, 462–468.

Lawler, Edward E. (1971). *Pay and Organizational Effectiveness: A Psychological View*. New York: McGraw-Hill.

Lawler, Edward E. (1973, 1994). *Motivation in Work Organizations*. Monterey, CA: Brooks/Cole.

Lawler, Edward E. (1981). *Pay and Organization Development*. Reading, MA: Addison-Wesley.

Lawler, Edward E. (1993). Understanding Work Motivation and Organizational Effectiveness: A Career-Long Journey. In Arthur G. Bedeian (Ed.), *Management Laureates: A Collection of Autobiographical Essays* (Vol. 2, pp. 81–109). Greenwich, CT: JAI Press.

Lawler, Edward E., & Porter, Lyman W. (1967). Antecedent Attitudes of Effective Managerial Performance. *Organizational Behavior and Human Performance*, 2, 122–142.

Lepper, Mark R.; Henderlong, Jennifer; & Gingras, Isabelle (1999). Understanding the Effects of Extrinsic Rewards on Intrinsic Motivation — Uses and Abuses of Meta-Analysis: Comment on Deci, Koestner, and Ryan (1999). *Psychological Bulletin*, 125, 669–676.

Lewin, Kurt (1938). The Conceptual Representation and the Measurement of Psychological Forces. *Contributions to Psychological Theory*, 1(4).

Lewin, Kurt (1951). *Field Theory in Social Science*. New York: Harper.

Locke, Edwin A. (1975). Personnel Attitudes and Motivation. *Annual Review of Psychology*, 26, 457–480.

Locke, Edwin A. (1980). Latham versus Komaki: A Tale of Two Paradigms. *Journal of Applied Psychology*, 65, 16–23.

Locke, Edwin A., & Henne, Douglas (1986). Work Motivation Theories. *International Review of Industrial and Organizational Psychology*, 1, 1–35.

Luthans, Fred (1973). *Organizational Behavior*. New York: McGraw-Hill.

Luthans, Fred (1990). Conversation with Lyman W. Porter. *Organizational Dynamics*, 18(3), 69–79.

Luthans, Fred (1996). A Common Man Travels "Back to the Future." In Arthur G. Bedeian (Ed.), *Management Laureates: A Collection of Autobiographical Essays* (Vol. 4, pp. 153–199). Greenwich, CT: JAI Press.

Luthans, Fred, & Davis, Tim R. V. (1982). An Idiographic Approach to Organizational Behavior Research: The Use of Single Case Experimental Designs and Direct Measures. *Academy of Management Review*, 7, 380–391.

Luthans, Fred, & Kreitner, Robert (1973). The Role of Punishment in Organizational Behavior Modification (O.B. Mod.). *Public Personnel Management*, 2(3), 156–161.

Luthans, Fred, & Kreitner, Robert (1975). *Organizational Behavior Modification*. Glenview, IL: Scott, Foresman.

Luthans, Fred, & Kreitner, Robert (1985). *Organizational Behavior Modification and Beyond: An Operant and Social Learning Approach*. Glenview, IL: Scott, Foresman.

Luthans, Fred, Maciag, Walter S., & Rosenkrantz, Stuart A. (1983). O. B. Mod.: Meeting the Productivity Challenge with Human Resources Management. *Personnel*, 60(2), 28–36.

Luthans, Fred, & Martinko, Mark (1987). Behavioral Approaches to Organizations. *International Review of Industrial and Organizational Psychology*, 2, 35–60.

Luthans, Fred, & Otteman, Robert (1973). Motivation vs. Learning Approaches to Organizational Behavior. *Business Horizons*, 16(6), 55–62.

Luthans, Fred; Paul, Robert; & Baker, Douglas (1981). An Experimental Analysis of the Impact of Contingent Reinforcement on Salespersons' Performance Behavior. *Journal of Applied Psychology*, 66, 314–323.

Luthans, Fred, & White, Donald D. (1971). Behavior Modification: Application to Manpower Management. *Personnel Administration*, 34(4), 41–47.

Lynd-Stevenson, Robert M. (1999). Expectancy-Value Theory and Predicting Future Employment Status in the Young Unemployed. *Journal of Occupational and Organizational Psychology*, 72, 101–106.

Mayer, Steven J., & Russell, James S. (1987). Behavior Modeling Training in Organizations: Concerns and Conclusions. *Journal of Management*, 13, 21–40.

Miller, Lynn E., & Grush, Joseph E. (1988). Improving Predictions in Expectancy Theory Research: Effects of Personality, Expectancies, and Norms. *Academy of Management Journal*, 31, 107–122.

Mitchell, Terence R. (1982). Expectancy-Value Models in Organizational Psychology. In Norman T. Feather (Ed.), *Expectations and Actions: Expectancy-Value Models in Psychology* (pp. 293–339). Hillsdale, NJ: Erlbaum.

Mitchell, Terence R. (1997). Matching Motivational Strategies with Organizational Contexts. *Research in Organizational Behavior*, 19, 57–149.

Nord, Walter R. (1969). Beyond the Teaching Machine: The Neglected Area of Operant Conditioning in the Theory and Practice of Management. *Organizational Behavior and Human Performance*, 4, 375–401.

O'Brien, Richard M.; Dickinson, Alyce M.; & Rosow, Michael P. (1982). *Industrial Behavior Modification: A Management Handbook*. New York: Pergamon.

Pinder, Craig C. (1998). *Work Motivation in Organizational Behavior*. Upper Saddle River, NJ: Prentice Hall.

Porter, Lyman W. (1993). An Unmanaged Pursuit of Management. In Arthur G. Bedeian (Ed.), *Management Laureates: A Collection of Autobiographical Essays* (Vol. 3, pp. 1–29). Greenwich, CT: JAI Press.

Porter, Lyman W. (1996). Forty Years of Organization Studies: Reflections from a Micro Perspective. *Administrative Science Quarterly*, 41, 262–269.

Porter, Lyman W., & Lawler, Edward E. (1968). *Managerial Attitudes and Performance*. Homewood, IL: Irwin.

Skinner, B. F. (1953). *Science and Human Behavior*. New York: Macmillan.

Skinner, B. F. (1971). *Beyond Freedom and Dignity*. New York: Knopf.

Skinner, B. F. (1974). *About Behaviorism*. New York: Knopf.

Skinner, B. F. (1975). The Steep and Thorny Way to a Science of Behavior. *American Psychologist*, 30, 42–49.

Skinner, B. F., & Dowling, William F. (1973). Conversation with B. F. Skinner. *Organizational Dynamics*, 1(3), 31–40.

Sorcher, Melvin (1971). A Behavior Modification Approach to Supervisory Training. *Professional Psychology*, 2, 401–402.

Stajkovic, Alexander D., & Luthans, Fred (1997). A Meta-Analysis of the Effects of Organizational Behavior Modification on Task Performance, 1975–95. *Academy of Management Journal*, 40, 1122–1149.

Stajkovic, Alexander D., & Luthans, Fred (1998). Social Cognitive Theory and Self-Efficacy: Going Beyond Traditional Motivational and Behavioral Approaches. *Organizational Dynamics*, 26(4), 62–74.

Steers, Richard M.; Porter, Lyman W.; & Bigley, Gregory A. (1996). *Motivation and Leadership at Work*. New York: McGraw-Hill.

Thierry, Henk (1990). Intrinsic Motivation Reconsidered. In Uwe Kleinbeck, Hans-Henning Quast, Henk Thierry, & Hartmut Häcker (Ed.), *Work Motivation* (pp. 67–82). Hillsdale, NJ: Erlbaum.

Thompson, Kenneth R., & Luthans, Fred (1983). A Behavioral Interpretation of Power. In Robert W. Allen & Lyman W. Porter (Eds.), *Organizational Influence Processes* (pp. 72–86). Glenview, IL: Scott, Foresman.

Tolman, Edward C. (1932). *Purposive Behavior in Animals and Men*. New York: Appleton-Century.

Tolman, Edward C. (1959). Principles of Purposive Behavior. In Sigmund Koch (Ed.), *Psychology: A Study of a Science* (Vol. 2, pp. 92–157). New York: McGraw-Hill.

Van Eerde, Wenderlein, & Thierry, Henk (1996). Vroom's Expectancy Models and Work-Related Criteria: A Meta-Analysis. *Journal of Applied Psychology*, 81, 575–586.

Vroom, Victor H. (1960). *Some Personality Determinants of the Effects of Participation*. Englewood Cliffs, NJ: Prentice Hall.

Vroom, Victor H. (1964). *Work and Motivation*. New York: Wiley.

Vroom, Victor H. (1966). Organizational Choice: A Study of Pre- and Postdecision Processes. *Organizational Behavior and Human Performance*, 1, 212–225.

Vroom, Victor H. (1993). Improvising and Muddling Through. In Arthur G. Bedeian (Ed.), *Management Laureates: A Collection of Autobiographical Essays* (Vol. 3, pp. 259–284). Greenwich, CT: JAI Press.

Vroom, Victor H., & Deci, Edward L. (1971). The Stability of Post-Decision Dissonance: A Follow-up Study of the Job Attitudes of Business School Graduates. *Organizational Behavior and Human Performance*, 6, 36–49.

Wanous, John P.; Keon, Thomas L.; & Latack, Janina C. (1983). Expectancy Theory and Occupational/Organizational Choices: A Review and Test. *Organizational Behavior and Human Performance*, 32, 66–86.

Welsh, Dianne H. B.; Luthans, Fred; & Sommer, Steven M. (1993). Managing Russian Factory Workers: The Impact of U. S.-Based Behavioral and Participative Techniques. *Academy of Management Journal*, 36, 58–79.

Wiersma, Uco J. (1992). The Effects of Extrinsic Rewards in Intrinsic Motivation: A Meta-analysis. *Journal of Occupational and Organizational Psychology*, 65, 101–114.

Williams, Scott (1997). Personality and Self-Leadership. *Human Resource Management Review*, 7, 139–155.

Wood, Robert E., & Bandura, Albert (1989). Social Cognitive Theory of Organization Management. *Academy of Management Review*, 14, 361–384.

Chapter 9

Theories of Motivation Rooted in Social Psychology

The theorists considered in this chapter often were influenced by noted social psychologists, but the nature of those ties differed substantially. J. Stacy Adams, who introduced equity theory to organizational behavior, has indicated a wide range of influences on his thinking, including a number of social psychologists, industrial social psychologists, and sociologists. How-

ever, his equity theory per se, as distinct from his work in other areas, appears to have been influenced largely by two individuals whose contributions were proximate in time to those of Adams (1963a). Foremost among these was the social psychologist Leon Festinger (1957), who served on the psychology faculties of several universities including in this period Stanford University, where Adams was also employed. Festinger's cognitive dissonance theory had a strong impact. So, too, did other proponents of social-exchange theories, including primarily the sociologist George Homans (1961), who set forth his ideas on distributive justice during a long career at Harvard University.

Edwin Locke (Locke & Latham, 1990a) has been influenced throughout his career by the philosophy of objectivism as set forth by Ayn Rand (1969). However, his theory of goal setting owes its primary debts to Thomas Ryan (1970), an experimental psychologist who became an industrial psychologist as well during an extended career on the faculty of Cornell University. Kurt Lewin (1935, 1938), the personality theorist and social psychologist whose work in the areas of level of aspiration and group decision-making are particularly relevant, also is in the direct line of descent. Locke traces goal-setting theory to other roots in psychology and in management (including management by objectives), but it is apparent that Ryan and Lewin deserve special acknowledgment. Starting in the latter 1970s Locke was increasingly joined by Gary Latham as the two further developed goal-setting theory.

EQUITY THEORY

Feelings of unfairness were the most frequently reported source of job dissatisfaction in the original Herzberg research. Although motivation-hygiene theory gave relatively little attention to this finding, other theories have made this desire or need for fairness, or justice, or equity their focus.

Theories of this kind have been articulated by a number of individuals in a variety of forms. Basically, they are concerned with exchange relationships among individuals and groups and with the motivating effects of a perceived imbalance in the exchange. Applications of this type of theory were extended beyond the organizational relationships that are of primary interest here to other areas, notably exploitative relationships, helping relationships, and intimate relationships (Walster, Berscheid, & Walster, 1973).

The theory developed by Adams (1963a, 1965) appears to be not only the most relevant for an understanding of employee motivation but also the most fully articulated. It has been the source of a sizable body of research designed to test its various propositions and has been given considerable attention by wage and salary administrators.

Background

Adams received all his degrees in psychology, at the undergraduate level from the University of Mississippi and as a graduate student from the University of North Carolina at Chapel Hill. After receiving his doctorate in 1957 he went to the psychology department at Stanford for 3 years and then served as a research psychologist with the General Electric Company in Crotonville, New York. This was as part of an effort to establish a basic social science program within the company, modeled on a small scale after the Bell Labs organization in the physical sciences. The Crotonville

program did not last beyond the 1960s, but while he was there, Adams developed his theory and carried out the initial test studies.

After General Electric, Adams returned to the University of North Carolina, this time with an appointment in the business school, where he remained the rest of his life. There he continued to publish on equity theory, but a long-standing interest in boundary spanning roles in organizations (Adams, 1976, 1980) absorbed much of his attention in the 1970s and 1980s. At the time of his death he had largely moved to more macro issues that were far removed from motivation.

Statement of the Theory

Although the term *equity* is usually used to describe the theory, it is at least as appropriate to describe it as *inequity* theory. The major motivating force considered is a striving for equity, but some degree of inequity must be perceived before this force can be mobilized.

Antecedents of Inequity

The theory starts with an exchange whereby the individual gives something and gets something in return. What the individual gives may be viewed as inputs to, or investments in, the relationship; examples are noted in table 9.1. For such inputs to function they must be recognized as existing by the individual and

TABLE 9.1 Possible inputs to and outcomes from an employment exchange (noted by J. Stacy Adams in various writings)

Input	Outcome
Education	Pay
Intelligence	Intrinsic rewards
Experience	Satisfying supervision
Training	Seniority benefits
Skill	Fringe benefits
Seniority	Job status
Age	Status symbols
Sex	Job perquisites
Ethnic background	Poor working conditions
Social status	Monotony
Job effort	Fate uncertainty
Personal appearance	Herzberg's dissatisfiers
Health	
Possession of tools	
Spouse's characteristics	

must be considered relevant to the relationship. They may or may not be recognized and perceived as relevant by the other party, for instance, an employer. If they are not, a potential for inequity exists.

On the other side of the exchange are various things the individual may receive, the outcomes of the exchange relationship. As with inputs, these must be recognized by the individual who receives them and considered relevant to the exchange if they are to function effectively. Shared concepts of what are fair relationships between these outcomes and various inputs are learned as part of the overall socialization process.

The third type of theoretical variable, in addition to inputs provided and outcomes received, is the reference person or group used in evaluating the equity of one's own exchange relationship. This reference source may be a coworker, relative, neighbor, group of coworkers, craft group, industry pattern, profession, and so on. It may even be the person involved in another job or another social role. For an individual or group to operate in this capacity there must be one or more attributes that are comparable to those of the comparer. The theory is not more precise in specifying how the appropriate reference source may be identified, although it is assumed that coworkers are commonly used.

Definition of Inequity

Inequity is said to exist when the ratio of an individual's outcomes to inputs departs to a significant degree from the ratio perceived for the reference source. Thus, people may feel that they are underrewarded in terms of what they put into a job in comparison with what other workers are getting for their contributions. This might happen when people consider themselves much harder workers than other employees but are paid the same as everyone else.

The theory is not limited to inequities that are unfavorable to the individual. Equity, balance, or reciprocity exists when outcome/input ratios for the individual and the reference source are equal, and the motivating force of inequity can arise when there is a departure either way from this steady state. Accordingly, people might consider themselves overrewarded, given their inputs, in comparison with others. This could be so should people perceive themselves as working as hard as their coworkers but, for reasons they consider irrelevant, are in fact paid much more.

Since most exchanges involve multiple inputs and outcomes, these must be summed across all factors perceived to be relevant to arrive at operative ratios. The various components of those outcome and input totals also may not have the same utilities or valence for the person; in the mind of a given individual, education may predominate among the inputs noted in table 9.1, and pay may predominate among the outcomes. In such a case education and pay would be given disproportionate weight in their respective totals. Finally, "the thresholds for equity are different (in absolute terms from a base of equity) in cases of under- and overreward. The threshold presumably would be higher in cases of overreward, for a certain amount of incongruity in these cases can be acceptably rationalized as 'good fortune' without attendant discomfort" (Adams, 1965, p. 282). Thus, the motivational effects of a favorable inequity may remain immobilized at a degree of disparity that would be motivating if the disparity were unfavorable.

This is an important consideration when testing the theory; overrewards must be sizable to have an effect.

Table 9.2 shows the relative amount of inequity that may be experienced by an individual under varying conditions of total inputs and outcomes; it may prove helpful in understanding the definition of inequity.

Reactions to Inequity

Inequity, when perceived, results in dissatisfaction, either in the form of anger (underreward) or guilt (overreward). A tension is created in proportion to the amount of inequity. In turn, this tension serves as a motivating force to reduce the inequity and move it to zero. A number of methods for reducing inequity tension are posited, as follows.

Altering inputs involves changing inputs either upward or downward to what might be an appropriately equitable level. In the employment context this means altering either the quantity or the quality of work to align them with reference source ratios. Certain inputs such as age cannot be modified in this manner, while others such as effort expansion or restriction can be. Input alteration is likely to occur when there is a variation from the perceived inputs of the reference source, as opposed to discrepancies in outcomes. Lowering inputs can also be anticipated when the inequity is unfavorable to oneself; when the inequity is favor-

TABLE 9.2 The amount of inequity experienced under various input and outcome conditions

	The perception of the reference source			
The perception of oneself	Inputs low — outcomes high	Inputs high — outcomes low	Inputs low — outcomes low	Inputs high — outcomes high
Inputs low — outcomes high	No inequity	Much inequity	Some inequity	Some inequity
Inputs high — outcomes low	Much inequity	No inequity	Some inequity	Some inequity
Inputs low — outcomes low	Some inequity	Some inequity	No inequity	No inequity
Inputs high — outcomes high	Some inequity	Some inequity	No inequity	No inequity

able, the inputs are likely to be increased. Restrictive production practices, as elaborated by the early human relations writers, then become a means of reducing inequity.

Another approach to reducing felt inequity is to attempt to shift outcomes. Increasing outcomes, if achieved, will serve to reduce unfavorable inequities. Theoretically, attempts to decrease outcomes would be expected in cases that involve favorable inequities. Charitable contributions often reflect this type of motivation, which, however, does not appear to be very common. The predominant mode in this instance appears to be the use of increased outcomes to reduce unfavorable inequity, as when union or other types of pressure are brought to bear to shift outcomes into balance with expectations.

As opposed to actually altering inputs and outcomes, a person may cognitively distort them to achieve the same results. To the degree that reality is important to an individual, distortions of this kind become difficult. Thus, the absolute level of one's education as an input, or the amount of one's pay as an outcome, may be hard to distort perceptually. Yet even in these cases distortion can occur, though less objective inputs and outcomes are much more easily perverted. Furthermore, shifts in the relative weighting of inputs and outcomes can be used to achieve the same result, as when the value of one's education is exaggerated or the personal utility (worth) of pay is misrepresented.

Leaving the field represents a way of dealing with inequity by reducing or entirely eliminating it through minimizing exposure to the inequity-producing context. This can occur through transfer, absenteeism, or even separation. Such responses are assumed to be relatively extreme and to occur only when the magnitude of inequity is sizable, or when the individual cannot deal with the inequity easily and flexibly.

Distortion may be applied not only to one's own inputs and outcomes but also to those attributed to a reference individual or group. Similarly, attempts may be made to eliminate a reference source from one's environment, as when a coworker who has been used as a reference person is harassed out of a job. Or the actual inputs or outcomes of the reference source may be altered, as when "rate busters" are induced to lower their efforts and productivity in response to strong individual and group pressure. Attempts to influence a reference source along these lines will vary considerably in their feasibility, but all are theoretically appropriate methods of reducing inequity.

It is also possible to shift to a new reference source to reduce inequity. Thus, a person who previously compared himself or herself to other similar professionals nationally may change from this cosmopolitan comparison to a local comparison utilizing only professionals within the company. This strategy may be least viable when a prior reference source has been used for a considerable time.

Choices among Reactions to Inequity

The theory is not as explicit as it might be about the circumstances under which the different reactions to inequity will emerge. However, Adams (1965) is well aware of the need for theoretical statements of this kind. He offers the following propositions:

1. Generally, an individual will attempt to maximize highly valued outcomes and the overall value of outcomes.
2. Inputs that are effortful and costly to change can be expected to increase only minimally.
3. Real and cognitively distorted changes in inputs that are central to one's self-concept and self-esteem will tend to be resisted. The same ap-

plies to the outcomes for a person when they have high relevance for the self.

4. The inputs and outcomes attributed to a reference source are much more easily distorted than those attributed to oneself.
5. Leaving the field will be used only when the inequity is sizable and other means of reducing it are unfavorable. Partial withdrawals such as absenteeism will occur at lower inequity levels than full withdrawals such as separation.
6. Changing the object of comparison, or reference source, will be strongly resisted once such a comparison has been stabilized over time.

Adams (1968b) also indicates that when the inequity tension is sizable, the probability that more than one method of reducing that tension will be utilized increases. However, individuals tend to differ in tolerances for tension. A person with a high tolerance level might not yet resort to multiple modes of inequity reduction at a point where a person with a low tolerance level would long before have mobilized more than one reaction. Adams notes further that these extensions to the theory remain speculative as long as direct measures of inequity thresholds, tolerance for inequity tension, and the tension itself are not available.

Extensions and Restatements

The nature and rationale of equity theory are expanded upon in a series of four propositions set forth by Elaine Walster et al. (1973). Since these propositions subsequently have been endorsed by Adams (Adams & Freedman, 1976), it seems appropriate to consider them part of the theory.

Proposition I. Individuals will try to maximize their outcomes (where outcomes equal rewards minus costs). The term *reward* refers to positive outcomes and the term *cost* refers to negative outcomes.

Proposition IIA. Groups can maximize collective reward by evolving accepted systems for "equitably" apportioning rewards and costs among members. Thus, members will evolve such systems of equity and will attempt to induce members to accept and adhere to these systems.

Proposition IIB. Groups will generally reward members who treat others equitably and generally punish (increase the costs for) members who treat others inequitably.

Proposition III. When individuals find themselves participating in inequitable relationships, they be-

come distressed (the more inequitable the relationship, the more distress). Anger and guilt are two of the major forms of distress.

Proposition IV. Individuals who discover that they are in an inequitable relationship attempt to eliminate distress by restoring equity. The greater the inequity, the more distress, and the harder they try to restore equity. There are two ways equity may be restored. People can restore actual equity by appropriately altering their own outcomes or inputs or the outcomes or inputs of others. People can restore psychological equity by appropriately distorting the perceptions of their own or others' outcomes or inputs.

Basic Research on Pay

Studies conducted by and in association with Adams in the early 1960s have had a major influence on subsequent research intended to test his theory. Although the theory is not restricted to matters of compensation, this early research did tend to establish such a focus. Furthermore, the type of experimental design formulated by the theory's author has had a strong influence on the designs used in subsequent investigations. There were five basic studies that tested the theory in the early period, and Adams did not publish any additional research in this area subsequently. All five studies deal with the most controversial aspect of the theory: the predicted effects of over-reward inequity.

Experiment I

Adams and William Rosenbaum (1962) reported a study conducted at New York University in which students referred by the university placement office were hired to conduct market research interviews. The advertised rate for the work was $3.50 per hour, and the initial implication was that the work would continue for several months.

The 22 students hired were split into two equal groups, and all were actually paid at the $3.50 per hour figure. At the time of hiring, the experimental subjects were exposed to treatment intended to make them feel inequitably overcompensated for their work. They were told, "You don't have nearly enough experience in interviewing or survey work of the kind we're engaged in," but nevertheless, after some agonizing, they were hired. In contrast, the control subjects were led to believe that their inputs were entirely appropriate to the pay and that they met all the qualifications. Thus, a condition of equity was established vis-à-vis "interviewers in general" as a reference source.

The interviewing job was terminated after roughly 2 1/2 hours. Productivity in the experimental group, where presumably guilt had been induced, was significantly higher than that in the controls. This is what the theory predicts: in order to justify their inequitably high outcomes (pay), the experimental subjects should exert more effort to compensate for their lack of experience as an input, thus conducting more interviews in the allotted time.

Experiment II

A subsequent study conducted by A. J. Arrowood and reported by Adams (1963a) was designed to deal with a possible confounding effect in Experiment I: it is possible that the experimental subjects worked harder, not to correct an inequity but to protect their jobs. The talk about their lack of qualifications may have made them feel insecure, with the result that they worked very hard to convince the experimenter to retain them.

To test this hypothesis, a study was conducted in Minneapolis using much the same approach as that used in Experiment I except that half of the subjects mailed their completed work in a pre-addressed envelope to New York rather than merely turning it over to the experimenter. It was made clear that under these circumstances the experimenter would never know how many interviews had been produced; accordingly, he would be in no position to fire anyone, and there would be no need to feel insecure.

Under the insecurity hypothesis, eliminating job insecurity should eliminate the difference between the experimental (inequity) and control (equity) groups. It did not. The tendency for experimental subjects to conduct more interviews than controls remained, regardless of whether the completed forms were returned to New York. Thus, the results of Experiment I do not appear to be attributable to insecurity; they are more likely to have been caused by attempts to reduce inequity tension.

Experiment III

Whereas the preceding studies used an hourly compensation rate, another investigation explored the effects of paying on a piece rate basis (Adams & Rosen-

baum, 1962). In most respects the procedure was the same as that in Experiment I. However, four groups were used, each containing nine subjects:

Group 1. Overreward inequity; paid $3.50 per hour

Group 2. Equity; paid $3.50 per hour

Group 3. Overreward inequity; paid 30 cents per interview

Group 4. Equity; paid 30 cents per interview

The use of piece rate payments adds a complicating factor in that exerting more effort to resolve the inequity will not solve the problem. Inputs do increase, but so do outcomes; thus the inequity remains and is exacerbated. As expected, the introduction of piece rate payment did have a markedly dampening effect on the tendency to produce more to eliminate inequity. In fact, the overreward piece rate workers completed the fewest interviews of any group; increasing their outcomes was apparently the last thing they wanted to do.

Experiment IV

The results of Experiment III tell much more about how people do not reduce inequity tension than about how they do. One hypothesis is that under this kind of inequity condition effort is increased but is put into improved quality of work that will not increase outcomes rather than into improved quantity that under piece rate payment will increase outcomes. Experiment IV attempts to test this hypothesis (Adams, 1963b). In this case procedures were introduced to permit measurement of interview quality, something that was not possible in Experiment III.

To do this, interviewers were encouraged to obtain as much information as possible from respondents in reply to several open-ended questions. Since lengthy responses (quality) inevitably limited the number of interviews obtained (quantity), following the directive to obtain more information should be an attractive approach to restoring equity. The results were indeed in accord with this expectation. Subjects in the overrewarded inequity condition obtained longer interviews on the average than those working under equitable payment, and they also completed fewer interviews.

Experiment V

The final study (Adams & Jacobsen, 1964) was conducted to provide a further check on the insecurity hypothesis considered in Experiment II. Sixty students from Columbia University who answered an advertisement for parttime summer work were hired to perform a proofreading task. Quantity of work was determined by the number of pages proofed and quality by the number of errors detected. Three different conditions related to equity were introduced:

1. Inequity was produced by such statements as, "you don't have nearly enough experience" and "your score on the proofreading test isn't really satisfactory," but payment was given at the full 30-cent per page rate initially quoted.
2. The same reduction of inputs as in no. 1 was combined with a compensating reduction of outcomes: "I can't pay you at the regular rate of 30 cents per page. I can pay you only 20 cents per page because your qualifications aren't sufficient."
3. Full equity was produced at the 30 cents per page figure: "You're just what we're looking for. You meet all the qualifications."

Within each of these three conditions, two alternatives related to prospects for continued employment were introduced as follows:

A. "The book is only one of a series . . . there is a lot of work ahead. . . . You may be able to help us in the future."
B. "Usually it isn't necessary to hire someone to proofread for us, but . . . we've got to get this particular book out, . . . The job will take a short time only."

Thus, there were six different conditions with 10 people in each.

Equity theory predicts better quality work and lower quantity for both conditions 1A and 1B. The insecurity hypothesis predicts that conditions 1A and 2B, where there was a job to be lost and every reason to believe it might be lost, would produce the higher quality, lower productivity response.

After 1 hour of work the study was terminated and the results reported in table 9.3 were obtained. Questions asked of the subjects at that point indicated that the desired perceptions regarding qualifications, pay levels, and opportunity for continued employment had, in fact, been induced by the various treatments. The data are fully in line with equity theory predictions; they do not support the insecurity hypothesis.

However, Adams (1968b) notes that under the inequity conditions there were a few subjects who produced large quantities of relatively low quality work. These individuals were found to be economically deprived, needing the money badly. As a result they maximized their outcomes even though they were aware of the inequity. Adams interprets these data as indicating that for some people economic motivation may be dominant over equity motivation. It is apparent that equity theory is not an all-encompassing motivational theory but rather deals with one particular type of motivation that has major implications for behavior in the workplace. In this connection Adams and Jacobsen note:

Overpayment by an employer need not necessarily increase his labor costs, provided he is primarily interested in quality, as opposed to production volume. If on the other hand the employer's objective is production volume, piecework overpayment may be very costly, especially for such work as inspection, quality control, finishing and other jobs

TABLE 9.3 Errors detected per page and number of pages proofed under varying conditions of equity

No.	Condition	Quality (errors detected)	Quantity (pages proofed)
1A	Inequity and insecure	7.9	8.7
1B	Inequity and secure	8.0	7.7
2A	Equity (at low pay) and insecure	4.7	11.3
2B	Equity (at low pay) and secure	4.9	11.8
3A	Equity and perhaps insecure	4.9	11.7
3B	Equity and secure	4.0	12.8

SOURCE: Adapted from J. Stacy Adams & Patricia R. Jacobsen (1964), Effects of Wage Inequities on Work Quality, *Journal of Abnormal and Social Psychology*, 69, 22–23

that inherently permit considerable latitude in work quality. (1964, p. 24)

Evaluation and Impact

A comprehensive review of the equity theory research indicates considerable support for the theory. This is not only my opinion, but the view of other scholars of the field as well (Greenberg, 1990; Mowday, 1996). In recent years the work on equity theory, which deals with what is called distributive justice (the fairness of outcome distributions), has been joined by a sizable outburst of research activity in the area of procedural justice, where the major concern is with the fairness of policies and procedures used to make decisions. This has led some to describe distributive justice research as on the decline. Yet research on equity theory in many of its aspects continues to be robust; activity dealing with *both* distributive and procedural issues is currently quite strong, and the distinction between the two is well established (Konovsky, 2000).

Research on Overreward

By no means has all of the research dealing with the effects of overreward inequity produced the same type of favorable results that Adams obtained originally. However, the theory itself posits a high threshold for overreward inequity, and there are data to support this. Thus, there is always the possibility (in a given study) that overreward thresholds were not consistently breached. Furthermore, a treatment or experimental manipulation might not be perceived as producing inequity at all, even though the researcher believed it should. Such could be the case, for instance, if what was thought to be an input manipulation (say changing the degree of job involvement) turned out to be an outcome manipulation (job involvement is considered a desirable opportunity for self-expression) for a sizable number of subjects. This kind of interchangeability among individual inputs and outcomes of the type noted in table 9.1 has been clearly established. Given the variety of possible mitigating circumstances, it is important to consider the overall weight of the evidence in evaluating the theory rather than relying on any individual study.

When this is done, there turns out to be considerable support for the overreward inequity proposition. In cases when the motivational effects of overreward

inequity are not demonstrated, strong feelings of inequity often appear not to have been mobilized.

Questions have been raised in some of the reviews as to whether it was inequity motivation that was aroused in the overreward studies; other motives have been suggested. There has been considerable wrestling with the issue over the years, and a number of studies have been conducted in an attempt to settle it. Adams (1968a) was quite critical of the approaches taken in some of this research. The upshot now appears to be that overreward inequity can be and has been aroused in many studies (Greenberg, 1990).

Another set of questions regarding overreward inequity has revolved around the time dimension. Given that the research has demonstrated the effects predicted by equity theory, it is still posited that these effects are transitory and have no real meaning in understanding ongoing motivation in organizations (Lawler, 1968).

Without question, much overreward research has been of short duration (under a week), and there is a distinct need for longitudinal studies (Cosier & Dalton, 1983). The possibility that in actual on-the-job practice overpayment only costs more and does not yield better performance is real. Initial improvements in performance may give way to cognitive adjustments that rationalize the overpayment into acceptability. Alternatively, the revised inputs provided by an employee may be in the form of good working relationships, friendliness, exemplary citizenship behavior, commitments to long-term employment, and the like (rather than direct performance-related effort), thus justifying the high pay on this basis. This appears to be a very likely reaction, and changes of this nature could be important enough to a company to warrant the overpayment. The problem is that for lack of appropriate research and precise theory we have no idea exactly what happens under circumstances of long-term overreward; performance effects can hold up as long as a week or so, however.

Evidence also exists that some people are more sensitive to overreward inequity effects than others (Vecchio, 1981). Those who are more morally mature and principled (with a greater propensity for experiencing guilt) are the ones who are particularly responsive to overpayment. The less morally mature do not exhibit the inequity reaction to nearly the same extent. This type of research begins to get directly at the underlying constructs of guilt and anger that account for equity tension; more such studies are needed.

Underreward Research

Although Adams did not create an underreward condition in his studies, other researchers have since conducted similar experiments that have extended the analysis to this condition. In addition to such pay-performance studies, there have been other research efforts that relate underreward to such inequity-reduction strategies as absenteeism and job separation.

With piece rate pay conditions, underrewarded individuals would be expected to increase the quantity of work in order to move total outcomes upward. At the same time, however, equity can only be achieved if inputs are not raised commensurate to the increase in outcomes. The most likely strategy for holding inputs down is to decrease the effort put into quality. The research data are entirely consistent with these expectations.

On an hourly pay schedule, underreward would be expected to result in less effort devoted to the work. Generally, this reduced input should yield a reduced quantity of work. On certain tasks, however, when quality is a major consideration, the reduced effort may well cause poorer quality work.

In general, the available research tends to support these equity-theory predictions for the pay underreward condition. Reviewers have consistently indicated that this conclusion is well-justified, based on the research findings.

Another more extreme way of dealing with underreward inequity noted by Adams is to leave the field. This response could theoretically occur under any inequity condition, but, given the differential thresholds involved, it might be expected to appear more widely in the underreward context. There, a common response is to achieve balance by increasing absenteeism. However, the turnover response represented by leaving the field is often in evidence as well (Summers & Hendrix, 1991). Organizations with undesirably high turnover would do well to look into perceptions of pay equity, and into the equitability of other aspects of the reward system.

Interestingly, and adding credence to the laboratory research, findings comparable to those obtained in the field have been obtained in simulated work studies that deal with pay and performance. It is not uncommon for some subjects in these studies to refuse further participation when faced with underreward inequity. Furthermore, if sizable inequities are made obvious and compelling through continued exposure

to reference individuals known to be receiving greater compensation for the same work, expressions of anger and highly disruptive behavior may well occur. When these more extreme methods of responding to perceived inequity are mobilized, they appear to supersede any performance effects.

Another line of research has tested the proposition that an individual will allocate rewards (outcomes) in a manner proportional to the inputs of the various parties. Designs call for some demonstration of actual inputs, usually for two people, and then as a dependent variable an allocation decision in accordance with perceptions of appropriate reward. The person making the allocation may be a third party or a person who has actually contributed inputs. The test of equity theory comes when the subject is given a chance to reallocate rewards. If an inequity has been created, will the subjects now act to restore equity? The answer appears to be that subjects will. Research of this kind has yielded strong support for equity theory (Leventhal, Weiss, & Long, 1969).

This raises a question as to how responsive people are to reports of injustice experienced by others vis-à-vis their own personal experiences in this regard. Clearly, people do take into account the experiences of others, but it takes a great deal of the reported injustice of others to equal even a little personally experienced injustice (Lind, Kray, & Thompson, 1998).

A very important application of equity theory in instances of underreward has emerged as a result of a research program initiated by Jerald Greenberg starting in the late 1980s (Greenberg & Scott, 1996; Giacalone & Greenberg, 1997). This research is important because the problem of theft by employees is widespread and represents a major cost to many businesses (Miner & Capps, 1996). For small firms it often results in business failure. In many such instances, theft of one kind or another turns out to be motivated by a desire to redress perceived grievances.

In equity theory terms, what the research shows is that theft represents an attempt to increase income to a point where an equitable balance is achieved relative to perceived input. Employees steal to pay themselves what they think is justly theirs for what they put into their work; thus, underreward tension is reduced and a source of dissatisfaction is alleviated. The greater the preexisting inequity tension, the more the stealing. However, the research also indicates that to the extent adequate explanations are provided for the inequity state, reflecting a degree of compassion and social sensitivity in dealing with the issue, theft tends to be less in evidence. Thus a procedural justice factor is added to the purely distributive. Also, high-status job titles and office locations can represent increased outcomes in the equity formula, thus reducing inequity tension and any proclivity for theft.

Referent Selection

Certain problems inherent in equity theory have been recognized for some time, going back to Adams and Freedman (1976); yet to a large extent they remain with us today. Terence Mitchell has this to say on the subject:

> It is still difficult to be precise about what constitutes an input and an outcome, or the standard being used for comparison. As Kanfer (1990) points out, standards and referents change over time and contexts. Kulik and Ambrose (1992) have elaborated on the importance of accurately determining the referent that people use. Also, it is still hard to predict exactly what will change as a result of inequity perceptions. One can change perceptions, comparisons, and actions and any combination of the three as a result of feeling unfairly treated. While theoretical work has helped to grapple with some of these issues . . . they still present problems. (1997, p. 91)

This indictment of the theory on grounds of lack of precision is entirely justified. Adams simply did not know how to be more precise, and for the most part neither has anyone else since. Some of these issues have been considered previously. The matter of referent selection, how people choose among those with whom their own inputs and outcomes may be compared, concerns us here. This is one issue on which some progress has been made.

Research indicates that people do make a wide range of comparisons, extending from self-evaluations, to others in the company, to those in the same job outside, to those of the same educational level or age, to what is expected from the company (Scholl, Cooper, & McKenna, 1987). All of these comparisons can contribute to pay dissatisfaction. Turnover, however, is particularly tied to perceived inequity in relation to external comparisons—people in the same job in other organizations and having similar education—as well as to self-evaluations. Investing extra effort in the job declines in the face of perceived inequity relative to others in the same job within the company. Thus, the nature of the comparisons made does have some differential impact; it matters which ones are chosen.

Another approach seeks to specify which referent choices will in fact be made. The model given in figure 9.1 is suggested for this purpose; it is theoretical in nature but induced from available research. This research indicates that most employees use one or two referent types and that choices tend to be fairly stable over time (Kulik & Ambrose, 1992). The key intervening constructs for choice are the availability of information regarding a referent and the relevance or acceptability of the referent for the person. In the latter instance similarity is a major consideration.

Propositions regarding the ways in which the variables of the model operate are set forth as follows:

1. Individuals in integrated fields will make more cross-sex comparisons than will those in sex-segregated fields.
2. Individuals in desegregated conditions will make more cross-race comparisons than will those in segregated conditions.
3. Individuals under the age of 65 will make more other comparisons than will individuals over the age of 65.
4. Individuals with longer tenure will make more other-external comparisons than will individuals with less tenure.
5. Upper-level individuals will make more other-external comparisons than will lower-level individuals.
6. Professionals will make more other-external comparisons than will nonprofessionals.
7. Individuals comparing extrinsic facets will make more other-comparisons than will individuals comparing intrinsic facets.
8. Individuals experiencing a procedural change will choose more self-past referents than will individuals who do not experience a procedural change.
9. Individuals who are physically proximate to other internal referents will make more comparisons to these referents than to individuals who are not physically proximate.

The authors also note that although similar referents are likely to be most relevant in the sense that they provide directly interpretable comparison data, dissimilar referents can well be preferred when the

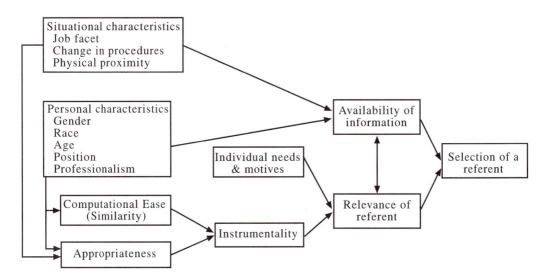

FIGURE 9.1 Model of the psychological processes involved in referent selection. From Carol T. Kulik & Maureen L. Ambrose (1992), Personal and Situational Determinants of Referent Choice, *Academy of Management Review*, 17, 216. Copyright 1992 by Academy of Management. Reproduced with permission.

comparer perceives those referents as at least minimally relevant and also has access to information about those referents.

Situational and Individual Differences

One issue that Adams did not envisage is that people from different backgrounds and operating in different contexts may develop different norms with regard to the appropriate distribution of rewards. The equity rule, and equity theory, are most appropriate to work situations where maximizing productivity and pay-for-performance are the norm. Historically this has been the situation in many companies in the United States. Yet cases exist where other distribution rules are supported by existing norms and are internalized by organization members. Among these, equality, where outcomes should be distributed equally to all participants with the objective of minimizing conflict, has been considered the most; here the extent of a person's inputs does not matter. Another similar possibility is the use of a need-based distribution rule, with outcomes allocated in terms of a person's perceived need for them; thus a type of social responsibility enters into the allocation process (Mowday, 1996). Where either equality or need-based norms dominate, equity theory will be less applicable.

Situations of the kind thus envisaged do exist. Different cultures at different points in time tend to adopt norms of one kind or another, at least with regard to certain aspects of the work process, and some cultures clearly do espouse equality and need-based norms. Chao Chen (1995) has compared China and the United States at different points in time and finds evidence for an equality norm in both cultures. In Israel need as a justice principle, although not a dominant factor, does serve as a guiding rule in the fairness evaluations of received pay (Dornstein, 1989). Other such national cultural variations have been noted. Elizabeth Mannix, Margaret Neale, and Gregory Northcraft (1995) have shown that variations in organizational cultures with regard to equity, equality, and need-based norms significantly influence which group members are perceived to be more powerful and thus most entitled and what distribution principles do in fact operate to determine resource allocations among members.

The point is that for whatever reasons some people do not behave in accordance with equity norms and their actions are not predictable from equity theory. Robert Vecchio (1981) found essentially the same thing in his study of the effects of overreward inequity on those who lack moral judgment and have little predisposition to experience guilt. People who gamble frequently are less committed to equity in allocations, and they appear more prone to accept reward distributions unrelated to norms of equity (Larwood, Kavanagh, & Levine, 1978). In these cases there appear to be individuals and groups of individuals who operate outside the boundaries of equity theory's domain.

Other studies identify wide individual and group variations among employees who nevertheless seem to be still operating within the domain of equity theory (see, for instance, Dulebohn & Martocchio, 1998). These individual differences do pose a major problem for equity theory. Adams clearly recognizes the role of individual differences, but specific propositions about them are lacking in the theory. Individuals differ not only in the utilities or valences they impute to various potential inputs and outcomes but also in their inequity thresholds, tolerances for inequity tension, and the strength of their equity motivation relative to other types of motivation. It is not possible to predict from the theory who will respond to a particular inequality induction and who will not, although it is apparent that such individual differences exist.

In response to this need for theory and research dealing with individual differences in inequity tension levels, thresholds, and tolerances, the concept of equity sensitivity has been advanced (Huseman, Hatfield, & Miles, 1987), and a measure has been developed. This theoretical extension posits three general types of individuals:

Benevolents—those who prefer their outcome/input ratios to be less than the outcome/input ratios of the comparison other; they are givers, and distress occurs with a departure from this preferred situation (equitable or overreward).

Equity sensitives—those who, conforming to the traditional norm of equity, prefer their outcome/input ratios to equal those of comparison others; distress occurs with both underreward and overreward.

Entitleds—those who prefer their outcome/input ratios to exceed the comparison others; they are getters, and experience distress in the face of equitable or underreward where they are not getting a better deal than others.

These formulations and others are expressed in a set of propositions:

1A. Benevolents prefer situations of high inputs for self compared to low inputs for self.
1B. Entitleds prefer situations of high outcomes for self compared to low outcomes for self.
2A. Benevolents prefer that their own inputs exceed their own outcomes.
2B. Entitleds prefer that their own outcomes exceed their own inputs.
2C. Equity sensitives prefer that their own inputs equal their own outcomes.
3A. Benevolents prefer that their outcome/input ratios be less that of the comparison other's.
3B. Entitleds prefer that their outcome/input ratios exceed that of the comparison others.
3C. Equity sensitives prefer that their outcome/input ratios be equal to that of the comparison other's.
4. A negative, linear relationship should exist between Benevolent's perceptions of equity and job satisfaction.
5. An inverted U-shaped relationship should exist between Equity sensitive's perceptions of equity and job satisfaction.
6. A positive, linear relationship should exist between Entitled's perception of equity and job satisfaction.

With regard to the question of when factors that are ambiguous on this score will be considered inputs and when they will be considered outcomes:

Benevolents are more likely to perceive ambiguous elements as outcomes.

Entitleds are more likely to perceive them as inputs.

Research indicates that even in identical situations, individuals do in fact choose different distribution norms, and in accordance with the expectations of equity sensitivity theorizing (King & Hinson, 1994). Also, comparisons of business students in the United States and the Czech Republic indicate that the likelihood of having an entitled orientation was consistently higher among the European students, the mean difference being on the order of half a standard deviation or more (Mueller & Clarke, 1998). To date at least, the equity sensitivity concept appears to be real, to yield valid results, and to provide useful information, but it is also complex and may demonstrate unexpected ties to personality characteristics (Mudrack, Mason, & Stepanski, 1999).

Equity and Expectancy

It would certainly appear that some of the concepts and research from equity theory, especially in the area of overreward inequity, are distinctly in conflict with expectancy theory. Under certain circumstances equity theory predicts (and the research seems to substantiate) that people do not strive to maximize rewards.

This problem has been given some attention by expectancy theorists. Their position is that the equity theory results can be incorporated within the larger framework of expectancy theory if certain assumptions are made regarding the way valences are formed or operate. In discussing this matter, Lawler says:

> There are two ways in which equity can come into play as a determinant of the valence of certain rewards. One way concerns the possibility that increasingly large piece-rate rewards could have a decreasing valence for subjects. That is, rewards that are seen as too large, and therefore inequitable, may have a lower valence than rewards which are perceived as equitable. A second point concerns the effect of the amount of a reward that has been received on the valence of additional amounts of the reward. It seems reasonable that once a perceived equitable level of rewards has been achieved future rewards will have lower valences. (1968, p. 609)

Formulations of this kind, whatever their attractiveness, are clearly post hoc. Expectancy theory is completely silent on what effects of this kind would be predicted, while equity theory is quite explicit. That certain phenomena can possibly be explained within a certain theoretical orientation does not mean that they are best explained in that manner. It would seem most appropriate to view the two theories as separate and distinct but with partially overlapping domains. This conclusion is reinforced by the fact that when equity and expectancy theories are tested together they tend to emerge as complementary, with each expanding the predictive power of the other. In fact, there is a possibility that the behavior of certain kinds of people may be predicted from expectancy theory, and that of others from equity theory. Vecchio's (1981) study of the effects of moral maturity is certainly consistent with this formulation, with equity theory clearly operating for the more mature and perhaps expectancy theory for the less so.

In the early 1990s, the majority of the research comparing equity and expectancy approaches was carried out with major league baseball and basketball players who were approaching free agency (see Harder, 1991, 1992; Bretz & Thomas, 1992). This research indicates that underreward performance effects will occur to the extent that they do not jeopardize future rewards, but if they do then avenues other than performance will be used to achieve equity. Overreward clearly has its effects, and over an extended period of time. Perceived inequities lead to discontent, can influence performance, and result in both trades and leaving the field (literally). But expectations of future rewards exert a motivational influence as well. The two theories seem to complement each other.

Equity Theory in Practice

Specifying what the effect of equity theory has been and is on practice is a difficult task. The theory is widely known among compensation specialists, and equity considerations typically are given major attention in setting pay scales, usually with a view to maintaining equity. Yet it is hard to determine cause-and-effect relationships, and there is no generally established or widely publicized procedure that can be directly linked to Adams or to equity theory. It would appear that compensation practitioners have been well aware of the importance of equity considerations for their work for many years. The more recent and precise formulations of Adams and those who have followed his lead have had an uncertain effect on existing practice. However, this situation says nothing about the *potential* utility of the theory in the future.

In view of the level of research support for equity theory, one could hope that it might provide the basis for major breakthroughs in management practice. This expectation is further increased because the two motives involved, guilt and anger reduction, are major influences on what people do. There can be little doubt that the theory deals with motivational processes that relate to large segments of human behavior, not only in the organizational context but also outside it.

One obvious application is to use the theory as a guide in introducing changed circumstances in the workplace, so that improved quality or quantity of work will result. This was Adams's objective when as an employee of the General Electric Company he undertook the early research on pay-performance relationships, and his writing clearly indicates his belief that this is feasible. Yet there appear to be no accounts of this type of application in the literature. As far as can be determined, feasibility studies have not been conducted, even though they could move us out of the laboratory and short-term simulation contexts into the ongoing work environment.

Thus, we can only guess at the results of such feasibility studies. It is doubtful whether overreward inequity could produce major performance changes. The amount of inequity would have to be sizable in order to exceed threshold, and thus the cost would be considerable; many businessmen would question this initial outlay.

Many of the research results have been obtained under highly structured circumstances with clearly established reference sources, input and outcome specifications, and rankings of inputs and outcomes. The experimenter has been free to adjust a wide range of factors and has chosen to hold many constant. In the ongoing organizational world these circumstances often do not exist because of union and competitive pressures. The ambiguity and uncertainty may be so great that it is very difficult to focus the inequity reaction on a performance-related response.

The conceptual leap from existing knowledge to practical application is sizable, and existing constraints may rule it out completely in many contexts. Without full knowledge of individual differences and their implications, it is doubtful whether inequities should be introduced to spark performance improvements. However, influences on citizenship behavior seem to be more easily achieved and knowledge of individual differences can be obtained.

In contrast to attempts to introduce inequities through variations in pay plans, compensation levels, input perceptions, and the like, traditional compensation administration has sought to achieve equity through an adjustment of outcomes to perceived inputs, thus reducing the probability of absenteeism, turnover, disruptive behavior, and the like. The major concern has been to avoid underreward inequity. In addition, equity theory can be of considerable value in understanding the behavior that follows unintentional inequities. Full comprehension of equity theory can be useful to a manager and can help to deal with individual circumstances. In particular, recent evidence regarding the influence that equity considerations exert on theft, and the ways in which procedural justice may operate in conjunction with distributive justice in this context, has major implications for cost reduction.

The procedures developed by Elliott Jaques (see Jaques & Cason, 1994), although incorporating an equity standard, do not assume an implicit motivational process. Jaques posits a single input, capacity, that is channeled through the amount of individual discretion that the person is allowed to exercise in the job. The longer the period of time a person is expected to exercise independent judgment in the work, the higher the pay level should be to be perceived as equitable. In general, this time span of discretion increases with occupational level.

Although Jaques's views have received criticism, and the measurement of time spans of discretion has proved difficult, the approach has much in common with equity theory and receives support from research. The major advance provided is the emphasis on time span of discretion, or freedom to act independently, as a major factor conditioning input perceptions. In this respect the theory has contributed a concept of considerable value for compensation administration. It is widely used in Europe and is deserving of more attention than it has received in U.S. practice.

GOAL-SETTING THEORY

Modern goal-setting theory, although it has multiple historical origins, owes much to the formulations of Kurt Lewin. Lewin's views resulted in a sizable amount of research on the determinants of the level of aspiration (or goal setting) as a dependent variable (Lewin, Dembo, Festinger, & Sears, 1944). The current resurgence of interest in this area (dating from the middle 1960s) delves primarily into the *effects* of goal setting on performance, however (Locke & Latham, 1990a).

Background

Edwin Locke was born in 1938 and attended Harvard University, where he majored in psychology and graduated in 1960. His graduate work was done at Cornell in industrial psychology with Patricia Cain Smith as his mentor. Upon receiving his doctorate in 1964 he joined the American Institutes for Research (AIR) in Washington, DC; this was a nonprofit research organization. There he continued the research on goal setting that he had begun in connection with his dissertation, under a grant from the U.S. Office of Naval Research (Locke, 1993).

At Cornell, Locke was exposed to the views of Thomas Ryan on the significant role that intentions play in human behavior. Although these views were not formally published until 1970, they were available in an early mimeographed version in 1964, and Locke was exposed to them well before that time. This debt to Ryan is acknowledged in numerous publications. Although the two never published together, Locke has continued the same line of work up to the present.

After 3 years at AIR Locke joined the psychology faculty at the University of Maryland. In 1970 he moved to the business school there and retained only a limited appointment in psychology. Ultimately the business school appointment became full time; he remained in this position until his recent retirement in 2001.

Gary Latham first published with Locke in 1975, but it was not until almost 5 years later that the collaboration began in earnest. Initially Latham's role involved testing goal-setting theory in the field, after many years when the theory had been exposed only to laboratory testing. Later this role expanded considerably, but his practical experience has always been a major contribution that he has been able to add to the partnership. Latham received his B.A. from Dalhousie University in Nova Scotia, his master's in industrial psychology from Georgia Tech, and his doctorate in the same field from the University of Akron (in 1974). His business experience has included work as a psychologist with the American Pulpwood Association, with the Weyerhaeuser Company, and as an independent consultant. His faculty employment began at the business school of the University of Washington in 1976. In 1990 he returned to Canada with an appointment in the business school at the University of Toronto.

Phase I Theory

The first theoretical statements on goal setting appear in published versions of Locke's doctoral dissertation. Initially the research objective was merely to determine "how the level of intended achievement is related to actual level of achievement" (Locke, 1966, p. 60), although there was an implicit hypothesis that higher levels of intended achievement would contribute to higher levels of performance. Soon thereafter this hypothesis was made explicit, with the added proviso that when an individual had specific goals or standards of performance to meet, the performance effects would be more pronounced than when specific goals were lacking (as with the instruction "do your best") (Locke & Bryan, 1966a).

Research-Guiding Hypotheses

Subsequently, this hypothesis about the superiority of specific over ambiguous goals was extended to task interest. "It was hypothesized . . . that working toward a determinate goal would lead to a higher level of task interest than would be the case with an abstract goal such as do your best" (Locke & Bryan, 1967, p. 121). Thus, the presence of specific hard goals should reduce boredom at work.

This emphasis on the significant motivational effects of specific goals that are difficult to achieve was extended to explain various other motivational phenomena. The first such extrapolation was to the area of knowledge of results or feedback on the effectiveness of performance. More specifically, it was hypothesized that knowledge of results achieves its motivational effects through the incorporating of goal setting and that in the absence of such performance intentions, knowledge of results does not contribute to the level of work output (Locke & Bryan, 1966b).

The popular Parkinson's Law is also explained as a goal-setting phenomenon (Bryan & Locke, 1967). This law indicates that work expands to fill the time available for its completion; more generally it can be hypothesized that "effort (or work pace) is adjusted to the perceived difficulty of the task undertaken." This process is said to be mediated by goal setting, and accordingly a goal-setting process is assumed to intervene between task perception and actual performance. The following quote not only explains how this might occur but also provides a first glimpse of the broader theoretical framework that emerged later:

> Adjustment (of effort to difficulty level) requires first that the subject perceive the task, that he be conscious of the fact that there is a task to be performed and that he have some idea or knowledge of what the task requires of him. Then, depending upon the situation and the individual's perception of it in relation to his own values, he will set himself a goal or standard in terms of which he will regulate and evaluate his performance. . . . This goal-setting procedure can vary widely in the degree to which it is conscious or subconscious, explicit or implicit . . . but once the goal is set, it is argued that effort and performance level will be regulated by and with reference to this goal. (Bryan & Locke, 1967, p. 260)

A similar explanation in terms of goal setting is applied to the relationships between monetary incentives and work performance. The specific hypotheses are these:

1. Goals and intentions will be related to behavior regardless of incentive conditions; that is, goals and intentions will be related to behavior both within and across different incentive conditions.
2. When incentive differences do correlate with behavior differences, these differences will be accompanied by corresponding differences in goals and intentions.
3. When goal or intention differences are controlled or partialed out, there will be no relationship between incentive condition and behavior. (Locke, Bryan, & Kendall, 1968, p. 106)

More Comprehensive Formulations

The theoretical statements considered to this point were all presented as hypotheses that were tested immediately in research. However, beginning in 1968 Locke began a series of attempts to pull his ideas together within a more comprehensive framework. That 7 years later he still had serious doubts as to whether these efforts had amounted to a true theory does not deny the fact that something more than a set of loosely related first-order hypotheses was achieved.

Clearly the formulations Locke presents are limited in various respects (Locke, 1968). Little attention is given to the developmental causes of particular goals, and thus to why people come to try consciously to do what they do. Furthermore, goals are viewed as having significance for performance only to the extent that they are actually accepted by the individual; thus the theory is one of accepted or internalized goals. Very difficult goals might well fail to achieve acceptance, and if this were the case the positive relationship between goal difficulty and performance would no longer be expected to hold. On almost any task there is a hypothetical level of difficulty beyond which goal acceptance will not occur. At this point a boundary condition of the theory has been reached. One of the key reasons monetary incentives work with regard to performance levels is that they contribute to task and goal acceptance, or commitment.

In the early statements, goal setting was introduced as an explanation not only of the effects of monetary incentives but also of knowledge of results and variations in available time. Later this list was expanded to several additional areas (Locke, 1968, 1970b). The

performance effects of participative management are attributed in part to explicit or implicit goal setting. Competition is viewed as a case in which the performance of others serves to establish goals that arouse individuals to higher levels of performance. Praise and reproof may well induce people to set hard performance goals, although it is apparent also that this need not necessarily occur; the theory is not specific as to when, under such circumstances, hard or easy goals will emerge.

Goals have two major attributes — content and intensity. Content refers to the nature of the activity or end sought. Intensity relates to the level of importance of the goal to the person. Goal content exerts a primarily directive influence, and it also serves to regulate energy expenditure because different goals require different amounts of effort. Goal intensity can also influence both the direction and level of effort. Important goals are more likely to be accepted, to elicit commitment, and thus to foster persistent striving.

Job Satisfaction Model

The theory treats job satisfaction in the short range as a function of the size of the perceived discrepancy between intended and actual performance. Goal achievement leads to the pleasurable emotional state we call satisfaction; failure to achieve a goal leads to the unpleasurable state of dissatisfaction (Locke, 1969, 1970a).

However, job satisfaction is usually viewed in a wider context than individual goal accomplishment. In this broader context, abstract job values serve in the manner of goals. "Job satisfaction and dissatisfaction are a function of the perceived relationship between what one wants from one's job and what one perceives it as offering or entailing" (Locke, 1969, p. 316). Values establish what one wants. Like the more immediate goals, they are characterized by content and intensity (importance). Thus the achievement of more important values (financial security, for instance) will yield greater satisfaction, and the same value-percept discrepancy will produce more dissatisfaction if the value is important than if it is not. Beyond these directional hypotheses, the theory does not indicate in specific detail the relationships that involve values, discrepancies, importance, and satisfaction-dissatisfaction. It does, however, view job satisfaction as primarily a product or outcome of goal- or value-directed effort, and thus a consequence of performance.

Locke, Norman Cartledge, and Claramae Knerr (1970) have proposed a theoretical model to explain how the various types of variables specified in Locke's theoretical formulations interact:

existents → cognition → emotional → goal → action
(such as (evaluation   reactions   setting
incentives against
or values)
previous
outcomes)

The most immediate determinant of action is the individual's goal. External incentives influence action through their impact on the individual's goal. Emotional reactions result from evaluations in which the person cognitively compares the existents against standards established by relevant values.

As an example of how these processes work, let us take an examination situation:

existent: → cognition: → emotion: → goal: → action:
grade of C+ dissatis- improve improved
C+ evaluated faction on next examina-
as too low examina- tion
relative to tion perfor-
B value mance
standard

Improved performance should result ultimately in greater satisfaction.

Locke et al. (1970) also extend this basic model to include anticipated existents and emotions, as well as the judged instrumentality of anticipated goals. Subgoal attainment is valued to the extent that it is seen as instrumental for an overall goal. Although these formulations regarding anticipatory states and subgoals add a degree of complexity to the model, they are nevertheless handled within the basic framework discussed in this chapter.

The Theory in Maturity

Throughout most of the 1970s, goal-setting theory was largely in hiatus. However, during this period Latham published a number of studies that moved research on setting goals from the laboratory out into the field. Then gradually activity on the theory front accelerated and culminated in Locke and Latham's A Theory of Goal Setting and Task Performance (1990a); this was Phase II.

Goals, Expectancies, Self-Efficacy, and Performance

A problem that arose early on was that because difficult goals are harder to reach, expectancy of success should show a negative linear relationship to performance; goal theory posits a positive linear relationship between goal difficulty and performance. In contrast, expectancy theory asserts a positive linear relationship between expectancy of success and performance level. The conflicting predictions involved here have elicited a number of proposed solutions.

In the 1990 version of their theory Locke and Latham introduce the concept of self-efficacy from Albert Bandura (1982) to yield their most recent solution (see also Bandura, 1997). Self-efficacy is a person's judgment of how well one can execute courses of action that are required to deal with prospective situations; it is positively related to future performance. It has a lot in common with the expectancy concept, but is much broader in scope. In summarizing this solution, Locke and Latham state the following:

> Goal setting theory is in full agreement, rather than conflict, with expectancy theory regarding the relationship of expectancy to performance. Expectancy is positively related to performance within any given goal group; self-efficacy and/or overall expectancy of performing well across the full range of possible performance levels is positively associated with goal level and performance, both within and across goal groups. Assigned goals facilitate performance because they influence both self-efficacy and personal goals. Self-efficacy affects goal choice, and both self-efficacy and personal goals affect performance. (Locke & Latham, 1990a, p. 85)

The means to the resolution is self-efficacy, and, in fact, this integration of goal-setting theory with Bandura's views has become increasingly evident since then (Bartol & Locke, 2000).

Goal Mechanisms

Why might goal setting work? On this score phase II theory represents a major advance over the early formulations. The basic propositions are (1) that goals energize performance by motivating people to exert effort in line with the difficulty of or demands of the goal or task (thus, they affect arousal by regulating intensity of effort); (2) goals motivate people to persist in activities through time; and (3) goals direct people's attention to relevant behaviors or outcomes and away from activities that are not relevant to the goals (thus, they orient people toward goal-relevant activities and they activate knowledge and skills perceived to be relevant to the task). If task strategies are held constant, and the goal mechanisms of effort, persistence, and direction are controlled or partialed out, goals should not affect task performance.

This raises the question of what task strategies are. The answer is that they are directional mechanisms with methods of performing a task that extend beyond the relatively automatic mechanisms inherent in effort, persistence, and direction as just discussed to conscious problem solving and creative innovation. They are an especially crucial link between goals and performance on complex tasks.

Why and how, then, are specific challenging goals hypothesized to lead to higher levels of performance? For the following reasons:

They are associated with higher self-efficacy (whether the goals are assigned or self-set).

They require higher performance in order for the individual to feel a sense of self-satisfaction.

They entail less ambiguity about what constitutes high or good performance.

They are typically more instrumental in bringing about valued outcomes.

They lead individuals to expend more effort.

They stimulate individuals to persist longer.

They direct attention and action better, and activate previously automatized skills.

They motivate individuals to search for suitable task strategies, to plan, and to utilize strategies that they have been taught. (Locke & Latham, 1990a, p. 108)

Determinants of Goal Choice

Although goal-setting theory has been primarily concerned with goals as independent variables, the earlier concern with goals as dependent variables (Lewin et al., 1944) has also been incorporated in the phase II theory. In this connection it should be recognized

that although assigned goals typically are accepted, even then the relationship between the assigned goal and a person's personal goal level is far from perfect. Thus the determinants of goal choice remain important even when goals are assigned.

In this connection the theory posits that people will typically raise their goals after failure as a compensation strategy; the operative motive is a desire to make up for past failure by dramatically increasing future performance. In this context goal choice is a function of what a person thinks can be achieved (perceived performance capability, given previous performance, ability levels, self-efficacy, and the like) and what a person would like to achieve or feels should be achieved (perceived desirability or appropriateness of performance, given group norms, competition, goal assignments, any money incentives, dissatisfaction occasioned by previous performance, and other such factors). The goal actually chosen represents a compromise between these two types of factors.

Goal Commitment

Commitment is expected to relate to performance as a direct positive effect. It should also serve to moderate the effects of goals on performance — goal level should be more highly (and positively) related to performance under conditions where the individuals involved have high commitment than where commitment is at a low level.

A number of factors are expected to influence commitment levels, some of which are the same as those previously noted for goal choice. One set of factors affects the perceived desirability or appropriateness (the valence) of trying for a given goal or goal level (such factors as authority, peer groups, publicness of goal statement, incentives, punishments, satisfaction, and goal intensity). Another set of factors affect the perceived ability of attaining (the expectancy of) a given goal or goal level (authority and goal intensity again, plus competition, attributions, and the like).

A commitment-related issue has to do with the relative effectiveness of assigned, participatively set, and self-set goals. Although there have been numerous positions taken on this score, goal-setting theory makes no a priori assumptions regarding the relative effectiveness of the different ways used to set goals. The importance of the matter from both practical and theoretical perspectives is recognized, however. The theory basically states that, insofar as the motivational mechanism of commitment is concerned, the differences among the various methods of setting goals are negligible—it does not matter which method is used. This is a topic that has spawned considerable research; we will consider this research shortly.

Further on Feedback

Phase I theory dealt with feedback. Phase II theory extends that treatment. With respect to feedback, goals are said to act as *mediators*—they are one of the key mechanisms by which feedback becomes translated into action. (This is a restatement of the phase I position.) With respect to goals, however, feedback is now designated as a moderator—goals regulate performance far more reliably when there is feedback present than when feedback is absent. Figure 9.2 sets forth a tentative model of how goal setting mediates feedback into performance under the phase II formulations. The net effects involved here should be as follows: (1) when goal setting is withheld, feedback should not work; (2) when feedback is withheld, goal setting should not work; (3) when goal setting plus feedback are explicitly invoked, the result should be more effective performance than with either one alone. In this and other contexts Locke has been quite critical of classical behaviorist interpretations on the grounds that they do not recognize the effects of the goal setting implicit in their studies:

> The probable reason why goal setting has been de-emphasized and feedback emphasized in the behavior modification literature is that goal setting is frankly an embarrassment to behavior modification theory. Behaviorism asserts that the key events controlling human action are *consequents*, things that occur after behavior. However, goals are things that occur before behavior; thus they are antecedents. . . . The key fallacy here is that a consequent cannot affect *action unless it becomes an antecedent.* How else can the past affect the future? Feedback does not result in anything unless the recipients do something with it, such as decide that they will try to improve their performance the next time they act. If consequent information is incorrectly interpreted or cannot be interpreted, it does not lead to any increase in the desired actions. . . . Nuttin (1984) identifies the fundamental behaviorist error as follows: "Human behavior does not consist of [automatically] repeating previously rein

forced responses; it involves setting immediate or distant goals, elaborating behavioral projects or plans, and working toward their realization by means of learned and readapted behavioral techniques and experiences" (p. 41). (Locke & Latham, 1990a, p. 187)

Goals and Ability, Task Complexity, Personality, Affect

If goals set in a situation are not within the ability level of the person, they will not be attained, irrespective of other considerations. The same is true if situational constraints block goal attainment. Essentially these are factors that set boundaries on the domain of goal-setting theory.

Complex tasks introduce demands that are expected to mute goal-setting effects to a degree and thus reduce the extent of the goal-performance relationship; thus performance will be less effective on complex tasks than on simple tasks, given the same goal input. At the same time, the relationship between task strategies and performance should be greater on complex tasks.

The phase I theory essentially held that individual differences in personality were not of concern for goal-setting theory; these factors should introduce only marginal amounts of variance into the components of the theory. At phase II this position has been modified. The current view is that a syndrome associated with achievement motivation (including need achievement, type A behavior, and internal locus of control) serves to characterize those who tend to set difficult goals. These are all characteristics found among the personal achiever type of successful entrepreneur (Miner, 1997). Also self-esteem, a close cousin to self-efficacy, should operate in the same manner. The hypothesis is that these factors affect the extent to which people take steps to increase their ability, find ways to overcome situational constraints, and deal effectively with complex tasks.

Job satisfaction or affect represents a major factor in phase I theory. Beyond this, phase II theory concerns itself with the aspects of the goal-setting process that should lead to positive appraisals (and satisfaction) or negative appraisals (dissatisfaction or anxiety). In the former category are success, the engagement of values, cognitive focus, and role clarity. In the latter category are failure, feelings of pressure, role conflict, and feelings of inequity.

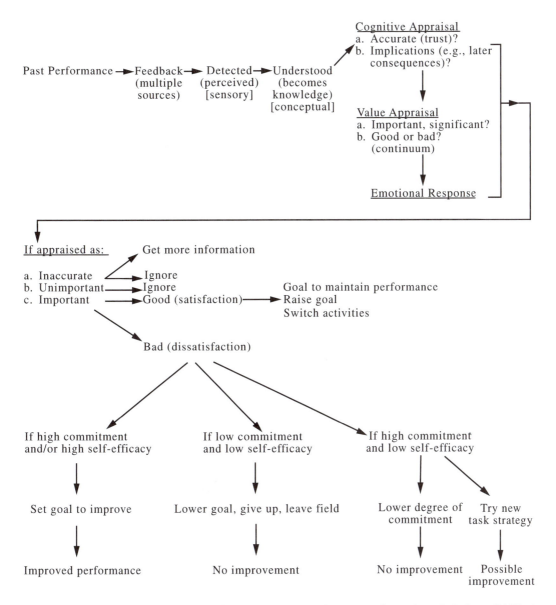

FIGURE 9.2 Model of how feedback leads to action. From Edwin A. Locke & Gary P. Latham (1990), *A Theory of Goal Setting and Task Performance* (Englewood Cliffs, NJ: Prentice Hall), 175. Copyright 1990. Reprinted by permission of Pearson Education, Inc.

The High-Performance Cycle

The ideas and concepts that we have been considering in phase II theory are combined in the model set forth in figure 9.3. This version (Locke & Latham, 1990c) differs somewhat from another published in the same year (Locke & Latham, 1990a). In the 1990a version

self-efficacy is moved from the moderator category to the demands category, which gives it somewhat higher billing; there it is designated "high self-efficacy." At the same time, expectancy is dropped from the model and situational constraint is added as a moderator. These two versions appear to have been produced at roughly the same time, although the paper in the

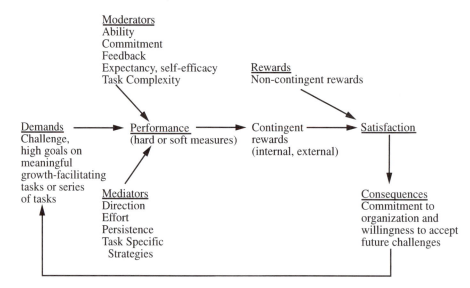

FIGURE 9.3 Model of the high-performance cycle. From Edwin A. Locke & Gary P. Latham (1990), Work Performance: The High Performance Cycle, in Uwe Kleinbeck, Hans-Henning Quast, Henk Thierry, & Hartmut Häcker (Eds.), *Work Motivation* (Hillsdale, NJ: Lawrence Erlbaum), 4. Copyright 1990 by Lawrence Erlbaum Associates. Reproduced with permission.

edited volume (1990c) must have been written first. There is another slightly different version as well (Locke & Latham, 1990b). Clearly, goal-setting theory is still undergoing development, at least to some extent.

In none of these versions of the model is personality given any billing at all. The theory still has not fully overcome the antipathy toward personality factors that characterized the phase I formulations, although it is gradually moving in that direction (see Locke, 2001).

In describing the high-performance cycle, the authors consider applications of their theory, a matter which will concern us in much greater detail in a subsequent section:

> The high performance model has important implications for the management of organizations. Effective organizations must expect a lot from their employees and must try to insure that they gain a sense of satisfaction in return for their efforts. Employee satisfaction will derive, in part, from giving employees personally meaningful work that they are capable of handling and, in part, from taking pains to reward good performance. Peters and Waterman (1982) have argued, consistent with

this model, that the best American organizations in the private sector have organizational philosophies that place a high premium on excellence in performance and on respect for employees. (Locke & Latham, 1990c, p. 18)

Goal Setting and Strategy Effects on Complex Tasks

Previously, in connection with the discussion of goal mechanisms, we considered task strategies, especially as they are used on complex tasks. These ideas are developed more fully in the model of figure 9.4, which deals with the relationships among goals, plans (task strategies), and performance.

Again there are two somewhat different versions of the theory in existence — the Wood and Locke (1990) version of figure 9.4 and the version contained in Locke and Latham (1990a). The theoretical tinkering continues. In the latter instance, the feedback loop at the bottom of the figure extending beyond (4a') to (1) is eliminated; thus this loop extends only to developing new task-specific plans. A link is also added running from these plans to (2a).

Phase III Developments

In the period since 1990 goal-setting theory has had relatively little new to say about its content, but a great deal to say about its domain. The focus has been on extending that domain in many directions. First was a concern with applying the theory to organization goals and business strategies, thus making an essentially micro theory into a macro one as well (Chesney & Locke, 1991). In addition, the theory entered the field of entrepreneurship with hypotheses about the effects of growth-oriented vision statements (read difficult goals) on business performance indices (Baum, Locke, & Kirkpatrick, 1998).

In addition to these macro emphases, the theory has moved in an exactly opposite direction, extending its domain to focus on self-set goals and self-management. Historically, goal setting has been primarily a social process, which is consistent with the theory's origins in social psychology; assigned goals were set with the aid of an authority figure, and participative goal setting was an even more distinctly social process. More recently, however, the theory has joined forces with organizational behavior modification (see chapter 8) to concentrate on the cognitive processes that are involved in self-management and on the role that self-set goals can play in the self-regulation of behavior (Latham & Locke, 1991). In this context, training for self-management, to set goals without the aid of others, becomes an important concern.

Finally, goal-setting theory has been extended in an attempt to join with other motivation theories, and thus achieve a degree of integration within the field. Figure 9.5 depicts this effort. The motivation hub and what happens thereafter represent a restatement of the high-performance cycle (see figure 9.3); this is where prediction of performance is said to be best achieved, because it is closest to the action. However, figure 9.5 also contains the motivation core (values and motives) and needs. These represent extensions of the theory's domain, along with the incorporation of previously separate ideas about motivation, most of which have been discussed in previous chapters of this book.

Applications

Latham is primarily responsible for bringing goal-setting theory into the world of practice. He has done

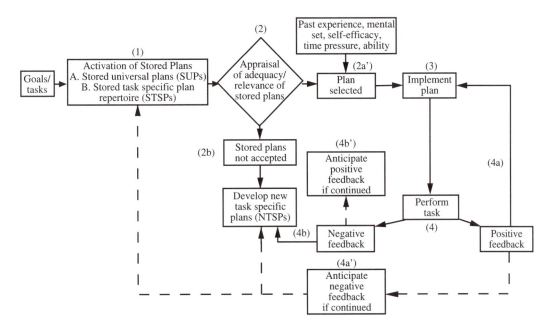

FIGURE 9.4 Model of the relationship among goals, plans, and performance. From Robert E. Wood & Edwin A. Locke (1990), Goal Setting and Strategy Effects on Complex Tasks, *Research in Organizational Behavior*, 12, 76. Copyright 1990. Reprinted with permission from Elsevier Science.

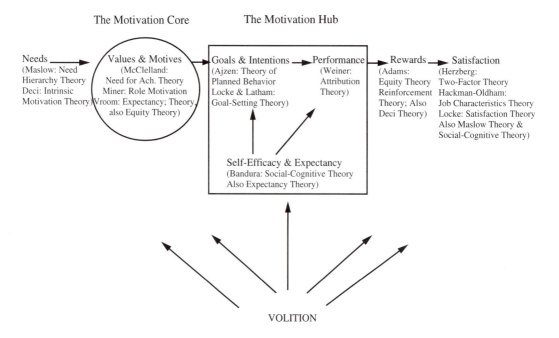

FIGURE 9.5 Model of the motivation sequence. From Edwin A. Locke (1991), The Motivation Sequence, the Motivation Hub, and the Motivation Core, *Organizational Behavior and Human Decision Processes*, 50, 289. Copyright 1991 by Academic Press. Reprinted with permission.

so through his work as a psychologist in various companies, both as an employee and as a consultant. However, goal setting existed in industry long before Latham arrived, in the form of management by objectives. We need to look at this phenomenon first.

Management by Objectives Approach

Management by objectives (MBO) dates its popularity to Peter Drucker's (1954) writings and to a later article by Douglas McGregor (1957). Its historical antecedents, however, may be traced back through the classical and scientific management literature and through management practice to the early 1900s, especially as the literature and practice deal with planning and its related activities. The term *management by objectives* itself appears to have been coined around 1950. This approach is identified strongly with General Electric and with Harold Smiddy, a long-time vice-president of that company (Greenwood, 1981). Goal-setting theory appeared in the mid-1960s and had its origins in the research laboratory.

Management by objectives involves a joint determination by subordinate and superior of common

goals, major areas of responsibility, and results expected; these measures are used as guides for operating the unit and assessing contributions of members. Usually a series of steps must be carried out, but the steps noted by different writers and used in different companies can vary widely. The key steps appear to be:

1. Setting objectives.
2. Working toward the goals.
3. Reviewing performance.

Beyond this basic goal-setting-feedback nexus, a tremendous amount of diversity emerges. Among the components of MBO are strategic planning, performance appraisal, management development, compensation administration, career planning, organization planning, job design, and coaching. A review of individual company programs suggests that the following should also be included: control systems design, organization development, human resource planning, job enrichment, leadership style change, and changes in organizational climate. It is clear that beyond its core elements, management by objectives is many things to many people. The degree to which goals are participatively set can vary considerably and so, too, can the extent of formalization in the sense of documentation or paperwork requirements.

This diversity can be a strength in that it is possible to tailor a program to the needs of a specific company. But from the point of view of evaluation, it creates major problems. Even if an MBO program is shown to yield positive results, it is very difficult to know what factors were responsible or to compare one study with others. In any given instance it may be goal setting that is the cause of a motivational effect, but it also may be any one of the other aspects of the program. Thus research on MBO must be viewed with some caution; variables are typically confounded, and implications for goal-setting theory tend to be indirect at best.

A problem for MBO is that the motivating effects of difficult goals appear to be particularly susceptible to dissipation over time, even among the particular kinds of individuals who are most responsive to them. To counteract this tendency, goal setting must be reinforced frequently. Thus if the need is for an immediate burst of energy due to declining profits or shrinking markets, MBO can prove very valuable. For the long term it is less likely to maintain effort levels unless it is possible to reactivate goals frequently and perhaps to shift the actual content of certain goals (and thus introduce new jobs) at periodic intervals.

These considerations suggest that goal setting for particular, relatively isolated operations is most likely to yield favorable results. In contrast, a comprehensive company-wide program can run into difficulties that will hamper its operations. Locke (1970b) has noted the value that goal setting may have when an individual supervisor deals with subordinates. In this limited context it can be adjusted to the individual characteristics of the subordinate to stay within the boundaries of theoretical application and establish appropriate priorities. An overall MBO program for a company, however, may well miss the mark with so many people that it ultimately loses its legitimacy, goal importance, and motivational impact for almost everyone. Many may feel they have been duped into setting certain goals only to have them "thrown in their face" months later (when they are almost forgotten) as justification for a denied promotion or salary raise.

Locke and Latham (1990a) review a number of reviews of research studies that attempted to evaluate MBO effectiveness. They conclude: "By every reason-

able method of counting, the overall MBO success rate hovers around the 90% success rate obtained for micro- and group-level studies" (p. 45). However, this does not mean success was achieved in all units or at all points in time considered in a given study or on all indices of success. There are many contingencies involved. A meta-analysis of evaluation studies indicates that a key contingency is the support of top management (Rodgers & Hunter, 1991); without this support the effects of MBO are negligible. Furthermore, it is often unclear what caused the success— goal setting may or may not be the key factor.

One thing, however, is clear and that is that MBO and goal-setting theory now have converged, to their mutual benefit, with the former thus acquiring a theoretical base and the latter being a popular arena of application.

Goal-Setting Theory Approach

Locke and Latham (1990a) note a number of applications of goal setting in human resource management. It may be used in job analysis to get people to contribute their knowledge of the work. It may be used to develop interview formats in connection with the situational interview approach, which is described as grounded in goal-setting theory. It may be used in connection with training, as for instance training in self-management, where goal setting is viewed as a core element. It may be used to establish mutual goals between management and labor as part of a relations by objectives program. It may be used as part of performance appraisal when feedback on performance is combined with setting specific improvement goals.

These are important applications, especially the use in connection with performance appraisal. However, the most important use of goal setting in organizations is as a stand-alone procedure for improving performance—much like MBO, but without the formalization that has come to characterize that approach. As with MBO there are certain steps that should be followed. Locke and Latham outline these steps as follows:

1. Specify the nature of the task(s) to be accomplished (that is, write a job description). This may be done in terms of work outcomes and/or in terms of work actions or behaviors.
2. Specify how performance is to be measured.
3. Specify the standard or target to be aimed for in quantitative terms based either on directly

measured output or on a Behavioral Observation Scale. Make the goal challenging; that is, difficult but attainable.

4. Specify the time span involved.
5. If there are multiple goals, rank them in terms of importance or priority. Get a consensus on this ranking.
6. If necessary, rate each goal quantitatively as to importance (priority) and difficulty. To measure overall performance, multiply importance by difficulty by degree of goal attainment, and then sum the products.
7. Determine the coordination requirements (especially lateral) for goal achievement. If the tasks are highly interdependent, use group goals. If group goals are used, be sure to develop a means of measuring each individual's contribution to the group's product. The goals should be modified only if employees clearly lack the ability or knowledge needed to reach them or when substantial changes in the job situation have occurred. (1984, p. 40)

Whether goals should be assigned by a superior or set participatively is an individual matter. Assigned goals appear to achieve much the same level of effect in hierarchic organizations as in the laboratory context, presumably because legitimate authority and the demand character of experiments operate in much the same manner. As with other human resource and organizational behavior approaches, findings with regard to goal setting seem to generalize from the research laboratory to the field rather well (Locke, 1986). Assigned goals work best with those who are already intrinsically motivated and who thus find the assigned goals less onerous. Participative goal setting works best if people are accustomed to and comfortable with it, and when intrinsic motivation to perform is at a low level, thus requiring an added inducement.

Overall, goal-setting procedures appear to have considerable motivational potential with the right people under the right circumstances. Difficulty, specificity, and acceptance of goals are important. Goal setting within the context of a comprehensive MBO program is a more uncertain matter, especially over the long term. The ideal approach seems to be to train individual supervisors of relatively independent jobs in the techniques of goal setting, as well as when to use them.

An idea of what the goal-setting theory approach can accomplish is provided by a study of the relationship between goal-setting activity and organizational profits (Terpstra & Rozell, 1994). A survey was sent to firms averaging approximately 6,000 employees inquiring about their use of goal-setting theory (61 percent used it) and also about firm profit levels and profit growth. Significant relationships were found. This does not establish causality, but the authors believe that the causal arrow runs from practice to profitability. Yet these findings are not always replicated. In one instance, within a single company, when goal setting was compared with indices of performance, goal setting and performance clearly were not positively related (Yearta, Maitlis, & Briner, 1995). Yet problems inherent in both the goal-setting program and the conduct of the research serve to emphasize not only the difficulties of doing goal setting right but also of doing research on goal setting right. In his analysis of prime movers in the business world, Locke (2000) documents many instances of the successful use of personal goal setting.

Evaluation and Impact

Goal-setting theory's formal statements emerged gradually and were intertwined closely with the research. This might represent a major problem in evaluating the theory against these research results were it not for several considerations. One is that Locke appears to have operated from an implicit theory that influenced the design of his research and the selection of research topics from the beginning, long before he made this theory explicit; this implicit theory clearly owes much to Ryan. Another is that Locke and Latham typically have conducted many studies in each area they have investigated, thus replicating their results several times. Accordingly, the theoretical hypotheses cannot be dismissed on the grounds that they incorporate empirical fluctuations attributable to chance on an ad hoc basis.

Examples of Research by the Theory's Authors

Both Locke and Latham have been involved in a large number of studies to test aspects of their theory. Describing all of these would be impossible, but it is possible to provide examples of the approaches taken. The highly inductive nature of the theory construction, going back and forth from research to theory to more research to theoretical refinement and so on, means that most theoretical statements were well established before they became true theory. Providing the full flavor of this process would carry us well beyond the space limitations of this chapter, but the following examples should help.

An initial series of studies used brainstorming tasks in which subjects were to list objects or things that could be described by a given adjective, or to give possible uses for certain objects (Locke, 1966). Goal levels (easy or hard) typically were set by the experimenter, and performance was measured in terms of numbers of objects or uses noted in a given time period over a number of trials. The subjects were all college students. Performance was consistently higher when harder goals existed. This was true even when the goals were set so high that they could actually be reached less than 10 percent of the time. In the one instance when subjects were permitted to set their own goals, they chose relatively easy ones, and their performance reflected this.

A similar experiment was conducted later using a complex psychomotor task that involved adjusting certain controls to produce a pattern of lights to match a standard. The more matches achieved in a set time period, the better the performance (Locke & Bryan, 1966a). Comparisons were made between the results achieved when specific, hard goals were set by the experimenter and those achieved when the student subjects were merely told to do their best. The results provided strong support for the hypothesis that specific hard goals improve performance.

These results were extended to various clerical tasks of a numerical nature in another series of studies (Locke & Bryan, 1967). In this instance, subject acceptance of goals was essential for goal-setting effects to occur. In certain instances when postexperimental questions indicated that subjects had not accepted the specific, hard goals assigned, performance was not superior. The introduction of a monetary incentive appears to have been effective in gaining the necessary commitment in one study, although other studies were able to produce similar results without incentives. Data obtained with an interest questionnaire indicated that subjects working for hard goals were significantly less bored than were subjects working without specific goals.

This is the laboratory approach to goal setting. It has been used in one form or another in many, many studies by the theory's authors and others. Usually, after substantial research, a theoretical synthesis is developed. Thus, the research on feedback effects resulted in the following theoretical statement:

> The present review found none of the evidence to be inconsistent with the notion that the effects of motivational knowledge of results depend upon the goals a subject sets in response to such knowledge. Most previous studies failed to separate the effects of knowledge qua knowledge from those of goal setting. . . . When the two effects are separated, there is no effect of knowledge of results over and above that which can be attributed to differential goal setting. (Locke, Cartledge, & Koeppel, 1968, p. 482)

The field research involving Latham started in the logging operations of wood products companies. In the first study, productivity (mean cords per day) was found to be highest not only when specific production goals were assigned but also when the crew supervisor stayed at the work site to encourage goal acceptance (Ronan, Latham, & Kinne, 1973).

In a second study, 10 matched pairs of logging crews were compared over a 14-week period. One of each pair was exposed to preliminary training in goal setting, and the other was not. Appropriate specific production goals were established for all crews each week, but only in the case of the previously trained crews were these goals communicated; thus only one of each pair was actively engaged in goal setting, although the performance of both crews could be measured relative to goals (Latham & Kinne, 1974). It is evident that the goal-setting crews exceeded their goals more often and usually outperformed the nongoal-setting crews in terms of a cords per man hour criterion (table 9.4).

A similar approach was used in a study by Latham and James Baldes (1975) to induce logging truck drivers to carry heavier loads to the mill. A goal of 94 percent of the legal weight limit was assigned. At the beginning of the period the trucks were averaging 60 percent. With the introduction of the goal, performance improved sharply and by the end of 9 months it had stabilized at over 90 percent: "Without the increase in efficiency due to goal setting it would have cost the company a quarter of a million dollars for the purchase of additional trucks in order to deliver the same quantity of logs to the mills" (Latham and Baldes, 1975, p. 124).

TABLE 9.4 Goal-setting and nongoal-setting logging crews compared in terms of cords per man hour relative to standard

Matched pair no.	Goal-setting crew	Nongoal-setting crew
1	+2.3	+.09
2	−0.9	−.09
3	+.05	−.08
4	+.05	−.07
5	+.04	+.01
6	+.13	−.02
7	+.08	−.16
8	+.22	+.24
9	+.08	−.07
10	+.11	+.13
Mean	+.09	−.002

Results such as these led to the conclusion that the goal-setting results obtained in the laboratory applied in the field as well.

Findings from Meta-Analytic Studies

I have been able to locate 14 meta-analyses of studies related to goal setting that have been published to date. Six of these appeared in the 1983–1987 period and were given attention in the Locke and Latham (1990a) volume. The early reviews tended to look at goal setting in conjunction with other approaches (Hunter & Schmidt, 1983; Guzzo, Jette, & Katzell, 1985); another was published in a proceedings volume (Chidester & Grigsby, 1984). Beginning in 1986, however, meta-analyses that were focused on goal setting became a feature of the major journals (Tubbs, 1986; Mento, Steel, & Karren, 1987; Wood, Mento, & Locke, 1987). This burst of activity was in part occasioned by the fact that meta-analysis was just finding its way into organizational behavior at this time. More significant was the fact that by then goal-setting theory had spawned sufficient research to justify meta-analyses. Over time, extending to the present, this output of related research has been tremendous; without the quantitative and qualitative reviews, comprehending and synthesizing this research becomes almost impossible.

The conclusion from these early meta-analyses is that goal difficulty and specificity do operate as the theory predicts in influencing performance, and that feedback combines with goal setting as hypothesized. Participation per se does not exhibit any special advantage in setting goals, and, again, this is in line with theoretical expectations. Goal-setting effects are most pronounced on relatively simple tasks; they decline on complex tasks such as business game simulations and scientific work.

Later meta-analyses have typically looked at more specific issues. Thus, Patrick Wright (1990) found that goal difficulty has in fact been operationalized in a number of different ways and that how it is operationalized has a substantial effect on performance outcomes. Nevertheless, the expected results are consistently obtained irrespective of the operationalization. Howard Klein (1991) identified similar problems in the measurement of expectancy theory variables; large variations were noted in different studies. When appropriate operationalization occurs, however, expectancy theory variables are significantly related to goal choice, goal commitment, and performance. These results confirm the compatibility of the two theories.

We have already noted the Rodgers and Hunter (1991) meta-analysis of management by objectives research. The key finding here was that MBO requires top management support and participation to work well.

J. C. Wofford, Vicki Goodwin, and Steven Premack (1992) were able to identify prior performance, ability, and—with somewhat less certainty—knowledge of results as antecedents of personal goals. Self-efficacy, expectancy of goal attainment, task difficulty, and task complexity (with a negative sign) were identified as antecedents of goal commitment. Goal commitment appeared to affect goal achievement. That certain hypothesized relationships did not emerge as expected seems to be due to the lack of a sufficient number of studies that often plagued this meta-analysis.

This dearth of research appears not to have been a problem in a meta-analysis of the effects of group goal setting (O'Leary-Kelly, Martocchio, & Frink, 1994). There, group goals were found to strongly influence performance with an effect size exceeding that typically found for individual goal setting.

A meta-analysis conducted by Alexander Stajkovic and Fred Luthans (1998) dealt specifically with self-efficacy, not goal setting, but this study is relevant because of the affinity that has developed between the two theoretical approaches. Self-efficacy is strongly related to performance, at a level that appears to exceed that often found for goal setting. As has been noted with goal setting, relationships between self-efficacy and performance decline as tasks move from simple to complex; yet significance does not disappear.

Another article provides the only meta-analytic results that bring any aspect of goal-setting theory into question (Donovan & Radosevich, 1998). Here, although goal commitment served to significantly moderate the relationship between goal difficulty and performance, it did not emerge as the powerful factor that theory would anticipate. This finding may reflect a shortcoming of the theory, but it may also reflect problems of definition and operationalization or limitations of the laboratory context used primarily to study the phenomenon. Research that identifies or introduces wide variations in goal commitment appears needed. Yet, as occasionally happens with meta-analytic studies, a later investigation of this same literature, but incorporating somewhat different studies, produced results more supportive of theory which are interpreted as refuting the Donovan and Radosevich (1998) conclusions (Klein, Wesson, Hollenbeck, & Alge, 1999). It still seems, however, that more research on the commitment factor is needed.

Proposition-Specific Evaluations

The meta-analyses overall provide very strong support for goal-setting theory. Yet there are aspects of the theory that they do not consider, often because there is insufficient research available as yet to use the approach.

As Locke and Latham (1990a) note, the theory suffers from ambiguity as regards the definition of its constructs, including goal difficulty and goal commitment, as well as in establishing certain boundary definitions, such as in the area of complex tasks. Nevertheless, a great deal of research of respectable quality has been conducted.

In general, the theoretical expectations of the phase I rubric have received strong support. There is reason to believe, however, that monetary incentives can involve motivational forces above and beyond goal setting (Locke & Latham, 1990a). Also, research on the job satisfaction formulations has not been as extensive as might be desired. However, confirmatory findings do exist (McFarlin & Rice, 1991).

The early concerns about conflicts between expectancy theory and goal-setting theory seem to have evaporated; in fact, expectancy concepts have been incorporated widely in goal-setting models. Self-efficacy represents a powerful addition to the goal-setting formulations as well, although there clearly is much common variance between the expectancy and self-efficacy concepts incorporated.

The elaboration of goal mechanisms in phase II has proved helpful in a number of respects. It fills a theoretical void that needed filling. The same can be said for the formulations regarding the determinants of goal choice. The recent review by John Donovan and David Radosevich (1998) raises questions about the role of goal commitment, but there is previous support for this construct, and variance restrictions inherent in the laboratory research may have limited the effectiveness of the tests utilized. Certain measurement advances offer promise with regard to goal commitment as well (Renn, Danehower, Swiercz, & Icenogle, 1999). The research on the ways in which goals are set — assigned, self, participative — for a while seemed to support motivational superiority for a participative approach. With the collaborative research of Latham, Miriam Erez, and Locke (1988) and the later discussion in the volume by Peter Frost and Ralph Stablein (1992), it became evident that assigned goals do as well as participative goals if they are properly sold to those doing the goal setting. The theory's position that differences are negligible appears to have been upheld.

Feedback is considered in both phase I and phase II theory. These hypotheses have considerable research support, although not all aspects of figure 9.2 have been the subject of study (Locke & Latham, 1990a). Ability and situational constraints also appear to operate as hypothesized. The theory recognizes the problems that are inherent in complex tasks, and the research supports the view that the basic theory works less well in this domain. Strategies exert a greater effect on performance in this context than do goals (Chesney & Locke, 1991). Personality factors have not been consistently incorporated in the theory, although there is increasing evidence that they should be (Campbell, 1982; Phillips & Gully, 1997). The strong demand character of the laboratory setting no doubt minimizes personality influences, but as complex problem solving, plans, and strategies become of increasing interest this is no longer true.

With regard to the different versions of the high-performance cycle model (figure 9.3), it now appears that self-efficacy (and expectancy) should be treated both as moderators *and* as demands, with direct effects on performance. Presumably the alternating versions represented attempts to find simpler presentations of the model, which in the end did not fully reflect the reality.

The phase III domain extensions are clearly incomplete. There is going to be a need for some new theory if such matters as real and stated organizational goals (Etzioni, 1964), business strategies, and the like are to be a major concern of the theory. Nevertheless, some progress has been made. For instance, the vision statements of entrepreneurs (as goals) do affect organizational performance and growth (Baum et al., 1998). Also the movement into the realm of self-management has struck a chord within organizational behavior (see Rousseau, 1997); it is still unclear as to how much new theory or cooptation of existing theory will be required by this thrust.

Mitchell (1997) notes that goal-setting theory has given insufficient attention to the context of goals, including multiple goals and goal priorities. Also lacking is concern with the actual process of setting goals — the political aspects of goal setting by managers for instance. These concerns are not merely reflective of research needs; they require theoretical extensions as well. Goal-setting theory now faces the problem that it has been so successful, and sparked so much research, that the research is in danger of overflowing the vessel that is its theory. It may no longer be possible to follow the inductive theory-research lockstep that Locke initiated in the 1960s. The problems unearthed seem to call for more expansive theorizing (Pinder, 1998).

Implications of the
Motivation Sequence Model

Figure 9.5 sets forth goal-setting theory within a larger theoretical picture. Edward Deci (1992) has criticized goal theory as representing only a partial theory of motivation in organizations, and he adds that it fails to address many of the most interesting and important questions regarding motivation. The motivation sequence represents an attempt to open up goal theory and integrate it with other theories of a similar nature. In doing so, it introduces needs, values, and motives that are not specifically tied to goals for consideration; Deci (1992) advocates introductions of this type.

Consider the following findings from research:

On complex tasks, specific challenging goals work to improve performance *only* if there is some type

of help in searching for strategies. (Earley, Connolly, & Lee, 1989)

On complex tasks, commitment to planning, and even to in-process planning, plays an important role in mediating the effects of goals on performance. (Weingart, 1992)

On a complex task, individuals — if they are given a creative goal — have lower productivity than those with *no goal*, presumably due to the fact that they are concentrating on creativity, not productivity. (Shalley, 1995)

These findings beg for information on the personality characteristics of the subjects; needs, values, and motive patterns become crucial as goal-setting theory moves to complex tasks of one kind or another. How would such characteristics as independence-dependence, the desire to plan, and a propensity for creative thought operate within the confines of the above studies? The motivation sequence makes such questions of legitimate concern for goal-setting theory and research.

It is evident that such factors as goal specificity, goal difficulty, and participation in setting goals affect various individuals differently. This finding could well be mediated by variations in the importance certain people attach to particular goals, or at a more abstract level, values. In any event, there are some distinct variations in the kinds of individuals who react differently to aspects of the goal-setting process. A thorough study of these variations in the context of adequate theoretical perspectives could, in fact, move goal-setting theory out of its current status, firmly constrained within the motivation hub of figure 9.5, to incorporate the motivation core, and beyond. There is indeed a glimmer here of the overarching motivation theory that Locke envisages.

CONCLUSIONS

These two motivation theories with roots in social psychology, the equity approach, and goal setting, do not appear to have much in common, other than a vaguely similar source of origin, but some commonalities can be noted. For one thing, both have survived over a considerable period of time and are still active today, goal-setting theory much more so, presumably because Locke and Latham are still alive and professionally involved, but equity theory clearly did not die with its author.

For another, both theories have moved, or seem to be moving, in similar directions. Personality considerations have become more important for both theories, although neither can be said to be truly personality-based at present. Yet as these theories become more closely integrated with other theories of motivation, they inevitably acquire constructs of a personality nature. Furthermore, the theorists — although not necessarily their theories — have moved in a macro direction: not away from their definitely micro base, but to study or incorporate certain macro variables. We do not know what this might have meant for equity theory, perhaps a theory of organizational membership and citizenship, but for goal theory it has meant a concern with complex organizational tasks and strategies.

As we complete our treatment of the motivation area, it is noteworthy that many, although certainly not all, of these theories are still active; they are first-generation theories that are affecting the second generation. Added to this is considerable evidence of convergence. The theories are not only moving, but they are moving toward each other. In this context, leadership theories would appear to be a long way off — far beyond the horizon. Yet as we will see, this is not really the case; leadership and motivation theories possess a number of common constructs and variables, and some common actors as well.

References

Adams, J. Stacy (1963a). Toward an Understanding of Inequity. *Journal of Abnormal and Social Psychology*, 67, 422–436.

Adams, J. Stacy (1963b). Wage Inequities, Productivity, and Work Quality. *Industrial Relations*, 3, 9–16.

Adams, J. Stacy (1965). Inequity in Social Exchange. In Leonard Berkowitz (Ed.), *Advances in Experimental Social Psychology* (Vol. 2, pp. 267–299). New York: Academic Press.

Adams, J. Stacy (1968a). Effects of Overpayment: Two Comments on Lawler's Paper. *Journal of Personality and Social Psychology*, 10, 315–316.

Adams, J. Stacy (1968b). A Framework for the Study of Modes of Resolving Inconsistency. In Robert P. Abelson, E. Aronson, W. J. McGuire, T. M. Newcomb, M. J. Rosenberg, & P. H. Tannenbaum (Eds.), *Theories of Cognitive Inconsistency: A Sourcebook* (pp. 655–660). Chicago: Rand, McNally.

Adams, J. Stacy (1976). The Structure and Dynamics of Behavior in Organizational Boundary Roles. In Marvin D. Dunnette (Ed.), *Handbook of Industrial and Organizational Psychology* (pp. 1175–1199). Chicago: Rand, McNally.

Adams, J. Stacy (1980). Interorganizational Processes and Organizational Boundary Activities. *Research in Organizational Behavior*, 2, 321–355.

Adams, J. Stacy, & Freedman, Sara (1976). Equity Theory Revisited: Comments and Annotated Bibliography. In Leonard Berkowitz & Elaine Walster (Eds.), *Advances in Experimental Social Psychology*, (Vol. 9, pp. 43–90). New York: Academic Press.

Adams, J. Stacy, & Jacobsen, Patricia R. (1964). Effects of Wage Inequities on Work Quality. *Journal of Abnormal and Social Psychology*, 69, 19–25.

Adams, J. Stacy, & Rosenbaum, William B. (1962). The Relationship of Worker Productivity to Cognitive Dissonance about Wage Inequities. *Journal of Applied Psychology*, 46, 161–164.

Bandura, Albert (1982). Self-efficacy Mechanism in Human Agency. *American Psychologist*, 37, 122–147.

Bandura, Albert (1997). *Self-Efficacy: The Exercise of Control*. New York: W. H. Freeman.

Bartol, Kathryn M., & Locke, Edwin A. (2000). Incentives and Motivation. In Sara L. Rynes & Barry Gerhart (Eds.), *Compensation in Organizations: Current Research and Practice* (pp. 104–147). San Francisco: Jossey-Bass.

Baum, J. Robert; Locke, Edwin A.; & Kirkpatrick, Shelley A. (1998). A Longitudinal Study of the Relation of Vision and Vision Communication to Venture Growth in Entrepreneurial Firms. *Journal of Applied Psychology*, 83, 43–54.

Bretz, Robert D., & Thomas, Steven L. (1992). Perceived Equity, Motivation, and Final-Offer Arbitration in Major League Baseball. *Journal of Applied Psychology*, 77, 280–287.

Bryan, Judith F., & Locke, Edwin A. (1967). Parkinson's Law as a Goal Setting Phenomenon. *Organizational Behavior and Human Performance*, 2, 258–275.

Campbell, Donald J. (1982). Determinants of Choice of Goal Difficulty Level: A Review of Situational and Personality Influences. *Journal of Occupational Psychology*, 55, 79–95.

Chen, Chao C. (1995). New Trends in Rewards Allocation Preferences: A Sino-U.S. Comparison. *Academy of Management Journal*, 38, 408–428.

Chesney, Amelia A., & Locke, Edwin A. (1991). Relationships among Goal Difficulty, Business Strategies, and Performance on a Complex Management Simulation Task. *Academy of Management Journal*, 34, 400–424.

Chidester, Thomas R., & Grigsby, W. Charles (1984). A Meta-Analysis of the Goal Setting-Performance Literature. *Academy of Management Proceedings*, 44, 202–206.

Cosier, Richard A., & Dalton, Dan R. (1983). Equity Theory and Time: A Reformulation. *Academy of Management Review*, 8, 311–319.

Deci, Edward L. (1992). On the Nature and Functions of Motivation Theories. *Psychological Science*, 3, 167–171.

Donovan, John J., & Radosevich, David J. (1998). The Moderating Role of Goal Commitment on the Goal Difficulty-Performance Relationship: A Meta-Analytic Review and Critical Reanalysis. *Journal of Applied Psychology*, 83, 308–315.

Dornstein, Miriam (1989). The Fairness Judgments of Received Pay and Their Determinants. *Journal of Occupational Psychology*, 62, 287–299.

Drucker, Peter F. (1954). *The Practice of Management*. New York: Harper, 1954.

Dulebohn, James, & Martocchio, Joseph J. (1998). Employee's Perceptions of the Distributive Justice of Pay Raise Decisions: A Policy Capturing Approach. *Journal of Business and Psychology*, 13, 41–64.

Earley, P. Christopher; Connolly, Terry; & Lee, Cynthia (1989). Task Strategy Interventions in Goal Setting: The Importance of Search in Strategy Development. *Journal of Management*, 15, 589–602.

Etzioni, Amitai (1964). *Modern Organizations*. Englewood Cliffs, NJ: Prentice Hall.

Festinger, Leon (1957). *A Theory of Cognitive Dissonance*. Evanston, IL: Row, Peterson.

Frost, Peter J., & Stablein, Ralph E. (1992). *Doing Exemplary Research* (pp. 142–176, Journey 5). Newbury Park, CA: Sage.

Giacalone, Robert A., & Greenberg, Jerald (1997). *Antisocial Behavior in Organizations*. Thousand Oaks, CA: Sage.

Greenberg, Jerald (1990). Organizational Justice: Yesterday, Today, and Tomorrow. *Journal of Management*, 16, 399–432.

Greenberg, Jerald, & Scott, Kimberly S. (1996). Why Do Workers Bite the Hands That Feed Them? Employee Theft as a Social Exchange Process. *Research in Organizational Behavior*, 18, 111–156.

Greenwood, Ronald G. (1981). Management by Objectives: As Developed by Peter Drucker, Assisted by Harold Smiddy. *Academy of Management Review*, 6, 225–230.

Guzzo, Richard A.; Jette, Richard D.; & Katzell, Raymond A. (1985). The Effects of Psychologically Based Intervention Programs on Worker Productivity: A Meta-Analysis. *Personnel Psychology*, 38, 275–291.

Harder, Joseph W. (1991). Equity Theory versus Expectancy Theory: The Case of Major League Baseball Free Agents. *Journal of Applied Psychology*, 76, 458–464.

Harder, Joseph W. (1992). Play for Pay: Effects of Inequity in a Pay-for-Performance Context. *Administrative Science Quarterly*, 37, 321–335.

Homans, George C. (1961). *Social Behavior: Its Elementary Forms*. New York: Harcourt, Brace, & World.

Hunter, John E., & Schmidt, Frank L. (1983). Quantifying the Effects of Psychological Interventions on Employee Job Performance and Work-Force Productivity. *American Psychologist*, 38, 473–478.

Huseman, Richard C.; Hatfield, John D.; & Miles, Edward W. (1987). A New Perspective on Equity Theory: The Equity Sensitivity Construct. *Academy of Management Review*, 12, 222–234.

Jaques, Elliott, & Cason, Kathryn (1994). *Human Capability*. Rockville, MD: Cason Hall.

Kanfer, Ruth (1990). Motivation Theory and Industrial and Organizational Psychology. In Marvin D. Dunnette & Leaetta M. Hough (Eds.), *Handbook of Industrial and Organizational Psychology* (Vol. 1, pp. 75–170). Palo Alto, CA: Consulting Psychologists Press.

King, Wesley C., & Hinson, Thomas, D. (1994). The Influence of Sex and Equity Sensitivity on Relationship Preferences, Assessment of Opponent, and Outcomes in a Negotiation Experiment. *Journal of Management*, 20, 605–624.

Klein, Howard J. (1991). Further Evidence on the Relationship between Goal Setting and Expectancy Theories. *Organizational Behavior and Human Decision Processes*, 49, 230–257.

Klein, Howard J.; Wesson, Michael J.; Hollenbeck, John R.; & Alge, Bradley, J. (1999). Goal Commitment and the Goal-Setting Process: Conceptual Clarification and Empirical Synthesis. *Journal of Applied Psychology*, 84, 885–896.

Konovsky, Mary A. (2000). Understanding Procedural Justice and Its Impact on Business Organizations. *Journal of Management*, 26, 489–511.

Kulik, Carol T., & Ambrose, Maureen L. (1992). Personal and Situational Determinants of Referent Choice. *Academy of Management Review*, 17, 212–237.

Larwood, Laurie; Kavanagh, Michael; & Levine, Richard (1978). Perceptions of Fairness with Three Different Economic Exchanges. *Academy of Management Journal*, 21, 69–83.

Latham, Gary P., & Baldes, J. James (1975). The Practical Significance of Locke's Theory of Goal Setting. *Journal of Applied Psychology*, 60, 122–124.

Latham, Gary P.; Erez, Miriam; & Locke, Edwin A. (1988). Resolving Scientific Disputes by the Joint Design of Crucial Experiments by the Antagonists: Application to the Erez-Latham Dispute Regarding Participation in Goal Setting. *Journal of Applied Psychology*, 73, 753–772.

Latham, Gary P., & Kinne, Sydney B. (1974). Improving Job Performance through Training in Goal Setting. *Journal of Applied Psychology*, 59, 187–191.

Latham, Gary P., & Locke, Edwin A. (1991). Self-Regulation through Goal Setting. *Organizational Behavior and Human Decision Processes*, 50, 212–247.

Lawler, Edward E. (1968). Equity Theory as a Predictor of Productivity and Work Quality. *Psychological Bulletin*, 70, 596–610.

Leventhal, Gerald S.; Weiss, Thomas; & Long, Gary (1969). Equity, Reciprocity, and Reallocating Rewards in the Dyad. *Journal of Personality and Social Psychology*, 13, 300–305.

Lewin, Kurt (1935). *A Dynamic Theory of Personality*. New York: McGraw-Hill.

Lewin, Kurt (1938). *The Conceptual Representation and the Measurement of Psychological Forces*. Durham, NC: Duke University Press.

Lewin, Kurt; Dembo, Tamara; Festinger, Leon; & Sears, Pauline S. (1944). Level of Aspiration. In J. McVicker Hunt (Ed.), *Personality and the Behavior Disorders* (Vol. 1, pp. 333–378). New York: Ronald Press.

Lind, E. Allan; Kray, Laura; & Thompson, Leigh (1998). The Social Construction of Injustice: Fairness Judgments in Response to Own and Others' Unfair Treatment by Authorities. *Organizational Behavior and Human Decision Processes*, 75, 1–22.

Locke, Edwin A. (1966). The Relationship of Intentions to Level of Performance. *Journal of Applied Psychology*, 50, 60–66.

Locke, Edwin A. (1968). Toward a Theory of Task Motivation and Incentives. *Organizational Behavior and Human Performance*, 3, 157–189.

Locke, Edwin A. (1969). What Is Job Satisfaction? *Organizational Behavior and Human Performance*, 4, 309–336.

Locke, Edwin A. (1970a). Job Satisfaction and Job Performance: A Theoretical Analysis. *Organizational Behavior and Human Performance*, 5, 484–500.

Locke, Edwin A. (1970b). The Supervisor as Motivator: His Influence on Employee Performance and Satisfaction. In Bernard M. Bass, R. Cooper, & J. A. Haas (Eds.), *Managing for Task Accomplishment* (pp. 57–67). Lexington, MA: Heath.

Locke, Edwin A. (1986). *Generalizing from Laboratory to Field Settings*. Lexington, MA: Lexington Books.

Locke, Edwin A. (1991). The Motivation Sequence, the Motivation Hub, and the Motivation Core. *Organizational Behavior and Human Decision Processes*, 50, 288–299.

Locke, Edwin A. (1993). Principled Ambition. In Arthur G. Bedeian (Ed.), *Management Laureates: A Collection of Autobiographical Essays* (Vol. 2, pp. 217–248). Greenwich, CT: JAI Press.

Locke, Edwin A. (2000). *The Prime Movers: Traits of the Great Wealth Creators*. New York: AMACOM.

Locke, Edwin A. (2001). Self-Set Goals and Self-Efficacy as Mediators of Incentives and Personality. In Miriam Erez, Uwe Kleinbeck, & Henk Thierry (Eds.), *Work Motivation in the Context of a Globalizing Economy*. Mahwah, NJ: Erlbaum.

Locke, Edwin A., & Bryan, Judith F. (1966a). Cognitive Aspects of Psychomotor Performance: The Effects of Performance Goals on Level of Performance. *Journal of Applied Psychology*, 50, 286–291.

Locke, Edwin A., & Bryan, Judith F. (1966b). The Effects of Goal Setting, Rule Learning, and Knowledge of Score on Performance. *American Journal of Psychology*, 79, 451–457.

Locke, Edwin A., & Bryan, Judith F. (1967). Performance Goals as Determinants of Level of Performance and Boredom. *Journal of Applied Psychology*, 51, 120–130.

Locke, Edwin A.; Bryan, Judith F.; & Kendall, Lorne M. (1968). Goals and Intentions as Mediators of the Effects of Monetary Incentives on Behavior. *Journal of Applied Psychology*, 52, 104–121.

Locke, Edwin A.; Cartledge, Norman; & Knerr, Claramae S. (1970). Studies of the Relationship between Satisfaction, Goal Setting, and Performance. *Organizational Behavior and Human Performance*, 5, 135–138.

Locke, Edwin A.; Cartledge, Norman; & Koeppel, Jeffrey (1968). Motivational Effects of Knowledge of Results: A Goal Setting Phenomenon. *Psychological Bulletin*, 70, 474–485.

Locke, Edwin A., & Latham, Gary P. (1984). *Goal Setting: A Motivational Technique That Works*. Englewood Cliffs, NJ: Prentice Hall.

Locke, Edwin A., & Latham, Gary P. (1990a). *A Theory of Goal Setting and Task Performance*. Englewood Cliffs, NJ: Prentice Hall.

Locke, Edwin A., & Latham, Gary P. (1990b). Work Motivation and Satisfaction: Light at the End of the Tunnel. *Psychological Science*, 1, 240–246.

Locke, Edwin A., & Latham, Gary P. (1990c). Work Performance: The High Performance Cycle. In Uwe Kleinbeck, Hans-Henning Quast, Henk Thierry, & Hartmut Häcker (Eds.), *Work Motivation* (pp. 3–25). Hillsdale, NJ: Erlbaum.

Mannix, Elizabeth A.; Neale, Margaret A.; & Northcraft, Gregory B. (1995). Equity, Equality, or Need? The Effects of Organizational Culture on the Allocation of Benefits and Burdens. *Organizational Behavior and Human Decision Processes*, 63, 276–286.

McFarlin, Dean B., & Rice, Robert W. (1991). Determinants of Satisfaction with Specific Job Facets: A Test of Locke's Model. *Journal of Business and Psychology*, 6, 25–38.

McGregor, Douglas (1957). An Uneasy Look at Performance Appraisal. *Harvard Business Review*, 35(3), 89–94.

Mento, Anthony J.; Steel, Robert J.; & Karren, Ronald J. (1987). A Meta-Analytic Study of the Effects of Goal Setting on Task Performance: 1966–1984. *Organizational Behavior and Human Decision Processes*, 39, 52–83.

Miner, John B. (1997). *A Psychological Typology of Successful Entrepreneurs*. Westport, CT: Quorum.

Miner, John B., & Capps, Michael H. (1996). *How Honesty Testing Works*. Westport, CT: Quorum.

Mitchell, Terence R. (1997). Matching Motivational Strategies with Organizational Contexts. *Research in Organizational Behavior*, 19, 57–149.

Mowday, Richard T. (1996). Equity Theory Predictions of Behavior in Organizations. In Richard M. Steers, Lyman W. Porter, & Gregory A. Bigley (Eds.), *Motivation and Leadership at Work* (pp. 53–71). New York: McGraw-Hill.

Mudrack, Peter E.; Mason, E. Sharon; & Stepanski, Kim M. (1999). Equity Sensitivity and Business Ethics. *Journal of Occupational and Organizational Psychology*, 72, 539–560.

Mueller, Stephen L., & Clarke, Linda D. (1998). Political-Economic Context and Sensitivity to Equity: Differences between the United States and the Transition Economies of Central and Eastern Europe. *Academy of Management Journal*, 41, 319–329.

Nuttin, J. R. (1984). *Motivation, Planning and Action: A Relational Theory of Behavioral Dynamics*. Hillsdale, NJ: Erlbaum.

O'Leary-Kelly, Anne M.; Martocchio, Joseph J.; & Frink, Dwight D. (1994). A Review of the Influence of Group Goals on Group Performance. *Academy of Management Journal*, 37, 1285–1301.

Peters, Thomas J., & Waterman, Robert H. (1982). *In Search of Excellence: Lessons from America's Best-Run Companies*. New York: Harper & Row.

Phillips, Jean M., & Gully, Stanley M. (1997). Role of Goal Orientation, Ability, Need for Achievement, and Locus of Control in the Self-Efficacy and Goal-Setting Process. *Journal of Applied Psychology*, 82, 792–802.

Pinder, Craig C. (1998). *Work Motivation in Organizational Behavior*. Upper Saddle River, NJ: Prentice Hall.

Rand, Ayn (1969). *Introduction to Objectivist Epistemology*. New York: The Objectivist.

Renn, Robert W.; Danehower, Carol; Swiercz, Paul M.; & Icenogle, Marjorie L. (1999). Further Examination of the Measurement Properties of Leifer & McGannon's (1986) Goal Acceptance and Goal Commitment Scales. *Journal of Occupational and Organizational Psychology*, 72, 107–113.

Rodgers, Robert, & Hunter, John E. (1991). Impact of Management by Objectives on Organizational Productivity. *Journal of Applied Psychology*, 76, 322–335.

Ronan, W. W.; Latham, Gary P.; & Kinne, Sydney B. (1973). Effects of Goal Setting and Supervision on Worker Behavior in an Industrial Situation. *Journal of Applied Psychology*, 58, 302–307.

Rousseau, Denise M. (1997). Organizational Behavior in the New Organizational Era. *Annual Review of Psychology*, 48, 515–546.

Ryan, Thomas A. (1970). *Intentional Behavior: An Approach to Human Motivation*. New York: Ronald Press.

Scholl, Richard W.; Cooper, Elizabeth A.; & McKenna, Jack F. (1987). Referent Selection in Determining Equity Perceptions: Differential Effects on Behavioral and Attitudinal Outcomes. *Personnel Psychology*, 40, 113–124.

Shalley, Christina E. (1995). Effects of Coaction, Expected Evaluation, and Goal Setting on Creativity and Productivity. *Academy of Management Journal*, 38, 483–503.

Stajkovic, Alexander D., & Luthans, Fred (1998). Self-Efficacy and Work-Related Performance: A Meta-Analysis. *Psychological Bulletin*, 124, 240–261.

Summers, Timothy P., & Hendrix, William H. (1991). Modeling the Role of Pay Equity Perceptions: A Field Study. *Journal of Occupational Psychology*, 64, 145–157.

Terpstra, David E., & Rozell, Elizabeth J. (1994). The Relationship of Goal Setting to Organizational Profitability. *Group and Organization Management*, 19, 285–294.

Tubbs, Mark E. (1986). Goal Setting—A Meta-Analytic Examination of the Empirical Evidence. *Journal of Applied Psychology*, 71, 474–483.

Vecchio, Robert P. (1981). An Individual-Differences Interpretation of the Conflicting Predictions Generated by an Equity and Expectancy Theory. *Journal of Applied Psychology*, 66, 470–481.

Walster, Elaine; Berscheid, Ellen; & Walster, G. William (1973). New Directions in Equity Research. *Journal of Personality and Social Psychology*, 25, 151–176.

Weingart, Laurie R. (1992). Impact of Group Goals, Task Component Complexity, Effort, and Planning on Group Performance. *Journal of Applied Psychology*, 77, 682–693.

Wofford, J. C.; Goodwin, Vicki L.; & Premack, Steven (1992). Meta-Analysis of the Antecedents of Personal Goal Level and Antecedents and Consequences of Goal Commitment. *Journal of Management*, 18, 595–615.

Wood, Robert E., & Locke, Edwin A. (1990). Goal Setting and Strategy Effects on Complex Tasks. *Research in Organizational Behavior*, 12, 73–109.

Wood, Robert E.; Mento, Anthony; & Locke, Edwin A. (1987). Task Complexity as a Moderator of Goal Effects: A Meta-Analysis. *Journal of Applied Psychology*, 72, 416–425.

Wright, Patrick M. (1990). Operationalization of Goal Difficulty as a Moderator of the Goal Difficulty-Performance Relationship. *Journal of Applied Psychology*, 75, 227–234.

Yearta, Shawn K.; Maitlis, Sally; & Briner, Rob B. (1995). An Exploratory Study of Goal Setting in Theory and Practice: A Motivational Technique That Works. *Journal of Occupational and Organizational Psychology*, 68, 237–252.

Part III

First-Generation Theories: Leadership

Chapter 10

Leadership Theories Built on
Motivational Constructs

The theories considered in this chapter were developed by authors who moved into the business schools in the first generation. The focus is on leadership theories that were built on existing motivation theo-

ries—specifically Abraham Maslow's need hierarchy theory (see chapter 6 in this volume) and expectancy theory, as proposed by Victor Vroom and by Lyman Porter and Edward Lawler (see chapter 8 in this volume). In addition, we will take up the formulations on consideration and initiating structure that emanated from Ohio State University, which, although not originally tied to any motivational theory, were incorporated into path-goal theory at an early point and thus became a component of that theory, which is motivationally based. The Ohio State formulations and research go back to the latter 1940s and, along with the University of Michigan program, represent the major thrusts of thinking on the subject of leadership in this early period.

Theory X and theory Y, as proposed by Douglas McGregor of MIT, adopted Maslow's need hierarchy theory, thus providing a motivational rationale for its views on leadership. McGregor was also influenced by numerous other proponents of participative management, which was widely espoused at the time he wrote in the 1950s and early 1960s. The heritage from Kurt Lewin is clearly in evidence.

Path-goal theory of leadership had a considerably later date of origin in the early 1970s. It is the product of independent but overlapping efforts by Robert House and Martin Evans. Both took their lead from the theoretical work on expectancy theory of motivation that had appeared during the 1960s. Of the two authors, House has been more active on a continuing basis and is generally considered the major contributor at present. However, Evans appears actually to have been the initial theorist in that his ideas were being developed before those of House. Not surprisingly, the path-goal line of theoretical thinking has close ties both to the University of Michigan (through expectancy theory) and to Ohio State University (through the consideration and initiating structure constructs).

THEORY X AND THEORY Y

The theories of McGregor were first formally expounded in 1957. However, the values that underlie these theories, and many of the ideas as well, can be traced back in various articles and speeches to the early 1940s (McGregor, 1966).

Background

Born in 1906, McGregor attended what is now Wayne State University and Oberlin College with the intention of becoming a minister. He ended up in psychology, however, and he obtained a doctorate in this subject from Harvard University in 1935 (Wren & Greenwood, 1998). After a brief teaching stint in social psychology at Harvard, he moved to Massachusetts Institute of Technology where he was promoted through the psychology department faculty ranks and eventually became executive director of the industrial relations section at a time when Lewin was also at MIT, although in a different university component. Subsequently he moved to the presidency of Antioch College, a position in which he remained for 6 years, until 1954, when he returned to MIT as a professor of industrial management. From 1948 to 1954 McGregor was an active participant in various industrial groups (see Meyer, 1997) and kept in close contact with the practitioner community as a consultant. He died in 1964.

To understand McGregor's views, it is important to put them in temporal perspective. McGregor was an advocate of humanism in the workplace. He wrote at a time when ideas of this kind were beginning to achieve considerable popularity, and he shared with a number of other theorists the task of promoting this popularity. Inevitably he was influenced by these people who shared his values and philosophical orientation—Maslow, Herzberg, Argyris, Likert, and others—and he drew heavily from them in his writings. This point is stressed by Warren Bennis, a former student of McGregor's and for many years a colleague at MIT:

> He (McGregor) was a genius, not necessarily for the originality of his ideas which were often "in the air" or developed by similarly creative spirits. He was a genius because he had clarity of mind, a rare empathy for the manager, and a flair for the right metaphor that established a new idea.... Theory X and Theory Y certainly existed before McGregor. But he named them, called them. (1972, p. 148)

Management historians have noted applications of the kind McGregor advocated in the business world dating back to 1910 (Wrege & Lattanzio, 1977). McGregor, however, took what was "in the air" and gave it a continuing reality that it had not possessed previously.

McGregor's Statements of His Theories

There are three major statements that deal with theory X and theory Y—first a 1957 article, then a full-scale book presentation in 1960, and finally some supplementary comments written in 1964 just before Mc-Gregor's death and published in a posthumous book (1967). Note that all three statements derive from the period after their author returned to MIT from Antioch.

Original Article (1957)

Theory X is set forth in a set of propositions and beliefs, hypothesized to be widely held in the ranks of management, that guide the formation of organization structures, policies, practices, and programs. It is thus a theory of the assumptions or working theories most managers use in carrying out their activities. The three propositions are as follow:

Theory X

1. Management is responsible for organizing the elements of productive enterprise — money, materials, equipment, and people — in the interest of economic ends.
2. With respect to people, this is a process of directing their efforts, motivating them, controlling their actions, and modifying their behavior to fit the needs of the organization.
3. Without this active intervention by management, people would be passive — even resistant — to organizational needs. They must therefore be persuaded, rewarded, punished, and controlled; their activities must be directed. This is management's task. (McGregor, 1957a, p. 23)

The five beliefs are the following:

4. The average man is by nature indolent — he works as little as possible.
5. He lacks ambition, dislikes responsibility, and prefers to be led.
6. He is inherently self-centered and indifferent to organizational needs.
7. He is by nature resistant to change.
8. He is gullible, not very bright, and the ready dupe of the charlatan and the demagogue. (p. 23)

McGregor views this "conventional" managerial theory of the nature of man as incorrect in spite of its widespread acceptance. Instead, he proposes Maslow's need hierarchy theory (see chapter 6) as a valid statement of man's motivational nature. Since lower-level needs have been largely satisfied, higher needs are activated, but under theory X managerial assumptions, these higher needs remain deprived. Accordingly, people at work act with the indolence, passivity, resistance to change, lack of responsibility, willingness to follow the demagogue, and unreasonable demands for economic benefits that theory X leads one to expect. No amount of reward and punishment focused at the level of lower needs will change the situation, because these needs being satisfied are no longer operative.

What is required is a different set of managerial assumptions and practices that are attuned to the higher-order needs of workers, the needs that have real behavior-producing potential at this point in time and which therefore reflect the nature of man as he currently is. The first proposition of this theory Y is the same as that of theory X; from that point on the two diverge sharply:

Theory Y

1. Management is responsible for organizing the elements of productive enterprise — money, materials, equipment, and people — in the interest of economic ends.
2. People are *not* by nature passive or resistant to organizational needs. They have become so as a result of experience in organizations.
3. The motivation, the potential for development, the capacity for assuming responsibility, the readiness to direct behavior toward organizational goals — all these are present in people. Management does not put them there. It is a responsibility of management to make it possible for people to recognize and develop these human characteristics for themselves.
4. The essential task of management is to arrange organizational conditions and methods of operation so that people can achieve their own goals *best* by directing *their own* efforts toward organizational objectives. (pp. 88–89)

Managing with a Y type working theory does not mean abdicating the managerial role or using a laissez-faire style. The shift from X to Y involves substituting self-control and self-direction for external control and thus treating people as adults rather than as children. Four different kinds of innovations in practice are discussed as consistent with theory Y: (1) decentralization and delegation, of the kind that might be expected when a flat organizational structure with wide spans of control is introduced; (2) job enlargement; (3) participation and consultative management, particularly as embodied in the Scanlon Plan; and (4) performance appraisal within a highly participative management by objectives framework, in which individuals set their own objectives and evaluate themselves.

Expanded Version (1960)

In his subsequent book McGregor (1960) elaborates on many of the themes contained in his original article. Theory X is stated in somewhat more muted terms, but the assumptions of dislike of work, preference for direction, desire to avoid responsibility, limited ambition, and need for security above all remain, along with the belief that the managerial role is to coerce and control people to devote their efforts to organizational objectives. This theory is described as materially influencing managerial strategy in industry and as the basis for the principles of management that have derived from classical management theory; it is real, not a straw man. Workers who operate in a theory X context with their higher-order needs deprived are being treated as children and exhibit symptoms of illness. In this discussion, as in certain other areas, McGregor draws heavily from the recently published theories of Chris Argyris (1957). Only in dealing with professionals in the research and development context does McGregor believe there has been any significant movement away from theory X.

In general, McGregor rejects the human relations approach either as involving pseudo-participation and thus actually continuing to maintain a theory X orientation or as an abdication. However, he does elaborate more fully than previously on the assumptions inherent in theory Y:

1. The expenditure of physical and mental effort in work is as natural as play or rest.
2. External control and the threat of punishment are not the only means for bringing about effort toward organizational objectives. Man will exercise self-direction and self-control in the service of objectives to which he is committed.
3. Commitment to objectives is a function of the rewards that are associated with their achievement. The most significant of such rewards — that is, the satisfaction of ego and self-actualization needs — can be direct products of effort directed toward organizational objectives.
4. The average human being learns under proper conditions not only to accept but also to seek responsibility.
5. The capacity to exercise a relatively high degree of imagination, ingenuity, and creativity in the solution of organizational problems is widely, not narrowly, distributed in the population.
6. Under the conditions of modern industrial life, the intellectual potentialities of the average human being are only partially utilized. (McGregor, 1960, pp. 47–48)

The central principle of theory Y is one of integration, whereby individuals "achieve their own goals best by directing their efforts toward the success of the enterprise"; this is in contrast to theory X, which operates according to the scalar principle of direction and control through the exercise of authority. McGregor's theory specifically states that operating on theory Y principles will create a more effective organization than will operating on theory X principles, which by its very nature thwarts the satisfaction of operative needs. In this connection, McGregor explicitly accepts both need hierarchy theory and motivation-hygiene theory as valid statements of human motivation.

Ultimately McGregor came to associate theory Y directly with participative management: "The principle of integration requires active and responsible participation of the individual in decisions affecting his own career" (1960, p. 103). Subsequently, the role of the manager in this participative relationship is specified: "the most appropriate roles of the manager vis à vis his subordinates are those of teacher, professional helper, colleague, consultant. Only to a limited degree will he assume the role of authoritative boss. The line manager who seeks to operate within the context of Theory Y will establish relationships with his subordinates, his superiors, and his colleagues which are much like those of the professional vis à vis his clients" (p. 174).

In certain respects this view, although consistent with McGregor's overall values, appears to be at variance with his stated position at the time he left the presidency of Antioch College:

> I believed, for example, that a leader could operate successfully as a kind of adviser to his organization. I thought I could avoid being a "boss." Unconsciously, I suspect, I hoped to duck the unpleasant necessity of making difficult decisions, of taking the responsibility for one course of action among many uncertain alternatives, of making mistakes and taking the consequences. I thought that maybe I could operate so that everyone would like me — that "good human relations" would eliminate all discord and disagreement. I could not have been more wrong. (McGregor, 1954)

By 1960 the impact of his prior experiences seems to have paled somewhat, and McGregor once again came to espouse an advisory, professional role for the manager rather than a hierarchic role. Yet there are hints of some uncertainties on this score throughout his writings.

The 1960 volume contains considerable elaboration on the author's views regarding management by objectives and on the Scanlon Plan as a method of participative management. In addition, McGregor endorsed various methods of improving managerial skills of social interaction, the kinds of skills a truly flexible, theory Y manager must possess. Psychotherapy is advocated, with the recognition that at the present time it is not practical for most managers. Laboratory or T-group training thus becomes the method of choice for developing skills of social interaction.

Finally, McGregor was realistic enough to recognize that there are subordinates who are incompetent, dishonest, and neurotically hostile, and there is such a thing as an incompatible relationship:

> Under such conditions, it is nonsense to talk about creating positive expectations, mutual confidence, a healthy climate. The only real solution is to end the relationship, by transfer under some circumstances, or by termination of employment under others. If this is impossible, all that remains is to recognize that effective management in such a relationship is impossible, and to make the best of the situation. (McGregor, 1960, p. 142)

Note that even in this situation a resort to approaches based on theory X assumptions is not advocated.

Supplementary Comments (1964)

As noted previously, the 1964 statements were actually published posthumously in 1967; they were edited by Warren Bennis and McGregor's wife, Caroline. This volume contains discussions of a variety of topics, many of them only tangentially related to theory X and theory Y. However, certain previous statements regarding those theories are reemphasized and elaborated upon. In McGregor's view, the best operating strategy out of a theory Y orientation is one that creates conditions in which subordinates can achieve their own goals, including self-actualization, most effectively by contributing to organizational goal achievement. This involves fostering integration, organizational commitment, and intrinsic motive satisfactions. It also means working to achieve conditions of mutual trust, support, and respect for the individual that will facilitate the emergence of self-actualizing behavior. McGregor clearly acknowledges that his espousal of this kind of managerial strategy is an outgrowth of his own strongly held values. These are said to be a belief in organized human effort, in the importance of meaningful work, in the undesirability of manipulation, and in the desirability of self-actualization.

McGregor also returns to the case of the individual who does not respond to such a theory Y–based strategy: "It is to be anticipated that some percentage of any employee group (perhaps of the order of 10 per cent) will not respond at all or will take advantage of such a strategy. For such people the firm enforcement of limits, followed if necessary by dismissal, is the only feasible course. Otherwise there is danger that indulgence toward such individuals will affect the whole organization negatively" (1967, p. 78). There is a definite ring of a more theory X–based approach in these statements than was evident in the 1960 discussion of the same topic.

The distinction between theories X and Y themselves, which are now referred to as cosmologies, and the various strategies that can grow out of them is clearly drawn. Theory X can yield a number of strategies, including the hard approach of scientific management and the soft approach of human relations; so can theory Y. Theory X and theory Y are not poles of a continuum; they are qualitatively different, and other distinct managerial working theories are also possible. The view that the theory X cosmology is much more widespread in the ranks of management than theory Y is reiterated.

The discussion of applications in the 1967 book focuses on the team building approaches that now are widely used in organization development. In this connection McGregor draws heavily on his experiences as a consultant to Union Carbide Corporation and Bell Telephone Company of Pennsylvania.

A recent book by Gary Heil, Bennis, and Deborah Stephens (2000) reviews many of McGregor's ideas and presents several selected essays taken from his speeches and writings. There is little new here.

Evaluation and Impact

There are very few direct tests of McGregor's formulations in the literature. In part, this is a consequence of the philosophical, highly value-laden nature of many of his statements. Certainly this is a philosophy-theory in every sense, and as such it becomes difficult if not impossible to test at some points; there are logical inconsistencies. Yet aspects of the theory certainly are testable. In all probability more has not been done because many researchers viewed McGregor's writings more as philosophical advocacy than as scientific theory. Furthermore, McGregor himself conducted no research related to his formulations, nor did he attempt to make his variables operational in any kind of measurement procedures. Under such conditions it is not uncommon for theories to fail to generate research.

Of course, there is considerable research evidence now bearing on the various theoretical positions that McGregor coopted and also on the applications he espoused. Of this research the most relevant is that dealing with need hierarchy theory, as discussed in chapter 6 of this volume. McGregor made need hierarchy theory a central aspect of his own theoretical position, and the current lack of clear-cut support for Maslow's views is thus a damaging blow to McGregor's position. The similar lack of support for motivation-hygiene theory (see chapter 7 of this volume) is not nearly as crucial, since McGregor merely added Herzberg's views to his own rather than incorporating them directly.

Among the large number of applications McGregor discussed and endorsed, only the highly participative, management by objectives (MBO) approach to performance appraisal appears to be an outgrowth of the theory per se (McGregor, 1957b). The discussion in chapter 9 of research on MBO and participative goal setting is relevant here, but that research does not provide the universal evidence for the superiority of participative over assigned approaches that McGregor anticipated. Job enlargement is advocated, although with relatively little description of specific approaches, and thus the treatments of orthodox job enrichment in chapter 7 of this volume — and of job characteristics theory as well — are both relevant.

Confusions over Tests of McGregor's Theorizing

There was a great deal of uncertainty in the literature of the time about what evidence could and could not be used to support McGregor's views. Even when a study is explicitly stated to be a test of McGregor's hypotheses, there is often a question as to whether it really is. With regard to this confusion Edgar Schein, a colleague at MIT, says, "I believe that McGregor himself muddied the conceptual waters when he linked to his analysis of managerial cosmologies a value position that it was management's obligation to create opportunities for self-actualization" (1975, p. 83). Without question, McGregor did present his views in a manner that was both persuasively compelling and conceptually confusing. In reviewing the evidence that surrounds the theory, therefore, every effort

must be made to determine whether the data cited are germane to the theory.

Ralph Stogdill (1974) draws on studies that show that, on occasion, greater job structure may be related to need satisfaction; that delegation is unrelated to either subordinate perception of supervisory consideration or job satisfaction; and that supervisor permissiveness does not relate consistently to either subordinate productivity or satisfaction; he uses these arguments against a "Theory Y type of leader behavior." On the latter point, at least, these conclusions may be questioned. On numerous occasions in his writings McGregor explicitly states that the strategies that emerge from theory Y assumptions — whatever else they may be — are not "soft," permissive, or laissez faire. Yet there are also many references to self-direction and self-control that imply a diminution of external forces of any kind; these may well have led Stogdill to interpret McGregor as he did.

Misconceptions regarding the exact type of leader behaviors that are manifestations of theory Y assumptions are so prevalent in the literature that it is almost impossible not to view a degree of theoretical imprecision as responsible. Thus, John Morse and Jay Lorsch (1970) take the theory to task because it does not allow for findings derived from contingency theory, which indicates that what is appropriate leader behavior in one context may not be in another. Schein (1975) points out, however, that one of the stated characteristics of a manager who operates from theory Y assumptions is greater flexibility in adapting to the needs of the situation, in contrast to the manager who works from a theory X orientation and who is more rigid. Schein correctly interprets McGregor in one sense: "The manager who finds the underlying assumptions of theory Y congenial will invent his own tactics provided he has a conception of the strategy involved. The manager whose underlying assumptions are those of Theory X cannot manage by integration and self-control no matter what techniques or forms are provided him" (McGregor, 1960, p. 75). Yet nowhere does McGregor clearly specify contingency variables and alternative behaviors. What should one do when? The theory leaves us hanging, and accordingly it is not surprising that others have put words in McGregor's pen.

Schein (1975) argues that theory X and theory Y, dealing as they do with managerial assumptions about the nature of man, have no necessary relationship to prescriptions that management should create conditions for higher-order need satisfaction and self-actual-ization, should foster integration of personal and orga-nizational goals, and should practice participative management. He points to his own findings in re-search with his students that indicate only a .60 corre-lation between theory Y assumptions and participative style, as measured by self-report questionnaires. But the point is that McGregor, as part of his overall theory, did move beyond the more descriptive theory of X and Y to a normative theory of leadership behavior, however imprecisely stated, and he did link his norma-tive formulations both to X and Y assumptions and to outcome variables such as organizational effectiveness and long-range profit. One can divorce theories X and Y from the rest of what McGregor said if one wishes, but then one has neither McGregor nor the reason for his sizable impact on management thought.

Non-Linear Systems Project

Starting in 1960, a small (225 employees) electronics firm in southern California began introducing proce-dures that were widely heralded as providing for a true test of the theory Y–based approach. The company, Non-Linear Systems, was profitable at the time, and the president was the initiator of the changes.

McGregor was familiar with the project and writes approvingly of the changes; clearly he viewed them as consistent with theory Y. He notes that "productivity increased over two years by about 30 per cent. With respect to quality, customer complaints decreased by 7 per cent. As of today, there are virtually no quality defects" (McGregor, 1967, pp. 88–89). Furthermore, the company was able to weather a fairly severe market crisis in the fourth year of the experiment. Within this context, the role of the supervisor is said to be that of "an expert source of help, a technical adviser, a teacher, a troubleshooter *by demand of the group*. He does not direct, control, or discipline in the con-ventional sense. He does not set standards of perfor-mance or exert pressure for improvement" (Mc-Gregor, 1967, p. 90).

Maslow spent a summer at Non-Linear Systems 2 years after the changes were first undertaken and wrote a book based on this experience (Maslow, 1965). He, too, endorsed the procedures introduced there, at least under favorable economic conditions, and considered them to be consistent with his own and McGregor's views. Yet initially there was some feeling that Mc-Gregor may have gone too far, since "a good deal of

the evidence upon which he [McGregor] bases his conclusions comes from my researches and my papers on motivations, self-actualization, etc. But I of all peo-ple should know just how shaky this foundation is" (Maslow, 1965, p. 55). However, Maslow viewed the evidence for theory X as even less acceptable and, later in the book, clearly takes theory Y to be proven fact (p. 148).

Arthur Kuriloff (1963) served as vice-president for manager performance and development at Non-Lin-ear Systems during the period of change. He, too, describes what was done as consistent with theory Y, noting the increases in mutual trust, the managerial emphasis on teaching and training rather than on directing and controlling, and the shift to team pro-duction and decision making. McGregor's reports of improved performance are generally endorsed, al-though the reduction in complaints from customers is stated to be 70 (not 7) percent. Clearly the company had grown in number of employees and product lines. Yet there was no claim of increased profits, although they were anticipated. Furthermore, at the outset all employees were placed on salary, at a level well above that prevailing in the surrounding community, thus creating an apparent condition of overpay inequity (see chapter 9 in this volume).

Five years into the project, the company experi-enced severe financial problems, and the president began to question many of the theory Y approaches. He attributes the company's financial problems to these very approaches (Kay, 1973). Recently several postmortem analyses of theory Y at Non-Linear Sys-tems have appeared in the literature that raise ques-tions regarding what actually happened. These analy-ses have been hampered, however, by the fact that practically no written records were maintained during the period of the change because of the concern that such records would be used for purposes of external control on performance.

Erwin Malone (1975) concludes that in all proba-bility no real increase in plant efficiency occurred at any point in the 5 years. He considers the reports of improved quality to be highly unreliable because of the lack of records. Job satisfaction appears to have increased for production workers but at the expense of those in management positions. Profits apparently declined over the 5 years, and bankruptcy was nar-rowly avoided at the time the company switched to a more traditional type of management. Overall, Ma-lone concludes that the experiment simply did not work and that similar results are to be expected whenever a firm is faced with highly competitive market conditions.

Another analysis leads to a somewhat different conclusion. Edmund Gray (1978) notes that the lack of records and the failure to introduce changes in a sequential manner with adequate control conditions for comparison make it practically impossible to determine what caused what. He also believes that McGregor's views were in fact misapplied, especially as reflected in a lack of vertical participation and communication. Accordingly, he feels that one can conclude nothing from the Non-Linear Systems experience at all, at least insofar as McGregor's theories are concerned.

By any interpretation the highly publicized Non-Linear Systems project did little to foster long term acceptance of McGregor's views.

Problem of Stereotyping

On the evidence, McGregor appears to have been more right than wrong about the prevailing managerial theory (cosmology) of his time. The data indicate that theory X-type thinking was widespread, although there was much more variation on this theme than McGregor recognized (Haire, Ghiselli, & Porter, 1966). Accounting managers appear to have been at the high end insofar as theory X is concerned (Caplan, 1971).

A problem arises, however, because both theory X and theory Y are broad strategies that do not take into account the huge variations to be found among employees. Managers may indeed think in such terms, but there is a real question as to whether they should, if they are to be effective. In this view, both theories are wrong, simply because people come in all varieties of individual differences and thus *all* stereotypes are wrong. There is ample evidence of the great range of human variation on a host of dimensions (Miner, 1985). The effective manager will recognize these variations and deal with each individual in terms of the kind of person he or she really is rather than placing all (or most) together in a single category, no matter how that category is defined. To do otherwise is to perceive almost every employee incorrectly to some degree, and at least some by a very large degree indeed.

Some will argue that McGregor can handle individual differences through the medium of need hierarchy theory. Yet that theory can explain only motivational differences at best, utilizes broad social stereotypes itself, and probably for just this reason has failed of research confirmation to date. In any event, McGregor does not spell out in any detail how need hierarchy theory would relate to individual differences in the workplace—such as the person who does not respond to a theory Y-based strategy, for instance.

The research evidence confirms that individual variation yields sufficiently wide fluctuations so that there are people who really want structure from above, authority relationships, hierarchic work contexts, and the like. Furthermore, there is no independent evidence that they are necessarily either emotionally ill or motivationally deprived. Clearly many people do want to work under theory Y managerial assumptions, but some want theory X also. Probably most individuals, given the choice, would prefer to work under assumptions (on the part of a superior) that are reasonably well meshed with the kind of people they actually are. That way unrealistic expectations would be avoided.

The problem here goes back to the issue originally raised by Schein (1975). If a theory Y manager means a person who operates (or uses a strategy, to follow McGregor's terminology) consistent with the professional model of adviser, teacher, or consultant, then there is a basic conflict with the managerial requirements of hierarchic systems, and it is hard to conceive of such a person being considered effective. Alternatively, if being a theory Y manager means having certain assumptions about one's subordinates only, and it so happens that the particular subordinates happen to match these assumptions reasonably well, then it is indeed possible to be an effective theory Y manager.

Unfortunately, there will inevitably be circumstances under which subordinates will not match theory Y assumptions, with the result that managerial expectations will be both quantitatively and qualitatively far removed from subordinate capabilities. As a result, it seems preferable to base one's assumptions about subordinates on what one knows about them as individuals and to develop strategies for dealing with them based on this knowledge. True, it is impossible to have the knowledge of each subordinate that a psychotherapist might have of each patient. But it is possible to approximate such conditions to some degree, and any such set of approximations will inevitably be superior to a single gross categorization applied to all subordinates.

This caveat against using stereotypes such as theory Y to describe employees in general, or the great majority of them, raises questions regarding the use of the leadership approach that McGregor advocated because it followed logically from this stereotype. On this point consider the following:

> Participative leadership becomes problematic when it is used as a technique to "share power," on the assumption that all employees seek and want power and its corresponding responsibilities. . . . Clearly such an assumption ignores the individual's motivational state. Since all employees do not have the identical salient needs, the indiscriminate adoption of the participative technique does not enhance the leader's effectiveness. On the other hand, the participative leader behavior is effective when the workers' belief in self-determination . . . or personal self-efficacy . . . is high. (Kanungo & Mendonca, 1996, pp. 275–276)

Clearly we need to look into how effective participative management is, and whether it is more effective with certain kinds of people (and in certain contexts) than others.

Does Participative Management Work?

In chapter 9 research on different approaches to goal setting, including a participative approach, was discussed. The evidence indicates that when other considerations are held constant, differences attributable to participative procedures are negligible; they have no special motivational value in goal setting (see Latham, Erez, & Locke, 1988). However, we need to look beyond goal setting to the wide array of organizational issues that McGregor had in mind to fully evaluate the participative management that he advocated.

There has been a substantial amount of research on this topic going back to the Hawthorne studies and the early research by Lewin (see chapter 2). These early investigations proved far from definitive, but they did provide the spark needed to initiate research of a more scientifically valid and organizationally relevant nature. The consequence at present is that meta-analyses, qualitative reviews, and even reviews of the reviews abound.

Correlations between participation and both performance and job satisfaction tend to be significant but low. The most comprehensive data are those used by John Wagner (1994), who reports that the average value for performance is in the range of .15 to .25 and for job satisfaction in the range of .08 to .16. Subsequently, based on a consideration of all factors involved, these figures were revised downward somewhat to a value of .11 for both performance and satisfaction (Locke, Alavi, & Wagner, 1997). Yet these analyses do not include all forms of participation, including in particular the use of delegation (Heller, Pusic, Strauss, & Wilpert, 1998). A number of studies are plagued by common methods variance, whereby measures of both the extent of participation and of outcomes are obtained from the same source, thus potentially inflating the correlations. A meta-analysis of recent vintage yields a correlation of .14 for all studies, using performance as a criterion (Sagie, 1994). In contrast to these figures of .20 or below, and by way of providing a benchmark for comparison, a recent meta-analysis of studies that investigate the effect of financial incentives on the quantity of performance produced a value of .32 (Jenkins, Gupta, Mitra, & Shaw, 1998). Clearly, if one wants to improve performance levels, incentive compensation appears to have more potential than participative management has. Yet combining the two could well do even better.

There seems to be little question that, across the board, the research on participative management has produced the kinds of results noted. However, there has been some controversy over how participative management should be defined for research purposes (see, for instance, Ledford & Lawler, 1994; Wagner, 1995). Robert Liden and Sharon Arad make the point that "one explanation for the lack of strong effects uncovered by literature reviews and meta-analyses is that the forms of participation studied did not include cases in which employees had full control over decision making" (1996, p. 217). Yet the fact that participation occurs within the confines of hierarchic, bureaucratic organizations places limits on what is possible. Probably the research merely samples the types of participation that can be carried out in such organizations. This would argue that the findings are of a kind best suited to testing McGregor's formulations, which are indeed stated for managers within corporate contexts. Higher levels of participation probably would produce stronger relationships, but they would also result in almost complete abdication of managerial authority.

The results obtained from participative management research in general do not yield support for McGregor's across-the-board prescriptions, or for the extent to which empowerment has become a key ingredient of the current business scene; the relationships to performance and satisfaction are not sufficiently strong. However, the data do support a view that, under appropriate circumstances, participative management can work quite well, and under other circumstances it can have profoundly negative effects (Sagie, 1994). Moderators that involve the type of people included and the existing situation can make a difference. We will take up this consideration in the next chapter, as we move to theories that deal with just these issues. For the moment, however, it is worth noting that participation as applied specifically within the performance appraisal context leads to greater satisfaction with the appraisal interview involved and with the appraisal system that spawned it (Cawley, Keeping, & Levy, 1998). This is not to say that greater overall job satisfaction results, but it does support McGregor (1957b) as far as it goes.

Theories X and Y Today

In spite of occasional support, such as the findings on participative practices in performance appraisal, McGregor's views have not fared well over the years. The idea of creating stereotypes such as X and Y to describe various managerial theories (or cosmologies) or philosophies (or ways of thinking) has not really caught on in the leadership area. William Ouchi's (1981) theory Z would seem to be in this vein, but theory Z, as a set of cultural norms, is not really on the same continuum as X and Y. The philosophies that Raymond Miles has described are more in the McGregor tradition—the traditional, human relations, and human resources models; the human investment philosophy (Miles, 1975; Miles & Creed, 1995). These, however, have not given rise to a significant body of research even now.

Other problems have arisen over the years. One involves McGregor's advocacy that managers assume a professional role in hierarchic organizations. From what we now know, as long as the organization remains hierarchic, doing this would require a kind of person with motives that would almost guarantee a high proportion of managerial failures (see Miner, 1993). McGregor appears to have been attempting to impose his own professional value system, which was entirely appropriate for him as a university professor, on managers with roles in organizations where it simply does not apply. In fact, he attempted to do just

this, using himself as a guinea pig, when he served as college president at Antioch; from his own statements, the results were exactly what more recent research would have led us to anticipate.

Along this line, a point that Bennis (1972) makes may be relevant. He feels that McGregor's ideal type theory Y manager is somehow not quite real or fully human. McGregor does not impute any motives or motive satisfactions to him, and thus it is not clear how a real human being would be able to function in accordance with the types of role prescriptions that might be established. It is difficult to reconcile this model with what is known about managerial motivation. The importance of this problem is accentuated by one point on which observers of the Non-Linear Systems situation do agree. Middle and upper-level management did not function well under the conditions of the project, and turnover at these levels was high. Many of these managers either did not assume the teacher-adviser role the theory prescribes, or, even further removed from expectations, they did not do much of anything and became totally bored.

When we add to all these difficulties the fact that Maslow's need hierarchy theory did not turn out to receive the high level of research substantiation that McGregor anticipated, thus leaving theory X and theory Y devoid of any motivational foundations at all, the only conclusion possible is that this was a theory for its times, more a philosophy than a theory, and is by now really outdated in any scientific sense. Symptomatic of this situation is the fact that Gary Yukl (1998), in the fourth edition of his widely used leadership textbook, makes no mention of theory X and theory Y and only passing reference to McGregor at all.

CONSIDERATION AND INITIATING STRUCTURE

If one were to extrapolate from a theory Y concept of managerial thinking to the way subordinates might perceive the behavior of such a manager, the likelihood is that something akin to the consideration factor would result; similarly for theory X thinking and initiating structure. Ties of this kind between McGregor's theorizing and the variables of the Ohio State studies have been recognized for some time (Beer, 1966). Yet it is unlikely that either approach was influenced directly by the other; these types of formulations were "in the air" during the 1950s and 1960s.

Background

The Ohio State studies began in 1945 under the direction of Carroll Shartle, who secured funding from the federal government for this purpose subsequent to his employment in government before and during World War II. However, Shartle was primarily an administrator. The actual development of the consideration and initiating structure measures and the research using them involved a number of people employed at Ohio State, often as graduate students, on the research grants that Shartle initially obtained (Shartle, 1979).

The original work was carried out by John Hemphill in the late 1940s as he moved to Ohio State from the University of Maryland where he had obtained his Ph.D. in psychology (Stogdill & Coons, 1957). The cooperative effort that ensued involved, in addition to Shartle and Hemphill, Ralph Stogdill, the associate director of the project. These three were the senior members (Fleishman, 1998). Others who worked on the studies at an early point as graduate students and who became well known in the field of organizational behavior include Edwin Fleishman and Bernard Bass.

Consideration and initiating structure are not theories. They are constructs that emerged from extensive item analyses and factor analyses (see dust-bowl empiricism, chapter 1) of a huge pool of items that represent descriptions of various aspects of leader behavior. They are thus names given to clusterings of items that resulted in measures of these constructs. Although apparently atheoretical in origin, the constructs may well have been determined in part by implicit theories that influenced the development and selection of items for the original item pool; the questions put into a factor analysis have considerable effect on what emerges.

Leadership Traits and Leader Behavior

The major thrust of the Ohio State measures and research has been to study the *behavior* of leaders, usually as described by those who work under them. This thrust has been consistent throughout, and it carries with it an explicit rejection of the idea that studying the personality characteristics (traits) of leaders might prove fruitful.

Early in the history of the Ohio State leadership studies Stogdill (1948) wrote a very influential review article and stated the position that the resort to trait research in studying leadership had not accomplished much; leaders and nonleaders could not be consistently differentiated. This review was followed by several others, to much the same effect. The net result was to move the leadership field away from the study of psychological factors within leaders to a type of leadership behaviorism, which continued to hold sway for several decades. These same psychological factors remained a subject for research, however, in other areas such as personnel selection and psychological assessment.

Clearly, the Ohio State researchers leapt into the void created by the abolition of trait research from the leadership field with a vengeance; thus behavioral studies came to dominate for many years. Personality research continued to be done, but it was typically neglected insofar as leadership was concerned. More recently, however, there have been some second thoughts on the wisdom of this approach.

For one thing, there are reasons to doubt Stogdill's (1948) original conclusions. When studies of non-adults are removed from that analysis, such characteristics as dominance, self-confidence, and high energy level, as well as task-relevant knowledge and intelligence, do appear to be associated with leadership (House & Aditya, 1997). Robert Lord, Christy De-Vader, and George Alliger (1986) worked with a different data set, but one interpreted as producing results analogous to Stogdill's (1948). They found in a meta-analysis that people perceived to be leaders did have certain associated characteristics—intelligence, dominance, and masculinity. They also found errors in the prior analysis.

Research out of the selection and assessment streams, rather than leadership, has continued to provide support for the significance of personality factors in managerial promotion and performance (see George, 1992; Miner, 1993). Further evidence that traits and individual differences are important in leadership derives from a study in which many of the same people emerged as leaders across multiple diverse leadership situations (Zaccaro, Foti, & Kenny, 1991).

I have argued that (1) consideration and initiating structure do not have any apparent basis in theory, and (2) they are not, as constructs, built on any foundation in motivation or personality theory. In fact, the Ohio State approach clearly rejects both of the above. Why then consider these constructs here? The answer, as noted earlier, is that the constructs are essential elements in various leadership theories, particularly, for our purposes, path-goal theory, which is a theory and is grounded in motivation theory.

Evaluation and Impact

In their original form, consideration and initiating structure were viewed as two independent dimensions rather than as opposite ends of a single continuum; thus, they were assumed to be uncorrelated with each other, either positively or negatively. Each was important to leadership success, so that being above average on both consideration and structure was particularly likely to bring about effective behavior in leadership situations. Furthermore, the appropriate method of measuring the key variables was assumed to be reports by qualified observers, primarily subordinates. It is in this basic form that the approach has been popularized.

Although originally simply a matter of two behavioral factors thought to make a difference in leadership outcomes, this idea has been extended so that more recent formulations have introduced a long list of moderators into the relationships between leadership behaviors and performance/satisfaction. Path-goal theory incorporates a number of these moderator variables, but others have been used as well.

The preferred method of obtaining evidence that bears on the consideration and initiating structure constructs has been some type of behavior description questionnaire. A leadership opinion questionnaire also has been used to elicit attitude data on how leaders believe they should behave in their roles. This latter measure has yielded few significant relationships with either performance or satisfaction measures over the years, and it is also somewhat peripheral in its relationship to the primarily behavioral thrust of the Ohio State research.

Leader Behavior Descriptions and Performance/Satisfaction

The early studies using behavior descriptions provided quite mixed results insofar as relationships to leader performance and employee satisfaction measures are concerned. A review by Abraham Korman (1966) made this widely apparent and sparked some new directions in research. There were sufficient instances of nonsignificant findings or even relationships in a direction opposite to those predicted so that considerable skepticism seemed warranted.

As a result, subsequent research began to take on a somewhat more positive coloration in that significant correlations were obtained with some consistency. This appears to have occurred, however, as a result of the introduction of numerous moderator variables into the research designs. In particular, the use of situational pressure, task-related satisfaction, subordinate need for information, job level, subordinate expectations, congruence of leadership styles in the hierarchy, subordinate's organizational independence, and leader upward influence served to enhance correlations between the leader behavior measures and outcome variables. The basic concept itself remained highly questionable, although there clearly were instances when it worked.

In the 1990s this variability of results remains. Richard Steers, Lyman Porter, and Gregory Bigley (1996) note that relationships between behavior description and outcomes are generally weak overall, with the only consistent finding being the tie between consideration and measures of satisfaction (which may to some degree be a function of common method bias). Other reviewers note the marked variability of results, but come to much the same conclusion (House & Podsakoff, 1994; Yukl, 1998; Bass, 1990; Clark & Clark, 1990). The most positive review cites evidence that the predictive power of consideration and initiating structure is moderate or low, adding that the parsimony inherent in the use of two summary scales may lead to a loss in descriptive accuracy (Fleishman et al., 1991). These reviews are all talking about unmoderated relationships; the data on moderated relationships will be of special concern in connection with path-goal theory.

A meta-analysis of this research, although not widely cited, should be considered as well (Fisher & Edwards, 1988). This review picks up in the later 1960s and thus does not deal with the earlier research on which the Korman (1966) review was based. The corrected mean correlation between consideration and performance was .29 and for job satisfaction .71; only the latter was significant. These correlation values for initiating structure were .16 and .41, neither of which achieve significance. There is considerable variation in correlations, depending on the particular behavior description instrument used, but the number of studies involved is relatively small in these analyses. Most of this research used a concurrent design.

Problem of Causality

In the early period it was generally assumed that when a correlation between leader behavior and subordinate performance levels was obtained, it reflected a causal flow from the leader to the subordinates. Over time, this assumption was questioned. There is now a sizable body of research indicating that the performance levels of subordinates can act on the leader and serve to bring about different kinds of behaviors toward the subordinates. This has been demonstrated for a wide range of leader behaviors, including consideration and initiating structure. However, just as these leader behaviors sometimes do and sometimes do not correlate with group performance indices, so also different performance levels may or may not produce changes in consideration and structuring.

The data of table 10.1 are reasonably typical of those obtained in other studies. In all three experiments, comparisons were made among behavior descriptions of leaders when the group performance was presented as either high or low to those providing the descriptions, and all other factors were held constant. Thus only the differences in performance levels could account for the changed descriptions. Although in this instance performance level was manipulated by leading the subjects to believe that a group had performed either well or poorly, similar results are obtained when actual group behavior is observed.

These findings do not permit one to conclude that leader behavior does not influence subordinate performance at all. The amount of covariation typically accounted for by the effects of performance on leader behavior descriptions is less than the total variation, and there is evidence that the causal flow occurs in both directions. Nevertheless, one can assume that when significant correlations between consideration (or initiating structure) and performance are obtained, a sizable component of the relationship can be attributed to the effects of subordinate performance on leader behavior, not the reverse. Thus, the basic hypotheses turn out to be much less powerful than the correlational data would suggest. This is a factor to keep in mind when interpreting the Fisher and Edwards (1988) meta-analysis where most of the studies were concurrent and did not address causality.

This discussion of causality in the Ohio State studies raises a question as to whether, in a broader sense, leadership really makes much of a difference. This is an important question bearing on all leadership theory. Does leadership account for a truly meaningful amount of variance in performance? The definitive studies on this topic have been concerned with succession situations where a new leader comes in and takes over a previously existing group or organization. In these situations, performance changes certainly do not always occur, but they can, and they do (Smith, Carson, & Alexander, 1984; Thomas, 1988). A particu-

TABLE 10.1 Mean consideration and initiating structure ascribed to leaders of high- and low-performing groups

	Leaders of	
Studies involved	High-performing groups	Low-performing groups
Study 1		
Consideration	33.4	29.3
Initiating structure	(25.6)	(20.8)
Study 2		
Consideration	(35.9)	(29.6)
Initiating structure	(31.2)	(26.1)
Study 3		
Consideration	42.2	40.0
Initiating structure	31.6	30.2

NOTE: Numbers in parentheses indicate statistically significant ($p < .05$) differences between high- and low-performing groups.

SOURCE: Adapted from Terence R. Mitchell, James R. Larson, & Stephen G. Green (1977), Leader Behavior, Situational Moderators, and Group Performance: An Attributional Analysis, *Organizational Behavior and Human Performance*, 18, 260, 262, 264

larly striking demonstration of leadership effects occurs in a study of succession among managers of major league baseball teams (Cannella & Rowe, 1995). Managers who had strong records of success and considerable prior experience as major league managers do tend to introduce performance improvements in their new teams, especially when the competition is intense. Yet under other circumstances, leadership on the baseball field can have little impact of any kind. There can be no certainty that leadership will matter in a specific instance.

Independence of Dimensions and Scale Variations

The consideration and initiating structure dimensions arose out of studies in which large numbers of items were subjected to factor analysis to determine what kinds of groupings emerged. Thus, the constructs of the theory are intimately related to the measurement procedures used. Accordingly, it is not surprising that a full evaluation of the Ohio State concepts requires an exploration of measurement factors.

The original view, for instance, that consideration and structure represent two independent dimensions has come into increasing question. Whether the theory is supported in this regard appears to depend on what measures are used. As noted previously, both leader opinion and behavior description questionnaires have been developed. However, there are at least three different versions of the behavior description questionnaire that have been used extensively in research.

These latter versions had been assumed to measure the same constructs. Evidence indicates that although this is largely true for consideration, it is not true for initiating structure (Schriesheim, House, & Kerr, 1976). The latter measures differ considerably in the extent to which they include items of a punitive, autocratic, or production-oriented nature. When these items are *extensively* included, consideration and structure typically do not emerge as significantly correlated; when they are included only *minimally*, a positive correlation on the order of .50 can be anticipated. These differences cannot be attributed to variations in the reliabilities of the measures, since there appear to be only small differences in this regard, and all measures yield quite satisfactory values. On balance, the evidence indicates that whether the dimensional independence hypothesis is supported depends on how the initiating structure construct is defined and

made operational. In any event, certain problems of construct validity exist.

These construct validity problems manifest themselves not only in correlations between measures but also in correlations between these measures and outcome criteria. Although the various consideration scales yield similar validities, this is not true of initiating structure. Contradictory results can be obtained when different measures are used; thus, at least part of the variation in validity results from one study to another may be attributed to measurement differences. A version that does not contain many autocratic, punitive, or production-oriented items has been found to correlate positively with job satisfaction, while a version with more of these items yields negative correlations (Schriesheim et al., 1976).

Problems with Subordinate Descriptions

The preferred method of measuring leader behavior that dominated the Ohio State research was the use of descriptions provided by subordinates, either individually or as a group. These tend to be summary statements based on what the subordinates remember and what they have perceived. Both memory and perception can be in error, and thus a potential source of bias exists.

One such problem is of a kind that is characteristic of performance-rating scales in general, which of course the Ohio State measures are. Halo errors, lenience, social desirability bias, even positive response sets are in evidence in the data (Bass, 1990). Leniency error is particularly typical on consideration measures and would appear to contribute to the positive correlations with job satisfaction.

A second problem arises out of considerations discussed in the following quote:

> People develop thought systems to deal with the complexities of organizational life. These "implicit theories of organizations" become manifest in the concepts and processes used to understand and give meaning to organizational events and occurrences, and to convey that understanding to others. . . . Leadership factors are of paramount importance in these shared, implicit organizational theories. (Meindl, 1990, pp. 197–198)

Implicit theories are simplifications, and we all use them. They have been shown to have a marked effect on responses to the Ohio State scales, to the point that what emerges may be as much or more a function of these implicit theories about leaders as of the actual behavior of a specific leader. It is often difficult to remember and summarize what a leader actually did, and even at the time perceptions can be uncertain and incorrect. Implicit theories serve to fill in the blanks when an answer is required and perceptions or memory do not provide it (Larson, 1982). To the extent this occurs, the Ohio State measures may provide better indices of common implicit theories than of leader behavior. The antidote to this kind of effect is to provide raters with detailed and specific, current information on the leader to be described. Behavior descriptions obtained at short intervals, which reduce demands on memory, could accomplish this, but unfortunately the Ohio State scales typically have not been used that way.

A third problem involves the ways in which leader behavior description data have been and may be analyzed. A common procedure is to take the scores from a leader's subordinates and average them to get an index for that leader and his or her group—a group level of analysis. This seems reasonable since the correlation between group members' ratings tends to be high. Yet, on occasion individual members respond quite differently from others, and this variance is not picked up in the group level procedure. Clearly an alternative is to use an individual level of analysis where the scores of individuals are used directly (not averaged across the group). These two procedures can say different things, or they may not, but in any event it is important to interpret them differently and appropriately, which has not always been the case (Schriesheim, Cogliser, & Neider, 1995). These problems of level of analysis are compounded by the fact that question wording may predispose responses to the individual or group levels, and different statistical approaches have been used from one study to another (yielding different results). In many ways it seems that the Ohio State measures and studies have become a resting place for almost every type of problem that can possibly plague research on organizational behavior.

High-High Hypothesis

The idea that leaders who are high on both consideration and initiating structure will be the most effective has been the subject of a sizable body of research (Larson, Hunt, & Osborn, 1976; Nystrom, 1978). In a wide range of organizations, this hypothesis has failed to achieve support. In all but a very few cases when leader behaviors did relate to criteria, either consideration alone or structure alone predicted about as well as the combination posited by this hypothesis. This is not surprising when the two factors themselves are correlated at the .50 level, as they are with certain versions of the Ohio State leader description measures; multiple regression adds little under these circumstances.

Generally, the approach in testing the high-high hypothesis has been to assume an independent, additive effect of the two factors on criteria. At best, these studies must be viewed as inconclusive. Another approach has been to use a multiplicative model, which assumes that consideration and initiating structure mutually facilitate each other. This approach has not been tested often, but on the evidence available it appears no more promising than the additive idea.

Although the high-high combination does not appear to have much relevance for real world outcomes, it does appear to be relevant for implicit theory formation. Faced with a high-performance situation, naïve subjects (students) provide leader descriptions that are of a distinctly high-high nature. Thus the high-high pattern tends to be viewed as characteristic of effective leaders, and behaviors of this kind are attributed to people known to be doing well in leadership positions (Butterfield & Powell, 1981). One cannot help wondering whether implicit theories of this type may not have been operating in those who developed the item pool for the original instrument to describe leaders.

Managerial Grid Theory of Leadership

Several true theories have been developed following the ideas inherent in consideration and initiating structure, but adding to them. One of these is managerial grid theory, which is, in fact, a theory of both leadership and organization development. The latter is considered later in this book. The leadership theory had its origins in the early 1960s and was formally and fully published several years later (Blake & Mouton, 1964). It has been through various iterations and elaborations into the 1990s (Blake & McCanse, 1991).

The grid approach is essentially a high-high one. The two dimensions are labeled *concern for people* and *concern for production*. Concern for people is manifested by an emphasis on getting results through trust and respect, obedience, sympathy, or understanding and support; both the nature and the intensity of concern for people are important. Concern for production is manifested by an emphasis on results, the bottom line, performance, profits, or mission; both quantity and quality of production are important. The two dimensions are not added together but, rather, are seen as interdependent, combining to form a particular leadership style.

The grid is a 9 by 9 picture that depicts the styles that result when concern for people and concern for production are related to one another. Five benchmark styles are described, from which leaders can select, depending on their proclivities and the situations they face.

> At 9,1, characterized as the "Authority Compliance" style, managers concentrate on maximizing production through the use of power, authority, and control.
>
> At 1,9, "Country Club Management," managers concentrate on good feelings among colleagues and subordinates even if production suffers as a result.
>
> At 1,1, "Impoverished Management," managers do the minimum required to remain employed in fulfilling the leadership role.
>
> At 5,5, "Middle-of-the-Road Management," managers concentrate on conforming to the status quo and maintaining middle-of-the-road positions.
>
> At 9,9, "Team Management," managers use a goal-centered approach that seeks results through broad involvement of group members; participation, commitment, and conflict resolution are emphasized.

This theory regards 9,9 as the preferred style, the one managers *should* select regardless of the situation. Recently, using much the same concepts, this grid approach has been extended to groups.

An important idea in the theory is that insofar as possible leaders should select forms of behavior that at one and the same time reflect both concern for production and for people. This is the 9,9 version of the high-high hypothesis. Note, however, that by virtue of the way in which the initiating structure and consideration scales were constructed (through factor analysis), items of this kind—if in the original pool at all—would be deleted because they load on two factors. The Ohio State measures simply do not have them. Thus grid theory goes beyond the high-high

formulations (see Sashkin & Fulmer, 1988). Consequently, the 9,9 team management score has an apparent upper bound of $9 \times 9 = 81$ (not $9 + 9 = 18$).

Given this situation, managerial grid theory needs independent testing. Yet no research that focuses directly on the superiority of 9,9 leadership, as measured by managerial grid scales and by organizational indices of performance effectiveness, has been published. However, there is evidence on the effectiveness of the 9,9 style as *judged* by groups of managers from various organizational contexts (Blake & Mouton, 1982). In most cases experienced managers clearly favor the 9,9 style. Yet this need not be an indication of the theory's worth. We have noted that people generally associate productive groups and high group output with the high-high style, which involves combining two types of activity, either additively or multiplicatively, at maximum levels. Thus the judged effectiveness of 9,9 leadership in all likelihood reflects the implicit theories of the judges much more than it proves the universal effectiveness of the approach. What is needed is solid performance-related research of the same kind that raised questions about the consideration and initiating-structure formulations. Such research is not available for the managerial grid itself, although many of the findings related to participative leadership theories do appear applicable. (They yield little support for the grid perspective.)

Situational Leadership Theory

Situational leadership theory represents another extension of the Ohio State concepts, and it introduces moderator variables in ways not unlike what occurs in path-goal theory. The theory appeared first in the late 1960s (Hersey & Blanchard, 1969). Thus it followed managerial grid theory by several years. Since then, there have been numerous cosmetic changes that involve the renaming of variables, and some substantive changes as well. At the present time, different versions of the theory are maintained in different published sources, with the result that considerable confusion exists (see Graeff, 1997). If anything, the trend over time has been to greater ambiguity and less theoretical consistency, presumably out of a desire to meet the demands of both the scholarly community and the practitioner community at one and the same time. This has been an immensely popular approach and has been used very widely in training programs for managers.

The following description of the theory is up to date (Hersey, Blanchard, & Johnson, 1996), but it cannot avoid being open to question as incongruent with some other version stated elsewhere:

> Situational leadership theory is based on the interplay among the extent of leader directive (task) behavior, leader socioemotional (relationship) behavior, and follower readiness/maturity for performing a certain function. In their view, followers are the most critical factor in leadership events. As followers vary, so does the appropriate style of supervision. Hence, there is no "one best way" to influence employees. More specifically, leader task behavior is defined as the extent to which the leader engages in specifying subordinate duties and responsibilities, while relationship behavior is defined as the extent to which the leader acts in a facilitative and supportive manner. Employee readiness/maturity is defined as the extent to which a follower has the ability and willingness to accomplish a given function. Ability is further defined as the knowledge, experience, and skill that an individual brings to a particular activity, while willingness is the extent to which an employee possesses confidence, commitment, and motivation for accomplishing a given task.
>
> Hersey and Blanchard identify four types of appropriate leader styles that correspond to four levels of subordinate maturity. As subordinate maturity progresses from very low to moderate, the appropriate leadership style shifts from a "low relationship and high task" style to a "high relationship and moderate task" style. Further increases in subordinate maturity (i.e., maturity of a comparatively high degree) are best dealt with by a "low relationship and low task" style. Instances where leadership style is appropriate for a given subordinate's level of maturity are termed "matches." For these "matched" cases, the theory should provide an accurate forecast of superior leader effectiveness, relative to "mismatched" cases. In essence, Situational Leadership predicts an interaction among leader relationship-behavior, leader task-behavior, and subordinate readiness/maturity in determining leader effectiveness. (Fernandez & Vecchio, 1997, p. 68)

This theory is intuitively appealing and, like the managerial grid, has been of particular interest to practitioners. The amount of published research testing the theory is limited, but some does exist. There are problems with the measurement instrument used with the theory, as well as with logical inconsistencies and ambiguities in the theory itself. What research evidence there is appears to indicate that the use of a more directive, structuring style with low-maturity employees yields the expected superior performance outcomes (see Fernandez & Vecchio, 1997). However, the theory does not appear to work well at higher levels of subordinate maturity.

The consensus at present is that the maturity moderator needs further work to provide an operational definition that can be used in research on the theory; without this, support for the theory is unlikely to be obtained consistently. Yet the focus on situational factors and the recognition of a need for leader flexibility in dealing with different subordinates represent major pluses.

The mixed research results for situational leadership theory match what has been obtained in the consideration and initiating structure research in general. With an understanding of this picture we can move on to a full exposition of path-goal theory.

PATH-GOAL THEORY

Path-goal theory has its origins in expectancy theory; in fact, it is in large part an expansion of expectancy theory concepts into the leadership domain. Thus the discussion in chapter 8 provides a backdrop for what is said here.

Two individuals have been the major contributors. Martin Evans first developed his ideas in the area as a doctoral student at Yale University and incorporated them in his dissertation, which was completed in 1968. Robert House presented his views first while a faculty member at Baruch College of the City University of New York in the early 1970s. Both the Evans and House versions have gone through several stages. Because of the strong roots in expectancy theory, all versions are more similar than they are different. Yet, it is meaningful to differentiate the contributions of the two major proponents of path-goal theory.

Background

Evans was born in 1939. After undergraduate and master's study in England at Manchester University, he received his Ph.D. from Yale University in administrative science in 1968; this was the time when Hackman, Lawler, Argyris, and others made this a very stimulating place to work—and to learn. After he received his degree, he spent 2 years at the London Business School, and in 1973 he settled permanently into a faculty position at the University of Toronto. He is still there as professor of management studies.

House has had a more varied career. After graduating from the University of Detroit, he worked for Chrysler and started on an MBA at his alma mater. Later he moved to the Ph.D. program in business at Ohio State University, where he obtained the degree in 1960, and continued on as a faculty member. During this period he got to know Shartle and Stogdill, but his basic education was in classical management with practically no organizational behavior included (House, 1993). In the latter respect, he has been self taught. House left Ohio State in 1963 for McKinsey and Company, and later moved to the City University of New York.

A combination of some research data obtained using the Ohio State scales, data which he really did not understand, and a reading of Evans's (1970a) article on path-goal theory led House to begin his work on the subject. In 1972 he moved to the University of Toronto, where he and Evans were colleagues for a number of years. More recently he has joined the faculty at the University of Pennsylvania's Wharton School.

Path-Goal Hypotheses by Evans

The basic model as originally set forth by Evans (1970a, 1970b) contained five steps. These are elaborated in figure 10.1. The process starts with the supervisor or leader behaving in certain ways. Two kinds of behavior are stressed, drawing on the conceptual scheme originally developed at Ohio State. The first type involves indications of trust, respect, warmth, concern for personal needs, and the like in dealing with subordinates and is reflected in considerable two-way communication and subordinate participation in decision making; this is *consideration*. The second type of behavior, *initiation of structure*, is focused more directly on organizational goals and includes organizing and defining work, establishing role prescriptions for subordinates, assigning tasks, planning work, and pushing for desired performances.

The behaviors affect the subordinate by influencing perceptions of path-goal instrumentalities—the extent to which following a certain path (behaving in a certain way) is seen as likely to lead to goal attainment or to hinder the achievement of goals. In turn, these perceived path-goal instrumentalities are multiplied with the importance of the goals involved to the subordinate (their valence) to yield the level of motivation to follow a path or engage in a specific behavior.

However, motivation is only one contributor to actual job behavior; environmental factors, including the nature of the task (as well as particular individual abilities), also exert an influence. The resulting frequency with which the subordinate does follow the path and exhibit a particular kind of behavior, when multiplied with the actual path-goal instrumentality (the extent to which that behavior really does contribute to attaining the goal and is not merely perceived as doing so), produces the level of goal attainment. In turn, goal attainment is viewed as a partial measure of job satisfaction.

Leadership Hypotheses

The focus of the theory is at the level of supervisory behavior. How can a supervisor influence path-goal instrumentalities? For one thing, the subordinate must perceive the superior as being in a position to influence rewards and punishments. Given this, a considerate supervisor would be seen as an abundant source of rewards and a source that fits the rewards given to the desires of the individual. An inconsiderate supervisor would differentiate less in terms of individual needs or goals.

Also, the subordinate must see these rewards as linked to, or contingent on, specific behaviors. Initiation of structure is the process by which rewards are tied to specific behavior paths. A supervisor who does not structure this way fails to indicate what paths should be utilized and distributes rewards without reference to the path followed.

To influence performance, a supervisor must make judgments as to which are high-performance paths and which are low. Although usually these judgments are easily made, there are instances in which only the highly considerate supervisor can make them. In particular, the considerate supervisor will perceive (1) being given suggestions by subordinates, and (2) helping fellow workers as high-performance paths; less considerate supervisors will not. Accordingly, these two so-called *variable* paths can be expected to be perceived as having higher path-goal instrumentalities when the supervisor is high in consideration.

The resulting hypotheses regarding the effects of

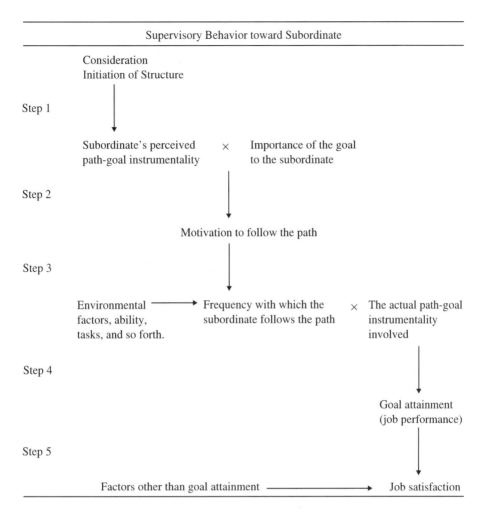

Supervisory Behavior toward Subordinate

Step 1

Consideration
Initiation of Structure

Step 2

Subordinate's perceived   ×   Importance of the goal
path-goal instrumentality   to the subordinate

Step 3

Motivation to follow the path

Step 4

Environmental ———→ Frequency with which the   ×   The actual path-goal
factors, ability,   subordinate follows the path   instrumentality
tasks, and so forth.   involved

Step 5

Goal attainment
(job performance)

Factors other than goal attainment ———————————→ Job satisfaction

FIGURE 10.1 Steps in the Evans path–goal model. Adapted from Martin G. Evans (1970), The Effects of Supervisory Behavior on the Path–Goal Relationship, *Organizational Behavior and Human Performance, 5,* 279–282.

different supervisory behaviors on perceived path-goal instrumentalities are as follows:

*For high-*performance paths:

1. High consideration and high structure → highly positive instrumentalities (following the high-performance path will help goal attainment)
2. High consideration and low structure → low positive or even neutral instrumentalities
3. Low consideration, regardless of structure → neutral instrumentalities for the high-performance paths

*For low-*performance paths:

1. High consideration and high structure → highly negative instrumentalities (following the low-performance path will hinder goal attainment)
2. High consideration and low structure → somewhat negative or neutral instrumentalities
3. Low consideration regardless of structure → neutral instrumentality for the low-performance paths

For the two variable paths:

1. High consideration and high structure → highly positive instrumentalities
2. High consideration and low structure → low positive instrumentalities

3. Low consideration regardless of structure → neutral instrumentality for the variable paths

The remaining hypotheses extend the theory to other aspects of the model set forth in figure 10.1:

1. The higher the sum of the products of path-goal instrumentality and goal importance, the higher the path frequency (steps 2 and 3)
2. The higher the sum of the products of path frequency and path-goal instrumentality, the higher the goal attainment (step 4)
3. When supervisory behavior is related to path-goal instrumentality (step 1) and when the product of path-goal instrumentality and path frequency is related to goal attainment (step 4), then supervisory behavior will be related to goal attainment—and to job satisfaction (the total model) (Evans, 1970a, p. 285)

Subsequent Extensions

Based on the results of research carried out to test the initial leadership hypotheses, Evans (1974) developed several extensions to his theory. These involve the introduction of three types of moderators into the relationships hypothesized at steps 1 and 2 of the model. The moderator variables are the degree of upward hierarchic influence with superiors that the supervisor has in the organization, the amount of role conflict the subordinate is experiencing, and the extent to which subordinates are predominantly internal or external in locus of control—that is, view themselves as masters of their own destiny or largely at the mercy of influence processes controlled outside the self.

These variables are incorporated in the theory as it relates to the prediction of motivation to follow a particular type of path through the following hypotheses:

1. The more considerate the supervisor, the higher the motivation is for high performance paths.
   a. The greater the upward influence of the supervisor, the more likely that he could offer and deliver many rewards (consideration) to the employees, thus influencing their expectancies and increasing their motivation.
2. The greater the initiation of structure, the higher the motivation is for high-performance paths.
   a. The higher the role conflict experienced by the subordinates (in that different role

senders had clearly different expectancies of how the individual should behave), the less effect the supervisor has on making the distribution of the rewards contingent on performance (initiating structure).
   b. The more internally controlled the subordinate, the stronger the relationship. (Evans, 1974, p. 173)

Subsequently the concern with personality considerations inherent in 2b above was expanded to include leader behaviors that are required to deal with low growth need strength, low tolerance for ambiguity, and low self-esteem in a subordinate (Evans, 1979).

Evans (1996) sets forth a long list of relevant behaviors that the theory has come to encompass, moving beyond consideration and initiating structure:

1. Reward variety
2. Diagnose differences in desired rewards
3. Maintain upward influence
4. Have charismatic behavior (articulates goal, competent, supportive, trustworthy)
5. Provide accurate feedback
6. Provide timely, clear, specific feedback
7. Discriminate between good and poor performance
8. Have courage to communicate feedback
9. Have accurate attributions about the causes of subordinate's behavior
10. Use participation in goal setting and measures
11. Communicate contingencies
12. Reward and punish contingent on performance
13. Recommend contingent organizational rewards
14. Stimulate contingent reward by group and by outsiders, supportive climate
15. Have visible performance
16. Provide group rewards
17. Articulate the value of the organization
18. Set difficult goals (directive, participative)
19. Show confidence
20. Provide coaching and training
21. Clarify paths (participative, directive)
22. Plan and organize
23. Be supportive
24. Maintain selection and placement

House's Path-Goal Theory

As originally presented, House's path-goal theory was said to differ from that of Evans "in that its [Evans's] predictions are not contingent on situational variables, and it is not an attempt to account for the conflicting findings" (House, 1971, p. 322). The two approaches moved closer together when Evans added his subsequent extensions, since both then utilized moderator variables.

In his first statement House (1971) presented a view of motivation as a combination of intrinsic and extrinsic valences and path instrumentalities of various kinds and then showed how these factors might be influenced by leader behaviors. A set of general propositions was then advanced, followed by certain illustrative hypotheses that were intended to show how the propositions might be made operational. These hypotheses dealt with leader consideration, initiating structure, closeness of supervision, hierarchical influence, and authoritarianism, as well as a number of other variables. As a theoretical statement this first effort is complex and at times difficult to follow; it is not at all clear why certain variables are introduced, and their role in the theory is often unclear.

Subsequent statements (House & Dessler 1974; House & Mitchell, 1974) have attempted to rectify these problems and do indeed present a much cleaner theoretical framework. It seems appropriate, therefore, to start our discussion with this revised version.

General Propositions

The general propositions of the theory are stated as follows:

1. Leader behavior is acceptable and satisfying to subordinates to the extent that the subordinates see such behavior as either an immediate source of satisfaction or as instrumental to future satisfaction.
2. The leader's behavior will be motivational, i.e., increase effort, to the extent that (1) such behavior makes satisfaction of subordinate's needs contingent on effective performance, and (2) such behavior complements the environment of subordinates by providing the coaching, guidance, support and rewards necessary for effective performance. (House & Mitchell, 1974, p. 84)

Thus, the inputs of the theory are various types of leader behaviors, and the outputs are the leader acceptance, job satisfaction, and motivation to performance of subordinates. Within this framework, the role of

the leader becomes one of recognizing and arousing subordinate desires for outcomes or goals that the leader can influence, increasing the personal payoffs to the subordinate for attainment of work goals, utilizing coaching and direction to make the paths to these personal payoffs easier to travel, helping subordinates clarify expectancies, reducing frustrating barriers, and increasing opportunities for personal satisfaction contingent on effective performance.

> Stated less formally, the motivational functions of the leader consist of increasing the number and kinds of personal payoffs to subordinates for work-goal attainment and making paths to these payoffs easier to travel by clarifying the paths, reducing road blocks and pitfalls, and increasing the opportunities for personal satisfaction en route. (House & Mitchell, 1974, p. 85)

This quote appears in almost identical form in other statements of the theory (House, 1971; House & Dessler, 1974) and represents the essence of the theoretical view. The types of leader behaviors through which these functions are performed are directive (initiating structure), supportive (consideration), achievement-oriented, and participative.

Contingency Factors

These leader behaviors influence subordinate outputs in different ways, depending on the manner in which certain contingency variables moderate the relationships. One set of contingency variables involves characteristics of subordinates. Typical hypotheses of this kind are the following:

> Subordinates with a high need for affiliation see high leader consideration as a source of satisfaction.

> Subordinates with a high need for achievement view leader behavior that clarifies path-goal relationships and provides feedback (achievement-oriented behavior) as more satisfying.

> Subordinates with a high need for extrinsic rewards (pay, for instance) perceive leader directiveness or coaching as more satisfying.

> Subordinates who perceive a strong internal locus of control experience a participative leadership style as more satisfying.

> Subordinates who are highly authoritarian are more receptive to directive leader behavior.

Subordinates who consider their ability relative to task demands to be high will find leader directiveness and coaching (initiating structure) less acceptable. (House & Dessler, 1974, pp. 31–32)

Although schematic statements of the theory note only subordinate authoritarianism, locus of control, and ability as personal moderators, it is clear from the preceding statements that the actual list is considerably longer.

A second set of contingency variables derives from pressures and demands in the work environment. Thus:

When the task is routine, clear group norms exist, and objective controls derive from the formal authority system, directive (structuring) leader behavior will be considered redundant and as representing excessively close supervision with resulting lowered subordinate satisfaction and leader acceptance. (House & Dessler, 1974, p. 33)

Theoretical statements tend to be consistent in emphasizing the task, the formal authority system, and the primary work group as environmental moderators.

In a later publication, certain contingency hypotheses are stated, using the four types of leader behavior specified in the theory as a starting point (Filley, House, & Kerr, 1976). The first of these behaviors, supportive leadership, is defined as "behavior that includes giving consideration to the needs of subordinates, displaying concern for their well-being, status, and comfort, and creating a friendly and pleasant climate" (p. 253). This type of leadership is hypothesized to yield its most positive effects on satisfaction when the work is stressful, frustrating, or dissatisfying.

Participative leadership involves the "sharing of information, power, and influence between supervisors and subordinates" (p. 253), thus treating subordinates largely as equals and allowing them to influence supervisory actions and decisions. It is hypothesized that when the task is clear and the subordinates are not ego-involved in the work, participative leadership will contribute to satisfaction and performance only for highly independent, nonauthoritarian subordinates. On ambiguous, ego-involving tasks, participative leadership will have positive effects, regardless of subordinate personality.

Instrumental leadership "features the planning, organizing, controlling, and coordinating of subordinate activities by leaders" (p. 253). Such directiveness is expected to yield positive results when the task is am-

biguous and when organizational procedures and policies are unclear or conflicting; with greater clarity and certainty, it will be a hindrance.

Achievement-oriented leadership "is characterized by leaders who set challenging goals, expect subordinates to perform at their highest level, continuously seek improvement in performance, and show a high degree of confidence that the subordinates will assume responsibility, put forth effort, and accomplish challenging goals" (p. 253). Leadership of this kind is expected to induce striving for high standards and confidence in meeting challenging goals, especially among individuals working on ambiguous, nonrepetitive tasks.

These hypotheses are often intertwined with research and in several cases are stated on an ad hoc basis. House is well aware of the problems associated with introducing contingency variables when needed rather than on a priori theoretical grounds. Accordingly, he views his approach as more of a useful theoretical framework than a fully developed, internally consistent theory.

The Reformulated Theory of Work Unit Leadership

Twenty-five years after the initial statement of his theory, House (1996) published a reformulation that was intended to supplement the original version. Only the axioms and propositions are given here in the interest of parsimony, but it should be understood that rationales for these statements are presented, based either on research findings or on logical deductions. The axioms are as follows:

1. Leader behavior is acceptable and satisfying to subordinates to the extent that the subordinates see such behavior as either an immediate source of satisfaction or as instrumental to future satisfaction. (This was the first general proposition previously.)
2. Leader behavior will enhance subordinate goal-oriented performance to the extent that such behavior (a) enhances the motivation of work unit members, (b) enhances task-relevant abilities of work unit members, (c) provides guidance, (d) reduces obstacles, and (e) provides the resources required for effective performance.
3. Leader behavior will enhance subordinate motivation to the extent that such behavior (a) makes satisfaction of subordinate's needs

and preferences contingent on effective performance, (b) makes subordinate's tasks intrinsically satisfying, (c) makes goal attainment intrinsically satisfying, (d) makes rewards contingent on goal accomplishment, and (e) complements the environment of subordinates by providing the psychological structure, support, and rewards necessary for effective performance.

4. Leader behavior will enhance subordinate task-relevant abilities to the extent that the leader engages in subordinate development efforts or serves as a role model from which followers can learn appropriate task-relevant behavior.

5. Leader behavior will enhance work unit performance to the extent that such behavior (a) facilitates collaborative relationships among unit members, (b) maintains positive relationships between the unit and the larger organizations in which it is embedded, (c) ensures that adequate resources are available to the work unit, and (d) enhances the legitimacy of the work unit in the eyes of other members of the organization of which the work unit is a part. (p. 335)

Axioms 4 and 5 broaden the theory. It now covers work unit performance overall, as well as individual subordinate performance.

The theory then states 26 propositions categorized under the leader behaviors involved, as follows.

I. Path-goal clarifying behaviors (capable of making subordinate needs and preferences contingent on effective performance by clarifying subordinate performance goals, the means by which tasks are effectively carried out, the standards by which performance is judged, and the expectancies held by others and how the subordinate should respond to them and by a judicious use of contingent rewards and punishments)

Proposition 1: When the task demands of subordinates are satisfying but ambiguous, path-goal clarifying behavior by superiors will be a source of clarification and subordinate satisfaction and therefore will be motivational.

Proposition 2: The higher the degree of subordinates' self-perceived ability relative to task demands, the less subordinates will view path-goal clarifying behavior by superiors as acceptable.

Proposition 3: When the task demands of subordinates are unambiguous and dissatisfying, path-goal clarifying behavior will be dissatisfying to subordi-

nates, will be seen as over controlling, will be resented and resisted, and therefore will be demotivational.

Proposition 4: When subordinates are highly personally involved in a decision or a task and the decision or task demands are ambiguous and satisfying, participative leadership will have a positive effect on the satisfaction and motivation of subordinates.

Proposition 5: Whether nonauthoritarian directive leadership or participative leadership will be most effective in providing path-goal clarification for subordinates who are not highly ego involved in their work will depend on the level of subordinates' preference for independence and self-directed behavior. Specifically:

Proposition 5a: Individuals with a low preference for independence and self-direction will find nonauthoritarian directive leadership to be valent. Therefore, when task demands are ambiguous and satisfying, for individuals with a low preference for independence and self-direction, directive leadership will be motivational.

Proposition 5b: Individuals with a high preference for independence and self-direction will find participative leadership to be valent. Therefore, when task demands are ambiguous and satisfying, for individuals with a strong preference for independence and self-direction, participative leader behavior will be motivational.

Proposition 6: Propositions 1 through 5 will be most predictive when it is possible to accurately assess the probability of attaining valued outcomes, contingent on high, medium, or low levels of effort, and will be less predictive when it is impossible to make such assessments accurately. (pp. 336–337)

II. Achievement-oriented behavior (as described previously, but to include stress on pride in work and on self-evaluation based on personal accomplishment)

Proposition 7: Achievement-oriented leader behavior will be effective when enacted by superiors who manage subordinates who have individual responsibility and control over their work.

Proposition 8: Achievement-oriented leader behavior will be most motivational for subordinates who are moderately or highly achievement motivated.

Proposition 9: Achievement-oriented leader behavior will enhance the valence of performance and increase the intrinsic satisfaction of moderately to highly achievement motivated subordinates. (pp. 338–339)

III. Work facilitation (consists of planning, scheduling and organizing work; coordinating; providing mentoring guidance, feedback; reducing obstacles and providing resources, authorizing subordinate actions)

Proposition 10: When the work of the unit is free of technological uncertainty, and the demands imposed on the work unit are predictable, leader planning, scheduling, organizing, and the establishment of formal prearranged coordination mechanisms will facilitate the work of the unit members.

Proposition 11: When the work of the unit is characterized by technological uncertainty or the external demands imposed on the unit are unpredictable, personal coordination of the work by the leader or reciprocal coordination by members of the work unit will facilitate work unit goal accomplishment.

Proposition 11a: When work unit members do not have task-relevant knowledge and experience, personal coordination of uncertain work by the leader will facilitate work unit goal accomplishment.

Proposition 11b: When work unit members have substantial task-relevant knowledge and experience, coordination of uncertain work by reciprocal coordination among work unit members will facilitate work unit goal accomplishment.

Proposition 11c: Under the conditions specified in Proposition 11b, work unit effectiveness will be enhanced by delegation of responsibility for reciprocal coordination to work unit members.

Proposition 12: When work unit members lack task-relevant knowledge and experience, developmental efforts on the part of superiors will enhance work unit effectiveness.

Proposition 13: When subordinates lack the necessary task-relevant knowledge and experience, supervisory efforts to reduce obstacles faced by subordinates will facilitate work unit accomplishment.

Proposition 13a: When subordinates have the necessary task-relevant knowledge and experience, supervisory delegation of authority to subordinates to reduce work-related obstacles will facilitate work unit accomplishment. (pp. 339–340)

IV. Supportive behavior (as described previously)

Proposition 14: When subordinates' tasks or work environments are dangerous, monotonous, stressful, or frustrating, supportive leader behavior will lead to increased subordinate effort and satisfaction by enhancing leader-subordinate relationships and self-confidence, lowering stress and anxiety, and compensating for unpleasant aspects of the work.

Proposition 15: When tasks are intrinsically satisfying or environmental conditions are not stressful, supportive leader behavior will have little effect on follower satisfaction, motivation, or performance. (pp. 340–342)

V. Interaction facilitation (consists of resolving disputes, facilitating communication, giving voice to a minority, emphasizing teamwork, and encouraging close relationships among members)

Proposition 16: Leader behavior directed toward interaction facilitation will increase work unit cohesiveness and reduce voluntary absenteeism and attrition.

Proposition 16a: Leader behavior directed toward interaction facilitation will increase work unit effectiveness when the work of the unit members is interdependent and the norms of the work group encourage unit members' performance.

Proposition 16b: Leader behavior directed toward interaction facilitation will be unnecessary, will increase social non-task-related communication, but will not increase work unit effectiveness when the work of the unit members is not interdependent. (p. 341)

VI. Group-oriented decision process (fostering decision quality and acceptance by posing problems not solutions, identifying mutual interests, encouraging participation, searching for alternatives, delaying evaluation, and ultimately combining advantages to achieve a solution)

Proposition 17: When mutual interests among work unit members with respect to solving problems or making effective decisions exists or can be established, the group decision process will increase both decision quality and decision acceptance.

Proposition 18: When decisions require acceptance by group members for implementation, inclusion of group members in the decision process whose acceptance is required will increase decision acceptance.

Proposition 19: When group members have expertise relevant to the technical or economic quality of decisions, inclusion of group members in the decision process who have relevant expertise will increase decision quality.

Proposition 20: A boundary condition for the successful application of propositions 17, 18, and 19 is that a mutual interest in making effective decisions exists or can be established among the group members involved. (p. 342)

VII. Representation and networking (presenting the group in a favorable manner and communicating the importance of the group's work; effective networking by maintaining positive relationships with influential others)

Proposition 21: Work unit legitimacy and ability to obtain resources will be enhanced by active representation and networking by work unit leaders.

Proposition 22: Active representation and networking by work unit leaders will have a more positive effect on work units with relatively lower interorganizational power than on other work units. (p. 342)

VIII. Value-based behavior (articulate a vision, display passion for the vision, demonstrate confidence in vision attainment, arouse nonconscious relevant follower motives, take risks to attain the vision, communicate high expectations, use symbolic behaviors to emphasize vision values, exhibit positive evaluations of followers frequently)

Proposition 23: Five conditions that facilitate the emergence and effectiveness of value-based leaders are (a) the opportunity for the leader to communicate an ideological vision; (b) an opportunity for substantial moral involvement on the part of both the leader and subordinates; (c) exceptional effort, behavior, and sacrifices required of both the leaders and subordinates; (d) values inherent in the leader's vision that are compatible with the deeply internalized values of work unit members; and (e) the experience of severe threat, crisis, stress, feelings of unfair treatment, persecution, or oppression induced by sources other than the leader.

Proposition 24: The emergence and effectiveness of value-based leadership will be enhanced to the extent that:

1. Extrinsic rewards cannot be, or are not made, contingent on individual performance.
2. There are few situational cues, constraints, and reinforcers to guide behavior and provide incentives for specific performance.
3. The leader refrains from the use of extrinsic rewards contingent on subordinate performance.

Proposition 25: When the values inherent in the vision of a value-based leader are in conflict with the dominant coalition of the larger organization or the prevailing culture of the organization, value-based leadership will induce substantial intergroup conflict or conflict between the leader's work unit and the dominant coalition of the organization. (pp. 345–346)

IX. Shared leadership

Proposition 26: When the work of work unit members is interdependent, encouragement by the leader of collaborative shared responsibility for the exercise of leader behaviors will enhance work unit cohesiveness and performance. (p. 346)

At various places in his article, House (1996) refers to both eight and 10 classes of leader behavior (but never the nine that are actually noted). Perhaps the intent is to delete shared leadership as a class to obtain the eight, but the implication is that some other class(es) of behavior is (are) intended that are not in fact discussed.

The new theory, while broader than previously, still has boundary limitations; its domain does not include emergent-informal leadership, leadership at several organizational levels, political behavior of leaders, strategic leadership of organizations, or leadership as it relates to organizational change. The new theory, like the previous one, has a strong rationality bias; thus, the absence of stress and of nonreducible uncertainty also constitute boundary conditions (House & Aditya, 1997).

Research by the Theorists

Both Evans and House use post hoc interpretations of prior studies as a basis for developing their own formulations. Although this approach has the advantage of placing the resulting theories at the forefront of knowledge, the studies thus used cannot be considered as providing evidence in support of hypotheses that were in fact derived from them. The present discussion will accordingly concern itself with a priori tests only.

Remember that after the Korman (1966) review of the literature involving the Ohio State measures, there was a burst of optimism as more consistent results began to appear using moderated relationships. This is the period in which path-goal theory emerged and also the period in which the authors of the theory carried out their own research.

Evans's Research

Evans (1970a) reports two studies, one conducted with blue-collar workers in a public utility company and one with nurses in a general hospital. In both cases a questionnaire was used to collect data relevant to certain goals, such as respect from one's supervisor, skill development, doing a good job, and pay. *Path-goal instrumentality* was measured by questions about the usefulness of such behaviors as performing well, giving suggestions to the boss, and doing low-quality work for goal attainment. *Path frequency* was indicated with reference to each of these paths, and estimates of *goal attainment* (How much is there now?) and *goal importance* (How important is it to you?) also were obtained. Indices of *job satisfaction* and supervisory *consideration and initiating structure* were included in the questionnaire.

The theory generally predicted path-goal instrumentalities in the utility company but failed to do so in the hospital. Predictions of path frequency from path-goal instrumentality (see figure 10.1) were highly successful in the utility company but less so in the hospital, although in neither case did goal importance make the expected contribution. Goal attainment was predicted from the combination of path-goal instrumentality and path frequency reasonably well in both organizations. The comprehensive hypothesis extending from supervisory behavior through to goal attainment and job satisfaction was supported strongly in the utility company but rarely in the hospital.

The subsequent extension of the theory through the addition of moderator relationships represented in large part an attempt to handle the disparate results obtained in the utility company and the hospital (Evans, 1974). To test these relationships, Evans carried out a study using employed MBA students, again using questionnaire measures that had been obtained from his subjects for all of the variables.

The overall results do not provide strong support for the extended theory. The self-rating of performance was not predicted differentially at different levels of any of the moderator variables.

There was some evidence that internal-external orientation moderated the relationship between consideration and job motivation in the expected manner, However, the hypothesis as stated deals with initiating structure, not consideration, while only consideration data are presented. It is not possible, in this instance, to determine whether the theory is confirmed.

House's Research

House (1971) conducted three studies to test hypotheses derived from his initial formulation of path-goal theory. In the first study, he was able to demonstrate that role ambiguity did moderate the relationship between supervisor initiating structure and subordinate satisfaction among individuals who performed quasi-professional or administrative work. However, the tendency for structuring to relate to greater satisfaction in ambiguous situations was far from strong.

The second study used task autonomy and job scope as moderators and tested the following hypotheses:

1. Initiating structure → high satisfaction (where autonomy is high)
2. Initiating structure → high performance (where autonomy is low)
3. Consideration → high satisfaction (where autonomy is low)
4. Consideration → high performance (where autonomy is low)
5. Consideration → high satisfaction (where job scope is low)
6. Consideration → high performance (where job scope is low)

The results obtained are summarized in table 10.2. Tests of significant differences between correlations indicate clear support for hypotheses 4 and 6, and some directional support for hypotheses 1, 2, and 3. Only hypothesis 5 involving job scope is clearly not supported. The results involving performance are particularly encouraging since the performance ratings were made independently.

TABLE 10.2 Correlations between leader behaviors and outcome variables (satisfaction and performance) when moderated by task autonomy and job scope

Relationships	Low group		Medium group		High group	
	Study 2	Study 3	Study 2	Study 3	Study 2	Study 3
Task Autonomy						
Initiating structure vs.						
Satisfaction (hypothesis 1)	.19	—	.21	—	.33	—
Performance (hypothesis 2)	.47	—	.18	—	.18	—
Consideration vs.						
Satisfaction (hypothesis 3)	.37	.45	.30	.28	.23	.36
Performance (hypothesis 4)	.42	−.15	.11	−.06	.08	−.06
Job Scope						
Satisfaction (hypothesis 5)	.36	.38	.30	.24	.30	.19
Performance (hypothesis 6)	.52	.33	.02	.18	.09	.04

NOTE: Correlations are for average satisfaction (over six components) and average performance ratings (over six factors).

SOURCE: Adapted from Robert J. House (1971), A Path-Goal Theory of Leader Effectiveness, *Administrative Science Quarterly*, 16, 331, 334, 336

A third study attempted to replicate the second with regard to hypotheses 3, 4, 5, and 6, all involving the consideration variable, using a different sample (see table 10.2). None of the correlation differences is significant, although hypothesis 6 and now also hypothesis 5 receive directional support, as does hypothesis 3 to a mixed degree. Hypothesis 4, which was strongly supported in the previous study, no longer is supported.

As a whole, this early research appears to provide some support for the path-goal theory, while suggesting that additional moderator variables may need to be considered. A second series of studies leads to much the same conclusion (House & Dessler, 1974).

In this latter research, the moderating effects of task structure were investigated for instrumental (similar to initiating structure), supportive (similar to consideration), and participative leadership behavior. In general, instrumental leadership was related to positive outcomes as hypothesized when there was little structure in the task, and supportive leadership was related similarly when there was considerable structure. As in the prior research, however, results did not always replicate from one sample to another, and significant differences between high and low task structure condition correlations occurred for only 9 of 22 comparisons.

Participative leadership was studied using certain items from the Ohio State measure of consideration plus additional, comparable items. The expectation

was that participative leadership might operate as a means of clarifying role expectations and thus would be most effective under conditions of low task structure. The data did not support this conclusion, and there was no real evidence that task structure moderated relationships between participative leadership and outcomes.

Research Void

Since the period of major research activity which characterized the theoretical start up years, the theory's authors have contributed nothing by way of directly relevant research. House has been working on a theory of charismatic leadership and, as indicated in propositions 23, 24, and 25 of the 1996 theory, ties between this work and path-goal theory have been developed. These ties are spelled out in more detail in House and Boas Shamir (1993). But the two theories are quite different in nature, and as of this writing they have been only tangentially related.

Why this research void has occurred is a meaningful question, given that both authors have actively contributed to the organizational behavior literature for many years. House in particular has been a prolific researcher. One possibility is that path-goal theory somehow lost its incentive value for the authors, perhaps because their initial results left them somewhat disenchanted. It is also possible that they simply did not know what to do next.

In any event, over many years the authors' contributions have been limited to commentaries. Evans (1996) argues that path-goal theory has not undergone reasonable testing, and he thus appears to remain committed to some version close to the original theory. House seems to have held a similar position for a number of years (see House & Baetz, 1979; House, 1987, 1988; Fiedler & House, 1988). However, by the 1990s there was clear evidence of disenchantment in his commentaries (House, 1993; House & Podsakoff, 1994; House, 1996). This disenchantment ultimately appears to have eventuated in the reformulated path-goal theory of work unit leadership.

Evaluation and Impact

I am not aware of any direct, a priori tests of the 1996 theory. Therefore what follows represents an evaluation of the initial theory as developed up to the mid-1970s. This will provide a view of the path-goal approach, but not of the specific theory currently on the table. The latter theory, however, is given attention subsequently.

Although path-goal theory proposes a wide range of moderators, House's concentration on task factors, and in particular task structure, appears to have exerted a strong influence on other researchers. Tests of the theory have been predominantly in this area and have focused on considerate or supportive, and directive or structuring leader behaviors much more than those of a participative or achievement-oriented type.

Quantitative Reviews

The first meta-analysis related to path-goal theory was conducted by Julie Indvik (1986), when this quantitative procedure was making its initial appearances in organizational behavior. Perhaps for this reason the published report is incomplete and difficult to evaluate. Path-goal theory presents a special problem for meta-analysis because of the large number of variables and hypotheses involved. As a result, the number of studies contributing to any one analysis tends to be low, and this problem clearly did plague the Indvik (1986) investigation, as did the fact that substitutes for the specific moderators of the theory are accepted on occasion. Indvik's conclusion is that the analyses support continued testing of the theory and that path-goal theory emerges largely intact from this meta-analysis. This conclusion was well received (Fiedler &

House, 1988), but as Indvik (1986) notes, the small number of studies in each moderator analysis provides grounds for caution.

A subsequent meta-analysis (Wofford & Liska, 1993) casts a much wider net, in part because it includes almost 10 more years of data and in part because unpublished studies were included. The results are best described in the authors' own words:

> The moderator analysis results . . . do not provide evidence that the nature of the existing moderator relationships are those proposed by the path-goal theories. A total of nineteen tests of potential moderator effects were conducted. Of these only six (32 percent) met the criteria of moderators in the hypothesized direction. . . . The number that met the criteria exceeds that to be expected by chance, but does not provide strong support for path-goal theories. Thus, although . . . test results strongly support the position that the relationships of leader behaviors with effectiveness measures are moderated ones, path-goal hypotheses regarding the nature of the moderators involved do not receive consistent support. (Wofford & Liska, 1993, pp. 872–873)

A problem with meta-analyses of this kind is that they pick up both well-conducted studies and not-so-well-conducted studies, then typically weight them equally. One might expect that after a new theory has been in the market for a number of years, many research problems would be ironed out; thus, the more recent research should contain the better-conducted studies. A look at path-goal theory research in the 1980s (there is little in the 1990s) should therefore prove informative. Two such studies provide predominant (but not total) support for the theory (Schriesheim & DeNisi, 1981; Fulk & Wendler, 1982). A third study found mixed support (but only for one of four hypotheses), although this one hypothesis held up in a longitudinal, as well as the concurrent, analysis (Keller, 1989). A fourth study did not support the theory at all (Schriesheim & Schriesheim, 1980), in spite of multiple analyses. There is something of the "glass is half full" versus "glass is half empty" phenomenon here, but overall these results would appear to be somewhat more supportive of the theory than most (and the research is better conducted, as well).

A final quantitative analysis was concerned with the appropriate establishing of moderator relationships in path-goal research (Podsakoff, MacKenzie,

Ahearne, & Bommer, 1995). The analysis indicated that approximately 25 percent of the moderator tests of path-goal theory produce significant results, although there are reasons to believe this might be an underestimate of reality. Replications of significant findings in additional samples are infrequent. In short, hypothesized moderator relationships are supported sufficiently often to exceed chance expectations, but they are not nearly as frequent as would be anticipated for a truly valid theory.

Measures, Moderators, and Motivation Theory

There can be no question that the research tests of path-goal theory provide equivocal results. A more basic question is whether the theory has really been tested at all. Almost without exception these tests have drawn in one way or another on the Ohio State scales. Yet it has been shown that these scales do not provide comparable measures of what might appear to be the same constructs. Untangling the confounding thus created appears difficult. Results previously reported to be supportive of the theory may not be if one uses a later operationalization of the variable, and so on. It is easy to accept positive results as positive, and negative as negative, regardless of the measures used, but when the measures are clearly not the same, the possibility of capitalization on chance through selection of measures is a real danger.

Furthermore, it now appears quite possible that leader behavior descriptions of the type the Ohio State measures provide may identify implicit theories and existing biases more often than true behaviors. Accordingly, there is a real prospect that studies using measures of this kind have not tapped the actual leader behaviors specified by the theory. An additional problem arises because the theory is considerably more comprehensive than the research on it. The outcomes specified are job satisfaction, acceptance of leader, and motivational behavior.

Although some researchers assume that motivational behavior includes only motivational components, the construct certainly has been tested primarily at the level of actual performance, and there appears to be sufficient theoretical support to justify testing at the performance level. Acceptance of the leader as an outcome has been given little attention. Among the various leader behaviors, published research on achievement-oriented behaviors is minimal, and research on participative behavior is much less than might be desired. Among the various environmental moderators noted, those of a task nature have been studied extensively, but such factors as existing authority systems and work group norms have received little attention. At the individual subordinate level, authoritarianism has received the most attention, while other factors have gone almost unrecognized.

Given this uncertainty regarding the nature and scope of the research, it is still possible to ask where the current research leads. Certainly there are sufficient findings that appear to support the theory, especially for task moderators, to rule out a purely chance explanation. However, the frequent negative findings have typically elicited a resort to additional moderators as explanations and thus added ad hoc extensions to the theory. Thus, job level differences have been added to explain contradictory findings with regard to task structure. Job level also has been used to explain similar disparities when role clarity is a moderator, but in this instance the relationships are completely reversed, even though task structure and role clarity would appear to be closely related concepts. The use of such ad hoc moderators on a case by case basis seems likely to fail on logical grounds alone, while making the theory so complex that it violates all meaningful concepts of parsimony.

The close tie that path-goal theory posits between leadership and subordinate motivation has a compelling logic to it that other theories have not achieved. One cannot help concluding that in this respect path-goal theory is on the right track, and it is probably for this reason that a number of significant findings have been obtained. However, the origins of path-goal theory in expectancy theory would appear to indicate that the limitations of that motivational theory should hold for leadership theory as well. As indicated in chapter 8, expectancy theory (whatever its pretensions) is bounded within a rather limited domain; it applies to the world of hedonistic, maximizing decisions and is concerned with a rational, conscious model of human behavior. So, too, is path-goal theory, and it is probably for just this reason that it often strikes out. A number of the research studies appear to have extended beyond the presumed boundaries of the theory, and if this is so, it is not surprising that they have failed to yield supportive results. One of the difficulties with path-goal theory is that its boundary conditions have not been clearly specified. Perhaps the goal of extending expectancy theory into the leadership domain has been achieved, and future contributions will derive primarily from the broader expectancy framework. Should this be the case, path-goal theory will still have made a contribution in melding leadership and motivation constructs and in pointing up the guiding, coaching role of leadership as it relates to motivation.

Thoughts on the 1996 Theory

House's (1996) major theoretical reformulation deals with many of the issues we have been considering. It is a response to criticisms and perceived deficiencies, and to the realities of research findings. As Chester Schriesheim and Linda Neider (1996) note, path-goal theory has survived for a long time based on its perceived "potential." There was a need to do something, and House has made a major contribution in that regard.

In the introduction to a special section of the *Leadership Quarterly* dealing with path-goal theory, which contains House's reformulations, James Hunt says, "We can all hope that this new article and the commentators' remarks . . . serve as a springboard for renewed research on the theory" (1996, p. 304). How likely is this? House still has not published any new research on the theory himself, other than the tangential work on the charismatic leadership aspects. Unlike the initial version, the theory is not introduced in conjunction with research on it. In fact, one gets the impression that House feels he made a mistake the first time by tying his theory to the Ohio State measures — a mistake subsequent researchers mimicked. He is not going to make that mistake again. Yet the consequence is that we have a new theory with many new variables — the behaviors for instance — that is completely devoid of operationalizations of those variables.

The chances are, when research is done in situations of this kind, that this research will take a considerable period to emerge and that the new measures will deviate substantially from what the theory's author had in mind. Given this, I would urge House to become involved in the construction of measures as quickly and as deeply as possible. Without this, it seems unlikely that Hunt's hoped for "springboard" effect will in fact occur. That would be unfortunate because on the surface it appears that, in fact, the new theory does overcome many of the deficiencies of its predecessor. But, being inductive from past research, the new theory requires substantial new research.

Applications?

An early statement by Evans (1970b) offered some promise that path-goal theory might make important contributions to managerial practice. However, the current state of affairs is best epitomized in the following statement:

> We are optimistic about the future outlook of leadership research. With the guidance of path-goal theorizing, future research is expected to unravel many confusing puzzles about the reasons for and effects of leader behavior that have, heretofore, not been solved. However, we add a word of caution: the theory, and the research on it, are [*sic*] relatively new to the literature of organizational behavior. Consequently, path-goal theory is offered more as a tool for directing research and stimulating insight than as a proven guide for managerial action. (House & Mitchell, 1974, p. 94)

Applications have not been developed and guidelines for managerial action have not been specifically spelled out. Given this situation, it appears premature to draw inferences about the use of the theory in management practice, especially as long as the 1996 theory remains untested.

CONCLUSIONS

The theories considered in this chapter raise questions about the practice of building leadership theories on motivational constructs. Surely, to date this approach has not been particularly successful, sometimes because of deficiencies in the underlying motivational theory and sometimes because of problems in constructing leadership theory on the motivational foundation.

Yet ultimately, to gain full understanding, it is going to be necessary to have theories of not only follower (subordinate) motivation but leader motivation as well, and also theories of leader and follower behavior. It seems unlikely that these will come from the same source, simply because motivation theorists and behavior theorists tend to have different backgrounds and areas of expertise. Thus the best theoretical strategy appears to be to build a number of separate theories and then link them to complete the whole. I believe that is what the fields of motivation and leadership are unwittingly struggling toward at the present time. Links to tie leadership of different kinds to different organizational forms will undoubtedly be required as well.

References

Argyris, Chris (1957). *Personality and Organization.* New York: Harper.

Bass, Bernard M. (1990). *Bass and Stogdill's Handbook of Leadership Theory, Research, and Managerial Applications.* New York: Free Press.

Beer, Michael (1966). *Leadership, Employee Needs and Motivation.* Columbus: Bureau of Business Research, College of Commerce and Administration, Ohio State University.

Bennis, Warren G. (1972). Chairman Mac in Perspective. *Harvard Business Review,* 50, 140–149.

Blake, Robert R., & McCanse, Anne A. (1991). *Leadership Dilemmas — Grid Solutions.* Houston: Gulf.

Blake, Robert R., & Mouton, Jane S. (1964). *The Managerial Grid.* Houston: Gulf.

Blake, Robert R., & Mouton, Jane S. (1982). Theory and Research for Developing a Science of Leadership. *Journal of Applied Behavioral Science,* 18, 275–291.

Butterfield, D. Anthony, & Powell, Gary N. (1981). Effect of Group Performance, Leader Sex, and Rater Sex on Ratings of Leader Behavior. *Organizational Behavior and Human Performance,* 28, 129–141.

Cannella, Albert A., & Rowe, W. Glenn (1995). Leader Capabilities, Succession, and Competitive Context: A Study of Professional Baseball Teams. *Leadership Quarterly,* 6, 69–88.

Caplan, Edwin H. (1971). *Management Accounting and Behavioral Science.* Reading, MA: Addison-Wesley.

Cawley, Brian D; Keeping, Lisa M; & Levy, Paul E. (1998). Participation in the Performance Appraisal Process and Employee Reactions: A Meta-Analytic Review of Field Investigations. *Journal of Applied Psychology,* 83, 615–633.

Clark, Kenneth E., & Clark, Miriam B. (1990). *Measures of Leadership.* West Orange, NJ: Leadership Library of America.

Evans, Martin G. (1970a). The Effects of Supervisory Behavior on the Path-Goal Relationship. *Organizational Behavior and Human Performance,* 5, 277–298.

Evans, Martin G. (1970b). Leadership and Motivation: A Core Concept. *Academy of Management Journal,* 13, 91–102.

Evans, Martin G. (1974). Extensions of a Path-Goal Theory of Motivation. *Journal of Applied Psychology,* 59, 172–178.

Evans, Martin G. (1979). Leadership. In Steven Kerr (Ed.), *Organizational Behavior* (pp. 207–239) Columbus, OH: Grid.

Evans, Martin G. (1996). House's "Path-Goal Theory of Leadership Effectiveness." *Leadership Quarterly,* 7, 305–309.

Fernandez, Carmen F., & Vecchio, Robert P. (1997). Situational Leadership Theory Revisited: A Test of an Across-Jobs Perspective. *Leadership Quarterly,* 8, 67–84.

Fiedler, Fred E., & House, Robert J. (1988). Leadership Theory and Research: A Report of Progress. *International Review of Industrial and Organizational Psychology,* 3, 73–92.

Filley, Alan C.; House, Robert J.; & Kerr, Steven (1976). *Managerial Process and Organizational Behavior.* Glenview, IL: Scott, Foresman.

Fisher, Bruce M., & Edwards, Jack E. (1988). Consideration and Initiating Structure and Their Relationships with Leader Effectiveness: A Meta-Analysis. *Academy of Management Proceedings,* 48, 201–205.

Fleishman, Edwin A. (1998). Patterns of Leadership Behavior Related to Employee Grievances and Turnover: Some Post Hoc Reflections. *Personnel Psychology,* 51, 825–834.

Fleishman, Edwin A.; Mumford, Michael D.; Zaccaro, Stephen J.; Levin, Kerry Y.; Korotkin, Arthur L.; & Hein, Michael B. (1991). Taxonomic Efforts in the Description of Leader Behavior: A Synthesis and Functional Interpretation. *Leadership Quarterly,* 2, 245–287.

Fulk, Janet, & Wendler, Eric R. (1982). Dimensionality of Leader Subordinate Interactions: A Path-Goal Investigation. *Organizational Behavior and Human Performance,* 30, 241–264.

George, Jennifer M. (1992). The Role of Personality in Organizational Life: Issues and Evidence. *Journal of Management,* 18, 185–213.

Graeff, Claude L. (1997). Evolution of Situational Leadership Theory: A Critical Review. *Leadership Quarterly,* 8, 153–170.

Gray, Edmund R. (1978). The Non-Linear Systems Experience: A Requiem. *Business Horizons,* 21(1), 31–36.

Haire, Mason; Ghiselli, Edwin E.; & Porter, Lyman W. (1966). *Managerial Thinking: An International Study.* New York: Wiley.

Heil, Gary; Bennis, Warren; & Stephens, Deborah C. (2000). *Douglas McGregor Revisited: Managing the Human Side of the Enterprise.* New York: Wiley.

Heller, Frank; Pusic, Eugen; Strauss, George; & Wilpert, Bernhard (1998). *Organizational Participation: Myth and Reality.* Oxford: Oxford University Press.

Hersey, Paul, & Blanchard, Kenneth H. (1969). Life Cycle Theory of Leadership. *Training and Development Journal,* 23(2), 26–34.

Hersey, Paul; Blanchard, Kenneth H.; & Johnson, D. E. (1996). *Management of Organizational Behavior: Utilizing Human Resources*. Englewood Cliffs, NJ: Prentice Hall.

House, Robert J. (1971). A Path-Goal Theory of Leader Effectiveness. *Administrative Science Quarterly*, 16, 321–338.

House, Robert J. (1987). Retrospective Comment. In Louis E. Boone & Donald D. Bowen (Eds.), *The Great Writings in Management and Organizational Behavior* (pp. 354–364). New York: Random House.

House, Robert J. (1988). Leadership Research: Some Forgotten, Ignored, or Overlooked Findings. In James G. Hunt, B. Rajaram Baliga, H. Peter Dachler, & Chester A. Schriesheim (Eds.), *Emerging Leadership Vistas* (pp. 245–260). Lexington, MA: Lexington Books.

House, Robert J. (1993). Slow Learner and Late Bloomer. In Arthur G. Bedeian (Ed.), *Management Laureates: A Collection of Autobiographical Essays* (pp. 41–78). Greenwich, CT: JAI Press.

House, Robert J. (1996). Path-Goal Theory of Leadership: Lessons, Legacy, and a Reformulated Theory. *Leadership Quarterly*, 7, 323–352.

House, Robert J., & Aditya, Ram N. (1997). The Social Scientific Study of Leadership: Quo Vadis? *Journal of Management*, 23, 409–473.

House, Robert J., & Baetz, Mary L. (1979). Leadership: Some Empirical Generalizations and New Research Directions. *Research in Organizational Behavior*, 1, 341–423.

House, Robert J., & Dessler, Gary (1974). The Path-Goal Theory of Leadership: Some Post Hoc and A Priori Tests. In James G. Hunt & Lars L. Larson (Eds.), *Contingency Approaches to Leadership* (pp. 29–55) Carbondale: Southern Illinois University Press.

House, Robert J., & Mitchell, Terence R. (1974). Path-Goal Theory of Leadership. *Journal of Contemporary Business*. 3(4), 81–97.

House, Robert J., & Podsakoff, Philip M. (1994). Leadership Effectiveness: Past Perspectives and Future Directions for Research.In Jerald Greenberg (Ed.), *Organizational Behavior: The State of the Science* (pp. 45–82). Hillsdale, NJ: Erlbaum.

House, Robert J., & Shamir, Boas (1993). Toward the Integration of Transformational, Charismatic, and Visionary Theories. In Martin M. Chemers & Roya Ayman (Eds.), *Leadership Theory and Research* (pp. 81–107) San Diego: Academic Press.

Hunt, James G. (1996). Citation Classics. *Leadership Quarterly*, 7, 303–304.

Indvik, Julie (1986). Path-Goal Theory of Leadership: A Meta-Analysis. *Academy of Management Proceedings*, 46, 189–192.

Jenkins, G. Douglas; Gupta, Nina; Mitra, Atul; & Shaw, Jason D. (1998). Are Financial Incentives Related to Performance? A Meta-Analytic Review of Empirical Research. *Journal of Applied Psychology*, 83, 777–787.

Kanungo, Rabindra N., & Mendonca, Manuel (1996). Cultural Contingencies and Leadership in Developing Countries. *Research in the Sociology of Organizations*, 14, 263–295.

Kay, Andrew (1973). Where Being Nice to Workers Didn't Work. *Business Week*, January 20, 98–100.

Keller, Robert T. (1989). A Test of Path-Goal Theory of Leadership with Need for Clarity as a Moderator in Research and Development Organizations. *Journal of Applied Psychology*, 74, 208–212.

Korman, Abraham K. (1966). Consideration, Initiating Structure and Organizational Criteria: A Review. *Personnel Psychology*, 19, 349–361.

Kuriloff, Arthur H. (1963). An Experiment in Management: Putting Theory Y to the Test. *Personnel*, 40(6), 8–17.

Larson, James R. (1982). Cognitive Mechanisms Mediating the Impact of Implicit Theories of Leader Behavior on Leader Behavior Ratings. *Organizational Behavior and Human Performance*, 29, 129–140.

Larson, Lars L.; Hunt, James G.; & Osborn, Richard N. (1976). The Great Hi-Hi Leader Behavior Myth: A Lesson from Occam's Razor. *Academy of Management Journal*, 19, 628–641.

Latham, Gary P.; Erez, Miriam; & Locke, Edwin A. (1988). Resolving Scientific Disputes by the Joint Design of Crucial Experiments by the Antagonists: Application to the Erez-Latham Dispute Regarding Participation in Goal Setting. *Journal of Applied Psychology*, 73, 753–772.

Ledford, Gerald, & Lawler, Edward E. (1994). Research on Employee Participation: Beating a Dead Horse? *Academy of Management Review*, 19, 632–644.

Liden, Robert C., & Arad, Sharon (1996). A Power Perspective of Empowerment and Work Groups: Implications for Human Resources Management Research. *Research in Personnel and Human Resources Management*, 14, 205–251.

Locke, Edwin A.; Alavi, Maryam; & Wagner, John A. (1997). Participation in Decision Making: An Information Exchange Perspective. *Research in Personnel and Human Resource Management*, 15, 293–331.

Lord, Robert G.; DeVader, Christy L.; & Alliger, George M. (1986). A Meta-Analysis of the Relation between Personality Traits and Leadership Perceptions: An Application of Validity Generalization Procedures. *Journal of Applied Psychology*, 71, 402–410.

Malone, Erwin L. (1975). The Non-Linear Systems Experiment in Participative Management. *Journal of Business*, 48, 52–64.

Maslow, Abraham H. (1965). *Eupsychian Management.* Homewood, IL: Irwin.

McGregor, Douglas (1954). On Leadership. *Antioch Notes,* 31(9).

McGregor, Douglas (1957a). The Human Side of Enterprise. *Management Review,* 46(11), 22–28, 88–92.

McGregor, Douglas (1957b). An Uneasy Look at Performance Appraisal. *Harvard Business Review,* 35(3), 89–94.

McGregor, Douglas (1960). *The Human Side of Enterprise.* New York: McGraw-Hill.

McGregor, Douglas (1966). *Leadership and Motivation: Essays of Douglas McGregor.* Cambridge, MA: MIT Press.

McGregor, Douglas (1967). *The Professional Manager.* New York: McGraw-Hill.

Meindl, James R. (1990). On Leadership: An Alternative to the Conventional Wisdom. *Research in Organizational Behavior,* 12, 159–203.

Meyer, Herbert (1997). An Early Stimulus to Psychology in Industry: A History of the Dearborn Conference Group. *Industrial-Organizational Psychologist,* 34(3), 24–27.

Miles, Raymond E. (1975). *Theories of Management: Implications for Organizational Behavior and Development.* New York: McGraw-Hill.

Miles, Raymond E., & Creed, W. E. Douglas (1995). Organizational Forms and Managerial Philosophies: A Descriptive and Analytical Review. *Research in Organizational Behavior,* 17, 333–372.

Miner, John B. (1985). *People Problems: The Executive Answer Book.* New York: Random House.

Miner, John B. (1993). *Role Motivation Theories.* London: Routledge.

Mitchell, Terence R.; Larson, James R.; & Green, Stephen G. (1977). Leader Behavior, Situational Moderators, and Group Performance: An Attributional Analysis. *Organizational Behavior and Human Performance,* 18, 254–268.

Morse, John J., & Lorsch, Jay W. (1970). Beyond Theory Y. *Harvard Business Review,* 48(3), 61–68.

Nystrom, Paul C. (1978). Managers and the Hi-Hi Leader Myth. *Academy of Management Journal,* 21, 325–331.

Ouchi, William G. (1981). *Theory Z: How American Business Can Meet the Japanese Challenge.* Reading, MA: Addison-Wesley.

Podsakoff, Philip M.; MacKenzie, Scott B.; Ahearne, Mike; & Bommer, William H. (1995). Searching for a Needle in a Haystack: Trying to Identify the Illusive Moderators of Leader Behavior. *Journal of Management,* 21, 422–470.

Sagie, Abraham (1994). Participative Decision Making and Performance: A Moderator Analysis. *Journal of Applied Behavioral Science,* 30, 227–246.

Sashkin, Marshall, & Fulmer, Robert M. (1988). Toward an Organizational Leadership Theory. In James G. Hunt, B. Rajaram Baliga, H. Peter Dachler, & Chester A. Schriesheim (Eds.), *Emerging Leadership Vistas* (pp. 51–65). Lexington, MA: Lexington Books.

Schein, Edgar H. (1975). The Hawthorne Group Studies Revisited: A Defense of Theory Y. In Eugene L. Cass & Frederick G. Zimmer (Eds.), *Man and Work in Society* (pp. 78–94). New York: Van Nostrand.

Schriesheim, Chester A.; Cogliser, Claudia C.; & Neider, Linda L. (1995). Is It "Trustworthy"? A Multiple-Levels-of-Analysis Reexamination of an Ohio State Leadership Study with Implications for Future Research. *Leadership Quarterly,* 6, 111–145.

Schriesheim, Chester A., & DeNisi, Angelo S. (1981). Task Dimensions as Moderators of the Effects of Instrumental Leadership: A Two-Sample Replicated Test of Path-Goal Leadership Theory. *Journal of Applied Psychology,* 66, 589–597.

Schriesheim, Chester A.; House, Robert J.; & Kerr, Steven (1976). Leader Initiating Structure: A Reconciliation of Discrepant Research Results and Some Empirical Tests. *Organizational Behavior and Human Performance,* 15, 297–321.

Schriesheim, Chester A., & Neider, Linda L. (1996). Path-Goal Leadership Theory: A Long and Winding Road. *Leadership Quarterly,* 7, 317–321.

Schriesheim, Janet F., & Schriesheim, Chester A. (1980). A Test of the Path-Goal Theory of Leadership and Some Suggested Directions for Future Research. *Personnel Psychology,* 33, 349–370.

Shartle, Carroll L. (1979). Early Years of the Ohio State University Leadership Studies. *Journal of Management,* 5, 127–134.

Smith, Jonathan E.; Carson, Kenneth P.; & Alexander, Ralph A. (1984). Leadership: It Can Make a Difference. *Academy of Management Journal,* 27, 765–776.

Steers, Richard M.; Porter, Lyman W.; & Bigley, Gregory A. (1996). *Motivation and Leadership at Work.* New York: McGraw-Hill.

Stogdill, Ralph M. (1948). Personal Factors Associated with Leadership: A Survey of the Literature. *Journal of Psychology,* 25, 35–71.

Stogdill, Ralph M. (1974). *Handbook of Leadership.* New York: Free Press.

Stogdill, Ralph M., & Coons, Alvin, E. (1957). *Leader Behavior: Its Descriptions and Measurement.* Columbus: Bureau of Business Research, College of Commerce and Administration, Ohio State University.

Thomas, Alan B. (1988). Does Leadership Make a Difference to Organizational Performance? *Administrative Science Quarterly,* 33, 388–400.

Wagner, John A. (1994). Participation's Effects on Performance and Satisfaction: A Reconsideration of Research Evidence. *Academy of Management Review*, 19, 312–330.

Wagner, John A. (1995). On Beating Dead Horses, Reconsidering Reconsiderations, and Ending Disputes: Further Thoughts about a Recent Study of Research on Participation. *Academy of Management Review*, 20, 506–509.

Wofford, J. C., & Liska, Laurie Z. (1993). Path-Goal Theories of Leadership: A Meta-Analysis. *Journal of Management*, 19, 857–876.

Wrege, Charles D., & Lattanzio, Bernice M. (1977). The Human Side of Enterprise: Forty-five Years before McGregor, the Work of Richard A. Feiss, Early Explorer in Human Relations. *Academy of Management Proceedings*, 37, 6–10.

Wren, Daniel A., & Greenwood, Ronald G. (1998). *Management Innovators: The People and Ideas That Have Shaped Modern Business*. New York: Oxford University Press.

Yukl, Gary (1998). *Leadership in Organizations*. Upper Saddle River, NJ: Prentice Hall.

Zaccaro, Stephen J.; Foti, Roseanne J.; & Kenny, David A. (1991). Self-Monitoring and Trait-Based Variance in Leadership: An Investigation of Leader Flexibility across Multiple Group Situations. *Journal of Applied Psychology*, 76, 308–315.

Chapter 11

Participative Leadership Theories

What came to be called the decision tree approach in leadership theory dates back to an article published by Robert Tannenbaum and Warren Schmidt in 1958. The article treats how managers select or decide on the behaviors they will use in different situations and with different subordinates. It also focuses on the degree to which these behaviors are boss-centered or subordinate-centered — that is, participative. These same concerns (the choice of leader behaviors and the degree of participativeness) also have characterized the theories that have followed.

The most comprehensive of these theories was proposed by Victor Vroom and various colleagues. The original work was done while Vroom was on the faculty at Carnegie-Mellon University (Vroom & Yetton, 1973); it was then expanded upon after Vroom moved to Yale University. Over much the same time period, starting in the late 1960s, another theoretical framework emerged with a quite similar orientation. This is Frank Heller's influence-power continuum theory, which began while Heller was on a visiting appointment at the University of California at Berkeley and continued after he moved to the Tavistock Institute in Great Britain (Heller, 1971).

NORMATIVE DECISION
PROCESS THEORY

As with his concern with motivation and expectancy theory (see chapter 8 in this volume), Vroom's interest in leadership, and particularly participative leadership, extends back to the period of his doctoral study at the University of Michigan (see Vroom, 1960). During this early period and subsequently in his formulation of a theory of leadership, Vroom was influenced strongly by the thinking of Norman Maier. This influence is manifest in the distinction between sharing decisions with individual subordinates and with the subordinate group as a whole, for instance, and in the differentiation between decision quality and decision acceptance (Maier, 1970). Yet Maier's formulations did not meld into a formal, cohesive theory of leadership of the kind Vroom and his coworkers have achieved.

Background

This is the same Victor Vroom who gave us his version of expectancy theory; chapter 8 here contains information on his career. There have been two major versions of normative decision process theory, both written by Vroom with two different doctoral students. The first version was written with Philip Yetton, who received his doctorate in 1972 from Carnegie-Mellon in industrial administration, having come to the United States from Great Britain. Subsequently, Yetton returned to England as a research fellow at the Manchester Business School. Most of his professional career, however, has been spent at the University of New South Wales in Australia on the faculty of the Graduate School of Management.

The second version of the theory was written with Arthur Jago, who received his Ph.D. in administrative science from Yale University in 1977. At about the time he received his doctorate he moved to the University of Houston, where he has remained since. This version of the theory had a long gestation period, as the two authors began working on related matters while they were together at Yale; the final product, however, was published much later (Vroom & Jago, 1988).

This presentation of normative decision process theory is introduced with a related article that was a product of a long-standing group at the University of California at Los Angeles. This group was active in promoting sensitivity training in the 1950s and later (see Tannenbaum, Kallejian, & Weschler, 1954; Kallejian, Weschler, & Tannenbaum, 1955). Tannenbaum headed up the group for many years. Schmidt was director of conferences and community services for the university Extension Service.

How to Choose a Leadership Pattern

Vroom and Yetton comment as follows on the Tannenbaum and Schmidt (1958) article:

> The most comprehensive treatment of situational factors as determinants of the effectiveness and efficiency of participation in decision-making is found in the work of Tannenbaum and Schmidt (1958). They discuss a large number of variables, including attitudes of the manager, his subordinates, and the situation, which ought to enter into the manager's decision about the degree to which he should share his power with his subordinates. But they stop at this inventory of variables and do not show how these might be combined and translated into different forms of action. (1973, p. 18)

Since the Vroom and Yetton theory and the extensions that have followed build on these views and do attempt to combine the variables and translate them into action, it is instructive to begin with the Tannenbaum and Schmidt formulations. In essence, these formulations deal with a range of leadership behaviors that a manager may draw on (see figure 11.1). The particular type of leadership behavior that a manager chooses to employ in a given situation depends on a variety of factors in the manager, the subordinates, and the situation itself, as follow:

Manager factors

The manager's value system, including the value placed on decision sharing

The manager's confidence and trust in subordinates

The manager's basic inclination toward directive or team leadership

The manager's security in the face of the uncertainty produced by delegation

Subordinate factors

The level of independence needs among subordinates

Range of Leader Behaviors Available

1. The manager makes and announces the decision.

2. The manager sells his decision to subordinates.

3. The manager presents ideas and invites questions.

4. The manager presents a tentative decision subject to change.

5. The manager presents a problem, invites suggestions, and then decides.

6. The manager defines the limits of a decision the group makes.

7. The manager permits his subordinates to function within the same limits imposed on him.

Boss-centered leadership

Subordinate-centered leadership

FIGURE 11.1 Range of leader behaviors available. Adapted from Robert Tannenbaum & Warren H. Schmidt (1958), How to Choose a Leadership Pattern, *Harvard Business Review*, 36(2), 96–97.

The readiness of subordinates to assume responsibility

The degree of tolerance for ambiguity possessed by subordinates

The extent to which subordinates are interested in the problem and believe it to be important

The understanding subordinates have of organizational goals and their identification with them

The knowledge and experience subordinates bring to the problem

The extent to which subordinates expect to share in decision making

Situation factors

The type of organization including, in particular, its values vis-à-vis participation, and the size and geographical dispersion of units

The effectiveness of the work group as a smoothly functioning team

The nature of the problem relative to the capabilities of the manager and the group

The degree to which time pressure exists, thus limiting subordinate involvement

Successful managers are defined as those who accurately and flexibly adjust their behavior to these various situational constraints on the choice of a leadership pattern.

Vroom (2000) continues to emphasize the impor-tant role these views have played in the development of normative decision process theory.

Initial Group Decision-Sharing Theory

In its original version, normative decision process the-ory differentiates between instances when, if decision sharing occurs, it will be with two or more subordi-nates and thus of a group nature, and cases when only a single subordinate would be involved (Vroom & Yetton, 1973). Under the group condition, the follow-ing leader behaviors are specified:

The manager solves the problem or makes the decision himself, using information available at the time. (A1)

The manager obtains the necessary information from subordinates, then decides the solution to the problem himself. (A2)

The manager shares the problem with relevant subordinates individually, getting their ideas and suggestions without bringing them together as a group, and then makes the decision himself. (C1)

The manager shares the problem with subordinates as a group, obtaining their collective ideas and suggestions, and then makes the decision himself. (C2)

The manager shares the problem with subordinates as a group, serves in a role much like that of a chairman in attempting to reach a consensus on a solution, and is willing to accept any solution that has the support of the group. (G2)

Decision Rules

A number of decision rules have been developed to guide the use of these leadership behaviors. The first three rules are intended to protect the quality of decisions and the last four their acceptance.

The information rule: If the quality of the decision is important, and if the leader does not possess enough information or expertise to solve the problem by himself, A1 behavior is eliminated.

The goal congruence (or trust) rule: If the quality of the decision is important and if the subordinates do not share the organizational goals to be obtained in solving the problem (cannot be trusted to base their efforts to solve the problem on organizational goals), G2 behavior is eliminated.

The unstructured problem rule: When the quality of the decision is important, the leader lacks the necessary information or expertise, and the problem is unstructured, A1, A2, and C1 behaviors are eliminated.

The acceptance rule: If acceptance of the decision by subordinates is critical to effective implementation, and if it is not certain that an autocratic decision made by the leader would receive acceptance, A1 and A2 behaviors are eliminated.

The conflict rule: If acceptance of the decision is critical, an autocratic decision is not certain to be accepted, and subordinates are likely to be in conflict or disagreement, A1, A2, and C1 behaviors are eliminated.

The fairness rule: If the quality of decision is unimportant and if acceptance is critical and not certain to result from an autocratic decision, A1, A2, C1, and C2 behaviors are eliminated.

The acceptance priority rule: If acceptance is critical, not assured by an autocratic decision, and if subordinates can be trusted, A1, A2, C1, and C2 behaviors are eliminated.

These decision rules incorporate certain of the factors noted by Tannenbaum and Schmidt, although by no means all of them; included are the importance of decision quality, the manager's level of information, the extent to which the problem is structured, the criticalness of subordinate acceptance, the probability of subordinate acceptance of an autocratic decision,

the degree to which subordinates are motivated to attain organizational goals, and the amount of subordinate conflict.

Decision Trees

When the decision rules are applied, they yield a feasible set of acceptable behaviors for different types of problems. To arrive at the feasible set for a given type of problem, one answers a series of questions either "yes" or "no." The process involved can be depicted as a decision tree. Several variants of this tree for the group situation may be found in the literature (Vroom, 1973, 1974, 1975, 1976b; Vroom & Yetton, 1973). The version given in figure 11.2 is somewhat easier to follow than some of the others. It yields 14 problem types and requires that answers be provided for seven questions:

Step 1: Is there a quality requirement such that one solution is likely to be more rational than another?

Step 2: Do I have sufficient information to make a high-quality decision?

Step 3: Is the problem structured?

Step 4: Is acceptance of the decision by subordinates critical to effective implementation?

Step 5: If I were to make the decision by myself, is it reasonably certain that it would be accepted by my subordinates?

Step 6: Do subordinates share the organizational goals to be attained in solving the problem?

Step 7: Is conflict among subordinates likely in preferred solutions?

The feasible sets of behaviors remaining after the decision rules are applied are noted in table 11.1 for each of the problem types, indicated by the numbers on the right in figure 11.2. The behaviors specified in the second column of table 11.1 are those that should be used to minimize the number of man hours devoted to the problem. As one moves to the right across the third column, time minimization is increasingly traded off against subordinate team development.

Initial Individual Decision-Sharing Theory

Like the group theory, the theory for dealing with individual subordinates specifies what kinds of man-

Questions

Step 1	Step 2	Step 3	Step 4	Step 5	Step 6	Step 7

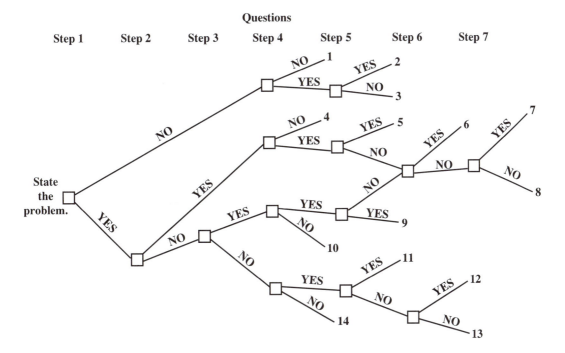

FIGURE 11.2 Decision tree for arriving at feasible sets of leader behaviors for different group problem types. Adapted from Victor H. Vroom & Philip W. Yetton (1973), *Leadership and Decision-making* (Pittsburgh, PA: University of Pittsburgh Press), 188.

ager behaviors are feasible in different problem situations; it, too, states what a manager should and should not do in a normative sense but specifically when the problem would affect only one subordinate.

The A1, A2, and C1 behaviors considered in the group theory are equally applicable to the individual situation. However, C2 and G2 are no longer appropriate, and two new behaviors become possible (Vroom & Yetton, 1973; Vroom & Jago, 1974):

The manager shares the problem with the subordinate, and together they analyze it and arrive at a mutually agreeable solution. (G1)

The manager delegates the problem to the subordinate, providing him with relevant information but giving him responsibility for solving the problem. (D1)

Decision Rules

With the change in relevant behaviors, certain changes in decision rules also become necessary. The goal congruence rule now serves to eliminate D1 and G1

behaviors. The unstructured problem rule eliminates A1 and A2 behaviors. The conflict rule is no longer relevant. A new rule, *the subordinate information rule*, indicates that if the quality of the decision is important and the subordinate lacks the information to solve the problem, D1 behavior is eliminated.

Decision Trees

The individual situation has not been depicted in a separate decision tree. However, various combined group and individual versions are available. Figure 11.3 presents a decision tree of this kind. In this instance, step 7 is not relevant for individual problems, since it relates to conflict among subordinates and only one subordinate exists for the individual case. A new question is added at the end:

Step 8: Do subordinates have sufficient information to make a high-quality decision?

The feasible sets for the 18 problem types noted in figure 11.3 for individual problems only are as in table

TABLE 11.1 Feasible sets of leader behaviors for each of 14 group problem types

Problem type	Total feasible set				
	Behavior calculated to minimize man hours spent	Behaviors providing for increasing amounts of team development			
1	A1	A2	C1	C2	G2
2	A1	A2	C1	C2	G2
3	G2				
4	A1	A2	C1	C2	G2[a]
5	A1	A2	C1	C2	G2[a]
6	G2				
7	C2				
8	C1	C2			
9	A2	C1	C2	G2[a]	
10	A2	C1	C2	G2[a]	
11	C2	G2[a]			
12	G2				
13	C2				
14	C2	G2[a]			

NOTE: A1 = the manager solves the problem or makes the decision himself, using information available at the time; A2 = the manager obtains the necessary information from subordinates, then decides the solution to the problem himself; C1 = the manager shares the problem with relevant subordinates individually, getting their ideas and suggestions without bringing them together as a group, and then makes the decision himself; C2 = the manager shares the problem with subordinates as a group, obtaining their collective ideas and suggestions, and then makes the decision himself; G2 = the manager shares the problem with subordinates as a group, serves in a role much like that of a chairman in attempting to reach a consensus on a solution, and is willing to accept any solution that has the support of the group.

a. Within the feasible set only when the answer to the step 6 question is "yes."

SOURCE: Adapted from Victor H. Vroom & Philip W. Yetton (1973), *Leadership and Decision-Making* (Pittsburgh, PA: University of Pittsburgh Press), 37

11.2. In the table, the minimum man-hour solution is given first and the most participative behavior is given last. Although figure 11.3 may be used with group problems, it is more cumbersome than figure 11.2 for that purpose.

Later Decision-Sharing Theory

The revision of the theory was available in some form in the mid-1980s, although it was not published until 1988. This new version is considerably more complex than the original, and it is claimed to be more valid as well.

Reasons for Revision

In Vroom and Jago (1988) a number of shortcomings of the original theory are stated, which served to guide the revision. The identification of these shortcomings is said to derive from prior research and from the experience of the authors in teaching the theory in management development programs. However, it appears that the latter has had more impact than the former. The shortcomings are as follows:

1. The original theory is not sufficiently specific on how to handle different situations, given that the feasible set can contain as many as five decision processes.
2. Also, there is no differentiation among behaviors outside the feasible set, even though the rules violated can vary in importance and number, and thus behaviors outside the set are not ineffective to the same degree.
3. The "yes" and "no" answers of a decision tree do not capture the shades of gray and the degrees of uncertainty that exist in reality.
4. Although the decision trees ask managers if they possess the information needed for a good quality decision, they do not ask the same question about subordinate information (in the group theory).
5. The original theory had difficulty dealing with situations where time to reach a decision is short.
6. The original theory could not handle circumstances where subordinates are geographically dispersed, making meetings impractical at best.
7. In its original version the theory fails to grasp the multiple complexities of organizational life; it is too primitive, too much an oversimplification.

Nature of the Revisions

The two models are the same in the decision processes specified (all seven of them) and in the criteria against which the effects of participation are evaluated (quality, commitment, time, and development). These latter, however, are combined in two equations:

$$D_{Eff} = D_{Qual} + D_{Comm} - D_{TP}$$

where D_{Eff} = decision effectiveness, D_{Qual} = decision quality, D_{Comm} = decision commitment, and D_{TP} = decision time penalty, and

Questions

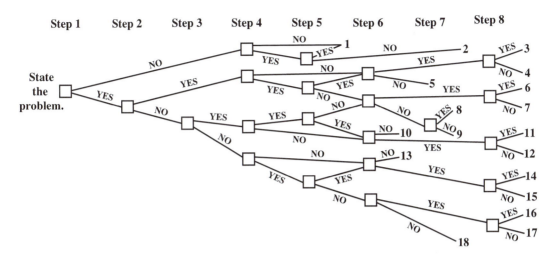

FIGURE 11.3 Decision tree for arriving at feasible sets of leader behaviors for different group and individual problem types. Adapted from Victor H. Vroom & Philip W. Yetton (1973), *Leadership and Decision-making* (Pittsburgh, PA: University of Pittsburgh Press), 194.

$$O_{\text{Eff}} = D_{\text{Eff}} - \text{Cost} + \text{Development}$$

where O_{Eff} = overall effectiveness, Cost = the time and energy used up in decision making, and Development = the value added to human capital by a decision-making process.

The prior decision rules are replaced by 12 problem attributes. Each of these is now stated initially as a question to be answered on a scale that extends over five points. The first eight of these attributes are essentially the same as noted previously, but the yes-no dichotomy has been replaced by the 5-point scale. However, the conflict question now has both group and individual versions:

Is conflict among subordinates over preferred solutions likely (group)?

Is conflict between you and your subordinate over a preferred solution likely (individual)?

The time and development factors are now handled as problem attributes as well:

Does a critically severe time constraint limit your ability to involve subordinates?

How important is it to you to minimize the time it takes to make the decision?

How important is it to you to maximize the opportunities for subordinate development?

The remaining question is entirely new:

Are the costs involved in bringing together geographically dispersed subordinates prohibitive?

Mathematical Functions

The function of the decision rules is also taken up by a number of equations. The two basic equations have already been stated. There are additional equations to provide input to the basic two; these provide values for D_{Qual}, D_{Comm}, D_{TP}, Cost, and Development. The equations for group decisions and individual decisions are different. The formulas for D_{Comm} for instance are as follow:

Group: $D_{\text{Comm}} = \text{CR} - \text{CR}/2\ [(f_1)(\text{CP}) - (f_3 + f_4 + 1)(\text{CO})(\text{CP})/2]$

Individual: $D_{\text{Comm}} = \text{CR} - \text{CR}\ [(f_1)(\text{CP})]$

where CR = the value for the rescaled problem attribute — commitment requirement, CP = the value for the rescaled problem attribute — commitment proba-

TABLE 11.2 Feasible sets of leader behaviors for each of 18 individual problem types

Problem type	Behaviors providing for increasing amounts of individual development				
1	A1	D1	A2	C1	G1
2	D1	G1			
3	A1	D1	A2	C1	G1
4	A1	A2	C1	G1	
5	A1	A2	C1		
6	D1	G1			
7	G1				
8	C1				
9	C1				
10	A2	C1			
11	D1	A2	C1	G1	
12	A2	C1	G1		
13	C1				
14	D1	C1	G1		
15	C1	G1			
16	D1	G1			
17	G1				
18	C1				

NOTE: A1 = the manager solves the problem or makes the decision himself, using information available at the time; A2 = the manager obtains the necessary information from subordinates, then decides the solution to the problem himself; C1 = the manager shares the problem with relevant subordinates individually, getting their ideas and suggestions without bringing them together as a group, and then makes the decision himself; G1 = the manager shares the problem with the subordinate, and together they analyze it and arrive at a mutually agreeable solution; D1 = the manager delegates the problem to the subordinate, providing him with relevant information but giving him responsibility for solving the problem.

SOURCE: Adapted from Victor H. Vroom & Philip W. Yetton (1973), *Leadership and Decision-Making* (Pittsburgh, PA: University of Pittsburgh Press), 194

bility, and CO = the value for the rescaled problem attribute — conflict.

The rescaling of the problem attribute scores designated by the manager on the 5-point scales is carried out using a table provided. The function values (f_3, f_4, f_1) vary with the decision process and are also derivable from a table; these latter have their origins in multiple regression analysis.

The equations (all of them) are applied five times in any given situation, once for each possible decision process. The theory's normative recommendation is the decision process, out of the five for either group or individual decision sharing, which yields the highest score for O_{Eff}. O_{Eff} is said to be a prediction of the overall effectiveness of a decision process, including its consequences on decision costs and subordinate

development. For a group problem these scores might be as follows:

Decision process:	A1	A2	C1	C2	G2
Overall effectiveness:	1.19	2.82	3.36	5.75	5.50

C2 has the highest score and is recommended. (You share the problem with your subordinates in a group meeting. In this meeting you obtain their ideas and suggestions. Then *you* make the decision, which may or may not reflect your subordinates' influence.)

For an individual problem the scores might be as follows:

Decision process:	A1	A2	C1	G1	D1
Overall effectiveness:	2.00	1.83	1.73	1.58	1.97

A1 has the highest score and is recommended. (You solve the problem or make the decision yourself using the information available to you at the present time.)

The process involved here — involving rescaling, determining functions, and calculating numerous values using multiple equations — is a complex one. It almost requires computer support. Decision trees have been developed to remove much of the complexity but still draw on the new theory. However, their simplicity eliminates much of the discriminating power from the theory as well.

Evaluation and Impact

In chapter 10 the rather negligible value of participation when applied across the board was noted. Vroom and Jago echo that conclusion but add the following:

> Participation cannot be studied without explicit attention to the context in which it is displayed. Leadership measures that try to capture a leader's style by asking a few questions about typical or average behavior are simply of little value. Certainly, there are those of us who are predisposed to be more autocratic or participative than another. However, the circumstances a person faces often dictate behavior other than that to which he or she is predisposed. And those situational forces have the larger effect when pitted against the person's inclinations or desires. (1995, p. 179)

These are the assumptions that guide normative decision process theory.

Early Descriptive Research

We now turn to the evidence on how valid the assumptions that guide normative decision process theory are and to the related issue of the validity of the theory overall.

Much of the early research on this topic was conducted by Vroom and his colleagues and used managers who were participating in management development programs (Vroom & Yetton, 1973). These managers typically reported how they would deal with a particular problem or how they had dealt with it in the past. The data are thus of a self-report nature; how a manager actually behaves in different problem situations is not known with certainty.

In one variant of the descriptive research procedure managers were asked to select a problem from their experience that affected at least two subordinates. Data were then obtained about which of the leader behaviors specified by the theory was utilized and about the various aspects of the problem situation that go into the decision tree. The results from a comprehensive study of all theoretical variables and from an earlier, less complete study that had been conducted as the theory was being developed are given in table 11.3.

The findings provide rather strong support for the view that the perceived locus of information is related to the degree of participation in the decision; to a lesser degree, decision-sharing appears to be a function of the extent to which subordinates can be trusted. The other findings tend to be equivocal, except for

some evidence indicating that when it appears probable that an autocratic decision will be accepted, participation is less likely. Subordinate conflict does not appear to be a relevant consideration.

A second research procedure early on utilized a set of standardized problem situations, and the managers were asked to place themselves in these situations. The various aspects of problem situations considered by the theory and built into the decision trees were incorporated deliberately in the problems, and the managers indicated for each problem which of the leader behaviors they would choose.

One important finding was that differences in the nature of the problem situations accounted for nearly three times as much variation in responses as differences between individuals. There was a tendency for managers to choose a more or less participative style with some consistency, but the tendency to vary one's style depending on the situation was much more pronounced. In all probability this situational effect was inflated in the research over what would be found in any one actual managerial situation, because the case problems covered an atypically large range of situations. Nevertheless, the theoretical expectation that situational factors do matter is supported. The problem or situation faced is a much better predictor of managerial behavior than the manager's basic style. People do vary their behavior to match the demands of the problems they face, and they do so over a wide range.

The research using standardized problems also in-

TABLE 11.3 Correlations between aspects of the problem situation and the degree of participativeness of the reported leader behavior

Aspects of the problem situation	Level of participation by leader	
	Comprehensive study	Partial study
Importance of a quality decision	(.12)	−.02
Amount of leader information	(−.36)	(−.34)
Amount of subordinate information	(.43)	Not measured
Degree to which the problem is structured	(−.15)	Not measured
Importance of subordinate acceptance	(.24)	.02
Probability of an autocratic decision being accepted	(−.23)	Not measured
Extent to which subordinates can be trusted to accept organizational goals	(.21)	(.18)
Amount of subordinate conflict	.08	−.01

NOTE: Numbers in parentheses are statistically significant at $p < .05$.

SOURCE: Adapted from Victor H. Vroom & Philip W. Yetton (1973), *Leadership and Decision-Making* (Pittsburgh, PA: University of Pittsburgh Press), 81–82

dicates that the various situational attributes of the theory are related to level of participation in the expected manner across eight different managerial samples. Among the variables of the theory, only the quality requirement failed to yield a significant relationship sufficiently often to bring the theoretical hypothesis into question. These latter results are in general agreement with other data obtained using a somewhat improved set of standardized problems as a measure (Jago, 1978). In this study the quality requirement also failed to show the predicted relationship on occasion, as did subordinate conflict.

Direct comparisons between what managers indicate as their behavior and what the theory recommends may be made, using both the recalled and standardized data. When this is done, the managers portray themselves as somewhat more participative and less variable in their behavior than the theory would prescribe. There is a strong tendency to avoid A1 behavior when it would be theoretically appropriate, and to a somewhat lesser extent G2 behavior; C1 behavior is clearly overstressed and so also is C2. In these comparisons the most time-conserving behavior alternative is taken as the ideal.

When the single most theoretically appropriate behavior is used in the comparison, agreement occurs in a little more than one-third of the cases; when the whole feasible set is used, this proportion is doubled. Violation of the various decision rules is much more likely to occur with regard to acceptance than quality. The fairness rule, the acceptance priority rule, and the conflict rule are often violated; the goal congruence rule and the information rule practically never are. Thus, it appears managers are much more likely to risk implementation of a decision by subordinates than risk the basic quality of the decision itself.

While the initial studies dealt entirely with group situations (Vroom & Yetton, 1973), another study used standardized problems of both a group and an individual nature (Vroom & Jago, 1974). The results from this study indicate that the individual situation elicits less participative behavior than does the group situation. Once again, situational differences were found to account for about three times as much variation on group problems as individual differences, but on individual problems this ratio jumped to 5 to 1, which indicates a much larger situational effect.

In general, the findings with regard to the effects of the various problem aspects are consistent with the theory for both group and individual problems. Still, there are certain departures from theoretical expectations in the case of the importance of a quality decision on individual problems (a low-quality requirement yields *more* participation) and subordinate conflict on group problems (more conflict yields *more* participation).

Agreement with the feasible set occurred 68 percent of the time on group problems, thus replicating prior findings. It rose to 83 percent for individual problems, wherein decision rule violation occurs predominantly with regard to the acceptance priority rule; agreement is quite rare for the rules designed to protect decision quality. On group problems the fairness and acceptance priority rules are again frequently violated, and the leader information rule is not. The most pronounced finding, however, is the much greater agreement with the theoretical model that is obtained with the individual problems.

A very likely problem with the methodology used in the descriptive research is that the reports of managers as to what they would do in the case situations might have little relationship to what they actually do in such situations. To investigate this hypothesis, responses to the cases were obtained from a group of managers and also from their subordinates (Jago & Vroom, 1975).

When the subordinates were asked to indicate how their superiors would respond in each situation, substantial agreement was found among subordinates of the same superior. However, the expected agreement between subordinates and superiors was not obtained. Further analysis suggested that several sources of bias existed in the subordinate descriptions, in particular a tendency to attribute behaviors to the superior that the subordinates also attributed to themselves. There was consistent underestimation of the variability of superior behavior and overestimation of the degree of autocratic behavior on the part of superiors, in comparison with the superior's own self-descriptions. A similar "autocratic shift" also has been noted by Vroom and Yetton (1973) and by Jago and Vroom (1977). On the evidence, this shift appears to be a function of perceptual error rather than behavioral fact.

The results of this study indicate that obtaining attributed descriptions of superiors from subordinates is a highly questionable method of determining the validity of the standardized case procedure. It may be that the problem is inherent in the use of situations not typically observed as such by the superiors or the subordinates. This line of research has neither proved nor disproved the value of the methodology used in the descriptive studies. Standardized observation of ongoing manager behavior appears to be needed.

More recently, the same problems with the use of subordinate data just noted have continued to be found (Heilman, Hornstein, Cage, & Herschlag, 1984; Field & House, 1990). Data of this kind do not mirror what is obtained from the managers themselves, nor do they provide the same high level of support for the theory.

Normative Tests

The real need in validating the theory (or theories) is not for descriptive findings, although these can prove useful in an inferential sense, but for normative findings that tie the theoretical variables to indices of managerial success and failure. A preliminary effort of this kind is reported by Vroom and Yetton (1973, p. 183). In this instance, managers were asked to describe a situation using the recalled problems design and then to rate both the quality and the acceptance of the decision. The expectation was that decisions outside the feasible set for the problem would be rated less effective.

The results indicated a tendency for decisions within feasible sets to be viewed as more effective. However, their superiority over decisions outside the feasible set was minimal and not statistically significant. A problem in interpreting these data is that the number of decision rule violations was minimal and the rated effectiveness level was consistently high. Thus, there was sufficient restriction of range on the criteria to make the lack of significant findings difficult to interpret. The study does not yield clear evidence one way or another. Subsequent research has attempted to overcome these difficulties.

Vroom and Jago (1988) report on six studies in which successful and unsuccessful decisions were identified and then the leader's behavior was established under each of these conditions. Table 11.4 summarizes the results of these studies. In the first three studies, all of the information came from the manager subjects, thus permitting common method bias. This was not true of the next two, which were laboratory studies. The downside here, however, is that the situations were of no real consequence to the subjects. The final study was like the first three but used small groups of managers to actually classify a decision (thus intervening in the common method sequence). Overall, these results are strongly supportive of the theory.

A study by Charles Margerison and R. Glube (1979) used franchisees to classify standardized problems and related the results to franchise performance and employee satisfaction. Those whose decisions more closely approximated the theory were more likely to have ventures that did well on both criteria. Similar findings were obtained in another study of retail salespeople and their managers (Paul & Ebadi, 1989). Managers who conformed closely to theoretical prescriptions had more productive sales personnel, and these people were more satisfied with their supervision and their work (but not with their pay or their coworkers).

Validity of Component Rules

A number of the studies noted previously provide information not only on the validity of the seven group decision rules in the aggregate, but individually as well. The results would seem to provide convincing support for all rules except the conflict rule (Vroom & Jago, 1988). This rule exhibited difficulties in the descriptive studies as well.

The problems identified in this area have served to stimulate more intensive research on the issue. One study (Ettling & Jago, 1988) seems to indicate that no problems exist with the conflict rule and that managers should resort to group participation when conflict exists among subordinates. The authors argue that previous failures to support the rule resulted from a lack of sufficient instances to adequately test the rule.

An additional study (Crouch & Yetton, 1987) finds that although the rule holds for managers with conflict management skills sufficient to deal with the conflict within the group, it does not hold for managers who lack conflict management skills. Such managers resort to participation at their own peril and may find themselves in the middle of a heated and escalating controversy. These authors argue that the Ettling and Jago (1988) study turned out as it did because the problems considered required very low levels of conflict management skills and did not challenge the managers in that regard. Crouch and Yetton's (1987) findings would seem to say that managers who are lacking in conflict management skills should undergo training in this regard before using the conflict rule. However, this assumes that the training would achieve its goal, a not altogether certain eventuality. In any event, this line of research places increased emphasis on individual differences as moderators for the theory. There

TABLE 11.4 Validity evidence from six studies representing normative tests

	Decision effectiveness (%)	
	Unsuccessful	Successful
Choice was within the feasible set		
Vroom & Jago (1978)[a]	32	68
Zimmer (1978)[b]	33	67
Tjosvold et al. (1986)[c]	39	61
Field (1982)[d]	51	49
Liddell et al. (1986)[e]	46	54
Böhnisch et al. (1987)[f]	33	67
Average	39	61
Choice was outside the feasible set		
Vroom & Jago	78	22
Zimmer	59	41
Tjosvold et al.	62	38
Field	64	36
Liddell et al.	71	29
Böhnisch et al.	56	44
Average	65	35

a. Victor H. Vroom & Arthur G. Jago (1978), On the Validity of the Vroom/Yetton Model, *Journal of Applied Psychology*, 63, 151–162.

b. R. J. Zimmer (1978), Validating the Vroom-Yetton normative model of leader behavior in field sales force management and measuring the training effects of TELOS on the leader behavior of district managers, unpublished doctoral dissertation, Virginia Polytechnic Institute and State University.

c. Dean Tjosvold, W. C. Wedley, & Richard H. G. Field, (1986), Constructive Controversy, the Vroom-Yetton Model, and Managerial Decision-Making, *Journal of Occupational Behavior*, 7, 125–138.

d. Richard H. G. Field (1982), A Test of the Vroom-Yetton Normative Model of Leadership, *Journal of Applied Psychology*, 67, 523–532.

e. W. W. Liddell, S. W. Elsea, A. E. Parkinson, & A. M. Hackett, (1986), A replication and refinement of "A test of the Vroom-Yetton normative model of leadership," manuscript submitted for publication.

f. W. Böhnisch, Arthur, G. Jago, & G. Reber (1987), Zur interkulturellen Validität des Vroom/Yetton Modells, *Die Betriebswirtschaft*, 47, 85–93.

SOURCE: Adapted from Victor H. Vroom & Arthur G. Jago (1988), *The New Leadership: Managing Participation in Organizations* (Englewood Cliffs, NJ: Prentice Hall), 80

may be room for more moderators of this type as the theory continues to develop. Past mentoring experience, for instance, has been found to influence the decision-making processes of the theory (Horgan & Simeon, 1990), when protégés are involved.

Construct Validity Issues

One approach to validation asks whether the constructs of a theory behave in ways that might be expected in their relationships with other variables. Vroom and Jago (1988, 1995) report data on this issue. Here responses to standardized problems are collapsed across situations to yield an individual difference measure of disposition toward autocratic versus participative decisions.

The data indicate that more autocratic predispositions characterize the military and that participative tendencies are more likely in academic settings and in government. Differences across industries in the private sector are minimal, but individual firms do vary in their characteristic approaches. Also higher-level managers are more participative than those at lower levels, perhaps because they are in a position to be. Sales/marketing and finance/accounting managers tend to be more autocratic, especially when compared with human resource managers, who are the most participative.

Cultural variations do exist. Within Europe, managers in Germany, Austria, and Switzerland are the more participative, while those from Poland and Czechoslovakia are the more autocratic. France is in between, along with the United States. Managers from lesser developed countries tend to be on the autocratic side.

Managers in their 20s are the most autocratic, with participativeness increasing up to a maximum during the 40s, where it levels off. Women are considerably more predisposed to participation, and this appears to be true of both managers and business students (Jago & Vroom, 1982). Thus the predisposition seems to antedate managerial experience. Yet other findings indicate that no gender differences exist, either in the desire for participation or in asking for such involvement (Kahnweiler & Thompson, 2000). This disparity in results is not easily explained.

Correlational analyses indicate that participativeness is more likely to be related to theory Y assumptions about subordinates, thus following Douglas McGregor (1960). It is also negatively correlated with a personality measure of authoritarianism and with initiating structure behavior as defined by the Ohio State scales; it is positively related to consideration behavior.

These latter findings provide good evidence for construct validity. Not all of the findings noted are equally supportive, but, in general, the data can be said to offer no serious threats to construct validity and several instances of clear substantiation.

Research on the Revised Theory

Several years before the 1988 publication of the later version of normative decision process theory, a laboratory study was conducted to provide a partial comparison of the new theory with the original (Jago, Ettling, & Vroom, 1985). The results are as follows, expressed in terms of the validity coefficients obtained:

	Initial Theory	Later Theory
Decision quality criterion.	.24	.38
Decision commitment criterion	.53	.84
Decision effectiveness	.29	.75

All of these validity coefficients are significant, but the major finding is the substantial improvement achieved with the new theory. Also, irrespective of the theory used, commitment is predicted much better than decision quality is. One real possibility is that the resort to participation has its major effect in facilitating acceptance of the decision. Quality may be changed less because the decision actually resulting is not very participative; the expert power of the managers often prevails in spite of efforts to do otherwise. Thus, the theory deals more with perceived than actual participation; accordingly, the main effect is on commitment.

Another study obtained solid evidence that the addition of the new decision attributes did bring about changes in the decision process; subjects did consider them (Field, Read, & Louviere, 1990), and they did so in a way that agreed with the theory. In this study, the conflict rule once again presented difficulty. Also, we have no data on the situation of manager-subordinate conflict posited in the individual model. Clearly the theoretical statements regarding conflict require more study.

Yet this and other research needs involving the new theory are not being satisfied in the 1990s. In part, of course, research answers provided previously for the initial theory, and there has been an abundance of these, are equally applicable to the later theory. But a research void seems to have set in now, to the disadvantage of a full evaluation of the new theory, which on the limited evidence available appears to represent a major advance, and to the detriment of the theory's overall testing and development. There is a definite problem when one compares the amount of research done on the two theoretical versions issued 15 years apart. Not only are the theories' authors conducting little research now, but also others are equally remiss in this regard.

As far as Vroom and Jago are concerned, the lack of research appears to be attributable to several factors: a marked escalation in long-simmering conflicts at Yale, which affected Vroom, and conflicts of a legal nature with the firm that has marketed a training program based on the theory for many years, which has affected both Vroom and Jago (Vroom, 1993). A more widespread concern, however, may be the effect of converting the theory into equations and burying it in a computer. From the viewpoint of scientific precision, this appears highly laudable, but from the viewpoint of user friendliness for researchers, it may be far less attractive. Recently (Vroom, 1999) a new program has been created, which is described as being "simple and very easy to use." Whether this will overcome the previously stated problem remains to be determined. In this connection, certain changes in the Al etc. taxonomy have been introduced as well.

Reviewer Reactions

At least relative to most theories, this one is free of ambiguities and stated with considerable precision. Much of it has been tested by both the authors and others, and with positive results. The 1988 book was written with three audiences in mind — managers, professional colleagues, and practitioners in the field of executive education and organizational development. This is a difficult balancing act to accomplish, perhaps an impossible one. So far, it has been only partially successful, with insufficient detail on the research for organizational behavior professionals and in addition a degree of overselling that on occasion amounts to exaggeration. Yet the book is an important one; if only it were longer and more detailed, and somewhat more objective.

But what do others have to say about the theory? Two sources considered in the last chapter came out in support of normative decision process theory (Wagner, 1994; Locke, Alavi, & Wagner, 1997). They are favorably disposed to the way in which moderator variables are used, as opposed to a pursuit of the main effects of participation, and they find the research evidence convincing.

Gary Yukl (1989, 1998) considers this "probably the best of the situational theories," but he also notes that it deals with only a small part of leadership, assumes that managers have the needed skills to put the theory into action, fails to consider decisions that extend over long periods of time while invoking multiple processes, does not consider some important decision procedures, and lacks the parsimony needed in a good theory (especially the 1988 version). Much of this is a matter of domain definition. Vroom and his colleagues are not trying to deal with many of the matters Yukl mentions, and the theory makes that clear. Theorists are justified in defining their domain as they see fit, but in doing so they risk the possibility that their theory will be considered trivial (because its domain is too small). Yukl does say the theory covers a small part of leadership, but neither he, nor anyone else to my knowledge, has accused it of being trivial.

A possibly more telling criticism involves the parsimony issue. Without question, normative decision process theory is complex, and it became more com-

plex with the 1988 version. Yet concluding that a theory lacks parsimony requires that making it simpler does not sacrifice understanding, prediction, and control. It is parsimony with all else being equal that is the criterion. Several more parsimonious approaches to the theory's domain have been proposed. However, when put to the test, two of these alternatives were found to achieve parsimony only at the expense of predictive power (Jago & Vroom, 1980). Until a less complex formulation can be developed that achieves the same effectiveness as the Vroom/Jago theory, we are going to have to accept the complexity that currently exists.

A review by Martin Chemers (1997) is more critical of the research evidence than the other reviews we have been considering, and it does not accept that the ability of managers to change behaviors at will has been proved. As to the former, the charge is that the validity of the theory rests on studies that use relatively weak methodologies. This criticism was entirely justified when all that was available was the descriptive research, but as more studies have accumulated, using a diverse array of methodologies, that situation has changed. It is hard to accept Chemers's (1997) negative views given the nature of the evidence. Moreover, Chemers is strongly identified with an alternative theoretical position that will be discussed in the next chapter. This does not mean that his arguments should be discounted, but they should be carefully evaluated relative to the evidence. On this score, and considering the research discussed in the previous pages, I have to disagree with Chemers's evaluation of the evidence.

A final review by Robert House and Ram Aditya (1997) is also by far the most critical. Their position is that research on normative decision process theory vastly overestimates support for the theory. As the author of path-goal theory, House is identified with a competing theory. But we need to consider his observations:

1. The theory assumes that the decision maker's goals are always congruent with the goal of the organization.
2. Since training is required in order to use the theory reliably, the population that may use it prescriptively is limited.
3. The theory ignores the discussion and conference skills required of the manager to actually solve problems on a group decision.
4. The theory is excessively complex.

5. Neither the underlying theory nor the models include consideration of manager or subordinate stress, intelligence, or experience.
6. Since the theory allows a million and a half combinations of possible relevant attributes, the theory appears to be untestable. (House & Aditya, 1997, p. 428)

Some of these criticisms deal with domain issues. For instance, the theorists' failure to consider decision making under stress is entirely justified, just as path-goal theory is justified in excluding stress on the ground that it violates the rationality boundary of that theory. Other criticisms deal with parsimony and complexity. Here we should note that no theory needs to be tested in the totality of its aspects. Because of the interconnectedness of most theories, there is added value in each test. If a number of tests are conducted across the full range of the theory, and they turn out to be supportive, then one can be increasingly convinced of the validity of the whole theory, even though many specific propositions have never been tested. Given the research that has been conducted to date, it seems realistic to conclude that normative decision process theory is rapidly approaching a point where it can be considered valid in most of its aspects.

Applications of the Theories

There are two related types of applications that have received attention in the literature. One is merely the use of the theory to guide managerial decisions in the hope of improving both their quality and acceptance. The second involves training in the use of the theory.

The 1988 theory was devised to be used in the former manner to guide on-the-job decisions. Although a method for that theory's use in training has been devised (Vroom & Jago, 1988), little information on that method is available. What research has been done on training, and almost all of the descriptions of use in both training and on-the-job decision making, involve the earlier version (Vroom & Yetton, 1973).

The essential argument for applying the theory in actual managerial decision making is, that in doing so a manager will achieve more effective decisions and thus better leadership. With regard to this point, the authors conclude the following:

Using the data collected in this investigation, we can estimate that agreement with the model in all cases would have increased the number of successful decisions from 52 percent to 68 percent in our sample and increased the overall effectiveness of decisions from 4.45 to 5.19 (on a 7-point scale). The latter effect is due more to the usefulness of the model in enhancing decision acceptance (where the expected increase would be from 4.62 to 5.41) as opposed to decision quality (from 4.56 to 4.97). It is of course difficult to translate these estimates into economic terms. . . . Although the use of the model is no guarantee of an effective decision and evidence obtained has already suggested avenues for its improvement, its use even in the present form can be expected to reduce many of the errors to be found in current managerial practice. (Vroom & Jago, 1978, p. 162)

To use the theory, a manager would answer the questions at steps 1 through 7 or steps 1 through 8 in a "yes" or "no" manner with reference to a particular problem faced. The selection of the particular decision tree to use would depend on whether a single subordinate or more than one was affected. Ultimately, this process yields a single problem type number. Using this number, a feasible set of decisions for the particular problem can be identified; these are the decisions that do not violate one or more decision rules. If minimizing the man-hours spent on the problem (and thus the time to decision implementation) is important, one selects the first alternative in the feasible set. To the extent participation is desired and time constraints are less important, one moves to the right in the feasible set.

The training program based on the initial theory has been described widely (Vroom, 1973, 1974, 1975, 1976a; Vroom & Yetton, 1973; see also Smith, 1979; Vroom & Jago, 1988). As provided by the consulting firm with which the theory's authors contracted it was called "TELOS" and more recently "Managing Involvement"; it lasts from 2 to 4 days.

Although the procedures used have varied somewhat over time, the following description provides an example of how the training may be conducted. It starts with a general familiarization with basic components of the theory and practice in using this information to describe oneself and others. Films are used in this phase. The participants then describe their own leadership behavior using one or another set of standardized cases. Next comes a certain amount of practice in simulated contexts in the use of different leadership behaviors, particularly G2, which is likely to be unfamiliar. Standard human-relations exercises are used to demonstrate the effects of participation on decision quality and acceptance. The normative model is then presented (including decision trees and feasible sets), and practice in using it is provided through application to another set of standardized cases.

Probably the key aspect of the training is the feedback of information on each manager's leadership style via computer printout, using data from responses to the standardized cases. A manual is provided to help in interpreting these data. The computer feedback provides answers to the following questions:

1. How autocratic or participative am I in my dealings with subordinates in comparison with other participants in the program?
2. What decision processes do I use more or less frequently than the average?
3. How close does my behavior come to that of the model? How frequently does my behavior agree with the feasible set? What evidence is there that my leadership style reflects the pressure of time, as opposed to a concern with the development of my subordinates? How do I compare in these respects with other participants in the class?
4. What rules do I violate most frequently and least frequently? How does this compare with other participants? On what cases did I violate these rules? Does my leadership style reflect more concern with getting decisions that are high in quality or with getting decisions that are accepted?
5. What circumstances cause me to behave in an autocratic fashion, and what circumstances cause me to behave participatively? In what respects is the way in which I attempt to vary my behavior with the demands of the situation similar to that of the model? (Vroom, 1973, pp. 79–80)

The results from the printout typically result in considerable soul searching and reanalysis of the cases. Small group discussions often are used to facilitate this process. Presumably this is the point at which change occurs, if it does occur, since the manager is inevitably under some pressure to shift behavior toward that of others and toward the normative model.

Evaluations of this training continue to present a problem. Vroom and Jago (1988) address this problem and present some evidence, but it is not adequate to

the need. Numerous testimonials, and posttraining evaluations from participants, indicate generally favorable reactions. Also, there is good evidence that the training moves managers in a participative direction, and that this change is maintained over time. Violations of decision rules decrease across the training.

However, we do not know whether the training actually makes participants better managers. What is needed is a design that compares trained and untrained managers on pretest-posttest measures of managerial performance. That kind of study has not been conducted, and it should be.

The theory has been criticized on the grounds that it stops at the level of the decision and does not proceed to skill development and application. Accordingly, a manager might learn how to make the right decision about leadership behavior without being able to execute that decision effectively, whether the intended behavior was autocratic or participative. Certainly this is an important problem in application, although not an insurmountable one, as Maier (1970) has shown. Skill training, in both autocratic and participative modes, should be introduced along with cognitive training.

A more difficult problem relates to whether under the stress of day-to-day activities managers actually can carry out the highly rational, conscious processes the theory requires. Doing so with hypothetical cases, stripped of personal emotional impact in an educational context far removed from the job is one thing; doing it in reality is another. Clearly, there is a great deal of research that needs to be done, especially with regard to the management development applications. We can only hope that the current void will end.

INFLUENCE-POWER CONTINUUM THEORY

A parallel theory to that of Vroom is Heller's theory of decision sharing, which, however, has concentrated more at the top management level. Although Heller's theoretical statements lack the precision achieved by Vroom, they have served to guide an extensive program of research. The Heller theory uses a decision-sharing continuum very similar to Vroom's, but the contingency variables are only partially overlapping. Furthermore, the theory is primarily, although not entirely, descriptive rather than normative.

Background

Heller started as an engineer in the automobile industry, but then earned an undergraduate degree in economics and sociology at the London School of Economics. His doctorate was obtained at University College, London, in psychology. After obtaining the degree, he was appointed head of the management studies department at the Polytechnic of Central London; that was in 1958. Three years later he became a consultant to the International Labor Office of the United Nations, serving in both Argentina and Chile. During this period he began his work on top management decision making.

The influence-power continuum theory really evolved, however, during several years beginning in 1966 when he was a visiting professor at the University of California at Berkeley and then at Stanford University. In 1968 Heller returned to England to join the staff of the Tavistock Institute of Human Relations. That has remained his home base ever since, although he has traveled extensively to conduct multinational research, much of it as part of various international research teams.

Theoretical Statements

To some extent, the Heller theory has been evolutionary, like so many other theories in the field of organizational behavior. The first preliminary statements in Heller and Yukl (1969) were followed by a major exposition (Heller, 1971) and then certain subsequent revisions and extensions (Heller, 1973, 1976; Heller & Wilpert, 1979, 1981). A new round of theoretical activity is most fully stated in Heller, Pieter Drenth, Paul Koopman, and Veljko Rus (1988).

Influence-Power Continuum

Originally Heller set forth a continuum with five different decision-making styles, extending from very high influence and power in the superior to a similar situation for subordinates:

The manager makes the decision without discussion or explanation.

The manager makes the decision but subsequently explains it.

The manager makes the decision but only after consultation with one or more subordinates.

The manager makes the decision jointly with subordinates, usually honoring a majority view.

The manager delegates the decision, so that it is actually made at the subordinate level.

Subsequently, following on an idea originally considered only in passing in a footnote (Heller & Yukl, 1969), the last delegation style was subdivided into short-term delegation, in which a review of the decision occurs rather quickly, and long-term delegation, in which review and evaluation occur much later and intervention is rare (Heller, 1976). Unlike Vroom, Heller does not specifically differentiate group and individual decision sharing.

Specific Hypotheses

A number of hypotheses are proposed to describe perceptions between superior and subordinate and how various factors influence the choice of a decision-making style (Heller, 1971):

1. Both superior and subordinate will believe more skills are necessary in their own jobs.
2. When superior and subordinate both estimate the time subordinates would need to acquire the skills and qualities necessary to perform the superior's job, the superior's estimates will be the larger.
3. Subordinates will see themselves as having more influence and power in relation to the superior's decision than the superiors do.
4. Superiors who perceive large differences in skills or skill requirements between themselves and subordinates will use more centralized, less participative decision procedures than in the absence of such a skill gap.
5. A large span of control for the superior will be associated with time-saving decision styles at the extremes of the continuum, either highly centralized or decentralized.
6. Superiors whose jobs have a small degree of freedom will use a more centralized decision-making style.
7. Superiors in the line function of management, having a smaller degree of freedom than those in staff, will use more centralized decision making.

8. The locus to which a decision applies (immediate subordinates, all those at any lower level, the subordinates of subordinates) will influence the superior's decision style (direction is not specified).
9. When decisions are more important to the business as a whole and to the superior than the subordinate, more centralized procedures will be used; when they are more important to a subordinate, power sharing will be greater.
10. The greater the experience (age, tenure in position, tenure with the company) of the superior, the more centralized his decision behavior.
11. The greater the experience of the subordinate, the more the superior will use power sharing styles.
12. Belief in participatory practices on the part of the superior will be associated with power sharing.

The concern with the moderating effects of such factors as skill level, experience, and importance of the decision to the business results in some similarities between the Heller and Vroom theories. However, there are major differences as well, and the Heller hypotheses are not stated in normative form.

Expanded Contingency Statements

In later publications Heller (1973, 1976) extended the list of contingency variables to cover a wide range of factors, many of them far removed from the immediate job situation. Thus, there are not only the various characteristics of the manager (experience, skill), situational variables close to the decision maker (job function, who the decision effects), and microstructural variables (span of control, department size) but also macrostructural variables such as organization size and workflow technology, and ecological variables such as environmental turbulence and level of economic development. The specific factors listed vary somewhat from one publication to another, and directional hypotheses are not stated consistently. Macrostructural and, in particular, ecological variables rarely are measured in actual research; the theory must be considered very loose in this expanded version.

This interpretation holds equally for the stated linkage between contingency variables and normative outcomes. Other things being equal, the power-sharing methods are to be preferred because they harness more of the existing reservoir of skills in the organization,

thus increasing motivation, satisfaction, and performance effectiveness. "Other things being equal" refers to the operation of the contingency variables. However, the specific manner in which these variables should moderate power sharing to produce desired outcomes is not indicated. Thus, the normative theory is incomplete.

Figure 11.4 represents one presentation of the contingency relationships of the theory. It is, in fact, more of a listing than a theoretical model; presumably that is why the word *assumed* is contained in the title. In another, earlier source the "managerial success" variable is not included under the core variables category (Heller & Wilpert, 1979, p. 51).

Heller and Wilpert (1981) discuss their decision not to specify causal relationships and state directional propositions at various points in their book. From a theoretical perspective these are important:

We make no simple assumptions about which factor *causes* participation, satisfaction, or managerial success. Organizational life is extremely complex. . . . The critical variables we have isolated in our research are in constant interaction. (pp. 6–7)

Our model . . . seeks to investigate, and it makes no rigid assumptions about causes and effects. (p. 19)

The terms 'core' and 'peripheral' (see figure 11.4) variables are used instead of 'dependent' and 'independent' variables to stress that our model does not make simple causal assumptions. It rather depends on the specific interest a social scientist may develop in analyzing a given body of data. (p. 54)

Hypotheses . . . were developed on the basis of ongoing theorizing and relevant research findings in the field of organizational behavior. . . . These hypotheses have been described in previous and more technical publications. . . . Here it is proposed to use a less formal approach by means of a series of research questions. (p. 61)

Formulating general research questions rather than specific hypotheses may overstrain the exploratory nature of the research. . . . We are probing into hitherto unexplored areas. (p. 65)

While our overall model does not presuppose or require causal links, direction can often be predicted. . . . The formulation of research questions is as good as specifying hypotheses. (p. 215)

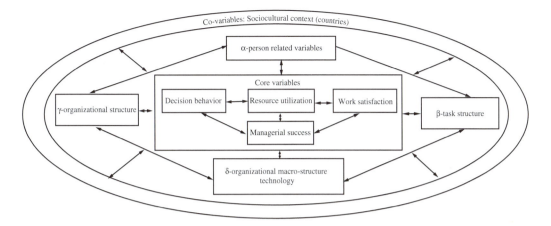

FIGURE 11.4 Model of assumed contingency relationships (all variables specified as outside the core variables grouping are considered peripheral). From Frank A. Heller & Bernhard Wilpert (1981), *Competency and Power in Managerial Decision Making* (Chichester UK: Wiley), 60. Copyright 1981, by John Wiley & Sons Limited. Reproduced with permission.

These statements speak to the very essence of theorizing, and I will return to them later. For the moment, it is important to indicate the research questions that were used instead of hypotheses:

1. Are there differences in the decision-making behavior of managers in different industrialized countries?
2. Will managers in different industrial branches and working in companies with different dominant technologies develop different decision-making patterns?
3. What is the relationship between experienced environmental turbulence and decision-making patterns?
4. Do different organizational levels differ in their respective decision making and leadership styles?
5. Do decision-making styles co-vary with different organizational and functional responsibilities of managers?
6. How is the immediate organizational job environment . . . related to managerial power- and influence-sharing?
7. What is the respective influence of different decision tasks and various person characteristics on the preferred choice of certain decision-making styles?
8. What is the role of objective and subjective skill requirements and skill availabilities in

influencing power- and influence-sharing between boss and subordinate?
9. What is the relationship between power- and influence-sharing on skill utilization and job satisfaction?
10. Do "successful" managers behave differently from "less successful" managers? (pp. 62–65)

The first eight of these questions deal with contingency variables that might influence or interact with power sharing; they are descriptive in nature. The last two questions relate power sharing to organizational outcomes and have a more normative quality.

In spite of the stated preference for questions rather than hypotheses, there does seem to be an implicit theory underlying the Heller and Wilpert (1981) studies, and this implicit theory rises to the surface on occasion. Thus there is a proposition to the effect that circumstances operating in close psychological proximity to a decision maker have a stronger effect on the choice of a decision method than circumstances that are more distant. The hierarchy of psychological distance is as follows:

1. personal attributes — age, experience, skill, training
2. situational characteristics (close to the person) — job function, hierarchical status

3. microstructure — span of control, decisional discretion
4. macrostructure — technology, environmental turbulence
5. the larger social system — national context

These are all components of figure 11.4.

The theoretical framework as developed to this point served to guide a concurrent study of the effects of legally mandated industrial democracy in different European countries (Industrial Democracy in Europe International Research Group, 1979, 1981). This work is largely peripheral to influence-power continuum theory and will not be given detailed attention here.

Variables Specified for Longitudinal Research

The theory as explicated to this point was tested using cross-sectional, concurrent designs usually involving a boss at the vice-presidential level and an immediate subordinate. The next round of research, however, moved to potentially predictive, longitudinal designs that extended over as much as 4 years. Here causal effects are more in evidence, and causal theorizing is clearly appropriate.

Yet the initial theoretical statements for the longitudinal research closely approximate those of Heller and Wilpert (1981). To this is added a four-stage view of the decision process over time (startup, developmental, finalization, implementation). Also the influence-power continuum is now modified somewhat (Heller, Drenth, Koopman, & Rus, 1977) and constitutes the independent variable:

No information (no information is given to subordinates)

Information (fairly detailed information is given to subordinates)

Opportunity to give advice (before the decision, the superior explains the problem and asks advice; subsequently, the superior makes the decision)

Advice is taken into consideration (as above, but the superior's choice usually reflects the advice received)

Joint decision making (superior and subordinate(s) together analyze the problem; everyone has equal influence on the final choice — a vote)

Complete control (subordinate(s) given authority to deal with the decision with superior intervention occurring only under exceptional circumstances)

The theory actually used in the longitudinal studies is set forth with varying degree of completeness in a number of sources (see, for instance, Decisions in Organizations Research Group, 1979; Decisions in Organizations Research Team, 1983; Heller, 1984; Heller & Misumi, 1987). A statement of the model and its variables is contained in figure 11.5. The most complete theoretical treatment is in Heller et al. (1988).

The variables specified in the latter source differ somewhat from those of figure 11.5. More specifically the contingency variables are broken into antecedent conditions (placed *before* the independent variable), consisting of organizational level, decision-making phases, nature of the issue, and meta power from figure 11.5 *plus* status power; and contingency variables, consisting of conflict and clarity of goal from figure 11.5 *plus* trust, acceptability, and achievement feasibility. Thus many former contingency variables no longer have that status.

Some of the variables of this model require explanation:

Metapower — external intervention in a decision from, for instance, corporate headquarters or government

Status power — the formal authority of a group, committee, or hierarchical level involved in a decision

Trust — the amount of confidence, openness, and trust that participants have during a decision

Acceptability — the extent to which a chosen solution is acceptable to a majority

Achievement feasibility — the likelihood of a solution being achieved

Satisfaction with process — degree of satisfaction with the process through which a decision is handled

Efficiency — the ratio of invested input to the decision quality output

Skill utilization — the extent to which relevant capacities and experiences of participants in a decision are utilized

Achievement — the extent to which expected goals, objectives, or desired outcomes are achieved by a decision; effectiveness

The other variables should be self-explanatory. Note that the dependent variables are specific to a decision, not of a more comprehensive organization-related nature.

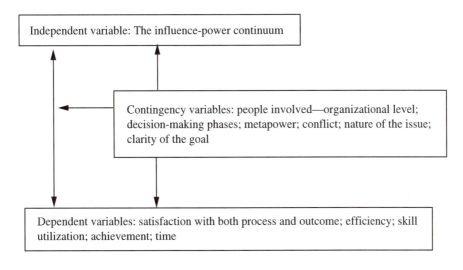

FIGURE 11.5 Variables used in the longitudinal studies of power relationships. Adapted from Decisions in Organizations Research Team (1983), A Contingency Model of Participative Decision Making: An Analysis of 56 Decisions in Three Dutch Organizations, *Journal of Occupational Psychology*, 56, 5.

Hypotheses: Specified and Not

Contrary to the earlier theoretical approach, the longitudinal research made very little use of specific hypotheses or even exploratory questions, although both are often implied. Thus, it is stated that variables such as influence, power, and conflict vary in different phases of a decision, but there is no indication of how they might be expected to vary.

In other cases, hypotheses are attributed to others, but whether they are being incorporated in influence-power continuum theory is not indicated. Thus, the fact that skill utilization (as defined above) serves to link participation to satisfaction, with greater participation increasing skill utilization and thus experienced satisfaction, is attributed to the "human resources" model, but its relevance for the present theory is left unstated.

The contingency variables of the model are considered to be important, yet "causal relationships cannot be clearly specified in advance but may be discovered in the course of a longitudinal study" (Heller et al., 1988, p. 114). Again, with regard to differences across phases of the decision process, previously said to be unspecified in nature: "Some of the results were hypothesized and will be analyzed when we combine all findings later; others were unexpected" (p. 160).

And "on the theoretical level we maintain that a high score on the influence-power continuum (IPC) in the start-up and finalization phase amounts to more power over a decision than high IPC scores in the development or implementation phase" (p. 206). The implication is that there was much more theoretical input to the longitudinal research than is in fact specified. There is a strange reluctance to make precise theoretical statements that leaves the reader both intrigued and unsatisfied.

Some insight into this situation is provided by the following statements made with reference to both the research we have been considering (Heller et al., 1988) and a study of an airport expansion project:

[These studies] do not aim at a theory of decision making or leadership. The objective is to use what can be called a transitional model, based on specific assumptions and capable of giving rise to testable hypotheses. In my view, scientific explanations require a theoretical framework: that is to say, a postulated pattern of variable interaction described by a model. They do not require a theory. This term should be reserved for a highly articulated and extensively tested system of predicted relationships that have received a substantial measure of acceptance by scientists working in the relevant disciplines. . . . The advantage of the less ambitious transitional model concept is its ability to adapt to the process of growth, refinement, and the inclusion of relevant complexities. The open-systems model used in the airport study has moved substantially from earlier formulations (Heller, 1971, 1976) without losing its essential contingency or basic variable framework. (Heller, 1984, p. 283)

Thus what was originally a theory has become an untheory, at least for purposes of formal exposition.

Competence Theory

Elsewhere, however, Heller (1987, 1992) has set forth a theoretical position of more limited range, which returns to certain aspects of the earlier formulations and builds on subsequent research.

The basic hypothesis is that influence and power sharing have positive consequences for an organization for three reasons: (1) they make use of members' existing competence-experience and skill; (2) they help develop new competence; (3) they liberate dormant motives. If attempts are made to use participation in the absence of relevant competence, however, inauthentic or manipulative results occur.

The essence of this hypothesis is that competence in subordinates may or may not be present and that thus competence operates as a contingency variable making for different results depending on its level; it is described as an antecedent to influence and power sharing in the decision process. Lacking necessary competence people are neither motivated or able to make contributions to a decision. However, such people may experience a feeling of being involved if influence and power sharing does occur, and increased satisfaction may result. This satisfaction should terminate when the inauthentic nature of the participation becomes evident. An intermediate position on the competence scale is specified where people engage in participative arrangements for the purpose of acquiring competence, which would then permit their changing to influence and power sharing based on new competence. Thus, training becomes an important prerequisite to influence and power sharing. Figure 11.6 sets forth the full model. Here, when sharing is used for developmental purposes (box 4), all people involved must be aware that this is the objective. Also figure 11.6 does not show the situation where participation is contraindicated.

A further aspect of competence theory is that influence and power sharing is hypothesized to have positive consequences manifest at the organizational level. Organizational efficiency is increased and, by inference, so are profits and productivity; thus, this is a normative theory. Previously, outcomes considered were limited to those close to the decision, and no impact at the organizational level was anticipated, the assumption being that other factors would overwhelm the effects of participation in the overall result (Heller et al., 1988). The move to organizational-level outcomes in competence theory is a clear break with the past.

In his more recent writings (in Heller, Pusic, Strauss, & Wilpert, 1998), Heller has continued to emphasize the importance of the role played by competence in participation.

Evaluation and Impact

The research on influence-power continuum theory, since Heller's early work in the United States, has been conducted by large multinational research teams. This has the advantage of permitting cross-national comparisons, but coordinating this type of effort to achieve common goals inevitably presents problems.

The early research uses questionnaire measures that are administered to a dyad consisting of a senior manager and a single immediate subordinate, usually the most senior subordinate. The questionnaires measure various theoretical variables and, in particular, the overall tendency to use power sharing along the influence-power continuum. Typically, the questionnaires are administered in a small group setting, and the results are fed back to the managers for discussion and interpretation.

The later longitudinal studies focused on decisions, not dyads, and used questionnaire data, as well as, in many cases, interviews and ratings on the variables made by researchers. There is a strong subjective element in this latter respect, and reliability questions emerge on occasion.

United States Study

The most comprehensive analysis of U.S. data used 130 managerial dyads from 15 companies located in California, the superiors being vice-presidents or major division heads (Heller, 1971). The findings consis-

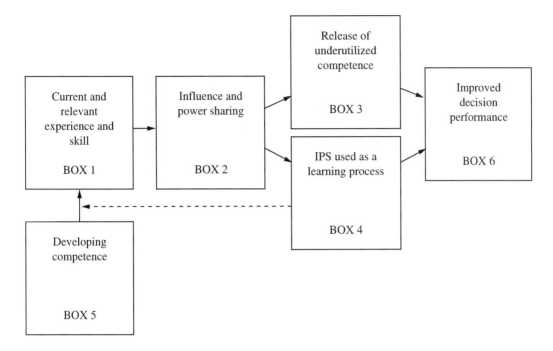

FIGURE 11.6 The competence model. From Frank A. Heller (1992), *Decision-Making and Leadership* (Cambridge: Cambridge University Press), 83. Copyright 1992 by Cambridge University Press. Reprinted with the permission.

tently support the first three hypotheses of the theory relating to perceptual differences within the dyad. Contingent effects on decision-making differences and span of control in line with hypotheses 4 also were obtained, and there was some support for hypothesis 6 in that general managers and personnel managers used the greatest amount of power sharing, while production and finance managers used the least. Hypothesis 7 relating to line-staff differences was not confirmed. Decisions that involved the subordinate's subordinates were more likely to be shared than were those that affected the subordinate only, consistent with hypothesis 8. The predicted relationships involving the importance of decisions to the business and to the subordinate (hypothesis 9) were demonstrated. With regard to the role of experience, the data are mixed; the role of superior experience is not confirmed, but the age of subordinates does operate in the expected manner. Hypothesis 12, which involves a belief in participatory practices, achieves little support.

The data indicate considerable variation in the degree of power sharing for the same manager, de-pending on the various contingent circumstances. The major stated reason for such sharing is to improve decision quality.

Subsequent International Research

This same research approach was applied subsequently in six European countries and Israel. Initial reports on these results in terms of support for the previous hypotheses continued to be predominantly positive (Heller, 1976; Heller & Wilpert, 1979).

The published findings provide further support for hypothesis 2 (that there are perceptual differences in the estimated time to learn the superior's job), hypothesis 3 (that subordinates perceive more power and influence in relation to superior's decisions), hypothesis 4 (that more centralized decision making goes with large perceived skill and skill-requirement differences), and hypothesis 8 (that the locus to which a decision applies makes a difference). In addition, the new hypotheses (that when skills and educational levels are high, decisions tend to be decentralized, and that when environmental turbulence and complexity are high, decentralization also occurs) receive support. The effects for education are quite strong; those for turbulence are much less so.

Finally, comparisons across nations indicate that differences are present. Managers from Great Britain, Germany, and Israel appear to use more centralized approaches, while managers from Sweden and France are more participative. When the United States data are added in, the U.S. managers appear to be in the more centralized category.

When the findings from this research were presented in final form (Heller & Wilpert, 1981), the format was one of providing answer to questions, as noted previously. The data bearing on these questions is extensive, but, summarizing, it appears that in most instances the importance of the contingency variables was substantial (see Miner, 1984). Support was minimal, however, for management level (question 4) and functional area (question 5). There was also some support for the view that power sharing relates to skill utilization and job satisfaction, although the findings are not very strong in either regard. Among other factors, greater use of participation was associated with managerial success (more rapid advancement). Since the data are cross-sectional, causal statements bearing on these final two questions cannot be made.

Longitudinal Research

The problem of excessive, unsynthesized data plagues this research, too; the results are difficult to get a handle on. Studies were conducted in seven organizations in Yugoslavia, the Netherlands, and the United Kingdom. The authors describe the following as the major results:

1. The importance of hierarchy in organizational life in general and in decision making in particular is fully confirmed.
2. The feasibility and empirical usefulness of the influence-power continuum is again demonstrated.
3. There is apparently no one method and no one superior way of making decisions. The distribution of influence varies (i) with the type of decision (it is different for budgeting and new product decisions for, instance); (ii) with the organization (there is something like an organizational culture which leads to more or less centralization); and (iii) country

differences are less important for policy purposes than the other findings we describe below.

4. Employees exert more influence over simple than over complex decisions. This is confirmed for operational, tactical and strategic decisions.
5. In general, the amount of influence exerted by the lower levels of organizations and by works councils is very limited. On average, it lies somewhere between being informed and being consulted. This means that, in practice, for most decisions there is no regular practice of prior consultation. The highest influence scores are achieved by the Yugoslav companies in all three categories of decision processes.
6. General satisfaction is not consistently or strongly affected by participative decision making, while other more specific measures like satisfaction with the style of participative leadership are.
7. Various measures of effectiveness show improvements when more participative methods are used.
8. Contrary to some previous research, we find that a moderate degree of conflict (perhaps better called disagreements) is consistently associated with more participative behavior.
9. The influence of people and bodies (like head offices and banks) outside the organization — which we call metapower — is more frequently than not supportive of the ongoing decision process. It supports not only management but at times lower levels.
10. Our assumption that the longitudinal process of decision-making can be divided into distinct phases which will show different patterns of behavior, has been substantiated.
11. The underutilization of available manpower skills is substantial and plays a very important role in the decision process. It is high if top management exercises considerable power or when the difference in influence between top management and the lowest levels is great. When status power at all levels is high, skill utilization is also greater.
12. Status power is highly predictive of the amount of influence exerted by the senior line and staff management as well as the lowest organizational level. Status power measures something like authority. (Heller et al., 1988, pp. 7–9)

These statements are made in a way that is almost entirely descriptive; there is little that is normative in these results. Correlations between participativeness and dependent variables are generally significant, but these variables are close to the decision and in most cases close to participation in the decision; they are not far removed from bordering on the tautological. The one instance where this is not true is when a measure of general satisfaction is used, and then the correlations drop into the teens; the average value is .15, which is consistent with what was reported previously for meta-analytic investigations. Contrary to what has often been assumed, skill utilization was not found to play a mediating role in increasing the effect of participation on either satisfaction or effectiveness of decision making.

Other findings are that managers are more participative with older, more experienced subordinates, as established in earlier studies, and that time pressure in a superior's job has no systematic relation to participativeness. On strategic decisions, control by top management and staff advisors is particularly pronounced. Differences in the degree of participativeness attributed to people by observers at different levels appear to be a function of the fact that status power and actual behavioral power tend to get confused in these judgments. Skill underutilization is associated with less influence and less satisfaction with participation. This whole matter of the use of skills is viewed as having important practical implications, and, accordingly, future research should focus on this factor.

In fact, competence theory does attempt to straighten out understanding of the role of skill utilization, and in this respect it moves in the direction of practical application. However, it has not reached that point as yet, simply because the extrapolation of the theory to the prediction of organizational level outcomes has not been tested, and it needs to be. None of the prior research on skill utilization has dealt with dependent variables of such a macro nature. We now have a truly normative theory, but we lack the type of research that could test it.

Theory and Untheory, Descriptive and Normative

Influence-power continuum formulations have had an uncertain and varying relationship to the world of theory. In the early period, during the 1960s and early 1970s, and in the 1990s theory is clearly in evidence.

In between, the picture shifts, and on occasion it moves all the way to outright denial of any attempt to achieve theory. Formal statements of hypotheses and propositions disappear and are replaced by an exploratory approach of a kind usually used to provide an inductive basis in research for subsequent theorizing. It is as if the prior theory has been wiped away, or perhaps has gone undercover to operate as implicit theory for the formulation of variables and sometimes the specification of their directionality. Propositions from other theories are often stated, but it is never clear whether they are stated for the purpose of testing them against the research evidence developed or to incorporate them in the influence-power continuum formulations; both seem to be the case on occasion.

In any event, for a period of almost 20 years the influence-power continuum view was either bad theory or no theory at all. This problem has been noted by others (see for example Slocum, 1984). During this time, the approach was overwhelmed with descriptive data that were not meaningfully tied together in any way. Consequently, any claims to providing normative direction for practice were lost.

Whether determining or not, it is relevant to note that the theory periods (in the 1960s and early 1970s, and in the 1990s) were ones when Heller was working largely alone. The untheory period, by contrast, was characterized by a number of group or team efforts where the participants in the research all had a claim on it, and thus Heller's own influence and power over the product were diluted. One might anticipate that the increased participation would have made for an improved product. Sadly, it has not. Yet Heller (1992) is clearly on the way to correcting this problem. Given the lengthy period of exploratory research, it should now be time to bring order out of chaos and use the mass of data to construct a new theory. This is what Heller began to do with competence theory. There is a need for more of the same, either in the form of other limited domain theories or of one overarching theoretical position.

Yet, unfortunately, when one writes good theory, the way opens for specific criticism and research testing that is difficult to question; all escape routes are closed. As noted previously, competence theory needs to be tested in its normative form. It also needs to be tested using alternative operationalizations of the competence variable. The problem is that skill underutilization has been identified almost entirely on the basis of subordinate judgments. If a person wants to exert more influence on a decision, one way of achieving this is to say, "I have unused skills that I can give you to create a better decision." The more such a person wants influence and power, the more competence he or she will claim that could be utilized. This potential source of distortion needs to be checked. Some objective, external measure of competence is required. Perhaps the approaches developed by David McClelland in connection with competency testing (see chapter 6 of this volume) could be applied; perhaps achievement tests could be utilized—but some such approach must be introduced to substantiate the claim that on average 20 percent of subordinate competence goes unutilized.

Until competence theory is tested adequately, it cannot provide a solid underpinning for practice. With all the research that has been conducted relevant to influence-power continuum theory, it is difficult to call for even more. The problem is that much of the research has not been conducted systematically in support of theory. That is unfortunate. Taken as a whole, Heller's theorizing comes close to achieving the breadth originally envisioned by Tannenbaum and Schmidt (1958). Yet in achieving that breadth, the theory often has become so loose and imprecise that conducting appropriate research tests become very difficult, if not impossible. The only hope for salvation is to return to the process of theory building and then undertaking new research to test that theory.

CONCLUSIONS

The two theories considered in this chapter ran concurrently over most of their histories and deal with very similar subject matter. Yet references one to the other by the theories' authors are minimal; they do occur, but there is little by way of building on each other's theorizing or research. Both theories use a similar participativeness continuum, which appears to draw much from Tannenbaum and Schmidt (1958). Both researches provide strong support for the view that participation is not a stable leadership style that characterizes certain managers but, rather, that it is a variable behavior that managers may or may not use, depending on the situation. There are many other similarities between the two sets of results as well. Both seem to support the idea of a prevailing organizational character or culture with regard to participation, for instance.

As readers may have noted, various countries are not always classified in the same way by the Vroom and Heller researches. This may reflect differences in measurement procedures, and thus may raise questions regarding construct validity, but more likely it occurs because of sampling differences within countries.

The matter of conflict among subordinates—how it relates to participativeness and its importance as a contingency variable—raises concerns for both theories. Clearly, skill in handling conflict is needed, and it may well be absent. This is an area that requires further study and perhaps theoretical elaboration as well. For instance, does the training envisaged by competence theory include training in handling conflicts?

Time pressures emerge as of differing significance for the two theories. Heller's research found no evidence that time pressure is related to the use of participation. Vroom makes this of central concern. The difference may be attributable to the measures used, but this is an area that needs study, especially since time pressure and a desire to foster subordinate development would appear to introduce conflicting demands.

Heller's finding that judgments of the degree of participation attributed to a person may be influenced by the status power of the position held by that person offers an approach to the problems the Vroom theory has had with conflicting ratings from managers themselves and their subordinates. Again, this is an area that requires new research.

Finally, there is the question of decision quality. This is crucial to competence theory, and it is rapidly becoming a key, if not the key, rationale for engaging in participative behavior. Yet acceptance of the decision is achieved at a much higher level than decision quality, given the same input of participativeness. Both the Vroom and the Heller researches raise questions about the extent to which major improvements in quality can be expected from decision sharing. This, too, is a subject that needs further study.

References

Böhnisch, W.; Jago, Arthur, G.; & Reber, G. (1987). Zur interkulturellen Validität des Vroom/Yetton Modells. *Die Betriebswirtschaft*, 47, 85–93.

Chemers, Martin M. (1997). *An Integrative Theory of Leadership*. Mahwah, NJ: Erlbaum.

Crouch, Andrew, & Yetton, Philip (1987). Manager Behavior, Leadership Style, and Subordinate Performance: An Empirical Extension of the Vroom-Yetton Conflict Rule. *Organizational Behavior and Human Decision Processes*, 39, 384–396.

Decisions in Organizations Research Group (1979). Participative Decision Making: A Comparative Study. *Industrial Relations*, 18, 295–309.

Decisions in Organizations Research Team (1983). A Contingency Model of Participative Decision Making: An Analysis of 56 Decisions in Three Dutch Organizations. *Journal of Occupational Psychology*, 56, 1–18.

Ettling, Jennifer T., & Jago, Arthur G. (1988). Participation under Conditions of Conflict: More on the Validity of the Vroom-Yetton Model. *Journal of Management Studies*, 25, 73–83.

Field, Richard H. G. (1982). A Test of the Vroom-Yetton Normative Model of Leadership. *Journal of Applied Psychology*, 67, 523–532.

Field, Richard H. G., & House, Robert J. (1990). A Test of the Vroom-Yetton Model Using Manager and Subordinate Reports. *Journal of Applied Psychology*, 75, 362–366.

Field, Richard H. G.; Read, Peter C.; & Louviere, Jordan J. (1990). The Effect of Situation Attributes on Decision Method Choice in the Vroom-Jago Model of Participation in Decision Making. *Leadership Quarterly*, 1, 165–176.

Heilman, Madeline E.; Hornstein, Harvey A.; Cage, Jack H.; & Herschlag, Judith K. (1984). Reactions to Prescribed Leader Behavior as a Function of Role Perspective: The Case of the Vroom-Yetton Model. *Journal of Applied Psychology*, 69, 50–60.

Heller, Frank A. (1971). *Managerial Decision-Making: A Study of Leadership Styles and Power-Sharing among Senior Managers*. London: Tavistock.

Heller, Frank A. (1973). Leadership Decision Making and Contingency Theory. *Industrial Relations*, 12, 183–199.

Heller, Frank A. (1976). Decision Processes: An Analysis of Power-Sharing at Senior Organizational Levels. In Robert Dubin (Ed.), *Handbook of Work, Organization, and Society* (pp. 687–745). Chicago: Rand, McNally.

Heller, Frank A. (1984). The Role of Longitudinal Method in Management Decision-Making Studies. In James G. Hunt, Dian-Marie Hosking, Chester A. Schriesheim, & Rosemary Stewart (Eds.), *Leaders and Managers: International Perspectives on Managerial Behavior and Leadership* (pp. 283–302). New York: Pergamon.

Heller, Frank A. (1987). Reality and Illusion in Senior Executive Decision Making. *Journal of Managerial Psychology*, 2(3), 23–27.

Heller, Frank A. (1992). *Decision-Making and Leadership*. Cambridge: Cambridge University Press.

Heller, Frank A.; Drenth, Pieter J. D.; Koopman, Paul; & Rus, Veljko (1977). A Longitudinal Study in Participative Decision-Making. *Human Relations*, 30, 567–587.

Heller, Frank A.; Drenth, Pieter J. D.; Koopman, Paul; & Rus, Veljko (1988). *Decisions in Organizations: A Three-Country Comparative Study*. London: Sage.

Heller, Frank A., & Misumi, Jyuji (1987). Decision Making. In Bernard M. Bass & Pieter J. D. Drenth (Eds.), *Advances in Organizational Psychology: An International Review* (pp. 207–219). Newbury Park, CA: Sage.

Heller, Frank A.; Pusic, Eugen; Strauss, George; & Wilpert, Bernhard (1998). *Organizational Participation: Myth and Reality*. Oxford: Oxford University Press.

Heller, Frank A., & Wilpert, Bernhard (1979). Managerial Decision Making: An International Comparison. In George W. England, Anant R. Negandhi, & Bernhard Wilpert (Eds.), *Organizational Functioning in a Cross-cultural Perspective* (pp. 49–71). Kent, OH: Kent State University Press.

Heller, Frank A., & Wilpert, Bernhard (1981). *Competence and Power in Managerial Decision-Making: A Study of Senior Levels of Organization in Eight Countries*. Chichester, UK: Wiley.

Heller, Frank A., & Yukl, Gary (1969). Participation, Managerial Decision-Making and Situational Variables. *Organizational Behavior and Human Performance*, 4, 227–241.

Horgan, Dianne D., & Simeon, Rebecca J. (1990). Mentoring and Participation: An Application of the Vroom-Yetton Model. *Journal of Business and Psychology*, 5, 63–84.

House, Robert J., & Aditya, Ram N. (1997). The Social Scientific Study of Leadership: Quo Vadis? *Journal of Management*, 23, 409–473.

Industrial Democracy in Europe International Research Group (1979). Participation: Formal Rules, Influence, and Involvement. *Industrial Relations*, 18, 273–294.

Industrial Democracy in Europe International Research Group (1981). *European Industrial Relations*. London: Oxford University Press.

Jago, Arthur G. (1978). A Test of Spuriousness in Descriptive Models of Participative Leader Behavior. *Journal of Applied Psychology*, 63, 383–387.

Jago, Arthur G.; Ettling, Jennifer T.; & Vroom, Victor H. (1985). Validating a Revision to the Vroom/Yetton Model: First Evidence. *Academy of Management Proceedings*, 45, 220–223.

Jago, Arthur G., & Vroom, Victor H. (1975). Perceptions of Leadership Style: Superior and Subordinate Descriptions of Decision-Making Behavior. In James G. Hunt & Lars L. Larson (Eds.), *Leadership Frontiers* (pp. 103–139). Kent, OH: Kent State University Press.

Jago, Arthur G., & Vroom, Victor H. (1977). Hierarchical Level and Leadership Style. *Organizational Behavior and Human Performance*, 18, 131–145.

Jago, Arthur G., & Vroom, Victor H. (1980). An Evaluation of Two Alternatives to the Vroom/Yetton Normative Model. *Academy of Management Journal*, 23, 347–355.

Jago, Arthur G., & Vroom, Victor H. (1982). Sex Differences in the Incidence and Evaluation of Participative Leader Behavior. *Journal of Applied Psychology*, 67, 776–783.

Kahnweiler, William M., & Thompson, Margaret A. (2000). Levels of Desired, Actual, and Perceived Control of Employee Involvement in Decision Making: An Empirical Investigation. *Journal of Business and Psychology*, 14, 407–427.

Kallejian, Verne J.; Weschler, Irving R.; & Tannenbaum, Robert (1955). Managers in Transition. *Harvard Business Review*, 33(4), 55–64.

Locke, Edwin A.; Alavi, Maryam; & Wagner, John A. (1997). Participation in Decision Making: An Information Exchange Perspective. *Research in Personnel and Human Resources Management*, 15, 293–331.

Maier, Norman R. F. (1970). *Problem Solving and Creativity — In Groups and Individuals*. Belmont, CA: Brooks/Cole.

Margerison, Charles, & Glube, R. (1979). Leadership Decision-Making: An Empirical Test of the Vroom and Yetton Model. *Journal of Management Studies*, 16, 45–55.

McGregor, Douglas (1960). *The Human Side of Enterprise*. New York: McGraw-Hill.

Miner, John B. (1984). Participation and Management. *International Yearbook of Organizational Democracy*, 2, 183–196.

Paul, Robert J., & Ebadi, Yar M. (1989). Leadership Decision Making in a Service Organization: A Field Test of the Vroom-Yetton Model. *Journal of Occupational Psychology*, 62, 202–211.

Slocum, John W. (1984). Commentary: Problems with Contingency Models of Leader Participation. In James G. Hunt, Dian-Marie Hosking, Chester A. Schriesheim, & Rosemary Stewart (Eds.), *Leaders and Managers: International Perspectives on Managerial Behavior and Leadership* (pp. 333–340). New York Pergamon.

Smith, Blanchard B. (1979). The TELOS Program and the Vroom-Yetton Model. In James G. Hunt & Lars

L. Larson (Eds.), *Crosscurrents in Leadership* (pp. 39–45). Carbondale: Southern Illinois University Press.

Tannenbaum, Robert; Kallejian, Verne; & Weschler, Irving R. (1954). Training Managers for Leadership. *Personnel*, 30, 254–260.

Tannenbaum, Robert, & Schmidt, Warren H. (1958). How to Choose a Leadership Pattern. *Harvard Business Review*, 36(2), 95–101.

Tjosvold, Dean; Wedley, W. C.; & Field, Richard H. G. (1986). Constructive Controversy, the Vroom-Yetton Model, and Managerial Decision-making. *Journal of Occupational Behavior*, 7, 125–138.

Vroom, Victor H. (1960). *Some Personality Determinants of the Effects of Participation*. Englewood Cliffs, NJ: Prentice Hall.

Vroom, Victor H. (1973). A New Look at Managerial Decision Making. *Organizational Dynamics*, 1(4), 66–80.

Vroom, Victor H. (1974). Decision Making and the Leadership Process. *Journal of Contemporary Business*, 3, 47–64.

Vroom, Victor H. (1975). Leadership Revisited. In Eugene L. Cass & Frederick G. Zimmer (Eds.), *Man and Work in Society* (pp. 220–234). New York: Van Nostrand.

Vroom, Victor H. (1976a). Can Leaders Learn to Lead? *Organizational Dynamics*, 4(3), 17–28.

Vroom, Victor H. (1976b). Leadership. In Marvin D. Dunnette (Ed.), *Handbook of Industrial and Organizational Psychology* (pp. 1527–1551). Chicago: Rand McNally.

Vroom, Victor H. (1993). Improvising and Muddling Through. In Arthur G. Bedeian (Ed.), *Management Laureates: A Collection of Autobiographical Essays* (Vol. 3, pp. 259–284). Greenwich, CT: JAI Press.

Vroom, Victor H. (1999). New Developments in Leadership and Decision Making. *OB News*, Spring, 4–5.

Vroom, Victor H. (2000). Leadership and the Decision-Making Process. *Organizational Dynamics*, 28(4), 82–94.

Vroom, Victor H., & Jago, Arthur G. (1974). Decision Making as a Social Process: Normative and Descriptive Models of Leader Behavior. *Decision Sciences*, 5, 743–769.

Vroom, Victor H., & Jago, Arthur G. (1978). On the Validity of the Vroom/Yetton Model. *Journal of Applied Psychology*, 63, 151–162.

Vroom, Victor H., & Jago, Arthur J. (1988). *The New Leadership: Managing Participation in Organizations*. Englewood Cliffs, NJ: Prentice Hall.

Vroom, Victor H., & Jago, Arthur G. (1995). Situation

Effects and Levels of Participation. *Leadership Quarterly*, 6, 169–181.

Vroom, Victor H., & Yetton, Philip W. (1973). *Leadership and Decision-Making*. Pittsburgh, PA: University of Pittsburgh Press.

Wagner, John A. (1994). Participation's Effects on Performance and Satisfaction: A Reconsideration of Research Evidence. *Academy of Management Review*, 19, 312–330.

Yukl, Gary (1989). Managerial Leadership: A Review of Theory and Research. *Journal of Management*, 15, 251–289.

Yukl, Gary (1998). *Leadership in Organizations*. Upper Saddle River, NJ: Prentice Hall.

Chapter 12

Further to the Contingency Approach in Leadership Theory

In this chapter the discussion focuses on two theoretical approaches that once again follow the contingency path that has prevailed in leadership since the Ohio State research failed to establish the dominance of consideration and initiating structure. Fred Fiedler's initial views were called *contingency theory*, reflecting the fact that his was the only such approach around at the time, and thus he had the contingency field all to himself. A subsequent, different formulation involving Fiedler has been labeled *cognitive resource theory*. Although direct concern with participation and power sharing in the beginning was minimal, such matters were considered ultimately as the theorizing progressed.

The formulations set forth by George Graen and his colleagues have focused on the dyad that is created by a superior and one subordinate, which was referred to initially as a *vertical dyad linkage* and later as a *leader-member exchange*. This is much like the individual situation considered in Victor Vroom's normative decision process theory (see chapter 11). It has in common with other leadership theories that it deals with differences in the way a manager behaves toward different subordinates and with the degree of participativeness that characterizes this behavior. In large part Graen's ideas represent a reaction against the tendency to consider leader behaviors as averages that apply to all subordinates (or all subordinate perceptions), as was done in the Ohio State University research on consideration and initiating structure (see chapter 10). In developing his own alternative views, Graen appears to have been influenced by the ideas of Daniel Katz and Robert Kahn (1966) regarding the processes of role taking in organizations and later by T. O. Jacobs's (1971) conceptions of the various kinds of exchange that occur in the leadership context.

CONTINGENCY AND COGNITIVE RESOURCE THEORIES

Contingency theory has had a long history, extending back to 1951, and has evolved slowly. Fiedler has been extremely responsive to research results, both those generated by himself and those of others. As a consequence, it is very difficult to separate research and theory as we have done in discussing other theories; there is a constant interplay back and forth. The theory is almost entirely inductive in nature, and, in fact, some scholars have questioned whether it should be labeled a theory at all. At least in the early period, contingency theory was a set of continually changing empirical generalizations.

Another distinguishing characteristic is that contingency theory has evolved around a measurement process. In fact, there was a measure before there was a theory. As a result, the usual procedures of theory construction have been reversed. Instead of proposing a set of theoretical constructs and then devising measures to match, Fiedler started with the measurement process and then sought to develop theoretical constructs to go with the measures and the research results obtained with them.

Background

Fiedler was born in Vienna in 1922 and moved to the United States shortly after Hitler invaded Austria in 1938. Ultimately he got to the University of Chicago, from which he received both his undergraduate degree and his Ph.D. in clinical psychology, replete with a personal psychoanalysis (Fiedler, 1992a). In 1951 he moved to the University of Illinois, where he eventually became a member of the psychology faculty. In this early period he spent a great deal of

time working on funded research projects, and this exposure served him well later when he needed to obtain his own research funding.

A major area of interest for many years was interpersonal perception; he pursued this subject in terms of, first, therapeutic relationships and, later, leadership. By the mid 1950s Fiedler's publications had shifted largely from clinical psychology to leadership and leader-follower relations. After his move from Illinois to the University of Washington in 1969, he began to work more closely with the business school, where he held an adjunct appointment, but his primary base has remained in psychology. He has worked extensively with graduate students and other faculty members throughout his career, thus generating a very large amount of research (see Hooijberg & Choi, 1999). Consistent with his international origins, he has remained interested in cross-cultural research and has held a number of visiting appointments at foreign universities. He retired from the University of Washington in 1992, although he has continued to publish since then (see, for instance, Fiedler, 1995, 1996; Fiedler & Macaulay, 1998).

Evolution of Contingency Theory

There have been two major stages in the development of contingency theory. The first, extending from the early 1950s to the early 1960s, was essentially exploratory. A sizable body of research data was collected, and various hypotheses were tried out in an attempt to explain the findings. During this period it is totally impossible to separate research from theory. The second stage began with the statement of contingency theory in a form much the same as that currently existing. This stage has continued to the present with the testing of these early propositions and of others that have emerged since. Thus, contingency theory overlaps with cognitive resource theory, which was first published in some form in 1979. The latter builds in part on the contingency theory foundation but adds a number of new variables and moves into new domains. In a real sense, cognitive resource theory represents stage three of the development of Fiedler's theorizing in the leadership area.

Exploratory Stage

Fiedler's original research interests involved the relationship between psychotherapist and patient, and the ways in which similarities and differences in ascribed self-concepts were related to effectiveness in such relationships (Fiedler, 1951). Self-concepts were measured originally using the Q-technique methodology, in which descriptive statements are sorted into categories in terms of the degree of approximation to perceived reality. This rather cumbersome approach was modified later as Fiedler's interests shifted to leader-member relationships in small task groups, but the concern with assumed similarities and differences among people remained.

Through a series of gradual transformations, the measurement process moved from the Q-technique to an approach of a semantic differential type (Fiedler, 1958). In this latter procedure the subject is asked to "think of the person with whom you can work best" and later to "think of the person with whom you can work least well." In both cases a description of that person then is obtained by having the subject place a mark on a 6-point graphic scale between two polar adjectives such as careless–careful, gloomy–cheerful, efficient–inefficient, and the like. The differences between the numerical descriptions applied to the most and least preferred coworkers are then used to compute an Assumed Similarity between Opposites Score (ASo) by summing over all the adjective pairs.

When the difference score is large, it means that the least and most preferred coworkers are seen as quite disparate, and thus assumed similarity is minimal; when it is small, the two are perceived as much the same. Essentially, what is involved is that when ASo is low, the person strongly rejects the least preferred coworker; job performance makes considerable difference in how people are judged.

The true meaning of the construct or constructs thus measured has presented difficulties from the beginning:

One of the main problems in the research program has been in finding an adequate interpretation of Assumed Similarity scores, especially ASo. While we have no difficulty in designating the operations which define these scores, we have encountered considerable problems in attempting to anchor their meaning within a more general framework of psychological theory. (Fiedler, 1958, p. 17)

The early resolution of this problem was as follows:

The Assumed Similarity Between Opposites Score measures an attitude toward others which may best be described as emotional or psychological distance. A person with high ASo tends to be concerned about his interpersonal relations, and he feels the need for the approval and support of his associates. In contrast, the low ASo person is relatively independent of others, less concerned with their feelings, and willing to reject a person with whom he cannot accomplish an assigned task. (Fiedler, 1958, p. 22)

The studies conducted during the 1950s used a variety of different approaches to the measurement of ASo, and thus it cannot be assumed that the findings are entirely comparable. The measures were related to indices of group effectiveness using basketball teams, surveying parties, bomber crews, tank crews, open hearth steel shops, farm supply cooperatives, and others (Fiedler, 1958; Godfrey, Fiedler, & Hall, 1959). The results indicated that ASo tends to relate to group performance only when it is moderated by some additional factor. These additional factors varied from study to study and were usually identified afterward. In some cases they were aspects of the task; in other cases they were aspects of the group's informal structure and sociometric choices or of the relationship between a leader and his key man.

Also, although generally the tendency was for the more psychologically distant, low-ASo leader to be associated with success, there were occasions when this was reversed. Thus in open hearth steel shops ASo was negatively correlated with effectiveness under certain task conditions (Cleven & Fiedler, 1956), and in farm supply cooperatives the ASo of the general manager was negatively related to success under certain sociometric conditions (Godfrey et al., 1959). However, in this 1959 study, the ASo of the informal leader of the board of directors was positively related to organizational success, again when appropriate sociometric moderators were operating.

After reading the reports of this early research, one comes away with a feeling that there is something there but with no clear conception of what that "something" is. The lack of comparability across studies; the variations in moderators, many of them identified after an extensive empirical search of possible alternatives; and the uncertainty as to whether ASo might not be subject to considerable influence by environmental circumstances including management development—all contribute to a sense of uneasiness. There is a clear need for a theoretical structure to guide research, rather than continuing to permit the research to generate a procession of short-lived theories.

Move to Formal Theory

In recognition of the need for a more stable theoretical structure, Fiedler articulated the major outlines of a contingency theory of leadership in the mid-1960s, drawing heavily on the research of the earlier, exploratory period. Fiedler's theory thus developed was first published in 1964, and its practical applications were elaborated in his 1965 work. The most comprehensive statement of this period appears in a subsequent book (Fiedler, 1967).

One change that occurred at this point is that ASo was dropped as a central theoretical variable, and one component of ASo—the least preferred coworker (LPC) rating—was substituted; descriptions of the most preferred coworker were no longer employed. Although the semantic differential approach to measurement had been used exclusively, the actual adjective pairs incorporated had tended to vary from study to study. Now the graphic scale was extended from six to eight points, and LPC was obtained by summing the values marked for each adjective pair in describing "the person with whom you can work least well." LPC and ASo are reported to correlate in the range of .80 to .90 (Fiedler, 1967).

The struggle with the meaning of the central constructs appears not to have been affected by the shift from ASo to LPC:

> It has been extremely difficult to develop an adequate and readily supportable interpretation of ASo and LPC scores. These scores do not measure attributes which correlate with the usual personality and ability tests or with attitude scales. Nor is there a one-to-one relationship between these scales and behaviors. . . . We visualize the high-LPC individual (who perceives his least-preferred coworker in a relatively favorable manner) as a person who derives his major satisfaction from successful interpersonal relationships, while the low-LPC person (who describes his LPC in very unfavorable terms) derives his major satisfaction from task performance. (Fiedler, 1967, p. 45)

Classification of Interacting Task Groups

Fiedler's theory is initially presented as applying within the domain of groups that have a task to perform or a goal to achieve, and in which this task accomplishment requires interaction among members, not a series of entirely independent efforts. Within this do-

main, groups may be classified with reference to three major factors: the leader's position power, the structure of the task, and the interpersonal relationship between leader and members.

Position power is a function of such considerations as legitimate authority and the degree to which positive and negative sanctions are available to the leader. It appears to assume the existence of an organization surrounding the group and a hierarchic means of conveying the power. The existence of position power makes the leader's job easier.

Task structure refers to the extent to which rules, regulations, job descriptions, and policies—role prescriptions—are clearly and unambiguously specified. It is easier to lead in highly structured situations because structured tasks are enforceable. Task structure is presumed to exist when decisions are subject to clear-cut verifiability in terms of correctness, goals are clearly stated and understood, multiple paths to attaining the goals are not present, and only one correct answer or solution exists. Like position power, task structure is derived from the organization.

The relationship between the leader and group members is much more an internal matter. It is reflected in the degree to which the leader is accepted and members are loyal to that person, and in the affective reactions of members to the leader. When leader-member relations are good, the leadership job is much easier. Good leader-member relations are reflected in a highly positive group atmosphere.

Using this set of classification factors, Fiedler developed a taxonomy for interacting task groups. The taxonomy does not deal with all possible alternatives. In keeping with the tendency to empirical generalization, it applies to groups of the kind that have been actually studied.

The results are as shown in table 12.1. The theoretical assumption is that these groups require different approaches to the leadership process to be effective. Subsequent analyses indicate that the degree of favorableness of the situation for the leader declines steadily from category 1 down. Actually, category 8-A was first labeled 5-A (Fiedler, 1964). However, it was later changed to 8-A to reflect its relative position on the favorableness scale (Fiedler, 1967).

Relations to Performance

Leader-member relations are the most important consideration in classifying groups, task structure is next,

TABLE 12.1 Fiedler's classification of interactive task groups

Group category	Leader-member relations	Task structure	Position power
1	Good	High	Strong
2	Good	High	Weak
3	Good	Low	Strong
4	Good	Low	Weak
5	Moderately poor	High	Strong
6	Moderately poor	High	Weak
7	Moderately poor	Low	Strong
8	Moderately poor	Low	Weak
8-A	Very poor	High	Strong

SOURCE: Adapted from Fred E. Fiedler (1967), A *Theory of Leadership Effectiveness* (New York: McGraw-Hill), 34

and position power is least important. Empirically based predictions about LPC-group effectiveness relationships are generated for each group using the degree of favorableness of the group situation for the leader as a moderator or contingency variable as in table 12.2.

In presenting this contingency model, Fiedler (1967) repeatedly refers to research data rather than to theoretical logic. Qualifications and uncertainties are numerous, again because findings from research raise questions about the influence of additional variables. There is no point at which Fiedler states exactly what his theory is, why it makes sense on logical grounds, and what its delimiting boundary statements are. In concluding his book, he cites the need for the following:

1. A better method of measuring the favorableness of the leadership situation.
2. A method of weighting leader-member relations, task structure, and position power.

TABLE 12.2 Performance relationships

Group category	Relationship of LPC to performance
1	Negative
2	Negative
3	Negative
4	Positive
5	Positive
6	Positive
7	Positive (but lower)
8	Negative
8-A	Negative

SOURCE: Adapted from Fred E. Fiedler (1967), A *Theory of Leadership Effectiveness* (New York: McGraw-Hill), 142

3. Knowledge of what really causes good or poor leader-member relations.
4. Information on the role of leader and member intelligence and ability.
5. Relating leader consideration, initiating structure, supportiveness, and so forth, to performance under varying degrees of situational favorableness.
6. Data on how task characteristics other than structure may operate.
7. Research on co-acting groups in which the members work independently.
8. Research on counteracting groups in which the members bargain with one another.
9. An understanding of individuals whose LPC scores fall in the middle range.
10. Specification of the influences of managers above the first level, line-staff status, and differing leadership styles among interacting managers.
11. Studies of the effects of training in diagnosing the favorableness of a leadership situation and in modifying it.

In none of these instances is a specific hypothesis stated, although hypotheses have been developed in some of the areas since. There is little attempt to posit a logically coherent theoretical system independent of the appeal to empirical data. The ambiguities surrounding the meaning of LPC make it almost impossible to make such an attempt.

Changes in the Basic Model

After the early statements of the theory in the mid 1960s there were a number of further developments, almost invariably as a result of subsequent research results. This continuing proliferation of both research findings and theoretical changes and extensions makes it difficult to determine which came first—and thus what is ad hoc theorizing and what is a test of theory. The following discussions focus on what at one time or another have been statements of theory; in later discussions an effort is made to identify true tests of these theoretical statements.

In subsequent presentations of the model, group category 8-A has typically been eliminated, and leader-member relations in categories 5 through 8 often have been referred to as poor rather than as moderately poor (Mitchell, Biglan, Oncken, & Fiedler, 1970). However, there are subsequent statements that the situation can be even less favorable for the leader than octant 8 indicates. There is some ambiguity on this whole matter of extreme unfavorableness.

In addition, there is some inconsistency as to which octants are predicted and which are not. Negative LPC-performance relations are anticipated for octants 1, 2, and 8 and positive relationships for octants 4 and 5. The other octants are variously ignored or even specifically not predicted; or they are predicted. When predictions are made, octant 3 is expected to yield a negative correlation, and octants 6 and 7 positive correlations (Fiedler, 1971; Fiedler & Chemers, 1974).

The original domain of the theory was that of interacting task groups. This subsequently has been extended to co-acting task groups but not to co-acting training groups that are said not to follow the contingency model (Fiedler, 1971; Fiedler & Chemers, 1974). The training groups referred to are those created to assist individuals in achieving their own goals, and in such groups a tentative suggestion is advanced that high LPC leaders consistently are more effective.

The situational favorableness dimension has been renamed *situation control and influence* in order to eliminate misunderstandings (Fiedler, 1978a). Also, a specific formula for weighting the three aspects of this dimension has been proposed. This formula calls for multiplying the leader-member relations score by 4, the task structure score by 2, and then adding these values to the position power score (Fiedler, 1978a, 1978b). Yet, it has been apparent for some time that situational control (or favorableness) is not simply a matter of the three basic factors:

It must be pointed out, of course, that the three major sub-scales of leader-member relations, task structure, and position power by no means represent the only factors which determine the leader's situational control and influence. Other studies have pointed to situational stress as affecting the leader's control; cross cultural studies have shown that linguistic and cultural heterogeneity also play a major role in determining leader control. And leader experience and training also increase control. In unusual cases this formula may thus require appropriate modification, and specific rules governing these modifications still need to be developed. (Fiedler, 1978a, p. 66)

Thus, in one study, the following hypothesis was tested:

As environmental stress increases, the relationship-oriented leader will become relatively more effective in promoting member adjustment than task-oriented leaders. Hence, under conditions of high stress, high LPC leaders should have better adjusted groups than low LPC leaders, while under conditions of low stress, low LPC leaders should have better adjusted groups than high LPC leaders. (Fiedler, O'Brien, & Ilgen, 1969)

As noted, the role of these additional factors is not stated specifically. Furthermore, there is ambiguity about the theoretical status of the middle LPC group, then estimated to be some 15 to 20 percent of the population. These individuals are considered to be different from either the high or low LPC groups and are labeled socioindependent, without a clear picture of their actual characteristics (Fiedler, 1978a). As in other areas where the theory lacks clarity, the problem is that no inherent theoretical logic exists, and therefore hypotheses await empirical findings. Each step of theory development must depend on the inductive theory generating processes of empiricism, or it does not occur.

Changing Meaning of LPC

In the early writings LPC (or ASo) was variously described as measuring psychological distance (Fiedler, 1958), controlling versus permissive attitudes in the leadership role (Fiedler, 1964), and task versus relationship orientations (Fiedler, 1967). Later, these categories were described as oversimplifications, although not necessarily totally incorrect, and two additional construct definitions were proposed.

Of these two, Fiedler most consistently has supported what he calls the *motivational hierarchy view* (Fiedler, 1972b, 1973, 1978a; Fiedler & Chemers, 1974). Essentially, this view states that leaders will manifest their primary motives under conditions over which they have little control and influence, but that when control and influence are assured (favorableness is high), primary motives are easily satisfied and it is possible to move down the hierarchy and seek to satisfy motives of secondary importance. Thus, high LPC leaders will seek relatedness under unfavorable circumstances and will seek to satisfy more task-related motives as conditions become more favorable. Low LPC leaders will manifest their primary task orientation in unfavorable situations but can be expected to shift to a more considerate, interpersonal relations-oriented pattern of behavior as their control and influence increase. In this view it is only under conditions of stress that the basic personality, or primary motive structure, reveals itself.

Sometimes, however, Fiedler is hesitant about the motivation hierarchy view:

> These findings favor a motivational hierarchy interpretation, although other interpretations, consistent with these findings, are also tenable. Whatever the precise and final interpretation of the LPC score might turn out to be, there is very little question that it measures a personality attribute which has very important consequences for organizational behavior. (Fiedler, 1978a, p. 103)

Consistent with this hesitancy is the fact that another formulation remains viable and is in fact frequently mentioned in favorable terms by Fiedler. This second view is considered to be "quite compatible with the interpretation of LPC as an index of motivational hierarchy" (Fiedler & Chemers, 1974, p. 77). It is stated in the greatest detail in Foa, Mitchell, and Fiedler (1971).

This second formulation is a cognitive interpretation. The LPC scale contains a variety of adjective pairs. Some are task oriented, some are interpersonal in nature, and some are mixed, although the majority are interpersonal. The cognitively complex individuals who differentiates among these types of adjectives are very likely to have high LPC scores because they describe their least preferred coworker positively on interpersonal adjectives and negatively on task adjectives. The low LPC, nondifferentiating people will describe their least preferred coworker negatively, not only with regard to task performance but also in interpersonal terms: as inefficient, cold, rejecting, and the like. Thus, the degree of differentiation among types of adjective pairs is the key to interpreting LPC.

A moderately favorable leadership situation is characterized by considerable differentiation among the various aspects: some are positive and some negative insofar as leader control and influence are concerned. Thus, a high LPC leader who is cognitively complex would provide a good match for such a moderately favorable situation and do well in terms of leadership performance. Very favorable or very unfavorable situations are much less differentiated in terms of the three major classification variables, and the low cognitive complexity of the low LPC leader should be a positive value. In fact, greater differentiation might well introduce problems. The key to success is a matching of differentiation levels in the leader and in the task situation.

Extensions to Leadership Dynamics

The first extensions of contingency theory into the domain of leadership dynamics involved changes that were introduced by training and increased experience. Fiedler (1972a) starts with the assumption that both leadership training and experience in the leadership role have not been shown to improve performance. He then uses an argument of the kind outlined in table 12.3 for training to show why this might be expected (Fiedler, Bons, & Hastings, 1975).

The primary consequence of the training is to increase leader influence and control through improved leader-member relations, task structuring, and position power. Such changes are equally likely to shift an individual into a good LPC-situation match or out of it, assuming that LPC itself is not changed. On the average, therefore, leadership performance will not be altered; an improvement in one person will be canceled out by the decreased effectiveness of another. In table 12.3 the extremely unfavorable situation beyond octant 8 is assumed to be rare but might occur with racially divided groups or when extreme stress is present; it appears to have much in common with the original category 8-A, although the hypothesized LPC relationship to performance is reversed.

One suggested approach to achieving effective results from training is teaching managers how to modify the favorableness of a situation to match their LPC

TABLE 12.3 Effects of leadership training on subsequent performance, as moderated by situational favorableness

Perception of situation		Effective performer	
Before training	After training	Before training	After training
1. Octant 4 ⟶ (Moderately favorable)	Octant 1 (Very favorable)	High LPC	Low LPC
2. Octant 8 ⟶ (Unfavorable)	Octant 4 (Moderately favorable)	Low LPC	High LPC
3. Beyond Octant 8 ⟶ (Extremely unfavorable)	Octant 8 (Unfavorable)	High LPC (speculative)	Low LPC

NOTE: Predicated on the hypothesis that training changes favorability as perceived by the leader to whatever next higher degree will reverse the leader effectiveness level.

SOURCE: Adapted from Fred E. Fiedler, P. M. Bons, & Limda L. Hastings (1975), New Strategies for Leadership Utilization, in W. T. Singleton & P. Spurgeon (Eds.), *Measurement of Human Resources* (New York: Halsted), 237

scores — how to engage in situational engineering. Another approach is to select for training only those individuals whose performance can be expected to improve because they will move into a good LPC-situation match, not out of it. Alternatively, all might be trained, but the training must be selectively combined with job rotation so that some return to more challenging jobs, thus offsetting the increased favorableness induced by the training for these particular individuals. Rotation of some kind, including promotion, may be the only way of offsetting the automatic increases in situational favorableness that come with increased managerial experience.

What the dynamic theory posits is that as leader control and influence (favorability) increase, for whatever reason, the performance level of the *high* LPC leader will change as in figure 12.1; the pattern is reversed for the *low* LPC leader. It should be noted that these statements (Fiedler, 1978a, 1978b) are not consistent with other statements of the theory insofar as octant 7 is concerned. Also, octant 6 is labeled as unfavorable (low control), although from the theory one would expect it to be included in the moderate range (with octant 7). These inconsistencies appear in schematic representations of the theory and are not discussed in the texts; thus the reasons for them are unclear.

The dynamic theory indicates that in selecting individuals for leadership positions, a decision should be made as to whether high initial performance is needed, or whether it is desirable to wait and permit training and experience to shift favorableness and performance levels. Also, as experience in a given job accumulates, there comes a point at which rotation

High LPC Leader

Octant:	8	7	6	5	4	3	2	1

Performance: Low ⟶ Low ⟶ High Medium ⟶ High ⟶ High ⟶ Low ⟶ Low ⟶ Low

Low LPC Leader

Octant:	8	7	6	5	4	3	2	1

Performance: High ⟶ High ⟶ Low Medium ⟶ Low ⟶ Low ⟶ High ⟶ High ⟶ High

FIGURE 12.1 Changes in performance level associated with changes in control and influence (favorability). Adapted from Fred E. Fiedler (1978), Situational Control and a Dynamic Theory of Leadership, in Bert King, Siegfried Streufert, and Fred E. Fiedler (Eds.), *Managerial Control and Organizational Democracy* (New York: Wiley), 114.

into a new, less familiar position is advisable. The theory is not specific in any general sense as to exactly how much experience is required before these hypothesized performance changes can be anticipated, although the degree of structure and complexity of the work and the intelligence of the leader are viewed as relevant (Fiedler, 1978b).

There is also some ambiguity about the effects of different kinds of training programs. Fiedler (1972a) describes human relations training as improving the leader-member relations factor and thus increasing favorableness, yet elsewhere (Fiedler, 1978a) he notes that training in participative management (which human relations training certainly is) reduces position power and accordingly decreases favorableness.

The theory also deals with changes in the degree of turbulence and instability in the organizational environment. With greater turbulence there is greater uncertainty and thus less leader control and influence. Personnel shakeups, reorganizations, new product lines, and the like introduce turbulence. Under continuing turbulent conditions the downward shift in favorableness can be expected ultimately to bring about a situation in which low LPC leaders are needed.

Multilevel and Multiple Sources Approach

Not too long ago, Roya Ayman, Martin Chemers, and Fiedler (1995) advanced the position that the strength of contingency theory is in its use of a multilevel and multiple-sources approach to defining leadership effectiveness. They note that measures of the leader's motivational orientation derive from leader responses (individual level); that aspects of the situation are determined by leader reports, as well as reports from subordinates and researchers (multilevel, multiple sources); and that outcomes are established primarily based on group performance (group level). Detailed evidence in support of this contention is set forth in table 12.4.

Evolution of Cognitive Resource Theory

Throughout the preceding discussion, and thus in the writings on contingency theory, there are references to intelligence, stress, and experience as variables that interested Fiedler and his coworkers; occasionally, they are incorporated in research, but they are never made part of contingency theory. The references to

intelligence go back at least to the 1967 book, to stress to the Fiedler et al. (1969) article, and to experience to Fiedler's (1972a) article. These three variables, however, ultimately came to serve as the core of cognitive resource theory.

Pre-Theory Views and Research

As is typical with Fiedler, a period of research dabbling preceded any resort to theorizing. The first signs of formal hypotheses, but not of the full theory, appeared in the latter 1970s. At this point Fiedler (1979) often with coworkers (Fiedler, Potter, Zais, & Knowlton, 1979) began to report on studies, carried out independent of contingency theory, which dealt with the interrelations among intelligence, stress, and experience. These studies tested formally stated hypotheses in this regard, hypotheses that had been developed out of induction derived from research that extended back at least 10 years.

The clearest statements of the two major hypotheses (other subsidiary hypotheses appeared to come and go) were the following:

1. The intelligence of staff personnel will be positively correlated with performance under stress-free conditions but uncorrelated or negatively correlated when stress with the immediate superior is high.
2. The experience of staff personnel will be uncorrelated with performance when stress with boss is low but positively correlated when stress with the immediate superior is high. (Potter & Fiedler, 1981)

Research to test these hypotheses was consistently supportive for leaders, as well as for staff personnel. However, there was evidence that stress from other sources, beyond stress with boss, could produce effects (Barnes, Potter, & Fiedler, 1983). This core of tested hypotheses later provided the basis for cognitive resource theory (Fiedler & Garcia, 1987), which then added a number of variables to this core — variables that at the time did not have the same empirical standing as intelligence, stress, and experience.

Formal Theory

The primary assumptions and hypotheses of cognitive resource theory relate to the decision tree set forth in figure 12.2. Once again, as with contingency theory,

TABLE 12.4 Contingency theory variables, level of analysis, measures used, and sources of data

Variables	Level	Measure	Source
Leader's motivational orientation	Individual	Least Preferred Coworker (LPC) Scale	Leader
Situational Control			
Group climate	Group	Group atmosphere, leader-member relationships, sociometric method	Leader or averaged group score
Task structure	Individual	Task structure scale or type of job	Leader or experimenter
Authority	Individual	Position power scale	Leader, experimenter, or superior
Effectiveness			
Satisfaction	Group or dyadic	Job Descriptor Index (JDI)	Subordinate
Performance	Group	Supervisory rating; archival data	Superior, experimenter, or org. records
Stress	Individual	Fiedler's job stress scale	Leader

SOURCE: Roya Ayman, Martin M. Chemers, & Fred E. Fiedler (1995), The Contingency Model of Leadership Effectiveness: Its Levels of Analysis, *Leadership Quarterly*, 6, 149. Copyright 1995. Reprinted with permission from Elsevier Science.

the hypotheses are stated in contingent form. The assumptions are as follows:

1. Intelligent and competent leaders make more effective plans, decisions, and action strategies than do leaders with less intelligence or competence.
2. Leaders of task groups communicate their plans, decisions, and action strategies primarily in the form of directive behavior.

These are followed by seven hypotheses dealing with the variables in figure 12.2:

1. If the leader is under stress, the leader's intellectual abilities will be diverted from the task, and the leader will focus on problems not directly related, or counter to the performance of the group task. Hence, under stress, and especially interpersonal stress, measures of leader intelligence and competence will not correlate with group performance.
2. The intellectual abilities of directive leaders correlate more highly with group performance than do intellectual abilities of nondirective leaders.
3. Unless the group complies with the leader's directions, the leader's plans and decisions will not be implemented. Hence the correlation between leader intelligence and performance is higher when the group supports

the leader than when the group does not support the leader.
4. If the leader is nondirective and the group is supportive, the intellectual abilities of group members correlate with performance.
5. The leader's intellectual abilities will contribute to group performance to the degree to which the task requires these particular abilities (i.e., is intellectually demanding).
6. Under conditions of high stress, and especially interpersonal stress, the leader's job-relevant experience (rather than his or her intellectual abilities) will correlate with task performance.
7. Directive behavior of the leader is in part determined by the contingency model elements, the leader's task motivation or relationship-motivation (determined by the Least Preferred Coworker scale), and situational control. (Fiedler & Garcia, 1987, p. 8)

Certain contingency theory variables provide the starting point, but the major goal is to identify links between leader personality (as indicated by LPC score), as well as situational control and influence, and group and organizational performance. The chain includes cognitive abilities (intelligence), stress, and experience, but directive behavior, group support, and external factors are added to this basic core.

Cognitive abilities may include measured creativity, as well as intelligence test score. Stress is most frequently a self-report of boss-induced stress. Experi-

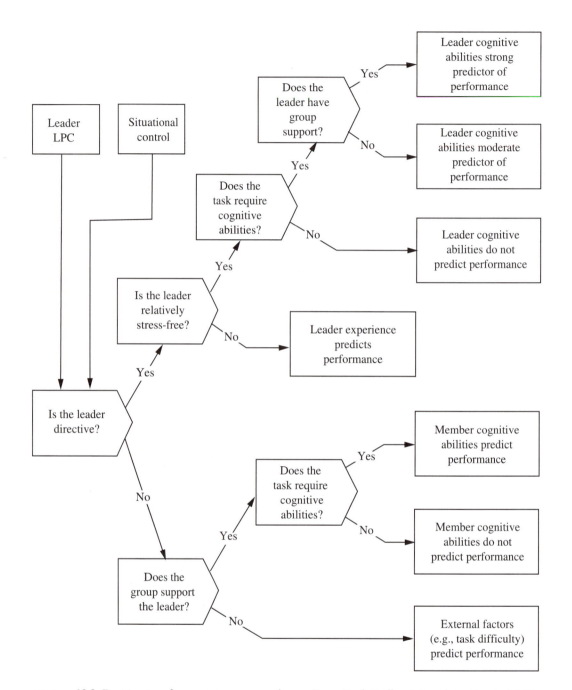

FIGURE 12.2 Decision tree for cognitive resource theory. From Fred Fiedler & Joseph E. Garcia (1987), *New Approaches to Effective Leadership: Cognitive Resources and Organizational Performance* (New York: Wiley), 9. Copyright 1987 by John Wiley. Reprinted with permission.

ence is the time served in an organization, position, or occupation; this type of index is generally unrelated to leadership performance. Directive behavior is observed behavior as reported by subordinates (often using initiating structure items from the Ohio State scales); considerate behavior, although measured, was not a powerful enough predictor to justify inclusion in the theory. Group support reflects a favorable group climate or atmosphere, and thus good leader-member relations.

The Fiedler and Garcia (1987) book contains, in addition to the theory just stated, descriptions of a large number of research studies. The amount of new theory presented is in fact quite thin (Neider & Schriesheim, 1988). However, in a later publication Fiedler (1993) attempts to remedy this problem by spelling out in more detail how LPC and situational control link to effective leader performance. The argument is as follows:

The basis for contingent relations in leadership theories lies in the nature of the situational factors, namely uncertainty and stress, which arouse leader anxiety. A change in the interaction between LPC and situational control from one of being "in match" (when the leader's LPC and situational control are likely to result in good leadership performance) to one of being not "in match" (when low-LPC leaders are in moderate-control situations and high-LPC leaders are in either high- or low-control conditions) causes the leader stress and anxiety, stemming . . . from a perceived inability to deal with situations of this nature.

Anxiety-arousing conditions cause the leader to fall back on previous successful reinforced behavior patterns. On a cognitive level these behaviors reflect what was learned from experience. On the affective level these behaviors reflect an earlier model of coping with interpersonal problems. Thus anxiety is associated with changes in leader behavior and performance; anxiety induces behavior that is simpler or represents a regression to an earlier stage in the leader's personality development.

The effectiveness of the leader's behavior and the resulting group and organizational performance depend on the degree to which the evoked leader reactions match the demands of the situation. (Fiedler, 1993, pp. 16, 19)

Theory-Forming and Theory-Testing Research

As noted, much of Fiedler and Garcia's (1987) book is devoted to descriptions of research. The status of this research in relation to the theory is at issue. The research is presented initially as an aid to theory construction. Elsewhere this same research is referred to as part of a 15-year research program that led to the development of cognitive resource theory (Fiedler & House, 1988). Thus this research would appear to be theory forming in nature. Yet there are questions as to whether this is what the theory's authors really mean—and believe.

Let us look at the nature of this body of research. There are 19 citations in the Fiedler and Garcia (1987) book that are marshaled to support cognitive resource theory and which appear to have been an outgrowth of Fiedler's research program funded primarily by grants from the U.S. military. The citations start in 1961 and spread over the period through 1983; all are pre-theory. There is a somewhat greater concentration in the latter 1970s and early 1980s because this is the period when the hypotheses dealing with intelligence, stress, and experience were tested. (Six of the citations are of this nature.)

More than two-thirds of the studies had military subjects as the focus; there are no studies conducted in the private sector. Of the 19 citations, seven are to unpublished sources (dissertations, theses, technical reports). In a number of instances the study sample is small, statistical significance is often marginal, and psychometric properties of measures are on occasion unreported. Many of the studies were originally designed for completely different purposes. All this is fine for exploratory research used to induce theory, but it is not appropriate for theory testing. On the evidence, except for the subprogram devoted to testing hypotheses that are limited to the domain of intelligence, stress, and experience, all of these indeed represent theory-forming research. Yet, as indicated in table 12.5, the authors tend on occasion to treat it as of a theory-testing nature. In what follows I do not accept this latter position; none of the research reported in the 1987 book is considered as evidence for or against the comprehensive cognitive resource theory. The book contains no new theory-testing research.

Evaluation and Impact

Fiedler's theories have in one way or another been a source of a great deal of research. He has had substantial funding, at both the universities of Illinois and Washington, and this made it possible to produce a continuing stream of studies; there have been a number of studies done on the outside as well, often initiated because someone did not believe Fiedler was

TABLE 12.5 Summary of major findings and conclusions and level of confidence in their generalizability

Hypothesis	Special limitations	Confidence level
Intelligent leaders make better plans and decisions	In low-stress conditions	Probable
Directive leaders use their intellectual abilities more	In high-control situations	High
Leaders' intelligence does not contribute to performance under stress	Especially if stress is interpersonal	High
Intellectual contribution of directive leaders is higher when group is supportive	Under low-stress conditions	Low to moderate
Group member intelligence is effectively used when the leader is nondirective and the group is supportive	Under low-stress conditions	Low to moderate
Intelligence is expected to contribute more as the intellectual demands of the task increase	General but weak; under low-stress conditions	High
Leaders' task-relevant abilities contribute to task performance	Complex	Needs further study
LPC and Situational Control predict leaders' directive behavior	Requires knowledge of task structure and other situational factors	Moderate to high

SOURCE: Fred E. Fiedler & Joseph E. Garcia (1987), *New Approaches to Effective Leadership: Cognitive Resources and Organizational Performance* (New York: Wiley), 204. Copyright 1987 by John Wiley. Reprinted with permission.

correct. As might be anticipated, this situation has sparked a great deal of controversy in the literature; commentaries, rejoinders, replies, and the like occur frequently, and Fiedler has almost invariably been in the midst of each such debate.

Status of Contingency Theory

In the early years, all this controversy, the frequent changes in theoretical position, and the uncertainty as to what was theory-forming and what was theory-testing research created a rather negative climate for contingency theory. The ideas were different (creative?) and intriguing. Yet organizational behavior as a whole was far from reaching a consensus, except perhaps to the effect that it was next to impossible to say what was going on, and that thus the most prudent approach was to delay a decision or perhaps not to express any views at all. This milieu of uncertainty prevailed up to the early 1980s when meta-analysis first came to the rescue. Figure 12.3 is presented to clarify the discussion as we now turn to these comprehensive, quantitative reviews.

The first meta-analysis was carried out by Michael Strube and Joseph Garcia (1981). This was very early in the application of the technique within organizational behavior, and the procedures used were not entirely up to the standards that have developed since. Nevertheless, the results produced substantial support for contingency theory overall and for all octants except two. There was a tendency for studies conducted by researchers who were affiliated with Fiedler to yield more positive results for the theory.

A subsequent meta-analysis reported by Lawrence Peters, Darrell Hartke, and John Pohlman (1985) appears to be somewhat more procedurally defensible. Their results, although generally supportive, indicated that the octant-specific findings in a number of cases required additional moderators beyond those of contingency theory to explain the data. Thus the theory appears to be to some degree incomplete. Octant 2 again presents problems. Support for the theory is considerably stronger when laboratory studies are used than from field studies.

Later, Chester Schriesheim, Bennett Tepper, and Linda Tetrault (1994) used meta-analysis to study the performance means in the various octants. Although the data obtained are not entirely consistent with expectations, the problems unearthed are most troublesome for the leader match application, which is discussed in a following section. In conjunction with the two previous meta-analyses, the findings from this study are interpreted as providing "more than sufficient evidence to conclude that the contingency model warrants further investigation and exploration (rather than abandonment)" (Schriesheim et al., 1994, p. 572). I take this to mean that the theory is more right than wrong, but that further adjustments and elaborations are needed.

In reviewing the research on contingency theory, including the meta-analyses, Bernard Bass (1990) notes that although they are outnumbered by the positive findings, a number of unsupportive studies do exist. In some of the latter, Fiedler has pointed to design problems that he feels invalidate the results. On the evidence, these criticisms appear justified in some cases, but not always. Nevertheless, there remain a goodly number of studies, usually of a field nature and not conducted by Fiedler's group, that do not support the theory. Bass also points to evidence indicating that the variability of validity coefficients within each octant is extremely large, presumably in part at least as a result of the inclusion of nonsupportive studies. The chance that a particular study will not produce the theoretically anticipated results in a given octant is substantial. Yet only the octant 2 data fail completely to support the theory. Fiedler contends, in the latter instance, that the theory is really one of

three zones as specified in figure 12.3, not eight octants (see House & Aditya, 1997). Thus, the results for octant 2 would average with those for octants 1 and 3 and obliterate the departure from theory. This appears to represent a post hoc adjustment in the theory to make it fit the data, however.

Overall, despite the evident support for contingency theory's validity, there are remaining problems. Yet attempts to develop alternative approaches to explain the findings generated around the theory have not produced anything better (Schriesheim et al., 1994). The alternatives considered to date do not predict the pattern of the data as well as contingency theory does.

LPC still represents a source of difficulties. Having a theory depend on one measure whose meaning is not clearly established cannot be a plus for any theory. Although Fielder now appears to have settled on the motivational hierarchy interpretation, there continues to be some disagreement within his camp (Ayman et al., 1995). In the early years, there were serious questions about the psychometric properties of LPC, but these have been largely resolved; the remaining problem is one of construct validity.

Perhaps the best evidence for an LPC problem is a study by John Kennedy (1982) that focused on the middle 25 percent of the population and the scores covered by this group. Fiedler typically identified such a group, although recently specifying it as smaller, at 10 percent or less of the population, and essentially

	Octants							
	1	2	3	4	5	6	7	8
When leader-member relations are	Good	Good	Good	Good	Poor	Poor	Poor	Poor
and task structure is	High	High	Low	Low	High	High	Low	Low
and position power is	Strong	Weak	Strong	Weak	Strong	Weak	Strong	Weak
	↓	↓	↓	↓	↓	↓	↓	↓
Effective group performance requires a leader motivated by	Task accomplishment (low LPC)			Good interpersonal relations (high LPC)				Task accomplishment (low LPC)

High ← SITUATIONAL CONTROL AND INFLUENCE → Low

FIGURE 12.3 The octants of contingency theory. Adapted from Fred Fiedler & Martin M. Chemers (1974), *Leadership and Effective Management* (Glenview, IL: Scott, Foresman), 80.

excluded it from contingency theory's domain. Kennedy finds, however, that his middle LPC group performs well in all leadership situations, and that in five of the eight octants these were the best-performing leaders. In octants 1, 5, and 7 the relationship between LPC and performance was significantly curvilinear, and these results are not consistent with the linear hypothesis that is posited by contingency theory. A possibility exists that LPC measures two aspects of personality: a dimension from strong to weak work motivation at the low end, and a dimension from sociophobia to sociophilia at the high end. In any event, Kennedy's findings deserve more research attention than they have received. It is possible that they contain the key to the meaning of LPC.

Fiedler's Own Evaluation

For many years Fiedler's personal view of what he had wrought was primarily manifest in his replies to attacks. He consistently defended his theory, and he did so by referring to research which he believed supported his positions. Later, in the 1990s, Fiedler became somewhat more reflective and in the process provided more insight into the underpinnings of his theory. He believes that the greatest contribution is "the conceptualization of leadership effectiveness as the product of an interaction between personality and situational factors and empirical support for this proposition" (Fiedler, 1991, p. 503). The criticism that he feels is particularly justified is that the contingency model itself is something of a "black box" that does not immediately reveal the reasons for the relationships it describes and predicts. As a result, true understanding is at a minimum.

Although he indicates an appreciation for deductive theorizing, Fiedler notes that this is impossible for him because he is constantly distracted by data: "For me, developing hypotheses has always been an inductive, messy, a posteriori process" (Fiedler, 1995, p. 453). Further to this point, he says:

> The model's greatest weaknesses arise from its inductive development. The LPC construct has little face or concurrent validity, and even evidence for its construct validity requires some faith. The lack of process-based explanations for performance effects makes both the understanding and application of the model more difficult. (Ayman et al., 1995, p. 162)

Yet major strengths are emphasized as well:

1. The conceptual and statistical independence of the theory's central constructs
2. The theory's emphasis on independent and, where possible, objective measures of important organizational outcomes such as group productivity
3. The theory's relatively lesser vulnerability to the invalidation of its constructs and findings as a result of information-processing biases and methodological weaknesses
4. The theory's proven predictive validity (p. 162)

Status of Cognitive Resource Theory

Cognitive resource theory has proved to be as diverse in the reactions it has elicited as contingency theory. House and Aditya (1997) feel that the empirical support for the theory is strong and that it has important implications for selection and situational management. Gary Yukl (1998) feels that the research results have been inconsistent across studies and that because a number of methodological weaknesses plague the studies, it is difficult to interpret them; he also points to various conceptual weaknesses.

The operationalization of experience and intelligence within the theory has produced particular problems. In the former instance, research suggests that prior experience that is *relevant* for performance in the present job is the factor that should be used, rather than merely organizational tenure (Bettin & Kennedy, 1990). With regard to intelligence, the argument is that relevant special abilities should be invoked rather than general intelligence. This has not been tested, but it is clear that Fiedler tends to underestimate the role of intelligence in managerial performance when he says that the relationship is low and weak. He draws on various publications of Edwin Ghiselli to support this interpretation, but, in fact, Ghiselli (1966) reports a highly significant correlation in the upper .20s and makes intelligence one of his more important indices of managerial talent.

There are also conceptual problems in the theory's handling of the stress variable. Fiedler, Earl Potter, and Mark McGuire (1992) make the point, which is emphasized elsewhere also, that the stress central to cognitive resource theory is the type generated by the boss for the leader. First, this does not take into account the fact that stress in this dyad is often occasioned by antiauthority attitudes in the leader; the cause is not always the boss. Second, no logical rationale is provided for the use of this particular type of stress. One would think that any stress that produced anxiety would impede functioning in the same manner. This interpretation is reinforced by the reported finding that stress-reduction training produces a major increase in the performance of more intelligent subjects over less intelligent ones (Fiedler, 1996).

Theory-testing research on cognitive resource theory has not been extensive and tends to deal with segments of the model rather than with the whole. The early research on the relationships among intelligence, stress, and experience continues to be given considerable attention (Fiedler, 1992b).

The importance of the directive behavior component of the model has also been demonstrated; this, incidentally, is entirely in line with Vroom's proposition from normative decision process theory (see chapter 11). The leader's cognitive resources contribute to group performance when the leader is knowledgeable and directive in getting that knowledge put to use (Murphy, Blyth, & Fiedler, 1992). In contrast, group members' task-related knowledge is used only if the leader is nondirective and participative. Thus, bright leaders should be directive, because they have ideas to convey (under low stress). Less bright leaders should be participative, because they need the ideas of the group. However, when bright leaders are under stress, they tend to impede group performance by talking a lot without contributing useful ideas (Gibson, Fiedler, & Barrett, 1993). All of this is germane to Frank Heller's competence theory and the underutilization of group member skills (see chapter 11).

Most of the research testing cognitive resource theory formulations has involved Fiedler, as the citations listed previously indicate (see also Fiedler & Macaulay, 1998). There is a need for data from other sources, and a study by Robert Vecchio (1990) provides some of this. The major positive finding from this research once again involved the directive behavior variable. When directive and nondirective situations were compared, the former produced more positive correlations between intelligence and group performance than the latter. Other aspects of the theory either could not be tested adequately or leave many questions about the procedures employed (see Fiedler, Murphy, & Gibson, 1992).

Overall, I believe that there is good support for the intelligence-stress-experience component of the theory in some form, although the specific nature of the variables needs further work. Also the role of the directive behavior segment appears to be well delineated. It would be desirable to see this role studied more, however, outside the military. It is possible that the military situation conditions people to be especially responsive to directive approaches. The ties to LPC and contingency theory have not been adequately studied, although cognitive resource theory could be cut loose from these ties with no great loss in understanding or prediction. Research that incorporates all of the theory's variables is lacking, and without it full support should be withheld.

At present, the major theoretical thrust appears to be toward getting into the "black box" that contains an understanding of why contingency theory is as it is. The previous quote from Fiedler (1993) dealing with the extent to which LPC and situational control are "in match" and reactions to this match (or lack of match) is a reflection of this thrust. In addition, Chemers (1993, 1997) has been developing an integrative theory of leadership that deals with these issues.

Leader Match Application

For some time contingency theorists have advocated a process of situational engineering whereby an individual leader is placed in a situation appropriate to his or her LPC score (Fiedler, 1965). For this approach to work for a given organization, LPC would have to be stable over time, and performance levels would have to be essentially the same across octants. In other words, with LPC appropriate to the situation, it should not matter whether octant 1 or 5 or 8 — or whatever — was used. Furthermore, this approach assumes that it is easier to change aspects of the situation, either by reengineering the job itself or by transfer to a different position, than it is to change the person, and in particular those aspects of the person that LPC measures. All of these assumptions and expectations are built into the leader match procedure, whereby individuals learn to modify their leadership situations to provide a degree of situational favorableness or control appropriate to their LPC.

Leader match training uses a programmed learning text. The process starts with a self-measurement of LPC and then with measures of the various aspects of the leadership situation — leader-member relations, task structure, and position power — to obtain an index of situational favorableness. Next, the individual learns how to match leadership style (LPC level) with the situation and subsequently to influence or self-engineer it to his or her personality. This may be done through the use of a variety of techniques, from influencing one's superior to actually moving to a new position. There is also a section on how to engineer the leadership situations of subordinate managers for those at the second level of supervision and above.

The training is self-paced with appropriate measurement instruments incorporated into the text. It adheres closely to the theory and uses theoretical discussions, problems, questions, and feedback statements. As a programmed learning text, it appears to be conceptually adequate. However, the real test is in the research on it.

There have been two editions of this training manual. The first was Fiedler, Chemers, and Mahar (1976). The second, which came eight years later (Fiedler & Chemers, 1984), is much the same as the first edition, except that there is a technical note on the effectiveness of leader match evaluation studies; some new normative data; and a new chapter that deals with intelligence, boss stress, job intellectual demands, and the like. It is reported that leader match in one of these two forms has been widely used for management development purposes.

Leader Match: Pro and Con

The amount of research conducted by Fiedler and his coworkers to evaluate the effects of leader match training is substantial (Fiedler & Mahar, 1979; Fiedler & Chemers, 1984; Fiedler & Garcia, 1985). Typically, this training has compared the subsequent performance of experimental (trained) and control leaders. The results quite consistently indicate that exposure to leader match theory or training does improve leader performance. In many instances, these are little studies with small samples and marginal significance. Occasionally leader match is bundled in with some other training program so that it is impossible to separate the effects of each. But there are studies of leader match only with samples of respectable size. That the sum total of these results from studies both strong and weak adds up to an impressive endorsement of leader match training is attested to by a meta-analysis of management development evaluation research that found leader match to be highly effective (Burke & Day, 1986). An additional point in its favor is that it costs little to conduct, being self-administered. This is the pro side.

On the con side, however, are a number of disturbing findings. Leader match does not always follow the same procedures for operationalizing variables that are used in the research to validate contingency theory. A question arises as to whether these departures from past practice, presumably intended to make the approach more palatable to practitioners, introduce a real change in such aspects as the classification into octants. The answer is that the changes do make a difference (Jago & Ragan, 1986). Leader match is not a direct offshoot of contingency theory, and thus it cannot legitimately claim that body of theory and research in its support. There has been some arguing back and forth on this matter, but the evidence indicating that leader match and contingency theory differ is quite compelling.

Another problem for situational engineering and leader match is inherent in the following quote:

> Data reported by Fiedler (1967, p. 259) show a steady decline in performance from favorable to unfavorable situations for an unstructured task and rather erratic variations for two structured tasks. Yet Fiedler (1965) has suggested situational engineering as an alternative to leadership training. In other words change the situation—shift a group up or down on the favorableness dimension—to fit the leadership style. But if mean productivity is not constant across situations, one might find that a leader who has the wrong leadership style in one situation may become even less effective when his group is changed to a second situation where, according to the model, his leadership style is right. (Shiflett, 1973, pp. 435–436)

Certain evidence makes it apparent that, indeed, "mean productivity is not constant across situations" (Schriesheim et al., 1994). Shifting people around across octants does not seem to be a very good idea.

Furthermore, there is reason to believe that those who experience leader match training often do not understand the material and thus are in no position to manipulate situational variables as the training prescribes. Also, the LPC score results may not be accepted, and, accordingly, adapting the situation to them may not even be attempted. All this means is that the positive training results may well have nothing at all to do with contingency theory and situational engineering (Kabanoff, 1981).

A more likely explanation, given what is now known, is that leader match training serves to increase personality factors such as the belief in one's ability to change things, self-confidence, self-efficacy, and managerial motivation, and that, in turn, these make for more effective managerial performance (Bass, 1990). It seems very unlikely that contingency theory is the cause of the results.

We have previously considered the stability of LPC. Under normal circumstances, it tends to remain stable, and it is because of this that Fiedler argues for the need to resort to situational engineering. But, clearly, there are conditions under which considerable variation can be expected (Rice, 1978), which suggest the possibility that concerted efforts to change LPC in a consistent manner might prove successful. The lack of reports of results from such efforts in the literature does not demonstrate that situational engineering is more easily accomplished. The problem is that as long as the true nature of LPC remains an enigma, it is hard to develop training programs to change it.

Although Fiedler has considered other possible applications of his theories, beyond leader match, particularly with regard to the use of LPC in selection, nothing specific has been formulated in this regard. Even on the leader match front, things were rather quiet during the 1990s and into the 2000s.

VERTICAL DYAD LINKAGE AND LEADER-MEMBER EXCHANGE THEORY

Theorizing about vertical dyad linkage and leader-member exchange is the product of George Graen, who has published with a number of different coworkers, primarily his doctoral students. In the very early period, Graen was concerned with the various roles people assume in organizations and with what he called the role-making process. As this approach increasingly began to focus on the superior-subordinate dyad, the term *vertical dyad linkage (VDL)* was adopted. Then in the early 1980s *leader-member exchange (LMX)* replaced VDL as more appropriately descriptive of the processes involved, although some publications of this period use the term *vertical exchange* as well, and some refer to *dyadic career reality theory*.

Background

Graen studied at the University of Minnesota and received his Ph.D. in industrial psychology from there in 1969. Subsequently, he took a faculty position in

the psychology department at the University of Illinois. In 1978 he moved to the business school at the University of Cincinnati, where he remained for a number of years. Recently, upon retirement from Cincinnati, he accepted a position at the University of Southwestern Louisiana. Earlier, in 1972, he held a visiting appointment at Keio University in Japan, and an interest in Japanese management that was kindled at that time has continued to exert an influence on his research.

Graen's initial research efforts involved expectancy theory (see chapter 8). He extended the Vroom model, moving beyond motivation into leadership and taking the aspect of role perception, which was also included in the Porter/Lawler theory, and developing it into a much more central theoretical concept (Graen, 1969). His idea of work roles, and the effective performer work role, led to the role-making formulations and thus to the beginnings of vertical dyad linkage theory.

Theoretical Statements on Vertical Dyad Linkages

Graen's concept of the vertical dyad refers to the relationship between a supervisor and an individual subordinate. There are as many such dyads in a work group as there are immediate subordinates to the unit's manager. For theoretical purposes, two types of dyadic relationships are important. These are variously referred to as relationships with informal assistants and ordinary members (Graen, 1976), leadership and supervisory relationships (Dansereau, Graen, & Haga, 1975), in-group and out-group relationships (Graen & Cashman, 1975), and high- and low-quality relationships (Graen & Schiemann, 1978).

Role of Dyadic Relationships

The essential concept is that when the relationship between manager and subordinate is of the informal assistant, leadership, in-group, high-quality type, very different kinds of outcomes in terms of job performance ratings, job satisfaction (including turnover), and experienced problems are to be anticipated. Specifically, under these circumstances, performance ratings will be higher, subordinate satisfaction greater (and turnover lower), and problems with supervision fewer.

The process involved has been summarized as follows:

The inputs to team development are the characteristics of each member and those of their leader. These characteristics are harnessed to outputs, such as member performance, satisfaction, and job problems, through their interactions with leader-member exchanges. Based on the compatibility of some combination of member's characteristics and some combination of leader's characteristics, a leader initiates either an in-group or an out-group exchange with his member early in the life of the dyadic relationship. (Graen & Cashman, 1975, pp. 154–155)

The major early indicator of what type of relationship will subsequently emerge is the degree to which negotiating latitude is extended by the manager. When the manager is relatively open in extending individualized assistance to work through job problems, an in-group relationship is likely:

[Such relationships] involve interlocking different task behaviors and forming different working relationships than do out-group exchanges. Specifically, in-group exchanges will involve, first, the interlocking of more responsible tasks accepted by members and higher levels of assistance provided by leaders; and second, working relationships will be characterized by greater support, sensitivity, and trust than occurs in out-group exchanges. Furthermore, the mechanism of this interlocking of member and leader behaviors probably is reciprocal reinforcement. . . . Once these structures emerge, they demonstrate high stability over time. Thus, until the nature of the linkage becomes altered, both member and leader behavior can be both understood and predicted over time. (Graen & Cashman, 1975, p. 155)

When an in-group relationship develops, leadership occurs in that behaviors depend on the interpersonal exchange, not formal authority. The leader gives resources at his or her command, and the member gives expanded effort and time. The leader loses control and becomes more dependent on the outcomes of negotiations with the member, while the member risks receiving less than equitable rewards and the unilateral institution of supervision. In contrast, under an out-group relationship supervision does exist, and the employment contract with its implicit acceptance of legitimate authority in exchange for pay and benefits governs.

The in-group relationship exhibits many of the characteristics of participative decision making and of job enrichment as well:

The superior for his part can offer the outcomes of job latitude, influence in decision making, open and honest communications, support of the member's actions and confidence in and consideration for the member, among others. The member can reciprocate with greater than required expenditures of time and energy, the assumption of greater responsibility, and commitment to the success of the entire unit or organization, among others. (Dansereau et al., 1975)

Extensions to the Vertical Dyad Model

Subsequently, the basic dyadic model was extended one level upward to include the manager's superior as well as subordinate (Cashman, Dansereau, Graen, & Haga, 1976). The hypothesis is that the nature of this manager-superior relationship (in-group or out-group) will affect the extent to which the manager can bring resources to the manager-subordinate relationship and thus exert an indirect effect on subordinate outputs such as satisfaction, job problems, termination, and the like.

A second extension relates to the matter of agreement between the manager and the dyadic subordinate. Two hypotheses are stated:

If a leader and a member have a high-quality dyadic relationship, the leader should be more aware of the problems confronting the member on the job. Hence, their perceptions should be more alike regarding the severity of job problems than those of a leader and a member in a low-quality relationship.

Another important set of variables . . . includes sensitivity of the leader to the member's job and attention, information, and support given the member by the leader. . . . If the quality of the interdependencies is high, leader and member should agree more accurately about these variables than those locked into lower quality relationships. (Graen & Schiemann, 1978, pp. 206–207)

Theoretical Statements about Leader-Member Exchanges

Initially at least, the shift to the leader-member exchange designation had relatively little meaning for the theory. However, it has come to have considerable significance in that the result has been to focus attention on the relationship in the dyad—the characteristics of that relationship and the ways in which the dyadic relationship is tied to organizational outcome variables (Graen & Uhl-Bien, 1991). In contrast, the vertical dyad linkage theory dealt with differential in-group and out-group member types within the work group, as well as with differentiation that resulted from resource constraints on managers, thus forcing them to develop one or more trusted assistants to aid in the functioning of the unit.

Relationship-Based Approach

One statement of the evolving theory introduces the concept of dyadic career reality to focus on the dyadic relationship (Graen & Scandura, 1986). This concept is defined as "a system of components and relationships; involving both members of a dyad; in interdependent patterns of behavior; sharing mutual outcome instrumentalities; and producing concepts of environments, cause maps, and value" (p. 150). This is a restatement of the former in-group process. Table 12.6 outlines the procedures through which dyadic career realities develop. Role concepts once again become central to the theory. Dyadic career realities often involve dyads of managers, and these managers exchange positional resources to their mutual benefit.—Resources noted include information, influence, tasks, latitude, support, and sensitivity (concern). The theory now includes not only vertical dyads, but horizontal and diagonal dyads as well, although little is said with regard to these latter.

A companion piece develops these ideas further, with special reference to the performance of unstructured tasks (Graen & Scandura, 1987). The authors invoke Chester Barnard's (1938) idea of an inducement-contributions balance to explain what happens within a vertical dyad. The exchange involved is depicted in figure 12.4, which shows how the relationship solidifies as it moves from role taking to role making to what is now called *role routinization*. Dyadic career reality implies an exchange of positional resources, as stated previously. When routinized and thus stabilized, the dyadic relationship involves trust, respect, loyalty, liking, intimacy, support, openness, and honesty.

The total process depicted in figure 12.4 may or may not move through to completion. If it does not, the leader-member exchange remains of low quality. When certain variables take high values the role-emergence process is more likely to reach completion.

TABLE 12.6 The normative model for the development of dyadic career realities

---

Role finding: The discovery of the (1) functional definitions of official duties and responsibilities, (2) the instrumental value of resources, and (3) the utility of formal written procedures

Procedure
1. Treat the official written role as problematic
2. Generate alternative definitions of duties and responsibilities, resources, and procedures
3. Reduce the alternative definitions to several multiple working hypotheses

Role making: The enactment of interlocking behaviors

Procedure
1. Treat dyadic working relationships as problematic
2. Generate alternative possibilities of task assignments, resource allocations, interdependencies, and inducements for contributions
3. Reduce the alternative possibilities to a feasible set
4. Enact interlocking behavior cycles

Role implementation: The assembly of interlocked behavior cycles into systems according to rules

Procedure
1. Treat systems as problematic
2. Generate alternative models of systems
3. Reduce the alternative models to prioritized set
4. Construct the systems according to the model as prioritized

---

SOURCE: George B. Graen & Terri A. Scandura (1986), A Theory of Dyadic Career Reality, *Research in Personnel and Human Resource Management*, 4, 153. Copyright 1986. Reprinted with permission from Elsevier Science.

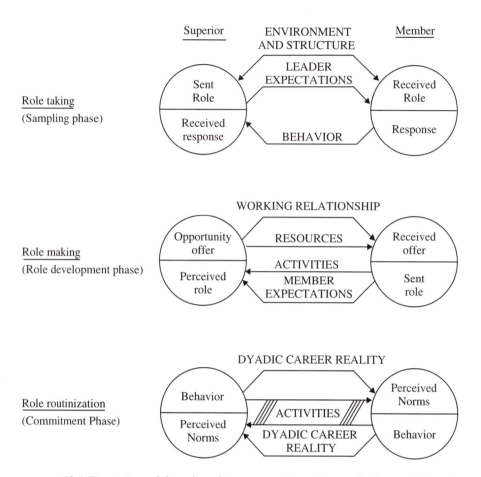

FIGURE 12.4 Description of the role-making process. From George B. Graen & Terri A. Scandura (1987), Toward a Psychology of Dyadic Organizing, *Research in Organizational Behavior*, 9, 180. Copyright 1987. Reprinted with permission from Elsevier Science.

For this to occur the superior should have the following: (1) adequate latitude in task assignment and a need to exercise it, (2) reasonably attractive positional and personal (power) resources and the imagination to employ them, and (3) some members possessing job growth potential (ability) and the motivation to accept challenges beyond their job description (Graen & Scandura, 1987, p. 185).

Leaders tend to select members for dyadic relationships who are dependable in that they can be counted on to complete tasks as the leader would if necessary, and who collaborate effectively (Graen, 1990). This selection may well eventuate in a productive leadership system that is said to expand the influence and commitment of a unit to capitalize on opportunities and available resources, as well as member abilities and motives, so as to integrate dyadic roles into cohe-

sive, coordinated management teams and larger networks. Once engaged in such a productive leadership system, managers are hypothesized to attempt to replicate it in new job situations in the future throughout their careers.

More recently, in the 1990s, leader-member exchange theory has begun to consider the role-making process in terms of a classification using stranger–acquaintance–maturity stages (Graen & Wakabayashi, 1994). At the initial stranger stage, the leader and member interact only on a limited basis and what interaction there is is of a strictly contractual nature. As the relationship moves to the acquaintance stage, it becomes more involved, but trust and loyalty remain less than fully developed. At the mature stage, a high degree of trust, respect, and obligation are achieved; now the potential for incremental influence is substantial, and members are encouraged to grow beyond the formal work contract and help redesign the unit. Role finding occurs at the stranger stage when LMX is low in the dyad. Role making occurs in the acquaintance stage when LMX is medium. Role implementation occurs at the mature leadership stage when LMX is high. Leadership making is said to occur as networks are built up, one relationship at a time, consisting of people both within and outside a team.

Dyadic Partnership Building

At this point leadership is defined as a partnership among dyadic members, a partnership that should (normatively) be developed if at all possible:

> Rather than managers treating some employees more favorably than others (as the "differentiation" approach of VDL suggests), this stage states that managers should provide all employees access to the process of LMX by making the initial offer to develop LMX partnerships to each subordinate. Making the partnership offer to every subordinate has a twofold effect: (1) the LMX process may be perceived as more equitable (and the model more palatable to practitioners and students who may have been uncomfortable with the inequity issue), and (2) the potential for more high-quality relationship development (partnerships) would increase the potential for more effective leadership and expanded organizational capability. (Graen & Uhl-Bien, 1995, p. 229)

Increasing the number of high-quality relationships in this way should improve unit performance. Although the theoretical objective is to teach and motivate leaders to develop high-quality partnerships with all group members, the reality that this may not in fact occur in every instance is recognized.

Expansion to Larger Components

Throughout the articles referenced in the preceding section there are relatively brief discussions of horizontal dyads, diagonal dyads, systems of interdependent dyads, combinations of dyads, network assemblies (of dyads), and the like. The idea is that one could map a complex interlocking leadership structure as an overlay on the task structure of an organization. Such a structure of multiple high-quality dyads should yield much added value in terms of organizational per-

formance. Self-directed teams are said to function most effectively when contrived out of the dyadic processes we have been considering (Graen & Uhl-Bien, 1991).

Expansion to this level, although contemplated, has not been the subject of empirical investigation (Graen & Uhl-Bien, 1995). This is the path down which leader-member exchange theory is headed, nevertheless, and the beginnings of a formal theory for this purpose have been proposed (Uhl-Bien, Graen, & Scandura, 2000). The idea is that multiple high-quality dyads offer a source of competitive advantage through the social capital thus created. This approach draws on the literature that deals with social capital, strategic human resource management, social network theory, and, of course, LMX theory.

Theory-Related Research in Which Graen Has Participated

Initial research by Graen and his coworkers used the leader behavior description measures of consideration and initiating structure but employed an individual subordinate level of analysis rather than average data for each work group, as in the original Ohio State studies. The nature of the analytical approach used in this research was highly consistent with the vertical dyad linkage model. However, the studies were not carried out as tests of that particular set of theoretical hypotheses; rather, they test certain hypotheses related to the relative predictive power of expectancy and equity theories (Dansereau, Cashman, & Graen, 1973), to the validity of the man-in-the-middle interpretation of managerial role stress (Graen, Dansereau, & Minami, 1972b), and to the nature of performance feedback (Graen, Dansereau, & Minami, 1972a; Graen, Dansereau, Minami, & Cashman, 1973). These studies are important, nevertheless, because they represent the empirical base from which vertical dyad linkage theory subsequently developed.

Studies Using Indirect Criteria

The next set of studies moved closer to actually testing vertical dyad linkage theory formulations without actually achieving this goal. In these cases actual measures of the quality of the dyadic relationships were not obtained, but other indices that yielded results consistent with theoretical expectations were used to differentiate the groups studied.

Thus, in one case newly hired clerical employees at a university were differentiated into those who separated relatively quickly and those who did not. Analysis of data obtained over a period of 16 weeks indicated that there was greater role conflict and ambiguity in relationships with superiors among those who subsequently left employment (Johnson & Graen, 1973). The design of this study does not permit direct extrapolation to vertical dyad linkage hypotheses, but the relationships are consistent with them.

The same is true of another analysis of additional data obtained from the same subjects (Graen, Orris, & Johnson, 1973). In this instance the group was differentiated not by job tenure but in terms of the extent to which the individual viewed the job as career relevant. Those who did not consider the job to be career relevant tended to have more turnover, but they also evidenced less communication with superiors, including less participation in decisions, as well as other responses consistent with an out-group status.

In another case, a group of university housing and food service managers was split in terms of their degree of professionalism and studied over a 9-month period subsequent to an extensive reorganization (Haga, Graen, & Dansereau, 1974). The findings are consistent with an interpretation that describes the professionals as possessing in-group status. In particular, they appear to be engaged in a sizable amount of role-making or role-altering behavior that is entirely consistent with theoretical expectations under conditions of negotiated roles.

Tests of Propositions

A subsequent analysis of data obtained from this same group of university managers is more directly supportive of the theory (Dansereau, Graen, & Haga, 1975). In this case, a measure of negotiating latitude perceived by the dyadic subordinate early in the relationship was used as a basis for differentiation. This early index of negotiating latitude proved to be a good predictor of in-group and out-group status throughout the 9 months of the study. In-group members received more supervisory attention and greater support, experienced fewer job problems, perceived their superior as more responsive to their needs and as communicating with them more, were evaluated as behaving in a manner closer to superior expectations, indicated more job satisfaction, and were less likely to separate. This pattern of results is quite congruent with the theory.

A replication study with a new sample that extended the measures to include communication frequency, bases of influence, and dyadic loyalty provides further support (Graen & Cashman, 1975). Clearly the in-group members were more involved in all aspects of their work and expended greater time and effort; they influenced decisions more and were in a better position to do so. Outcomes such as rated performance, job satisfaction, and job problems were all more positive for in-group members, and, as expected, dyadic loyalty and trust were greater in these exchanges. In this study data were obtained on the use of various bases of influence or power. Referent and expert power characterize the in-group exchanges, consistent with their more participative, negotiated nature. There is also some basis for concluding that coercive or legitimate (bureaucratic) influence characterizes the out-group exchanges. In any event, these findings are consistent with the hypothesized leadership-supervision distinction.

A study by Graen and Steven Ginsburgh (1977) partially replicates the earlier study involving the career relevance of the job (Graen, Orris, & Johnson, 1973) and extends it by investigating the quality of the dyadic relationship, in this instance as perceived by the superior, not the subordinate, as in previous studies. Although university clerical employees also were used in this study, they were not new employees. The sample is essentially the same as that used in the Graen and James Cashman (1975) research.

The findings indicate that in-group subordinates were given greater amounts of sensitivity and self-determination by their superiors. They also were rated as better performers. However, the anticipated job satisfaction differences did not emerge, even though turnover was greater among out-group subordinates. Taken as a whole, the data show that the quality of the dyadic relationship is associated with work outcomes but that the career relatedness of the work accounts for additional variance.

Research on the Extended Model

A reanalysis of the original data derived from university housing and food managers (Dansereau et al., 1975) extends those findings to the level of the superior's superior (Cashman et al., 1976). The data provide some support for the view that whether a superior has an in- or out-group relationship with the person above affects the outcomes from dyadic relationships with subordinates. In particular, when the upward exchange is of an out-group nature, subordinates tend to perceive job problems, especially problems in bringing about change. They are also less satisfied with their rewards and the technical competence of their superior. Although the findings with regard to the various effects of higher-level relationships on job satisfaction are less pervasive than those for the immediate dyad, significant results do occur. This study did not yield the expected results for the turnover outcome, however.

A later study, also conducted within the administrative components of a university, yields similar support for the effect of the quality of the upper-level dyadic relationship at lower levels (Graen, Cashman, Ginsburgh & Schiemann, 1977). However, the specific types of job problems and other factors affected are frequently quite different. These differences in results in the two settings are attributed to variations in the organizational contexts of the studies — in flux in the first instance and stable in the second.

An investigation carried out to determine whether greater perceptual agreement within the dyad was to be anticipated as a function of the quality of the relationship provides generally supportive results (Graen & Schiemann, 1978). In this case, quality was measured at the subordinate level with a measure of known good reliability. Again the samples were obtained within the administrative contexts of universities and overlapped prior studies. The findings indicate that perceptual agreements are consistently less pronounced when out-group dyads are involved.

During the 1970s, research that did not involve Graen appears to be nonexistent. Also this research tended to draw on a very small number of subject pools, most of them apparently from one university. In many respects the development of vertical dyad linkage theory seems to reflect the use of grounded theory in that the formulations emerged from concentrated study of a single context. Subsequently, data to test the theory were obtained from a substantially different university setting, but still a university (Liden & Graen, 1980). This study yielded strong support for vertical dyad theory, except in the case of satisfaction measures. Perceptual agreement was also found in accordance with the extended model.

Measurement of Leader-Member Exchange

Over the years the instrument used to determine the quality of a leader-member exchange as perceived by either member of a dyad has grown in length from 2 items to 14; there are at least seven versions. Most recommended is the 7-item measure that correlates well with the longer versions (Graen & Uhl-Bien, 1995). LMX appears to be constituted out of three dimensions: (1) mutual respect for the capabilities of the other, (2) anticipation of deepening trust with the other, and (3) expectation that interacting obligation will grow over time. These dimensions are highly related so that development of separate measures does not appear justified. A core item reads, "How would you characterize your working relationship with your leader (your member)?" It is rated on a 5-point scale from ineffective to effective.

An example of the use of such a leader-member exchange scale involved a comparison of LMX with average leadership style in predicting the turnover criterion among computer personnel of a public utility. In this instance the 5-item measure was used, and turnover was high. Leader-member exchange proved to be a much stronger predictor of turnover than average leadership style, accounting for three times more variance. The unique exchange between leader and member appears to be what influences a person to remain in the organization (Graen, Liden, & Hoel, 1982).

Research on Dyadic Partnership Building

This research involved efforts to improve the quality of all dyad relationships with the objective of increasing performance levels; thus it is a test of the normative theory, not just the descriptive theory.

The first such effort was carried out in a department of a government installation where the employees processed case data at computer terminals (Graen, Novak, & Sommerkamp, 1982). Managers in the department received training that included lectures, discussion, and role modeling. Topics covered were the leader-member exchange model, active listening, exchanging mutual expectations, exchanging resources, and practicing one-on-one sessions with subordinates. Actual treatment sessions followed this training and involved conversations between leaders and their members:

During the training sessions the general structure of the conversations as well as the specific questions and techniques to facilitate the conversations were devised by the managers with the help of the trainer: (1) the manager was to spend time asking about and discussing each person's gripes, concerns, and job expectations about (a) the member's job, (b) the supervisor's job, and (c) their working relationship; (2) using "active listening" skills learned in the training, the manager was to be particularly attentive and sensitive to what issues were raised and how they were formulated by each subordinate; (3) the manager was to refrain from imposing his/her frame of reference or management's frame of reference about the issues raised; and (4) the manager was to share some of his/her own job expectations about (a) his/her own job, (b) his/her member's job, and (c) their working relationship. Increasing the level of reciprocal understanding and helpfulness within dyads regarding job issues and behaviors was the goal of the treatment. (Graen et al., 1982, p. 114)

These sessions were conducted with all participants in the treatment group. Before and after results, in terms of performance, were compared for this group and for other groups from the department, which were not exposed to the LMX treatment.

Productivity increases measured in terms of the quantity of cases handled showed a significant advantage in favor of the group that was trained in LMX. Furthermore, this gain was primarily a function of effects that occurred in a high-growth need group of subjects. This latter index was included in the study because a job enrichment treatment based on job characteristics theory was introduced, along with the LMX treatment (see chapter 7). Any job enrichment effects per se, however, were negated by certain policy changes that were introduced by the organization unknown to the experimenters; thus job characteristics theory was not, in fact, tested.

A subsequent publication (Scandura & Graen, 1984), based on data from the same context, was aimed at determining whether low or high initial LMX subjects were most responsive to the treatment effects. The results clearly indicated that the low LMX subjects responded most positively to the treatment in terms of both the quality of their leader-member exchanges and the quantity of their productivity. This analysis did not include any consideration of growth need effects.

Another report on this project (Graen, Scandura, & Graen, 1986) substantiates the moderator effects of growth need strength, but makes no mention of the finding that low-quality leader-member exchange translates into greater productivity with the appropriate training. This latter result is most consistent with theory in that it means that dyadic partnership building applied across the board should result in both low- and high-quality dyads initially moving with training to high-quality relationships. However, if growth need strength is a moderator of the training effect, one would anticipate that it would also moderate the initial dyadic choices as well. In such an event low-quality dyads would not contain many high-growth need strength people and thus would offer little potential for upward movement. This seeming contradiction is neither explained nor even confronted. Growth need strength is not a component of the theory as stated in comprehensive forms.

Japanese Research

On his first visit to Japan in 1972 Graen began a research project with various Japanese corporations, which—at least in the case of one company—extended for 13 years (Wakabayashi & Graen, 1989). The results of this longitudinal analysis indicate that the establishment of high-quality exchanges in the early period after joining a company was a strong predictor of promotion and subsequent career success as a manager. Those with initial low-quality relationships did not do nearly as well.

When leader-member exchanges, measured organizational commitment, potential as determined from assessment centers, and performance appraisals by supervisors were compared in terms of their capacity to predict promotions and success subsequently, the performance appraisals were most effective (Graen, Wakabayashi, Graen, & Graen, 1990). However, LMX was almost as good, and it was a better predictor of satisfaction measures. The assessment center predictions and organizational commitment were much less effective. Overall, the Japanese research provides a strong endorsement for the vertical dyad linkage/leader-member exchange theory.

Evaluation and Impact

Many of the criticisms and questions applied to the vertical dyad linkage model and the research on it no longer hold. Subjects outside of universities have been used extensively now. Research by others besides Graen and his coworkers has expanded rapidly in the 1980s and 1990s. Varied criterion measures have been used in research studies, to a point where concerns about common method biases cannot be invoked to dismiss the theory's validity. The theory has become more normative in nature, thus supplementing its initial purely descriptive emphasis. The fact of in-group and out-group relationships (or high- and low-quality LMX) has been demonstrated with sufficient frequency so that the existence of such relationships is no longer in doubt; they appear to occur in roughly 90 percent of all groups. Yet criticisms do remain, especially on the grounds that theory statements have been inconsistent over time, measures have varied widely, and analyses have not adequately considered the levels at which phenomena occur (see, for example, Schriesheim, Castro, & Cogliser, 1999).

Leader-Member Exchange and Outcome Relationships

Like a number of theories we have been considering, vertical dyad linkage theory has now grown to the point where the research generated by it is sufficient to justify meta-analysis. To my knowledge only one such application has been undertaken (Gerstner & Day, 1997), and in that instance the focus is primarily on the relationship between LMX indices and a wide variety of outcome variables. The research considered extends up through 1996. The results obtained and the number of separate samples on which each correlation is based are given in table 12.7.

From table 12.7 it is apparent that LMX is more strongly related to subjective than to objective factors. The only outcome not predicted is actual turnover.

Objective performance is predicted, but at a marginal level; it is doubtful that this finding has much practical significance. However, objective measures of performance and turnover were used as criteria in relatively few studies.

A review conducted by Liden, Sparrowe, and Wayne (1997) without benefit of the meta-analytic results reaches much the same conclusions as those indicated in table 12.7. In this instance, however, the objective performance results were considered to be nonsignificant, thus placing them in the same category as actual turnover. In spite of the positive results found using a promotion criterion in Japan, it has not been possible to replicate these findings in the United States.

A thorough review by House and Aditya (1997), also without benefit of the meta-analytic findings, points to the fact that although studies involving Graen have found significant relations with turnover, a number of other studies have not. It appears likely that natural inclinations to separate among low-quality LMX employees are stifled by other considerations in many situations. House and Aditya (1997) also note the problems LMX has had in predicting performance, and they conclude that the theory can be most accurately viewed as one that deals with dyadic relationships and their subjective consequences, rather than being a true theory of leadership.

Yet recent reports suggest it is too early to dismiss the idea that there are hard performance data consequences of high-quality LMXs. These reports postdate

TABLE 12.7 Relationships between LMX and outcome variables

Outcome measure	No. of samples	Correlation (corrected for unreliability)
Performance		
Objective measure	8	.11*
Rating of leader in LMX	12	.55*
Rating of member in LMX	30	.30*
Satisfaction		
Overall	33	.50*
With supervision	27	.71*
Turnover		
Actual	7	−.04
Intention	8	−.31*
Organizational commitment	17	.42*

*Significant at the $p < .05$ level or better.

SOURCE: Adapted from Charlotte R. Gerstner & David V. Day (1997), Meta-analytic Review of Leader Member Exchange Theory: Correlates and Construct Issues, *Journal of Applied Psychology, 82,* 832–833

the meta-analytic review and thus were not included in it (Klein & Kim, 1998; Vecchio, 1998). Both studies yield correlations in the mid to upper .20s using performance criteria that are centrally focused on the specific work done, a matter that has been of concern in previous studies. Also, there is reason to believe that because greater opportunities for negotiating role latitude allow for a more pronounced association between LMX and performance, the LMX-performance relationship may be more likely to manifest itself in higher-level positions (Fernandez & Vecchio, 1997). This needs further study, but it does seem that, given appropriate circumstances, both turnover and performance data should yield the predicted relationships with LMX; this is not an entirely subjective theory.

Validity of Other Theoretical Propositions

A problem for leader-member exchange theory, as for other theoretical positions, is that the perceptions of subordinates do not match up well with those reported by their superiors. Gerstner and Day's (1997) meta-analysis finds a corrected correlation between the two LMX values of .37, significant but by no means sufficient to say the two are measuring the same thing. Chemers (1997) takes this disparity to mean that at least in some cases leader-member exchanges reflect perceptions and assumptions more than factual realities. It is possible that the problem reflects in part that subordinates tend to report on their perceptions of the position and its status-based relationships as much as on their perceptions of the person. This is the possibility that Heller raised (see chapter 11 of this volume).

Theory states that high-quality dyadic relationships tend to form based on similarities. Although the matter of demographic similarity has produced mixed results to date, perceived attitudinal similarity does characterize these dyads (Engle & Lord, 1997), as does emotional similarity (Bauer & Green, 1996). Liking for each other is also tied into this constellation, and agreement with leaders is stronger for those members in a high-quality LMX (Gerstner & Day, 1997). Thus the similarity proposition receives considerable support, at least insofar as particular types of similarity are involved.

Several studies have considered the longitudinal development of dyadic relationships from their inception and thus the role-making process (Liden,

Wayne, & Stilwell, 1993; Bauer & Green, 1996). It appears that as high-quality relationships emerge, and they do so very quickly, the leader grants considerable latitude to the member and delegation occurs frequently. The importance of delegation in the exchange has been noted by Schriesheim, Neider, and Scandura (1998) as well. This pattern involving delegation is consistent with the trust-building and testing features of the role-making component of leader-member exchange theory. In this manner role routinization occurs.

However, it is also apparent that performance is not the only factor that is operating in high-quality dyadic relationships (Liden et al., 1993, 1997). Affective reactions most frequently manifest in mutual liking are closely intertwined with the performance aspect; there may well be an ingratiatory feature. This nonperformance component of LMX appears to account for its multidimensional nature.

Graen's international research has focused on Japanese applications of the theory. Others, however, have found that the theory generalizes to China, as well. Thus, LMX predicts both performance and organizational citizenship behavior, the extra-role component of performance, in that context (Hui, Law, & Chen, 1999). In general, the theory appears to exhibit good validity with Chinese subjects. Another extension based on research has to do with the conceptually similar mentoring construct. It appears that as perceived by subordinates, mentoring and high-quality LMX relationships are indistinguishable. Yet the superiors involved react to the two differently, and for them they appear to be empirically distinct (Scandura & Schriesheim, 1994). Presumably, the superiors are influenced by the fact that mentoring often occurs across the boundaries of the immediate work group.

Although certainly not part of leader-member exchange theory in its present form, there are findings that link that theory with goal-setting theory (Klein & Kim, 1998). It has been found that LMX can operate to exert a strong positive influence on goal commitment. This influence occurs for high LMX people but disappears completely when the LMX is low. There is a substantial correlation between goal commitment and performance with high LMX, but this linkage is nonexistent with low LMX. This finding is important in that it raises the possibility of linking two powerful theories across their respective domains. Also, there is some evidence to the effect that high LMX and transformational leadership (see chapter 25 of this volume) are positively related, thus extending the domains of both these theories (Howell & Hall-Merenda, 1999).

The research considered in this section provides considerable support for the validity of leader-member exchange theory in a number of its component aspects. This research is primarily of recent origin, and the recent research is generally superior with regard to design and measurement features to the research conducted during the 1970s and 1980s. We have not as yet touched on the extension of the theory beyond the within-group vertical dyadic relationship to networks of dyads, to horizontal and diagonal dyads, and to higher levels of aggregation within the focal organization and even across organizational boundaries, however. Graen and Uhl-Bien (1995) envisage such an extension beyond leadership, perhaps to create macro theory; House and Aditya (1997) view the prospects here as promising; and Uhl-Bien et al. (2000) present one limited approach of this type.

Nevertheless, the fact is that no really comprehensive theory of this kind exists, and the subject has been raised intermittently for a number of years. Is it likely that expanded, valid macro theory of this kind will emerge from leader-member exchange theory as it currently exists? I do not think so. The domain of the theory now is narrow and specifically delimited. The relationships involved have been shown to be almost entirely within-groups in nature; they do not support the average leadership style, or a between-groups model (Schriesheim et al., 1998). The phenomenon is real enough, but using it to understand macro organizational functioning represents a large theoretical leap. Dyadic linkages could well be part of such a theory, but that leader-member dyads actually drive organizational level processes and structure seems unlikely. If this were the case, one would think that more real theory along these lines would have appeared as Graen and his coworkers have grappled with the issue over the years. The social capital views have much in common with the human resource accounting concepts proposed by Rensis Likert (see chapter 13 of this volume), but they are only a partial answer even here; and they are untested.

New Theoretical Directions and Their Prospects

Leader-member exchange theory does not lack for alternative or supplementary theorizing, much of it serving the purpose of expanding the domain of the basic theory in some way, just as Graen has been trying to do. Bass (1990), for instance, has emphasized that dyadic phenomena need to be supplemented with group level analyses if total group functioning in relation to the leader is to be understood.

Certainly there is more to what is involved here than the processes and outcomes of dyadic relationships. Leaders do deal consistently with all members of the group on occasion, and thus the concept of an average leader-group relationship does have meaning, as Fiedler's contingency theory posits. Leader-member exchange theory had its origins in the idea that there is more to within group functioning than average leadership style, and that is clearly true, but it does not mean that dyadic relationships are the whole story. A theory that went beyond dyads simply at the group level, not into organization-level phenomena and complex networks, would seem to offer the prospect of achieving greater understanding without requiring a major domain expansion. Such a theory would need to add new constructs to those of leader-member exchange theory, however. Group goal commitment might be one such related construct.

As it has become evident that high-quality LMXs involve something more than a purely work-based relationship and that in this regard LMX is multidimensional, there has been increasing concern with affective considerations and the liking that develops between two people. This has eventuated in theory development that deals with how friendship relationships enter into leader-member exchanges (Boyd & Taylor, 1998). Propositions have been set forth and research questions have been proposed. The idea is that by using the concept of a developing friendship, new insights into the nature of LMX may be obtained. This remains to be demonstrated. It gets into such matters as romances that develop at work, matters which Graen and his coworkers have avoided by emphasizing the work-based rather than friendship-based nature of the vertical dyad relationship.

Certainly, extensions of this kind are warranted, given the direction research findings have taken, and they may even prove quite fruitful in understanding how organizations operate. The propositions—which involve similarity, extent of contact, power distance, quality of reward levels, attribution processes, charismatic features, overly close or exploitative relationships, and their ties to LMX, appear promising and worthy of testing. But, to date, research tests have not been carried out, and without them we cannot determine how useful this line of theorizing really is.

A related extension to the theory involves diversity issues, specifically gender and race but also perhaps age and disability (Scandura & Lankau, 1996). It is argued that more attention should be given to these factors as they relate to the various stages of role development. To date, the theoretical position is that demographic similarity should foster high-quality LMX relationships; yet the research is decidedly mixed as to its support for this proposition. Similarity clearly operates in other respects to foster high quality relationships, but not necessarily demographic similarity.

Scandura and Lankau (1996) argue that because LMX is fundamentally based on the connectedness of one person to another, it should incorporate diversity variables to reflect the nature of today's workforce. It is not entirely clear whether this view stems from a value-based position or a scientific one. No formal theory on the matter is proposed, although suggestions along these lines are offered. Whether the specific inclusion of diversity issues in leader-member exchange theory might prove fruitful from a scientific perspective is inevitably dependent on how the issues are formulated, what variables are included and what relationships involving them are posited, and how the research tests turn out. At present we appear to be a long way from having answers in any of these areas.

Fred Dansereau, a major participant in the early development of vertical dyad linkage theory, has proposed a theoretical position that, in a number of respects, is more an alternative to Graen's theorizing than an extension to it. The development of Dansereau's (1995) thinking is outlined here:

Stage 1. Allowing for More than the Traditional (ALS) View (1972–1977).
Although an individual may be a leader, in part due to his or her individual style or individual difference, this is only one possible component of leadership. This traditional individual difference view is sometimes referred to as the average leadership style (ALS) approach.

Stage 2. Development of the (VDL) Vertical Dyad Linkage (Dyad-Group) Approach (1978–1983).
An individual may be a leader for some individuals (in-group members) and not for others (out-group members). Leaders discriminate among individuals against the backdrop of the formal assignment of subordinates to leaders.

Stage 3. Development of the Individualized Leadership Approach (1984–1989).
Individuals link with other individuals on a one-to-one independent dyadic basis. A leader may link with many other individuals, as well as with only a few individuals and not others. It depends on the two individuals: the leader and the other individual. It does not depend on the formal assignment of subordinates to groups or on the style or individual differences of the leader.

Stage 4. Source of Linkages in the Individualized Leadership Approach (1990–1995).
Individuals become leaders by providing a focal person with a sense of support for the focal person's self-worth as an individual. Individuals become followers from receiving a sense of self-worth from the leader and perform in ways that satisfy the leader and themselves; in the process, they validate their own sense of self-worth. For other individuals (nonfollowers), leaders do not provide a sense of self-worth. Nonfollowers may or may not be located in a formal supervisory unit (that is, in-groups and out-groups are not required in each formal group). (Dansereau, 1995, p. 482)

The break with leader-member exchange theory appears to have occurred in late stage 2. The key concepts here are a view of leadership as individualized, operating differently with each other member of a dyad (consistent with a clinical approach to superior-subordinate relationships) and the emphasis on the leader's role in providing a sense of self-worth (consistent with the concept of self-efficacy; see chapter 9 in this volume). This approach takes a different direction from leader-member exchange theory, although it stems from the same origins, and the two are not necessarily fully contradictory. It appears to have very good prospects as a way to gaining a more complete understanding of a leader's relationships with others.

A final derivative theory is in part the product of another of Graen's coworkers, Robert Liden. The approach has been stated somewhat differently in various sources as it attempts to focus on somewhat different problems, but the key features remain the same (see Liden et al., 1997; Sparrowe & Liden, 1997). The central idea is to put exchange theory back into leader-member exchanges and to use the concept of reciprocity to accomplish this. Furthermore, the context of these exchanges is viewed as important, and social network analysis is invoked to deal with this context. Roles are viewed as multidimensional, and affect, loyalty, contribution, and professional respect are considered to be the key dimensions of the roles inherent in the LMX relationship. Like Dansereau's theory, Liden's theory also represents a domain expansion of the leader-member exchange approach. Both theories offer good prospects and appear to break important new ground, although the horizons opened by the Dansereau formulations appear to be somewhat more far-reaching.

Applications for Organizations and Individuals

We have already considered one type of intervention arising out of leader-member exchange theory. This intervention is described in three publications (Graen, Novak, & Sommerkamp, 1982; Scandura & Graen, 1984; Graen et al., 1986). It appears to offer promise, but there has been little by way of follow-up to this work. The intent is to create as many dyadic relationships of a high-quality nature as possible, and the normative theory involved states that expanding the opportunity for high-quality exchanges to everyone should improve performance overall.

It is apparent that in the research reported, when high LMX formation was facilitated by the training and treatment, performance did improve. However, there are remaining uncertainties that have never been resolved. It appears that an initial increase in performance levels was followed by a return to base line conditions, suggesting that the effects were short-lived. It is possible that the facilitated relationships were not maintained, although the data indicate that at least for a time high-quality exchanges were induced on a widespread basis.

The problem discussed previously—involving the apparent moderator effects of high growth need strength coupled with the finding of improvements focused among those with former low-quality exchanges—is perplexing. Furthermore, although an argument in favor of the approach is that it acts to deal with feelings of inequity by making high-quality exchanges available to all, it also serves to eliminate any elitist motivations that may have driven the behavior of high LMX people previously. These individuals may well have considered themselves winners before, but with the intervention this status is taken away from them.

All in all, at present the value of an across the board high-quality exchange intervention must be considered promising but uncertain. It has not had widespread application, and it should not until the uncertainties are resolved. This area contains some of the greatest research needs surrounding LMX theory. In particular, studies should be conducted over considerable periods of time to resolve the questions involving continuing effects. Also the role of growth need strength needs to be established, both in normal dyad formations and in facilitated relationships. Until these questions are resolved, applications of the training to practice on other than an experimental basis do not seem warranted.

A related application is concerned not with what organizations should do to improve their effectiveness, but with what individual members should do to achieve their personal ends (Graen, 1989). The focus is on things a person should do to achieve fast track status in management, what unwritten rules exist in organizations, and how to become an insider who understands these rules and follows them to move up the hierarchy. These unwritten rules are part of the informal organization and constitute the secrets of organizational politics. There are 15 such secrets of the fast track:

1. Find the hidden strategies of your organization, and use them to achieve your objectives. (This involves forming working relationships— networks—with people who have access to special resources, skills, and abilities to do important work.)
2. Do your homework in order to pass the tests. (These tests can range from sample questions to command performances; you should test others, as well, to evaluate sources of information.)
3. Accept calculated risks by using appropriate contingency plans. (Thus, learn to improve your decision average by taking calculated career risks.)
4. Recognize that apparently complete and final plans are merely flexible guidelines to the actions necessary for implementation. (Thus, make your plans broad and open-ended so that you can adapt them as they are implemented.)
5. Expect to be financially undercompensated for the first half of your career and to be overcompensated for the second half. (People on the fast track inevitably grow out of their job descriptions and take on extra duties beyond what they are paid to do.)
6. Work to make your boss successful. (This is at the heart of the exchange between the two

of you and involves a process of reciprocal promotion.)

7. Work to get your boss to promote your career. (This is the other side of the coin and involves grooming your replacement as well.)

8. Use reciprocal relationships to build supportive networks. (It is important that these be competence networks involving effective working relationships and competent people.)

9. Don't let your areas of competence become too narrowly specialized. (Avoid the specialist's trap by continually taking on new challenges.)

10. Try to act with foresight more often than with hindsight. (Be proactive by identifying the right potential problem, choosing the right solution, and choosing the best implementation process.)

11. Develop cordial relationships with your competitors: Be courteous, considerate, and polite in all relationships. (You need not like all these people, but making unnecessary enemies is an expensive luxury.)

12. Seek out key expert insiders, and learn from them. (Have numerous mentors and preserve these relationships of your reciprocal network.)

13. Make sure to acknowledge everyone's contribution. (Giving credit can be used as a tool to develop a network of working relationships.)

14. Prefer equivalent exchanges between peers instead of rewards and punishments between unequal partners. (Equivalent exchanges are those in which a resource, service, or behavior is given with the understanding that something of equivalent value will eventually be returned; this requires mutual trust.)

15. Never take unfair advantage of anyone, and avoid letting anyone take unfair advantage of you. (Networks cannot be maintained without a reputation for trustworthiness.)

To aid in achieving the goals of these secrets, there are discussions of reading the unwritten rules, finding out whether you're on the fast track, methods of getting on the fast track, outgrowing your present job, developing resources with superiors and competent peers, solving problems, obtaining inside information, developing fast-track leadership, and discovering the broader organizational picture. This is a comprehensive manual for playing the hierarchy, with many appealing ideas.

Graen does not present this manual as being a direct product of his research. However, there are frequent references to studies and the results of studies.

Some of what is said is clearly based on research, but there are normative statements that go beyond the research as well. The ideas are intriguing, and they have the ring of truth. Not all are supported by research, and Graen does not claim that they are. All in all, efforts of this kind would seem to be a useful contribution to organizational behavior practice, although one could wish for a somewhat more solid empirical underpinning. For instance, is it the high growth need people who are most likely to take these ideas and run with them?

CONCLUSIONS

As we saw with first-generation motivation theories, a number of first-generation leadership theories remain active to the present, both with continually evolving theory and by providing a continuing impetus for new research. This is particularly true for the theories considered in this chapter — contingency theory and the more recent cognitive resource theory, as well as leader-member exchange theory. Path-goal theory has seen some revival after a hiatus, normative decision process theory is in something of a recession but still active, and influence-power continuum theory appears to be returning to the realm of theory. Only theory X and theory Y and the consideration-initiating structure formulations have definitely passed their prime and are in the process of becoming of primarily historical interest. Plus several new leadership theories have taken a prominent position in the second-generation agenda. Leadership remains an active theoretical field.

Convergence with motivation theory has had a rather rocky past, but solutions in this regard still seem viable. Convergence within leadership theory itself seems more immediately possible, however. In particular, leader-member exchange theory appears capable of providing insights within the leader-member relations component of contingency theory, the aspect of situational favorableness that exerts the greatest influence. Also cognitive resource theory is most likely to be activated in response to stress with the boss, a context on which leader-member exchange theory would seem to have something to say (although the current emphasis on high- rather than low-quality exchanges is inconsistent with this expectation). Perhaps a fruitful next focus for leader-member exchange theory would be to look at low-quality exchanges more closely, thus following the route proposed by Dansereau (1995).

Another question that requires explanation is why training procedures like leader match and the facilitation of high-quality exchanges are as effective as they are in the absence of strong ties to the theories from which they derive. One possibility is that they work because they produce increased managerial motivation by sensitizing participants to the nature and characteristics of the managerial role in hierarchic organizations (see chapter 5 in this volume). Other training that seeks to improve leadership capabilities in a bureaucratic context may do the same thing (Miner, 1986).

In any event, there appears to be no lack of significant issues to consider and study in the leadership area. The field has advanced considerably in the past 25 years. I believe this has occurred because it has broadened its perspective to incorporate topics and approaches moving far beyond the limited subject matter that characterized its early years.

References

Ayman, Roya; Chemers, Martin M.; & Fiedler, Fred E. (1995). The Contingency Model of Leadership Effectiveness: Its Levels of Analysis. *Leadership Quarterly*, 6, 147–167.

Barnard, Chester I. (1938). *The Functions of the Executive*. Cambridge, MA: Harvard University Press.

Barnes, Valerie; Potter, Earl H.; & Fiedler, Fred E. (1983). Effect of Interpersonal Stress on the Prediction of Academic Performance. *Journal of Applied Psychology*, 68, 686–697.

Bass, Bernard M. (1990). *Bass and Stogdill's Handbook of Leadership: Theory, Research, and Managerial Applications*. New York: Free Press.

Bauer, Tayla N., & Green, Stephen G. (1996). Development of Leader-Member Exchange: A Longitudinal Test. *Academy of Management Journal*, 39, 1538–1567.

Bettin, Patrick J., & Kennedy, John K. (1990). Leadership Experience and Leader Performance: Some Empirical Support at Last. *Leadership Quarterly*, 1, 219–228.

Boyd, Nancy G., & Taylor, Robert R. (1998). A Developmental Approach to the Examination of Friendship in Leader-Follower Relationships. *Leadership Quarterly*, 9, 1–25.

Burke, Michael J., & Day, Russell R. (1986). A Cumulative Study of the Effectiveness of Managerial Training. *Journal of Applied Psychology*, 71, 232–245.

Cashman, James; Dansereau, Fred; Graen, George; & Haga, William J. (1976). Organizational Understructure and Leadership: A Longitudinal Investigation of the Managerial Role-Making Process. *Organizational Behavior and Human Performance*, 15, 278–296.

Chemers, Martin M. (1993). An Integrative Theory of Leadership. In Martin M. Chemers & Roya Ayman (Eds.), *Leadership Theory and Research: Perspectives and Directions* (pp. 293–319). San Diego: Academic Press.

Chemers, Martin M. (1997). *An Integrative Theory of Leadership*. Mahwah, NJ: Erlbaum.

Cleven, Walter A., & Fiedler, Fred E. (1956). Interpersonal Perceptions of Open-Hearth Foremen and Steel Production. *Journal of Applied Psychology*, 40, 312–314.

Dansereau, Fred (1995). A Dyadic Approach to Leadership: Creating and Nurturing This Approach under Fire. *Leadership Quarterly*, 6, 479–490.

Dansereau, Fred; Cashman, James; & Graen, George (1973). Instrumentality Theory and Equity Theory as Complementary Approaches in Predicting the Relationship of Leadership and Turnover among Managers. *Organizational Behavior and Human Performance*, 10, 184–200.

Dansereau, Fred; Graen, George; & Haga, William J. (1975). A Vertical Dyad Linkage Approach to Leadership within Formal Organizations: A Longitudinal Investigation of the Role Making Process. *Organizational Behavior and Human Performance*, 13, 46–78.

Engle, Elaine M., & Lord, Robert G. (1997). Implicit Theories, Self-Schemas, and Leader-Member Exchange. *Academy of Management Journal*, 40, 988–1010.

Fernandez, Carmen F., & Vecchio, Robert P. (1997). Situational Leadership Theory Revisited: A Test of an Across-Jobs Perspective. *Leadership Quarterly*, 8, 67–84.

Fiedler, Fred E. (1951). A Method of Objective Quantification of Certain Countertransference Attitudes. *Journal of Clinical Psychology*, 7, 101–107.

Fiedler, Fred E. (1958). *Leader Attitudes and Group Effectiveness*. Urbana: University of Illinois Press.

Fiedler, Fred E. (1964). A Contingency Model of Leadership Effectiveness. In Leonard Berkowitz (Ed.), *Advances in Experimental Social Psychology* (Vol. 1, pp. 149–190). New York: Academic Press.

Fiedler, Fred E. (1965). Engineer the Job to Fit the Manager. *Harvard Business Review*, 43(5), 115–122.

Fiedler, Fred E. (1967). *A Theory of Leadership Effectiveness*. New York: McGraw-Hill.

Fiedler, Fred E. (1971). Validation and Extension of the Contingency Model of Leadership Effectiveness: A

Review of Empirical Findings. *Psychological Bulletin*, 76, 128–148.

Fiedler, Fred E. (1972a). The Effects of Leadership Training and Experience: A Contingency Model Interpretation. *Administrative Science Quarterly*, 17, 453–470.

Fiedler, Fred E. (1972b). Personality, Motivational Systems, and Behavior of High and Low LPC Persons. *Human Relations*, 25, 391–412.

Fiedler, Fred E. (1973). Personality and Situational Determinants of Leader Behavior. In Edwin A. Fleishman and James G. Hunt (Eds.), *Current Developments in the Study of Leadership* (pp. 41–61). Carbondale: Southern Illinois University Press.

Fiedler, Fred E. (1978a). The Contingency Model and the Dynamics of the Leadership Process. In Leonard Berkowitz (Ed.), *Advances in Experimental Social Psychology* (Vol. 11, pp. 59–112). New York: Academic Press.

Fiedler, Fred E. (1978b). Situational Control and a Dynamic Theory of Leadership. In Bert King, Siegfried Streufert, & Fred E. Fiedler (Eds.), *Managerial Control and Organizational Democracy* (pp. 107–131). New York: Wiley.

Fiedler, Fred E. (1979). Organizational Determinants of Managerial Incompetence. In James G. Hunt & Lars L. Larson (Eds.), *Crosscurrents in Leadership* (pp. 11–22). Carbondale: Southern Illinois University Press.

Fiedler, Fred E. (1991). Review of *A Theory of Leadership Effectiveness* by Fred E. Fiedler. *Journal of Management*, 17, 501–503.

Fiedler, Fred E. (1992a). Life in a Pretzel-Shaped Universe. In Arthur G. Bedeian (Ed.), *Management Laureates: A Collection of Autobiographical Essays* (Vol. 1, pp. 303–333). Greenwich, CT: JAI Press.

Fiedler, Fred E. (1992b). Time-Based Measures of Leadership Experience and Organizational Performance: A Review of Research and a Preliminary Model. *Leadership Quarterly*, 3, 5–23.

Fiedler, Fred E. (1993). The Leadership Situation and the Black Box in Contingency Theories. In Martin M. Chemers & Roya Ayman (Eds.), *Leadership Theory and Research: Perspectives and Directions* (pp. 1–28). San Diego: Academic Press.

Fiedler, Fred E. (1995). Reflections by an Accidental Theorist. *Leadership Quarterly*, 6, 453–461.

Fiedler, Fred E. (1996). Research on Leadership Selection and Training: One View of the Future. *Administrative Science Quarterly*, 41, 241–250.

Fiedler, Fred E.; Bons, P. M.; & Hastings, Limda L. (1975). New Strategies for Leadership Utilization. In W. T. Singleton & P. Spurgeon (Eds.), *Measure-ment of Human Resources* (pp. 233–244). New York: Halsted.

Fiedler, Fred E., & Chemers, Martin M. (1974). *Leadership and Effective Management.* Glenview, IL: Scott, Foresman.

Fiedler, Fred E., & Chemers, Martin M. (1984). *Improving Leadership Effectiveness: The Leader Match Concept.* New York: Wiley.

Fiedler, Fred E.; Chemers, Martin M.; & Mahar, Linda (1976). *Improving Leadership Effectiveness: The Leader Match Concept.* New York: Wiley.

Fiedler, Fred E., & Garcia, Joseph E. (1985). Comparing Organization Development and Management Training. *Personnel Administrator*, 30(3), 35–47.

Fiedler, Fred E., & Garcia, Joseph E. (1987). *New Approaches to Effective Leadership: Cognitive Resources and Organizational Performance.* New York: Wiley.

Fiedler, Fred E., & House, Robert J. (1988). Leadership Theory and Research: A Report of Progress. *International Review of Industrial and Organizational Psychology*, 3, 73–92.

Fiedler, Fred E., & Macaulay, Jennifer L. (1998). The Leadership Situation: A Missing Factor in Selecting and Training Managers. *Human Resource Management Review*, 8, 335–350.

Fiedler, Fred E., & Mahar, Linda (1979). The Effectiveness of Contingency Model Training: A Review of the Validation of Leader Match. *Personnel Psychology*, 32, 45–62.

Fiedler, Fred E.; Murphy, Susan E.; & Gibson, Frederick W. (1992). Inaccurate Reporting and Inappropriate Variables: A Reply to Vecchio's (1990) Examination of Cognitive Resource Theory. *Journal of Applied Psychology* 77, 372–374.

Fiedler, Fred E.; O'Brien, Gordon E.; & Ilgen, Daniel R. (1969). The Effect of Leadership Style upon the Performance and Adjustment of Volunteer Teams Operating in a Stressful Foreign Environment. *Human Relations*, 22, 503–514.

Fiedler, Fred E.; Potter, Earl H.; & McGuire, Mark A. (1992). Stress and Effective Leadership Decisions. In Frank A. Heller (Ed.), *Decision-Making and Leadership* (pp. 46–57). Cambridge: Cambridge University Press.

Fiedler, Fred E.; Potter, Earl H.; Zais, Mitchell M.; & Knowlton, William A. (1979). Organizational Stress and the Use and Misuse of Managerial Intelligence and Experience. *Journal of Applied Psychology*, 64, 635–647.

Foa, Uriel G.; Mitchell, Terence R.; & Fiedler, Fred E. (1971). Differentiation Matching. *Behavioral Science*, 16, 130–142.

Gerstner, Charlotte R., & Day, David V. (1997). Meta-Analytic Review of Leader-Member Exchange Theory: Correlates and Construct Issues. *Journal of Applied Psychology*, 82, 827–844.

Ghiselli, Edwin E. (1966). *Explorations in Managerial Talent*. Pacific Palisades, CA: Goodyear.

Gibson, Frederick W.; Fiedler, Fred E.; & Barrett, Kelley M. (1993). Stress, Babble, and the Utilization of the Leader's Intellectual Abilities. *Leadership Quarterly*, 4, 189–208.

Godfrey, Eleanor P.; Fiedler, Fred E.; & Hall, D. M. (1959). *Boards, Management, and Company Success*. Danville, IL: Interstate Press.

Graen, George (1969). Instrumentality Theory of Work Motivation: Some Experimental Results and Suggested Modifications. *Journal of Applied Psychology Monograph*, 53(2), Part 2, 1–25.

Graen, George (1976). Role-Making Processes within Complex Organizations. In Marvin D. Dunnette (Ed.), *Handbook of Industrial and Organizational Psychology* (pp. 1201–1245). Chicago: Rand, McNally.

Graen, George B. (1989). *Unwritten Rules for Your Career: 15 Secrets for Fast-track Success*. New York: Wiley.

Graen, George B. (1990). Designing Productive Leadership Systems to Improve Both Work Motivation and Organizational Effectiveness. In Uwe Kleinbeck, Hans-Henning Quast, Henk Thierry, & Hartmut Häcker (Eds.), *Work Motivation* (pp. 133–167). Hillsdale, NJ: Erlbaum.

Graen, George, & Cashman, James F. (1975). A Role-Making Model of Leadership in Formal Organizations: A Developmental Approach. In James G. Hunt & Lars L. Larson (Eds.), *Leadership Frontiers* (pp. 143–165). Kent, OH: Kent State University Press.

Graen, George; Cashman, James F.; Ginsburgh, Steven; & Schiemann, William (1977). Effects of Linking-Pin Quality on the Quality of Working Life of Lower Participants. *Administrative Science Quarterly*, 22, 491–504.

Graen, George; Dansereau, Fred; & Minami, Takao (1972a). Dysfunctional Leadership Styles. *Organizational Behavior and Human Performance*, 7, 216–236.

Graen, George; Dansereau, Fred; & Minami, Takao (1972b). An Empirical Test of the Man-in-the-Middle Hypothesis among Executives in a Hierarchical Organization Employing a Unit-Set Analysis. *Organizational Behavior and Human Performance*, 8, 262–285.

Graen, George; Dansereau, Fred; Minami, Takao; & Cashman, James (1973). Leadership Behaviors as Cues to Performance Evaluation. *Academy of Management Journal*, 16, 611–623.

Graen, George, & Ginsburgh, Steven (1977). Job Resignation as a Function of Role Orientation and Leader Acceptance: A Longitudinal Investigation of Organizational Assimilation. *Organizational Behavior and Human Performance*, 19, 1–17.

Graen, George B.; Liden, Robert C.; & Hoel, William (1982). Role of Leadership in the Employee Withdrawal Process. *Journal of Applied Psychology*, 67, 868–872.

Graen, George; Novak, Michael A.; & Sommerkamp, Patricia (1982). The Effect of Leader-Member Exchange and Job Design on Productivity and Satisfaction: Testing a Dual Attachment Model. *Organizational Behavior and Human Performance*, 30, 109–131.

Graen, George; Orris, James B.; & Johnson, Thomas W. (1973). Role Assimilation Processes in a Complex Organization. *Journal of Vocational Behavior*, 3, 395–420.

Graen, George B., & Scandura, Terri A. (1986). A Theory of Dyadic Career Reality. *Research in Personnel and Human Resources Management*, 4, 147–181.

Graen, George B., & Scandura, Terri A. (1987). Toward a Psychology of Dyadic Organizing. *Research in Organizational Behavior*, 9, 175–208.

Graen, George B.; Scandura, Terri A.; & Graen, Michael R. (1986). A Field Experimental Test of the Moderating Effects of Growth Need Strength on Productivity. *Journal of Applied Psychology*, 71, 484–491.

Graen, George, & Schiemann, William (1978). Leader-Member Agreement: A Vertical Dyad Linkage Approach. *Journal of Applied Psychology*, 63, 206–212.

Graen, George B., & Uhl-Bien, Mary (1991). The Transformation of Professionals into Self-Managing and Partially Self-Designing Contributors: Toward a Theory of Leadership-Making. *Journal of Management Systems*, 3(3), 33–48.

Graen, George B., & Uhl-Bien, Mary (1995). Relationships-Based Approach to Leadership: Development of Leader-Member Exchange (LMX) Theory of Leadership over 25 Years: Applying a Multi-level Multi-domain Perspective. *Leadership Quarterly*, 6, 219–247.

Graen, George B., & Wakabayashi, Mitsuru (1994). Cross-Cultural Leadership Making: Bridging American and Japanese Diversity for Team Advantage. In Harry C. Triandis, Marvin D. Dunnette, & Leaetta M. Hough (Eds.), *Handbook of Industrial and Organizational Psychology* (Vol. 4, pp. 415–446). Palo Alto, CA: Consulting Psychologists Press.

Graen, George B.; Wakabayashi, Mitsuru; Graen, Michael R.; & Graen, Martin G. (1990). International Generalizability of American Hypotheses about Japanese Management Progress: A Strong Inference Investigation. *Leadership Quarterly*, 1, 1–23.

Haga, William J.; Graen, George; & Dansereau, Fred (1974). Professionalism and Role Making in a Service Organization: A Longitudinal Investigation. *American Sociological Review*, 39, 122–133.

Hooijberg, Robert, & Choi, Jaepil (1999). From Austria to the United States and from Evaluating Therapists to Developing Cognitive Resources Theory: An Interview with Fred Fiedler. *Leadership Quarterly*, 10, 653–665.

House, Robert J., & Aditya, Ram N. (1997). The Social Scientific Study of Leadership: Quo Vadis? *Journal of Management*, 23, 409–473.

Howell, Jane M., & Hall-Merenda, Kathryn E. (1999). The Ties That Bind: The Impact of Leader-Member Exchange, Transformational and Transactional Leadership, and Distance on Predicting Follower Performance. *Journal of Applied Psychology*, 84, 680–694.

Hui, Chun; Law, Kenneth S.; & Chen, Zhen X. (1999). A Structural Equation Model of the Effects of Negative Affectivity, Leader-Member Exchange, and Perceived Job Mobility on In-role and Extra-role Performance: A Chinese Case. *Organizational Behavior and Human Decision Processes*, 77, 3–21.

Jacobs, T. O. (1971). *Leadership and Exchange in Formal Organizations*. Alexandria, VA: Human Resources Research Organization.

Jago, Arthur G., & Ragan, James W. (1986). The Trouble with Leader Match Is That It Doesn't Match Fiedler's Contingency Model. *Journal of Applied Psychology*, 71, 555–559.

Johnson, Thomas W., & Graen, George (1973). Organizational Assimilation and Role Rejection. *Organizational Behavior and Human Performance*, 10, 72–87.

Kabanoff, Boris (1981). A Critique of Leader Match and Its Implications for Leadership Research. *Personnel Psychology*, 34, 749–764.

Katz, Daniel N., & Kahn, Robert L. (1966). *The Social Psychology of Organizations*. New York: Wiley.

Kennedy, John K. (1982). Middle LPC Leaders and the Contingency Model of Leadership Effectiveness. *Organizational Behavior and Human Performance*, 30, 1–14.

Klein, Howard J., & Kim, Jay S. (1998). A Field Study of the Influence of Situational Constraints, Leader-Member Exchange, and Goal Commitment on Performance. *Academy of Management Journal*, 41, 88–95.

Liden, Robert C., & Graen, George B. (1980). Generalizability of the Vertical Dyad Linkage Model of Leadership. *Academy of Management Journal*, 23, 451–465.

Liden, Robert C.; Sparrowe, Raymond T.; & Wayne, Sandy J. (1997). Leader-Member Exchange Theory: The Past and Potential for the Future. *Research in Personnel and Human Resources Management*, 15, 47–119.

Liden, Robert C.; Wayne, Sandy J.; & Stilwell, Dean (1993). A Longitudinal Study on the Early Development of Leader-Member Exchanges. *Journal of Applied Psychology*, 78, 662–674.

Miner, John B. (1986). Managerial Role Motivation Training. *Journal of Managerial Psychology*, 1(1), 25–30.

Mitchell, Terence R.; Biglan, Anthony; Oncken, Gerald R.; & Fiedler, Fred E. (1970). The Contingency Model: Criticisms and Suggestions. *Academy of Management Journal*, 13, 253–267.

Murphy, Susan E.; Blyth, Dewey; & Fiedler, Fred E. (1992). Cognitive Resource Theory and the Utilization of the Leader's and Group Members' Technical Competence. *Leadership Quarterly*, 3, 237–255.

Neider, Linda L., & Schriesheim, Chester A. (1988). Review of Fiedler and Garcia's *New Approaches to Effective Leadership*. *Administrative Science Quarterly*, 33, 135–140.

Peters, Lawrence H.; Hartke, Darrell D.; & Pohlman, John T. (1985). Fiedler's Contingency Theory of Leadership: An Application of the Meta-Analysis Procedures of Schmidt and Hunter. *Psychological Bulletin*, 97, 274–285.

Potter, Earl H., & Fiedler, Fred E. (1981). The Utilization of Staff Member Intelligence and Experience under High and Low Stress. *Academy of Management Journal*, 24, 361–376.

Rice, Robert W. (1978). Psychometric Properties of the Esteem for Least Preferred Coworker (LPC) Scale. *Academy of Management Review*, 3, 106–117.

Scandura, Terri A., & Graen, George B. (1984). Moderating Effects of Initial Leader-Member Exchange Status on the Effects of a Leadership Intervention. *Journal of Applied Psychology*, 69, 428–436.

Scandura, Terri A., & Lankau, Melenie J. (1996). Developing Diverse Leaders: A Leader-Member Exchange Approach. *Leadership Quarterly*, 7, 243–263.

Scandura, Terri A., & Schriesheim, Chester A. (1994). Leader-Member Exchange and Supervisor Career Mentoring as Complementary Constructs in Leadership Research. *Academy of Management Journal*, 37, 1588–1602.

Schriescheim, Chester A.; Castro, Stephanie L.; & Cogliser, Claudia C. (1999). Leader-Member Exchange (LMX) Research: A Comprehensive Review of Theory, Measurement, and Data-Analytic Practices. *Leadership Quarterly*, 10, 63–113.

Schriesheim, Chester A.; Neider, Linda L.; & Scandura, Terri A. (1998). Delegation and Leader-Member Exchange: Main Effects, Moderators, and Measurement Issues. *Academy of Management Journal*, 41, 298–318.

Schriesheim, Chester A.; Tepper, Bennett J., & Tetrault, Linda A. (1994). Least Preferred Co-Worker Score, Situational Control, and Leadership Effectiveness: A Meta-Analysis of Contingency Model Performance Predictions. *Journal of Applied Psychology*, 79, 561–573.

Shiflett, Samuel C. (1973). The Contingency Model of Leadership Effectiveness: Some Implications for Its Statistical and Methodological Properties. *Behavioral Science*, 18, 429–440.

Sparrowe, Raymond T., & Liden, Robert C. (1997). Process and Structure in Leader-Member Exchange. *Academy of Management Review*, 22, 522–552.

Strube, Michael J., & Garcia, Joseph E. (1981). A Meta-Analytic Investigation of Fiedler's Contingency Model of Leadership Effectiveness. *Psychological Bulletin*, 90, 307–321.

Uhl-Bien, Mary; Graen, George B.; & Scandura, Terri A. (2000). Implications of Leader-Member Exchange (LMX) for Strategic Human Resource Management Systems: Relationships as Social Capital for Competitive Advantage. *Research in Personnel and Human Resources Management*, 18, 137–185.

Vecchio, Robert P. (1990). Theoretical and Empirical Examination of Cognitive Resource Theory. *Journal of Applied Psychology*, 75, 141–147.

Vecchio, Robert P. (1998). Leader-Member Exchange, Objective Performance, Employment Duration, and Supervisor Ratings: Testing for Moderating and Mediation. *Journal of Business and Psychology*, 12, 327–341.

Wakabayashi, Mitsuru, & Graen, George (1989). Human Resource Development of Japanese Managers: Leadership and Career Investment. *Research in Personnel and Human Resources Management.*, Suppl. 1, 235–256.

Yukl, Gary (1998). *Leadership in Organizations*. Upper Saddle River, NJ: Prentice Hall.

Part IV

First-Generation Theories: Systems Concepts of Organization

Chapter 13

Organizational Level Theories with Roots in Group Dynamics and Group Leadership

At the beginning of chapter 10 it was noted that in the early years formulations and research that ema-nated from Ohio State University and from the University of Michigan represented the major thrusts of thinking on leadership. At that time leadership was conceived of as a component of group dynamics; it was a type of group process. Gradually this early emphasis began to be infused with ideas about organizations as a whole that were part of the existing atmosphere elsewhere in organizational behavior. The focus on group processes remained, but organization level concepts were added.

Much the same type of expansions to theory occurred at both the University of Michigan and at Ohio State, but because the starting points in group dynamics were somewhat different, the organization level theories differed also. At Michigan the guiding light for this development was Rensis Likert, whose theory of system 4 and 4T evolved in the behavioral humanist tradition with a strong and continuing emphasis on participative processes within work groups that resulted in shared leadership. Control theory, which also developed from Michigan, was the product of

Arnold Tannenbaum. It came into being somewhat later than Likert's initial formulations and attempted to deal with certain topic areas in which Tannenbaum felt the early Michigan work was conceptually insufficient. Thus it was a separate, but related, line of theorizing that produced its own set of research studies.

The origins of the Ohio State approach to organization level theorizing were in the atheoretical consideration and initiating structure constructs (see chapter 10 in this volume). Ralph Stogdill was heavily involved in this approach to leadership behavior research, and his thinking on organizations was clearly influenced by it. Group-focused systems theory is the result. Unlike the Michigan theories, it did not place strong emphasis on participation and humanism.

THEORY OF SYSTEMS 1–4 AND 4T

The theoretical formulations of Rensis Likert are among the best known in the behavioral humanist tradition. His constructs overlap in a number of respects with those of other participative management advocates, such as Abraham Maslow, Douglas McGregor, and Chris Argyris, but there are important differences as well. In particular, Likert's theory strongly emphasizes work groups and their interactions, as well as practical considerations of profit and loss. The major focus initially was on leadership within the group, but the theory quickly expanded to incorporate lateral and vertical intergroup relationships, organizational climates, and social systems. Ultimately it became a full-blown theory of organizational process and in certain respects of structure as well.

Background

Likert's theoretical contributions evolved during his long career as director of the Institute for Social Research at the University of Michigan (Likert, 1978). He started as a civil engineering major at Michigan, then shifted to sociology for his degree. After a year at the Union Theological Seminary, he entered the psychology department at Columbia University, where he obtained a doctorate in social psychology in 1932. After a period teaching psychology at New York University, he moved to a research position at the Life Insurance Agency Management Association in Hartford, Connecticut. In 1939 he went to Washington with the Agriculture Department to head up the Divi-

sion of Program Surveys, an organization that expanded substantially during the war years.

With cutbacks after the war, the senior staff component of this group negotiated an arrangement to move en masse to the University of Michigan (Likert, 1979). Thus, the Survey Research Center was born as a self-supporting research entity. In 1948 the Research Center for Group Dynamics from MIT became a partner in this endeavor, thus creating the combined entity called the Institute for Social Research, which Likert directed until he retired from the university. In the early years, the institute received key support from the Office of Naval Research, but as the institute evolved, the major source of funds was private industry.

At age 67 Likert formed Rensis Likert Associates, with which he remained active until his death in 1981 at the age of 78. He indicates that his thinking initially was influenced by a number of people, including Elton Mayo and the Hawthorne researchers, as well as Mary Parker Follett (Likert, 1979). It is also apparent that his thinking was very much in reaction to the ideas advanced by the classical management writers, Frederick Taylor in particular. Likert did not serve on a business school faculty, but he wrote widely in the business literature.

Likert's Theory of the Participative Organization

The theory to be considered is set forth primarily in three books: *New Patterns of Management* (Likert, 1961), *The Human Organization* (Likert, 1967), and *New Ways of Managing Conflict* (Likert & Likert, 1976). These books were supplemented by a number of journal articles. The program of research conducted by the Institute for Social Research served as both an inductive source and an empirical testing ground for Likert's theoretical formulations. In fact, this grounding in observation and research is so strong that Likert often wrote as if describing established fact or presenting empirical elaborations, rather than formulating theory. Yet it remains advisable to scrutinize his views in the light of scientific theory in the same manner as the other conceptualizations are explored in this book. Certainly there are places in his writings where Likert clearly indicates that he is presenting theory.

New Patterns of Management

The first comprehensive statements of Likert's views (Likert, 1961) contained extensive discussions of research that had been conducted by the staff of the Institute for Social Research during the late 1940s and the 1950s. Such sequencing might give the impression that the 1961 theory was an outgrowth of prior research and that this research cannot legitimately be viewed as a test of the theory. Yet Likert's earlier writings, extending back to the 1940s (Likert & Willets, 1940–1941), contain many statements that are analogous to those set forth more formally in the 1961 volume. Thus key concepts such as the principle of supportive relationships and the value of participative management appear to have guided the research of the University of Michigan group from the beginning. The concepts were clearly enunciated in external publications by the early 1950s (Likert, 1953; Mann & Likert, 1952). Though the early theory and research are not entirely free of "the chicken and the egg" problems, certain significant research specifically designed to test Likert's hypotheses was conducted in this period.

The principle of supportive relationships is stated in somewhat varied forms in Likert's writings, but the meaning changes very little:

> The leadership and other processes of the organization must be such as to ensure a maximum probability that in all interactions and all relationships with the organization each member will, in the light of his background, values, and expectations, view the experience as supportive and one which builds and maintains his sense of personal worth and importance. (Likert, 1961, p. 103)

Elsewhere Likert refers to such a statement as the "fundamental concept" and "general formula" of the theory (Likert, 1959). As a theoretical hypothesis, it should be prefaced with "If a high-producing organization is desired . . .".

This basic principle assumes an extremely important and influential role for leadership in the organization. Effective leaders are those who are employee-centered, in that they behave in ways that create a perception of supportiveness. At the same time, they transmit high-performance goals through a kind of "contagious enthusiasm" and possess the needed technical competence.

The major source of supportive relationships lies in the work group. Thus a derivation from the basic principle states:

> Management will make full use of the potential capacities of its human resources only when each person in an organization is a member of one or more effectively functioning work groups that have a high degree of group loyalty, effective skills of interaction, and high performance goals. . . . An organization will function best when its personnel function not as individuals but as members of highly effective work groups with high performance goals. Consequently, management should deliberately endeavor to build these effective groups, linking them into an overall organization by means of people who hold overlapping group membership. The superior in one group is a subordinate in the next group and so on through the organization. (Likert, 1961, pp. 104–105)

Individuals who are in these positions of dual group membership ideally should exert influence in both groups—both upward and downward, as members and as leaders. In doing so they perform the linking pin function and open up channels of communication through the organization. Failure to perform the linking pin function effectively results in work group failure at the subordinate level. To the extent that there are many such failed groups, and to the extent that groups of this kind exist toward the top of the hierarchy, the organization as a whole will function less effectively. Thus, open, two-way communication and influence are essential to organizational effectiveness. Group and intergroup meetings facilitate two-way communication and influence. Lateral or horizontal groupings and committees act as buffers against failures in the vertical linking pin system and are therefore recommended. The overall, overlapping group structure tends to bind group goals into those of the organization and creates unity of effort and a capacity to deal with conflict.

The key to an effective organization is an integrated system of overlapping groups. Therefore it becomes crucial to establish the conditions that make for effective group functioning. Likert (1961) notes 24 such characteristics, virtually all of which involve some application of the principle of supportive relationships.

1. Members are skilled in the roles required for interaction.
2. The group has existed long enough to have established stable, positive relationships.
3. The members and leader are attracted to the group and are loyal to each other.
4. There is high confidence and trust.
5. The group's values and goals adequately reflect those of individual members.

6. Individuals performing linking functions attempt to harmonize the values and goals of their groups.
7. Important group values have a high likelihood of member acceptance.
8. Members strive to contribute to group values and goals out of a desire to maintain a sense of personal worth.
9. Group activities occur in a supportive atmosphere.
10. The superior has considerable influence on the group atmosphere, making it supportive and cooperative.
11. The group fosters the development of members to their full potential.
12. Members accept the goals established by the group.
13. Group-set goals stretch members to the maximum.
14. There is considerable mutual help in achieving goals.
15. The atmosphere of the group fosters creativity.
16. The group fosters "constructive" conformity.
17. Open communication, especially of information that is important to the group, is facilitated.
18. The communication process is utilized in the interest of the group.
19. Members receive information from other group members and trust it.
20. There is a strong desire to influence other group members and to be receptive to influence.
21. Considerable influence is exerted by members on the leader, and needed information is transmitted to the leader.
22. In spite of the stability created by common goals and values, flexibility exists.
23. Appropriate individual decision making is facilitated by the common group goals and values.
24. Leaders are selected carefully, often through a peer nomination process.

Likert distinguishes three sets of variables that have major significance for organizational functioning: causal, intervening, and end-result. Figure 13.1 presents these variables and their relationships. Likert particularly emphasizes the intervening variables and their measurement. He comes to this position via the following logic: There is often a sizable lag between a change in the causal variables and any resultant change in end-result variables. This lag, like that associated with technological innovation, may well be measured in years. Accordingly, to determine within a reasonable period of time what effects have been

set in motion by a change and thus to establish a short feedback cycle, one must obtain measures of intervening variables. Effects may not show at the end-result point for years.

An important example of the need for a focus on intervening variables is provided by autocratic, production-oriented supervision. Such supervision can obtain results, but at the expense of squandering human assets, a process similar to liquidating physical assets. If the accounting system measures end-result variables only, these may be unaffected for some time, and the manager involved may be promoted to repeat the process before the consequences emerge. However, an accounting system that deals with intervening variables will identify the nature and extent of the decline in human assets, and thus in the quality of the human organization, and will cost these changes against the productivity figures, making them look much less impressive (Likert, 1958). Consequently, the manager who violates the principle of supportive relationships is less likely to be promoted, and the organization will benefit as a result.

Although the principle of participation is emphasized as the best guide for managerial action throughout the 1961 book, Likert does not explicitly relate it to other alternative management systems until the next to the last chapter. Here he describes what he calls exploitive authoritative, benevolent authoritative, and consultative systems and sets them against the participative group system that embodies the principle of participation. The four systems are differentiated with regard to motivational forces, communication, interaction-influence, decision making, goal setting, control, and performance. The participative group system is said to operate toward the end of a single continuum on which the other systems also fall. Under the participative group system greater total influence is exerted in the organization as a whole, and, consequently, performance is more effective overall. However, "the amount and character of participation need to be geared to the values, skills, and expectations of the people involved if productive results are to be obtained. . . . Participation should not be thought of as a single process or activity, but rather as a whole range of processes and activities" (Likert, 1961, p. 242).

The Human Organization

The second of Likert's books (1967) covers much the same ground as the first, but a number of concepts are

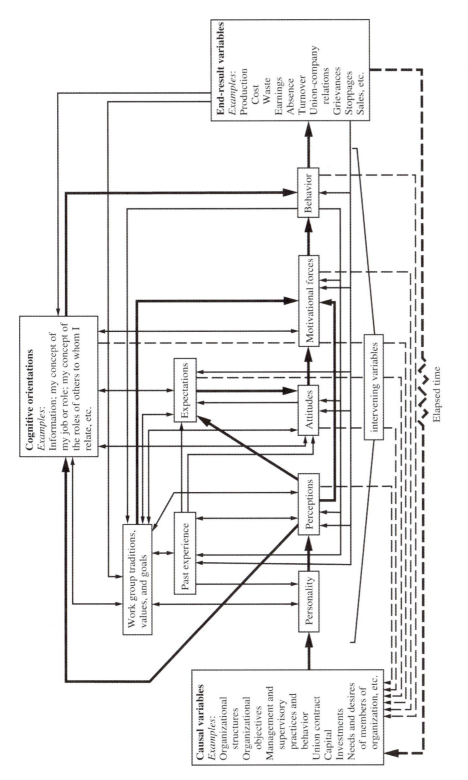

FIGURE 13.1 Pattern of relationships between causal, intervening, and end-result variables, showing measurements yielding prompt and delayed information. From Rensis Likert (1961), *New Patterns of Management* (New York: McGraw-Hill), 201. Copyright 1961. Reproduced with permission of The McGraw-Hill Companies.

elaborated more fully, and there is a more pronounced emphasis on certain facets such as establishing high goals, structuring the organization, and accounting for human assets.

Exploitive authoritative, benevolent authoritative, consultative, and participative group systems are now labeled systems 1, 2, 3, and 4 for the first time, and the list of characteristics of these systems is extended in the areas of leadership, communication, decision making, control, goal setting, and training. Furthermore, the total list, minus the performance items, is converted into a questionnaire that may be used to obtain reports on the current organization, past states of the organization, ideal circumstances, and so on. This Profile of Organizational Characteristics provides an index of how closely an organization approximates the theoretically superior system 4. Shifts toward that system are expected to result in long-range improvements in productivity, labor relations, costs, and earnings.

By contrast, shifts away from system 4, as occur in most cost reduction efforts, will set in motion strong negative influences on intervening variables, even though the immediate results may be favorable. These negative influences are related to a definite sequence of events that does not manifest itself fully in end-result variables for three or four years, or even longer. The human relations approach to management often is introduced at this point as a salve for the existing system 2 organization. Because it does not actually shift the organization toward system 4, however, it does not work. A shift can best be achieved by teaching managers system 4 principles.

Changes in an organization toward a new system should be internally consistent. One cannot achieve the desired results by changing only certain aspects of the system, as when sensitivity training is introduced but everything else remains the same. The whole system needs to be shifted over a wide range of causal variables. The list of such variables in Likert's 1967 book is expanded considerably beyond those noted in the 1961 volume, as is the list of intervening variables. Such variables should be measured periodically to monitor the progress and comprehensiveness of change.

Elsewhere Likert lists five "principles of effective management" that characterize the approach hypothesized to lead to favorable organizational outcomes:

1. The highest levels of productive and cooperative motivation are obtained when the non-economic motives are made compatible with the economic motives.

2. High levels of cooperative motivation can be attained by applying the principle of supportive relationships.
3. High levels of cooperative motivation and the linking of such motivation to the goals of the common enterprise are achieved mainly through informal processes in face-to-face work groups.
4. The setting of goals and priorities and the assessment of accomplishments must be a continuing activity of the various groups.
5. In applying these ideas to a particular organization, management should take account of the unique problems, objectives, conditions, and traditions of the company. (Likert & Seashore, 1963, p. 103)

Likert (1967) rejects the classical management view that an individual should have only one boss. He advocates horizontally overlapping groups with linking pins for many purposes and comprehensive group decision making for resolving any conflicts that may develop. Cross-function work groups that are product-related should be introduced at both higher and lower levels in the organization. Geographic cross-function groups also may be introduced.

For effective coordination the whole organization must consist of multiple, overlapping groups that are skillful in group decision making. Such a structure is not consonant with systems such as 2 but is compatible with system 4. Product management and similar work forms can be introduced successfully by extremely able managers in systems other than 4, but these forms will produce much better results in their natural environment.

New Ways of Managing Conflict

Likert's third book dealing with system 4 theory, written with his wife, Jane (Likert & Likert, 1976), contains considerably less organization theory that is original than its predecessors. However, the continuum of systems 1 through 4 is extended to cover a larger number of organizational forms. This elaboration generally follows some ideas developed earlier (Likert & Dowling, 1973).

System 0 covers permissive, laissez-faire organizations with little functional differentiation, large spans of control, and considerable confusion regarding roles. As might be expected from its position on the continuum, an organization of this kind is not hypothesized to be effective. However, the system 5 organization of the future will be extremely effective: the authority of hierarchy will disappear, and authority will accrue entirely from group relationships and linking pin roles. Whereas system 4 organizations operate from an interplay of group and hierarchical forces, system 5 organizations will function almost entirely as overlapping groups.

The central thesis of the Likert and Likert (1976) book is that system 4 is the best method currently available for dealing with conflict, not only in the organizational context but in other contexts as well. The essential propositions are that:

1. Conflict involves interactions among people or social units and occurs in a social system.
2. Conflict resolution depends on the effectiveness of the social system used.
3. The closer the social system is to system 4, the greater the probability of constructive conflict resolution.
4. System 4 can be used in every conflict situation by those who wish to achieve resolution. Applying system 4 to conflict situations requires an understanding of system 4 principles, skill in their use, and the passage of time.

Thus one would anticipate that a move to system 4 in an organization ultimately would not only improve productivity and profits (Likert says by 20 to 40 percent), but also cause a marked reduction in conflict.

In system 4T the designation T refers to *total*. System 4T theory states that there are additional factors beyond position on the system 1 through 4 continuum that contribute to organizational effectiveness. Likert had previously mentioned a number of these factors without specifically incorporating them into his theory. The aspects of the human organization above and beyond the system continuum now include:

1. The levels of performance goals held by the leader and transmitted to subordinates
2. The levels of knowledge and skill of the leader with regard to the technical field, administration, interaction processes, and problem solving
3. The capacity and motivation of the leader to provide planning, resources, equipment, training, and help to subordinates
4. The degree to which the structure provides for optimum differentiation and for sufficient linkages
5. The extent to which stable working relationships exist within units

With the addition of these variables, the theory explicitly incorporates certain factors previously proposed by David Bowers and Stanley Seashore (1966) in their four-factor theory of leadership: support, interaction facilitation, goal emphasis, and work facilitation. The theory as now stated is clearly much more than a theory of the effects of participation. In fact, system 4 loses its preeminent role. Likert and Likert note that "if an organization, or a department, scores high on the system 1 to 4 scale and low on one or more of the other dimensions, such as technical competence or level of performance goals, the probabilities are great that it will not be highly effective in conflict management or performance" (1976, p. 50).

System 4T also introduces the concept of peer leadership and organizational climate. Peer leadership occurs when subordinate group members engage in leadership behavior. Such behavior tends to reflect the style of the leader. Under system 4T, peer leadership tends to strengthen the organization and has positive effects. In systems 1 or 2 it may well restrict output.

Organizational climate is defined as a composite state that is influenced by group member perceptions of the situation in the department, or some larger organizational entity, in which their group resides. It is influenced most by behavior toward the top of the organization and can severely constrain the type of management possible at lower levels. In system 4T, organizational climate is hypothesized to be a positive force.

In essence, Likert believed that there are general principles applicable to all managerial situations, though actual applications may vary with the particular culture involved. Bowers (1976), in interpreting Likert, states three reasons why management contains universal and transferable properties:

1. Human nature in its inherited essence is the same everywhere.
2. The scientific method is the same everywhere.
3. Culture, though it may influence the application of management principles, is not in itself a principle.

The implication is that the situational variations discussed by the organizational contingency theorists, who are considered later in this book, are mere cultural variants in the application of basic principles (Likert & Dowling, 1973; Likert & Likert, 1976). It is not at all clear that this is what the contingency theorists mean, nor does Likert spell out in any specific detail what cultural variations would be expected to have what effects under what circumstances. As a result, any findings that fail to support Likert's may be attributed to cultural variations on an ad hoc basis.

Applications of the Theory

Likert wrote extensively in the more popular management literature. This usually means that a theorist is interested in promoting applications, and this clearly was the case with Likert. The following applications are of interest to us here.

Accounting Approach to Human Resource Valuation

Throughout his writings Likert expressed concern over the liquidation of the human organization to obtain short-term increases in productivity. His thinking in this regard appears to have been stimulated by certain findings from research conducted by Nancy Morse and Everett Reimer (1956) and by his experiences with hierarchically initiated cost reduction programs. Any attempt to demonstrate that certain approaches squander the human organization, while others preserve and develop it, requires that appropriate measures of the value, or at least of change in the value, of human assets be developed. By this logical route Likert became one of the very early proponents of so-called human resource or human asset accounting. Starting with a chapter in *The Human Organization* (1967), Likert has proposed a number of extensions to practice in this area.

Initially, Likert (1967) defined human assets in terms of "the value of the productive capacity of a firm's human organization and . . . the value of its customer goodwill." Goodwill was subsequently expanded to include shareholder and supplier loyalty, as well as reputation in both the financial and local communities (Likert & Bowers, 1969). However, at the level of application the focus has been primarily on internal, human organization variables.

A wide range of different approaches to the valuation of the human organization has been developed. Though Likert emphasizes an approach that is grounded in his own theoretical views, he advocates the utilization of other approaches on the grounds that they provide different types of information. Two of these are specifically noted: one based on measuring the costs invested in the human organization for re-

cruiting, selection, training, and the like; the other based on estimating the replacement costs of the human investments (Likert & Bowers, 1973).

The essential and distinguishing aspect of Likert's own approach to human resource accounting is its heavy reliance on survey-type research using questionnaire measures. Two types of causal variables are stressed (Likert, 1973; Likert & Bowers, 1973):

1. Managerial behavior as reflected in support, team building, goal emphasis, and work facilitation (help with work)
2. Organizational climate as reflected in communication flow, decision-making practices, concern for persons, and influence on department, technological adequacy, and motivational conditions

At the level of intervening variables, measures are obtained for:

1. Peer leadership as reflected in support, team building, goal emphasis, and work facilitation
2. Group process as reflected in planning together, making good decisions, knowing jobs, sharing information, wanting to meet goals, member trust, and the meeting of unusual demands
3. Satisfaction with fellow workers, superiors, jobs, the organization, pay, progress, and chances for getting ahead

These causal and intervening variables are important because, according to theory, they determine the level of end-result variables in the future. Thus the future value of the human organization may be assessed by measuring causal and intervening conditions today.

To determine increases or decreases in the value of the human organization, causal and intervening measures are taken at two points in time, and difference indices are computed after the measures are standardized to eliminate differences in variability. These difference indices are then multiplied by the correlation coefficient for the relationship between the particular causal or intervening variable and the end-result variable to give greater weight to changes in the variables that have greater causal impact. Finally, the estimate of performance change is converted into units of the performance measure, preferably dollars. Combined results may be obtained by using multiple correlation techniques. What emerges is a statement of the consequences of various changes in the causal and intervening variables for productive efficiency. One can say what the consequences of a given change will be in terms of total cost decreases or increases for a given amount of production.

The information derived from these calculations may be used to determine whether a particular plant manager, for instance, is a human organization builder or a liquidator. It may also be used to determine whether a shift toward system 4 is recommended as a means of offsetting a trend that anticipates declines in future productivity.

Questions about Human Resource Accounting

Although human resource accounting has considerable practical appeal, application of the Likert approach or any other similar approach has not been widespread. One inherent problem is the very diversity of human resource accounting approaches. It is difficult to determine which approach to introduce, and the cost of introducing several approaches may be too large to justify.

There are also measurement problems, especially in the Likert approach. Should measurements really be restricted to the variables of system 4 theory? Are the assumptions that underlie the calculations justified, especially if we weight the data according to the size of the correlation coefficients? Is the measurement of change, as opposed to the measurement of absolute value, sufficient?

Without doubt, these considerations have contributed to the problems human resource accounting has had in winning acceptance by practitioners. But another factor that must be considered is the widespread skepticism over whether greater precision of measurement would really make any difference in the way organizations operate. What are the consequences of installing a human resource accounting system for organizational effectiveness and investment decisions? Is the Likert approach better or worse than others? for what purposes? These are research questions, but little such research has been conducted. Human resource accounting has an inherent practical appeal, and Likert has made a very real creative contribution, but there are many unanswered questions that have hampered its acceptance.

Organization Development Applications

Although certain of the early attempts to introduce participative management in various companies might well qualify as organization development, certain other approaches that are identified with Rensis Likert and the Institute for Social Research are even more clearly addressed to organization development. Two of these approaches seem to have originated in other contexts and to have been given limited attention by Likert and his associates. The introduction of cross-functional teams, making extensive use of horizontal linking pins, is in fact closely allied with project management and the matrix structure and goes back many years. Likert (1975) views the cross-functional team approach as a means of moving toward system 4.

Another approach, management by group objectives (MBGO), had its origins in the management by objectives (MBO) literature of the 1950s. The added element in MBGO is that objectives are set by the work group as a whole in problem-solving sessions (Likert & Fisher, 1977). The intent is to eliminate the tendency toward competition that is fostered by the more traditional type of MBO. There are several examples of the successful incorporation of MBGO in more comprehensive organization development efforts. Among these, Likert and Fisher (1977) note successful applications in a retail sales division and an automotive plant.

However, the primary organization development procedure introduced by Likert and his associates is the survey feedback method or, more broadly, survey-guided development. This approach has a long history at the Institute for Social Research, extending back to early work at the Detroit Edison Company (Mann & Likert, 1952). It is a natural outgrowth of the survey methodology that has characterized the work of the institute from its beginnings.

The essential element of survey-guided development is the use of questionnaire data, aggregated both for work groups and for larger units, to induce change toward system 4. Since the data are fed back to the groups from which they were gathered for purposes of identifying problems and developing group solutions, the approach itself is system 4 in nature and therefore provides an experiential model for the type of management system desired as an end result. In early applications the questionnaire feedback moved down through the organization, level by level, like a waterfall. However, simultaneous feedback at all levels is now considered acceptable. The ideal appears to be a top-down approach, emphasizing overlapping group or linking pin relationships that nevertheless move the information rapidly.

The steps in the overall process are as follows:

1. Initial planning sessions involving key members of the outside consulting staff, plant management, and representatives from nonmanagerial personnel within the organization
2. Administration of the questionnaires to all members of the organization
3. Training for some members of the organization to act as internal resource persons in the feedback meetings
4. Training for organizational members in basic concepts describing how organizations function
5. The return of data to group supervisors
6. Group feedback meetings
7. The presentation of a systematic diagnosis
8. The allocation of resources in accordance with needs, as indicated by the systematic diagnosis and feedback meetings
9. Gathering, organizing, and evaluating intermediate feedback to monitor progress in the change activity
10. A formal reassessment of the organization to examine progress (Bowers & Franklin, 1977, p. 117)

Thus questionnaires are administered in successive waves to provoke, monitor, and reassess change.

This organization development process was set forth in detail in a manual by D. Hausser, P. Pecorella, and Anne Wissler (1977) and in somewhat more general form in David Nadler (1977). The training in organizational functioning noted in step 4 has a strong system 4 flavor and is described in Jerome Franklin, Wissler, and Gregory Spencer (1977).

The questionnaire used almost exclusively in organization development efforts carried out with the assistance of the Institute for Social Research is the Survey of Organizations. This instrument has gone through a number of revisions. Its basic measures are those for establishing the status of causal and intervening variables — managerial behavior or leadership, organizational climate, peer leadership, group process and satisfaction. As a survey instrument, the Survey of Organizations appears to be well prepared and useful (see Hausser et al., 1977). However, it is clearly a special product of the converging influences of Likert's system 4 theory and Bowers and Seashore's (1966) four-factor theory of leadership. Thus, to the extent these theories are wrong, the instrument is less useful.

Practical Impact

Data bearing on the effectiveness of survey feedback as an intervention in organization development are somewhat limited. An early study conducted by Bowers (1973) compared organization development approaches used in 23 organizations on measures from the Survey of Organizations. Of the approaches considered, survey feedback produced the most positive changes. Other similar studies comparing pre- and posttest findings on the Michigan instrument tend to support the wide applicability of the survey feedback approach.

However, the strength of this support must be tempered somewhat. No data on end-result variables are included. The findings indicate that changes did occur, but there is no way of knowing how much difference they made in the long run. Furthermore, the fact that the change measures, and the measure yielding the data that were fed back to and discussed in the groups, were one and the same, contaminates the results; only the survey feedback data were so contaminated. It would have been desirable to use as a pretest and posttest some measure other than the Survey of Organizations.

As research results have accumulated, the early superiority of survey feedback over other organization development techniques has been less in evidence; the approach seems to produce significant changes under some circumstances, but not others, and it is not fully apparent exactly what the conducive circumstances are.

The status of survey feedback procedures today is certainly not what Likert would have desired. There has been a merging with other approaches, often under the quality of work life label, so that the survey emphasis is less pronounced even among the Michigan based practitioners (Nurick, 1985). Some have added numerous other diagnostic tools to the survey data so that it is no longer appropriate to describe their approach as being genuine survey feedback (see Walton & Nadler, 1994).

Among organizational development practitioners, survey feedback remains one of the many approaches used, but it is not among those most preferred (Church, Burke, & Van Eynde, 1994). For reasons that are not entirely clear, Likert's theory is not currently very attractive to organization development practitioners as a theoretical orientation on which to base their work (Bazigos & Burke, 1997). It appears that this practical rejection of system 4 theory has hurt the survey feedback application as well.

Evaluation and Impact

For a considerable period of time, almost all of the research on Likert's theory was conducted by staff members of the Institute for Social Research at the University of Michigan or by individuals who were closely associated with the institute. Although this organization continued to be a major source of studies of the theory during the 1970s, a number of others have tested the theory since, often using instruments developed at Michigan. Likert's books, particularly the 1961 and 1967 volumes, contain extensive reviews of the research conducted by members of the Michigan group. As presented, the research is almost universally favorable to the theory, though questions have been raised subsequently about some of the studies. Of these studies, a number have been cited and reprinted often enough to justify referring to them as classics.

Comparing High- and
Low-Producing Groups

A major research strategy in the early period was to enter organizations to identify high- and low-producing work groups and then administer extensive questionnaires to the members for the purpose of establishing leadership practices that differentiated the effective and ineffective groups (Likert, 1961), It is apparent that the questions used were developed with some idea of the value of the participative approach. Nevertheless, Likert's formal specification of concepts, such as the principle of supportive relationships, also appears to have been influenced by the results of the research. Thus the studies may be viewed as tests of the theory only in a general form.

Though the best known of these investigations were those conducted with clerical groups in an insurance company and with railroad section gangs, a summary of the results by Robert Kahn and Daniel Katz (1960) includes other research. In high-producing groups it was found that leaders whose more differentiated role often included planning and interpersonal activities did not do the same things as their subordinates. High production also was associated with general rather than close supervision; with an employee-oriented, supportive approach; and with a high level of group involvement among members.

The data on which these conclusions are based vary considerably in the degree to which they differentiate the high and low groups. In several cases the support claimed for the conclusions is based on comparisons that are, at best, of marginal statistical significance. Furthermore, the concurrent, correlational nature of the research design makes causal interpretation inappropriate. All in all, this research appears now to have been of greater value for theory building than for theory testing.

Harwood Research

The Harwood Company was described in chapter 2 in this volume in connection with the discussion of Kurt Lewin's influence on organizational behavior. The company served as the site of significant research from the late 1930s. One early finding derived from a case study conducted during World War II that drew on Lewin's ideas. The study demonstrated the use of participative decision making in overcoming managerial resistance to hiring women over the age of 30 during a labor shortage (Marrow & French, 1945). This study was followed by a more sophisticated experiment, which dealt with the use of participation in overcoming resistance to the introduction of new production processes (Coch & French, 1948).

For some time Harwood had suffered increases in turnover and grievances, and decreases in production, whenever changes in job activities were introduced. In the experiment, job changes were undertaken among groups of 18 hand pressers, 13 pajama folders, 8 pajama examiners, 7 pajama examiners, and 2 sewing operators. The hand pressers, serving as a control group, were merely told that certain job changes would be made. The pajama folders were persuaded that a change was needed and were then asked to select their own representatives to undergo training. These representatives subsequently trained the others. The remaining groups were treated essentially the same as the pajama folders, but being smaller groups, all members underwent the initial training. The groups approved the plans for change by consensus, after lengthy discussions of possible approaches.

Before the change, all groups had been producing at approximately 60 units per hour, which was the plant norm. All experienced the usual drop in production after the change. The control group of hand pressers never did recover and stabilized at about 50 units. The pajama folders whose representatives participated in initial training recovered gradually and ultimately moved up to between 65 and 70 units per hour. The remaining, full-participation groups recovered more rapidly and stabilized at 70 to 75 units. Data on aggressive acts toward management, grievances, and turnover are generally in line with the production findings. In a subsequent study, the original control group of hand pressers was broken up and after several months reconstituted (with only 13 members remaining). After changing to the new pressing procedures introduced by means of the total participation approach, their production also rose to over 70 units per hour. Though no statistical tests are presented, the differences among the groups appear to be sizable.

Although the results of this research seem clear enough, their interpretation is another matter. It can be argued that, as a designated social science research site, Harwood was atypical in a number of respects, thus making generalization of the findings unwarranted. There is a real question as to whether a causal impact of participation on motivation can be assumed, given that no measures of motivation or of the effects of participation manipulations on the various groups were obtained. A number of other factors might account for the results, including differences in jobs and job changes, group sizes, methods of presenting the need for change, competition levels, quality of training, and knowledge of results.

A subsequent study, conducted in Norway, which seemed to have eliminated a number of possible confounding effects and included a measure of how well the experimental manipulations "took," generally failed to yield significant findings (French, Israel, & Ås, 1960). The comparison of the United States and Norwegian results led Likert to conclude that participation must be culturally relevant if it is to work effectively. However, a subsequent attempt to replicate the Harwood study in the United States also failed to support the superiority of direct participation (Fleishman, 1965). These two studies suggest that generalization from the Harwood situation should be approached with considerable caution. Yet it is apparent that the Harwood results are not time bound. Findings similar to those of Lester Coch and John French (1948) were reported 10 years later for a more extensive change in the production process at Harwood (French, Ross. Kirby, Nelson, & Smyth, 1958).

Pelz's Research on Upward Influence

The empirical basis for Likert's linking pin hypothesis was certain research conducted by Donald Pelz (1952). This research produced evidence that supervisors with considerable influence on their superiors who also "side with employees" and exhibit "social closeness to employees" elicit greater employee satisfaction than other supervisors. When the supervisor does not have much upward influence, behavior supportive of employees tends to make little difference and, in fact, can have negative consequences because it raises false expectations,

The results on which these conclusions are based are not strong, but they are consistent. Furthermore, these results appear to be an outgrowth of ad hoc data analysis and thus require further independent study. In contrast to Likert, whose linking pin theory extends the role of two-way influence to all levels of the organization and to a wide range of end-result variables, Pelz is concerned only with first-level supervision and satisfaction with the supervisor. Yet, based on his findings, Pelz does advocate increasing the amount of influence given to these supervisors.

Morse and Reimer Experiment

In the Morse and Reimer (1956) experiment, within a single department decision making was shifted downward to increase employee participation considerably in two divisions and upward to emphasize top-level, hierarchical decisions in two other divisions. Pretests were administered prior to a 6-month period during which the changes were introduced by means of training programs for supervisors. The divisions operated for a full year under the conditions thus created before the posttest was administered. There is considerable evidence that the experimental treatments did take.

In general there was an increase in satisfaction in the participative divisions and a decrease in satisfaction in the hierarchical divisions, though not all the changes were statistically significant. Productivity increased in both contexts, but the increase was significantly greater in the hierarchical groups. Job-related turnover was greater in the hierarchical divisions but was relatively low in both situations.

The authors of the report, and subsequently Likert (1961), suggested that the greater productivity increases in the hierarchical groups would not be maintained over time. The Likert hypothesis is that higher productivity was achieved at the expense of squandering human assets, a practice that ultimately would result in decreased productivity, as well as the decline in satisfaction already noted. This hypothesis is, of course, post hoc, and the study neither supports nor refutes it.

Clearly the productivity findings were not as expected, and questions can be raised about the use of a clerical cost index here rather than a unit production measure. Furthermore, the effects of interactions across divisions within the department are not known. Nevertheless, the study remains one of the most impressive yet on participative management, and data from a computer simulation study suggest that Likert was right about the time-lag effects (Brightman, 1975). At the end of 5 simulated years, democratic groups were more productive. However, this was a simulation, and the results in these cases depend on the assumptions built into the computer program.

A later study, similar to that of Morse and Reimer, focused in much the same manner on introducing numerous aspects of the Likert theory (Seashore & Bowers, 1963). The results are open to question because the experimental and control groups were essentially self-selected, and hard data on absenteeism and productivity could not be interpreted. Nevertheless, there was evidence that the experimental treatments did take and that they contributed to greater satisfactions in many areas, as in the Morse and Reimer study.

Weldon Studies

The research reported in this section represented an extension of the earlier Harwood work. It compares changes made at Weldon, also a textile firm, where participative procedures were first introduced during the period after Weldon's acquisition by Harwood and at the main plant of Harwood where participation had been a way of life for some years (Marrow, Bowers, & Seashore, 1967; Seashore & Bowers, 1970). The changes were carried out between 1962 and 1964; a follow-up analysis was conducted in 1969.

The results of the Weldon research are perplexing. On the Likert profile, Weldon appears to have moved over the period of study from the borderline between systems 1 and 2 to early system 4. Yet in other respects the evidence that the workers perceived a major shift

in their work is far from convincing. On balance, one cannot say with certainty to what extent the experimental manipulations as they relate to system 4 theory really took, yet very clearly something happened. The Likert profile results may have been a reaction to newly learned expectations, but a major increase in efficiency and productivity did occur, bringing Weldon very close to Harwood in these respects. Satisfaction increased with regard to the work done, but decreased insofar as immediate supervision was concerned; the overall pattern of motivational and attitudinal change was mixed and varied from measure to measure. In general, the follow-up data closely matched the results obtained in 1964, after the changes had been completed.

Weldon was in serious difficulty at the time of its acquisition and, accordingly, researchers had no time to introduce changes one at a time and study the effects of each separately. A whole battery of changes, extending well beyond the diversity of even system 4T, was introduced almost simultaneously. The researchers tried to isolate the effects of the various changes, which included coaching low performers, terminating chronic low performers, introducing group problem solving, and providing supervisory training. But the confounding of effects was so pronounced that this analysis must be considered very tentative. A major review concludes:

> The authors must be commended for trying to sort out the contribution of the various factors, but their estimates cannot be taken at face value, since their method of determining the various effects ignores such possibilities as delayed effects and interactions among the changes. While it seems almost certain that the sum total of the organizational changes made were responsible for the effects observed, isolating the precise degree of effect produced by each change is virtually impossible from the methodology employed. . . . Thus the title used for the book which summarized this project, Management by Participation, must be viewed as somewhat misleading at best. (Locke & Schweiger, 1979, pp. 301–302)

Beyond the Classics

The classic studies noted previously from the University of Michigan group are the most widely cited with regard to system 4 theory. There is some additional research, however, that focused directly on the theory, although often on only part of it. Again, the studies tend to have ties to the University of Michigan, but not always.

A study conducted within the National Aeronautics and Space Administration validated various aspects of system 4 theory against criteria of unit effectiveness and also compared the theory with other theories of a similar nature (Mott, 1972). Questionnaire measures indicated good validity for the principle of supportive relationships and some validity for high-performance goals, but group methods of supervision and participation were unrelated to effectiveness. Of the four theories considered, Likert's predicted the criteria least often.

Research conducted in development banks in Brazil using the Profile of Organizational Characteristics indicated that banks closer to system 4 were viewed as more effective by their employees and generally elicited higher levels of satisfaction (Butterfield & Farris, 1974). However, no relationships with external indices of bank effectiveness were identified. Alternatively, a study that compared divisions within a single California company found system 4 conditions to be related positively, not only to satisfaction but also to objective measures of division performance (Roberts, Miles, & Blankenship, 1968). Similarly, a comparison of 10 high-performing plants in Yugoslavia with an equal number of less successful plants indicated that the high performers approximated system 4 more closely (Mozina, Jerovsek, Tannenbaum, & Likert, 1970).

Other research, which was conducted by individuals associated with the Institute for Social Research, has also tended to support the theory. Thus a comparison of the geographically dispersed departments of a nationwide company indicated that supportive behavior on the part of the supervisor, an overlapping group form of organization, and better use of group processes (including meetings) were associated with higher productivity (Likert, 1961). A similar study in the sales offices of an insurance company found that success was related to supportive behavior, high goals, group methods of supervision, peer-group loyalty, and an effective interaction-influence system (Likert, 1967). Likert and Likert (1976) describe a number of studies conducted in the United States and in other parts of the world that indicate a strong association between system 4 and productivity.

Composite results are reported by Likert (1973) for data in the Institute for Social Research files at that time. The nature of the productive efficiency measure is not stated, but the correlation coefficients appear unusually high. Elsewhere, Likert and Bowers (1973) note that the productivity correlations reported were not obtained from the whole data base but from a single organization "where the performance measurements have a minimum of noise or error." A subsequent report by Bowers (1975) that does utilize the whole database indicates a much lower level of correlation in analyses of hard data from the operating records of a number of firms. In these studies, measures of causal and intervening variables are known to have been obtained from a single questionnaire index, and this factor would be expected to contribute to high common method-based variance and inflated correlations among variables.

The results considered in this section are primarily concurrent in nature. This introduces two types of problems. One cannot establish, as the theory predicts, that system 4 conditions *caused* greater satisfaction and productivity; it might have been just the reverse. Furthermore, the theory incorporates a time-lag factor, and without some knowledge of temporal relationships one cannot say whether or not the research results are valid. A lack of significant findings may only mean that the time to achieve impact has not yet passed.

There is some evidence from predictive research to answer these criticisms. A comparative study of two General Motors plants in the Atlanta, Georgia, area showed a rapid movement toward system 4 in the experimental plant, followed a year or so later by improved productivity as well (Dowling, 1975). System 4 was introduced with intensive training. Though job enrichment was not involved and participation was, it is also true that the employees in the experimental plant acquired considerable job-related knowledge during the training, that an elaborate performance feedback system was introduced, and that certain staffing changes were made. Though these changes were all consistent with system 4T, their concomitant introduction makes it impossible to establish specific causes.

Linking Pin Approach

Research that takes its departure from the early work of Pelz (1952) dealing with the moderating effects of supervisory upward influence has yielded variable support for Likert's linking pin concept. The concept was not supported in one company study, but was supported in another (House, Filley, & Gujarati,

1971). It is not entirely clear why these disparate results occur, although upward influence may only operate as a moderator when the employee is quite dependent on the immediate superior.

Several other lines of investigation suggest that linking pin relationships can yield positive consequences. Research has emphasized consistently that two-way communication is more satisfying and more accurate than one-way, downward communication, but that it is also very time consuming. This may account in part for the long lag times associated with system 4 implementation. The data of chapter 12, which deal with leader member exchange theory, indicate that good linking pin relationships can be associated with a variety of positive outcomes. Franklin (1975), using the Institute for Social Research database, finds that the quality of group process at the superior level is related closely to organizational climate, managerial leadership, peer leadership, and group process at the subordinate level when measured roughly a year later. The data not only support the lag-time concept but also show, as do the vertical dyad linkage results, that relationships at higher levels can have a strong influence on lower-level functioning. This is a necessary condition if linking pin structures are to enhance end-result variables.

Computer simulations—conducted to test the view that a linking pin structure will lead to greater and more accurate upward communication (Ono, Tindale, Hulin, & Davis, 1988)—raise questions about this idea. It appears that under most circumstances successive decisions moving up the hierarchy tend to distort the information conveyed; in particular, they tend to suppress the influence of minority views, with the result that democracy is not fostered. This counterintuitive result needs empirical testing, but as it stands it places participative management and the linking pin approach in conflict with one another. A question is also raised by the finding that upward influence attempts most frequently use reason, as subordinates bring data and information to bear in support of requests to achieve their ends (Chacko, 1990). The survey feedback approach is certainly consistent with an approach of this kind in that it puts data in the hands of a subordinate, but under many circumstances the superior will have more relevant information and thus be in a position to negate any possible influence of a subordinate based on reason.

All in all, for a concept that bears almost the entire weight of the organizational level component of

system 4, above the work group level, the linking pin approach used across multiple levels of hierarchy clearly needs more research study and support. It seems likely that it can be made to work as Likert proposed, but, based on the evidence available to date, this does not appear to be by any means a certain outcome.

System 4 in Light of Research on Participation

Chapter 10 presented a detailed discussion of whether participation works and concluded that, overall, outcomes are affected to only a rather small degree. It is evident, that under certain circumstances, however, participation can serve to predict outcomes rather well. Chapter 11 helps delineate some of those circumstances. The question remaining is whether systems 4 and 4T represent specific circumstances under which participation works. Although on an ad hoc basis Likert did propose culture as a moderator, his position generally was that his theory applied widely, in much the same way as classical management theory held its principles to be universal. If we hold to this universalistic, or near universalistic, position, then the appropriate test is the one provided by meta-analysis, and there system 4 theory comes up short, being at best a weak predictor of the desired outcomes it intends to predict.

Though Likert has tended to emphasize the widespread, if not universal, value of participation, there are data from the Institute for Social Research databank itself that are at variance with such a view (Bowers, 1975). Within this database, participation appears to be ineffective at the top of the organization but more effective in the middle and at the bottom; it is also ineffective in organizations whose purpose is to conduct research or to serve as administrative headquarters for a decentralized firm or both; and participation varies in effectiveness in other contexts. Bowers (1975) also found, as have others, that satisfaction was predicted more effectively than productivity and that prediction with a 1-year lag produced better results than did concurrent analysis.

Many of the difficulties with system 4 theory relate to its origins in group dynamics. Basically it is a small group or work group theory extrapolated to the total organization. It often appears to extend beyond the domain to which it is most applicable. Almost all the research supporting the theory has come from the lower organizational levels. Survey research, based on the Profile of Organizational Characteristics and on the Survey of Organizations, extends to higher levels, but the sheer weight of the data from lower levels tends to obscure results at higher levels, where relatively fewer people are involved. When top-level data are analyzed separately, they do not to support the theory.

The major conceptual problem relates to the role of hierarchy. Under system 5, hierarchy is eliminated, but this system has not been elaborated fully, and, accordingly, it is inappropriate to assess the theory on the basis of system 5. However, the very nature of system 5 suggests why Likert is so unspecific about the role of hierarchy in system 4 — he appears not to have really wanted it there, either. Though Likert invokes the linking pin concept to explain how group goals are kept consonant with organizational goals, he gives little attention to the specific organizational processes involved. Furthermore, the research on upward influence and vertical linking pin relationships supports the theory only with regard to relatively circumscribed, dyadic interactions — again at the level of leadership and group dynamics, not organizational theory. We know nothing from the research about how failed groups at the top influence bottom-level groups, for instance.

A related difficulty with system 4 theory involves role conflict. Likert recognizes the need for clear definition of roles in an organization, but at the same time he advocates vertical and horizontal linking pin structures, cross-functional teams, and matrix designs that would be expected to increase uncertainty and conflict. The answer to this apparent paradox appears to lie in the implicit assumption that hierarchy is sufficiently weak and unimportant in system 4 to minimize its impact as a source of role conflict. Yet this whole area remains theoretically vague.

This same failure of Likert's theory to deal adequately with hierarchy increases competition from an alternative explanation of the research. Mauk Mulder (1977) has shown that participation provides fertile ground for the unilateral exercise of influence based on perceived expertise and proficiency. Given that the more competent individuals are selected for managerial roles and then provided with more training and information, the introduction of participation may only enhance the effective operation of hierarchy. This source of confounding permeates all the organizational research. Failure to explicate the role of hierarchy has led to inadequate concern for the nature and characteristics of managers in the organizational chain. As a consequence, the effects of managerial knowledge, information, training, and the like have not been controlled, and the effects of supportive supervision, participation, and so on, may well have been overestimated.

The problem of confounding in the research on system 4 theory in general is compounded by the way in which the theory itself is stated. System 4T incorporates not only supportiveness and participation but also goal setting, technical knowledge and skill, resource availability, and structural differentiation. All these variables have been shown on occasion to relate to group or organizational effectiveness. But then what is the role of the original system 4 constructs? A theory to which more and more variables are added is more likely to violate the principle of parsimony. Are there some variables in system 4T theory that neither predict outcomes nor advance understanding? Is it possible that the system 4 variables are unnecessary? We do not know, primarily because the research results are so frequently open to alternative interpretation.

Likert tends to deal with disconfirming results by adding to his theory on an ad hoc basis, rather than thoroughly revising it. The results of this approach have been mixed. The hypothesis of lag from causal to intervening to end-result variables appears to have considerable validity, but the lack of specific time intervals provides an "escape hatch" when the theory appears not to have been confirmed — usually the elapsed time is said to have been too short.

A similar escape hatch is ascribing research failures to situational and cultural variables that were not specified before the research was conducted. The theory is mute on when system 4 may be expected to be consonant or not consonant with situational demands and thus when the theory would be expected to work. To specify such circumstances would turn the theory into a contingency theory or perhaps a limited domain theory, rather than the general theory of organizational functioning to which Likert aspires. Yet without this specification of circumstances, it is a much less powerful theory.

Indeed, there is sufficient evidence to indicate that the effectiveness of system 4 type theories is contingent upon circumstances in the form of both individual differences and other contextual components (Glew, O'Leary-Kelly, Griffin, & Van Fleet, 1995). The theory appears to work best at the level of the individual work group; this would seem to be its practical, if not its intended, domain. Within this domain a number of circumstances that can enhance or mitigate the effects of system 4 have been noted. Certainly neither theory nor research has charted this area adequately as yet. It seems possible, however, that many of the moderator or contingency variables now proposed may be reduced to the level of personality of work group members — that is, for some types of people, the group control approach of system 4 generates considerable satisfaction and energy output, while for others it does not. The more positive consequences would tend to occur when members want to interact with others and to do so effectively, like to have a sense of belonging to a group, have favorable attitudes toward peers generally, prefer collaboration to competition, and enjoy participating in the democratic process. In any event it seems that a scaled down theory, which established a smaller domain of application and perhaps specified certain contingency variables as well, would fare better than system 4 theory has to date.

Certain additional conclusions for theories of participation such as system 4 theory derive from ethnographic studies that involve a completely different body of literature than what we have been considering. Here depth of understanding may be obtained, but often at the risk that research controls over theoretically unspecified variables can be deficient. Nevertheless, this is a literature worth considering. One such analysis finds that, contrary to what some have maintained, participation does not act to undermine the type of solidarity of work groups that supports union activity. The argument here is that participation lowers worker solidarity by displacing conflicts away from management to lateral conflicts among workers. The data refute this; in fact, participation makes what was previously unofficial and covert, official and overt (Hodson, Welsh, Rieble, Jamison, & Creighton, 1993).

This ethnographic finding is joined by another which indicates that participation results in increased worker effort, greater pride in work, more insider knowledge, and more job satisfaction. The net result is greater worker power that can be used to bargain for more freedom and a sense of dignity (Hodson, 1996). This positive shift from a worker perspective is not all it might be, but it is significant nevertheless. In general, on the ethnographic evidence, participation works to the advantage of workers and unions alike. Whether this happens at the expense of management and stockholders is not considered.

If we relax the rules of science further, beyond ethnography, the result eventually becomes philosophy. And participation such as that proposed by system 4 theory has not lacked for philosophical advocates. These appeals take the form of ethical arguments. They typically find that participation is ethically superior to other forms, but they may come to this conclusion from more than one direction (see, for example, Sashkin, 1984; Collins, 1997). Arguing philosophical issues such as this is beyond the purview of this book, but the reader should be aware of what is science and what is not in this area.

Finally, with the increase in the number of laws that constrain corporate action, the number of legal actions against companies, and the size of the judgments rendered in recent years, the risks of autonomous functioning by either individuals or work groups can be sizable. Accordingly, many managers simply do not consider it advisable to shift control downward or even to expand lower-level control for fear that the whole future of the firm will be jeopardized.

This matter of control within the organization is the major focus of the next section of this chapter. The theory set forth there also emanates from the Institute for Social Research and is closely allied with that of Likert. Research related to this theory has some bearing on the validity of system 4 theory as well. Consequently, it appears appropriate to suspend further consideration of Likert's theory until the data relating to control theory have been considered. It is important to recognize, however, that from a managerial perspective, adoption of the major tenets of system 4 theory can involve high risk.

CONTROL THEORY

Certain aspects of control theory were incorporated into system 4 theory. Both were clearly part of the thinking at the Institute for Social Research during the same period. Yet control theory was from the beginning, and remains, the unique product of Arnold Tannenbaum, who was at the University of Michigan throughout almost all of his professional career. This should not be confused with the theory based on the tenets of cybernetics, which carries the same name; that theory is a completely different matter.

Background

Tannenbaum's first degree was in electrical engineering from Purdue University in 1945. He became associated with the Center for Group Dynamics when it moved from MIT to Syracuse University after Lewin's death. After completing his doctorate in social psychology with Floyd Allport at Syracuse University in 1954, Tannenbaum moved with the Center for Group Dynamics to the Institute for Social Research at Michigan, where he remained as program director and professor in the psychology department. Like Likert, he was not in the business school.

In Tannenbaum's (1956) own view, his theory emerged from the early Michigan studies that contrasted leadership behaviors in high- and low-producing work groups; from the Morse and Reimer research, in which he played an active role (Morse, Reimer, & Tannenbaum, 1951); and from the early work on hierarchical influence done by Pelz. Tannenbaum interprets all these studies as analyses of the effects of variations in the amount and distribution of control. They are limited in scope, however, to the work group and to supervisory practices. Tannenbaum extended the framework of control to the total organization.

Much of Tannenbaum's thinking about the role of control in organizations was influenced by Allport's views on interpersonal control and dominance relationships. However, Tannenbaum was interested in theory at the organizational level from an early time (Morse et al., 1951). As a formal entity, control theory was created as a framework for a study of four local unions.

Evolution of Control Theory

Much of the development of control theory is set forth in a series of articles bound together after their original publication and republished as a book. This edited volume (Tannenbaum, 1968) contains material extending back to 1956.

Theory as Articulated for the Union Research

This first theoretical statement sets forth the basic conceptual framework (Tannenbaum & Kahn, 1957; Tannenbaum, 1968). Control is defined in a number of publications as "the capacity to manipulate available means for the satisfaction of needs." It is concerned with the allocation of rewards and punishments in an organization, and for this reason differences in control systems strongly influence the way organizations function.

Control may vary both in total amount within the organization, from whatever source, and in distribution. Characteristically, distribution is considered in terms of groups at different levels in the organizational hierarchy. Within the union context, high control at the rank-and-file level and low control at the officer level is associated with *democracy*. In contrast, high officer and low membership control reflects an *autocratic* or oligarchic system. In the *laissez-faire* or anarchic model, the amount of control in the organization is low at all levels; no one exercises much control. Where the amount of control in the organization is high for both officers and rank-and-file members, the system is *polyarchic*.

Several postulates describe the way control works.

1. There must be both a subject and an object, in that someone must control something. Controlling is the active aspect; being controlled, the passive.
2. Controlling must be motivated to occur. Thus there must be a perception of worthwhile rewards associated with the behavior.
3. Internal control within an organization and external control of the environment are closely related.
4. Control involves several phases of activity: the *legislative*, in which policies and courses of action are decided; the *administrative*, in which policies and courses of action are interpreted and implemented; the *sanctions*, in which rewards and punishments are given or withheld.

Tannenbaum does not offer clear-cut statements of his hypotheses. Nevertheless, they can be gleaned from a close reading of his articles and books. In the union research, member control was hypothesized to be positively related to member participation, as reflected in such activities as attendance at meetings, for instance. A similar relationship was expected to exist for total amount of control.

The amount of control in the organization consistently plays a more important role in the theory than does the distribution. Thus the amount of control is hypothesized to relate positively to organizational power over the environment, competition and intraorganizational conflict, member loyalty, interorganizational conflict (with management, for instance), militancy, member conformity, and receipt of sanctions. Though total control is expected to exert a causal influence on these variables, reciprocal relationships are anticipated as well. A factor such as organizational power can contribute to total control, in addition to being caused by it.

Tannenbaum refers to the set of variables considered in this section as the *organizational power syndrome*. Although these variables are expected to yield increased order and uniformity in an organization, within this syndrome it is the total amount of control that matters. High total control is associated with a strong organization that is effective in the pursuit of its goals. However, a variety of distribution patterns can yield this same result. Even in discussing employee-centered leadership in this early period, Tannenbaum only goes so far as to state that this style fosters membership control and member participation; he does not extend the hypothesis to organizational effectiveness, as Likert has:

> In the typical evaluation of democracy in organizations and communities, great emphasis is put upon the distribution of control and all too little on the total amount of control exercised. . . . We should think less in terms of the autocratic-democratic dichotomy and more in terms of the basic dimensions of control, within which an infinite number of patterns can be found. (Tannenbaum & Kahn, 1958, p. 237)

The specific hypotheses stated in relation to elevated member control and a democratic model involve member participation in union activities and a greater member interest in broad social goals, as opposed to bread-and-butter issues. In addition, the widely observed tendency for unions to become less democratic over time is attributed primarily to a relative decrease in member control in the later, more stable period.

Extensions during the 1960s

During the 1960s, control theory was increasingly extended from its original focus on local unions into the domain of organizations in general. These developments are documented in an early review article (Tannenbaum, 1962) and in *Control in Organizations* (Tannenbaum, 1968).

One major change introduced early in the decade was to relate increases in relative amounts of control at lower levels, and thus a particular control distribution, to organizational effectiveness. This was a step that Tannenbaum had not taken when the theoretical focus was on unions only. It puts him much more in line with Likert's views on the superiority of democratic (system 4) forms over more autocratic forms,

and Tannenbaum (1968, p. 57) acknowledges his debt to Likert in this regard.

At the same time, the theory continued to stress the importance of the total amount of control. The relationship with effectiveness is reciprocal: greater control yields greater organizational effectiveness, and effectiveness contributes to greater control. The hypothesis is qualified as follows, however:

> Too much control may be as dysfunctional as too little, and a hypothesis more general than that offered above would specify an optimum level of control above or below which the organization would function below its potential. We are not yet in a position to specify the optimum for specific organizations. We can safely assume, however, that many . . . organizations are operating at a level considerably below it. (Tannenbaum, 1968, p. 58)

Another new hypothesis states that "across areas of experience, satisfaction will be a positive function of control" (Tannenbaum, 1968, p. 241). On the average, people who have greater control over an aspect of their work will be more satisfied in that regard, though for some few individuals control may not have this significance.

The view that the total amount of control in an organization is not a fixed sum is elaborated on at some length, particularly with reference to how expansion may occur:

1. There may be an expansion into the organization's external environment, such that greater influence over competitors, governments, and the like occurs.
2. There may be certain kinds of internal changes — either in the structural factors that determine member interactions and influence, or in the motivational factors that cause members to exercise control and to become amenable to control.

Control may expand as a function of increased interpersonal exchange, greater personal inclusion in the organization, cooptation of new members, and the like. Participative approaches of the kind represented by system 4 are particularly likely to increase the amount of control in this manner. The "influence pie" is expanded from within, as more organizational members exert influence on each other.

Participation and Control

The matter of the nature of various types of participative systems and their relationships to the total influence pie has become of increasing concern for control theory in recent years:

> Participation is often thought to imply taking power from managers and giving it to subordinates, but in fact managers need not exercise less control where there is participation. A reduction in managerial power *may* occur, but it need not. . . . The participative organization may be one in which the *total amount of control* is higher than in the nonparticipative organization. . . . The success of participative approaches hinges not on reducing control, but on achieving, a system of control that is more effective than that of other systems. In fact, many participative schemes are really designed implicitly, if not explicitly, to legitimize, if not enhance, the control exercised by managers. (Tannenbaum, 1974, pp. 78–79)

As an outgrowth of this view, specific hypotheses have been formulated (Rosner, Kavcic, Tannenbaum, Vianello, & Wieser, 1973):

1. The degree of workers' participation in decision making is related positively to the amount of total control in the organization, and more specifically to the amount of control by the workers as a whole and by management.
2. The relationship between workers' participation in decision making and the amount of management control is mediated both by the frequency of communication between subordinates and superiors and by the amount of the workers' control.
3. A rise in the amount of workers' control increases trust in management, which in turn increases management control.
4. A rise in the amount of workers' control contributes to a sense of worker responsibility, which in turn increases management control.

According to these formulations, shifts in the direction of participative management would not be expected to eradicate hierarchy. Control would increase in the ranks of management also, though probably the *relative* amount would be somewhat less than under a less participative system. For control theory, participation effects of this kind are not restricted to approaches such as system 4; they may occur as a result of a socialist economy as well (Tannenbaum, Kavcic, Rosner, Vianello, & Wieser, 1974). Thus the general hypothesis is that people at the upper level in organizations will have consistently greater control than those below, but that in organizations designed on the basis of socialist ideological principles this hierarchic differential will be smaller than elsewhere (Tannenbaum & Rozgonyi, 1986).

Control Graph Method

Most research on control theory has used a measurement procedure that was developed at the inception of the theory: the control graph The existence of this method has been a boon to researchers. Nevertheless, such extensive reliance on a single procedure for operationalizing theoretical variables raises questions about construct validity and the specificity of results to the particular measure used.

Nature of the Method

The control graph method uses survey methodology. A questionnaire asks members of the organization to indicate how much control they believe individuals at various levels exert. Thus, in the union research, questions cast in the format "In general, how much do you think _____ has to say about how things are decided in this local?" were asked for the president, the executive board, the plant bargaining committee, and the membership (Tannenbaum & Kahn, 1958). Responses were given on a 5-point scale, ranging from "a great deal of say" to "no say at all."

These scale values are averaged for all respondents to obtain scores that reflect the amount of control exercised at each organizational level. A graph is then constructed on which the amount of control reported for each level is plotted against the hierarchical level involved. Figure 13.2 illustrates various possible results. Line 1 is positively sloped and reflects a democratic control structure. Line 4 is negatively sloped and reflects an autocratic or centralized structure. Both lines indicate the same amount of control, but the control distributions vary dramatically. Line 3 reflects an essentially laissez-faire structure with very little control at any level. Line 2 reflects a polyarchic system. A comparison of these two lines reveals sizable differences in the amount of control exercised in the organizations, even though the distributions are iden-

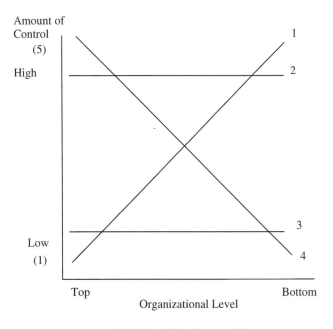

FIGURE 13.2 Hypothetical control lines

tical. The lines of figure 13.2 have been selected to portray hypothetically pure cases. In actual practice, the lines drawn to connect the various points on the hierarchical scale may yield a great variety of curves. Straight-line relationships occur only rarely.

Although control graphs typically are constructed to reflect the control that is actually exerted (or active control), there are several alternative measures in the literature. One alternative is an index of passive control, which indicates the extent of control over each hierarchical level (Tannenbaum, 1968). The basic data derive from essentially the same questions used to measure active control. However, in this instance respondents rate on a 5-point scale the amount of influence exerted by each level on all levels, including the level in question, as in figure 13.3. The scores for the levels are then averaged in terms of influence perceived from all sources, and the points are plotted just as with active control. In general, these passive control curves tend to be flatter than active control curves: being controlled is more equally distributed across hierarchical levels. The data of figure 13.3 also permit the construction of separate curves, which show the amount of control exerted by each level on the various levels (top management, management below the top level, rank-and-file), although such a detailed approach is not commonly used.

Another measure deals with ideal or desired control (Tannenbaum, 1968). In this variant the word *should* is substituted for *does* in the questions of figure 13.3. Comparisons characteristically are made between actual and ideal curves. The ideal values tend to be higher than the actual, with the discrepancy being greatest at the lower levels.

On occasion, specific questions are asked about control in various areas (wages and salaries, hiring, pricing, investments, and so on) as a supplement to or replacement for the more global questions (Tannenbaum, 1968). The responses to a number of specific questions may be summed to obtain a total measure. In this approach, as with the other measures discussed, question wording has not been completely standardized. There are variations from study to study, and it is not entirely clear what effects these variations may have on results. Also the verbal descriptors applied to the 5 points on the scale have not always been the same.

Difficulties

The reliability of the control graph has received only limited attention. The use of large numbers of raters whose reports are averaged would tend to argue for good reliability; the use of a very limited number of

1. In general, how much say or influence does top management have on what the following groups do in the company?

	Little or no influence	Some influence	Quite a bit of influence	A great deal of influence	A very great deal of influence
Top management	_____	_____	_____	_____	_____
Management below the top level	_____	_____	_____	_____	_____
The rank-and-file workers	_____	_____	_____	_____	_____

2. In general, how much say or influence does management below the top level have on what the following groups do in the company?

	Little or no influence	Some influence	Quite a bit of influence	A great deal of influence	A very great deal of influence
Top management	_____	_____	_____	_____	_____
Management below the top level	_____	_____	_____	_____	_____
The rank-and-file workers	_____	_____	_____	_____	_____

3. In general, how much say or influence do the rank-and-file workers have on what the following groups do in the company?

	Little or no influence	Some influence	Quite a bit of influence	A great deal of influence	A very great deal of influence
Top management	_____	_____	_____	_____	_____
Management below the top level	_____	_____	_____	_____	_____
The rank-and-file workers	_____	_____	_____	_____	_____

FIGURE 13.3 Typical set of questions for constructing active and passive control curves

questions to fix points on a curve suggests that reliability may not be as great as desired. Tannenbaum and Cooke (1979) note a lack of predicted correlations between the perceptions of various groups about the influence exerted by these groups. The problem is great enough to suggest low reliability in a measure that combines responses. In one study, judgments by the rank and file and by board members regarding the control of the president correlated .50, but the correlations for the control of the rank and file itself and of the board were .25 and .18, respectively (Tannenbaum, 1968). Findings of this kind suggest that the composition of the sample used to determine control values may exert considerable influence on the results obtained.

Tannenbaum (1968) also contains data on the split-half reliabilities (corrected for group size) of various control indices. These range from .53 to .84, with a median of .67. Here, as elsewhere, the argument for reliability is predicated on the use of large numbers of respondents whose ratings are averaged. Ideally, however, data from repeat administrations would be used to determine reliabilities. Such data do not exist in the published literature. Furthermore, other investigators have reported split-half reliabilities well below .67 (Pennings, 1976).

To this problem with reliability may be added certain other difficulties that the authors themselves raised at an early point (Tannenbaum & Kahn, 1957):

1. There is no provision for scaling the hierarchical level and amount of control dimensions to achieve equal units of measurement. As a result, unknown biases may be introduced into the findings.
2. The theory assumes a measure of actual control in organizations, while the measure is a perceptual one. The measures may not be analogous with the theory's constructs.
3. The control graph does not deal with the means through which control is exercised and thus may be insufficient.
4. It may be more appropriate to deal with specific areas in which control is exercised, rather than to use a global index.
5. The roles of passive and ideal control curves need to be explored further.

Among these points, matters of construct validity and difficulties in global measurement have received the most attention. In addition, certain aspects of the reliability problem, which Tannenbaum tends to deemphasize, have been given consideration.

On Construct Validity

The question of whether actual control, as opposed to mere perception of control, is represented in the control graph has been the subject of considerable research. Tannenbaum (1968) presents evidence that, though individual perceptions influence the results obtained, group or structural factors also tend to operate. The latter are interpreted as specific structural effects of actual control, with the following qualification:

It must be noted, however, that this particular interpretation does not follow necessarily from the logic of our analysis. It is possible, for example, that our measures have tapped some cultural stereotype common to the office as a whole, rather than the actual behaviors assumed to be associated with control and bases of power. (Tannenbaum, 1968, p. 222)

Overall, the results from this line of research are consistent with the idea that a sizable amount of variance in control graph measures is attributable to actual control, but they do not extend to the point of certain proof.

One problem with the control graph method is that respondents are free to interpret "say or influence" in their own way. Thus what is said to be influence at one level may not be the same thing as influence at another. There is evidence that this is the case:

Influence is specific as to hierarchic level. This indicates that the levels not only are perceived to have a different degree of influence, but that there is also a qualitative difference. . . . The questions measure influence in three dimensions, one for each hierarchical level. This means that it is not possible to draw a control curve as this requires unidimensional variables. (Gundelach & Tetzschner, 1976, pp. 59–60)

Conclusions such as these appear somewhat extreme, based on the data; at the very least, one can use measures of slope and total control to test the theory, whether or not a graph actually is constructed. Yet questions as to what the control graph measures mean are raised by this type of analysis—questions that are given further credence by the fact that, in the measurement of control, different hierarchical groups often yield different outcomes. It appears that control under one circumstance is not the same as control under another, and that the control graph method lacks the capacity to differentiate.

Evidence indicates that a majority of individuals respond to the questionnaire in a theoretically appropriate manner, although this is certainly not true of all. Attempts to correlate control graph measures with other measures that appear to tap the same constructs have produced favorable results. Thus the distribution measures do correlate (averaging in the .50s) with other indices of centralization (Tannenbaum, 1968), and both slope and total control show the expected relationships with independent measures of participation (Tannenbaum et al., 1974). All in all, it appears that the global questions yield only very rough measures of actual control, and do so with considerable "noise," and that the underlying constructs tapped by given measures may vary considerably, depending on the specific question, the respondent sample, the organization, and other circumstances.

Many problems associated with the control graph method might be solved by substituting a series of questions about influence in specific decision areas for the global questions. This approach should establish constructs with greater precision and at the same time increase reliability, because scores are based on a greater number of items. Yet, when one gets down to the matter of predicting criteria, there appears to be no difference between the standard global measure and an index based on eight specific items. The latter is more reliable, and results are not significant on all criteria for either measure, but the data do not support an outright rejection of the global measure for the more specific index (Patchen, 1963).

Variations in Concordance

It has been noted that the control curves produced by representatives of different hierarchical levels often do not agree—there is a lack of agreement or integration within the organization. Tannenbaum gave this phenomenon little attention. Subsequent research indicates that organizations can differ considerably in the degree of concordance between the control curves that emanate from different levels. Furthermore, variations in concordance can be good predictors of outcome criteria, especially criteria that emanate from employees rather than from managers (McMahon & Perritt, 1973; McMahon & Ivancevich, 1976).

This matter of concordance or agreement between the control ratings of various levels is not a direct derivative of control theory. In fact, for that theory, concordance is an index of measurement error or unreliability. Nevertheless, the fact that variations in concordance do exist among organizations and may have significant consequences has implications for control theory. In one sense, the fact that such a measure derives from theoretical concepts supports the usefulness of control theory. In another sense, the fact that the measure is not explicated by the theory and in fact is considered to reflect error indicates limitations in the power of the theory. As will be seen in later chapters, certain organizational theories that use integration as a control construct explain the concordance results better than does control theory.

Evaluation and Impact

Much of the research on control theory has been conducted by Tannenbaum and his associates. This research often has been international in character, with particular focus on socialist economic systems. However, a number of studies, both domestic and international, have been conducted without any involvement of the author of the theory.

Union Research

Questionnaire data to include control graph measures were obtained from rank-and-file members of four union locals in Michigan. The number of respondents per local varied from 163 to 223 (Tannenbaum & Kahn, 1958). In general, the control curves sloped positively toward greater control in the membership and bargaining committee than in the president and executive board, although there were sizable variations from local to local. The more democratic the local (the greater the member control), the more member participation as reflected in attendance at meetings. As hypothesized, a similar relationship held for total control. The greater the positive slope of the control curve for the local, the more likely members were to endorse broad social goals. However, this finding did not apply to political action and appeared to reflect primarily a desire for expanded organizing activity.

Analyses dealing with the organizational power syndrome produced consistently supportive results. Total control proved to be related to union power, union-management conflict, intralocal conflict, loyalty, conformity, and participation in union affairs. High total control was associated with uniformity in a wide range of areas.

Overall, these results support control theory, but in several respects the union research must be viewed as a pilot study. The findings are presented as comparisons between ranks for four organizations, too few for appropriate statistical testing. Furthermore, the data are concurrent and do not yield evidence to support the causal hypotheses of the theory. Though the authors advance suggestions as to the relative effectiveness of the locals, they report no direct tests of hypotheses related to effectiveness and control in the original study.

Predicting Organizational Effectiveness

Among the theory's hypotheses, those dealing with the prediction of organizational effectiveness have received the greatest research attention subsequent to the union studies. Researchers have focused on the view that the total amount of control in an organization contributes in an important way to an effective organization. However, a number of studies also have dealt with the hypothesis that a more positive, or at least a less negative, control curve, and thus a more democratic system is a source of success.

Total amount of control has been found to correlate positively with independent measures of organizational effectiveness in a wide range of situations. A review and reanalysis of early University of Michigan studies reports a significant relationship for five out of six studies (Smith, 1966). Similarly, a report on early research conducted in Yugoslavia indicates consistently positive results with the total control index, although measures of control distribution did not produce the hypothesized relationship in any instance (Rus, 1970).

A review by Tannenbaum and Robert Cooke (1979) of many more studies yielded essentially the same conclusions. Over 20 studies were considered, many of them unpublished. Only a small fraction of the studies failed to yield some evidence of a significant positive relationship between total control and organizational effectiveness. Negative relationships between total control and several effectiveness indices were found in one study (McMahon & Ivancevich, 1976). However, this research differed from most other studies in that the control measures were obtained from management personnel and the effectiveness measures from operating employees. An analysis, apparently based on a largely overlapping sample and using effectiveness measures that were derived from first-level managers, produced results much more consistent with the literature as a whole (McMahon & Perritt, 1973).

Research that deals with the distribution of control, or slope of the control curve, has not produced the same consistent results as total amount of control. Often the correlations never attain statistical significance. When they do, it may be that the more democratic systems are more effective, but this is by no means always true. On the evidence, Tannenbaum's early hesitation in endorsing democratic control structures seems justified. He would have done well to hold to this position after the union research.

Tannenbaum summarizes the findings presented in *Control in Organizations*:

1. Organizations with influential rank-and-file members *can be* as effective as organizations with relatively uninfluential members (contrary to the traditional view).
2. Organizations with powerful officers can be as effective as organizations in which the officers are less influential (contrary to most participative views).
3. Organizations with influential rank-and-file memberships are likely to be more effective than those with uninfluential memberships *provided* the officers are not less influential (contrary to the traditional views).
4. Organizations with powerful officers are likely to be more effective than those with less powerful officers, *provided* the memberships are not less influential (contrary to most participative views).
5. Organizations with influential leaders *and* members are likely to be more effective than organizations with less influential members and/or leaders (contrary to both traditional and participative views).
6. Differences in power between persons of different rank are *not* likely to be associated with criteria of performance. This statement sharply contradicts some arguments for participative organization to the extent that these arguments identify participation with "power equalization." (Tannenbaum, 1968, pp. 309–310)

Control theory hypothesizes not only a relationship between amount of control and effectiveness but also a causal relationship. Increased control should produce greater effectiveness; yet, at the same time, greater effectiveness should increase control. Studies that deal with causation are few in number, but they do exist. In one instance measures of the amount of control taken in one year correlated significantly with a number of performance criteria obtained a year later. Criteria obtained at the same time as the control data yielded much lower and generally nonsignificant results (Tannenbaum, 1968). In this particular study, significant predictions from performance to control level were not obtained.

A longitudinal study conducted by George Farris (1969), by contrast, yields evidence of a stronger effect of performance on control than of control on performance. The generally low correlations in this instance, however, make interpretation difficult.

One of the few laboratory studies that deal with control theory further supports the view that greater control can contribute to greater effectiveness (Levine, 1973). The control levels in three-person problem-solving groups were experimentally manipulated. Groups with a high total amount of control performed consistently better and were more satisfied. Accordingly, it seems appropriate to conclude that high levels of control can be a source of effectiveness.

Control and Satisfaction

In a number of studies, total amount of control is positively related to measures of satisfaction, loyalty, morale, and the like. Positive slope, or its approximation, also tends to be related to variables of this kind, but not to the degree that amount of control is. Unlike the analyses that involve organizational effectiveness criteria, however, those that use satisfaction criteria typically risk contamination due to common method variance, since the same questionnaire was used to measure both the control variables and the criteria. Correlations as high as .90 between total amount of control and satisfaction suggest that common method variance may well be a problem, given the relatively low reliability of control measures.

In any event, though control theory anticipates a positive overall relationship between amount of control and satisfaction, it further hypothesizes that individuals will experience greater satisfaction in areas where their control is greater. In general, this appears to be true (Tannenbaum, 1968). Workers tend to report greater satisfaction in areas in which, on independent evidence, they would be expected to exert greater control. In one instance where control was expanded in certain areas and not others, the changes in control correlated .46 with increases in satisfaction.

Participation and the Expandable Influence Pie

Control theory posits that increases in control at lower levels through the introduction of participative procedures can, and frequently do, result in increases in control at upper levels also, thus expanding the total amount of control in the organization considerably. As a consequence, a resort to participative management would not be expected to eliminate hierarchy, although the degree of negative slope in the control curve might be reduced somewhat.

An early study cited by Likert (1961) compared control curves for departments that varied in the extent to which participative procedures were applied in them. Differences in control at the worker level reflected the participation differences. Furthermore, the same rank ordering was maintained at the higher man-

agement level. Participative approaches were correlated with a greater amount of control in general, as the theory would anticipate, and with greater productivity as well. All the control curves exhibited a negative slope, irrespective of the level of participation.

This and other concurrent evidence tends to substantiate the expandable pie concept (Tannenbaum & Cooke, 1974). Studies of industrial firms consistently indicate that hierarchical control systems predominate even in socialized societies (Tannenbaum et al., 1974; Tannenbaum & Rozgonyi, 1986). Exceptions involving positive slopes appear to occur in voluntary organizations and local unions where the departure from bureaucratic organization is sizable. There is also some basis for anticipating a less hierarchical curve in professional organizations (Farris & Butterfield, 1972).

Measures of participation tend to correlate positively with the total amount of control in the organization (Tannenbaum et al., 1974). Yet the reverse also may be true in some cases:

> Data from the international study also show that coercion as a "basis of power" for the supervisor tends to be negatively correlated with the total amount of control in organizations. However, these correlations are not always large, and an exception occurs in 10 Yugoslav plants where, for reasons that we do not understand, a high level of control is associated with coercive leadership practices. (Tannenbaum and Cooke, 1974, p. 40)

Furthermore, the international research finds that the greater total control in participative systems is primarily a function of differences at lower levels, not all levels:

> The major contribution to the enhanced influence in the participative, compared to the nonparticipative, plants appears to result from the greater influence of workers. . . . This power equalization, however, does not mean a reduction in the control exercised by managers — managers, on the average, hold their own. (Rosner et al., 1973, p. 207)

Although this outcome is not entirely consistent with theoretical predictions and the earlier Likert (1961) data, other hypotheses regarding participation are supported in this study. Frequency of superior-subordinate communication and amount of worker control tend to mediate the relationship between worker participation and management influence in a positive manner. Similarly, trust in management and a sense of worker responsibility (and thus, presumably, a lack of worker-management conflict) mediate the relationship between worker and manager control.

The studies considered to this point do not indicate that increasing participation at lower levels will *cause* an expansion of total control, although the results generally are consistent with such an interpretation. To answer the causal questions, longitudinal research to observe the effects of expanded participation over time is needed.

An effort to obtain longitudinal data of this kind was incorporated in the Harwood and Weldon research. Control graphs, obtained at Weldon in 1962, 1963, and 1964, during the period of a concentrated effort to increase participation, indicate that very little change in control actually occurred. If anything, there was a diminution of control at higher levels and an increase at lower levels; no expansion of the influence pie occurred. Data from Harwood over the same period indicated that an increase in total control did occur there, which was in evidence at all levels (Marrow et al.,1967). However, Harwood had already shifted to a participative system by 1962, and the Harwood measures taken from 1962 to 1964 were intended as controls for those at Weldon.

This suggests that delayed response may be characteristic of increases in control, and, indeed, the data collected at Weldon in 1969 indicate an increase in total control over the earlier period (Seashore & Bowers, 1970). The change was most pronounced at the highest level and quite minimal at the employee level. Thus the role played by participation in the 1969 results becomes problematic. The findings from the Weldon research as a whole are subject to multiple interpretations; this appears to be no less true of the control graph findings.

Other attempts at longitudinal analyses carried out in conjunction with early University of Michigan studies also fail to yield the anticipated results. In one instance comparisons of data collected in 1958 and in 1961 during a period of intensive efforts to introduce participative procedures in experimental groups produced only very weak evidence of an increase in total control. The increases that were found occurred entirely at the upper levels; actual employee control did not increase, though the results for desired control were consistent with expectations for a program to increase employee participation (Tannenbaum, 1968).

Control graphs in Yugoslavia were compared over a 5-year period. Since the laws in that country had been moving progressively to define enterprises as essentially participative in nature, sizable increases in control were anticipated over the period of the study. Once again the changes in actual total control were minimal, though positive, and primarily attributable to increases in control at the top of the organizations. At the same time, desired control increased more substantially, especially at the worker level. In this case the time spans involved appear broad enough to have captured any lag effects that might have been present.

In another study, control graphs were constructed from the responses of all personnel in branch offices of an insurance company to questionnaires administered before and 3 months after a management development program for branch managers was carried out (Baum, Sorensen, & Place, 1970). The program was human relations oriented and stressed power equalization. This emphasis was clearly evident in the scores on desired control, which shifted sharply in a power-equalized direction in the experimental branches where the managers received the training and failed to shift in the control branches where managers did not receive the training.

Nonetheless, total actual control did not increase after training, and although control at lower levels shifted upward, the control exercised by the branch managers decreased. These effects were still in evidence after the control group data were used to correct for apparent regressions toward the mean. In this instance no expansion in the influence pie occurred: what the workers won, the managers lost.

The pattern of a high positive correlation between participative approaches and total control in concurrent studies, combined with little evidence that participation *causes* increased control, suggests that high levels of control may result in managers deciding to use a participative approach. This would seem particularly feasible if control contributes to organizational effectiveness (as it apparently does) and in organizations where there is considerable control at high levels. High-level managers who exert a sizable influence on their organizations and who are well entrenched by virtue of managing an effective organization may simply be in the best position to risk introducing participative procedures.

It has been suggested also that the expandable influence pie concept will hold only where intraorganizational conflict (as, for instance, between management and workers) is at a minimum. In the presence of conflict, what one level wins, the other loses, as in the insurance firm (Gundelach & Tetzschner, 1976). In the absence of conflict, trust, responsibility, two-way communication, and the like can operate to permit greater control at all levels. Data presented by Clagett Smith (1966) indicate that in bureaucratic systems such as industrial organizations, high levels of conflict are likely to be associated with low levels of overall control, with the result that laissez-faire (or anarchy) is approached. In contrast, less conflict is associated with greater overall control. Here, also, we cannot identify cause-and-effect relationships, but since the expandable pie hypothesis is not always valid, it seems reasonable to posit internal conflict as a moderator.

In describing such a conflict-laden situation where the results do not fit the theory, Tannenbaum notes:

> Democratic control (i.e., positive slope) does not have the predicted effect. . . . While the pattern of control may lead to high rank-and-file morale, it does not appear to promote basic identification with organizational objectives and practices or motivated action leading to high performance. It appears that in this organization, high rank-and-file control relative to the leaders may have the effect of members acting simply in terms of their own self-interests and not accepting the contributions of leaders. . . . In the absence of shared organizational norms and a system of high mutual influence (i.e., high total control) to regulate and coordinate member action with respect to these norms, it is not surprising that democratic control is not conducive to high organizational performance. (1968, p. 163)

Role of Hierarchy

The discussion previously led to the conclusion that system 4 theory had not been successful in developing a conceptually sound method of dealing with hierarchy. Because the roots of the theory were in group dynamics, the whole matter of hierarchical relationships was not well integrated with other constructs. In many respects, control theory may be viewed as an attempt to fill this gap in the system 4 theory. Control theory focuses primarily on hierarchy and attempts to integrate it with participative management.

Control theory has been only partially successful in integrating hierarchy with participative management. The difficulties have been in handling participation.

The simplest hypothesis is that the concept of slope can be used to represent participation and that the more positive or less negative the slope, the more democratic and effective the organization. Support for this hypothesis was obtained only rarely and then typically not in business firms.

The more complex hypothesis that deals with participation left hierarchy intact (and the negative slope that goes with it), while tying participation into the finding that total control consistently was related to effectiveness. Here, too, however, the participation part of the hypothesis runs into difficulty. Attempts to introduce participative approaches have the expected impact on levels of desired control, but not on other aspects of the control graph. If anything, the data appear to be explained best by the following hypothesis: where considerable control in an absolute sense exists above the worker level, there is a greater willingness to expand worker control, and the total amount of organizational control is likely to expand only in those instances where conflict between workers and management is at a minimum.

In spite of its failures (or very limited success) in dealing with the concept of participation, control theory has made a sizable contribution to the understanding of organizational functioning. The finding that satisfaction tends to be greater in areas where the individual experiences greater control provides new insights into job enrichment research. Knowing that organizations can vary in total amount of control — that control is not a fixed sum and that therefore control gained by some members need not be control lost by others — is valuable in understanding both organization-member and organization-environment relationships.

However, the most important contribution of control theory is the hypothesis (now soundly grounded in research) that a greater amount of control overall contributes to a more effective organization. This finding has emerged from study after study, in spite of major imperfections in the questionnaire used. Because most imperfections — such as unreliability of measurement — would tend to void the finding of any significant results, the underlying phenomenon in this case must be very powerful indeed. The only report of results opposite to those hypothesized above occurred when the control measures were obtained at the managerial level exclusively (McMahon & Ivancevich, 1976). In other studies the emphasis on the shared perceptions among worker respondents (and their concordance with perceptions at higher levels, as well) that the organization exercises considerable control may be the key construct. Presumably, these perceptions of organizational control would have some validity.

Control theory thus provides a basis for understanding how organizational effectiveness is obtained. Effectiveness appears to be a product of control processes that produce uniformity and coordinate effort behind goals. The result is a type of conformity. However, the pressures toward conformity need not come only from the top for the organization to be effective; ideally, control comes from all directions. It is important to recognize in this connection that control at any level includes control from within one's own group. Thus rank-and-file groups can exert very strong influence on their members, resulting in a greater amount of control than bureaucracy can produce (Barker, 1993).

Tannenbaum has indicated that the relationship between control and effectiveness might be curvilinear. Yet tests of the theory have continued to treat the hypothesis as linear, and that is the hypothesis the research supports. It seems reasonable that an organization might experience too much control, but the theory lacks specificity in this area and relevant research is nonexistent.

Application

Control theory has not generated any applications that are uniquely its own. However, the theory clearly implies that anything that can be done to increase the amount of organizational control and/or the perception of it will contribute to a more effective organization. Although guidelines for accomplishing this have not been developed and the introduction of participative management seems insufficient, several recommendations can be made.

For one thing, control in the sense that Tannenbaum uses the term is not the same as managerial control in the traditional literature. There managerial control is defined as the steps a manager takes to assure that actual performance conforms as nearly as practical to plan. Control of this kind invariably involves evaluation and feedback. In contrast, Tannenbaum is concerned with a much broader concept, which encompasses managerial control, as well as other types of influence. Accordingly, increasing the total amount of control should not be equated with

introducing an expanded array of managerial control systems. This may be part of the process, but it is certainly not all that Tannenbaum intended or that the research supports.

Furthermore, expanding control may well require increasing control at the lower levels—that is, not only the receipt of control, but also its exercise. As Tannenbaum (1966) notes, managers may resist this on the strength of a fixed-pie assumption. If conflict is rampant in the organization, the managers' assumption that their own control will suffer may be correct. Accordingly, it may be essential to develop mutual trust and a sense of responsibility before expanding control levels.

Control theory does not concern itself with how to increase organizational control, and this is one of its major deficiencies from the viewpoint of the practitioner. In contrast, the theory has produced one conclusion that has tremendous practical significance: organizations do need to be well controlled, and this does not have to be accomplished through centralization and a steep slope of hierarchy.

GROUP-FOCUSED SYSTEMS THEORY

Probably more than the two theories just considered group-focused systems theory is truly in the systems tradition. Its author Ralph Stogdill is a psychologist, but he acknowledges a major debt to sociologist Talcott Parsons (1951) in developing his ideas about organizations. Nevertheless, Stogdill's formulations contain a degree of emphasis on individual and group variables that is not found in the more sociological systems approaches to be considered later in this book.

Background

Stogdill was born in 1904 and attended Ohio Wesleyan University before shifting to Ohio State University. There he received his undergraduate, master's, and doctoral degrees, the latter in 1934. His early training was in clinical psychology, and he was initially employed by the Ohio Bureau of Juvenile Research, where he worked until 1942. His writing in this period dealt with clinical subject matter. He worked as a psychologist in the maritime service during World War II. In 1946 he returned to Ohio State and became associated with the Ohio State Leadership Studies, an association that lasted until his retirement in 1975.

Stogdill was associate director of the leadership program for many years and became a professor of business organizations in 1960; later, in 1968, he was named professor of management sciences and psychology. His writing from the late 1940s on dealt with leadership (see chapter 10 in this volume) and organizations. He developed a number of measurement scales and authored the first *Handbook of Leadership* (Stogdill, 1974a). Thus Stogdill's career path was from clinical psychology to leadership research to theorizing about organizations. He died in 1978.

From Leadership of Groups to Systems Theory of Organization

Stogdill (1959) opens his book with the statement, "It is the purpose of this book to develop a theory of organization achievement." He then writes for more than a hundred pages about groups and group members, with little reference to organizations. Basically, the theory represents a direct extrapolation from the group to the organization. The only difference is that "an organization is a group in which the positions in the system are differentiated relative to function and status. . . . It is found convenient to differentiate organizations from groups only in terms of degree of structure, since both must be regarded as groups" (Stogdill, 1959, p. 125). As a consequence, the variables of the theory tend to be drawn to a considerable degree from individual psychology and group dynamics; the reader must substitute the word *organization* for *group* at numerous points.

A second caution with regard to terminology: Stogdill tends to define his terms with an admirable degree of precision, but his definitions are not always in line with common usage among either lay or professional readers. As a result, it becomes important to pay close attention to Stogdill's definitions. In addition, Stogdill's whole theory is not easy to comprehend.

Individual Behavior and Group Achievement

In his 1959 book Stogdill describes three major theoretical variables and hypothesizes relationships among them. As is common with systems concepts, the three variable types are inputs, mediating variables (or mediators), and outputs. Inputs are associated with individuals as members; outputs, with the group (organization). Mediating variables are structures or processes

within the group. The group itself is defined as an "*open interaction system* in which actions determine the *structure* of the system and successive interactions exert coequal effects upon the *identity* of the system":

> By *interaction* is meant that, in a system composed of two members, A reacts to B and B reacts to A in such a manner that the response of each is a reaction to the behavior of the other. By *open system* is meant that, within limits necessary to maintain interaction, members may leave or enter the system without destroying the identity of the system. By *structure* is meant that the system is so differentiated or ordered that member A is not identical with member B, and the reaction of A to B is not identical with the reaction of B to A. By *identity* is meant the continuity of interaction which permits the system to be recognized as the same group during successive periods of observation. (Stogdill, 1959, pp. 18–19)

In a group of minimum structure, where members successively exchange positions while still maintaining system identity, individual freedom of action is limited to staying in the system or leaving it. Similarly, freedom of action is hypothesized to be highly constrained under conditions of maximum structure; in between is an optimum degree of structure that maximizes freedom.

There are three types of member inputs: performances, interactions, and expectations. A performance is perceived by members of a group as an act that identifies an individual as a participant in the group's operations. The performances of members taken together describe the task being carried out by the group. These individual performances, as well as interaction behaviors, are inputs under the theory; so, too, are expectations—defined as readiness for reinforcement.

The expectations of members form the basis of group purpose. Members are prepared or unprepared to experience various possible outcomes. They have ideas about both the probability of occurrence and the desirability of these outcomes. Values represent a special type of expectation:

> A personal *value system* may be defined as a highly generalized set of expectations in which desirability estimates are mutually confirmed with little reference to probability estimates, and which serve as a referent or criterion for evaluating the

desirability of alternative outcomes. . . . These value systems . . . are reinforced by satisfying as well as unsatisfying outcomes, and are little diminished by the failure of outcomes to confirm their validity. (Stogdill, 1959, pp. 72–73)

Groups tend to exert strong influences on the expectations of members. The goals and norms of the group serve as counterparts to individual value systems. Such group structures of expectation are highly stable over time. Member interactions tend to reinforce these expectations, with the result that considerable singleness of purpose in pursuit of valued outcomes tends to emerge within the group.

Formal structure within the group differentiates positions in such a way that members exhibit predictable patterns of performance and response. Positions have status and function:

The *status* of a position defines the degree of freedom granted its occupant in initiating and maintaining the goal direction and structure of the system in which the position is located. . . . The function of a position defines the general nature of the contribution that its occupant is expected to make toward the accomplishment of the group purpose. (Stogdill, 1959, p. 123)

Role structures, in contrast to formal structures, attach to the person rather than to the position. They represent a set of expectations conditioned in part by the status and function of the position occupied, but also by the demands made on the individual by other members and by the members' view of the individual as a person. Role structures involve authority and responsibility:

Authority may be defined as the degree of freedom that the occupant of a position is expected to exercise in initiating performance and interaction within a formally acknowledged structure. . . . *Responsibility* may be defined as the specific set or range of performances that a member is expected to exhibit by virtue of the operational demands made upon his position in a formally acknowledged structure. (Stogdill, 1959, p. 129)

Because roles are not always clearly defined and role expectations may vary among members of a group, role confusion and conflict represent distinct possibilities. The result is a diminution of the power of the group. The group's power is dependent not only on

unity of purpose, strength of effort, and coordination of operations but also on integration of its structure.

Outputs, in contrast to inputs, are group achievements, not individual behaviors. The three output types are productivity, integration, and morale:

Group *productivity* is defined as the degree of change in expectancy values created by the group operations. Group *integration* is defined as the extent to which structures and operations are capable of being maintained under stress. Group *morale* is defined as degrees of freedom from restraint in action toward a goal. (Stogdill, 1959, p. 198)

The three types of group outputs can vary simultaneously, but only when there are comparable variations in inputs. When inputs are held constant, an increase in one output must occur at a cost to one or both of the other outputs. Productivity is hypothesized to be high when function and status are clearly defined, when group structure and goal direction are maintained, and when responsibility and authority are enlarged to the degree permitted by the need to control operations. Under these circumstances, mediator variables contribute the most to the utilization of inputs.

Integration is analogous to group cohesion, but the definition is behavioral, not subjective. Integration requires a clearly defined role structure and is influenced by the level of member satisfaction, although integration is not identical with satisfaction. Integration tends to be high when:

1. Members are loyal to the group, support it, and are closely agreed on group goals and methods of obtaining them.
2. Subgroups support the structure and goals of the larger group, and their activities are coordinated with these goals.
3. The structure and operations of the larger group (organization) are supported by both individual members and subgroups.

Morale also is defined behaviorally, in terms of freedom of action, rather than subjectively, in terms of feelings. Morale can be either too high or too low for the group's own welfare. Morale, like freedom of action, is a curvilinear function of the degree of group structure. Thus bureaucracies can become so rigid that they restrict individual freedom of action, group morale, and adaptive initiative. Success also can contribute to high morale. Operations control, like structure, is hypothesized to stand in a curvilinear relationship to morale. When freedom to act and morale are high, motivation will be high also, but when morale is low, action can be so constrained that motivation is not manifested in behavior.

Four hypotheses regarding group outputs are stated:

1. Productivity and morale are positively related.
2. Morale can be related either positively or negatively to integration.
3. Integration and productivity are negatively related.
4. Morale, productivity, and integration may be positively related when the group is strongly motivated in striving toward goal achievement or when motivation is very low. (Stogdill, 1959, p. 222)

Hypothesis 4 assumes changes in member inputs; the first three hypotheses do not. The final theoretical model, devoid of hypothesized relationships among variables, is given in table 13.1. The model is said to portray an open system exchanging members and values with its environment, though Stogdill devotes relatively little attention to exchange between the system and the environment.

Intragroup-Intergroup Theory

After 1959, Stogdill elaborated on his theory in several respects. One early development is described in table 13.2 (Stogdill, 1962). The model attempts to account for individual accomplishments and individual and group reputation as outputs, in addition to the group

achievements of productivity, integration, and morale. Performances, interactions, and expectations are inputs common to all mediators and outputs. The primary direction of effects is from inputs through mediators to outputs, but there are also feedback effects. There is considerable mixing across the individual attributes, interpersonal relations, and group attributes due to their common input pool. A secondary set of effects runs from reference groups to norms to group purposes and from personality to role structure to formal structure.

In the same publication (1962) Stogdill considers the matter of intergroup relations, setting forth a partial model for this purpose. This model specifies certain environmental and cultural factors (resources, institutions, mores, social classes, philosophy, science, technology, coalitions, and alliances) that influence the relations between groups. The variables of table 13.2 are assumed to interact as they operate within the two groups and to produce intergroup outcomes. The extent of the involvement between groups is a function of the type of group involvement (total groups, subgroups, or individuals), the formality of the contact, and whether the contact is authorized, unauthorized, or accidental. This intergroup model, as contrasted with the basic group model, admittedly is incomplete and lacks hypotheses regarding relationships among variables.

Dimensions of Organization Theory

In a later statement Stogdill (1966) deals primarily with the scope of organization theory. Here he is clearly more concerned with organizations than with groups, but at the same time, dynamic relationships

TABLE 13.1 The structure of the theory of organizational achievement

Member inputs	Mediating variables		Group outputs
Behaviors	Formal structure	Role structure	Achievement
Performances	Functions	Responsibility	Productivity
Interactions	Status	Authority	Morale
Expectations	(Purpose, Norms)	(Operations)	Integration
Group Structure and Operations			Effects

NOTE: The terms in parentheses (Purpose, Norms) (Operations) refer to factors that condition or stabilize the particular mediating variables with which they are listed.

SOURCE: Ralph M. Stogdill (1959), *Individual Behavior and Group Achievement* (New York: Oxford University Press), 13. Copyright 1959 by Oxford University Press. Reprinted with permission.

TABLE 13.2 Model for a person, interperson, and group system in the intragroup-intergroup theory

Inputs	Mediating variables	Outputs
		Individual Attributes
Performances:	1. Individual's reference groups	Individual accomplishments
	2. Individual personality, values	
		Interpersonal Relations
Interactions:	1. Group norms	Individual and group reputation
	2. Role structure	
	Responsibility	
	Authority	
		Group Attributes
Expectations:	1. Group purposes, goals	Group achievements
	2. Formal structure	Productivity
	Functions	Integration
	Status	Morale

SOURCE: Adapted from Ralph M. Stogdill (1962), Intragroup-Intergroup Theory and Research. In Muzafer Sherif (Ed.), *Intergroup Relations and Leadership* (New York: Wiley), 52

are treated as secondary to variable listings. The group-organization differentiation becomes much more pronounced:

> We may define a group as a social interaction system with minimum structure. We shall regard an organization as a social interaction system in which the differentiation of expectations defines the structure of positions and roles in the system. Most of the groups and subgroups with which we shall be concerned will exhibit characteristics of organization. (Stogdill, 1966, p. 13)

The basic model is stated as follows:

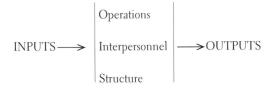

The input and output variables are now essentially the same, but there is a concern with measured inputs, both human (skill, effort, expectation, time, knowledge, and motivation) and material (money, materials, and facilities). Furthermore, the specific hypotheses about output relationships are stated somewhat more generally:

> In view of the number of variables and the complexity of the interrelationships among the variables that affect the output, it is difficult to formulate any all-inclusive statements of relationships among the output variables. If inputs are held constant and operations become stabilized over a given period of time, it would appear that an increase in one output must necessarily be accomplished at the expense of one or both of the other outputs. (Stogdill, 1966, p. 39)

The number of mediating variables is expanded to include operations (individual task performance, and technical processes), interpersonnel (a term coined by Stogdill to include interaction, intercommunication, interexpectation, interpersonal affect, and intersocial comparisons), and structure (purpose and policies, positions, roles, communication nets, work group structures and norms, and other subgroup structures and norms). Although extensions of this kind do increase the inclusiveness of the theory, they also confuse inputs and mediators somewhat, while raising questions regarding the parsimoniousness of theoretical statement. The precise definitions that were invariably given in earlier explications no longer hold in the 1966 statement.

Stogdill's move to an open systems perspective is increasingly in evidence in 1966. External, environmental constraints are listed as climate and material resources, folk mores and religious norms, common law and political philosophy, governmental and legal regulations, economic institutions and norms, professional and craft norms, fraternal and philanthropic norms, and family and community norms. Stogdill lists a number of survival mechanisms for coping with these environmental factors, though without adequate explication. Stogdill is clearly trying to combine a number of approaches to organization theory, particularly including the classical management and behavior concepts. It is also apparent that integrating them is not easy.

Basic Concepts

Certain variables in the Stogdill statement of 1966 did not survive in the next version, while some new variables were added (Stogdill, 1967a). Furthermore, some variables are renamed, although the definitions remain much the same. The model now includes specific feedback loops from mediators to inputs and from outputs to mediators and inputs, as well as the major progression from inputs to mediators to outputs.

Inputs are actions (performances), interactions, and expectations, plus task materials; outputs are product (productivity), drive (morale), and cohesiveness (integration). The differentiation of mediators into operations, interpersonnel, and structure is retained from the 1966 version, but within these categories there are major changes. Operations are divided into human performances and technical processes; structures into the familiar positions (status and function) and roles (responsibility, authority, plus delegation), to which are added formal and informal subsystems and departmentation. New structural variables are added, and other variables are dropped without explanation.

The greatest changes, however, occur in the area of interpersonnel, which covers "a large complex of behaviors and relationships that account for exchanges between member and member, and between member and organization" (Stogdill, 1967a, p. B671). The components of this category are completely recast to include the following:

Interpersonal relations (superior, subordinate, peer)

Personal-organizational exchange relations

Reinforcement, satisfactions, and dissatisfactions

Internal-external relations (reference groups)

Subgroup norms and pressures

Subsystem interrelations

Finally, the original hypotheses regarding output relationships are reinstated. One condition for a posi-

tive relationship between morale and integration is external threat to the group; this relationship can be negative when the group is divided into cliques and when there are differences in loyalties.

Behavioral Model of Organization

In speeches given at the American Psychological Association meetings in 1969 and the Eastern Academy of Management meetings in 1973, Stogdill attempted to reformulate his theory in mathematical terms. The resulting paper represents the most sophisticated of his theoretical statements (Stogdill, 1974b). For this purpose he used finer categories of analysis in restating the input variables. He also formally incorporated the concept of satisfaction into the theory: "Satisfaction, although a characteristic of individuals, is not an input. It varies as a result of reinforcement or nonreinforcement, and should be regarded as a subtype of mediating variable that can feed back as an input as the group progresses in its activities" (Stogdill, 1974b, p. 8). The subcategories introduced are listed in table 13.3.

Formulas for the major mediating and output variables are set forth in figure 13.4. In these formulas, specific outputs are tied directly to specific types of mediators. The concept of drive (morale) also is delineated somewhat more fully than it had been in the past:

> Drive is defined as degree of group arousal. Mutually reinforced expectations define an area of freedom for the group and determine to a large degree the objective or objectives toward which drive will be directed. Under conditions of high commitment to group goals and freedom from restraint, drive is likely to be expended in effort toward goal achievement. However, under high restraint, drive may become directed toward the reduction of restraint as a secondary objective. (Stogdill, 1974b, p. 12)

As in the early formulation of the theory, the influences of environmental factors are recognized, but no attempt is made to incorporate them directly into the mathematical statements.

Evaluation and Impact

Like a number of other systems theories, Stogdill's group-focused approach has generated little research.

TABLE 13.3 Subcategories under member inputs and the mediating variable of satisfaction

Performances	Expectations (regarding) (*Cont.*)
Nontask	Mutual liking
Task	Nontask performances
Specialized	Task specialization
Interactions	Returns from the organization
Mutual (reciprocated)	Task performance
Nontask-related	Task urgency
Task-related	Reference group support
Bypassing immediate superiors	Satisfaction (with)
Expectations (regarding)	Status
Contributions to be made	Contributions to organization
Freedom to act and decide	Freedom of action
Goal (outcome) values	Organization and supervision
Freedom to interact	Returns from the organization
Discontinuity of membership	

SOURCE: Adapted from Ralph M. Stogdill (1974), *A Behavioral Model of Organization* (unpublished ms., Ohio State University, Columbus)

In many of its early forms the theory produced more static models and lists of variables than testable hypotheses, though there were some of the latter, too. The later mathematical formulations were never formally published and are not widely known. So, though they constitute highly testable hypotheses, no evidence bearing on them exists.

Related Literature

Stogdill's 1959 volume contains extensive reviews of research related to the theory. However, it is clear that this research was the base from which the theory was generated. Stogdill tends to extrapolate from and reinterpret studies that were originally conducted to test hypotheses differing considerably from those of his own theory. Given this background, research conducted before 1959 cannot be used as evidence for the theory.

In a later review of relationships among the output variables, Stogdill (1972) cites studies carried out before 1959 and later studies that were not typically intended as direct tests of the group-focused theory. Six of the more recent studies related productivity to drive (morale), and three of these reported positive correlations as hypothesized. Fourteen correlations from nine studies since 1959 bear on the association between productivity and cohesiveness (integration). Five of the correlations were negative (as hypothesized), but another five were positive, and four were

not significantly different from zero. Research on the drive-cohesiveness relationship was practically nonexistent in the more recent period, but when the earlier studies were subdivided, they indicated a negative relationship under conditions of threat, a finding that appears inconsistent with the 1967 statement of the theory.

Stogdill's Research

Stogdill (1965) carried out extensive research in 27 organizational units using rating and questionnaire measures of mediator and output variables (but not inputs). The measures were developed with the constructs of the theory in mind and are of satisfactory reliability. The organizational units were taken from metals, chemical, aircraft, textile, and retailing firms, as well as state government. Stogdill's own statement of the findings from factor analyses as they relate to the group-focused theory is as follows:

The theory predicts the following findings in the present research:

1. Group productivity and cohesiveness are negatively related in several types of organizations.
2. Employee satisfaction is more highly related to group cohesiveness than to group productivity.

Operations = Task performances × Expectations regarding task performance × $\dfrac{\text{Task-related interactions}}{\text{Mutual interactions}}$

Interpersonnel = Nontask performances × Expectations regarding nontask performances × Nontask-related interactions

Structure = Specialized performances × Expectations regarding task specialization × $\dfrac{\text{Mutual interactions}}{\text{Interactions bypassing immediate superiors}}$

Productivity = Operations × $\left(\text{Expectations regarding goal values} + \text{Expectations regarding contributions to be made}\right)$ × $\left[\text{Expectations regarding task urgency} + \dfrac{\text{Expectations regarding discontinuity of membership}}{\text{Satisfaction with contributions to organization}}\right]$ with $\dfrac{\text{Satisfaction with status}}{}$

Cohesiveness (Integration) = Structure × $\left(\text{Satisfaction with status} + \text{Expectations regarding mutual liking}\right)$ × $\left[\dfrac{\text{Expectations regarding reference group support}}{\text{Expectations regarding task urgency}} + \dfrac{\text{Satisfaction with organization and supervision}}{\text{Expectations regarding discontinuity of membership}}\right]$

Drive (Morale) = Interpersonnel × $\left(\text{Expectations regarding freedom to act and decide} + \text{Expectations regarding task urgency} + \text{Satisfaction with freedom of action}\right)$ × $\left[\dfrac{\text{Expectations regarding contributions to be made}}{\text{Satisfaction with contributions to organization}} + \dfrac{\text{Expectations regarding returns from the organization}}{\text{Satisfaction with returns from the organization}}\right]$

FIGURE 13.4 Mathematical relationships between mediating variables and outputs in group-focused systems theory. Adapted from Ralph M. Stogdill (1974), *A Behavioral Model of Organization* (unpublished ms., Ohio State University, Columbus).

The theory did not predict the following findings:

1. Supervisory leadership is more highly related to employee satisfaction than to group performance.
2. One aspect of employee attitudes (satisfaction with freedom on the job) is related to group drive.
3. Group drive and group cohesiveness are more highly related than was previously thought to be true. (Stogdill, 1965, pp. 292–293)

Mediators such as responsibility and authority generally showed little relationship to output variables.

A subsequent correlational analysis of the output measures used in this research (Stogdill, 1972) produced significant negative relationships between productivity and cohesiveness (integration) in 38 percent of the units; there were no significant positive correlations. However, the expected positive correlation between productivity and drive (morale) occurred only 15 percent of the time, and there was one significant negative value. Drive and cohesiveness did not exhibit a consistent pattern, as hypothesized, though 58 percent of the correlations were positive in direction; only three values were significant, and these varied in sign.

In another study conducted within a single company, Stogdill (1967b) found varied levels of support and nonsupport for the output relationship hypotheses, depending on the particular measures of output variables that were used. Since many different measures of the same construct were used in the different studies considered in Stogdill's (1959, 1972) literature reviews, measurement factors may well account for the extremely variable results noted there. Still, these findings do raise questions about construct validity. Either the constructs of the theory lack sufficient precision of definition, or Stogdill has fitted measures to them too loosely.

In a final study Stogdill (1966) hypothesizes that under conditions of increased inputs, rather than the stable input states assumed (but not actually measured) in preceding studies, output variables may be positively intercorrelated. The study covered six football games and related coach's ratings of morale and integration and yards lost or gained (productivity) to each other. Morale, integration, and productivity were highly positively correlated on offense. Under game conditions, when major investments of effort (performances) and expectations can be anticipated over short periods of time, this result would be expected. However, this study, like all others, did not actually measure inputs.

Overview

In general, psychologists, and those with a psychological orientation to macro organizational behavior, have viewed Stogdill's formulations favorably (Filley & House, 1984; Tosi, 1987). These publications provide summaries of the Stogdill (1959) volume as well. The solid base of research evidence that underlies the construction of the theory makes it extremely attractive and leads one to forget the sparsity of posttheory tests. To some degree, the undeniable excellence of the author's underlying scholarship may have fostered uncritical acceptance of his theory. In any event, sociologists appear to have been much less impressed. Starting with the individual and the group, as the psychological theorists considered in this chapter do, does not make much sense to most sociologically ori-

ented organizational behaviorists, especially when the domain under consideration is the total organization.

Stogdill struggled with these and other problems with his theory for over 20 years. He revised it constantly. The original statement assumed a close parallel between group and organization that does not now appear warranted, and it neglected the environment. Stogdill was clearly more comfortable theorizing about individuals and groups, and leadership. He tried to work up through an intergroup model, but that effort was admittedly incomplete. Then he began listing variables at the organization and environment levels with the prospect of moving from this to a full-blown theory. The result was confusing. It was not clear how the old and new variables related to each other, and true theoretical hypotheses never were developed. The problems of measurement became even more acute.

Ultimately, Stogdill appears to have recognized that the broad, abstract definitions of variables in the early theory were unlikely to produce confirming research evidence — the gap from theory to research was too great. So he attempted to develop precise hypotheses in mathematical form, using variables of much more limited scope. He broke down the original constructs into smaller units and, accordingly, was able to bridge the gap between model construction and theory building. Such an effort runs a high risk of being wrong; the hypotheses really can be tested. Stogdill did not publish this version of the theory, though he did write it out in a working paper. No research has been done on it, though it has enough logical coherence and related evidence to justify a research investment in it.

Certainly, Stogdill's final theory is the most promising. Earlier versions, insofar as they have been tested, still lack research support. The most extensive work has been done on the hypothesized relationships among output variables. The data do not consistently support these hypotheses. However, the hypotheses are predicated on the stability of inputs. Since input measures have not been devised, it is impossible to know whether the inputs might have varied in any given study. Accordingly, the research that has been conducted cannot be considered an adequate test of the theory. Satisfactory tests of Stogdill's theory are simply too sparse to justify conclusions. As a scientist, one must keep an open mind and say, "I don't know."

Application

As Stogdill (1959) noted at an early point, a theory need not define an applied technology, and indeed his has not done so. Nevertheless, there is inherent in the theory a prescription that productivity should not be overemphasized — that a delicate balance between outputs is necessary to an effective organization. About obtaining this optimum balance between, productivity, morale, and integration, Stogdill says, "the methods for accomplishing this desirable state of affairs on a rational basis are yet to be developed. The most effective managers appear to obtain the balance intuitively" (1972, p. 40). This would suggest that a technology might be developed by studying effective and ineffective managers, as defined by their capacity to approximate the theoretical ideal. Yet this has not been done to date.

CONCLUSIONS

Systems theory has had a broad impact on thinking in a number of fields. For organizational behavior it was a whole new way of looking at organizations and their environments. Its arrival was widely heralded, and many predicted that it would be the source of new and important breakthroughs in knowledge. Yet the breakthroughs have not come, or at least not on the scale anticipated. The problems seem to lie in the theory's extremely wide-ranging and highly abstract constructs and in its inability to spawn a significant body of research. In psychological systems theory at least, these factors are closely related.

A general principle in systems theory is that everything relates to everything else. In practice, at least for psychological systems theories, this has meant that causal hypotheses are minimized; the theories tend to be static rather than dynamic. Although the theories considered in this chapter state hypotheses, as often as not these hypotheses lack a clear tie to the basic open systems model. Rather, these hypotheses derive primarily from work in the field of group dynamics and are then extrapolated to the organizational level, where they may well not apply. The hypotheses of the theories are not logically embedded in the systems models, and thus their research confirmation, when it does occur, provides little by way of value added, insofar as the larger theory is concerned.

References

Barker, James R. (1993). Tightening the Iron Cage: Concertive Control in Self-Managing Teams. *Administrative Science Quarterly*, 38, 408–437.

Baum, Bernard H.; Sorensen, Peter F.; & Place, William S. (1970). The Effect of Managerial Training on Organizational Control: An Experimental Study. *Organizational Behavior and Human Performance*, 5, 170–182.

Bazigos, Michael N., & Burke, W. Warner (1997). Theory Orientations of Organization Development Management (OD) Practitioners. *Group and Organization Management*, 22, 384–408.

Bowers, David G. (1973). OD Techniques and Their Results in 23 Organizations: The Michigan ICL Study. *Journal of Applied Behavioral Science*, 9, 21–43.

Bowers, David G. (1975). Hierarchy, Function, and the Generalizability of Leadership Practices. In James G. Hunt & Lars L. Larson (Eds.), *Leadership Frontiers* (pp. 167–180). Kent, OH: Kent State University Press.

Bowers, David G. (1976). *Systems of Organization.* Ann Arbor: University of Michigan Press.

Bowers, David G., & Franklin, Jerome L. (1977). *Survey Guided Development I: Data-Based Organizational Change.* La Jolla, CA: University Associates.

Bowers, David G., & Seashore, Stanley E. (1966). Predicting Organizational Effectiveness with a Four-Factor Theory of Leadership. *Administrative Science Quarterly*, 11, 238–263.

Brightman, Harvey J. (1975). Leadership Style and Worker Interpersonal Orientation: A Computer Simulation Study. *Organizational Behavior and Human Performance*, 14, 91–122.

Butterfield, D. Anthony, & Farris, George F. (1974). The Likert Organizational Profile: Methodological Analysis and Test of System 4 Theory in Brazil. *Journal of Applied Psychology*, 59, 15–23.

Chacko, Harsha E. (1990). Methods of Upward Influence, Motivational Needs, and Administrators' Perceptions of Their Supervisors' Leadership Styles. *Group and Organization Studies*, 15, 253–265.

Church, Allan H.; Burke, W. Warner; & Van Eynde, Donald F. (1994). Values, Motives, and Interventions of Organization Development Practitioners. *Group and Organization Management*, 19, 5–50.

Coch, Lester, & French, John R. P. (1948). Overcoming Resistance to Change. *Human Relations*, 1, 512–532.

Collins, Denis (1997). The Ethical Superiority and Inevitability of Participatory Management as an Organizational System. *Organization Science*, 8, 489–507.

Dowling, William F. (1975). At General Motors: System 4 Builds Performance and Profits. *Organizational Dynamics*, 3(3), 23–38.

Farris, George F. (1969). Organizational Factors and Individual Performance: A Longitudinal Study. *Journal of Applied Psychology*, 53, 87–92.

Farris, George F., & Butterfield, D. Anthony (1972). Control Theory in Brazilian Organizations. *Administrative Science Quarterly*, 17, 574–585.

Filley, Alan, & House, Robert J. (1984). Ralph M. Stogdill's "Individual Behavior and Group Achievement." In Henry L. Tosi (Ed.), *Theories of Organizations* (pp. 105–117). New York: Wiley.

Fleishman, Edwin A. (1965). Attitude versus Skill Factors in Work Group Productivity. *Personnel Psychology*, 18, 253–266.

Franklin, Jerome L. (1975). Down the Organization: Influence Processes across Levels of Hierarchy. *Administrative Science Quarterly*, 20, 153–164.

Franklin, Jerome L.; Wissler, Anne L.; & Spencer, Gregory J. (1977). *Survey Guided Development III: A Manual for Concepts Training*. La Jolla, CA: University Associates.

French, John R. P.; Israel, Joachim; & Ås, Dagfinn (1960). An Experiment on Participation in a Norwegian Factory: Interpersonal Dimensions of Decision-Making. *Human Relations*, 13, 3–19.

French, John R. P.; Ross, Ian C.; Kirby, S.; Nelson, J. R.; & Smyth, P. (1958). Employee Participation in a Program of Industrial Change. *Personnel*, 35(6), 16–29.

Glew, David J.; O'Leary-Kelly, Anne M.; Griffin, Ricky W.; & Van Fleet, David D. (1995). Participation in Organizations: A Preview of the Issues and Proposed Framework for Future Analysis. *Journal of Management*, 21, 395–421.

Gundelach, Peter, & Tetzschner, Helge (1976). Measurement of Influence in Organizations: Critique of the Control-Graph Method. *Acta Sociologica*, 19, 49–63.

Hauser, D. L.; Pecorella, P. A.; & Wissler, Anne L. (1977). *Survey Guided Development II: A Manual for Consultants*. La Jolla, CA: University Associates.

Hodson, Randy (1996). Dignity in the Workplace under Participative Management: Alienation and Freedom Revisited. *American Sociological Review*, 61, 719–738.

Hodson, Randy; Welsh, Sandy; Rieble, Sabine; Jamison, Cheryl S.; & Creighton, Sean (1993). Is Worker Solidarity Undermined by Autonomy and Participation? Patterns from the Ethnographic Literature. *American Sociological Review*, 58, 398–416.

House, Robert J.; Filley, Alan C.; & Gujarati, Damodar (1971). Leadership Style, Hierarchical Influence, and the Satisfaction of Subordinate Role Expectations: A Test of Likert's Influence Proposition. *Journal of Applied Psychology*, 55, 422–432.

Kahn, Robert L., & Katz, Daniel (1960). Leadership Practices in Relation to Productivity and Morale. In Dorwin Cartwright & Alvin Zander (Eds.), *Group Dynamics: Research and Theory* (pp. 554–570). Evanston, IL: Row, Peterson.

Levine, Edwin L. (1973). Problems of Organizational Control in Microcosm: Group Performance and Group Member Satisfaction as a Function of Differences in Control Structure. *Journal of Applied Psychology*, 58, 186–196.

Likert, Rensis (1953). *Motivation: The Core of Management*. American Management Association Personnel Series, No. 155, 3–21.

Likert, Rensis (1958). Measuring Organizational Performance. *Harvard Business Review*, 36(2), 41–52.

Likert, Rensis (1959). A Motivational Approach to a Modified Theory of Organization and Management. In Mason Haire (Ed.), *Modern Organization Theory* (pp. 184–217). New York: Wiley.

Likert, Rensis (1961). *New Patterns of Management*. New York: McGraw-Hill.

Likert, Rensis (1967). *The Human Organization: Its Management and Value*. New York: McGraw-Hill.

Likert, Rensis (1973). Human Resource Accounting: Building and Assessing Productive Organizations. *Personnel*, 50(3), 8–24.

Likert, Rensis (1975). Improving Cost Performance with Cross-Functional Teams. *Conference Board Record*, 12(9), 51–59.

Likert, Rensis (1978). Managing an Interdisciplinary Research Institute: The Institute for Social Research. *Academy of Management Proceedings*, 38, 384–388,

Likert, Rensis (1979). From Production- and Employee-Centeredness to System 1–4. *Journal of Management*, 5, 147–156.

Likert, Rensis, & Bowers, David G. (1969). Organization Theory and Human Resource Accounting. *American Psychologist*, 24, 585–592.

Likert, Rensis, & Bowers, David G. (1973). Improving the Accuracy of P/L Reports by Estimating the Change in Dollar Value of the Human Organization. *Michigan Business Review*, 25(March), 15–24.

Likert, Rensis & Dowling, William F. (1973). Conversation with Rensis Likert. *Organizational Dynamics*, 2(1), 33–49.

Likert, Rensis, & Fisher, M. Scott (1977). MBGO: Putting Some Team Spirit into MBO. *Personnel*, 54(1), 40–47.

Likert, Rensis, & Likert, Jane G. (1976). *New Ways of Managing Conflict*. New York: McGraw-Hill.

Likert, Rensis, & Seashore, Stanley, E. (1963). Making Cost Control Work. *Harvard Business Review*, 41(6), 96–108.

Likert, Rensis, & Willets, J. M. (1940–41). *Morale and Agency Management*. Hartford, CT: Life Insurance Agency Management Association.

Locke, Edwin A., & Schweiger, David M. (1979). Participation in Decision-Making: One More Look. *Research in Organizational Behavior*, 1, 265–339.

Mann, Floyd C., & Likert, Rensis (1952). The Need for Research on the Communication of Research Results. *Human Organization*, 11(4), 15–19.

Marrow, Alfred J.; Bowers, David G.; & Seashore, Stanley E. (1967). *Management by Participation*. New York: Harper & Row.

Marrow, Alfred J., & French, John R. P. (1945). Changing a Stereotype in Industry. *Journal of Social Issues*, 1(3), 33–37.

McMahon, J. Timothy, & Ivancevich, John M. (1976). A Study of Control in a Manufacturing Organization: Managers and Non-Managers. *Administrative Science Quarterly*, 21, 66–83.

McMahon, J. Timothy, & Perritt, G. W. (1973). Toward a Contingency Theory of Organizational Control. *Academy of Management Journal*, 16, 624–635.

Morse, Nancy C., & Reimer, Everett (1956). The Experimental Change of a Major Organizational Variable. *Journal of Abnormal and Social Psychology*, 52, 120–129.

Morse, Nancy C.; Reimer, Everett; & Tannenbaum, Arnold S. (1951). Regulation and Control in Hierarchic Organizations. *Journal of Social Issues*, 7(3), 41–48.

Mott, Paul E. (1972). *The Characteristics of Effective Organizations*. New York: Harper & Row.

Mozina, Stane; Jerovsek, Janez; Tannenbaum, Arnold S.; & Likert, Rensis (1970). Testing a Management Style. *European Business*, 27(Autumn), 60–68.

Mulder, Mauk (1977). *The Daily Power Game*. Leiden, the Netherlands: Martinus Nijhoff.

Nadler, David A. (1977). *Feedback and Organization Development: Using Data-Based Methods*. Reading, MA: Addison-Wesley.

Nurick, Aaron J. (1985). *Participation in Organizational Change: The TVA Experiment*. New York: Praeger.

Ono, Kaoru; Tindale, R. Scott; Hulin, Charles L.; & Davis, James H. (1988). Intuition vs. Deduction: Some Thought Experiments Concerning Likert's Linking-Pin Theory of Organization. *Organizational Behavior and Human Decision Processes*, 42, 135–154.

Parsons, Talcott (1951). *The Social System*. Glencoe, IL: Free Press.

Patchen, Martin (1963). Alternative Questionnaire Approaches to the Measurement of Influence in Organizations. *American Journal of Sociology*, 69, 41–52.

Pelz, Donald C. (1952). Influence: A Key to Effective Leadership in the First-Line Supervisor. *Personnel*, 29, 209–217.

Pennings, Johannes M. (1976). Dimensions of Organizational Influence and Their Effectiveness Correlates. *Administrative Science Quarterly*, 21, 688–699.

Roberts, Karlene; Miles, Raymond E.; & Blankenship, L. Vaughn (1968). Organizational Leadership, Satisfaction, and Productivity: A Comparative Analysis. *Academy of Management Journal*, 11, 401–414.

Rosner, Menachem; Kavcic, Bogdan; Tannenbaum, Arnold S.; Vianello, Mino; & Wieser, Georg (1973). Worker Participation and Influence in Five Countries. *Industrial Relations*, 12, 200–212.

Rus, Veljko (1970). Influence Structure in Yugoslav Enterprise. *Industrial Relations*, 9, 148–160.

Sashkin, Marshall (1984). Participative Management Is an Ethical Imperative. *Organizational Dynamics*, 12(4), 4–22.

Seashore, Stanley E., & Bowers, David G. (1963). *Changing the Structure and Functioning of an Organization: Report of a Field Experiment*. Ann Arbor: Institute for Social Research, University of Michigan.

Seashore, Stanley E., & Bowers, David G. (1970). Durability of Organizational Change. *American Psychologist*, 25, 227–233.

Smith, Clagett G. (1966). A Comparative Analysis of Some Conditions and Consequences of Intra-Organizational Conflict. *Administrative Science Quarterly*, 10, 504–529.

Stogdill, Ralph M. (1959). *Individual Behavior and Group Achievement*. New York: Oxford University Press.

Stogdill, Ralph M. (1962). Intragroup-Intergroup Theory and Research. In Muzafer Sherif (Ed.), *Intergroup Relations and Leadership* (pp. 48–65). New York: Wiley.

Stogdill, Ralph M. (1965). *Managers, Employees, Organizations*. Columbus: Bureau of Business Research, Ohio State University.

Stogdill, Ralph M. (1966). Dimensions of Organization Theory. In James D. Thompson (Ed.), *Approaches to Organizational Design* (pp. 3–56). Pittsburgh, PA: University of Pittsburgh Press.

Stogdill, Ralph M. (1967a). Basic Concepts for a Theory of Organization. *Management Science*, 13, B665–676.

Stogdill, Ralph M. (1967b). The Structure of Organization Behavior. *Multivariate Behavioral Research*, 2, 47–61.

Stogdill, Ralph M. (1972). Group Productivity, Drive, and Cohesiveness. *Organizational Behavior and Human Performance*, 8, 26–43.

Stogdill, Ralph M. (1974a). A Behavioral Model of Organization. Columbus: Ohio State University (unpublished).

Stogdill, Ralph M. (1974b). *Handbook of Leadership: A Survey of Theory and Research.* New York: Free Press.

Tannenbaum, Arnold S. (1956). The Concept of Organizational Control. *Journal of Social Issues,* 12(2), 50–60.

Tannenbaum, Arnold S. (1962). Control in Organizations: Individual Adjustments and Organizational Performance. *Administrative Science Quarterly,* 7, 236–257.

Tannenbaum, Arnold S. (1966). *Social Psychology of Work Organization.* Belmont, CA: Wadsworth.

Tannenbaum, Arnold S. (1968). *Control in Organizations.* New York: McGraw-Hill.

Tannenbaum, Arnold S. (1974). Systems of Formal Participation. In George Strauss et al (Eds.), *Organizational Behavior: Research and Issues* (pp. 77–105). Madison, WI: Industrial Relations Research Association.

Tannenbaum, Arnold S., & Cooke, Robert A. (1974). Control and Participation. *Journal of Contemporary Business,* 3(4), 35–46.

Tannenbaum, Arnold S., & Cooke, Robert A. (1979). Organizational Control: A Review of Studies Employing the Control Graph Method. In Cornelis J. Lammers & David Hickson (Eds.), *Organizations Alike and Unlike* (pp. 183–210). London: Routledge & Kegan Paul.

Tannenbaum, Arnold S., & Kahn, Robert L. (1957). Organizational Control Structures: A General Descriptive Technique as Applied to Four Local Unions. *Human Relations,* 10, 127–139.

Tannenbaum, Arnold S., & Kahn, Robert L. (1958). *Participation in Union Locals.* Evanston, IL: Row, Peterson.

Tannenbaum, Arnold S.; Kavcic, Bogdon; Rosner, Menachem; Vianello, Mino; & Wieser, Georg (1974). *Hierarchy in Organizations: An International Comparison.* San Francisco: Jossey-Bass.

Tannenbaum, Arnold S., & Rozgonyi, Tomás (1986). *Authority and Reward in Organizations: An International Research.* Ann Arbor: Survey Research Center, Institute for Social Research, University of Michigan.

Tosi, Henry L. (1987) Review of *Individual Behavior and Group Achievement. Academy of Management Review,* 12, 563–565.

Walton, Elise, & Nadler, David A. (1994). Diagnosis for Organization Design. In Ann Howard (Ed.), *Diagnosis for Organizational Change: Methods and Models* (pp. 85–105). New York: Guilford Press.

Chapter 14

Comprehensive Psychological
Open Systems Theories

The failure to generate research from the systems components of the organizational level theories rooted in group dynamics of the preceding chapter is in part a consequence of the lack of hypotheses to test and in part a consequence of the highly abstract and general nature of those hypotheses that are generated. In this chapter, two additional psychological systems theories

are considered, which also have certain ties to group dynamics and leadership, although not in as pronounced a manner as the theories just considered. The theories in chapter 14 focus much more on the environment of the organization and thus are more clearly *open* systems theories. We need to see whether under these circumstances the systems approach yields more and better research support. Can systems theorizing overcome its inherent problems and contribute major advances in understanding, prediction, and application? That is the question to which we turn now.

The two theories considered in this chapter have in common that they move further from their roots in group dynamics than the theories treated in chapter 13. They are closely allied to those theories in many respects, but they make much more comprehensive use of the systems concept, eventually incorporating major formulations regarding the environment and its interaction with organizations. Thus these are truly open systems theories in a sense that the system 4, control, and group-focused systems theories really are not. The distinction here is between using system concepts and developing full-blown systems theories. The theories of chapter 13 do the former; those now to be discussed are the latter.

Daniel Katz and Robert Kahn propose a social psychology of organizations that developed out of the same origins as those of Rensis Likert's and Arnold Tannenbaum's theories at the University of Michigan. Both Katz and Kahn were involved in the early research on participative management that was conducted by the Institute for Social Research at the University of Michigan. Both acknowledge a clear debt to Likert. Yet in many respects their theory provides an alternative to system 4 theory, while it maintains the same orientation in behavioral humanist values.

Sociotechnical systems theory started far away in England, but its value orientation was much the same as that of the Michigan group and it came to parallel the Michigan theories in a number of other respects as well. Its major and initial author was Eric Trist, a psychologist, whose early work was of a clinical nature and who came to organizational behavior via the same kind of focus on group processes that the other psychological systems theorists evinced. He was joined in his work, particularly the theoretical aspects, by Fred Emery. The two collaborated on a number of the more important statements of the theory as it evolved.

SOCIAL PSYCHOLOGY OF ORGANIZATIONS

The Katz and Kahn theory is set forth primarily in two editions of a book entitled *The Social Psychology of Organizations*, published in 1966 and 1978. These books enjoyed considerable popularity during the 1970s and the 1980s as the most sophisticated statements of the Michigan way of thinking.

Background

Katz was born in 1903. His undergraduate degree was from the University of Buffalo, and his doctorate in social psychology was obtained from another upstate New York school, Syracuse University. That was in 1928, and his mentor was Floyd Allport. Next he spent 15 years in the psychology department at Princeton

University. During World War II he was a member of the federal government group with Likert, working on survey research studies. After the war ended, Katz took a position as chairman of the psychology department at Brooklyn College, but by 1947 he had followed the other members of the Likert group to the newly founded Institute for Social Research at the University of Michigan. He remained there for the rest of his career, holding an appointment in the psychology department as well. Katz did not have a relationship with the business school at Michigan; in fact, he was well into his career as a social psychologist and in his 50s when organizational behavior was born. He died at age 95 in 1998.

Kahn was born in 1918 and received his education from the University of Michigan, culminating in a doctorate in social psychology in 1952. He remained at Michigan throughout his career with appointments in the Institute for Social Research's Survey Research Center, as well as the psychology department and in public health. The latter was an outgrowth of his work on role conflict, stress, and related health matters. He is currently an emeritus professor from Michigan.

The Michigan theorists appear to have found in the Institute for Social Research the same type of multidisciplinary melting pot function that the business schools provided for many others of organizational behavior's contributors. Both Likert and Katz had well-established careers in other areas as organizational behavior came into being, and thus the business schools offered them little by way of unique opportunity. Their situation was much like that of David McClelland in that regard. Tannenbaum and Kahn were of a somewhat younger age cohort, but followed the role models provided for them, in large part because the Institute for Social Research served many of the functions a business school might have offered.

Initial Systems Theory

The book that first presents the social psychology of organizations is in part a theoretical statement and in part a review of organizational literature in certain areas (Katz & Kahn, 1966). The theory is covered largely in the first seven chapters and reviewed in the last, although several important theoretical statements occur in the intervening chapters on power and authority and on leadership.

Systems Concept

The basic model involves energic inputs (sources of energy), the transformation of these inputs within the system, and an output that recycles or returns as energic input to keep the system going. In many cases, outcomes are converted to money, which, in turn, provides the needed input. The defining characteristics of such open systems are as follows:

1. The importation of *energic inputs* from the social environment
2. Transformation of available energy as *throughput,* so that work is done within the system
3. The exportation of a product or *output* into the environment
4. A *cycle of events* in which the product exported to the environment provides the energy for repetition of the cycle
5. The development of *negative entropy* whereby more energy is imported from the environment than is expended in work, thus counteracting the entropic imperative, which inevitably tends toward disorganization and death
6. The existence of *information inputs* or signals about how the environment and the system are functioning; *negative feedback* from internal functioning, which provides information to correct deviations from course; and a *coding* process that simplifies energic and information inputs and permits their selective reception
7. A *steady state* that preserves the character of the system and is marked by a stable ratio of energy exchanges and relations between the parts
8. Movement in the direction of increasing *differentiation,* elaboration, or specialization
9. The operation of the principle of *equifinality* under which a system can achieve the same final state from different initial conditions and by various paths

Defining Characteristics and Structures

Energic inputs are differentiated between maintenance inputs that sustain the system and production inputs that are processed and yield productive outputs. System integration is achieved through the operation of roles, or standardized patterns of behavior that are required of all who perform a function or set of tasks; norms, or expectations of role incumbents that serve to verbalize and sanction role requirements; and values that are even more general ideological justifica-

tions and aspirations. The theory posits five basic types of subsystems:

Production or technical — concerned with the throughput and the work done

Supportive — concerned with procurement of inputs, disposal of outputs, and institutional functions related to the environment

Maintenance — concerned with tying people to their roles, either through selection of personnel or through rewards and sanctions, thus preserving the system

Adaptive — concerned with adaptive change to environmental variations

Managerial — concerned with direction, coordination, and control of other subsystems and activities. This system operates through the use of regulatory mechanisms that utilize feedback about output as related to input, and through authority structures that legitimize directives in some manner.

A number of other constructs and processes are proposed, the most theoretically relevant of which are system boundaries (those barriers between system and environment that determine degrees of openness for the system) and leading systems (those that exert greater influence over the inputs of other component systems, and thus control interactions).

The authors describe the developmental process in organizations as follows:

> At Stage 1 certain characteristics of a human population and some common environmental problem interact to generate task demands and a primitive production structure to fulfill them. At Stage 2 devices for formulating and enforcing rules appear. An authority structure emerges and becomes the basis for managerial and maintenance subsystems. Stage 3 sees the further elaboration of supportive structures at the organizational boundaries — structures for procurement, disposal, and institutional relations. (Katz & Kahn, 1966, p. 109)

As set forth in table 14.1, the consequence of this evolution is a set of structures, each with its own dynamic, or common motivation, for the group, and mechanisms for achieving this dynamic. Within the managerial structure a maximization principle is hypothesized, which as a dynamic often tends to override the maintenance of a steady state. This is so because:

TABLE 14.1 The dynamics and mechanisms of subsystem structures

Subsystem structure	Dynamic (common motivation)	Mechanisms
Production	Technical proficiency	Division of labor Job specifications and standards
Supportive (boundary)		
Procurement and disposal	Focused manipulation of environ- ment	Control of sources of supply Creation of image
Institutional	Social manipulation and integration	Contributing to community Influencing social structure
Maintenance	Maintaining steady state; predict- ability	Standard legitimized procedures System rewards Socialization
Adaptive	Pressing for change	Recommending changes to manage- ment
Managerial		
Conflict resolution within hier- archy	Control	Sanctions of authority
Coordinating functional struc- tures	Compromise vs. integration	Alternative concessions Adjudication machinery
Coordinating external requirements with resources and needs	Long-term survival Optimization Improving resource use Increasing capabilities	Increasing business volume Adding functions Controlling environment Organization planning

SOURCE: Adapted from Daniel Katz & Robert L. Kahn (1966), *The Social Psychology of Organizations* (New York: Wiley), 86

1. The proficiency dynamic leads to an increase in organizational capabilities.
2. Expansion is the simplest method of dealing with problems of internal strain.
3. Expansion is also the most direct solution in coping with problems of a changing social environment.
4. Bureaucratic role systems in their nature permit of ready elaboration.
5. Organizational ideology encourages growth aspirations. (Katz & Kahn, 1966, pp. 99–100)

Organizational Typology and Effectiveness

Organizations fall into four major types, based on the functions they perform for society. Productive (economic) organizations create wealth, manufacture goods, and provide services. Maintenance organizations socialize people for their roles in society, including other organizations. Adaptive organizations create knowledge and often apply it as well. Managerial (political) organizations adjudicate, coordinate, and control resources and people.

In addition, organizations may be classified in terms of many secondary characteristics. Among these

are throughput as it relates to products or to people; maintenance through intrinsic or extrinsic rewards; degree of permeability of organizational boundaries; extent of structural elaboration; and steady state or maximization as the dominant dynamic.

A condition for organizational survival is negative entropy whereby more energy is brought into the organization than emerges as output. Some energy is consumed by the organization in creating and maintaining itself. If this amount is large, the organization is inefficient; thus, efficiency is defined in terms of the ratio of energic output to energic input.

Organizational effectiveness, in contrast, is defined as the maximization of energic return to the organization by all means. To the extent that economic and technical means are employed for energic return, efficiency is affected as well. But maximization by political means is also possible and often is of considerable significance. Here the maximization typically occurs at some cost to the environment, either in the form of other organizations (such as competitors) or individuals. However, the authors also define as political certain processes that are carried out within the organization's boundaries, such as paying lower wages than other firms. As they themselves indicate, their distinction between efficiency and political effectiveness as components of organizational effectiveness is somewhat arbitrary.

Organizational Roles

Katz and Kahn (1966) define an organization as an open system of roles, thus emphasizing a view of organizations as contrived in nature and consisting of a structure of acts or events. This role-related component of the theory was first proposed and defined at an earlier date (Kahn, Wolfe, Quinn, Snoek, & Rosenthal, 1964), as were other concepts and constructs.

Roles are made up of certain recurrent activities within the total, interrelated pattern that yields the organizational output. Specifically, roles are those activities that exist within a single subsystem and a single office. An *office* is a point within organizational space and consists of one or more roles to be performed by individuals. Individuals are surrounded by others, including superiors and subordinates, who operate as role senders to them and constitute the role set. This process of role sending and receiving is described in figure 14.1. *Role conflict* occurs when compliance with role sendings of one type would make it difficult or impossible to comply with role sendings of another type. *Role ambiguity* arises from a lack of role-related information or inadequacies in the communication of such information. In an ongoing organization, the simplicity of figure 14.1 is often disturbed when one role involves many activities, when multiple roles exist in a single office, or when one person occupies several offices.

Though Katz and Kahn tend to deemphasize hypothesis formulation, they offer four statements that they call interesting speculations or predictions about organizational roles:

1. The more activities contained within a role, the more likely it is to be varied and satisfying, the more likely it is to involve coordination among the activities it comprises, and the less immediate will be the necessity for coordination with other roles and offices.
2. The more interrole coordination an organization requires, the more the achievement of coordination is assigned to offices high in the organizational structure.
3. The more coordinative demands that are concentrated in a given office, the more the incumbent seeks a generalized, programmed solution. . . . Such a programmed solution

is sought because it can be set up to hold for a considerable period of time, thus relieving the incumbent of the continuing press of certain types of decisions.
4. The greater the programming of interjob coordination, the greater will be the use of organizational authority and sanctions. (Katz & Kahn, 1966, pp. 181–182)

Hierarchic and Democratic Systems

One other area in which specific hypotheses are formulated with regard to organizational process and structure is that of hierarchic versus democratic organization. Hierarchic systems are said to survive longer and to be more efficient:

1. When the tasks do not require creativity and when identification with organizational goals is not essential
2. When environmental demands are clear and obvious so that information about them is redundant and multiple processors of this information are not needed
3. When rapid decision making is necessary
4. When the environment is such that it requires little adaptive change, thus approximating the conditions of a closed system

Essentially the opposite set of conditions argue for a democratic organizational structure. With regard to formal, hierarchic structure the authors conclude:

It is an instrument of great effectiveness; it offers great economies over unorganized effort; it achieves great unity and compliance. We must face up to its deficiencies, however. These include great waste of human potential for innovation and creativity and great psychological cost to the members. . . . The modification of hierarchical organization to meet these criticisms is one of the great needs of human life. (Katz & Kahn, 1966, p. 222)

Hierarchic Position and Leadership

Leadership theory in the 1960s, and for a considerable period of time thereafter, rarely gave much attention to position in the hierarchic organization as a variable of importance; the focus was on leadership of a group. The work of Katz and Kahn (1966) is one exception. Effective leaders are differentiated by position level and by the types of relationships and role expectations

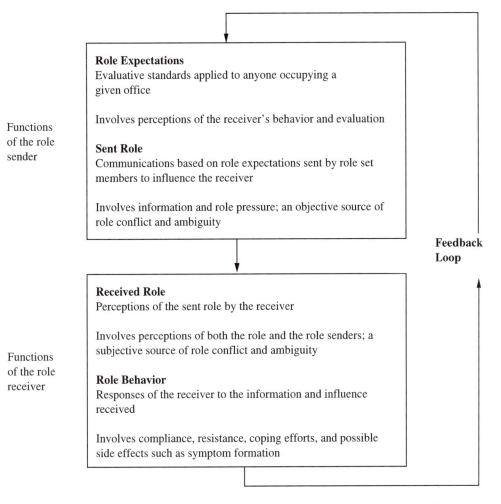

Functions
of the role
sender

Role Expectations
Evaluative standards applied to anyone occupying a
given office

Involves perceptions of the receiver's behavior and evaluation

Sent Role
Communications based on role expectations sent by role set
members to influence the receiver

Involves information and role pressure; an objective source of
role conflict and ambiguity

**Feedback
Loop**

Functions
of the role
receiver

Received Role
Perceptions of the sent role by the receiver

Involves perceptions of both the role and the role senders; a
subjective source of role conflict and ambiguity

Role Behavior
Responses of the receiver to the information and influence
received

Involves compliance, resistance, coping efforts, and possible
side effects such as symptom formation

FIGURE 14.1 Model of the role episode. Adapted from Robert L. Kahn, Donald M. Wolfe, Robert
P. Quinn, J. Diedrick Snoek, & Robert A. Rosenthal (1964), *Organizational Stress: Studies in Role
Conflict and Ambiguity* (New York: Wiley), 26; Daniel Katz & Robert L. Kahn (1966), *The Social
Psychology of Organizations* (New York: Wiley), 182.

associated with that level. These leadership requirements are outlined in table 14.2. Presumably an organization staffed to meet these requirements at each
level would be more effective than one not so staffed.

Opening the Theory Up

The theory set forth in the 1978 edition of the Katz
and Kahn book is largely unchanged from the 1966
edition, although there are some important additions,
as well as many embellishments and expanded examples. The book grew by over 60 percent, but many of
the additions were nontheoretical in nature.

Principle of Integration

One change in 1978 is the explicit inclusion of integration as a characteristic of open systems. Thus the list
of nine defining characteristics of open systems is
extended to include integration and coordination.
These characteristics counter differentiation and unify
the system. Integration may be achieved through
shared norms and values; unification through coordination involves fixed control arrangements, such as
setting the speed of an assembly line.

As organizational structures grow, there is a tendency toward increased differentiation or specializa-

TABLE 14.2 Leadership requirements at different hierarchic levels

Hierarchical level	First-level supervision	Middle management	Top management
Nature of leadership required	Administration — the use of existing structure	Interpolation — supplementing and piecing out the structure	Origination — change, creation, and elimination of structure
Required cognitive abilities and skills	Technical knowledge; understanding of rules	Subsystem perspective — two-way orientation of leader	Systemic perspective — external and internal
Required emotional abilities and skills	Equity and fairness in applying rules and using sanctions	Integration of the immediate work group with the larger system (good human relations)	Charisma

SOURCE: Adapted from Daniel Katz & Robert L. Kahn (1966), *The Social Psychology of Organizations* (New York: Wiley), 312

tion, followed by a complementary tendency toward increased integration or coordination. As the structure divides, integration is increasingly needed. Both differentiation and integration can be pushed beyond the point of maximum system return, however. An optimum point, and thus a curvilinear relation to efficiency, is posited. In particular, the use of fixed coordination devices is questioned when they are applied at high levels across many units of the system. Making decisions at lower levels, where they can apply to a smaller slice of the organization, is considered preferable.

Environmental Factors

Katz and Kahn's 1978 treatment devotes considerably more attention to the environment and to organizational methods of coping with it than did their 1966 version, thus countering a potential source of criticism for an open systems theory. Though much of the discussion draws heavily on the theory and research of others, some original theory is included. Five environmental sectors within which organizations function are identified:

1. The value patterns of the cultural environment
2. The political structure or pattern of legal norms and statutes
3. The economic environment of competitive markets and inputs
4. The informational and technological environment
5. The natural or physical or ecological environment, including geography, natural resources, and climate

Each of these sectors may vary along four dimensions that are drawn largely from sociotechnical systems

theory: stable to turbulent, homogeneous to diverse, random to clustered, and scarce to munificent. Thus an organization may have a stable natural environment and a turbulent economic one, and so on. Generally, Katz and Kahn do not hypothesize about relationships among dimensions across sectors, but instead stress the need for measurement and empirical study. However, the sectors are thought to reflect a hierarchy of complexity, especially with regard to turbulence. As a lower-level sector such as the natural environment fails to provide stability, each higher-level sector is mobilized for that purpose. If all else fails, including political stabilization, turbulence may be reduced by a resort to common cultural values in the manner advocated by sociotechnical systems theory.

Organizational response in coping with environments may be summarized as follows:

> The lack of assurance of sustained inputs and continuing markets for outputs leads to various forms of organizational response to reduce uncertainty. The first attempt is to control the environment directly and to incorporate it within the system. Then come efforts at indirect control through influencing other systems by means of political manipulation or economic bargaining. Or the organization may move to change its own structure to accord with environmental change. The concept of the temporary society can be considered in this context for it calls for adaptive, problem solving task forces. (Katz & Kahn, 1978, p. 141)

After The Social Psychology of Organizations

Subsequent to the second edition of their major statement on organization theory, and given the trends from the first to the second volume, it would seem likely that more theorizing of an open systems, environment-related nature would follow. This did not happen. An edited book of readings on which Stacy Adams collaborated was published that organized its subject matter in a manner roughly parallel to that used in *The Social Psychology of Organizations* and operated as a supplement to the 1978 volume (Katz, Kahn, & Adams, 1980), but no new theory was introduced. At this point Katz was nearing the end of his professional career, and Kahn's interests shifted almost entirely to matters of stress and health.

Essentially, Kahn followed the lead that emanated from his early work on role phenomena to study the difficulties associated with role processes that produce stress and subsequently health problems. There were several publications on the topic of stress, including, in particular, Kahn (1981), Robert Sutton and Kahn (1987), and Kahn and Philippe Byosiere (1992). This last contains the most specific statements of how role difficulties fit into the process of stress development in organizations. Figure 14.2 outlines this process; see particularly item 2, Stressors in organizational life.

Evaluation and Impact

Except in the area of role processes, the authors of the social psychology of organizations theory have not conducted research to test their ideas. That has been left to others.

Status of Research

The consequence of the authors' failure to conduct research on their own theory, as is so often the case, has been that only limited research is available. A number of studies such as Jeffrey Pfeffer's (1972) investigation of mergers take their lead from open systems concepts. But such studies typically cite several related theoretical positions at once. The most that can be said about the theory from this type of research is that environmental factors are important for organizations and that organizations attempt to cope with these factors. There is nothing, other than general support for an open systems concept, that bears specifically on the constructs and hypotheses of the Katz and Kahn (1966 and 1978) theory as distinct from similar theories, some of which precede by a number of years the first Katz and Kahn statement. The problem appears to be that psychological open systems theory

is stated abstractly without any indication of how to measure the variables operationally. Such circumstances almost invariably stifle research on a theory, because researchers cannot be sure they are really testing the theory.

A rare instance of research that appears to relate specifically to the theory is a study by Barry Staw and Eugene Szwajkowski (1975). This study tests the general proposition that organizations must import resources from the environment to survive and that in less munificent environments organizations will exert greater effort to obtain these resources. The specific hypothesis tested was that in scarce environments companies will be more likely to engage in unfair market practices or restraint of trade to procure added resources. This hypothesis represented an extrapolation from the Katz and Kahn (1966) statements. The research was subsequently used in Katz and Kahn (1978) in the formulation of more specific statements on the effects of environmental scarcity or munificence.

Staw and Szwajkowski (1975) found that companies involved in litigation over practices such as price fixing, illegal merger, refusal to deal, and the like had not only been less profitable over the preceding 5 years, but also came from industries that were equally low in profitability. The data do not unequivocally support a causal interpretation from environmental scarcity to increased effort to secure inputs, but they are entirely consistent with such a hypothesis.

Hierarchic Concepts

A striking aspect of the Katz and Kahn theory is its segmented nature. With many theories, verification of one hypothesis leads to the assumption of truth for other logically related hypotheses. This often cannot be done with Katz and Kahn's formulations. The role-related concepts have no necessary relationships to open systems concepts; they could be embedded in a quite different theoretical milieu and still operate in the same manner. Similarly, the theoretical statements regarding hierarchic versus democratic systems and the hierarchic concept of leadership have no necessary relationships to the rest of the theory. Accordingly, the research evidence that follows must be considered applicable only within very narrow limits.

Hierarchic systems are expected to function best when creativity is not required, environments are obvious, rapid decisions are needed, and closed system

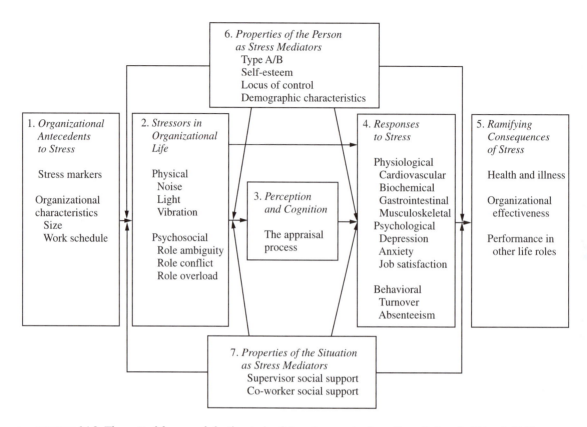

FIGURE 14.2 Theoretical framework for the study of stress in organizations. From Robert L. Kahn & Philippe Byosiere (1992), Stress in Organizations, in Marvin D. Dunnette & Leaetta M. Hough (Eds.), *Handbook of Industrial and Organizational Psychology*, 2nd ed., Vol. 3 (Palo Alto, CA: Consulting Psychologists Press), 592. Copyright 1992 by Consulting Psychologists Press. Reprinted with permission.

conditions apply. John Baum (1978) tested the effects of a strongly rules-oriented procedure for handling absenteeism under circumstances he interpreted as hierarchically ideal. The objective was to compare the effects on chronic absentees of hierarchically controlled procedures and preestablished punishments with decentralized, flexible control conditions. The results clearly support the hierarchic approach under the circumstances specified. Absenteeism was reduced substantially more under experimental conditions than under control conditions.

These Baum (1978) findings support the Katz and Kahn theory as long as one assumes that conditions appropriate for a hierarchic approach existed. In a previous study that compared the effects of a similar legalistic approach on classroom attendance with a laissez-faire approach, the results were similar. Both

attendance and performance improved under the standardized attendance rules (Baum & Youngblood, 1975). The two studies combined suggest that preestablished, hierarchic approaches with high legitimacy may be effective, irrespective of circumstances. It is not at all certain that a classroom environment meets the theoretical requirements for a hierarchic system, although some might contend that an intermediate accounting class of the kind used in this research does.

Another of the generally rare tests of the hierarchic formulations is the study by Paul Mott (1972) that contrasted various leadership theories. Measures of the required cognitive and emotional abilities and skills were developed specifically for this study following the lead of table 14.2. These were related to effectiveness measures obtained at the branch and division levels of an organization.

None of the measures was related to branch effectiveness, so the theory fails to gain support there. Furthermore, technical skill and fairness were significantly related to division effectiveness, which they should not have been according to the theory. Significant relationships were also obtained at the division level for subsystem perspective and integration. These correlations were in accord with the theory and were the highest obtained in the study. Systemic perspective did not achieve a satisfactory level of significance. Overall, the data indicate that the variables of the Katz and Kahn theory are related to organizational effectiveness, but not necessarily in the manner specified by the theory.

Kahn Studies of Role Stress

Given the segmented nature of the Katz and Kahn theory, it is possible to test parts of the theory without saying much about the remainder. This is particularly true of the formulations about organizational roles that antedated the major theoretical statement by 2 years. Actually, the role-related concepts have been the subject of considerable research, which often has supported the theory.

Kahn et al. (1964) studied role processes that were associated with various offices in the managerial subsystems of seven firms. They conducted standardized interviews with role receivers to get at role perceptions and responses and with role senders for each receiver to get at role expectations and pressures. In addition, a nationwide survey on role conflict and ambiguity was used to determine the generalizability of the intensive study results. This survey involved 725 employed individuals.

The findings indicate widespread role conflict and ambiguity. Both phenomena have negative consequences for the individual, including reduced job satisfaction, low confidence, and tension, as well as a tendency to withdraw from the sources of tension. Role conflict tends to be high in boundary-spanning positions, those extending both outside the company and outside the department, in innovative problem-solving positions, and in management positions. Individuals differ not only in the degree of objective role conflict they elicit from senders, but also in the degree of role stress they actually experience.

Though organizational performance was not measured in this research, the authors argue strongly for the desirability of reducing role stress. This need appears to increase as organizations grow in size up to about 5,000 persons; beyond that point, the stress curve levels off. The increase with size is attributed to burgeoning coordination devices, which, in turn, increase the potential for role conflict. The solution recommended is giving each work group as much autonomy as possible. When the principle of coordinative economy is followed, the organization is "decentralized, flat, and lean, a federated rather than a lofty structure" (Katz et al., 1964, p. 395). Whether such organizations are more effective is, of course, an empirical question, extending well beyond the bounds of the research into roles actually conducted.

Role-Related Research

The finding that negative consequences for both the individual and the organization are associated with role conflict and ambiguity is one of the best substantiated in the organizational behavior literature (see, for example, King & King, 1990; Grover, 1993; Smith & Tisak, 1993). Lynda and Daniel King say that reviews and meta-analyses "all concur that role conflict and role ambiguity are associated with dissatisfaction, tension and anxiety, lack of commitment and involvement, propensity to leave the organization, and to a lesser extent performance" (1990, p. 58). In this respect, then, the Katz and Kahn theory receives strong support. There is sufficient recent evidence on this point to allay possible concerns about post hoc theorizing (see, for example, Siegall, 2000). Yet the effects on job performance overall are much more evident for role ambiguity than for role conflict (Tubre & Collins, 2000).

There are studies that do not support the theory, but the negative results usually can be accounted for by special features of the particular investigation, including measurement considerations. Measurement concerns have abounded in this area with much of the controversy involving arguments for and against specific instruments (see, for example, Netemeyer, Johnston, & Burton, 1990; Harris & Bladen, 1994). Yet the research uses a variety of instruments while reaching much the same conclusions. At times the arguments over measurement methodology seem overly esoteric and to have lost their ties to the original theory. Nevertheless, it has been possible to establish relationships with indices of organizational effectiveness, thus extending the scope of the findings even beyond that of the original research (Kahn et al.,

1964). In one study, for example, a significant correlation of .37 was obtained between a role clarity measure and the effectiveness of 20 regional offices of an insurance company (Posner & Butterfield, 1978).

Reformulations at the Subsystem Level

A series of publications (Doll & Melcher, 1976; Doll, 1977a, 1977b) report on attempts to operationalize certain constructs of the Katz and Kahn theory and relate the constructs to behavior. In this research the independent variables are role expectations, norms, and values as measured by questionnaire items. The dependent variables are commitment to membership, dependability of role performance, and the degree of extra-role performance that spontaneously supports organizational goals; these three contribute to an overall index of individual behavior. Independent and dependent variables seem to have been measured within the same questionnaire. Reliabilities are said to be satisfactory but are not reported.

In operationalizing variables, this research often moves beyond the Katz and Kahn (1966) statements. In addition, new hypotheses are occasionally derived from the theory. These procedures are justified on the grounds that the original theory is too loosely stated to be tested. However, one wonders if the Katz and Kahn theory or some other explanation was in fact tested. Still, this research indicates how useful the

theoretical constructs and variables may be as building blocks in the development of more precise and sophisticated theories.

Table 14.3 shows the correlations between certain aspects of production and maintenance subsystems and overall individual behavior. Subjects were 226 individuals who occupied various roles in 25 organizations. As hypothesized, the increasing complexity of the production subsystem that accompanied increasing size was associated with less efficient behavior. The only departure from this pattern was the lack of a significant relationship between unpredictable role behavior and overall behavior. Within the maintenance subsystem the hypothesized relationships consistently occurred, but role expectations regarding intrinsic satisfactions in the work appeared to be most important. Overall, the data clearly support the reformulated theory. Similar results were obtained when communication processes were studied (Doll, 1977b).

Applications

Like Stogdill's version of systems theory, the Katz and Kahn approach has not been a major source of applications for practice. However, applications are discussed, and certain possible potential uses are inherent in the authors' other work.

In their writing about open systems theory the authors endorse several applications, particularly cer-

TABLE 14.3 Correlations between aspects of production and maintenance subsystems and overall behavior

Independent variable	Dependent variable: overall behavior
Production subsystem	
Complexity of the role set	−.35*
Degree to which functional specialization is extensive (many role restrictions)	−.41*
Unpredictability of role behavior	.09
Degree to which role expectations regarding task demands are high	−.32*
Maintenance subsystem	
Degree to which role expectations relate extrinsic rewards to performance and seniority	.23*
Degree to which role expectations associating intrinsic satisfactions with role performance are extensive	.51*
Degree to which role expectations associate undesirable behavior with institutionalized rather than capricious punishments	.28*
Degree to which values and norms are explicit	.36*

*Correlations statistically significant at $p < .05$.

SOURCE: Adapted from William J. Doll & Arlyn S. Melcher (1976), The Production Subsystem of the Katz and Kahn Framework: A Reformulation and Empirical Evaluation, *Midwest Division of the Academy of Management Proceedings*, 292; William J. Doll (1977), The Maintenance Subsystem of the Katz and Kahn Framework, *Midwest Division of the Academy of Management Proceedings*, 340

tain change procedures (Katz & Georgopoulos, 1971; Katz & Kahn, 1966 and 1978). They note the general need for an enlargement of adaptive subsystems to cope with changing environments and new social inputs.

In this connection Katz and Kahn advocate a much greater application of democratic principles. They recommend the use of project teams that combine service and production functions, sensitivity training, and organization development programs of various kinds. The objective is to move toward a system with broader, more flexible roles and more open subsystem boundaries—in short, debureaucratization. At the same time, value changes are needed:

> The task for the adaptive processes of an organization is one of the creative adaptation of central values to changing inputs. . . .
> Adaptation through genuine participation and active involvement based upon democratic principles and processes can still be successful. The great need of our time is a reformulation of social values that would make possible a higher level of integration for all social systems. (Katz & Georgopoulos, 1971, pp. 365–366)

With regard to legislated placement of worker representatives on corporate boards as a step toward representative democracy along lines that have become commonplace in Europe, the authors have this to say:

> The movement toward legislated worker representation in the conduct of enterprise is both a significant force for future organizational change and a reflection of changes that have already occurred at the organizational level. An employing organization is a system that exists in a larger social context, and that context includes both labor unions and legislative bodies. Organizational change can be extended or contained, accelerated or retarded, demanded or denied by these contextual agencies. (Katz & Kahn, 1978, p. 746)

These endorsements of democratization within organizations do not represent a necessary logical outgrowth of open systems theory, even though they are stated in the terminology of the theory. In fact, the attendance control system developed by Baum (1978), which appears to be a logical development from the theory, clearly moves in the direction of hierarchic rather than democratic processes. Other theories considered in this volume contain inherent rationales for the generally democratizing change procedures that they have either generated or embraced. The theories may be wrong, but if they are right, the applications proposed follow logically. This is much less true of the psychological open systems theories that are inherently neutral in the hierarchy-democracy debate. Given this situation, it is difficult to understand why Katz and Kahn recommend democratization, except as a value as opposed to a scientific conclusion.

Since the social psychology of organizations formulations were first published, its constructs often have been used to interpret organizational phenomena and the results of research studies. In these instances the theory has not been tested but, rather, used as a framework for explaining organizational processes.

Thus, Katz and Naphtali Golomb (1974–1975) used the concepts of integration (role expectations, norms, and values), effectiveness, and adaptive value modification at the individual, systemic, and societal levels to analyze the kibbutzim communities in Israel. The authors also used their constructs of boundary transactions and environmental feedback systems as a framework for a study of the reactions of recipients of government services to their "bureaucratic encounters" (Katz, Gutek, Kahn, & Barton, 1975; Kahn, Katz, & Gutek, 1976) and for an analysis of feedback as it operates in social systems in general and in governmental program evaluation in particular (Katz, 1975). Similarly, Clagett Smith and James King (1975) used open systems concepts in their study of the effectiveness of different mental hospitals. Ned Rosen (1970) did not originally formulate his study of the effects of rotating foremen across work groups in open systems theory terms, but he found the theory useful in developing an ad hoc interpretation of the results.

These examples suggest that the theory, or at least certain constructs of the theory, might be useful to practitioners in developing working theories to cope with day-to-day decisions in ongoing organizations. Managers in particular need such working theories to filter and organize the information that comes to them. Inevitably they will develop some theories, and the Katz and Kahn framework offers some promise for this purpose. However, if the theory is to be widely applied in this way, it must be restated and transmitted with this purpose in mind, either in published form or through management development programs.

Contributions from the Systems Approach

In the beginning of this chapter, it is noted that the systems approach to theorizing tends to be static rather than dynamic, to thwart hypothesis formation, and thus to limit rather than to accelerate research on a theory. The Katz and Kahn theory does nothing to rebut these conclusions. Clearly these authors are well aware of the problem:

> In some respects open-system theory is not a theory at all; it does not pretend to the specific sequences of cause and effect, the specific hypotheses and tests of hypotheses which are the basic elements of theory. Open-system theory is rather a framework, a meta-theory, a model in the broadest sense of that overused term. Open-system theory is an approach and a conceptual language for understanding and describing many kinds and levels of phenomena. (Katz & Kahn, 1966, p. 452; 1978, p. 752)

An article by Donde Ashmos and George Huber (1987) provides a good discussion of the limitations and potential of the systems approach.

The strength of systems thinking — and this is apparent in the social psychology of organizations formulations — is that it provides a classification system and framework for organizing important variables. In the literature, one encounters frequent references to the Katz and Kahn formulations, but they are more often cited for conceptual clarification than for research hypotheses. When the theory is considered in formulating hypotheses, it tends to be used at such a high level of abstraction that it cannot be differentiated from a number of similar theories. Often the concepts are stated so broadly they contribute very little to prediction and understanding.

Yet the organizing properties of the systems approach should not be underestimated. As an example I would cite the systems model of human resource management activities that I have used in various forms for more than 25 years. The most recent version is contained in figure 14.3. Models of this kind provide a useful way of thinking about human resource processes. However, in spite of repeated efforts, I have never been able to generate a true theory of human resource management, replete with useful and testable hypotheses, from such a systems-based classification approach. My impression is that Katz and Kahn had this same type of experience.

SOCIOTECHNICAL SYSTEMS THEORY

In many respects sociotechnical systems theory is the European counterpart of system 4 theory. It has been associated closely from its beginnings with the Tavistock Institute of Human Relations in London, just as system 4 theory has been with the Institute for Social Research at the University of Michigan. Collaboration between these two organizations has been considerable over the years, including joint editorial responsibility for the journal *Human Relations*.

The Tavistock Institute was an outgrowth of the Tavistock Clinic that was formed in 1920 to provide psychotherapy to those who could not otherwise afford it. The institute emerged as a separate, incorporated entity when the clinic entered the British national health service after World War II (Dicks, 1970). One major figure in the institute and its chairman for many years was Eric Trist, who is the primary author of sociotechnical systems theory. Trist was joined in his theoretical efforts and in his research by others, who were either employed by the institute or strongly influenced by it. Thus in many respects sociotechnical systems theory is a product of the same kind of group interaction on which the theory itself often focuses.

Background

Trist was born in 1909. Thus he is of the same age cohort as Likert, Katz, and Stogdill. He attended Cambridge University and obtained his first degree in English literature. Subsequently, in 1933, he earned a second degree in psychology from the same source. His emphasis was on a mix of social psychology and psychoanalysis (Trist, 1993). The next 2 years were spent in the United States at Yale University, where he studied social anthropology. On returning to England Trist worked primarily as a researcher at the University of St. Andrews, investigating unemployment problems. When World War II broke out, he went into the army and became a clinical psychologist at the Tavistock Clinic, an association which in one form or another lasted for many years. His interest in groups was kindled by this early exposure to group psychotherapy from a psychoanalytic perspective (Fox, 1990).

Trist himself notes four phases in his career in England. First he was a social psychologist, then a specialist in group dynamics with a psychoanalytic orientation, then a specialist in sociotechnical systems,

Organizational Boundary

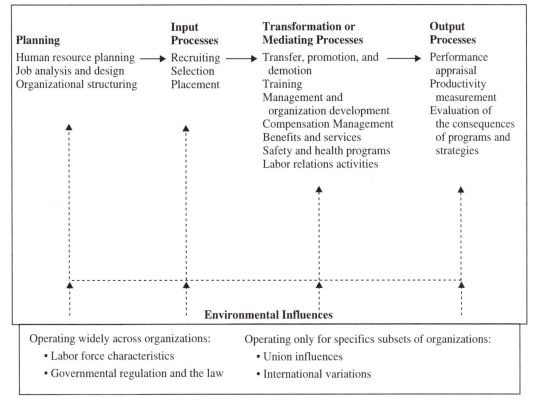

FIGURE 14.3 A systems model of the human resource management process

and finally he turned to socioorganizational ecology (Trist, 1993). His major theorizing covers the last two phases. It arose out of influences from psychoanalysis, from Lewin, from the personality-culture approach, and from open systems theory (Trist & Murray, 1990). He was also influenced by a set of values that appear to have much in common with those of Lewin: responsible self-regulation, freedom from oppression, democracy, self-determination of work activities, fair treatment, and workplace dignity for all (Pasmore & Khalsa, 1993). He was a humanist, and his approach to research was essentially that of ethnography, a combination that allowed him to focus his research efforts where his strong values could be engaged.

In 1966 Trist left Tavistock for the business school at UCLA. Then, 3 years later, he moved to the Wharton School at the University of Pennsylvania. On retiring from Wharton in 1978 he went to York University in Canada, from which he retired in 1985. He died in 1993.

Sociotechnical theory was a group product, consistent with its authors' commitment and the commitment of the Tavistock organization to democracy and participative principles. Trist has noted 10 other contributors, but among these Fred Emery, an Australian, stands out (Fox, 1995). Especially in the later years, when Trist devoted much of his energy to applied action research projects, Emery became the major theoretical contributor. He was born in Australia in 1925 and entered into the sociotechnical work when he joined Tavistock as a UNESCO fellow in 1951. He remained at Tavistock until 1969 when he returned to Australia to join the faculty of the Australian National University in Canberra. He died in 1997.

Statements of the Theory

Sociotechnical systems theory dates from the description of the change from a system of coal mining that emphasized autonomous work groups to a more mechanized system that was extrapolated from factory procedures (Trist & Bamforth, 1951). It is the thesis of Trist and of Bamforth, who had been a miner himself, that the introduction of the new longwall methods broke up the existing sociotechnical whole and created an imbalance:

> A qualitative change will have to be effected in the general character of the method so that a social as well as a technological whole can come into existence. Only if this is achieved can the relationships of the cycle work-group be successfully integrated and a new social balance be created. . . . It is difficult to see how these problems can be solved effectively without restoring responsible autonomy to primary groups throughout the system and ensuring that each of these groups has a satisfying sub-whole as its work task, and some scope for flexibility in work-pace. . . . It is likely that any attempts in this direction would require to take advantage of the recent trend of training face-workers for more than one role, so that interchangeability of tasks would be possible within work teams. (Trist & Bamforth, 1951, p. 38)

Open Systems and the Causal Textures of Environments

Sociotechnical theory began with the idea that there must be a best match, or joint optimization, between the task or technical environment and the social system. The theory at this stage operated at the work-group level primarily and gave little attention to the functioning of the organization as a whole. However, at least as early as 1959, the theory was extended through the introduction of open systems concepts (Trist, 1969).

An enterprise is an open system that engages in continuing exchanges with other enterprises, institutions, and individuals in its external environment. Its sociotechnical system must permit it to maintain a steady state in which work can be done in the face of changing environmental circumstances. This open systems approach contrasts with that of closed systems, which regard the enterprise as "sufficiently independent to allow most of its problems to be analyzed with reference to its internal structure and without reference to its external environment" (Trist, 1969, p. 270).

With the introduction of open systems concepts, sociotechnical theory became concerned with the total organization, including top management. Its authors also began creating a typology of environments that organizations (or segments of organizations) might face. The typology focuses on the different causal textures of environments—"the extent and manner in which the variables relevant to the constituent systems and their inter-relations are, independently of any particular system, causally related or interwoven with each other" (Emery & Trist, 1973, p. 41). Four ideal types of environments are described in various publications (Emery & Trist, 1965, 1973; Emery, 1967; Trist, 1976b, 1977).

In the *placid random* environment, the interconnectedness of elements is at a minimum and change is slow, if it occurs at all. Factors that may help or hinder goal achievement are randomly distributed, so that the optimal strategy is simply trying to do the best one can on a local basis; planning in any real sense is not possible. Learning occurs, but only at the level of simple conditioning.

Placid random environments are said to typify pre-agricultural, primitive societies and to occur only in certain specialized subsystems of modern societies—certain types of small job shops, surviving general stores, typing pools, and assembly lines. Other examples of a placid random environment are "an old-fashioned mad-house" and a concentration camp, where the prediction of events is almost impossible. In discussing such environments, the theorists treat the organizational context surrounding an individual or work unit and the environmental context surrounding an enterprise or organization as interchangeable concepts.

Although *placid clustered environments*, too, change slowly, the grouping of factors within them follows some logic. As a result, goal achievement is either helped or hindered, and strategies to deal with the environment may be developed. Organizations in such environments can develop environmental knowledge and use that knowledge to position themselves effectively. Traditional agricultural and business societies were of this type. Firms of limited size that possess a distinctive competence and fill a stable market demand have placid clustered environments in the present business structure. Such firms tend to be highly specialized and relatively invulnerable to economic cycles.

With the advent of industrialism, environmental change accelerated and large-scale bureaucracies emerged to cope with this change. The *disturbed reactive* context is characterized by competitive challenge, and organizations in such environments must develop strategies to deal with other organizations of the same kind having the same goals. Each firm in an industry must counteract power moves by other firms in the industry at the same time it is establishing its own strategies. As a result, organizations in such an environment are continually engaged in a complex set of reactions to each other.

Disturbed reactive environments are said to have reached their peak after World War II. The predominant form since then increasingly has been the *turbulent field*. Though definitions of the other three environments are not always as precise as might be desired, from a theoretical perspective only the turbulent environment is of central significance to the theory. The other types are posited primarily for purposes of contrast. Unlike the placid environments, and like the disturbed reactive environments, change is rampant in turbulent fields. But this change arises "not simply from the interaction of the component organizations, but also from the field. . . . The 'ground' is in motion" (Emery & Trist, 1965, p. 26).

Turbulent fields have emerged as a consequence of the development of huge organizations that exert effects beyond their industries, the increasing significance of public and governmental actions for economic organizations, the rapid change occasioned by increased research and development, and the expanded scope and speed of communication. Such fields introduce so much greater uncertainty than their predecessors that individual organizations can no longer cope with it through their own independent efforts. Strategic planning, as it was utilized in other environments, is inadequate when change is rampant.

Just as system 4 theory introduced a possible fifth system without elaborating on it, so sociotechnical theory merely touches on a fifth type of environment in a footnote:

> Any attempt to conceptualize a higher order of environmental complexity would probably involve us in notions similar to vortical processes. We have not pursued this because we cannot conceive of adaptation occurring in such fields. In case there may be something to the hunch that a type V environment has the dynamics of a vortex, it is worthwhile noting that vortices develop at system boundaries when one system is moving or evolving very fast relative to the other. (Emery & Trist, 1973, p. 41)

Postindustrial Society

Emery and Trist contend that society is still using an organizational structure that, in coping with the more complex turbulent environments of the present, is appropriate only to disturbed reactive environments. This cannot possibly work, because turbulent environments are too fast-changing, complex, interdependent, and uncertain for the essentially rigid and uncreative bureaucratic form. This theme is elaborated from a variety of viewpoints (Emery & Trist, 1965, 1973; Emery, 1967, 1974; Trist, 1973, 1975a, 1976a, 1976b, 1977, 1985; Trist, Emery, & Murray, 1997). A key concept of bureaucracy is redundancy of parts, whereby the work is broken down to the simplest and least costly elements possible. Individuals who perform such work are easily trained and replaced, but reliable control systems (requiring additional redundancy) are needed to make the system operate effectively. Such systems are so cumbersome that they are unresponsive to turbulent environments.

By their nature organizations require redundancy to minimize error in the face of environmental change. However, an alternative design to redundancy of parts is redundancy of functions among individuals and units that have wide repertoires of activities and are self-regulating. "Only organizations based on the redundancy of functions have the flexibility and innovative potential to give the possibility of adaptation to turbulent conditions" (Trist, 1977, p. 273).

In addition, turbulent environments require a set of simplifying values, much like systems of professional ethics, to foster intraorganizational and interorganizational collaboration rather than competition. Accordingly, organizations, become institutionalized and act in accord with the needs of the larger society. Hierarchy is reduced, if not eliminated, and alternatives such as composite, autonomous groups, matrices, and networks are fostered (Herbst, 1976). Because organizational design principles imply certain values, the movement toward these nonhierarchical forms and toward redundancy of functions can only occur within a value system that stresses the worth of individuals and of democratic processes.

Moving toward a postindustrial society that is capable of coping with a turbulent world requires active intervention:

1. The *object of intervention* is to increase the probability of the advent of one of the more

rather than one of the less desirable of the "alternative futures" which seem to be open.

2. The *instrument of intervention* is "adaptive planning"—the working out with all concerned of plans subject to continuous and progressive modification which are what have to be made when what has to be done cannot be decided on the basis of previous experience.

3. The *agency of intervention* is government—but in collaboration with other key institutional groups—for adaptive planning will require the active participation as well as the free consent of the governed. (Emery & Trist, 1973, p. 124)

As a result of this planned intervention, the changes noted in table 14.4 will occur. A new set of values, congruent with postindustrialism, will replace the Protestant ethic values of industrialism: "The core relevant values involved are those associated with organizational democracy" (Trist, 1976b, p. 18).

Autonomous Work Groups

Much of this argument for organizational democracy must be considered social philosophy rather than

TABLE 14.4 Changes associated with the move to a postindustrial society

Changing cultural values
  From achievement to self-actualization
  From self-control to self-expression
  From independence to interdependence
  From endurance of distress to capacity for joy

Changing organizational philosophies
  From mechanistic to organic forms
  From competitive to collaborative relations
  From separate to linked objectives
  From a view of one's resources as owned absolutely to a
    view of one's resources as shared with society

Changing ecological strategies
  From responsive to crisis to crisis-anticipation strategies
  From specific to comprehensive measures
  From requiring consent to requiring participation
  From damping conflict to confronting conflict
  From short to long planning horizons
  From detailed central control to generalized control
  From small local government to large area government
  From standardized to innovative administration
  From separate to coordinated services

SOURCE: Adapted from Fred E. Emery & Eric L. Trist (1973), *Toward a Social Ecology* (London: Plenum), 174, 182, 186

testable scientific theory, but at the level of organizational design, sociotechnical theory contends that a turbulent world has already arrived and that democratic alternatives to hierarchy will be more effective than bureaucracy. Here, hypotheses of a scientific nature are indeed advanced, and they indicate a very specific type of democratic organization.

In writing about sociotechnical systems theory as applied to work groups, Trist typically credits certain hypotheses developed by Emery (Trist, 1973, 1975a). Though formulated much earlier, these hypotheses were first published in Emery and Einar Thorsrud (1976). They state how a sociotechnical system should be organized and operated to produce positive outcomes in the modern world.

In this context the primary task of management is to cope with the environment across the boundary of the organization. To the extent management must "coordinate internal variances in the organization" it will be less effective. Organization members must be given considerable autonomy and selective independence if the enterprise is to achieve the steady state it needs for effectiveness in its environment (see Emery & Thorsrud, 1976, pp. 4–5).

This inevitable theoretical commitment to autonomous work groups appears inconsistent with the contingency concepts of sociotechnical theory. The explanation given is as follows:

> It seemed that there was "The Myth of the Machine." The organization theory opposing ours was not "a machine theory of organization" but a general theory of bureaucracy. . . . In the first and older perspective our task was to prove for each technology that organizational choice was possible; as each new technology emerged our task was on again. In the second perspective, the relevance of our approach could be established by asking a single question: Is management necessary to the organization? If the answer is yes, then, regardless of technology, some degree of self-management of groups of members is possible. Sociotechnical theory does not thereby go out of the door. To go from what is organizationally possible to what is viable one must answer such critical questions as "what groups should be formed around what tasks"; "how semi-autonomous"; "what degree of multiskilling is necessary." These questions can be answered only by some form of socio-technical analysis in each practical instance. (Emery & Thorsrud, 1976, p. 7)

At best this view assigns the theory's sociotechnical aspects a role secondary to environmental determinism and antibureaucracy.

Much of the theory deals with job enrichment — challenging job content, opportunity to learn, individual decision making, recognition in the work place, the opportunity to relate work to social life, and a sense that the job leads to a desirable future. In a more specific sense this means task variety, tasks forming meaningful wholes, optimum length of work cycle, individual goal setting coupled with feedback, inclusion of auxiliary and preparatory tasks, inclusion of tasks worthy of community respect, and the perception of a contribution to product utility. These hypotheses for positive outcomes are not unlike those of other job enrichment views

But "the redesigning of jobs leads beyond the individual job to the organization of groups of workers and beyond into the revision of our notions about supervision and the organization of support services. . . . The implications were even wider . . . a challenge to traditional management style and philosophy" (Emery & Thorsrud, 1976, p. 17). At the group level this calls for interlocking tasks, job rotation, or physical proximity where there is task interdependence or stress, or where individual jobs do not create a perception of contribution to product utility. Multiskilling of operators, according to the principle of redundancy of functions, is necessary for job rotation and is a key concept of the theory. Information for self-control should be made immediately available to the operators themselves. Meetings and contacts that foster group formation should be institutionalized. Foremen should be trained to deal with groups rather than individuals. Incentives should be of a group nature. The group must monitor and control individual contributions and assign tasks. In essence the system is one of group rather than hierarchical control, and effort is induced by group processes rather than superior managers. Thus group productivity is fostered by:

1. Communicating quickly, directly, and openly the needs for coordination arising from task or individual variability
2. Allocating tasks and other rewards and punishments to control what they consider to be a fair contribution by members (Emery & Thorsrud, 1976, p. 163)

Although the term *autonomous work group* is typically used to describe this type of organization, the groups are in fact only semiautonomous, since they depend on the company for resources, and the company remains responsible for compliance with legal constraints. The degree of autonomy will vary with the circumstances. At a minimum the group will decide on working methods and work allocation. Beyond this the members may control changes in the composition of the group, the equipment and tools used, maintenance, planning, quality standards, and at the highest level the defining of work goals. Thus much of the traditional supervisory task is taken over by the group. What remains to supervision is not the exercise of power over individuals, but the coordination of the group with the resources and objectives of the larger organization.

P. G. Herbst (1976) extended the theoretical treatment of nonbureaucratic structures designed to cope with turbulent environments. His *composite autonomous group* comes closest to what has been discussed previously. In such a context all members can perform all tasks. Consequently there is no special leadership function, and members can adopt whatever work structures and procedures seem desirable. Because of complete multiskilling, group size must remain small, although sets of autonomous groups linked by rotation of membership are possible.

The *matrix group* contains members who have a primary specialist function but some overlapping competencies with other members. The lack of complete multiskilling introduces some structural constraints, but permits much larger group sizes. Such groups may produce a variety of products and may choose their own procedures and even input needs. Generally, members work in small subsets, with those subsets "directively correlated" toward specified goals.

A *network group* tends to be widely dispersed. Long-term, directive correlations that are accepted by members focus their efforts on particular aims; correlations of this kind exist in the professions. Network groups typically find ways to go beyond what is already established. Members are maximally autonomous, but they build on and extend each other's work. In principle, such groups are temporary systems set up to achieve particular goals; competencies are overlapping, and size is limited.

To deal with larger organizational structures, the theory posits linked, composite, autonomous groups; networks of networks; and matrices of organizational units. All these nonbureaucratic structures are hypothesized to be superior to the bureaucratic hierarchy. However, Herbst makes the following statement:

There are conditions, especially in the field of public administration, where bureaucratic organizations function well. . . . Relevant conditions for this are:

1. That the task be decomposed into independent parts
2. Both the nature and requirements for task performance are stable over fairly long periods of time
3. Sufficient areas of discretion and responsible autonomy with respect to task performance exist at all levels so that even the lowest level provides the opportunity for the performance of a relatively autonomous professional role.

At the present time these conditions are decreasingly met. (1976, p. 19)

Such a theoretical statement appears consistent with the contingency aspects of sociotechnical theory but inconsistent with the Emery and Thorsrud (1976) statements of the inevitable superiority of autonomous work groups over bureaucracy. One could avoid the contradiction by reference to alternative types of environments, but Herbst does not do this. Indeed, if government is to be the key source of interventions for adaptive planning and changes to cope with turbulent environments, it would be hard to argue that government itself does not face such an environment.

Alternative and Elaborated Positions

The scientists concerned with sociotechnical systems theory constitute a network group, as described by Herbst. Trist and Hugh Murray (1990) note 17 organizational members of this network in eight countries, primarily in Europe but also in the United States, Canada, Australia, and India. The individuals whose ideas have been considered to this point constitute the core of the group, but there are others whose contributions either extend the theory or, in a few instances, provide alternative explanations. The status of these contributions relative to the basic theory is not clear. In some cases the core group seems to have granted its stamp of approval, as when Trist endorses a book in its foreword (Kingdon, 1973; Susman, 1976), but even then agreement on all points is not certain. In some areas even Trist and Emery appear to have disagreed with each other (Trist et al., 1997).

Alternative and elaborated positions have developed and extended sociotechnical theory as it relates to the causal textures of environments and to the turbulent field in particular. Among others, Shirley Terreberry (1968), J. L. Metcalfe (1974), and Dennis Mileti and David Gillespie (1976) have made contributions in this area. The last set forth a number of formal propositions that deal with organization-environment relationships. These and other statements appear to be aimed at greater theoretical specificity than are earlier statements by Emery and Trist. An essay by Joseph McCann and John Selsky (1984) develops the idea of a type 5 environment and hyperturbulence more fully.

This same specificity of theoretical statement appears to be the objective in a number of contributions that deal with autonomous work groups — in particular the contributions of Thomas Cummings and Suresh Srivastva (1977), Louis Davis (1977), and Gerald Susman (1976). Donald Kingdon (1973) devotes particular attention to the matrix group and to organizations that incorporate this structure. Eric Miller and A. K. Rice (1967) extend the theory to ways in which commitment can be achieved in sociotechnical systems and to the importance of group and organizational boundary definitions. These alternative and elaborated positions are of too great a range to deal with in any detail here, and it is not clear in all cases that the contributions would warrant such attention in any event. However, it is important to note the scope of the sociotechnical systems theory network.

The subject of commitment, however, has been picked up at various points by both Emery and Trist and elaborated most fully in Lyman Ketchum and Trist (1992). This discussion is closely allied to the job enrichment literature considered in chapter 7 in this volume and extends the previous discussions in this regard. Employee commitment is a goal of sociotechnical systems and it is achieved by satisfying the following intrinsic needs:

1. The need for the job to be reasonably demanding in terms other than sheer endurance and to provide a minimum of variety (not necessarily novelty, which is too much for some people though the spice of life for others). This is to recognize enfranchisement in problem solving as a human right.
2. The need to be able to learn on the job on a continuing basis. Again, this is a question

of neither too much nor too little, but of matching solutions to personal requirements. This is to recognize personal growth as a human right.

3. The need for some area of decision making that the individual can call his own. This recognizes the opportunity to use one's own judgment as a human right.

4. The need for some degree of social support and recognition in the workplace, from both fellow workers and bosses. This recognizes "group belongingness" as a human right.

5. The need to be able to relate what one does and what one produces to one's social life. That is, to have a meaningful occupational identity that gives a man or woman dignity. This recognizes the opportunity to contribute to society as a human right.

6. The need to feel that the job leads to some sort of desirable future (not necessarily promotion). It may involve training or redeployment—a career at shop floor level leading to the development of greater skill. It includes being able to participate in choosing that future. This recognizes hope as a human right. (pp. 10–11)

Beyond these intrinsic motivations it is important to provide for certain extrinsic satisfactions. Thus sociotechnical system design should include steps to assure fair and adequate pay, job security, appropriate benefits, safety in the work environment, good health, and due process to protect rights. To this list Trist added that *gainsharing* should eventually be provided, so that employees may share in the added material fruits made possible by the developing partnership between workers and managers, and thus to prevent perceptions of inequity by workers (see Fox, 1995). Thus sociotechnical systems theory came to incorporate the multitude of factors that system 4T also included.

Sociotechnical Research

Almost without exception, the research generated by sociotechnical systems theory has involved, either the introduction of autonomous work groups in situations where they did not previously exist or the study of such groups after they emerged spontaneously. Most of these studies have come from Europe and the United States, though some are from India and other parts of the world. Unfortunately, many of these investiga-

tions are better classified as case studies or demonstration projects than as scientific research studies, since systematic measurement and controls are lacking. (These studies are considered as examples of applications in the next section.) The following discussion focuses on research that can be considered legitimate tests of the theory.

Coal-Mining Studies

Although the original work on the mining of coal in England was ethnographic and involved merely describing what happened (Trist & Bamforth, 1951), subsequent investigations in the same context have taken a more scientific form.

In one instance comparisons were made between two groups of approximately 40 workers. One group used the then conventional longwall method of mining that was technology-dominated, highly specialized, and segmented. The other group—a more sociotechnically balanced, composite, autonomous group—used the same technology (Trist, Higgin, Murray, & Pollock, 1963; Trist, 1969). The composite, autonomous group was characterized by (1) multiskilling so that task continuity could be maintained from shift to shift; (2) self-selected teams that allocated tasks among themselves; (3) payment based on a bonus allocated by the group in equal shares; and (4) a generally high degree of group autonomy and self-regulation. None of these factors was present in the conventional group. An attempt was made to match the coal panels mined by the two groups so that only differences in work organization would be reflected in the results. Although the findings as given in table 14.5 were not subjected to statistical test, the pattern for the sociotechnical system was clearly superior.

A second study compared two groups, organized to varying degrees according to composite autonomous principles (Trist et al., 1963). Here, the differentiation was less pronounced than in the previous study, but the matching of coal panels to eliminate differences attributable to the difficulty of the work was good. The more autonomous group was found to be more productive, even though the comparison group exercised a degree of autonomy. A factor in this result appears to be the greater creativity in dealing with work problems exhibited by the more autonomous group.

In interpreting the results of this and the preceding

TABLE 14.5 Comparisons of results of conventional and composite autonomous group systems of coal mining

Criteria	Conventional longwall system	Composite, autonomous group system
Productivity as a percentage of estimated face potential	78	95
Percentage of shifts lagging behind the established production cycle	69	5
Absenteeism without reason as a percentage of possible shifts	4.3	.4
Absenteeism because of sickness or other reasons as a percentage of possible shifts	8.9	4.6
Absenteeism because of accidents as a percentage of possible shifts	6.8	3.2

NOTE: No statistical tests were conducted.

SOURCE: Adapted from Eric L. Trist, G. W. Higgin, Hugh Murray, & A. B. Pollack (1963), *Organizational Choice: Capabilities of Groups at the Coal Face under Changing Technologies* (London: Tavistock), 123, 125

research it is important to recognize that an autonomous group approach had been characteristic in the industry before the longwall technology was introduced. In fact, the early sociotechnical systems theory hypotheses were derived from study of these early autonomous groups. Many miners had had long experience with this approach and tended to revert to it in some situations, even after the longwall technology was introduced. Accordingly, the experimental groups were more emergent than contrived and appear to be particularly congruent with sociotechnical concepts. The authors note: "In pits where there is no composite tradition resistance to the introduction of composite working is likely to be considerable" (Trist et al., 1963, pp. 292–293). Given this situation, the extent to which the early coal mining findings can be generalized is left in doubt.

More recent research with the Rushton Mining Company in Pennsylvania deals directly with this problem (Goodman, 1979). Autonomous group procedures were introduced in some sections and not in others. Furthermore, the procedures were introduced in the various sections with a time lag to further facilitate control comparisons. There was no previous history of autonomous group functioning in this situation. The experimental procedures were introduced by a research team headed by Eric Trist and were generally comparable to those of the early British studies (Susman, 1976; Trist, Susman, & Brown, 1977).

The initial reports appear to have been favorable (Mills, 1976). However, comprehensive comparisons of experimental and control sections prior to and during the first 17 months of the study are mixed:

1. *Productivity.* The experiment did not significantly increase productivity.
2. *Safety.* The experiment did not significantly affect accident rates. There were significant reductions in the number of violations of . . . mining regulations. Safety practices and attitudes toward better safety practices improved. . . .
3. *Job Skills.* Miners in the experimental section reported that the programme had substantially increased their job skills.
4. *Job Attitudes.* Greater feelings of responsibility, more interest in work, more positive feelings about one's work group seem to be attributable to the experiment.
5. *Communication.* There was much more communication both vertically and horizontally, whereas previously communication had been primarily from top to bottom.
6. *Managerial Stress.* The programme increased stress for the supervisors of the experimental crew and some middle managers.
7. *Labour-Management Relations.* There were no changes in traditional indicators of labour-management relations such as the number or content of grievances. (Goodman & Lawler, 1979, p. 152)

Two additional points are important. The top wage was introduced in experimental sections for all members, which is consistent with the concept of multiskilling. Because of a variable wage scale, significant earnings differences existed in the control sections. This fact appears to have been a source of some conflict within the mine, but also it may have fostered more positive attitudes in the autonomous groups. In addition, it is apparent that without a historical background favorable to the approach, sociotechnical systems procedures may be resisted. There were several votes against installing autonomous groups and other evidence of resistance from certain quarters, including some members of management (Trist et al., 1977).

Eventually, after several years, the experimental interventions disappeared from Rushton. A major factor was a strike by the union, but multiple sources of resistance actually combined gradually to thwart the program.

Indian Textile Mill Studies

In addition to the British coal-mining studies, probably the best known investigation that emanated from the Tavistock group is an analysis of the introduction of autonomous work groups into two textile mills in India. Since the beginning of the research in 1953, the Ahmedabad Manufacturing and Calico Printing Company was involved in several studies, and data are available for a 17-year period (Rice, 1958, 1963; Miller, 1975). Because production figures were obtained for a period before the creation of the experimental groups and because certain comparisons are made both between autonomous and nonautonomous groups within the company and between the company and the industry as a whole, this research seems to qualify as an experiment.

In the 2 years after the autonomous groups were formed there was an increase in productivity from approximately 80 percent to 95 percent of potential, and this change is attributed to the sociotechnical procedures on the basis of control comparisons. At the same time, the quality of work improved significantly, by a factor of 59 percent. Follow-up data through 1960 indicate that the company assumed a position of considerable competitive advantage over other leading mills after the autonomous groups were introduced.

Some 10 years later one group formed on an autonomous basis was still functioning in that manner and maintaining its high performance (Miller, 1975). However, other autonomous groups were not doing as well. Furthermore, these groups appear to have backed away

from the sociotechnical procedures over the years under the pressures of environmental change (a result that was not predicted by the theory because autonomous groups should be ideally suited to cope with change and uncertainty). In one group it now seemed that the experimental induction never really took at all, except briefly to impress the researchers. Unfortunately there were no measures to determine exactly how autonomous various groups were at different times; data on this point are essentially impressionistic.

Interpretations of this research tend to vary widely. Katz and Kahn indicate that "by and large the history of the effects of the experimental plan is an amazing success story" (1978, p. 709). Many others have taken a similar position, although characteristically without considering Miller's (1975) follow-up data. Of particular interest are Miller's comments on the use of experimental and control comparisons within the company: "Comparisons of performance data need to be treated with a good deal of caution. It is virtually impossible to make precise comparisons between different types of looms weaving different types of cloth. Before and after comparisons on the same looms weaving a similar type of cloth are more reliable" (1975, p. 356). Yet, even in this instance, variations in the quality of yarn and supplies and in the criteria of measurement cloud the attribution of change over time to worker performance.

This matter of what caused the changes has been a major source of concern. S. K. Roy (1969) argues that a key factor may well have been the sizable pay increases instituted with the introduction of the sociotechnical system. He presents evidence from his own research to support this interpretation. Certainly a confounding of experimental changes and pay increases has characterized sociotechnical research. However, it is not possible to account for the *continued* high performance of the one autonomous group on this basis, given changes in the payment system that occurred over the years (Miller, 1975).

Research in Norway and Sweden

Sociotechnical theory was next extended to studies in Norway and subsequently in Sweden. Here the applications were widespread because they were facilitated by positive government interventions and a friendly social climate. Yet the emphasis was on demonstration projects and case applications rather than on scientific studies. There was a tendency to assume that industrial democracy was good and then move on to problems of dissemination, rather than to question basic theoretical hypotheses.

One exception to this generalization involved a study conducted in a Swedish tobacco company (Agervold, 1975). Comparisons of an autonomous group with a similar nonautonomous group in another factory tended to support the hypothesis of more positive attitudes in the sociotechnical context. However, it is apparent that plant differences per se account for part of the differential, and the experimental effects must be discounted proportionately. Because the results of statistical tests are not provided, it is difficult to evaluate these attitudinal findings, but it would appear that the effect of introducing autonomous work groups was not pronounced. Data on productivity changes indicate a 14 percent increase at the very least in the experimental group, but it is difficult to evaluate this because control figures are not given.

In studies such as this the question of the extent to which the dictates of sociotechnical systems theory really were followed is important. If the experimental interventions did not take or were somewhat less than what the theory would anticipate, any failure to achieve hypothesized results would be expected. A first attempt at dealing with this measurement problem was proposed by Jon Gulowsen (1972).

Figure 14.4 shows a scale of items indicating the degree to which a group is autonomous. The scale has been applied to eight different work groups, and based on these data, it appears to be unidimensional or cumulative in that a positive response to a higher-level item implies a positive response to all lower-level items. Unfortunately, scales such as this have not been used widely in research on sociotechnical systems theory. As a result, unfavorable findings often are explained post hoc as incomplete experimental induction, and no solid evidence is offered of the degree to which an autonomous system was in fact created.

Additional Research

A number of studies have been conducted in various locations around the world that speak to the validity of sociotechnical theory. There are not a great many such studies, but several bear noting; they are spread over a considerable time span. Pasmore (1978) carried out one of the few studies that compared alternative approaches to organizational change in two parallel units of a food processing firm. One unit was first surveyed, then fed the results of the survey in accordance with the Michigan approach discussed in chapter 13 in this volume, then redesigned along sociotechnical lines and surveyed again. During this same period, the second unit experienced the same survey interventions but did not shift to a sociotechnical form. Subsequently, both units had the second survey results fed back to them, and the second unit then experienced a sizable amount of job enrichment, though not enjoying other benefits of the autonomous group approach. Finally, both units were surveyed again. Significant improvements in employee attitudes were

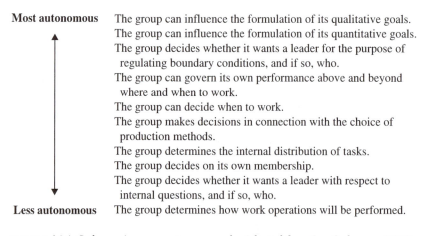

FIGURE 14.4 Gulowsen's group autonomy scale. Adapted from Jon Gulowsen (1972), A Measure of Work-Group Autonomy, in Louis E. Davis & James C. Taylor (Eds.), *Design of Jobs* (Baltimore: Penguin), 376–378.

found, but they could not be attributed to any particular intervention technique; all three procedures produced positive results. In terms of productivity and cost savings, however, the autonomous group procedure was clearly superior. In particular, there was a sizable savings in labor costs due to a 19 percent reduction in personnel required to operate the unit.

Research reported by Cummings and Srivastva (1977) produced much less positive results. In one instance, sociotechnical procedures were introduced into the estimating and die engineering components of an aluminum forging plant. Control comparisons were made with data obtained from the personnel, engineering, and information systems groups in the same plant. The overall effects of the autonomous group procedure appear to have been a significant negative shift in attitudes, a decrease in productivity (at least as experienced by those involved), and a generally more negative evaluation of the experimental groups by outside departments using their services. The experiment was terminated by management after 6 months.

A second study in the same company compared two wheel line production units: one organized on a sociotechnical basis, and the other not so organized (Cummings & Srivastva, 1977). There was little attitudinal change, other than a greater amount of insecurity in the experimental group. Absenteeism was higher in the autonomous groups, and the members of these groups perceived their performance as poorer. Their supervisors rated their performance higher than did the supervisors of the control subjects, but these measures appear to be biased.

Although the overall results of the second study were perceived more positively by the company's management, neither set of findings supports sociotechnical theory. Cummings and Srivastva (1977) attribute the results to the failure of sociotechnical interventions to take fully under the impact of individual resistance and the economic crisis position of the company at the time of the study. Though the authors used no comprehensive measure of experimental take such as Gulowsen's (1972), there is some evidence to support their contentions. Still, the theory would not have predicted the results obtained. If anything, sociotechnically organized groups should ultimately emerge as more effective, not less effective, in coping with turbulent environmental circumstances.

Other research that was conducted in a more favorable economic milieu does yield more positive outcomes. The initial results, obtained when autonomous groups were introduced in one of the company's plants, appear to be very favorable, although control data were not available (Bramlette, Jewell, & Mescon, 1977). Subsequently, two sociotechnically organized plants in the company were compared with plants of a more traditional nature (Beldt, 1978). The data indicate that the experimental plants were distinctly superior in terms of absenteeism, production volume per worker hour, labor costs per unit of output, and employee satisfaction.

It is not entirely clear what caused these outcome differences. The sociotechnical plants had younger workers who were somewhat better educated, and one plant used an exceptionally advanced technology. Furthermore, the workers in the experimental plants did not exhibit the value structures one might anticipate. Such factors as trust, cooperation, autonomy, creativity, and equality were not more highly valued in the autonomous groups; compassion, tolerance, individuality, and risk actually were valued less. But skill and success were valued highly, and the few managers required in these plants were strongly managerially motivated individuals. It may be that for some reason the experimental plants attracted people who were more motivated toward, and more capable of, outstanding productivity.

More recently, research has been able to use better controls and longitudinal analyses to achieve more definitive results. A study conducted in a confectionery company in England used a consultant from Tavistock and was particularly well designed (Wall, Kemp, Jackson, & Clegg, 1986). It extended well beyond the initial period during which positive results have been most likely to be obtained. There is no question that stable and lasting changes occurred: perceived work autonomy and intrinsic job satisfaction both shifted in a positive direction. But job motivation, commitment, mental health, and job performance did not improve. Turnover increased, although external labor force factors may have been involved. Although productivity levels appear to have been unchanged, certain cost savings were realized because the need for managers was less and indirect labor costs decreased. All in all, the changes were viewed as less than anticipated.

A comparable study that was conducted in a minerals processing company in Australia provides further evidence (Cordery, Mueller, & Smith, 1991). Once again, job satisfaction appears to have been increased — and more broadly now to include commitment — but trust in management showed no differences. Both turnover and absenteeism were higher under autonomous conditions. Productivity differences could not be determined with certainty but appear not to have been present. There clearly was a reduction in managerial and support personnel, with a resulting decline in labor costs. Contiguous units that were not provided the opportunity to participate in the sociotechnical program were clearly adversely affected by it (high turnover, work stoppages, etc.). The results overall were mixed; there were clear changes, but they were both positive and negative in their effects.

Demonstrations and Applications

Interpreting the results of research conducted to test sociotechnical theory is not easy, even when the researcher makes a serious effort to use adequate scientific controls. In the projects considered in this section, however, interpretation is practically impossible. The projects are important because they demonstrate the nature of and sometimes the pitfalls associated with sociotechnical systems design, and not because they contribute to evaluation of the underlying theory. In this respect the term *experiment* as applied to these projects is often inappropriate and misleading.

Principles of Sociotechnical Systems Design

Among individuals presenting guidelines or principles for undertaking sociotechnical interventions are some of the original theorists—for example, Emery and Trist (1978), Trist (1975b), Herbst (1976), and Ketchum and Trist (1992). Cummings and Srivastva (1977) describe a systematic procedure for implementing sociotechnical systems. The principles presented by Albert Cherns are comprehensive:

1. *Comparability.* The means to design must be consistent with the end to be achieved. If people in the organization are to share in decision making, they must share in the design.
2. *Minimal critical specification.* At each stage of the design what is critical should be identified and only that should be specified. . . . Precision about what has to be done may be necessary, but rarely precision about how it is to be done. . . . If you specify more than you need, you foreclose options that should be kept open.
3. *Variance control.* If variances cannot be

eliminated, they should be dealt with as near to their point of origin as possible. A variance is an unprogrammed event. . . . Applying the principle of variance control would lead us to incorporate inspection with production, allowing people whenever possible to inspect their own work.
4. *Multifunction.* Design the organization so that it can achieve its objectives in more than one way. Allow each unit a repertoire of performance . . . redundancy of functions.
5. *Boundary location.* Roles that require shared access to knowledge or experience should be within the same departmental boundaries.
6. *Information flow.* Information systems should be designed to provide information to the organizational unit that will take action on the basis of the information. . . . Sophisticated information systems can supply a work team with exactly the right kind and amount of feedback, thus enabling the team to learn to control the variances that occur in its spheres of responsibility.
7. *Support congruence.* The system of social support should be designed to reinforce the behaviors that the organization structure is designed to elicit. If an organization is designed on the basis of group or team operations with team responsibility, a payment system based on individual performance would be incongruent.
8. *Design and human values.* A prime objective of organizational design should be to provide a high quality of working life to its members.
9. *Transitional organization.* There is a changeover period from old to new that requires a transitional organization. . . . What is required is a careful rehearsal of the roles that have to be performed during the changeover, especially the continuing training role of the supervisor.
10. *Completion.* Design is an iterative process. The closure of options opens new ones. . . . The multifunctional, multilevel, multidisciplinary team required for the original design is also needed for its evaluation and review. (1977, pp. 55–63)

An application concern that has arisen out of experience with the history of actual interventions is that the program may dissipate over time, often after a promising early period. This was the experience at

Rushton. Or diffusion to other locations may be stifled so that the intervention site becomes a walled enclave. Failures of these kinds may be associated with the flow of business cycles, and formulations to that effect have been offered (De Greene, 1988). However, the authors of sociotechnical systems theory have tended to emphasize the peripheral nature of most interventions. The projects are carried out in new plants or other locations that are far removed from headquarters, and they tend to receive little or no attention from top management.

To counteract this, Ketchum and Trist (1992) proposed that a center-out rather than a periphery-in strategy be used when projects are first introduced into a firm. In reality this is a top-down strategy; support for change is obtained from top management first, and this group then goes public, establishing beachheads for sociotechnical innovations at strategic points in the company. This center-out principle clearly calls for use of the hierarchy and in doing so assumes that hierarchy exists—which is somewhat strange for a theory that elsewhere has placed strong emphasis on providing substitutes for hierarchy. There is a logical inconsistency here.

Another point that bears mention involves an area in which one might think principles might operate but none is stated. Experience appears to indicate that certain types of people perform better under sociotechnical conditions than others, and, in fact, there is evidence to this effect (Neuman, 1991). Given the clinical background of the theory's authors, principles specifying how individual differences should operate in the staffing of sociotechnical interventions would be expected. Yet such principles do not exist, thus implying that the theory works with everyone. The frequent finding of high turnover belies that conclusion. This appears to be an instance in which theoretical opportunity has been foregone.

A wide range of applications based on the existing principles is reported in the literature (see, in particular, Trist & Dwyer, 1982; Trist, 1985; Trist & Murray, 1993). Fox (1995) notes some 30 organizations so involved. The examples that follow are among the most widely discussed.

Norwegian Industrial Democracy Program

The Norwegian projects are unusual in that they represent a concerted effort on the part of industry,

unions, and, eventually, government to change a whole society. The first four projects considered here were undertaken in the early 1960s with active assistance from the Tavistock group (Emery & Thorsrud, 1976). Subsequent diffusion has been slow within Norway, and the massive social change originally envisaged has not occurred (Thorsrud, Sorensen, & Gustavsen, 1976). Yet there have been other applications, some of the most interesting being in the shipping industry (Herbst, 1974).

The first project, undertaken in the wire drawing department of a steel mill (Christiana Spigerverk), met with considerable resistance at the shop floor level initially and had continuing problems with union manning requirements throughout. Except for 2 weeks in the middle of the project when conditions were optimal, little success was in evidence. A major problem was that multiskilling and the introduction of a group bonus system brought earnings of the autonomous groups to a level that disrupted the overall factory pay structure. As a result, strong pressures against "rate busting" were exerted on the groups, pressures to which they responded. In this first effort the groups seemed unable to cope with strong environmental forces.

Autonomous groups were introduced among operators in the chemical pulp department and considerably later in a paper machines department of a pulp and paper company (Hunsfos). Overall, this project appears to have been a qualified success. Major improvements occurred in the initial period, but there was a subsequent loss of momentum: "Considerable resistance occurred among foremen and production management and among some operators who previously held protected, high status jobs" (Thorsrud et al., 1976, p. 434). However, a degree of management acceptance did develop, and efforts to expand the project into other areas were undertaken. It is not entirely clear from the published report what the long-term consequences for the Hunsfos firm were.

Initial changes were introduced in a small plant in a rural location (NOBO Factories), and within that plant in a new department producing electric panel heaters. The project was apparently a major success:

The company management were well experienced in making these sorts of measures of worker productivity and well aware of the sorts of allowances that have to be made, often intuitively, for the effects of equipment change. They believed the observed changes were real and were significant. Their calculations also led them to believe that quality standards had improved and maintenance costs dropped. (Emery & Thorsrud, 1976, p. 96)

When the production process was transferred to a new location and expanded, the autonomous group procedures went with it and have continued in use. Diffusion to the main company did not occur, however.

Another project initially involved the introduction of sociotechnical approaches throughout a new fertilizer plant (Norsk Hydro). The plant was manned at a level that was sharply below comparable plants without autonomous work groups, at sizable cost savings. These savings existed even though compensation levels rose with multiskilling and bonus payments. Yet, in spite of the generally favorable evaluation of the fertilizer plant results, diffusions to other existing plants did not progress on schedule. Management resistance to revised roles has been considerable. In one instance a plant that had initiated autonomous groups was shut down because of market factors. There have been union sources of resistance as well. All in all, the results, though favorable, did not achieve the breadth of application that was originally envisaged.

Swedish Extensions

Diffusion in Norway, though it continued, was slow; in Sweden, by contrast, diffusion was rapid (Peterson, 1976). Apparently the idea of industrial democracy on the shop floor is particularly consonant with Swedish culture. Furthermore, it is in Sweden that some of the most dramatic shifts away from assembly line technology have occurred.

The initial pilot project (Saab-Scania) was undertaken in 1969 in units of a truck plant. The results of this effort were then used in 1972 to start up an engine manufacturing plant that was organized on a sociotechnical basis. In this latter instance there was no assembly line in the conventional sense; the plant was designed to permit parallel groups to assemble complete engines at their own pace. The results of the pilot project were generally favorable. It is difficult to evaluate the total plant project and difficult as well to turn back from the sociotechnical commitment embodied in the design of the plant itself:

By the conventional criteria of management, the system is a success. Quantity of production is within the expectation (worker minutes per engine) of conventional assembly methods. Absence and turnover, which were special problems in the assembly operation, are now no higher than in other worker categories. . . . Changes of this kind require investment, in many senses of that word. The system of parallel workshops requires more space than the conventional assembly line. The method of conveying engines and materials was more costly to install. To these costs must be added the time of the committees that labored to invent and create the system. (Katz & Kahn, 1978, pp. 726, 728)

A project very similar to Saab-Scania occurred at the Volvo plant at Kalmar, except that the scale was larger. Again a new factory is involved, but in this case a total automobile is the product. The assembly process is broken down into a series of group operations, with inspections built into each group (Gyllenhammar, 1977). The Kalmar plant appears to have been somewhat more expensive to build than conventional plants and was about as efficient. However, a major objective was to deal with the company's labor supply problems, and that has been accomplished. Also fewer supervisors are needed, and the technology permits greater flexibility in introducing new models. The company clearly is satisfied with the results, and the sociotechnical approach has diffused to other operations.

General Foods at Topeka, Kansas

The Topeka project was carried out in a new General Foods plant of small size. It was generally considered to be a success from the beginning (Walton, 1972). As in many such projects, staffing could be maintained at a low level due to multiskilling. Costs were consistently low, although the extent to which this was a function of the new equipment is unknown.

Subsequent events at the Topeka plant did not follow as positive a course (Walton, 1977). Commitment to the sociotechnical approach within the work force was cyclical, but some erosion was in evidence overall. Problems with the payment system continued, particularly problems with the group-based allocations of rewards. Plantwide issues were not dealt with as effectively as they could be. Though opposition from within has grown, the autonomous groups remained solidly in place. Furthermore, production costs continued to be low, absenteeism and turnover rates acceptable, and overall job satisfaction high.

The Topeka project received considerable coverage in the business press. Nevertheless, diffusion within General Foods did not occur, and it remains unclear what caused the success that was obtained. There have been arguments that the interpretations developed from the available evidence extend well beyond what the data justify, to the point that they represent advocacy much more than science (Yorks & Whitsett, 1985). Reports on other sociotechnical projects, such as the one at Shell Oil, have also been criticized as not fully and truly presenting the facts, with the result that an overly rosy picture emerges (see Blackler & Brown, 1980).

Evaluation and Impact

Much of what has been said about systems 4 and 4T and the Michigan theorizing in general is equally applicable to sociotechnical systems theory. Both originated at the work group level and seem to work best there. In larger organizational and environmental contexts they tend to run into difficulties.

Theory at the Level of Environments and Management

As it deals with causal textures of environments, sociotechnical theory has been the subject of considerable criticism. J. L. Metcalfe (1974) considers it excessively vague and lacking in rigor. In part for this reason, research has not focused directly on the environmental aspects of the theory. Eric Rhenman takes issue with several of the theory's basic propositions in the environmental area:

1. All environments contain some random elements, some clustering, some risk of reaction, and a certain amount of structural change.
2. The four classes of environment suggested by Emery and Trist leave no room for distinguishing between different types of value environments.
3. Structural change in the environment need not always be a disadvantage. For organizations that can dominate their environment in particular, such changes can be of positive

value. In this context I question Emery and Trist's claim that some sort of matrix organization is needed to deal with the turbulent environment. (1973, p. 190)

In fact, there is little evidence that bureaucratic organizations are inherently incapable of coping with turbulent environments or that sociotechnical organizations are particularly adept in this regard. Arthur Stinchcombe (1974) argues that, through appropriate adjustment of line-staff relationships, bureaucracies can function as a major source of innovation, and he presents evidence to support this view. The position that bureaucracies are inevitably too rigid and bound by tradition to cope with rapid change through innovation is not supported by the evidence. Furthermore, there is no logical reason why the processes and procedures generated by autonomous groups cannot become equally entrenched over time; in fact, there is reason to believe that they do (Barker, 1993). Nor is there any basis for concluding that autonomous groups are necessarily inherently creative. In line with this position is the finding that autonomous work groups often are vulnerable to turbulent forces and changing conditions in their environments, not only in the startup phase but also after they are established. Evidence to this effect comes from Miller (1975), Cummings and Srivastva (1977), and Walton (1977).

The role of management in a sociotechnical system presents certain problems. There appears to be no place in the theory for the manager who coordinates internal variances in the organization. Theoretically this should be done closer to the variances themselves, by the workers. Seemingly, this argues for a positively sloped control curve and flies directly in the face of much evidence generated by control theory, as discussed in chapter 13 in this volume. The theory's hypotheses about management have never been tested adequately. Rice (1963) devotes considerable attention to changes at this level but does not make them a subject of research investigation.

The introduction of autonomous groups tends to generate considerable managerial stress, presumably as a result of the role ambiguity that results. In one apparently successful application, plant managers were found to be of a type who usually perform very well in bureaucratic settings (Beldt, 1978). Although government is considered to be the intervention agent of choice, in fact, top management has filled that role much more frequently and apparently with greater success. These and other considerations related to the role of management are not handled in a logically consistent manner by sociotechnical systems theory, if they are handled at all.

The original emphasis on organizational designs that are contingent on an optimal social-technical fit seems inconsistent with the subsequent advocacy of autonomous work groups as the one best (and bureaucracy as the one worst) design. As Herbst (1976) suggests, there must be situations where bureaucracy is appropriate, given the technological context. Working up from a kind of technological determinism does not necessarily produce the same result as working down from a corresponding kind of environmental determinism. The inconsistencies that may result are, at least in part, a function of the theory's network form of authorship, but they are real, nevertheless.

Level of Work Groups

The foregoing discussion yields a rather dismal picture for sociotechnical systems theory. However, when one moves to the workgroup level where the theory began, the picture brightens. This is the level at which the research has been done, and the results often are positive. It is hard to predict whether the outcome will be greater output, better quality, less absenteeism, reduced turnover, fewer accidents, greater job satisfaction, or what, but the introduction of autonomous work groups is often associated with improvements.

It is difficult to understand why a particular outcome such as increased productivity occurs in one study and not another, and why on some occasions nothing improves. Sociotechnical systems theory is of little help in explaining these variations. Furthermore, what actually causes the changes when they do occur is not known. It is tempting to assert that change is caused by industrial democracy per se, but the sociotechnical approach calls for making so many changes at once that it is almost impossible to judge the value of the individual variables, including those of industrial democracy. Increased pay, self-selection of work situation, multiskilling with its resultant job enrichment, and decreased contact with authority almost invariably occur in studies of autonomous work groups. The compounding of experimental variables makes interpretation very hazardous.

Even among work groups, sociotechnical theory has faced its share of criticism, primarily on grounds of incompleteness. Thus, Richard Hackman contends:

1. The theory does not specify the attributes of group tasks that are required for creation of effective autonomous work groups . . . because key task attributes are not specified, it is not possible to devise measures of those attributes for use in theory guided diagnoses of work systems prior to change, in evaluations of the effects of changes on the work, or in tests of the conceptual adequacy of the theory itself.
2. Individual differences among people are not explicitly dealt with in the sociotechnical approach. . . . The theory does not deal with the fact that social needs vary in strength among people. Such differences may affect whether individuals seek to participate in an autonomous group.
3. The theory does not address the internal dynamics that occur among members of work groups. . . . The assumption apparently is that members of autonomous work groups will develop on their own satisfactory ways of working together. . . . Given the substantial evidence about ways that groups can go "sour," the validity of that assumption must be considered questionable. (1978, p. 64)

Certainly sociotechnical theory has suffered as a consequence of inattention to measurement. Except for an instrument developed by John Oliver (1982), little has been done to follow up on Gulowsen's (1972) initial work. Accordingly, it is often impossible to determine whether an appropriate test of the theory has actually been carried out.

Hackman's second point about individual differences is equally well taken. Apparently, autonomous work groups are not for all, just as bureaucratic authority systems seem not to be for all. Many may view the forced social interaction with distaste and rebel against the tyranny of group decision. Theoretical extension and research into individual differences seem curiously lacking, given the clinical background of the original Tavistock unit.

Hackman's final point, though largely correct, cannot be considered a valid criticism of the theory. It is hypothesized that, to the extent they are left alone, groups will develop effective solutions; they may need some training and structuring initially but not in the continuing work situation. That such groups may go sour is not necessarily attributable to failures of internal group dynamics. The theory would attribute such phenomena largely to external forces that limit autonomy, to inappropriate sociotechnical fit, and the like.

Such hypotheses should certainly be viewed as theoretically justified. Whether they are valid is a matter for research.

Pros and Cons of Application

The basic question insofar as application is concerned is whether autonomous groups should be introduced. That the theory itself has run into difficulties is of little managerial significance. The theory has spawned an approach that may well be justified in its own right. If anything, the techniques of sociotechnical application appear to have outdistanced the theory, much as, for instance, psychoanalytic therapy has moved beyond psychoanalytic theory.

It seems apparent that sociotechnical approaches are more likely to work in certain contexts than in others. Small-town environments, small work forces, new locations (startup situations, greenfield sites), geographic separation from the rest of the company, and extensive planning horizons seem to help, although they do not guarantee diffusion to other locations. The absence of a union, or at least of a militant union, represents a favorable situation as well. Converting an existing workforce to sociotechnical approaches and dealing with more authoritarian cultures can introduce problems (Anderson & Terborg, 1986; Fairhurst, Green, & Courtright, 1995). Organizational and national cultures that are favorable to job autonomy and participative process provide fertile ground for sociotechnical approaches. The early coalfield research benefited from the former. Evidence indicates that the Nordic countries, such as Norway and Sweden, as opposed to the United States, Canada, and Australia, provide a favorable climate for interventions of this type (Dobbin & Boychuk, 1999). In addition, certain technologies seem to foster sociotechnical approaches and others to thwart them (Sorensen, 1985).

Sociotechnical interventions certainly can produce resistance, either in the short run or over long periods, and this resistance can escalate. Yet these innovations can also work, and major negative consequences are rare. Accordingly, the approach can be recommended where there is a reasonable chance of success and where the company faces a basic problem that sociotechnical concepts can reasonably be calculated to solve, as in the instance of Volvo's labor supply problems. This is not to say that autonomous work groups are an all-purpose solution. At present at least, autonomous work groups are best advised as a solution

to special problems, except in such countries as Sweden where there is extensive cultural support. In other contexts there is a real risk that too widespread an application will exhaust the resources that are needed for success and will undermine the whole endeavor. Success has occurred consistently where the scale is small and the context is isolated enough to permit social pressures to operate uncontested, or where social pressures are supported by external forces.

Management should consider two additional factors. Sociotechnical systems in the United States often have operated as nonunion enclaves in unionized companies. Even pro-labor advocates admit the resilience of autonomous work groups in the face of organizing attempts. Whether this is good or bad depends on one's point of view, but introducing autonomous work groups does seem to eliminate or at least temporarily reduce pressures from a union. Whether the approach is worth the investment depends on the relative costs involved.

Second, the sociotechnical approach appears to reduce manpower needs. Because of multiskilling, more flexible work organization, and the assumption of managerial tasks by the work group, fewer people are needed. Thus, even though each person is typically paid more, total costs tend to be reduced. This is a major managerial advantage, but for unions it means fewer potential dues-paying members, and for society as a whole it may mean increased unemployment. Under conditions of substantial business growth, neither of these considerations should represent a problem. But without growth, adoption of sociotechnical approaches on a major scale could raise a whole new set of problems, no matter how streamlined and efficient the resulting organization might be.

We end with a generally favorable vote for the sociotechnical approach, given the right circumstances and the right people, although it is not necessarily a favorable vote for sociotechnical theory and the reasons it espouses for introducing autonomous work groups. Even more, the apparent success of applications of the sociotechnical approach calls for expanded research. The number of unanswered questions is staggering.

Future Directions

While the sociotechnical approach antedates the concept of organization development, the two have tended to merge in recent years so that autonomous work groups are now often introduced as organization development interventions, just as survey feedback is. In fact, during the 1990s this kind of merging has become so prevalent that it is very difficult to determine what approach in practice is an application of what theory. One thing is certain: teams in some form under some name have been widely adopted. This phenomenon is often attributed to the influence of Jon Katzenbach and Douglas Smith's book *The Wisdom of Teams* (1993), but it clearly has multiple origins that existed before publication of that book. In any event, teams are now widespread (Cohen & Bailey, 1997; Varma, Beatty, Schneier, & Ulrich, 1999), and they travel under a great many different names; examples are autonomous work groups and sociotechnical systems, but also self-managing work teams, self-organizing teams, empowered groups, self-regulating work groups, self-directed teams, high-performance work systems, bossless teams, and, on occasion, such entities as quality circles, task forces, communication teams, new venture teams, and business brand teams, even though these last may well have somewhat different characteristics (Barry, 1991). It seems that each company and each consulting firm uses a different combination of these words in an effort to differentiate its product.

The expansion of these approaches appears to reflect competitive pressures and the need to reduce costs much more than the compelling logic of theoretical statements, but nevertheless there are theoretical factors at work. In fact, sociotechnical systems theory is often credited with providing the underpinnings for the current burst of activity on the team front (see, for example, Kirkman & Shapiro, 1997; Moorhead, Neck, & West, 1998). Yet roots of the current developments extend back into social learning theory and organizational behavior modification, especially the concept of self-control or self-regulation, as well (see chapter 8 in this volume). This theoretical source appears equally credible (Cohen, Chang, & Ledford, 1997). In any event, the future of sociotechnical theory and its applications would seem to be inexorably tied now to developments of a team nature. This thrust for the future seems inevitable with the deaths of the theory's major authors during the 1990s.

CONCLUSIONS

The parallels between the theoretical developments initiated from the Institute for Social Research at the University of Michigan and those coming out of the Tavistock Institute are many. These include the fact that both organizations appear to have operated in lieu of business schools for their members, serving many of the same functions in fostering the growth of organizational behavior's theories.

Yet the two organizations differed also. This became manifest at an early meeting between the two groups, in 1949 (Trist, Emery, & Murray, 1997). There was some tension generated because the Tavistock people "wanted to get on with things which were of practical interest" while perceiving the Michigan group as having "gone into methodology and concept development." As Trist (in the Trist et al., 1997, volume) notes: "We were moving into the society and they were moving away from it" (p. 677). The Michigan approach was too academic for the action-oriented Tavistock consultants. This difference persevered for many years; it is clearly manifest in the different types of significant contributions that the two organizations have made.

The unifying theme between Michigan and Tavistock has been participation at the group level, a theme that has extended to a number of other theories as well. Our treatment of participation here has been from the perspective of the various *theories* that endorse participation in some form. A more comprehensive coverage of the topic is provided by Frank Heller, Eugen Pusic, George Strauss, and Bernhard Wilpert (1998). This book looks at the subject from multiple positions and provides a balanced discussion of the pros and cons involved.

References

Agervold, Mogens (1975). Swedish Experiments in Industrial Democracy. In Louis E. Davis & Albert B. Cherns (Eds.), *Cases and Commentary*. Vol. 2: *The Quality of Working Life* (pp. 46–65). New York: Free Press.

Anderson, Roger L., & Terborg, James R. (1986). Managing Employee Beliefs in Work Redesign Interventions. *Academy of Management Proceedings*, 46, 225–228.

Ashmos, Donde P., & Huber, George P. (1987). The Systems Paradigm in Organization Theory: Correcting the Record and Suggesting the Future. *Academy of Management Review*, 12, 607–621.

Barker, James R. (1993). Tightening the Iron Cage: Concertive Control in Self-Managing Teams. *Administrative Science Quarterly*, 38, 408–437.

Barry, David (1991). Managing the Bossless Team: Lessons in Distributed Leadership. *Organizational Dynamics*, 20(1), 31–47.

Baum, John F. (1978). Effectiveness of an Attendance Control Policy in Reducing Chronic Absenteeism. *Personnel Psychology*, 31, 71–81.

Baum, John F., & Youngblood, Stuart A. (1975). Impact of an Organizational Control Policy on Absenteeism, Performance, and Satisfaction. *Journal of Applied Psychology*, 60, 688–694.

Beldt, Sandra F. (1978). An Analysis of Values in Traditional Organizations and Nontraditional Organizations Structured Using Socio-Technical Systems Design, Ph.D. Dissertation, Georgia State University, Atlanta.

Blackler, Frank H. M., & Brown, Colin A. (1980). *Whatever Happened to Shell's New Philosophy of Management? Lessons for the 1980s from a Major Socio-Technical Intervention of the 1960s*. Westmead, UK: Teakfield.

Bramlette, Carl A.; Jewell, Donald O.; & Mescon, Michael H. (1977). Designing for Organizational Effectiveness: A Better Way; How It Works. *Atlanta Economic Review*, 27(5), 35–41; 27(6) 10–15.

Cherns, Albert B. (1977). Can Behavioral Science Help Design Organizations? *Organizational Dynamics*, 5(4), 44–64.

Cohen, Susan G., & Bailey, Diane E. (1997). What Makes Teams Work: Group Effectiveness Research from the Shop Floor to the Executive Suite. *Journal of Management*, 23, 239–290.

Cohen, Susan G.; Chang, Lei; & Ledford, Gerald E. (1997). A Hierarchical Construct of Self-Management Leadership and Its Relationship to Quality of Work Life and Perceived Work Group Effectiveness. *Personnel Psychology*, 50, 275–308.

Cordery, John L.; Mueller, Walter S.; & Smith, Leigh M. (1991). Attitudinal and Behavioral Effects of Autonomous Group Working: A Longitudinal Field Study. *Academy of Management Journal*, 34, 464–476.

Cummings, Thomas G., & Srivastva, Suresh (1977). *Management of Work: A Socio-Technical Systems Approach*. Kent, OH: Kent State University Press.

Davis, Louis E. (1977). Evolving Alternative Organizational Designs: Their Sociotechnical Bases. *Human Relations*, 30, 261–273.

De Greene, Kenyon B. (1988). Long Wave Cycles of Sociotechnical Change and Innovation: A Macropsychological Perspective. *Journal of Occupational Psychology*, 61, 7–23.

Dicks, Henry V. (1970). *Fifty Years of the Tavistock Clinic*. London: Routledge & Kegan Paul.

Dobbin, Frank, & Boychuk, Terry (1999). National Employment Systems and Job Autonomy: Why Job Autonomy Is High in the Nordic Countries and Low in the United States, Canada, and Australia. *Organization Studies*, 20, 257–291.

Doll, William J. (1977a). The Maintenance Subsystem of the Katz and Kahn Framework. *Midwest Division of the Academy of Management Proceedings*, 334–345.

Doll, William J. (1977b). The Regulatory Mechanisms of the Katz and Kahn Framework. *Academy of Management Proceedings*, 37, 188–197.

Doll, William J., & Melcher, Arlyn S. (1976). The Production Subsystem of the Katz and Kahn Framework: A Reformulation and Empirical Evaluation. *Midwest Division of the Academy of Management Proceedings*, 285–296.

Emery, Fred E. (1967). The Next Thirty Years: Concepts, Methods and Anticipations. *Human Relations*, 20, 199–237.

Emery, Fred E. (1974). Bureaucracy and Beyond. *Organizational Dynamics*, 2(3), 3–13.

Emery, Fred E., & Thorsrud, Einar (1976). *Democracy at Work*. Leiden, the Netherlands: Martinus Nijhoff.

Emery, Fred E., & Trist, Eric L. (1965). The Causal Texture of Organizational Environments. *Human Relations*, 18, 21–32.

Emery, Fred E., & Trist, Eric L. (1973). *Toward a Social Ecology*. London: Plenum.

Emery, Fred E., & Trist, Eric L. (1978). Analytical Model for Sociotechnical Systems. In William A. Pasmore & John J. Sherwood (Eds.), *Sociotechnical Systems: A Sourcebook* (pp. 120–131). La Jolla, CA: University Associates.

Fairhurst, Gail T.; Green, Stephen; & Courtright, John (1995). Inertial Forces and the Implementation of a Socio-technical Systems Approach: A Communication Study. *Organization Science*, 6, 168–185.

Fox, William M. (1990). An Interview with Eric Trist, Father of the Sociotechnical Systems Approach. *Journal of Applied Behavioral Science*, 26, 259–279.

Fox, William M. (1995). Sociotechnical System Principles and Guidelines: Past and Present. *Journal of Applied Behavioral Science*, 31, 91–105.

Goodman, Paul S. (1979). *Assessing Organizational Change: The Rushton Quality of Work Experiment*. New York: Wiley.

Goodman, Paul S., & Lawler, Edward E. (1979). United States. In *New Forms of Work Organization*, 1 (pp. 141–173). Geneva, Switzerland: International Labour Office.

Grover, Steven L. (1993). Why Professionals Lie: The Impact of Professional Role Conflict on Reporting

Accuracy. *Organizational Behavior and Human Decision Processes*, 55, 251–272.

Gulowsen, Jon (1972). A Measure of Work Group Autonomy. In Louis E. Davis & James C. Taylor (Eds.), *Design of Jobs* (pp. 374–390). Baltimore: Penguin.

Gyllenhammar, Pehr G. (1977). How Volvo Adapts Work to People. *Harvard Business Review*, 55(4), 102–113.

Hackman, J. Richard (1978). The Design of Self-Managing Work Groups. In Bert King, Siegfried Streufert, & Fred E. Fiedler (Eds.), *Managerial Control and Organizational Democracy* (pp. 61–91). New York: Wiley.

Harris, Michael M., & Bladen, Amy (1994). Wording Effects in the Measurement of Role Conflict and Role Ambiguity: A Multitrait-Multimethod Analysis. *Journal of Management*, 20, 887–901.

Heller, Frank; Pusic, Eugen; Strauss, George; & Wilpert, Bernhard (1998). *Organizational Participation: Myth and Reality*. New York: Oxford University Press.

Herbst, P. G. (1974). *Sociotechnical Design: Strategies in Multidisciplinary Research*. London: Tavistock.

Herbst, P. G. (1976). *Alternatives to Hierarchies*. Leiden, the Netherlands: Martinus Nijhoff.

Kahn, Robert L. (1981). *Work and Health*. New York: Wiley.

Kahn, Robert L., & Byosiere, Philippe (1992). Stress in Organizations. In Marvin D. Dunnette & Leaetta M. Hough (Eds.), *Handbook of Industrial and Organizational Psychology* (Vol. 3, pp. 571–650). Palo Alto, CA: Consulting Psychologists Press.

Kahn, Robert L.; Katz, Daniel; & Gutek, Barbara (1976). Bureaucratic Encounters: An Evaluation of Government Services. *Journal of Applied Behavioral Science*, 12, 178–198.

Kahn, Robert L.; Wolfe, Donald M.; Quinn, Robert P.; Snoek, J. Diedrick; & Rosenthal, Robert A. (1964). *Organizational Stress: Studies in Role Conflict and Ambiguity*. New York: Wiley.

Katz, Daniel (1975). Feedback in Social Systems: Operational and Systemic Research on Production, Maintenance, Control, and Adaptive Functions. In C. A. Bennett & A. A. Lumsdaine (Eds.), *Evaluation and Experiment: Some Critical Issues in Assessing Social Programs* (pp. 465–523). New York: Academic Press.

Katz, Daniel, & Georgopoulos, Basil S. (1971). Organizations in a Changing World. *Journal of Applied Behavioral Science*, 7, 342–370.

Katz, Daniel, & Golomb, Naphtali (1974–1975). Integration, Effectiveness and Adaptation in Social Systems: A Comparative Analysis of Kibbutzim Communities. *Administrative Science Quarterly*, 6, 283–315, 389–421.

Katz, Daniel; Gutek, Barbara A.; Kahn, Robert L.; & Barton, Eugenia (1975). *Bureaucratic Encounters: A Pilot Study in the Evaluation of Government Services*. Ann Arbor: Institute for Social Research, University of Michigan.

Katz, Daniel, & Kahn, Robert L. (1966 and 1978). *The Social Psychology of Organizations*. New York: Wiley.

Katz, Daniel; Kahn, Robert L.; & Adams, J. Stacy (1980). *The Study of Organizations*. San Francisco: Jossey-Bass.

Katzenbach, Jon R., & Smith, Douglas K. (1993). *The Wisdom of Teams: Creating the High-Performance Organization*. Boston: Harvard Business School Press.

Ketchum, Lyman D., & Trist, Eric L. (1992). *All Teams Are Not Created Equal: How Employee Empowerment Really Works*. Newbury Park, CA: Sage.

King, Lynda A., & King, Daniel W. (1990). Role Conflict and Role Ambiguity: A Critical Assessment of Construct Validity. *Psychological Bulletin*, 107, 48–64.

Kingdon, Donald R. (1973). *Matrix Organization: Managing Information Technology*. London: Tavistock.

Kirkman, Bradley L., & Shapiro, Debra L. (1997). The Impact of Cultural Values on Employee Resistance to Teams: Toward a Model of Globalized Self-Managing Work Team Effectiveness. *Academy of Management Review*, 22, 730–757.

McCann, Joseph E., & Selsky, John (1984). Hyperturbulence and the Emergence of Type 5 Environments. *Academy of Management Review*, 9, 460–470.

Metcalfe, J. L. (1974). Systems Models, Economic Models and the Causal Texture of Organizational Environments: An Approach to Macro-Organization Theory. *Human Relations*, 27, 639–663.

Mileti, Dennis S., & Gillespie, David P. (1976). An Integrated Formulation of Organization-Environment Interdependencies. *Human Relations*, 29, 85–100.

Miller, Eric J. (1975). Socio-Technical Systems in Weaving, 1953–1970: A Follow-up Study. *Human Relations*, 28, 349–386.

Miller, Eric J., & Rice, A. K. (1967). *Systems of Organization: The Control of Task and Sentient Boundaries*. London: Tavistock.

Mills, Ted (1976). Altering the Social Structure in Coal Mining: A Case Study. *Monthly Labor Review*, 99 (10), 3–10.

Moorhead, Gregory; Neck, Christopher P.; & West, Mindy S. (1998). The Tendency toward Defective Decision Making within Self-Managing Teams: The Relevance of Groupthink for the 21st Century. *Organizational Behavior and Human Decision-Processes*, 73, 327–351.

Mott, Paul E. (1972). *The Characteristics of Effective Organization*. New York: Harper & Row.

Netemeyer, Richard G.; Johnston, Mark W.; & Burton, Scot (1990). Analysis of Role Conflict and Role Ambiguity in a Structural Equations Framework. *Journal of Applied Psychology*, 75, 148–157.

Neuman, George A. (1991). Autonomous Work Group Selection. *Journal of Business and Psychology*, 6, 283–291.

Oliver, John E. (1982). An Instrument for Classifying Organizations. *Academy of Management Journal*, 25, 855–866.

Pasmore, William A., & Khalsa, Gurudev S. (1993). The Contributions of Eric Trist to the Social Engagement of Social Science. *Academy of Management Review*, 18, 546–569.

Pasmore, William A. (1978). The Comparative Impacts of Sociotechnical System, Job-Redesign, and Survey-Feedback Interventions. In William A. Pasmore & John J. Sherwood (Eds.), *Sociotechnical Systems: A Sourcebook* (pp. 291–301). La Jolla, CA: University Associates.

Peterson, Richard B. (1976). Swedish Experiments in Job Reform. *Business Horizons*, 19(3), 13–22.

Pfeffer, Jeffrey (1972). Merger as a Response to Organizational Interdependence. *Administrative Science Quarterly*, 17, 382–394.

Posner, Barry Z., & Butterfield, D. Anthony (1978). Role Clarity and Organizational Level. *Journal of Management*, 4(2), 81–90.

Rhenman, Eric (1973). *Organization Theory for Long-Range Planning*. London: Wiley.

Rice, A. K. (1958). *Productivity and Social Organization: The Ahmedabad Experiment*. London: Tavistock.

Rice, A. K. (1963). *The Enterprise and Its Environment*. London: Tavistock.

Rosen, Ned A. (1970). Open Systems Theory in an Organizational Sub-system: A Field Experiment. *Organizational Behavior and Human Performance*, 5, 245–265.

Roy, S. K. (1969). A Re-examination of the Methodology of A. K. Rice's Indian Textile Mill Work Reorganization. *Indian Journal of Industrial Relations*, 5(2), 170–191.

Siegall, Marc (2000). Putting the Stress Back into Role Stress: Improving the Measurement of Role Conflict and Role Ambiguity. *Journal of Managerial Psychology*, 15, 427–439.

Smith, Carlla S., & Tisak, John (1993). Discrepancy Measures of Role Stress Revisited: New Perspectives on Old Issues. *Organizational Behavior and Human Decision Processes*, 56, 285–307.

Smith, Clagett G., & King, James A. (1975). *Mental Hospitals: A Study in Organizational Effectiveness*. Lexington, MA: Heath

Sorensen, Knut H. (1985). Technology and Industrial Democracy: An Inquiry into Some Theoretical Issues and Their Social Basis. *Organization Studies*, 6, 139–160.

Staw, Barry M., & Szwajkowski, Eugene (1975). The Scarcity-Munificence Component of Organizational Environments and the Commission of Illegal Acts. *Administrative Science Quarterly*, 20, 345–354.

Stinchcombe, Arthur L. (1974). *Creating Efficient Industrial Administration*. New York: Academic Press.

Susman, Gerald I. (1976). *Autonomy at Work: A Sociotechnical Analysis of Participative Management*. New York: Praeger.

Sutton, Robert I., & Kahn, Robert L. (1987). Prediction, Understanding, and Control as Antidotes to Organizational Stress. In Jay W. Lorsch (Ed.), *Handbook of Organizational Behavior* (pp. 272–285). Englewood Cliffs, NJ: Prentice Hall.

Terreberry, Shirley (1968). The Evolution of Organizational Environments. *Administrative Science Quarterly*, 12, 590–613.

Thorsrud, Einar; Sorensen, Bjorg A.; & Gustavsen, Bjorn (1976). Sociotechnical Approach to Industrial Democracy in Norway. In Robert Dubin (Ed.), *Handbook of Work, Organization, and Society* (pp. 421–464). Chicago: Rand McNally.

Trist, Eric L. (1969). On Socio-Technical Systems. In Warren G. Bennis, Kenneth D. Benne, & Robert Chin (Eds.), *The Planning of Change* (pp. 269–282). New York: Holt, Rinehart & Winston.

Trist, Eric L. (1973). A Socio-Technical Critique of Scientific Management. In D. O. Edge & J. W. Wolfe (Eds.), *Meaning and Control* (pp. 95–119). London: Tavistock.

Trist, Eric L. (1975a). The New Work Ethic in Europe and America. In Carl A. Bramlette & Michael H. Mescon (Eds.), *Man and the Future of Organizations* (Vol. 4, pp. 45–64). Atlanta: Department of Management, Georgia State University.

Trist, Eric L. (1975b). Planning the First Steps toward Quality of Working Life in a Developing Country. In Louis E. Davis & Albert B. Cherns (Eds.), *Problems, Prospects, and the State of the Art*. Vol. 1: *The Quality of Working Life* (pp. 78–85). New York: Free Press.

Trist, Eric L. (1976a). Action Research and Adaptive Planning. In A. W. Clark (Ed.), *Experimenting with Organizational Life* (pp. 223–236). London: Plenum.

Trist, Eric L. (1976b). *A Concept of Organizational Ecology*. Philadelphia: Management and Behavioral Science Center, University of Pennsylvania.

Trist, Eric L. (1977). Collaboration in Work Settings: A Personal Perspective. *Journal of Applied Behavioral Science*, 13, 268–278.

Trist, Eric L. (1985). Intervention Strategies for Interorganizational Domains. In Robert Tannenbaum, Newton Margulies, & Fred Massarik (Eds.), *Human Systems Development: New Perspectives on People and Organizations* (pp. 167–197). San Francisco: Jossey-Bass.

Trist, Eric L. (1993). Guilty of Enthusiasm. In Arthur G. Bedeian (Ed.), *Management Laureates: A Collection of Autobiographical Essays* (Vol. 3, pp. 193–221). Greenwich, CT: JAI Press.

Trist, Eric L., & Bamforth, K. W. (1951). Some Social and Psychological Consequences of the Longwall Method of Coal-Getting. *Human Relations*, 4, 3–38.

Trist, Eric L., & Dwyer, Charles (1982). The Limits of Laissez-Faire as a Sociotechnical Change Strategy. In Robert Zager & Michael P. Rosow (Eds.), *The Innovative Organization: Productivity Programs in Action* (pp. 149–183). New York: Pergamon.

Trist, Eric L.; Emery, Fred; & Murray, Hugh (1997). *The Social Engagement of Social Science: A Tavistock Anthology*. Vol. 3: *The Socio-Ecological Perspective*. Philadelphia, PA: University of Pennsylvania Press.

Trist, Eric L.; Higgin, G. W.; Murray, Hugh; & Pollock, A. B. (1963). *Organizational Choice: Capabilities of Groups at the Coal Face under Changing Technologies*. London: Tavistock.

Trist, Eric L., & Murray, Hugh (1990). *The Social Engagement of Social Science: A Tavistock Anthology*. Vol. 1: *The Socio-Psychological Perspective*. Philadelphia: University of Pennsylvania Press.

Trist, Eric L., & Murray, Hugh (1993). *The Social Engagement of Social Science: A Tavistock Anthology*. Vol. 2: *The Socio-Technical Perspective*. Philadelphia: University of Pennsylvania Press.

Trist, Eric L.; Susman, Gerald I.; & Brown, Grant R. (1977). An Experiment in Autonomous Working in an American Underground Coal Mine. *Human Relations*, 30, 201–236.

Tubre, Travis C., & Collins, Judith M. (2000). Jackson and Schuler (1985) Revisited: A Meta-Analysis of the Relationship Between Role Ambiguity, Role Conflict, and Job Performance. *Journal of Management*, 26, 155–169.

Varma, Arup; Beatty, Richard W.; Schneier, Craig E.; & Ulrich, David O. (1999). High Performance Work Systems: Exciting Discovery or Passing Fad? *Human Resource Planning*, 22(1), 26–37.

Wall, Toby D.; Kemp, Nigel J.; Jackson, Paul R.; & Clegg, Chris W. (1986). Outcomes of Autonomous Work Groups: A Long-term Field Experiment. *Academy of Management Journal*, 29, 280–304.

Walton, Richard E. (1972). How to Counter Alienation in the Plant. *Harvard Business Review*, 50(6), 70–81.

Walton, Richard E. (1977). Work Innovation at Topeka: After Six Years. *Journal of Applied Behavioral Science*, 13, 422–433.

Yorks, Lyle, & Whitsett, David A. (1985). Hawthorne, Topeka, and the Issue of Science versus Advocacy in Organizational Behavior. *Academy of Management Review*, 10, 21–30.

Chapter 15

Sociological Open Systems Theories

Chapters 13 and 14 deal with systems theories of a very specific type: those that start from group level phenomena and thus have their origins in microorganizational behavior and social psychology, even though they ultimately extend into the macro domain. In chapter 15 the discussion now turns to two systems theories of a sociological nature that start at the organizational level without the ties to group dynamics. The question to be considered is whether under these circumstances the systems approach fares better as a basis for theory construction.

The organizational theories of James Thompson and Tom Burns draw from a wide range of organizational behavior contributors, but the primary influences in both cases are sociological in nature. Both were educated as sociologists, Thompson in the United States and Burns in Great Britain. Both wrote a single book that represents their major theoretical contribution. These are theorists who drew on the intellectual ideas around them to produce a product that in certain respects codified those ideas but also went beyond them to introduce considerable innovative content. Neither person was associated with any particular school, as the theorists considered previously were with the behavioral humanist position. Thus strong humanist values did not play an important role in these formulations. The two wrote separately during the 1960s and apparently were not aware of each other's work. They were both influenced by Max Weber's theory of bureaucracy, but only as one among several such influences. Certainly, systems concepts are pronounced components in both theories. If there are sociological open systems theories of organizational behavior, these are such theories.

THEORETICAL PROPOSITIONS OF JAMES THOMPSON

Although the field of sociology has spawned more than one theory of organizational functioning and structure that uses systems concepts, the work of Thompson is more centrally focused on the open systems approach than is any other. Thompson's theory is tied to the theories considered in chapters 13 and 14 in this volume. In its concern with technological variables, it is also related to the theories to be discussed in chapter 16. Moreover, in its concern with decision making it has much in common with the theories to be treated in part VI. Above all, however, Thompson's is an open systems theory that deals with organization-environment relationships and their effects.

Background

Thompson was one of a group of behavioral scientists brought together on the faculty of Cornell University's business school as organizational behavior was beginning to emerge as a distinct field. The prime mover in this development was Edward Litchfield, dean of the school. After military service during World War II and an aborted and brief career in journalism, Thompson entered the doctoral program in sociology at the University of North Carolina in 1949. There he worked on an Air Force research project, obtained his degree, and remained in a research capacity with funding from the Ford Foundation.

His first regular faculty appointment was the one at Cornell. While there he became the founding editor of *Administrative Science Quarterly*, which began publication in 1956. When Litchfield moved on to the University of Pittsburgh as its president, Thompson went with him, again with an appointment in the business school. This association proved to be rather short-lived, and from there Thompson went to Indiana University for a 6-year stint. As his interest in the study of organizations began to wane, he moved to the sociology department at Vanderbilt in 1968. Thompson died in 1973 at the age of 53.

Throughout most of his career, Thompson was a conceptualizer and theorist rather than a researcher,

though he did conduct some original organizational research at an early point (Thompson, 1956). His later research derived from secondary sources and was not focused on the major hypotheses of his theory (McNeil & Thompson, 1971). He wrote sparingly and succinctly. Two books contain practically all his theoretical writings, and those who read these books typically find themselves going back over sentences again and again to glean their full meaning.

Thompson's Propositions

Thompson presented many of his ideas initially in various essay-type articles. These ideas subsequently were polished and extensively supplemented in his major work, *Organizations in Action* (Thompson, 1967). He published a textbook dealing with the behavioral sciences in general (Thompson & Van Houten, 1970), and after his death, editors prepared a volume containing the papers that led up to *Organizations in Action*, selections from that book, and certain subsequent contributions, not all of which are focused on organizational issues (Rushing & Zald, 1976).

Thompson's primary approach to theory construction was the conceptual inventory—a series of parallel propositions, usually stated in somewhat abstract terms; the propositions were conceptually derived rather than drawn from an extensive perusal of existing research. This conceptual emphasis distinguishes Thompson from James March and Herbert Simon (1958) and from Bernard Berelson and Gary Steiner (1964), whose approaches to proposition formulation involved much greater empirical generalization. The theoretical variables are not tightly interrelated logically, however; the propositions do not derive from a common set of postulates and assumptions, as is the case with the most rigorous deductive theories. Rather, sets of propositions are developed to deal with various areas of major concern in the study of organizations.

Early Writings

Although we will rely on Thompson (1967) for a formal statement of the theory, knowledge of the variables considered in previous publications should facilitate understanding. Early on, Thompson established propositions that were based on such variables as the abstractness of the organization's goal as reflected in its product, the ease of using the technology for new purposes, and the degree of mechanization as opposed to professionalization of the technology (Thompson & Bates, 1957).

Subsequently, Thompson and William McEwen (1958) analyzed organizational decision making in the goal-setting context. Organizations must gain support from their environments in setting goals, and this is accomplished by using the strategies of *competition* (rivalry between two or more organizations for the exchange of goods and services), *co-optation* (absorbing outsiders into the policy-making structure of the organization to avert threat), and *coalition* (combining organizations for a common purpose). As one moves up the scale from competition to coalition, environmental conditioning becomes increasingly costly, with coalition being the most extreme strategy.

Thompson and Arthur Tuden (1959) look at the internal processes of organizational decision, using the proposition that the role of administration is often to manage the decision process, as well as to make the decisions. The key variables are the degree of agreement or disagreement among decision makers in their beliefs about the causation of alternative actions and in their preferences for possible outcomes. When agreement is high on both dimensions, decisions are made by specialists' *computations* and the appropriate structure is *bureaucracy*. When agreement about causation is lacking, decisions arc made by majority *judgment* (voting) and the appropriate structure is a *collegium*. When agreement about outcomes is lacking, decisions are made by bargaining and *compromise* within a *representative body*. When disagreement rules on both dimensions, an *inspirational* decision, perhaps made by a charismatic leader, is needed, and the ideal structure involves the randomness and disorganization of *anomie*. Again, organizational costs associated with decision making increase as one moves from computation, through judgment and compromise, to inspiration.

Conflict in organizations is in part a function of the differentiations and interactions required by their technologies, but organizations also can exercise some control over these processes and thus have a degree of discretion in handling conflict (Thompson, 1960). In addition to technology, the labor force and the heterogeneity of the task environment (the part of the environment that is not indifferent to the organization) can be sources of conflict. Technology produces conflict based on administrative allocations, and defense against conflict is achieved through varying organizational structures. The labor force produces conflict because employees bring latent roles to the job, as with nepotism and patronage; defense is achieved by limiting diversity through recruitment and selection. The task environment yields conflict as a result of competing pressures, and the defense against this is manipulating the exposure of members to these pressures.

Introduction of Systems Concepts

The preceding statements do not use systems concepts explicitly, although they certainly imply them. However, in 1962 Thompson wrote an article in which he focused on output roles and the nature of boundary-spanning transactions. The major variables considered were the degree to which the output role incumbent was armed with set routines for dealing with individuals in the environment, such as customers, and the degree to which these nonmembers were compelled to participate in a relationship with the output role occupant. Thompson and Robert Hawkes (1962) also use the open system concept explicitly in discussing reactions to community disaster.

By 1964 Thompson had begun to incorporate these systems formulations into his propositions on organizational functioning:

1. Variations in environmental conditions will bring about changes in decision strategies for input and output components of the firm.
2. Variations in environmental conditions can penetrate the input and output "buffers" and cause changes in the technical core of the organization (thus violating the ideal isolation of the technical core in its mediating role).
3. Variations in environmental conditions will alter the dependence of input, technical core, and output components relative to one another.
4. When input or output components transfer uncertainty rather than absorb it, there will be conflict among input, technical core, and output components. (Thompson, 1964, pp. 341–342)

At this point what had been a series of segmented theories of decision making, conflict, boundary roles, and the like was beginning to fuse into a more comprehensive statement under the open systems rubric.

The theory that resulted is presented in *Organizations in Action* (Thompson, 1967). It spans a wide domain but does not include voluntary organizations. The organizations covered operate as open systems that face uncertainty, but at the same time they need certainty; it is in this latter sense that they are said to be subject to criteria of rationality. Both the environment and technology are sources of uncertainty. Certainty is introduced in various ways:

Rationality. Organizations engage in input activities. To be rational they strive to make their core technologies function as well as possible, and to accomplish this they seek to seal off these technologies from environmental influences — thus approximating closed system conditions.

Buffering. On both the input and output sides buffering is one way to stabilize the environment of the technical core. Examples of input buffering are stockpiling of raw materials and preventive maintenance; an example of output buffering would be using warehoused product inventories to deal with market fluctuations.

Smoothing. To the extent buffering is insufficient, smoothing, or leveling, activities are invoked to reduce environmental fluctuations. Reduced late-night airline fares and the scheduling of nonemergency operations for low-use periods by hospitals represent attempts to smooth input and output transactions.

Forecasting. When smoothing activities are inadequate, organizations resort to forecasting to anticipate fluctuations and adapt the technical core to them. Peak load periods are thus known in advance and may be treated as constraints. Staffing or other input levels can be increased to anticipate needs, and an essentially closed-system logic can be maintained.

Rationing. Finally, should all else fail, organizations must resort to rationing, whereby services or products are provided on some preestablished basis. Major environmental fluctuations, as for instance a community disaster facing a hospital or a sudden fad facing a manufacturer, can necessitate rationing. This strategy is less than ideal because the organization must forego opportunities.

Domains of Organized Action

Organizations typically stake out a domain within which certain goods or services are provided. When this domain is recognized by those in the task environment — those who can provide needed support for the organization — a degree of domain consensus exists. Thus organizations develop dependencies on components of their environment, which vary with the degree of need (for a raw material, for instance) and the number of alternative sources of supply. For the organization, dependence and power relative to various environmental components are inversely related.

Under a competitive strategy, organizations seek to establish and hold power by maintaining multiple alternatives, by seeking prestige, and by focusing their efforts to achieve power on those components of the task environment that otherwise are most likely to place them in a dependent position. As noted previously, support from the environment, or power over it, may also be obtained by bargaining, cooptation, and coalition.

To the extent an organization is constrained from action in the various sectors of its environment, it will seek increasing degrees of power over those sectors in which it remains free to act. Thus a firm operating in an impoverished market will seek to exercise power over sources of raw materials and labor to adjust them to market demand for the product. To the extent such efforts fail, there is likely to be an attempt to enlarge the task environment — for instance, by involving previously uninvolved governmental units or by resorting to the courts.

Design

Organizations may deal with environmental problems by placing their boundaries around activities that could be performed by other task environment components. In organizations where the technology is *long-linked*, as with an assembly line, domains tend to expand through vertical integration, perhaps expanding backward into raw material production or forward into direct marketing. Organizations in which the technology is *mediating*, as with commercial banks that mediate between depositors and borrowers, expand their domains by increasing the populations served. *Intensive* technologies that draw on a variety of techniques to achieve a change in a person (as in a general hospital) or an object (as in the construction industry) require that the domain be expanded by incorporating the person or object involved. Intensive technology yields a custom-made output, and problems are reduced to the extent the client can be controlled.

These types of growth often yield a lack of balance in that capacities vary considerably from one component to another. To deal with such situations, (1) multicomponent organizations subject to rationality norms will seek to grow until the least reducible component is approximately fully occupied, and (2) organizations with capacity in excess of what the task environment supports will seek to enlarge their domains.

Technology and Structure

Components within an organization may be interdependent in various ways. Under *pooled* interdependence, each part makes a separate contribution to the whole and is in turn supported by the whole, as with branch sales offices. Under *sequential* interdependence, one part must act before another can, as in the relationship of production to marketing. Under *reciprocal* interdependence, the interdependence is two-way and thus symmetrical. Operations and maintenance units are reciprocally interdependent in that maintaining equipment in good repair is an input to operations, while equipment needing repair is an input to maintenance. As one moves from pooled to sequential to reciprocal interdependence, coordination becomes more difficult and costly. The appropriate approach for pooled interdependence is *standardization*; for sequential interdependence, *planning* and scheduling; and for reciprocal interdependence, coordination by *mutual adjustment*.

Because coordination is costly, the ideal is to use standardization if possible, then planning, and finally mutual adjustment only if absolutely necessary. Components also are grouped to minimize coordination costs. Thus reciprocally interdependent units are placed together in small, relatively autonomous, local groups. If only sequential interdependence is involved, then these units are so grouped. With only pooled interdependence, positions are grouped homogeneously to facilitate the use of standardization.

Problems of reciprocal interdependence, if present, are dealt with at the lowest organizational levels possible. Groups higher up are developed to deal with sequential interdependence, and finally toward the top, homogeneous units are created to facilitate standardization among components that have pooled interdependence, as in a divisionalized structure. As a result of these priorities, similar positions may not be grouped together, and standardized rules must be used to blanket homogeneous positions across divisions.

Liaison positions with staff designations are created to link the rule-making agency with these positions. When departments cannot handle all sequential interdependence, committees tend to be invoked to deal with the remaining coordination, and when departments cannot encompass all reciprocal interdependence, project teams are created.

Rationality and Structure

The logic of organizational design based on technology must be supplemented by a concern with environmental characteristics. To the extent that the task environment is heterogeneous, an attempt will be made to identify homogeneous segments and create boundary-spanning units to deal with each. These units are further subdivided if the amount of interaction across the boundary requires it.

Organizations will rely heavily on standardized rules in coping with stable environments and with environments in which the range of variation is known. If the range of variation is very large or unknown, localized boundary-spanning units are needed to monitor and plan effectively.

Thompson specifies environments in terms of their homogeneity-heterogeneity and stability-variability, and he indicates organizational forms for boundary-spanning units to match these different environments:

Homogeneous-stable — a few functional divisions utilizing standardized rules or adaptation

Heterogeneous-stable — a variety of functional divisions matched to homogeneous segments of the task environment and utilizing rules extensively

Homogeneous-variable — geographic, decentralized divisions concerned with planning responses to change

Heterogeneous-variable — divisions functionally differentiated to match segments of the task environment and decentralized to monitor and plan

What has been said about the effects of technology and environment on structure requires some integration. Propositions dealing with the joint effects of the two forces are as follows:

When technical-core and boundary-spanning activities can be isolated from one another except for scheduling, organizations under norms of rationality will be centralized with an overarching layer composed of functional divisions.

Under conditions of complexity, when the major components of an organization are reciprocally interdependent, these components will be segmented and arranged in self-sufficient clusters, each cluster having its own domain. (. . . a product division or a profit center, or it may in general usage be known as a decentralized division). (Thompson, 1967, pp. 75–76)

Assessment

Sociological systems theory is more concerned than most theories about how organizations assess themselves and are assessed by others. One proposition states that assessments based on *efficiency* tests that involve input-output calculations are most preferred, followed by *instrumental* tests (whether a desired state of affairs is achieved), and finally *social* tests, which involve the judgments of reference groups. Often efficiency tests cannot be applied due to insufficient knowledge and ambiguous standards.

Other hypotheses to deal with the assessment process have been proposed: given stable task environments, organizations seek to demonstrate historical improvement; in dynamic environments, they seek to demonstrate success relative to comparable organizations. Generally the demonstration of improvement along dimensions of particular concern to sectors of the environment on which the organization is most dependent is considered to be of greatest value.

In evaluating internal units, organizations are guided by the unit's method of coordinating interdependence. Accordingly, those units that use standardized rules are assessed in terms of degree of adherence to those rules; those units that follow plans and schedules are assessed in terms of filling the previously established quotas; and units that rely on mutual adjustment are assessed in terms of the expressed confidence of reciprocally dependent units.

The "Variable Human"

Thompson (1967) devotes considerable attention to the inducement-contribution bargain, whereby organizational members either explicitly or implicitly agree to contribute effort in various forms and amounts in return for inducements such as pay. This bargain is determined through power processes. Where the

technology is routine, collective bargaining is the method of choice. In intensive technologies, whether one achieves the occupational ceiling early or late is important. Those in early-ceiling occupations seek leverage to upgrade the occupation through collective action. Under late-ceiling conditions such as those obtaining in the professions, the key element in bargaining is the person's visibility among occupational colleagues. Within management, the bargain is strongly influenced by the individual's reputation for having scarce abilities to solve organizational problems. In roles that are boundary-spanning, the bargain is determined by the power of the environmental segment on which the organization depends and by the person's ability to handle this dependence effectively.

Discretion

The exercise of discretion in organizations is not always viewed as attractive. Discretion tends to be avoided when uncertainty seems to outweigh the organization's predictive capacity and when the consequences of error appear to be great. Organizations themselves foster avoidance of discretion by using inappropriate structures and assessment criteria and by assessing performance on various incompatible criteria. Several of Thompson's propositions deal with multiple consequences of discretion:

1. Organizations seek to guard against deviant discretion by policing methods.
2. Where workloads exceed capacity and the individual has options, he is tempted to select tasks which promise to enhance his scores on assessment criteria.
3. Where workloads or resource supplies fluctuate, the individual is tempted to stockpile (empire build).
4. Where alternatives are present, the individual is tempted to report successes and suppress evidence of failure. (Thompson, 1967, pp. 122–124)

Individuals in highly discretionary positions such as top management characteristically seek to maintain power that exceeds their dependence on others in the organization. When this is not possible, the individual will seek a coalition that may include essential segments of the task environment. Certainly, changes in environmental dependencies can serve to restructure coalitions.

The number of political positions or power bases in an organization increases with the number of sources of uncertainty and with the degree of decentralization. However, power bases and organizational goals can change rapidly under conditions of a dynamic task environment or technology. Generally such changes are functional for the organization, and for that reason commitments to entrenched power, as in the case of a founding entrepreneur, should be avoided.

Control

The propositions that deal with control draw heavily on the concept of coalition—primarily the dominant coalition—and on Thompson and Tuden's (1959) typology of decision making. The dominant coalition increases in size with increases in the number of areas in the organization where it is necessary to rely on a judgmental decision; thus a shift in one area from the predominance of computational to judgmental decisions can be expected to place a representative of that area in the dominant coalition. Similarly, imperfections in the core technology and heterogeneity in the task environment foster coalition membership for task-environmental and technological specialists.

Conflict within the dominant coalition can be expected to increase (1) as interdependence increases, (2) as environmental forces require compromises on outcome preferences, and (3) as the variety of professions represented increases. When power is widely distributed within the dominant coalition, an inner circle emerges, without which the coalition would be immobilized. Under such circumstances the dominant coalition as a whole becomes a ratifying body. To the extent there is a central power figure, this individual is the one who can manage the dominant coalition.

At the conclusion of his book Thompson (1967) reemphasizes the importance of the open systems approach and of the dimension of certainty-uncertainty. Uncertainties come from inside and outside the organization. There are three major sources:

Generalized uncertainty, or lack of cause-effect understanding in the culture at large

Contingency, in which the outcomes of organizational action are in part determined by the actions of environmental elements

Internal interdependence of components

As used by Thompson, the uncertainty concept is highly congruent with an open systems approach that emphasizes exchanges across organizational boundaries.

Later Writings

Thompson's writings after 1967 focus on two major themes. One involves extrapolating some of his ideas about organizations to other social units—in particular, to society at large. The other involves speculations about social and organizational forms of the future. There is some minor reworking or reformulating of earlier views, but by and large the *Organizations in Action* propositions stand as the statements of the theory.

Thompson (1974b) extends his concept of technological determinism in organizations to society at large. In this view technology determines the type of interdependence, which, in turn, is a major factor in political orientations and societal identification. In considering interdependence, however, Thompson (1974a, 1974b) now uses a somewhat different set of categories. Pooled and sequential interdependence remain essentially unchanged, but the concept of *intensive* interdependence is drawn from the previous categorization of technologies and is substituted for reciprocal interdependence. Intensive interdependence is concerned with knowledge generation and application, and a major characteristic is its lack of permanence. As with reciprocal interdependence, units need to adjust to feedback from others, and, indeed, mutual adjustment remains the essential method of coordination.

Thompson (1974a) believes the future will see much greater use of intensive interdependence and of temporary systems, often involving the actions of sets of organizations, not merely sets of individuals. In many respects, his views parallel those of certain organization development theorists. Of the organizational world of the year 2000, a time that is now a reality, he predicted:

Many of us, or our successors, will hold regular jobs in formal organizations with geographic identities and regularities, with recognized clienteles and functions.... But I believe such things will be routine, taken for granted, unproblematic. Our preoccupations as a society, I believe, will not be in this arena, but rather with what I have tried to designate as *complex organizations* of a much more fluid, ad hoc, flexible form. Perhaps these should not be designed organizations at all, and the emphasis should instead be placed on the administration of temporarily organized activities . . . with the development of administration teams or cadres to specialize in a continuous process of synthesizing. Perhaps complex organizations of the future will be known not for their components but by their cadres, with each cadre devoted to mobilizing and deploying resources in shifting configurations, to employ changing technologies to meet changing demands. (Thompson, 1973, as stated in Rushing & Zald, 1976, p. 245)

Evaluation and Impact

Obviously Thompson intended to state his propositions so that they might be tested. Nevertheless, he is aware that he has not provided operational definitions of his variables, and he seems to have anticipated what has since turned out to be true — research tests have been few and far between:

> The propositions . . . have been stated in the form which allows them to be negated if incorrect. . . . Testable form is not enough, however. We must have operations which will enable us to say the specific conditions do or do not exist. Hopefully our propositions seem plausible and important, but it is unlikely that many will be treated as hypotheses for extensive testing, for in the process of the necessary conceptual refinement, more specific and subtle hypotheses will be generated. (Thompson, 1967, p. 163)

Though there are some direct tests of one or more of Thompson's propositions, these are few. More commonly, certain theory concepts have been used in testing hypotheses that differ from, but are entirely consistent with, the hypotheses that Thompson formulated. On occasion it seems that Thompson's propositions have been stretched to the breaking point to achieve consonance between them and the design or results of a particular study.

Cooptation and Coalition

The theory posits a hierarchy of procedures for dealing with environmental uncertainty that runs from the least costly, which is competition, through bargaining or contracting and cooptation, to the most costly,

which is coalition or coalescing (Thompson & McEwen, 1958; Thompson, 1967). Although the preference hierarchy as such has not been studied, there is research evidence to support the hypothesis that cooptation and coalition are methods of dealing with uncertainty and interdependence.

Thus, for example, Jeffrey Pfeffer (1972a) studied corporate board memberships, relating board composition to such factors as need for access to capital markets and the extent of governmental regulation. The expectation was that representatives of financial institutions, attorneys, and other outsiders would be coopted onto boards to deal with these external dependencies. Data are presented that are consistent with this expectation. Furthermore, companies that deviated from an optimum board structure commensurate with the dependency requirements existing in their particular industries were less profitable.

In another study Pfeffer (1972b) looked at the use of merger as a method of coping with uncertainty and interdependence. He found that merger behavior was better explained as an attempt to deal with input and output dependencies than it was by any competing hypotheses. Evidence is also presented to show that mergers are often used to reduce the effect of competition within an industry and to achieve diversification that will reduce the company's dependence on a limited set of other organizations.

Analyses such as these, dealing with cooptation, coalescing, and related concepts, are probably best viewed as supporting the open systems approach generally, rather than Thompson's theory specifically. The findings fit well with Thompson's views, but they can be explained equally effectively by other theories of a similar nature.

Protecting the Technical Core

An example of research that attempts to study the use of buffering and forecasting to protect the technical core is the work of William Williams (1977), who hypothesized that investment in these mechanisms will be greater when they are particularly needed because of a high degree of mechanization of the technical core. Hypotheses of this kind are more specific than the Thompson propositions but are entirely consonant with them.

Consistent with the hypotheses, it was found that the use of buffering systems — as represented by disproportionately larger employment in the areas of facility maintenance, employee acquisition, and supervision — was associated with various measures of throughput mechanization; the relationships are particularly strong for the extent of supervisory employment, with correlations in the .60s and .70s. Also, employment of individuals to deal with output transactions and to survey and forecast the environment was associated with greater throughput mechanization, but only under conditions of high environmental competition. Where competition was minimal, heavy investment in boundary personnel of this kind apparently was not needed to protect the technical core.

There is also evidence that the degree of smoothing in input and output transactions such as sales, capital expenditures, and dividend payments is associated with uncertainty reduction, as reflected in the lower volatility of various common stock return measures (Lev, 1975). To the extent a company can achieve smooth flow across its boundaries from year to year, objective indexes of risk appear to be relatively low also.

Research of this kind that deals with methods of protecting the technical core tends to substantiate Thompson's hypotheses about specific mechanisms. However, nothing has been done to investigate priorities of usage along the lines that the theory's hypotheses posit.

Varieties of Technology

Numerous studies draw on Thompson's typology of technologies to test various hypotheses about organizations and their members. These hypotheses often extend well beyond what Thompson actually said, and while they are typically confirmed by the research, the findings support his theoretical propositions only in a very general sense. Thus, Thomas Mahoney and Peter Frost (1974) found differences in criteria of effectiveness that were associated with the dominant technology of a unit. Scheduling and coordination were important in achieving productivity in long-linked technology, and effectiveness was assessed without reference to interactions with other units. Interactions with other units became increasingly significant in assessing effectiveness as the technology changed to mediating and then to intensive; so, too, did quality of staff.

Clearly, the various technologies have differential effects on numerous aspects of an organization and its employees. This way of considering technologies

can prove useful (Mackenzie, 1986). Technology, as Thompson conceived it, can make a difference in organizations; whether it makes a difference in exactly the way Thompson proposed is another question. On that point, the evidence is extremely sparse. The following quotation reflects one major problem inhibiting research in this area: "Thompson's concepts are quite abstract, thus making them difficult to apply unambiguously even in a classification of organizations where one is provided with a great deal of information" (Morrissey & Gillespie, 1975, p. 331).

Interdependence and Coordination

Evidence exists that supports Thompson's propositions about coordination. Thus, Tom Reeves and Barry Turner (1972) report that mutual adjustment appears to be the appropriate method of coordination under conditions of reciprocal interdependence. They base this conclusion on intensive case studies of batch production factories. However, they also report that high levels of uncertainty and complexity require the use of mutual adjustment and that mutual adjustment may well be appropriate under uncertain conditions, irrespective of the nature of the interdependence. If anything, they believe that the uncertainty effects are greater than the interdependence effects. Other evidence also gives credence to the important role played by uncertainty in determining modes of coordination (Argote, 1982).

Similarly, John Baumler (1971) found in a simulation study that a coordination approach that approximated standardization yielded very positive results when interdependence was low, as in the pooled situation, but actually had a negative effect when interdependence was greater. In contrast, a more informal approach that approximates mutual adjustment worked well under conditions approaching reciprocal interdependence.

All in all, Thompson appears to have been right more often than not. Yet there is more to coordination than the interdependence relationships the theory proposes.

Environmental Stability and Homogeneity

Research such as that reported by Robert Duncan (1972) offers considerable support for the homogeneity-heterogeneity and stability-variability dimensions of the environment formulated by Thompson. These dimensions appear to be important in managers' perceptions of environmental uncertainty. Thus in homogeneous-stable contexts, little uncertainty is experienced, while in heterogeneous-variable situations it is considerable. Of the two dimensions, stability-variability seems to contribute more to uncertainty perceptions.

When one moves to the theory's more specific statements that relate environmental characteristics to organizational structure, there is less support, however. For instance, a study conducted by Stuart Schmidt and Larry Cummings (1976) failed to establish any relationship between environmental variability and structural differentiation. Initial analyses did suggest a relationship between environmental heterogeneity and differentiation. However, the size of the organization was found to mediate this relationship, and when these size effects were removed, heterogeneity and differentiation proved to be unrelated.

The general problem of how uncertainty about the environment affects organizational structure is a matter of concern for several theories that are considered in subsequent chapters of this volume. However, Thompson's propositions in this area are relatively specific. There is little research bearing on them, and what does exist is nonconfirming.

Assessment

Although research on Thompson's propositions about assessment of organizational effectiveness is minimal, some findings support the differentiation among efficiency, instrumental, and social tests and the relationship of the use of these tests to such matters as decision certainty, change, and technology (Mahoney & Weitzel, 1969).

A study by Carl Schramm (1975) deals with the ways organizations such as universities seek to compete when they are forced to use social tests in comparisons with reference groups. From faculty salary information reported to the American Association of University Professors over a 10-year period it was apparent that reporting universities attempted to improve their relative positions along this dimension over time. Since salary levels have much to do with recruiting quality faculty (an area of much environmental dependence), competition on this variable is highly consistent with Thompson's hypotheses.

In addition, universities that paid higher salaries and that had other, higher-quality standards as well tended to join in the salary survey process at an earlier date, thus attempting to make their favorable assessment position visible. Universities that were not able to demonstrate a favorable rate of improvement in compensation tended to drop out of the survey process, presumably with a view to emphasizing other dimensions on which they could compete more effectively. Though not uniquely derivable from Thompson's propositions on assessment, Schramm's findings do support them in a number of respects.

Discretion and Control

The theory posits that changes at the top levels of the hierarchy should reflect a responsiveness to organizational demands. In this view one would expect organizations that are facing unstable and hostile environments to experience greater turnover at the top simply to adjust to new contingencies. Furthermore, these personnel changes should be consonant with the problems faced. Data on turnover for hospital administrators support this. Although the relationships are not strong, they do reflect a consistent tendency for problem environments to be associated with low tenure (Pfeffer & Salancik, 1977). Also, when the operating budget is obtained primarily from payments by private insurers, chief administrators with training in hospital administration tend to be brought in. There is a similar tendency to call in accountants. However, when private donations or government funds are critical to hospital operation, other personnel with more appropriate backgrounds are called in. Clearly, organizational contingencies do relate to top-level staffing, as Thompson hypothesized.

There is other evidence that supports Thompson's propositions on discretion and control. Inner, elite circles are a reality in many organizations and serve as a major source of organizational innovation. The case analyses of batch production firms yield results that are consistent with the hypothesis that less perfect technologies are likely to be represented in the dominant coalition (Reeves & Turner, 1972). However, the authors believe that the power of production management is as much a consequence of the critical role that is played in meeting market demand contingencies as it is a consequence of imperfections in the technology. All the evidence does not appear to be in on this proposition.

Application

Certainly, Thompson's theory is an applied theory of organizational structuring and operation; it deals with practical problems that range from strategy formulation to unit staffing. To the extent one wishes to be rational (under norms of rationality), it is a normative theory that tells us what to do in a wide range of areas to make an organization more effective. But that is where it ends.

Thompson was not a consultant to organizations (Perrow, 1976), and he did not implement his ideas to determine how they worked. Neither has anyone else. Except for a few laboratory studies, the research into Thompson's theory has not been experimental. It looks at what is, rather than what happens when experimental changes are introduced. Causation is therefore difficult to establish. It should be possible to develop a technology of organizational intervention that matches the theory, but Thompson did not do it, and as is typically the case under such circumstances, no one else has moved his theory across the application gap.

Yet a ray of hope is introduced by Emily Schultheiss (1991) a Westinghouse Electric manager. In reviewing *Organizations in Action* she says:

> Over the past decade I have often been called upon to help other managers who have organizational problems or who desire to make some change or improvement in their organizations. Over and over again I have found myself relying on the meat of Thompson's theory in these situations. Thompson laid the groundwork for understanding the basics of organizational behavior and for helping managers detect when the components of their organization are out of alignment. (p. 498)

There is a suggestion here that the theory could provide a working theory for managerial decision making, perhaps to supplant classical management theory, which has lingered on too long in serving that purpose. Yet Thompson's writings are too sparse to do this for most managers. Someone needs to elaborate on them, if their practical utility is to be fully engaged.

Critiques

Due to its high level of abstraction and the lack of operationalized constructs, Thompson's theory has inspired little research, and in those studies that have been done, it is difficult to determine whether they are true tests of the theory. Furthermore, because the theory lacks logical interconnectedness, the verification of one theoretical proposition often does not increase confidence in the truth of other propositions not yet tested. As Graham Astley (1991) notes in a companion review to that of Schultheiss, scholars have tended to use Thompson's work as a conceptual starting point and as a vehicle for interpreting theoretical inquiry rather than as a basis for empirical testing. For many it has provided a whole host of valuable concepts and a framework for the rational understanding of organizations and their actions, even if the hypothesized relationships remain untested or in some cases appear untenable.

There can be no question that Thompson's theoretical work is widely respected. Conceptually, it represented a major leap forward. Thompson used the deductive approach far more than any previous theorist to develop new constructs and new relationships. His work was, and remains, a tremendous creative accomplishment.

Against this background it is appropriate to consider not only the research evidence, but also the logical or conceptual criticisms that have been lodged against the theory. One such view is that Thompson is too uncritically accepting of current organizations and current organizational forms. He fails to deal with such problems as socially irresponsible behavior and illegal acts, the frustration of needs of lower-level employees by management, and the quality of work life (Perrow, 1976). Charles Perrow contends that Thompson was wrong in being so uncritical and that his contribution would have been much richer had he been less detached (rational?). Perrow's criticism is in many ways more philosophical than scientific; in his writings Thompson was not the humanist others might have wished him to be. From a scientific viewpoint a theorist has a right to define his domain, and as long as the domain is not trivial (and Thompson's clearly was not), he cannot be faulted on that score. Thompson chose to ignore voluntary organizations and to emphasize management and top-level strategy formulation over individual employee concerns. Such domain limitations are often good theoretical strategy; some would even argue that Thompson attempted to cover too large a theoretical domain.

Chris Argyris (1972) has lodged a similar set of criticisms. He maintains that one must deal with the irrational and the rational, the informal and the formal, the psychological and the sociological if one is to understand organizations. Furthermore, he views sociological open systems theory as "an explication of scientific management and engineering economics" (1972, p. 26). He continues:

> Although Thompson aspires to present a more realistic integration of the formal and natural system, the integration actually made favors the closed system, traditional management, economically oriented model which he rejects as incomplete. The "variable human" seems to be minimally variable and minimally human. . . . Man turns out to be the closed system Thompson so cogently describes as ineffective for existing living systems. Group dynamics and interpersonal relations are not included. (pp. 33–34)

In line with his own theoretical formulations, Argyris maintains that all organizations use reciprocal interdependence and coordinate by mutual adjustment; those that do not cannot cope with a dynamic environment. On this latter point, Thompson would argue that "under norms of rationality" change should occur as environmental concerns and internal interdependencies require and that to use a more costly level of coordination than the current situation requires is not rational. In view of the fact that mutual adjustment can on occasion actually increase interdependence, excessive use of this approach of the kind Argyris suggests can escalate interdependence to a point where most organizations cannot cope, producing a state of near anarchy.

Wanting a sociological open systems theory to be and to do things that it cannot be and do is a pervasive problem. An article by Louis Pondy and Ian Mitroff (1979) takes the theory to task for not being open enough. In fact, the authors view the theory as essentially closed and controlled because it uses such concepts as standardization, buffering, and smoothing, which are attempts to introduce high degrees of certainty and stability into the organization. Pondy and Mitroff maintain that organizations need variety in their environments and without it they experience the equivalent of sensory deprivation; thus organizations should not strive for certainty but, rather, should seek uncertainty and even evoke it in their environments. Under some circumstances this is probably correct, but the level of uncertainty can be so high that it threatens to overwhelm both organizations and indi-

vidual human beings, and it was to such situations that Thompson addressed his theory.

At the level of what Thompson's theory is, rather than what it might be, there remain some definite problems. Perrow (1976) has raised questions about mediating technology and how it differs from long-linked technology. The two are actually much the same, with the major difference being that one deals with service industries and the other with production industries. With regard to Thompson's proposed differences, Perrow advances some very cogent arguments:

> Both have standardization and repetition as their basic characteristics. The only difference is that mediating technologies operate extensively with "multiple clients or customers distributed in time and space." But that is also true of firms with long-linked technologies, such as General Motors. And doesn't A. T. and T. or the post office (mediating technologies) use a highly standardized and repetitive technology, characteristic of the long-linked form? He says the organization with a mediating technology will handle uncertainty by increasing the populations served, while those with long-linked technologies integrate vertically. But Alcoa and G. M. certainly seek to increase the population served, and A. T. and T. has a significant degree of vertical integration. (1976, p. 719)

Apparently those who have attempted to classify technologies according to Thompson's system also have had difficulties. The system is very abstract and should have been elaborated on with many more specific examples. Because the varieties of interdependence and of technology are so closely related, this matter of ambiguity and insufficient differentiation spills over into the interdependence formulations. Are intensive and reciprocal interdependence the same thing? What does pooled interdependence really mean? Users need a detailed guide for classifying organizations (or their units) by these typologies. Had Thompson applied his system he might have found that differences that appeared clear to him at a high level of abstraction were not nearly so clear at an operational level.

Many of Thompson's propositions have not as yet been adequately tested; we simply do not know if they are true or not. Yet other propositions have been supported, and even more *seem* to have been supported, though the hypotheses actually tested often are not the same as those proposed by Thompson.

Only in the area of environmental effects on structure are there data that definitely question Thompson's propositions. The relationships with differentiation do not support his theory of environmental determinism. Many other studies raise serious questions about the validity of so-called structural contingency models of the kind discussed in this chapter and the chapters that follow (Pennings, 1992). These are also sometimes called strategic contingencies theories (see Fligstein & Freeland, 1995).

Yet in spite of the problems associated with obtaining research support for this approach to theorizing, it should be recognized that there are strong proponents as well (see Donaldson, 1995), who believe the research support is there. We will return to this issue after having considered the other theories typically placed under the structural contingency umbrella. These theories use contingency variables, such as the factors of environmental uncertainty and modes of technology that Thompson employs, to moderate between dimensions of organizational structure and effectiveness. Clearly, however, numerous other factors, including the amount of internal organizational control (see chapter 13 in this volume), operate in this area.

Without much more research into the propositions of Thompson's open systems theory as they extend across the whole span of its domain, one cannot be sure where the theory's most pronounced weak spots lie. Such research has been distinctly on the wane in recent years, to the point where our questions may never be answered. Thompson's creative genius deserves a better empirical response than it is now receiving. At the same time, the abstract, unrelated hypotheses generated by systems theories appear to be self-defeating insofar as research confirmation is concerned.

MECHANISTIC AND ORGANIC SYSTEMS

Mechanistic and organic systems theory has much in common with Likert's differentiation of systems 1 to 3 as opposed to system 4 (see chapter 13). Since its original publication in 1961 by Tavistock, mechanic and organic systems theory has been credited by its author, Tom Burns (in Burns & Stalker, 1994), with close parallels to the theoretical positions developed by Joan Woodward (1965) about various technologies,

to Michel Crozier's (1964) analyses of political processes in bureaucracies, and to March and Simon's (1958) treatment of programmed and nonprogrammed decision making (both the Woodward and the March and Simon theories are discussed in later chapters of this book). Yet Burns indicates that at the time of its formulation his theory was uninformed from any of these sources. It does appear to be a product of many forces that were "in the air" during the 1950s and early 1960s when the theory was developed, however, particularly forces of this kind that existed in the social science intellectual community of Europe.

Background

As discussed in chapter 5, organizational behavior in Europe during the early period did not involve business schools much, because few existed. The field focused on macrostructural issues and was largely dominated by sociologists who were working in either sociology departments or independent research units, or both. Most of their research involved comparative case analysis, and direct ties to practice were limited.

Burns was typical of this group. He spent more than 30 years at the University of Edinburgh in Scotland, from which he retired in 1981. His base was in what became the department of sociology, although he was also associated with the Social Science Research Center of the university. Before joining the Edinburgh faculty, he worked during the postwar years in the area of urban sociology with the West Midland Group on Post-war Reconstruction and Planning in the United Kingdom.

Although the major statement of mechanistic and organic systems theory is to be found in one book, *The Management of Innovation* (Burns & Stalker, 1994), Burns made other contributions to both sociology and organizational behavior. Noteworthy in the latter regard is his work on communication patterns in organizations (see Burns, 1954) and on clique formation in organizations (see Burns, 1955). Subsequent to the publication of his major theoretical work in 1961, Burns (1977) undertook a lengthy study of the BBC. This book expands on the earlier one, providing more detail on the idea that organizations possess formal authority and task systems, career systems that are laced with considerable competitive striving, and political systems that are focused on power relationships. It did not change the theoretical position stated previously, however.

G. M. Stalker, a psychologist, worked with Burns in conducting interviews and carrying out observations for the Scottish phase of the research reported in *The Management of Innovation*. Subsequently, he left the academic world and became a consultant. He has not contributed to the professional literature since.

Development of the Theory of Two Systems

Burns's theory was derived inductively from a series of case studies of firms that were operating primarily in the electronics industry in Great Britain. Thus, to understand the theory, it is necessary to start back with this qualitative research and the circumstances surrounding it.

Qualitative Research

The research was initiated as part of a project to monitor the progress of Scottish engineering firms as efforts were made to facilitate their entry into the new field of electronically controlled machinery and equipment. This project was carried out under the aegis of a voluntary association that was supported financially by industrial firms, local governments, and the unions, which, in turn, worked closely with the government of Scotland. Ultimately, this effort was extended to England and included a number of firms that were more fully committed to electronics development than had been the case in Scotland.

The final sample of 20 firms (or segments of firms) included primarily these electronics firms that were faced with a changing technology, but also included several companies from other industries, most of which had research and development interests in other fields. In addition to the changing technology of electronics engineering, many of these firms in the 1950s were forced to face the prospect of changing markets as a result of the government's decreased defense contracting after the war. This defense market was variable over a number of years, but eventually it became evident that to survive, most firms would have to develop the unfamiliar commercial market that existed beyond government. At the time of the study, these firms were attempting to do this.

The sample thus accumulated was entirely opportunistic in nature—firms were gradually found over a period of several years that were willing to participate in the study. Each was studied separately using the case method. Outside observers came in and conducted unstructured interviews, attended meetings, and listened to conversations. Notes were made on the spot. The methodology was essentially that of the field sociology or social anthropology of the day. As the data were being collected, the observers tried to construct a systematic explanatory description of the company situation, a description that was not just internally consistent but congruent with explanatory descriptions derived from other social systems as set forth in the literature.

This approach yielded no quantitative data; it was entirely qualitative. As the authors themselves state: "All this is very far removed from any method of investigation which could possibly be called scientific" (Burns & Stalker, 1994, p. 13). Thus the only value of the studies themselves is in the theory they generated; they *prove* nothing. With regard to the method employed, the authors state further: "It does not share the principal advantage of the anthropological field method, which lies in a lengthy period of residence in the community being studied" (p. 13). In fact, the authors provide no information on how much time they actually spent within each company.

Contingency Factors

The theory of mechanistic and organic (or sometimes organismic) systems uses change rather than the nature of the technology itself as a contingency variable (Burns, 1963; Burns & Stalker, 1994). Although the major emphasis is on technological change, market change is also a consideration. Both exert certain pressures on the organization that make particular organizational forms desirable:

> As the rate of change increases in the technical field, so does the number of occasions which demand quick and effective interpretation between people working in different parts of the system. As the rate of change increases in the market field, so does the need to multiply the points of contact between the concern and the markets it wishes to explore and develop. (Burns & Stalker, 1994, p. 231)

This position emerges from the situation in which the authors found the firms they studied. The technological changes were inherent in the accelerating developments that were occurring in the knowledge base of the electronics field external to the firms and thus in their environments. But these external changes were reflected in technological changes that were occurring within the firms as well, although to varying degrees. The market changes were not consequences of strategic choices made within the firms as much as they were forced responses to external factors that were associated with governmental actions. It is important to understand that the theory really dealt with these two specific and rather limited contingency variables, which in this instance happened to be highly correlated.

The status of other states of technological market change (such as those induced entirely by internal initiatives) in the theory is not clarified. Furthermore, technology and market are assumed to move as one, even though it is apparent that in many other cases this is not what happens. The theory is mute, for instance, about the situation where markets change and technology remains stable or vice versa.

Ideal Types of Organization

Mechanistic systems, which are suited to stable conditions, and organic systems, which are appropriate to changing conditions that introduce new problems and unforeseen requirements for action, are posited as polarities, not as a dichotomy. Thus intermediate stages may occur between the extremes, as described in table 15.1, and firms may operate within both systems at the same time.

Organic organizations are stratified primarily in terms of expertise, and leadership accrues to those who are the best informed and capable. There is much more commitment to the organization, with the result that formal and informal systems become indistinguishable. A framework of values and beliefs, much like those characterizing a profession, develops that becomes an effective substitute for formal hierarchy. Yet the ambiguity and lack of structure can become a source of anxiety for many. Even when the organic system arises as a planned response to a rapidly changing technology that is little understood, managers often yearn for a greater degree of structure.

The authors also note that members of organic systems frequently act in such a way as to openly or tacitly reject attempts to exercise authority over them (see as well Burns, 1957). This almost never happens in mechanistic systems. It appears to reflect the authority of expertise and knowledge that prevails in organic systems irrespective of designated rank.

In many respects organic systems have the characteristics of professional systems that operate to serve a client, which in this instance is the larger organization. And from the descriptions in the Burns and Stalker book, it appears that the organic systems are primarily staffed with professionals; they may, however, exist in a larger organizational context which has few professionals and more real managers, and which represents a more mechanistic system. This is why a concern is said to operate frequently with a management system that includes both the mechanistic and the organic forms.

Pathological Forms of the Mechanistic System

The need for structure, combined with certain political and personal career factors, can block change from mechanistic to organic forms, when such a change would be appropriate; the result is often some pathological form of the mechanistic system and less effective organizational performance (Burns, 1963). Individuals in mechanistic systems may fail to adapt because they are committed to sectional groups or departments, and internal politics may serve to perpetuate existing forms. Similarly, it may be in the interests of individuals and their long-term career plans to maintain the status quo.

Three possible pathological responses to change and the consequent uncertainty are noted. First is the *ambiguous figure* system, in which increasing numbers of exceptions to policy are referred to top-level managers and lower-level managers start to bypass those above them to get decisions made. The result is an overloaded chief executive, considerable conflict, and a highly politicized organization. A second response is the *mechanistic jungle*, in which more and more branches are added to the bureaucratic tree and increasing numbers of specialized positions are created to deal with new problems. Since the problems are often related to communication, the new positions tend to be of a liaison type, and the communication system becomes too complex to function. Finally, there is the *super-personal* or committee system response to change and uncertainty that temporarily grafts committees on the mechanistic structure to deal with special problems, rather than making the needed change to an organic system.

The theory does not indicate when each of these responses might be anticipated, but all are considered nonfunctional under conditions of change.

TABLE 15.1 Characteristics of mechanistic and organic systems

Mechanistic system (appropriate to stable conditions)	Organic system (appropriate to changing conditions)
1. The *specialized differentiation* of functional tasks into which the problems and tasks facing the concern as a whole are broken down	1. The *contributive nature* of special knowledge and experience to the common tasks of the concern
2. The *abstract nature* of each individual task, which is pursued with techniques and purposes distinct from those of the concern as a whole	2. The *realistic nature* of the individual task, which is seen as set by the total situation of the concern
3. The reconciliation, for each level in the hierarchy, of these distinct performances by the *immediate superiors*	3. The adjustment and *continual redefinition* of individual tasks through interaction with others
4. The *precise definition* of rights, obligations, and technical methods attached to each functional role	4. The *shedding of responsibility* as a limited field of rights, obligations, and methods. Thus problems may not be avoided as someone else's responsibility
5. The *translation of rights*, obligations, and methods into the responsibilities of a functional position	5. The *spread of commitment* to the concern beyond any technical definition
6. The *hierarchic structure* of control, authority, and communication	6. A *network structure* of control, authority, and communication. Sanctions derive from presumed community of interest with the rest of the organization
7. A reinforcement of the hierarchic structure by the location of *knowledge* of actualities exclusively *at the top* of the hierarchy	7. *Knowledge* about the technical or commercial nature of the task may be located *anywhere*. This location becomes the ad hoc center of authority and communication
8. A tendency for *interaction* between members of the concern to be *vertical*	8. A *lateral* direction of *communication* through the organization, resembling consultation rather than command
9. A tendency for operations and working behavior to be governed by the instructions and decisions issued by *superiors*	9. A content of communication which consists of *information and advice* rather than instructions and decisions
10. *Insistence on loyalty* to the concern and obedience to superiors as a condition of membership	10. *Commitment* to the concern's tasks and to the technological ethos of material progress and expansion is more highly valued than loyalty and obedience
11. A greater importance and prestige attaching to *local* than to cosmopolitan knowledge, experience, and skill	11. Importance and prestige attach to *affiliations and expertise* valid in the industrial and technical and commercial milieu external to the firm

SOURCE: Tom Burns & G. M. Stalker (1994), *The Management of Innovation*, revised edition (London: Oxford University Press), 120–122. Copyright 1994 by Tom Burns and G. M. Stalker. Reprinted with permission.

Evaluation and Impact

As indicated previously, the case studies that underlie the development of mechanistic and organic systems theory do not constitute scientific evidence in favor of the theory. The authors do not claim this, but later interpretations have on occasion taken such a position. In this connection it should be noted that most of the firms (or parts of firms) studied were in the rapidly changing electronics industry and thus according to

theory should at least strive to become organic in nature. However, a few firms were in other industries, and these appear to provide the examples of companies operating in stable environments for whom their mechanistic systems are entirely appropriate (and yield profitable operations). Thus in the research the theoretical continuum from mechanistic to organic seems to be fully confounded with industry representation (other than electronics versus electronics). Similar research design problems are manifest frequently.

Given the inductive nature of the theory, it seems likely that these problems have carried over from research to theory.

Research Tests

Because the authors do not present theory testing research in *The Management of Innovation*, and have conducted no such research since, it becomes necessary to look elsewhere for evidence on the validity of mechanistic and organic systems theory. There is not a great deal of this kind of research, but some does exist.

Ideally, the hypothesis on technological change would be tested longitudinally. One such investigation compares increases in the scope of the technology in social service organizations with various structural changes (Dewar & Hage, 1978). The data are consistent with the view that technological change produces more diversified and specialized occupational structures, but the anticipated effects of technological change on levels of hierarchy and factors associated with spans of control were minimal at best.

In another series of studies, various indices of technological change that took place over considerable periods of time before the study were related to measures of centralization, specialization, formalization, spans of control, levels of hierarchy, and various staff personnel indices (Reimann, 1975, 1980). Though not specifically formulated in terms of the mechanistic-organic concept, many of the structural indexes clearly relate to it. Yet no significant relationships were found, nor were the variables of the study related to measures of organizational effectiveness. Robert Keller, John Slocum, and Gerald Susman (1974)—using a measure of the number of product changes in continuous process manufacturing organizations—also failed to find support for the Burns and Stalker theory, even though they made the mechanistic-organic differentiation explicit. Organic firms did prove to be more successful in process industries, but this was totally unrelated to the amount of technological change.

An earlier study by Edward Harvey (1968) had used the product change measure and obtained more favorable results, even though it did not include data on organizational effectiveness. The findings, given in table 15.2, clearly indicate that greater technological change is associated with a more organic organizational form. These results cannot be attributed to size effects.

On balance, this evidence is not strongly supportive of the Burns and Stalker hypotheses regarding technology. The Harvey (1968) study provides the most positive evidence, but since it does not test the hypotheses on success, even this support is only partial. Studies that deal with market change are nonexistent.

Bringing the Research up to Date

In the 1990s there were many studies of the relations between technology and structural variables (Goodman & Sproull, 1990; Miller, Glick, Wang, & Huber, 1991), but there was a dearth of research on technological change, as would be needed to test the Burns and Stalker theory in its comprehensive form. As others have noted, developments around the theory are essentially stagnant (Pennings & Harianto, 1992). This state of affairs continues to the present. Yet the Burns and Stalker volume is one of the most widely cited in organizational behavior (Pennings, 1992). It appears that the field has accorded the theory a degree of uncritical acceptance that the research evidence would not justify. The following quotation offers a possible reason for this reaction:

> So Burns' work is very appealing to me and also, because of its complexity and subtlety, is of lasting value. *Management of Innovation* pulls off the difficult trick of offering a simple message, suitable for summarizing in overhead transparencies or examination questions, while at the same time qualifying and complicating this message in an enormous variety of ways, many of which are both provisional *and* dependent upon the concerns and the point of view of the observer. (Turner, 1995, p. 283)

What research has been conducted on mechanistic and organic systems concepts in the past couple of decades has dealt with the theory in a piecemeal fashion. Thus, a study by Robert Russell and Craig Russell (1992) has looked at the relation between innovation and organic structure—considered to be represented by decentralization, informality, and complexity of work. What it found, however, was that innovation (as represented by two separate measures) was related only to decentralization, not at all to formality or complexity. This suggests that the total organic system may not be required for innovation to occur, a result which is not what one would have expected from a reading of mechanistic-organic systems theory.

TABLE 15.2 Relationships between frequency of product changes and aspects of structure in manufacturing firms

Structural variable	Frequency of product changes (%)		
	Few	Intermediate	Many
Number of subunits (division of labor)			
Few	0	13	64
Intermediate	31	56	36
Many	69	31	0
Levels of hierarchy			
Few	0	19	64
Intermediate	38	44	36
Many	62	37	0
Number of managers per employee			
Few	0	6	79
Intermediate	31	63	21
Many	69	31	0
Extent of programming of roles, output, and communications			
Low (organic)	0	6	72
Intermediate	23	81	21
High (mechanistic)	77	13	7

SOURCE: Adapted from Edward Harvey (1968), Technology and the Structure of Organizations, *American Sociological Review*, 33, 255

Because mechanistic systems are clearly capable of certain types of innovation on occasion (Daft, 1982), the conceptual foundation of the organic type system as a distinct purveyor of innovation is brought into doubt.

A second relevant piece of research looked at communication patterns in two plants of the same company—one said to be mechanistic and the other organic (Courtright, Fairhurst, & Rogers, 1989). In this instance the mechanistic plant was without question operating with a bureaucratic, hierarchic structure. The organic plant used self-managed teams and participatory decision making extensively. The focus on communication patterns seems entirely appropriate, given Burns's prior interest in this matter and the attention given to it in the Burns and Stalker book. There organic communications are said to be horizontal or lateral, consultative, focused on information and advice, and rejecting of the exercise of authority over the individual.

In the study, competitiveness and evidence of manager dominance were less pronounced in the organic context, as were disagreements, conflict, order-giving, and attempts at control. The interactions appear to have been more frequently consultative in the organic plant. Overall, these findings seem to have much in common with what Burns and Stalker (1994) describe. However, conflict over the exercise of authority seems to be less rather than more prevalent in the organic plant. There is just enough disagreement inherent in the findings from the two sources to suggest that the two were not defining organicity in quite the same way. The fact that teams and group decision making, as well as participation, were not part of the Burns and Stalker description of organic systems, even though their book and Likert's appeared in the same year, reinforces this conclusion.

Organic Systems as Professional Forms

There has been a tendency to view organic systems as encompassing anything that is not bureaucratic and to differentiate mechanistic from organic systems on the basis of the degree of social formality vis-à-vis informality present (Morand, 1995). Yet it is apparent that nonbureaucratic forms include at least three other types: the group system that the Michigan and sociotechnical theorists envisaged, professional systems, and at least some varieties of entrepreneurial systems (see chapter 5 and Miner, 1993). Lumping all three of these under the organic umbrella does not seem justified, and from the descriptions in *The Manage-*

ment of Innovation it does not appear to be what Burns and Stalker intended, either.

As indicated previously, group systems differ considerably from what Burns and Stalker described. Entrepreneurial or task systems tend to be smaller than many of the firms they studied, and these systems can well incorporate more structuring (Schoonhoven, Eisenhardt, & Lyman, 1990). From the descriptions provided, it appears that the organic systems of Burns and Stalker were, in fact, professional in nature. The people described in the organic organizations were typically research scientists and engineers who were engaged in a process of innovation whereby the boundaries of firm knowledge were to be extended into new areas. The managers in such contexts were often professional leaders. Although the studies of these firms usually extended beyond the research or professional component into top management, the organic system concept appears to have had its home among the professionals where the actual innovations occurred (see Miner, Crane, & Vandenberg, 1994). That the theory's authors focused on this particular context and described it with considerable flare is not surprising, given their university (professional) backgrounds.

While the organic structure described appears to be primarily professional in form and staffed with professionals, the mechanistic firms came from outside the electronics industry and thus were not experiencing major technological and market changes. More important, they do not appear to be of a kind where many professionals would be employed. That the mechanistic firms with capable managers and few professionals, and thus no meaningful professional components to deal with, tended to do well is not surprising—the manager-mechanistic fit is strong. Similarly, the organic systems (professional forms) with many competent professionals appear to have done well—the professional-organic fit is strong. The firms that did not do well were those with a mechanistic, hierarchic system but many professionals in the electronics industry—the mechanistic-professional misfit involved is an inherently poor one, and firm success should suffer, as it did, as a result.

This analysis suggests that, in fact, technological and market changes were not the determining factors that the theory takes them to be. It is possible to explain the Burns and Stalker results in a more parsimonious fashion without resort to environmental variables. The data provided by the theory's authors are inadequate to fully test this hypothesis, but they appear consistent with it, and the research results obtained from tests of the environmental change component of the theory do little to support that component's viability. There is a very good chance that mechanistic-organic theory made the mistake of interpreting concomitant events as causal agents.

Value of Conceptual Typologies

In chapter 1 of this volume, conceptual typologies were discussed as a particular kind of approach to theorizing. In macroorganizational behavior there appears to be considerable commonality in the types of organizations described by these typologies, although certain differences exist as well. Thus Cornelis Lammers (1988) finds that some variant of the organic type can be traced back through various writers in Germany to as early as 1921. He also notes certain similarities to other types of more recent origin.

Typologies such as that of Burns and Stalker have been a subject of some controversy in organizational behavior. There are those who argue against the typological approach, both as to its value and as to its characterization as theory (see, for example, Donaldson, 1996). In so arguing, they attempt to demolish the general case that underlies the mechanistic-organic typology and thus indirectly, and sometimes not so indirectly, that typology itself. I have stated my position on this matter in chapter 1. An article by Alan Meyer, Anne Tsui, and C. R. Hinings (1993) discusses the issues involved at some length and comes to the conclusion that typologies are theories and have the potential to make valuable contributions to our knowledge of organization behavior—which view I strongly endorse. However, the literature does contain criticisms of mechanistic and organic systems theory based on the fact that a conceptual typology is utilized; this is one type of criticism that, in my opinion, is unwarranted.

Application

The Burns and Stalker theory would seem to provide useful guidelines for organizational structuring. It has the advantage of considerable parsimony, although the professional organization interpretation suggests even more is possible. Yet it falls short of this goal in a number of respects. It fails to specify when the various pathological forms will emerge, and to that extent it is incomplete. The mechanistic-organic differentiation appears to be useful conceptually, but research evidence that this variable operates as hypothesized (at least in response to technological change) is sparse indeed. The kind of specifics required to generate mechanistic and particularly organic structures are lacking. There are no demonstration projects that the authors can point to as examples of what the theory espouses in a normative sense, and the contrast with sociotechnical theory in this regard is striking. Furthermore, no recommendations are provided as to what should be done when technology and market considerations move in different directions.

Mechanistic and organic systems theory has not provided a basis for practice in any specific sense, and there is a real question as to whether it could or should do so in its present form. In fact, the theory's authors give little attention to the matter of application; they merely describe what they found in the organizations they studied.

CONCLUSIONS

At the beginning of this chapter a question was posed as to whether sociological open systems theories, free from the encumberment with group dynamics that is so evident in their psychological counterparts, are able to gain a better return on their investment in the systems approach. On the evidence from the two theories that are discussed here, one would have to say that any improvement is minimal. Although more potentially researchable hypotheses do appear, they operate at such an abstract level and with an abundance of vagueness that serves to mystify the construction of operational measures; thus, very little relevant research has been conducted. In recent years this drought has reduced the research stream to little more than a few puddles.

Not only has the sociological version of open systems theory lacked research, but also the common problem of an application void continues. And there has been a special problem in that the literature on these theories has tended to generate a complex web of esoteric arguments, apparently as a substitute for doing the kind of research that would provide factual evidence on the issues. In fact, such research results as there are often tend to be lost in the heat of partisan debate.

This has been a particular problem with regard to contingency approaches of the kind utilized by Thompson and by Burns and Stalker (see Fry & Smith, 1987). The abstractions and ambiguity of the theorists seem to escalate in the hands of the critics, rather than producing attempts to overcome problems and yield acceptable measures that can be used in research. It should be emphasized that, in addition to their systems qualities, these are theories of a contingency nature that have much in common with Fred Fiedler's contingency theory of leadership (see chapter 12). But in this macrocontext, the contingency approach has accumulated an order of controversy and esoteric elaboration that did not appear in the leadership area, where the major questions have had to do with the legitimacy and interpretation of research results.

References

Argote, Linda (1982). Input Uncertainty and Organizational Coordination in Hospital Emergency Units. *Administrative Science Quarterly*, 27, 420–434.

Argyris, Chris (1972), *The Applicability of Organizational Sociology*. Cambridge: Cambridge University Press.

Astley, W. Graham (1991). Review of *Organizations in Action*. *Journal of Management*, 17, 499–500.

Baumler, John V. (1971). Defined Criteria of Performance in Organizational Control. *Administrative Science Quarterly*, 16, 340–349.

Berelson, Bernard, & Steiner, Gary A. (1964). *Human Behavior: An Inventory of Scientific Findings*. New York: Harcourt, Brace, & World.

Burns, Tom (1954). The Directions of Activity and Communication in a Departmental Executive Group. *Human Relations*, 7, 73–97.

Burns, Tom (1955). The Reference of Conduct in Small Groups: Cliques and Cabals in Occupational Milieux. *Human Relations*, 8, 467–486.

Burns, Tom (1957). Management in Action. *Operational Research Quarterly*, 8, 45–60.

Burns, Tom (1963). Industry in a New Age. *New Society*, 31 January, 17–20.

Burns, Tom (1977). *The BBC: Public Institution and Private World*. London: Macmillan.

Burns, Tom, & Stalker, G. M. (1961). *The Management of Innovation*. London: Tavistock.

Burns, Tom, & Stalker, G. M. (1994). *The Management of Innovation*. Oxford: Oxford University Press.

Courtright, John A.; Fairhurst, Gail T.; & Rogers, L. Edna (1989). Interaction Patterns in Organic and

Mechanistic Systems. *Academy of Management Journal*, 32, 773–802.

Crozier, Michel (1964). *The Bureaucratic Phenomenon*. Chicago: University of Chicago Press.

Daft, Richard L. (1982). Bureaucratic versus Nonbureaucratic Structure and the Process of Innovation and Change. *Research in the Sociology of Organizations*, 1, 129–166.

Dewar, Robert D., & Hage, Jerald (1978). Size, Technology, Complexity, and Structural Differentiation: Toward a Theoretical Synthesis. *Administrative Science Quarterly*, 23, 111–136.

Donaldson, Lex (1995). *American Anti-management Theories of Organization: A Critique of Paradigm Proliferation*. Cambridge: Cambridge University Press.

Donaldson, Lex (1996). *For Positivist Organization Theory*. London: Sage.

Duncan, Robert B. (1972). Characteristics of Organizational Environments and Perceived Environmental Uncertainty. *Administrative Science Quarterly*, 17, 313–327.

Fligstein, Neil, & Freeland, Robert (1995). Theoretical and Comparative Perspectives on Corporate Organization. *Annual Review of Sociology*, 21, 21–43.

Fry, Louis W., & Smith, Deborah A. (1987). Congruence, Contingency, and Theory Building. *Academy of Management Review*, 12, 117–132.

Goodman, Paul S., & Sproull, Lee S. (1990). *Technology and Organizations*. San Francisco: Jossey-Bass.

Harvey, Edward (1968). Technology and the Structure of Organizations. *American Sociological Review*, 33, 247–259.

Keller, Robert T.; Slocum, John W.; & Susman, Gerald I. (1974). Uncertainty and Type of Management System in Continuous Process Organizations. *Academy of Management Journal*, 17, 56–68.

Lammers, Cornelis J. (1988). Transience and Persistence of Ideal Types in Organization Theory. *Research in the Sociology of Organizations*, 6, 203–224.

Lev, Baruch (1975). Environmental Uncertainty Reduction by Smoothing and Buffering: An Empirical Verification. *Academy of Management Journal*, 18, 864–871.

Mackenzie, Kenneth D. (1986). *Organizational Design: The Organizational Audit and Analysis Technology*. Norwood, NJ: Ablex.

Mahoney, Thomas A., & Frost, Peter J. (1974). The Role of Technology in Models of Organizational Effectiveness. *Organizational Behavior and Human Performance*, 11, 122–138.

Mahoney, Thomas A., & Weitzel, William (1969). Managerial Models of Organizational Effectiveness. *Administrative Science Quarterly*, 14, 357–365.

March, James G., & Simon, Herbert A. (1958). *Organizations*. New York: Wiley.

McNeil, Kenneth, & Thompson, James D. (1971). The Regeneration of Social Organizations. *American Sociological Review*, 36, 624–637.

Meyer, Alan D.; Tsui, Anne S.; & Hinings, C. R. (1993). Configurational Approaches to Organizational Analysis. *Academy of Management Journal*, 36, 1175–1195.

Miller, C. Chet; Glick, William H.; Wang, Yau-de; & Huber, George P. (1991). Understanding Technology-Structure Relationships: Theory Development and Meta-analytic Theory Testing. *Academy of Management Journal*, 34, 370–399.

Miner, John B. (1993). *Role Motivation Theories*. London: Routledge.

Miner, John B.; Crane, Donald P.; & Vandenberg, Robert J. (1994). Congruence and Fit in Professional Role Motivation Theory. *Organization Science*, 5, 86–97.

Morand, David A. (1995). The Role of Formality and Informality in the Enactment of Bureaucratic versus Organic Organizations. *Academy of Management Review*, 20, 831–872.

Morrissey, Elizabeth, & Gillespie, David F. (1975). Technology and the Conflict of Professionals in Bureaucratic Organizations. *Sociological Quarterly*, 16, 319–332.

Pennings, Johannes M. (1992). Structural Contingency Theory: A Reappraisal. *Research in Organizational Behavior*, 14, 267–309.

Pennings, Johannes M., & Harianto, Farid (1992). Technological Networking and Innovation Implementation. *Organization Science*, 3, 356–382.

Perrow, Charles (1976). Review of *Organizations and Beyond*. *Administrative Science Quarterly*, 21, 718–721.

Pfeffer, Jeffrey (1972a). Size and Composition of Corporate Boards of Directors: The Organization and Its Environment. *Administrative Science Quarterly*, 17, 218–228.

Pfeffer, Jeffrey (1972b). Merger as a Response to Organizational Interdependence. *Administrative Science Quarterly*, 17, 382–394.

Pfeffer, Jeffrey, & Salancik, Gerald R. (1977). Organizational Contexts and the Characteristics and Tenure of Hospital Administrators. *Academy of Management Journal*, 20, 74–88.

Pondy, Louis R., & Mitroff, Ian I. (1979). Beyond Open Systems Models of Organization. *Research in Organizational Behavior*, 1, 3–39.

Reeves, Tom K., & Turner, Barry A. (1972). A Theory of Organization and Behavior in Batch Production Factories. *Administrative Science Quarterly*, 17, 81–98.

Reimann, Bernard C. (1975). Organizational Effectiveness and Management's Public Values: A Canonical Analysis. *Academy of Management Journal*, 18, 224–241.

Reimann, Bernard C. (1980). Organizational Structure and Technology in Manufacturing: System versus Work Flow Level Perspectives. *Academy of Management Journal*, 23, 61–77.

Rushing, William A., & Zald, Mayer N. (1976). *Organizations and Beyond: Selected Essays of James D. Thompson*. Lexington, MA: D. C. Heath.

Russell, Robert D., & Russell, Craig J. (1992). An Examination of the Effects of Organizational Norms, Organizational Structure, and Environmental Uncertainty on Entrepreneurial Strategy. *Journal of Management*, 18, 639–656.

Schmidt, Stuart M., & Cummings, Larry L. (1976). Organizational Environment, Differentiation, and Perceived Environmental Uncertainty. *Decision Sciences*, 7, 447–467.

Schoonhoven, Claudia B.; Eisenhardt, Kathleen M.; & Lyman, Katherine (1990). Speeding Products to Market: Waiting Time to First Product Introduction in New Firms. *Administrative Science Quarterly*, 35, 177–207.

Schramm, Carl J. (1975). Thompson's Assessment of Organizations: Universities and the AAUP Salary Grades. *Administrative Science Quarterly*, 20, 87–96.

Schultheiss, Emily E. (1991). Review of *Organizations in Action*. *Journal of Management*, 17, 497–498.

Thompson, James D. (1956). Authority and Power in Identical Organizations. *American Journal of Sociology*, 62, 290–298.

Thompson, James D. (1960). Organizational Management of Conflict. *Administrative Science Quarterly*, 4, 389–409.

Thompson, James D. (1962). Organizations and Output Transactions. *American Journal of Sociology*, 67, 309–324.

Thompson, James D. (1964). Decision-making, the Firm, and the Market. In William W. Cooper, Harold J. Leavitt, & Maynard W. Shelley (Eds.), *New Perspectives in Organization Research* (pp. 334–348). New York: Wiley.

Thompson, James D. (1967). *Organizations in Action: Social Science Bases of Administrative Theory*. New York: McGraw-Hill.

Thompson, James D. (1973). Society's Frontiers for Organizing Activities. *Public Administration Review*, 33, 327–335.

Thompson, James D. (1974a). Social Interdependence, the Polity, and Public Administration. *Administration and Society*, 6, 3–21.

Thompson, James D. (1974b). Technology, Polity and Societal Development. *Administrative Science Quarterly*, 19, 6–21.

Thompson, James D., & Bates Frederick L. (1957). Technology, Organization, and Administration. *Administrative Science Quarterly*, 2, 325–343.

Thompson, James D., & Hawkes, Robert W. (1962). Disaster, Community Organization, and Administrative Process. In George W. Baker & Dwight W. Chapman (Eds.), *Man and Society in Disaster* (pp. 268–300). New York: Basic Books.

Thompson, James D., & McEwen, William J. (1958). Organizational Goals and Environment: Goal-Setting as an Interaction Process. *American Sociological Review*, 23, 23–31.

Thompson, James D., & Tuden, Arthur (1959). Strategies, Structures, and Processes of Organizational Decision. In James D. Thompson, P. B. Hammond, Robert W. Hawkes, & B. H. Junker (Eds.), *Comparative Studies in Administration* (pp. 195–216). Pittsburgh, PA: University of Pittsburgh Press.

Thompson, James D., & Van Houten, Donald R. (1970). *The Behavioral Sciences: An Interpretation*. Reading, MA: Addison-Wesley.

Turner, Barry A. (1995). A Personal Trajectory through Organization Studies. *Research in the Sociology of Organizations*, 13, 275–301.

Williams, William W. (1977). Organizational Size, Technology, and Employment Investments in Ancillary Specialisms. *Academy of Management Proceedings*, 37, 224–228.

Woodward, Joan (1965). *Industrial Organization: Theory and Practice*. Oxford: Oxford University Press.

Chapter 16

The Technological Imperative

In this chapter and in chapter 17 we look at additional contingency theories of a sociological and systems nature. Here in chapter 16 the theories of Joan Woodward and of Charles Perrow attempt to use technology as a contingency variable. We will see how well this works when technology itself, not change, operates alone without other contingency variables present.

Woodward and Perrow have in common not only an interest in the role of technology in organizations, but also a commitment to the use of technological variation as a contingency variable. They agree that there is no one best way to structure organizations — that structure should and often does vary with particular conditions. Though they emphasize different aspects of technology and vary in their conceptualization of the varieties of technology to some degree, the two theories are much more alike than they are different. The causal link between technology and organization that they emphasize has come to be known as the *technological imperative*. The theorists who espouse it in one form or another have had a significant effect on the study of organizations.

Technological contingency theory and the more comprehensive environmental approach to contingency theory are both based on an open systems view of organizations (Wren, 1994). The contingency approach to organizational design represents an outgrowth or extension of systems theory, combined with a reaction against any "one best way" of organizing and managing, in particular the classical management positions.

WOODWARD'S TECHNOLOGICAL DETERMINISM

The Woodward theory is an outgrowth of an extensive research project that used data from 100 firms and, to a somewhat lesser degree, of a series of case studies. It is therefore inductive in nature. As with many organizational theories, the formulations represent post hoc interpretations of the research. Thus the research, though important in its own right, cannot be considered a validation of the technological theory. Nevertheless, the research fails to support many hypotheses of classical management theory, which it was originally designed to test, and it was this outcome that sparked the search for an alternative interpretation.

Background

Woodward was born in 1916. Her scholarly career began at the University of Liverpool. She was educated in philosophy and worked in the personnel field and in the British Civil Service before taking a research position at Liverpool. She had a strong commitment to social and public service, which has been compared to that of Mary Parker Follett (Turner, 1995). In fact, she was well aware of Follett's writings.

The research and theory that are of concern to organizational behavior began in 1953 when Woodward became director of the Human Relations Research Unit at the South East Essex Technical College. Subsequently, she moved to head up the Industrial Sociology Unit of the Production Engineering Section of the Mechanical Engineering Department in Imperial College of Science and Technology, London, where she remained throughout the 1960s. She died in 1971 after a period of illness. Throughout her career in industrial sociology and organizational behavior she was housed in various research units and served quite extensively as a consultant to British industry.

The research from which the theory derived was conducted in the same time period as the research by Tom Burns and G. M. Stalker (1961), and several of the firms involved were used in both studies.

Theory and Its Empirical Base

Both the theory and the research are presented in three major publications: *Management and Technology* (Woodward, 1958), *Industrial Organization: Theory and Practice* (Woodward, 1965), and *Industrial Organization: Behavior and Control* (Woodward, 1970). The 1958 version is a brief and preliminary version of the 1965 report. The 1970 book contains some theoretical extensions, as well as additional case studies and certain reanalyses of the earlier data. In that book technology is defined as "the collection of plant, machines, tools, and recipes available at a given time for the execution of the production task and the rationale underlying their utilization" (Woodward, 1970, p. 4).

Study of Manufacturing Firms

The Woodward study (1958, 1965) dealt with 100 manufacturing firms in the South Essex area of England. Roughly one-third of these firms were branch factories of larger companies. Although firms with fewer than 100 employees were excluded, the sample still focused on smaller organizations, and almost three-quarters of them had fewer than 500 employees. Data dealing with the background and objectives of the firm, manufacturing processes, organizational structure and processes, and financial success were obtained from records and interviews.

The initial analyses compared such factors as the number of levels of management, spans of control, managerial ratios, staff ratios, ratios of direct to indirect labor, and the use of organizational planning to financial success. The essential objective was to test certain principles of management that had been derived from classical management theory. However, the Burns and Stalker organic-mechanistic classification was also used, in the expectation that organicity would be associated with success because of pervasive, rapid, technological change in the area studied. Both successful and less successful firms differed widely on the variables studied, and none of the predicted relationships was identified. Moreover, quantitative data on success relationships are not provided, nor are significance tests reported.

In exploring the data for some benefits to be salvaged from an extremely time-consuming data collection process, the researchers noted certain differences when the technological categories of table 16.1 were

TABLE 16.1 Original and revised systems for classifying technologies

Original system (Woodward, 1958)	Revised system (Woodward, 1965)
Unit and Small Batch Production	
1. Production of simple units to customers' orders	1. Production of units to customers' requirements
2. Production of technically complex units	2. Production of prototypes
3. Fabrication of large equipment in stages	3. Fabrication of large equipment in stages
4. Production of small batches	4. Production of small batches to customers' orders
Large Batch and Mass Production	
5. Production of large batches, assembly-line type	5. Production of large batches
6. Mass production	6. Production of large batches on assembly lines
	7. Mass production
Process Production	
7. Process production of chemicals in batches	8. Intermittent production of chemicals in multipurpose plant
8. Continuous flow production of liquids, gases, and solid shapes	9. Continuous flow production of liquids, gases, and crystalline substances
Combined Systems	
9. Production of components in large batches, subsequently assembled diversely	10. Production of standardized components in large batches, subsequently assembled diversely
10. Process production combined with the preparation of a product for sale by large batch or mass production methods	11. Process production of crystalline substances, subsequently prepared for sale by standardized production methods

SOURCE: Adapted from Joan Woodward (1958), *Management and Technology, Problems of Progress in Industry*, No. 3 (London: Her Majesty's Stationery Office), 8; Joan Woodward (1965), *Industrial Organization: Theory and Practice* (Oxford: Oxford University Press), 39

used. In subsequent analyses by technological category, combined systems were eliminated and other cases had insufficient data. The reported findings were consistent, of course, with the stated hypotheses, since the hypotheses derive from the findings. In general, these findings are given in verbal terms only. The exceptions are shown in table 16.2. Additional support for the theory is adduced from a limited number of case analyses (Woodward, 1965, 1970). A reanalysis of the data formed the basis for the control hypotheses of the theory.

Technological Classification Systems

Woodward used three major classes of technologies: unit and small batch, large batch and mass production, and process. The scales to which these categorizations were applied varied slightly from the 1958 to the 1965 versions, as noted in table 16.1. However, the scale used was one of increasing technical complexity in that the production process was more controllable and yielded more predictable results. No necessary relationship was assumed between this scale and either progressiveness or organizational size.

In essence, the theory states that there is a causal impact of the system of production on organizational patterns:

Different technologies imposed different kinds of demands on individuals and organizations, and these demands had to be met through an appropriate form of organization. There were still a number of differences between firms — related to such factors as history, background, and personalities — but these were not as significant as the differences between one production group and another and their influence seemed to be limited by technical considerations. (Woodward, 1958, p. 9)

Organizational Patterns

Certain effects that technology has on organization are a direct function of increasing complexity. Thus, as one moves up the scale from unit through large batch to process production, the number of levels of management would be expected to increase; so, too, would the span of control of the chief executive. Committees increasingly are needed toward the process end of the scale, thus reducing authoritarianism; there

TABLE 16.2 Relationships between technology and organizational variables

| | Technological category | | | | | |
| | Unit and small batch | | Large batch and mass | | Process production | |
Organizational variables	n	Median	n	Median	n	Median
Levels of management	24	3	31	4	25	6
Span of control of CEO	—	4	—	7	—	10
Percentage of costs allocated to wages	23	36	28	33	20	15
Ratio of managers to nonmanagers	—	1:23	—	1:16	—	1:8
Number of direct workers to one indirect	24	9	28	6	23	1
Number of industrial workers to one staff	24	8	28	6	23	2
Span of control of first-line supervisors	24	23	31	49	25	13

| | Relative successfulness of firms by category | | | | | |
Percentage with each first-line span	More (n = 5)	Less (n = 5)	More (n = 5)	Less (n = 6)	More (n = 6)	Less (n = 4)
Fewer than 10	0	20	0	0	17	25
11 to 20	0	20	0	17	83	0
21 to 30	80	0	0	17	0	25
31 to 40	20	0	0	17	0	50
41 to 50	0	40	60	0	0	0
51 to 60	0	20	40	0	0	0
61 to 70	0	0	0	0	0	0
71 to 80	0	0	0	17	0	0
81 to 90	0	0	0	32	0	0

NOTE: — = not reported.

SOURCE: Adapted from Joan Woodward (1965), *Industrial Organization: Theory and Practice* (Oxford: Oxford University Press), 52–55, 59–60, 69

is more delegation and decentralization. Spans of control in middle management are expected to decrease with increasing technological complexity.

Labor costs should be relatively much lower and the proportion of managerial personnel higher in process firms. There are also likely to be more industrial relations specialists, and educational levels should be higher. Direct production work is the predominant source of employment in unit and small batch firms, with clerical and administrative employment increasing as one moves up the scale.

Additional factors are assumed to show a curvilinear relationship to technological complexity. One such factor is the span of control of production supervisors. This span should be greatest and the use of skilled workers least in large batch and mass production.

In terms of the mechanistic-organic differentiation developed by Burns and Stalker (1961), mechanistic patterns with highly formalized structures should predominate in the middle of the technological complexity scale, while organic patterns with greater participativeness and flexibility in the production categories should predominate at the extremes. The traditional line-staff structure is also associated with firms in the middle range of technologies. At the extremes, either line domination or a functional form with specialists who make many of the key decisions should prevail. Written communication is expected to be more frequent in the large batch and mass production firms, while verbal communication is expected to predominate in firms at the ends of the scale. Quality and other pressures generally should be greater in the middle range, producing more negative attitudes and poorer labor relations.

Technology, Organization, and Success

The basic hypothesis of technological theory is that the firms most nearly approximating the typical structure for their technology should be the most successful. Firms that deviate in either direction from the ideal specified by their technology should be less successful. Thus success is a function of an appropriate fit between technology and structure. Although this fit may be consciously planned, and should be in the large batch and mass production category, it arises spontaneously in many cases.

Success in the middle range of technology is thus associated with a mechanistic system:

> In general, the administrative expedients associated with success in large-batch production firms were in line with the principles and ideas on which the teaching of management subjects is based. In all the successful large batch production firms there was not only a clear definition of duties and responsibilities . . . but also an adherence to the principles of unity of command; a separation (at least on paper) of advisory from executive responsibilities, and a chief executive who controlled no more than the recommended five or six direct subordinates. The tendency to regard large batch production as the typical system of modern industry may be the explanation of this link between success and conformity with management theory. (Woodward, 1965, p. 71)

In this view the application of classical management principles at the extremes of the technological complexity scale should be frequent but associated with ineffective organizational performance.

Technological change must be radical enough to influence the production system before structural change should be anticipated. Should the structure not be adapted to the new technology, however, technological innovations cannot be expected to bring success. Structural changes of an appropriate nature are made more difficult by the fact that development plays the dominant role in unit and small batch systems, while manufacturing dominates in large batch and mass production industry, and marketing is most important in process systems. Thus, entrenched power positions may well have to change.

Role of Control

The theory as set forth so far is logically consistent and in many respects logically compelling. However, like many such inductive theories, Woodward's is highly responsive to data, and here difficulties arise:

> Production organization did not appear to be as closely related to the scale of technology [see table 16.1] as other aspects of organization. In the categories at the extremes of the scale there were no problems. . . . But between these two extremes a relationship between production organization and technology was difficult to establish. The general impression obtained from the background survey — that there was greater variation in the way production operations were planned and controlled in firms in the middle ranges of the scale — was confirmed by the follow-up studies. (Woodward, 1965, p. 155)

Attempts to deal with this conclusion within the theory have taken several forms, but the role of the control system as an intervening variable between technology and structure has been of continuing concern. The need for some additional theoretical construct was accentuated by the failure of the technology-structure fit to influence success consistently within the middle range of technology. At the same time, it was within the middle range that social and technical objectives were at variance most frequently and complex control systems were most likely to appear. Accordingly, structure in the production component itself hypothetically reflected the control system as much as it did the technology, and the control system was often influenced by social and economic factors.

On logical grounds alone one might expect the technological imperative to operate with greatest strength close to the technology within the production component. Yet it is precisely at this point, at least in large batch and mass production systems, that an additional variable is introduced. Nevertheless an attempt is made to specify the relationships between different control systems and different organizational structures and processes (Woodward, 1970).

Control systems fall along two major dimensions: (1) the degree to which they are unitary as opposed to fragmented, and (2) the degree to which they are personal (hierarchical) as opposed to impersonal (mechanical). Controls in unit and small batch production would be expected to be unitary and personal, and in process production, unitary and impersonal (as a function of the technology itself). Within the more heterogeneous large batch and mass production category more diversity is expected, but fragmentation frequently should occur. Here the theory hypothesizes that firms with personal controls should be structured like unit and small batch organizations and those with impersonal controls like process firms.

The research findings on which these hypotheses about control are based derive from a reanalysis of the original management study data carried out some time after the results presented in table 16.2 were obtained. Table 16.3 presents the figures from this subsequent reanalysis.

Technological Determinism Revisited

With the introduction of control concepts, Woodward's theory appears to be moving away from pure technological determinism. Control and technology together are said to determine uncertainty levels, and uncertainty influences structure. The technology scale (table16.1) covers a range of complexity or predictability, with uncertainty decreasing in the production process as one moves up the scale. Thus the creation of a common metric for technological and control variables seems feasible, but now one has an uncertainty imperative, not a technological imperative.

Woodward's theory was not entirely consistent on this matter at the time of Woodward's death. However, her commitment to technological determinism certainly was less strong than it had been at an earlier time:

It is important to emphasize that the approach is not technological determinism. It is not suggested

that technology is the only, or even the main, determinant of organizational behavior. All that is implied is that technological differences . . . provide a better basis for comparing organizational behavior from firm to firm than do the other comparative frameworks that currently are being used. (Woodward, 1973, p. 60)

Although . . . technology is regarded as a basis for comparison and not as the sole or even the major determinant of behavior, there is little doubt that an approach of this nature does suggest a degree of determinism. (Woodward, 1973, p. 63)

Aston Studies and Technology

A series of studies dealing with a wide range of variables, but bearing on technology, was initiated in the early 1960s at what was to become the University of Aston in Birmingham, England. The discussion here will focus on the relevance for technology and the Woodward theory. However, we will return to these Aston studies later to consider the wider findings.

The Aston research was a group effort, and it continued through the 1960s into the 1970s, but with a changing cast of characters (Pugh & Hickson, 1976). The primary members of the initial group were Derek Pugh, who assumed a leadership role and was educated as a psychologist; David Hickson, who was something of a social science generalist; and Robert Hinings, a sociologist. Structurally the research unit involved was located in what amounted to a business school, although such schools were rarely so designated in Europe at that time. The history of this group, and how it came to be, has been widely chronicled (see

TABLE 16.3 Woodward's reanalysis of management study data by technological category and type of control

	Technological category (%)		
Controls	Unit	Large batch	Process
Unitary and personal ($n = 28$)	75	15	0
Fragmented and personal ($n = 21$)	25	35	0
Fragmented and impersonal ($n = 18$)	0	40	5
Unitary and impersonal ($n = 33$)	0	10	95

SOURCE: Adapted from Joan Woodward (1970), *Industrial Organization: Behavior and Control* (Oxford: Oxford University Press), 48

Pugh & Hickson, 1993; Pugh, 1996; Greenwood & Devine, 1997; Hickson, 1998).

The research conducted has been quite influential in macroorganizational behavior generally. The unifying links in these studies are the use of relatively large samples of diverse organizations, often drawn to represent a given area, and the scoring of these organizations on standardized measures related to context and structure. Information for these latter scales was provided by top-level managers and existing records.

Original Study

The initial Aston study used a composite measure of technology that dealt with the degree of automation, the rigidity of the workflow processes, the interdependence of workflow, and the extent to which operations were evaluated against precise specifications or plans. This primary measure of technology was considered to be an index of workflow integration (Hickson, Pugh, & Pheysey, 1969). An attempt also was made to develop a scale analogous to that originally devised by Woodward (1958), which applied to manufacturing organizations only. This latter measure, considered to be an index of production continuity, correlated .46 with the basic Aston measure.

Table 16.4 contains data for workflow integration, production continuity, and size as measured by number of employees, correlated with three composite measures of structure (structuring of activities, concentration of authority, control of workflow by line managers), their major component scales, and other indices considered by Woodward. The findings do not provide strong support for the technological imperative. In manufacturing organizations, where one would expect the theory to apply, there are few significant correlations with any technology measure, and the significant correlations with technology that do emerge can be explained in terms of the larger and more frequently significant size correlations. Only a marginally significant curvilinear relationship to the first-line supervisor's span of control is as hypothesized.

Within the much more diverse total sample, technology does yield significant correlations, but those for size are usually larger. In general, technology tends to be the better predictor only when structural factors close to the workflow are considered. Given that most of their organizations were larger than Woodward's

(none under 250 employees and 60 percent over 500), the authors hypothesize:

> Structural variables will be associated with operations technology only where they are centered on the workflow. The smaller the organization the more its structure will be pervaded by such technological effects; the larger the organization, the more these effects will be confined to variables such as job counts of employees on activities linked with the workflow itself, and will not be detectable in variables of the more remote administrative and hierarchical nature. (Hickson et al., 1969, pp. 394–395)

Limited Scale Replications

There have been several replication studies conducted on a more limited scale that support the original Aston finding that size-structure correlations typically exceed those for technology and structure. Data from two such studies are given in table 16.5. Again the correlations obtained with the Aston workflow integration measure of technology tend to shrink when the sample is limited to manufacturing firms only. Also, although size yields larger correlations, and more significant values as well, one cannot conclude that technology is unrelated to important structural dimensions.

National Study

The most comprehensive attempt at replicating the original Aston results involved 82 firms that were distributed throughout England and Scotland, thus the designation "national study." All were in the business sector, and a predominant number were autonomous. The size scale was extended downward to 100 employees. The results relating to technology characteristically confirm the earlier Aston findings (Child & Mansfield, 1972; Child, 1973a, 1973b, 1975). Size continues to yield high correlations with structural variables, but those for technology are not negligible. Although significant correlations with technology occur close to the technology in various staffing ratios, they also emerge in relation to structuring activities generally.

In contrast to all preceding studies, the national research included measures of organizational performance bearing on Woodward's hypothesis that organizations in the middle range of structure for a technology group would be more successful. The data on this

TABLE 16.4 Statistically significant correlations of technology measures and size with structural variables

Structural variables	All organizations (n = 46)		Manufacturing organizations (n = 31)		
			Technology		
	Technology (Aston)	Size (employees)	Aston	Woodward	Size (employees)
Degree of structuring of activities	.34	.69	—	.41(.07)[a]	.78
Role specification	.38	.75	—	.52(.26)[a]	.83
Functional specialization	.44	.67	—	—	.75
Standardization of procedures	.46	.56	—	—	.65
Formalization of documentation	—	.55	—	—	.67
Degree of concentration of authority	−.30	—	—	—	—
Standardization of selection/ promotion	−.38	.31	—	.43(.29)[a]	.42
Centralization of decisions	—	−.39	—	—	−.47
Organizational autonomy	—	—	—	—	—
Degree of control of workflow by line managers	−.46	—	—	—	—
Formalization of role performance recording	.41	.42	—	—	.45
First-line span of control	.35	—	—	−(.36)[b]	—
Percentage of workflow managers	−.53	—	—	—	—
CEO span of control	—	.32	—	—	—
Levels of management	—	.67	—	.51(.26)[a]	.77
Percentage of direct workers	—	—	—	—	−.46
Percentage of nonworkflow personnel	.34	.36	—	—	.53
Size (number of employees)	—		—	.47	
Woodward technology measure			.46		

NOTE: Correlations are statistically significant at $p < .05$ or better.

a. Figures in parentheses are partial correlations with size removed—none are statistically significant.

b. Curvilinear correlation in parentheses—significant ($p < .05$) and in accord with Woodward theory.

SOURCE: Adapted from David J. Hickson, Derek S. Pugh, & Diana C. Pheysey (1969), Operations Technology and Organization Structure: An Empirical Reappraisal, *Administrative Science Quarterly*, 14, 386, 391

point are not particularly encouraging. Lex Donaldson (1976) indicates that analyses of the relationships involving organizational structure show little association with performance; however, there are some positive findings, though not necessarily of the exact type Woodward anticipated:

> Correlations were computed separately for above and below average performance companies between a measure of rigidity in the main workflow and organizational variables. . . . Although in both high and low performance companies maintenance roles become more specialized along with the use of more rigid technology (generally characterized by heavier and more specialized plant), it was only in faster growing and more profitable companies that the requirements of the more rigid technologies were met by allocating a larger per-

centage of total employment to maintenance services. A comparable distinction was apparent with dispatch and transport activities. In higher performance companies there was a significant positive relationship between rigidity of technology and a greater proportion of total employment being given over to these activities; in low performance companies there was no relationship. . . . Among the companies securing an above average level of income to sales, as rigidity of technology increased so did the proportion of employment devoted to market research activities and the level of specialization among employees in that function. (Child, 1975, pp. 24–25)

The Aston researchers have consistently interpreted all of their findings as evidence against the technological imperative. Yet they report numerous relationships between technology and structure. Though the size correlations are often larger, they are rarely significantly larger. Furthermore, whether the technological effects are considered to be swamped by those of size is a consequence of one's assumptions about the causal processes involved (Aldrich, 1972; Pugh & Hickson, 1972). Longitudinal research that sorts out the causal sequencing among technology, size, and various aspects of structure is clearly needed. Aside from a small and inconclusive study by J. H. K. Inkson, Pugh, and Hickson (1970), the Aston researchers have focused on concurrent data. This appropriate first step has not answered all the questions.

Evaluation and Impact

The Aston research was in large part a response to the Woodward hypotheses, although ultimately it moved well beyond them. In dealing with technology it considered organizational, as opposed to subunit or work group, processes and structures. The total literature related to the technological imperative concerns itself with a diverse range of organizations and includes both subunit and total system levels of analysis (Reimann & Inzerilli, 1981). However, that portion of the literature that has used a measure of technology analogous to that employed by Woodward and accordingly purports to test the Woodward theory has continued the focus on manufacturing industry at the firm level.

Zwerman Study

The most ambitious attempt to replicate the Woodward findings involved 55 firms in the Minneapolis area (Zwerman, 1970). This sample was restricted to organizations with more than 100 employees, but it contained disproportionately more large firms than did the Woodward study.

The data indicate that organic systems predominate at the extremes of the technology scale whereas mechanistic systems predominate in the intermediate, large-batch and mass production category. However, only when mechanistic systems are used with intermediate technologies is there any relationship to organizational success. Additional data on structural relationships are given in table 16.6. With the exception of the span of control of first-line supervisors, the reported medians for technology groups follow a pattern that is consistent with the Woodward hypotheses. Thus the CEO span of control increases with technological complexity, and so on. The differences are smaller than they were in the Woodward study, and significance levels are not reported. When success is considered, the expected pattern of more successful firms falling close to the median for the technology group and the less successful falling at both extremes (see table 16.4) is not obtained, although data on less successful process firms were not available. Overall, even though the author interprets his findings as strongly

TABLE 16.5 Correlation of technology and size with structural variables in two studies

Structural variables	Forty organizations in the English midlands		Twenty-five midlands manufacturing firms		Twenty-one U.S. (Ohio) manufacturing firms	
	Technology (Aston measure)	Size (employees)	Technology (Aston measure)	Size (employees)	Technology (Aston measure)	Size (employees)
Degree of structuring of activities	.51*	.61*	.30	.71*	.59*	.72*
Functional specialization			.27	.80*	.64*	.82*
Formalization of documentation			.26	.51*	.45*	.48*
Degree of concentration of authority	−.39*	.11	−.25	.00	.30	.35
Size	.23		.31		.75*	

*Correlations statistically significant ($p < .05$ or better).

SOURCE: Adapted from J. H. K. Inkson, Derek S. Pugh, & David J. Hickson (1970), Organization Context and Structure: An Abbreviated Replication, *Administrative Science Quarterly*, 15, 321; J. H. K. Inkson, J. P. Schwitter, Diana C. Pheysey, & David J. Hickson (1970), A Comparison of Organization Structure and Managerial Roles: Ohio, U.S.A. and the Midlands, England, *Journal of Management Studies*, 7, 361

TABLE 16.6 Relationships (%) among technology, success, and structure in the Zwerman sample

	Technology					
	Unit and small batch		Large batch and mass		Process	
Structural variable	Successful	Less successful	Successful	Less successful	Successful	Less successful
Span of control of CEO						
1–3	22	11	8	13	0	0
4–5	56	22	15	54	17	0
6–7	11	45	46	20	17	0
8–10	11	22	15	13	33	0
11+	0	0	15	0	33	0
Medians	5		6		8.5	
Ratio of nonmanagers to managers						
1–6	10	0	46	27	80	0
7–12	50	45	15	20	20	0
13–18	10	45	15	40	0	0
19+	30	10	24	13	0	0
Medians	12		10.5		5	
Levels of management						
2–3	45	45	0	6	0	0
4	22	11	20	40	0	0
5	33	22	33	27	17	0
6+	0	22	47	27	83	0
Medians	4		5		6	
Ratio of production to nonproduction workers						
–1	50	0	13	13	83	0
2–3	30	33	54	54	17	0
4–5	20	33	13	20	0	0
6+	0	33	20	13	0	0
Medians	3		2		.6	
Percentage of costs allocated to wages						
12½%	11	20	0	22	0	0
12½–25%	11	0	10	0	60	0
26–50%	33	40	70	45	20	0
>50%	45	40	20	33	20	0
Medians	36		35		25	
Span of control of first-line supervisors						
10	22	0	15	7	25	0
11–20	45	50	38	53	50	0
21–30	0	0	8	13	0	0
31–40	33	50	23	13	25	0
41–50	0	0	8	7	0	0
51+	0	0	8	7	0	0
Medians	20		20		17	

SOURCE: Adapted from William L. Zwerman (1970), *New Perspectives on Organization Theory* (Westport, CT: Greenwood), 67, 71, 73, 100, 108, 184

supportive of the Woodward theory, this support is, in fact, rather weak (Donaldson, 1976).

Additional Research

In general, the limited research tests of Woodward's hypotheses on organizational effectiveness have not confirmed the theory. Some findings indicate an interplay between technology, structure, and effectiveness, however. Thus, Pradip Khandwalla (1974) found the hypothesized relationships between technology and structural dimensions—such as decentralization—among the more successful firms, but not among the less successful.

Tests that deal with the technological imperative itself yield extremely mixed results. There is some support for the Aston finding that certain personnel ratios and spans of control at the lowest level are related to technology (Blau, Falbe, McKinley, & Tracy, 1976). Yet these investigators did not find support for the views that structural variables directly linked to production are affected most or that technology exerts its most pervasive influence in small organizations. Characteristically, size relationships were greater than those involving technology.

A study by Bernard Reimann (1980) used an index of technology that was modeled on that of Woodward and found a limited number of relationships. Of 11 correlations with structural variables, 3 were significant with formalization, centralization of operations, and size of the maintenance staff. Variables such as number of levels in the hierarchy and the various spans of control were unrelated to the technology measure. Surprisingly, the presence or absence of an in-house computer yielded 7 significant correlations, while size produced only 5.

In reviewing the literature in this area, Reimann and Giorgio Inzerilli conclude:

> Findings with respect to the technology-structure relationship are difficult to compare, and, where they are comparable, often inconsistent. This, of course, was to be expected since many of the complex organizations studies may have been operating with several different workflow technologies (e.g., some unit, some mass, and some process production) and the aggregate measures used generally did not reflect this possible variety. (1981, p. 258)

One finding that appears to support the Woodward view with some consistency is that at the level of first line supervision the relationship between span of control and technical complexity is curvilinear, with maximal spans in the middle range of technology (Collins & Hull, 1986). This says nothing about the causal determinism of the technological imperative, however. In fact, what emerges from subsequent research is that technical complexity is not the cause. The variations in span of control now appear to be a consequence of the interacting forces of production unit size and, to a lesser degree, of the complexity of the task. When these factors are controlled, the curvilinearity virtually disappears. Thus the complexity of the technology does not appear to be the cause of the structural variations.

Also presenting a problem for the Woodward formulations is that as new technologies have emerged they do not appear to fit neatly into the hypothesized framework (Hull & Collins, 1987). Thus, a type of high-technology batch production system has emerged in recent years, but it does not conform empirically to the Woodward categories as it is much more complex than batch systems are hypothesized to be. It would seem that some modification of the technical complexity measure would be needed each time technologies change.

This raises the whole issue of construct validity. As noted in table 16.4, the Aston researchers found a correlation of .46 between their own measure of technology and another measure that was developed to coincide with Woodward. Subsequent research suggests that values above .46 can be expected only rarely, even when essentially comparable technology constructs are involved. In general, the rather low correlations between measures of technology do not appear to reflect an underlying unreliability of these measures. That is not the problem. Rather, when advocates of the technological imperative get down to measuring what they mean by technology, the operational results may be only very minimally related.

Attempts to integrate the research results in a overall manner appear to be influenced in a number of instances by preconceived views, with the result that important studies are often left out and variations in methodological precision are given insufficient attention. This is where meta-analysis can prove most valuable. When meta-analysis is applied to studies that use the Woodward index of technical complexity, the relationship between technology and structural variables proves to be significant in 3 of 11 instances. There are positive correlations with vertical differentiation, formalization, and chief executive span of control (Tehrani, Montanari, & Carson, 1990). However, these correlations are low, varying between .13 and .20. By way of contrast, measures of interdependence based on Thompson's theoretical formulations (see chapter 15) yield 2 significant correlations (of the 7 with sufficient research to justify inclusion) and the Aston workflow integration measure yields 6 significant correlations out of 11.

The support for the Woodward approach is far from impressive. Furthermore, this analysis did not take into account the organizational effectiveness factor, which is clearly part of the Woodward theory. Had it been possible to add this factor into the calculations, support would have been even less manifest in all probability.

Problems with the Theory and Research

Research on Woodward's technology determinism has produced results that have been described as bewildering, confusing, and contradictory (Miller, Glick, Wang, & Huber, 1991).

In coming to this same conclusion Collins, Jerald Hage, and Hull offer some suggestions as to why the technology thesis has floundered:

> *First,* many of the sociotechnical and industrial relations studies never developed measurable concepts and are still waiting to be codified [see chapter 14].
>
> *Second,* researchers who advanced beyond the detail of descriptive case studies either went in the direction of a set of categorical concepts that proved difficult to measure [see chapter 15] or to more narrowly conceived unidimensional concepts. The former approach is conceptually rich but subject to all sorts of coding disagreement, whereas the latter (as represented by the Aston approach) is operationally promising but less profound in breadth and insight.
>
> *Third,* while technology is multifaceted, it has been diversely conceptualized and measured at several analytical levels; this inconsistency of measurement has made it difficult to determine the validity and reliability of the findings.
>
> *Finally,* few comparative theorists have treated technology as a separate "system" in its own right, resulting in a conceptual narrowness that misses the original contributions of the sociotechnical tradition and the early comparative theorists who were strongly influenced by the sociotechnical tradition [i.e., Woodward]. (1988, p. 82)

This view considers the problem to exist at the interaction between theoretical conceptualization and measurement. For instance, when the Woodward theory and research are considered in these terms, it is apparent that the theory is incomplete in the middle range of technology, and the later resort to control systems as the explanatory variable (Woodward, 1970) introduces considerable theoretical confusion. It is not at all clear whether control procedures are part of technology, of structure, or of some other category of variable such as organizational process, and measurement becomes equally confounded.

Another such problem is that most organizations of any size have multiple technologies. To the degree that this is true, striking an average or defining a dominant technology misrepresents the true state of affairs (Scott, 1990). Furthermore, the theory does not tell us exactly how to identify a dominant technology in order to measure it or what to do when there is no apparent dominant technology (other than dropping that firm from the study).

Segmenting the organization by subunits and testing the theory within units can well reduce this source of error, but it fails to achieve a theory of *organization.* Furthermore, it appears that these subunit (or individual) level studies often do not deal with technology as Woodward originally used the term. Rather, they measure task or job design factors at a micro level. The result is a considerable dilution of construct validity.

The dilution of construct validity is exaggerated by the fact that different definitions of technology and structure appear to overlap so that a given variable may be considered part of technology in one instance and of structure in another; we saw this with Woodward's concept of control. Classification problems are particularly pronounced when the technology is not of a manufacturing nature and with variables that reflect individual role prescriptions. As a result of inconsistencies in the applications of category boundaries, it is difficult to determine the comparability of different study results.

Another problem is the tendency to use limited sets of variables or even single variables to stand for the whole technology or structure construct. Generalization of this kind is risky in that different aspects of technology and of structure may, in fact, operate differently. The Woodward theory hypothesizes different forms of relationships, even within the span of control concept, and in numerous instances aspects of formalization and centralization have acted differentially. Denise Rousseau (1979) has shown that studies have dealt in various instances with input characteristics, input control, conversion processes, output control, and output characteristics, while treating each of these as a proxy for technology as a whole. Similarly studies conducted at the individual, subunit, and organizational levels are used interchangeably to demonstrate relationships between organizational technology and organizational structure. Most of the research is much less generalizable than it has been made out to be. Thus failure to find a relationship may not sound the death knell of technological imperative theory as a whole, but finding one does not prove all versions to be true, either.

Perhaps the most perplexing problem is causality. The theory includes a causal arrow. Yet we have little that even approximates a controlled study where a technology is introduced in one setting and not in another and structural changes then are measured. In no research has the technology-structure fit been manipulated and effectiveness then measured. Such studies are difficult to conduct, but tests of this kind have been applied to other theories. They are needed in the case of the technological imperative.

Some longitudinal research has been done, and path analysis has been used to extract causal generalizations from concurrent data. Path analysis appears to be less useful than longitudinal studies, depending as it does on certain very limiting assumptions. In fact, two different applications have produced what appear to be directly antithetical conclusions: that technology causes structure (Aldrich, 1972) and that structure causes technology (Glisson, 1978). One is left with a feeling that something other than concurrent data are needed.

Longitudinal data indicate that technology does not have much causal impact. Thus a shift in a large hospital kitchen from batch to mass production technology was found to produce certain changes in job characteristics for those close to the change, but no other structural alterations (Billings, Klimoski, & Breaugh, 1977). Other research indicates that technological changes can be accompanied by the introduction of new specialists and thus a more differentiated work force. To the extent these specialists are able to exercise expert power of the kind typically invoked by professionals, it appears that some decentralization close to the technology may occur. There is no reason why, in the case of a major upgrading of technology, these structural effects might not reverberate out to

more distant parts of the organization, but the findings to date indicate this is not a very common occurrence.

If the causal impact of technology is as limited as the data appear to imply, how can one account for those findings that emerge from certain concurrent studies, indicating that relationships between technological and structural variables do exist? One possibility is that micro variables need to be introduced into what have been essentially macro equations, and, in fact, Child (1972) and others have emphasized the role of choice in organizational structuring.

The point here is that both the technologies and the structures of an organization are chosen at a point in time by an individual or individuals who have sufficient control over resources to implement these technologies and structures. Once chosen, both sets of variables may exert controls on organization members and operate as constraints on further change. As noted, the choices involving technology may carry with them certain implications for structure, as when professionals are needed. Also choices regarding structure—for instance, the introduction of small autonomous work groups—may carry implications for technology. However, at a higher level both technology and structure are chosen and thus caused by the same third factor. Until changes in either technology or structure are introduced, the original choices are continually reaffirmed, and when changes do occur, they also come about as a result of choice.

In this view, the primary causal variable is a decision or choice, not technology or structure. To the extent certain correlations between technological and structural variables exist in the minds of the choosers, these will be perpetuated in organizations and found in research. Though some such correlations in the minds of decision makers may yield patterns that make for more effective organizations, research focused on technological considerations has produced little to confirm this hypothesis.

When we give the primary emphasis to the causal effects of choice, which operates conjointly on technology and structure, we severely limit the role of the technological imperative. To the extent the choosers in organizations are influenced by common philosophies or achieve a degree of consensus as a result of interorganizational communications, patterns of relationships may emerge with some consistency, as they did in the Aston studies. Such a theory suggests a change in research strategy to focus on organizational decision makers and the procedures they use to make choices about technology and structure. Pursuing the technological imperative alone seems no more likely to be fruitful in the future than it has been in the past.

Applying the Theory

Up to now, we have given scant attention to applications. This is not an oversight; rather, it reflects the realities in this area of theory construction. The Woodward research was originally undertaken to influence the content of management courses and thereby management practice. In reporting on that research the author notes:

> It was hoped that this research would produce findings on which the management course offered in the South East Essex Technical College could be appraised. At first sight this report may suggest that these courses have limited usefulness and can in some circumstances be misleading to students. The danger lies in the tendency to teach the principles of administration as though they were scientific laws. (Woodward, 1958, p. 34)

Although the research generated caution in teaching the principles of classical management theory, it did not generate a new course based on the technological imperative or a new design to help organizations fit their structures to their technologies more appropriately. Clear-cut guides to action are almost totally lacking. In this sense this technological imperative theory has not generated the technology even for its own application.

Moving On

Given the current state of affairs, it is not surprising that theorists recently have come to abandon Woodward's version of technologically imperative theory and to propose new ways of using the technology construct, including the human choice factor (see for example Orlikowski, 1992). One trend of the future, building on the Woodward base, appears to be reflected in the following quotation:

> Technology is . . . a mechanism capable of bridging constructs important to macro-organizational theory and individual's perceptual, affective, and behavioral responses. The potential effects of core technologies on organizational structures are . . .

only a part, perhaps even an overemphasized part, of the total influence of technologies. (Hulin & Roznowski, 1985, p. 80)

According to this view, different technologies have different effects on those exposed to them, as sociotechnical theory would anticipate, and these effects may be more important than any structural ones. In fact, what is proposed is the creation of some type of meso theory that would bring micro and macro variables together. With an expanded array of predictor variables, it should be possible to explain a larger proportion of outcome variance. But that this sort of thing is being considered says a great deal about the current status of Woodward's theory.

PERROW'S COMPARATIVE FRAMEWORK

Perrow is a sociologist who began to write about the technological imperative intensively in the middle 1960s, somewhat later than Woodward. His concern with technology as a central factor in theorizing about organizations appears to have been sparked by James Thompson's early work (see chapter 15 in this volume).

Background

After 3 years of military service, Perrow entered Black Mountain College near Asheville, North Carolina, but ultimately he received his degree from the University of California at Berkeley in sociology. His doctoral work was done under Philip Selznick, one of the major figures in the early development of organizational study and macro organizational behavior (Selznick, 1949). On completing the degree in 1958, Perrow went to the University of Michigan in the sociology department. His contacts with the Institute for Social Research while there led him to believe that the institute served management much more than the workers. From Michigan he moved to the University of Pittsburgh, with appointments in sociology and public administration. It was there that the work on technology began; his prior work had concentrated primarily on hospitals. He stayed 3 years. Next came a stint at the University of Wisconsin, in sociology, and after a few years a longer stay at the State University of New York at Stony Brook. In the early 1980s Perrow moved to Yale, where he has remained.

Other than the partial appointment in public administration at Pittsburgh and a visiting year at the London Graduate School of Business, Perrow worked in sociology departments. Among the American theorists of organizational behavior who were in his age cohort his failure to move into a continuing business school position is unusual. The reason appears to be related to some strongly held values. He describes himself as a person with "inchoate liberal or even radical instincts" and "an organization theorist with an uncertain macro-leftist tilt" (Perrow, 1993). He wrote a book (Perrow, 1972b) titled *The Radical Attack on Business*, which he describes as presenting a sympathetic interpretation of the new left. He was a participant in the activist, radical demonstrations on campus during the 1960s and 1970s. Yet he has dabbled with business schools throughout his career and has written for business publications. One would have to assume that his values were too strong to permit him to actually make the move to business, however, although he must have had opportunities. On the evidence, it seems best that he remained in sociology; there would inevitably have been value clashes otherwise.

Statements of Technical Theory

Perrow's concern with technology in organizations appears to have manifested itself first in an article that dealt with the goal-setting process in organizations where technology was portrayed as influencing the operative goals—those goals reflected in the observed operating policies and day-to-day decisions of the organization (Perrow, 1961).

This way of thinking was developed further in an extensive review of the literature on hospitals (Perrow, 1965). In this article he sets forth a view of organizations, emphasizing that:

the work [is] performed on the basic material which is to be altered, rather than focusing upon the interaction of organizational members or the function for society. From this perspective, organizations are viewed as systems which utilize energy (given up by humans and nonhuman devices) in a patterned, directed effort to alter the condition of basic materials in a predetermined manner. . . . Technology is a technique or complex of techniques employed to alter materials (human or nonhuman, mental or physical) in an anticipated manner. (Perrow, 1965, pp. 913, 915)

Technology is a major factor in determining structure, dominance relationships, and consequently operative goals. Thus, in hospitals, trustees would be expected to play the key role when the technology is simple, physicians when medical technology is central, and administrators when multiple technologies must be coordinated. Views of this kind clearly cast Perrow as a proponent of the technological imperative.

Dimensions of Technology

Building on these beginnings, Perrow set forth his basic theory in somewhat different forms in several publications (1966, 1967, 1968, 1970b). Two aspects of technology are viewed as having major importance for organizational structure. One is the *number of exceptions* encountered in the work. Do the stimuli lack variability so that they can be handled in a highly programmed manner, or do they pose a constant variety so that every task seems to be a new one? Second, if there are exceptions, *search* must be instituted to determine the appropriate response. The search may be quite analyzable in that it involves routine and logical analysis: one can determine a response by looking it up in a book or by drawing on some other programmed solution. With unanalyzable search, ready-made solutions do not exist. Intuition, insight, experience, and the like are needed. Highly rationalized, programmed responses are not available.

Using this cognitive concept of technology, Perrow places organizations at various points in the two-dimensional space created by the two variables: the number of exceptions and the analyzability of search. Table 16.7 summarizes the results and indicates which of the four quadrants (1, craftsman; 2, nonroutine; 3, engineering; and 4, routine) contains each type of organization. The two dimensions tend to be positively correlated. Thus one would not expect to find many instances of tasks that have very few exceptions where search is distinctly unanalyzable or cases of tasks with a great many exceptions where search is almost completely analyzable.

Paralleling the distinctions Perrow made with regard to technology is another set that deals with the characteristics of the raw material, which in certain cases may be human beings, as in educational institutions. This raw material may vary in the extent to which it is perceived as uniform and stable by members of the organization, paralleling the number of exceptions variable in technology. It may also vary in

TABLE 16.7 Positions of types of firms on Perrow's dimensions of technology

No. of exceptions	Type of search
Many	Unanalyzable
R and D firms (2)	Custom craftsmanship (1)
Engineering prototypes (3)	R and D firms (2)
Nonroutine manufacturing (aerospace) (2)	Craftsmanship (1)
Engineering (heavy equipment) (3)	Nonroutine manufacturing (aerospace) (2)
Custom craftsmanship (1)	Engineering prototypes (3)
Craftsmanship (1)	Routine manufacturing (tonnage steel mills) (4)
Routine manufacturing (tonnage steel mills) (4)	Engineering (heavy equipment) (3)
Continuous processing (4)	Continuous processing (4)
Few	Analyzable

NOTE: Figures in parentheses are the quadrant designations: (1) craftsman (few exceptions—unanalyzable search); (2) nonroutine (many exceptions—unanalyzable search); (3) engineering (many exceptions—analyzable search); (4) routine (few exceptions—analyzable search).

SOURCE: Adapted from Charles Perrow (1968), The Effect of Technological Change on the Structure of Business Firms, in B. C. Roberts (Ed.), Industrial Relations: Contemporary Issues (New York: Macmillan), 211

the degree to which it is well understood (analyzable). Organizations generally seek to standardize raw materials, making them as uniform and stable as possible to minimize the number of exceptions.

Technology and Structure

In relating technology to structure, Perrow makes a major distinction between quadrant 4 with its routine technology, which should foster bureaucratic organization, and quadrant 2 with its nonroutine technology, which requires nonbureaucratic forms. He also relates quadrant 4 to the mechanistic system posited by Burns and Stalker and quadrant 2 to the organic system. With regard to the Woodward classification of firms (see table 16.1) he has this to say:

> Most of those in the general category "small batch and unit" are probably involved in nonroutine production; those in the "large batch and unit" are probably involved in routine production; those in the "large batch and mass production" category have a mixture of routine and nonroutine technologies, but are predominantly routine. If so, her findings would be consistent with our perspective. However, her analysis of continuous process firms unfortunately cannot easily be incorporated in the scheme advanced here. (Perrow, 1967, p. 207)

In addition to these general statements about the routine to nonroutine continuum, Perrow extends his analysis to quadrants 1 and 3 and attempts to deal

with task structure in more precise terms. The results of this process are presented in table 16.8. The structural dimensions relate to control and coordination. The extent of interdependence of groups is also considered, though it is said to be high only in the flexible, polycentralized firms needed in quadrant 2, where a nonroutine technology predominates.

Control is defined in terms of the degree of discretion an individual or a group has in making decisions about how the work should be organized and carried out and in terms of the power to call on resources and establish goals. Coordination is viewed as occurring either through planning, where the interaction of tasks is programmed in advance (by rules or by the mechanical processes involved) or through feedback where there are negotiated alterations in tasks that involve two units (mutual adjustment).

These aspects of control and coordination are specified separately for middle management, which is understood to include technical staff control and support functions, and for direct, first-level supervision of production and marketing. In addition, there is some consideration of the top management level where major strategies and policies are formulated, although specifics of structure are not stated in the same manner for this level and thus are not included in table 16.8. All other things being equal, top management should have routine tasks and techniques in quadrants 4 and 1, nonroutine tasks in quadrant 2, and somewhat nonroutine tasks in quadrant 3. However, because the product environment (competitors, customers, suppliers, unions, and regulatory agencies) can have a major effect on top management structure, nonroutine tasks may be introduced at this level by environmental forces, and major departures from technological determinism may result. The processes involved here are not spelled out in great detail; in some respects, top management structure appears to be outside the domain of the theory.

Attention is also given to the social, as opposed to task, structure of the organization. Differences in organizationally relevant interactions are posited in relation to technology. In nonroutine firms (quadrant 2), these interactions deal with the long-range goals and direction of development of the organization. In craftsman firms (quadrant 1) the emphasis is on communal and personal satisfactions born of long and close associations. In quadrant 4 with its routine technology, the social structure has an instrumental identity, stressing job security, protection from arbitrary authority, pay, and other matters often of concern to unions. In engineering firms (quadrant 3) there is primarily work or task identification, with its allied satisfactions.

Technology and Goals

As one moves from task structure to social structure to goals, correlations with technology may be expected

TABLE 16.8 Characteristics of firms in Perrow's four quadrants (technological types)

Variables	Quadrant 1 (craftsman)	Quadrant 2 (nonroutine)	Quadrant 3 (engineering)	Quadrant 4 (routine)
Technology	Few exceptions — unanalyzable search	Many exceptions — unanalyzable search	Many exceptions — analyzable search	Few exceptions — analyzable search
Raw material	Uniform and stable — not well understood	Nonuniform and unstable — not well understood	Nonuniform and unstable — not well understood	Uniform and stable — well understood
Appropriate task structure	Decentralized	Flexible — polycentralized	Flexible — centralized	Formal — centralized
Interdependence of groups	Low	High	Low	Low
Discretion				
Middle management	Low	High	High	Low
Direct supervision	High	High	Low	Low
Power				
Middle management	Low	High	High	High
Direct supervision	High	High	Low	Low
Coordination method within groups				
Middle management	Planning	Feedback	Feedback	Planning
Direct supervision	Feedback	Feedback	Planning	Planning
Appropriate social structure	Social identity (communal)	Goal identification (mission, distinctive competence)	Work or task identification (technical satisfactions)	Instrumental identification (job security, pay)
Appropriate goals				
System	Stability / Few risks / Moderate to low profit emphasis	High growth / High risks / Low emphasis on profit	Moderate growth / Some risks / Moderate profit emphasis	Stability / Few risks / High profit emphasis
Product	Quality / No innovations	High quality / Innovation	Reliability / Moderate innovations	Quantity / No innovations
Derived	Conservative	Liberal	Liberal	Conservative

SOURCE: Adapted from Charles Perrow (1967), A Framework for the Comparative Analysis of Organizations, *American Sociological Review*, 32, 196, 198–200, 203

to decrease appreciably. Thus technology sets only broad limits on possible goals. These goals are considered in three categories. System goals, the first category, relate to the organization as a whole, but do not include its products, on which the second category of goals is based. The third category, the derived goals, define the uses to which power generated by the organization may be put in the larger society. Hypotheses with regard to these three types of goals as they operate in different technologies are given in table 16.8.

Perrow (1967) is less certain about his statements on goals than he is about his statements on technology and structure. The influences of individual personalities and environmental forces on goals may be considerably greater than that of technology. The theory is indeed very tentative at this point.

Subsequent Developments

Shortly after the presentation of his theory, Perrow wrote a book dealing with organizations and their functioning. In it he devoted very little space to the technological imperative. A footnote is revealing: "For a not very successful attempt to spell out four models [of technology], rather than just two see Perrow, 'Framework for Comparative Organizational Analysis'" (Perrow, 1972a, p. 170). Sometime in the early 1970s Perrow evidently became somewhat disillusioned with technological theory and the research on it. His only major work in the area in the mid-1970s was an article refuting the view that technological change has been widespread and rapid (and thus environments turbulent) in recent years (Perrow, 1974).

Later, however, he began to give attention to a theme that he had noted almost as an aside a number of years before: "For many purposes of organizational analysis technology might not be an independent variable but a dependent one" (Perrow, 1966, p. 163). More specifically, on the basis of a historical analysis of the literature surrounding the industrial revolution, he concludes:

> The techniques of doing the work, the technology, the machines, the work flow, the layout, was designed to fit in with and to maximize the potential of this new social system. In contrast to present-day contingency theory, structure predicts to technology, not the other way around (I might add, as an aside, that it still does in its basic sense). Machines were designed, in part, to be unobtrusive control devices, limiting discretion of the opera-

tive, pacing her or him faster, demanding continuous attendance, signaling a lapse of attention. The skilled worker was anathema to the factory system: her or his skills had to be dissolved in a machine, or, in Taylorism after the turn of the century, extracted from the worker and placed in the hands of management. . . . The organization came first, the technology second. (Perrow, 1978, pp. 6–8)

Though typically not fully committed to this position either, Perrow clearly does have doubts about technological determinism. He raises the question of whether "structural determinism" is not a more defensible position. His openness of mind is clearly intellectually admirable. But it is still important to establish the validity of the technological imperative.

This idea that structure can affect technology, and that conscious choice can shift technology in one direction or another, has been stated since as well (see, for example, Perrow, 1983). In looking back on his 1967 article Perrow (1981) feels that the ideas are still fairly sound, but that power, along with institutional and cross-cultural factors, has weakened the value of the theory. In his autobiography Perrow likens the 1967 article to a vintage wine and says that the theory "aged delightfully over the next ten years until reservations, problems with empirical demonstration, complexities and new interests eroded it" (1993, p. 420). With regard to empirical demonstration, he notes "only some of the organizations fitted the mold; too many other variables, unmeasured but still known to us, entered in to reduce the requisite correlation levels and significance tests. The results did not play out in the pattern that we had predicted" (p. 422). What then is this research evidence?

Evaluation and Impact

The preceding quotation had reference to Perrow's own research conducted to test his theory. There are other studies to consider as well.

Perrow's Measures and Research

Perrow (1970a, 1970c, 1973) conducted studies in 14 firms or divisions of firms to investigate relationships between technology and structure. The data were obtained from questionnaire measures that were administered at the managerial level. This questionnaire contained a number of questions that intended to get at dimensions of technology. However, in the final analysis Perrow rejected certain of these questions as inappropriate to the study of technology as he defined it. As a result, he ended with a measure focused on the single dimension running from routine (cell 4) to nonroutine (cell 2) of his theory, and he did not operationalize the engineering and craftsman components. The questions in the final technology index asked for a rating of (1) the percentage of time the respondents were not sure whether what they did would work or not, and (2) the probability that there was someone else in the organization who could help them should they face a problem in their work that they could not handle.

Reports of the study do not systematically relate the findings to the theory, and the structural dimensions considered are neither consistently the same as those in table 16.8 nor always differentiated by managerial level. The measures used deal with the following:

Clarity — clear lines of authority, written rules, precise duties and authority, and delegation

Strictness — following orders, consistent use of procedures, and consistent reporting relationships

Openness — use of group decisions, lower-level suggestions, interdepartmental teams, and individual initiative and judgment

Influence — within the whole company and with supervisors

Coordination — whether by planning and routine or by mutual adjustment and feedback

Power — of management levels and functional areas

Relationships were found that tied nonroutine technology with feedback coordination, low strictness, and possibly low clarity, but not with openness, individual influence, or power. These findings are summarized as follows:

The relationship between technology and task-related aspects of structure was high, but the relationship between technology and subordinate power, influence, and discretion was attenuated. Apparently, considerations of organizational history and leadership variables, which were not measured, played an increasing role here. (Perrow, 1970a, p. 82)

No findings related to social structure and goals are reported by Perrow, but Karl Magnusen (1973) indi-cates there was some directional support for the goals formulations, but little for those regarding social structure.

Other Tests of the Theory

In contrast to the research on the Woodward theory, research on the Perrow theory has focused on service rather than on manufacturing organizations and frequently has considered subunits rather than total systems as the basis for analysis. Within this primary context that involves subunit-level analyses of service organizations, measures of Perrow's routine-nonroutine dimensions have shown consistent relationship to structural factors (Reimann & Inzerilli, 1981). At this subunit level, sizable variations in technology within the unit are less likely to occur, and thus one potential source of error in organization-wide studies is eliminated.

Furthermore, there is some evidence that technology can actually cause the structural effects (Van de Ven, 1977). Longitudinal analyses indicated that as the technology became more nonroutine, supervisory decision making decreased and employee and group decision making increased — and thus a certain type of decentralization occurred. These technological effects exceeded those for size. Alternatively, there are also data, though less powerful because they derive from concurrent analyses, which suggest that structural factors (in this case, division of labor) may influence the degree of routinization of work (Glisson, 1978). Actually, there is no reason why the primary direction of causation could not vary from one structural variable to another.

Perrow's routine-nonroutine dimension was included in the meta-analysis of theoretically based technology constructs that was discussed previously in this chapter (Tehrani et al., 1990). The correlations of this dimension with aspects of structure were more likely to be significant than for any other technological operationalization — four out of the six calculated. These calculations were not small and included values of .50 with formalization and of −.49 with an index of education/professionalism. However, this analysis does not contain data on the degree of effectiveness that results from the technology-structure fit.

Yet there are data that clearly support such a hypothesis (see, for example, Alexander & Randolph, 1985; Keller, 1994). Research of this kind has tended to fall only within the general framework of the Perrow theory, however, without focusing on its specific content; it, too, has been conducted at the subunit or micro level. The study by Robert Keller (1994) used technology scales measuring both the number of exceptions and the type of search dimensions; an index of structure appropriate to the Perrow theory; multiple criteria of success; and a longitudinal, predictive design. The results were strongly supportive for the dimension "number of exceptions" and predicted results a year later; the second dimension did not produce significant relationships with the outcome variables.

When measurement focuses on the Perrow dimensions of technology and is concerned with the micro level where unitary technologies can be expected, the evidence for construct validity is much more encouraging than is that found for technology in other contexts (Withey, Daft, & Cooper, 1983). The two dimensions load differentially on two separate factors, although they tend to be highly correlated with one another. There is evidence for convergent and discriminant validity. Reliabilities for the different measures studied are generally satisfactory and with appropriate attention to item wording and test length can be in the .80s. Measures with good psychometric properties clearly are available for the Perrow variables.

Although the evidence bearing on the theory is in many respects quite positive, a comparison of the findings with table 16.8 indicates that only limited aspects of the basic theory have been tested. There is certainly room for a great deal more work in this regard, and, given current trends, the likelihood of the necessary research being conducted is not high.

Implications for Practice

Like the Woodward version, Perrow's technological imperative theory has failed to generate guides for application; the technology needed to put the theory into practice simply does not exist. Actually, however, Perrow did envisage the development of such a technology at an early point:

Students must not only learn discrete techniques or even analytical skills, but also acquire the ability to see when a technique is or is not applicable because of the technological and structural situation in which it might be applied. More generally, the perspective has implications for management practices: Why do you have so much trouble when you try to combine routine and nonroutine production techniques in the same plant? Not just because

metallurgists and old time production men won't mix. When should you isolate production lines or even phases of production? Classical management theory will not help here. When should you buy the latest book by McGregor, Bennis, or Argyris and order participative management to come into effect, by next Thursday? Not if you have a routine operation, and only in some units if it is a craft or engineering operation. (Perrow, 1966, pp. 161–162)

Perrow's ideas could have been extended in practice, and research could have been designed to test their utility. But one could seriously question whether the scientific foundation is strong enough to support a sound technological superstructure.

Technological Imperative — Micro and Macro

The Perrow theory is something of an enigma. It is presented as a theory of organization level functioning and the examples cited are of this type (see table 16.7). Yet the theoretical variables appear to deal more with individual or at best work group level concepts. This is manifest not only in the theoretical definitions but also in Perrow's own operationalizations and in the level at which research designed to test the theory has been carried out. It is questionable whether the theory or the research that has been generated by it should be extrapolated to the organizational level. Ultimately, Perrow (1972a) appears to have recognized these problems also.

At the micro level Perrow's theory has received considerable support. In this research it emerges not so much as a broad theory of organization but as a theory of job design that is focused on the routine-nonroutine dimension. Other aspects of the theory simply have not been tested sufficiently. Although these studies tend to aggregate data obtained from individuals, they do so within units where considerable task homogeneity exists. In addition, they focus on only one aspect of the job — routineness — ignoring even the engineering-craftsman dimension that Perrow also proposed. Accordingly, it seems best to consider the Perrow theory as it has been operationalized and tested: a limited-scale, micro-level theory of organizational behavior, rather than a theory of macro organizational process and structure. This conclusion is reinforced by Perrow's own tentativeness in hypothesizing about organizational social structure and goals and his indication that organizational technology operates more as a dependent than as an independent variable.

For the past two decades or more Perrow has been working on other issues, in most cases issues with greater inherent value appeal for him than the technology-structure relationship. This commitment to social issues is reflected in his book with Mauro Guillen titled *The AIDS Disaster: The Failure of Organizations in New York and the Nation* (1990) and in his own *Normal Accidents: Living with High Risk Technologies* (1984). Coupled with his developing ambivalence regarding his technological imperative theory, this shift in the author's interests has served to leave the theory at something of a dead end. There are many unanswered questions, including the micro-macro issue, that beg for answers from the author, and from research. At present, the best guess is that these questions will remain unanswered.

CONCLUSIONS

The literature related to the technological imperative is about as confused as any in the area of organizational theorizing. Major reviews of research come to almost diametrically opposed conclusions (Donaldson, 1976; Reimann & Inzerilli, 1981). Even the theorists themselves have basic disagreements. Thus, Woodward has the following to say:

> Although, however, Perrow develops his ideas as a basis for comparison, his attempts at measurement are of an elementary kind. . . . His attention seems to be focused on the perception by organization members of the constraints in the work environment. . . . Indeed he does what the Imperial College team had tried to avoid from the outset: he classifies technology in terms that are themselves social. (1970, p. 33)

And Perrow indicates: "It is impossible to determine how Woodward or Burns and Stalker arrived at their classifications of companies" (1967, p. 208). Certain problems in the technological imperative literature relate to the individual theories and their approach to measurement, but others relate to the general concept of a technological imperative itself. Woodward and Perrow came very close to rejecting their own theories in the early 1970s. Often the theorists have had difficulty making the theories work subsequently, either in individual case contexts or in more comprehensive organizational research.

The most appropriate conclusion appears to be that the technological imperative defined as an implicit, causal, unilateral determinant has not held up under close scrutiny. There are circumstances in which it operates, usually on a limited scale, but we know little as yet about what those circumstances are. Where it can be clearly seen, at the micro level, we have glimpses of a strong dynamic, but above this level for most organizations multiple technologies continue to cloud our vision. Technology clearly can make a difference in organizations. Yet at present it is a construct in search of a good theory to mobilize it.

References

Aldrich, Howard E. (1972). Technology and Organizational Structure: A Reexamination of the Findings of the Aston Group. *Administrative Science Quarterly*, 17, 26–43.

Alexander, Judith W., & Randolph, W. Alan (1985). The Fit between Technology and Structure as a Predictor of Performance in Nursing Subunits. *Academy of Management Journal*, 28, 844–859.

Billings, Robert S.; Klimoski, Richard J.; & Breaugh, James A. (1977). The Impact of a Change in Technology on Job Characteristics: A Quasi-Experiment. *Administrative Science Quarterly*, 22, 318–339.

Blau, Peter M.; Falbe, Cecilia M.; McKinley, William; & Tracy, Phelps K. (1976). Technology and Organization in Manufacturing. *Administrative Science Quarterly*, 21, 20–40.

Burns, Tom, & Stalker, G. M. (1961). *The Management of Innovation.* London: Tavistock.

Child, John (1972). Organizational Structure and Strategies of Control: A Replication of the Aston Study. *Administrative Science Quarterly*, 17, 163–177.

Child, John (1973a). Predicting and Understanding Organization Structure. *Administrative Science Quarterly*, 18, 168–185.

Child, John (1973b). Parkinson's Progress: Accounting for the Number of Specialists in Organizations. *Administrative Science Quarterly*, 18, 328–348.

Child, John (1975). Managerial and Organizational Factors Associated with Company Performance. Part II: A Contingency Analysis. *Journal of Management Studies*, 12, 12–27.

Child, John, & Mansfield, Roger (1972). Technology, Size and Organizational Structure. *Sociology*, 6, 369–393.

Collins, Paul D.; Hage, Jerald; & Hull, Frank M. (1988). A Framework for Analyzing Technical Systems in

Complex Organizations. *Research in the Sociology of Organizations*, 6, 81–100.

Collins, Paul D., & Hull, Frank M. (1986). Technology and Span of Control: Woodward Revisited. *Journal of Management Studies*, 23, 143–164.

Donaldson, Lex (1976). Woodward, Technology, Organizational Structure and Performance: A Critique of the Universal Generalization. *Journal of Management Studies*, 13, 255–273.

Glisson, Charles A. (1978). Dependence of Technological Routinization on Structural Variables in Human Service Organizations. *Administrative Science Quarterly*, 23, 383–395.

Greenwood, Royston, & Devine, Kay (1997). Inside Aston: A Conversation with Derek Pugh. *Journal of Management Inquiry*, 6, 200–208.

Hickson, David J. (1998). A Surprised Academic: Learning from Others While Walking on Thin Ice. In Arthur G. Bedeian (Ed.), *Management Laureates: A Collection of Autobiographical Essays* (Vol. 5, pp. 93–128) Stamford, CT: JAI Press.

Hickson, David J.; Pugh, Derek S.; & Pheysey, Diana C. (1969). Operations Technology and Organization Structure: An Empirical Reappraisal. *Administrative Science Quarterly*, 14, 378–397.

Hulin, Charles L., & Roznowski, Mary (1985). Organizational Technologies: Effects on Organizations' Characteristics and Individuals' Responses. *Research in Organizational Behavior*, 7, 39–85.

Hull, Frank M., & Collins, Paul D. (1987). High-Technology Batch Production Systems: Woodward's Missing Type. *Academy of Management Journal*, 30, 786–797.

Inkson, J. H. K.; Pugh, Derek S.; & Hickson, David J. (1970). Organization Context and Structure: An Abbreviated Replication. *Administrative Science Quarterly*, 15, 318–329.

Inkson, J. H. K.; Schwitter, J. P.; Pheysey, Diana C.; & Hickson, David J. (1970). A Comparison of Organization Structure and Managerial Roles: Ohio, U.S.A., and the Midlands, England. *Journal of Management Studies*, 7, 347–363.

Keller, Robert T. (1994). Technology-Information Processing Fit and the Performance of R&D Project Groups: A Test of Contingency Theory. *Academy of Management Journal*, 37, 167–179.

Khandwalla, Pradip N. (1974). Mass Output Orientation of Operations Technology and Organizational Structure. *Administrative Science Quarterly*, 19, 74–97.

Magnusen, Karl O. (1973). Perspectives on Organizational Design and Development. Research Paper No. 21, Graduate School of Business, Columbia University.

Miller, C. Chet; Glick, William H.; Wang, Yau-de; & Huber, George P. (1991). Understanding Technology-Structure Relationships: Theory Development and Meta-analytic Theory Testing. *Academy of Management Journal*, 34, 370–399.

Orlikowski, Wanda J. (1992). The Quality of Technology: Rethinking the Concept of Technology in Organizations. *Organization Science*, 3, 398–427.

Perrow, Charles (1961). The Analysis of Goals in Complex Organizations. *American Sociological Review*, 26, 854–866.

Perrow, Charles (1965). Hospitals: Technology, Structure, and Goals. In James G. March (Ed.), *Handbook of Organizations* (pp. 910–971). Chicago: Rand McNally.

Perrow, Charles (1966). Technology and Organizational Structure. *Industrial Relations Research Association Proceedings*, 19, 156–163.

Perrow, Charles (1967). A Framework for the Comparative Analysis of Organizations. *American Sociological Review*, 32, 194–208.

Perrow, Charles (1968). The Effect of Technological Change on the Structure of Business Firms. In B. C. Roberts (Ed.), *Industrial Relations: Contemporary Issues* (pp. 205–219). New York: Macmillan.

Perrow, Charles (1970a). Departmental Power and Perspectives in Industrial Firms. In Mayer Zald (Ed.), *Power in Organizations* (pp. 59–89). Nashville: Vanderbilt University Press.

Perrow, Charles (1970b). *Organizational Analysis: A Sociological View*. Belmont, CA: Wadsworth.

Perrow, Charles (1970c). Technology and Structure. Working Paper, University of Wisconsin, Madison.

Perrow, Charles (1972a). *Complex Organizations: A Critical Essay*. Glenview, IL: Scott, Foresman.

Perrow, Charles (1972b). *The Radical Attack on Business*. New York: Harcourt Brace Jovanovich.

Perrow, Charles (1973). Some Reflections on Technology and Organizational Analysis. In Anant R. Negandhi (Ed.), *Modern Organizational Theory: Contextual, Environmental, and Socio-Cultural Variables* (pp. 47–57). Kent, OH: Kent State University Press.

Perrow, Charles (1974). Is Business Really Changing? *Organizational Dynamics*, 3(1), 31–44.

Perrow, Charles (1978). The Emergence of a Society of Organizations. Working Paper, State University of New York at Stony Brook.

Perrow, Charles (1981). This Week's Citation Classic. *Current Contents*, 14, 14.

Perrow, Charles (1983). The Organizational Context of Human Factors Engineering. *Administrative Science Quarterly*, 28, 521–541.

Perrow, Charles (1984). *Normal Accidents: Living with High Risk Technologies.* New York: Basic Books.

Perrow, Charles (1993). An Almost Random Career. In Arthur G. Bedeian (Ed.), *Management Laureates: A Collection of Autobiographical Essays* (Vol. 2, pp. 399–438) Greenwich, CT: JAI Press.

Perrow, Charles, & Guillen, Mauro (1990). *The AIDS Disaster: The Failure of Organizations in New York and the Nation.* New Haven, CT: Yale University Press.

Pugh, Derek S. (1996). A Taste for Innovation. In Arthur G. Bedeian (Ed.), *Management Laureates: A Collection of Autobiographical Essays* (Vol. 4, pp. 235–276) Greenwich, CT: JAI Press.

Pugh, Derek S., & Hickson, David J. (1972). Causal Inference and the Aston Studies. *Administrative Science Quarterly,* 17, 273–276.

Pugh, Derek S., & Hickson, David J. (1976). *Organizational Structure in Its Context: The Aston Programme I.* Lexington, MA: D. C. Heath.

Pugh, Derek S., & Hickson, David J. (1993). *Great Writers on Organizations: The Omnibus Edition.* Aldershot, UK: Dartmouth.

Reimann, Bernard C. (1980). Organization Structure and Technology in Manufacturing: System versus Work Flow Level Perspectives. *Academy of Management Journal,* 23, 61–77.

Reimann, Bernard C., & Inzerilli, Giorgio (1981). Technology and Organization: A Review and Synthesis of Major Research Findings. In George W. England, Anant R. Negandhi, & Bernhard Wilpert (Eds.), *The Functioning of Complex Organizations* (pp. 237–274). Cambridge, MA: Oelgeschlager, Gunn & Hain.

Rousseau, Denise M. (1979). Assessment of Technology in Organizations: Closed versus Open Systems Approaches. *Academy of Management Review,* 4, 531–542.

Scott, W. Richard (1990). Technology and Structure: An Organizational-Level Perspective. In Paul S. Goodman & Lee S. Sproull (Eds.), *Technology and Organizations* (pp. 109–143). San Francisco: Jossey-Bass.

Selznick, Philip (1949). *TVA and the Grass Roots.* Berkeley: University of California Press.

Tehrani, Minoo; Montanari, John R.; & Carson, Kenneth P. (1990). Technology as Determinant of Organization Structure: A Meta-analytic Review. *Academy of Management Proceedings,* 50, 180–184.

Turner, Barry A. (1995). A Personal Trajectory through Organization Studies. *Research in the Sociology of Organizations,* 13, 275–301.

Van de Ven, Andrew H. (1977). A Panel Study on the Effects of Task Uncertainty, Interdependence, and Size on Unit Decision Making. *Organization and Administrative Sciences,* 8, 237–253.

Withey, Michael; Daft, Richard L.; & Cooper, William H. (1983). Measures of Perrow's Work Unit Technology: An Empirical Assessment and a New Scale. *Academy of Management Journal,* 26, 45–63.

Woodward, Joan (1958). *Management and Technology.* Problems of Progress in Industry, No. 3. London: Her Majesty's Stationery Office.

Woodward, Joan (1965). *Industrial Organization: Theory and Practice.* Oxford: Oxford University Press.

Woodward, Joan (1970). *Industrial Organization: Behavior and Control.* Oxford: Oxford University Press.

Woodward, Joan (1973). Technology, Material Control, and Organizational Behavior. In Anant R. Negandhi (Ed.), *Modern Organizational Theory: Contextual, Environmental, and Socio-Cultural Variables* (pp. 58–68). Kent, OH: Kent State University Press.

Wren, Daniel A. (1994). *The Evolution of Management Thought.* New York: Wiley.

Zwerman, William L. (1970). *New Perspectives on Organization Theory.* Westport, CT: Greenwood.

Chapter 17

Differentiation and Integration in the Contingency Theory of Organization

In this chapter we turn to an expanded contingency formulation, and move back outside the organizational boundaries, in an effort to find the critical contingency process that will provide a true understanding of organization structuring and success.

Certainly theories related to the technological imperative are contingency theories, as are numerous other theories that fall under the broad systems rubric. All these theories say there is no one best way to structure organizations. But the term *contingency theory* as used in macro organizational behavior has become associated primarily with the formulations of Paul Lawrence and Jay Lorsch.

The basic statements of the theory appear in an article (Lawrence & Lorsch, 1967a) and in a book (Lawrence & Lorsch, 1967c), although reports on pilot studies and preliminary hypotheses that exerted considerable influence on these formulations were published earlier (Lorsch, 1965; Lorsch & Lawrence, 1965). Since the 1960s, several extensions to the theory have been published, some of them growing out of the participation of individuals working on their dissertations at Harvard University under the major theorists.

Background

Lawrence was born in 1922 and graduated from Albion College. A lifelong association with the Harvard Business School began in 1942, interrupted only by military service during World War II. Lawrence was at Harvard during some of Elton Mayo's tenure there and was strongly influenced in the early years by Fritz Roethlisberger (see chapter 2 in this volume). He was educated in the post-Hawthorne period when the case tradition was developing. His primary disciplinary identification, before the emergence of organizational behavior, was with applied sociology, although anthropology, especially in its methods, exerted a strong influence. He received his doctorate from Harvard Business School in 1950.

Throughout his career Lawrence followed various emerging social problems, did field research on them typically in collaboration with others, and then wrote books on what was found (Lawrence & Lawrence, 1993). The work on contingency theory of organization represented one such instance of delving into a specific problem area and arose out of prior fieldwork and analyses in the area of job enrichment (see chapter 7 in this volume; see also Turner & Lawrence, 1965). Lawrence describes himself as a political liberal, and his humanism is reflected both in his selection of problems for study and in his approach to them. He retired from Harvard Business School in 1991.

Lorsch was a doctoral student at Harvard University when the contingency theory research was beginning and joined in the project as a research assistant to Lawrence. The collaboration has been a fruitful one, and Lorsch has remained at Harvard on the business school faculty throughout his career.

Lawrence and Lorsch Theory

Although the contingency theorists acknowledge a number of debts in presenting their views, their most influential sources, other than the prior field research in the job enrichment area, appear to be Joan Woodward (see chapter 16) and the Burns and Stalker work (see chapter 15). In its emphasis on the importance of environmental change and uncertainty, and in other respects as well, contingency theory has much in common with the mechanistic-organic formulations; however, contingency theory is much more complex.

Initial Hypotheses

The first formal statement of contingency theory defined an organization as follows: "A system of interrelated behaviors of people who are performing a task that has been differentiated into several distinct subsystems, each subsystem performing a portion of the task, and the efforts of each being integrated to achieve effective performance of the system" (Lawrence & Lorsch, 1967a, p. 3).

The task was to account for a whole input-transformation-output cycle, and the early formulations were focused on research, production, and sales subsystems. Unique to the definition, however, is the inclusion of differentiation and integration, which are defined as follows:

Differentiation . . . the state of segmentation of the organizational system into subsystems, each of which tends to develop particular attributes in relation to the requirements posed by its relevant external environment.

Integration . . . the process of achieving unity of effort among the various subsystems in the accomplishment of the organization's task. (Lawrence & Lorsch, 1967a, pp. 3–4)

Differentiation of subsystems was viewed in terms of four factors. In addition to the frequently cited *formalization of structure*, these were *orientation of members toward others*, *time orientation* of members, and *goal orientation* of the subsystem members. The three orientation factors are behavioral attributes. Hypotheses stating the relationships of these factors to the environment are as follows:

1. The greater the certainty of the relevant subenvironment, the more formalized the structure of the subsystem.
2. Subsystems dealing with environments of moderate certainty will have members with more social interpersonal orientations, whereas subsystems coping with either very certain environments or very uncertain environments will have members with more task-oriented interpersonal orientations.
3. The time orientations of subsystem members will vary directly with the modal time required to get definitive feedback from the relevant subenvironment.
4. The members of a subsystem will develop a primary concern with the goals of coping with their particular subenvironment. (Lawrence & Lorsch, 1967a, pp. 6–8)

Three additional hypotheses include the concept of integration and relate it to the environment and to differentiation:

5. Within any organizational system, given a similar degree of requisite integration, the greater the degree of differentiation in subsystem attributes between pairs of subsys-

tems, the less effective will be the integration achieved between them.

6. Overall performance in coping with the external environment will be related to there being a degree of differentiation among subsystems consistent with the requirements of their relevant subenvironments and a degree of integration consistent with requirements of the total environment.

7. When the environment requires both a high degree of system differentiation and a high degree of integration, integrative devices will tend to emerge. (Lawrence & Lorsch, 1967a, pp. 10–12)

In these formulations no distinction was made between the actual environment and the environment as perceived by management.

Early Elaboration

The more extensive publication of the theory in book form (Lawrence & Lorsch, 1967c) does not formally restate the seven hypotheses, though it does not clearly depart from them. However, differentiation and integration are defined somewhat differently:

Differentiation . . . the difference in cognitive and emotional orientation among managers in different functional departments. This was later amended to include "and the differences in formal structure among these departments." (Dalton, Lawrence, & Lorsch, 1970, p. 5)

Integration . . . the quality of the state of collaboration that exists among departments that are required to achieve unity of effort by the demands of the environment. (Lawrence & Lorsch, 1967c, p. 11)

Among functional specialists, differentiation almost invariably creates a potential for conflict. Integration is the means by which conflicts are resolved. At the simplest level, integration is achieved through adjudication within the management hierarchy. However, sizable demands created by the environment, which are typically mediated through the degree of differentiation, require the use of more extensive integration devices at lower levels. Among these integrative positions are product manager, program coordinator, project leader, planning director, and systems

designer that cut across and link major subsystems (Lawrence & Lorsch, 1967b).

The environment includes not only forces external to the organization but also "the physical machinery, the nonhuman aspect of production" (Lawrence & Lorsch, 1967c, p. 27). The authors maintain that uncertainty may reside in equipment performance, as well as in factors that remain outside the firm's boundaries. Uncertainty is a product of unclear information, uncertain causal relationships, and long feedback spans from the environment. Accordingly, uncertainty would be greater for the research components of an organization than for the production subsystem. Highly uncertain environments require high degrees of differentiation and integration for effective performance (a state of unstable equilibrium). More certain environments typically require neither.

Integration is most appropriately achieved through confrontation or negotiated problem solving, rather than through the smoothing over of differences or the forcing of resolutions through the use of power or authority. Thus in uncertain environments, where the demand for integration is high, effective organizations will use confrontation. In addition, influence should be based on competence and expertise, and insofar as special integrator positions have emerged, incumbents in those positions should maintain a balanced orientation toward the separate subsystems and convey a feeling that conflict resolution will be rewarded.

Lorsch and Allen Extensions

Although the original theory dealt with differentiation among departmental subsystems that are organized on a functional basis, Lorsch and Stephen Allen (1973) subsequently extended it to cover corporate-divisional and interdivisional relationships in firms that are organized into multiple product divisions. This extension provided hypotheses for the authors' own research. After carrying out this research, they formulated a set of hypotheses based on their findings and on the earlier hypotheses of Lawrence and Lorsch (1967c).

In all, Lorsch and Allen stated 39 hypotheses. Many of these represent extensions of the earlier concepts to the more complex relationships of product division organization. Thus the environment for a division comes to include the corporate headquarters, and the complexity of the interdependence between headquarters and the division becomes a consideration in integration.

Lorsch and Allen add some new concepts to the theory. One factor that influences the extent of differentiation is the *cognitive limitation* imposed by individual information processing capabilities. Also, *economic risk* influences integration:

> Within a firm the greater the differentiation between any division and the corporate headquarters and the greater the economic risk posed by that division, the greater the difficulties of achieving integration between these two units. (Lorsch & Allen, 1973, p. 179)

The concept of *integrative effort* is introduced in the following hypothesis:

> Either an excess or a deficit of integrative effort relative to the degree of interdependence and of differentiation required at the corporate-divisional interface will tend to lead to less effective relationships among these units. (Lorsch & Allen, 1973, p. 182)

Certain hypotheses are stated in such general terms it would be difficult to test them. For example: "Corporations will tend to develop divisional performance evaluation systems which are broadly consistent with the overall uncertainty and the patterns of diversity and interdependence which characterize their total environments" (Lorsch & Allen, 1973, p. 187).

The Lorsch and Allen (1973) volume, like certain other more recent writings (Lorsch, 1976), gives somewhat less emphasis to environmental uncertainty as a contingency variable, while it extends the contingency concept to other aspects of the environment. In partic-

ular, the homogeneity versus heterogeneity, or the diversity aspect of the environment is emphasized. Heterogeneity may be correlated with uncertainty, but it is not the same thing.

Lorsch and Morse Extensions

The formulations and extensions of contingency theory considered to this point deal with organization and environment and with the fit between the two. The work of Lorsch and John Morse (1974) extends this theory to individual members of organizations. Previously people's predispositions were considered only as one among several environmental factors. Now the domain of the theory is extended to include microorganizational behavior. Lorsch and Morse view organizational and unit effectiveness as dependent on a total fit between environment, organization, and the individual. The original pattern is depicted as shown in figure 17.1.

To this framework, Lorsch and Morse add as organizational factors the amount of *control* or *influence* members are expected to have over their own and others' activities and the degree to which members are expected to *coordinate* their activities. Table 17.1 gives the essence of the resulting theory. Manufacturing plants operating in environments with high certainty should exhibit the pattern shown on the left in the table; to the extent they depart from that pattern, they should be less effective. Similarly, the pattern on the right fits uncertain environments of the kind research units often face; if the organization and its members do not operate as indicated, effectiveness should be low.

When organizational subsystems are structured and staffed in a manner appropriate to their environments, differentiation will result, given that the environments differ insofar as the hypothesized con-

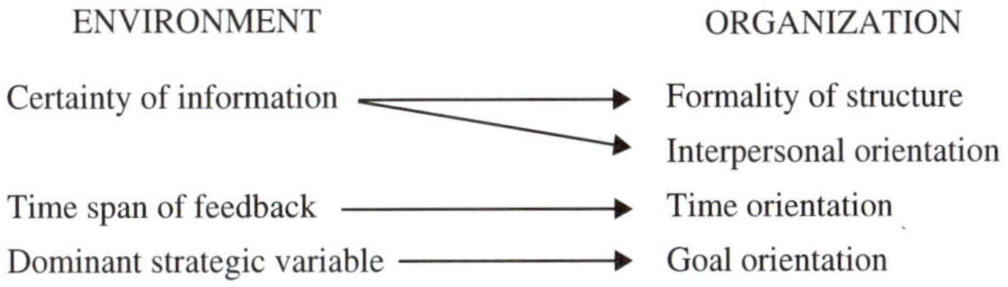

ENVIRONMENT   ORGANIZATION

Certainty of information ───────────▶ Formality of structure
                        ╲────────────▶ Interpersonal orientation
Time span of feedback ──────────────▶ Time orientation
Dominant strategic variable ────────▶ Goal orientation

FIGURE 17.1 Lorsch and Morse statement of the original environment-organization fit. Adapted from Jay W. Lorsch & John J. Morse (1974), *Organizations and Their Members: A Contingency Approach* (New York: Harper & Row), 9.

tingency variables are concerned. Thus, if the manufacturing plant and the research laboratory of table
17.1 were in the same company, the differentiation
would be appropriate because the company environment contains uncertainty as well as diversity (certainty and uncertainty) (Lorsch, 1977). Alternatively,
in a highly uncertain environment the uncertainty
might be diffused through all subsystems (at least in
this sense, diversity would be minimal). Under these
circumstances, all subsystems would tend to approximate the right side of table 17.1 and differentiation
would be low. Yet the theory argues for differentiation
in the face of uncertainty. There appears to be a logical
problem here. Under conditions of high uncertainty
in all subsystems of the organization, should one differentiate the subsystems in terms other than goals, and
if so how?

In any event, Lawrence (1975) has subsequently
endorsed the Lorsch and Morse extensions and formulated that theory as indicated in figure 17.2. The level
of competence motivation is said to be a function of
the fit or lack of fit between the certainty of the task,
the personal characteristics of employees, and the organizational structure. In connection with this formulation Lawrence postulates that the level of uncertainty
faced has escalated sharply over the past 50 years but
that the human capacity to cope with uncertainty has
expanded as well.

Lawrence and Dyer Extensions

In *Renewing American Industry* Lawrence and Davis
Dyer (1983) present a major extension of the original
theory, which unfortunately has not been given the
attention it deserves. The presentation starts with a
set of propositions and definitions that partially overlap
with previous statements but ultimately go well beyond them:

- The difficulty organizations experience in
  coping with their *resource domain* and with
  their *information domain* depends on the degree of uncertainty in these areas.
- The number of variations in an organization's immediate environment which directly
  influence its choice of which goods and services to supply is called its *information complexity* (I C).
- The degree of difficulty an organization experiences in securing the resources it needs to
  survive and grow is called its *resource scarcity*
  (RS).
- An organization is defined as being in a state
  of *readaptation* when its performance is simultaneously efficient and innovative.
- The process by which organizations repeatedly reconcile efficiency and innovation is
  called the *readaptive process.*
- For the readaptive process to be sustained,

TABLE 17.1 Examples of high environment-organization-individual fit in production and research and
development units

Variables	Manufacturing plant	Research laboratory
Nature of environment	Certain	Uncertain
Organizational structures and processes	Short time orientation	Long time orientation
	Strong technoeconomic goals	Strong scientific goals
	High formality of structure	Low formality of structure
	Influence concentrated at the top — directive	Influence diffused through many levels — participative
	High coordination	Low coordination
	Confrontation to resolve conflicts	Confrontation to resolve conflicts
Individual characteristics	Low cognitive complexity	High cognitive complexity
	Low tolerance for ambiguity	High tolerance for ambiguity
	Dependency in authority relation- ships	Independence in authority relation- ships
	Preference for group interaction	Preference for working alone
	High feeling of competence	High feeling of competence
Performance outcome	Effective	Effective

SOURCE: Adapted from Jay W. Lorsch & John J. Morse (1974), *Organizations and Their Members: A Contingency Approach* (New
York: Harper & Row), 52, 112

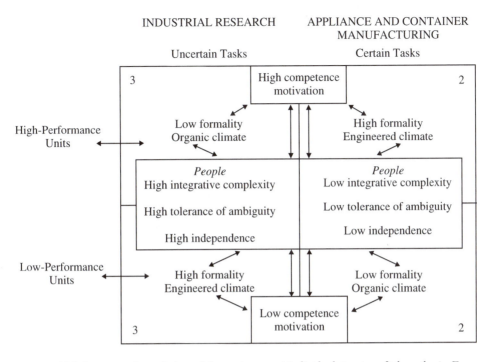

FIGURE 17.2 Lawrence formulation of the environment-individual-structure fit hypothesis. From Paul R. Lawrence (1975), Individual Differences in the World of Work, in Eugene L. Cass & Frederick G. Zimmer (Eds.), *Man and Work in Society* (New York: Van Nostrand Reinhold), 24. Copyright 1975 by Van Nostrand Reinhold. Reprinted with permission.

organizational members need to *learn* in order to be innovative and need to *strive* in order to be efficient.

• Readaptation, characterized by continuing efficiency and innovation, is most likely to occur when information complexity and resource scarcity both fall in the intermediate range of the Framework of Adaptation, or in area 5 [see figure 17.3].

• The readaptive process depends on an organization's entire membership being made cognizant of the broad purpose, ethical standards, and operating principles of the firm with emphasis given throughout to the value of both efficiency and innovation.

• As information complexity increases, organizations must, within the limits of their resources, employ new kinds of specialists if they are to learn and innovate in regard to the new, incoming information. This is the process of *organizational differentiation* (D).

• As resource scarcity increases, organizations must increase the number of mechanisms

available for coordinating their activities if they are to be efficient—up to the point, that is, that the scarcity of resources itself acts as a constraint. This is the process of *organizational integration* (I).

• Within a given firm readaptation will be most likely when both organizational differentiation and organizational integration are high.

• The readaptive process depends on an organization making balanced use of three kinds of human resource practices affecting the involvement of their employees: *market mechanisms* offering tangible financial rewards (M); *bureaucratic mechanisms* encouraging stability in the organization (B); and *clan mechanisms* encouraging a sense of membership (C) [see figure 17.4].

• The readaptive process depends on the organization's structure reflecting overall a relatively even distribution of power; there must be a reasonable balance in the vertical hierarchy as well as among the operating functions and/or divisions positioned horizontally

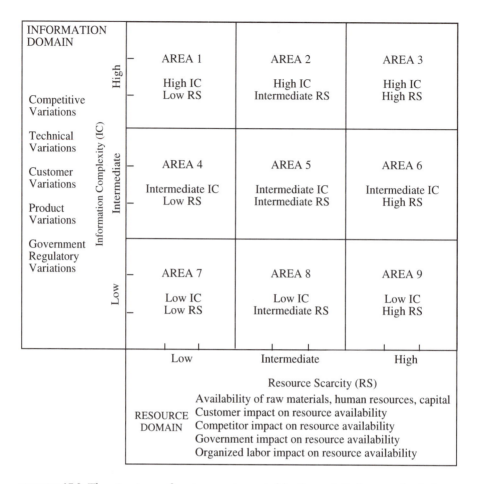

FIGURE 17.3 The nine types of environments created by the analytic framework of adaptation. From Paul R. Lawrence & Davis Dyer (1983), *Renewing American Industry: Organizing for Efficiency and Innovation* (New York: Free Press), 6. Copyright 1983. Reprinted with permission of The Free Press, a Division of Simon & Schuster, Inc.

throughout the organization. (Lawrence & Dyer, 1983, pp. 5–12)

This framework does not assume any type of determinism — environmental, technological, or other. Choice is central to the formulations, both from within the organization and on the part of components of the environment such as government and unions. The concept of readaptive strategy in figure 17.4 incorporates this idea of choice. Also in the figure the reference to power balance seems to have much in common with Arnold Tannenbaum's ideas regarding organizational control (see chapter 13 in this volume).

Like sociotechnical theory (see chapter 14 in this volume), contingency theory in its extended version gives an important role to government. Government

can act to facilitate movement of total industries and specific organizations toward area 5 from other environmental locations in figure 17.3. Thus the theory does not advocate totally free enterprise. Figure 17.5 uses the nine-environment matrix to show how the government might act to promote movement to an area 5 environment from various other locations.

The Lawrence and Dyer (1983) extensions include certain explicit and potentially testable hypotheses (H). The first three of these deal with the relationships among resource scarcity, information complexity, and readaptive outcomes:

H.1   Innovation has an inverted U-curve relation to information complexity in the organization's domain.

H.2 Efficiency has an inverted U-curve relation to resource scarcity in the organization's domain.

H.3 Member involvement has an inverted U-curve relation to environmental uncertainty generally. (Lawrence & Dyer, 1983, p. 301)

Next, hypotheses are advanced regarding the specific forms the variables of the theory (see figure 17.4) will take when a firm is in a particular environmental context and faced with a given uncertainty constellation. These hypotheses represent the results of qualitative research conducted on various industries. Figure 17.6 sets forth the seven variants involved. An example covering the linkage for area 1 is as follows:

H.4 Firms in an industry cluster that centers on Area 1 will tend to manifest the organizational form of adhocracy, characterized by a prospector strategy, high differentiation, low integration, predominantly clan human resource practices, and higher relative power for research groups. Outcomes will tend to be high innovation, low efficiency, and moderate involvement. (Lawrence & Dyer, 1983, p. 324

The terminology used here draws heavily on the literature of management strategy (Miles & Snow, 1978; Mintzberg, 1979; Ouchi, 1981).

A final set of hypotheses involves the relationships between existing uncertainty and perceived uncertainty:

H.5.1 Firms experiencing high levels of RS and/or IC will tend to overly simplify and minimize their environmental uncertainties.

H.5.2 Firms experiencing low levels of RS and/or IC will tend to exaggerate their environmental uncertainties. (Lawrence & Dyer, 1983, p. 329)

Organizational adaptation and the more theoretically important readaptation are distinguished as follows:

Adaptation . . . the process by which an organization and its environment reach and maintain an equilibrium ensuring the survival of the system as a whole.

Readaptation . . . a form of organizational adaptation in which the organization and its relevant

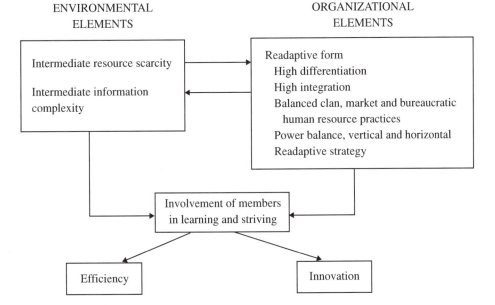

FIGURE 17.4 Schematic of the readaptive process showing the interaction between the environment and readaptive form and strategy. From Paul R. Lawrence & Davis Dyer (1983), *Renewing American Industry: Organizing for Efficiency and Innovation* (New York: Free Press), 13. Copyright 1983. Reprinted with permission of The Free Press, a Division of Simon & Schuster, Inc.

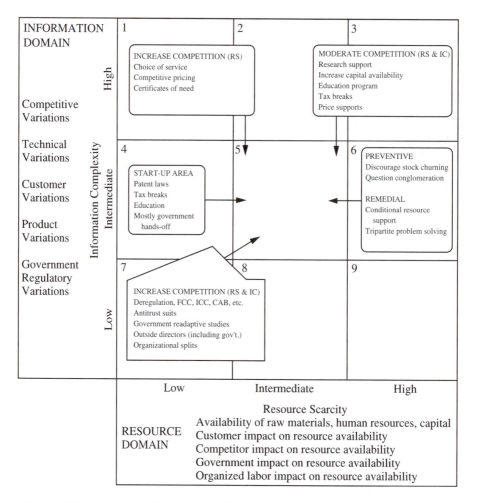

FIGURE 17.5 Summary of theoretical implications for government action. From Paul R. Lawrence & Davis Dyer (1983), *Renewing American Industry: Organizing for Efficiency and Innovation* (New York: Free Press), 288. Copyright 1983. Reprinted with permission of The Free Press, a Division of Simon & Schuster, Inc.

environment interact and evolve toward exchanges that are more acceptable to the internal and external stakeholders as evidenced by high levels of innovation, efficiency, and member involvement. (Lawrence & Dyer, 1983, p. 295)

These definitions clearly evidence the open systems nature of the contingency theory formulations.

Harvard-Based Research

The unfolding of contingency theory has in each instance coincided with a major research study con-

ducted by the theorists. The usual pattern has been to undertake an exploratory study on a very limited sample, firm up the hypotheses on the basis of that work, and then extend the research to a larger sample as a full test of the theory. To the extent that the hypotheses tested in the final study are influenced by the pilot study findings and the organizations involved in the pilot study also are used in the final study, there is potential contamination in this strategy. This appears to have been the case in the Harvard studies, and so they cannot be considered full tests of the theory. Yet the studies constitute an important and widely cited body of research.

Studies in the Plastics, Foods, and Containers Industries

The pilot work for the research done in the plastics, foods, and containers industries made use of two firms in the plastics industry (Lorsch, 1965; Lorsch & Lawrence, 1965). The final study involved six firms in the plastics industry (Lawrence & Lorsch, 1967a, 1967c) and two firms each in the foods and containers industries (Lawrence & Lorsch, 1967c). Data were gathered on theoretically relevant variables using questionnaires and interviews with 30 to 50 managers in each company.

Within the plastics industry, uncertainty was found to be at medium levels for the technoeconomic (manufacturing) and market environments but very high for the scientific environment. For the foods companies, technoeconomic uncertainty was also medium but market and scientific uncertainty were both considerably higher. As a result, the total environmental uncertainty for the foods companies was only slightly below that for plastics. However, the containers firms were

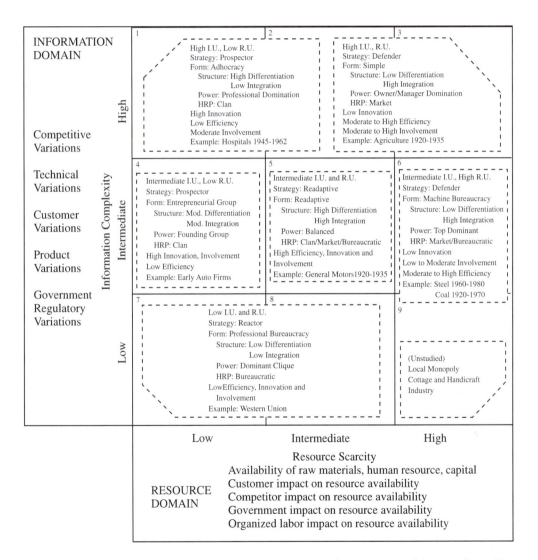

FIGURE 17.6 Hypotheses regarding the fit between environmental uncertainty and theoretical variables. From Paul R. Lawrence & Davis Dyer (1983), *Renewing American Industry: Organizing for Efficiency and Innovation* (New York: Free Press), 257, 325. Copyright 1983. Reprinted with permission of The Free Press, a Division of Simon & Schuster, Inc.

TABLE 17.2 Data on environmental uncertainty, effectiveness, differentiation, and integration in three industries

Environment	Financial effectiveness rank of firms	Extent of differentiation		Effectiveness of integration	
		Rank	Score	Rank	Score
Plastics industry	1	4	8.7	2	5.6
(Relatively uncertain;	2	1	9.4	1	5.7
considerable diversity of	3	5	7.5	3	5.3
uncertainty)	4	2.5	9.0	4	5.1
	5	6	6.3	6	4.7
	6	2.5	9.0	5	4.9
Foods industry	1	1	8.0	1	5.3
(Relatively uncertain;	2	2	6.5	2	5.0
considerable diversity of uncertainty)					
Containers industry	1	1.5	5.7	1	5.7
(Low to medium	2	1.5	5.7	2	4.8
uncertainty; less diversity of uncertainty)					

SOURCE: Adapted from Paul R. Lawrence & Jay W. Lorsch (1967), *Organization and Environment: Managing Differentiation and Integration* (Boston: Graduate School of Business Administration, Harvard University), 50, 103

found to operate in a more homogeneous environment of medium to low uncertainty throughout.

Table 17.2 contains the results of the research insofar as differentiation and integration are concerned. In the plastics industry, differentiation should be highly correlated with financial effectiveness; it is not. However, the relationship between differentiation and effectiveness in the foods industry is as hypothesized, although a somewhat higher differentiation score might have been expected in the more successful firm. In the containers industry, differentiation is low, but the anticipated difference in financial effectiveness does not emerge. Thus, the more successful company does not fit its environment any better than the less successful. These data do not strongly support the differentiation hypotheses, even though the authors cite more impressionistic findings that do.

The results involving integration are different. The findings are in accord with the theory for the plastics industry, and to a somewhat lesser degree for the foods industry. But in the more certain containers industry the original theory would have predicted that success would be associated with low integration. This is clearly not the case. The data from all three industries are consistent with the view that integration helps performance, and this appears to be true irrespective of any possible contingencies introduced by environmental uncertainty.

The major role of integrating units and individuals is hypothesized to be resolving conflicts among functional departments. These conflicts were expected to be greatest in more effective firms in highly uncertain environments; thus the influence of integrators should be greater there. The data indicate, however, that integrator influence was high in all six plastics firms, irrespective of performance level. This appears consistent with the similarity of differentiation scores among these firms.

The findings do suggest that integrators in the more successful plastics firms tend to be intermediate with regard to goal, time, and interpersonal orientations, as well as formality of structure between the functional departments they integrate. They are also more likely to feel rewarded for resolving conflicts. There was a highly significant tendency for more effective plastics companies to use confrontation to resolve conflicts, although the smoothing over of differences was used less in these more effective firms. However, in the foods industry, confrontation was most pronounced in the low-performance company, and differences in smoothing scores were nonexistent. In the containers industry, the successful firm used both confrontation and smoothing more and forcing less.

Studies in Conglomerates and
the Paper Industry

The pilot study for research done among six multidivisional firms made use of two conglomerates (Lorsch, 1968). The research was then extended to include two more conglomerates and two paper companies. The divisions in all six firms handled different product lines (Lorsch & Allen, 1973). Data were collected by interviews and questionnaires.

Findings on the major theoretical variables are given in table 17.3 The data indicate that integrative effort cannot be substituted for integration in the theory; in fact, it is difficult to interpret these data in any manner. In a division-by-division analysis, integrative effort was correlated −.70 with differentiation, the reverse of what might have been expected.

Among the three effective firms, the first appears to fit the theory, the second is generally satisfactory though it lacks integration, and the third is too integrated and probably too differentiated to be as effective as it is in its homogeneous and clearly very certain environment. The fourth firm also requires low differentiation and integration, but its moderate success level would lead one to expect somewhat higher differentiation scores. The fifth firm has a performance pattern consistent with its uncertainty scores, but totally inconsistent with the degree of environmental diversity. The final firm exhibits the reverse pattern — the performance results fit well for diversity, but one would expect a higher level of performance, given the uncertainty level.

Overall, the data do not provide any greater support for environmental diversity as a contingency variable than for uncertainty. Any way one computes it, the theory fails in two instances, succeeds in two, and yields somewhat equivocal results in the other two. Generally the straight, noncontingent relationships between differentiation and integration scores and effectiveness appear considerably more promising than the contingency hypotheses. However, division-by-division analyses within the conglomerates yield a significant relationship ($p < .05$) for integration only (.62), not for differentiation. Across the two industrial environments it is clearly integration and not differentiation that is associated with success (Miner, 1979).

One problem with the Lorsch and Allen (1973) report is that a great volume of data is presented, but not necessarily in a manner that makes it easy to relate the findings to the theoretical hypotheses. However, confrontation of conflict is associated with effective integration as expected, and confrontation also is related positively to firm effectiveness. Smoothing had no relationship to effectiveness, and forcing predominated in the less effective firms. In general this indicates the value of rationality in decision making. High performance in both the conglomerates and paper firms was reported to be associated with the following:

1. Intermediate orientation toward time, goals, and interpersonal relations, and high influence of linking functions
2. Corporate-divisional influence balance

TABLE 17.3 Data on environments, effectiveness, differentiation, and integration based on rankings for six firms

| Firm no. | Environments | | Financial effectiveness | Differentiation | | Integration | | |
| | Diversity | Uncertainty | | Corporate-divisional | Total firm | Corporate-divisional | | Interdivisional effort |
						Actual	Effort	
1	1	1	1 (High)	3	1	1	6	5
2	3	3	2 (High)	1	2	4	5	6
3	4	5	3 (High)	2	4	2	2	1
4	5	6	4 (Moderate)	4	5	3	3	4
5	6	2	5 (Low)	6	6	6	1	3
6	2	4	6 (Low)	5	3	5	4	2

NOTE: Firms 1, 2, 5, and 6 are conglomerates; firms 3 and 4 are paper companies.

SOURCE: Adapted from Jay W. Lorsch & Stephen A. Allen (1973), *Managing Diversity and Interdependence: An Organizational Study of Multidivisional Firms* (Boston: Graduate School of Business Administration, Harvard University), 143, 153

3. Modes of resolving conflicts—the degree to which confrontation or problem solving was used
4. Overall quality of upward and downward information flows

These findings support the idea that integration is a source of effectiveness, but since the variables involved are not related to environmental characteristics, it is impossible to consider them in the context of contingency theory itself.

Studies in Manufacturing and Research and Development (R&D)

The pilot research for the Harvard study of manufacturing and R&D divisions in five companies was conducted in two container plants of a single company and in two communications research laboratories of another company (Morse & Lorsch, 1970). Subsequently the sample was extended to include a pair of plants that were manufacturing household appliances, two research laboratories that were working with proprietary drugs, and two medical technology laboratories (Lorsch & Morse, 1974). In each company pair, one installation was considered to be effective and the other less so. Certain early analyses of the relationship between uncertainty and personality considered only the four manufacturing plants and four of the research laboratories (Morse & Young, 1973). In addition to interviews and questionnaires, psychological tests were administered to a cross section of managers in the plants, and managers and professionals in the laboratories.

The manufacturing plants were originally selected to represent an environment of some certainty, and their mean score of 6.3 on the uncertainty measure supports this conclusion. In contrast, the research laboratories had a mean uncertainty score of 15.4. The two groups were sharply distinguished on this index.

If one contrasts the data of table 17.4 with the hypotheses embodied in table 17.1, some striking disparities appear. Effective plants do not have lower scores than the ineffective plants on the personality variables, and the effective laboratories do not have higher scores. The only differences associated with organizational effectiveness are the scores on the feeling of competence measures, and these are as hypothesized. Since those who work in the more effective systems presumably are more competent, a finding that they feel so is not unexpected.

What emerges from these data is a clear indication that people who work in research laboratories are more cognitively complex, more tolerant of ambiguity, more independent of authority, and more individualistic. Presumably, that is a function of some combination of self-selection, professional selection, and acculturation.

In the manufacturing plants, time orientation did not differentiate the effective and ineffective organizations—in both, the time orientation was short. But all other structure and process variables in table 17.1 did differentiate effective and ineffective organizations and in the predicted direction. The more effective plants had stronger technoeconomic goals, more formality of structure, greater influence at the top exercised in a more directive manner, a higher degree of coordination, and a greater use of confrontation to resolve conflicts.

In the research laboratories, the pattern is almost completely reversed, as suggested by the hypotheses of table 17.1. The more effective laboratories exhibit a longer time orientation, a greater commitment to scientific goals, less formality of structure, more influence at lower organizational levels, a more participative style, less coordination, and a greater use of confrontation. Clearly, success is associated with very different organizational characteristics in the research and manufacturing contexts.

These results say nothing about the original *organizational* theory of differentiation and integration. The data are for single subsystems only. Furthermore, being concurrent, they are subject to multiple explanations. Although the authors emphasize the role of the fit between environment and organization, the findings may be explained without recourse to the environmental level and thus to the dimension of certainty-uncertainty:

1. The effective research units appear to have relied strongly on professional norms to induce and control individual efforts toward goal achievement. The less effective research units appear to have confounded the already existing professional system of norms by adding in a sizable amount of hierarchic pressures as well. That this should create role conflict and lower performance levels is entirely consistent with research findings.
2. The effective manufacturing plants clearly place strong reliance on hierarchic authority to induce goal contributions. . . . The low-performing manufacturing plants are often

TABLE 17.4 Individual characteristics in effective and ineffective organizations in certain and uncertain environments

Individual characteristic	Certain (plants)		Uncertain (laboratories)		Certain total	Uncertain total
	Effective	Ineffective	Effective	Ineffective		
Cognitive complexity	4.2	4.2	5.2	5.2	(4.2	5.2)
Tolerance for ambiguity	2.6	2.5	2.9	2.9	(2.6	2.9)
Independence in authority relationships	2.2	2.1	2.8	2.9	(2.2	2.8)
Preference for working alone	2.4	2.4	3.0	3.0	(2.4	3.0)
Feeling of competence						
Measure 1	(1.2)	(.5)	(1.2)	(.2)	.8	.7
Measure 2	(2.4)	(1.2)	(2.3)	(1.0)	1.8	1.7

NOTE: Numbers in parentheses are statistically significant at $p < .05$ between effective and ineffective organizations.

SOURCE: Adapted from Jay W. Lorsch & John W. Morse (1974), *Organizations and Their Members: A Contingency Approach* (Boston: Graduate School of Business Administration, Harvard University), 40–41, 43–44, 53–55

characterized by a basically laissez-faire approach, where strong inducements of any kind are lacking. Extrapolation from research on leadership would indicate that just such performance problems should occur in a laissez-faire context.

3. On occasion low performance in the manufacturing context was associated with a confounding of a hierarchic authority system with an inducement system which made use of group norms and pressures (participative decision making of a kind) to induce contributions. Again, the potential for role conflict was sizable, and the likelihood that this contributed to the performance deficiencies considerable. (Miner, 1979, pp. 290–291)

Case Studies

In addition to the full-scale studies noted previously, Lorsch and Lawrence (1970) edited a volume of studies, primarily doctoral dissertations, dealing with contingency theory. Included are the pilot studies for the Lorsch and Allen (1973) and Lorsch and Morse (1974) investigations.

The remaining articles, to the extent they report research at all, are case studies of one or, at most, two organizations. Quantitative data are rarely included. Even though this volume provides considerable insight into the intellectual climate contingency theory created at Harvard during the 1960s, it does not contain any generalizable findings that bear directly on the contingency theory hypotheses. For this reason

the specific case studies are not considered individually here.

There is, however, one exception, among the Harvard studies of that period, which did report new and relevant quantitative results. Eric Neilsen (1974) studied two rather small firms that were using the Lawrence and Lorsch measures and reported his findings in quantitative terms. Both firms were highly effective, but one faced an environment that was more uncertain and, at the same time, contained a greater diversity of uncertainty levels. This greater uncertainty and diversity would have been expected to elicit more differentiation and integration to achieve such high effectiveness, but it did not. Overall, the two firms were equally differentiated. On the integration measures the firm that was facing the somewhat more certain and less diverse environment scored the highest. Since actual effectiveness data are not given, one cannot say whether this greater integration was related to better financial results. In any event, the pattern of the findings does not fit theoretical expectations.

Industry Studies

The Lawrence and Dyer (1983) book is devoted in large part to a set of historical studies about the development of the auto, steel, hospital, agriculture, residential construction, coal, and telecommunications industries in America. Davis Dyer is a historian, and the analyses are well done. But they are not scientific research; no original data are included, and conclusions are drawn through judgments based on secondary sources. The results of these industry studies are the findings of figure 17.6, and the variants of hypothesis 4. This is a perfectly appropriate use of qualitative research to generate theory.

Support for the propositions and hypotheses of the extended theory derives not only from the industry studies, but from extensive literature reviews. Again, however, the objective is theory generation, not theory testing. Such constructs as information complexity and resource scarcity remain unmeasured; only judgments of their levels are contained in the industry studies. Operationalizing the variables of the extended theory is admitted to be a difficult task and it is left to others. Thus, in the end, the theory simply is not tested by its authors.

Lawrence and Dyer recognize the problem here. In fact, at the very end of their book they report on an attempt to develop systematic ratings of the components of information complexity and resource scarcity on a scale of 0 to 2. These ratings were made for various key periods in the development of each industry and for the time of the study (1981). Of this effort at a more systematized approach the authors say:

> The mental gymnastics we went through in assigning these scores were complex, and in the last analysis they represent a series of judgments. It is interesting, however, to compare ratings made in this manner with the broader judgments we had earlier made for each industry. . . . The correspondence . . . is fairly close and the deviations are interesting. . . . The correspondence is strong enough to suggest that further measurement work in this direction is warranted. (Lawrence & Dyer, 1983, pp. 333–334)

These efforts are worthy of applause. One could only hope that more had been done, with applications to new samples and appropriate attention to psychometric properties.

Applications of the Theory

From its beginnings contingency theory of organization has been closely tied to application. The original studies were part of organizational change programs that were first described in an article written in 1965, though not published until later (Lorsch & Lawrence, 1969). The theory rapidly became associated with the organization development movement (Lawrence &

Lorsch, 1969). In general, Lorsch remained involved in the development of such applications (Lorsch, 1977). Lawrence increasingly focused on the development of matrix organization structures, which, although they are in no sense a derivative of contingency theory, fit well with the differentiation and integration concepts (Davis & Lawrence, 1977).

Applications in
Organization Development

The approach taken in the initial change programs is described as follows:

> Our general approach, then, has been to spend considerable time and effort through the use of questionnaires, and a systematic interviewing program in gathering data to be analyzed in terms of a conceptual framework developed in our research efforts [contingency theory]. Having collected and analyzed these data we have then educated management to our conceptual scheme and have fed the data back to them, working through with them the meanings and the limitations of the data. The managers themselves have worked out whatever structural changes seemed required and have collaborated with us in the formulation of specific development programs to alleviate specific reorganizational problems. (Lorsch & Lawrence, 1969, p. 471)

One frequently mentioned type of specific development program is a training effort in which members of differentiated departments are brought together for the purpose of gaining a better understanding of each other's roles. The objective is to confront sources of conflict and attempt to resolve them through mutual understanding (Lawrence & Lorsch, 1967c; Lorsch & Lawrence, 1969). In general, these descriptions deal with the high differentiation and integration situation that is associated with high uncertainty. Although it is recognized that an environmental fit may require little differentiation or integration and that a change toward such a situation may also be facilitated through training, little attention is given to this type of contingency. It clearly is not what the authors are interested in.

Dealing with Interfaces

For purposes of organization development there are three important interfaces: organization-environment, group-group, and individual-organization (Lawrence & Lorsch, 1969). First, sources of uncertainty in the environment and the needs of organization members are diagnosed and a picture of what the organization should be is drawn up. Then data are obtained on existing differentiation levels, integration methods, conflict resolution processes, and sources of dissatisfaction. By comparing what is with what should be, one can obtain a blueprint for change that is tailored to the specific organization.

To initiate change at the organization-environment interface, many different approaches may be employed, ranging from training, to internal realignments of departments, to major structural reorganizations. Realignments and reorganizations are intended to overcome pressures for consistency across departments, to adjust unit differentiation to changes in the environment, to create new departments to cope with new environmental elements, and to adapt to growth. At this interface the major goal is the appropriate type and degree of differentiation. As a result, a major structural intervention may be introduced at an early stage of the organization development program, rather than after extensive process interventions, as in most other approaches to organization development.

However, once appropriate differentiation is achieved, there arises a need to effect integration and collaboration among the diverse elements. The basic sequence of activities is diagnosis, design, action planning, implementation, and evaluation. Diagnostic data are fed back to organization members in much the same manner as they are with other organization development approaches. This typically eventuates in a *differentiation laboratory* that is designed to provide understanding of the varying outlooks of different units. It is focused on the group-group interface and constitutes both action planning and implementation. Business games may also be used for this purpose. The intended outcome is the development of new behavior patterns that will facilitate collaboration and integration.

The authors contrast their contingent approach at this interface to the more universalistic approach of other practitioners:

> They argue that all organizations need . . . the development of trust and understanding between groups and the confrontation of conflict. . . . Our model also leads us to see confrontation of conflict as necessary. Where we differ from these other practitioners is in placing emphasis on the requirement for other conflict-management variables which

are contingent on environmental demands; on the required state of differentiation; and also on the design of appropriate structural devices for achieving integration. They focus on educational interventions which emphasize face-to-face group process and interpersonal skill. We recognize these as important, but again would go further. . . . We have also used diagnostic data and have encouraged managers to use other means to alter expectations and behavior (i.e., formal organizational changes, redefinition of tasks, and other educational techniques). (Lawrence & Lorsch, 1969, pp. 58–59)

As application moves to the individual-organization interface, it abandons contingency theory as its conceptual base and begins to draw more heavily on the views of another Harvard-based theorist, David McClelland (see chapter 6 in this volume).

Organization Development Extensions

In his writing during the 1970s Lorsch tended to emphasize the implications of theory and research for applications, rather than additional approaches to organization development. Lorsch and Allen (1973) deal with differentiation within the hierarchy (decentralization), as well as with differentiation among functional departments. In Lorsch and Morse (1974), concepts from achievement motivation theory are replaced with other individual constructs such as cognitive complexity, tolerance for ambiguity, and independence in authority relationships in matters that involve the individual-organization interface. These books contain some interesting chapters on applications in the areas of organizational structure and process, but little is said about specific procedures and techniques. Almost every statement follows directly from the theory.

After greater experience in undertaking organization development applications, Lorsch (1977) seems less inclined to rely on precise measurement instruments and more favorably disposed toward diagnosis based on clinical insights derived from top-level interviews. He also emphasizes that organizational design changes must be congruent with the preferences of top management to be effectively implemented. Finally, changes must be consistent with each other so that they all move toward the same objective. All too often, changes prove to be offsetting, and nothing actually happens.

Though the change sequence proposed includes an evaluation phase, little has been done to determine the effectiveness of the contingency approach to organization development. The authors cite case studies in support of their procedures but offer no solid evaluation research of a longitudinal nature.

In recent years neither Lawrence nor Lorsch has been a contributor to the literature on organization development. The approaches they proposed are certainly part of many practitioners' armamentaria but activities such as redesigning organization structures are not at the forefront of organization development practice (Church, Burke, & Van Eynde, 1994). Over the years, contingency theory — with its emphasis on structural change and the consideration of environmental factors before undertaking an intervention — has been popular with practitioners in organization development (Bazigos & Burke, 1997). However, there appears to have been some falloff as a source of undergirding for practice in the more recent period; in fact, systemwide theories in general have exhibited limited attractiveness. Furthermore, knowledge of contingency theory of organizations among managers overall does not appear to be at a high level at the present time (Priem & Rosenstein, 2000).

Introducing Matrix Organization

In a sense, contingency theory of organization has adopted matrix organization; certainly it did not create it. The matrix structure was noted in the early theoretical publications as congruent with the needs created by a highly uncertain environment, but later Lawrence focused major attention on the matrix form (Davis & Lawrence, 1977, 1978; Lawrence, Kolodny, & Davis, 1977). In these writings matrix is defined as "any organization that employs a *multiple command system* that includes not only a multiple command structure but also related support mechanisms and an associated organizational culture and behavior pattern" (see Davis & Lawrence, 1977, p. 3).

The value of the matrix form is inherent in its potential for greater flexibility in responding to environmental pressures. Since environments vary in the pressures they produce, there are conditions under which matrix organization may not be needed, or may even be dysfunctional. Accordingly, one would not expect to find this type of structure emerging in all organizations.

There are three conditions (all of which must be present) under which the matrix is the preferred mode. First, two or more critical sectors such as functions, products, services, markets, or geographical areas must be highly salient for goal accomplishment at the same time. Second, the need to perform uncertain, complex, and interdependent tasks must exist so that a sizable information-processing capacity is required. Third, there must be a need to realize economies of scale by using scarce human resources effectively.

Although these conditions are not specified in terms of contingency theory, they clearly assume a complex, uncertain, and perhaps highly competitive environment. The theory would posit a need for differentiation to process various types of information and for integration to coordinate the differentiation. The matrix organization contains both. Such an organization is specified, as one would expect from contingency theory, in terms of not only its structure but also its systems, culture, and behaviors — just as differentiation is.

The matrix emerges from the classical pyramidal form in which all members have one boss. In the next phase a temporary overlay is added to the functional structure in the form of project management. Typically these projects do not contain their own resources and draw on a variety of outside sources for this purpose. The key aspects of organization are a project manager, decentralized resource support, and centralized planning and control. Clearly the project aspect is not yet the coequal of the functional.

In phase three the overlay becomes permanent, with a product or brand manager whose task is to maintain product viability in the marketplace and stable membership. Yet the overlay is still complementary to functional organization. Finally, in the mature matrix, a dual authority relationship emerges in which the power is balanced. There are two bosses representing two bases of organization. Typically these are function and product, but other bases may be used, even to the point of extending the matrix beyond two dimensions. The key roles are top leadership, which actually is outside the matrix, matrix managers who share subordinates with other matrix managers, and subordinate managers, who have two bosses.

Matrix forms involve increased interdependencies and thus increased communication and opportunity for conflict. As in contingency theory, confrontation is proposed as the best method of dealing with this conflict. The matrix structure requires collaboration to function, and the key ingredient for collaboration is said to be trust.

All this means that new patterns of behavior must be learned if people are to function effectively in the new structure. This is facilitated through a team-banding process that may have a staff professional or a process consultant in the role of catalyst. Team-building meetings are held that appear to have much in common with the differentiation laboratories previously discussed. These are aimed at identifying expectations and dealing with such matters as objectives, frequency of meetings, leadership, roles and responsibilities, decision modes, communication and conflict resolution patterns, and interpersonal problems.

In addition to such group procedures there is a need for individual development to provide knowledge and skills relevant to the matrix form. A training program for matrix managers involving skill training, experiential learning, and team building is recommended. The elements are as follows:

1. Knowledge input about matrix organizations and information about why their organization is adopting matrix. This would include top management's philosophy.
2. Lecture, discussion, and exercises about effective communication and group process.
3. Lecture and exercises on concepts and techniques relevant to the kind of business problem solving expected.
4. A simulation in which individuals are randomly placed in groups and given a business task. Each member is given a role to play and each experiences directly the problem of making and implementing decisions. Each examines the experience with the help of a trainer and learns from it.
5. The actual teams are brought together to work on a number of exercises to create a low-risk setting for self-examination and learning.
6. A team-building meeting is conducted, with a professional, as a process consultant, to go over the important startup questions. (Davis & Lawrence, 1977, p. 113)

At this point implementation of the matrix takes on many qualities of traditional organization development.

Potential Problems with Matrix

Many things can go wrong in organizations as they move to the matrix structure (Davis & Lawrence, 1978). A state of confusion may develop where no clear lines of authority are recognized (anarchy). An excessive amount of conflict related to a state of free-floating power (power struggles) may emerge. Matrix management may become equated with group decision making to an inappropriate degree (severe groupitis). Under conditions of business decline, the matrix may be blamed for what is in fact poor management and may be eliminated (collapse during economic crunch). Failure to realize possible economies of scale may occur, with the result that costs become excessive (excessive overhead). The matrix structure may gravitate from the higher levels of the organization downward, so that it exists only at the group and division levels (sinking to lower levels). Matrices within matrices within matrices often develop out of power fights rather than the logic of design (uncontrolled layering). Internal preoccupations may become so compelling that contact with the realities of the market is lost (navel gazing). There may be so much democracy that action is not taken when needed (decision strangulation).

These problems can be overcome if the organization is aware of them, but to some extent they are inherent in the form itself. To these must be added the very real possibility of major role conflicts (see chapter 14).

Research Evidence on Matrix

With the exception of their own work in several medical centers, the authors cite practically no research on the matrix form. Even the authors' medical center research does not actually test the matrix form (Charns, Lawrence, & Weisbord, 1977; Weisbord, Lawrence, & Charns, 1978).

Interviews and questionnaires explicitly based on contingency theory were administered in nine medical centers. Differentiation and integration were found to be inadequate to environmental demands. Differences associated with technical specialties (departments) and functions (M.D. education, Ph.D. education, internship and residency training, research, and patient care) were in evidence, but there was considerable blurring in perceptions of them. Confrontation was not widely used to resolve conflicts.

The three conditions for the use of matrix organization appeared to be present. Greater differentiation and integration were needed, and the matrix form seemed to be an ideal method of accomplishing this. However, the research did not relate differentiation and integration measures to the effectiveness of the centers. Nor is there a report on the consequences of introducing a matrix structure. In essence, the research stops at the diagnostic stage, and the implications drawn must be accepted on the basis of faith in the underlying contingency theory and in the matrix application of it.

Although extensively used in organizations, matrix structures have not been extensively tested by anyone; the problem is not unique to those who approach the matter from a contingency theory perspective. Even today there is still much to learn about what makes for a successful application (Ford & Randolph, 1992). What research has been done suggests that the contingency theorists were wrong in positing a developmental sequence as the matrix evolves. Rather, the form appears to be structurally stable once it is introduced (Burns & Wholey, 1993). However, consistent with the contingency view, the matrix structure does appear to be introduced to meet problems of increased diversity.

The problems inherent in the matrix form take on added concerns because the result appears to be that contingency theory is pitted against the Katz and Kahn theory of the social psychology of organizations and its subcomponent of role processes. It would appear that matrix organization can yield considerable role conflict and ambiguity, as might be expected, and that negative consequences such as increased anxiety levels can be anticipated. Whether other advantages such as increased flexibility outweigh these negative considerations and whether the role conflict can be neutralized under certain circumstances simply are not known. At present and as things stand, we have a situation in which contingency theory appears to advocate an approach that is essentially untested in any scientific sense, against the opposition of role theory, which has been widely tested and supported.

Introducing the Readaptive Process

The Lawrence and Dyer (1983) formulations have not produced applications on nearly the same scale as the organization development and matrix approaches.

Essentially what is advocated is that companies take steps to engage in readaptation and move to an area 5 environment if they are not already there and to keep themselves in area 5 if they are there. Examples of the authors' experiences in working with companies to accomplish these outcomes are not provided, but certain general implications of the theory for managerial action are set forth:

1. Although organizations can get by for a time being only efficient or only innovative, over the long term there must be a simultaneous achievement of both efficiency and innovation.

2. Achieving and sustaining readaptive results is difficult for an organization, but it is by no means impossible.

3. Member involvement is essential to the simultaneous achievement of both efficiency and innovation.

4. The current circumstances of any given organization determine what particular actions will best foster readaptation.

5. Overall, both industry and government have a part to play in any drive toward achieving strong readaptive outcomes; the degree and nature of the initiative each takes will depend on the particular environmental pressures and possibilities of a given situation.

6. Readaptation can be achieved only if industry as well as government see their goals in terms of concrete sources of wealth rather than in terms of money which is only a symbol for wealth.

7. If both government and industry are aware that intermediate levels of resource scarcity and information complexity favor readaptation, the destructive suspicion and animosity usually associated with debate on broad economic issues will be significantly lessened and the focus of discussion turned to questions amenable to constructive solution.

8. In addition to being production systems, organizations have great potential for being learning and social systems as well.

9. In their efforts to achieve innovation and efficiency, managers who understand the readaptive process can identify and employ a wide variety of organizational mechanisms that may not have been recognized or fully utilized.

10. Industrial managers and government offi-

cials who achieve readaptive results perform a difficult and valuable service that deserves recognition. (Lawrence & Dyer, 1983, pp. 267–269)

These are certainly not specific guidelines for action. They are informed by the industry studies and the theory, not hands-on experience. Yet they are a useful first approximation and can help to provide managers with a way of thinking about problems.

Evaluation and Impact

The Harvard research suffers from a potential source of contamination in moving from pilot study to theory to a research test that included the pilot data. The research considered now does not suffer from this problem.

Early Research on Measurement and Construct Validity

The initial methodological analyses of the Lawrence and Lorsch (1967c) environmental uncertainty operationalization were carried out on a sample of managers at the middle and top levels (Tosi, Aldag, & Storey, 1973). The overall reliability of the scale was found to be .51, and the subscale values were .11 for research, .38 for manufacturing, and .52 for marketing. These values are low but not surprising, considering the shortness of the instrument.

To get at construct validity, measures of volatility in the external environment were established from the range of fluctuations over a 10-year period. Technological, income, and sales volatility measures were calculated for the industry as a whole and for the firm in which each manager-respondent worked. The correlations between the uncertainty scale and these measures of actual environmental variation were uniformly low and, to the extent they were statistically significant, negative. A reanalysis of specific functions and their relevant environments did little to improve the degree or direction of the correlations.

In reply, Lawrence and Lorsch (1973) argue that the volatility measures do not tap what they meant by uncertainty and that the Tosi et al. (1973) findings do not adequately reflect construct validity. Furthermore, the theorists note that they confirmed the results from the uncertainty scale in other ways in their research and that the subjects in the study by Tosi et al. were

not the best qualified to complete the scale. Overall, the results of this first methodological investigation appear to be a standoff, but they raise serious questions about scale reliability and the degree of match between uncertainty as perceived by managers and as reflected in the actual environment.

Lawrence and Lorsch (1967c) clearly use a measure of uncertainty as perceived by organizational decision makers, but in this early period they viewed the measure as roughly equivalent to the external circumstances and thus as providing a proxy for some not-easily-obtained objective index. Others have tended to emphasize the perceptual aspects more and the realities of the environment somewhat less, while noting that individual characteristics may also play a role in uncertainty perception (Downey & Slocum, 1975).

Kirk Downey, Don Hellriegel, and John Slocum (1975) report low reliabilities for the uncertainty scale as utilized by Lawrence and Lorsch among the division managers of a conglomerate. They also analyzed industry volatility data and the managers' perceptions of a number of variables such as competition that are related to uncertainty. Overall, the data provide no evidence of construct validity. Even an alternative measure of the Lawrence and Lorsch uncertainty construct proved to be unrelated to the original scale. Nevertheless, in an extension of this study the authors found that a specific characteristic of the individual manager—the degree of cognitive complexity—was positively associated with the perception of uncertainty (Downey, Hellriegel, & Slocum, 1977).

Other data indicate a more positive relationship between perceived uncertainty and environmental aspects—change rate, in particular, but also complexity and routineness (Tung, 1979). However, all these variables were measured by one questionnaire administered at one time to one individual per organizational unit. The possibility that common method variance may have confounded the results cannot be excluded. Thus these results require further external substantiation before they can be accepted, especially in view of conflicting findings from other studies.

It becomes increasingly clear that individual differences can influence perceptions of uncertainty. One laboratory study developed evidence that preexisting tolerance for ambiguity can be an important determinant of these perceptions (McCaskey, 1976). The following quotation raises important new questions regarding contingency theory relationships:

A person high in tolerance for ambiguity may take the same situation and make it into something more complex and uncertain than a person low in tolerance for ambiguity does. . . . Organization members seem to adjust the level of environmental uncertainty they perceive to fit their own needs for stimulation and closure. People more tolerant of ambiguity seem to want the challenge of working with greater uncertainty, even to the point of creating it themselves. For some jobs, for some organizations, greater tolerance for ambiguity is desirable. In other cases, if high tolerance for ambiguity people see and maybe create uncertainty even in relatively well-defined situations, high tolerance for ambiguity can be dysfunctional. (McCaskey, 1976, p. 75)

Processes such as these, if they operate among top-level executives, could create havoc for the hypotheses of the Lawrence and Lorsch theory simply because environmental uncertainty (as perceived) now becomes a function of what the individual desires.

Although the operationalization of environmental uncertainty has been the focus of most concerns about the Lawrence and Lorsch (1967c) measures, there have been other such measurement problems as well. Louis Fry, Aryeh Kidron, Richard Osborn, and Richard Trafton (1980), for example, conducted analyses of the scale used to differentiate conflict resolution methodologies into confrontation, smoothing, and forcing approaches. They were unable to replicate the Lawrence and Lorsch findings and concluded that the scale does not provide valid and reliable measures of conflict resolution modes.

Evolving Conceptualization of Environmental Uncertainty

Given the confusion surrounding the uncertainty construct in the 1970s, it would not have been surprising to find work on the subject virtually abandoned in the 1980s and 1990s. Yet this has not happened. We know that Lawrence was still trying to refine his own views in the early 1980s, and others have continued to make contributions since then (Bluedorn, 1993). There has been some real progress, although not always of a kind that supports the Lawrence and Lorsch theory and measurement.

Several researchers, notably Gregory Dess and Donald Beard (1984) and Mark Sharfman and James Dean (1991), have developed useful objective measures of various components of environmental uncertainty. Certain of these measures appear to tap variables very much like the information complexity and resource scarcity constructs posited by Lawrence and Dyer (1983). However, there is always the possibility that a theorist will disavow an operationalization advanced by others, and, in fact, this sort of thing has occurred with regard to some of the objective uncertainty indices that have been developed (Dess & Rasheed, 1991). We need to hear from Lawrence and Lorsch with their reactions to these new measures; to date, they have been silent on the subject. Position statements from the theorists are particularly needed in view of the divergences among the various objective measures.

Lawrence and Dyer (1983) in their hypotheses 5.1 and 5.2 clearly indicate that perceived environmental uncertainty may be distorted in the perceptual process. Thus they would appear to be opting for objective indices. Yet Lawrence and Lorsch (1967c) used a measure of perceived uncertainty. Work in this latter area has resulted in the differentiation of various types, in much the same manner as objective uncertainty has been differentiated. Under such a scheme the Lawrence and Lorsch measure has been identified with *effect* uncertainty, whereby difficulty is experienced in predicting what the impact of environmental events on the organization might be (Milliken, 1987). However, others have seemed to view the same measure as more an index of *state* uncertainty, where one does not understand how components of the environment might be changing (Miller & Shamsie, 1999). There seems to be a great deal of uncertainty about what the original Lawrence and Lorsch uncertainty construct is.

In general, scale reliabilities in the perceptual area have been low, as were those for the Lawrence and Lorsch scale (Buchko, 1994). Construct validity has been a continuing problem. It appears that using a measure of perceived environmental uncertainty as a proxy for objective reality (as Lawrence and Lorsch did) is not warranted in most cases (Boyd, Dess, & Rasheed, 1993; Boyd & Fulk, 1996). The correlations tend to be marginal at best, and sometimes nonexistent, although if sources of distortion in perceptions can be minimized, this does help. There is no reason to believe that the Lawrence and Lorsch measure was particularly effective in this latter regard.

All in all, even though both the conceptualization and measurement of environmental uncertainty have seen sizable improvements, this has done little to improve the situation insofar as contingency theory is concerned. We still have what appears to be a poor measure as far as the Lawrence and Lorsch (1967c) index is concerned, and no measure at all for the Lawrence and Dyer (1983) constructs.

Research Yielding Partial Theoretical Support

There is little research that might be considered a true replication of the Harvard studies. One exception is a study conducted in three banks that follows the original Lawrence and Lorsch (1967c) design closely (Herbert & Matthews, 1977). In general, data at the subunit level for operations, customer service, and marketing are compatible with expectations. As a group, the banks operate in a moderately uncertain environment—below the plastics industry but by no means as certain as containers—and the marketing environment appears particularly uncertain. In this context one would expect moderate degrees of both differentiation and integration to yield financial success.

In actuality, the most successful bank was the least differentiated but the most integrated. The differentiation level of this high performer might well be theoretically appropriate, and the low-performing bank's high differentiation excessive, as the authors suggest. Yet the uncertainty score for the low performer was right up with the plastics firms, suggesting a possible need for its high differentiation. Differentiation and integration ranks were perfectly negatively correlated across the three banks, and in this instance, as in prior studies, it was integration that was correlated positively with success. The parsimonious explanation is that effective integration contributes to success, that differentiation matters little, and that environmental uncertainty as measured is not relevant.

In a series of widely cited studies Robert Duncan attempted to add a greater degree of precision to the uncertainty construct and to investigate various methods of adaptation. In the process Duncan (1972) developed a new measure of uncertainty that differentiated simple-complex and static-dynamic dimensions of the environment. He found, as hypothesized, that perceived uncertainty was greatest where the environment was experienced as dynamic and complex. Of the two environmental components, the static-dynamic contributed more to the perception of uncertainty. However, the

uncertainty measure used, though conceptually similar to the measure used by Lawrence and Lorsch, does not appear to be closely related empirically (Downey et al., 1975). Furthermore, Downey et al. were unable to replicate Duncan's findings on the role of the simple-complex dimension in perceived environmental uncertainty.

Duncan (1973) also studied structural differences at the subunit level (not the total organization) as related to environmental uncertainty. He found that when uncertainty was high, the more effective units were more likely to use different structures to deal with routine and nonroutine decisions. Thus there was differentiation within the same department. Though consistent with the perspective of Lawrence and Lorsch, this finding clearly goes beyond their actual theoretical statements. As anticipated, uncertainty was associated with a less-structured hierarchy of authority, more participation, fewer rules and procedures, and less division of labor for nonroutine decisions (Duncan, 1974).

In another study Anant Negandhi and Bernard Reimann (1973) considered 30 diverse manufacturing firms that were operating under pervasive growth-market conditions in India. Construing the environment as stable and relatively certain overall, and extrapolating from contingency theory of organization, the authors hypothesized that centralization of decision making would be associated with organizational effectiveness. However, the results showed just the reverse: there was a marked tendency for the decentralized firms to be more effective. In the more effective firms, decentralization was particularly likely to be accompanied by formalized systems to handle manpower planning, employee selection, compensation, appraisal, and training (Reimann & Negandhi, 1975).

Although the results discussed here provide little support for contingency theory, an analysis in terms of market competition yields somewhat more favorable results (Negandhi & Reimann, 1972). Under competitive circumstances, decentralization was strongly associated with effectiveness. However, a significant though smaller relationship of the same kind was found under conditions of little competition. The authors interpret this as a reflection of the cultural context in India, thus adding another contingency variable to the theory.

Research conducted in Mexico and Italy yields support for the original theory without the need for cultural modification (Simonetti & Boseman, 1975). In Italy decentralization was related positively to economic effectiveness in competitive markets and negatively under conditions of minimal competition. No significant differences were found in Mexico under limited competition; only the positive relationship between decentralization and effectiveness with high competition was significant.

Working from an initial finding that companies operating under conditions of high environmental uncertainty tended to use uncertainty reduction mechanisms such as staff services and vertical integration extensively, Pradip Khandwalla (1972, 1973) correlated these uncertainty-related variables with various indices of differentiation and integration for high- and low-profit firms. Though the measures of variables are different from those of Lawrence and Lorsch, in part because they were obtained from a mail survey, there is enough conceptual similarity to view the research as relevant for contingency theory. Under that theory one would expect higher levels of uncertainty to be compensated with greater differentiation and integration in the more effective firms, but not in the less effective.

The data of table 17.5 yield mixed support for that expectation. As in other studies, uncertainty relates to decentralization, but the additional relationship to profitability is minimal. Only in the case of the vertical integration index can structural differentiation be said to be functional in the face of uncertainty. With regard to integration, the use of team decision making at the top level, and not the use of sophisticated controls, follows the theory. In this sense, uncertainty, coupled with integration, is associated with profitability; a lack of association is not. The total theory—that uncertainty requires differentiation and then, in turn, integration to produce effectiveness—appears to be supported in 2 of 12 variable sets. Neither differentiation nor integration appears to be related consistently in a noncontingent manner to effectiveness. However, such noncontingent relationships do appear to exist for the decentralization measure of differentiation and the controls measure of integration—two of the five indices.

Research That Is Nonsupportive

I have presented the partially supportive research in some detail because the various studies are supportive in different ways, and understanding the research approach is a necessary precondition for understanding the findings. In the case of nonsupportive studies this more comprehensive approach is not needed, the tests of contingency theory simply do not yield support, and there are a goodly number of these studies.

Johannes Pennings (1975), for example, studied 40 brokerage offices of a single firm and found no evidence of a tie between various uncertainty-related environmental variables, indices of structure, and effectiveness. The environmental measures exhibited no consistent relationship with structure, and with uncertainty no relationship at all; neither did these variables relate to effectiveness. However, structure alone was closely tied to effectiveness:

TABLE 17.5 Relationships of uncertainty with differentiation and integration indexes in firms with varying profitability

| | Uncertainty index | | | |
| | Use of staff services | | Vertical integration | |
Organizational variables	Profit high	Profit low	Profit high	Profit low
Differentiation indexes				
Decentralization	.56*	.51*	.55*	.31*
Functional departmentalization	.07	−.07	.36*	−.09
Divisionalization	.57*	.32*	.28*	−.01
Integration indexes				
Use of sophisticated controls	.34*	.30*	.22	.33*
Participative management at the top level	.43*	.00	.38*	.00

*Values statistically significant (p .05 or better).

SOURCE: Adapted from Pradip N. Khandwalla (1973), Viable and Effective Organizational Designs of Firms, *Academy of Management Journal*, 16, 490

If the employees of the organization were left on their own, did not share ideas, were not informationally integrated, did not participate in decisions, and did not receive support, the effectiveness on any criterion will be below average. This is probably the best single statement that could summarize the relationship between structural variables and effectiveness. . . . From the results obtained, one questions the usefulness of the structural-contingency model. (Pennings, 1975, p. 405)

Barbara Keats and Michael Hitt describe their results, in the one area where significance was obtained, from a comprehensive study of manufacturing firms as follows:

Firms in this study that had unstable, and thus uncertain, environments reacted by divesting businesses and developing a simpler structure. . . . The decision focus among the firms was on the reduction of uncertainty by retreating to a better-understood environment and creating a simpler organization rather than on risk reduction through increasing diversification. (1988, p. 587)

Elsewhere these authors say:

Although early theorists argued that firms' structures should become more complex in the face of volatile environments (e.g. Lawrence and Lorsch), the results of this study suggest that firms develop simpler, more centralized structures when facing unstable environments. However, the differences between this study and earlier work might relate to differences in construct definition and measurement. (p. 590)

In this study neither complexity nor resource scarcity exhibited any relationships in support of theory.

Authors' Current Views

On several occasions Lawrence or both authors together have offered comments on their previous contingency theory work. Lawrence (1987) notes that the early enthusiasm evoked by the theory has waned. Further, he feels that the contingency approach overall can be extremely variable in its effectiveness. At the low end are attempts to specify every possible contingency; such multicontingency formulations serve only to trivialize and are not useful. At the high end are broadly powerful uniformities of the kind that

the Lawrence and Lorsch theory and its elaborations attempt; this alternative may provide somewhat less universal propositions, but in the appropriate domains it can be very useful for practice.

Later Lawrence and Lorsch (1991) reiterate that their theory's influence is waning, not because it has been refuted but because it is aging. In general they feel that contingency theory has been supported by the bulk of the research that followed it. They note that problems have been identified in their environmental uncertainty measure. However, this is not a crucial failure since other evidence supported their conclusion in this area: "We . . . hope that someone with a greater interest and aptitude for instrument development than ourselves will undertake the difficult task of developing a better instrument" (p. 492).

Lawrence, in his autobiography (Lawrence & Lawrence, 1993), continues to reiterate his belief in the basic validity of contingency theory. He feels that the new, extended version of contingency theory presented in the book with Dyer has been underappreciated, a judgment with which I would concur.

Unfortunately, nowhere in these commentaries is there a detailed, systematic response to the developing literature related to contingency theory. Yet I must concur with the theory's authors in their belief that the theory represents a major contribution to the field of organizational behavior. It introduces several advances over its sister theory, the technological imperative. For one thing, it deals with organizational subunits and their environments separately, thus avoiding the pitfalls of organizational averaging and abstractions; differentiated subunits are, in fact, a major component of the theory. Second, it addresses the problem of achieving organized effort toward goals through the introduction of the integration concept. This concept in one form or another has shown much promise in organization theory. Finally, contingency theory has spawned and lent support to applications, which though inadequately tested have the merit of bridging the gap between theory and practice. To this list others have made a number of additions (see, for example, Bluedorn, 1991). However, these three strike me as particularly important against the backdrop of other theories that use the systems and contingency approach.

Status of Environmental Uncertainty

In one respect, however, contingency theory exhibits much the same vulnerability as technological imperative theory, and that is in the area of its contingency variable. Environmental uncertainty suffers from most of the difficulties that technology does, plus a few of its own. The overwhelming problem is that of construct validity. What is uncertainty? It is not environmental change, as the mechanistic-organic formulations might suggest, because with improvements in forecasting techniques, many changes have become highly predictable and thus no longer a source of uncertainty. Uncertainty is not environmental diversity either, as some extensions to contingency theory might suggest. On logical as well as empirical grounds this equation breaks down. Under conditions of high uncertainty across all organizational subunits, uncertainty is at a maximum, but diversity (at least on the uncertainty variable) is low.

Contingency theory has been criticized for confusing internal technological uncertainty with its external environmental counterpart and for inappropriately equating subjective and objective uncertainty. Though the scope of the uncertainty variable Lawrence and Lorsch envisaged may well have been so great as to make it unmanageable, the greatest difficulties seem to revolve around the perceived uncertainty concept. Empirically it has proved almost impossible to demonstrate construct validity, and unreliable measures have emerged often enough to suggest an underlying ambiguity in the basic construct. The Lawrence and Dyer elaborations do help on this score, but without operationalizations it is difficult to know how much or in what ways. The rating approach to measurement here suffers from the fact that it is presented in such a manner as to make replication impossible, and reliability concerns must inevitably remain.

Perceived uncertainty is part of the original Lawrence and Lorsch measurement process, and it seems to have a place in their construct as well. Yet it is not a direct match with the objective environment. It is strongly influenced by characteristics of the perceiver. Some people desire uncertainty and create it by stirring up the environment or by penetrating more deeply into it so that there is more of it to cope with; they may also distort their world. Others become extremely anxious in the face of uncertainty and eliminate it wherever possible, not only by controlling the environment but also by limiting it drastically, or by ignoring and even denying aspects of it. Clearly, organizations can fail because key decision makers distort uncertainty levels both upward and downward to an excessive degree and adjust organization structures and functioning inappro-

priately to something that is not really there. Numerous cases in the business policy and business strategy area demonstrate this again and again. It is particularly common to keep perceived uncertainty low by totally ignoring major threats in the environment until it is too late. Here subjective and objective uncertainty are far from being the same thing.

To the extent the same individuals in a firm report on certainty levels in the environment and actually determine internal structures, there is a good probability that environmental uncertainty will be matched with internal structural uncertainty (organic forms) and environmental certainty with structural certainty (mechanistic forms). This is simply because those who prefer one or the other are likely to prefer it everywhere and to create a world to match. There is no reason why all this should have much to do with organizational effectiveness, and it typically does not.

At present it would appear that environmental uncertainty, at least as Lawrence and Lorsch conceived it, is a construct that is no longer theoretically useful. There may very well be something here that can contribute to a greater understanding of organizational functioning, but to get at that something requires breaking the global construct down into constituent parts that can be defined, measured, and validated with sufficient precision. Progress has indeed been made on this score. What is needed now is precise specification of new theory regarding how the components of uncertainty relate to other variables, including aspects of structure and effectiveness.

One additional problem clouds the understanding of differentiation-integration-uncertainty relationships as set forth by the theory. Several writers have noted that in a mature context concurrent studies should yield high levels of differentiation and integration in an environment of *low* perceived uncertainty, because the organizational variables should have acted over time to tame the environment. Such effects, coupled with a sampling of organizations at different stages of adaptive change, could completely confound concurrent research results. The theory does not deal with such matters as time lags and reciprocal effects between organization and environment. Others, including Lawrence and Lorsch (1991), have noted that there is a need for longitudinal research to confront these issues, but there is also a need for theoretical extensions that indicate what to expect if such research were conducted.

Numerous environmental factors within a rather

wide band of variation currently may have little relevance for many organizations. Certainly this is true for the company that has established a monopoly, or carved out a solid market niche, or operates in a pervasive growth market. Furthermore, a variety of structures may be adequate to the demands of any given environmental context. To the extent these conclusions are valid, contingency theory needs considerable revision to match the realities of the organizational world.

CONCLUSIONS

Contingency theory of organization, like other comprehensive systems theories and theories that use the contingency approach, has suffered from severe problems related to the measurement of its major constructs. These measurement problems are not fully divorced from difficulties inherent in the constructs themselves and the way they are defined. Given this situation, the tendency has been to look beyond systems theory to other types of formulations.

The primary alternative thus introduced has been some variant of Weber's concept of bureaucracy (see chapter 3). Theories of this type start with the idea of bureaucracy and then seek to extend it in some way to deal with the issues that systems theories have considered.

References

Bazigos, Michael N., & Burke, W. Warner (1997). Theory Orientations of Organization Development (OD) Practitioners. *Group and Organization Management*, 22, 384–408.

Bluedorn, Allen C. (1991). Review of *Organization and Environment. Journal of Management*, 17, 494–496.

Bluedorn, Allen C. (1993). Pilgrim's Progress: Trends and Convergence in Research on Organizational Size and Environments. *Journal of Management*, 19, 163–191.

Boyd, Brian K.; Dess, Gregory G.; & Rasheed, Abdul M. A. (1993). Divergence between Archival and Perceptual Measures of the Environment: Causes and Consequences. *Academy of Management Review*, 18, 204–226.

Boyd, Brian K., & Fulk, Janet (1996). Executive Scanning and Perceived Uncertainty: A Multidimensional Model. *Journal of Management*, 22, 1–21.

Buchko, Aaron A. (1994). Conceptualization and Measurement of Environmental Uncertainty: An Assessment of the Miles and Snow Perceived Environmental Uncertainty Scale. *Academy of Management Journal*, 37, 410–425.

Burns, Lawton R., & Wholey, Douglas R. (1993). Adoption and Abandonment of Matrix Management Programs: Effects of Organizational Characteristics and Interorganizational Networks. *Academy of Management Journal*, 36, 106–138.

Charns, Martin P.; Lawrence, Paul R.; & Weisbord, Marvin R. (1977). Organizing Multiple-function Professionals in Academic Medical Centers. In Paul C. Nystrom & William H. Starbuck (Eds.), *Prescriptive Models of Organizations* (pp. 71–88). New York: Elsevier North-Holland.

Church, Allen H.; Burke, W. Warner; & Van Eynde, Donald F. (1994). Values, Motives, and Interventions of Organization Development Practitioners. *Group and Organization Management*, 19, 5–50.

Dalton, Gene W.; Lawrence, Paul R.; & Lorsch, Jay W. (1970). *Organizational Structure and Design*. Homewood, IL: Irwin-Dorsey.

Davis, Stanley M., & Lawrence, Paul R. (1977). *Matrix*. Reading, MA: Addison-Wesley.

Davis, Stanley M., & Lawrence, Paul R. (1978). Problems of Matrix Organizations. *Harvard Business Review*, 56(3), 131–142.

Dess, Gregory G., & Beard, Donald W. (1984). Dimensions of Organizational Task Environments. *Administrative Science Quarterly*, 29, 52–73.

Dess, Gregory G., & Rasheed, Abdul M. A. (1991). Conceptualizing and Measuring Organizational Environments: A Critique and Suggestions. *Journal of Management*, 17, 701–710.

Downey, H. Kirk; Hellriegel, Don; & Slocum, John W. (1975). Environmental Uncertainty: The Construct and Its Application. *Administrative Science Quarterly*, 20, 613–629.

Downey, H. Kirk; Hellriegel, Don; & Slocum, John W. (1977). Individual Characteristics as Sources of Perceived Uncertainty Variability. *Human Relations*, 30, 161–174.

Downey, H. Kirk, & Slocum, John W. (1975). Uncertainty: Measures, Research, and Sources of Variations. *Academy of Management Journal*, 18, 562–578.

Duncan, Robert B. (1972). Characteristics of Organizational Environments and Perceived Environmental Uncertainty. *Administrative Science Quarterly*, 17, 313–327.

Duncan, Robert B. (1973). Multiple Decision-Making Structures in Adapting to Environmental Uncertainty: The Impact on Organizational Effectiveness. *Human Relations*, 26, 273–291.

Duncan, Robert B. (1974). Modifications in Decision Structure in Adapting to the Environment: Some Implications for Organizational Learning. *Decision Sciences*, 5(4), 122–142.

Ford, Robert C., & Randolph, W. Alan (1992). Cross-Functional Structures: A Review and Integration of Matrix Organization and Project Management. *Journal of Management*, 18, 267–294.

Fry, Louis W.; Kidron, Aryeh G.; Osborn, Richard N.; & Trafton, Richard S. (1980). A Constructive Replication of the Lawrence and Lorsch Conflict Resolution Methodology. *Journal of Management*, 6, 7–19.

Herbert, Theodore T., & Matthews, Ronald D. (1977). Is the Contingency Theory of Organization a Technology-Bound Conceptualization? *Journal of Management*, 3, 1–10.

Keats, Barbara W., & Hitt, Michael A. (1988). A Causal Model of Linkages among Environmental Dimensions, Macro Organizational Characteristics, and Performance. *Academy of Management Journal*, 31, 570–598.

Khandwalla, Pradip N. (1972). Environment and Its Impact on the Organization. *International Studies of Management and Organization*, 2, 297–313.

Khandwalla, Pradip N. (1973). Viable and Effective Organizational Designs of Firms. *Academy of Management Journal*, 16, 481–495.

Lawrence, Paul R. (1975). Individual Differences in the World of Work. In Eugene L. Cass & Frederick G. Zimmer (Eds.), *Man and Work in Society* (pp. 19–29). New York: Van Nostrand.

Lawrence, Paul R. (1987). Historical Development of Organizational Behavior. In Jay W. Lorsch (Ed.), *Handbook of Organizational Behavior* (pp. 1–9). Englewood Cliffs, NJ: Prentice Hall.

Lawrence, Paul R., & Dyer, Davis (1983). *Renewing American Industry: Organizing for Efficiency and Innovation.* New York: Free Press.

Lawrence, Paul R.; Kolodny, Harvey F.; & Davis, Stanley M. (1977). The Human Side of the Matrix. *Organizational Dynamics*, 6(1), 43–61.

Lawrence, Paul R., & Lawrence, Anne T. (1993). Doing Problem-Oriented Research: A Daughter's Interview. In Arthur G. Bedeian (Ed.), *Management Laureates: A Collection of Autobiographical Essays* (Vol. 2, pp. 111–148). Greenwich, CT: JAI Press.

Lawrence, Paul R., & Lorsch, Jay W. (1967a). Differentiation and Integration in Complex Organizations. *Administrative Science Quarterly*, 12, 1–47.

Lawrence, Paul R., & Lorsch, Jay W. (1967b). New Management Job: The Integrator. *Harvard Business Review*, 45(6), 142–151.

Lawrence, Paul R., & Lorsch, Jay W. (1967c). *Organization and Environment: Managing Differentiation and Integration.* Boston: Graduate School of Business Administration, Harvard University.

Lawrence, Paul R., & Lorsch, Jay W. (1969). *Developing Organizations: Diagnosis and Action.* Reading, MA: Addison-Wesley.

Lawrence, Paul R,. & Lorsch, Jay W. (1973). A Reply to Tosi, Aldag, and Storey. *Administrative Science Quarterly*, 18, 397–398.

Lawrence, Paul R., & Lorsch, Jay W. (1991). Review of *Organization and Environment. Journal of Management*, 17, 491–493.

Lorsch, Jay W. (1965). *Product Innovation and Organization.* New York: Macmillan.

Lorsch, Jay W. (1968). Organizing for Diversification. *Academy of Management Proceedings*, 28, 87–100.

Lorsch, Jay W. (1976). Contingency Theory and Organization Design: A Personal Odyssey. In Ralph H. Kilman, Louis R. Pondy, & Dennis P. Slevin (Eds.), *The Management of Organization Design: Strategies and Implementation* (pp. 141–165). New York: Elsevier North-Holland.

Lorsch, Jay W. (1977). Organizational Design: A Situational Perspective. *Organizational Dynamics*, 6(2), 2–14.

Lorsch, Jay W., & Allen, Stephen A. (1973). *Managing Diversity and Interdependence: An Organizational Study of Multidivisional Firms.* Boston: Graduate School of Business Administration, Harvard University.

Lorsch, Jay W., & Lawrence, Paul R. (1965). Organizing for Product Innovation. *Harvard Business Review*, 43(1).

Lorsch, Jay W., & Lawrence, Paul R. (1969). The Diagnosis of Organizational Problems. In Warren G. Bennis, Kenneth D. Benne, & Robert Chin (Eds.), *The Planning of Change* (pp. 468–476). New York: Holt, Rinehart, and Winston.

Lorsch, Jay W., & Lawrence, Paul R. (1970). *Studies in Organizational Design.* Homewood, IL: Irwin-Dorsey.

Lorsch, Jay W., & Morse, John J. (1974). *Organizations and Their Members: A Contingency Approach.* New York: Harper & Row.

McCaskey, Michael B. (1976). Tolerance for Ambiguity and the Perception of Uncertainty in Organization Design. In Ralph H. Kilman, Louis R. Pondy, & Dennis P. Slevin (Eds.), *The Management of Organization Design: Research and Methodology* (pp. 59–85). New York: Elsevier North-Holland.

Miles, Raymond E., & Snow, Charles C. (1978). *Organizational Strategy, Structure and Process.* New York: McGraw-Hill.

Miller, Danny, & Shamsie, Jamal (1999). Strategic Responses to Three Kinds of Uncertainty: Product Line

Simplicity at the Hollywood Film Studies. *Journal of Management*, 25, 97–116.

Milliken, Frances J. (1987). Three Types of Perceived Uncertainty about the Environment: State, Effect, and Response Uncertainty. *Academy of Management Review*, 12, 133–142.

Miner, John B. (1979). The Role of Organizational Structure and Process in Strategy Implementation: Commentary. In Dan E. Schendel & Charles W. Hofer (Eds.), *Strategic Management: A New View of Business Policy and Planning* (pp. 289–302). Boston: Little, Brown.

Mintzberg, Henry (1979). *The Structuring of Organizations: A Synthesis of the Research*. Englewood Cliffs, NJ: Prentice Hall.

Morse, John J., & Lorsch, Jay W. (1970). Beyond Theory Y. *Harvard Business Review*, 48(3), 61–68.

Morse, John J., & Young, Darroch F. (1973). Personality Development and Task Choices: A Systems View. *Human Relations*, 26, 307–324.

Negandhi, Anant R., & Reimann, Bernard C. (1972). A Contingency Theory of Organization Re-Examined in the Context of a Developing Country. *Academy of Management Journal*, 15, 137–146.

Negandhi, Anant R., & Reimann, Bernard C. (1973). Task Environment, Decentralization, and Organizational Effectiveness. *Human Relations*, 26, 203–214.

Neilsen, Eric H. (1974). Contingency Theory Applied to Small Business Organizations. *Human Relations*, 27, 357–379.

Ouchi, William (1981). *Theory Z: How American Business Can Meet the Japanese Challenge*. Reading, MA: Addison-Wesley.

Pennings, Johannes M. (1975). The Relevance of the Structural-Contingency Model for Organizational Effectiveness. *Administrative Science Quarterly*, 20, 393–410.

Priem, Richard L., & Rosenstein, Joseph (2000). Is Organization Theory Obvious to Practitioners? A Test of One Established Theory. *Organization Science*, 11, 509–524.

Reimann, Bernard C., & Negandhi, Anant R. (1975). Strategies of Administrative Control and Organizational Effectiveness. *Human Relations*, 28, 475–486.

Sharfman, Mark P., & Dean, James W. (1991). Conceptualizing and Measuring the Organizational Environment: A Multidimensional Approach. *Journal of Management*, 17, 681–700.

Simonetti, Jack L., & Boseman, F. Glenn (1975). The Impact of Market Competition on Organizational Structure and Effectiveness: A Cross-Cultural Study. *Academy of Management Journal*, 18, 631–638.

Tosi, Henry; Aldag, Ramon; & Storey, Ronald (1973). On the Measurement of the Environment: An Assessment of the Lawrence and Lorsch Environmental Uncertainty Questionnaire. *Administrative Science Quarterly*, 18, 27–36.

Tung, Rosalie L. (1979). Dimensions of Organizational Environments: An Exploratory Study of Their Impact on Organization Structure. *Academy of Management Journal*, 22, 672–693.

Turner, Arthur N., & Lawrence, Paul R. (1965). *Industrial Jobs and the Worker: An Investigation of Response to Task Attributes*. Boston: Harvard Graduate School of Business Administration.

Weisbord, Marvin R.; Lawrence, Paul R.; & Charns, Martin P. (1978). Three Dilemmas of Academic Medical Centers. *Journal of Applied Behavioral Science*, 14, 284–304.

Part V

First-Generation Theories: Bureaucracy-Related Concepts

Chapter 18

Theory and Research That Remain Close to the Weberian Origins

Elaborations of Weber's theory of bureaucracy (see chapter 3) have taken a variety of forms. A major theoretical thrust has been toward the specification of dysfunctional side effects of bureaucracy. Another has formulated more precise theoretical hypotheses and developed operational definitions of variables. And yet another has differentiated various types of bureaucracies within the broad framework that was established by Weber.

As we will see later (see chapter 20), certain theorists have viewed the dysfunctions of the bureaucratic form as so overriding as to argue against its use altogether; others have remained content to point up the difficulties in bureaucratic systems without abandoning the underlying theory. Early examples of this latter approach, which emerged from intensive case studies, were Philip Selznick's (1949) analysis of the Tennessee Valley Authority and Alvin Gouldner's (1954) study of a gypsum plant. These two formulations and a similar model developed by Robert Merton (1940) were analyzed by James March and Herbert Simon (1958) as examples of the dysfunctions type of theory.

The two theories considered in this chapter both remain relatively close to Weber's formulations, although they recognize dysfunctions and elaborate on Weber's theory in ways beyond dysfunctions as well. The theories developed by the Aston researchers and by Peter Blau also have in common that each is closely intertwined with a large body of research that was conducted by the theorists and those closely associated with them.

THEORY BEHIND
THE ASTON STUDIES

Chapter 16 contained an introduction to the Aston research but focused only on its implications for Joan Woodward's theory and the technological imperative. Certainly Woodward's views on the role of technology in organization structuring stimulated the Aston work initially. But there is much more to the program than that, and much more to the theorizing than the position that organizational size is a more potent contingency variable than technology is.

The comprehensiveness of the Aston approach, in terms of both personnel and scope is reflected in the following:

The first generation of Aston scholars included Derek Pugh (who went on to become professor at the London Business School and subsequently to the Open University), David Hickson (who became professor at the University of Bradford), and C. R. (Bob) Hinings (who became professor at the University of Birmingham and is now at the University of Alberta). The focus of the first generation was upon the relationship between organization structure and contingency variables such as technology, size, and environment. Their articles are early statements of structural contingency theory.

The second generation of Aston scholars included Diane Pheysey (who remained at Aston), Kerr Inkson (who moved to the University of Auckland), and Roy Payne (who became professor at the University of Sheffield). The second generation focused on the relationship between organizational structure and organizational climate.

The third generation of Aston scholars involved Lex Donaldson (now at the Australian Graduate School of Management), John Child (now at the University of Cambridge), and Charles McMillan (now at York University, Canada). This generation broadened the scope of the Aston Studies to include organizational performance and cross-cultural analysis. (Greenwood & Devine, 1997, p. 201)

The genesis of all this, as noted in chapter 16, was in the collaboration of Pugh, Hickson, and Hinings. Pugh is generally recognized as the senior member of the group at the time; he was also the intellectual leader and the most experienced researcher. Hickson (1996) says that his lead authorship of the initial articles was "well merited by intellectual contributions." Elsewhere Hickson (1998) refers to Pugh's "massive input" to the research.

Background

Pugh was born in 1930. He was educated at the University of Edinburgh, while Tom Burns was on the faculty, and majored in psychology; he remained at the university after receiving his master's degree, doing some teaching and conducting research on absenteeism. Subsequently he moved to the Birmingham College of Technology in the department of industrial administration, which was essentially a business school appointment. Several years later the college became the University of Aston in Birmingham, and Pugh received his doctorate from that university. In 1968 he accepted an appointment at the London Business School at a time when the Aston research group was beginning to break up. He remained there for 15 years and then shifted to the Open University in London, from which he retired in 1995.

Initiated in 1961, the Aston studies were carried out by a group that was transformed several times as generations came and went. The unit was formally terminated in 1973, but it had not been active for several years before that time. In fact, after 1968 the major work was conducted by a group that was reconstituted at the London Business School; this too ultimately lost out to turnover.

From Aston Studies to Aston Theory

There is no one place where the Aston theory is formally stated. It is intertwined with the research and spread over a number of years and publications. As Malcolm Warner said in 1981, "there is a potentially brilliant empirical theory of organizations to be written by the Aston gurus" (p. 450). This void remains unfilled today. Thus we are left with the need to pick from here and there, and hopefully to adequately represent the Aston position.

Fortunately, however, the Aston researchers compiled their major publications (extending from 1963 to 1981) in a series of four books. The first volume (Pugh & Hickson, 1976) deals with the original studies on organizational structure and context that had been conducted in the English midlands; Pugh is author or co-author of all of the papers. The second volume (Pugh & Hinings, 1976) includes papers that deal with extensions and replications of the original work; Pugh co-authored only one of the nine papers, but he does contribute to the introduction and the concluding remarks. The third volume (Pugh & Payne,

1977) goes beyond the organizational level to consider research on roles and groups as they relate to organization; here Pugh co-authored two of the nine papers plus the introductory and concluding materials. The fourth volume (Hickson & McMillan, 1981) presents a number of studies using the Aston methodology and conducted in various countries around the world; Pugh is not represented here at all.

These are the sources from which I have distilled the Aston theory. With very few exceptions this theory is to be found in the papers to which Derek Pugh contributed. In the following discussion I often use citations to the four-volume series.

Constructs of the Theory

The Aston research began with a set of assumptions, as follows:

1. In order to find which organizational problems are specific to particular kinds of organizations, and which are common to all organizations, comparative studies are needed that include organizations of many types.
2. Meaningful comparisons can only be made when there is a common standard for comparison — preferably measurement.
3. The nature of an organization will be influenced by its objectives and environments, so these must be taken into account.
4. Study of the work behavior of individuals or groups should be related to study of the characteristics of the organization in which the behavior occurs.
5. Studies of organizational processes of stability and change should be undertaken in relation to a framework of significant variables and relationships that is established through comparative studies. (Pugh & Hickson, 1976, pp. vi–vii; Pugh, 1976, p. 63)

Thus comparative research using measures of preestablished variables was to be emphasized. This represented a reaction against the ambiguity of the case approach that had heretofore prevailed in the European study of organizations (see chapter 15 on Tom Burns and G. M. Stalker's mechanistic and organic systems). However, to conduct the research it was necessary to have measures, and measures presupposed constructs. This part of the theory came from a reading of the existing management and social science literature and was thus a priori; a major influence within this literature was Max Weber.

The major structural variables that emerged from this process were as follows:

Specialization — the degree to which activities are divided into specialized roles, the number of different specialist roles established

Standardization of work flow activities — the degree to which standard rules and procedures for processing and controlling work exist

Standardization of employment practices — the degree to which standardized employment practices in, for example, recruiting, promoting, and disciplining employees exist

Formalization — the degree to which instructions, procedures, and the like are written down and documented, then filed

Centralization — the degree to which authority to make decisions is located at the top of the management hierarchy

Configuration — a blanket concept used to cover factors derived from the organization chart: (1) the length of the chain of command, (2) the size of spans of control, (3) the percentage of specialized or support personnel

In addition, dimensions were established for the context within which this structure operated, as follows:

Origin and history — whether the organization was privately founded and the changes in such factors as ownership and location experienced

Ownership and control — type of ownership, whether private or public, and the degree of concentration of ownership

Size — the number of employees, net assets held, extent of market position, and the like

Technology — the degree of integration in the organization's work process

Location — the number of geographically dispersed operating sites

Dependence — the extent of dependence on customers, suppliers, trade unions, owning groups, and the like

These are the constructs entered into the macro analyses, which are the source of the most important contributions from the Aston research. There are additional more micro variables; we will consider these shortly.

Based on factor analysis, groupings of the basic variables were established as follows:

Structuring of activities—combining specialization, standardization, and formalization into one construct

Centralization of decisions (concentration of authority)—combining centralization with the existence of considerable decision-making power in a higher-level chief executive, board, or council (in the case of a subsidiary); standardization of employment activities loads on this factor

Line control of workflow—combining aspects of configuration (high percentage of line subordinates, low ratio of subordinates to superiors) with impersonal control through formalization of role performance (a component of formalization); operational (but not personnel) control resides in the line hierarchy

Pugh and Hickson confirmed that "these basic dimensions . . . are very much the stuff of which bureaucracy is made. Conceptually they stand in the Weberian tradition" (1976, p. 4). And again, "we must first of all isolate the conceptually distinct elements that go into Weber's formulation of bureaucracy. . . . The insights of Weber can then be translated into a set of empirically testable hypotheses" (p. 28). This is what the Aston researchers attempted to do.

Certain other constructs beyond those noted previously are used on occasion:

Flexibility—a structural variable involving the determination of changes over a period of time: the amount, the speed, the acceleration and so on

Charter—a contextual variable describing the purpose and ideology of the organization

Resources—a contextual variable dealing with the human, ideational, financial, and material resources at an organization's disposal

Performance is considered to be represented by an organization's success in reaching its stated goals in various areas. In fact, however, little use is made of performance variables in the research. There is also some variation in the specific constructs designated and the nature of their operationalization.

Macro Relationships and Hypotheses

In contrast to the theoretical constructs, which were established in advance of the research, the theory's hypotheses have an empirical derivation; they arose

out of the original Aston research and thus cannot be tested using it. The one exception to this statement occurs in the case of technology. A test of the technological imperative was carried out by using an operationalization of Woodward's technology construct and also a measure of integration in the work process; this test was designed for use beyond the manufacturing context (see chapter 16) and, in fact, was a test of a theory that derived from outside Aston, not of Aston theorizing.

Figure 18.1 presents the framework for the Aston hypotheses. In itself, however, this framework lacks precision and is more of a variable listing than a theoretical statement. It does say, nevertheless, that organization structure is the central factor.

The next step is a summarization of the findings from the initial Aston study as follows:

1. The division of labor (specialization), the existence of procedures (standardization) and the use of written communication and role definition (formalization) are highly related and can be summarized by a single structural dimension called 'structuring of activities'. This dimension is primarily related to the size of the organization, and secondarily to its technology. Large organizations with automated and integrated technologies will have more specialists, and more procedures, and they will use written means of communication and role definition. Size is quite clearly the most important factor here.

2. The locus of authority (centralization) is negatively related to specialization, and a number of measures of centralization can be summarized by a single structural dimension called 'concentration of authority'. This is primarily related to the dependence of the organization on other organizations. Those organizations which are dependent on other organizations by virtue of ownership ties or economic integration will centralize many decisions.

3. Various aspects of role structure such as the number of employees in the direct line hierarchy, the span of control of the first-line supervisor, and so on, are related and can be summarized by a single structural dimension called 'line control of workflow'. Organizations with integrated and automated technologies will control work by means of procedures and specialists outside the line chain of command, and vice versa. (Pugh & Hinings, 1976, pp. ix–x)

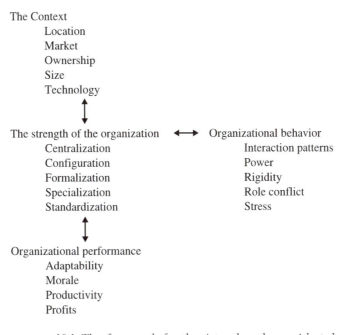

The Context
    Location
    Market
    Ownership
    Size
    Technology

The strength of the organization ⟷ Organizational behavior
    Centralization   Interaction patterns
    Configuration   Power
    Formalization   Rigidity
    Specialization   Role conflict
    Standardization   Stress

Organizational performance
    Adaptability
    Morale
    Productivity
    Profits

FIGURE 18.1 The framework for the Aston hypotheses. Adapted from Derek S. Pugh & David J. Hickson (1976), *Organizational Structure in Its Context: The Aston Programme I* (Lexington, MA: D. C. Heath), 186.

These findings relate context variables to organization structure and provide "a set of hypotheses for testing in further studies" (p. x). Thus the theory's hypotheses are direct empirical generalizations. These hypotheses may be outlined as follows:

Size is related to structuring of activities, with larger organizations likely to be highly structured.

Dependence is related to concentration of authority, with organizations that have greater dependence more likely to have a greater concentration of authority (centralization).

Technology is related to some configurational features, with organizations having more integrated technologies likely to have less line control of the workflow. (Pugh & Hickson, 1976, pp. 10–13)

Causation and Determinism

Note that the preceding hypotheses state context-structure relationships, but they do not specify causation. Yet causation is of concern to the researchers: "The Aston studies were designed . . . to bring us nearer to

the study of generalizable causal relationships" (Pugh & Hickson, 1976, p. 189).

At one point (Pugh & Hickson, 1976, pp. 13–14) the authors seem to be tendering causal hypotheses running from the contextual aspects of the hypotheses just stated to the structural, at least in the sense that decisions on contextual matters serve to constrain choices on structure. Later, however (pp. 107–108), they are much more tentative on this score. The discussion uses words such as "*tempting to* argue," "*can be* hypothesized," "*may be* hypothesized," "*can be* suggested." It ends with the following statement:

But a cross-sectional study such as this can only establish relationship. Causes should be inferred from a theory that generates a dynamic model about changes over time. The contribution of the present study is to establish a framework of operationally defined and empirically validated concepts. (p. 108)

Furthermore, these relationships are viewed as potentially reciprocal in that causation can run from context to structure and/or structure to context. This is what the two-headed arrow in figure 18.1 means. The exact nature of the causation is not specified there.

Choice, as in the choice of a growth strategy, can clearly enter into the relationships. The idea of complete determination from context to structure (as with the technological imperative) is firmly rejected: "If we could make perfect predictions in every case it would mean that context entirely determines the structure of the organizations, and that the views and strategic choices of top managers are irrelevant (Child, 1972a). This is obviously not so" (Pugh & Hickson, 1976, p. 187). Without evidence from longitudinal studies as a basis, the authors are unwilling to theorize about causation, but they do posit that complete determinism using such factors as size, dependence, and technology as contingency variables is not their theory; there must be some room for choice. They end by saying, "Where causal imagery is used, it is put forward hypothetically to initiate further study" (p. 187).

Taxonomy of Bureaucratic Structures

While Weber set forth a single concept of bureaucracy, the Aston authors propose a taxonomy that differentiates several forms within the overall bureaucratic concept. In this regard they break with Weber and enter into new territory.

In its simplest form the taxonomy may be characterized on the two dimensions of centralization of decisions (concentration of authority) and structuring of activities to yield four basic forms (Pugh & Hickson, 1993). Thus, we have figure 18.2. The taxonomy, as the name implies, is empirically based and is derived

from factor analysis using the data from the original study. In its more complete form (figure 18.3) three dimensions interact to produce seven different forms. Potentially there are 12 types, but empirically only 7 cells are occupied by clusters of organizations.

In figure 18.2 the implicitly structured organizations of figure 18.3 are labeled *nonbureaucracies*. Nonbureaucracies are typically rather small firms, whereas workflow bureaucracies tend to be large. The authors recognize that the theory might be influenced by its empirical base; there was only one full bureaucracy, for instance, in the original sample and no autonomous professional organizations. Empirically derived theoretical statements of this kind definitely need to be cross-validated on a new sample.

In addition to the taxonomy, the terminology of figure 18.3 implies certain hypotheses about the form of the developmental sequence. This sequencing is based on size and runs from "implicit" to "pre-" to "nascent," and then eventually to "full," the complete bureaucratic type. Thus a movement over time toward bureaucracy is hypothesized.

Theory as Extended in a Micro Direction

It is interesting to note that although Pugh was trained as a psychologist and identifies himself as such (Pugh, 1996), the publications of the Aston studies, with only a few exceptions, were in the literature of organizational behavior and of sociology. The few exceptions occur when the studies move in a micro direction.

Figure 18.1 includes a component labeled "organizational behavior." The intent in this regard is to consider relationships between context/structure and aspects of group and role structure, as well as individ-

		Low	High
Centralization	High	Personnel bureaucracy	Full bureaucracy
	Low	Non-bureaucracy	Workflow bureaucracy
		Low	High

Structuring

FIGURE 18.2 Simplified Aston taxonomy. Adapted from Derek S. Pugh & David J. Hickson (1993), *Great Writers on Organizations: The Omnibus Edition* (Aldershot, UK: Dartmouth), 16.

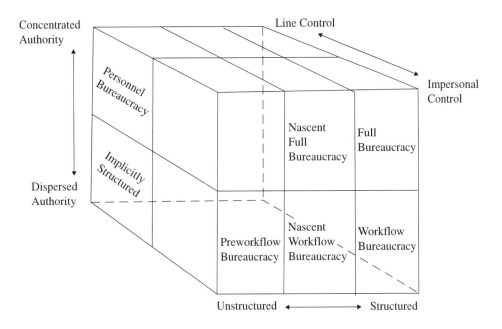

FIGURE 18.3 The Aston bureaucratic taxonomy. From Derek S. Pugh, David J. Hickson, & C. Robert Hinings (1969), An Empirical Taxonomy of Structures of Work Organizations, *Administrative Science Quarterly*, 14(1), 123. Copyright 1969. Reprinted with permission.

ual attitudes and behavior. Figure 18.4 outlines a framework for theory of this nature.

The major hypothesis advanced is labeled the "administrative reduction of variance thesis." This may be stated as follows:

> The two main structural variables (structuring of activities and concentration of authority) increase the degree of specificity of role-prescriptions characteristic of the organization, and, in an environment thus formally defined in terms of highly prescribed roles, relatively cautious and conformist behaviour becomes most appropriate. Thus, in the role sending activities described by Kahn et al. (1964), where formal roles are mediated by interpersonal role-conceptions and expectations, conformity and stability become highly valued. In this relatively stable organizational and social environment interpersonal conflict is less likely. Thus a single explanatory causal chain is hypothesized, whereby administrative factors in structured and/ or concentrated authority organizations reduce the amount of variance in roles, and thereby the amount of innovation and flexibility encouraged in interpersonal relations and conflict engendered by interpersonal behaviour. Organizational variables, role

> variables, and interpersonal variables are linked. (Pugh & Payne, 1977, pp. 15–16)

This is the idea that bureaucracy and the classical management form constrain innovation, which emerged so frequently in the first-generation literature of organizational behavior.

A variation on this theme is subsequently posited as related to climate within an organization and to group structure, using the Burns and Stalker terminology (see chapter 15 in this volume):

> A mechanistic structuring of activities, through division of labour, standardized procedures and written specification over-prescribes the tasks of managers and is, therefore, not likely to produce a developmental climate where people are stimulated to be innovative. Secondly, the centralization and the high ratio of superordinates characteristic of such organizations are likely to lead to an emphasis on control. At the group level, a mechanistic structure is likely to result in low task complexity, especially at lower levels, and in greater formality of relationships, with emphasis on memos, minutes, written instructions and agendas limiting the opportunity for spontaneous, informal communication.

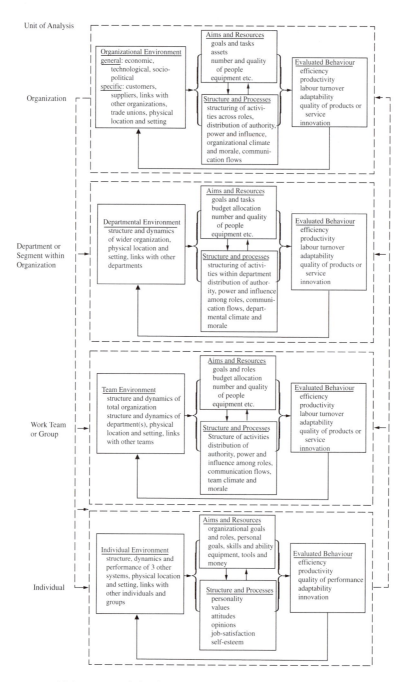

FIGURE 18.4 Framework for theory and research dealing with the micro level. Adapted from Derek S. Pugh & Roy L. Payne (1977), *Organizational Behavior in Its Context: The Aston Programme III* (Lexington, MA: D. C. Heath), viii.

Lack of autonomy may accompany the formality, since authority in a mechanistic organization tends to be concentrated at the top of the hierarchy.

Many writers have argued that top executives are likely to have great influence on the climate of the organization, and, once the top policy makers have made decisions, they exert pressure on subordinates to execute them. Members under such pressure and control, who must execute decisions in which they have not participated, are not likely to have a high sense of involvement in the group's activities and goals, and therefore are not likely to take great satisfaction in their work. (Pugh & Payne, 1977, pp. 72–73)

Domain Extensions

A number of studies have been undertaken with the objective of extending the generalizability of the original Aston findings beyond the cross-sectional analysis of work organizations in the English midlands from which they derived. These extensions do not have a broad theoretical underpinning, but there are some hypotheses to be considered.

One set of extensions involves the movement of the theoretical domain outward from work organizations of a business and governmental nature to include organizations that incorporate voluntary members. These would include occupational interest associations, local government departments, churches, and colleges with their unpaid councillors, pupils, laity, and rank and file members. The implicit hypothesis is that the bureaucratic findings can be extended into this domain, and thus the theory would cover organizations with voluntary members, as well as work organizations (Pugh & Hinings, 1976). Remember that James Thompson (see chapter 14) explicitly excluded voluntary organizations from the domain of his theory.

A second extension applies to the international arena and appears to have preceded the research that extends beyond England's borders. This is referred to as the bold culture-free hypothesis; in fact, it is the widely held convergence hypothesis. Under this view, relationships between the structural characteristics of work organizations and organizational context variables will be stable across societies throughout the world. Societies converge on certain common features of their work organizations as related to structure and context.

This formulation was subsequently modified to a degree as follows: "The traditionalism of industrialized societies is negatively related to the formalization of their work units, but not otherwise to the organizational structures of these units" (Hickson & McMillan, 1981, p. 47). The idea here is that a highly traditionalized society will not require the high degree of formalization in its organizations that a less traditionalized society does; the two factors serve in lieu of one another. It is not entirely clear whether this hypothesis was generated before the initial research related to it or afterward.

Insofar as cultural variations across societies enter into the macro level process of organizations they are expected to do so through the medium of choice.

Finally, although relatively little is hypothesized with regard to the operation of dynamic processes over time, based on the argument that almost all of the Aston research was cross-sectional, the theoretical domain is extended in time in one respect. Based on a small-scale pilot study, a ratchet mechanism is proposed, whereby increases in the size of an organization over time would bring about increasing structuring, but decreases in size would not result in decreasing structuring. This hypothesis clearly seems to say something about the way that size *causes* structuring and thus seems to be an exception to prior disclaimers.

Evaluation and Impact

The Aston theory is a refinement of Weber's theory of bureaucracy. In many respects, research on one is research on the other. Yet as we have seen, there are departures as well between the two theories. Given the preceding theoretical statements, the original Aston studies may be viewed in large part as theory testing for Weber's theory, but as theory forming for the Aston theory. The research results are indeed incorporated in the latter theory, and in reviewing the theory we have reviewed the results as well. Nevertheless it may prove helpful to look at these findings more closely, in part to substantiate the support for Weber; in part to indicate the size of the relationships.

Initial Aston Research on Macro Variables

The initial study was conducted in the English midlands in the area around Birmingham. The measures were developed with considerable sophistication, using standardized interviews with knowledgeable personnel and corroboration from organizational documents.

Specialization, standardization, and formalization are highly correlated with each other, although the particular measure that deals with standardization of selection procedures, advancement, and the like does not always follow the expected pattern (see table 18.1). However, centralization is, if anything, negatively related to the other criteria, again with the exception of the index of standardization of personnel procedures. Size of organization tends to reinforce these patterns: larger size is associated with more specialization, standardization, and formalization, but less centralization. The magnitude of the correlations in this study is impressive, although there may be some overlap in the content of certain measures. Further data on technology and size relationships are contained in table 16.4.

Data bearing on hypotheses relating context to structure are given in table 18.2. As one would expect, the findings are congruent with the hypotheses; the correlations in the .60s are substantial.

Aston Replications

Findings from two major British replication studies are summarized in table 18.3. The variables considered are those hypothesized as characteristics of bureaucracy by Peter Grinyer and Masoud Yasai-Ardekani (1980) in their study of 45 companies located in southeast England. Data are also given in table 18.3 for John Child's (1972b) national study of 82 manufacturing concerns (see chapter 16 in this volume). With the exception of the proportion of managers, the variables are all consistently intercorrelated, but in contrast to the data of table 18.1 the overall centralization results are not only all negative but also all statistically significant. Further breakdown of the centralization variable indicates that this departure from theory occurs in production, personnel, buying, and organizing decisions. The departure from theory is much less for marketing and financial decisions, though these correlations are not significantly positive either.

In the national study the stability of the factor structure underlying the theory reflected in figure 18.3 was analyzed. Primarily because of the centralization findings, the structure did not remain stable. The data bring the concentration of authority dimension into question and suggest that decentralization is a component of structuring: "The solution whereby structuring of activities and concentration of authority represent underlying dimensions of organization structure requires further empirical examination. . . . The taxonomy . . . should be utilized with caution" (Child, 1972b, p. 174). Based on his analysis of the national study data, Roger Mansfield (1973) goes so far as to suggest that the Weberian concept of a single bureau-

TABLE 18.1 Correlations among structural measures from the original Aston study

	Specialization		Standardization		Formalization	
	Functional	Overall	Personnel procedures	Overall	Performance recording	Overall
Specialization						
Functional						
Overall	.87*					
Standardization						
Personnel procedures	−.15	.09				
Overall	.76*	.80*	.23			
Formalization						
Performance recording	.66*	.54*	−.12	.72*		
Overall	.57*	.68*	.38*	.83*	.75*	
Centralization	−.64*	−.53*	.30*	−.27	−.27	−.20

*Correlations statistically significant (*p* < .05 or better).

SOURCE: Adapted from Derek S. Pugh & David J. Hickson (1976), *Organizational Structure in Its Context: The Aston Programme I* (Lexington, MA: D. C. Heath), 57

TABLE 18.2 Correlations involving contextual variables from the original Aston study

Contextual variables	Structuring of activities	Concentration of authority (centralization)	Line control of workflow
Size of organization (employees)	.69*	−.10	.15
Workflow integration (technology)	.34*	−.30*	−.46*
Dependence	−.05	.66*	.13

*Correlations statistically significant ($p < .05$ or better).

SOURCE: Adapted from Derek S. Pugh & David J. Hickson (1976), *Organizational Structure in Its Context: The Aston Programme I* (Lexington, MA: D. C. Heath), 100, 103, 141

cratic type should not be abandoned in favor of the empirical taxonomy.

Figure 18.5 presents the results of the national study in a form that amounts to a set of empirically derived hypotheses for further study. Note that the arrows tend to be unidirectional, reflecting "the likely directions of dominant influence" (Child, 1976, p. 62) and thus a commitment as to causality. Also, decentralization is now bound directly into the bureau-

cratic concept, rather than separated out as in the original Aston study.

The different results on centralization between the Aston and national studies—and also the Southeast England study—have been the subject of considerable discussion (Donaldson, Child, & Aldrich, 1975). Random fluctuations and differences in degree of organizational diversity likely have combined to produce the disparity.

TABLE 18.3 Significant ($p < .05$ or better) correlations among structural variables in two studies, National and Southeast England

Structural variables	Functional specialization	Formalization	Proportion of managers	Levels of hierarchy
Formalization				
National	.69			
Southeast	.70			
Proportion of managers				
National	—	—		
Southeast	.31	.28		
Levels of hierarchy				
National	.51	.48	—	
Southeast	.63	.56	—	
Centralization — overall				
National	−.28	−.53	—	−.41
Southeast	−.63	−.43	—	−.46
By decision type (all Southeast)				
Production	−.63	−.46	—	−.52
Marketing	−.30	—	—	—
Budget change	—	—	—	—
Personnel and buying	−.58	−.48	—	−.63
Organizational change	−.42	−.34	—	—

SOURCE: Adapted from John Child (1972), Organization Structure and Strategies of Control: A Replication of the Aston Study, *Administrative Science Quarterly*, 17, 169, and Peter H. Grinyer & Masoud Yasai-Ardekani (1980), Dimensions of Organizational Structure: A Critical Replication, *Academy of Management Journal*, 23, 412–413

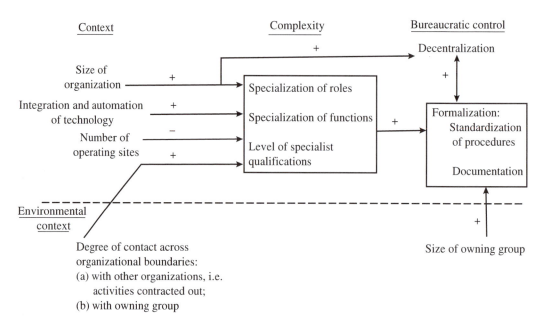

FIGURE 18.5 Summary of relationships suggested by the national study. Adapted from John Child (1976), Predicting and Understanding Organization Structure, in Derek S. Pugh & C. Robert Hinings (Eds.), *Organizational Structure Extensions and Replications: The Aston Programme II* (Lexington, MA: D. C. Heath), 63.

Pugh and Hinings (1976), however, hold to the original view that centralization should be handled separately and not considered part of the structuring of activities factor. They add to this the following statement:

> Discussion of centralization using the Aston schedule needs to be handled with care. The Aston measures had low reliability in the initial study. . . . Centralization is a more complex concept than standardization (and formalization). . . . In the case of centralization, the original measure has clear weaknesses, and subsequent findings based on it are confusing. (p. 172)

If reliability and construct validity problems are present, this would normally be expected to lower correlations. This, too, may account for the results obtained in the original study.

A final point relates to the extent to which managerial and organizational variables predict company performance. This factor was incorporated in the national study, and several different indices of company economic performance were considered; the original As-

ton studies did not deal with performance. No strong relationships were found, however. A number of possible reasons for these disappointing results are considered, but the bottom line is that company performance could not be incorporated in the model.

Aston Research Extending in a Micro Direction

The framework of figure 18.4 is only partially reflected in the Aston research. At the individual level very little was done; most of the studies relate macro variables to group structure and aspects of climate (Pugh & Payne, 1977). The former results are outlined in the context of the research as a whole, and the hypotheses involved, in figure 18.6. They do not support the administrative reduction of variance thesis. Innovative role-sending while associated with structuring of activities, relates positively, not negatively as hypothesized. Similarly, high structuring does not produce a negative correlation with interpersonal conflict.

The research on organizational climate and the climate of line subgroups is equally disappointing. Evidence for the idea that bureaucracies in their true form produce dysfunctions that limit innovation and development was nowhere to be found. The conclusion seems to be that climate is independent of context and structure. The authors conclude from this line of research that:

> The negative psychological consequences of bureaucracy predicted by many writers on organizations do not appear in any strong and consistent way. . . . The administrative reduction of variance thesis does not apply in any simple way at the lower levels of management and supervision. . . . Bureaucratic structures can provide satisfying work environments. . . . The climate studies show no evidence that less attractive climates consistently occur in bureaucratic structures. (Pugh & Payne, 1977, pp. 160–162)

Some of these findings might be accounted for on the basis of measurement unreliability, but there are significant findings in a direction opposite to those hypothesized, and the results have been established in multiple studies. All in all, attempts to extend the Aston research in a micro direction have not been very successful. Perhaps this is why this research thrust remains so abbreviated.

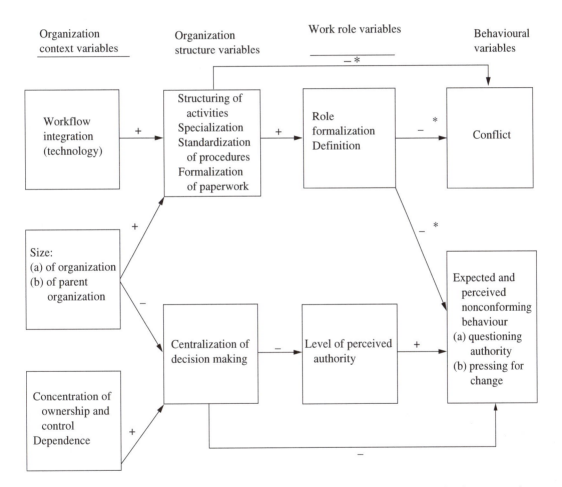

FIGURE 18.6 Hypotheses and research results linking context, structure, work roles, and behavior. *In these three relationships, a negative value was hypothesized and a positive value found. All other hypothesized relationships were supported in varying degrees of strength. From Derek S. Pugh (1976), The Aston Approach to the Study of Organizations, in Geert Hofstede & M. Sami Kassem (Eds.), *European Contributions to Organization Theory* (Amsterdam: Van Gorcum, Assen), 74. Copyright 1976 Royal Van Gorcum, Assen, The Netherlands. Reprinted with permission.

TABLE 18.4 Patterns of relationships between contextual and structural variables in international studies

Contextual variables	Structural variables		
	Formalization	Specialization	Centralization
Size	Plus	Plus	Minus
Size of parent organization	Plus	Plus	Not indicated
Dependence	Usually plus	Not indicated	Plus

SOURCE: Adapted from David J. Hickson & Charles J. McMillan (1981), *Organization and Nation: The Aston Programme IV* (Hampshire, UK: Gower), 193

Aston Research on Domain Extensions

In its first extension the Aston theory was expanded to cover voluntary organizations and in some cases to professional units as well. Does the research support this kind of domain extension? This research looked at trade unions, professional associations, local government units, churches, colleges, and technological institutes (Pugh & Hinings, 1976). Although there is evidence of bureaucracy in this type of situation, the patterns of variables do not always follow the Aston theory, and the extent of influences from voluntary and professional components appears to exert a strong effect on the amount and form of bureaucratization. Size continues to be an important factor. The findings appear to be not unlike those reported in a study of voluntary organizations by Celeste Wilderom and Miner (1991). In any event, one cannot assume that the Aston theory, to the extent it has been supported by research, is equally applicable to organizations beyond its original domain of bureaucratic work organizations; sometimes in certain respects it is, sometimes not.

The second extension was international in nature. These studies were conducted beyond England in Canada, the United States, Germany, Poland (under Communism), Jordan, Egypt, India, Japan, and Sweden (Hickson & McMillan, 1981). The results indicate that although there are cultural variations in context and structure and their relationships, the differences between organizations within nations are greater than the differences between nations, thus supporting the convergence hypothesis. The prevailing pattern of relationships found in these international studies is indicated in table 18.4. A meta-analysis of the relationships involving size supports these findings for specialization and formalization, but found no relationship for centralization (Miller, 1987); a much larger number of studies strengthen one's faith in these results. Research on the interchangeability of societal traditionalism and organizational formalization is more limited than that on the convergence hypothesis. It is, in fact, restricted to the finding that in England—with its strong traditionalism—formalization scores tend to be low; in Canada, formalization scores are intermediate; in the United States—with relatively little societal traditionalism—organizational formalization has been found to be high. No actual measures of traditionalism were obtained. Clearly this hypothesis needs more research.

The third extension, longitudinally over time to create dynamic knowledge of organizations, as incorporated in the ratchet mechanism, has not been the subject of published research by the Aston group. However, Pugh (1976) refers to a comparative longitudinal study in a number of firms involving interviews with a group of managers every 2 weeks and extending over several months. Although it was indicated to be in process, I can find no subsequent report on this study.

Handling Professionalism

The preceding treatment of the role Aston-related studies played in evaluating Aston theory suggests that much of what is known about the theory's value derives from this source. However, there are several areas in which additional research and comments are relevant. One of these is the role of professionals in relation to the Aston concept of bureaucracy.

For Weber, knowledge was the key to power in bureaucracies and should be positively related to the other indices. Those who question that conclusion have focused on professional knowledge, not the kind of knowledge that is indigenous to the organization itself. Within the professional domain, however, a good case can be made that knowledge does not follow the path Weber proposed. Not only are organizations in which professional components predominate structured differently than bureaucracies are, but within bureaucracies themselves professionalization, like centralization, often does not exhibit the expected relationships.

Perhaps the diversity of the Aston sample permitted a degree of nonbureaucratic contamination, thus influencing the centralization results. In any event, the finding that variables do not relate in the same manner in professional and semiprofessional organizations as they do in bureaucracies appears characteristic (Hage & Aiken, 1967). Within bureaucracies the evidence is that decentralization tends to occur in conjunction with bureaucratization; in professional systems this pattern does not emerge. Furthermore, in industrial bureaucracies larger size appears to foster this emphasis on decentralization and indirect control (Mahoney, Frost, Crandall, & Weitzel, 1972).

An extensive review of the research by Richard Hall (1991) emphasizes the incompatibility of bureaucratic and professional systems. There clearly are instances in which bureaucracy incorporates professional components effectively, but that does not mean that the two are part of the same process. Also educational attainment, especially when the bachelor's degree is the highest degree earned, is not an adequate surrogate for professionalism. The point that is being made is well illustrated in table 18.5. Professionalism and the characteristics of bureaucracy are either unrelated, or

perhaps negatively related, depending on how one interprets the data. In large accounting firms, for instance, bureaucracy and a professional orientation represent an antithesis (Sorensen & Sorensen, 1974). John Oliver (1982) has shown that professional systems may be identified as separate entities, even though on occasion they may be incorporated within bureaucracies. This same point is made by Miner, Donald Crane, and Robert Vandenberg (1994; see also the discussion of role motivation theory in chapter 5 in this volume).

The Aston researchers and Aston theory do not clearly distinguish bureaucratic and professional systems. This would be expected to dilute the results and make the theory less powerful. It appears to have produced major problems for the taxonomy of bureaucratic subtypes.

In the area of bureaucratic subtypes it is important to distinguish between taxonomies of forms within the overall bureaucratic concept and taxonomies that extend beyond bureaucracy. The Aston formulations lack theoretical precision in this regard. Furthermore, like so many theories based on factor analysis, they do not hold up in subsequent investigations. Accepting the Aston theory as an alternative to Weberian bureaucracy does not seem warranted. Nevertheless, nothing in what Weber said would preclude the existence of subtypes within the ideal concept of bureaucracy; he simply did not deal with this issue.

Yet approaches of more recent vintage that have much in common with the Aston taxonomy have not fared well at the hands of research. A case in point

TABLE 18.5 Correlations between indices of professionalism and bureaucracy

	Professional indices			
Bureaucratic criteria	Degree of commitment to professional organizations	Belief in service	Belief in self-regulation	Sense of professional calling
Hierarchy of authority	−.03	−.26	−.15	−.15
Division of labor	−.24	−.26	−.23	−.12
Rules	−.14	−.12	−.11	.11
Procedures	−.36*	−.21	−.10	.00
Impersonality	−.26	−.10	−.02	−.34*

*Correlations statistically significant ($p < .05$).

SOURCE: Adapted from Richard H. Hall (1977), *Organizations: Structure and Process* (Englewood Cliffs, NJ: Prentice-Hall), 169

is Henry Mintzberg's (1983) typology, which clearly spreads beyond bureaucracy. It, like the Aston approach, has failed to achieve validation from research (Doty, Glick, & Huber, 1993).

Normative Findings

Although the results from the national study did not yield encouraging evidence for the hypothesis that structure relates to organizational success indices, there are some other data that provide a more positive picture. Remember that the original Aston theory did not posit anything regarding relationships extending to outcome variables, but one certainly comes away from a reading of the theory with the impression that positive findings in this regard would be welcome.

Weber clearly did consider monocratic bureaucracy superior to other organizational forms. To test this position would require comparisons that pit bureaucracy against various other types of organizations. In such studies the influence of factors other than the organizational system, such as resource inputs and environmental forces, would have to be controlled. For example, the influences of human resource inputs such as intellectual abilities and appropriate personality characteristics (bureaucratic and professional motivation, for instance, each in its own context) would have to be removed. The difficulty of conducting such comparative research is obvious, and accordingly data of this kind are lacking. There are some studies in which variations along some dimension of bureaucracy are related to success, however. Research of this type does not really test Weber's superiority hypothesis, but it does provide insights into the effectiveness of bureaucracy in attaining desired goals.

An early review of research dealing with relationships between organization size, hierarchical levels, administrative proportion, specialization, formalization, and centralization and effectiveness yields consistently inconsistent results (Dalton, Todor, Spendolini, Fielding, & Porter, 1980). However, classical management theory aspires to address all forms of organization, and this review is similarly unrestricted. It is not clear what would have been the result if the review had been limited to bureaucratic forms. Furthermore, the review draws on certain measures not implied by bureaucratic theory. Overall, the analysis by Dalton et al. is not particularly helpful in providing a test of the Aston formulations.

Steven Paulson (1974) studied a number of health-related organizations, many of which were clearly non-bureaucratic in nature. Although public agencies were analyzed separately from voluntary and professional organizations, it is still not clear that a purified bureaucratic sample was obtained. Nevertheless, high formalization and low centralization are most likely to relate to effectiveness, and structural factors in any event are generally rather weak predictors of organizational outcomes in this health-related context.

However, a study by Selwyn Becker and Duncan Neuhauser (1975) of 30 community hospitals yields somewhat stronger conclusions. Standardization or formalization of procedures and a variable referred to as visibility of consequences, which appears to reflect organizational rationality, both showed substantial positive relationships to various effectiveness indices in the administrative (bureaucratic) components of the hospitals. In the medical (professional) components, standardization related negatively to effectiveness, but the rationality variable remained positively correlated; once again the disparity between bureaucratic and professional systems is emphasized. In a subsequent study of insurance companies that focused only on the visibility of consequences concept, positive relationships with efficiency measures were obtained.

Bernard Reimann and Anant Negandhi (1975) found in their study in India that formalized process (manufacturing) and particularly personnel controls, coupled with decentralization, promoted organizational effectiveness. The combination of high formalization in the form of controls and low centralization is associated with greater effectiveness than either alone (Negandhi, 1975). A recent study by Peter Evans and James Rauch (1999) found that resort to bureaucratic processes in state economic agencies was highly correlated with country economic growth in a sample of 35 developing nations.

Thus, there are data that support the view that aspects of bureaucracy are related to organizational success, or at least can be found so under appropriate circumstances. It would appear that aspects of other organizational forms, such as the professional, yield the same result. Thus, the superiority of the bureaucratic form has not been demonstrated; but the Aston theorists did not say this, only Weber did.

Role of Size

Research on relationships that involve organizational size has continued since the Aston studies and is generally supportive of the Aston theory, although longitudinal research tends to yield somewhat smaller relationships (Bluedorn, 1993). Research conducted by Barbara Keats and Michael Hitt (1988) seems to be at variance with this conclusion, in that size was found to play only a small role in structuring. However, this study did not use the full range of structural variables considered by the Aston researchers, and the one such variable employed was measured in a substantially different manner. Thus any relevance for the Aston theory is minimal. The ratchet mechanism has generally been found to operate as hypothesized, at least in the sense that decreases in organizational size do not produce declines in structural variables commensurate with the increases produced by growth (Meyer, Stevenson, & Webster, 1985).

It becomes increasingly apparent that, to really understand size and its influence on structuring and other organizational variables, it is important to conduct longitudinal studies. Size at a point in time is a product of cycles of growth and decline; growth in particular is important, since most organizations start small (Weinzimmer, Nystrom, & Freeman, 1998). The Aston approach with its emphasis on cross-sectional analyses represents a good beginning, but it needs to be supplemented with longitudinal work as Pugh recognized. This is the route to more sophisticated, dynamic theory; research of this kind will be invoked in connection with Blau's theory.

Application

Applications of bureaucratic theory are difficult to discuss, given their widespread nature, although perhaps it is best to consider the current scene more a demonstration of this particular organizational phenomenon than an outgrowth of any theory itself. Probably our organizational world would be much the same had Weber never written, but we would understand it much less well.

Perhaps the major strength of bureaucracy is its capacity to structure large systems. Through Weber's law of the small number, coupled with hierarchy, it is possible for what would otherwise be small group processes to be expanded throughout huge organizations. The individual units and subunits serve partial goals that become their own total goals, but the composite result is an effective organization. The processes involved are not unlike those of regulated capitalism.

Each component seeks its own ends, but the overall result redounds to the benefit of the whole.

Given our current knowledge, bureaucracy becomes the structure of choice for large organizations, and the greater the rationality, formalization, standardization, specialization, and decentralization, the more effective it will be. This does not mean there will not be negative side effects for individuals, but these can combine to subvert the structure only where the bureaucratic system was improperly designed and operated in the first place.

The choice of bureaucracy is made easy for large systems because few alternatives are available. One could draw on patrimonial and charismatic forms, but they seem ill adapted to the needs of the modern world, as Weber so effectively argued. The nonbureaucratic forms that do appear appropriate to current needs — professional, task, and group systems — are primarily suited to small organizations. With the exception of representative democracy for group systems, we have not devised methods of applying these systems to large numbers of people. Typically, as organizations grow, bureaucracy is superimposed on the existing system to deal with the expanded size. In such cases, the original professional, task, or group system that is not sufficiently robust can easily disappear under the onslaught of the new bureaucracy. If organizations are to grow and achieve economies of scale and speed, some degree of bureaucratization appears inevitable, at least until other methods of handling large organizations can be created.

Given this as background, what has Aston theory contributed to organization planning and design? From the perspective of practice the greatest contribution appears to be inherent in the scales and measures of organizational characteristics. These have been published widely in appendices to articles and book chapters. They indicate exactly what to do if one wishes to achieve greater standardization, or formalization, or whatever. Thus within the range of discretion available they say how choices may be carried out. There is no evidence that I am aware of as to how widely the measures may be used in this manner, but they are available and can be used to help design organizations. A close reading of them will certainly contribute to a practitioner's understanding of design considerations.

Perusal of Pugh's contributions clearly indicates that he was aware of the practical value inherent in producing measures of bureaucracy. Yet others with a different orientation to the field have been critical on this score, considering the measures unexciting and really of little practical value (see Marsden & Townley, 1996). Yet constructing them took a great deal of work, and it is partly for that reason that bureaucracy and its constructs remained unoperationalized for so long.

A final point on applications has to do with the findings with regard to the administrative reduction of variance thesis, and thus the frequently posited dysfunctions of bureaucracy. It appears that these dysfunctions do not emerge as nearly the problem some have contended. The Aston research in this micro area did not confirm theory, but it should not be ignored. It says that bureaucracy is not so bad, and that when appropriate in terms of the size of the organization and relationships to external entities, it should be implemented, not avoided.

Structural Contingency Theory

In chapter 15 structural contingency theory was briefly mentioned in connection with the discussion of James Thompson's theoretical propositions. This approach is relevant for the Aston theory and in important respects is an outgrowth of Aston. Although it is endorsed in varying degrees, from mildly to quite strongly, by a number of scholars (see for example Pennings, 1992, and Hall, 1991), the major advocate who has done the most to systematize the approach is Lex Donaldson.

Donaldson was mentioned previously as one of the third generation of Aston scholars. He worked with John Child and to a lesser extent Derek Pugh at Aston and at the London Business School, where he received his doctorate, but he never published with Pugh. He has been in Australia for many years at the University of New South Wales in the Australian Graduate School of Management. Thus he is both of the Aston studies, and yet rather far removed from its research and theoretical origins. Although he has been primarily a theorist and critic, he has published several reports of his own research that is related to structural contingency theory (Donaldson, 1982, 1987).

Scope and Coverage

Structural contingency theory is rooted in the contingency theory approach as treated in chapters 15, 16, and 17 and in this chapter. Which specific theories are involved has not been consistently indicated, and this may be related to the fact that the theory has changed somewhat through a number of statements and restatements.

Initially Donaldson (1985a) appears to have had the Aston theory in mind, when he discussed structural contingency theory, and thus the contingency variables of size, dependence, and technology. Later, however (Donaldson, 1990), he notes only the Paul Lawrence and Jay Lorsch version of contingency theory (see chapter 17), thus emphasizing environmental uncertainty as a contingency variable, but without reference to the subsequent, more differentiated, views of Lawrence and Davis Dyer.

In a more comprehensive treatment, Donaldson (1995) stresses a much wider range of contingency and systems theorists, most of whom are discussed in this book, including Joan Woodward (chapter 16), Burns and Stalker (chapter 15), Lawrence and Lorsch (chapter 17), Pugh and the other Aston theorists (this chapter), Fred Emery and Eric Trist (chapter 14), Charles Perrow (chapter 16), Thompson (chapter 15), and Peter Blau (this chapter). Accordingly, a great variety of contingency factors appear to become part of the theory, and a much larger range of potential supporters is marshaled.

This particular theoretical presentation, however, draws heavily on Alfred Chandler (1962), thus emphasizing strategy (and in particular growth strategy) as a contingency variable that influences structure. Chandler's theory of strategy and structure is much more a part of the strategic management field than of organizational behavior, and consequently it is not considered here. It is discussed at length in Miner (1982), in a manner commensurate with the approach used in this book, and a large part of the research on it is considered there also. Donaldson's selection of strategy and structure theory to illustrate structural contingency theory seems somewhat strange in that the theory is not nearly as closely identified with organizational behavior as others that might have been chosen, and the introduction of strategy (read: choice) as a contingency variable creates certain problems for the theory, as we will see subsequently. A major consideration appears to have been the relevance of Donaldson's (1987) own research on the subject.

Elsewhere, in presenting a list of contingency theorists whose work underlies structural contingency theory, and by implication in endorsing the contingency variables thus involved, Donaldson (1996a) notes most of the names listed here. Yet for some reason, Emery and Trist, and thus sociotechnical theory, and Perrow's version of the technological imperative are omitted. Donaldson's (1996b) chapter in the *Handbook of Organization Studies* continues to omit Emery and Trist, presumably because their theory is more of an open systems than truly contingency nature, but Perrow is now included again.

These variations in inclusions and exclusions are of considerable importance because we need to know what contingency variables are theoretically significant. Different presentations provide different emphases in this regard, but the following from Donaldson (1996b) is most relevant. He notes that several contingency factors—strategy, size, task uncertainty, and technology—represent characteristics of the organization, but also reflect influences from the environment. Then he says that "task uncertainty is the core contingency concept that has implications for second-order contingency concepts such as innovation and size" (p. 58). One would assume that strategy and technology are of a second-order nature as well. The stress on the role of task uncertainty appears to reflect a reemphasis on the Lawrence and Lorsch theory as the basic underpinning of structural contingency theory.

Statements of the Theory

The exact nature of structural contingency theory has to be gleaned from statements sprinkled throughout Donaldson's writings. In this he is consistent with his Aston origins.

The theory views the organization as adaptive in its structuring to the particular states of the contingency variables. Changes in structure occur incrementally to achieve this adaptation. The causal flow is clearly stated to be from contingency factor to structural factor; there is no equivocating in this regard. Furthermore, it takes a fit between contingency and structural variables to achieve positive outcomes. When the two are out of fit, organizational performance will suffer. A structural adaptation to regain fit occurs as follows:

1. There is . . . a fit between the organizational structure and the contingency which affects organizational performance.
2. There is the idea that a change by the organization in its contingency variables causes it to move from fit to misfit.
3. There is the idea that misfit causes structural change.

4. There is also the idea . . . that the organization by changing its organization structure moves from misfit into fit. (Donaldson, 1995, p. 33)

At stage 2 the misfit eventually operates to degrade performance. This triggers an incremental process of structural change to adapt to the new contingency state. The structural changes are in degree of bureaucratization, divisionalization, organicness, and the like, depending on the contingency variable involved.

According to Donaldson (1995), structural contingency theory is the base onto which aspects of other theories may be added to fill in holes in the structural contingency formulations; thus a single theory of organization, at least at the macro level, is created. The result is an overarching theoretical integration, which the field needs at the present time. Newer theories would contribute only in limited and localized ways, building on the central core of structural contingency theory.

In discussing the theory thus created, Donaldson sets forth six characteristics:

1. It is *nomothetic*, meaning that the phenomena are analyzed using a general framework with factors that apply to all organizations, both for the contingency factors (such as size and strategy) and for the organizational structure (like specialization and centralization). General causal relationships in the form of law-like regularities are sought between contingency and structural factors.
2. The research associated with the theory is *methodologically positivist* in that there is much use of comparative empirical research, often with the measurement of variables and statistical analysis of data.
3. The theory explains organizational structure by *material factors* such as size, technology and so on, rather than by ideationalist factors such as ideas, ideologies, perceptions, norms and the like. (Even in the work of Chandler the "strategy" that affects structure refers to the degree of diversification and vertical integration existing in the organization; a mere plan or intention of diversifying that was not implemented would not require a change of structure.)
4. The theory is *deterministic* in that managers are seen as having to adopt the organizational structure that is required by the contingency factors, in order to gain organizational effectiveness.

5. The theory is closely *informed by empirical research* rather than armchair speculation or extended theorizing prior to empirical data collection. It is built upon the data patterns and arguments of the pioneering works.
6. The theory is consciously scientific in style, with *the aim being to produce scientific knowledge of the type achieved in the natural sciences.* (1996a, p. 3)

Structural contingency theory uses objective *determinism* to state the causal flow from contingency variables to structural. It uses *functionalism* and thus holds that structure is determined ultimately by functional necessity and the drive for organizational effectiveness. It uses *Cartesianism* in that organizations are seen as taking many different positions in multidimensional space; thus it employs continuous variables rather than types of organizations. It assumes that *generalization* is possible, desirable, and can be demonstrated for organizational structures.

The contingency variables emphasized by the theory have changed in different presentations. Another area of change is determinism and its alternative — human choice. At an early point Donaldson adopted a view much like that of Child (1972a), which incorporated strategic choice in the contingency process. Over time this has changed to a strict determinism or imperative (comparable to the technological imperative view, but extrapolated to all contingency factors). It thus extends well beyond the original Aston view that contingency factors set constraints on managerial discretion. Causation from structure to contingency, and thus the idea of a proactive organization producing changes in its environment, is rejected. With regard to choice Donaldson says the following:

Specifically, there appears to be little scope for the effect of contingency on structure to be mediated by cognitive or political or other social processes. Managers choose the new structure and this involves cognition, perception and problem-solving. But these are mainly intervening variables between contingency and structure; that is, the decision processes seem to be largely determined by the contingency and other objective, situational factors. Once the contingency changes and produces a misfit, then problems ensue and problem-solving initiated by the managers results in a recommended new structure. This recommendation becomes accepted when the problems grow into increasingly poor performance. The structure which emerges is predetermined by the objective contingency, misfit and performance variables. Once the contingency changes, organizations adapt their structure in highly predictable ways. Organizational structural change moves according to laws which are deterministic. (1996a, pp. 160–161)

Of course, this position creates problems vis-à-vis previous statements about the role of strategy as a contingency variable, which follow from Chandler (1962). That Donaldson has wrestled with this problem is evident in number 3 of the previously stated characteristics of structural contingency theory. His most recent position is to define Chandler's growth strategy as simply diversification, or elsewhere as corporate development (Donaldson, 1997). This interpretation appears to depart from Chandler, from Child's (1997) position, and from usual understandings in the field of strategic management.

Donaldson also recognizes a problem around the concept of fit when multiple contingency variables are involved; this is the matter of what he calls Cartesianism. On this he says the following:

Structural contingency theory is multivariate in the sense that many contingency and structural factors are continuous variables. The fit between a structural value and a contingency value is also a continuous line connecting each point of fit. There are a number of such fit lines between each of the pairs of contingency and structural variables. Thus fit is a curve that connects all of these fit lines within the multidimensional space formed by all the contingency and structural variables. Hence there are very many points of fit in this space. And any one point of fit connects with the next points of fit in each direction, so that the organization can move from one fit to another. This allows the organization to change greatly over time by a series of incremental steps. Growth from small business to large multinational corporation is made possible in this way. (1996a, p. 165)

Criticism of Other Positions

Donaldson's objective from an early point was not only to state structural contingency theory but also to refute critics and alternative positions that threatened aspects of the theory. Initially this involved no more than dealing with attacks from the critical theory, poststructuralism, or postmodernism perspective, all of which were of a basically anti-science nature. In this context, Marxist ideology was also viewed as a threat (Donaldson, 1985a). These positions were particularly salient for Donaldson because they originated outside the United States and had strong currency in England. He was clearly much more aware of the threat involved in these positions than were most scholars in the United States at the time. He has remained concerned about this matter, however, and has continued to mount a counterattack (Donaldson, 1988, 1992). After all, structural contingency theory is a social science theory rooted in empirical investigation in a scientific mode and aspires to create scientific laws comparable to those of the physical sciences.

This first round of critiques focused on radical positions and, accordingly, had a primarily British flavor, although positions of a similar type originating from the United States were also included. The second book in the series (Donaldson, 1995) is intended to redress this balance and concentrate on U.S. theories. It takes up a number of second-generation theories that will be covered in later parts of this book: population ecology theory, neo-institutional theory, and resource dependence theory. There are also critiques of economics-based theories that are beyond the purview of this book, such as agency theory and transaction cost economics.

These critiques are conducted from the perspective of structural contingency theory and tend to point up areas of theoretical conflict. They also emphasize aspects of the theories that tend to denigrate or paint a negative picture of corporate managers; this aspect comes into play in particular with regard to organizational economics. Donaldson feels that the anti-management orientation of many U.S. theories is to be deplored. Also the approach taken in his 1995 volume is to advocate relegating the theories discussed to a secondary position where they would provide possible adjuncts or add-ons to structural contingency theory. Thus the coverage of macro organizational behavior theory is narrowed as large segments of these other theories are placed out of bounds or considered to be of only very limited interest.

The third book (Donaldson, 1996a) contains another round of criticisms of what are viewed as competing positions. These serve to narrow the theoretical field even further, and, in fact, if they are followed in terms of their implications for the use of various approaches to theory development, they would severely constrain the range of theory available. One approach that is attacked is the strategic choice type

of theory, which is viewed as antithetical to determinism. Political explanations of organizational structure are rejected because they are in opposition to functionalism. Organizational typologies are brought into question as a consequence of structural contingency theory's commitment to Cartesianism and the use of continuous quantitative variables. Types imply quantum changes, not incremental shifts along a continuum, to move from a fit with one type to another; thus quantum change is rejected as well. Finally, organizational systematics, whereby an organization is viewed as fitting a near-unique niche which must be studied in detail so that homogenous taxonomies can be developed across many such distinct niche-based organizations, is considered to inhibit generalization and thus to threaten the creation of general laws.

More recently Donaldson (1997) has again taken issue with the structure action approach in theory development, which serves to emphasize the primary role of strategic choice. He also has deplored the use in practice of approaches that serve to downgrade the position of managers within the large corporation — attempts to replace hierarchy, flatten the organization so that very few managers remain, minimize company management representation on the board of directors, and the like (Donaldson & Hilmer, 1998). Whatever one's position on the many matters that Donaldson has critiqued, there can be no question that the net result of his recommendations would be a severe limitation of the alternatives available to both theorists and practitioners.

Evaluation and Impact

The advent of structural contingency theory and its promulgation by Donaldson has had the effect of keeping the Aston theory and research visible and stimulating further discussion. Aston theory fell off noticeably in its impact as its major proponents moved on to other locations and areas of interest. By the early 1980s scientific interest had clearly peaked. The writings of Donaldson and others have reversed this trend to a meaningful degree, although they do not appear to have done much in reactivating the research stream.

The deliberate narrowing of the field of study and approaches to it, as well as the simplification of theory, that Donaldson advocates — in fact, the whole idea of a core supertheory to which other theories become secondary — has not gone unchallenged. Critics have converged on this narrowing aspect of structural contingency theory from a variety of directions and philosophical perspectives (see, for example, Aldrich, 1988; Child, 1988; Clegg, 1988). The consensus appears to be that we are not yet at a point in macro organizational behavior where we can afford to forego innovation, creativity, and the development of new ideas, and perhaps we never will be. To put blinders on numerous theoretical positions and approaches to theory development before testing has occurred does not appear likely to yield benefits equal to the potential costs. Reducing the great variety of theoretical positions is laudable only after the theories have been created and found wanting in the crucible of research, not before the theories are born. If structural contingency theory is indeed the supertheory, then research will establish it as such, when studied in comparison to other positions.

This brings us to the validity of the theory. Since structural contingency theory is in large part a composite of contingency theories already considered, the evidence on these theories is relevant. Donaldson consistently claims substantial support for these theories, while admitting to several problem areas. The evidence presented in the last few chapters of this volume is not nearly as forgiving. The theories typically have strong research support in certain respects, but there are other areas of major failure and a goodly ground that has not been investigated. The Aston findings on the relationship between size and the structuring of activities variables, with average correlations corrected for unreliability ranging from .59 to .82 (Donaldson, 1996a), are among the most impressive. Yet these correlations alone do not prove anything about the direction of causation, or determinism.

A particularly weak feature in the research on contingency theories is the tie between structural fit and outcomes. Research in this area has been far less frequent than might be desired, as Donaldson (1995) recognizes, and when this matter has been investigated, the results often have not produced significant relationships. This problem exists in the research on strategy-structure theory (Miner, 1982), as it does in organizational behavior's contingency theories. Also the very limited support for the Burns and Stalker formulations has been acknowledged by Donaldson (1995). The ratchet mechanism, which research appears to support, would seem to argue that when organizational size decreases, and a misfit with structure is created, the original high structuring is often maintained, not reduced to regain fit as the theory would

predict. All in all, one must question the overwhelming research validation of the theory that Donaldson claims; at no point does he work through the various contingency theories citing the evidence and weighing it, as has been done in previous chapters of this book.

In fact, the status of the various component theories and their contingency variables within structural contingency theory is left rather uncertain. The tendency to cite various theories at different times is a clear problem. To what has been said previously should be added Donaldson's (1996b) statement that environmental hostility as proposed by Pradip Khandwalla (1977) and the product life-cycle (Donaldson, 1985b) are also contingency factors within the theory. Also, uncertainty, which is obviously an important factor in the theory, is viewed at different points as environmental uncertainty and task uncertainty; there is a clear need for construct clarification.

As the list of contingency variables grows, the complexity of the multiple fits involved and the relationships among them grows as well. This matter, which presumably involves the dominance of certain contingency variables over others under certain circumstances, has not been addressed by Donaldson or anyone else, although the problem is recognized:

> Clarifying the exact few contingencies that apply to each different aspect of structure and including them in multivariate models that exhaustively capture fit and then measuring this multivariate fit and its impact on performance is the next step in fit research. It constitutes an important agenda item for future contingency research. (Donaldson, 1996b, p. 69)

In the key area of its contingency variables, the theory is very muddy at the present time.

Given the nature and number of these difficulties, foreclosing the study of other macro organizational behavior theories in favor of structural contingency theory simply is not warranted on the evidence. Major theoretical development and research tasks remain to be completed, and there is no strong reason to believe that such efforts will necessarily produce the results the theory's supporters anticipate. Nevertheless, as an outgrowth of the Aston work, structural contingency theory has done a great deal to keep a very important line of theoretical and research endeavor active and has served to bring into focus many of the issues raised by the Aston efforts.

The foregoing has been written without benefit of access to a very recent book by Donaldson (2001) dealing with this subject matter. The reader may wish to check this source for a statement of the structural contingency theory position that goes beyond what is contained in this volume.

BLAU'S THEORY OF DIFFERENTIATION

Blau's theory was developed in parallel with the Aston theory, but on a different side of the Atlantic, and it lead to somewhat different questions. Both theories represent attempts to formulate precise theoretical hypotheses based on Weber and, having converted Weber to more readily testable form, to actually carry out the necessary research. The two programs were both initiated during the 1960s and reached the publication phase at much the same time. Both cite each other, but the two theories appear to have evolved independently.

In addition to Weber, Blau appears to have been influenced indirectly in his approach by other classical sociological theorists—Georg Simmel, Emile Durkheim, and to a degree Karl Marx (Calhoun & Scott, 1990). The most important direct influences seem to have come from Robert Merton and Paul Lazarsfed, the latter primarily in the area of research methodology, both of whom were Blau's mentors when he was a graduate student at Columbia University (Merton, 1990).

Background

Blau has always been a sociologist. He was president of the American Sociological Association in 1974, and he has written on a variety of sociological topics throughout his career. Thus his contributions are often identified more with sociology than with organizational behavior, and are indeed more central to sociology than those of the Aston theorists. Yet Blau's theorizing is of considerable importance for macro organizational behavior as well.

His sociological education began at Elmhurst College, near Chicago, which he entered upon coming to the United States in 1939 at the age of 21 from Vienna, Austria (Blau, 1995). He, like several other of the theorists we have considered, was a Jew who escaped from the Nazis to emigrate to the United States. After college and several years in the army, he entered graduate study in sociology at Columbia

University. He obtained his doctorate there in 1952; there were stints as a faculty member at Wayne State University and at Cornell University in between, while he was writing his dissertation. In 1953 he began his regular professorial career in the sociology department at the University of Chicago, where he remained for 17 years. Then in 1970 he returned to Columbia. Since then he has been on the sociology faculties at the State University of New York at Albany and, most recently, at the University of North Carolina in Chapel Hill.

Blau's contributions to the study of organizations have been intermittent through his career. His graduate study did focus in that area, and the outgrowth was a dissertation, later published as a book (Blau, 1955), that utilized the Hawthorne studies as a model and considered interpersonal and group relationships in two government agencies. This, and most of Blau's work in the organization area over the next few years, was primarily micro in nature. The initial signs of a more macro orientation began to appear in a text published with Richard Scott (Blau & Scott, 1962), but even then the primary focus was at the micro level. Later in the 1960s Blau began research (and formal theory construction) of a more basic structural type, building on the 1962 groundwork. Yet this did not come to fruition in the form of a fully developed theory for some time (Blau, 1970b). Later in the 1970s Blau's interests shifted from differentiation within organizations to differentiation within societies and to problems of inequality.

Thus, Blau's status as an organization theorist did not become established until the middle of his career, and he did not produce his theory of organizational differentiation until he was more than 50 years old. Before that time he was at least as well known for his other contributions to sociology—to social exchange theory and to the understanding of occupational mobility, for example. He was approaching 40 as the field of organizational behavior came into being in business schools. Given the nature of his career in sociology and the timing of events, it is little wonder that Blau was not attracted to a business school position. The fact that he had an interest in Marxian theory of class differences and a socialist background (Blau, 1995) may have been a contributing factor as well.

Theoretical Positions

Many of Blau's writings on organizations originally appeared as articles in the sociological literature.

These have been compiled in a volume entitled *On the Nature of Organizations* (Blau, 1974), and it is to this volume that primary reference is made here.

Blau on Weber

Blau accepts a number of the criticisms of Weber that were developed by others. He agrees that Weber failed to recognize certain dysfunctions created by bureaucracy, such as the encouragement of less personally responsible behavior. Basically, Weber focused on the functions of bureaucratic institutions within the larger society and failed to deal effectively with many problems of their internal workings. In discussing promotion he emphasized the use of objective, rational procedures, but he failed to deal with the relative worth of seniority and merit. In the same vein, while noting numerous departures from the bureaucratic ideal, Weber does not recognize the existence and role of informal organization as a social entity.

Blau notes certain difficulties inherent in Weber's concept of authority—his use of the ideal type or pure case and his handling of the interface between bureaucracy and democracy. These difficulties are exacerbated by the fact that Weber is not entirely consistent in his treatment of these matters.

The theory recognizes both a voluntary element and imperative control in rational-legal authority, but it does not attempt to reconcile the two. Blau proposes that the key factor is the development of norms of compliance within the subordinate group. The individual complies in part because the power to orchestrate sanctions resides in the superior and creates subordinate dependence, but in the context of group norms subordinates may obey even when they would not otherwise voluntarily comply.

One difficulty with the use of ideal types such as bureaucracy is that they freeze relationships so that factors must covary together, when, in fact, these factors may vary independently under certain conditions. As an approach to theory construction, the ideal type is at one and the same time a conceptual scheme and a set of hypotheses. It specifies aspects of a bureaucracy that are highly salient, and criteria for identifying bureaucracy in terms of these aspects. But it also states hypotheses about relationships among the aspects and their relation to efficiency that are empirically testable. If the empirical facts do not confirm the hypotheses in all respects, the ideal type becomes meaningless. Blau argues for abandoning ideal type constructs in bureaucratic theory in favor of a set of hypotheses relating key variables under specified circumstances.

Weber discusses democracy and collegiality on numerous occasions, but he never distinguishes between them and bureaucracy in any systematic manner. It is almost as if Weber does not know quite what to do with democracy within his historical framework. He borders on, but does not actually deal with, the distinction posed by sociotechnical theory (chapter 14 in this volume). Blau suggests that bureaucratic and democratic (group) systems are different and should be treated as such.

At various points in other writings Blau takes up dysfunctions of bureaucracy that Weber did not recognize. He notes the tendency for impersonal government agencies to provide inappropriate or insensitive treatment to clients (Blau, 1955); the nonresponsiveness to membership interests characterizing certain oligarchies (Blau, 1956); the ways in which corporate structures mobilize power in support of purposes that may be inimical to human welfare, as well as that threaten individual liberties and democratic institutions (Blau & Schoenherr, 1971); and the fact that overly centralized bureaucracies may have deleterious consequences for the exercise of professional discretion (Blau, 1973).

Clearly Blau departs from Weber in a number of respects, but he also recognizes that bureaucratic structures are indispensable for using complex technologies and for supporting arrangements that involve advanced division of labor, both of which yield major social benefits. Of Weber himself he says: "Perhaps the most difficult task for a scholar is to develop a new approach to the study of reality. . . . It is no exaggeration to say that Weber was one of the rare men who has done just this" (Blau, 1974, p. 57).

In addition, Blau has given particular attention to operationalizing the constructs of bureaucratic theory: size, complexity, specialization, expertness, administrative staff, hierarchy, rules, impersonality, and career stability. This is not done in the same manner as that of the Aston researchers, but it is done effectively nevertheless.

Professionalism, Expert Knowledge, and Bureaucracy

As noted previously in this chapter, Weber held that the major source of rational-legal authority was expert knowledge, which accrued to those at higher levels in the bureaucratic system in increasing proportions. In many respects Weber was right. Communication comes down through a bureaucracy, and thus each higher level can know more. Knowledge that is idiosyncratic to the particular organization — knowledge of rules and information related to strategic decision making — is clearly a function of hierarchical position. But Weber failed to reckon with the organizational value of professional knowledge (legal, scientific, medical, and the like), which enters the organization through professional components and often at relatively low levels. Under such circumstances a hierarchical superior may be expert on strictly organizational issues, but not on professional knowledge relevant to the concern.

The relationship between expertise and hierarchy may not be quite as Weber viewed it, and thus rational-legal authority may flow in somewhat different directions. Blau recognized this problem and viewed professional authority as a separate entity that need not covary with bureaucratic variables such as the specialized division of labor. In this he follows a number of sociologists dating back to Talcott Parsons and A. M. Henderson in their translation of Weber (1947).

Certainly, there are marked similarities between bureaucratic and professional systems — among them, impersonality, rational decision making, and an emphasis on technical expertness. But there are many differences also. In stressing the differences and noting the potential sources of conflict between the two types of authority, Blau departs significantly from Weber's theory.

At the same time, Blau (1973) uses bureaucratic concepts in his analysis of colleges and universities, just as the Aston researchers did. Wolf Heydebrand (1990) contends that, by using these concepts he introduces a number of inconsistencies and anomalies that are at variance with the very nature of bureaucracy. There is indeed reason to believe that Blau did not fully resolve the theoretical problems to be found at the interface between bureaucratic and professional systems.

Differentiation in Organizations

Building on the results of a study of government employment security units, Blau developed a largely deductive theory of differentiation in organizations that primarily extends Weber's position rather than opposes it. Differentiation occurs when the number of geographical branches, occupational positions, hierarchical levels, and divisions, or units within branches or divisions, increases. The hypotheses are as follows:

1. Increasing size generates structural differentiation in organizations along various dimensions at decelerating rates.
    1A. Large size promotes structural differentiation.
    1B. Large size promotes differentiation along several different lines.
    1C. The rate of differentiation declines with expanding size.
    1.1. As the size of organizations increases, its marginal influence on differentiation decreases.
    1.2. The larger an organization is, the larger is the average size of its structural components of all kinds.
    1.3. The proportionate size of the average structural component, as distinguished from the absolute size, decreases with increases in organizational size.
    1.4. The larger the organization is, the wider the supervisory span of control.
    1.5. Organizations exhibit an economy of scale in management.
    1.6. The economy of scale in administrative overhead itself declines with increasing organizational size.
2. Structural differentiation in organizations enlarges the administrative component.
    2.1. The large size of an organization indirectly raises the ratio of administrative personnel through the structural differentiation it generates.
    2.2. The direct effects of large organizational size lowering the administrative ratio exceed its indirect effects raising it owing to the structural differentiation it generates.
    2.3 The differentiation of large organizations into subunits stems the decline in the economy of scale in management with increasing size. (Blau, 1974, pp. 302–317)

These propositions have been restated more recently as follows:

First, the large size of organizations increases their differentiation in various dimensions at decelerating rates. This is the case whether the division of labor, vertical levels, horizontal subdivisions, or other forms of differentiation are examined. For every form of differentiation, in other words, the size of an organization is positively related to the extent of differentiation, but all these correlations are most pronounced for smaller organizations and become increasingly attenuated for those in the larger size range. In mathematical terms, the influence of size on differentiation is indicated by a polynomial with a positive main and a negative squared term.

Second, large size reduces administrative overhead (the proportion of administrative personnel), which implies an administrative economy of scale. Third, degree of differentiation, which entails greater structural complexity, is positively related to administrative overhead. Finally, large size directly reduces yet indirectly (mediated by its influence on differentiation) increases administrative overhead; but the direct negative exceeds the indirect positive effect on administrative cost; this produces the net negative effect that finds expression in the administrative economy of scale.

The theory seeks to explain why the rate of differentiation with the increasing size of organizations declines for larger organizations. The inference made is that the feedback effect of the rising administrative cost of increasing organizational differentiation, and hence complexity, with growing size are responsible. To sustain the economy of scale in administrative cost from which large organizations benefit, they must not become so differentiated that the administrative cost of complexity absorbs this economy of scale; this is effected by dampening the influence of expanded size on enhancing differentiation and complexity. (Blau, 1995, p. 12)

The theory as stated is deductively derived but the deductive process starts with an induction from the Blau and Schoenherr (1971) research finding that organizational membership size is highly correlated with the extent of differentiation (Slater, 1985).

Decentralization in Bureaucracies

Blau (1974) makes a distinction between managing through direct and indirect controls. Direct control involves close observation and corrective orders. Indirect control relies more on impersonal procedures that automatically limit behavior. Examples of indirect controls are automation and merit personnel standards. Clearly, indirect control has been expedited with the aid of computers. Direct control reflects centralization, while indirect control indicates standardization or formalization.

Weber leads one to expect that both centralization

and formalization increase with greater bureaucratization; the two go together. Blau (1970a) proposes, however, that formalization through indirect controls actually restricts the manager and serves as a means of decentralization. In this view, direct and indirect controls are alternatives and define two different types of bureaucracies. Modern bureaucracies stress the formalization of indirect control and are more decentralized. These variables do not covary in the manner Weber appears to have envisaged.

Whether this is a true departure from Weber depends on whether one interprets the use of indirect controls as formalization or simply as another type of authority. Comments by discussants after the presentation of Blau's (1970a) paper reflect uncertainty on this point and raise questions of construct validity for the Weber theory. Note that this is an area in which the Aston theory ran into difficulty as well. In any event, Blau's theory of alternative control procedures can stand on its own merits. It parallels Chandler's (1962) formulations rather closely.

Evaluation and Impact

Much of the research on Blau's theorizing has been conducted by Blau himself in conjunction with others. These studies were all cross-sectional in nature. However, a body of research does exist that goes beyond this, in that others not directly involved with the theory have conducted the studies and changes over time have been considered.

Blau's Comparative Studies

Blau's (1955) early research focused on informal relationships within individual bureaucracies, such as consultations between federal enforcement agents on different problems, even when this practice was officially proscribed. However, his most important contributions to the theory of bureaucracy are comparative analyses across multiple organizations (Blau & Schoenherr, 1971; Blau, 1974; Blau, Falbe, McKinley, & Tracy, 1976). Blau assumed that bureaucratic characteristics are actually variables and that therefore real-world (as contrasted with ideal type) bureaucracies are bureaucratic to varying degrees.

The theory of organizational differentiation evolved from a study of employment security units, so that study cannot be used to test the theory. However, subsequent research on samples drawn from government finance departments, department stores, universities and colleges, teaching hospitals (Blau, 1974), and manufacturing plants (Blau et al., 1976) consistently supports the theoretical hypotheses across all types of differentiation. The role of size in organizational structure appears to be important, and correlations with differentiation are substantial, rising as high as the .80s in certain instances. This is consistent with the Aston findings.

Clearly, Weber viewed size as a major correlate of bureaucracy, though he did not rule out bureaucratization of small organizations. Weber's predominant position on centralization appears to be that it occurs in conjunction with bureaucracy; yet some of Weber's statements may be and have been interpreted differently on occasion. This makes the relationship between centralization and other indices of bureaucratization such as formalization and control particularly important. Blau and Schoenherr's (1971) research has addressed this issue.

The data from state employment agencies shown in table 18.6 indicate a generally negative relationship in that increases in formalization are accompanied by less centralization. The only meaningful exceptions relate to hiring decisions in which there is a tendency for more standardized performance ratings and more managers (more control) to be associated with more centralization. Blau and Schoenherr (1971) conclude that top management needs to decentralize decisions as the organization grows and the levels of hierarchy increase, but that top management actually does this only when the risks of decentralization can be minimized. The indirect control made possible by standardized procedures, rules, computerized systems, and the like becomes a necessary condition for moving decisions downward. These results certainly go beyond Weber and seem to run counter to his hypothesis that rationalization and centralization increase in tandem.

Early External Research on Differentiation Theory

Blau (1995) concludes from his own research on organizations of varied types that, irrespective of type, (1) large organizations are more differentiated than small, (2) large organizations have less administrative overhead than small ones, and (3) more differentiation raises administrative overhead. These conclusions are consistent with theory, but they derive from cross-sectional studies only. They may be diagrammed as shown in figure 18.7. Blau (1995) recognizes, however, that evidence from other sources, using different approaches, does not always support these conclusions. It is to this evidence, particularly that which accumulated up to the early 1980s, that we now turn.

It seems apparent that the strong positive correlation between size and differentiation has been found often enough to be taken seriously. There have been exceptions, as Hall (1991) notes, but these are most likely to occur when measures based on perceptual rather than on objective data are used, and when the studies include organizations that have large nonbureaucratic components, such as professional and voluntary groups. There is a problem as to the direction of causation also. A number of investigators, among whom Meyer (1982) is typical, indicate that size increases may well result

TABLE 18.6 Correlation between various indices of formalization or control and indices of centralization in state employment agencies

	Centralization			
Formalization or control	Of hiring decisions	Of budget proposals	Of organization change decisions	Of other decisions
Extent of personal rules and regulations	−.18	−.34*	−.10	−.19
Number of civil service appointments	−.02	.05	−.18	−.33*
Extent of computerization	−.34*	−.29*	−.22	−.12
Degree of standardization of performance ratings	.27*	.07	−.09	−.28*
Proportion of managers	.29*	.22	.07	−.29*

*Correlations statistically significant ($p < .05$).

SOURCE: Adapted from Peter M. Blau & Richard A. Schoenherr (1971), *The Structure of Organizations* (New York: Basic Books), 416–417.

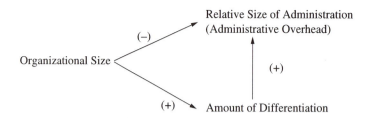

FIGURE 18.7 Relationships among organization size, administrative overhead, and differentiation

from a proliferation of hierarchic levels and specialized subunits, rather than the reverse.

As to the negative correlation between size and administrative overhead, the results of numerous studies are mixed. Henry Travers (1978) reviewed 27 such studies and could not identify any consistent pattern. There certainly are some substantial negative relationships that have been established in particular investigations, but these are matched by equally large positive correlations, and a number of nonsignificant findings as well. Travers believes that the major factor contributing to this inconsistent pattern is the extreme variation of operationalizations of administrative overhead, as well as of size. In both instances, certain peripheral groups such as unpaid members, part-time employees, seasonal workers, and the like may or may not be included. The problem appears to be inherent in the lack of clearly defined theoretical constructs.

Furthermore, and perhaps even more important, is the fact that the studies reviewed contained extremely diverse types of organizations. Only half of the studies focused on distinctly bureaucratic samples of organizations in business and government. The others used schools, colleges and universities, and voluntary organizations, all of which contained sizable components of a nonbureaucratic nature; these latter components were not excluded from the analyses. In spite of Blau's (1995) contention that his theory applies widely to organizations of any type, it seems quite possible that it is limited to the domain of bureaucratic systems. If so, this could well account for the inconsistent results.

Regarding the relationship between differentiation and administrative overhead, Blau's research clearly established a positive correlation. Subsequent studies have not typically dealt with this segment of the theory, perhaps because the results were viewed as self-evident. However, nothing that would challenge Blau's positions appeared in the early period.

Longitudinal Studies

Like the Aston researchers, Blau used cross-sectional studies in his own investigations, but the two theories differ in that the Blau formulations have sparked longitudinal investigations by others. Although a certain amount of research of this nature was published in the early period, research designs have improved steadily, and some of the more recent contributions have been much more definitive in their findings. These later studies do not directly test the hypotheses advanced by Blau because organizational growth and decline were not explicitly included in his formulations. Yet implicitly the theory does seem to apply to the processes of change that get organizations to their current status.

One significant finding from this longitudinal line of research is that not merely size but organizational age and change in size affect organizational restructuring processes (Baker & Cullen, 1993). Current size is the best predictor, but it is joined in important ways by the period over which the organization has survived and by periods of growth and decline. These results were obtained in a study of colleges and universities.

Going beyond the prediction of restructuring, John Cullen, Kenneth Anderson, and Douglas Baker (1986) look at the relationships among the three theoretical variables of the differentiation theory under conditions of change in a sample of universities. The results for periods of decline in size were as follows:

1. Differentiation decreased in 60% of the universities, but sometimes proportionately slower than the decline, and subunits were added in some cases.
2. Administrative staff decreases occurred with either greater or less than proportional reductions in roughly 40% of the universities,

but more typical was an actual increase in administrative overhead.

3. Decreasing differentiation did not lead to a decrease in administrative staff; on the contrary over 50% of the universities added administrators with reduced differentiation. (based on Cullen et al., 1986, pp. 223–224)

In all three instances, these results are interpreted as running contrary to Blau's theory.

The results for periods of growth were no more encouraging, although cross-sectional analyses did replicate Blau's findings, and the theory, in most respects. Accordingly, the theory is interpreted as a theory of scale, but not of change. Interestingly, it also appears to apply under conditions of very rapid organizational growth. The failure to support theory insofar as size-administrative relationships (#2 above) are concerned has also been found in school districts (Ford, 1980). There is something of a ratchet mechanism involved here.

A study by William McKinley (1987) looked into the differentiation-administrative overhead relationship specifically, and did so in a clearly bureaucratic context of manufacturing firms. Under conditions of decline in size, the theory once again was not confirmed; the expected strong positive relationship was no longer in evidence when decline occurred.

Finally, compelling evidence that size can be a consequence of changes in organization resulting in differentiation has been developed (Meyer et al., 1985). Thus, the countertheoretical position that had been advocated previously now appears to be correct. The evidence comes from a study of financial components in three city governments over many years. Apparently, added components drive the size of the organization upward somewhat later. This does not always happen, but it is the more likely situation.

Critiques of Blau's Theory

In reviewing the evidence on differentiation theory, Allen Bluedorn (1993) concludes that the major challenge to the theory comes from longitudinal studies such as those just considered. These studies raise questions that move well beyond the content of the original theory and, in fact, indicate that a more comprehensive theory dealing with change as well as scale is now needed.

Donaldson (1996a) interprets Blau's theory and research as consistent with structural contingency theory, and accordingly he endorses the theory of differentiation. In the process, he reviews a number of countervailing studies and offers arguments to refute them. In addition, he presents the results of a meta-analysis covering some 17 studies (8 of them the Blau studies) on the relationship between size and administrative overhead. This meta-analysis yields an average correlation of −.45, which is consistent with theory but heavily weighted by the results from Blau's research on government organizations.

This review by Donaldson (1996a) fails to treat a number of the longitudinal studies that I have included in the previous section primarily because they seem to me to have something new and important to say; he does consider other longitudinal studies, however. The meta-analysis of the relationship between size and administrative overhead is heavily weighted with Blau's own research and appears to incorporate at most 3 of the 27 studies on the subject reviewed by Travers (1978). Of the 9 studies included that do not derive from the Blau research program, 4 yield positive correlations and 5 negative.

Chris Argyris (1972), in contrast to Donaldson, takes a negative position on Blau's theory and research. He emphasizes Blau's failure to consider the informal organization (although Blau, 1955, had done this in his dissertation). He also takes issue with the way in which variables were operationalized in the research (using official descriptions of organization structures) on the grounds that these may well be invalid. To some extent, Blau has answered Argyris's arguments with his research outside the civil service context. On one point, however, this is clearly not the case. Although Blau's theory of differentiation specifies causal influences from size to the structural variables, his tests of the theory are cross-sectional, rather than longitudinal, and thus do not bear directly on the causal hypotheses. Clearly, additional research is needed that considers what organizations do as they increase in size and what temporal relationships are involved. As we have seen, this early criticism has been answered by more recent longitudinal tests of the theory, but not entirely to the satisfaction of the theory's advocates.

Stephen Turner (1977) takes Blau to task on philosophical grounds, questioning the role of explanation and Blau's claim to deductive rigor. His critique is aimed as much at all of the theoretical approaches of modern sociology as at Blau's theory specifically. It fails to deal with the argument that, irrespective of its construction or its level of explanation, a theory that generates empirical support and deals with important questions may be valuable as a source of understanding, prediction, and/or control.

Blau's views of professional knowledge and decentralization have received considerable support. There is also reason, based on the research, to favor his concept of bureaucratic theory as a set of interrelated hypotheses over the ideal type construction proposed by Weber. Blau raises certain questions about Weber's handling of democratic or collegial systems as opposed to bureaucracy. Such systems, like the professional, appear to be different, and there is substantial evidence, which has been reviewed previously at some length, to support this position. In view of this situation, the next step in research would seem to require disentangling bureaucratic systems from other types of systems to carry out tests of bureaucratic theories, such as Blau's and that of the Aston researchers, in organizations that are predominantly bureaucratic in nature or in the bureaucratic components of mixed organizations.

A final point has been raised by Richard Scott (1990). His view is that structures are often determined not by size, but by cultural forces such as belief systems, laws, and regulatory frameworks, as well as professional norms and pressures to conform to existing modal models. Thus size arguments must compete with a variety of alternative explanations. To evaluate these types of claimants, comparative research beyond what has been considered here is needed.

Application

Almost everything that has been said with regard to the Aston theory is equally applicable to Blau's theory of differentiation and his related views. Both of these theories relate to organization planning and designing organization structures. They yield measures that can be used to diagnose current organization structures and to change them. To the extent the theories have been found valid, they should be followed in structuring and restructuring bureaucratic systems. Research on Blau's theory suggests that, in periods of organizational decline in particular, bureaucracies may remain overstructured in ways that are costly and may even threaten organizational survival. This is something that those who design organizations may find useful to keep in mind and consider as their organizations

undergo change. In this way, choice may be applied to overcome barriers and move to the type of fit that structural contingency theory advocates.

CONCLUSIONS

The Aston theory and Blau's theory have much in common in the variables they emphasize and in the type of research they have fostered. They also agree in that they both use a contingency framework. In this latter respect they have much in common with the contingency theories considered in part IV of this volume; in fact, structural contingency theory tends to lump all of these positions together.

This raises a question as to why the Aston and Blau theories have been separated from other contingency theories in this volume. I must admit that the decision appears somewhat arbitrary. However, the explicit introduction of Weber's concept of bureaucracy into the theoretical equation seems to me to represent a new and important element that deserves emphasis. The contingency theories of part IV arose out of an open systems theory orientation and acknowledge little debt to Weber. Those considered in this chapter are quite different in this particular regard. Thus my decision was based on a consideration of the ways in which ideas have originated and developed, which is consistent with the approach taken throughout this book.

References

Aldrich, Howard (1988). Paradigm Warriors: Donaldson versus the Critics of Organization Theory. *Organization Studies*, 9, 19–25.

Argyris, Chris (1972). *The Applicability of Organizational Sociology*. Cambridge: Cambridge University Press.

Baker, Douglas D., & Cullen, John B. (1993). Administrative Reorganization and Configurational Context: The Contingent Effects of Age, Size, and Change in Size. *Academy of Management Journal*, 36, 1251–1277.

Becker, Selwyn W., & Neuhauser, Duncan (1975). *The Efficient Organization*. New York: Elsevier.

Blau, Peter M. (1955). *The Dynamics of Bureaucracy: A Study of Interpersonal Relations in Two Government Agencies*. Chicago: University of Chicago Press.

Blau, Peter M. (1956). *Bureaucracy in Modern Society*. New York: Random House.

Blau, Peter M. (1970a). Decentralization in Bureaucracies. In Mayer N. Zald (Ed.), *Power in Organizations* (pp. 150–174). Nashville, TN: Vanderbilt University Press.

Blau, Peter M. (1970b). A Formal Theory of Differentiation in Organizations. *American Sociological Review*, 35, 201–218.

Blau, Peter M. (1973). *The Organization of Academic Work*. New York: Wiley.

Blau, Peter M. (1974). *On the Nature of Organizations*. New York: Wiley.

Blau, Peter M. (1995). A Circuitous Path to Macrostructural Theory. *Annual Review of Sociology*, 21, 1–19.

Blau, Peter M.; Falbe, Cecilia M.; McKinley, William; & Tracy, Phelps K. (1976). Technology and Organization in Manufacturing. *Administrative Science Quarterly*, 21, 20–40.

Blau, Peter M., & Schoenherr, Richard A. (1971). *The Structure of Organizations*. New York: Basic Books.

Blau, Peter M., & Scott, W. Richard (1962). *Formal Organizations: A Comparative Approach*. San Francisco: Chandler.

Bluedorn, Allen C. (1993). Pilgrim's Progress: Trends and Convergence in Research on Organizational Size and Environments. *Journal of Management*, 19, 163–191.

Calhoun, Craig, & Scott, W. Richard (1990). Introduction: Peter Blau's Sociological Structuralism. In Craig Calhoun, Marshall W. Meyer, & W. Richard Scott (Eds.), *Structures of Power and Constraint: Papers in Honor of Peter M. Blau* (pp. 1–36). Cambridge: Cambridge University Press.

Chandler, Alfred D. (1962). *Strategy and Structure: Chapters in the History of the American Industrial Enterprise*. Cambridge, MA: MIT Press.

Child, John (1972a). Organizational Structure, Environment and Performance: The Role of Strategic Choice. *Sociology*, 6, 1–22.

Child, John (1972b). Organization Structure and Strategies of Control: A Replication of the Aston Study. *Administrative Science Quarterly*, 17, 163–177.

Child, John (1976). Predicting and Understanding Organization Structure. In Derek S. Pugh & C. Robert Hinings (Eds.), *Organizational Structure Extensions and Replications: The Aston Programme* II (pp. 45–64). Lexington, MA: D. C. Heath.

Child, John (1988). On Organizations in Their Sectors. *Organization Studies*, 9, 13–19.

Child, John (1997). Strategic Choice in the Analysis of Action, Structure, Organizations and Environment: Retrospect and Prospect. *Organization Studies*, 18, 43–76.

Clegg, Stewart R. (1988). The Good, the Bad, and the Ugly. *Organization Studies*, 9, 7–13.

Cullen, John B.; Anderson, Kenneth S.; & Baker, Douglas D. (1986). Blau's Theory of Structural Differenti-

ation Revisited: A Theory of Structural Change or Scale? *Academy of Management Journal*, 29, 203–229.

Dalton, Dan R.; Todor, William D.; Spendolini, Michael J.; Fielding, Gordon J.; & Porter, Lyman W. (1980). Organizational Structure and Performance: A Critical Review. *Academy of Management Review*, 5, 49–64.

Donaldson, Lex (1982). Divisionalization and Diversification: A Longitudinal Study. *Academy of Management Journal*, 25, 909–914.

Donaldson, Lex (1985a). *In Defense of Organization Theory: A Reply to the Critics*. Cambridge: Cambridge University Press.

Donaldson, Lex (1985b). Organization Design and the Life-Cycles of Products. *Journal of Management Studies*, 22, 25–37.

Donaldson, Lex (1987). Strategy and Structural Adjustment to Regain Fit and Performance: In Defense of Contingency Theory. *Journal of Management Studies*, 24, 1–24.

Donaldson, Lex (1988). In Successful Defense of Organization Theory: A Routing of the Critics. *Organization Studies*, 9, 28–32.

Donaldson, Lex (1990). The Ethereal Hand: Organizational Economics and Management Theory. *Academy of Management Review*, 15, 369–381.

Donaldson, Lex (1992). The Weick Stuff: Managing beyond Games. *Organization Science*, 3, 461–466.

Donaldson, Lex (1995). *American Anti-Management Theories of Organization: A Critique of Paradigm Proliferation*. Cambridge: Cambridge University Press.

Donaldson, Lex (1996a). *For Positivist Organization Theory: Proving the Hard Core*. London: Sage.

Donaldson, Lex (1996b). The Normal Science of Structural Contingency Theory. In Stewart R. Clegg, Cynthia Hardy, & Walter R. Nord (Eds.), *Handbook of Organization Studies* (pp. 57–76). London: Sage.

Donaldson, Lex (1997). A Positivist Alternative to the Structure-Action Approach. *Organization Studies*, 18, 77–92.

Donaldson, Lex (2001). *The Contingency Theory of Organizations*. Thousand Oaks, CA: Sage.

Donaldson, Lex; Child, John; & Aldrich, Howard (1975). The Aston Findings on Centralization: Further Discussion. *Administrative Science Quarterly*, 20, 453–460.

Donaldson, Lex, & Hilmer, Frederick G. (1998). Management Redeemed: The Case against Fads That Harm Management. *Organizational Dynamics*, 26(4), 7–20.

Doty, D. Harold; Glick, William H.; & Huber, George P. (1993). Fit, Equifinality, and Organizational Effectiveness: A Test of Two Configurational Theories. *Academy of Management Journal*, 36, 1196–1250.

Evans, Peter, & Rauch, James E. (1999). Bureaucracy and Growth: A Cross-National Analysis of the Effects of Weberian State Structures on Economic Growth. *American Sociological Review*, 64, 748–765.

Ford, Jeffrey D. (1980). The Administrative Component in Growing and Declining Organizations: A Longitudinal Analysis. *Academy of Management Journal*, 23, 615–630.

Gouldner, Alvin (1954). *Patterns of Industrial Bureaucracy*. New York: Free Press.

Greenwood, Royston, & Devine, Kay (1997). Inside Aston: A Conversation with Derek Pugh. *Journal of Management Inquiry*, 6, 200–208.

Grinyer, Peter H., & Yasai-Ardekani, Masoud (1980). Dimensions of Organizational Structure: A Critical Replication. *Academy of Management Journal*, 23, 405–431.

Hage, Jerald, & Aiken, Michael (1967). Relationships of Centralization to Other Structural Properties. *Administrative Science Quarterly*, 12, 72–92.

Hall, Richard H. (1977). *Organizations: Structure and Process*. Englewood Cliffs, NJ: Prentice Hall.

Hall, Richard H. (1991). *Organizations: Structures, Processes, and Outcomes*. Englewood Cliffs, NJ: Prentice Hall.

Heydebrand, Wolf (1990). The Technocratic Organization of Academic Work. In Craig Calhoun, Marshall W. Meyer, & W. Richard Scott (Eds.), *Structures of Power and Constraint: Papers in Honor of Peter M. Blau* (pp. 271–320). Cambridge: Cambridge University Press.

Hickson, David J. (1996). The ASQ Years Then and Now through the Eyes of a Euro-Brit. *Administrative Science Quarterly*, 41, 217–228.

Hickson, David J. (1998). A Surprised Academic: Learning from Others While Walking on Thin Ice. In Arthur G. Bedeian (Ed.), *Management Laureates: A Collection of Autobiographical Essays* (pp. 93–128). Greenwich, CT: JAI Press.

Hickson, David J., & McMillan, Charles J. (1981). *Organization and Nation: The Aston Programme IV*. Hampshire, UK: Gower.

Kahn, Robert L.; Wolfe, Donald M.; Quinn, Robert P.; Snoeck, J. Diedrich; & Rosenthal, Robert A. (1964). *Organizational Stress: Studies in Role Conflict and Ambiguity*. New York: Wiley.

Keats, Barbara W., & Hitt, Michael A. (1988). A Causal Model of Linkages among Environmental Dimensions, Macro Organizational Characteristics, and Performance. *Academy of Management Journal*, 31, 570–598.

Khandwalla, Pradip N. (1977). *The Design of Organizations*. New York: Harcourt, Brace, Jovanovich.

Mahoney, Thomas A.; Frost, Peter; Crandall, Norman F.; & Weitzel, William (1972). The Conditioning Influence of Organizational Size upon Managerial Practice. *Organizational Behavior and Human Performance*, 8, 230–241.

Mansfield, Roger (1973). Bureaucracy and Centralization: An Examination of Organizational Structure. *Administrative Science Quarterly*, 18, 477–488.

March, James G., & Simon, Herbert A. (1958). *Organizations*. New York: Wiley.

Marsden, Richard, & Townley, Barbara (1996). The Owl of Minerva: Reflections on Theory in Practice. In Stewart R. Clegg, Cynthia Hardy, & Walter R. Nord (Eds.), *Handbook of Organization Studies* (pp. 659–675). Thousand Oaks, CA: Sage.

McKinley, William (1987). Complexity and Administrative Intensity: The Case of Declining Organizations. *Administrative Science Quarterly*, 32, 87–105.

Merton, Robert K. (1940). Bureaucratic Structure and Personality. *Social Forces*, 18, 560–568.

Merton, Robert K. (1990). Epistolary Notes on the Making of a Sociological Dissertation Classic: *The Dynamics of Bureaucracy*. In Craig Calhoun, Marshall W. Meyer, & W. Richard Scott (Eds.), *Structures of Power and Constraint: Papers in Honor of Peter M. Blau* (pp. 37–66). Cambridge: Cambridge University Press.

Meyer, Marshall W. (1982). Bureaucratic versus Profit Organization. *Research in Organizational Behavior*, 4, 89–125.

Meyer, Marshall W.; Stevenson, William; & Webster, Stephen (1985). *Limits to Bureaucratic Growth*. New York: Walter de Gruyter.

Miller, George A. (1987). Meta-analysis and the Culture-free Hypothesis. *Organization Studies*, 8, 309–326.

Miner, John B. (1982). *Theories of Organizational Structure and Process*. Hinsdale, IL: Dryden.

Miner, John B.; Crane, Donald P.; & Vandenberg, Robert J. (1994). Congruence and Fit in Professional Role Motivation Theory. *Organization Science*, 5, 86–97.

Mintzberg, Henry T. (1983). *Structure in Fives: Designing Effective Organizations*. Englewood Cliffs, NJ: Prentice Hall.

Negandhi, Anant R. (1975). *Organization Theory in an Open System*. New York: Dunellen.

Oliver, John E. (1982). An Instrument for Classifying Organizations. *Academy of Management Journal*, 25, 855–866.

Paulson, Steven K. (1974). Causal Analysis of Interorganizational Relations: An Axiomatic Theory Revisited. *Administrative Science Quarterly*, 19, 319–337.

Pennings, Johannes M. (1992). Structural Contingency Theory: A Reappraisal. *Research in Organizational Behavior*, 14, 267–309.

Pugh, Derek S. (1976). The Aston Approach to the Study of Organizations. In Geert Hofstede & M. Sami Kassem (Eds.), *European Contributions to Organization Theory* (pp. 62–78). Amsterdam, the Netherlands: Van Gorcum, Assen.

Pugh, Derek S. (1996). A Taste for Innovation. In Arthur G. Bedeian (Ed.), *Management Laureates: A Collection of Autobiographical Essays* (Vol. 4, pp. 235–276). Greenwich, CT: JAI Press.

Pugh, Derek S., & Hickson, David J. (1976). *Organizational Structure in its Context: The Aston Programme I*. Lexington, MA: D. C. Heath.

Pugh, Derek S., & Hickson, David J. (1993). *Great Writers on Organizations: The Omnibus Edition*. Aldershot, UK: Dartmouth.

Pugh, Derek S.; Hickson, David J.; & Hinings, C. Robert (1969). An Empirical Taxonomy of Structures of Work Organizations. *Administrative Science Quarterly*, 14, 115–126.

Pugh, Derek S., & Hinings, C. Robert (1976). *Organizational Structure Extensions and Replications: The Aston Programme II*. Lexington, MA: D. C. Heath.

Pugh, Derek S., & Payne, Roy L. (1977). *Organizational Behavior in Its Context: The Aston Programme III*. Lexington, MA: D. C. Heath.

Reimann, Bernard C., & Negandhi, Anant R. (1975). Strategies of Administrative Control and Organizational Effectiveness. *Human Relations*, 28, 475–486.

Scott, W. Richard (1990). Introduction to Part II: Formal Organization. In Craig Calhoun, Marshall W. Meyer, & W. Richard Scott (Eds.), *Structures of Power and Constraint: Papers in Honor of Peter M. Blau* (pp. 181–189). Cambridge: Cambridge University Press.

Selznick, Philip (1949). *TVA and the Grass Roots*. Berkeley: University of California Press.

Slater, Robert O. (1985). Organizational Size and Differentiation. *Research in the Sociology of Organizations*, 4, 127–180.

Sorensen, James E., & Sorensen, Thomas L. (1974). The Conflict of Professionals in Bureaucratic Organizations. *Administrative Science Quarterly*, 19, 98–106.

Travers, Henry J. (1978). *Organization: Size and Intensity*. Washington, DC: University Press of America.

Turner, Stephen P. (1977). Blau's Theory of Differentiation: Is It Explanatory? In J. Kenneth Benson (Ed.), *Organizational Analysis: Critique and Innovation* (pp. 19–34). Beverly Hills, CA: Sage.

Warner, Malcolm (1981). Review of *Organization and Nation: The Aston Programme IV. Journal of Management Studies*, 18, 448–450.

Weber, Max (1947). *The Theory of Social and Economic Organization*. Trans. and ed. Talcott Parsons & A. M. Henderson. New York: Free Press.

Weinzimmer, Laurence G.; Nystrom, Paul C.; & Freeman, Sarah J. (1998). Measuring Organizational Growth: Issues, Consequences, and Guidelines. *Journal of Management*, 24, 235–262.

Wilderom, Celeste P. M., & Miner, John B. (1991). Defining Voluntary Groups and Agencies within Organization Science. *Organization Science*, 2, 366–378.

Chapter 19

Theoretical Variants on the Bureaucratic Theme

Chapter 18 considered certain variants on Max Weber's theory that set forth precise hypotheses and developed operational definitions of the constructs involved. In the process, dysfunctional consequences of bureaucracy were sometimes noted, and types of bureaucracies were introduced to some degree as well. In this chapter, this emphasis is reversed. Either dysfunctions or types are at the forefront of the discussion; measurement and operationalization of theoretical variables take a secondary position. However, the positive emphasis on Weber's contribution remains strong. Both

Victor Thompson, a political scientist, and Amitai Etzioni, a sociologist, take their start from Weber's theory of bureaucracy.

THEORETICAL ELABORATIONS OF VICTOR THOMPSON

While the Aston group and Peter Blau moved back and forth between theory and research, Thompson devoted himself primarily to theory. He largely emphasized the dysfunctions and inadequacies of bureaucracy, while considering variants that might help overcome these problems. Like the preceding theorists, Thompson remains generally committed to the genius of Weber. His ideas are presented in a series of books and a few articles.

Background

Thompson was born in 1912. He obtained his B.A. from the University of Washington in 1939 and a doctorate in political science from Columbia University in 1949. In between, he served in Washington, D.C. during World War II as an administrator for the rationing program, and as a teacher at the University of Texas while working on his dissertation.

His first regular faculty appointment was at the Illinois Institute of Technology, where he remained until 1961, serving as chairman of the political and social science department throughout most of his tenure. After a visiting year in Uganda, Thompson moved to the political science department at Syracuse University for 4 years and then became head of that department at the University of Illinois in 1966. By 1971 he was off to the University of Florida, again in political science, where he also became department chairman; he retired from that institution. Throughout the 1950s and 1960s he built on his Washington contacts to serve in a variety of part-time and temporary positions with various federal agencies and councils.

Thompson's first book was based on his experience with price administration and rationing programs in Washington, D.C. (Thompson, 1950). In this same period he also published a text in public administration with Herbert Simon and Donald Smithburg, his colleagues at IIT (Simon, Smithburg, & Thompson, 1950). The department at IIT also administered a graduate program in public administration (Simon, 1991). Thus, with his administrative duties and other writing, Thompson did not begin to publish his theoretical ideas until the early 1960s. He continued to publish them for over 15 years.

At the time of organizational behavior's arrival on the scene Thompson was in his mid-40s, a department head, and well established in political science. Thus, he too is one of those who did not move into a business school. He was heavily involved in public administration activities, however, and published in the organizational behavior literature, not only in books but with articles as well.

Dysfunctions of and Variants on Bureaucracy

Thompson was at Columbia as a graduate student during the same period as Blau, but in political science, not sociology. He began to actively study and write about organizations in the same period as the Aston researchers and Blau. He was a colleague and co-author with Simon. Blau and Simon appear to have influenced his early thinking on organizations, along

of course with Weber. But he was well aware of the developing literature of the time in organizational behavior, both micro and macro, especially U.S. literature. Despite Thompson's basic commitment to political science and public administration, his work was centrally positioned within organizational behavior (Tosi, 1984).

Modern Organization

According to Thompson (1961b), the major problem for many modern bureaucracies is the imbalance between ability and authority. Increasingly, the knowledge needed to operate the organization is found among specialists and professionals who do not have significant positions of authority. At the same time, bureaucracy by its very nature places the right to exercise authority and the responsibility for outcomes in the hands of hierarchic superiors. The result is continuing confusion and conflict.

The characteristics of bureaucracy listed by Thompson are similar to Weber's, but with a somewhat different emphasis:

1. A spirit of rationalism, with science and technology as major contributors
2. Highly trained specialists appointed by merit to a system of assured careers
3. Routinization of organizational activities
4. Factoring of the general goal of the organization into subgoals for units along the lines of differentiation
5. Apparent inversion of ends and means such that the total organizational goal becomes lost to view and the subgoals of units become ends in themselves
6. A formalistic impersonality
7. Categorization of data in accordance with the needs of specialists
8. Classification of clients to minimize discrimination
9. Seeming slowness to act or change as a result of resistance to change and preoccupation with hierarchy
10. Concern with the monistic ideal, including a strong emphasis on legitimizing the superior-subordinate relationship, authority-responsibility, and hierarchy; thus organizational conflict, divergent goals, and divergent interests are precluded as lacking legitimacy.

Those who come into contact with bureaucracies must adjust to these characteristics. Certain people

(Thompson calls them *bureautics*) are too immature to adjust and react with an overwhelming suspicion. Bureausis is considered a disease that normally prevents people from rising in the hierarchy.

In addition to bureausis and adaptive bureaucratic behavior, Thompson describes bureaupathic behavior that is created by anxiety and insecurity. This phenomenon results in large part from the gap between the rights and duties of the hierarchical superior and the specialized ability to solve problems, a gap which in turn makes the superior dependent on specialist subordinates. Often superiors react to this situation with an excessive need for control, an overemphasis on compliance with rules, exaggerated aloofness, resistance to change, and insistence on the rights of office. Such bureaupathology is a function of the insecurity of authority that is produced in large part by increasing specialization.

In this concern with problems of the pathology of bureaucracy and the resort to personality-based metaphors Thompson appears to have much in common with Tom Burns (see chapter 15 in this volume). However, the two views appear to have arisen completely independently of one another, although at essentially the same time.

Thompson does not give a great deal of attention to solving the problems of bureaucracy that he notes. What he does suggest are certain variants on the basic bureaucratic theme made necessary when the presence of specialists must be accommodated. These approaches involve changes in processes and in structures, as follows:

1. Give most persons in supervisory positions some specific instrumental functions in addition to the exercise of authority, such as the factory foreman and the college department chairman have.
2. Establish two equal salary scales, one for specialists and one for the hierarchy.
3. Reexamine the division of labor in each organization to bring it into line with the needs of specialization. Wherever machine technology allows, the microdivision of labor should be ended.
4. Ensure that all organizational processes and arrangements have as a manifest purpose the furthering of cooperation. (Thompson, 1961b, pp. 195–197)

In this early period Thompson (1961a) gave a great deal of attention to the problems of intraorganizational conflict and to the need to minimize them. This con-flict is said to be a function of several factors as reflected in the following propositions:

1. Conflict is a function of disagreement over the reality of interdependence.
   1.1 Lack of agreement about the reality of interdependence arises from lack of acceptance of specialties. Lack of acceptance of specialties results from lack of accreditation of specialties, which, in turn, is a function of
      1.1.1. their newness, or
      1.1.2. the creation of specialties by acts of authority in defiance of technical criteria.
   1.2. Lack of agreement about the reality of interdependence is also a function of differing perceptions of reality. These differing perceptions are a function of position in
      1.2.1. the authority system,
      1.2.2. the status system, and
      1.2.3. the system of person-to-person communication (the group system).
2. Conflict is a function of the degree of disparity between authority (the right to be consulted) and the ability to contribute to goals. This disparity arises from
   2.1. Growing dependence upon specialists (a function of the process of specialization) while hierarchical role definitions change more slowly; and
   2.2. The allocation of rights (delegation) in disregard of the needs of specialization (acts of sheer authority).
3. Conflict is a function of the degree of status violation involved in interaction.
   3.1. Status violation results from advancing specialization and consequent growing interdependence of high- and low-status positions—from positional claims to deference, on the one hand, and the fact of dependence upon specialists, on the other.
4. Conflict is made more or less intense by the relative importance of the interdependence to the success of the organization.
5. Finally, conflict is a function of the lack of shared values and reality perceptions (identifications), which are, in addition to personalities,
   5.1. A function of the lack of spontaneity and freedom in communicative interaction, which is
      5.1.1. a function of the resistance to penetration from without of the principal behavior systems—the authority system, the status system, and the technical system (specialization).

In short, conflict arises from growing inconsistencies between specialist and hierarchical roles. Whereas there are other bases for conflict, it is likely that they could be easily managed under a regime of specialist solidarity that is based on the mutual recognition of the need for interdependence. (Thompson, 1961a, pp. 518–519)

Bureaucracy and Innovation

It is Thompson's (1969) thesis that bureaucracies are under-innovative and that they need to perform a more entrepreneurial function for society than they do. He treats creativity and innovation as essentially the same and the rigidity of bureaucracy as a bar to either.

Much the same as Blau did, Thompson considered professionalism an alternative to bureaucracy. Furthermore, he calls professional systems more innovative than bureaucratic systems. This is because they are "pluralistic and collegiate rather than monocratic and hierarchical" (Thompson, 1969, p. 93). Professionalizing an organization decreases administration, top-down command, unquestioning obedience, constriction of communication, and interunit conflict. The associated shift to professional peer control should yield increased flexibility, variety, and receptivity to change, and thus innovation. Structurally there would be greater use of certain project forms,

Innovative, professional organizations would dispense with performance ratings by superiors and with most job descriptions. Thompson (1965) views the small technical organization headed by a creative entrepreneur and staffed with a small group of "able and personally loyal" peers as the prototype for innovation. To the extent this structure can be incorporated into or grafted onto them, large organizations might be expected to become more innovative.

Without Sympathy or Enthusiasm

In a small book aptly entitled by paraphrasing Weber's wording, Thompson (1975) takes up another potential dysfunction of bureaucracy—its lack of compassion for the individual. As Weber stated, bureaucracy by its very nature is impersonal—it lacks sympathy (affection) and enthusiasm, but also hatred and passion. It is not disposed to bend its rules positively in favor of individually perceived equity, but neither is it vindictive and personally punitive.

Thompson discusses a wide range of procedures that are intended to make bureaucratic systems more compassionate and more sensitive to the needs of individuals, including compassionate personnel administration, organization development, sensitivity training, small units, combined roles, "corrupt" political machines and prefectural administration, the ombudsman, and egalitarian ("new left") administration. In the end, Thompson rejects all of these as mere gimmicks.

The ultimate solution is an evolution of organizational structures and individual personalities to the point where they are mutually adjusted. Individuals must grow so that they can delay gratification and recognize the social dysfunctions of personal favors. Organizations must adapt, with an assist from an advancing technology, to individual needs. As in other instances, Thompson is more persuasive and specific about techniques that will not work than in outlining solutions that will work. He makes the point that in today's world bureaucracy generates considerable resentment.

Bureaucracy and the Modern World

Subsequently Thompson (1976) distinguishes more fully between natural (informal) and artificial (bureaucratic) systems. In particular, he is concerned with the relations of each to innovation and change. Following Weber, Thompson develops the idea that artificial systems are tools to carry out the goals of their owners (the charismatic leader, the electorate, etc.). As tools, they are subject to evaluation and control in light of the goals. Artificial systems are monocratic in that only owner goals are relevant, not the goals of other possible claimants such as employees. Norms of rationality prevail.

Natural systems exist alongside the artificial and are an inevitable concomitant of bureaucracy. They are not tools of the owner, but spontaneously emergent entities serving only themselves. They are not rational systems, and their referent is internal—their members. Thus, a bureaucratic *organization* is pluralistic, even though the bureaucratic system per se is monocratic. Although the natural and artificial systems have inherent conflicting interests, on occasion and in certain respects, the natural system may complement the artificial. Thus the natural system may provide needed redundancy and reliability, flexibility and innovation, and, under certain circumstances, additional rewards and motivation. At the same time, the natural system is primarily devoted to survival-oriented adaptation to the artificial system, and norms of rationality are not relevant for it.

Thompson states in a number of places that the natural system, not the artificial, is the source of innovation, flexibility, and change in bureaucratic organizations:

> Innovative adaptations, if they occur, are largely products of natural system conditions. (1976, p. 19)

> The more organizations are rationalized, the more scientific management is applied to them, the "tauter the ship," and the more romanticism and falsified or erroneous calculations are needed, if there are to be any innovations at all. (1976, p. 90)

> Because the artificial system, or plan, of the organization can only provide extrinsic rewards, it cannot motivate to innovation. (In fact, innovations cannot even be legitimate, because their actual relation to the owner's goal cannot be known in advance.) Innovation for the most part, therefore, must occur outside the formal artificial system. (1976, p. 95)

Yet the theoretical role of natural systems is muddied by statements such as the following:

> An example of a natural system claim is the almost universal resistance to innovation found in bureaucracy. . . . A dynamic artificial system (for example one associated with a dynamic technology) will be associated with a dynamic natural system, and *vice versa*. Where technological change is minimal, as in education, natural systematic development is so strong as to render the organization unchangeable. (Thompson, 1976, p. 24)

Given the above, it becomes difficult to identify the hypothesized source of innovation in bureaucratic organizations. Thompson does not draw on the research in this area in developing his theory. He does favor project teams and venture teams for this purpose, however.

Venture Structures

During the 1970s Thompson working with James Hlavacek developed his ideas regarding innovation and venture teams in a series of articles. In the first of these (Hlavacek & Thompson, 1973), the authors start with a statement regarding the environment for innovation: (1) security and freedom are important considerations; (2) a rich and varied background of ideas, at the boundaries of a field, are required, and thus a specialist rather than a generalist; (3) strong personal commitment to the creative process tends to exist. This set of conditions is contrasted with bureaucracy, which is said to yield an environment that is hostile to innovation and creativity:

> The bureaucratic strategy has a strong tendency to individualize work and to reduce it in scope and responsibility. By these effects on work, reliability, control, and productivity are all increased. . . . Reliability, control, and productivity, *ceteris paribus*, are also promoted by reducing work to simple repetitive *routines* — by avoiding the insecurities and risks of actual problem solving. Routinization, in turn, depends upon stabilizing the organization's conditions of operation. . . . Far from a drive to innovate, the bureaucratic organization has many reasons for fostering the opposite condition — a tendency to stifle innovations. (Hlavacek & Thompson, 1973, pp. 364–365)

Product management and venture team structures are hypothesized as a way of modifying bureaucracy to reduce this tendency to stifle innovation.

Another such approach is the joint venture, where two firms combine a portion of their assets to create a new organization intended to engineer, produce, and market a product innovation (Hlavacek & Thompson, 1975). This approach is also favored for the purpose of initial innovation, but steps must be taken to minimize the impact of bureaucracy.

In a final article, Hlavacek and Thompson (1978) place greater emphasis on internal venture structures, but they view success as problematic because of venture conflict with more permanent divisions or departments:

> Bureaucratization of authority over venturing would defeat the whole new concept of venture groups — namely, an end run around corporate bureaucratic obstacles by way of a small, inter-disciplinary project group freed from most of the corporate restrictions. (Hlavacek & Thompson, 1978, p. 245)

Freedom to create and operate as the dominant motivation behind ventures is hypothesized to be the key ingredient, and if it is lost, the venture will fail.

Evaluation and Impact

Research initiated specifically for the purpose of testing Thompson's propositions regarding bureaucracy and its variants is rare. The major exceptions are the author's studies of venture structures. However, the issues Thompson raises are important ones, and they have been the subject of considerable research, quite independent of any relationships to Thompson's theory. Thus there is a sizable literature to which we can turn for evidence on his views.

Personality Considerations

Thompson's theory dealt with the problem of individual adaptation to bureaucracy. Arthur Stinchcombe (1974) and others going back to Weber have maintained that an effective bureaucracy requires certain motivational patterns. The research data indicate that there are people who can and cannot adjust to bureaucratic systems in various roles. Furthermore, based on personality data, bureaucratic systems differ significantly from professional systems.

Sally Baker, Etzioni, Richard Hansen, and Marvin Sontag (1973) developed a measure of worker tolerance for bureaucratic structure based on attitudes toward rules and regulations, attitudes toward the legitimacy of authority, attitudes toward performing limited and structured tasks, and the capacity to delay gratification. This measure differentiates among organizational contexts in a manner that appears to be positively related to their degree of bureaucratization. It also predicts turnover within bureaucracies and performance ratings.

Leonard Gordon (1970) developed a similar instrument that tapped willingness to comply with a superior's wishes, confidence in expert judgment, preference for impersonal relationships, a desire for the security provided by rules and standard procedures, and a desire for the security of organizational identification. Correlations with other measures suggest considerable construct validity. This measure also differentiates among contexts with varying degrees of bureaucratization and predicts turnover in bureaucracies.

I have developed a somewhat different approach to this matter in connection with the specification of managerial role motivation theory (see chapter 5 in this volume), which focuses on the personality characteristics that are required of managers in bureaucratic systems. Included are measures of characteristics that are related to functioning within the hierarchy — positive attitudes upward, competitiveness horizontally with peers, and the exercise of power downward; characteristics related to size of organization — assertiveness and desire to stand out from the group or be visible; and characteristics related to carrying out the functions of management. Research results indicate that these personality characteristics are a source of behavior and decisions appropriate to the bureaucratic managerial context (Miner, 1993, 2002). However, these results do not mesh nearly as well with nonmanagerial work and nonbureaucatic systems. Apparently there are people who cannot adapt to and thus experience considerable anxiety in bureaucratic managerial roles. Furthermore, the kinds of characteristics that make for managerial effectiveness in bureaucracies are generally distinct from those making for professional effectiveness.

On the evidence, although this research does not prove Thompson's specific formulations, it does support his view that there are people who have a great deal of difficulty adjusting to bureaucracy. More broadly, it also appears that certain other individuals have difficulty adjusting to other organizational forms, such as the professional and entrepreneurial, as well (Miner, 1993).

Organizations can produce anxiety and insecurity in their members, and they can arouse resentment and anger in particular individuals as well. Whether bureaucracies produce these emotional reactions more than other types of organizations is an open question, but being larger, they are likely to affect more people in this way. There is substantial evidence that during the late 1960s and early 1970s this type of reaction against bureaucracy increased rather dramatically among college students (Miner, 1971, 1993).

That these personality phenomena may amount to a sickness or emotional pathology, as Thompson indicates, is supported by the findings of table 19.1. The theory states that many such individuals cannot adjust to positions in the bureaucratic hierarchy and thus are restricted to lower-level bureaucratic employment or employment outside of bureaucracies. Most of the neurotics and psychotics considered in table 19.1 became emotionally ill while serving in a military bureaucracy. As a group, they did not achieve nearly the same levels of employment as would have been anticipated from population data over the 10 years subsequent to discharge (Miner & Anderson, 1958). Though this downward shift in employment level can-

TABLE 19.1 Proportion (%) of emotionally disturbed individuals (discharged from the Armed Forces as neurotic or psychotic) last working at upper and lower occupational levels

Groups	Upper-level employment, including managerial and professional	Lower-level employment, including semiskilled and unskilled
Employed population as a whole	44	56
Discharged as neurotic	24	76
Discharged as psychotic	21	79

SOURCE: Adapted from John B. Miner & James K. Anderson (1958), The Postwar Occupational Adjustment of Emotionally Disturbed Soldiers, *Journal of Applied Psychology*, 42, 320

not be attributed entirely to failures of bureaucratic adjustment, a sizable proportion of the differential does appear to have been caused by such factors, as Thompson's theory would anticipate.

Conflicts with Professionals

The matter of difficulties stemming from the mix of bureaucracy and professionalism in organizations is not new with Thompson's theory; we have visited it on a number of occasions previously—in connection with mechanistic/organic systems theory in chapter 15, with contingency theory in chapter 17, and with both Aston theory and Blau's differentiation theory in chapter 18, for example. However, the extent to which Thompson focuses his theoretical propositions on conflict between bureaucratic and professional systems is new, especially the concern with interdependence in joint decision making as between bureaucratic and professional (specialized) segments of an organization.

One view is that not only is conflict with professionals well established but also professional systems are losing out to bureaucratic control (Leicht & Fennell, 1997). Another formulation involves the fact that many of the older professions have been imported into bureaucratic organizations, while others—such as librarians, computer programmers, financial managers, and many health care professionals—are organizationally generated, and have shorter professional training periods. In this view, only the imported professions represent a source of conflict; the professions with origins within bureaucracy and less professional training are much more compatible (Barley & Tolbert, 1991). A third position holds that professional segments within bureaucracies allow professionals to consolidate considerable authority over their own af-

fairs and over nonprofessionals who work within this segment, even though control of the organization as a whole remains in the hands of bureaucracy (Derber & Schwartz, 1991). This idea of a legitimized professional island within bureaucracy suggests somewhat reduced conflict, but it does not preclude it.

The view that the two forms of authority, bureaucratic and professional, can exist in the same organization, and that when they do, conflict is to be expected is widely held, based on the evidence from a number of case studies (Zucker, 1991). Furthermore, this conflict increases as a function of the length of professional training. Perhaps this is why professions with origins within bureaucracy, and with shorter training periods, provoke less conflict. The evidence is clear that conflict is not inevitable when professions operate within bureaucracies (Hall, 1991). Yet, as table 19.2 shows, the potential for conflict is sizable simply because the two groups involved are trying to accomplish different things, using different means, and operating from different assumptions.

The pattern of conflict found appears to be one of long-term fluctuation based on conditions in the professional labor market and thus the power of professionals. Both administrators and professionals are dependent on one another. When one needs the other more, the negotiating balance shifts and power shifts with it into one camp or another (Bacharach, Bamberger, & Conley, 1991). At these extremes there is less conflict because one party is in control and the other must adjust. When the power balance is more equal, the fight for control escalates. This cyclical pattern is documented from case studies conducted by Bacharach et al. (1991) and by others (see, for example, Schellenberg & Miller, 1998). It may help explain the claim at certain times that one system or the other is achieving a permanently dominant position.

Overall, it appears that Thompson was largely right in his view of the nature and the extent of professional-bureaucracy conflict. A lot more is known now than when Thompson wrote on the subject, but this knowledge is not inconsistent with the idea that a substantial potential for conflict exists.

Innovation within Bureaucracies

Within the context of what has been said previously, Thompson appears to be contending that by nature bureaucracies cannot innovate and yet that, as Paul Lawrence and Davis Dyer say (see chapter 17), many of them need innovation. Professional systems can innovate, and this situation places bureaucracies in a dependent mode vis-à-vis their professional components. Accordingly, professionals gain negotiating leverage in the balance of power when the bureaucratic need for innovation intensifies.

The best evidence on these matters derives from a meta-analysis of a rather extensive literature dealing with the determinants of innovation rates in organizations. The results are given in table 19.3. Included there are not only the average correlations, but the author's expected relationships derived from theory and in some instances prior research (Damanpour,

1991). In large part these hypotheses posit a positive relationship between professional factors and innovation but a negative relationship between bureaucratic factors and innovation.

Where positive relationships are expected, they are in fact obtained with only one exception, and that involves a characteristic (managerial tenure) that does not concern professionals. Note, however, that significant positive results occur for managerial attitude toward change and administrative intensity, which also are not professional in nature. In any event, the truly professional factors all yield correlations that fit with the expected higher levels of innovation. Thus, in this respect, Thompson's theory is confirmed: the presence and effective use of professionals does make for a higher innovation rate.

As to the negative effect of bureaucracy, the data present a different picture. As noted, some factors associated with managers, and thus the bureaucratic component, yield positive correlations with innovation. Even more important, support for the bureaucratic hypotheses (at the bottom of table 19.3) is minimal: only one fit out of four possible is obtained, and that, involving centralization, is far from strong. All in all, there is little here to confirm Thompson's concept of the inhibiting effect of bureaucracy on innovation.

One possible explanation for these types of findings is that professional systems generate technical innova-

TABLE 19.2 Bureaucracy versus professionals—sources of conflict

| Parameter | Managerial strategies sought | |
	By administrators	By professionals
Task	Partial; interdependent with other tasks	Complete task
Training	Short; on-the-job; specialized skill	Extensive; external; total skills learned
Loyalty	To the organization	To the profession
Career	Ascent in organizational hierarcy	Ascent in the professional "hierarchy"
Structure and organization	By organizational product/process/project	By professional specialty/discipline
Projection selection	Limit individual choice to ensure results/profit	Full choice based on interest and contribution to profession
Rules and regulations	Accountability, administrative authority, and sanctions; tight controls and direction	Collegial influence and advice or rituals and ideology
Autonomy	Underspecification of ends and overspecification of means	Extensive autonomy and participation in determination of ends as well as means
Supervision	Close supervision	General supervision only; professional standards of evaluation

SOURCE: Samuel B. Bacharach, Peter Bamberger, & Sharon C. Conley (1991), Negotiating the See-Saw of Managerial Strategy: A Resurrection of the Study of Professionals in Organizational Theory, *Research in the Sociology of Organizations*, 8, 220. Copyright 1991. Reprinted with permission of Elsevier Science.

TABLE 19.3 Findings from meta-analysis on the determinants of innovation rate

Characteristics hypothesized	Meta-analytic finding	Fit
Have Positive relationship with innovation rate		
Specialization	.39	Yes
Funcational differentiation	.34	Yes
Professionalism	.17	Yes
Managerial attitude toward change	.27	Yes
Managerial tenure	NS	No
Technical knowledge resources	.47	Yes
Administrative intensity	.22	Yes
Slack resources	.14	Yes
External communication	.36	Yes
Internal communication	.17	Yes
Have Negative relationship with innovation rate		
Formalization	NS	No
Centralization	−.16	Yes
Vertical differentiation	NS	No
Size	.32	No

SOURCE: Adapted from Fariborz Damanpour (1991), Organizational Innovation: A Meta-Analysis of Effects of Determinants and Moderators, *Academy of Management Journal*, 34, pp. 558–559, 568

tions and bureaucratic systems generate administrative innovations (Daft, 1982). Thus, each segment has its own special type of proclivity in this regard. Since administrative innovations have been studied less, they would weigh in less strongly in any composite analysis. This type of moderator effect is not supported, however, in the Damanpour (1991) meta-analysis; both types of system appear to be capable of generating innovations of either kind. Truly innovative organizations apparently introduce a prevailing climate in all their components, which fosters innovation of any kind.

The literature on innovation has continued to produce mixed results and theoretical dead-ends over a considerable period of time (see Anderson & King, 1993; Hage, 1999). In this context the Damanpour (1991) results, based as they are on quantitative findings and relatively free of theoretical preconceptions, stand out as providing the best indication of the state of current knowledge. They support Thompson as regards professional innovation, but they do not portray bureaucracy as necessarily being the innovative wasteland that Thompson envisioned.

Dual Hierarchy Application

Thompson (1961a) recommends dealing with problems created by the presence of professional specialists in bureaucracies by creating a dual hierarchy with separate salary scales for the specialists. A review by Mary Ann Von Glinow (1988) raises serious questions about dual hierarchies, however. Most applications have been within the research and development context, and in practice many anticipated advantages do not materialize. The professionals may experience a lack of power, they may view their position as indicative of failure, there may be a lack of equity with the managerial hierarchy, professional hierarchy positions may be too few in number, and evaluative criteria may be inequitable.

One alternative is a triple hierarchy that incorporates liaison personnel with circumscribed areas of authority that are closely related to professional matters. Another approach is the separation of professional and hierarchical systems, as found in many universities where the spheres of influence of faculty and central administration are clearly differentiated. In any event, Thompson's dual hierarchy concept is very difficult to operationalize effectively in primarily bureaucratic organizations. It has not been the subject of research by the theory's author.

Venture Structure Applications

Thompson (1976) advocates the incorporation of an entrepreneurial system within the broad confines of

TABLE 19.4 Comparison of staff product managers and venture team managers in the same company on indices of bureaucracy

	Means scores[a]	
Indices of bureaucracy	Staff product managers	Venture team managers
Division of labor	4.1	4.2
Hierarchy of authority	(3.3)	(4.2)
Procedural specifications	(3.4)	(4.6)
Rules	(3.1)	(4.4)
Impersonality	3.8	3.7

NOTE: Numbers in parentheses indicate statistically significant difference between the columns at $p < .05$.

a. Larger values indicate a lesser degree of bureaucracy.

SOURCE: Adapted from James D. Hlavacek & Victor A. Thompson (1973), Bureaucracy and New Product Innovation, *Academy of Management Journal*, 16, 370

bureaucracy. Such venture efforts have been the subject of some research on his part (Hlavacek & Thompson, 1973, 1975, 1978). The objective is to graft innovation onto a bureaucratic structure that is assumed to be noninnovative by its very nature.

Evidence presented in table 19.4 indicates that venture teams can be less bureaucratized than personnel carrying out similar efforts totally within the firm, as is the case with product management (Hlavacek & Thompson, 1973). Yet venture teams, like dual hierarchies, are hard to implement well. They typically exist in a highly unstable state. There are major problems at the interface between the entrepreneurial and bureaucratic systems, and conflict between the two is frequent.

An analysis of 21 venture efforts that did not survive into profitability yielded the following conclusions:

Venture teams do not easily fit into going concerns. They frequently fail, for multiple reasons, including:

a. increased costs, uncertainty, or underfinancing;
b. failure to win acceptance within the firm;
c. insufficient operating freedom for the venture team;
d. internal power struggles;
e. a short-term top management perspective;
f. technically rather than commercially oriented venture managers;
g. lack of financial or organizational resources for commercial success; and
h. the established divisions' neglect or resistance to them. (Hlavacek & Thompson, 1978, p. 248)

Hlavacek and Thompson (1975) also undertook an analysis of various features of joint ventures between two firms where one supplies the technology and the other the marketing capability. Typically the technology contributor was the smaller. Here, too, evidence of a conflict between the two components was found.

A good deal has been written about venture structures and their operation (see, for example, the literature reviews and research reports of Burgelman & Sayles, 1986; Block & MacMillan, 1993). The most appropriate conclusion appears to be that venture structures can survive and grow, and be profitable, but not easily, and many do not achieve any of these results. Their dependence on the parent company is part of the problem, and this may be a function of bureaucracy conflicts. Yet similar problems arise between venture capitalists and the ventures they fund, and there bureaucracy cannot be invoked as the villain. More likely it is simply a matter of diverse goals, diverse people, power balances, and pressures for joint decision making. In any event, it remains true that corporate ventures often do not prosper as much as do independent entrepreneurial startups.

Evidence also indicates that although entrepreneurial characteristics make for success as a corporate venture leader, success is most likely to occur when these are combined in the same person with certain characteristics of a good manager (Miner, 1996, 1997). This combination appears to mitigate the clash that often occurs between entrepreneurs and managers when the two are entirely distinct types of people. Given the evidence in this area of personality differences and potential for personality conflicts, the most appropriate conclusion appears to be that Thompson was right in emphasizing the conflict-laden nature of the corporate-venture interface, and the threats to innovation thus created, but that he was wrong in attributing these problems to bureaucracy primarily. Here, as in other areas we have considered, Thompson appears to have overemphasized certain dysfunctions of bureaucracy.

With the exception of bureaucracy itself, most bureaucracy theorists have not spawned or endorsed other organizational forms. The major exception is

Victor Thompson. However, Thompson has uncovered more potential problems of bureaucracies than he has solved. No doubt dual hierarchies for professionals in bureaucratic organizations and venture teams for entrepreneurs can be made to work, but before this can happen the integrity of the nonbureaucratic system must be protected. Experience indicates that this does not happen spontaneously. A nonbureaucratic system is more likely to survive when it is the basis for organization to begin with than when it is added as an appendage to an existing bureaucracy. Clearly, there are major challenges to both practice and research inherent in combining multiple systems in a single organization.

ETZIONI'S COMPLIANCE THEORY

Etzioni's theory focuses on the compliance processes that operate on lower participants in organizations. The result is a typology of bureaucracies that takes a considerably different approach than the theories we have been considering. The variables are different and the questions addressed are new. Like Thompson, Etzioni has been primarily a theorist, leaving the conduct of research on his theory to others. On occasion he has carried out studies, but these have been somewhat peripheral to the major thrust of his theorizing.

Background

Etzioni was born in Germany in 1929 but spent most of his early life in Israel. He received his undergraduate education from Hebrew University there, from which he graduated in 1954. Much of his early work focused on the organizational structure of kibbutzim; both his master's thesis and his doctoral dissertation dealt with this topic. He was awarded a Ph.D. in sociology by the University of California at Berkeley in 1958.

From Berkeley Etzioni went to Columbia University in the sociology department, which he subsequently headed for a number of years. In 1980 he moved to George Washington University to be more involved in the Washington scene, and he has remained there ever since. Throughout his career Etzioni has identified primarily with sociology; he was president of the American Sociological Association in 1995. Yet he has maintained close ties with organizational behavior. In the late 1980s he spent a period

visiting at the Harvard Business School and published in the *Harvard Business Review* (Etzioni, 1989).

Although the study of organizations has been a prevailing theme since his early analyses of kibbutz structure, Etzioni has branched out into other areas of sociology and the social sciences in general, especially in recent years. Thus his major contributions to organizational behavior occurred in the 1960s and 1970s. Among his other areas of activity are a detailed analysis of the assumptions that underlie classical economic theory (Etzioni, 1988,1989) and a continuing study of societal level processes (Etzioni, 1968a, 1996). He has been quite politically active with agendas related to this latter interest, including world peace.

The major influences on Etzioni's work, in addition to Weber and his interpreter Talcott Parsons, came from the Berkeley period—Reinhard Bendix, Philip Selznick, and, in particular, Seymour Lipset— all well-known sociologists.

Typology for the Study of Bureaucracies

The theoretical formulations we will consider evolved initially immediately after Etzioni's kibbutzim period in the late 1950s, in article form (see for instance Etzioni, 1959). The major comprehensive statement, *A Comparative Analysis of Complex Organizations*, however, was published in 1961. A number of years later this volume was followed by a re-publication of the same theory, combined with a review and analysis of the research that had emerged in reaction to the original statement (Etzioni, 1975). There is some minimal new theory in this book as well. Over the years, the author published a number of abbreviated restatements of his theory (Etzioni, 1964, 1968b; Gross & Etzioni, 1985). The latter of these also contain some review and analysis of research tests. Etzioni (1975) notes and endorses several summaries of his theory, including those most recently available in Edgar Schein (1980) and Derek Pugh and David Hickson (1993). For a summary that converts Etzioni's terminology into a somewhat different set of labels, see Robert House (1984).

Compliance theory is not an inductive product of Etzioni's own research efforts. Rather, he describes it as an interaction of theoretical concepts that were developed by others and the analysis of a large number of empirical studies, also conducted by others. Barney Glaser and Anselm Strauss (1967) relate this approach to their concept of grounded theory and find it more grounded than some others of the period, but still not grounded enough. They would have preferred detailed, first-hand analyses of existing organizations to the use of secondary sources. Many of Etzioni's sources, however, represent what amount to case studies of specific organizations; they are largely observational in an anthropological sense.

Toward an Analytical Typology

An organization is defined as a social unit that is devoted primarily to the attainment of specific goals; it is a complex bureaucracy for purposes of the theory. Weber's model was developed with reference to business and government organizations and, to some extent, hierarchical churches and the military. Etzioni moves beyond this to many other organizational types with bureaucratic components. Thus, in regard to the domain of his theory, he provides a considerable extension. He also subdivides bureaucracy, thus extending bureaucratic theory in another sense, using the nature of the compliance involved as a basis. Compliance is defined as a relationship that is established both by the power of superiors to control subordinates and by the orientation of subordinates to this power of the superior.

The theory assumes three major sources of control: coercion, economic assets, and normative values. No source is inherently superior or yields more power under all circumstances. The resulting types of compliance provide a basis for comparisons among organizations. These types are coercive, utilitarian, and normative; this in contrast to Weber's legitimate and illegitimate power. Etzioni also differs from Weber in that he replaces the ideal type concept with a set of variables that are used to create all three types. At least in the initial statement of his theory, Etzioni makes no assumptions about the causal direction of relationships.

We now turn to some definitions.

Power is a person's ability to influence or induce someone else to carry out the person's directives or the norms that person supports; power positions give incumbents regular access to some means of power.

Coercive power is based on the use or threat to use physical sanctions (pain, hunger, etc.).

Remunerative power is based on control over material resources and rewards (pay, benefits, etc.).

Normative power is based on the dispensation and manipulation of symbolic rewards (moral involvement, social acceptance, etc.). (Etzioni, 1961, pp. 4–5)

Most organizations are assumed to operate from one major means of power, relying somewhat less on the other two. In response to these types of power, subordinates display some type of involvement—for instance, the cathectic-evaluative orientation of the person—and this involvement is characterized by both intensity and direction. The involvement may take several forms:

Alienative, indicating an intense negative orientation

Calculative, indicating either a positive or negative orientation of low intensity

Moral, indicating an intense positive orientation (Etzioni, 1961, p. 10).

The compliance relationship is defined in terms of the type of power applied to the lower participants of an organization and the type of involvement developed by these same lower participants (table 19.5). All nine types of compliance relationships are possible and do occur. However, "b" relationships are less common than those of the "a" type. This is because only the "a" form exhibits congruence or fit, and is therefore more effective. These congruent relationships may be labeled as follows:

Normative—normative, moral

Utilitarian—remunerative, calculative

Coercive—coercive, alienative

It is hypothesized that organizations tend to shift their compliance structures from "out of fit" to "in fit," and

TABLE 19.5 The compliance relationship determined by power and involvement

Type of power	Type of involvement		
	Alienative	Calculative	Moral
Normative	b	b	a
Remunerative	b	a	b
Coercive	a	b	b

a = congruent; b = noncongruent.

SOURCE: Adapted from Amitai Etzioni (1961), *A Comparative Analysis of Complex Organizations* (New York: Free Press) 12

thus from "b" to "a" forms, and that they resist pressures pushing them to "b" forms if they are already in a congruent "a" structure.

Questions arise as to the nature of the lower participants to which this typology applies and regarding why these people are so important. In the latter respect, the answer is that normally the control of lower participants is especially problematic because the lower a person is in the organizational hierarchy, the fewer the rewards of whatever kind obtained. Lower participants are those with titles such as inmate, client, customer, member, employee, and the like. They are defined as participants who are high on only one of the following: involvement, subordination, or performance obligations. Thus not all customers and clients are included. Included lower participants, not necessarily merely employees, set the lower boundary of an organization.

Predominantly coercive organizations include prisons, custodial hospitals, concentration camps, and certain unions. Predominantly utilitarian organizations include blue-collar and white-collar industries, business unions, and farmer's cooperatives. Predominantly normative organizations include religious entities, general hospitals, colleges and universities, schools, professional organizations, social unions, voluntary associations, and political organizations with an ideological program. There are some dual compliance structures that employ two bases with similar frequencies, but either these organizations are ineffective or they have developed special mechanisms for coping.

Correlates of Compliance

Organizational goals are specified as a state of affairs the organization is attempting to realize. They may be either stated or actual, and the two need not be the same. Three types are considered:

> Order goals represent attempts to control people who are deviant from the perspective of some social unit the organization is serving, such as society, by segregating these people and blocking further deviant activity.
>
> Economic goals represent efforts to produce commodities and services for outside users.
>
> Culture goals represent attempts to institutionalize conditions required to create and preserve symbolic objects, to apply them, and to reinforce commitment to these objects. Social goals are a subtype of culture goals. (Etzioni, 1961, pp. 72–73)

TABLE 19.6 Goals and compliance structures

Type of compliance	Type of goal		
	Order	Economic	Culture
Normative	b	b	a
Utilitarian	b	a	b
Coercive	a	b	b

a = congruent; b = noncongruent.

SOURCE: Adapted from Amitai Etzioni (1961), A Comparative Analysis of Complex Organizations (New York: Free Press), 74

Although organizations may have multiple goals, one is usually predominant. These goals line up with the various compliance structures as shown in table 19.6. Most organizations fall on the "a" diagonal, although the "b" positions are occupied on occasion. The congruent "a" types are more effective; the incongruent "b" types less so, even though they may survive. At the same time "b" organizations tend to strive toward the more effective "a" types, either by shifting their goals or their compliance structures, or both.

The term *elites* refers to people in organizations who have power. Lower elites are those who possess direct power over lower participants. The source of elite power may be inherent in the position held and accordingly may be coercive, remunerative, or normative; such people are referred to as *officers*. *Leaders* are those who derive power from their personal characteristics. The relationships involved here are shown in table 19.7. Under crisis conditions only leaders of one type or the other can maintain compliance, but with only personal power to rely on informal leaders remain vulnerable.

Elites control both *expressive* activities, thus meeting organizational needs for social and normative integration, and *instrumental* activities, thus fulfilling

TABLE 19.7 Elites and sources of power

Power derived from personal characteristics	Power derived from position	
	Yes	No
Yes	Formal leaders (officers)	Informal leaders
No	Officers	Nonelite

SOURCE: Adapted from Amitai Etzioni (1961), A Comparative Analysis of Complex Organizations (New York: Free Press), 90

needs of input and allocation. The former is comparable to consideration, as measured by the Ohio State scales, and the latter to initiating structure (see chapter 10 in this volume) (Gross & Etzioni, 1985). Expressive activities tend to require moral involvement on the part of lower participants and thus are appropriately supervised by elites who hold normative power; power based on personal characteristics is particularly appropriate and effective. Instrumental activities tend to require calculative involvement and are best supervised by those with utilitarian power over those who do the performing; here power derived from one's position is most effective. These relationships are depicted in table 19.8.

The effective elite hierarchy is one in which the structure of the elites and the hierarchy of goals, or means, are congruent (Etzioni, 1959):

> In normative organizations it is functional for the expressive elite to subordinate the instrumental one. . . . In utilitarian organizations, high productivity is associated with subordination of the expressive elite by the instrumental elite, and cooperation between the two. In coercive organizations the antagonism between organizational and informal elites makes for an unstable relationship instead of a clear pattern of subordination. (Etzioni, 1961, p. 126)

Further Correlates of Compliance

Etzioni discusses a number of additional correlates of compliance, each of which is important to the theory in varying respects and degrees.

The degree of *consensus* is an index of the extent to which groups within an organization differ in orientation and thus the extent to which the organization is integrated. Consensus may be on general values, organizational goals, means to goals, participation in the organization, performance obligations, and cognitive perspectives. The degree of consensus as among different statuses presents a special problem. Consensus should be highest in normative organizations and least in coercive ones. Normative organizations need both a high degree and a wide range of consensus. Utilitarian organizations, with their emphasis on production goals and contributions by lower participants, require consensus on performance obligations, participation, and cognitive perspectives. Coercive organizations can function even in the face of a widespread lack of consensus.

Etzioni's treatment of *communications* operates from only a very limited empirical base. Instrumental and expressive communications use different networks. The former distributes information and knowledge, and influences cognitive orientations—much of it has the character of formalization. The latter changes or reinforces attitudes, norms, and values. Not surprisingly, normative organizations tend to stress downward expressive communications, utilitarian organizations emphasize vertical instrumental communication, and coercive organizations often operate with blocked vertical channels combined with considerable horizontal expressive communication. Because these propositions lack a solid empirical base, the need for relevant research is apparent.

Socialization refers to the acquisition of the requisite orientations for satisfactory functioning in a role (Parsons, 1951). Normative organizations are characterized by the greatest amount and scope of socialization; this socialization may be mostly expressive in some, but in other instances instrumental elements are also included. Utilitarian organizations rely heavily on expressive (particularly motivational) socialization. Coercive organizations operate with relatively little by way of socialization; what there is, is instrumental or occurs entirely within the lower participant culture. Socialization overall may be viewed as a mechanism whereby the existing consensus structure and communication practices of the organization are transmitted to each new generation of participants.

The next set of compliance correlates—recruitment, scope, and pervasiveness—deals with concepts that have some direct relationship to the organization's environment.

Organizational recruitment provides new members from the outside environment. Coercive organizations

TABLE 19.8 Activity type related to leader type

Activity type	Leader type		
	Informal leaders	Formal leaders	Officers
Instrumental	+	++	+++
Expressive	+++	++	+

NOTE: + frequency indicates likeliness from least (+) to most (+++).

SOURCE: Adapted from Amitai Etzioni (1961), *A Comparative Analysis of Complex Organizations* (New York: Free Press), 93

accomplish this through the efforts of the courts, police, and the like. Utilitarian organizations compete
for human resources in the labor market. Normative
organizations rely in large part on expressive communication and socialization for their lower participants,
although professional organizations resort to market
competition as well. Thus, in general, the methods
used to obtain participants from the environment parallel those used to control participants once acquired.
This consequence between recruitment and the compliance structure is not a necessary outcome, however.
The flow from recruitment to effectiveness may be
depicted as in figure 19.1. Frequently selectivity in
recruitment and socialization operate as substitutes
for one another. However, the highest levels of organizational quality are achieved when both socialization
effort and recruiting selectivity are at a high level.
When only recruitment or only socialization is high,
the results would be expected to be of medium quality.
If both are low, quality is low.

Organizational scope refers to the number of activities in which participants are jointly involved. Scope
is measured by the extent that participants' activities
are limited to other participants versus involving non-
participants as well. In total organizations, of high
scope, practically all activities are carried out within.
When scope is narrow, participants share few activities
relative to what is shared with outsiders.

Organizational pervasiveness refers to the number
of activities both inside and outside the organization
for which the organization establishes norms. Pervasiveness may cover more or less activities than scope;
thus the normative boundary and the action boundary
need not be the same. In general, both coercive and
utilitarian organizations have quite similar ranges of
scope and pervasiveness, but this is not true of normative organizations. The relationships involved are as

TABLE 19.9 Compliance as related to scope and pervasiveness

| | Pervasiveness | |
Scope	Low	High
Broad	Coercive organizations	Normative organizations
Narrow	Utilitarian organizations	Normative orgainzations

SOURCE: Adapted from Amitai Etzioni (1961), *A Comparative Analysis of Complex Organization* (New York: Free Press) 164

shown in table 19.9. Both scope and pervasiveness
exhibit characteristic relationships to compliance.

Cohesion is defined as a positive expressive relationship among two or more participants. It reduces the
variation in group members' behavior, but it has no
necessary relation to the direction of involvement of
lower participants. It is likened to a pipe through
which normative content of any kind may flow. Higher
cohesion means better flow, but it says nothing about
the substance of that flow. Thus cohesion is not a
correlate of compliance. The more homogeneous a
group on a variety of characteristics, the more likely
group cohesion is to develop; similarly, the greater
the cohesion, the more the group is likely to become
homogeneous. In addition to group or peer cohesion,
there may also be hierarchical cohesion across organizational ranks involving officers and lower participants. In this case, if the officers are committed to
organizational norms, the cohesion may operate to
produce positive involvement in the organization on
the part of lower participants. Thus, it is important to
differentiate group cohesion from hierarchical cohesion.

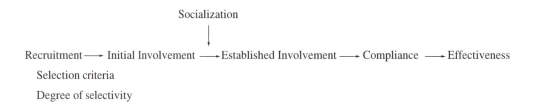

FIGURE 19.1 Flow from recruitment to effective performance. Adapted from Amitai Etzioni (1961),
A Comparative Analysis of Complex Organizations (New York: Free Press), 157.

Compliance and Charisma

We move to the compliance structure of higher participants or elites. Several points may be made in this regard: (1) the control of lower elites by higher elites is influenced by the control higher elites exercise over lower participants; (2) the compliance structure of elites varies from one organization to another much less than with lower participants, primarily because coercive power is rarely used at this level and because pure moral involvement is uncommon as well; (3) the higher the rank, the more normative the control exercised over it. In line with this third point, as we move to the compliance of higher participants, the study become restricted to matters of diffuse and intensive normative power, what is called charisma.

Weber made charisma, defined as an extraordinary quality of a person, a central concern for bureaucracy. Etzioni defines it as the ability of a person in an organization to exercise diffuse and intense influence over the normative orientations of other participants. This charisma may be developed in a variety of organizational positions:

> When charisma is concentrated at the *top*, this is referred to as the *T-Structure*; only utilitarian organizations follow this model (many companies).
>
> When charisma is characteristic of all *line* positions, this is referred to as the *L-Structure*; normative organizations emphasizing pure normative compliance follow this model (many churches).
>
> When charisma is limited to one or more *ranks* other than the top level, this is referred to as the *R-Structure*; normative organizations stressing social compliance follow this model (many professional organizations).
>
> There are in addition organizations (such as prisons) in which charisma is not required at all. (Etzioni, 1961, pp. 208–209)

Although Weber tended to emphasize the dysfunctional role of charisma in leading bureaucracies away from their established functions, Etzioni emphasizes the functional role. This functional role for charisma becomes manifest as long as it follows the pattern depicted in table 19.10.

The use of charisma in this manner as a source of compliance strains organizational discipline on occasion, simply because certain members assume a highly personalized type of power. This is less of a problem in the utilitarian T-Structures because charisma is minimal and to be found in a safe place at the top. It is a problem for L-Structures such as churches and for R-Structures of a professional nature. In these organizations extensive controls must be instituted to keep the personalized power of widespread charisma from contributing to deviance.

Additional Propositions

Using the theoretical framework we have been considering, Etzioni (1961, 1975) sets forth several additional propositions. One such statement proposes that most executives are more effective in one type of compliance structure than the other two, since each type of compliance requires a distinctive pattern of personality characteristics, aptitudes, and inclinations. Variations in authoritarianism are cited as one example in this regard (Etzioni, 1961).

Another proposition focuses on the need for both instrumental and expressive leadership roles in most organizations. The relationship between these two should be compatible with the goals of the organization and the compliance structure. All things considered, separating the roles so that both an instrumental leader and an expressive leader exist seems to recommend itself. Dual leadership of this kind is endorsed (Etzioni, 1975).

On an issue that had previously been left unresolved, Etzioni (1975) proposes that in the modern world a clear secular trend, and signs of a similar human yearning as well, exist toward increasing reliance on normative organizations and reduced reliance on coercive and utilitarian ones. This trend derives theoretical support from the work of Abraham Maslow and from need hierarchy theory (see chapter 6 in this volume). The trend toward a normative dominance in society is discussed at length in Etzioni (1968a).

Finally, Etzioni has the following to say about a definition of effectiveness:

> It seems wiser, then, to define organizational effectiveness not merely as a level of goal realization but as a pattern of relationships among the elements of an organizational system which enhances its service of one or more goals. . . . The suggested definition . . . allows taking into account system needs which ensure effectiveness beyond the short . . . run. (1975, p. 133)

TABLE 19.10 Location of charisma in relation to rank and compliance structure

Organizational rank	Type of compliance structure			
	Coercive	Utilitarian	Normative (L)	Normative (R)
Highest	Not charismatic	Charismatic	Charismatic	Not charismatic
Middle	Not charismatic	Not charismatic	Charismatic	Charismatic

SOURCE: Adapted from Amitai Etzioni (1961), *A Comparative Analysis of Complex Organizations* (New York: Free Press) 224

Etzioni's compliance theory is in large part a dictionary of terms and variables for the study of organizations. Yet in 1961 Etzioni was well aware that he had not solved the problem of developing instruments that could be used to test his propositions. He felt the propositions had been stated in testable form, but he was unsure of what would happen next. Without operationalization of his constructs, research could not progress very far, and few operationalizations were available at the time. Etzioni himself is primarily a theorist and only a researcher to a limited degree. He did not see exactly how the bridge to validated theory could be constructed. In fact, the 1961 book ends on a somewhat pessimistic note in this regard.

Evaluation and Impact

In spite of Etzioni's initial misgivings, compliance theory did generate considerable research in the years immediately after its publication. This research is reviewed at length in the revised edition (Etzioni, 1975). It is reviewed further, but with little reference to new studies in Gross and Etzioni (1985). The failure to incorporate research published in the ensuing 10 years seems to reflect a sharp reduction in research on the theory. This impression is reinforced by a continuing void in the years since 1985. It appears that as Etzioni left the study of organizations, the field of organizational behavior left the study of Etzioni's theory. This is unfortunate, but somewhat predictable from experience with other theories. Yet we do have roughly a 15-year stock of research on compliance theory to draw on.

This research as reviewed by Etzioni (1975) is widely dispersed, and over half of his citations did not appear in regular published sources. Furthermore, the specific relevance of a number of the studies for compliance theory is subject to some question. There is a tendency in this literature to take the compliance theory concepts and use them in the testing of hypotheses that go well beyond Etzioni's own formulations, delving into problem areas of specific interest to the individual researchers. As one might expect from the large number of unpublished studies, the methodology in some instances is questionable; for example, there are reports on purely qualitative case analyses that are treated as theory testing. Yet in an overall sense the research product is impressive.

Compliance Thesis Revisited

The analytical typology has been tested quite extensively — in hospitals, business firms, prisons, infantry training units, governmental agencies, and mixed samples of organizations, for instance. It has been tested at the comprehensive organization level and at the level of distinctive components, such as R&D departments.

Methods of operationalizing the power and involvement dimensions have been developed, and thus it has been proven possible to operationalize the basic compliance typology. Problems in placing organizations within the typology have been experienced, however, especially when the normative type seems to be involved (Hall, 1991). Public schools represent an example; different students may comply on any of the bases, depending on their situation and relation to the organization. When large professional components are present in an organization and when clients, patients, students, and the like are involved, it seems inappropriate to treat these organizations, or the nonhierarchic component, as a type within bureaucracy.

Empirically, the compliance typology has proven useful for studying compliance, but it is less useful for studying the factors that have been the focus of many other macro theories. Thus, it would seem that different typologies, and thus ways of classifying organizations, can be useful for different purposes; multiple valid typologies may stand at the same time. When compliance is a major issue for an organization, Etzioni's approach can prove very helpful. But there are organizations for which compliance is not a real concern. In such circumstances typologies dealing with other problem areas, such as growth and size, may have greater value.

One feature of compliance theory is that certain organizations exhibit power-involvement fit and others do not. It is hypothesized that this fit is not only a source of effectiveness, but organizations that do not possess fit move toward it and those that do possess it resist movement that would damage this relationship. This latter, dynamic feature of the theory has received little research attention. Once again, we find that needed longitudinal research is lacking.

Goals and Effectiveness Revisited

As hypothesized, stated and actual goals have been found to differ. This research, conducted in a mental health complex, also indicates that for purposes of compliance analysis it is the actual goals that need to be studied. Furthermore, the classification of goals as order, economic, and culture can be empirically demonstrated.

The fit between type of goal and compliance has been studied in normative, utilitarian, and coercive organizations. Although some of the findings are rather weak, the overall results provide support for the idea that compliance-goal fit is associated with greater organizational effectiveness. Thus, the typology appears to be useful. However, there is a need for research in situations where goals are perceived as unclear and difficult to measure, which appears to be most likely in coercive and normative organizations.

Compliance and Elites Revisited

Research indicates that elite roles may be characterized as expressive or instrumental within utilitarian organizations. This finding has been extended to normative organizations where expressive roles were found to dominate. However, data on the relationships between compliance structures and the instrumental-expressive balance among elites is far from conclusive. Often studies have used proxies for effectiveness, and it is not possible on the data to conclude for or against the hypothesis.

A study in which the theory's author collaborated (Etzioni & Lehman, 1968) seems to support the position that effectiveness is fostered if expressive and instrumental leadership are separated and allocated to different people, at least in normative organizations. However, it appears that this research preceded the formulation of the dual leadership hypothesis and may well have exerted considerable influence on it.

Other Correlates Revisited

Most of the studies of correlates, beyond those dealing with goals and elites, have been conducted in normative organizations. There, selectivity often has been found to play an important role in effectiveness. Socialization does not necessarily trade off with selectivity to compensate for deficiencies in recruitment; nevertheless, high selectivity requires a degree of socialization to produce effectiveness. Evidence from another source indicates that when selectivity and socialization are both high, effectiveness is greatest; when both are low, it tends to be minimal. Some evidence for a selectivity-socialization tradeoff derives from this research as well. Thus compliance theory gains what amounts to mixed support from research in this area. There is also some evidence that pervasiveness tends to be high in normative organizations, as hypothesized, and that consensus is positively associated with effectiveness.

Studies in the utilitarian context dealing with correlates are limited. The major finding has been that, as expected, hierarchical cohesion is associated with positive involvement on the part of lower participants; this fits with the results obtained with leader member exchange theory (see chapter 11 in this volume).

Research in coercive organizations appears to indicate that broad scope and high pervasiveness create severe tensions that require special mechanisms if the organization is to survive. This conclusion, however, is based on historical analyses of the relationship of slaves to their plantations. It cannot qualify as controlled research.

Some work has also been done looking at causal relations involving correlates as established from path analysis. Since compliance theory itself does not state causal hypotheses, this clearly goes beyond the theory, but Etzioni (1975) nevertheless considers it relevant. It has the advantage that it deals with a number of correlates. Reports on these results have been presented in both unpublished and published sources (see for example Mulford, Klonglan, Warren, & Schmitz, 1972).

The initial work was done within the U.S. Civil Defense system in three states; this was considered to be a normative organization (largely voluntary). A simplified version of the predominant causal flow would look as shown in figure 19.2. Pervasiveness and selectivity also played some role, although selectivity in this particular organization was not a primary factor (consensus and cohesion were not measured in this study). The path coefficients for scope are both the highest and most frequently significant.

A subsequent study of utilitarian farm cooperatives yielded a somewhat different causal picture, as would be expected, given the fact that a different type of compliance is involved. The most striking new finding is that selectivity in recruitment now plays a very important role. Also pervasiveness is consistently related to effectiveness.

These findings required certain causal assumptions that Etzioni does not always accept, and the techniques of path analysis are somewhat suspect in any event. However, the data clearly indicate that some path to effectiveness is present, that these paths do not look the same for the two compliance types, and that the variables considered, in some combination, play an important role in organizational functioning.

All in all, with regard to correlates, the research that focuses on Etzioni's hypotheses directly appears to be somewhat spotty. It is unfortunate that no more has been done. The variables do appear to be measurable, in contrast to Etzioni's (1961) initial concerns on this score, and they do appear to play important roles in the different types of organizations. Yet this does not always occur in exactly the ways compliance theory anticipates. Etzioni himself is more optimistic about the degree to which the research supports compliance theory than I have been, in large part because he draws on qualitative, historical analyses for this purpose. For the reasons stated in chapter 1, I cannot

accept this type of study as a research test, however interesting, even fascinating, the data may be.

Personal and Charismatic Considerations

Charisma is a major concern in both Weber's and Etzioni's theories. Beyond this, however, the two theories depart considerably both as to definitions and with regard to the number of organizational positions in which charisma is expected to appear. Thus, to adequately test the compliance theory formulations, a measure of charisma specifically designed for that purpose is needed. Such a measure has not been created, and without it Etzioni's views remain essentially untested. Several studies in this area are cited in support of compliance theory, but lacking a measure of charisma, they cannot be considered to provide adequate evidence with regard to the charisma propositions.

A proposition on which some evidence is available is the one that states that most executives are more effective in one type of compliance structure than the other two, because of differences in the personality make-up required for performance in different types of organizations and their roles. Finding no research on this subject, Etzioni undertook a small pilot study in the area (Etzioni, 1961). Only 24 subjects were utilized, all ex-military, and data were obtained from newspaper articles. The military careers of these people were analyzed to place them in groups where high normative power was needed (combat) and little normative power was involved (desk). Then this classification was broken down by whether their subsequent civilian careers were of a high or low normative nature. Consistent with the hypothesis, 79 percent of the cases fell on the diagonal, in which high military normative orientation was matched with high civilian and low with low. In spite of the small sample, this was statistically significant.

Other evidence that differential personality patterns are associated with career success in different

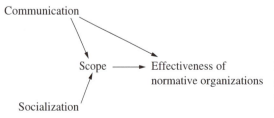

FIGURE 19.2 Predominant causal flow influencing effectiveness. Adapted from Amitai Etzioni (1975), A *Comparative Analysis of Complex Organizations* (New York: Free Press), 410.

types of organizations derives from role motivation theory (see chapter 5 in this volume). There the organizational typology is not exactly the same as that employed by Etzioni, but his normative type would seem to match up well with the professional, and his coercive and utilitarian types both appear to have much in common with the hierarchic form. Evidence on the relationships among measures of the personality characteristics that make for success in different types of organizations is reviewed in Miner 1993 and is presented in more detail in Miner 1980 and 1990. A particularly important study in this regard, because it deals with whole careers, is Miner 2002. On this evidence it seems safe to conclude that managers and professionals (and entrepreneurs as well) have distinct personality patterns that provide a special capacity to achieve success in the different types of organizations. Thus, Etzioni's proposition in this regard is supported, although the data were not obtained with the specific purpose of testing his theory in mind.

Application

Etzioni says little about the application of his theory to organizational practice until the last two pages of his 1975 book. There he writes briefly on the subject of guidability, by which he means something much akin to organization development. This change process is viewed as a joint product of efforts by organizational elites and lower participants. Coercive organizations, although dominated by elites, lack the support of lower participants and thus are capable of little collective, guided action. The substantial cross-rank integration in normative organizations permits more collective action, but guidability is another matter because the relationships are often too expressive and nonrational for this purpose. Utilitarian organizations are intermediate in their capacity for collective action, while exhibiting the most guidability of the three types. Etzioni ends with the following statement:

> Change may occur . . . as a result of deliberate elite policies and various degrees of organizational consensus and mobilization of the lower participants. . . . The purpose here is neither to summarize the guidance theory nor to work out the details of its application to organizational analysis in general or to compliance theory in particular, but to indicate a direction in which, I suggest, fruitful theoretical as well as empirical explorations of compliance may develop. (Etzioni, 1975, p. 505)

This does not provide much to go on insofar as application is concerned.

CONCLUSIONS

A prevailing concern of the theories considered in this chapter, and in chapter 18 as well, is the handling of professionals and professional components within the context of bureaucracy. To a degree, this concern extends to entrepreneurs and entrepreneurial components. All of the theories subsume these nonbureaucratic features under a concept of bureaucracy. Thus bureaucratic theory from Weber comes first, and then the troublesome elements are added in to form variants on bureaucracy or special types. The problem keeps coming up in these theories, and yet it remains only partially solved.

A different approach is to treat bureaucracy as one type of organization and the professional, and entrepreneurial types as others. All may in fact represent freestanding types and on this basis would seem to be co-equals for whom independent theories may be derived. Accordingly, when the different types are conjoined, as they are when bureaucratic and professional systems come together, the ideal approach would seem to be to develop a theory of the interaction, working from the two limited domain theories as a base; this is in contrast to working from bureaucratic theory alone and modifying it, an approach which to date has not proved entirely satisfactory. What I suggest is in line with role motivation theory, but would require going beyond that theory as it exists at present, to deal with the interaction per se.

References

Anderson, Neil, & King, Nigel (1993). Innovation in Organizations. *International Review of Industrial and Organizational Psychology*, 8, 1–34.

Bacharach, Samuel B.; Bamberger, Peter; & Conley, Sharon C. (1991). Negotiating the See-Saw of Managerial Strategy: A Resurrection of the Study of Professionals in Organizational Theory. *Research in the Sociology of Organizations*, 8, 217–238.

Baker, Sally H.; Etzioni, Amitai; Hansen, Richard A.; & Sontag, Marvin (1973). Tolerance for Bureaucratic Structure: Theory and Measurement. *Human Relations*, 26, 775–786.

Barley, Stephen R., & Tolbert, Pamela S. (1991). Introduction: At the Intersection of Organizations and

Occupations. *Research in the Sociology of Organizations*, 8, 1–13.

Block, Zenas, & MacMillan, Ian C. (1993). *Corporate Venturing: Creating New Businesses within the Firm.* Boston: Harvard Business School Press.

Burgelman, Robert A., & Sayles, Leonard R. (1986). *Inside Corporate Innovation: Strategy, Structure, and Managerial Skills.* New York: Free Press.

Daft, Richard L. (1982). Bureaucratic versus Nonbureaucratic Structure and the Process of Innovation and Change. *Research in the Sociology of Organizations*, 1, 129–166.

Damanpour, Fariborz (1991). Organizational Innovation: A Meta-Analysis of Effects of Determinants and Moderators. *Academy of Management Journal*, 34, 555–590.

Derber, Charles, & Schwartz, William A. (1991). New Mandarins or New Proletariat? Professional Power at Work. *Research in the Sociology of Organizations*, 8, 71–96.

Etzioni, Amitai (1959). Authority Structure and Organizational Effectiveness. *Administrative Science Quarterly*, 4, 43–67.

Etzioni, Amitai (1961). *A Comparative Analysis of Complex Organizations: On Power, Involvement, and Their Correlates.* New York: Free Press.

Etzioni, Amitai (1964). *Modern Organizations.* Englewood Cliffs, NJ: Prentice Hall.

Etzioni, Amitai (1968a). *The Active Society: A Theory of Societal and Political Processes.* New York: Free Press.

Etzioni, Amitai (1968b). Organizational Dimensions and Their Interrelationships: A Theory of Compliance. In Bernard P. Indik & F. Kenneth Berrien (Eds.), *People, Groups, and Organizations* (pp. 94–109). New York: Teachers College Press,.

Etzioni, Amitai (1975). *A Comparative Analysis of Complex Organizations: On Power, Involvement, and Their Correlates*, rev. and enl. ed. New York: Free Press.

Etzioni, Amitai (1988). *The Moral Dimension: Toward a New Economics.* New York: Free Press.

Etzioni, Amitai (1989). Humble Decision Making. *Harvard Business Review*, 67(4), 122–126.

Etzioni, Amitai (1996). The Responsive Community: A Communitarian Perspective. *American Sociological Review*, 61, 1–11.

Etzioni, Amitai, & Lehman, Ethna (1968). Dual Leadership in a Therapeutic Organization. *International Review of Applied Psychology*, 17, 51–67.

Glaser, Barney G., & Strauss, Anselm L. (1967). *The Discovery of Grounded Theory: Strategies for Qualitative Research.* Chicago: Aldine.

Gordon, Leonard V. (1970). Measurement of Bureaucratic Orientation. *Personnel Psychology*, 23, 1–11.

Gross, Edward, & Etzioni, Amitai (1985). *Organizations in Society.* Englewood Cliffs, NJ: Prentice Hall.

Hage, Jerald T. (1999). Organizational Innovation and Organizational Change. *Annual Review of Sociology*, 25, 597–622.

Hall, Richard H. (1991). *Organizations: Structures, Processes, and Outcomes.* Englewood Cliffs, NJ: Prentice Hall.

Hlavacek, James D., & Thompson, Victor A. (1973). Bureaucracy and New Product Innovation. *Academy of Management Journal*, 16, 361–372.

Hlavacek, James D., & Thompson, Victor A. (1975). The Joint Venture Approach to Technology Utilization. *IEEE Transactions on Engineering Management*, EM-23(1), 35–41.

Hlavacek, James D., & Thompson, Victor A. (1978). Bureaucracy and Venture Failures. *Academy of Management Review*, 3, 242–248.

House, Robert J. (1984). Amitai Etzioni's *A Comparative Analysis of Complex Organizations*. In Henry L. Tosi (Ed.), *Theories of Organization* (pp. 85–91). New York: Wiley.

Leicht, Kevin T., & Fennell, Mary L. (1997). The Changing Organizational Context of Professional Work. *Annual Review of Sociology*, 23, 215–231.

Miner, John B. (1971). Changes in Student Attitudes toward Bureaucratic Role Prescriptions during the 1960s. *Administrative Science Quarterly*, 16, 412–428.

Miner, John B. (1980). The Role of Managerial and Professional Motivation in the Career Success of Management Professors. *Academy of Management Journal*, 23, 487–508.

Miner, John B. (1990). Entrepreneurs, High Growth Entrepreneurs, and Managers: Contrasting and Overlapping Motivational Patterns. *Journal of Business Venturing*, 5, 221–234.

Miner, John B. (1993). *Role Motivation Theories.* New York: Routledge.

Miner, John B. (1996). *The Four Routes to Entrepreneurial Success.* San Francisco: Berrett-Koehler.

Miner, John B. (1997). *A Psychological Typology of Successful Entrepreneurs.* Westport, CT: Quorum.

Miner, John B. (2002). The Role Motivation Theories of Organizational Leadership. In Francis J. Yammarino & Bruce J. Avolio (Eds.), *Transformational and Charismatic Leadership: The Road Ahead.* New York: Elsevier.

Miner, John B., & Anderson, James K. (1958). The Postwar Occupational Adjustment of Emotionally Disturbed Soldiers. *Journal of Applied Psychology*, 42, 317–322.

Mulford, Charles L.; Klonglan, Gerald E.; Warren, R.; & Schmitz, P. (1972). A Causal Model of Effectiveness in Organizations. *Social Science Research*, 1, 61–78.

Parsons, Talcott (1951). *The Social System*. Glencoe, IL: Free Press.

Pugh, Derek S., & Hickson, David J. (1993). *Great Writers on Organizations: The Omnibus Edition*. Aldershot, UK: Dartmouth.

Schein, Edgar H. (1980). *Organizational Psychology*. Englewood Cliffs, NJ: Prentice Hall.

Schellenberg, Kathryn, & Miller, George A. (1998). Turbulence and Bureaucracy. *Journal of Applied Behavioral Science*, 34, 202–221.

Simon, Herbert A. (1991). *Models of My Life*. New York: Basic Books.

Simon, Herbert A.; Smithburg, Donald W.; & Thompson, Victor A. (1950). *Public Administration*. New York: Knopf.

Stinchcombe, Arthur L. (1974). *Creating Efficient Industrial Administrations*. New York: Academic Press.

Thompson, Victor A. (1950). *The Regulatory Process in OPA Rationing*. New York: Kings Crown Press.

Thompson, Victor A. (1961a). Hierarchy, Specialization, and Organizational Conflict. *Administrative Science Quarterly*, 5, 485–521.

Thompson, Victor A. (1961b). *Modern Organization*. New York: Knopf.

Thompson, Victor A. (1965). Bureaucracy and Innovation. *Administrative Science Quarterly*, 10, 1–20.

Thompson, Victor A. (1969). *Bureaucracy and Innovation*. University: University of Alabama Press.

Thompson, Victor A. (1975). *Without Sympathy or Enthusiasm: The Problem of Administrative Compassion*. University: University of Alabama Press.

Thompson, Victor A. (1976). *Bureaucracy and the Modern World*. Morristown, NJ: General Learning Press.

Tosi, Henry L. (1984). *Theories of Organization*. New York: Wiley.

Von Glinow, Mary Ann (1988). *The New Professionals: Managing Today's High-Tech Employees*. Cambridge, MA: Ballinger.

Zucker, Lynne G. (1991). Markets for Bureaucratic Authority and Control: Information Quality in Professions and Services. *Research in the Sociology of Organizations*, 8, 157–190.

Chapter 20

Goal Congruence Theory and the
Route to Organization Development

As we will see in this chapter, our discussion is not yet done with the problems of professionals and bureaucracies. Now, however, the orientation shifts 180 degrees from one that strongly emphasizes bureaucracy to one that deemphasizes it. The dysfunctions considered are viewed as so great that bureaucracy must be destroyed as an organizational form.

Organization development is not new to the readers of this volume. Rensis Likert, and system 4 theory (see chapter 13 in this volume), created an organization development application that we considered at some length. Eric Trist and Fred Emery, and their sociotechnical systems theory (see chapter 14), produced applications that were rapidly absorbed by organization development. Paul Lawrence and Jay Lorsch, and the contingency theory of organization (see chapter 17), spawned an organization development intervention approach that, as we have seen, had considerable impact. In this chapter two additional theories that are closely linked to organization development are discussed, the theories of Chris Argyris and Warren Bennis. In both instances the theorists' ideas led them first to embrace laboratory or sensitivity training as a method of interpersonal skill development and subsequently to expand from there into the broader arena of organization development. The two are similar also in their strong and continuing emphasis on humanist values, which caused them to condemn Max Weber's bureaucracy and the classical management theories of Henri Fayol and Frederick Taylor (see chapter 3). For them, at least in the early period, bureaucracy was unacceptable because it deprived participants of their dignity and their capacity for growth. Some alternative organizational form was needed, and organization development was the means to transformation.

GOAL CONGRUENCE
AND ITS ANALOGUES

Background

Born in 1923, Argyris did his undergraduate work in psychology at Clark University, from which he graduated in 1947. After obtaining a master's degree in psychology and economics at Kansas University, he moved on to the School of Industrial and Labor Relations at Cornell University and obtained his Ph.D. from there in 1951. During this period he appears to have been initially influenced most by Roger Barker and Fritz Heider, and in particular by the action research perspective of Kurt Lewin (see chapter 2 in this volume); all of these people were psychologists. At Cornell, however, his mentor was William Foote White, a sociologist and applied anthropologist (Argyris, 1992a). From that time onward he has been something of an all-purpose social scientist with publications in varied fields, but organizational behavior has been a major part of his identity since the field emerged.

From Cornell Argyris went to Yale University, initially in the Labor and Management Center but later in the administrative sciences department (Putnam, 1995), at the time when Clayton Alderfer, Richard Hackman, Greg Oldham, Edward Lawler, and Martin Evans were there; he headed that unit for a while. Then in 1971 he moved to Harvard University, with appointments in education and business. Throughout the Yale period he was actively involved in the laboratory education movement and in T-groups. He has now retired from Harvard, but he continues to write and consult extensively.

An idea of Argyris's somewhat iconoclastic approach to the field may be gained from his stated methodology for research, which is to engage in active intervention within organizations. This intervention approach is guided by three "realizations":

1. The application of knowledge is the most robust empirical test of validity.
2. The rule that scientific research is descriptive can be the basis for limiting its validity and actionability.
3. The methodology for conducting rigorous empirical research is a methodology for controlling ideas and people. (Argyris, 1998a, p. 877)

Clearly this iconoclasm is not the concept of research endorsed in this volume, but it does help explain the case-oriented brand of ethnography, as opposed to more controlled experimental designs, that Argyris has pursued in much of his work.

Stages of Goal Congruence
Theory Development

During the 1950s, when his goal congruence theory was crystallizing, Argyris was strongly influenced by the thinking of E. Wight Bakke (1950, 1959) with whom he worked at the Yale Labor and Management Center. As we will see, this influence was temporary, however.

Although Argyris has written extensively throughout his career, three major statements appear to represent milestones in the exposition of goal congruence theory. The first is *Personality and Organization* (Argyris, 1957), the second is *Integrating the Individual and the Organization* (Argyris, 1964), and the third is an article in *Administrative Science Quarterly* entitled "Personality and Organization Theory Revisited" (Argyris, 1973). These three publications provide the framework around which the hypotheses of goal congruence theory may be developed.

Personality and Organization

Argyris's investigation of the effects of budgets on managers reveals the issues with which he was concerned in his early theorizing and the direction of his thinking. Argyris reached the following conclusions after extensive, unstructured interviews with financial and operating managers in four manufacturing plants:

1. Budget pressure tends to unite the employees against management and tends to place the factory supervisor under tension. This tension may lead to inefficiency, aggression, and perhaps a complete breakdown on the part of the supervisor.

2. The finance staff can obtain feelings of success only by finding fault with factory people. The feelings of failure among factory supervisors lead to many human relations problems.
3. The use of budgets as "needlers" by top management tends to make the factory supervisors see only the problems of their own department. . . . They are not "plant-centered" in outlook. (Argyris, 1952, p. 25)

In building a theory to deal with such problems, Argyris first followed Bakke (1950) very closely (Argyris, 1954). Subsequently, however, though retaining many of his earlier concepts, he developed goal congruence theory as a distinct entity in its own right (Argyris, 1957).

A basic concept of Argyris's theory is that of the healthy adult personality, as distinguished from the personality of an infant or small child. Table 20.1 shows the dimensions of personality that are relevant; the individual's plotted scores (or profile) along these dimensions are equated with self-actualization. This is a much more specific formulation of the self-actualization construct than other theorists have offered. Individuals develop or progress to varying degrees along these dimensions. Various forces within society, including organizations, and within the individuals themselves inhibit this process. Here the influence of Maslow (chapter 6) is clearly evident, and Argyris, like so many at the time, appears to have been guilty of uncritical acceptance of aspects of need hierarchy theory.

A second theoretical building block of the theory is the concept of organization as epitomized in classical management theory (and bureaucratic theory). The principles of that theory are accepted as given because "to date no one has defined a more useful set of formal organization principles" (Argyris, 1957, p. 58). Included are the principles of task specialization, chain of command, unity of direction, and span of control.

Such a formal organization is viewed as incongruent with development to a healthy, mature state as set forth in table 20.1; it operates to inhibit members, forcing them back toward an infantile state. The potential incongruency between the developmental needs of individuals and the requirements of formal organization is exaggerated to the extent that

1. Employees are more mature than the organization assumes
2. The organization structure follows classical principles closely
3. One moves downward in the organization
4. The jobs approach an assembly line character

As a result of the incongruency, healthy employees often become passive, dependent, and submissive over time. In the process they experience the kinds of problems Argyris noted in his analysis of the effects of budgets. Frustration, conflict, failure, and a short time perspective prevail. Among other reactions the employee may leave the organization (only to face the same problems elsewhere), attempt to move to high levels in the organization (though there are few such positions), adapt by resorting to emotional defense mechanisms such as escape from reality and psychosomatic illness, or become apathetic and uninvolved. The employee may also express aggression in the context of the informal work group by restricting output.

In reaction to the high turnover and absenteeism, low productivity, and lack of organizational identification thus produced, management often introduces more controls and becomes more directive. As a result, the undesired behavior is increased. These processes

TABLE 20.1 Developmental trends to a mature, healthy, self-actualizing personality

From (as infants)	To (as adults)
A state of passivity	A state of increasing activity
A state of dependence on others	A state of relative independence
Being capable of behaving in only a few ways	Being capable of behaving in many ways
Having erratic, casual, shallow, quickly dropped interests	Having deeper interests
Having a short time perspective (primarily in the present)	Having much larger time perspective (extending into the past and future)
A lack of awareness of self	An awareness and control over oneself

SOURCE: Adapted from Chris Argyris (1957), *Personality and Organization* (New York: Harper & Row), 50

are summarized in a set of 10 basic theoretical propositions:

1. There is a lack of congruency between the needs of healthy individuals and the demands of the formal organization. An administrator, therefore, is always faced with an inherent tendency toward continual disturbance.
2. The resultants of this disturbance are frustration, failure, short-time perspective, and conflict.
3. Under certain conditions the degree of frustration, failure, short-time perspective, and conflict will tend to increase (among these conditions are those previously noted—greater employee maturity, structure follows classical principles, etc.).
4. The nature of the formal principles of organization cause the subordinate, at any given level, to experience competition, rivalry, and intersubordinate hostility and to develop a focus toward the parts rather than the whole.
5. The employee's adaptive behavior maintains self-integration and impedes integration with the formal organization.
6. The adaptive behavior of the employees has a cumulative effect, feeds back into the organization, and reinforces itself.
7. Certain management reactions tend to increase the antagonisms that underlie the adaptive behavior. These actions tend to be (1) increasing the degree of directive leadership, (2) increasing the degree of management controls, (3) increasing the number of pseudo human relations programs.
8. Other management actions can decrease the degree of incongruency between the individual and formal organization. One way is to use a new input of individuals who do not aspire to be healthy, mature adults. A second way is to change the nature of the formal organizational structure, directive leadership, and management controls. Job and/or role enlargement is one effective method to change the organization structure. Employee-centered leadership is one possible way to modify the directive leadership.
9. Job or role enlargement and employee-centered leadership will not tend to work to the extent that the adaptive behavior has become embedded in the original culture and the self-concept of the individuals.
10. The difficulties involved in proposition 9 may be minimized by the use of reality-oriented leadership (i.e., the leader ought to first diagnose what is reality and then use the appropriate leadership pattern). (Argyris, 1957, pp. 233–237)

Integrating the Individual and the Organization

Following the publication of his 1957 volume, Argyris expanded and modified his theory. Although this process appears to have been gradual, the outcome was a new comprehensive, theoretical statement (Argyris, 1964). In this book he replaces his maturity or infant–adult dimension with certain formulations about psychological energy. Argyris maintains that psychological energy exists in all people, cannot be blocked permanently, and varies with the state of mind of the individual. Furthermore:

The potential energy an individual has available to him will be a function of the degree of self-esteem: the higher the self-esteem the greater the *potential energy*. The actual energy an individual has will be a function of the degree to which he can experience psychological success. Psychological success (and its derivatives of self-esteem, etc.) is therefore defined as the conditions for creating the proper state of mind. (Argyris, 1964, p. 29)

Among other factors, a climate of trust serves to enhance opportunities for psychological success.

In restating his first theoretical proposition on the sources of incongruency, Argyris now substitutes "individuals aspiring for psychological success" for the former "healthy individuals." He no longer uses the specific statements given in table 20.1. Not everyone desires psychological success, and it is the incongruency between individual needs and organizational form that causes disturbance and unintended consequences (such as passivity, aggression, etc.). This incongruency may result as much from placing a person who does not aspire to psychological success in a context where aspirations of this type are required as from placing a person who does desire psychological success in the typical pyramidal organization. In any event, wherever such incongruencies exist, people will consume energy-producing unintended consequences of the organizational form and thus divert energy from organizational goals.

Dropping the maturity dimension set forth in table 20.1 creates a problem in defining self-actualization, which is retained in the theory. The solution is to view self-actualization as having no specific content. People have a need to actualize themselves that can be identified from their behavior: "The actualization can be in the direction of maturity. . . . However, in this scheme, the actualization could be toward apathy and alienation" (Argyris, 1964, p. 142). This shift to a view of self-actualization as having no set content actually appeared several years earlier and was reflected in a procedure developed for scoring self-actualization as revealed in interviews (Argyris 1959, 1960b).

The next step was to set forth what Argyris (1964) calls the mix model. Here he proposes that problems associated with incongruency are best overcome by modifying pyramidal organizations to provide more meaningful challenges and opportunities for psychological success. At the same time, individuals must be changed to make them less fearful of the opportunity for psychological success. These and other changes must be made to reduce disturbances and unintended consequences. The mix model presents a set of six hypotheses about how organizations should be changed to achieve these ends and make them "axiologically good," to use Argyris's term:

1. The direction of core activities such as achieving objectives, internal maintenance, and environmental adaptations should be spread in an interrelated manner throughout the organization, rather than concentrated in a single component such as top management.
2. The members of the organization should be aware of the organization as a totality in all its patterned interrelationships, rather than as a random set of parts.
3. The objectives that guide the organization should be those of the whole, rather than of individual components.
4. The organization should be able to influence goal attainment and internal maintenance in accordance with its own desires, rather than lacking influence in these respects.
5. The organization should be able to influence its externally oriented activities in its environment in accordance with its own desires, rather than lacking influence in this respect.
6. The nature of the organization's core activities should be influenced by considerations that extend into both the past and the future, rather than being determined only by the present. (Argyris, 1964, pp. 151–154)

These hypotheses for integrating organizational and individual goals appear to have much in common with the hypotheses regarding individual development toward health and maturity set forth in table 20.1 In fact, this relationship is made explicit in an earlier statement:

> As long as complex organizations use people, it may be possible that they will tend to obtain greater commitment, flexibility, responsibility, and openness and thereby enhance their chances for survival and growth if they strive to create conditions wherein the individual is able to actualize his potential as much as possible. . . . A first step toward integrating the individual and the organization is for both to aspire toward the conditions represented by the axiologically good organization. (Argyris, 1962a, p. 76)

The mix model is a statement of conditions for organizational effectiveness. However, the theory anticipates that the degree to which the organization's structure should fully match these conditions depends on the kinds of decisions to be made. Argyris's statements on organizational structures are given in table 20.2. He indicates a clear need for varying structures in accordance with decision types:

> If one asks the individual in the organization of the future to see the company organizational chart, he will be asked, "For what type of decision?" In order to accomplish this, "decision rules" will have to be defined to guide our choice of the proper structure.

But the power to choose among structures remains democratic:

> The task of defining the decision rules to tell the participants which organization structure should be used under a given set of conditions will be assigned to as many participants as possible. . . . If autocracy is to be used, the use of it will be defined under participative conditions (Structure IV). (Argyris, 1964, pp. 211–212)

Table 20.2 represents Argyris's initial effort to provide guidelines for the participative selection of structures.

The Theory Revisited

In its earliest version goal congruence theory carried a message that was distinctly anti-formal organization.

TABLE 20.2 Conditions for the use of structures having varying degrees of axiological goodness

Degree of axiological goodness	Type of organizational structure	Conditions for use
Low ↑	Pyramidal	When time is important and subordinate acceptance is assured
		When decisions are routine and the use of authority is legitimized
		When the decision does not affect the distribution of power, reward, controls, work specialization, or the centralization of information
		When a large number of people are involved and it is difficult to bring them together
		When the individuals do not desire psychological success
	Overlapping groups (Likert)	When the decision is not routine, but does not affect the distribution of power, control, information, and the specialization of work
		When time is important
		When the decision to make a change cannot be delegated to all
	Power according to functional contribution	Anywhere there are differences in competence—individuals receive their power according to the perception that other members have of their potential contribution
↓ High	Power according to inevitable organizational responsibilities (each individual has equal power)	When decisions involve high responsibility and are basic to the organization
		When the decision affects the distribution of power, control, information, and the specialization of work
		When the decision defines rules for the conditions under which a particular structure would be used

SOURCE: Adapted from Chris Argyris (1964), *Integrating the Individual and the Organization* (New York: Wiley), 198–210

Subsequently, this message was muted somewhat, although it remained in evidence. In the third version (Argyris, 1973, 1974b) there is some return to a more militant organizational position.

Actually, by 1972 Argyris had revived the infant–adult dimensions of table 20.1. While infant individuals in adult organizations and adult individuals in infant organizations both yield incongruence, the latter circumstance represents "the predominant conditions in 'real' life." Congruence between person and organization was presumed to be rare (Argyris, 1972).

In this later, more formal restatement of the theory, the six infant–adult dimensions of table 20.1 are reduced to four. These new dimensions are not entirely consistent with those stated previously, especially with regard to the development of abilities. Thus:

Infants begin as—

dependent and submissive

having few abilities

having shallow abilities

having a short time perspective

While adults strive toward—

independence, autonomy, and control over the immediate world

developing many abilities

developing a few abilities in depth

developing a longer time perspective (Argyris, 1973, p. 142)

Pyramidal organizations now are characterized by specialized and fractionalized work, established production rates and speed of work, order giving, performance evaluation, the use of rewards, and perpetuated membership. These are associated with bureaucracy and scientific management, rather than with classical management theory, as previously stated. The consequences of incongruence for organization members are fighting the organization, leaving it, apathy and indifference, or becoming market- (or pay-) oriented in dealing with the organization. References to upward mobility as a response have been consistently ignored after the first theoretical statements. In tone the revisited theory is not a great deal different from the original version. However, there are specific variations that require somewhat different empirical tests. In particular the future of formal organizations is viewed more negatively:

> None of the theories discussed (primarily those of bureaucracy and rational systems), with the exception of personality and organization theory and those similar . . . would predict the single most important trend about public and private organizations, namely, their increasing internal deterioration and lack of effectiveness in producing services or products. (Argyris, 1973, p. 159)

Organizational Learning and Defensive Routines

Starting in the mid-1970s Argyris began to promulgate a view of organizational learning that has concerned him over the years since. This view appears to represent a whole new approach with a new nomenclature, new constructs, and new collaborations. Yet the implicit humanism is still in evidence, and although anti-bureaucracy statements are less manifest, they are not gone. Furthermore, the goal congruence formulations have never been repudiated. In fact, they have reemerged on several occasions. The characteristic infant–adult designation and the concept of psychological success are explicitly endorsed (Argyris, 1990), and in several articles Argyris (1994, 1998b) has invoked aspects of goal congruence theory to make a point. Thus the two theories seem to stand side by side, not fully integrated, but still with the same humanistic values behind them and, as we will see, with a similar approach to application resulting.

From the mid-1970s onward Argyris has stated and restated his theory of organizational learning and defensive routines many times, often with the same examples and much the same wording, but with an orientation apparently intended to reach different audiences. Thus his books on the subject have typically been the products of different publishers and are presented with a somewhat different thrust—for example, Argyris 1980 seeks to engage organizational behavior and other social science researchers; Argyris 1982 and

1993 speak to organization development practitioners; Argyris 1985 packages the theory for those in the field of strategic management; Argyris 1990 focuses on managers and managers-to-be, thus coming closest to providing a textbook coverage of the theory; Argyris and Schön 1996 review an earlier statement, now with a strong emphasis on the organizational as opposed to individual nature of the theory; and Argyris 2000 talks to human resource managers who use advice from consultants and gurus. Another volume of recent vintage (Argyris, 1992b), brings together a number of articles and book chapters related to the theory, most of them originally published in the period 1975 to 1991. I draw heavily on this source in presenting the theory.

Learning and Its Types

Organizational learning is desirable. It is a means to detect and correct errors, as well as a source of innovation. An important barrier to learning is some type of organizational defense. These anti-learning defenses are represented by policies, practices, or actions that prevent participants in the organization from experiencing embarrassment or threat, and also from discovering the causes of embarrassment or threat. Errors occur as plans and policies reach the implementation phase, and they are present by design rather than because of ignorance; they are designed to protect people from embarrassment and threat and are thus part of the defensive routine. As Peter Dachler puts it:

> Argyris has repeatedly shown how hierarchical structures and their emphasis on control . . . bring about defensive reactions and therefore limit effective organizational learning. . . . He seeks the solution in the "re-education" of (primarily powerful) individuals and in changes of structural and policy issues. (1994, p. 463)

In the latter vein Argyris says "social science should . . . pay attention to producing knowledge about virtual worlds that provide liberating alternatives . . . that endow human beings with competencies to reverse and undo the self-fueling, anti-learning, overprotective processes" (the organizational defenses) (1992b, p. 4).

An important distinction is made between espoused meaning, or theory, and people's views as reflected when they actually behave, their theories in use. This is much like the separation between stated and actual goals that Amitai Etzioni makes (see chapter 19). Any real, meaningful behavior change requires changes in people's theories in use and in the learning system of the organization; espoused theories are merely window dressing.

Figure 20.1 sets forth two types of theories in use behind learning that are significant for the theory—single loop and double loop. Single loop learning may occur when matches are created, so that the consequences of actions are what was intended. More frequently, however, single loop learning is a result of a mismatch in which actions are corrected through feedback to align with consequences, and then create a match; only the actions are changed, not the factors behind the actions. In double loop learning the change is deeper in that the governing variables are changed—the variables that can be inferred, by observing the actions of individuals who are acting as agents for the organization (top management), to drive and guide actions of others. Double loop learning is particularly relevant when an issue is complex and nonprogrammable, when the long-range effectiveness of the organization is involved.

When double loop learning is engaged by a mismatch or error, matters of trust and mistrust often arise, which make correction difficult. Also, if the focus remains at the single loop level, people may become servants of the status quo, a phrase Argyris

uses often. Unfreezing the models of organizational structures and processes now in good currency is essential to engage double loop learning. Inherent in the move to double loop learning are problems related to unawareness, suppression of feelings, and the need to alter reasoning processes. Achieving this type of learning is not easy.

Models I and II

Individuals design their actions, and to do so they bring to bear theories in use, which they mobilize for given situations. Under single loop learning conditions, this theory in use has the characteristics of Model I, although in general people are not aware of this model in themselves. Table 20.3 sets forth Model I in a comprehensive form. Argyris presents this figure on numerous occasions in somewhat different forms, although the basic format and message remain the same. Typically these versions represent abbreviations of what is contained in table 20.3.

Model I tends to inhibit double loop learning, and organizations whose structure is congruent with that model are unlikely to be characterized by double loop learning. Such organizations have a pyramidal form with specialization of work, unity of command, and centralization of power. These conditions, which are essentially those of bureaucracy, are said to be congruent with the governing variables of Model I.

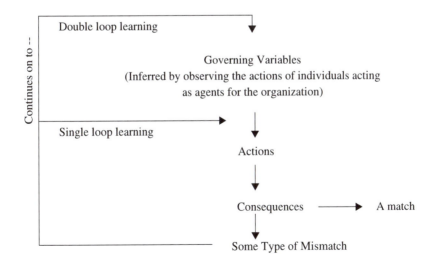

FIGURE 20.1 The distinction between single loop and double loop learning. Adapted from Chris Argyris (1992), *On Organizational Learning* (Cambridge, MA: Blackwell), 8, and other sources by the same author.

TABLE 20.3 Model I theory in use

Governing variables ⟶	Action strategies ⟶	Behavioral world consequences ⟶	Learning consequences ⟶	Consequences on effectiveness
Define goals; achieve them Maximize winning; minimize losing Suppress negative feelings in self and others Be rational; minimize emotionality	Design and manage the environment unilaterally Own and control the task Protect self unilaterally Protect others unilaterally; so they are not hurt	Actor seen as defensive Group and interpersonal relationships defensive Defensive norms exist Low freedom of choice; little risk taking or commitment	Self-sealing processes Single loop learning Escalating error Little testing of theories publicly; much testing privately	Decreased effectiveness over long term

Model II is not the opposite of Model I, nor does it completely replace Model I. Model I theories in use continue to be appropriate when programmable, routine decisions are involved and when a crisis must be handled. Furthermore, structural changes congruent with Model II do not actually work unless the individuals involved adopt Model II theories as their own.

Under Model II there is a continuous testing of the status quo; such situations are rare currently. The model represents an ideal state and involves sharing power with anyone who has relevant competence. People do not move to Model II without help. Argyris is much more tentative in depicting Model II than Model I, and the early publications did not provide a clear picture of it at all. However, table 20.4 is based on recent statements plus several abbreviated versions proposed earlier. It provides a comprehensive cover-

age of Model II, comparable to that of table 20.3 for Model I. Note that a major aspect of Model II is that power is dispersed. It requires unfreezing of a type that permits reexamining the underlying values and assumptions at both the individual and organizational levels. For a discussion of Model I and Model II in action, see George Roth and Art Kleiner (2000).

Originally in numerous publications Argyris took the position that only double loop learning and Model II could lead to "liberating alternatives and changing status quo." However, more recently he has come to question that conclusion based on field experience with certain methodologies in areas such as financial reporting:

I began to observe examples where technical theories that were implemented correctly reduced the likelihood of embarrassment and threat in the first

TABLE 20.4 Model II theory in use

Governing variables ⟶	Action strategies ⟶	Behavioral world consequences ⟶	Learning consequences ⟶	Consequences on effectiveness
Valid and confirmable information Free and informed choice Commitment to a choice; monitoring of implementation	Design situations and encounters such that participants can be origins and experience personal causation Task is jointly controlled Protection of self is joint; oriented to growth Protection of others is bilateral	Actor seen as minimally defensive Group and interpersonal relationships minimally defensive Learning-oriented norms High freedom of choice; much risk taking and commitment	Reduction of self-fulfilling, self-sealing, error escalating processes Double loop learning Frequent public testing of theories Effective problem solving	Increased effectiveness over long term

place. The routine single-loop features of technical theories also created liberating alternatives. Although they did not create double-loop learning, it appeared that they prevented the need for double-loop learning in the first place. (Argyris, 1996, p. 80)

It is not clear how widespread these exceptions to previously existing theory may be.

Individual and Organizational Levels

At many points Argyris presents his ideas in such a way as to suggest he is writing personality theory, not organizational behavior theory. Yet this is not his intent. In a number of places he takes pains to differentiate organizational defensive routines from those of individuals. He notes that (1) people behave in a manner consistent with their organization's defensive routines, even though from personality research a much greater diversity of personalities would be expected; (2) although people move in and out of organizations, the defensive routines in place do not change over time; (3) the defensive routines appear to have the character of products of socialization; and (4) since the actions used to create or trigger the routines are used by most people, their source cannot be individual psychological anxiety (Argyris, 1992b). Thus individuals act as agents for organizations, as well as for themselves, to produce defensive routines that prevent or distort valid information, are not discussible, and whose undiscussability is not discussible. All this is part of the organization's culture. Such a pattern is depicted in figure 20.2.

The truly organizational nature of the theory is particularly manifest in Argyris and Schön (1996). There organizational learning is defined in terms that serve to emphasize the level at which the process occurs:

> Organizational learning occurs when individuals within an organization experience a problematic situation and inquire into it on the organization's behalf. They experience a surprising mismatch between expected and actual results of action and respond to that mismatch through a process of thought and further action that leads them to modify their images of organization or their understandings of organizational phenomena and to restructure their activities so as to bring outcomes and expectations into line, thereby changing organizational theory-in-use. In order to become organizational, the learning that results from organizational inquiry must become embedded in the images of organization held in its members' minds and/or in the epistemological artifacts (the maps, memories, and programs) embedded in the organizational environment. (p. 16)

> Inquiry becomes organizational when individuals inquire on behalf of the organization, within a community of inquiry governed, formally or informally, by the roles and rules of the organization. (p. 33)

Organization Development Applications

Argyris's theoretical views call for a movement to organizational forms that are less formalized, pyramidal,

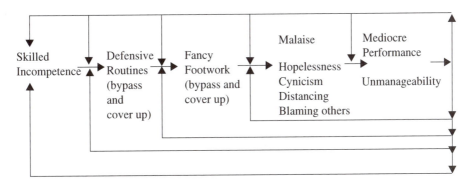

FIGURE 20.2 Organizational defense pattern. From Chris Argyris (1990), *Overcoming Defenses: Facilitating Organizational Learning* (Boston: Allyn & Bacon), 64. Copyright 1990. Reprinted by permission of Pearson Education, Inc.

and bureaucratic. He advocates various methods for achieving this objective, extending from laboratory (or T-group, or sensitivity, or human growth) training in the early period to learning seminars or workshops later, but these approaches are consistently part of an overall organization development effort, almost always starting at the top of the organization. For Argyris, organization development in some form became not only an application of his theories to practice but a means to testing these theories against his experiences in the field, and thus to refining the theories in various ways.

Laboratory Training

Argyris became involved with laboratory training at an early point in its history. In his early use of the approach he hypothesized that if executives could become more authentic, could increase their interpersonal competence, could change their values, and ultimately change their behavior, their organizations would shift to forms more appropriate than those in the pyramidal form. The objectives of training then are to increase:

1. Giving and receiving nonevaluative descriptive feedback
2. Owning and helping others to own to their values, attitudes, ideas, and feelings
3. Openness to new values, attitudes, and feelings, as well as helping others to develop their degree of openness
4. Experimenting (and helping others to do the same) with new values, attitudes, ideas, and feelings
5. Taking risks with new values, attitudes, ideas, and feelings (Argyris, 1962b, p. 26)

Shifts in accordance with the objectives did occur among 11 top-level executives from the same division of a major company who trained together under Argyris. Changes in values and interpersonal competence were achieved. However, there also was evidence that the managers had considerable difficulty applying the new values and skills at work and that they experienced some fadeout. The impact at the organizational level appears not to have been great (Argyris, 1962b). A second application study with members of a board of directors also suggests that individual changes occurred, and these changes appear to have carried over from the laboratory sessions to the regular board meetings (Argyris, 1965).

In spite of his initial enthusiasm for laboratory training in its various forms, Argyris (1992b) ultimately came to have serious doubts about it. The on-the-job effects anticipated were rarely in evidence. Furthermore, by the early 1970s both the business world and the scientific community had become disenchanted with the approach. Opportunities to apply skills as a facilitator were drying up.

Organization Development

As Argyris presents it, organization development focuses more directly on organizational problems and change than does laboratory training. The basic cycle moves from collecting information to making an organizational decision, and finally to developing a commitment to that decision. The role of the interventionist is a relatively active one: "The interventionist should attempt to create norms of individuality, concern, and trust. He should attempt to draw out conflict, threat, or confusion so that they may be dealt with openly. . . . The interventionist should intervene so that the clients may experience psychological success" (Argyris, 1970, p. 221).

Clearly, even where laboratory training is not used in the traditional manner, the commitment to its values and to goal congruence theory remains strong. In many cases Argyris (1971) advocates the use of confrontation meetings in which important organizational problems of an interpersonal nature are faced openly. His reported examples deal almost exclusively with top management groups. This pattern is particularly evident in a book dealing with an organization development project carried out with the staff of a major newspaper:

> The first step in the study was to conduct a diagnosis of the client system. This produced a map of the living system which identified some major internal factors causing organizational ineffectiveness. The factors were fed back to top management. . . . After obtaining valid information about the client system the next step was for the executives to decide if they wanted to take action to begin to correct the problems identified. . . . After the top executives chose to attempt to correct some of the problems, they faced the task of becoming internally committed to the actions implicit in the decision. The first step was to agree to attend a learning seminar. (Argyris, 1974a, pp. 276–277)

In this approach to organization development Argyris clearly views interpersonal change as a necessary prelude to organizational change. Furthermore, much of the original laboratory training is retained in the learning seminars. In the particular instance of the newspaper, this approach did not eventuate in basic organizational changes, and, at least in a relative sense, the change program was a failure.

Learning Seminars as Organization Development

The learning seminars have evolved into an overall approach labeled *action science* (Argyris, Putnam, & Smith, 1985). The characteristics of this approach are outlined in table 20.5. The learning level is high, thus challenging the premises that underlie theories in use and management's governing values.

The activities in a seminar may be elucidated with reference to the learning paradox—the actions taken to promote productive organizational learning often actually inhibit deeper learning of the Model II type. To deal with this paradox the facilitator is advised to do the following:

1. Describe the defensive patterns that underlie the learning paradox.
2. Design, jointly with the participants, ways to interrupt the circular, self-reinforcing processes that inhibit double loop learning.
3. Help the participants assess the degree to which their action strategies are likely to limit the implementation of the solutions they have designed.
4. Help the participants realize how they have participated in creating and maintaining a behavioral world where the strategies they redesign to correct the situation are unlikely to be effective.
5. Involve the participants in sessions . . . where they can develop the concepts and skills they need in order to escape from this bind.
6. Reduce the use of defensive reasoning and increase the use of productive reason.
7. Reduce . . . organizational defensive routines, and replace them with high quality inquiry, good dialectic, and double loop learning. (Argyris & Schön, 1996, pp. 282–284)

What is involved here is a process of using interpretations to help participants gain insight, thus following the model inherent in much psychotherapy. In the process participants will exhibit considerable emotionality, beginning with bewilderment and frustration but extending to anger and fear; the facilitator should respond with empathy, while not allowing these emotions to become an excuse for backing off from the situation.

The steps in this organization development process go something like this:

1. Help participants (at the top level now) to become aware of their Model I theories in use and automatic counterproductive reasoning processes.

TABLE 20.5 Characteristics of action science

Criteria	Action science response
Philosophical basis	Humanism and action research (Lewin)
Purpose	Behavioral change through articulation of reasoning processes and improved public disclosure
Time focus	Long term
Type of change	Interpersonal and intrapersonal
Epistemology	Making explicit tacit theories in use
Nature of discourse	Personally emancipatory, through exploring the premises of beliefs
Ideology	Subscribing to double loop learning that is concerned with elicitation of mental models
Methodology	Processing of here-and-now reasoning or of on-line interactions
Role of the facilitator	Active, demonstrating and orchestrating on-line Model II learning skills
Personal risk	Psychological, involving exposure of personal defenses and vulnerabilities
Organizational risk	Heavy, requiring all management levels to expose their assumptions
Assessment	In terms of management and organizational effectiveness resulting from systemic change
Learning level	High, thus challenging premises underlying theories in use and management's governing values

SOURCE: Adapted from Joseph A. Raelin (1997), Action Learning and Action Science: Are They Different? *Organizational Dynamics*, 26(1), 32

2. Help these participants to see how they create and maintain learning systems that feed back to sanction Model I.
3. Mix in the various organizational consequences such as organizational defensive routines so that participants come to see what is happening in their organization.
4. Help the top level participants connect these kinds of knowledge with the actual business decisions they are making.
5. Help these participants learn the Model II theory in such a way as to be able to use it under low to moderate stress; thus, with practice, Model II becomes both an espoused theory and a theory in use.
6. Once the top people begin to behave consistently in a Model II mode, move the learning process down through lower management levels by conducting learning seminars there for those who want to participate. (Fulmer & Keys, 1998; Argyris, 1992b)

This process can be quite lengthy, but as Argyris notes most people do not learn to play tennis overnight, either. As Model II is introduced, alternative governing values and behavioral strategies are given attention so that the status quo no longer exerts a binding influence; all this takes considerable time.

Put somewhat differently, these steps to overcoming organizational defenses run as follows: (1) make a diagnosis of the problem, (2) connect the diagnosis to the actual behavior of the participants, (3) show them how their behavior creates organizational defenses, (4) help them change their behavior, (5) change the defensive routine that reinforced the old behavior, and (6) develop new organizational norms and a culture that reinforce the new behavior (Argyris, 1990, p. 155). This is a version of Lewin's unfreezing-moving-refreezing model (see chapter 2 in this volume).

Techniques of Action Science

One aspect of the action science organization development approach is the process of serial interpretation just noted, but there are other techniques as well, most of them founded in some variant of the case method.

One such technique is for the facilitator to use preselected cases as a basis for group discussion, thus moving participants to particular issues that are considered important. Much more frequent, however, is the use of participant-written cases. These are presented

to the group by one participant at a time; their form is as follows:

1. In one paragraph describe a key organizational problem as you see it.
2. Assume you could talk to whomever you wish to begin to solve the problem.
3. Next split your page into two columns. On the right-hand side write how you would begin the meeting; what you would actually say. Then write what you believe the other(s) would say. Then write your response to their response. Continue writing this scenario for two or so double-spaced written pages.
4. On the left hand column write any idea or feeling that you would have that you would not communicate for whatever reason. (Argyris, 1995, p. 23)

This case becomes a basis for lengthy discussion. Sometimes other participants are asked to provide a new version of the meeting in the case. Sometimes the participants role-play the meeting in various versions. The objective is to get the case writer to redesign his or her actions so as to move from the Model I that is invariably inherent in the original case to something closer to Model II. In this process the top management group comes to learn about its own group dynamics (Argyris, 1991). This resultant is not unlike that obtained from laboratory training. Generally these sessions are tape recorded so that participants can listen to them later and continue their learning.

Another technique involves the construction of a diagram or action map by each participant (following the lead of Lewin). This map depicts the interdependence between governing conditions, action strategies and several orders of counterproductive consequences, plus the feedback processes that maintain the pattern. It is intended to help participants determine the relevant variables, to link them in a causal chain, and to see the pattern established, thus making it easier to assess plausibility. The causal chain of such a map (with examples appended) might be as shown in figure 20.3.

There is a great deal here, and in the learning seminars and action science as a whole, that harks back to laboratory training. Although the terminology is new, the basic concerns are similar—authenticity, openness, confrontation, and the like. Once again Argyris emphasizes questioning basic premises, cutting through defensiveness, getting at the realities for the individual and the organization. In many respects

Governing conditions (low trust on interpersonal issues)
↓
Generic action strategies (craft attributions to be untestable)
↓
Consequences for group dynamics (become polarized)
↓
Consequences for group dynamics (exhibit low confidence in group effectiveness)
↓
Consequences for organization (exhibit bad-mouthing outside group)
↓
Consequences for problem solving (experience cynicism about effectiveness)
↓
Consequences for leadership (keep leadership style consistent with defenses)
↓
(earn criticism by acting out organizational defenses)
↓
(feel pulled apart)

FIGURE 20.3 The causal chain of an action map. Adapted from Chris Argyris & Donald A. Schön (1996), *Organizational Learning II: Theory, Method, and Practice* (Reading, MA: Addison-Wesley), 160–161.

the role of the facilitator or change agent has changed little over the years.

However, in one respect Argyris has introduced a major change—his concern for organizational effectiveness has now taken center stage, which is consistent with changes in the organization development field as a whole (Church, Burke, & Van Eynde, 1994). Perhaps as a result, his theoretical orientation is now one of the more popular underpinnings for organization development practice (Bazigos & Burke, 1997).

Evaluation and Impact

In noting that Argyris's theories have exerted a strong influence on organization development practice I do not wish to imply that this is the only arena in which they have had an impact. Mainstream organizational behavior has on occasion found them quite appealing (see, for instance, Porter, 1989), especially the treatment of goal congruence issues. And Argyris's organizational learning formulations have elicited positive reactions from a variety of sources, including scholars with a psychoanalytic orientation to the field (see, for example, Diamond, 1986). The newer theory even has spawned a concept of triple loop learning to be added to the single and double loop varieties (Nielsen, 1993; Foldy & Creed, 1999). Triple loop learning goes beyond the actor's own values to question the

basic values of the societal traditions in which the actions take place. My point simply is that these theories have proven influential in a variety of contexts; they are not trivial.

To understand what has happened fully we need to look at the historical development of research, and of ideas about research, much as we have considered the development of theory.

Argyris's Interview-Based Studies

In the 1950s and the early 1960s Argyris conducted several studies to test his views. In one such study, members of various departments of a bank were interviewed to determine the degree of fusion or goal congruence they experienced in their jobs and to relate this index to other factors in accordance with the theory (Argyris, 1954). Though this study precedes Argyris's (1957) first formal statement of goal congruence theory, it tests certain hypotheses that are part of that theory.

Measures of the degree to which individual members actualize themselves in the organization and of the degree to which the organization appeared to express itself were obtained. When both indices were high, as they were in three departments, the departments appeared to be effective; when the indices were lower, as they were in one instance, the department exhibited more conflict and less organizational commitment. There was some evidence that low personal actualization scores were predictive of voluntary turnover. The reliability of the coding of interview data to obtain this personal actualization score was satisfactory, but the organizational measure yielded marginal reliability at best.

In subsequent research Argyris concerned himself less with the congruence of goals than with personal actualization. The emphases in the reports on these studies, which were carried out in two plants of a manufacturing firm, are somewhat different from one publication to another (Argyris, 1958, 1959, 1960a, 1960b).

In this instance the coding reliability of the self-actualization index was rather low (roughly 70 percent agreement). Nevertheless, this score did operate as hypothesized, with high scores characterizing the more effective plant. In addition, the self-actualization data support a number of theory-based predictions about differences between the two plants and between components within them.

In the less effective plant, employees report more widespread pressure, and though the foremen do not exhibit the same pattern, those who experience pressure, experience it more intensely. The foremen also place greater emphasis on promotion and pay, in accordance with the theory, but neither plant has much turnover at the foreman level. Among employees there is less concern with quality, less friendliness, and more pro-union sentiment in the less effective plant. These are, of course, concurrent findings; they do not establish cause and effect.

Early Research by Others

Argyris marshaled a considerable amount of research, the results of which could be predicted or explained by goal congruence theory (Argyris, 1957, 1964, 1972, 1973). This was an impressive scholarly undertaking, as Lyman Porter (1989) has indicated; these findings appear convincing in that the studies consistently support the theory. Yet the use of ad hoc explanation, selective coverage of relevant research, and the fact that alternative theories might also predict and explain the same results raise a note of caution. In reality, only research that is directly focused on theoretical hypotheses can establish the validity of the theory. In his reviews Argyris does note several studies that directly support the goal congruence hypotheses, although not with total consistency. In particular, posi-

tive consequences are likely to accrue from fusion or goal congruence. Unfortunately, most of these studies have not been published in the regular professional literature and cannot be evaluated adequately on the basis of Argyris's descriptions. What follows here represents a sampling of the research from the 1960s and 1970s that appears particularly relevant.

Charles Bonjean and Gary Vance (1968) developed a questionnaire measure of self-actualization that correlated .61 and .72 with Argyris's index in two separate samples. Those individuals who were found to experience low self-actualization reported getting angry with supervisors more, making more errors in their work, thinking more about earning money, feeling less satisfied with their jobs, and thinking more about seeking other work. All these findings are consistent with goal congruence theory predictions. Yet high and low self-actualization subjects did not differ with regard to restriction of output, aggression toward co-workers, and lack of interest in work.

Johannes Pennings (1976) related measures of organizational autonomy and participation to various criterion indices in 40 offices of a brokerage firm to test certain hypotheses set forth by Argyris. The results generally supported the theory. The only major departure was that "good" organizational structures were not associated with reduced anxiety levels; in fact, additional analyses indicate a significantly higher level of anxiety under participative conditions, a finding that is inconsistent with an expectation of greater mental health.

A somewhat similar study by Robert Dewar and James Werbel (1979) was conducted in 13 consumer reporting agencies. As goal congruence theory would predict, high levels of formalization and routinization of the technology were associated with reduced job satisfaction, and neither formalization nor routinization showed any relationship to the amount of conflict. In contrast, extensive surveillance and rule enforcement were related to conflict. The implication is that conflict arises not so much out of specific organizational structures as from directive leadership. However, it may well be that the presence of conflict elicited the directive leadership rather than the leadership eliciting the conflict.

Goal congruence theory hypothesizes that the tendency to oppose bureaucratic procedures increases at each lower organizational level. However, Robert Rossel (1971) found that such negative orientations are most pronounced just below top management; they are much less in evidence at the top, but also at levels down into first-level supervision. These findings appear to be related to opportunities for promotion, a topic that Argyris considered in his early theories, but subsequently dropped.

Finally, a study by Ronald Burke and Tamara Weir (1978) indicates that the "good" organization in Argyris's sense creates a climate in which members not only help each other more but are more likely to solicit help from each other. However, this mutual helping operates more with regard to personal than to work-related problems, which suggests that direct impact on work outcomes such as the quantity and quality of production may be minimal.

In reviewing related literatures, Argyris consistently comes to conclusions that support goal congruence theory. In many instances he reinterprets studies carried out without reference to his theories. It seems appropriate here to look at the conclusions reached by others who have reviewed the same literature.

Lawrence James and Allan Jones (1976) note a paucity of research dealing with relationships between organizational structure and the individual but conclude that structural factors may influence attitudes and behavior as Argyris anticipates. Yet the evidence does not seem to support the view that formal organization has a direct linear impact on attitudes and behavior:

A high degree of formalization and standardization was found to be positively related to satisfaction and behavior because it reduced role ambiguity in one set of studies. However, formalization and specialization were described as deleterious to satisfaction and behavior when important task characteristics were deleted from jobs. . . . Nonlinear relationships exist between formalization, specialization, standardization and behavior and attitudes where a certain level of structure is conducive to positive attitudes and behavior, but too much or too little structure has a negative connotation. (James & Jones, 1976, p. 106)

Much the same conclusion emerged from a review by Alan Bryman (1976). He points to considerable evidence that many people desire and prosper under a far greater degree of structure than Argyris would advocate. Structure provides stability and order, with the result that uncertainty and anxiety are reduced. There is no basis for concluding that individuals with needs of this kind are necessarily immature and emotionally unhealthy, nor that they constitute a small minority.

Inner Contradictions of Rigorous Research

By the mid-1960s at the latest, Argyris had concluded that the research pattern emerging in organizational behavior was not of a kind that he wished to continue to endorse. He came to believe that scientific research has an authoritarian bias that is analogous to the effects of pyramidal organizations (Argyris 1968). Subjects react to experimental controls as they would to organizational controls, and the findings are distorted accordingly. His solution for this situation also derives from his theory that one should

reduce the researcher's control over the subject . . . to provide the subject with greater influence, with longer time perspective regarding, and greater internal involvement in, the research project . . . having worker representative groups (in organizations) and student representative groups (in universities) to help in the design and execution of research. (Argyris, 1968, p. 193)

These ideas are intriguing. Yet certain assumptions are inherent in Argyris's position. First, he assumes the validity of goal congruence theory. If employees do not react to organizational controls as hypothesized, then the extension to experimental controls is not likely to be valid, either, following Argyris's own logic. Second, he assumes that certain apparent similarities between the two situations make the theoretical extension from organization to research warranted. Both of these assumptions require evidence. On the latter there is almost no evidence. We do not know whether goal congruence theory works within the domain of scientific research because no one, including Argyris, has tested it there, with or without subject participation in the research design.

This issue has not gone away. It appears in a major statement somewhat later (Argyris, 1980), and aspects of the problem are taken up after that (see for instance Argyris, 1982). Subsequently Argyris seems somewhat ambivalent on the matter, frequently introducing statements such as "the systematic study of the program's effectiveness will have to wait for the results of the research" (Argyris, 1989, p. 15). In no case are these references to research in progress followed later by reports of completed, systematic, scientific research studies. It appears that somewhere in the 1960s Argyris stopped any attempt at truly verifiable research of a scientific nature; it is not clear what he meant by his research-in-progress statements, but these appear to have been references to qualitative, ethnographic studies following upon various kinds of interventions. Even these have never been fully reported.

The consequence of all this has been that Argyris no longer conducted, or reported, research on his theories after his initial studies. Furthermore, others have moved away from his theories out of a concern that their research might be viewed as inappropriate as against the criteria for legitimate investigation Argyris had established. Let me elaborate.

Argyris's position is that—

1. The conditions of unilateral control embedded in rigorous research procedures create, for the subjects, conditions of dependence, submissiveness, and short time perspective.
2. The abstractions required for precision and quantification tend to lead to instruments whose meanings are not based on the action context experienced by subjects in their everyday life (hence the meanings may be confusing, unclear, and ambiguous).
3. The axiom that the purpose of science is to understand or explain while prediction and control are tests of our understanding and explanation leads to a social science of the status quo.
4. The consequences previously described, coupled with their undiscussability, could lead people to misperceive the experimental manipulation and/or to unrealizingly distort what they report in instruments and during interviews as well as what they exhibit in their actual behavior. (Argyris, 1980, pp. 51–52)

To avoid these consequences of the Model I situation created, subjects must be involved in all phases of research design and planning so that they truly understand what is going on.

Argyris clearly has reference to the kinds of research utilizing self-report questionnaires and interviews that he himself has conducted. There are many other kinds of research. Furthermore, research can be devoted to normative ends, not just descriptions and understanding, and thus with a little ingenuity the researcher may produce findings which foster change, not just reinforcement of the status quo; much medical research on new treatments provides vivid examples.

In the process of arguing for this position Argyris attacks aspects of a number of theories considered in this book. In particular, theories that are closely intertwined with research, such as Fred Fiedler's contingency theory of leadership, the Ohio State perspective on leadership, and Peter Blau's differentiation theory, come in for criticism; so too do competing theories, such as James March's views related to organizational learning (see Argyris, 1996). These attacks are wide-ranging and cover much of organizational behavior theory and its research base.

Yet it makes no sense to include research subjects in the test development and item selection phase of a study that involves the use of an intelligence test, or to include subjects who have no knowledge of such matters in the planning of research that would ideally require a complex experimental design and sophisticated statistical analyses. It makes no sense that is, *unless* the objective is to undermine and block research of these kinds entirely. That may well be what Argyris is attempting to do. He argues for the use of qualitative, case material (often derived from recorded transcripts), without either experimental or statistical controls, to test his theories. At one point (Argyris, 1982), he dismisses the use of control groups in testing the effectiveness of his interventions as unwarranted; using participants as their own controls would be sufficient. He does not indicate a recognition of the fact that the results achieved by the two approaches are not the same, or note that some of his own early research did use a control group.

In this latter vein it is important to recognize that Argyris marshaled many studies in support of goal congruence theory, including some of his own, which, based on his subsequent position as to the conduct of valid research, would have to be brought into question. There is something of the "having your cake and eating it too" factor operating here. If Argyris changed his thinking as to the conduct of research at some point, he should say so, and explain how his prior interpretations are affected; this has not occurred.

In any event it is apparent that these views on what is required to conduct acceptable research have not only served to stifle any meaningful scientific research on Argyris's part, but research on the part of others as related to his theories as well. The risk that any such studies would be rejected as invalid, if they did not support theory, would seem to be too high.

Future of Goal Congruence Formulations

Goal congruence theory has been criticized for dealing only with individual-organization relationships and ignoring the effects of the organization's environment. Nevertheless, good theory should be written to apply within a specific domain, and Argyris is certainly justified in establishing theoretical boundaries for his constructs.

Even within its domain, however, goal congruence theory faces many conceptual and empirical difficulties. A basic problem is the contention that bureaucracy *causes* emotional illness, infantile behavior, dependent personalities, and the like. The concept of human maturity as set forth in table 20.1 appears to be essentially valid. However, many personality theorists, including the writer, would add to the list a capacity to deal with authority relationships effectively, so that overreactions, either positive or negative, are minimized. In this view, then, learning to function in a bureaucratic system and to delay immediate gratification for future reward is a sign of maturity, not infantilism.

There is evidence that bureaucratic organizations tend to attract emotionally disturbed individuals at the lower levels, presumably because these people can function effectively in such positions and not at higher levels. But this does not mean the organization *caused* the pathology. It seems probable that Argyris, observing organization members within a limited time span and noting the contiguity of pathology and formal structure, incorrectly attributed direct causation to the structure, when in fact it was often the ambiguity- and anxiety-reducing structure itself that permitted particular individuals to function in an organizational setting at all (Diamond, 1986).

Actually, Argyris is not consistent as to whether immature people (those lacking psychological success) are created by formal organizations and thus can mature in an alternative structure, or whether they are of a personality type that functions well only in congruent systems (bureaucracies); he says both at different points. Obviously the implications for organizational design differ considerably in the two instances. Possibly both processes occur in different individuals, but then the theory should deal clearly with methods of identifying the two classes of people, which it does not.

A special problem arises with goal congruence theory in regard to the relationship between bureaucratic authority and dependency. The theory appears to confuse objective and subjective (personality-based) dependency. Hierarchical systems do create objective dependency relationships to varying degrees for most, if not all, members. But because one individual is

dependent on another for rewards does not mean that that person constantly craves the support, help, approval, instruction, and domination of others, and becomes angry when they are not received, in the manner of the dependent personality. Certainly, bureaucratic systems do attract dependent personalities; they may well create some dependent personalities under certain circumstances; but they clearly attract a great many nondependent people, even though all work under a degree of objective dependency.

In his earliest theoretical statements Argyris did consider alternative responses to formal structure other than regression into passive dependency, including upward mobility in the organizational hierarchy. The theory did not specify how to identify such people, however, or mention alternative responses of this kind later.

Argyris has been criticized for neglecting individual differences and offering a "one best way" prescription that is analogous to scientific management. Argyris (1973) disputed this, and, indeed, such concepts as his reality-centered leadership and mix model do require contingent hypotheses. However, these contingent hypotheses are given relatively little attention, have not been tested empirically, and at times are completely ignored. Often they are treated more as escape valves than as formal parts of the theory. To be useful, these contingency variables and hypotheses need to be much more clearly stated—they need to spell out where, when, and how various structures and leadership behaviors are to be used.

Individual personalities come in a great variety of forms. Some fit well and thrive in one type of organization, generating considerable energy for movement toward organizational goals, while others fit in another type. Some personalities may not fit any known organization. A society that is to use its human talent effectively must generate a variety of organizational forms. The mix model approaches this problem, but goal congruence theory as a whole tends to bypass it.

Lest I be considered as critical of Argyris as he has been of many other theorists, let me hasten to add an additional point, which I consider to be the saving grace of goal congruence theory. The essence of the theory is that when individual members and organizations fit each other—when their goals are congruent—organizational effectiveness will be fostered because members will devote their efforts to organizational goal achievement. This is an integration hypothesis, and it is consistently supported by the research of

Argyris and of others cited in this chapter. Similar integration formulations are reinforced by the findings on concordance cited in chapter 13 and by findings noted in other chapters of this book. Goal congruence theory emphasized, if it did not create, one of the most important concepts in organizational theory at an early time. For this Argyris deserves considerable credit.

As Argyris moved from laboratory training, and an organization development approach in which this training was central, to learning seminars and action learning, he abandoned his past terminology and substituted many new terms. He also added new techniques, although aspects of his past practice were retained. This explicit abandonment of laboratory training in the practice area was not matched by a similar move away from goal congruence formulations in the theory area. Yet on the evidence, it probably should have been. In most, but not all respects, the theory has become outmoded.

Future of the Organizational Learning Formulations

As Argyris moved on to a theory devoted to organizational learning and defensive routines, the ties to a single approach to practice become much closer. There simply is no research on the theory itself and no marshaling of other's research. The theory rises or falls with what can be demonstrated in practice.

Perhaps because of this strong practice emphasis early on, the new theory often lacks precision. Exactly when Model I should be invoked and when Model II should be brought to bear is never clearly stated; all we know for sure is that one is bad and one is good. In fact, there is a certain amorphous quality about Model II that is never fully overcome, even with later efforts to achieve more precision. At times one gets the feeling that there is some kind of hidden agenda here that is never explicitly developed. This ambiguity in formulating Model II has been noted by many reviewers of Argyris's numerous books. As Lipshitz (2000, p. 471) notes, "it is difficult to understand in depth and extremely difficult to implement."

An even greater problem, however, is the total reliance on qualitative research evidence that has not been reported fully. I believe there is something to be said for involving subjects more directly in the whole research process on occasion, but not always,

and not with a rigidity that severely limits the domain of scientific research. Argyris's theory can be and should be tested using rigorous research techniques—pretests and posttests, control groups, reliable measures, and direct ties to effectiveness criteria. Without this we will never know whether the interventions work or whether the theory has any validity. Argyris certainly can rebut the findings from such research, but it needs to be made available for those who may wish to use it. Unfortunately, the way things are headed, the future does not look promising from this perspective.

THEORY OF BUREAUCRATIC DEMISE

The theoretical contributions of Warren Bennis are less fully developed than those of Argyris, but they have had a considerable effect and their influence on the emergence of organization development is at least equal to that of Argyris. Building on certain earlier views, Bennis first formally presented his theory in a speech to the American Psychological Association in 1964 and followed this with a number of publications on the subject that frequently overlapped. We will pursue the course of theoretical development as evidenced in these publications.

Background

Born in 1925, Bennis had a brief stint at UCLA during military service, but really did his undergraduate work at Antioch College in Ohio after World War II. Douglas McGregor arrived there as president during this period, and Bennis was strongly influenced by him, to the point of going to MIT for graduate work on his recommendation (Bennis, 1991, 1992). There he majored in economics but took courses in other social science subjects as well. He received a doctorate in economics in 1955, but subsequently taught in psychology departments, briefly at MIT, and then for 3 years at Boston University. He returned to MIT in 1959 in the business school at McGregor's behest (the latter having left the presidency of Antioch in the interim) and completed a lengthy psychoanalysis.

In 1967 Bennis began an 11-year period in academic administration, emulating his mentor McGregor in many respects. He started at the State University of New York (SUNY) at Buffalo, and then moved to the presidency of the University of Cincinnati. At the age of 53 he experienced a heart attack and left administration for a position in the business school at the University of Southern California, where he has remained since. He has published a number of books on a range of organizational behavior topics, among them two posthumous volumes of McGregor's writings (see chapter 10 in this volume). Like McGregor and Argyris, Bennis was, and remains, a strongly committed humanist, and he became involved early in the laboratory training movement.

Bureaucracy and Its Alternatives

Like the sociotechnical theorists discussed in chapter 14, Bennis considered bureaucracy unsuited to the demands of the times. As a structural solution to problems of human organization, bureaucracy fails to deal effectively with its own internal realities or with factors in the current external environment. Therefore, through a process that is comparable to natural selection, bureaucracy will ultimately become extinct: "Within the next twenty-five to fifty years, we should all be witness to, and participate in, the end of bureaucracy and the rise of new social systems better able to cope with twentieth-century demands" (Bennis, 1966a, p. 4).

Problems with Bureaucracy

For Bennis, bureaucracy means essentially the same thing as it did for Argyris: division of labor along functional lines, hierarchy, rules, impersonality, a system of procedures, and promotion based on technical competence. In rating bureaucracy's internal inadequacies, Bennis draws on Argyris's views, but adds other considerations as well:

Bureaucracy does not adequately allow for personal growth and the development of mature personalities.

It develops conformity and "group-think."

It does not take into account the "informal organization" and the emergent and unanticipated problems.

Its systems of control and authority are hopelessly outdated.

It has no adequate judicial process.

It does not possess adequate means for resolving differences, and conflicts among ranks and, most particularly, among functional groups.

Communication (and innovative ideas) are thwarted or distorted because of hierarchical divisions.

The full human resources of bureaucracy are not being utilized because of mistrust, fear of reprisals, etc.

It cannot assimilate the influx of new technology or scientists entering the organization.

It will modify the personality structure such that man will become and reflect the dull, gray, conditioned "organization man." (Bennis, 1966a, p. 6)

Although these inadequacies are viewed as real and important, they can be handled, at least in part, through the emergence of a pervasive ethic of productivity. Thus the key problems causing the demise of bureaucracy are environmental. The environmental changes that concern Bennis are the rapid growth of science, the growth of intellectual technology, and the growth of research and development. In line with the turbulent field concepts of the sociotechnical theorists, he points to the "scientific and technological revolution" as the major threat to bureaucracy. Adapting to such rapid environmental change is beyond the innovative capacity of that structure.

Elsewhere, Bennis (1967) and Bennis and Philip Slater (1968) formulate the problems of bureaucracy somewhat differently, citing four basic sources of vulnerability. Again the emphasis is on change and complexity and on the difficulty bureaucracy has in coping with them. First, there is the knowledge and population explosion, and the concept of bureaucracy as efficient only in dealing with the routine and predictable. Second, the growth in organizational size and international scope, while not necessarily sounding a death knell for bureaucracy, "is leading to a neo-Jeffersonian approach" (Bennis, 1969a, p. 21). Third, the need for diverse, specialized competencies, often of a professional nature, has increased, bringing into the labor force individuals who are not easily absorbed by bureaucratic structures.

Finally, Bennis describes a philosophic shift in management itself that is essentially antithetical to bureaucratic precepts:

A new concept of man based on increased knowledge of his complex and shifting needs, which replaces an oversimplified, innocent, push-button idea of man.

A new concept of power, based on collaboration and reason, which replaces a model of power based on coercion and threat.

A new concept of organizational values, based on humanistic-democratic ideals, which replaces the depersonalized, mechanistic value system of bureaucracy. (Bennis, 1969a, p. 22)

These changes in philosophy are hypothesized to result from a need for religious experience coupled with the secularization of religion. The position taken here is very similar to that subsequently utilized by Robert Dubin (1976) to explain the widespread appeal the various humanistic philosophy theories have for practicing managers.

Bennis hypothesized first five (1966b) and then six (1969a) core problem areas for organizations. The solutions used by bureaucracies and the "new twentieth-century conditions" that organizations of the future will face point up further deficiencies of the bureaucratic form. This line of argument is set forth in table 20.6.

Organizations of the Future

Seemingly influenced by his long association with the Massachusetts Institute of Technology, Bennis's analysis of bureaucracy's inadequacies focuses heavily on its inability to adapt to accelerating scientific and technological change. In proposing solutions that are more in tune with the "new twentieth-century conditions," he turns to the world of science and research and couples this scientific orientation with a strong commitment to organizational democracy.

In projecting the type of organization that will function effectively in the world of the future, Bennis draws heavily on the professional model as reflected in universities, hospitals, research and development organizations, and the like. Given that the major problem is to cope with technological change, more and more professionals will enter all kinds of organizations. However, professionals are committed to their professions and to professional organizations, not to the employing organization per se. Thus their very presence tends to foster structures other than those of a bureaucratic nature.

With regard to the labor force of the future the following distribution of employment is projected:

40% of the work force will have positions in problem-solving organizations, most of them technologically based.

40% will be social change agents, that is, individu-

TABLE 20.6 Core problem areas for organizations, bureaucratic solutions, and future conditions

Core problem areas	Bureaucratic solutions	New twentieth-century conditions
Integrating individual and organization goals	No solution—the tension involved is disregarded	Scientific understanding of man's complexity; rising aspirations; humanistic ethos
Distributing social influence and the sources of power and authority	Explicit reliance on rational, legal power; implicit use of coercive power	Separation of management and ownership; rise of trade unions and educational level; negative effects of authoritarian rule
Producing mechanisms for the control of conflict—collaboration	Resolving conflicts through vertical hierarchy and horizontal coordination; use of loyalty	Professionalization creates need for interdependence; leadership too complex for one-man rule
Adapting to environmental change	Environment stable and tasks routine; adapting haphazard, with many unanticipated consequences	Turbulent environment; rapid technological change
Dealing with growth and decay—revitalization	Assumptions of future similar to past	Rapid changes make constant attention to revisions imperative
Achieving identity through commitment to organizational goals (added subsequently)	Primary goal clear, simple, and stable	Increased goal complexity due to diversity and multiple capabilities; creates role conflict and ambiguity

SOURCE: Adapted from Warren G. Bennis (1969), *Organization Development: Its Nature, Origins, and Prospects* (Reading, MA: Addison-Wesley), 26, 27

als working on revitalization of our institutions or with those problems people feel in times of transition, including moral and ethical problems.

20%, to my despair, will do the remaining unprogrammed, low-level jobs of the society. . . . Perhaps there are enough people with physical or mental handicaps, or people with low aspirations, to do them. It's difficult to think about. (Bennis, 1969b, p. 237)

Thus some 80 percent will be either professionals or employed in professional organizations. The reduction in nonprofessional employment will be made possible by automation and computerization; intellectual power will be substituted for muscle power.

In the 1960s Bennis appears to vacillate between predicting the virtual elimination of the nonprofessional component in society and ignoring this component as irrelevant to his theorizing.

Temporary Systems

In describing the organizational structures suited to the times, Bennis drew heavily on his knowledge of the project structures that had become widespread in research and development organizations:

1. The key will be "temporary": there will be adaptive, rapidly changing *temporary systems*.
2. These will be organized around *problems-to-be-solved*.
3. The problems will be solved by groups of relative *strangers* who represent a set of diverse professional skills.
4. The groups will be conducted on *organic* rather than mechanical models; they will evolve in response to the problem rather than programmed role expectations.
5. The function of the "executive" thus becomes *coordinator*, or "linking pin" between various project groups. He must be a man who can speak the diverse languages of research and who can relay information and mediate among the groups.
6. People will be differentiated not vertically according to rank and role but flexibly according to skill and professional training. (Bennis, 1966a, p. 12)

This structure, which is labeled *organic-adaptive*, is presumed to operate within a society that is also characterized by relationships of a largely temporary nature

(Bennis & Slater, 1968). Motivation is fostered as individual-professional and organizational goals come closer together. Commitment to work groups will be at a minimum with temporary systems, thus reducing one manifestation of individual-organizational goal incongruence.

The hypotheses for the "good organization" set forth by Bennis lack the diversity of Argyris's mix model. They differ in a number of respects from the autonomous group concepts of the sociotechnical theorists (chapter 14 in this volume) and from system 4 (chapter 13). What is in fact distinctive about Bennis's views is his emphasis on the professional and on professional forms of organization.

Revisions in the 1970s

Just as Douglas McGregor came to modify some of his views on theory X and theory Y after serving as a university president, so Bennis changed his theories after similar administrative experiences:

The 1964 paper I mentioned earlier was written within the liberal-democratic framework, and it contained many of the inherent problems and advantages of that perspective. . . . I feel far less certainty and closure at this time than I did five years ago. (Bennis, 1970, p. 597)

Bureaucracy is the inevitable—and therefore necessary—form for governing large and complex organizations. (Bennis, 1973, pp. 144–145)

The temporary system has its place, but it's not going to occupy a paramount or pervasive position. There will always be a bureaucracy; the sun will never set on bureaucracies. (Bennis, 1974, p. 57)

At first glance the author would appear to be totally rejecting his own theory. However, a closer reading of many of his statements during the 1970s suggests another interpretation: Bennis considered it necessary to limit the domain of his theory, and thus to shift it from organizations in general to a particular type of essentially professional organization.

Yet Bennis has not accepted this more limited role for his theory with consistency either. The following statement is clearly at variance with those quoted previously:

Ten years ago, I predicted that in the next twenty-five to fifty years we will participate in the end of bureaucracy as we know it and the rise of new systems better suited to twentieth century demands of industrialization. . . .

I have no reason to believe differently today. On the contrary I realize now that my prediction is already a distinct reality so that the prediction is foreshadowed by practice. By "bureaucracy," I mean the typical organizational structure that coordinates the business of most every human organization we know of. (Bennis, 1975, p. 330)

Continuing Ambiguity

Increasingly, and almost completely in recent years, Bennis has moved to writing for a popular, not scholarly, audience. The books have been more frequent, but the previous balance between philosophy and theory has shifted sharply in a philosophic direction. There is little if any testable theory. A persistent theme has been to describe role models of bureaucratic leadership and group process using unstructured interviews and published sources. Actual data or means of analysis are not stated, only interpretations; replication would be impossible. Science has been left behind. This is fine for its purpose, but it is important to recognize it for what it is.

In this writing Bennis continues to manifest his humanism and his commitment to the democratization of the workplace (Bennis, Parikh, & Lessem, 1994). He steadfastly holds to his view of a complex, rapidly changing, turbulent environment that imposes certain imperatives on the organizations caught up in its tide. But what does he say about the demise of bureaucracy? How does he view events of the past 30 years or more since he propounded his theory? Has the theory passed the test of time? Is it valid now? We know that in the 1970s this picture was muddied. The short answer now is that it still is. In a *Harvard Business Review* retrospective (Bennis, 1990) on his earlier statements (Slater & Bennis, 1964) we find the following:

It's wonderful to reread something you wrote 26 years ago and discover you were right. . . . Democracy was, and is, more effective than autocracy, bureaucracy, and other nondemocratic forms of organization. . . . In international politics, democratization is a very recent phenomenon, although a profound one. . . . The democratization of the workplace has made fewer headlines, but has been no less dramatic. . . . Now most major corporations

practice some form of egalitarian management. (Bennis, 1990, p. 174)

And elsewhere, somewhat more recently:

Post-bureaucratic organization requires a new kind of alliance between leaders and led. Todays organizations are evolving into federations, networks, clusters, cross-functional teams, temporary systems, ad hoc task forces, lattices, modules, matrices—almost anything but pyramids with their obsolete top-down leadership. (Bennis, 1999, p. 76)

All this is quite clear—bureaucracy is dying (if not as yet quite dead), as it should be, and the theory of bureaucratic demise is still alive and well.

Yet other statements give pause:

The normative goal of organizational development is to humanize bureaucracy. . . . But values (or normative goals) are only one consideration and perhaps not the most important one. . . . Problems of leadership, coordination, collaboration and communication force themselves on our attention. Most knowledge utilization efforts have to do with maintaining the virtues of bureaucracy—its speed, precision, predictability, and efficiency—while trying to preserve an adaptability to change and a climate of creativity, personal growth, and satisfaction for the workforce. (Bennis, 1987, p. 41)

This seems to say that there are virtues of bureaucracy worth maintaining, not exactly what we have become used to hearing. Furthermore, there are times when Bennis is not sure that democracy has come to prevail in the workplace:

I see the notion of empowerment on a collision course with many of the ideas associated with downsizing, restructuring, and reengineering. . . . You alter the culture dramatically . . . the trust of the personnel begins to wane . . . people start looking for other jobs. . . . Rather than feeling empowered, people feel disempowered, frightened, anxious, and scared. . . . Trust continues to be a major concern for the employees. If leaders can't establish that trust, then participation and empowerment will be cynical relics of a distopian nightmare. (quoted in Hodgetts, 1996, pp. 73–74, 78)

This does not sound like a trendline to a utopia of workplace democracy. Perhaps the theory should be amended to adopt the contingent hypothesis that bureaucracy will be eliminated only under conditions of growth, but that hypothesis was not stated at any point.

The current status of bureaucratic demise theory remains uncertain in view of statements by the theory's author over a long period since the first formulations in the 1960s. We will return to this issue later in this chapter, but it is important at this point to establish the existing state of affairs. Also, this problem of ambiguity is not limited to the status of bureaucracy. At one point Bennis indicates his endorsement of Argyris's ideas about the inclusion of subjects "as coinvestigators if the research is to have any meaning and ultimately lead to change" (Bennis, 1985, p. 352). This raises a question as to whether he is invoking Argyris's dictate against conducting any research without subject participation in the design. Is this true for all research, for applied research, or for research on organization development? Given that Bennis, like Argyris, now has given up any involvement in research studies, this is an important matter. Yet there remains nothing but ambiguity.

Contributions to Organization Development

Bennis's concern with changing organizations and with laboratory training preceded his formal statement of the theory of bureaucratic demise (Bennis, Benne, & Chin, 1961; Burke & Bennis, 1961). Thus his recommendations for practice were not so much an outgrowth of his organizational theory as a development parallel with it.

Laboratory Training

In the early period Bennis appears to have been interested in laboratory training primarily as a means to individual and group change rather than organizational change. His focus is on internal group processes, group development, trainer behavior, and the like; the T-group is concerned with what is happening now within the group itself, not with the outside world (Bennis, 1964). Accordingly, learning is based on experience.

Yet the stated values underlying the training are clearly consistent with an unfreezing of commitment to current structures and a shift to nonbureaucratic forms of organization (Schein & Bennis, 1965):

Values of science

Spirit of inquiry

Expanded consciousness and choice

Authenticity in interpersonal relations

Values of democracy

Collaboration

Conflict resolution through rational means

Laboratory groups are temporary systems in the fullest sense of that concept. Thus laboratory training represents an ideal method of moving to the type of organization Bennis advocated.

Not surprisingly, Bennis (1966a) came to a position much like that of Argyris in which laboratory training of "family groups" within organizations was favored as a method of planned organizational change. This commitment to laboratory training as a component of organizational change programs remained strong, but Bennis recognizes that it is not appropriate under all circumstances:

> In undertaking any planned social change using lab training, the core of the target system's values must not be too different from the lab training values.... Legitimacy for the change must be gained by obtaining the support of the key people. ... Voluntary commitment of the participants may be a crucial factor in the success of the program. ... The state of cultural readiness must be assessed. (Bennis, 1977, pp. 211–215)

Organization Development

Bennis (1969a) lists a number of characteristics of organization development, as he views it:

1. An educational strategy intended to produce organizational change that focuses on "people" variables such as values and interpersonal relationships
2. The changes desired are associated with specific organizational problems such as growth, member satisfactions, and effectiveness
3. An educational strategy such as laboratory training, confrontation meetings, or learning seminars, which stresses experienced behavior
4. A change agent, usually external, who is in a collaborative relationship with the organization and who holds values of a kind that will lead to a less bureaucratic and more humane and democratic system

5. Objectives of the change effort that are congruent with the change agent values and
that include:
   a. improved interpersonal competence
   b. changed values that emphasize human
   factors and feelings
   c. increased understanding within and across
   groups with reduced tensions resulting
   d. development of effective team management
   e. more open and rational forms of conflict
   resolution
   f. more organic systems characterized by
   mutual trust and shared responsibility (pp.
   10–15)

In spite of his belief that the T-group is far from
universally appropriate, Bennis notes the existence of
"the T-group coloration that almost all organization
development programs take on" (1969a, p. 78). Given
this coloration, he outlines certain problems that seriously limit the applicability of organization development:

> The organization development consultant tends to
> use the truth-love model when it may be inappro-
> priate and has no alternative model to guide his
> practice under conditions of distrust, violence, and
> conflict. Essentially this means that in pluralistic
> power situations, in situations which are not easily
> controlled, organization development practice may
> not reach its desired goals. (Bennis, 1969a, p. 78)

> Organization development pays lip service only to
> structural (or technological) changes while relying
> only on a change in organizational "climate." . . .
> The organization development literature is filled
> with vague promises about "restructuring" or "orga-
> nizational design" but with some exceptions few
> outcomes are actually demonstrated. . . . Far more
> has to be done in bridging an engineering design
> approach with organizational development change
> strategies. (Bennis, 1969a, p. 80)

Bennis did not develop a distinctive approach to
organization development, as Argyris did with his
learning seminars and action science. The approach
Bennis emphasized, involving a heavy reliance on
laboratory training and T-groups, was essentially mainstream (if it is possible to apply that term to organization development at all) for the period in which it
was invoked. Since we will be looking at several similar
theories and several similar approaches to organization

development in the next chapter, any empirical assessment of organizational development generally, as rooted
in laboratory training, needs to await these later treatments. However, it should be apparent that Bennis's
views often reflected a considerable degree of realism
about the limits of applicability of his approach. This
may have derived from his previous exposure to psychoanalysis, a procedure that has much in common
with laboratory training.

Evaluation and Impact

Bennis's theory of bureaucratic demise has not generated a great deal of research—in part because of its
sizable infusion of philosophy, in part because of uncertainty over the true meaning of the hypotheses, in
part because certain hypotheses could be fully tested
only at some point in the future, and in part because
of a lack of measures of key variables. Bennis himself
has neither contributed measures of his own nor carried out studies related to his theory, although he did
do earlier research on the effects of the laboratory
training carried out under the National Training Laboratories program at Bethel, Maine, on participant
self-perceptions (Burke & Bennis, 1961). However,
there are some findings that bear on the theory.

Failure of Innovation

A central theme in the theory of bureaucratic demise
is that bureaucracies cannot mobilize innovative strategies to cope with rapid environmental changes such
as those produced by modern scientific and technological developments. This view has been argued from
somewhat different premises by a number of others
and has surfaced several times in preceding chapters
of this volume, most notably by Victor Thompson in
chapter 19. There the evidence reviewed supported
the value of professional systems as sources of innovation, but it did not support the conclusion that bureaucracy is inevitably antithetical to innovation.

Early research indicates that the decentralized, participative, organic-adaptive structures that Bennis advocates are well suited to the generation of innovations, but within such structures adoption—actually
putting the innovation into effect—appears to be more
difficult (Pierce & Delbecq, 1977). Organic-adaptive
structures, especially when staffed with professionals,
tend to foster a search for ideas and to create a positive

intellectual climate, but nothing may happen after that, or in some cases the implementation that does occur represents a distorted version of the original idea. For purposes of effective implementation, a more formalized system can prove helpful and, on occasion, may be badly needed. The tendency for high-technology firms staffed with scientists to fail to carry their innovations through into the marketplace, and even to devalue the implementation of marketing efforts, is a case in point (Roberts, 1991; Miner, 1997).

Bureaucracies, even highly formalized ones, can be innovative. A national interview study dealing with this topic conducted in the period Bennis was writing about concluded as follows:

> There is a small but consistent tendency for -[people] who work in bureaucratic organizations to be more intellectually flexible, more open to new experience, and more self-directed in their values than are [people] who work in nonbureaucratic organizations. This may in part result from bureaucracies' drawing on a more educated work force. In large part, though, it appears to be a consequence of occupational conditions attendant on bureaucratization—notably, far greater protections, somewhat higher income, and substantively more complex work. (Kohn, 1971, p. 461)

One problem with the nonbureaucratic forms of the Bennis theory is that they tend to elicit considerable anxiety and tension in many people (Bryman, 1976). This anxiety, if sufficiently high, can block creativity; it can also so inhibit action that innovative ideas are not implemented. The greater predictability and protection against arbitrary action that is provided by truly bureaucratic organizations should reduce anxiety levels for many people and, at least for them, foster innovation.

Formalized bureaucracies can be challenging and innovative, as the Aston researchers found (see chapter 18 in this volume). One contributing factor to this result is a value system that supports innovation operating in the organization, especially in the leadership group. If values favoring innovation exist at the top, innovations are likely to occur and to be implemented, even in more formalized systems.

One can conclude that a number of considerations determine whether an organization will adapt to environmental change in an innovative and effective manner and that a resort to bureaucratic determinism to explain organizational demise represents a gross oversimplification at best. Yet Bennis's views on temporary systems, the professional model, and the like do appear to be useful. As part of a theory of professional organizational structures, his formulations in these areas appear to have considerable validity.

Ambiguity Factor

There can be little doubt that Bennis has vacillated widely over the years since his theory of bureaucratic demise was proposed, and the ambiguity is now so great that it is impossible to say where the theory stands at the present time. Of one thing we can be certain: The contention that democracy has triumphed over bureaucracy in the workplace, and that this is because democracy is more effective, simply is not justified by the data (Collins, 1997; Lawler, Mohrman, & Ledford, 1992). Democracy at work seems to go up and down like a seesaw, depending on various factors, but no markedly greater effectiveness has been demonstrated for it (see chapters 10 and 13). To the extent democracy has increased at any point in time, this has characteristically involved its addition to existing forms, not its replacement of them. Bureaucracy continues to be very much a reality. Perhaps Bennis will be right at the 50-year point; no one can say for sure. But as of 35 years out, at this writing, the evidence that bureaucracy is dead does not exist.

This leaves us with a question as to how and why Bennis got to the ambiguity that now permeates his theory. A reading of the sources from which the ambiguity stems suggests that in each instance he was coming at his theory from a different perspective, with a different objective. It is easy under such circumstances to get caught up in the logic of the moment and say things that are not consistent with some prior logic. This becomes doubly easy if the theory of concern is not the major focus of one's thought processes but, rather, is secondary to the philosophy and values (humanist) that drove the theory in the first place. Surely Bennis has moved away from science and theory toward philosophy, drama, and even poetry over the years. The sum total of his statements over time is now distinctly lacking as a body of logically consistent and scientifically verified or verifiable theory, but perhaps this is not the way the theory should be evaluated; it is certainly persuasive philosophy and good theater. This may well have become Bennis's primary intent.

CONCLUSIONS

The theories considered in this chapter and the applications associated with them have proved controversial. The theorists have been accused both of leaning too far to the left and of offering token solutions to organizational problems while covertly supporting the industrial status quo to an unwarranted degree. These matters are more philosophic than scientific or practical and are unlikely to be resolved here. Even the veiled (and sometimes not so veiled) implications that these theorists have personal problems with authority or are engaged in an unwarranted imposition of their professional values on others are not really important. All of us generate our theories out of personal experiences and values. The crucial questions are whether theories are right or wrong and whether their applications are useful or not, not how the theorists arrived at their views. It is possible to develop very right theories out of very wrong (bad) motivations.

It would appear that Argyris and Bennis have used bureaucratic and classical management forms as straw men for their alternative structures. From the evidence, bureaucracy need not be as rigid, uncreative, oppressive, and incapable of environmental adaptation as these theorists contend. It does not lead to organizational degeneration and failure any more than any other form. It seems unlikely to disappear from the face of the earth in the immediate future, largely because it is the only structure that has adequately dealt with the kinds of problems and decisions that occur at the upper levels of large organizations.

Surely there are bureaucracies that deserve all the criticisms Argyris and Bennis heap on them; many have withered and died, as a review of the *Fortune* 500 firms over the years will clearly indicate. However, these failures appear to be more a function of a wide range of managerial errors than a function of the inadequacies inherent in bureaucratic structure. A number of firms that have effectively used bureaucracy for many years have remained high on the list of corporate performers throughout their existence. Whether bureaucracies cope effectively and prosper seems to depend largely on such factors as the values of the leadership group, individual member capabilities, and adequate incorporation of staff-level positions. Contrary to the original Bennis view, bureaucracies handle conflicts within the realm of legitimate hierarchical authority (which functions in much the same manner as the judicial process), and they have ad-justed in many cases to sizable infusions of professionals and professional structures under an overall bureaucratic umbrella.

The Argyris and Bennis theories may also be faulted for a lack of internal consistency, which makes testing them difficult. Both authors tend to introduce new concepts over time in response to new influences on their thinking without indicating exactly how these concepts relate to prior theory. Alternative hypotheses are sometimes left standing side by side without any theoretical integration.

However, it should be understood that this is criticism from a much later vantage point. These theories appeared during a period of rapid growth in the service and professional occupations and just before major shifts in the balance of personality types within the population, primarily away from those types that fit bureaucracies best (Miner, 1974). The theories, especially Bennis's, fostered the development and expansion of professional structures at a time when they were greatly needed. The theories also contributed, as did the system 4 and sociotechnical theories, to organizational changes of other kinds that appear to have been consonant with shifting personality constellations. In this sense the Argyris and Bennis theories performed an extremely useful societal function, whatever their long-term scientific imperfections. They helped introduce organization development, which is without question the major practical application generated so far by the new field of organizational behavior.

References

Argyris, Chris (1952). *The Impact of Budgets on People.* New York: Controllership Foundation.

Argyris, Chris (1954). *Organization of a Bank: A Study of the Nature of Organization and the Fusion Process.* New Haven, CT: Labor and Management Center, Yale University.

Argyris, Chris (1957). *Personality and Organization.* New York: Harper & Row.

Argyris, Chris (1958). The Organization: What Makes It Healthy? *Harvard Business Review*, 36(6), 107–116.

Argyris, Chris (1959). Understanding Human Behavior in Organizations: One Viewpoint. In Mason Haire (Ed.), *Modern Organization Theory* (pp. 115–154). New York: Wiley.

Argyris, Chris (1960a). Organizational Effectiveness under Stress. *Harvard Business Review*, 38(3), 137–146.

Argyris, Chris (1960b). *Understanding Organizational Behavior*. Homewood, IL: Dorsey.

Argyris, Chris (1962a). The Integration of the Individual and the Organization. In George B. Strother (Ed.), *Social Science Approaches to Business Behavior* (pp. 57–98). Homewood, IL: Irwin.

Argyris, Chris (1962b). *Interpersonal Competence and Organizational Effectiveness*. Homewood, IL: Irwin.

Argyris, Chris (1964). *Integrating the Individual and the Organization*. New York: Wiley.

Argyris, Chris (1965). *Organization and Innovation*. Homewood, IL: Irwin.

Argyris, Chris (1968). Some Unintended Consequences of Rigorous Research. *Psychological Bulletin*, 70, 185–197.

Argyris, Chris (1970). *Intervention Theory and Method: A Behavioral Science View*. Reading, MA: Addison-Wesley.

Argyris, Chris (1971). *Management and Organizational Development: The Path from XA to YB*. New York: McGraw-Hill.

Argyris, Chris (1972). *The Applicability of Organizational Sociology*. Cambridge: Cambridge University Press.

Argyris, Chris (1973). Personality and Organization Theory Revisited. *Administrative Science Quarterly*, 18, 141–167.

Argyris, Chris (1974a). *Behind the Front Page: Organizational Self-Renewal in a Metropolitan Newspaper*. San Francisco: Jossey-Bass.

Argyris, Chris (1974b). Personality vs. Organization. *Organizational Dynamics*, 3(2), 3–17.

Argyris, Chris (1980). *The Inner Contradictions of Rigorous Research*. New York: Academic Press.

Argyris, Chris (1982). *Reasoning, Learning, Action: Individual and Organizational*. San Francisco: Jossey-Bass.

Argyris, Chris (1985). *Strategy, Change, and Defensive Routines*. Boston: Pitman.

Argyris, Chris (1989). Strategy Implementation: An Experience in Learning. *Organizational Dynamics*, 18(2), 5–15.

Argyris, Chris (1990). *Overcoming Organizational Defenses: Facilitating Organizational Learning*. Boston: Allyn & Bacon.

Argyris, Chris (1991). Teaching Smart People How to Learn. *Harvard Business Review*, 69(3), 99–109.

Argyris, Chris (1992a). Looking Backward and Inward in Order to Contribute to the Future. In Arthur G. Bedeian (Ed.), *Management Laureates: A Collection of Autobiographical Essays* (Vol. 1, pp. 41–64). Greenwich, CT: JAI Press.

Argyris, Chris (1992b). *On Organizational Learning*. Cambridge, MA: Blackwell.

Argyris, Chris (1993). *Knowledge for Action: A Guide to Overcoming Barriers to Organizational Change*. San Francisco: Jossey-Bass.

Argyris, Chris (1994). Litigation Mentality and Organizational Learning. In Sim B. Sitkin & Robert J. Bies (Eds.), *The Legalistic Organization* (pp. 347–358). Thousand Oaks, CA: Sage.

Argyris, Chris (1995). Action Science and Organizational Learning. *Journal of Managerial Psychology*, 10(6), 20–26.

Argyris, Chris (1996). Unrecognized Defenses of Scholars: Impact on Theory and Research. *Organization Science*, 7, 79–87.

Argyris, Chris (1998a). Award for Life Achievement in the Application of Psychology. *American Psychologist*, 53, 877–878.

Argyris, Chris (1998b). Empowerment: The Emperor's New Clothes. *Harvard Business Review*, 76(3), 98–105.

Argyris, Chris (2000). *Flawed Advice and the Management Trap*. New York: Oxford University Press.

Argyris, Chris; Putnam, Robert; & Smith, Diane M. (1985). *Action Science: Concepts, Methods, and Skills for Research and Intervention*. San Francisco: Jossey-Bass.

Argyris, Chris, & Schön, Donald A. (1996). *Organizational Learning II: Theory, Method, and Practice*. Reading, MA: Addison-Wesley.

Bakke, E. Wight (1950). *Bonds of Organization*. New York: Harper.

Bakke, E. Wight (1959). Concept of the Social Organization. In Mason Haire (Ed.), *Modern Organization Theory* (pp. 16–75). New York: Wiley.

Bazigos, Michael N., & Burke, W. Warner (1997). Theory Orientations of Organization Development (OD) Practitioners. *Group and Organization Management*, 22, 384–408.

Bennis, Warren G. (1964). Patterns and Vicissitudes in T-Group Development. In Leland P. Bradford, Jack R. Gibb, & Kenneth D. Benne (Eds.), *T-Group Theory and Laboratory Method* (pp. 248–278). New York: Wiley.

Bennis, Warren G. (1966a). *Changing Organizations*. New York: McGraw-Hill.

Bennis, Warren G. (1966b). Changing Organizations. *Journal of Applied Behavioral Science*, 2, 247–263.

Bennis, Warren G. (1967). Organizations of the Future. *Personnel Administration*, 30(5), 6–19.

Bennis, Warren G. (1969a). *Organization Development: Its Nature, Origins, and Prospects*. Reading, MA: Addison-Wesley.

Bennis, Warren G. (1969b). The Temporary Society. *Journal of Creative Behavior*, 3, 223–241.

Bennis, Warren G. (1970). A Funny Thing Happened on the Way to the Future. *American Psychologist*, 25, 595–608.

Bennis, Warren G. (1973). *The Leaning Ivory Tower.* San Francisco: Jossey-Bass.

Bennis, Warren G. (1974). Conversation with Warren Bennis. *Organizational Dynamics*, 2(3), 51–66.

Bennis, Warren G. (1975). The Problem: Integrating the Organization and the Individual. In William G. Monahan (Ed.), *Theoretical Dimensions of Educational Administration* (pp. 317–346). New York: Macmillan.

Bennis, Warren G. (1977). Bureaucracy and Social Change: An Anatomy of a Training Failure. In Philip H. Mirvis & David N. Berg (Eds.), *Failures in Organization Development and Change: Cases and Essays for Learning* (pp. 191–215). New York: Wiley.

Bennis, Warren G. (1985). Observations on What We Have Learned about Useful Research. In Edward E. Lawler, Allan M. Mohrman, Susan A. Mohrman, Gerald E. Ledford, & Thomas G. Cummings (Eds.), *Doing Research That Is Useful for Theory and Practice* (pp. 351–357). San Francisco: Jossey-Bass.

Bennis, Warren G. (1987). Using Our Knowledge of Organizational Behavior: The Improbable Task. In Jay W. Lorsch (Ed.), *Handbook of Organizational Behavior* (pp. 29–49). Englewood Cliffs, NJ: Prentice Hall.

Bennis, Warren G. (1990). Retrospective Commentary (On the Occasion of the Republication of Slater & Bennis, 1964). *Harvard Business Review*, 68(5), 174–175.

Bennis, Warren G. (1991; 1992). Autobiography—Part 1; Part 2. *Journal of Applied Behavioral Science*, 27, 413–424; 28, 318–330.

Bennis, Warren G. (1999). The End of Leadership: Exemplary Leadership Is Impossible without Full Inclusion, Initiatives, and Cooperation of Followers. *Organizational Dynamics*, 28(1), 71–80.

Bennis, Warren G.; Benne, Kenneth D.; & Chin, Robert (1961). *The Planning of Change.* New York: Holt, Rinehart & Winston.

Bennis, Warren G.; Parikh, Jagdish; & Lessem, Ronnie (1994). *Beyond Leadership: Balancing Economics, Ethics and Ecology.* Cambridge, MA: Blackwell.

Bennis, Warren G., & Slater, Philip E. (1968). *The Temporary Society.* New York: Harper & Row.

Bonjean, Charles M., & Vance, Gary G. (1968). A Short-Form Measure of Self-Actualization. *Journal of Applied Behavioral Science*, 4, 299–312.

Bryman, Alan (1976). Structure in Organizations: A Reconsideration. *Journal of Occupational Psychology*, 49, 1–9.

Burke, Richard L., & Bennis, Warren G. (1961). Changes in Perception of Self and Others during Human Relations Training. *Human Relations*, 14, 165–182.

Burke, Ronald J., & Weir, Tamara (1978). Organizational Climate and Informal Helping Processes in Work Settings. *Journal of Management*, 4(2), 91–105.

Church, Allan H.; Burke, W. Warner; & Van Eynde, Donald F. (1994). Values, Motives, and Interventions of Organizational Development Practitioners. *Group and Organization Management*, 19, 5–50.

Collins, Denis (1997). The Ethical Superiority and Inevitability of Participatory Management as an Organizational System. *Organization Science*, 8, 489–507.

Dachler, H. Peter (1994). Review of *On Organizational Learning. Organization Studies*, 15, 460–464.

Dewar, Robert, & Werbel, James (1979). Universalistic and Contingency Predictions of Employee Satisfaction and Conflict. *Administrative Science Quarterly*, 24, 426–448.

Diamond, Michael A. (1986). Resistance to Change: A Psychoanalytic Critique of Argyris and Schön's Contributions to Organization Theory and Intervention. *Journal of Management Studies*, 23, 543–562.

Dubin, Robert (1976). Theory Building in Applied Areas. In Marvin D. Dunnette (Ed.), *Handbook of Industrial and Organizational Psychology* (pp. 17–39). Chicago: Rand, McNally.

Foldy, Erica G., & Creed, W. E. Douglas (1999). Action Learning, Fragmentation, and the Interaction of Single-, Double-, and Triple-Loop Change: A Case of Gay and Lesbian Workplace Advocacy. *Journal of Applied Behavioral Science*, 35, 207–227.

Fulmer, Robert M., & Keys, J. Bernard (1998). A Conversation with Chris Argyris: The Father of Organizational Learning. *Organizational Dynamics*, 27(2), 21–32.

Hodgetts, Richard M. (1996). A Conversation with Warren Bennis: On Leadership in the Midst of Downsizing. *Organizational Dynamics*, 25(1), 72–78.

James, Lawrence R., & Jones, Allan P. (1976). Organizational Structure: A Review of Structural Dimensions and Their Conceptual Relationships with Individual Attitudes and Behavior. *Organizational Behavior and Human Performance*, 16, 74–113.

Kohn, Melvin L. (1971). Bureaucratic Man: A Portrait and an Interpretation. *American Sociological Review*, 36, 461–474.

Lawler, Edward E.; Mohrman, Susan A.; & Ledford, Gerald E. (1992). *Employee Involvement and Total Quality Management.* San Francisco: Jossey-Bass.

Lipshitz, Raanan (2000). Chic, Mystique, and Misconception: Argyris and Schön and the Rhetoric of

Organizational Learning. *Journal of Applied Behavioral Science*, 36, 456–473.

Miner, John B. (1974). *The Human Constraint*. Washington, DC: BNA Books.

Miner, John B. (1997). *A Psychological Typology of Successful Entrepreneurs*. Westport, CT: Quorum.

Nielsen, Richard P. (1993). Triple-Loop Action-Learning as HRM Method: Two European Cases. *Research in Personnel and Human Resources Management*, Supplement 3, 75–93.

Pennings, Johannes M. (1976). Dimensions of Organizational Influence and Their Effectiveness Correlates. *Administrative Science Quarterly*, 21, 688–699.

Pierce, Jon L., & Delbecq, André L. (1977). Organizational Structure, Individual Attitudes and Innovation. *Academy of Management Review*, 2, 27–37.

Porter, Lyman W. (1989). A Retrospective Review: Argyris's *Personality and Organization*. *Academy of Management Review*, 14, 284–285.

Putnam, Robert (1995). A Biography of Chris Argyris. *Journal of Applied Behavioral Science*, 31, 253–255.

Raelin, Joseph A. (1997). Action Learning and Action Science: Are They Different? *Organizational Dynamics*, 26(1), 21–34.

Roberts, Edward B. (1991). *Entrepreneurs in High Technology: Lessons from MIT and Beyond*. New York: Oxford University Press.

Rossel, Robert D. (1971). Autonomy in Bureaucracies. *Administrative Science Quarterly*, 16, 308–314.

Roth, George, & Kleiner, Art (2000). *Car Launch: The Human Side of Managing Change*. New York: Oxford University Press.

Schein, Edgar H., & Bennis, Warren G. (1965). *Personal and Organizational Change through Group Methods: The Laboratory Approach*. New York: Wiley.

Slater, Philip E., & Bennis, Warren G. (1964). Democracy Is Inevitable. *Harvard Business Review*, 42(2), 51–59.

Chapter 21

The Mix of Organization Development and Leadership

In this chapter we take up several additional theories that are related to organization development practice. They are not as blatantly anti-bureaucracy as those we have been considering in the preceding two chapters, but in espousing humanist values and fostering the use of procedures that are intended to change organizations to make them less bureaucratic, they implicitly assume a position alongside the theories of Chris Argyris and Warren Bennis.

The origins of organization development were in a humanist anti-bureaucracy/classical management philosophy that is clearly manifest in the theories initially expounded by Argyris and Bennis (chapter 20 in this volume). The theories considered in this chapter are organizational in nature, but they are closely tied to more micro-level leadership theories. Each micro theory contains within it aspects that appear to reflect components of bureaucratic leadership. Thus there is a certain mitigation of the attack on bureaucracy in these theories, as contrasted with the theories proposed by Argyris and Bennis.

Grid organization development theory is a straightforward extrapolation of the managerial grid theory of leadership (Blake & Mouton, 1964), which was discussed in chapter 10 as an outgrowth of the consideration and initiating structure formulations that emanated from Ohio State University. To be more specific, grid leadership theory is a derivative of the high-high hypothesis and carries with it some of the burdens of that approach. Yet it is important to look into the organization development theory, not only because it extends to the macro level and thus introduces new variables, but because it was at the forefront of the organization development movement and exerted considerable influence.

Edgar Schein's ties to leadership theory follow a very different course. Initially his concern was with the change process and with his own particular approach to organization development (process consultation). Only as it became evident that this approach would benefit from a broader theoretical perspective did he delve into the area of leadership and its role in influencing organizational culture (Schein, 1985). In the end what emerged was a comprehensive culture theory in which top managers were significant actors. In this theory culture served in a number of respects as a substitute for hierarchy (and thus bureaucracy). Thus Schein's theory offers an alternative to bureaucracy, not only in its early and continuing focus on organization development but also in its subsequent elaboration of the culture construct as a tool for human organization that can in certain respects replace aspects of bureaucracy.

As we move to a discussion of these two theories, it is important to recognize that the two theorists had in common not just their concern with leadership issues but a background in laboratory training that included a lengthy association with the National Training Laboratories in Bethel, Maine. In this latter regard they join Argyris and Bennis.

GRID ORGANIZATION DEVELOPMENT

Background

Robert Blake was born in 1918. At Berea College in Kentucky, he majored in psychology and philosophy, Next came a master's degree in psychology at the University of Virginia, service during World War II in a psychological research unit, and a doctorate in social psychology from the University of Texas in 1947. He remained in the psychology department at Texas until 1964, but with frequent leaves of absence—to Tavistock in London, to the Harvard Department of

Social Relations, and to what is now the Exxon Corporation. From 1964 on Blake headed Scientific Methods Inc., a professional firm that was engaged in consulting, conducting seminars, and publishing, which he founded with his coauthor Jane Mouton. After 1984 he cut back on his managerial activities with the firm, concentrating on the professional side (teaching, consulting, and writing), which he preferred (Blake, 1992).

Blake has been a prolific publisher of both articles and books, beginning in 1943. Early on, these were primarily of a scholarly nature in various areas of psychology. Later, most were focused on a more popular audience, which was consistent with the marketing needs of his company. After several articles on laboratory training, the first publications on grid leadership training appeared in 1962. By 1964 organization development applications began to appear in print. Both the micro and macro theories continued to receive frequent attention from the mid-1960s on.

From 1954 on Blake published frequently with Jane Mouton, who 10 years later became his partner at Scientific Methods. Mouton was a graduate student with Blake in the psychology department at Texas and received her doctorate there in 1954. She died in 1987.

From Leadership Theory to Organization Development

The story of grid organization development evolved from laboratory training and was combined with certain early research on intergroup conflict and its resolution (Blake, Shepard, & Mouton, 1964). Out of this combination came both the grid theory of leadership and only slightly later the organization development approach, which incorporates the grid ideas. The latter had its temporal origins in a consulting project conducted for Exxon in an effort to improve their leadership effectiveness.

The first publications on grid organization development appeared in the mid-1960s in several articles and book chapters (see for example Blake & Mouton, 1964; Blake, Mouton, Barnes, & Greiner, 1964; Blake & Mouton, 1965). Next came two book-length treatments in the latter 1960s (Blake & Mouton, 1968, 1969). More recent updates occur in major volumes published by Blake and Mouton (1985), Blake, Mouton, and McCanse (1989), and Blake and McCanse (1991). All of these sources present some version of the six-phase model that underlies the approach. In the process and with varying degrees of specificity, they cover the managerial grid theory of leadership.

Framework

Figure 21.1 represents an advanced version of the original grid and recapitulates what was said here in chapter 10 on this score. The goal of grid organization development is to produce a 9,9 organization, and thus to move an organization from that which is repetitious, mechanical, arbitrary, or senseless toward one that is meaningful, purposeful, problem-solving, and goal-oriented; interactions should change from those that arouse distrust and disrespect to those that use problem-solving to create mutual trust, support, and feelings of personal worth. These changes are not unlike those sought by laboratory training, but the grid procedure takes a somewhat different route to achieve that end.

The six phases are intended to solve problems of communication initially, and then problems of planning. The process as a whole takes from 3 to 5 years, or even longer—which is not surprising in view of the fact that a major culture change is envisioned.

There is an inherent inconsistency in using top-down authority to install a procedure that is basically participative, and this problem is compounded by the fact that the outside consultants involved typically approach the organization through top management. The proposed solution is to provide an opportunity to test the approach through reading, pilot exposure to aspects of the procedure, and special training for key individuals. After this, a steering committee, with

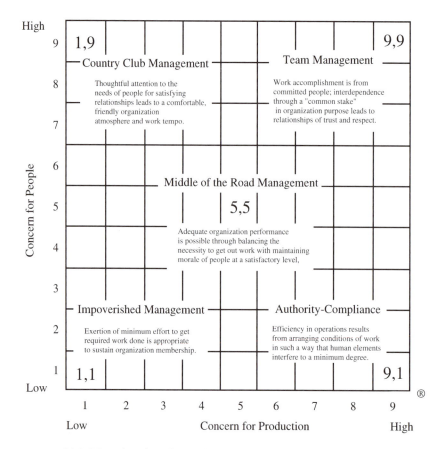

FIGURE 21.1 Major benchmarks on the leadership (managerial) grid. From Robert R. Blake & Anne Adams McCanse (1991), *Leadership Dilemmas—Grid Solutions* (Houston: Gulf Publishing Company), 29. Copyright 1991 by Grid International Inc. Reproduced by permission of the owners.

all levels represented, can make the decision to go ahead with adequate knowledge to make that decision. Top management is represented here, but the decision to commit is essentially participative.

Regarding organizational culture, the authors say:

> If communication is clear and unobstructed and problem solving is approached in the light of the firm's objectives one kind of culture is present. . . . Another kind of culture is present when interactions are tentative, political, or opportunistic, when organization members . . . salute the tenets of bureaucracy. Corporate excellence can only be achieved when (1) a culture is created within which organization members are motivated to become involved in corporate problems . . . (2) teamwork characterized by a genuine sense of participation produces synergistic results, (3) conflicts are brought out into the open . . . (4) solutions that fall short of soundness are rejected. (Blake & Mouton, 1968, pp. 275–277)

Grid organization development has at its heart six variables that may serve as the source of organizational difficulties. These six appear to have been identified originally in the small group context (Blake, 1992). They are:

1. Power/Authority—differences in the strength of influence exerted by members
2. Norms/Standards—the traditions that groups come to accept as second nature
3. Cohesion/Morale—the extent to which people feel drawn to the group
4. Differentiation/Structure—the extent to which member roles are made detailed and explicit
5. Goals/Objectives—the identified purposes toward which a group strives
6. Feedback/Critique—the ability of a group to make use of member reactions to determine how future action should be directed

The origins of grid organization development in group dynamics are clearly manifest in these variables. Of the six the first, power/authority, is considered to be the most likely barrier to corporate effectiveness.

Phase 1: Managerial Grid Laboratory— Seminar Training

The first two phases of the Blake and Mouton approach represent management development, not nec-

essarily organization development. In phase 1 the training is actually conducted by organization line managers who have attended public seminars of the same type, which also were designed to teach the benefits of the 9,9 style. Each group within the organization can have up to 50 participants, with a mix of levels involved, but no superior-subordinate dyads. The idea is to include everyone in the organization in one of the groups so that all know what the grid is and are exposed to the norms of openness inherent in any laboratory training.

The training itself extends over 50 hours. There are numerous exercises, and feedback is given regarding one's own personal style. This latter is focused on grid considerations, rather than having the broad agenda characteristic of laboratory training generally. Topics given special attention are power in supervision and conflict resolution. Those who conduct the training do little formal lecturing; they manage the learning process (clarify goals, provide explanations, aid in learning the grid, critique success). The stated goals of the grid training are increasing self-understanding, experiencing problem-solving effectiveness, learning about managing conflict, and comprehending the organizational implications of what has been learned in terms of overall culture.

Phase 1A Projects

Once a sizable number of people have completed the phase 1 training, and before all have completed it, back on-the-job projects of a culturewide, but not work group nature, may be undertaken. Quality and safety are cited as problems subject to this approach; these are problems that result from cultural norms. The projects attempt to change norms that defeat effectiveness. They do so by using an approach that does not rely on power and authority. The latter tend to create resistance and alienation; thus becoming self-defeating.

The conditions necessary to the success of norm-changing projects of this kind are as follow:

1. All norms carriers actively participate.
2. Leadership is by those responsible for ultimate decisions.
3. Participants are involved with the problem.
4. Facts and data are provided about the objective situation.
5. Ventilation and catharsis are provided as needed.
6. Reasons for the current problems are identified.

7. Implicit agreements are made explicit.
8. Changes in norms are subject to follow-up.
(Blake et al., 1989, pp. 136–137)

These projects may be set up in the final sessions of the grid seminar training. Later, as the organization moves to phase 2, they may be brought in as evidence of concrete change, adding further motivational force to the thrust emanating from the phase 1 seminars.

Phase 2: Team Development

At this point, when all organization members have completed the phase 1 training, the results of that training are transferred back to the job situation via meetings of bosses and their immediate subordinates. This process starts at the top where the operating practices of this group are examined and group goals are set. Lower-level teams then follow, with the result that vertical linking occurs as in Rensis Likert's system 4 (see chapter 13 in this volume).

The focus in phase 2 is on the team and implementing 9,9 at that level. A moderator from some other team, usually a prior instructor in phase 1, is brought in to intervene and provide interpretations of group processes that are obstructing problem solving. After this process of removing blocks to action has been worked through, the team turns to day-to-day operating problems. In phase 2 feedback/critique takes on a particularly important role.

The objectives of this team development phase are to (1) replace outmoded traditions and practices with a problem-solving culture, (2) increase personal objectivity in self-assessment of work behavior, (3) set standards for excellence, (4) establish objectives for team and individual achievements, (5) increase teamwork skills, and (6) use critique for learning. More broadly the goal appears to be to build on the grid seminar learning and to prevent fadeout of the kind that usually occurs after training has been terminated.

Phase 2 activities are facilitated by instrumentation such as diagnostic questionnaires. The activities take 5 days for each team, but may be spread over considerable time if necessary. In the more recent period, this phase has been preceded by a reading of *Spectacular Teamwork* (Blake, Mouton, & Allen, 1987). Also recently this phase appears to have been reduced to 3 days, with the final session devoted to setting team objectives. Later follow-up in several months is desirable.

Phase 3: Horizontal and Vertical Intergroup Linking

This phase is referred to with different terms at various points in time. Horizontal and vertical intergroup linking is the initial terminology and is the most all-encompassing, but intergroup development, horizontal linking, and interface development are also used. There has been some change in emphasis over time, but the shift from an intragroup focus in phase 2 to an intergroup focus in phase 3 remains paramount. The objective is to use methods of team coordination that go beyond the relatively ineffective invoking of hierarchy.

Phase 3 is designed to foster better intergroup problem solving. Each team in conjunction with one other develops an image of itself and of the other team. These images are stated in both existing and ideal terms and are presented at joint meetings as a basis for discussion. Conflicts are surfaced and blockages are removed so the groups can move on to real operational joint problem solving. A second approach involves bringing together a level of hierarchy, such as first-level supervisors to achieve horizontal linking and thus create a strong normative culture around the horizontal reference group. Often representatives are used who meet and then return to report to their groups back home; this cycle may be repeated many times as problems are explored and solved.

Intergroup procedures may be focused on managers who exert considerable influence only. They may include union representatives when union-management conflict is involved. The tendency in phase 3 is to focus on parts of the organization where intergroup cleavages exist. The services of a grid organization development specialist may well be required at this point to coordinate the working out of conflicts. In this process the underlying grid learning and the 9,9 idea are used to establish a common ground.

More recently, the activities of phase 3 have been described in terms of the interface conflict-solving model, which operates in six steps (Blake et al., 1989). These steps are (1) developing the optimal model—each group separately, (2) consolidating the optimal relationship—joint effort, (3) describing the actual relationship—each group separately, 4) consolidating the actual relationship—joint effort, (5) planning for change—joint effort, (6) progress review and replanning. Confrontation is used extensively throughout this process to get problems out in the open where they can be solved.

Phase 4: Setting Organizational Improvement Goals

This goal setting phase initially used task groups comprised of a vertical slice–like phase 1, with no immediate superior-subordinate dyads, but multiple levels. Goals might also come from existing organizational teams. The intent was to deal with problems that could best be solved by concerted efforts throughout the organization and to identify attainable goals on which there appeared to be considerable agreement. This approach has the advantage that it draws heavily on lower-level input. However, as originally stated, it was not clearly explicated and appears not to have worked very well. In particular, needed knowledge did not always exist at lower levels and there was a marked tendency to stick within the boundaries established by the existing status quo.

From the late 1960s on, the focus in phase 4 shifted to the top-level team and a top-down approach. The objective was to design an ideal strategic corporate model of what the organization should become. The elements of this model are key corporate financial objectives, the nature of business activities, the character of markets, organizational structure, basic policies of the business, and development requirements. The authors, having tried moving to phase 4 without the other phases, feel that challenging traditions is difficult without having gone through phases 1 to 3 (Blake & Mouton, 1968).

The design of the ideal model is done by the top team as a group, with the assistance of a grid specialist. Then it is transmitted downward for review, evaluation, and critique. Recommendations for revision are sought. The number of levels of management involved in this exercise is a function of local considerations. Ideally, however, this process will mobilize lower-level commitment. Yet it reflects much less involvement of the organization as a whole than does the original use of vertical slice task forces.

Phase 5: Implementing Planned Change by Attaining Established Goals

The phases conducted up to this point may take as long as 2 years; implementation can involve a similar period. It is carried out with the aid of a grid organization development specialist who intervenes with the authority of ideas to counteract the pull of cultural traditions and to foster the goals of phase 4.

A technique intended to foster commitment based on full understanding of the problems involved uses an educational process with classes of 40 members each, repeated until the whole organization, or all managers, have participated. The steps are (1) assessment of individual knowledge of the problem, (2) individual study of the related facts, (3) definition of the study topic through task paragraph instructions, (4) team agreement as to the facts of the case, (5) agreement with and commitment to the problem solution.

This early technique appears to have been superseded by an approach that is more top-down in nature. It appears to be difficult to change hierarchically structured organizations without using the hierarchy. In the early years the grid approach was to ignore hierarchy if at all possible. Later, hierarchy was directly co-opted in the change effort, as the issues of concern moved to the total organizational level. The considerations involved in this shift in organization development strategy are not discussed. However, the new technique now promulgated involves the initial establishment of a phase-5 coordinator and a top-level strategy implementation committee. Below these are various implementation planning teams for each profit center constituted to contain the needed knowledge. The top-level committee receives reports from and monitors these planning teams to foster coordination.

More recently still, even this technique has disappeared from the discussions and the goals of phase 5 become the central concern. These are as follow:

1. Examining existing activities to identify gaps between how the organization is now being operated and the way it is expected to operate according to the ideal strategic model
2. Specifying which activities are sound, which can be changed and retained, which are unsound and need to be replaced or abandoned, and what new or additional activities are needed to meet the requirements of the ideal model
3. Designing the specific actions necessary to change the ideal model
4. Continuing to run the business while simultaneously changing it toward the ideal model (Blake & McCanse, 1991, p. 353)

The emphasis here is on feasibility analysis, return on investment, and costing.

Phase 6: Stabilization

The tendency in phase 6 is for the old culture to reassert itself in certain respects. The goal of this phase, and of the grid specialist, is to identify and correct these throwbacks. Scientific Methods has developed instruments that can be used for this purpose. Phase 6 extends over at least a year, but in one sense organization development is never completed. During the year after phase 5, a process of critiquing against previous benchmarks is carried out to determine how far the company has come. Monitoring environmental changes should be instituted on a continuing basis; when these reach a significant high point, a new cycle of grid organization development should be considered.

Evaluation and Impact

As we move now to an evaluation of this approach to organization development, it is important to recognize two considerations. One is that Blake and Mouton, for whatever reason, have never published full reports of grid-related research in the scholarly literature of psychology or organizational behavior. This in spite of the fact that in the 1950s and early 1960s they published extensively in the literature of scientific psychology on various other topics, including sources of intergroup conflict and conflict resolution. As they moved to grid topics, however, these authors published what research they did conduct only in sources oriented to a more popular and practitioner audience, and thus their reports are much less complete than good scientific reporting would require.

The second consideration is that, although the grid underlies the total organization development experience, it does so in an uneven manner. Grid theory is most manifest in phases 1 and 2. In phase 3 conflict resolution considerations take center stage (see Blake & Mouton, 1984), and here a solid grounding in research does exist, but it is not grid research. In phases 4 through 6 there has been a pronounced movement away from grid-based activities to more conventional management consulting approaches since the early period. The implication is that the more micro, grid-oriented activities initially introduced in these latter phases did not work well, although the authors never

say this. In any event, grid organization development is not fully a derivative of grid leadership theory.

Research at the Micro Level

In chapter 10, in discussing the managerial grid theory of leadership, I concluded that research that would clearly validate the theory is lacking. What evidence is provided is incomplete and impossible to evaluate. Implicit theories of what constitutes good leadership seem to confound much of the research that is based on judged effective behavior. Blake and Mouton (1982) invoke research reported by Likert (see chapter 13) and Argyris (see chapter 20) in support of their theory, but as I have indicated previously, this support is weak at best.

Several studies that deal with career accomplishment and managerial promotion rates seem to present a more favorable picture (Blake & Mouton, 1964; Hall, 1976), and in fact they have been noted by the theory's authors as providing supportive evidence (Blake & Mouton, 1982). However, the published reports of these studies are inadequate to permit a scientific evaluation. Either statistical analyses are not reported at all, or they are insufficient. In particular, experiment-wise analyses are lacking. There do appear to be some encouraging results, but unfortunately the data to fully evaluate the research are not made available.

Research at the Micro-Macro Level

Given that grid theory of leadership provides the base on which grid organization development is built, the failure to find clear support for the leadership theory presents the organization development theory with major problems. Nevertheless, the two are not inextricably linked, and a body of research on macro applications does exist.

The list of such research is headed by a group of studies featured by Blake and Mouton (1988). These were conducted at Exxon, Unilever, and United Airlines. In some cases the evaluation research covered the full six phases of the program; in other instances somewhat less than that were included. However, the authors contend that the full range of the organization development effort is not required for positive results to emerge.

The first study involved the initial refinery work at what is now Exxon. This research was reported on first by a group, including several outside evaluators from Harvard Business School (Blake, Mouton et al., 1964). Changes were monitored at least into the fifth year of the program (Blake & Mouton, 1964). Over this period the refinery shifted from a serious deficit position to one in which it returned a substantial profit. There were many changes in technology and other factors involved, but knowledgeable managers attributed at least 30 percent of the gain to the organization development effort.

Other changes included a decrease in refinery labor force that exceeded the industry average, a revised organization structure, reduced internal conflict and improved cooperation, increased skill in the use of team action, and a number of other interpersonal or intergroup improvements. Bennis (1987) points to the Exxon story as an example of a highly successful organization development program.

Nevertheless, there are problems here. For one thing, the grid approach did not spread widely within Exxon and, in fact, had largely ceased by the mid-1960s; this could be due to many factors. More important, the research design was not sufficiently controlled to attribute causation to the grid program with any degree of certainty. What is needed in these cases is a pre–post measurement on criterion variables coupled with sufficient control group measurement so that any changes attributable to factors other than the intervention can be subtracted from those found in the experimental group. Unfortunately, nothing approximating this degree of precision is reported for the Exxon research.

The Unilever study involved the full range of a grid organization development program. It used both experimental and control conditions, and data are reported from a pretest period through to the end of phase 6. Reports on this study are contained in a number of sources (see, for example, Blake & Mouton, 1982, 1985, 1988; Blake & McCanse, 1991). Comparisons were made between the Canadian and United States companies where one received the organization development program and the other did not. The findings for profitability are given in figure 21.2; they are striking. It is not clear from the reports what versions of the phase 4 through 6 interventions were introduced, nor do we know whether these advanced phase efforts actually caused the sharp improvements later in the program or whether lagged effects from the earlier phases were responsible. In any event, the program as a whole appears to have had a major effect

on profits. Concomitant with the profit changes, a number of improvements in conditions within the grid-active subsidiary are reported, especially in the area of union-management relationships.

The two components of Unilever appear to be matched on a number of factors that could affect these results, given the similarity in the operative policies that stem from the parent company and affect both. The one thing that we do not know is the extent to which the varying economies, and cultures, of the two countries involved might have influenced the findings. Since information on which country was the grid country and which was not is not provided, there is no way of checking on this hypothesis. There could have been a confounding of country differences with grid-created differences such that some or all of the profitability change is attributable to something other than the organization development program.

The third study involves United Airlines and appears to be restricted to an intervention focused on cockpit flight crews. Thus, although described as a macro organization development effort (Blake & Mouton, 1988), it probably was more micro in nature and involved only the early phases of the total grid program. In any event, pre–post comparisons indicate a 50 percent decrease in mistake rates on FAA proficiency checks (Blake & McCanse, 1991). This comparison does not involve a control group. However, such data are reported for another comparison. Across the period of the intervention the hull loss index, reflecting the miles flown without unscheduled down time for repair and maintenance, increased from 2.5 to 5.0 at United while the industry average of 2.2 remained about the same (Blake & Mouton, 1988). The data provided on this study are limited, but as far as they go they clearly appear to support the validity of the grid approach to organization development.

Evaluations in the literature other than those reported by people associated with Scientific Methods are few in number. One such study conducted in Australia focused on attitudinal changes across a 3-year grid organization development effort that appears to have progressed at least through phase 2 (Yetton & Crawford, 1992). Although control data are lacking, the findings suggest that the intervention increased dissatisfaction because it fostered participation as a one best way for everyone when, in fact, there were numerous situations where participation was unwarranted or infeasible. Thus a change in espoused behavior and company norms was created that was not

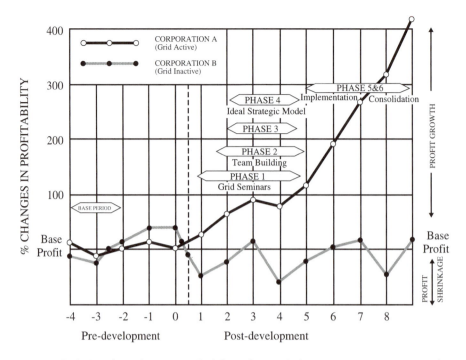

FIGURE 21.2 Timeline showing profitability of two Unilever corporate entities in the United States and Canada. From Robert R. Blake & Anne Adams McCanse (1991), *Leadership Dilemmas — Grid Solutions* (Houston: Gulf Publishing Company), 354. Copyright 1991 by Grid International Inc. Reproduced by permission of the owners.

matched by the level of participation that could realistically be achieved; the result of this disparity was considerable disenchantment and a tendency to blame the CEO who had initiated the grid program in the first place. Certainly in the CEO's eyes the intervention had been less than successful, and he was clearly not alone in this view.

Problem of Missing Data

On the evidence it would seem that grid organization development can be a success, and apparently it can also fail. What is not clear is how often one or the other of these outcomes is likely to occur. The people from Scientific Methods, and specifically the authors of grid theory, report only positive results, consistent with their desire to market their services and products and with the fact that studies are reported only in sources likely to come to the attention of potential clients. However, these same authors also report a long list of clients, and Scientific Methods is an organization with offices all over the world. In short, there appear to have been many, many opportunities to test the theory at both the micro and macro levels. Furthermore, the changes that have been introduced in the various phases of the organization development program would seem to indicate that at least some less than optimal results have been obtained.

Certain questions have been raised about the three engagements that are reported, but even greater questions would be raised if these were only the best of some 50 or so instances where, in other engagements, events did not appear to be evolving in quite as positive a manner. There is a certain confounding of marketing and scientific goals here, and realistically one has to recognize that situation. What would the missing engagements tell us if the full story were available?

Grid organization development looks to have the potential for positive consequences. Yet any such endorsement must be qualified with a healthy dose of caution. There is so much that the authors have not told us about their research efforts.

FROM PROCESS CONSULTATION
TO ORGANIZATIONAL CULTURE
AND LEADERSHIP THEORY

Edgar Schein was influenced in his approach to practice and in his theoretical thinking by a number of people, but among these he gives special credit to certain specific sources. First among these is Douglas McGregor (see the discussion of theory X and theory Y in chapter 10), who was in many respects his mentor in the early days at MIT (Schein, 1975; Luthans, 1989). The second source singled out is what is referred to as the Chicago school of sociology by which Schein (1989b) says he means Everett Hughes, Melville Dalton, and Erving Goffman. These people tried to articulate a clinical approach to their work during the late 1950s by emphasizing careful observation, sensemaking, and theories built on observational underpinnings. Schein was much impressed by this approach, and he tried to emulate it in his own work.

Background

Schein is another of those who escaped to the United States from a Hitler-dominated Europe. He was born in Switzerland in 1928 and lived in several European countries before moving to the United States in 1938. He attended the University of Chicago and graduated in 1947. Then, after a master's degree from Stanford University in 1949, he went to Harvard University, where he obtained a doctorate in social and clinical psychology in 1952. From Harvard he moved to the Walter Reed Institute of Research for a 4-year stint in the military, which included an opportunity to study released prisoners who had been brainwashed during the Korean War.

In 1956 Schein joined the faculty of the newly formed Graduate School of Management at MIT. He was hired by Douglas McGregor, who also introduced him to T-groups at the Bethel, Maine center of the National Training Laboratories and to consulting work (Schein, 1993a). He has remained at MIT throughout his career, served on the Bethel faculty during the summer months for many years, and continues as an active consultant.

The interrelationships among the various areas of Schein's interest, and his publishing, are important to an understanding of the ideas to be discussed here. His initial work was the study of how prisoners were influenced by the Chinese Communists to do and

say things that without this coercion would have been out of the question for them (Schein, 1957; Schein, Schneier, & Barker, 1961). Taking up on the issue of organizational participants' reactions to influences exerted on them by their organizations, Schein next studied the effects of companies on MIT graduates as they moved on into the labor force. This concern with processes of organizational socialization continued for some time (Schein, 1968; Van Maanen & Schein, 1979). Gradually it merged into the subsequent formulations on organizational cultures and then into a broader concern with career dynamics and career anchors (Schein, 1978, 1987b, 1996a), which became a distinct theoretical thrust of its own.

However, Schein is best known for his contributions in the areas of process consultation and organizational culture (Luthans, 1989), and it is these that are given primary attention here. The process consultation ideas represent a direct contribution to practice and they came first. They were an outgrowth of Schein's early experience with laboratory training but were colored by other influences as well (Schein & Bennis, 1965). The theory of organizational culture, and leadership influences on it, came later. The latter reflects a desire to provide a broader underpinning for the process consultation ideas and was, in addition, a natural outgrowth of the work on socialization. Also involved was an intensified exposure to other cultures worldwide through a series of visiting appointments and consulting engagements (Schein, 1993a).

Process Consultation
and Organizational Practice

The approach to practice that Schein developed was in its origins initially anti-bureaucracy simply because the laboratory training movement was of that nature. However, the idea of helping the client system help itself rapidly became central to process consulting, and with this there developed a more accepting approach to organizations in their current forms (Schein, 1990a). Yet bits and pieces of humanism and anti-bureaucracy continue to manifest themselves. There are references to bureaucracy as ineffective (Schein, 1981b), to the need to empower employees and eliminate dependence on the hierarchy (Schein, 1995), and to the uselessness of studying bureaucratic structural variables such as centralization and formalization (in Luthans, 1989). Humanistic values are frequently noted as a guiding force, although not always with positive consequences (see Schein, 1990b). The possibility of abandoning hierarchy in the world of the future is given serious consideration (Schein, 1989a).

Early Process Consultation

The initial public presentation of process consultation (Schein, 1969) had a long history in the author's existing consulting practice, but not a long gestation period. The 1969 book was a first attempt to explain what was already an established approach. The definition of process consulting, along with the assumptions behind it, which derive from laboratory training, are as follows:

Definition. Process consulting is a set of activities on the part of the consultant which help the client to perceive, understand, and act upon process events which occur in the client's environment.

1. Managers often do not know what is wrong and need special help in diagnosing what their problems actually are.
2. Managers often do not know what kinds of help consultants can give to them.
3. Most managers have a constructive intent to improve things, but need help in identifying what to improve and how to improve it.
4. Most organizations can be more effective if they learn to diagnose their own strengths and weaknesses. . . . every . . . organization will have some weaknesses.
5. A consultant could probably not . . . learn enough about the culture . . . to suggest reliable new courses of action. . . . He must work jointly with members of the organization who do know the culture.
6. One of the process consultant's roles is to provide new and challenging alternatives. . . . Decision-making . . . must, however, remain in the hands of the client.
7. It is of prime importance that the process consultant be expert in how to *diagnose* and . . . *establish effective helping relationships* with clients. Effective process consultation involves passing on . . . these skills. (Schein, 1969, pp. 8–9)

The human processes involved here that contribute to organizational effectiveness include communication, member roles and functions in groups, group problem-solving, group norms and growth, leadership and authority, and intergroup cooperation or competition. The approach clearly operates primarily at the group level.

The stages of process consultation tend to overlap one another. However, they may be specified as follows:

1. Initial contact with the client organization—indication of the perceived problem
2. Defining the relationship, including the formal and psychological contract—focus on how the group gets its work done
3. Selecting a setting (what and when to observe, as near the top of the organization as possible, one in which it is easy to observe group processes, one in which real work is involved) and a method of work (as congruent as possible with process consultation values, thus making the consultant maximally visible to develop trust)
4. Data gathering and diagnosis, which inevitably are interventions—use of observation and interviews, but not questionnaires and survey measures, which are too impersonal
5. Intervention—in declining order of likelihood, the use of agenda-setting interventions, feedback of observations or data, coaching or counseling, and structural suggestions (which occur rarely)
6. Evaluation and disengagement—looking for evidence of changes in values as related to concern for human problems and process issues, as well as in interpersonal skills

Throughout, efforts are concentrated on helping the organization to become aware of organizational processes and to engage in self-diagnosis. Much of what is described represents extending laboratory training into the real, working groups of an ongoing organization.

Process Consultation in Maturity

While Schein's first presentation was intended largely to tell his colleagues what he did out in the corporate world, his initial writing in the 1980s was directed much more at managers. The intent was to show them how they could exert influence without resort to power and authority (Schein, 1987c) and, thus, to demonstrate the value of assuming the same helping role that process consultants assume. When this happens, the organization achieves its goals and subordinates are helped to grow and develop. In discussing these process interventions, Schein has the following to say:

1. Process is always to be favored as an intervention focus over content.
2. Task process is always to be favored over interpersonal process.
3. Structural interventions are in principle the most powerful . . . but they are also likely to be most resisted. (1987c, p. 52)

The list of human processes that contribute to organizational effectiveness is extended to include intrapsychic processes, cultural rules of interaction, and change processes as epitomized by Lewin's unfreezing-moving-refreezing model. The intervention process is expounded in much greater detail; four basic types are noted: exploratory interventions (What do you have in mind?), diagnostic interventions (Why is this more of a problem now?), action alternative interventions (Have you considered either of these alternatives?), confrontive interventions (It sounds to me like you feel angry at this person, is that right?). Also a variety of techniques that may be built into process consultation with the assistance of key client members are noted: intergroup exercises, survey feedback, role playing, educational interventions, responsibility-charting, and many others. In dealing with structural issues, process consultants should limit themselves to raising questions that make structural options clear.

In a small book written in this period, Schein (1987a) makes a distinction between the clinical perspective that characterizes process consultation and the ethnographic perspective of the cultural anthropologist. The former focuses on helping and producing change, while the latter is concerned with obtaining valid data for science and leaving the system undisturbed. To really understand an organization, both approaches must be combined in some manner.

Schein (1988) is a revision of the 1969 volume with considerable expansion of the discussion. The definition of process consultation noted previously is amended by adding the phrase "in order to improve the situation as defined by the client" (p. 11). A chapter is added on performance appraisal and feedback on the grounds that both appraisal and process consultation require skills in giving feedback. The general structure of this book, however, is much the same as that of its predecessor.

Revisitation

In returning one more time to the topic of process consultation Schein (1999b) covers many of the same matters that were considered in previous volumes. But there are additional points made as well. Process consultation, for instance, is likened to Argyris's double loop learning in that the intent is to increase the client system's capacity for learning. Furthermore, a set of principles is set forth with the intent of providing guidance to the process consultant:

1. Always try to be helpful.
2. Always stay in touch with the current reality.
3. Access your ignorance.
4. Everything you do is an intervention.
5. It is the client who owns the problem and the solution.
6. Go with the flow.
7. Timing is crucial.
8. Be constructively opportunistic with confrontive interventions.
9. Everything is a source of data; errors will occur and are the prime source of learning.
10. When in doubt, share the problem. (Schein, 1999b, p. 60)

Although these principles are amplified with much more specific detail, their listing here helps to provide a feeling for what process consultation entails.

Schein (1999b) now places considerable stress on a technique called dialogue, which may be used with quite large groups and which he contrasts with the sensitivity training approach that came more directly out of the laboratory training at Bethel. The following quotes reflect a certain distancing from the positions Schein took in the 1960s:

Sensitivity training is focused more on hearing others' *feelings* and tuning in on all the levels of communication; dialogue is focused more on the *thinking* process and how our perceptions and cognitions are preformed by our past experiences. (1999b, p. 203)

In the typical sensitivity-training workshop, participants explore relationships . . . through giving and receiving deliberate feedback. . . . In dialogue, the participants explore *all* the complexities of thinking and language. (1999b, pp. 203–204)

In sensitivity training the goal is to use the group process to develop our *individual* interpersonal skills, whereas dialogue aims to build a group that can think generatively, creatively, and most importantly *together*. . . . Dialogue is thus a potential vehicle for creative problem identification and problem solving. (1999b, p. 204)

It is this latter feature that makes dialogue particularly attractive for use within the context of process consultation; it now appears to have taken center stage.

Theory of Organizational Culture and Leadership

The concept of organizational culture can be found in Schein's earlier writings, and in Blake's too, but in the 1980s this is a topic that suffused the field of organizational behavior. Schein was at the forefront of this onslaught, starting with a number of articles that dealt with components of his theory. These often derived from the work on socialization and careers, but they were also informed by their author's experiences as a process consultant (Schein, 1981a, 1983, 1984a, 1984b). This all came together in a subsequent book that represents the most comprehensive theoretical statement (Schein, 1985). This book is the primary source for the following discussion.

Basic Statement

Leadership comes in the front door of any discussion of culture because what leaders actually do, as distinct from managers, is to create and change cultures. Culture, in turn, means

> a pattern of basic assumptions—invented, discovered, or developed by a given group as it learns to cope with its problems of external adaptation and internal integration—that has worked well enough to be considered valid and, therefore, to be taught to new members as the correct way to perceive, think, and feel in relation to those problems. (Schein, 1985, p. 9)

Figure 21.3 depicts the levels of culture; the essence of organizational culture is at the level of basic assumptions. These assumptions set limits on corporate strategies such that if the alignment is not appropriate the strategies cannot be implemented. Thus, cultures, like structures, are a means to strategic implementation, and, in fact, cultures incorporate structures as one of their components.

Schein's knowledge of cultures and his ideas about them derive primarily from his clinical experience with them, and thus from process consultation. This may be a limited perspective in certain respects, but it is a rich source as well. However, just as Schein's consulting has been focused at the group level, his concept of culture has a similar focus:

> Culture formation is . . . identical with the process of group formation in that the very essence of "groupness" or group identity—the shared patterns of thought, belief, feelings, and values that result from shared experience and common learning—is what we ultimately end up calling the "culture" of that group. . . . So group growth and culture formation can be seen as two sides of the same coin, and both are the result of leadership activities.
>
> What we need to understand, then, is how the *individual* intentions of the founders, leaders, or conveners of a new group or organization, their own definitions of the situation, their assumptions and values, come to be a *shared, consensually validated* set of definitions that are passed on to new members as "the correct way to define the situation." (Schein, 1985, p. 50)

Cultures are interrelated sets of assumptions and thus multidimensional. They are far superior to typologies, such as those involving bureaucracy, as bases for understanding organizations; two organizations with the same structures may otherwise have totally different cultures.

The recommended approach to deciphering culture is observation and interviews. Artifacts are used only to check hypotheses that are derived from other sources. Culture questionnaires are not recommended because they get at espoused values at best. They do not tap the basic assumptions that represent the essence of culture. Also Schein has serious doubts about the efficacy of feeding back written culture descriptions to the organization involved. To do this is often interpreted as akin to an invasion of privacy. It may remove the defenses against anxiety that the culture provides for its members and thus leave them emotionally exposed.

Culture and Leadership

Culture is the result of group learning experiences in which a number of people face a problem and work out a solution together. To the extent the solution is effective, it and the factors associated with it become embedded in the emerging culture. Variations in cultures reflect differences in the personalities of leaders,

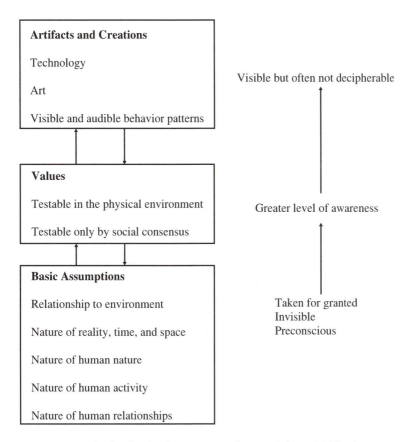

Artifacts and Creations

Technology

Art

Visible and audible behavior patterns

Visible but often not decipherable

Values

Testable in the physical environment

Testable only by social consensus

Greater level of awareness

Basic Assumptions

Relationship to environment

Nature of reality, time, and space

Nature of human nature

Nature of human activity

Nature of human relationships

Taken for granted
Invisible
Preconscious

FIGURE 21.3 The levels of culture. From Edgar H. Schein (1985), *Organizational Culture and Leadership* (San Francisco: Jossey-Bass), 14. Copyright 1985 by Jossey-Bass. Reprinted by permission of Jossey-Bass, Inc., a subsidiary of John Wiley & Sons, Inc.

members, and the circumstances of early problem solutions. It is assumed that all organizations start as small groups, and that therefore organizational cultures inevitably have their origins in the development of group norms.

Both at the level of the initial group and as organizational dynamics are added with growth, founders and leaders are a key ingredient of culture formation. Founders have a vision for the organization and they bring in others who share this vision. Founders also have strong assumptions in the areas noted in figure 21.3, and many of these assumptions survive in the culture because they contribute to effective problem solutions. If this is not the case the venture fails. As certain founder assumptions prove effective, they reduce the anxieties of members, and this reinforces learning of specific ways of thinking and doing things. Thus a process of cultural embedding occurs.

The primary mechanisms for embedding are (1) the things leaders pay attention to, measure and control; (2) leader reaction to critical incidents or crises; (3) deliberate leader role modeling and teaching; (4) the criteria for allocation of rewards and status applied; and (5) the criteria for recruitment, selection, promotion, and termination applied. In addition, there are certain secondary mechanisms for embedding that work only if they are logically consistent with the primary ones; to obtain this reinforcing effect, leaders attempt to control these secondary mechanisms. They are (1) organizational structure and design, (2) organizational procedures and systems, (3) the design of buildings and physical space, (4) stories and myths about important people and events, and (5) formal statements of organizational philosophies and missions.

The cultures thus constructed can be very strong, so that much change can occur within an organization, even though the basic culture remains unmoved. When culture change does become an issue, however, the change mechanisms that are mobilized, and the unfreezing forces which begin to operate, appear to be a function of the firm's age. Table 21.1 demonstrates how the growth stages of an organization influence culture changes.

At both stage I and stage II, organizational theory and development are noted as change mechanisms on the ground that culture is in part a defense mechanism to protect against anxiety, and, consequently, these approaches should be appropriate to helping organizations change themselves. Organization devel-

opment, although not totally of a therapeutic nature, does start with therapeutic interventions intended to promote self-insight. In this connection Schein (1985) indicates doubts as to whether Blake and Mouton's grid approach is sufficient to produce culture change. To achieve change it is necessary to bring the buried assumptions of culture to the surface in such a way that they are confronted and evaluated; this is rare.

In closing the 1985 discussion Schein emphasizes various "do nots" for managers. Such concepts as values, climate, and corporate philosophy are determined by culture, but managers should not assume that they *are* the culture; culture operates at a deeper level.

TABLE 21.1 Growth stages, functions of culture, and change mechanisms

Growth stage	Function of culture/issue	Change mechanisms
I. *Birth and early growth* Founder domination, possible family domination	Culture is a distinctive competence and source of identity Culture is the "glue" that holds organization together Organization strives toward more integration and clarity Heavy emphasis on socialization as evidence of commitment	Natural evolution Self-guided evolution through organizational therapy Managed evolution through hybrids Managed "revolution" through outsiders
Succession phase	Culture becomes battleground between conservatives and liberals Potential successors are judged on whether they will preserve or change cultural elements	
II. *Organizational midlife* Expansion of products/ markets Vertical integration Geographical expansion Acquisitions, mergers	Cultural integration declines as new subcultures are spawned Loss of key goals, values, and assumptions creates crisis of identity Opportunity to manage direction of cultural change is provided	Planned change and organization development Technological seduction Change through scandal, explosion of myths Incrementalism
III. *Organizational maturity* Maturity or decline of markets Increasing internal stability and/or stagnation Lack of motivation to change	Culture becomes a constraint on innovation Culture preserves the glories of the past, hence is valued as a source of self-esteem, defense	Coercive persuasion Turnaround Reorganization, destruction, rebirth
Transformation option	Culture change is necessary and inevitable, but not all elements of culture can or must change Essential elements of culture must be identified, preserved Culture change can be managed or simply allowed to evolve	
Destruction option Bankruptcy and reorganization Takeover and reorganization Merger and assimilation	Cultural changes at fundamental paradigm levels Culture changes through massive replacement of key people	

SOURCE: Edgar H. Schein (1985), *Organizational Culture and Leadership* (San Francisco: Jossey-Bass), 271–272. Copyright 1985 by Jossey-Bass. Reprinted by permission of Jossey-Bass, Inc., a subsidiary of John Wiley & Sons, Inc.

Assuming that culture applies to the human side of the organization only is also a mistake; products, markets, missions, and the like are also important aspects of culture. Culture cannot easily be manipulated, and to assume otherwise can produce trouble; managers are controlled by culture much more than they control it. No culture should be assumed to be inherently better than others, and strong cultures are not better than weak ones. Do not assume that culture relates only to the matter of organizational effectiveness; it is much more than that.

Subcultures and the Learning Leader

In the preface of his second edition, Schein says that "the major changes are in dropping various materials that were peripheral to culture and in adding a number of chapters on subculture, culture deciphering, and the learning leader and culture" (1992, p. xvii). There is less attention to theory and more concern with subcultures.

The proposed method of deciphering culture is a considerable extension of the earlier procedures. It starts with establishing the commitment of leadership to deal with some problem (usually strategic) that is assumed to require culture change. A group of up to 50 members from the culture is then constituted, and the process consultants works with them by giving an initial lecture on the nature of culture, eliciting values, and probing into the area of shared underlying assumptions. The last process involves looking for disparities between identified artifacts and proclaimed values. Next, the large group is split into subgroups, which, if possible, represent subcultures within the whole. These subgroups work on identifying more assumptions and on categorizing assumptions as to whether they will help or hinder solution of the problem at hand. The subgroups report back to the whole where consensus is ironed out. The change process is then initiated with a lecture on that subject, new subgroups, and the development of a change strategy by the whole.

Subcultures tend to form around areas of differentiation within the organization—functional units, geographical divisions, acquisitions, and the like. Usually the people in these components carry with them an outside culture that becomes melded into the prevailing organizational culture to form a subculture. Professional identifications, geographical variations, customer characteristics, and such may thus intrude into the process of culture formation. Subcultures also form at various levels of the managerial hierarchy, where they are influenced by the types of tasks to be performed. Sometimes subcultures arise that are deliberately countercultural vis-à-vis the main culture; diversity on ethnic, racial, gender, and other such grounds can also be a source. A particularly salient subculture at present often develops around the information technology component.

An especially intriguing challenge for leadership is to develop a learning organization that can continue to make its own diagnoses and self-manage the change process. Such a culture institutionalizes learning and innovation. Schein's (1992) theory of the assumptions inherent in such a culture is set forth in table 21.2. This is a very difficult type of culture to establish and maintain.

As stated previously, leadership is the capacity to understand and change cultures; this applies to subcultures as well as main cultures. Different stages of organizational development (see table 21.1) require different approaches to handling culture, as do different strategic issues. Dealing with cultural transformations requires a leader who is a perpetual learner. Leaders of this kind must possess the following:

1. New levels of perception and insight into the realities of the world and also into themselves
2. Extraordinary levels of motivation to go through the inevitable pain of learning and change
3. The emotional strength to manage their own and others' anxiety as learning and change become more and more a way of life
4. New skills in analyzing and changing cultural assumptions
5. The willingness and ability to involve others and elicit their participation
6. The ability to learn the assumptions of a whole new organizational culture (Schein, 1992, pp. 391–392)

Schein (1996c) provides a particularly insightful analysis of how leaders can create and nurture an organizational culture, with special reference to the role that Singapore's Economic Development Board has played in the economic success of that country.

Cultural Learning and Change

More recently Schein has concentrated on giving his theory wider exposure and on fine-tuning some of

TABLE 21.2 Assumptions required for a perpetually learning culture

Assumption regarding	Learning culture response
Relationships to the environment	Organization dominant
Nature of reality (truth)	Pragmatic
Nature of time	Near-future oriented, medium units of time
Nature of human nature	Basically good, mutable
Nature of human activity	Proactive
Nature of human relationships	Blend of groupism-individualism, blend of authoritative-collegial
Information and communication	Fully connected
Subcultural uniformity vs. diversity	High diversity
Task vs. relationship orientation	Blend of task and relationship orientation
Linear vs. systemic field logic	Systemic thinking

SOURCE: Adapted from Edgar H. Schein (1992), *Organizational Culture and Leadership*, 2nd ed. (San Francisco: Jossey-Bass), 364–372.

the ideas. A small book (Schein, 1999a) is the major vehicle for these latter purposes, although there are several significant theoretical extensions noted there also. Among these is a treatment of the anxiety that is associated with learning, and particularly with the learning that occurs during culture change. This learning anxiety can be disruptive, and, accordingly, leaders must create a sense of psychological safety by providing a compelling positive vision, formal training such as team building, for involvement of the learner, practice opportunities and feedback, positive role models, support groups, and consistent systems and structures. Without these conditions, change programs will fail.

Culture change normally requires establishing a temporary parallel learning system where new assumptions are practiced and learned in comparative safety. The establishment of various groups to foster change is inherent in this parallel learning procedure. The steps involved are (1) to ensure that before anything else the leaders have learned something new, (2) for the leaders to create a change management group or steering committee, (3) for this steering committee to go through its own learning process, (4) for the steering committee to design the organizational learning process to include various task forces focused on the major issues, (5) for these task forces to learn how to learn, (6) for the task forces to create specific change programs, (7) for the steering committee to maintain communication through the change process, and, finally, (8) for the steering committee to develop mechanisms for continuous learning (Schein, 1993b). Pro-

cess consultants work with these various groups to facilitate the learning and change processes.

Previously we have considered the dialogue approach as it relates to process consultation. Schein (1993c, 1996d, 1999a) also introduces the dialogue concept into his discussion of culture. He feels it is a particularly appropriate technique for bridging the gaps between organizational cultures when companies are joined via merger and acquisition, or when subcultures are in conflict. Among the latter situations are those involving different levels of the management hierarchy, as well as the perennial disparities between the executive, engineering, and operating cultures in manufacturing firms. Dialogue is the method of choice for dealing with differences that extend across culture boundaries, especially differences that need to be ironed out during periods of culture change.

Evaluation and Impact

Schein (in Luthans, 1989) notes that somewhere in the 1960s he largely gave up on experimentation because he felt work of this kind was not adequate to explain the real world variables with which he was dealing in process consultation. The result has been that he has neither carried out research to evaluate the results of his process consulting engagements nor conducted tests of his culture and leadership theory. In fact, there is little by way of discussion of research in Schein's writing on these subjects; he appears to perceive himself as a clinician, not a researcher, and at times he seems to be unsure as to whether he is a theorist, either. Yet he has contrived a logically tight and compelling theory, as well as methods of approaching the measurement of many of its variables. It is simply that he prefers to leave the whole matter of conducting related research to others, if they feel that is what is needed, or possible. He, himself, has not published research in the scholarly literature since the 1960s, although he has made contributions of other kinds to this literature (see for example Schein, 1996b). For a statement of his current thinking on research, which is basically unchanged, see Schein (2000).

Status of Research on
Process Consultation

As so often happens, the author of this approach to organization development has served as a role model for others in the field of organizational behavior. His failure to conduct research on process consultation has been emulated by others. There is no research to my knowledge that one can point to and say "this is a test of the effectiveness of Schein's procedure for carrying out organization development." Schein does not mention any such studies, although there are investigations that attempt to assess procedures of a *human processual* nature, to include team building, T-groups and other techniques that Schein has used on occasion. We will consider these shortly. The problem is that without specific guidance on the matter, it is impossible to determine whether a given application was carried out in a manner that Schein would accept as an appropriate instance of his process consultation. Thus a particular study may or may not be suitable for consideration as a test. Lacking guidance from Schein we cannot know.

There is some evidence that relates to the viability and impact of process consultation, however. A study conducted by Allan Church, Warner Burke and Donald Van Eynde (1994) indicates that approaches to organization development other than process consultation have achieved greater popularity in the field; nevertheless, process consultation ranks fifth among 22 interventions and activities considered. Another study (McMahan & Woodman, 1992) uses broader categories of analysis and focuses only on internal OD consultants, but seems to indicate that roughly one-third of the time of these individuals is devoted to something that would pass as process consultation. Although indicative of substantial popularity, comparisons with data for 10 years earlier suggest a considerable decline in the use of process consultation procedures.

A final point is made in a discussion of the use of organization development approaches in relatively small entrepreneurial firms. W. Gibb Dyer (1997), who has had considerable experience with process consultation, reports that in his experience these firms require content consulting in addition to a process approach. This focus on both the content of the problem and the process used to solve it appears to be spreading into some applications in larger firms as well. Relying entirely on the knowledge base of the firm involved in the manner of process consultation would appear to be on the decline.

Status of Research on Cultures
and Leadership Theory

There is a dearth of solid research testing Schein's theory of cultures and leadership, but not for the same reasons. The often unconscious or preconscious nature of cultural assumptions, combined with the fact that the study of culture has its origins in clinical and ethnographic approaches that are primarily based in anthropological observations, has made for a situation where qualitative procedures far outweigh the quantitative. As a result, numerous theories of organizational culture have emerged, often with diverse viewpoints (Martin, 1992), but little by way of quantitative testing. Thus Schein's theory is in the position of being merely one among many such theories whose validity is unknown, even though it was received with considerable acclaim and appears to have substantial potential.

The study of organizational culture has been described as in a state of chaos at present (Martin & Frost, 1996), and with good reason. There is no science to sort out truth from fantasy, and stridency of protestation becomes the major criterion for fleeting acceptance. This state of affairs appears to be primarily attributable to the strong qualitative orientation of the field, and this is readily evident from a reading of edited volumes on organizational culture (see, for example, Frost, Moore, Louis, Lundberg, & Martin, 1991).

Although many have argued that organizational culture is not amenable to quantitative research, and some view it as outside the realm of science as well, these positions do not seem tenable. Just as projective techniques can be used to get at unconscious motivation in micro organizational behavior, they can be used to get at cultural assumptions in macro organizational behavior. The Thematic Apperception Test has been proposed as particularly applicable for this purpose (Trice, 1991). Furthermore, observations and field notes can be categorized and scored to get at dimensions of culture, and these procedures can be repeated to determine reliability of measurement. My point is that techniques are available to test the hypotheses of culture theories. The preference of those who work in the field for producing what amounts to fiction (Trice, 1991) cannot be an excuse for leaving theories untested. Unfortunately, the theory of organizational culture and leadership that Schein has proposed has become caught up in all this. As a consequence, we cannot know its validity.

Effectiveness of Organization Development in the Early Period

Organization development comes in many colors, as we have seen. In addition, researchers in the field have not always described in sufficient detail either the techniques used or the theories that underlie these efforts. Thus, reviews of the research literature often provide a good indication of the effectiveness of organization development as a whole, while leaving the specifics of what changed what and what theory worked best rather uncertain. Nevertheless, by looking at these reviews, we can reach some conclusions about the effectiveness of the various approaches and theories considered in this and the preceding chapter, and particularly those of Edgar Schein.

In fact, the amount of research on the topic is quite extensive, going back a number of years. The quality of this research has been questioned on occasion, but it appears to be adequate and it is improving. Roughly 75 percent of early studies, and by that I mean those conducted before the mid-1970s, used procedures related to laboratory training at some point in the overall process and thus had something in common with process consultation. There clearly have been major changes in the nature of organization development practice over the years (Esper, 1990; Sanzgiri & Gottlieb, 1992), which were particularly pronounced during the 1970s as T-groups and sensitivity training fell into disrepute. Thus, it is appropriate to separate the reviews conducted before and after the middle of that decade; they deal with different types of interventions.

In chapter 13, reference was made to an analysis by David Bowers (1973) of data from organization development programs carried out in 23 organizations. Laboratory training had a predominantly negative impact using the system 4–oriented Survey of Organizations variables. Related approaches along the lines of process consultation yield somewhat more positive results, or at least somewhat less negative. Overall, the results are not favorable to the kinds of interventions we have been considering. Importantly, however, all these studies were carried out in conjunction with the Survey Research Center at the University of Michigan and relied entirely on a single change measure that dealt primarily with climate.

Analyses that cast a wider net tend to yield somewhat more favorable results. Clayton Alderfer (1977) considers a still limited range of studies and finds evidence for changes in work attitudes, production rates, quality of production, turnover, and absenteeism—all in an organizationally positive direction. The results of a much more extensive research survey by Jerry Porras and Per Berg (1978) are outlined in table 21.3. Their most striking finding is the high frequency of change in performance indices, as contrasted with factors such as individual job satisfaction. Although these results do not allow us to isolate the effects of procedures based on laboratory training only, the results cannot be entirely independent of laboratory training procedures simply because some 75 percent of the studies used them. When traditional laboratory training was the dominant intervention, however, the percentage of significant results obtained was the lowest among the five approaches considered and a more task-focused version of laboratory training was only slightly superior. Overall, the data suggest that positive results can be anticipated approximately half the time and that organizationally significant factors such as profits, performance, and output are most likely to be affected.

An additional review by Peter Smith, which focuses on the effects of laboratory training as well as its use in organization development, concludes:

> Of the studies reviewed in this article, 100 permit the drawing of a conclusion as to whether or not an effect of training was obtained. Of these studies, 78 did show an increase in one or more scores after training which was significantly greater than any change the controls may have shown. . . . Only 31 studies permitted the drawing of a conclusion

TABLE 21.3 Changes resulting from organization development interventions ($N = 35$ studies)

Type of measure	Proportion of studies where a type of measure was used yielding significant changes (%)
All studies[a]	
Individual satisfaction	38
Group performance	63
Organizational economic performance	65
Turnover and absenteeism	50
People-oriented process variables (i.e., motivation)	46
Task-oriented process variables (i.e., goal emphasis)	45
Individual process variables (i.e., openness)	62
By type of dominant intervention	
Laboratory training	
Outcome variables (satisfaction, performance, etc.)	44
Process variables (motivation, goal emphasis, etc.)	44
Task-focused laboratory training—team building	
Outcome variables	53
Process variables	45

a. Approximately three-quarters of these studies used some form of laboratory training.

SOURCE: Adapted from Jerry I. Porras & Per O. Berg (1978), The Impact of Organization Development, *Academy of Management Review*, 3, 254–259

as to persistence of change at follow-up. Of these 21 did show persistence of change. (Smith, 1975, p. 615)

In the organization development context, changes of some kind were found with even greater frequency, but not always in total alignment with the trainers' intentions:

The use of sensitivity training within organizational development can frequently achieve effects. These effects have not always been the intended ones, but the existing studies do not make it possible to formulate any hypotheses as to what differentiates the projects which fail to achieve their purpose. More intuitive data would suggest a wealth of historical and cultural factors with which organizational change agents need to contend. (Smith, 1975, p. 615)

In short, the approach pioneered by Argyris, Bennis, and Schein can work, but it is difficult to predict either the exact nature of the effect, or even when an effect will occur. The possibility of organizationally undesirable outcomes must be considered real.

More Recent Studies of Organization Development Effectiveness

As we move beyond the 1970s, the number of studies increases and so does the number of reviews. However, the most pronounced change is the diversity of types of interventions introduced. A recent handbook covers a wide range of approaches but makes practically no mention of process consultation or of Schein's work at all (Holman & Devane, 1999). Therefore it is quite possible for a research review to cover a varied set of studies, only a few of which fall within the purview that we have been considering; this is in marked contrast to the situation that existed in the early period. There clearly has been a shift to other approaches beyond process consultation, as was documented previously.

A review by Marshall Sashkin and Burke (1990) dealt with publications of the 1980s. They conclude that there can be little doubt that organization development overall has major positive effects on performance measures. However, there is also some evidence that these results may be obtained at the cost of performance pressures, which, in turn, create negative satisfaction and attitude changes. They note that team building using established employee groups has become a key ingredient of practice and that organizational culture is increasingly discussed in the literature, although with little by way of systematic research to support it. No theory of organization development processes was found to have achieved consensus support within the field.

Porras and Peter Robertson (1992) carried out a literature review that permits breakdown by several types of interventions. What are called social factor interventions—which includes process consultation—had the highest proportion of positive outcomes at 51 percent (only 6 percent were negative). Figures at or above the 50 percent level were obtained for a number of types of criteria, including individual behavior, organizational outcomes, social factors, and organizing arrangements. These results for social factor interventions may be contrasted with the figure of 38 percent obtained for organization development interventions of all types. These results appear to be much the same, insofar as human processual interventions are concerned, as those obtained in the early period. This occurs in spite of the fact that there would seem to have been a reduced emphasis on the need to resort to participation in the more recent period.

Porras and Robert Silvers (1991) provide an extensive review of the literature up to that point, including several meta-analyses that were conducted during the 1980s. Their conclusions are consistently positive, except that organization development does not appear to work well in professional contexts; it works best within the bureaucratic confines that it was originally intended to supplant.

Team building has been a feature of many process consultation interventions over the years. The research evidence has generally indicated a positive influence on satisfaction and attitudes but has been somewhat mixed insofar as improved productivity is concerned. A recent meta-analytic review was undertaken with the specific intent of dealing with the latter issue (Svyantek, Goodman, Benz, & Gard, 1999). The studies involved were published over a period from 1967 to 1986. The conclusion was that team building did have a significant positive impact on productivity, whether measured in objective or subjective terms. Interestingly, however, participation by the group in developing the plan for team building and the use of action research procedures decreased the effect of team building; this appears to be inconsistent with Argyris's expectations (see chapter 20 in this volume).

Overall, the results of evaluation research seem to be consistent with the claims for process consultation. We cannot know for sure whether process consultation per se produced these results because the data are expressed in terms that seem to overrepresent (social factors, human processual) or underrepresent (sensitivity training, team building) the totality of the process consulting approach. Nevertheless, the findings are distinctly encouraging. If they were otherwise, this research would almost certainly be used to argue that process consultation does not work well.

Golembiewski's Concept of Alpha, Beta, and Gamma Change

Robert Golembiewski has developed with others a theory of the change process that occurs with organization development. It is not a theory of organizational structure or process, comparable to those we have been considering. Rather, it is more limited in scale and focuses on the nature and measurement of the changes that occur as organization development programs are implemented. Nevertheless, it is important for Schein's views and for other approaches to organization development.

Golembiewski received his doctorate from Yale University in political science in 1958. He first entered a business school at the University of Illinois in 1960, and toward the middle of that decade, having been introduced to laboratory training as a result of a visiting appointment at Yale arranged by Argyris, he began to concentrate in the area of organization development (Golembiewski, 1992). He has continued to work in that area since, primarily as a faculty member at the University of Georgia, where he has remained for many years. His approach to practice appears to be similar to Schein's in many respects, and, in fact, he has endorsed process consultation in its early applications (Golembiewski, 1989).

One of Golembiewski's major concerns has been the evaluation of the success achieved by various organization development programs. He has written on this subject from various perspectives, including his own studies (see, for example, Boss & Golembiewski, 1995), reviews of studies conducted by others (as in Golembiewski, 1991), and reviews of closely related literatures (Golembiewski & Sun, 1990). He concludes that organization development is successful in achieving its objectives roughly 70 percent of the time based on the typical review, with a lower bound of

50 percent among the numerous analyses (Golembiewski, 1989). This appears somewhat optimistic, based on the data presented previously.

From this line of work emerged a question as to what really changes as a result of organization development interventions. The major contribution to answering this question was an article describing alpha, beta, and gamma change (Golembiewski, Billingsley, & Yeager, 1976); subsequent restatements followed shortly thereafter (see, for example, Golembiewski, 1977), and there have also been elaborations of a more recent vintage (as, for instance, Golembiewski, 1986). The definitions of the three types of change are as follows:

> *Alpha change* involves a variation in the level of some existential state, given a constantly calibrated measuring instrument related to a constant conceptual domain.
>
> *Beta change* involves a variation in the level of some existential state, complicated by the fact that some intervals of the measurement continuum associated with a constant conceptual domain have been recalibrated.
>
> *Gamma change* involves a redefinition or reconceptualization of some domain, a major change in the perspective or frame-of-reference within which phenomena are perceived and classified, in what is taken to be relevant in some slice of reality. (Golembiewski et al., 1976, pp. 134–135)

Alpha changes, then, occur along relatively stable dimensions defined in terms of discrete and constant intervals. Beta changes are characterized by shifts in the intervals used and involve restandardization of a measure in the mind of the respondent. Gamma changes involve a redefining of the psychological space covered by a measure, such as shifting from one construct to another or expanding the domain envisaged by a given construct; thus new meanings are introduced.

Alpha change is what we normally assume to occur across the process of an intervention when we repeat measurements over time. Yet there is convincing evidence that beta and gamma changes can occur as well, and usually without their effects being evident to the researcher; thus we have a potential source of error.

This potentiality for error is particularly pronounced in organization development evaluations for three reasons. First, most interventions are intended to produce gamma change, and probably beta change

as well. Organization development is typically viewed as a process for introducing a new social order or a new culture. It intends to change values and ways of perceiving; concepts of ideal states are expected to shift. If these changes do not occur, then the effort is likely to be considered ineffectual, but if they do occur, beta and gamma changes are introduced, which, in turn, confound the measurement process.

Second, beta and gamma change are most likely to influence self-report measures when meanings and standards within the individual tend to determine the data; this is in contrast to projective measures or hard data outcome measures of productivity. These self-reports are often used to evaluate the results of organization development interventions, either in the form of survey questionnaires or, less often, standardized interviews. To the extent these approaches are used, conclusions regarding organization development success rates are placed in jeopardy.

Third, procedures of various kinds aimed at detecting beta and gamma change have been developed; some are statistical in nature, and some involve innovations in research design. There are numerous remaining problems in this regard, but procedures do exist (Porras & Robertson, 1992). The problem is that beyond the research employed to develop them, they are not used in the actual conduct of evaluation studies (Porras & Silvers, 1991; Sashkin & Burke, 1990). Thus, in spite of the substantial increase in knowledge that has occurred as a result of Golembiewski's theory of change processes, there has been little impact on evaluation practice. Beta and gamma changes continue to lie there, suspected now, but still undetected.

Consequences of the Tripartite Theory

What then does Golembiewski's theory mean for the success rates noted previously, which are predicated on the incorrect assumption that all change is alpha in nature? The original instigation for the theory came from a deviant case when an evaluation by the usual self-report methods indicated failure, as indicated by no change from pretest to posttest. Yet participants in the intervention insisted on its overall success. This type of situation would suggest that the research reports may represent underestimates. Others have reached this same conclusion:

> While beta change is a phenomenon relevant only to variables measured through reports of organiza-

618 FIRST-GENERATION THEORIES: BUREAUCRACY

tional members, sufficient number of the variables in these studies were measured in this manner that we believe beta change could be partly responsible for the frequent occurrence of a lack of change in the dependent variables. (Porras & Robertson, 1992, p. 808)

Gamma change is another matter, but given the thrust of organization development in general, one might anticipate that if this type of change occurs at all, it would be of a kind to foster the intervention's values and new meanings. This remains to be empirically demonstrated, however.

An example of how beta and gamma changes might operate is provided by Bowers's (1973) comparative study of interventions in 23 organizations using the Survey of Organizations developed by Likert at the University of Michigan. If an intervention produced recalibration, that recalibration could serve to shift the ideal against which judgments are made upward toward system 4. Accordingly, the self-report of current circumstances made relative to the new, not the old, ideal would be less positive than would have been the case had the old ideal been used. Similarly, one intervention approach, such as survey feedback, might be dominated by alpha change, while another, such as laboratory training, might reflect primarily gamma change; this gamma change would not be picked up at all by the pre–post self-report measures.

One solution to the problems thus identified is to use measures other than those of a self-report nature. This has been done with measures of performance, including productivity, absenteeism, turnover and the like; positive results have been obtained with these kinds of measures, thus providing confidence in the success rates reported. Another alternative would be to use projective measures that call for individuals to provide responses which are interpreted by the researcher, not the individuals themselves as in the self-report techniques; this approach has not been used to my knowledge.

There is also the question of whether beta and gamma changes—if they do operate to decrease the amount of recognized change—do so to a meaningful degree. Some beta change and most gamma change would seem to require basic cultural changes before their mechanisms are activated. Yet Schein contends that such changes are difficult to achieve and probably occur rarely; most interventions produce their results within the flexibility allowed by the existing culture.

If this is the case, we are dealing with a real phenomenon, yet one that has only minimal effects on the results obtained. Clearly there remains a great deal for research to tell us. However, it does appear that if the variables of the tripartite theory do have a meaningful influence, it is to increase the size of positive success findings in most instances. Since the effects of approaches akin to process consultation are often evaluated using self-report measures, this would seem to provide increased support for this type of approach to organization development.

CONCLUSIONS

Because different approaches to organization development are now driven by very different organizational behavior theories, even if they had similar origins in laboratory training, it is important to consider and evaluate each separately on its own ground. When this is done, we often come up with a limited amount of research, many questions, and, in particular, many doubts about the validity of the theoretical base. This is certainly the current state of affairs with regard to the theories and applications proposed by Blake and Mouton and Schein.

Yet comprehensive reviews of the effectiveness of organization development interventions indicate a success rate that is sufficient for us to be fairly certain that projected changes are occurring quite often, although by no means always. What this state of affairs seems to indicate to me is that practice has outdistanced theory—that organization development practitioners are mixing approaches and adopting techniques to situations so they may get better results than the basic theories would warrant. In some cases the theories may be better than this, but until they are more adequately tested we cannot be sure. In the meantime, organization development seems to be progressing nicely, moving away from its origins in humanism and anti-bureaucracy, and focusing more on the bottom line. What we need now is a theory that will catch up with practice in these respects and provide the driving force for a new round of advances in practice, hopefully in conjunction with improvements in the approaches taken to evaluating practice.

References

Alderfer, Clayton P. (1977). Organization Development. *Annual Review of Psychology*, 28, 197–223.

Bennis, Warren G. (1987). Using Our Knowledge of Organizational Behavior: The Improbable Task. In Jay W. Lorsch (Ed.), *Handbook of Organizational Behavior*, (pp. 29–49). Englewood Cliffs, NJ: Prentice Hall.

Blake, Robert R. (1992). The Fruits of Professional Interdependence for Enriching a Career. In Arthur G. Bedeian (Ed.), *Management Laureates: A Collection of Autobiographical Essays* (Vol. 1, pp. 109–165). Greenwich, CT: JAI Press.

Blake, Robert R., & McCanse, Anne A. (1991). *Leadership Dilemmas: Grid Solutions*. Houston: Gulf.

Blake, Robert R., & Mouton, Jane S. (1964). *The Managerial Grid*. Houston: Gulf.

Blake, Robert R., & Mouton, Jane S. (1965). A 9,9 Approach for Increasing Organizational Productivity. In Edgar H. Schein & Warren G. Bennis (Eds.), *Personal and Organizational Change through Group Methods* (pp. 169–183). New York: Wiley.

Blake, Robert R., & Mouton, Jane S. (1968). *Corporate Excellence through Grid Organization Development*. Houston: Gulf.

Blake, Robert R., & Mouton, Jane S. (1969). *Building a Dynamic Corporation through Grid Organization Development*. Reading, MA: Addison-Wesley.

Blake, Robert R., & Mouton, Jane S. (1982). A Comparative Analysis of Situationalism and 9,9 Management by Principle. *Organizational Dynamics*, 10(4), 20–43.

Blake, Robert R., & Mouton, Jane S. (1984). Overcoming Group Warfare. *Harvard Business Review*, 62(6), 98–108.

Blake, Robert R., & Mouton, Jane S. (1985). *The Managerial Grid III: The Key to Leadership Excellence*. Houston: Gulf.

Blake, Robert R., & Mouton, Jane S. (1988). Follow-up with Unique Insights on Program Evaluation. *Group and Organization Studies*, 13, 33–35.

Blake, Robert R.; Mouton, Jane S.; & Allen, Robert L. (1987). *Spectacular Teamwork: How to Develop the Leadership Skills for Team Success*. London: Sidgwick & Jackson.

Blake, Robert R.; Mouton, Jane S.; Barnes, Louis B.; & Greiner, Larry E. (1964). Breakthrough in Organization Development. *Harvard Business Review*, 42(6), 133–155.

Blake, Robert R.; Mouton, Jane S.; & McCanse, Anne A. (1989). *Change by Design*. Reading, MA: Addison-Wesley.

Blake, Robert R.; Shepard, Herbert A.; & Mouton, Jane S. (1964). *Managing Intergroup Conflict in Industry*. Houston: Gulf.

Boss, R. Wayne, & Golembiewski, Robert T. (1995). Do You Have to Start at the Top? The Chief Executive Officer's Role in Successful Organization Development Efforts. *Journal of Applied Behavioral Science*, 31, 259–277.

Bowers, David G. (1973). OD Techniques and Their Results in 23 Organizations: The Michigan ICL Study. *Journal of Applied Behavioral Science*, 9, 21–43.

Church, Allan H.; Burke, W. Warner; & Van Eynde, Donald F. (1994). Values, Motives, and Interventions of Organization Development Practitioners. *Group and Organization Management*, 19, 5–50.

Dyer, W. Gibb (1997). Organization Development in the Entrepreneurial Firm. *Journal of Applied Behavioral Science*, 33, 190–208.

Esper, Jane L. (1990). Organizational Change and Development: Core Practitioner Competencies and Future Trends. *Advances in Organization Development*, 1, 277–314.

Frost, Peter J.; Moore, Larry F.; Louis, Meryl R.; Lundberg, Craig C.; & Martin, Joanne (1991). *Reframing Organizational Culture*. Newbury Park, CA: Sage.

Golembiewski, Robert T. (1977). *Public Administration as a Developing Discipline: Part II. Organization Development as One of a Future Family of Miniparadigms*. New York: Marcel Dekker.

Golembiewski, Robert T. (1986). Contours in Social Change: Elemental Graphics and a Surrogate Variable for Gamma Change. *Academy of Management Review*, 11, 550–566.

Golembiewski, Robert T. (1989). *Organization Development: Ideas and Issues*. New Brunswick, NJ: Transaction Publishers.

Golembiewski, Robert T. (1991). OD Applications in Developmental Settings: Four Perspectives on Action Research in an Important Locus. *Research in the Sociology of Organizations*, 9, 201–263.

Golembiewski, Robert T. (1992). Mid-Career Perspectives. In Arthur G. Bedeian (Ed.), *Management Laureates: A Collection of Autobiographical Essays* (Vol. 1, pp. 371–416). Greenwich, CT: JAI Press.

Golembiewski, Robert T.; Billingsley, Keith; & Yeager, Samuel (1976). Measuring Change and Persistence in Human Affairs: Types of Change Generated by OD Designs. *Journal of Applied Behavioral Science*, 12, 133–157.

Golembiewski, Robert T., & Sun, Ben-Chu (1990). Positive Findings Bias in QWL Studies: Rigor and Outcomes in a Large Sample. *Journal of Management*, 16, 665–674.

Hall, Jay (1976). To Achieve or Not: The Manager's Choice. *California Management Review*, 18(4), 5–18.

Holman, Peggy, & Devane, Tom (1999). *The Change Handbook: Group Methods for Shaping the Future*. San Francisco: Berrett-Koehler.

Luthans, Fred (1989). Conversation with Edgar H. Schein. *Organizational Dynamics*, 17(4), 60–76.

Martin, Joanne (1992). *Cultures in Organizations: Three Perspectives.* New York: Oxford University Press.

Martin, Joanne, & Frost, Peter (1996). The Organizational Culture War Games: A Struggle for Intellectual Dominance. In Stewart R. Clegg, Cynthia Hardy, & Walter R. Nord (Eds.), *Handbook of Organization Studies* (pp. 599–621). London: Sage.

McMahan, Gary C., & Woodman, Richard W. (1992). The Current Practice of Organization Development within the Firm. *Group and Organization Management*, 17, 117–134.

Porras, Jerry I., & Berg, Per O. (1978). The Impact of Organization Development. *Academy of Management Review*, 3, 249–266.

Porras, Jerry I., & Robertson, Peter J. (1992). Organization Development: Theory, Practice, and Research. In Marvin D. Dunnette & Leaetta M. Hough (Eds.), *Handbook of Industrial and Organizational Psychology*, (Vol. 3, pp. 719–822). Palo Alto, CA: Consulting Psychologists Press.

Porras, Jerry I., & Silvers, Robert C. (1991). Organization Development and Transformation. *Annual Review of Psychology*, 42, 51–78.

Sanzgiri, Jyotsna, & Gottlieb, Jonathan Z. (1992). Philosophic and Pragmatic Influences on the Practice of Organization Development, 1950–2000. *Organizational Dynamics*, 21(2), 57–69.

Sashkin, Marshall, & Burke, W. Warner (1990). Organization Development in the 1980s. *Advances in Organization Development*, 1, 315–346.

Schein, Edgar H. (1957). Patterns of Reactions to Severe Chronic Stress in American Army Prisoners of War of the Chinese. In *Symposium No. 4—Methods of Forceful Indoctrination: Observations and Interviews* (pp. 253–269). New York: Group for the Advancement of Psychiatry.

Schein, Edgar H. (1968). Organizational Socialization and the Profession of Management. *Sloan Management Review*, 9(2), 1–16.

Schein, Edgar H. (1969). *Process Consultation: Its Role in Organization Development.* Reading, MA: Addison-Wesley.

Schein, Edgar H. (1975). The Hawthorne Group Studies Revisited: A Defense of Theory Y. In Eugene L. Cass & Frederick G. Zimmer (Eds.), *Man and Work in Society*, (pp. 78–94). New York: Van Nostrand Reinhold.

Schein, Edgar H. (1978). *Career Dynamics: Matching Individual and Organizational Needs.* Reading, MA: Addison-Wesley.

Schein, Edgar H. (1981a). Does Japanese Management Style Have a Message for American Managers? *Sloan Management Review*, 23(1), 55–68.

Schein, Edgar H. (1981b). Improving Face-to-Face Relationships. *Sloan Management Review*, 22(/2), 43–52.

Schein, Edgar H. (1983). The Role of the Founder in Creating Organizational Culture. *Organizational Dynamics*, 12(1), 13–28.

Schein, Edgar H. (1984a). Coming to a New Awareness of Organizational Culture. *Sloan Management Review*, 25(2), 3–16.

Schein, Edgar H. (1984b). Culture as an Environmental Context for Careers. *Journal of Occupational Behavior*, 5, 71–81.

Schein, Edgar H. (1985). *Organizational Culture and Leadership: A Dynamic View.* San Francisco: Jossey-Bass.

Schein, Edgar H. (1987a). *The Clinical Perspective in Fieldwork.* Newbury Park, CA: Sage.

Schein, Edgar H. (1987b). Individuals and Careers. In Jay W. Lorsch (Ed.), *Handbook of Organizational Behavior* (pp. 155–171). Englewood Cliffs, NJ: Prentice Hall.

Schein, Edgar H. (1987c). *Process Consultation. Vol. 2: Lessons for Managers and Consultants.* Reading, MA: Addison-Wesley.

Schein, Edgar H. (1988). *Process Consultation. Vol. 1: Its Role in Organization Development.* Reading, MA: Addison-Wesley.

Schein, Edgar H. (1989a). Reassessing the "Divine Rights" of Managers. *Sloan Management Review*, 30(2), 63–68.

Schein, Edgar H. (1989b). A Social Psychologist Discovers Chicago Sociology. *Academy of Management Review*, 14, 103–104.

Schein, Edgar H. (1990a). Back to the Future: Recapturing the OD Vision. *Advances in Organization Development*, 1, 13–26.

Schein, Edgar H. (1990b). A General Philosophy of Helping: Process Consultation. *Sloan Management Review*, 31(3), 57–64.

Schein, Edgar H. (1992). *Organizational Culture and Leadership.* 2nd ed. San Francisco: Jossey-Bass.

Schein, Edgar H. (1993a). The Academic as Artist: Personal and Professional Roots. In Arthur G. Bedeian (Ed.), *Management Laureates: A Collection of Autobiographical Essays* (Vol. 3, pp. 31–62). Greenwich, CT: JAI Press.

Schein, Edgar H. (1993b). How Can Organizations Learn Faster? The Challenge of Entering the Green Room. *Sloan Management Review*, 34(2), 85–92.

Schein, Edgar H. (1993c). On Dialogue, Culture, and Organizational Learning. *Organizational Dynamics*, 22(2), 40–51.

Schein, Edgar H. (1995). Process Consultation, Action Research and Clinical Inquiry: Are They the Same? *Journal of Managerial Psychology*, 10(6), 14–19.

Schein, Edgar H. (1996a). Career Anchors Revisited: Implications for Career Development in the 21st Century. *Academy of Management Executive*, 10(4), 80–88.

Schein, Edgar H. (1996b). Culture: The Missing Concept in Organization Studies. *Administrative Science Quarterly*, 41, 229–240.

Schein, Edgar H. (1996c). *Strategic Pragmatism: The Culture of Singapore's Economic Development Board*. Cambridge, MA: MIT Press.

Schein, Edgar H. (1996d). Three Cultures of Management: The Key to Organizational Learning. *Sloan Management Review*, 38(1), 9–20.

Schein, Edgar H. (1999a). *The Corporate Culture Survival Guide: Sense and Nonsense About Culture Change*. San Francisco, CA: Jossey-Bass.

Schein, Edgar H. (1999b). *Process Consultation Revisited: Building the Helping Relationship*. Reading, MA: Addison-Wesley.

Schein, Edgar H. (2000). When Will We Learn? In Art Kleiner & George Roth (Eds.), *Oil Change: Perspectives on Corporate Transformation* (pp. 189–198). New York: Oxford University Press.

Schein, Edgar H., & Bennis, Warren G. (1965). *Personal and Organizational Change Through Group Methods: The Laboratory Approach*. New York: Wiley.

Schein, Edgar H.; Schneier, Inge; & Barker, Curtis H. (1961). *Coercive Persuasion*. New York: Norton.

Smith, Peter B. (1975). Controlled Studies of the Outcome of Sensitivity Training. *Psychological Bulletin*, 82, 597–622.

Svyantek, Daniel J.; Goodman, Scott A.; Benz, Lori L.; & Gard, Julia A. (1999). The Relationship between Organizational Characteristics and Team Building Success. *Journal of Business and Psychology*, 14, 265–283.

Trice, Harrison M. (1991). Comments and Discussion. In Peter J. Frost, Larry F. Moore, Meryl R. Louis, Craig C. Lundberg, & Joanne Martin (Eds.), *Reframing Organizational Culture* (pp. 298–308). Newbury Park, CA: Sage.

Van Maanen, John, & Schein, Edgar H. (1979). Toward a Theory of Organizational Socialization. *Research in Organizational Behavior*, 1, 209–264.

Yetton, Philip, & Crawford, Mike (1992). Reassessment of Participative Decision-making: A Case of Too Much Participation. In Frank Heller (Ed.), *Decision-Making and Leadership* (pp. 90–112). Cambridge: Cambridge University Press

Part VI

First-Generation Theories:
Organizational Decision Making

Chapter 22

Theories of Decision Process

We turn now to a topic that has been with organizational behavior since its early beginnings. Theories of organizational decision making have played an important role in the field, not only in their own right but also in their implications for other topic areas. Thus, it is appropriate to take these theories up last among those of a first-generation nature. They cast a wide net across the field, spanning both micro and macro variables, and thus achieving a solid status as meso theories as well.

This chapter derives much of its content from a handful of seminal books. These books are Herbert Simon's (1947) *Administrative Behavior*, James March and Simon's (1958) *Organizations*, Richard Cyert and March's (1963) *A Behavioral Theory of the Firm*, and two books by Karl Weick—*The Social Psychology of Organizing* (1969, 2nd edition 1979) and *Sensemaking in Organizations* (1995). We will cover much more ground, but these books are the major sources.

Weick's work represents a separate theoretical thrust, but Simon's and March's theorizing were at one point closely intertwined. However, for many years now they have been involved in quite distinct types of theoretical efforts.

Although the theories to be considered tend to focus on decision making, and in recent years to focus on that subject more and more, they cover a number of conventional components of organizational functioning that they characteristically relate to the decision process. Initially we will take up Simon's theoretical work and his joint efforts with March; here the emphasis on rational decision making within the bounds of possibility is pronounced. Next we take up March's independent work and then Weick's formulations; in both instances decision making well beyond the bounds of rationality becomes of major concern.

ADMINISTRATIVE BEHAVIOR AND ORGANIZATIONS

Simon is by no means new to these pages. Chapter 2 considers the influence that Chester Barnard exerted on his views, particularly in the area of decision making. Chapter 3 notes Simon's criticisms of classical management theory on the grounds of both ambiguity of statement and logical inconsistency. In chapter 4 there is a brief discussion of the role that the Graduate School of Industrial Administration at Carnegie Tech, of which Simon was a founding member, played in the development of the field of organizational behavior. A much more extended discussion of the Carnegie situation and Simon's changing status there is contained in chapter 5. Chapter 19 considers Simon's collaboration with Victor Thompson when both were on the faculty at Illinois Institute of Technology.

Background

It is now time to fill in the gaps between these glimpses of Herbert Simon's thinking and career. He was born in 1916 and received his doctorate in 1942 from the University of Chicago in political science, the same school and discipline that awarded his undergraduate degree as well (in 1936). For the 3 years before obtaining the Ph.D., he worked on public administration research at the University of California at Berkeley. His first regular faculty appointment was back in Chicago at Illinois Institute of Technology, again in politi-

cal science, but with a developing interest in economics. After 7 years at IIT—and because of the economics interest, publication of *Administrative Behavior* in 1947, and a continuing mathematical orientation to social science—Simon moved to the School of Industrial Administration, then in the process of being founded, at what is now Carnegie Mellon University. At this point any formal identification with political science ended, but by his own admission Simon has always been something of a politician within the intellectual community, and his original choice of a field of study reflects this (Simon, 1991).

The years at Carnegie, at least the early ones, were marked by considerable controversy and ultimately by movement from the developing field of organizational behavior to psychology, a move that was formally consummated in 1970. This was both a departmental transfer and a shift in primary field, but both had been in process for a number of years. Much of Simon's research and publication from the early 1960s on has been in cognitive processes, artificial intelligence, and computer modeling. His appointment in psychology became joined with another in computer science. He became emeritus from Carnegie Mellon in 1993, and died in 2001.

March was born in 1928. He did his undergraduate work at the University of Wisconsin. Serving at Stanford University since 1970, he has an equally diverse array of discipline associations, including appointments in political science, education, sociology, and business administration. He, too, started in the field of political science with a degree from Yale University in 1953. From 1953 to 1964 he was with Simon at Carnegie Mellon before taking an administrative position at the University of California (Irvine) for 6 years. He has been emeritus from Stanford since 1995. Unlike Simon, March has remained largely within the field of organizational behavior, insofar as his intellectual contributions are concerned, throughout his career, although his approach to the field has drawn on many different literatures (see Augier & Kreiner, 2000).

Theory of Administrative Behavior

Simon's *Administrative Behavior* (1947), which was developed from his dissertation, is unusual in a number of respects. For one thing, it contributed substantially to his winning the Nobel Prize in economics. Like so many others, Simon also attempts to demolish classical management theory, but instead of arguing primarily on grounds of humanism or adaptive inflexibility, he attacks it for logical inconsistency and failure to measure up to the demands of scientific theorizing. While rejecting the normative principles of classical theory, Simon (1946) does not then advocate a new normative theory to replace them. Instead, he takes only a first step toward reconstruction by setting forth a vocabulary and conceptual framework. His clear intent is to focus primarily on decision-making processes.

Limits to Rationality

A central thesis in Simon's thinking is that rational decision making is limited to or bounded by (1) a person's skills, habits, and reflexes; (2) the values and concepts of purpose that influence the decision; and (3) the person's knowledge, particularly of the consequences of alternatives. Inherent in this view is the idea that decisions involve not only factual judgments but also ethical or value judgments that relate to the goals and purposes to be served. In a very rough sense, *administration* relates to factual judgments and *policy* to value judgments. In the same sense, facts more often tend to be related to means and values to ends.

Simon's views in this area must be set against the prevailing concept of a highly rational, maximizing decision maker, as epitomized by "economic man":

It is impossible for the behavior of a single, isolated individual to reach any high degree of rationality. The number of alternatives he must explore is so great, the information he would need to evaluate them so vast that even an approximation to objective rationality is hard to conceive. Individual choice takes place in an environment of "givens"—premises that are accepted by the subject as bases for his choice; and behavior is adaptive only within the limits set by these "givens." (Simon, 1947, p. 79)

Behavior thus fails of objective rationality in several respects:

1. Rationality requires a complete knowledge and anticipation of the consequences that will follow on each choice. In fact, knowledge of consequences is always fragmentary.
2. Since these consequences lie in the future, imagination must supply the lack of experienced feeling in attaching value to them. But values can be only imperfectly anticipated.
3. Rationality requires a choice among all possible alternative behaviors. In actual behavior, only a very few of all these possible alternatives ever come to mind. (Simon, 1947, p. 81)

Within an organization, the decision process begins with *substantive planning*—the broad decisions that affect values, methods of attaining those values, and needed knowledge, skills, and information. Second, there is *procedural planning*, which involves decisions about mechanisms to direct attention and channel information in accordance with the substantive plan. Finally, there is *execution* based on day-to-day decisions. The hierarchy of steps increasingly restricts alternatives and limits the decision process. Consistent with this objective, work is divided among members, standard practices are introduced, decisions are transmitted through the organization, and members are trained in matters related to their decisions. Thus much of organizational structure and process is explained in relation to making decisions manageable.

Simon (1947) devotes considerable attention to the criterion of efficiency, which requires that the alternative selected be the one that will yield the greatest net return. If costs are fixed, the decision should maximize income, and if income is fixed, it should minimize costs. When efficiency is the accepted criterion, rationality governs decision making, much as it does in economic theory when an attempt is made to maximize utility. Given the limits to rationality, Simon does not assert that managerial decisions are characteristically dominated by the criterion of efficiency. Yet, Simon seems to favor that end highly and to argue for maximization of efficiency and rational decisions to the extent that available data permit. On occasion he even seems to imply that rationality often is attainable. In subsequent treatments, however, he is less optimistic (Simon, Smithburg & Thompson, 1950; Simon, 1957a).

Inducements-Contributions Equilibrium

Business organizations have at least three kinds of participants—entrepreneurs, employees, and customers. Entrepreneurs enter into contracts with employees to obtain their time and effort and with customers to obtain their money to pay wages and thus maintain the employment contract. Though in businesses the inducement—money—is indirect, in some organizations such as churches the inducement for members may be some direct personal value. In any event, a necessary condition for gaining and continuing to belong to an organization is some form of inducements-contributions agreement.

When the contributions are adequate to attract what is needed to provide the appropriate kinds and amounts of inducements, the organization prospers. One kind of contribution in such situations is a willingness to accept authority. This willingness extends over a zone of acceptance whose width is determined by the nature and extent of inducements. If the employment contract terms, implicit or explicit, are favorable, an employee can be expected to contribute willingly over a broad range of activities. But if the inducements provide little satisfaction of personal goals, contributions and the zone of acceptance shrink.

In these relationships authority is defined as "the power to make decisions which guide the actions of another" (Simon, 1947, p. 125). Authority is only one form of influence, which also includes persuasion and suggestion. Authority exists only as long as it is accepted, and thus only as long as what is required falls within the zone of acceptance.

Models of Man and Other Extensions

In the period after the first publication of *Administrative Behavior* Simon developed his concepts more fully in a number of articles. These articles, as well as others unrelated to organizational structure and process, were brought together in a single volume entitled *Models of Man* (Simon, 1957b). In the same year *Administrative Behavior* (1957a) was republished, with a lengthy introduction that qualified and extended Simon's earlier views. In both publications the term *satisficing* is now used to refer to the behavior of those who "have not the wits to maximize."

In elaborating on the idea that administrative theory is, in fact, synonymous with the theory of intended and bounded rationality, Simon amended his prior views to include the satisficing concept:

1. While economic man maximizes—selects the best alternative from among all those available to him, his cousin, whom we shall call administrative man—satisfices—looks for a course of action that is satisfactory or "good enough."

2. Economic man deals with the "real world" in all its complexity. Administrative man recognizes that the world he perceives is a drastically simplified model of the buzzing, blooming confusion that constitutes the real world. He is content with this gross simplification because he believes that the real world is mostly empty—that most of the facts of the real world have no great relevance to any particular situation he is facing. He makes his choices using a simple picture of the situation that takes into account just a few of the factors that he regards as most relevant and crucial. . . . Administrative man is able to make his decisions with relatively simple rules of thumb that do not make impossible demands upon his capacity for thought. (Simon, 1957a, pp. xxv–xxvi)

In publication after publication Simon attacks the economic theory that assumes perfect knowledge and ignores the reality of bounded rationality. Under bounded rationality the decision maker, instead of maximizing, searches only until he finds an alternative where the payoff is good enough. There is no need to look beyond this point for an alternative that will yield an even higher payoff. In formulating the satisficing concept, Simon assumes a sequential pattern of choice:

The aspiration level, which defines a satisfactory alternative, may change from point to point in this sequence of trials. A vague principle would be that as the individual, in his exploration of alternatives, finds it easy to discover satisfactory alternatives, his aspiration level rises; as he finds it difficult to discover satisfactory alternatives, his aspiration level falls. . . . Such changes in aspiration level would tend to bring about a "near-uniqueness" of the satisfactory solutions, and would also tend to guarantee the existence of satisfactory solutions. For the failure to discover a solution would depress the aspiration level and bring satisfactory solutions into existence. (Simon, 1957b, p. 253)

Elaborating further on the inducements-contributions equilibrium, Simon notes that employment contracts and sales contracts differ in that the former specify only a zone of acceptance of authority (and perhaps areas of nonacceptance), rather than specific terms and actions for each party. Yet, as Simon himself recognizes, his theory tends somewhat inconsistently to assume rational, utility-maximizing behavior in the employment relationship:

> Each participant will remain in the organization if the satisfaction (or utility) he derives from the net balance of inducements over contributions (measured in terms of their utility to him) is greater than the satisfaction he could obtain if he withdrew. The zero point in such a "satisfaction function" is defined, therefore, in terms of the opportunity cost of participation. (Simon, 1957b, p. 173)

Theory of Organizations

The book *Organizations* (March & Simon, 1958) has much in common with James Thompson's *Organizations in Action* (1967). However, March and Simon's inventory of propositions is largely induced from empirical research, while Thompson's derives from conceptual premises. Many March and Simon hypotheses deal with variables such as motivation, group behavior, and leadership that fall entirely within the confines of organizational behavior at the micro level. But at the micro level March and Simon's theory is now primarily of historical interest, having been superseded by other, more sophisticated formulations. The following discussion focuses on the theory's more comprehensive concepts and propositions as they relate to the organization as a whole, including its processes of decision making.

Satisficing and Bounded Rationality

The March and Simon (1958) discussion of decision making follows already familiar lines. However, some new concepts are added and old ones are developed more fully. The concept of performance program, which appears to be roughly analogous to role prescription, is invoked in the discussion of control and coordination systems. Performance programs, although intended to make behavior within an organization more predictable, are themselves selected on a satisficing basis, thus making it difficult to predict which performance programs will be chosen. Programs differ in their degree of stress on means and ends and thus in the amount of discretion they permit.

Division of work is viewed as a means of simplifying the decision process. Units are established on the basis of purpose, and subgoals are introduced so that decision makers may face problems with which they can cope. Once units are created, the problem of interdependence arises. In stable, predictable environments there is considerable tolerance for interdependence, and process specialization can be carried quite far. In more rapidly changing environments specialization carries much higher risks. Thus organizations attempt to stabilize their environments by homogenizing materials, using interchangeable parts, holding buffer inventories, and the like to maintain specialization. Yet coordination problems remain:

> We may label coordination based on pre-established schedules *coordination by plan*, and coordination that involves transmission of new information *coordination by feedback*. The more stable and predictable the situation, the greater the reliance on coordination by plan; the more variable and unpredictable the situation, the greater the reliance on coordination by feedback. (March & Simon, 1958, p. 160).

The influence of March and Simon on Thompson (1967) becomes very apparent in such formulations.

In general, highly programmed tasks drive out unprogrammed tasks. Organizations that do not give special consideration to this fact will fail to plan and innovate. To obtain unprogrammed action, organizations must establish specially budgeted planning units with their own specific goals or introduce hard-and-fast deadlines for the completion of unprogrammed tasks. Whether innovation occurs at the top levels of an organization depends on the type of coordination used. Feedback coordination facilitates, and coordination by plan limits, innovative decision making at the top.

The concept of bounded rationality provides a rationale not only for the division of work but also for the decentralization of decision making. Given existing limits on human capacity, decentralized systems in which decisions are moved down and out to larger numbers of individuals are preferred over centralized systems.

Decision to Participate

A stable inducements-contributions equilibrium is posited as a necessary condition for organizational survival. Increases in inducements decrease the tendency for an individual to leave the organization. The inducements-contributions balance is influenced by both perceived desirability and perceived ease of leaving. Propositions relating various factors to both perceived desirability of movement and perceived ease of movement are shown in figure 22.1.

Conflict

Conflict in organizations may be within the individual, in that known, acceptable, decision alternatives are not available, or between individuals (or groups), in that different individuals make different choices. Conflict of the latter type is of prime concern here. Conflict within the individual is important, too, in that it retards choice, and choice is a necessary condition for intergroup conflict.

Figure 22.2 outlines the major propositions involving intergroup conflict. The formulations relating to joint decision making are of particular interest. Sharing a common service unit and being adjacent to another unit in a flow-chart sense are given as examples of situations calling for joint decision making. Conflict is expected to be high in these instances. Conflict is most likely to be related to budgeting and monetary allocations and will tend to increase when overall resources are reduced.

Reactions to conflict include (1) problem solving, often with a search for new alternatives; (2) persuasion, often with a search for previously unconsidered superordinate objectives; (3) bargaining, where goal disagreements are taken as inevitable; and (4) politics, where the conflict arena is expanded to include other groups and constituencies. Typically, managerial hierarchies prefer problem solving and persuasion to bargaining and politics and will prefer to use them in conflict resolution. Problem solving and persuasion put less strain on the status and power systems.

Theoretical Extensions

Simon has continued to build on this theory in varied ways and in a somewhat intermittent manner. Much of his effort has been devoted to extending the concepts of bounded rationality in areas of human problem solving and computer science. In some cases these

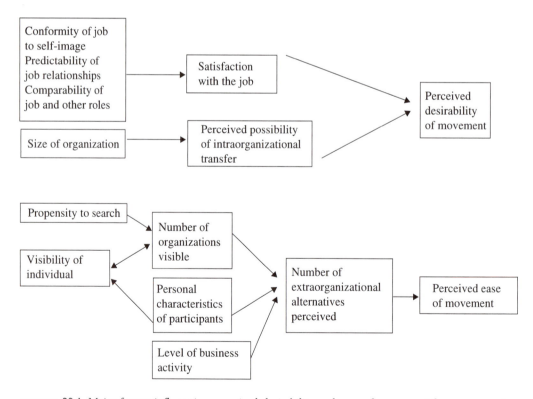

FIGURE 22.1 Major factors influencing perceived desirability and ease of movement from an organization. Adapted from James G. March & Herbert A. Simon (1958), *Organizations* (New York: Wiley), 99, 106.

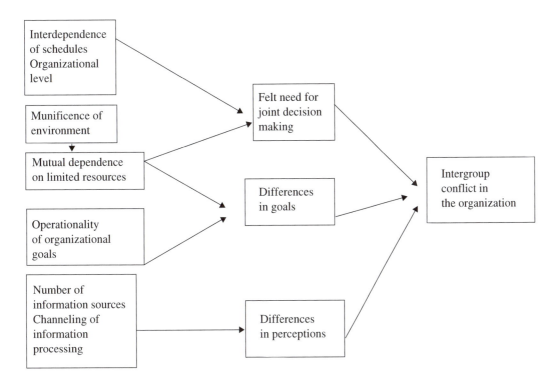

FIGURE 22.2 Major factors influencing intergroup conflict. Adapted from James G. March & Herbert A. Simon (1958), *Organizations* (New York: Wiley), 128.

activities are clearly within the confines of organizational behavior, sometimes they are of only tangential relevance, and more often they are not of the field at all. The present discussion focuses on the organizational behavior end of this continuum.

Organizational Goals

In 1964 Simon published an article dealing with goals that he subsequently included in the third edition of *Administrative Behavior*. His discussion is described as "generally compatible with, but not identical to, that of my colleagues, R. M. Cyert and J. G. March" (Simon, 1976, p. 257). In fact, it appears to be the beginning of a separation in viewpoints that has taken Simon and March in different directions since their collaboration on *Organizations* in 1958.

For Simon, goals are value premises for decisions and must be clearly distinguished from individual motives. In his view goals become synonymous with constraints:

A course of action, to be acceptable, must satisfy a whole set of requirements, or constraints. Some-

times one of these requirements is singled out and referred to as the goal of the action. But the choice of one of the constraints, from many, is to a large extent arbitrary. For many purposes it is more meaningful to refer to the whole set of requirements as the (complex) goal of the action. This conclusion applies both to individual and organizational decision-making. (Simon, 1976, p. 262)

These goals/constraints can serve to generate alternatives or, in the more traditional role of goals, to test alternatives. If the goals are used in the sense of generating alternatives, there appears to be little goal congruence among the subunits of an organization, and goal conflict seems rampant. If the goals are used in the traditional sense, the sharing of constraint sets becomes much more widespread.

Simon (1976) gives less emphasis to bargaining and loosely bound coalitions than Cyert and March (1963) do. The goals/constraints emerge out of the inducements-contributions equilibrium, but they are also strongly influenced by the system of organizational roles in which decisions made in one unit serve as constraints for other parts of the organization. The coupling here is loose, but the decisions that produce the role structure can be measured against various organizational goals (other constraints) and corrected accordingly. Personal motives become much less important than programmed organizational roles in organizational decisions. Furthermore, given a hierarchical system, it is logical to use the term *organizational goal* to refer to "the constraint sets and criteria of search that define roles at the upper levels" (Simon, 1976, p. 277) and "to describe most business firms as directed toward profit making—subject to a number of side constraints" (p. 278).

Computers, Decisions, and Structures

From an early period Simon was concerned with the influence of computers on organizational decision making and, because decisions are the raison d'être for structure, on organizational design as well. His views appear in what is essentially the third edition of a book first published in 1960 entitled *The New Science of Management Decision* (Simon, 1977). In this book Simon describes programmed and nonprogrammed decisions and the techniques applicable to each. Simon's views in this regard are contained in table 22.1.

Basically, Simon (1977) views hierarchy as an essential feature of large, complex systems of any kind. Applying this concept to organizations, nonprogrammed decision making is characteristic at the top levels, programmed decision making at the mid-

dle level, and the basic work processes—the actual doing—at the bottom level. The same hierarchical structure and subdivision into units is ascribed to computer systems, and this is a natural outgrowth of the decision-making focus involved: "Hierarchy is the adaptive form for finite intelligence to assume in the face of complexity" (Simon, 1977, p. 114). Thus, adding computers to the decision process should not change the essentially hierarchical nature of organizations.

Earlier, March and Simon (1958) espoused decentralization to facilitate coping with complex decisions. Later Simon says:

> In the first twenty years after the Second World War there was a movement toward decentralization in large American business firms. This movement was probably a sound development, but it did not signify that more decentralization at all times and under all circumstances is a good thing. It signified that at a particular time in history, many American firms, which had experienced almost continuous long-term growth and diversification, discovered that they could operate more effectively if they brought together all the activities relating to individual products or groups of similar products and decentralized a great deal of decision making to the departments handling these products or product groups. . . . In the past ten years we have heard less about decentralization. . . . Some of this reversal of trend was produced by second thoughts after the earlier enthusiasm for product-group divi-

TABLE 22.1 Techniques of decision making used in programmed and nonprogrammed approaches

Types of decisions	Techniques applicable

Programmed
  Repetitive and routine
  A definite procedure has been worked out so that decisions do not have to be handled de novo each time they occur
	Traditional
	  Habit
	  Standard operating procedures
	  Organizational structure
	
	Modern
	  Operations research
	  Electronic data processing

Nonprogrammed
  Novel, unstructured, and unusually consequential
  No cut-and-dried method for handling the problem because it has not arisen before, or because its precise nature and structure are elusive and complex, or because it is so important that it deserves a custom-tailored treatment
	Traditional
	  Judgment, intuition, and creativity
	  Selection and training of executives
	
	Modern
	  Heuristic problem solving applied to training humans
	  Constructing heuristic computer programs

SOURCE: Adapted from Herbert A. Simon (1977), *The New Science of Management Decision* (Englewood Cliffs, NJ: Prentice Hall), 46, 48

sionalization. . . . A second force working toward recentralization of decisions has been the introduction of computers and automation. (Simon, 1977, p. 116)

In short, computers now make it unnecessary to decentralize to handle complex decisions, and, combined with operations research techniques, computers tend to foster coordination and planning at superordinate levels—thus centralization. The result is a greater rationalization of the system, perhaps with fewer levels of hierarchy but with a greater broadening through the addition of staff positions: "For some managers, important satisfactions derived in the past from certain kinds of interpersonal relations with others will be lost. For other managers, important satisfactions from a feeling of the adequacy of their professional skills will be gained" (Simon, 1977, p. 133). It is clear, though he does not say so explicitly, that Simon views strategy/structure theory as deficient in its failure to include the computer variable.

Role of Expertise and Intuition

More recently Simon's contributions to organizational behavior have focused on expert decision making—expert systems, intuitive competence, organizational learning, and the like (Simon, 1987, 1991; Prietula & Simon, 1989). These are ideas that come out of his work in cognitive science, artificial intelligence, and computer systems. The goal of much of this work was to create computer systems that can perform expert professional tasks competently.

Simon's thesis is that intuition is really not much different from other problem solving, but it is problem solving embedded in years of experience so that it has become automatic and not easily accessible to consciousness:

The intuitive skills of managers depend on the same kinds of mechanisms as the intuitive skills of chessmasters or physicians. . . . The experienced manager, too, has in his or her memory a large amount of knowledge, gained from training and experience and organized in terms of recognizable chunks and associated information. (Simon, 1987, p. 61)

This kind of intuition yields competent decisions because of its origins in lengthy learning. It should be contrasted with intuition that is embedded in stress and emotion and thus is much more likely to yield irrationality. Failure of expert intuition may also result from insufficient attention, so that the necessary chunks of knowledge are not built up in memory.

Organizational learning occurs either as a consequence of the learning of existing members or by bringing in new members with new knowledge to contribute. The experts that possess this essential learning include top management, but they may be found anywhere in the organization. Organizational memories are built up out of such learning. To understand organizations it is important to

explore the contents of important organizational memories, the way in which these contents are accessed (or ignored) in the decision making process, and the ways in which they are acquired by organizations and transmitted from one part of an organization to another. Among the contents of organizational memories perhaps the most important ones are the representations of the organization itself and its goals, for it is this representation (or representations, if it is not uniform throughout the organization) that provides the basis for defining the roles of organization members. (Simon, 1991, p. 133)

Here it sounds very much like Simon is describing the deciphering of culture.

A further point in this connection is that organizational learning may be lost if key experts leave the organization. One way of protecting against this is the creation of computerized expert systems that contain the problem-solving capabilities of the experts.

Commentaries

In 1957 Simon updated *Administrative Behavior* via a lengthy introduction; in 1976 he added a set of articles reprinted from his past publications. In 1997, however, he appended commentaries, some quite extensive, to the original 11 chapters. Although they contain a substantial number of references, the commentaries do not focus on the current status of the field; rather, the references are spread about equally over the five decades of the past 50 years and the discussion is similarly dispersed in time. Thus, much of what is said there has already been considered here. Yet there are some significant additions to theory.

One such addition has to do with the role of authority and structuring:

People are more creative, and most capable of self-actualizing, when their environment provides them with an appropriate amount of structure, not too much and not too little. (Simon, 1997, pp. 203)

It also deals with the consequences of participation:

At least two crucial conditions must be satisfied in order for participation to increase production: (1) the basic attitude of the employees to the organization must be sufficiently positive . . . (2) the employees must, through observation or otherwise, have access to information about the manufacturing process. (Simon, 1997, p. 205)

Unless these two conditions are met, employees are unlikely to be either willing or able to increase output.

Simon also devotes considerable discussion to organizational structuring when it is viewed as a decision-making and information-processing system. He suggests dividing an organization not on the basis of the usual departmentalization, but according to the principal components into which the decision-making process divides (elsewhere these are said to be setting the agenda, representing the problem, finding alternatives, and selecting alternatives). This is consistent with the constraints of bounded rationality. Beyond this, decision problems should be factored to minimize interdependence among components and to conserve attention. It is not division of labor that is important in the modern organization, but factorization of decision making. Thus one should start by examining the information system and the decisions it supports, quite independent of the existing department structure. Unfortunately, Simon does not move beyond this to give specific normative guidelines for organizational design.

Decision makers acquire a representation of their situation that takes from operative goals that part that reflects the information to which they typically attend. Thus decision makers in one unit, focused on a particular type of information, come to identify with a set of goals and worldview that differ sharply from those held by decision makers in other units. Similarly chief executives from different functional backgrounds may see different things as they face the same problem, and derive different solutions; this is a process of selective perception.

Evaluation and Impact

For many years now, Simon's research has been conducted outside the field of organizational behavior.

However, he did engage in research of an organizational behavior nature in the early years. As to applications, there has been little explicit emphasis of this kind, which is consistent with the basically descriptive nature of the theory. Occasionally normative statements do appear in Simon's writings, but rarely to the point of positing a technology for practice. However, Simon et al. (1950), a text in public administration, were strongly influenced by Simon's theoretical views on the process and role of decision making.

Simon's Early Studies

Initially, Simon conducted studies in the field of government administration that, although applied in nature, had little relationship to his theories. For instance, there were analyses of optimal case loads for welfare workers (Simon & Devine, 1941) and of the fiscal factors associated with consolidating local governments (Simon, 1943). A later study dealt with the organization of the accounting function in seven companies (Simon, Guetzkow, Kozmetsky, & Tyndall, 1954). Although the research provides some qualified support for segmentation and decentralization, it does not relate these factors to the need to simplify decision making. In fact, the research appears to have been conducted without reference to theoretical concepts of any kind.

Subsequent studies were more closely related to the theory. A laboratory investigation of behavior in varied communication networks demonstrated the effect of programming differences on problem solving (Guetzkow & Simon, 1955). A detailed analysis of the decision processes employed by a company that was investigating the feasibility of using electronic data processing equipment demonstrated both a tendency to break down the decision into more manageable units and the use of extensive search procedures, which were treated in accordance with the theory of satisficing (Cyert, Simon, & Trow, 1956). A study of executives who were working in different functional areas of a business indicated, as expected, that the executives' departmental identifications exerted considerable influence on the ways in which they perceived problems (Dearborn & Simon, 1958). Although limited by small sample sizes and other considerations, and thus far from conclusive in and of themselves, these studies begin to build a structure of support for the theory.

Bounded Rationality and Satisficing

Writing in the third edition of *Administrative Behavior*, Simon (1976) notes:

> In view of the substantial body of evidence now available in support of the concept of bounded rationality, of satisficing, and of the limited rationality of administrative man, I do not regard the description of human rationality . . . as hypothetical but as now having been verified in its main features. (p. xxxi)

In this connection he mentions a study by G. P. E. Clarkson described in Cyert and March (1963) and another by Peer Soelberg (1966), as well as research conducted by the theorists themselves. The Clarkson study compared predictions made from a model developed from the Cyert and March (1963) theory with actual portfolio decisions made by a bank trust officer. Insofar as quasi resolution of conflict and uncertainty avoidance are concerned, the model agrees almost perfectly with the theory. Problemistic search and organizational learning are less clearly represented (Clarkson, 1962). Yet the decision-making process modeled is, in a sense, simple-minded, constrained in its computations, and adaptively rational. Such a theory-based model comes close to depicting reality.

The Soelberg (1966) study confirms the theory only in part. What emerges from this and other studies is a frequent tendency to search beyond the point of choice, but not with a view to maximizing; rather, the objective is to validate or confirm the choice. Furthermore, there are sizable differences between individuals in the degree to which their decisions approach the maximizing, validating or confirming, and satisficing modes. To the extent evidence is available, goals other than profit appear to influence top-level decisions, and firms in which the rationality is less bounded are more likely to be profitable, in spite of the frequent use of satisficing. Managers are more likely than unskilled and semiskilled workers to approximate rationality in their decision making (Arroba, 1978). It seems apparent that bounded rationality and satisficing in one form or another are indeed important aspects of the decision-making process, but that more complex, specific, and probably more normative formulations are needed to improve understanding, prediction, and practice (Taylor, 1975; Park, 1978; Bowen & Qiu, 1992).

In the 1990s certain attacks on the theory appeared under what might broadly be construed as the post-modernist banner. The first of these (Mumby & Putnam, 1992) reinterprets *Administrative Behavior* and the concept of bounded rationality in ways that I am sure Simon would not recognize. In several respects this interpretation is incorrect, and in placing the label of sexism on the author it appears to do an injustice. The presentation is an instance of philosophy with an unabashedly political agenda, not of science or testable theory. A similar article by Martin Kilduff (1993) similarly attacks *Organizations*. Although the intellectual vendetta is somewhat more muted here than in the previous article, and the claim that the March and Simon theory suffers from some logical inconsistency does have a certain justification, the issues involved are not central to the theory. Both articles are presented as intended to open debate and raise new considerations, and in that spirit it seems important to mention them. However, their contribution to science and to theoretical evaluation is minimal at best.

Against this backdrop I feel it is only just to mention that others have found the theories involved to be valid and useful — both the satisficing concept (Koopman & Pool, 1990) and aspects of the *Organizations* theory (Bowen & Siehl, 1997). It is not clear to me why certain people feel compelled to attack this particular theoretical approach on nonscientific grounds; yet as we will see, the story does not end with what has been considered to this point. Perhaps this type of attack is an inevitable consequence of developing a widely known and influential theory.

Inducements and Contributions

The inducements-contributions component of the theory can be derived from a number of theories of organizational behavior, at least as it relates to individual satisfaction, turnover, and performance. There are no comparative studies available that would indicate that the theory, as stated here, is superior. Nevertheless, some studies do establish some validity for the inducements-contributions formulations (see Staw, 1974). Changes, and particularly reductions, in inducements tend to increase turnover and reduce overall contributions.

Research relating this factor to organizational survival is lacking. Furthermore, there have been few attempts to identify the limits of the zone of acceptance under specific circumstances. How do variations in inducements actually influence contributions? For whom? When? What kinds of inducements and contributions? The theory as stated is difficult to test because of its broad nature. There is a need for specific hypotheses that go beyond the general framework.

Selective Perception

Several studies have been conducted bearing on the Dearborn and Simon (1958) study and the theoretical view that experience in a functional area influences aspects of problem solving. None of these studies completely replicates the Dearborn and Simon research; in fact, questions have been raised about the interpretation of that particular study as well. The best conclusion available at present, based on studies that seem to deal most effectively with confounding factors, is that functional background does exert an influence on perceptual processes and approaches in problem solving (Waller, Huber, & Glick, 1995; Beyer et al., 1997). However, this influence does not always take the exact form that Simon's theory would anticipate. Selective perception in the organizational context appears to be a reality, but at present not a well-understood reality.

Other Research Issues

Figures 22.1 and 22.2 present flow charts showing theoretical variables that are related to turnover and intergroup conflict. These subjects have been and are being researched consistently. The March and Simon formulations have provided a framework for developments in these fields, and much of the work being done builds on this beginning. We have considered turnover at a number of points previously, and intergroup conflict research was a major activity for Robert Blake before he embarked on organization development (see chapter 21 in this volume). Theory and research in these areas have now moved well beyond the March and Simon theory, but the influence of that theory is still manifest.

Turning now to the more recent theoretical extensions, the theory as it relates to expertise and intuition has been given a certain amount of research attention. Simon (1987) notes a study by Marius Bouwman (1978) in which the decision processes of expert financial analysts were computer modeled as the analysts attempted to detect company problems from examination of financial statements. The model is then compared to behavioral results: "a close match is usually found." A second study by R. Bhaskar (1978) computer modeled the thinking of business students and experienced business managers as they considered a business case. The two groups solved the case about equally well, but the business managers accomplished this result much more rapidly; they identified the key features quickly with the appearances of intuition, while the students engaged in more conscious, explicit analysis.

These results appear to confirm Simon's theory in many of its aspects. However, research carried out by Alessandro Lomi, Erik Larsen, and Ari Ginsberg (1997), also using computer modeling, raises questions about the efficacy of experience in moving toward an optimal solution. Experts may learn from experience, but that does not ensure that the experience will be interpreted correctly. The theory clearly needs to be more explicit as to who will benefit from experience sufficiently to reach expert status and achieve valid intuition; many people apparently do not.

Overview

Chris Argyris (1973, 1976) has been a consistent critic of the Carnegie Mellon theorizing as a whole. His initial concern, consistent with his own theoretical position as elucidated in chapter 20, was that these theorists espoused a traditional, pyramidal organization that did not adequately consider man's self-actualizing and often nonrational nature. Theory of this type, though said to be descriptive, inevitably becomes normative and incorrectly perpetuates the status quo.

In reply to this attack Simon (1973) cites a number of instances in which Argyris (1973) misrepresents or misinterprets his views. More important, however, Simon seriously questions Argyris's essential assumption:

> The charge is not that the theories are wrong, but that, right or wrong, they are anti-revolutionary and reactionary. We are not to describe social phenomena as they are, because describing them legitimizes them, and makes them harder to change. . . . Argyris' argument that we must not describe the world as it is lest we prevent its reform is of a piece with the general antirationalism of the contemporary counter culture. . . . Knowledge about the world and about ourselves is better than ignorance. Nothing in human history refutes that belief, or suggests that we can save mankind by

halting descriptive research on the rational aspects of human behavior. (Simon, 1973, p. 351)

A balanced view of the theories proposed by Simon and March would be to recognize that considerable research support exists for many of the theoretical propositions, but that certain shortcomings exist as well. Simon first set out to establish a descriptive framework and a vocabulary for dealing with organizations. He, and March, were highly successful in this endeavor. But the framework is still only a framework; few details between the supporting timbers have been filled in, either by research or by further theorizing. Descriptive theory can give rise to normative theory, but except for a certain implicit, normative flavor that Argyris detected, this has not happened. The framework appears solid and awaits further construction. Of all the theoretical orientations considered in this volume, the one arising originally from the collaboration at Carnegie Institute of Technology (now Carnegie Mellon University) is one of the most promising, but it has not been fully developed, or used.

BEHAVIORAL THEORY OF THE FIRM, THE GARBAGE CAN, AND ORGANIZATIONAL LEARNING

As we have seen Simon and March began to go separate ways in the early 1960s; their views diverged initially on the commitment to rationality and regarding the nature of organizational goals. However, the major disparity was that in large part Simon left organizational behavior for cognitive psychology and computer science, while March remained within the field, although with some return to political science as well, as reflected in two books (March & Olsen, 1989, 1995) which contain only limited discussion of aspects of organizational behavior theory.

Background

The major features of March's background have been described previously. He was hired by Simon at Carnegie Mellon right out of his Yale University doctorate in political science. But he only remained at Carnegie until 1964, right after the publication of A Behavioral Theory of the Firm with Richard Cyert.

In contrast to Simon and March, Cyert has remained much more closely associated with Carnegie and with the discipline of economics. Since obtaining his doctorate from Columbia University, Cyert has served both as dean of the graduate school of industrial administration and as president of Carnegie Mellon University. Subsequent to the publication of his book with March, Cyert worked on relating the basic formulations to economic theory per se (Cyert & Hedrick, 1972), on using those formulations as a framework for looking at organization theory (Cyert & MacCrimmon, 1968), and on commenting on the field of university administration (Cyert, 1975). The result was not so much a further extension of the theory as a placing of its major concepts in perspective. His major focus throughout most of his career has been on performing as a university administrator.

March has also collaborated extensively with Johan Olsen, who was first professor of political science at the University of Bergen in Norway and more recently research director at Advanced Research on the Europeanization of the Nation-State in Norway, as well as professor of political science at the University of Oslo. He obtained his doctorate from the University of Bergen in 1971. As a result of this association and others, March has spent considerable time in scholarly circles in Scandinavia.

Behavioral Theory of the Firm

Building on a collaboration begun a number of years before, Cyert and March (1955, 1956) extended their early ideas in various articles and ultimately published the most fully developed version of their theory in A Behavioral Theory of the Firm (1963). The theory takes the firm as its basic unit; attempts to predict firm behavior with regard to pricing, output, resource allocation, and the like; and focuses on the actual processes of organizational decision making.

Goal Formation

The firm is viewed as a coalition of managers, workers, stockholders, customers, and others, each with their own goals. The objectives that emerge from this coalition are determined by bargaining, are stabilized by various internal control processes, and are adjusted over time in response to environmental change. Within the coalition, some members exert greater influence and make greater demands for policy commitments than others. Such commitments, once made, become stabilized in the form of budget allocations, particular divisions of labor, and the like. At the same time, clear, logical conflicts between the demands of different coalition members often remain unresolved in the goal structure. Conflicts may remain unresolved because attention tends to focus sequentially on first one goal and then another, thus skirting the need to deal with incompatibilities.

A coalition is viable, and thus an organization exists, if the payments (inducements), including influence over goals, are adequate to keep coalition members in the organization. These demands of members tend to be roughly correlated with the resources available to the organization, but the correlation is indeed rough:

> Because of these frictions in the mutual adjustment of payments and demands, there is ordinarily a disparity between the resources available to the organization and the payments required to maintain the coalition. This difference between total resources and total necessary payments is what we have called *organizational slack*. Slack consists in payments to members of the coalition in excess of what is required to maintain the organization. (Cyert & March, 1963, p. 36)

Examples cited are excessively high dividends or wages, unnecessary public services, overstaffing, and the like. Such slack tends to absorb variability in the firm's environment; it increases when the environment is munificent and decreases as the cycle shifts toward barrenness.

Although the goals that emerge from bargaining within the coalition may vary widely, a limited set is considered sufficient to account for most of the variance. These are classifiable as production goals (with regard to both the smoothing and the level of production), inventory goals, sales goals, market share goals, and profit goals. Goal conflict in these areas is rarely fully resolved. Rather it tends to be suffered through mechanisms such as decentralization of goal attention, sequential attention to various goals, and adjustments in slack.

Expectations and Choice

The concepts of organizational expectations and choice set forth by Cyert and March (1963) closely follow those considered previously. However, the authors provide certain more specific formulations. They

develop an executive decision-tree model as follows:

1. Forecast competitors' behavior
2. Forecast demand
3. Estimate costs
4. Specify objectives

These four steps are taken in no particular order. When all four are completed, the organization moves to:

5. Evaluate plan by examining the results of steps 1 to 3 to see if at least one alternative meets the objectives of step 4. If one does, the organization immediately moves to step 9.
6. Reexamine costs if step 5 does not yield a satisfactory alternative. After reexamination, return to step 5.
7. Reexamine demand if step 5 still fails to yield a satisfactory alternative. Again, return to step 5 after the reexamination.
8. Reexamine objectives, following the same pattern as that followed in steps 6 and 7. There is a tendency to revise objectives downward as necessary.
9. Select alternative.

Such a decision system is viewed as adaptive in the following sense:

1. There exist a number of states of the system. At any point in time the system in some sense "prefers" some of these states to others.
2. There exists an external source of disturbance or shock to the system. These shocks cannot be controlled.
3. There exist a number of decision variables internal to the system. These variables are manipulated according to some decision rules.
4. Each combination of external shocks and decision variables in the system changes the state of the system. Thus, given an existing state, an external shock, and a decision, the next state is determined.
5. Any decision rule that leads to a preferred state at one point in time is more likely to be used in the future than it was in the past. (Cyert & March, 1963, p. 99)

The decision rules or standard operating procedures are both general and specific. Three basic principles appear to govern at the general level: avoid uncertainty, maintain the rules, and use simple rules. At

the specific level there are four major types of procedures: task performance rules, continuing records and
reports, information-handling rules, and plans. Plans
are defined at one and the same time as goals, schedules, theories, and precedents.

These standard operating procedures exert a major
impact on decision-making behavior within the firm
as follows:

1. *Effects on individual goals within the organization.* The specification of a plan or other
   rule has a direct effect on the desires and
   expectations of organizational members.
2. *Effects on individual perceptions of the state
   of the environment.* Different parts of the organization see different environments, and the
   environments they see depend on the rules
   for recording and processing information.
3. *Effects on the range of alternatives considered*
   by organization members in arriving at operating decisions. The way in which the organization searches for alternatives is substantially a function of the operating rule it has.
4. *Effects on the managerial decision rules used*
   in the organization. In fact, these rules frequently are specified explicitly. (Cyert &
   March, 1963, p. 112)

What these theorists have done is develop more
fully the idea that various "rules of thumb" are used
in reaching decisions when satisficing occurs.

Relational Concepts

Underlying the formulations on organizational goals,
expectations, and choice are four major relational concepts: (1) *quasi resolution of conflict*, which involves
goals that operate as aspiration-level constraints imposed by the demands of coalition members; (2) *uncertainty avoidance*, which is accomplished by focusing
on more predictable short-term environments and
short-run feedback or by arranging a negotiated environment; (3) *problemistic search*, which is concerned
with engineering a solution to a specific problem—a
solution that is motivated, simple-minded to the degree possible, and biased by the prior training, hopes,
and conflicting goals of those involved; (4) *organizational learning*, which results in changes and adaptations in goals, in attention rules, and in search rules.
The way these concepts enter into the organizational
decision process is outlined in the decision tree of
figure 22.3.

As developed, the theory is essentially descriptive
in nature. It attempts to understand and predict what
executives do and will do, rather than to state what
they should do. To the extent there are normative
implications, these appear to have emerged as an after-
thought; they have clearly not been the central focus
of the theorists' efforts.

An updated description of the search process envisioned is contained in figure 22.4.

Garbage Can Model

Throughout Simon's writings there runs an implicit
normative underpinning that says some type of rationality, to the extent it is possible, is always to be desired.
In contrast, March has increasingly moved away from
such a position. The following statement appears to
epitomize his views:

> Interesting people and interesting organizations
> construct complicated theories of themselves. In
> order to do this, they need to supplement the
> technology of reason with a technology of foolish-
> ness. Individuals and organizations need ways of
> doing things for which they have no good reason.
> Not always. Not usually. But sometimes. They
> need to act before they think. (March, 1972,
> p. 423)

From this orientation the so-called garbage can model
of organizational choice emerged (Cohen, March, &
Olsen, 1972; Cohen & March, 1974; March & Olsen,
1976), as discussed in the following sections.

Organized Anarchies

The garbage can model applies in situations where
organized anarchies exist, and the university setting
is cited as a prime example of such a context. The
characteristics of an organized anarchy are:

1. *Problematic goals*—preferences are ill-defined
   and inconsistent, and are discovered most frequently through action rather than serving as a
   basis for action.
2. *Unclear technology*—the organization does not
   understand its own processes and thus operates
   from trial and error, learning from accidents of
   the past, imitation, and the power of necessity.
3. *Fluid participation*—participants change fre-

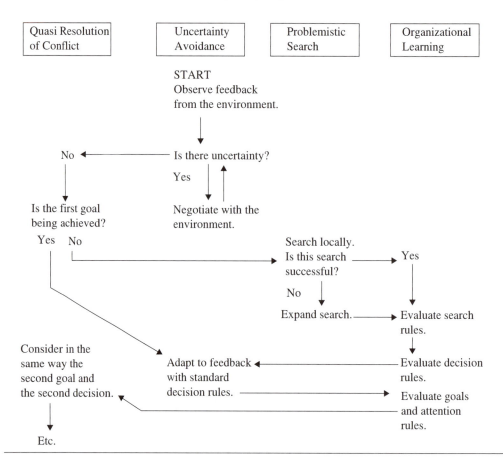

FIGURE 22.3 Organizational decision process at an abstract level ("Start" is at the point of receiving feedback from past decisions). Adapted from Richard M. Cyert & James G. March (1963), *A Behavioral Theory of the Firm* (Englewood Cliffs, NJ: Prentice Hall), 126.

quently and the amount of attention given to the organization by any one participant can vary significantly.

In such an organization issues tend to have low salience for most participants, being important primarily for symbolic reasons; there is a great deal of inertia; the occasion of a decision provides a garbage can into which all types of problems of current concern may be thrown; choice processes are easily overloaded; and the information base available for search and learning tends to be very limited. Ambiguity permeates not only the goal structure and the understanding of technologies and environments, but also the interpretation of past events, the organization's history, and even the concept of organizational membership.

Organizational Choice

The concept of organizational choice is described as follows:

Although organizations can often be viewed as vehicles for solving well-defined problems and as structures within which conflict is resolved through bargaining, there are also sets of procedures through which organizational participants arrive at an interpretation of what they are doing and what they have done while doing it. From this point of view, an organization is a collection of choices looking for problems, issues and feelings looking for decision situations in which they might be aired, solutions looking for issues to which they might be the answer, and decision makers looking for work.

. . . A key to understanding the processes within organizations is to view a choice opportunity as a garbage can into which various problems and solutions are dumped by participants. (Cohen & March, 1974, p. 81)

Among the hypotheses proposed are the following:

1. As the load on the decision system increases, so too does the number of decisions made by flight (problems leaving choices, thus making a choice which solves nothing possible) and oversight (choices being activated without being attached to problems, with the result that there is speedy acceptance).

2. Which problems and solutions are attended to in the context of which choices depends on the timing of appearance and who is available at the time to participate.
3. Problems, solutions, and attitudes that are persistently present are attended to more consistently than those that are sporadic.
4. Rules limiting the flow of problems to choices and the flow of participants to choice (controlling who may participate in the decision) change the process and the outcomes.
5. Given the widespread use of flight and oversight, the movement of certain problems to certain choices affects not only the choices

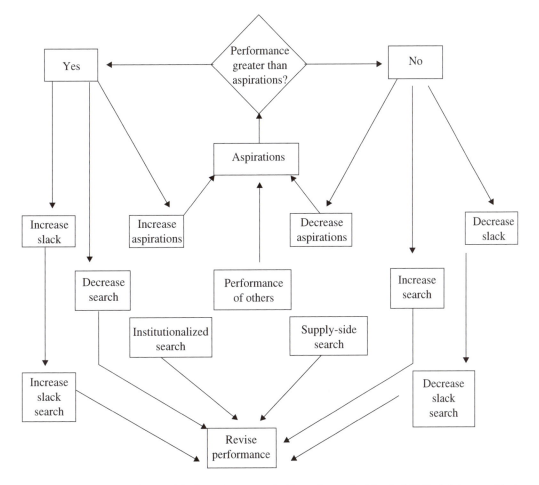

FIGURE 22.4 An expanded model of satisficing search. From James G. March (1994), *A Primer on Decision Making: How Decisions Happen* (New York: Free Press), 33. Copyright 1994 by James G. March. Reprinted with permission of The Free Press, a Division of Simon & Schuster, Inc.

8

to which the problems move, but the choices left alone as well.

6. Problems and solutions are debated to a degree because of the positive rewards associated with participation in the process of debate, rather than with decision outcomes. (March & Olsen, 1976)

The elements of the theory are best understood in the context of a computer simulation (Cohen et al., 1972). In this simulation certain factors are fixed: the number of time periods considered, the number of choice opportunities, the number of decision makers involved, the number of problems, and the solution coefficient for each time period. Entry times for choices and problems were varied across time periods using randomly generated sequences. Net energy load on the organization, which was defined as the difference between the participant energy required to solve all problems and the total amount of such energy available to the organization, varied from light to moderate to heavy. The relation between problems and choices (access structure) was established in three ways: (1) any active problem has access to any active choice; (2) important problems have access to many choices, and important choices are accessible to important problems only; (3) access between problems and choices is highly constrained and specialized. A similar structuring process was used to establish the relation between decision makers and choices (the decision structure), and the categories were again unsegmented, hierarchical, and specialized. The distribution of energy among decision makers, reflecting the amount of time spent by each on organizational problems, varied from important people with low energy, through equal energy for all decision makers, to important people with high energy.

When such a simulation is run, certain consistencies appear that might best be considered specific hypotheses for subsequent empirical investigation:

1. Resolution of problems as a style for making decisions is not the most common style, except under conditions where flight is severely restricted (for instance, specialized access) or a few conditions under light load. Decision making by flight and oversight is a major feature of the process in general.
2. The process is quite thoroughly and quite generally sensitive to variations in load.... An increase in the net energy load on the system generally increases problem activity,

decision maker activity, decision difficulty, and the uses of flight and oversight.

3. A typical feature of the model is the tendency of decision makers and problems to track each other through choices.... Both decision makers and problems tend to move together from choice to choice.
4. There are some important interconnections among three key aspects of the efficiency of the decision processes specified. The first is problem activity ... a rough measure of the potential for decision conflict.... The second aspect is problem latency, the amount of time problems spend activated but not linked to choices. The third aspect is decision time, the persistence of choices. Presumably a good organizational structure would keep both problem activity and problem latency low through rapid problem solution in its choices. In the garbage can process such a result was never observed.
5. The process is frequently sharply interactive. ... Phenomena are ... dependent on the particular combination of structures involved.... High segmentation of access structure generally produces slow decision time.... A specialized access structure, in combination with an unsegmented decision structure, produces quick decisions.
6. Important problems are more likely to be solved than unimportant ones. Problems which appear early are more likely to be resolved than later ones.
7. Important choices are less likely to resolve problems than unimportant choices. Important choices are made-by oversight and flight. Unimportant choices are made by resolution.
8. Although a large proportion of the choices are made, the choice failures that do occur are concentrated among the most important and least important choices. Choices of intermediate importance are virtually always made. (Cohen et al., 1972, pp. 9–11)

Organizational Attention

Such concepts as net energy load refer to the matter of participant attention. What happens in a decision situation is strongly dependent on who pays attention to what, and when (March & Olsen, 1976). Organizational structures, rules, and role expectations have a lot to do with this process; they serve as constraints on attention, while normally specifying only upper and lower limits for involvement. As with access and decision structures, attention may be organized so that all are affected equally by constraints, on a specialized basis, or on a hierarchical basis. Which attention structure will predominate is a function of the interdependencies of individual and group actions and the distribution of competencies, values, and resources.

Attention is often a consequence of competing demands on an individual's time, and as a result those who end up making a decision tend to be those who have nothing better to do. This is particularly true in unsegmented, permissive attention structures. Since status tends to attach more to the right to attend to a particular decision than to actual participation in it, individuals often compete for the right and then fail to attend. Nevertheless, more than any other factor, attention is predictable from a knowledge of standard operating procedures and administrative roles.

Learning under Ambiguity

The preceding theory of organizational attention contains a number of concepts and variables, but the theoretical relationships are not fully developed. The same may be said of formulations that relate to organizational learning (March & Olsen, 1976). The major focus of organizational learning is on the individual, and thus all but a few of the formulations are of more relevance for the study of micro organizational behavior than of organizational structure and process.

A primary point is that organizational learning is not necessarily adaptive or a source of wisdom and improved performance under conditions of ambiguity. Learning may well yield myths, fictions, folklore, and illusions rather than improvement. This is because it is not always obvious what happened, or why it happened, or whether what happened is a good thing. Given this ambiguity, learning can get far removed from what rationality would indicate.

Under such circumstances a theory of organizational learning would need to include the following ideas:

1. The ways in which information exposure, organizational memory, and the retrieval of history vary across individuals and subunits
2. How incentives and motivation for various forms of learning operate
3. How preexisting understandings, beliefs, and attitudes may condition learning
4. How the timing, order, and context of information influence the development of beliefs. (March & Olsen, 1976, pp. 59–60)

Specific hypotheses at the organizational level regarding such variables are not presented.

Domain Considerations

As originally formulated, the garbage can model applied to decision making in universities, and that was its domain. Gradually this domain has expanded, especially into public bureaucracies, although there never has been any claim that all decision making is of this type. There do appear to be many situations outside universities in which garbage can processes exist while still being constrained in some manner by social norms, organizational structures, and networks of connections that restrict the entry of decision makers, problems, choices, and solutions (March, 1994b). In a hierarchic system, for instance, important decision makers have access to many choices that are not available to less important decision makers. Similar types of access structures can be specified for solutions and problems. After all, the garbage can model is not a system of total disorder; it may only seem so when considered from a standard means-ends perspective (March, 1988).

Out of extended exposure to naval operations and personnel, certain limiting propositions bearing on the garbage can model as applied to this context were developed. Similar propositions might be set forth for other domain extensions:

Proposition 1: In order to accommodate important features of military organizations and situations, garbage can models need to include significant elements of structure that are absent from most discussions of the model in the theoretical literature.

Proposition 2: Although military decision making is rarely, if ever, a pure case of unsegmented garbage can decision making, there are significant garbage can elements in even the most operational decisions.

Proposition 3: Although military decision making cannot be managed effectively by assuming a pure garbage can, significant insights into managerial problems and possibilities can be obtained by combining a more traditional view with some elements of garbage can thinking. (March & Weissinger-Baylon, 1986, pp. 4–5)

Another possible extension of the garbage can approach involves participative decision making in groups, which is not a large extension but an important one. March concludes in this regard:

Participation is very likely to be frustrating. . . . A natural sequence to be expected is one in which participation first increases the attraction to decision making and then gradually decreases it. . . . One person's effects on a decision are lost in the effects of others, and one decision's effects are lost in the general confusions of history. . . . Experience is likely to teach that participation is a fraud and a waste. (1994b, pp. 166–168)

These hypotheses take a more negative tone than those Simon proposed for participation, but both envisage the real possibility of nil effects.

In concluding his primer on decision making March (1994b) argues for the need to suspend—at least temporarily—the operation of the system of reasoned consistency in an organization. He suggests such things as treating the self as a hypothesis, treating intuition as real, treating hypocrisy as a transition, treating memory as an enemy, and treating experience as a theory. Organizations need both playfulness and consistency, and they tend to come down hard on the consistency style. To get more organizational play, periods of temporary relief from control, coordination, and communication should be introduced.

Further to Organizational Learning

Of the various topics related to organizational decision making we have been considering, organizational learning has received the greatest amount of attention from March and his associates in the past 15 years or so.

Roles of History, Experience, and Memory

Learning occurs in organizations by encoding inferences that have been derived from history into a variety of routines that guide behavior (Levitt & March, 1988). These routines can persist, even though considerable turnover in personnel occurs; thus, they are organizational, not individual, in nature. They can change as a result of further experience, which is viewed as successful. There is a potential problem, however, in that favorable performance with an inferior procedure leads the organization to accumulate even more experience with that procedure while minimizing the amount of experience with a superior procedure, which, because of this lack of experience, is not learned and used. This is termed a *competency trap*. In all of this it is important to recognize that

history is not guaranteed to have any optimal result or certain destiny (March, 1994a).

Actually what is learned is determined less by history than by the way history is interpreted, and this can vary in different parts of an organization. These interpretations of history are stored in organizational memory, or at least some of them are. Memory tends to be orderly, but it can be inconsistent and ambiguous, too. Furthermore, errors may arise out of the ways in which memory is maintained and accessed. In many respects, organizational memory appears to have much the character of organizational culture.

Some organizations, in some manner, learn to learn and some do not. They learn from experience, but this process is confounded by such problems as paucity, redundancy, and complexity, which are inherent in this experience base. Learning does not by any means assure intelligent behavior. Yet history and its lessons as encoded in routines do lead to useful learning of some kind. Furthermore, as compared with alternatives such as bargaining, learning may do quite well; the alternatives make mistakes also.

When Experience Is Limited

The preceding discussion deals with generalities. There are not a great many testable hypotheses, although a framework for generating hypotheses is provided. Although there are instances in which March becomes more specific, again hypotheses may not follow. The case where organizations attempt to learn from history, even though the amount of experience available is quite limited, is one such instance (March, Sproull, & Tamuz, 1991).

One approach in these situations is to experience the available history more richly—to look at more aspects of the experience, consider more observations or interpretations, and experience more preferences. A second approach is to expand the experience base by considering near-histories (events that almost happened) and hypothetical histories (events that might have happened, given certain reasonable conditions). Both of these approaches are suspect, however, in terms of their reliability and validity. These two criteria can conflict in that the stable, shared knowledge required for reliability can restrict discovering contrary experience of a kind that permits valid learning.

Certainly, it is hard to justify many of the ways organizations handle small histories, even though many people appear to consistently believe they can do so. In the end, we are left with four basic questions that need to be resolved before this belief in the capacity to justify small histories can be supported:

1. What is the evidential standing of imagination (near and hypothetical histories)?
2. What is the proper process for combining expectations and interrelated, cumulated aspects of rich description into an interpretation of history?
3. What is the proper trade-off between reliability and validity in historical interpretation?
4. What are the relative values of multiple observations of events and multiple interpretations of them? (March et al., 1991, pp. 10–11)

Exploration and Exploitation

Exploration involves learning through experimentation with new approaches—the returns are uncertain, distant, and likely to be negative. Exploitation involves learning through a process of refining and extending existing competencies—the returns are predictable, proximate, and positive. Yet an emphasis on exploitation can compromise competitive position in such a way that finishing near the top is precluded (March, 1991).

Organizations that resort to exploration almost exclusively create the risk that they will run up major costs and gain few benefits; there may be too many undeveloped, unimplemented ideas. But an exclusive reliance on exploitation can lead to being trapped in a status quo that is suboptimal. Clearly, maintaining some type of balance between the two is to be desired, since they compete for scarce resources, and few organizations will be able to afford heavy investments in both directions. Thus, the need for a trade-off, which is somehow balanced, is hypothesized, although the exact point of balance is not stated, nor is a method for determining it.

Simplification and Specialization

Many of the cognitive limits that restrict rationality also restrict learning. These individual limitations are also joined by those of an organizational nature. Two mechanisms are specified to facilitate learning under such circumstances. One is *simplification*, whereby experience is restricted to the environment in which action occurs. Isolated subunits can be the site of learning, which is impossible when there are several simultaneously interacting units. Thus buffers around units are created and environments are enacted—for example, departmental boundaries are created—in order to facilitate learning. *Specialization* seeks the same result. Learning tends to focus attention and to narrow down the scope of competence. Thus several different, small learning locales often become substitutes for one another.

These two mechanisms can improve organizational performance, but they can limit performance as well because they tend to mean that both the long run and the larger picture are ignored. They also create a tendency to overlook failures because successes are magnified, thus driving out understanding of the risks of failure:

> As learners settle into these domains in which they have competence and accumulate experience in them, they experience fewer and fewer failures. Insofar as they generalize that experience to other domains, they are likely to exaggerate considerably the likelihood of success.... Confidence finds confirmation in its own imagination.... Learning is less self-correcting than might be expected. (Levinthal & March, 1993, p. 104)

The theory of learning as set forth by March is more extensive than what is covered here, but it is set forth in chunks in different locations at different points in time; I have covered what I believe to be the major chunks. Also March is much more adept at framing problems and unearthing competing tendencies than at establishing hypotheses for experimental testing. This difficulty has been noted before, and it affects the ease with which the theory may be evaluated.

Evaluation and Impact

Simon, March, and Cyert all carried out studies related to their theories in the early years, sometimes in collaboration with each other. March continued doing research in organizational behavior long after the others had ceased to do so, but even he moved away from empirical analyses some 20 years ago, roughly at the point he became engaged primarily with problems related to organizational learning.

Research on Behavioral Theory of the Firm

Studies in the context of the behavioral theory of the firm appear to have contributed primarily to the development of the behavioral theory rather than to testing it. Throughout the middle and late 1950s March conducted a number of studies related to group processes and the dynamics of influence (for example, see March, 1956), but it was only toward the very end of the decade that he and Cyert began to collaborate on the research that provided an underpinning for their theory.

In one instance a series of decisions dealing with renovating old equipment, finding new working quarters, selecting a consulting firm, and choosing a data processing system were studied in much the same manner as Cyert et al. (1956) had done. It was found that marginal advantages of alternatives were considered only in the grossest sense, search was carried out in a bargaining context, computations were simple and focused on feasibility considerations, and individual and unit biases permeated the decisions (Cyert, Dill, & March, 1958). A subsequent laboratory study substantiated the existence of bias in sales and cost estimates, but found in addition that those obtaining the false information tended to apply a suitable bias discount (Cyert, March, & Starbuck, 1961). This finding, that bias may not be a significant factor in overall organizational decisions, as opposed to individual decisions, is not fully congruent with the theory, and the authors note the need for further study on this point.

Cyert and March (1963) report on several studies in which their formulations about expectation and choice processes were used to develop computer models. The results obtained were then compared with actual empirical data. A duopoly model was used to generate profit figures, which were then compared with longitudinal results reported for the American Can Company and the Continental Can Company. The fit, though by no means perfect, is reasonably good. This was also true of a model that was constructed to predict price and output decisions in a department store. Actual decisions were predicted accurately in 88 to 96 percent of the cases, depending on the particular output or price index used. Although the behavioral theory of the firm was not compared with alternative theories in these studies, its predictive power appears to be considerable.

Working from several case studies, Feldman and March (1981) present evidence that organizations systematically collect more information than they use in the decision process; they act first and receive requested information later, they solicit reports and do

not read them. The authors interpret this phenomenon as reflecting the symbolic value that information has in portraying a commitment to rational choice.

Research in the Garbage Can

March originally viewed educational institutions as the prime examples of organized anarchies, and he has conducted considerable research on educational organizations. Much of this research is tangential to the garbage can model, however, and some is totally unrelated. The original presentation of the model discussed extensively the expected consequences of reduced slack for universities that were rich and poor, small and large (Cohen et al., 1972). Specific predictions were made in a computer model for universities in the various categories. The results are interesting and provocative, but they say little about the validity of the theory. In the words of the authors:

> The application of the model to this particular situation among American colleges and universities clearly depends upon a large number of assumptions. Other assumptions would lead to other interpretations of the impact of adversity within a garbage can decision process. Nevertheless, the derivations from the model have some face validity as a description of some aspects of recent life in American higher education. (Cohen et al., 1972, p. 15)

Unfortunately, hard data were not available to the authors.

Similarly, March's basic studies of college administrators, though intended to illustrate the garbage can model, fail to prove its validity (Cohen & March, 1974; March & Olsen, 1976). They simply were not designed for this purpose. In contrast, certain case studies described by March and Romelaer in the March and Olsen volume deal with decisions such as eliminating a program in speech, transferring a program in architecture, changing a grading system, and introducing a new doctoral field in economics that are clearly understandable within the garbage can framework.

Several investigations by March also touch on the garbage can model without really testing it. Thus a study extending over more than 30 years of the positions held by school superintendents indicates an almost random pattern, with the performance of individuals having practically no significance. This finding is at least consistent with the concept of the nonheroic, somewhat powerless top administrator in organized anarchies (March & March, 1977), but it does not deal with why the results occur. In another study it was found that university departments attempt to change their curriculums to make them more attractive to students when the university is experiencing financial difficulty, but that this effect is less pronounced in departments with greater research reputations (Manns & March, 1978). These results say something about coalitions, bargaining power, and the like, but they do not provide direct support for the garbage can model.

Thus research evidence in support of the theory remains inadequate, awaiting studies by individuals other than March. The following prescription for action in university settings also must be held in abeyance for lack of evidence:

> One of the complications in accomplishing something in a garbage can decision-making process is the tendency for any particular project to become entwined with a variety of other issues simply because those issues exist at the time the project is before the organization. A proposal for curricular reform becomes an arena for a concern for social justice. . . . A proposal for bicycle paths becomes an arena for discussion of sexual inequality. It is pointless to try to react to such problems by attempting to enforce rules of relevance. . . . The appropriate tactical response is to provide garbage cans into which wide varieties of problems can be dumped. The more conspicuous the can, the more garbage it will attract away from other projects. . . . On a grand scale, discussions of overall organizational objectives or overall organizational long-term plans are classic first-quality cans. . . . On a smaller scale, the first item on a meeting agenda is an obvious garbage can. (Cohen & March, 1974, p. 211)

Decisions in Coalitions

The concept of an organization as a coalition in which goals and decision outcomes are determined by bargaining and slack plays an important role has been studied primarily through analyses of actual decisions in organizations. One area of study has been budget decisions in universities. Budget allocations to departments have been found to be closely related to power position within the coalition, irrespective of actual departmental needs as reflected in work load, number

of faculty, and the like (Pfeffer & Moore, 1980). The power of a department was particularly manifest under conditions of scarcity.

Other research indicates that repetitive, programmable decisions in business firms tend to coincide closely with expectations from the Cyert and March (1963) theory. Factors such as multiple goals, constraints, satisficing, uncertainty avoidance, bargaining, standard operating procedures, and rules of thumb were all in evidence in the weekly advertising decisions of a supermarket chain, and these factors tended to operate as the theory would predict (Rados, 1972).

Alternatively, to predict top-level strategy decisions that are one of a kind, the Cyert and March (1963) theory, though still applicable, needs considerable elaboration. In a field study of decisions related to investments and acquisitions by a rapidly growing computer firm it was found that sequential bargaining across hierarchical levels played an important role, that uncertainty of outcome tends to elicit a greater number of criteria or goals, and that search may be elicited by factors other than problems, and by opportunities in particular (Carter, 1971). The original theory seems to need a greater degree of specification if it is to be applied to strategic decisions.

The important role that slack plays in maintaining coalitions has been documented. Both too much slack and too little can prove detrimental to innovation, however (Nohria & Gulati, 1996). Slack does serve to foster more experimentation and thus innovative breakthrough, but it can also produce a lack of discipline over innovative projects to the point where they become nonproductive and fail in their implementation.

Organized Anarchies

Previously in this chapter we have noted case studies of decisions in which observation, interviews, and occasionally records were used to obtain data. In these instances the data collection is characteristically unstandardized and replication of the research would be difficult, even if exactly the same decision situation could be identified. Such analyses of small numbers of cases are very useful for constructing descriptive theories but much less useful for testing them. Unfortunately, the research on organized anarchies and the garbage can model tends to be of this kind.

The March and Olsen (1976) volume contains descriptions of a university dean selection decision (by Olsen), a medical school location decision (by Kare Rommetveit), decision making in an experimental free school (by Kristian Kreiner and Soren Christensen), a racial desegregation decision in a school district (by Stephen Weiner), and a university reorganization decision (by Olsen). These decisions are said to be consistent with the garbage can model, and they appear to have much in common with that model, as does the R&D department decision making described by Michael McCaskey (1979). The model unquestionably "rings a bell" when held up against the realities of these decision situations. Still, none of these studies explicitly tests hypotheses derived from the theory.

One study in the March and Olsen volume does test hypotheses based on the theory in a context that could well qualify as organized anarchy. This research (by Per Stava, 1976) deals with certain college location decisions in Norway that were inherently political in nature. Various demographic indexes were used to predict where the colleges would be located, and these predictions were then compared with the actual decisions made by the Norwegian parliament. The results are rather surprising:

> Our analysis supports legal-bureaucratic theories of political choice. . . . Not power, not interest groups, not voters, but some simple, even sensible, rules come to dominate—without explicit computation. . . . The system pursues a political solution within highly restrictive normative rules of equity. Although, as far as we know, no one in the system calculated anything approximating our weighted distance criterion, the process constrained itself to solutions consistent with such a conception of fairness and need. . . . Our analysis indicates a case for treating decisions as explainable in terms of stable, structural elements in the situation. (Stava, 1976, p. 217)

If the context was that of organized anarchy, then the findings do not fit the hypothesized garbage can model.

Since the 1970s there has been considerable study and use of the garbage can concepts, although attention tended to drop off during the 1990s. There have been several reviews, of which March and Roger Weissinger-Baylon (1986) and Richard Magjuka (1988) are typical. It now seems apparent that the garbage can as originally proposed is atypical in bureaucratic organizations. It tends to be constrained and channeled

by structure in numerous respects, including the degree to which participation is fluid; hierarchic positions tend to force participation in certain decisions. There clearly are elements of the garbage can in these contexts, as reflected in the three propositions set forth by March and Weissinger-Baylon (1986) for the military, but even these theoretical modifications may overstate the case for deviations from rationality. For instance, Frank Heller, Pieter Drenth, Paul Koopman, and Veljko Rus (1988) found no support for the garbage can model in their multinational study of decision making in bureaucracies, and they cite additional research to this same effect.

The initial computer simulations advanced when the garbage can idea was proposed left out people in structures and thus were incomplete. Several attempts to remedy this situation have been published, and progress is evident (Masuch & LaPotin, 1989). Yet as a method of testing the theory for validity, this approach appears to be inadequate at the present stage of our knowledge; the model has become hugely complex, and external validation is very difficult.

Evidence from a study of college textbook publishing decisions (Levitt & Nass, 1989) indicates also that this complexity may well have been understated. In this study, the environment beyond the publishing company, not just company structure, was found to exert an influence on decision processes that were inherently of a garbage can nature. Orderliness was introduced as a function of the actions of competitors, professional characteristics, and customer (university) arrangements.

What emerges from the research is that situations that give every indication of being examples of garbage can decision making often turn out to be much more ordered and rational than first appeared. The basis for the rationality is by no means self-evident, but with sufficient study it tends to reveal itself. This does not mean necessarily that the garbage can elements are entirely eliminated, but they are reduced. Given this situation, it may be best to consider garbage can decision making as an ideal or pure case, appropriate for theoretical analysis, but not often adequate to the task of understanding and predicting the actual outcomes of a decision process without considerable supplementing and restructuring. This is not to say that viewing decisions from a garbage can perspective may not provide useful information. What is needed now are data on where, when, how often, and to what extent the garbage can model fits.

Research on Organizational Learning

Organizational learning is defined differently by different authors and occurs in a variety of types (Miller, 1996). One result is that the limited research on the topic is spread over a wide range of areas. We have already seen that Argyris's approach (see chapter 20) has not evoked much research; the same is true of March's. As Anne Miner and Stephen Mezias note: "Historically, learning articles have consisted primarily of (1) general schematic models of organizational learning, (2) field-based qualitative insights, and (3) simulation studies" (1996, p. 95). There is a "dramatic need for more systematic empirical learning research with special emphasis on longitudinal studies" (p. 94). Expressions of need such as this are to be found throughout the organizational learning literature.

Yet there is good reason to believe that organizational learning is a "hot topic" right now, not only among scholars, but for practitioners as well, in spite of the lack of an empirical base. In fact, there has been research on why this has occurred. The antecedents appear to be as follows:

1. The shift in the relative importance of factors of production away from capital toward labor, particularly intellectual labor
2. The ever more rapid pace of change in the business environment
3. Widespread acceptance of knowledge as a prime source of competitive advantage
4. The greater demands being placed on all businesses by customers
5. Increasing dissatisfaction among managers and employees with the traditional, command-and-control management paradigm
6. The intensely competitive nature of global businesses (Harvey & Denton, 1999, p. 897)

It is hoped that these forces will eventually drive the conduct of research on March's theory, which is arguably the most promising theory of organizational learning that is currently available. Yet it is sobering that a search of the recent literature has turned up only one study, as of mid-2000, focused directly on that theory with acceptable sample size and design—a study primarily in the strategic management domain dealing with the fate of expansion efforts. The finding with regard to the theory was that "learning is not confined to identifiable points of feedback such as net present value or actual dissolution, but in fact is far more continuous, haphazard, and idiosyncratic" (Pennings, Barkema, & Douma, 1994, p. 635). This relates to the idea that learning can occur even from near-decisions and failures.

Overview

March's emphasis on the value of foolishness in organizational decision making is distinctly at variance with Simon's stress on the intendedly rational. In fact, foolishness appears to be strongly aligned with Chester Barnard's appeal to intuition, which Simon rejected. Similarly, the organized anarchy view of universities that March propounds does not fit well with the much more rational view that Cyert (1975) came to espouse as a university president. Cyert himself explains the difference in viewpoint as largely temporal, with the organized anarchy concepts applying in times of high slack and his own current views (1975) being more descriptive of what happens under low-slack conditions. However, March does not propose that slack be used as a contingency variable, and the research on university budgeting only partially supports Cyert's suggestion.

Thus, there is some disparity among the Carnegie theorists. However, Argyris (1976) is consistently critical. He accuses Cohen and March (1974) of Machiavellian tactics, such as the suggestion that garbage cans be created to attract problems away from other projects, and of sanctioning deceit. Again, the charge is that the theory fosters the status quo, although now the status quo is organized anarchy. But to this is added a charge of thwarting openness and trust. To know how the organizational world is and to develop tactics for coping with reality hardly seem to be undesirable scientific goals. In fact, we often must understand reality before we can decide whether it should be and can be changed. One must question whether Argyris's criticisms here are consistent with the goals of science as considered in chapter 1 of this volume.

Yet, Argyris has continued his attacks more recently. He is concerned about a blindness to double loop learning and a tendency to place core concepts beyond the requirements of empirical falsifiability, as well as a resort to defensive reasoning (Argyris, 1996). These concerns are developed at some length; a rebuttal is contained in Miner and Mezias (1996). It appears that March's sin is that he failed to use Argyris's variables and terminology, even though he began developing his ideas on organizational learning well before Argyris published on the subject.

Any treatment of March's theorizing has to consider the early work up through the garbage can separately from the treatment of organizational learning. Much of what was said with regard to Simon's theorizing in the overview applies to the early March as well. The concepts are useful, many have empirical support, they provide a solid foundation for the study of organizational decision making, but there is need for much more extensive research to fill in holes in the support and to answer important questions.

The theorizing on organizational learning is a quite different matter. What seems to have happened in this instance is that the theory has gravitated to a locale on the theoretical terrain map and is now situated very close to organizational culture (see chapter 21 in this volume). Much that can be said about one approach applies to the other as well; the problems appear to be similar. Whether March's organizational learning theory, and culture too, will be able to move to a new, more nourishing location on the theoretical map is anybody's guess at this point, but time does appear to be running out. Furthermore, March's championing of foolishness and his naming of garbage can decision making have been somewhat less than popular in some quarters. There appears to be an orientation to theater more than science here that tends to make some serious researchers wish to distance themselves from it.

As guides for organizational action, one would expect all of the theories considered to this point in this chapter to provide little help. They are essentially descriptive theories, not normative. March does move occasionally into the realm of strategic management, but not very far. His primary role in this regard has been to show that there are good reasons for things being as they are. At best, his theories give organizational members a way to look at and talk about their organizational world and to understand it better.

Cohen and March (1974) provide a set of rules for operating in a garbage can context. Briefly, these rules are as follows: spend time, persist, exchange status for substance, facilitate opposition participation, overload the system, provide garbage cans, manage unobtrusively, and interpret history—guidelines that Argyris considered Machiavellian. These guidelines appear to make sense, given a controlled anarchy. But such face validity, rather than true empirical evidence, suggests caution. No studies have been done where

interventions of these kinds have been introduced and the consequences measured. In fact, although it appears that garbage can decision situations do exist, we have no way of scaling the extent of their presence and knowing when these types of interventions might be appropriate.

ORGANIZING AND SENSEMAKING

As we shift now to the theory developed by Karl Weick, we move into what looks to be another world. In fact, decision making is not even the explicit matter of concern. Yet the theory deals with the same domain covered by decision-making theorists and is concerned with many of the same issues. That is why it belongs in the same chapter as the theories of Simon and March.

Weick's original theorizing appears primarily in three books, although there are important theoretical contributions contained in some of the essays that he has so frequently sprinkled across the journal and book chapter literature of organizational behavior. The books, however, form the framework through which the theory is presented here. These are the first (Weick, 1969) and second (Weick, 1979) editions of the *Social Psychology of Organizing* and *Sensemaking in Organizations* (Weick, 1995).

Background

Born in 1936, Weick is somewhat younger than most of organizational behavior's first-generation theorists. He did his undergraduate work at Wittenberg College and went on to Ohio State University, where he was strongly influenced by Harold Pepinsky, a counseling psychologist with diverse interests. Although he was originally enrolled in the industrial psychology program at Ohio State, his Ph.D. in 1962 was actually granted in organizational psychology. His early writing out of the doctorate was often concerned with issues related to cognitive dissonance and involved considerable reporting of empirical research.

From Ohio State Weick went to Purdue University, where he taught industrial psychology, then to the University of Minnesota, moving increasingly toward social psychology, and finally with his first business school appointment to Cornell University in 1972. There he edited *Administrative Science Quarterly* and stayed for the longest stint to this point in his career.

In 1984 Weick moved again, to the business school at the University of Texas, and then in 1988 back to the Midwest at the University of Michigan, where he has remained. Increasingly, his writing has concentrated on books and essays, not empirical research any longer. He says he studies "interpretation, sensemaking, equivocality, stress, dissonance, and crises behavior" (Weick, 1993c, p. 312).

This is not a listing that one would find often, and the subject matter is presented in ways that are often difficult to understand. John Van Maanen, who admires this work immensely, says "Weick . . . has produced a substantial body of work. It is a body of work I have tried to enter and understand (not always successfully)" (1995, p. 135). Derek Pugh, who is much less of an admirer, says:

> In the early 70s there was a conference, and we had Karl Weick over because he was a big name in process in those days. Somehow or other I can't relate to what he has to say. At that time, I said "I don't understand what the second half of the book is about." And he said, "Well I don't think I understand what the second half of the book is about." . . . Karl Weick's paradigm doesn't relate to me, and I don't understand it. It think its interesting, but the things he talks about are not things that interest me. I'm working in a different paradigm. (quoted in Greenwood & Devine, 1997, p. 207)

Not surprisingly Weick's name is not to be found in Pugh and David Hickson's (1993) *Great Writers on Organizations*. Weick's writing tends to elicit a bimodal distribution on the favorability-unfavorability dimension, and he recognizes that fact. But on any rating of ease to difficulty of understanding much more unanimity exists—this is not an easy read. At an earlier point I took an approach similar to Pugh's and did not include Weick's work in my discussions of major theories in large part because I was not sure I could reflect his ideas correctly. Now, I feel compelled to tackle them, but I do so with some sense of uncertainty.

Organizing Theory

Weick's *Social Psychology of Organizing* (1969) seems to have been titled to reflect both its similarity to and differences from a very influential book with much the same name published 3 years earlier (Katz and Kahn's *The Social Psychology of Organizations*; see chapter 14 in this volume). The disparity in title serves to point up the fact that Weick's focus is indeed on the *process* of organizing. Furthermore, his book is introduced as directed to the student with no prior background in social psychology; this would seem to place an undue burden on the introductory student.

Concepts of Organization

Weick does not place strong emphasis on organizational goals. In fact, actions may well precede goals, and, accordingly, goal statements become essentially retrospective. Rationality is attributed primarily to small groups, with the result that organizations are characterized by multiple, often contradictory, rationalities. Groups are the key to understanding organizations. Organizations are to be understood in terms of processes under way, and thus organizing activities; there are regularities in such activities, but structure at a point in time is unimportant.

Organizing involves adapting to an environment that, in fact, is enacted by interdependent human actors within the organization. This environment is closely tied to that to which the organizational actors pay attention. Organizing focuses on removing uncertainty so that equivocality is reduced and information is obtained. Actions come first and provide the content for cognition; thus, planning does not control actions, but actions control plans. This type of formulation leaves planning with a very limited role in organizational functioning (and strategy, too).

These and other concepts of organization may be summarized as follows:

1. Processes involved in organizing must continually be reaccomplished.
2. Control is a prominent process within organizations, but it is accomplished by relationships, not by people.
3. Goal consensus is not a precondition of order and regularity.
4. Triads are the basic unit of analysis in organization theory.
5. Attentional processes are a crucial determinant of human organizing.
6. Organizations continue to exist only to the degree that they are able to maintain a balance between flexibility and stability (attainment of one is at the expense of the other).
7. Organizing is directed toward removing equivocality from the information environment (the equivocality of processes must

match the equivocality of their informational inputs). (Weick, 1969, pp. 36–41)

Processes are individual behaviors interlocked among people; thus the behaviors of one person become contingent on those of another. These interlocked behaviors stabilize and are repeated. This regularity is what is called organizational structure, and people try to preserve it as long as it remains rewarding. These interlocked behaviors are the basic elements of organizing; each process within organizing contains sets of interlocked behaviors that can serve to remove a certain amount of equivocality from the information fed to the process.

Processes of Organizing

The organizing processes are developed from a view derived from theories of sociocultural evolution. These processes are related using the model of figure 22.5. I will attempt to explain that model. The basic processes are enactment, selection, and retention. Assuming that actors can modify the ways in which the model unfolds, and thus exert control over at least some aspects, it is not unreasonable to expect that

these choice points occur at the output side of the retention process; thus the feedback loops in figure 22.5. The basic questions are "Knowing what I know now, should I (1) notice something new and (2) act differently?" Nevertheless, it is rules that determine the course of these evolutionary processes; organizing is in fact the set of rules that govern the ways in which elements interact to produce predictable outcomes.

With regard to the enacted environment—

1. The creation of meaning is an attentional process, but it is attention to that which has already occurred.
2. Since the attention is directed backward from a specific point in time, . . . whatever is occurring at the moment will influence what the person discovers when he glances backward.
3. Memory processes . . . influence meaning.
4. Only when a response occurs does the stimulus become defined.

It is these primitive meanings, these bits of enacted information, that constitute the informational input for subsequent processes of selection and retention. (Weick, 1969, pp. 65, 69)

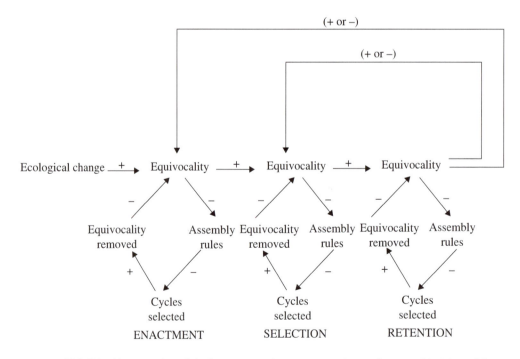

FIGURE 22.5 Weick's original model of organizing (– = inverse path; + = direct path). Adapted from Karl E. Weick (1969), *The Social Psychology of Organizing* (Reading, MA: Addison-Wesley), 93.

These informational inputs derive from collective, not individual, actions. Ecological change sparks collective actions, and ecological change gains its control over organizations in this manner. These actions are the raw material from which the primitive meanings are derived. The selection process then sorts these equivocal outputs from enactment to make them less equivocal. Equivocality is constantly removed as we progress through the model.

The three processes all contain both assembly rules and interlocked behavior cycles. The assembly rules deal with such matters as effort (select cycles that require the least effort), frequency (select cycles that have occurred most often previously), success (select cycles that have worked to remove equivocality), permanence (select cycles that will yield the most stable change), and so on. Ten are listed—these four, plus duration, availability, personnel, relevance, reward, and disturbance. The greater the equivocality operationalized, the fewer the rules activated to compose the process. This is so because when the input is less equivocal, more certainty exists and therefore more rules can be activated in assembling a process to deal with this input. The interlocked behavior cycles consist of an action by one person (assembles a set of criteria for application to the input), a response by another person (accepts or rejects assemblage), and a double interact (abandons, revises, or maintains assemblage). When behaviors are thus selected for a process, interpersonal networks are in fact selected and stable interaction patterns are activated.

In figure 22.5, since the equivocality-to-assembly-rules path is inverse, it is given the minus sign. The path from assembly rules to behavior cycles is similar, and thus also is designated with a minus sign. The path from the behavior cycles selected to equivocality removal is direct, and thus it is given a plus sign (the more the cycles, the more the removal). The equivocality-removed-to-equivocality-remaining path is, of course, inverse (minus sign). Remaining equivocality is passed along to the next process. The three processes function similarly, but they differ in the kinds of assembly rules operating and in the amount of equivocality that exists in the typical inputs involved.

Returning to the feedback loops, choices may be made that hold largely equivocal or largely unequivocal content in the retention process:

Unless the actor treats retained content as both equivocal and unequivocal, the system in which he is involved will not survive. In order to maintain the balance between stability and flexibility necessary for system survival, he must treat retained content as equivocal in one of his two decisions about future acts or choices, and treat it as unequivocal in the other decision. (Weick, 1969, p. 80)

Thus both deviation-amplifying and deviation-counteracting loops are necessary. A system will survive only if an odd number of negative cycles exist.

Based on these statements and the model of figure 22.5, Weick sets forth a definition as follows: "Organizing consists of the resolving of equivocality in an enacted environment by means of interlocked behaviors embedded in conditionally related processes" (1969, p. 91). Organizing is thus a matter of information processing. Equivocality must be registered prior to its removal. For registry to occur, the order inherent in the input must match that of the process to which the information is an input. For equivocality to be removed, the order must be greater than that inherent in the input to the process. All this is accomplished within a process by the number of behavior cycles applied, thus removing equivocality, and the number of assembly rules used, thus registering equivocality. In enactment, the interstructured behavior cycles are concerned with doing, acting, and performing. In selection, these cycles are concerned with choosing which among the previous actions should be "repeated, acknowledged, and given the status of beneficial experience" (Weick, 1969, p. 95).

Consequences

In concluding his statement of the theory Weick says:

The basic point here is that once the particular pattern of relationships is specified, predictable consequences should be observed. . . . Once the observer specifies the elements and relationships, he can test, refine, and even refute the ideas mentioned here. Even though the model is general it is still refutable. If a system with an odd number of negative cycles disintegrates, or if a system with an even number of negative cycles survives, then we are wrong. If the relationships not under the control of human actors (i.e. enactment + selection + retention) do not exhibit direct causal ties, then we are wrong. And if any of the other assumed causal relationships are nonexistent, then we are wrong. (1969, p. 96)

Thus the theory is said to be empirically testable. So, too, are certain hypotheses derived from the theory, such as "if the actor's performance of an assigned task removes equivocality in the informational inputs he attends to, then productivity and satisfaction should become more closely tied together, and both should be high" (p. 99).

For decision making, the theory implies that past experience and satisficing are much less important than the state of the informational input (its equivocality). For planning, the important factor is the form of reflection produced by the plan, not the form of anticipation: "A dyad in which members cooperate should be *less* satisfying than a dyad in which they alternate between cooperation (socialized action) and competition (individual action)" (p. 105).

Guidelines for action are also set forth, predicated on some degree of validation of the theory:

1. Don't panic in the face of disorder—disorder is needed to handle equivocality of input.
2. You never do one thing all at once—it takes time for the self-correcting nature of the system to unfold.
3. Chaotic action is preferable to orderly inaction—only action can provide a basis for learning.
4. The most important decisions are often the least apparent—the key decisions are those influencing the feedback loops from retention.
5. You should coordinate processes rather than groups—locate the three organizing processes, determine the direction of their causal ties, and then adjust the linkages to assure an odd number of negative cycles. (Weick, 1969, pp. 106–108)

Ten Years Later

The second edition of the *Social Psychology of Organizing* (Weick, 1979) is a much expanded (from 121 pages to 294), grossly reordered version with many more examples and quotes, along with some new content. Things are often worded differently. Organizing, for instance, is now defined as "a consensually validated grammar for reducing equivocality by means of sensible interlocked behaviors" (Weick, 1979, p. 3).

The concept of a cause map is introduced to describe what goes on in a group discussion. It indicates which events affected which others and the direction of this affect (plus or minus). Such a map facilitates determining the number of negative signs involved in interactions and thus whether the odd number required for stability and deviation-counteraction is present. The list of possible assembly rules is expanded from the 10 noted previously to 16 (adding uncertainty, obligations, precedent, absorption, enhancement, and mutilation). The sequence within a process set forth in the lower part of figure 22.5 is changed as shown in figure 22.6. The raw material moving from enactment to selection as its input consists of equivocal enactments and also cause maps of varying equivocality.

Although Weick continues to emphasize process, he does feel it is possible to state where the organization resides:

> The organization consists of plans, recipes, rules, instructions and programs for generating, interpreting, and governing behavior that are jointly managed by two or more people. . . . You look at the contents of the retention process, you identify the dominant assembly rules, you pinpoint the interpersonal cycles that tend to be most salient and incorporated into the largest number of processes, and you try to articulate the cause maps that recur. . . . These several properties constitute the stability, continuity, and repetition that produces the impression of similarity across time in the processes that occur. (Weick, 1979, p. 235)

Yet elsewhere there is a statement to the effect that the complexity of organization can only be described by sets of differential equations, which in turn require measures of the variable elements. Constructing such measures is said to be "next to impossible and probably not worth doing any way" (p. 212). In the second edition references to testability, refutability, and hypotheses of the kind noted in the first edition (dealing with satisfaction and productivity) have completely disappeared.

Nevertheless, the guidelines for actions are retained and expanded. The first four of these remain the same, but the fifth is replaced by six new guidelines:

5. There is no solution—origins are typically impossible to discover because they are often remote from the symptom.
6. Stamp out utility—when people adapt to one situation they lose resources needed to adapt to other situations in the future.

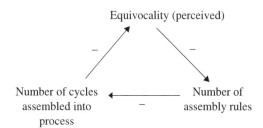

FIGURE 22.6 Revisions to Weick's model. Adapted from Karl E. Weick (1979), *The Social Psychology of Organizing* (Reading, MA: Addison-Wesley), 133.

7. The map is the territory—the cause maps produced do in fact create the territory the organization inhabits.
8. Rechart the organizational chart—do this by replacing people with variables (assertiveness, compliance, delegation, demand for control, rigidity of behavior, and the like).
9. Visualize organizations as evolutionary systems—this has much the quality of the previous fifth guideline.
10. Complicate yourself—for instance, for a period of time discredit all that has been known previously by resort to some procedure such as randomization; thus introducing new equivocality. (Weick, 1979, 246–263)

Finally, as part of a much expanded vocabulary introduced into the theory, the concept of loose coupling (among enactment, selection, and retention processes for instance) is invoked. This concept was initially introduced several years earlier to describe the operation of educational organizations. There the following points were made:

Concepts such as loose coupling serve as sensitizing devices . . . to notice and question things that had previously been taken for granted. . . . Preoccupation with rationalized, tidy, efficient, coordinated structures has blinded many . . . to some of the attractive properties of less rationalized . . . events. . . . By loose coupling, the author intends to convey the image that coupled events are responsive, but that each event also preserves its own identity and some evidence of its physical and logical separateness. . . . Loose coupling also carries connotations of impermanence, dissolvability, and tacitness. (Weick, 1976, pp. 2–3)

For a number of reasons Weick clearly favors loose coupling of organizational elements and processes; innovation tends to be fostered.

Sensemaking Theory

No third version of the organizing theory has been presented, but several essays during the 1980s and early 1990s elucidate on the earlier statements. One such is a discussion of enactment as it occurs under crisis conditions (ecological change) (Weick, 1988). Here enactment is described as a process in which "first, portions of the field of experience are bracketed and singled out for closer attention on the basis of preconceptions. Second, people act within the context of these bracketed elements, under the guidance of preconceptions, and often shape these elements in the direction of preconceptions" (p. 307). Because actions tend to be somewhat further along than understanding of these actions, crises may be intensified before we know what we are doing. Loose coupling can help here. So, too, can improvisation, which can correct blind spots inherent in an existing design (Weick, 1993b).

One of these interim essays seems to question previously stated theory (Daft & Weick, 1984) and consequently introduces certain logical inconsistencies. The proposed model sets forth enacting, discovering, undirected viewing, and conditioned viewing as top management interpretation modes. Thus, enactment is downplayed at the expense of three other processes given equal billing. Furthermore, strategy formulation and decision making, formerly relegated to subsidiary status, are now placed center stage. It is not clear whether this formulation represents a new theory (intended to replace parts of organizing theory) or an aberration (occasioned by the particular joint authorship involved). In any event, the next book (Weick, 1995) does not restate organizing theory but, rather, sets forth a new but related perspective.

Properties of Sensemaking

The book *Sensemaking in Organizations* may be viewed as one long (200-page) response to the sentence completion stem "Sensemaking is . . . " The process is first described in terms of seven characteristics:

1. Grounded in identity construction—and thus in the creation of individual and organizational identity
2. Retrospective—in the same manner as enactment
3. Enactive of sensible environments—as with enactment
4. Social—basically a social, not individual, process embedded in conversation, group discussions, and the like
5. Ongoing—based on continued bracketing and segmenting of moments in the flow of life
6. Focused on and by extracted cues—these cues from the environment are both the targets and the grist of the process
7. Driven by plausibility rather than accuracy—based on reasonable explanations of what might be happening (Weick, 1995, pp. 18–61)

Three quotes from Weick may help set the scene:

The dominance of retrospect in sensemaking is a major reason why students of sensemaking find forecasting, contingency planning, strategic planning, and other magical probes into the future wasteful and misleading if they are decoupled from reflective action and history. (1995, p. 30)

Once people begin to act (enactment), they generate outcomes (cues) in some context (social), and this helps them discover (retrospect) what is occurring (ongoing), what needs to be explained (plausibility), and what should be done next (identity enhancement). (1995, p. 55)

If accuracy is nice but not necessary in sensemaking, then what is necessary? The answer is, something that preserves plausibility and coherence, something that is reasonable and memorable, something that embodies past experience and expectations, something that resonates with other people, something that can be constructed retrospectively but also can be used prospectively, something that captures both feeling and thought, something that allows for embellishment to fit current oddities, something that is fun to construct. In short . . . a good story. . . . Sensemaking is about plausibility, coherence, and reasonableness. (1995, pp. 60–61)

Sensemaking in Organizations

Much of Weick's discussion of sensemaking is generic in that it applies well beyond the bounds of organizational behavior. However, he does speak at times to organizational issues specifically. In this connection he marshals support from some 55 sources in the literature of organizations extending back to Fritz Roethlisberger and William Dickson, Barnard, and Weber, as well as March and Simon.

Both organizing and sensemaking are of the same nature in that they are concerned with imposing order, counteracting deviations, simplifying, and connecting. Organizational forms represent bridging operations between "the intersubjective and the generically intersubjective" (Weick, 1995, p. 73). These bridging operations form a common ground between organizing and sensemaking. Furthermore, organizations must retain certain common meanings and joint understandings as people come and go. If this capability for mutually reinforcing interpretation disappears as people are replaced, then neither organization nor sensemaking can be maintained.

Using concepts such as these, Weick develops "a common core that enables us to represent the setting in which organizational sensemaking occurs" (1995, p. 75). Steps toward a picture of the common core would include the following:

1. A basic focus of organizing is the question, how does action become coordinated in the world of multiple realities?
2. One answer to this question lies in a social form that generates vivid, unique, intersubjective understandings that can be picked up and enlarged by people who did not participate in the original construction.
3. There is always some loss of understanding when the intersubjective is translated into the generic. The function of organizational forms is to manage this loss by keeping it small and allowing it to be renegotiated.
4. To manage a transition is to manage the tension that often results when people try to reconcile the innovation inherent in intersubjectivity with the control inherent in generic subjectivity. Organizational forms represent bridging operations that attempt this reconciliation on an ongoing basis.
5. Reconciliation is accomplished by such things as interlocking routines and habitu-

ated action patterns, both of which have their origin in dyadic interaction.

6. And finally, the social forms of organization consist basically of patterned activity developed and maintained through continuous communication activity, during which participants evolve equivalent understandings around issues of common interest. (1995, p. 75)

What Weick is doing here is providing a bridge that was previously lacking between the small group level and the organization. Yet there is no restatement of organizing theory to make this contribution clear.

With regard to organizational forms, Weick posits that they tend to be devised starting at the bottom of the hierarchy and working upward. The result is a potentially incoherent assortment of issues that is supposed to be managed at the top because of the great diversity that exists at the bottom. Making sense of this ambiguity may well be beyond human capability. Accordingly, "the best organizational design is to do away with the top-management team. Because the organization makes sense, literally and figuratively, at the bottom, that is all the design that is necessary." (1995, p. 117). This would appear to represent a degree of loose coupling well beyond anything envisaged previously; it also puts an end to hierarchy. Toward the end of his 1995 book Weick comes out strongly for movement away from hierarchy to horizontal structuring; generic subjectivity becomes meaningless in a system of unit change and flux, and intersubjective sensemaking becomes the defining property of organizations. Thus, Weick both specifies the procedures for generic subjectivity (as reflected in processes of arguing, expecting, committing, and manipulating that define roles and produce premises for action) and questions the need for generic subjectivity in organizations of the future.

Guidelines for practice emerging out of the extended definition of sensemaking are as follows:

1. Talk the walk—walking (action) sets the means for finding things worth talking about.
2. Every manager an author—the words that are chosen make a big difference.
3. Every manager a historian—any decision maker is only as good as the memory that can be brought to bear and the history that can be constructed retrospectively.
4. Meetings make sense—they are the main place where sensemaking occurs.
5. Stamp in verbs—verbs, not nouns, capture action and thus establish the path for sensemaking.

6. Encourage shared experience—stories about shared experience engage culture.
7. Expectations are real—expectations provide filters and guidance for the actions that permit sensemaking. (Weick, 1995, pp. 182–191)

Research on Sensemaking

A reviewer who read an early draft of the 1995 book is quoted by Weick as being surprised by the lack of empirical, quantitative research invoked in support of the theory. The clear implication is that such research is needed to test these ideas. Weick's reply is typically equivocal, but he does note that "close to 50% of the items in the reference list are qualitative empirical studies" (1995, p. 169). He argues that sensemaking is best understood using methodologies such as naturalistic inquiry, grounded theory, critical incidents, case scenarios, dialectical analysis, field observations, laboratory study, and participative observation. An example of a study of this kind, described as using iterative grounded theory as its research method, is presented by James Orton (2000).

The emphasis in these approaches is on the qualitative, although certain of these methodologies may be cast to provide quantitative tests of theory as well. Weick emphasizes characteristics such as preserving action that is situated in context, deemphasizing researcher-specified measures, observing close in and not from the armchair, participants defining the work environment, deemphasizing hypotheses, testing against common sense rather than a priori theories, subordinating precision and replicability to vividness of meaning, examining a small number of cases in detail, choosing settings less for representativeness than for access to phenomena, and dealing with meanings rather than frequency counts. These are the mindsets for methodology associated with the study of sensemaking. There is no definite specification as to whether they are intended to generate theory or to test it, but the implication is that both are being invoked. If so, this is distinctly at variance with the position set forth in chapter 1 of this book.

Theory Post-1995

Weick has continued to produce essays since the sensemaking book, but with no specific pattern of focus. Weick and Frances Westley (1996) stress the fact that organizing creates opportunities for learning.

What is learned are intersubjective meanings embedded in a culture. Thus learning and organizations conceptualized as cultures are closely related.

Weick (1998) further develops his previous statements on the value of organizational improvisation, as modeled after jazz improvisation. Improvisation is a response to an inability to plan and can be a major source of innovation. Yet it produces surprises, and that can represent a problem. Thus, improvisation can be both a benefit and a liability for organizations. It does appear to be close to the root process in organizing, however. This particular essay seems to be more a matter of thinking out loud than of true theory formulation. It is best understood as pretheory in nature, what is often referred to by a title containing "Toward a Theory of . . . ."

Weick, Kathleen Sutcliffe, and David Obstfeld (1999) argue that high reliability organizations, which must constantly cope with the potential for devastating error, can provide a model for mainstream organizations, especially those emphasizing quality, resorting to major decentralizations, engaged in considerable outsourcing, participating in interorganizational networks, or driven to minimize slack in their operations—in short, a very large number of organizations. A model for such high reliability organization is in figure 22.7.

The key concept here is *mindfulness*, which is

as much about the quality of attention as it is about the conservation of attention. It is as much about what people do with what they notice as it is about the activity of noticing itself. Mindfulness involves

interpretive work directed at weak signals, differentiation of received wisdom, and reframing, all of which can enlarge what is known about what was noticed. (Weick et al., 1999, pp. 89–90)

Notice that all of these essays in the latter 1990s are related primarily to aspects of organizing, not sensemaking per se, although aspects of the sensemaking vocabulary may be introduced. Also, very recently Weick and Sutcliffe (2001) have published a book that presents the high reliability organization arguments in expanded form and packages them for a practitioner audience.

Evaluation and Impact

It should be evident that Weick's commitment to the testing of his theories via the usual scientific approaches has waned over the years, to the point where a legitimate question can be raised as to whether he is writing untestable philosophy or testable scientific theory. He himself would probably opt for the latter, but with the proviso that something other than the usual scientific approaches should be applied. In actual fact, he has moved increasingly closer to the philosophy of postmodernism and its methods of confirmation. All this is something we need to look at more closely.

Weick's Own Evidence

Michel Bougan, Weick, and Din Binkhorst (1977) report on a quantitative study of cause maps generated

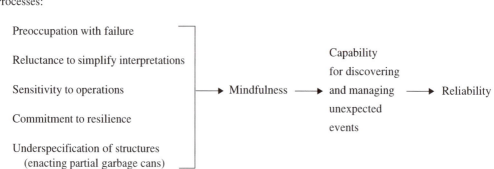

FIGURE 22.7 Model for a high reliability organization. Adapted from Karl E. Weick, Kathleen M. Sutcliffe, & David Obstfeld (1999), Organizing for High Reliability: Processes of Collective Mindfulness, *Research in Organizational Behavior*, 21, 89.

by the 19 members of the Utrecht Jazz Orchestra. This study involves measurement and ranking of variables, cross-validation of results in a holdout sample, regression analysis, and tests of significance. The findings are consistent with certain statements from organizing theory, to the effect that the structure of causality among variables (the pattern of relations), rather than variable content, determines the fate of the system and that what ties thought together among members ties the organization together. Cause maps generated by members are useful means of studying these phenomena, and rankings of variables provided by these maps explain a sizable amount of an individual participant's perceived influence over the variables. This is a solid and ingenious beginning toward unraveling the empirical basis for organizing theory. Indeed, measures of theoretical variables are constructed from the cause maps.

Yet this is where the research program ended. Subsequently, Weick moved to qualitative case data, consistent with his prescriptions in Weick (1995), often data provided by other authors and sources. One such instance is an analysis of the airplane collision that occurred on the runway at Tenerife airport. In this article Weick (1990) appears to be not so much testing theory as groping toward the creation of theory. Another instance involves an analysis of the process of operating nuclear-powered Navy aircraft carriers (Weick & Roberts, 1993). Here the data are used to provide examples for the development of theoretical constructs such as collective mind and heedful interrelating. In Weick (1993a) the case of a group of firefighters who parachuted into a remote area in an attempt to control a forest fire, and in a number of instances died as a result, is interpreted according to organizing theory. Yet this interpretation is no more compelling than those that might have been derived from other, competing theories. There is no actual test of Weick's theory involved.

In essays of these kinds Weick presents a story interwoven with theory, which is driven by plausibility, but not necessarily by accuracy. On the latter score we simply do not have the data to reach a determination. Weick wants us to accept his explanations, and what he says makes sense, but that is the end of it. Other possible explanations are not considered, and certainly none is ruled out. A common practice is to actually use the case information to move on to further theory development, leaving the matter of testing the prior theory completely up in the air. Weick emerges as an inveterate theorizer who cannot resist a theorizing opportunity; constructing theory is what he finds interesting, and he is creative in what he does. The cases provide an ideal incubator for his skill, and this is an entirely appropriate use of this material. However, the Weick of the past 20 years appears very unlikely to return to the mundane matter of empirical testing that characterized his earlier years. He is now hooked on theorizing.

Some idea of how he goes about this process is provided by an analysis of Weick's work carried out by Craig Lundberg (1999). This analysis is entitled to indicate how Weick approaches the selection of *research* topics, but in actual fact, since there has been no research recently, it deals with setting agendas for theorizing. What Weick appears to do is use one or more of six approaches:

1. Notice an anomaly, and try to explain it.
2. Notice the level of analysis that dominates the explanation of something, and try an explanation at another level.
3. Notice (or create) language that may enrich explanation and explore it.
4. Notice common or simple activities or things and exploit them as metaphors.
5. Notice the context of an explanation, and apply the explanation to another context.
6. Notice commonly accepted knowledge or practices, and pursue possible counter intuitive explanations. (Lundberg, 1999, pp. 34–37)

This is how Weick engages his very considerable creative capabilities.

Evidence Adduced by Others

Weick's writings contain frequent citations to a wide range of literature, but these sources do not necessarily contain research evidence in direct support of the point being made. In fact, an extensive search reveals no studies conducted by others to indicate that a direct test of hypotheses derived from Weick's theories has been carried out and the theory confirmed, in whole or in part. This is presumably because of difficulties in understanding and interpreting what Weick has written and in measuring his variables. Ambiguity, whatever its other benefits may be, does not attract scientific research.

However, Weick's theories are frequently cited by others, and it may prove useful to understand how this occurs. One instance involves a research study that deals with a related topic (such as relationships between cognition and action), but does not directly test Weick in this regard. At the same time, Weick's concepts are invoked, and research focused on them is urged (see for example Thomas, Clark, & Gioia, 1993). This approach, which makes use of Weick's ideas, not to generate research hypotheses but to aid in the interpretation of results, is found not just before the sensemaking volume but afterward as well (Gioia & Thomas, 1996).

Another approach is to publish a review or analysis that attests to the tenability of some position Weick has taken, even though no clear empirical evidence or compelling argument is provided. Thus a construct or a way of approaching a problem may be promoted. An example is the article by Lloyd Sandelands and Ralph Stablein (1987), which argues for the potential value of the concept of organizational mind (mindfulness). Weick then subsequently used this article to support his development of related theory.

Another tack takes Weick's theorizing as a major input to the expounding of some new theory, which goes well beyond what Weick said and often takes a completely new direction as well. Examples of this approach are a view of entrepreneurship that builds on organizing theory (Hill & Levenhagen, 1995), a theory of creativity in organizations that draws from both the organizing and the sensemaking theories (Drazin, Glynn, & Kazanjian, 1999), and a theory of organizational technology implementation that takes its lead primarily from sensemaking theory (Griffith, 1999).

In many respects Weick's theorizing is used in much the same way as James Thompson's theory was at an earlier point in time (see chapter 15 in this volume). It does not seem to provoke research directly, but it often gets wound into an exposition in one manner or another.

Overview

Weick's writing has been described as insightful, innovative, artsy, having the character of montage, lacking sharp definition, possessing an unsettling order, devoid of descriptive certainty, and failing to provide detachable conclusions (Van Maanen, 1995). The "unusual phrases, labels, titles, reversals, sweeps and swoops of wordplay [suggest] something of a protest and an example of how to break from the frozen

technical writing codes" (p. 139). Certainly Weick does not make it easy for the researcher to formulate a study to determine the validity of what he is saying. At times, there appears to be a deliberate effort to thwart research on the ideas presented. For some, all this is frustrating and thoughtless; for others, it reflects genius at work. I have tried to provide sufficient quotes from Weick's books and essays so that readers may make their own determination in this regard.

Another question that has been posed is whether Weick really believes and intends that sensemaking is an entirely retrospective process. His failure to make room for prospective sensemaking seems to fly in the face of everyday experience (Gioia & Mehra, 1996). Does Weick's position on enactment reflect the totality of his views, or is he merely trying to make a point? Is strategic planning pointless, as Weick most typically implies? Is meaning always a retrospective attribution, and are decision making and intention unimportant? What about the evidence for goal setting theory (see chapter 9), which Weick does not consider? I must admit that Weick seems to be wrong in his rejection of intention, prospective goals, and such matters as vision and planning, but then it is possible that he is a bit tongue in cheek on this score. I wish I felt more certainty regarding what he really thinks.

A final point relates to the extent to which Weick has come to embrace the philosophy of postmodernism. Certainly he has moved in that direction over the years, and postmodernists often welcome him as one of their own. Yet Weick has not repudiated his ties to science, even though these ties often seem to have more of a dotted line quality than one could hope for. And there are those who clearly want more postmodernity from Weick than he appears willing to give (see Magala, 1997). Again we are left with a high degree of ambiguity. Probably Weick would not have it any other way.

CONCLUSIONS

This ends our discussion of first-generation theories in organizational behavior. These are theories that emerged out of the equivocality and new mixes of literatures and disciplines created by the behavioral revolution that brought social scientists of varying types into, or closer to, the business schools and to each other. In many respects, these theorists worked from an agenda very similar to the one that Weick has typically used. The key in this approach to theorizing is to juxtapose elements that have not previously been seen together. The emergence of organizational behavior as a field served this purpose well.

Theorizing in this mode involves a type of decision making in a context where garbage can elements and renewed equivocality have been introduced, not necessarily for the purpose of stimulating theory, but certainly with some purpose in mind. In contrast, the theories to be considered next, the second-generation theories, were generated out of a somewhat more stable scholarly context. It will be instructive not only to compare the results achieved from the two generational contexts, but to see how greatly they do in fact differ.

References

Argyris, Chris (1973). Some Limits of Rationale Man Organizational Theory. *Public Administration Review*, 33, 253–267.

Argyris, Chris (1976). Single-Loop and Double-Loop Models in Research on Decision Making. *Administrative Science Quarterly*, 21, 363–375.

Argyris, Chris (1996). Unrecognized Defenses of Scholars: Impact on Theory and Research. *Organization Science*, 7, 79–87.

Arroba, Tanya Y. (1978). Decision-Making Style as a Function of Occupational Group, Decision Content and Perceived Importance. *Journal of Occupational Psychology*, 51, 219–226.

Augier, Mie, & Kreiner, Kristian (2000). An Interview with James G. March. *Journal of Management Inquiry*, 9, 284–297.

Beyer, Janice M.; Chattopadhyay, Prithviraj; George, Elizabeth; Glick, William H.; ogilvie, dt; & Pugliese, Dulce (1997). The Selective Perception of Managers Revisited. *Academy of Management Journal*, 40, 716–737.

Bhaskar, R. (1978). *Problem Solving in Semantically Rich Domains*. Doctoral dissertation. Pittsburgh, PA: Carnegie Mellon University.

Bougan, Michel; Weick, Karl; & Binkhorst, Din (1977). Cognition in Organizations: An Analysis of the Utrecht Jazz Orchestra. *Administrative Science Quarterly*, 22, 606–639.

Bouwman, Marius J. (1978). *Financial Diagnosis*. Doctoral dissertation. Pittsburgh, PA: Carnegie Mellon University.

Bowen, David E.; & Siehl, Caren (1997). The Future of Human Resource Management: March and Simon (1958) Revisited. *Human Resource Management*, 36(1), 57–63.

Bowen, James, & Qiu, Zi-lei (1992). Satisficing When Buying Information. *Organizational Behavior and Human Decision Processes*, 51, 471–481.

Carter, E. Eugene (1971). The Behavioral Theory of the Firm and Top-Level Corporate Decisions. *Administrative Science Quarterly*, 16, 413–428.

Clarkson, G. P. E. (1962). *Portfolio Selection: A Simulation of Trust Investment*. Englewood Cliffs, NJ: Prentice Hall.

Cohen, Michael D., & March, James G. (1974). *Leadership and Ambiguity: The American College President*. New York: McGraw-Hill.

Cohen, Michael D.; March, James G.; & Olsen, Johan P. (1972). A Garbage Can Model of Organizational Choice. *Administrative Science Quarterly*, 17, 1–25.

Cyert, Richard M. (1975). *The Management of Nonprofit Organizations*. Lexington, MA: D. C. Heath.

Cyert, Richard M.; Dill, William R.; & March, James G. (1958). The Role of Expectations in Business Decision Making. *Administrative Science Quarterly*, 3, 307–340.

Cyert, Richard M., & Hedrick, Charles L. (1972). Theory of the Firm: Past, Present, and Future: An Interpretation. *Journal of Economic Literature*, 10, 398–412.

Cyert, Richard M., & MacCrimmon, Kenneth R. (1968). Organizations. In Gardner Lindzey & Elliot Aronson (Eds.), *Handbook of Social Psychology* (pp. 568–611). Reading, MA: Addison-Wesley.

Cyert, Richard M., & March, James G. (1955). Organizational Structure and Pricing Behavior in an Oligopolistic Market. *American Economic Review*, 45, 129–139.

Cyert, Richard M., & March, James G. (1956). Organizational Factors in the Theory of Oligopoly. *Quarterly Journal of Economics*, 70, 44–64.

Cyert, Richard M., & March, James G. (1963). *A Behavioral Theory of the Firm*. Englewood Cliffs, NJ: Prentice Hall (1992, Oxford, UK: Blackwell).

Cyert, Richard M.; March, James G.; & Starbuck, William H. (1961). Two Experiments on Bias and Conflict in Organizational Estimation. *Management Science*, 7, 254–264.

Cyert, Richard M.; Simon, Herbert A.; & Trow, Donald B. (1956). Observations of a Business Decision. *Journal of Business*, 29, 237–248.

Daft, Richard L., & Weick, Karl E. (1984). Toward a Model of Organizations as Interpretation Systems. *Academy of Management Review*, 9, 284–295.

Dearborn, DeWitt C., & Simon, Herbert A. (1958). Selective Perception: A Note on the Departmental Identifications of Executives. *Sociometry*, 21, 140–144.

Drazin, Robert; Glynn, Mary Ann; & Kazanjian, Robert K. (1999). Multilevel Theorizing about Creativity in Organizations: A Sensemaking Perspective. *Academy of Management Review*, 24, 286–307.

Feldman, Martha S., & March, James G. (1981). Information in Organizations as Signal and Symbol. *Administrative Science Quarterly*, 26, 171–186.

Gioia, Dennis A., & Mehra, Ajay (1996). Review of *Sensemaking in Organizations*. *Academy of Management Review*, 21, 1226–1230.

Gioia, Dennis A., & Thomas, James B. (1996). Identity, Image, and Issue Interpretation: Sensemaking during Strategic Change in Academia. *Administrative Science Quarterly*, 41, 370–403.

Greenwood, Royston & Devine, Kay (1997). Inside Aston: A Conversation with Derek Pugh. *Journal of Management Inquiry*, 6, 200–208.

Griffith, Terri L. (1999). Technology Features as Triggers for Sensemaking. *Academy of Management Review*, 24, 472–488.

Guetzkow, Harold, & Simon, Herbert A. (1955). The Impact of Certain Communication Nets upon Organization and Performance in Task-Oriented Groups. *Management Science*, 1, 233–250.

Harvey, Charles, & Denton, John (1999). To Come of Age: The Antecedents of Organizational Learning. *Journal of Management Studies*, 36, 897–918.

Heller, Frank; Drenth, Pieter; Koopman, Paul; & Rus, Veljko (1988). *Decisions in Organizations: A Three-Country Comparative Study*. London: Sage.

Hill, Robert C., & Levenhagen, Michael (1995). Metaphors and Mental Models: Sensemaking and Sensegiving in Innovative and Entrepreneurial Activities. *Journal of Management*, 21, 1057–1074.

Kilduff, Martin (1993). Deconstructing *Organizations*. *Academy of Management Review*, 18, 13–31.

Koopman, Paul L., & Pool, Jeroen (1990). Decision Making in Organizations. *International Review of Industrial and Organizational Psychology*, 5, 101–148.

Levinthal, Daniel A., & March, James G. (1993). The Myopia of Learning. *Strategic Management Journal*, 14, 95–112.

Levitt, Barbara, & March, James G. (1988). Organizational Learning. *Annual Review of Sociology*, 14, 319–340.

Levitt, Barbara, & Nass, Clifford (1989). The Lid on the Garbage Can: Institutional Constraints on Decision Making in the Technical Core of College-Text Publishers. *Administrative Science Quarterly*, 34, 190–207.

Lomi, Alessandro; Larsen, Erik R.; & Ginsberg, Ari (1997). Adaptive Learning in Organizations: A System Dynamics-Based Exploration. *Journal of Management*, 23, 561–582.

Lundberg, Craig C. (1999). Finding Research Agendas: Getting Started Weick-Like. *Industrial-Organizational Psychologist*, 37(2), 32–39.

Magala, Slawomir J. (1997). The Making and Unmaking of Sense (Book Review Essay—*Sensemaking in Organizations*). *Organization Studies*, 18, 317–338.

Magjuka, Richard (1988). Garbage Can Theory of Organizational Decision Making: A Review. *Research in the Sociology of Organizations*, 6, 225–259.

Manns, Curtis L., & March, James G. (1978). Financial Adversity, Internal Competition, and Curriculum Change in a University. *Administrative Science Quarterly*, 23, 541–552.

March, James C., & March, James G. (1977). Almost Random Careers: The Wisconsin School Superintendency, 1940–72. *Administrative Science Quarterly*, 22, 377–409.

March, James G. (1956). Influence Measurement in Experimental and Semi-Experimental Groups. *Sociometry*, 19, 260–271.

March, James G. (1972). Model Bias in Social Action. *Review of Educational Research*, 42, 413–429.

March, James G. (1988). *Decisions and Organizations*. Oxford: Blackwell.

March, James G. (1991). Exploration and Exploitation in Organizational Learning. *Organization Science*, 2, 71–87.

March, James G. (1994a). The Evolution of Evolution. In Joel A. C. Baum & Jitendra V. Singh (Eds.), *Evolutionary Dynamics of Organizations* (pp. 39–49). New York: Oxford University Press.

March, James G. (1994b). *A Primer on Decision Making: How Decisions Happen*. New York: Free Press.

March, James G., & Olsen, Johan P. (1976). *Ambiguity and Choice in Organizations*. Bergen, Norway: Universitetsforlaget.

March, James G., & Olsen, Johan P. (1989). *Rediscovering Institutions: The Organizational Basis of Politics*. New York: Free Press.

March, James G., & Olsen, Johan P. (1995). *Democratic Governance*. New York: Free Press.

March, James G., & Simon, Herbert A. (1958). *Organizations*. New York: Wiley (1992, Oxford, UK: Blackwell).

March, James G.; Sproull, Lee S.; & Tamuz, Michal (1991). Learning from Samples of One or Fewer. *Organization Science*, 2, 1–13.

March, James G., & Weissinger-Baylon, Roger (1986). *Ambiguity and Command: Organizational Perspectives on Military Decision Making*. Marshfield, MA: Pitman.

Masuch, Michael, & LaPotin, Perry (1989). Beyond Garbage Cans: An AI Model of Organizational Choice. *Administrative Science Quarterly*, 34, 38–67.

McCaskey, Michael B. (1979). The Management of Ambiguity. *Organizational Dynamics*, 7(4), 31–48.

Miller, Danny (1996). A Preliminary Typology of Organizational Learning: Synthesizing the Literature. *Journal of Management*, 22, 485–505.

Miner, Anne S., & Mezias, Stephen J. (1996). Ugly Duckling No More: Pasts and Futures of Organizational Learning Research. *Organization Science* ,7, 88–99.

Mumby, Dennis K., & Putnam, Linda L. (1992). The Politics of Emotion: A Feminist Reading of Bounded Rationality. *Academy of Management Review*, 17, 465–486.

Nohria, Nitin, & Gulati, Ranjay (1996). Is Slack Good or Bad for Innovation? *Academy of Management Journal*, 39, 1245–1264.

Orton, James D. (2000). Enactment, Sensemaking and Decision Making: Redesign Processes in the 1976 Reorganization of U.S. Intelligence. *Journal of Management Studies*, 37, 213–234.

Park, C. Whan (1978). A Seven-Point Scale and a Decision-Maker's Simplifying Choice Strategy: An Operationalized Satisficing-Plus Model. *Organizational Behavior and Human Performance*, 21, 252–271.

Pennings, Johannes M.; Barkema, Harry; & Douma, Sytse (1994). Organizational Learning and Diversification. *Academy of Management Journal*, 37, 608–640.

Pfeffer, Jeffrey, & Moore, William L. (1980). Power in University Budgeting: A Replication and Extension. *Administrative Science Quarterly*, 25, 637–653.

Prietula, Michael J., & Simon, Herbert A. (1989). The Experts in Your Midst. *Harvard Business Review*, 67(1), 120–124.

Pugh, Derek S., & Hickson, David J. (1993). *Great Writers on Organizations: The Omnibus Edition*. Aldershot, UK: Dartmouth.

Rados, David L. (1972). Selection and Evaluation of Alternatives in Repetitive Decision Making. *Administrative Science Quarterly*, 17, 196–206.

Sandelands, Lloyd E., & Stablein, Ralph E. (1987). The Concept of Organization Mind. *Research in the Sociology of Organizations*, 5, 135–161.

Simon, Herbert A. (1943). *Fiscal Aspects of Metropolitan Consolidation*. Berkeley: Bureau of Public Administration, University of California.

Simon, Herbert A. (1946). The Proverbs of Administration. *Public Administration Review*, 6, 53–57.

Simon, Herbert A. (1947, 1957a, 1976, 1997). *Administrative Behavior: A Study of Decision-Making Processes in Administrative Organizations*. 1st, 2nd, 3rd, and 4th ed. New York: Free Press.

Simon, Herbert A. (1957b). *Models of Man: Social and Rational*. New York: Wiley.

Simon, Herbert A. (1964). On the Concept of Organizational Goals. *Administrative Science Quarterly*, 9, 1–22.

Simon, Herbert A. (1973). Organization Man: Rational or Self-Actualizing? *Public Administration Review*, 33, 346–353.

Simon, Herbert A. (1977). *The New Science of Management Decision*. Englewood Cliffs, NJ: Prentice Hall.

Simon, Herbert A. (1987). Making Management Decisions: The Role of Intuition and Emotion. *Academy of Management Executive*, 1, 57–64.

Simon, Herbert A. (1991). Bounded Rationality and Organizational Learning. *Organization Science*, 2, 125–134.

Simon, Herbert A., & Devine, William R. (1941). Controlling Human Factors in an Administrative Experiment. *Public Administration Review*, 1, 485–492.

Simon, Herbert A.; Guetzkow, Harold; Kozmetsky, George; & Tyndall, Gordon (1954). *Centralization vs. Decentralization in Organizing the Controller's Department*. New York: Controllership Foundation.

Simon, Herbert A.; Smithburg, Donald W.; & Thompson, Victor A. (1950). *Public Administration*. New York: Knopf.

Soelberg, Peer (1966). Unprogrammed Decision Making. *Academy of Management Proceedings*, 26, 3–16.

Stava, Per (1976). Constraints on the Politics of Public Choice. In James G. March & Johan P. Olsen, *Ambiguity and Choice in Organizations* (pp. 206–224). Bergen, Norway: Universitetsforlaget.

Staw, Barry M. (1974). Attitudinal and Behavioral Consequences of Changing a Major Organizational Reward: A Natural Field Experiment. *Journal of Personality and Social Psychology*, 29, 742–751.

Taylor, Ronald N. (1975). Psychological Determinants of Bounded Rationality: Implications for Decision-Making Strategies. *Decision Sciences*, 6, 409–429.

Thomas, James B.; Clark, Shawn M.; & Gioia, Dennis A. (1993). Strategic Sensemaking and Organizational Performance: Linkages among Scanning, Interpretation, Action, and Outcomes. *Academy of Management Journal*, 36, 239–270.

Thompson, James D. (1967). *Organizations in Action*. New York: McGraw-Hill.

Van Maanen, John (1995). Style as Theory. *Organization Science*, 6, 133–143.

Waller, Mary J.; Huber, George P.; & Glick, William H. (1995). Functional Background as a Determinant of Executives' Selective Perception. *Academy of Management Journal*, 38, 943–974.

Weick, Karl E. (1969, 1979). *The Social Psychology of Organizing*. 1st ed., 2nd ed. Reading, MA: Addison-Wesley.

Weick, Karl E. (1976). Educational Organizations as Loosely Coupled Systems. *Administrative Science Quarterly*, 21, 1–19.

Weick, Karl E. (1988). Enacted Sensemaking in Crisis

Situations. *Journal of Management Studies*, 25, 305–317.

Weick, Karl E. (1990). The Vulnerable System: An Analysis of the Tenerife Air Disaster. *Journal of Management*, 16, 571–593.

Weick, Karl E. (1993a). The Collapse of Sensemaking in Organizations: The Mann Gulch Disaster. *Administrative Science Quarterly*, 38, 628–652.

Weick, Karl E. (1993b). Organizational Redesign As Improvisation. In George P. Huber & William H. Glick (Eds.), *Organizational Change and Redesign: Ideas and Insights for Improving Performance* (pp. 346–379). New York: Oxford University Press.

Weick, Karl E. (1993c). Turning Context into Text: An Academic Life as Data. In Arthur G. Bedeian (Ed.), *Management Laureates: A Collection of Autobiographical Essays* (Vol. 3, pp. 285–323). Greenwich, CT: JAI Press.

Weick, Karl E. (1995). *Sensemaking in Organizations*. Thousand Oaks, CA: Sage.

Weick, Karl E. (1998). Introductory Essay: Improvisation as a Mindset for Organizational Analysis. *Organization Science*, 9, 543–555.

Weick, Karl E., & Roberts, Karlene H. (1993). Collective Mind in Organizations: Heedful Interrelating on Flight Decks. *Administrative Science Quarterly*, 38, 357–381.

Weick, Karl E., & Sutcliffe, Kathleen M. (2001). *Managing the Unexpected: Assuring High Performance in an Age of Complexity*. San Francisco: Jossey-Bass.

Weick, Karl E.; Sutcliffe, Kathleen M.; & Obstfeld, David (1999). Organizing for High Reliability: Processes of Collective Mindfulness. *Research in Organizational Behavior*, 21, 81–123.

Weick, Karl E., & Westley, Frances (1996). Organizational Learning: Affirming an Oxymoron. In Stewart R. Clegg, Cynthia Hardy, & Walter R. Nord (Eds.), *Handbook of Organization Studies* (pp. 440–458). London: Sage.

Part VII

Second-Generation Theories: Motivation and Perception

Chapter 23

Theories of Behavior
in Organizations and
of Attribution Processes

The second-generation theories of organizational behavior did not emerge out of quite the degree of uncertainty that characterized the milieu of the first-generation theories. The date that marks the beginning of this new grouping is 1974. This is not an arbitrary designation but merely reflects the empirical point at which change appears to have occurred in the literature. By this point the movement of behavioral scientists into the business schools had been consolidated, and a new group of scholars began to enter the field; often they had been educated in organizational behavior by the business schools themselves.

The theorists of the second generation to be considered here are, in fact, an eclectic group. Some are from business schools, where they were educated in organizational behavior, and some are psychologists and sociologists who remained outside the prime setting for organizational behavior although they were still substantially influenced by events that were occurring in the business schools. A number of these theorists were in fact of the first generation, but the theories to be discussed here are second generation—created in the mid to late 1970s and 1980s out of a quite different context than that of their predecessors. As we will see, why these theories appeared later, even though their authors were on the organizational behavior scene at a considerably earlier point, is an individual matter. The background experiences of each particular theorist appear to make much more difference here than does any overarching effect of the times.

As the reader may have noted, certain of the theories considered previously under the first generation designation were strictly speaking second generation in nature, according to the time of their emergence. These are theories that had clear ties to earlier first generation theories, and thus seemed most appropriately treated in conjunction with them, but which appeared later; most were in fact authored by first generation theorists or their students. These seven "bridging theories" between generations are listed below with their chapter citations:

Edward Deci and Richard Ryan's cognitive evaluation theory of intrinsic and extrinsic motivation (chapter 8)

Fred Fiedler and Joseph Garcia's cognitive resource theory of leadership (chapter 12)

Lex Donaldson's structural contingency theory (chapter 18)

Chris Argyris's theory of organizational learning and defensive routines (chapter 20)

Edgar Schein's theory of organizational culture and leadership (chapter 21)

Robert Golembiewski's concept of alpha, beta, and gamma change in organizational development (chapter 21)

James March's organizational learning concepts (chapter 22)

The specific theories considered in this chapter are appropriately viewed in conjunction with part II of this book. The theory of behavior in organizations is the joint product of James Naylor, Robert Pritchard, and Daniel Ilgen, who presented their views in a major work (Naylor, Pritchard, & Ilgen, 1980). This theory derives its constructs from a number of sources, but expectancy theory appears to have exerted a strong influence; perceptions play an important role also. Attribution theory came into organizational behavior from psychology. It is essentially a way of thinking about perceptual process. However, the major such theory within organizational behavior has to do with perceptions of poor or ineffective employees and is related to leadership in certain of its aspects. This more specific attribution theory is the product of Terence Mitchell, whom we have met previously in several contexts, including, once again, expectancy theory.

THEORY OF BEHAVIOR IN ORGANIZATIONS

The theory of behavior to be considered here is a product of the joint efforts of three people who spent 5 years discussing their ideas before putting them together in book form (Naylor et al., 1980). The three did not publish any previous statements of these ideas, and they have not published together since. Most of Naylor's research has been in the area of human judgment and how people cope with uncertainty. Pritchard has specialized in motivation and satisfaction, as has Ilgen, but with added expertise in role relationships. The three brought a common interest in cognitive processes to their joint endeavor. At the same time, each contributed in a separate way as well.

Background

Naylor was born in 1932 and obtained all of his degrees from Purdue University, with the Ph.D. being granted in psychology in 1960. From his doctorate he went to Ohio State University, still in psychology, where he progressed up the academic ranks to professor. In 1968 he returned to Purdue as chair of the psychology department, and then in 1986 he moved back to Ohio State, where he chaired the psychology department for many years. In 1966 Naylor founded the *Journal of Organizational Behavior and Human Performance* (later, the phrase *Decision Processes* was substituted for *Performance*). He remained editor for 33 years, and in the process developed an extremely influential interdisciplinary publication (Weber, 1998). Ilgen succeeded him as editor in 1999.

Pritchard was born in 1945 and received his Ph.D. in industrial psychology from the University of Minnesota in 1969. From there he went to Purdue for 5 years, then to the University of Houston (1974 to 1988), and finally to Texas A&M, where he remains. His major appointments all have been in psychology departments.

Ilgen was born in 1943. After an undergraduate degree in psychology at Iowa State University, he went to the University of Illinois and received his doctorate in industrial psychology there in 1968. He remained at Illinois for several years, but by 1972 he had joined Naylor and Pritchard at Purdue, where he remained until 1983. His first business school appointment came in 1983, at Michigan State University; he is still there.

Note that all three authors were at Purdue together in the early 1970s for a period of time. However, Pritchard left for Houston before the work began on A *Theory of Behavior in Organizations*. Also, Naylor is not only the first author, but was more senior at the time of writing. Without question, his influence was the most pronounced.

Conscious, Rational Theory of Behavior

Although like expectancy theory in its concern with conscious processes and with rational choice, the theory of behavior in organizations is both more comprehensive and different in certain key aspects.

Elements of Behavior

The theory deals in some way with individual behavior, the environment, individual differences, perceptions, motivation, learning, and affect. Behavior has as its basic unit the *act*, which is characterized by both *amplitude* (the commitment to the act in terms of the individual resources—time and effort—allocated) and *direction* (the specific kind of activity involved). Acts produce products, which are, in turn, perceived either by the actor or by others; these *perceived products* are critical to the theory.

Environments conceived in terms of types, dimensions, or enacted properties are rejected in favor of an approach that emphasizes the process through which the environment influences individual behavior. Key are the processes by which environmental features come into existence (called *attribute creation*) and the process by which these features affect behavior (called *attribute influence*). Attribute creation may be a function of an individual's own behavior, or it may be totally noncontingent in this sense. Attribute influence may occur as a result of the reward properties that are perceived in certain environmental features by the individual (called *influence through affect*). In addition, these features may limit behavior and thus operate through what is called *influence through constraint*.

Individual differences, to include needs, aptitudes, personality characteristics, and abilities, are seen as setting constraints in the same manner as certain environmental features. Although considered pervasive, the theory also tends to downplay them: "We believe the conceptual problems involved in describing individual differences in a definitive way are extremely difficult and beyond the scope of the present theory" (Naylor et al., 1980, p. 15).

Perceptual process refers to the way that specific perceptions or cognitions are formed. *Cognitions* are conscious perceptions of a state of the environment, or of a state of the self (retrieved from memory or formed through thought), or of relationships between such states (contingencies). Motivational process refers to a temporary need deprivation that provides the force for behavior. This occurs as positive or negative valences are attached to perceived available outcomes, which result in utilities for products (when the valence is combined with perceptions of contingencies relating products and evaluations of products, as well as contingencies between evaluation of products and received outcomes). It also occurs as there are modifications in the temporary motivational state as a function of perceived outcomes. Both outcomes and motivation may be specified as intrinsic or extrinsic.

Three kinds of contingencies are central in the theory:

1. That a particular act will result in a particular product or amount of that product
2. That a particular product or amount of that product will result in a particular evaluation
3. That a particular evaluation will result in a particular outcome or reward

Note that these are not the contingencies of expectancy theory. Learning occurs as individuals modify their knowledge of these contingencies and then alter their behavior accordingly. No explicit memory mechanism is presented within the theory, although some such process is assumed.

Affect is necessary for the motivational system to function. Affect is defined as a psychological state (a cognition) of pleasure or satisfaction, both positive and negative. The theory typically is concerned with affect in relation to outcomes. This affect may be actual or anticipated (expected), and in the latter case it is referred to as either a valence or utility.

Constructs of the General Theory

Figure 23.1 provides an overall view of the theory. Moving from left to right, we take up the various states or constructs noted in the figure:

> *Objective products* are the external environment's measured perceptions of the products produced by an individual.

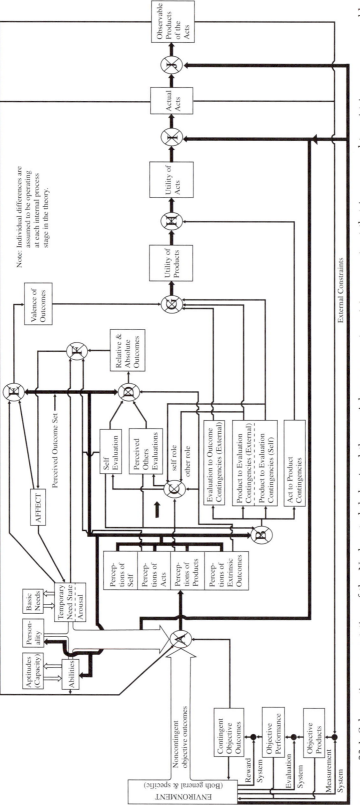
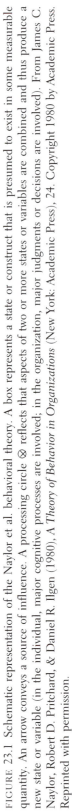

Note: Individual differences are assumed to be operating at each internal process stage in the theory.

FIGURE 23.1 Schematic representation of the Naylor et al. behavioral theory. A box represents a state or construct that is presumed to exist in some measurable quantity. An arrow conveys a source of influence. A processing circle $\otimes$ reflects that aspects of two or more states or variables are combined and thus produce a new state or variable (in the individual, major cognitive processes are involved; in the organization, major judgments or decisions are involved). From James C. Naylor, Robert D. Pritchard, & Daniel R. Ilgen (1980), *A Theory of Behavior in Organizations* (New York: Academic Press), 24. Copyright 1980 by Academic Press. Reprinted with permission.

Objective performance reflects the fact that a subset of the objective products is placed on an evaluative continuum. Once evaluated, these products become objective performance.

Contingent objective outcomes are what the environment provides to an individual as a function of the evaluation system (such as pay raises, promotions, feedback, and recognition); these outcomes are based on objective performance. (Naylor et al., 1980, pp. 27–30)

At this point the theory moves from the environment to within the individual:

Individual differences are divided into several classes, although a fully developed conceptual scheme is not provided. Some distinctions are required because different classes of variables influence behavior differently. Distinctions are made between aptitudes-abilities, personality, and needs.

Aptitudes and abilities refer to the potential capacity to perform an act.

Personality is a powerful moderator of behavior at all levels of the theory.

Basic needs imply a fairly permanent preference for certain kinds of outcomes.

Temporary need states refer to differences at a specific point in time and reflect the current level of satisfaction of the more permanent needs. (Naylor et al., 1980, pp. 31–35)

Next come a set of perceptions formed by an individual in response to the environment:

Perceptions of self refer to a person's own characteristics and attributes.

Perceptions of acts refer to a person's own behavior.

Perceptions of products refer to a person's own products.

Perceptions of extrinsic outcomes refer to the subset of the totality of environmental stimuli actually perceived by a person and to how much of that outcome is received. (Naylor et al., 1980, pp. 35–36)

Next, the following constructs get at the basic components that lie entirely within the individual:

Affect is the pleasure or satisfaction experienced by an individual at a point in time. It is an attractive-

ness-related variable that does not in and of itself have motivating properties.

The various *contingencies* refer to complex sets of perceptions or cognitions or belief states built from cognitive processing of the various types of perceptions.

Act-to-product contingencies are the perceived contingencies between a person's own acts and the results of those acts.

Product-to-evaluation contingencies are the perceived contingencies between products produced by a person and the evaluation of that person's performance. There are a number of evaluators here, and the evaluation system used by a person is related to, and in fact defines, the role that person has for an individual.

Evaluation-to-outcome contingencies are composed of a person's perceptions of the way the evaluation received is translated into actual outcomes by others in the environment.

Self-evaluation is a person's evaluation of that person's own performance.

Perceived others' evaluations are the perceptions a person has of the variety of others' evaluations in the environment.

Outcomes may be perceived in terms of how much has been received—the absolute outcome. These absolute levels may be compared to expectations of the level that should be received or to the level that other people in the environment have received—relative outcomes.

Valence of outcomes refers to the affect that is anticipated to be experienced when a particular outcome is received. This anticipated affect carries with it motivating properties that are derived from the connection to need satisfaction.

Utility of products is the anticipated value that an individual perceives as associated with the products that person could generate. The utility of a particular product is formed by combining product-to-evaluation contingencies, evaluation-to-outcome contingencies, and valence of outcomes and may be viewed as the extent to which a product will lead to valued extrinsic and intrinsic outcomes.

Utility of acts is the anticipated value a person perceives to be associated with different behaviors and is formed by combining the utility of products and the act-to-product contingencies. (Naylor et al., 1980, pp. 37–44)

At this point the theory moves outside the individual again, back into the environment.

Actual acts are behaviors a person emits in terms of both their amplitude and direction. Although capable of being measured, they typically are not.

Observable products of the acts reflect the consequences of the actual acts in terms of the things produced by the acts. These products are what is typically observed and measured by the environment. (Naylor et al., 1980, pp. 44–45)

Relationships of the General Theory

The interrelationships expressed by the arrows in figure 23.1 state the determinants and consequences of variables; these relationships are causal in nature.

An individual can affect the environment (as represented by the arrows from the three boxes in the lower left corner of figure 23.1). However, the major effects flow from the environment to the person. These are of several kinds:

1. There is the large number of stimuli produced by the general and specific environment—the noncontingent objective outcomes. These do not include the outcomes given to the individual by the environment on a contingent basis in reaction to performance; these derive from the contingent objective outcomes. All converge at process point A.
2. A set of influences flows from the environment, operating as moderators or constraints at the process points to the far right of figure 23.1 (I and J).
3. The environment affects the individual through three systems used by the environment to process information received from the individual and to respond to that information:
   a. The *measurement system*—a judgment process through which an evaluator selects a subset of products and determines how much of each has been produced.
   b. The *evaluation system*—a process through which the evaluator determines how good or bad the performance of the individual is. The evaluator combines objective products into classes, after defining the products that warrant attention, and then establishes relations between products and evaluations. Taken together, these processes serve to define the role the evaluator has for the individual.
   c. The *reward system*—the rules evaluators use to attach outcomes to individual performance. (Naylor et al., 1980, pp. 47–53)

Individual differences also influence behavior in a number of ways:

1. Individual differences influence the way that a person perceives stimuli (at process point A).
2. Influences also flow to moderate and constrain the translating of the utility of acts to actual acts (at process point I).
3. Individual differences affect the attaching of affect to outcomes received already and the attaching of valence to outcomes anticipated in the future (processing points F and E).
4. Since this is basically a cognitive theory, whenever a person must process information (which occurs at all of the processing points) individual difference variables are activated. This is shown in the note to figure 23.1. (Naylor et al., 1980, pp. 53–55)

The various classes of perceptions are influenced by noncontingent objective outcomes, contingent objective outcomes, and the acts and products of the individual, all coming together at processing point A, and all, in turn, conditioned by individual differences. These perceptions affect a number of other constructs of the theory, in particular, the various perceived contingencies.

Processing point C brings together the factors that influence individuals' evaluations of their own performances. This includes self-evaluation (how well the person perceives the role established for the self is being fulfilled) and perceived others' evaluations (how well the person perceives the roles established by others are being fulfilled). Inputs here are several types of perceptions and the various product-to-evaluation contingencies.

Processing point D is the place where perceptions of relative and absolute outcomes are formed. Absolute outcomes flow from the perceptions of extrinsic outcomes. Relative outcomes result from equity and expectation comparisons. The attachment of affect to these two types of outcomes occurs at processing point F. This is basically a matter of comparing the outcome level with the temporary need state. There are several ways outcomes influence affect:

1. Externally controlled outcomes are processed to yield perceptions of outcome levels before affect is attached.

2. The outcome, which is intrinsic, comes directly from performing the act and is by its nature pleasurable or painful.
3. The outcome, also intrinsic, is based on the self-evaluation of performance. (Naylor et al., 1980, pp. 61–62)

Valences are formed at processing point E. In addition to affect, the other source of influence is what is labeled the perceived outcome set, which essentially is the combined set of perceptions.

Processing point G provides input to the utility of products, which is a complex set of perceptions that are derived from valence of outcomes, evaluation-to-outcome contingencies, and product-to-evaluation contingencies. The individual must determine how valuable the various products that could be generated are, taking these factors into account. Once the utility of products is formed, it continues to guide the remainder of the person's behavior, subject to moderators and constraints from the environment. The perceptions regarding utility of acts form the individual's behavioral intentions.

Judgment

The general theory is first applied to the subject of judgment. Two types of distinctions are noted:

1. Judgments are either *descriptive* in nature (involve ordering or locating stimuli on a continuum without reference to affective concerns) or *evaluative* (involve an indication of preference regarding stimuli, which reflects an affective response).
2. Judgments are either *concurrent* (apply to the present state of stimuli) or *predictive* (concern the state of the stimulus expected to exist at some future time). (Naylor et al., 1980, pp. 73–77)

These distinctions are then used to assist in describing what happens at the process points in figure 23.1. At point

A. People form their initial perceptions of the stimulus world via descriptive judgments.
B. People form contingency relationships among various cognitions by using descriptive judgments and probability learning.
C. The process of evaluation, and attaching affects, occurs (evaluative judgment).
D. People make descriptive judgments concerning the absolute magnitude of outcomes, which

may be converted to relative magnitudes through comparisons.
E. People attach anticipated affect to anticipated outcomes using predictive judgment.
F. Affect is attached to perceived outcomes already received. These processes (at E and F) constitute the core of motivation.
G. Predictive judgments (anticipations) are established concerning the utility of products.
H. The utility established at point G is converted through evaluative judgments into the overall commitments to acts.

The authors note that

The theory should be viewed as an explanation of behavior of the most idealized kind. It represents our view of how man ought to perform if man is truly rational. . . . Unfortunately . . . people do not utilize the cognitive system in its pure . . . sense. (Naylor et al., 1980, p. 110)

Most . . . behavior is accomplished through the use of heuristic techniques . . . designed to simplify one's existence and help to avoid the complexities of having to perform each of the . . . processes in every behavioral act. (p. 92)

Although there is some discussion of heuristics, and what such a "degraded" version of the theory might look like, no real theory of heuristics is presented. Most heuristics are simply written off as representing individual difference characteristics (and thus not subject to coverage within the theory).

Roles and Role Behaviors

Roles may be considered to be cognitive structures within individual's belief systems and thus are highly relevant for any cognitive theory. In developing their position, Naylor et al. (1980) draw heavily on Daniel Katz and Robert Kahn (see chapter 14 in this volume), and they invoke expectancy theory (chapter 8) to deal with matters of role compliance. The key propositions advanced are as follows, given that products are the basic units of measured behavior:

1. If the product of a focal person is evaluated by either the focal person or some specified other, that product is relevant to either the

self-role or the role held for that focal person by the specified other.

2. A role is defined as a pattern or set of nonzero contingencies between a perceived set of products for the focal person and the evaluation of those products on the part of some person (either self or other).

3. These role contingencies may be viewed appropriately as weights that are somehow indicative of the degree of relevance or importance of the individual products related to the evaluation judgment of the observer. (pp. 121–122)

The value of using contingencies to define roles is that they provide recognition of the fact that higher-level evaluations may go with increasing amounts of product.

The steps in the development of a role received from some other are set forth in figure 23.2. This figure follows upon the extreme right-hand side of figure 23.1. A similar diagram for self-role may be devised from the upper portion of figure 23.2.

Motivation Defined

Although the previous discussion has dealt with motivation at some length in the context of the general theory, a more detailed statement is also provided. Here "motivation is defined as the process of allocating personal resources in the form of time and energy to various acts in such a way that the anticipated affect resulting from these acts is maximized" (Naylor et al., 1980, p. 159). Resources are consciously committed in a goal-directed manner.

This is a maximizing conceptualization and seems to ignore the evidence for satisficing. The authors recognize this, but they argue that the distinction

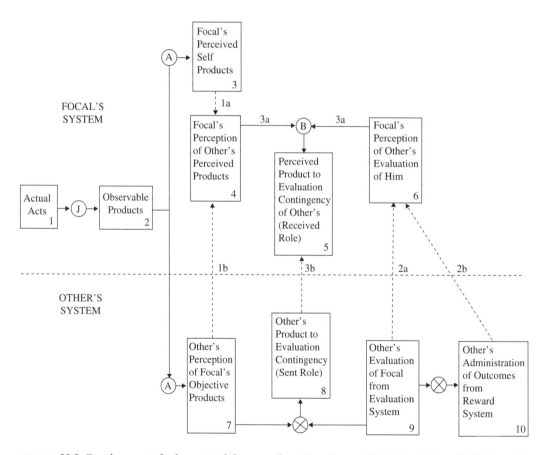

FIGURE 23.2 Development of role received from another. From James C. Naylor, Robert D. Pritchard, & Daniel R. Ilgen (1980), *A Theory of Behavior in Organizations* (New York: Academic Press), 130. Copyright 1980 by Academic Press. Reprinted with permission.

between an outside observer's point of view and the focal person's perspective is important here. The theory is concerned with the latter, and from this viewpoint, considering the costs and affects associated with all possible behaviors, the person does maximize the anticipated affect that results from behavior.

Commitment to acts is important in this motivational process. This commitment reflects the person's general level of activation, which is measured by the ratio of commitment to all acts (trivial and relevant) to the maximum possible commitment. Individual differences produce wide variations in the general level of activation or arousal. Within the person, this level tends to be quite stable in, say, the job context. What is interpreted as an increase in motivation is in reality a consequence of a choice to increase the proportion of relevant to not relevant acts. There is no increase in total effort or commitment level, but rather a change in the direction of behavior.

Supplements to the Motivation Model

In the general theory a number of the constructs relate to motivation—basic needs, temporary need state (arousal), affect, valence of outcomes, the three sets of contingencies, the utility of products, utility of acts, and actual acts. To these components of figure 23.1 the theorists add certain supplemental constructs not depicted there. The rationale for this theoretical extension appears to be a desire to deal with certain perceived deficiencies of expectancy theory, particularly the fact that expectancy theory seems to ignore the way in which the total set of resources is allocated to different acts—the direction issue.

The first supplemental construct considered is motivational force, which operates when different levels of resources committed to an act result in different levels of anticipated affect. Motivational force is equal to the ratio of change in anticipated affect to change in commitment to the act. Stated somewhat differently, it is

> the slope of the function describing a composite contingency relationship between resources committed to an act and the amounts of affect anticipated from the committing of various levels of resources to that act. This composite contingency is actually a composite of the three specific contingency relationships; namely the act-to-product, product-to-evaluation, and evaluation-to-outcome contingencies. (Naylor et al., 1980, p. 189)

This composite contingency relationship is the utility of an act. When the slope is steep (the ratio of change in anticipated affect to change in commitment is large) strong motivational force is activated. If the slope is flat, the reverse is true.

Several additional propositions follow:

> A person will commit additional resources to that act perceived as having the largest ratio (or steepest slope) for the specific amount of additional resources that the individual is willing to consider committing. (p. 193)

> To retain the motivational force notion in the utility of products . . . the motivational force of a product is the degree to which variations in the quantity-quality of the product are accompanied by variations in amount of anticipated affect. A product for which large changes in quantity-quality result in large changes in perceived affect anticipated to result will have strong motivational force. (p. 197)

The next new construct is *utility of evaluations*, which may be viewed as the functional relationship between evaluation level and the anticipated affect tied to each level. The proposition states that "the utility of a given level of evaluation is the valence of the level of outcomes expected to be received from that level of evaluation, summed across outcomes . . . the total anticipated attractiveness of the outcomes that will follow from that level of evaluation" (p. 198).

The utility of evaluation function says a good deal about how much power the evaluator possesses; if an evaluator has strong evaluation-to-outcome contingencies for those particular outcomes that are valued by a person, that evaluator has power over the person. Thus power considerations are tied in with motivational processes.

At the end of this treatment of motivation, the authors return to the matter of simplifying strategies, heuristics, and degraded courses of action. Simplifying behaviors are acts that have their own utility functions, and they are attractive because of the huge effort and time (resource) expenditures that are required to carry out the complex calculations we have been considering. The contention is that among the components of the theory products are the most salient for people and that people *focus on products* as a simplifying strategy by attempting to produce a pattern of products that will ultimately result in maximum positive affect. As long as the contingencies . . . and the valence of outcomes remain fairly constant, focusing on products with their associated motivational force works rather nicely. . . . The person does not need to be aware on a regular basis of all of the other elements. (p. 222)

Leadership and Organizational Climate

In addition to the topics considered previously, the authors look at leadership and also organizational climate through the lens of their theoretical position. The leadership field receives the most attention. Leadership effectiveness is defined as the degree to which a leader can influence subordinates in such a manner as to result in group goal accomplishment. The behavior of a leader in this context may be understood in the same manner as the behavior of any other person. However, because of distortions introduced by implicit leadership theories, the contingencies of measurement and evaluation systems for leaders tend to be particularly inaccurate.

In general, the treatment of leadership "owes a major intellectual debt to the notions of path-goal theory." This is the version of that theory that stood in 1980 (see chapter 10), and the authors indeed do not present anything significant that moves far beyond that theory insofar as the understanding of leadership is concerned. However, the formulations by Naylor et al. (1980) of the processes involved, especially of the links between acts and evaluations, is more complex than in path-goal theory. (This is reflected in the presentations already covered.) Also, their theory addresses *any* behavior of the leader, not merely consideration and initiating structure or some expanded but specific set of behaviors. Basically, the theoretical argument is that leader influence depends on leader control over the three sets of subordinate contingencies, as well as on the subordinate's perceived value for those outcomes that the leader can control.

The discussion of organizational climate is more limited, largely because the authors have doubts about the usefulness of the construct. They start with a definition: "Climate can be viewed as the judgment process involved in attributing a class of humanlike traits to an entity outside the individual where this entity may be a work group or even an entire organization" (p. 254). Thus, it reflects a set of generalized attributions about the environment. They conclude that this construct has little value in predicting individual behavior within an organization, although it may be related to certain withdrawal or avoidance behaviors (absenteeism, turnover, tardiness). The theory does not really deal with climate in any meaningful manner, and it is not entirely clear why this topic is introduced at all.

Finally, it should be emphasized that the basic presentation of the theory is just that. It does not contain any research on the theory of behavior in organizations. The authors note in this regard: "We think there are many fascinating questions to be asked and researched to see if the general and specific linkages and concepts developed here are empirically viable" (p. 273). They do present a listing of many such questions, although these are not stated in hypothesis form. Even more disappointing is the failure to include any data.

Addendum on Goal Setting

Several years after the publication of the basic theory Naylor and Ilgen (1984) presented an extension of that theory that dealt specifically with the motivational effects of goal setting. What they had to say was not really new, but it did represent at the time a more precise conceptualization of the goal setting process. Their theoretical framework to explain why goals work views goal setting as a motivational effect that exerts influence initially on anticipated evaluations of performance or product levels and later on the utility of commitment of effort to accomplish the performance at the level desired.

Locke and Latham (1990) take issue with the Naylor and Ilgen (1984) formulations in certain respects, and have presented considerable research dealing with why goals achieve the motivational effects they do (see chapter 9 in this volume). The way of looking at goal setting presented by Naylor and Ilgen has not served to spark research efforts concentrated directly on their theoretical framework.

Evaluation and Impact

Testing the theory of behavior in organizations is complicated by the very complexity of the theory. It is very unlikely that anyone could devise a study that would encompass the totality of the theory (Kanfer, 1990). The net result has been that research has tended to focus on segments of the whole and, as it turns out, has emphasized certain components at the expense of others.

Measurement-Oriented Research

Of the theory's three authors, Pritchard has contributed most toward a research evaluation of the validity of the constructs and hypothesized relationships. The other two authors have certainly remained active in the field, but for some reason they have chosen not to make the theory of behavior in organizations the focus of their efforts.

Dougherty and Pritchard (1985) initiated the measurement efforts by developing scales to deal with the various role-based constructs; these scales use products as their central inputs. A study with attorneys as subjects indicated that the product-based measures were psychometrically sound and useful, but they predicted outcome variables only slightly better than did existing role measures. Although it is not a direct test of the underlying theory, this research indicates that certain of the constructs involved are viable and worthy of further investigation.

Another such effort involved developing theory-based measures to be used in a study of productivity and productivity enhancement among Air Force personnel (Pritchard, Jones, Roth, Stuebing, & Ekeberg, 1988; Pritchard, 1990). Again, products and product indicators were used, and indices of contingencies between the level of evaluation and amount of an outcome were developed. The findings indicated that the steeper the slope of these contingencies, the greater the contribution to overall effectiveness; as also hypothesized, the contingencies involved did not typically exhibit direct linear relationships. As far as it goes, this research is clearly consistent with theoretical expectations; however, the major focus of the research was on the use of a feedback system to stimulate productivity, not on testing theory.

More recently, the data from this study have been reanalyzed using an approach judged to be more appropriate to the purposes at hand (Sawyer, Latham, Pritchard, & Bennett, 1999). The findings provide strong support for the contingencies aspect of the theory in a work group context, and for the motivational force construct in certain of its aspects as well.

Laboratory Studies

Most of the research bearing on the theory of Naylor et al. (1980) is of a laboratory nature and uses under-graduates as subjects. This research has been quite focused in nature, but it permits considerable control and thus more certain conclusions than the field research.

A study by Larson and Callahan (1990) provides strong inferential evidence that conceptualizing motivation as a resource allocation process is a useful and valid approach. Furthermore, this study indicates that redirection of resources is a major factor in improved productivity, although it does not rule out the possibility that increased effort may occur under certain circumstances.

The results of another laboratory study are well described as follows:

> Sawyer (1990) considered the effect of risk and uncertainty on individuals' judgments of contingencies (in this case, the relationship between acts and products from Naylor et al.'s 1980 theory of motivation) and their decisions to allocate time to an activity. When contingencies were learned under uncertain conditions, individuals judged contingencies to be more linear than they actually were. Additionally, individuals preferred to allocate resources to the more certain contingencies. In conditions where functions were equally uncertain, individuals used the optimal allocation rule. Sawyer's (1990) study provides one of the few empirical tests of Naylor et al.'s (1980) theory. His results suggest the theory, which is a refinement and extension of expectancy theory, may not be any more successful in predicting resource allocations or behavior in uncertain environments than the traditional expectancy theory approach. (Ambrose & Kulik, 1999, p. 240)

One interpretation of this result is that the degraded (less complex) expectancy theories tap into the same heuristics as the Naylor et al. (1980) theory when actual human cognitive processes are applied, and thus the two approaches yield similar results. In both instances, errors or biases occur because the operating heuristics are the same.

In fact, there is considerable evidence that when the behavior in organizations framework is used in research, considerable departures from the predicted judgmental patterns may be anticipated (Sniezek, May, & Sawyer, 1990; Switzer & Sniezek, 1991). Furthermore, there is reason to believe that these distortions (in the act-to-product contingency judgment) are a function of the use of a heuristic that serves to simplify the process of judging. Exactly how these judgment biases influence behavior is not well-established in these studies, but the possibility exists that goal setting may achieve its effects by anchoring behavior in much the same way that heuristics anchor cognitive processes.

Research in Context

Reviewers have consistently viewed the theory of Naylor et al. (1980) as innovative, especially in its aspects of resource allocation, and highly complex (Staw, 1984; Kanfer, 1990, 1992). This complexity is evident in figure 23.1, and a comparison of that figure with the research reported serves to emphasize how limited the research really is. This becomes even more apparent when the extensions of the general theory into areas such as leadership and role behavior are considered. It is not that the theoretical statements are of uncertain meaning or ambiguous, but they are complex and cover a great deal of ground. The result appears to have been that only those with a background in the field of judgment and decision making have been willing to tackle the task of empirically assessing the theory—and unfortunately not a large number of these people, either.

One conclusion that does result from the research to date is that heuristics, degraded judgments, satisficing, and the like play an important role in organizational motivation. The theory's authors recognize this, but they prefer to pursue an optimizing type of theoretical statement. The alternative would be to develop a theory of what human beings actually do, rather than a theory of ideal processes. Such a theory might well encompass the present approach, as well as expectancy formulations and much of the goal setting process. It also should permit a much better understanding of how motivation actually unwinds in the organizational context than we have at present.

The Naylor et al. (1980) theory is anything but a theory for practice. It was clearly written for scholars, not practitioners. There is little mention of how these ideas might be brought to bear in actual application. In fact, as Larry Cummings indicates, "a reading of Naylor, Pritchard, and Ilgen suggests that there is relatively little unique about behavior that is contextual, social, or organizational. The 'in organizations' represents a weak main effect" (1981, p. 663).

Since the publication of the theory, Pritchard has developed productivity measures that are based in part on the theory's concepts, and he has used these measures in a program of group-based feedback and goal setting that has been found quite effective in stimulating productive output. Although the Air Force program that used this approach was subsequently discontinued for reasons external to the program itself, this effort must clearly be judged a success. However, its theoretical ties are multiple, and only certain aspects of the way in which productivity was measured appear to be directly attributable to the theory of behavior in organizations.

As we move now to discussion of a new theory, it is useful to recognize that the effort by Naylor, Pritchard, and Ilgen tends to be labeled differently by different discussants, depending on the particular orientation of the person involved. Some view it as a theory of motivation; others say it is a theory of perception or cognitive process, while still others place it in the context of decision making or judgment. In reality, in its complexity, it is all of these. However, for present purposes, it fits best in the line of succession from motivation theories that focus on needs, expectancies, valences, and the like.

ATTRIBUTION THEORY APPLIED TO POOR PERFORMANCE

Attribution theory had a long history in psychology, particularly social psychology, before it found its way into organizational behavior (Harvey & Weary, 1984). Theorists who make attributions the core constructs of their thinking are concerned with the perceived causes of events and the consequences of the particular types of perceptions involved. There is no one attribution theory; many different forms have emerged. Within organizational behavior, however, approaches to assignment of responsibility have prevailed; these approaches are concerned with how people make attributions for the behavior and outcomes of other individuals (Martinko, 1995). The most widely known and extensively researched of these theories is the approach developed by Terence Mitchell and others to indicate how leaders perceive and explain the poor performance of subordinates. This is an interpersonal attribution model concerned with explanations for the actions of others. Within psychology there has been much more concern with intrapersonal attributions— explanations of and for one's own behavior. Thus in organizational behavior, attribution processes tend to be viewed as perceptual in nature, not motivational, although elements of both are involved. The Mitchell theory adds a leadership component as well.

Background

Born in 1942, Mitchell obtained his undergraduate degree in psychology from Duke University in 1964 and completed subsequent work in public administration at the University of Exeter in England. His graduate study was in social psychology at the University of Illinois, but with a minor in public administration. He received the Ph.D. in 1969. Immediately thereafter he took a position at the University of Washington with a joint appointment in organizational behavior (in the business school) and psychology.

In 1969 Fred Fiedler moved from Illinois to Washington also (see chapter 12 in this volume), and it is no coincidence that both had a major interest in interpersonal perception: They conducted research and published together for several years, although their interests have taken them in different directions since the early 1970s. Mitchell was promoted to full professor at Washington in 1977 and has remained there since.

Consistent with his wide range of scholarly activities, Mitchell has published with many different individuals. This is also true of his contributions to attribution theory. His major coauthor in the early period was Stephen Green, who was then with him at the University of Washington and subsequently spent many years on the faculty of the business school at the University of Cincinnati. Green now holds a similar appointment at Purdue University. Green became increasingly involved in the study of poor and ineffective performance, however, as distinct from its fusion with attribution processes. He did not continue to publish with Mitchell after the early 1980s.

Attribution Theory

Mitchell's theory has its roots in a background of work in two areas—attribution theory and the management of ineffective performance. The attribution theory component is the most extensive and goes back further in time. The beginning is generally considered to be the work of Fritz Heider (1958); later work was influenced by Edward Jones, Harold Kelley, and Julian Rotter (Martinko, 1995). Mitchell cites all of these as sources of his own thinking. Jones contributed in particular to the distinction between actors and ob-servers (Jones & Davis, 1965; Jones & Nisbett, 1971). Kelley provided views of the attribution process that were later formally built into Mitchell's theory, as we will see (Kelley, 1967, 1973). Rotter (1966) was primarily an input to Mitchell's early research, which was on the developmental path leading up to the actual creation of the attribution theory of poor performance.

In addition to these formulations, Mitchell drew on certain ideas related to achievement motivation (see chapter 6 in this volume) put forth by Bernard Weiner. In relating achievement motivation to attribution processes, Weiner at that time was attempting to enlarge on McClelland's view that people motivated by achievement prefer to attribute credit for outcomes to their own efforts rather than to chance or luck.

Weiner's (1972) theory deals with the degree to which people ascribe their successes and failures to the following:

1. Their own ability—viewed as a stable characteristic and inside oneself
2. Their effort level—viewed as a variable factor, also inside oneself
3. The difficulty of the task—viewed as stable and given, but external to the self
4. Luck—viewed as variable and unstable, also external to the self (p. 356)

Wide individual differences are postulated in the tendency to attribute what happens to a person to each of these factors. In particular, achievement-motivated people are expected to attribute their successes to their own efforts and their failures to not trying hard enough. If they fail, they are likely to try again because they tend to believe that with greater effort they can succeed. Thus, they consistently perceive their ability levels as being quite high. When they do succeed, it is because they tried hard and used their abilities.

In contrast, those with a low need for achievement view effort as irrelevant. They attribute failure to other factors, in particular lack of ability, a condition that they believe is generally characteristic of themselves. Success is viewed as primarily a consequence of the external factors of easy tasks and luck.

Obviously, if one is interested in motivating a person to do something, what will work in dealing with an achievement-oriented person may be absolutely useless in dealing with a person who lacks achievement motivation. This suggests, as Weiner has indicated, that educational programs attempting to bring about motivational change and development in the achievement area should focus first on teaching the participants that effort does make a difference and that internal causation is a key factor mediating between a task and the level of performance on that task.

Although relevant research at the time was not extensive, there was a degree of support for an explanation of the dynamics of achievement motivation in terms of attribution mechanisms (Weiner, 1972; Weiner & Sierad, 1975). If nothing else, these findings served to demonstrate to Mitchell that attribution theory was a useful vehicle for explaining many phenomena within organizational behavior (Weiner, 1974). An essay by Calder (1977) served to demonstrate more directly the ways in which attributional thinking could contribute to an understanding of leadership processes.

Management of Ineffective Performance

The second line of development leading to Mitchell's theory of attribution and poor performance harks back to my own personal experiences in developing a diagnostic scheme to aid managers in determining the causes of (making attributions regarding) the ineffective performance of subordinates (see chapter 5). The key writings here that appear to have influenced Mitchell are John Miner (1963), Lawrence Steinmetz (1969), and Miner and Frank Brewer (1976). The idea in these early statements was that, faced with an instance of poor performance, a manager should try to figure out (diagnose) the various causes that contribute to failure. Only with this knowledge could a suitable treatment or corrective action be determined, which would establish effective performance where failure had existed before. What Mitchell's theory added to this is that it viewed the diagnostic process as one of making attributions, with all the potential for error inherent in perceptions of this type.

Theoretical Statements

Before actually moving to the presentation of the basic theory, Mitchell participated in several studies that dealt with attributional subject matter, but in a manner somewhat tangential to the theory that finally evolved. These studies considered Rotter's (1966) locus of control construct (Mitchell, Smyser, & Weed, 1975) and attributional biases in ratings of leader behavior (Mitchell, Larson, & Green, 1977). In his *An-*

nual Review article, Mitchell concludes: "While the work on applying attribution theory to the organizational context is rather recent, what has been done seems promising" (1979, p. 251). Shortly thereafter he began the presentation of his own theory.

Attributional Processes in Leader-Member Interactions

In the first presentation of the theory (Green & Mitchell, 1979), leaders are considered to be information processors where the naïve causal attributions serve as mediators between the behaviors of subordinates and the leaders' behaviors. Following Kelley (1967, 1973), these attributions may be categorized as grounded in a perception (1) of the employee (person) as cause, (2) of the task (entity) as cause, or (3) of the external circumstances surrounding the event (context) as cause. The cause of an event (behavior of subordinate) will in all likelihood be found in something that varies during and after the event occurs, rather than remaining stable—the principle of covariation. The information sought by the leader (and this too follows Kelley) is of three kinds:

> *Distinctiveness*—Did the behavior occur on this task, but not others?
>
> *Consistency*—How consistent is this behavior with the other behavior of the person?
>
> *Consensus*—Is the behavior unique to this particular person as opposed to being widespread among others?

These and other factors are brought together in the model of the attributional process set forth in figure 23.3. This identical model appears in a later publication as well (Mitchell, Green, & Wood, 1981). The organizational and/or personal policy loop refers to mechanisms that circumvent the attributional process so that if it occurs at all it has no impact on leader behavior. A variety of hypotheses related to factors in figure 23.3 are sprinkled through the Green and Mitchell (1979) essay and are brought together toward the end. These represent the essential original contribution of the theory.

> I. Leaders can be seen as scientists engaging in a process of hypothesis testing by gathering information and seeking causal explanations

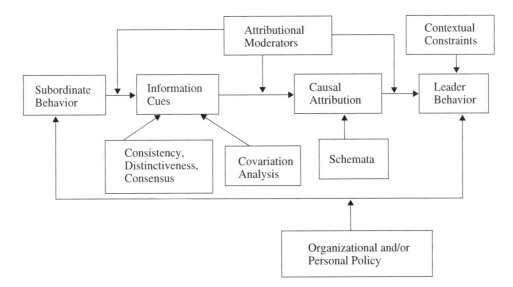

FIGURE 23.3 The basic attributional model in leader-member interactions. From Stephen G. Green & Terence R. Mitchell (1979), Attributional Processes of Leaders in Leader-Member Interactions, *Organizational Behavior and Human Performance*, 23, 450. Copyright 1979 by Academic Press. Reprinted with permission.

about the behavior and performance of their group members.

II. A leader's behavior is likely to depend more on consistency and distinctiveness information about a member's performance than on consensus information.

   A. When consensus information is used, it is likely to be self-based consensus.

III. Because a leader is more likely to explain member performance with internal causes than external causes, leader behavior is more likely to be directed at the member than at situational factors.

   A. Since a member is more likely to explain his or her own performance with external causes, this basic difference in causal explanations and the resultant leader behavior serves as a major source of leader-member conflict and miscommunication.

IV. Locus of control and stability are two critical dimensions of causal attributions which mediate leaders' responses to member performance.

   A. A leader is likely to focus his or her actions on the member when performance is seen as due to internal causes (e.g., suggest training when performance is seen as due to lack of knowledge).

   B. A leader is likely to focus his or her actions on situational factors when the member's performance is seen as due to external causes (e.g., changing a job procedure if it is too difficult for most employees).

   C. A leader's evaluations of a member's present performance are heavily influenced by effort (internal, unstable) attributions.

   D. A leader will be both more rewarding and more punishing of present performance which is attributed to effort.

   E. A leader's expectancies about a member's future performance are heavily influenced by the stability of attributions; the more stable the cause is seen to be (e.g., ability) the more future performance of the member is expected to be consistent with present performance.

V. Attributional processes are directly related to how much uncertainty a leader experiences in attempting to manage subordinates.

   A. Multiple causation tends to result in leader uncertainty. This uncertainty may intensify the testing of the member by the leader and result in less extreme actions by the leader.

   B. Unstable causal explanations create uncertainty, with unstable, external attributions presenting the most uncertainty for the leader.

VI. The relationship between leader and member is a critical moderator of the leader's attributions and subsequent behavior.
   A. The more a leader is empathetic with the member, sees the member as similar, respects and/or likes the member, the more likely the leader is to form "favorable" causal attributions for the member's performance (e.g., attributing success to internal causes and failure to external causes).
   B. The more removed the leader (e.g., the greater the power), the more likely the leader is to make "unfavorable" causal attributions about the member's performance.
   C. Favorable attributions will enhance rewarding behavior and reduce punishing behavior on the part of the leader. Unfavorable attributions will result in the opposite type of behavior on the part of the leader.
VII. Leader expectations about member performance interact with actual performance to determine the leader's attributions.
   A. The leader will attribute member performance to internal causes (e.g., effort) when expectations and performance are consistent.
   B. The leader will attribute member performance to external causes (e.g., luck) when expectations and performance are inconsistent.
VIII. The effects of the subordinate's behavior and the degree of responsibility inferred by the leader will influence the action selected.
   A. The more extreme the effect, the more extreme the response.
   B. The greater the perceived responsibility of the member, the more likely the leader is to take action concerning the member and the more extreme the response. (Green & Mitchell, 1979, pp. 451–452)

Model of Leader Response to Poor Performance

The next theoretical statement was the presentation of the model in figure 23.4. In conjunction with this model, which is more theoretically focused than figure 23.3, certain propositions are set forth:

At link #1 high distinctiveness, low consistency, and high consensus should result in internal attributions.

The more severe the consequences of the poor performance, the greater the probability that the leader will make internal attributions and respond with punishment.

When an internal attribution is made, the leader should respond by attempting to change the subordinate's behavior through feedback, punishment, or training; when the attribution is external, the response should be directed at changing the situation or task.

Leaders in general will attribute poor performance in subordinates to internal rather than external causes. (Mitchell & Wood, 1980)

In a subsequent publication, the model of figure 23.3 is presented, but the discussion suggests that figure 23.4 was actually in mind (see Mitchell et al., 1981). Here attention is focused on moderators of the attributional process:

A number of factors other than the classical attributional factors (e.g., Kelley or Weiner's work) may moderate the informational processes. Some of these moderators such as individual characteristics seem likely to alter or distort the causal explanation the leader believes. Other moderators such as the effects of the subordinate's behavior seem likely to alter the leader's behavior so it does not follow directly from prior attributions. In either case, it is clear that factors outside of the classical information processing models have real implications for the extent to which attributions affect leader behavior toward the member. (Mitchell et al., 1981, p. 209).

The moderators noted are—

At link no.1:

Self-serving attributions by the leader (taking responsibility for positive outcomes, but not for negative)

Relationship of leader and member (whatever decreases psychological distance between the two increases the leader's tendency to make attributions similar to the subordinate's self-attributions)

Personal characteristics (race and sex, among other personal factors, can serve to increase biases inherent in the attributional process)

Leader expectations (behavior consistent with leader expectations tends to elicit internal attributions, while behavior that is inconsistent with ex-

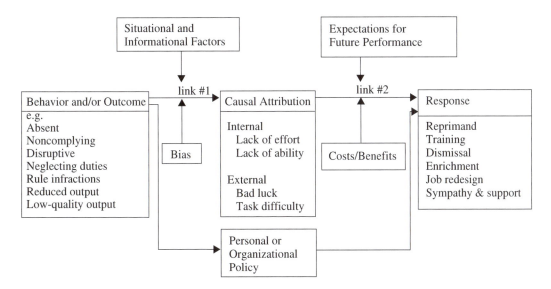

FIGURE 23.4 The attributional model of leader response to subordinate poor performance. From Terence R. Mitchell & Robert E. Wood (1980), Supervisor's Responses to Subordinate Poor Performance: A Test of an Attributional Model, *Organizational Behavior and Human Performance*, 25, 124. Copyright 1980 by Academic Press. Reprinted with permission.

pectations tends to elicit external attributions—i.e., difficult task).

At link no. 2:

Leader's perceptions of responsibility (the more a subordinate is judged responsible for an outcome, the greater the likelihood that the leader will take action toward the subordinate and the greater the degree of that action)

The effects of behavior (the effects or impact of the behavior will be taken into account in determining the leader response)

Accounts (the subordinate's explanation of the event can exert an influence on the leader response)

Ease of change (believing that the behavior of people is easier to change than the environment, a leader faced with uncertainty will opt for changing the subordinate) (Mitchell et al., 1981, pp. 205–209)

Certain of these moderators were considered in the 1979 paper, but others are new. In addition, various boundary conditions for the attribution process are noted: these include restrictions on leader behaviors,

replacing attributional processes with organizational policy, and the use of rigid personal policy decision rules. The eventual goal of the theorizing and research is not only to establish sources of error that influence practice but also to determine ways of reducing these errors; training may be a means to this latter end.

Variants of the model set forth in figure 23.4 have been published since, although the basic structure remains the same (Mitchell, 1982; Mitchell & O'Reilly, 1983). The major changes appear to be an emphasis on the fact that biases may enter at both links no. 1 and no. 2 and on the fact that at these same points rational inputs occur as well (the terminology of situational and informational factors and expectations for future performance is replaced by rational inputs).

Impression Management

An article by Robert Wood and Mitchell (1981) picks up on the matter of accounts noted previously and elaborates the theory more fully in this regard. This area was not adequately considered in initial presentations of the model. The hypotheses read as follows:

Accounts of external causes, when given by the subordinate, will lead a supervisor to discount internal causes as explanations for poor performance.

Accounts of external causes will reduce the likelihood of the manager directing a disciplinary action at the subordinate and the punitiveness of any disciplinary action chosen.

Accounts of prior external causes should lead the manager to have lower expectations of future failure by the subordinate and to be less likely to closely supervise the subordinate after the event. (Wood & Mitchell, 1981, pp. 359–360)

Also, with regard to apologies, which are statements of remorse and thus are self-punitive in nature:

Apologies by the subordinate should . . . reduce the likelihood of the manager directing a disciplinary action at the subordinate and, in particular, should reduce the punitiveness of disciplinary action. (Wood & Mitchell, 1981, pp. 359–360)

Group Poor Performance

The development work on the theory in the area of group poor performance was done by Karen Brown (1984), but it was done at the University of Washington, with Mitchell's assistance, and using funds from a research grant awarded to Mitchell. Thus, this extension legitimately may be considered a part of the Mitchell theory, especially since Mitchell and Brown subsequently published research on the subject together (Brown & Mitchell, 1986).

The essence of the theory is contained in the propositions listed in the left column of table 23.1. The propositions at the right involve individual performance failure and are provided to facilitate contrasting the two concepts. It is apparent that dealing with poor performance failure at the group level introduces some new considerations.

Introducing Ingratiation into the Theory

Ingratiation represents an attempt by a person to increase his or her attractiveness in the eyes of others. It is a social influence process that comes to organizational behavior from social psychology where it has previously been integrated with attribution processes (Jones & Wortman, 1973). Robert Liden and Mitchell (1988) attempt to extend this integration of ingratiation and attribution theories to create a more comprehensive theory of leader reactions to poor performance.

The article in which this theory is presented contains 18 propositions dealing with ingratiation, and a number of them have multiple variants. Most of these propositions are rather general in nature, and only a limited set deal directly with the application of the ingratiation concept to attribution theory as applied to poor performance. Within this set, some propositions deal with strategies to defend oneself against criticism and others with strategies to promote or assert oneself. The propositions that are clearly relevant for prior theory read as follows:

Ingratiation strategies used to defend oneself following poor performance will tend to be short-term, reactive, and designed to manipulate target attributions concerning the poor performance.

Assertive strategies used to promote oneself will tend to be long-term, proactive, and either designed to manipulate target attributions or to simply be liked by the target.

Targets will be less likely to alter their attributions for the ingratiator's poor performance when the ingratiator has a history of poor performance or if the outcome of the poor performance is serious.

The more frequent and serious a performance problem, the more likely a leader will have a policy for handling the problem; leaders who have chosen to bypass the attributional process by developing policies for handling performance problems will ignore apologies, accounts, and excuses. (Liden & Mitchell, 1988, pp. 577–578, 580)

From these propositions it becomes apparent that the extension of the theory into the realm of ingratiation builds on prior work in the area of impression management.

Effects of Group Performance and Leader Power

A recent extension to the basic theory builds on the group level work by Brown (1984) and also on a program of research by David Kipnis (1987) that deals with the consequences of leader power. The hypotheses involved are as follows:

1a. Individuals (members and leaders) in high-performing groups will make more internal attributions for performance than will individuals in low-performing groups.

1b. Individuals (members and leaders) in low-performing groups will make more external attributions for performance than will individuals in high-performing groups.

TABLE 23.1 Managerial attributions regarding poor group and individual performance hypothesized from theory at link no. 1 of the Attributional Model

Attributions about poor group performance	Attributions about poor individual performance
External attributions are made about the work environment	Internal attributions are made about the poorly performing subordinate
Internal attributions are made about employees' poor attitudes. These attitudes are viewed as having developed because of the negative influence of one or more "bad apples" in a cohesive or interdependent group.	External attributions are made about the work environment. Attitude problems are viewed as being more likely as causes of group poor performance and less likely as causes of individual poor performance.
Internal attributions are made by upper-level managers, regardless of whether poor performance is associated with one individual or an entire group. This results from a lack of task experience and direct contact and also from the fact that these upper-level managers take a broader system perspective and compare groups rather than individuals in assessing performance.	
Attributions are made that remove blame from the supervisor. These can include internal attributions about employees and external attributions about system factors that are outside of the supervisor's control.	External attributions are more likely here because individual poor performance is less relevant to the supervisor and, therefore, less likely to elicit a defensive or self-protecting diagnosis.
Internal attributions about group members escalate over time when poor performance persists, particularly when group failure is viewed as a personal failure by the supervisor.	External attributions about system or supervisory factors may be more comfortably made because the accumulated failures of one employee are less likely to be viewed as personal failures for the supervisor.

SOURCE: Adapted from Karen A. Brown (1984), Explaining Group Poor Performance: An Attributional Analysis, *Academy of Management Review*, 9, 58

2a. High-power leaders will make more internal attributions for success than will low power leaders.
2b. High-power leaders will make more external attributions for failure than will low-power leaders.
3a. Leaders who experience a gain in power will increase their level of internal attributions for success; leaders who experience a loss in power will decrease their level of internal attributions for success.
3b. Leaders who experience a gain in power will increase their level of external attributions for failure; leaders who experience a loss in power will decrease their level of external attributions for failure. (Ferrier, Smith, Rediker, & Mitchell, 1995, p. 318)

There are several other hypotheses dealing with power, but these do not relate to the basic attributional theory.

Evaluation and Impact

Statements of the theory consist essentially of a few models that show relationships among constructs, as well as a long list of propositions and hypotheses spread over a period from 1979 to 1995. This list does not represent a parsimonious theoretical formulation, but to date it is the best we have. Mitchell has not written a book distilling his theory, perhaps because he views the theory as still developing. However, we do have the advantage of a large number of research studies that Mitchell has conducted with a diverse array of coauthors, many of them students and colleagues at the University of Washington.

Early Mitchell Studies

Not all of the hypotheses of the theory have been subjected to research testing by Mitchell, and some of the tests that have been conducted offer rather indirect evidence, primarily because non-theory variables and relationships were incorporated. Nevertheless, operationalizations of the major constructs are available, and a good deal of information has accumulated about the conduct of research into the attributional aspects of the analysis of ineffective performance—primarily via laboratory study.

Biases are clearly evident: when performance is held constant, performance evaluations are influenced by whether attributions are made to effort or ability (Knowlton & Mitchell, 1980). There is also a bias toward attributing causality for poor performance to internal factors generally, and this bias is accentuated when a history of poor performance exists and the outcome is serious (Mitchell & Wood, 1980). Furthermore, attributions play a role in determining leader responses; internal attributions make for responses directed at the poor performer, not the context. Low-, as compared to high-, performing subordinates elicit more negative attributions, more negative attitudes, a preference for closer supervision, less feedback, and reduced financial compensation (Ilgen, Mitchell, & Fredrickson, 1981). However, these consistently negative reactions were mitigated somewhat when the leader's rewards depended on the performance level of the subordinate. While leaders tend to focus on internal attributions, subordinates see their poor performance as externally caused, thus creating conditions for conflict (Mitchell et al., 1981).

These early findings lend considerable support to the basic theory. There is a problem, however, in that the results stem from research which consistently is of a laboratory nature and uses reactions to cases and simulations. The subjects are mostly students, playing both leader and subordinate roles. We know little from this research about how attributions operate in the world of practice. Furthermore, Mitchell interjects certain concerns of his own:

> Not only are attributions only one contributor to action . . . according to our findings attributions play a *minor* role. . . . There are many settings where actions may be simply determined by personal, social or organizational policies. Attributions would be completely bypassed. In many other settings it appears that contextual, task, social, and cost/benefit type factors are as important or more important than attributions. Therefore, in many settings attributions may be weekly related to action at best. (1982, p. 71)

This suggests that attributional biases may be counteracted in many instances, or they may simply be replaced by other biases.

Mitchell's Expanded Research Agenda

Studies since the early ones on the basic theory cover considerable ground, including some looking back at the initial hypotheses. The Wood and Mitchell (1981) studies dealing with impression management are generally supportive of the theory. Although subordinate accounts do operate as hypothesized to reduce leader negative reactions, expectations of future failure did not operate consistently as hypothesized, and apologies appeared to have a minimal effect. Research on the specific hypotheses dealing with ingratiation, beyond what is discussed here, has not been reported.

Research conducted to determine how prior experience in the same job as the poor performer, and thus less psychological distance, influences attributions indicates that the result is a greater resort to external causes (Mitchell & Kalb, 1982). Field data tend to support this laboratory finding. Evidence also indicates that subjects will react more positively to feedback when the feedback implies that an external cause for performance problems exists (Liden & Mitchell, 1985).

Studies on the group theory indicate that multiple poor performers, as opposed to a single one, do have an effect on the diagnosis of reasons for poor performance (Brown & Mitchell, 1986), thus tending to shift attributions away from internal causes and toward external ones. In another study (Ferrier et al., 1995) it was found that members from high-performing groups tend to resort to more internal attributions than do those from low-performing groups. External attributions follow the reverse pattern. This result is as hypothesized. However, attempts to test hypotheses on leader power did not provide consistent support and suggest a need for theoretical revisions. Gain and loss of power did not have the expected consequences, and the theory proved defective with regard to power use in other respects as well. Perhaps adding in the power variable served to overextend the basic theory.

Research on a resort to company policy, as opposed to personal diagnosis, in handling instances of poor performance indicates that even when an appropriate policy is available, there is a 50-50 chance that the policy will not govern. Following policy has the benefit of saving time, and when managers feel judged and pressured they are more likely to opt for this approach. Concern with matters of fairness prompts individual diagnosis and thus the use of attributions. Staying with company policy tends to foster more severe actions (Liden, Mitchell, & Maslyn, 1998). Faced with large numbers of subordinates and many instances of performance problems, it appears that the balance often shifts sharply toward a manager holding closely to policy.

Closely Related Research

What I have in mind here is research on either attributions or ineffective performances conducted by people who have at one time or another been closely allied to the theory. My intent is to merely note these contributions rather than to treat them in detail when they do not provide evidence for the theory's evaluation. In general, however, they do say something about the network that has evolved around Mitchell's work, and thus its impact.

After participating in the early theoretical efforts, Green has devoted himself to the study of ineffective performance, and this is largely independent of ties to attribution theory. There was an early, and only partially successful, effort to relate the causes of performance failure set forth by Miner (1963) and Steinmetz (1969) to the attribution framework (in Mitchell & O'Reilly, 1983). And Stephen Green and Liden (1980) carried out a study looking into attributional and company policy factors in leader responses (control decisions):

> As hypothesized when the subordinate was seen as causal, vis-à-vis situational factors, control responses were directed at the subordinate, were more punitive, and included more change to his/her job. Also, as expected, the supervisors complied with policy least when it disagreed with their causal beliefs or was severe. (Green & Liden, 1980, p. 457)

More recently, however, Green has been concerned with poor performance extending over a period of time as it occurs in actual field situations rather than with the single episodes and laboratory conditions that have been the focus of Mitchell's work. These efforts (Green, Fairhurst, & Snavely, 1986; Gavin, Green, & Fairhurst, 1995) raise questions about some of the practical implications of the basic theory, especially as it relates to the development of leader responses at link no. 2. However, they do not deal with the attributional formulations that represent the core of the theory.

Liden has cooperated with a number of others to study the disciplinary process applied to poor performance and the role of group decision making in this regard (Liden et al., 1999). Mitchell himself has joined forces with others at the University of Washington with a primary interest in the self-efficacy concept

to study the relationships among attributions, self-efficacy, and performance (Silver, Mitchell, & Gist, 1995). This work considers self-attributions rather than the attributions to others that characterize almost all of Mitchell's prior theorizing and research; it finds sizable interrelationships.

Finally mention should be made of a study conducted with Judith Heerwagen (Heerwagen, Beach, & Mitchell, 1985), which attempted to use a film to sensitize people to internal and external causes of poor performances and thus remove biases. However, when the costs and benefits associated with different leader responses were introduced as a factor, these nonattributional aspects come to dominate the situation and the responses. Mitchell concludes: "More research is clearly needed on how the social and situational factors influence appraisal and how errors or biases can be removed" (1983, p. 55).

Outside Research on the Basic Theory

Probably the most extensive research program on the theory, besides those involving Mitchell or those closely allied with him, has been carried out by Neal Ashkanasy in Australia (see Ashkanasy & Gallois, 1994; Ashkanasy, 1995). This research has studied the role of distinctiveness, consistency, and consensus in relation to attributions for performance failure and success. The results indicate that poor performance does foster complex cognitive processes aimed at developing causal explanations. Furthermore, these processes tend to follow the pattern established by the Mitchell theory, although the findings from field research are more consistently supportive than those obtained in the laboratory. The use of varied designs and samples in this program yields considerable confidence in the conclusions.

Another field study indicates that at link no. 2, leader responses tend to be tied to the attributions made at link no. 1 (Judge & Martocchio, 1995). When the attributions for poor performance are of an external nature, disciplinary responses tend to be less severe than when an internal attribution is made. This study also looked into the moderating role of an individual difference variable (fairness orientation), thus moving beyond what Mitchell and colleagues have considered in their theorizing. The findings indicate that a strong sense of fairness serves to make for the use of more severe punishment, although this factor accounts for only a modest effect on disciplinary decisions. Dean Tjosvold (1985) also finds a tie between attributions and leader responses, in that superiors who make internal attributions to effort respond to poor performance with threats, assertions of power, dislike, increased social distance, and dissatisfaction, while attributions to ability yield more encouragement and favorable conclusions. As hypothesized, the existence of an interdependent relationship between superior and subordinate, where the superior receives rewards based on the subordinate's behavior, serves to produce more assistance and open-mindeness toward the subordinate. Earl Pence, William Pendleton, Greg Dobbins, and Joseph Sgro (1982) provide evidence to support the idea that the specific causal attribution involved, not merely whether it is internal or external, determines leader responses. A lack of effort elicits the most coercive corrective action.

These findings confirm the basic theory with a good deal of consistency, and this support comes from both laboratory and field studies. However, some disparity from theoretical expectations is introduced by a study conducted in a casino setting (Smither, Skov, & Adler, 1986). As the data of table 23.2 indicate, relationships at link no. 2 were much what would be expected, but the correlations are rather low. Furthermore, the expected tendency for supervisors to pick internal attributions and performers to favor external ones was not clearly evident. Effort and task difficulty showed differential tendencies in the expected directions, but the two sources (supervisors and performers) did *not* differ significantly. Supervisors attributed causation to the quality of supervision (an *external* factor) more frequently than the performers. Control subjects without task experience attributed causation to the external factors of task difficulty and working conditions *more* than the performers did. The authors conclude that the attributions made often depend on the specific context and, accordingly, may deviate from theoretical expectations; biases may or may not operate, depending on context.

Outside Research on Psychological Distance

A number of studies have been conducted on the definition of psychological distance between leader and poor performer. Of particular interest has been the matter of the effects of gender and race differences, when the leader is a white male and the performer is a female or black, or both. One expectation here is that attributions to ability will be less likely for women and blacks. Among women overall, however, this does not appear to be the case, although it does appear to be true when analyses are restricted to the most highly successful performers—a post hoc analysis (Greenhaus & Parasuraman, 1993). Blacks did show the expected pattern, and in addition their performance was attributed less to effort and more to the effects of help. Taken as a whole, the effects of psychological distance were much more in evidence for blacks than for women. This tendency for differences in subordinate gender to exhibit minimal effects has been found in other studies as well (Dobbins, 1985).

Another aspect of psychological distance considered is the liking the leader has for the poor performer. Less liking (more distance) should result in attributions to internal factors and more punitive responses.

TABLE 23.2 Significant ($p < .05$) correlations between attributions for performance and corrective actions recommended

	Attributed cause of poor performance				
Corrective response	Effort	Ability	Task difficulty	Working conditions	Quality of supervision
Additional training	—	.24	—	—	.21
Transfer to less difficult task	—	.31	.16	—	—
Disciplinary warning	.31	—	—	−.22	—
Modified work environment	—	—	.19	.30	—
Encouragement and support from supervisor	—	−.19	—	.16	.21
Hiring people with more ability	.23	.20	—	—	—

SOURCE: Adapted from James W. Smither, Richard B. Skov, & Seymour Adler (1986), Attributions for the Poorly Performing Blackjack Dealer: In the Cards or Inability? *Personnel Psychology*, 39, 129, 134

Both of these expectations were supported in a field study, but only the latter in a laboratory study (Dobbins & Russell, 1986). Certain deficiencies in the realism of the laboratory research appear to account for the failure to identify effects of liking on attributions in the laboratory context. A variant on the study of liking here is to consider ingroup and outgroup status, as defined by leader member exchange theory (see chapter 12 in this volume). When this approach to the psychological distance factor is invoked, the following results are obtained:

> Internal attributions were significantly higher for ingroup members than for outgroup members when performance was effective. Internal attributions were significantly higher for outgroup members than for ingroup members when performance was ineffective. Supervisors appear to be less consistent in assigning external attributions to ingroup and outgroup members than they are in making internal attributions. None of the mean differences in external attributions were significant. (Heneman, Greenberger, & Anonyuo, 1989, p. 471)

Insofar as they go, these findings are consistent with theory, but the failure to find expected results for external attributions (luck and task difficulty) does give some pause.

Outside Research on Accounts

A body of research has developed that relates in one way or another to the accounts concept. Dennis Gioia and Henry Sims (1986) studied performance-related conversations between managers and subordinates, finding that the subordinates tend to present self-serving arguments which apparently were heard. The face-to-face interactions resulted in considerable information seeking by the managers, and, ultimately, an attributional shift to greater leniency—less blame for failure and more credit for success.

Kathleen Dugan (1989) reports a similar leniency shift, but only when the original attribution for poor performance was to lack of effort. Under such conditions more problem solving occurred, there was more attributional change, agreement was more common, and salary raises were more frequently granted. When lack of ability was at the core of attributions, leniency effects and attributional change were not in evidence. Thus the expected consequences of subordinate ac-counts were found only when effort was the attributional focus.

A more recent series of studies looked into the extent to which newness on the job might serve as an excuse for poor performance (Greenberg, 1996). Using newness and lack of experience for impression management purposes did serve to evoke more positive evaluations as long as the observer was unaffected by the poor performance. However, if the observer bears some cost as a result of the poor performance, the use of newness for impression management purposes tends to backfire and actually reduces performance evaluations, as well as shifting attributions in an internal direction.

Thus it appears that accounts and related phenomena can well change attributions and raise evaluations through a leniency effect, but there are conditions under which these hypothesized consequences do not occur. The variable impact of accounts at link no. 2 would seem to be a factor in the relatively low correlations between attributions and leader response (see table 23.2). Brian Klaas and Hoyt Wheeler (1990) also report substantial variations in the policies that are employed by managers in selecting corrective actions. All in all, there appears to be somewhat more variability in the approaches taken to ineffective performance than attribution theory would anticipate.

Concerns about Attributional Approaches

As we have seen, the attribution theory advanced by Mitchell and his colleagues has considerable research support, although there are certain departures from theoretical expectations. Biases of the kind hypothesized are inherent in perceptual processes, and the major propositions of the theory have been confirmed to a large extent. These conclusions are now generally recognized (see Chemers, 1997; Yukl, 1998). Yet certain concerns, and even disagreements, with the theory have been noted.

One such concern relates to the degree of convergence between leader and subordinate attributions. In general, it is assumed that the most likely occurrence in the face of subordinate poor performance is that the leader attribution will be internal, and somewhat biased in that regard, while the subordinate's self-attribution will be external and self-serving. The resulting disagreement can mean undesirable conflict with negative consequences for all involved.

However, another possible consequence is that the supervisor's influence serves to bring about convergence, not conflict, with the internal attribution being adopted by both. This can happen because of the authority role the supervisor holds; it can mean reduced self-efficacy for the subordinate and worse, if the assessment is essentially inaccurate (Sankowsky, 1989), which it may well be due to operative biases. Should inaccuracy be present in the now joint attribution, corrective actions are unlikely to work, and the problem will escalate. This line of reasoning argues for accurate assessments, removal of biases, and actions fitted to real causes, whether attributions converge or not.

Another concern of a similar nature is that Mitchell's presentation of attribution theory in the leader-member dyad places too much emphasis on leader attributions at the expense of a full elaboration of member attributions (Martinko & Gardner, 1987). In this approach an expanded theory of attribution processes in the dyad is proposed replete with its own models and propositions. Unfortunately, although these ideas have merit, they have not elicited much research attention. In this respect they are similar to the theoretical extension dealing with group poor performance that was proposed by Brown (1984). Neither attempt to expand the domain of the theory has yielded the research response that appears warranted.

These concerns call for theoretical modifications and extensions, but they do not attack the basic formulations of attribution theory. In contrast, Robert Lord (1995) and Lord and Jonathan Smith (1983) express what amount to core disagreements with the theory as developed by Mitchell and colleagues. In this view the highly rational, perceiver-as-scientist view of the attribution process should be reconsidered. The more likely process is one that is automatic, implicit, and so rapid that reasoning has not yet had time to occur. This perceiver-as-primitive-processor view is very different from that proposed by Mitchell. Explicit, rational problem solving may well occur only after implicit information processing, with its high potential for error, has already occurred. These implicit types of attributions are based on primitive categorizations, are prelinguistic, and are affect laden. As we will see in the next chapter, they have been found to operate widely in the leadership domain, although those who use them often are not aware of what is happening. For this reason, training is unlikely to influence these implicit processes.

Steven Cronshaw and Lord (1987) present evidence in support of this alternative view of what happens at the point of attribution. However, a study by Richard Gooding and Angelo Kinicki (1995), using practicing managers, indicates that implicit categorizations are most likely to be mobilized when events have positive outcomes. The more explicit, reasoned problem-solving approach envisioned by Mitchell is characteristic in the case of events with negative outcomes, such as poor performance. Implicit theories were not found to operate in the latter instance. Thus, insofar as the Mitchell theory remains one of attributions under conditions of ineffective performance, the evidence available to date seems to support it and to reject Lord's alternative interpretation. An expanded theory, however, which dealt in detail with effective performance, would have to give serious attention to implicit categorization processes.

Although the basic theory speaks to the matter of multiple causes in the sense that greater uncertainty is anticipated, most of the theory, and the research, assumes a single incident of poor performance and a single cause. Yet, as Green and his colleagues have shown, in actual practice poor performance is typically an ongoing affair. Furthermore, the causation of ineffective performance tends to be overdetermined with a number of different types of factors impinging at the same time. Evidence from clinical practice indicates that this number can range from one to eight with an average of four (Miner, 1991). Rarely is it a matter of just effort, or ability, or task difficulty. The point is that attribution theory focuses on a small microcosm of the underlying reality, which is much more complex. This is cause for concern as well.

As Mitchell (1982) has indicated, attributions are only part of a much larger process. They are bypassed by personal and organizational policies, do not account for any substantial amount of variance in outcomes, and deal with only a limited aspect of the diagnosis and correction of ineffective performance. Yet because it serves to identify sources of bias and error, attribution theory remains important. Furthermore, from our knowledge of the nature of the process, it is apparent that training can operate to intervene to change what happens at links no. 1 and no. 2. Probably managerial role motivation training, as discussed in chapter 5, serves to reduce bias in this manner. However, although motivation-increasing effects have been demonstrated for this training, bias-reducing effects have not been considered specifically.

Mitchell's group has looked into other types of training, but without definitive conclusions. The need for further research on how training may be used to rid the diagnosis and correction of ineffective performance of attributional biases is apparent. Without such research, extensive application of the theory is unwarranted and seems unlikely.

CONCLUSIONS

If comparisons are made between the first-generation period in the motivation area and the second, it is apparent that new theories are relatively few in number in the more recent period. New need theories are virtually nonexistent, and other types of truly innovative theorizing on motivational topics are limited in number (Pinder, 1998). In part, this situation may be occasioned by the staying power of the first-generation theories such as goal setting and organizational behavior modification, which have been transformed but certainly not abandoned. There is a clear need for renewed attention to the development of new theories that deal with motivational topics.

Nevertheless, perception and cognitive process theories have seen major advances. The cognitive revolution (Ilgen, Major, & Tower, 1994) has expanded out of psychology and joined forces with the problem areas and functioning of complex organizations to the distinct advantage of the field of organizational behavior. Whole new areas of knowledge and investigation have opened up. We have seen something of this phenomenon in the present chapter with the theories discussed here, and we will consider more such cognitive theorizing in the chapter that follows. It is apparent that the issues raised in organizational behavior as the field seeks to understand the operation of organizations provide fruitful ground for cognitive types of explanations.

References

Ambrose, Maureen L., & Kulik, Carol T. (1999). Old Friends, New Faces: Motivation Research in the 1990s. *Journal of Management*, 25, 231–292.

Ashkanasy, Neal M. (1995). Supervisory Attributions and Evaluative Judgments of Subordinate Performance: A Further Test of the Green and Mitchell Model. In Mark J. Martinko (Ed.), *Attribution Theory: An Organizational Perspective* (pp. 211–228). Delray Beach, Fl: St. Lucie Press.

Ashkanasy, Neal M., & Gallois, Cynthia (1994). Leader Attributions and Evaluations: Effects of Locus of Control, Supervisory Control, and Task Control. *Organizational Behavior and Human Decision Processes*, 59, 27–50.

Brown, Karen A. (1984). Explaining Group Poor Performance: An Attributional Analysis. *Academy of Management Review*, 9, 54–63.

Brown, Karen A., & Mitchell, Terence R. (1986). Influence of Task Interdependence and Number of Poor Performers on Diagnoses of Causes of Poor Performance. *Academy of Management Journal*, 29, 412–424.

Calder, Bobby J. (1977). An Attributional Theory of Leadership. In Barry M. Staw & Gerald R. Salancik (Eds.), *New Direction in Organizational Behavior* (pp. 179–204). Chicago: St. Clair Press.

Chemers, Martin M. (1997). *An Integrative Theory of Leadership*. Mahwah, NJ: Lawrence Erlbaum Associates.

Cronshaw, Steven F., & Lord, Robert G. (1987). Effects of Categorization, Attribution, and Encoding Processes on Leadership Perceptions. *Journal of Applied Psychology*, 72, 97–106.

Cummings, Larry L. (1981). Review of *A Theory of Behavior in Organizations. Contemporary Psychology*, 26, 661–663.

Dobbins, Gregory H. (1985). Effects of Gender on Leader's Responses to Poor Performers: An Attributional Interpretation. *Academy of Management Journal*, 28, 587–598.

Dobbins, Gregory H., & Russell, Jeanne M. (1986). The Biasing Effects of Subordinate Likeableness on Leaders' Responses to Poor Performers: A Laboratory and Field Study. *Personnel Psychology*, 39, 759–777.

Dougherty, Thomas W., & Pritchard, Robert D. (1985). The Measurement of Role Variables: Exploratory Examination of a New Approach. *Organizational Behavior and Human Decision Processes*, 35, 141–155.

Dugan, Kathleen W. (1989). Ability and Effort Attributions: Do They Affect How Managers Communicate Performance Feedback Information? *Academy of Management Journal*, 32, 87–114.

Ferrier, Walter J.; Smith, Ken G.; Rediker, Kenneth J.; & Mitchell, Terence R. (1995). Distributive Justice Norms and Attributions for Performance Outcomes as a Function of Power. In Mark J. Martinko (Ed.), *Attribution Theory: An Organizational Perspective* (pp. 315–330). Delray Beach, FL: St. Lucie Press.

Gavin, Mark B.; Green, Stephen G.; & Fairhurst, Gail T. (1995). Managerial Control Strategies for Poor Performance over Time and the Impact on Subordinate Reactions. *Organizational Behavior and Human Decision Processes*, 63, 207–221.

Gioia, Dennis A., & Sims, Henry P. (1986). Cognition-Behavior Connections: Attribution and Verbal Behavior in Leader-Subordinate Interactions. *Organizational Behavior and Human Decision Processes*, 37, 197–229.

Gooding, Richard Z., & Kinicki, Angelo J. (1995). Interpreting Event Causes: The Complementary Role of Categorization and Attribution Processes. *Journal of Management Studies*, 32, 1–22.

Green, Stephen G.; Fairhurst,, Gail T.; & Snavely, B. Kay (1986). Chains of Poor Performance and Supervisory Control. *Organizational Behavior and Human Decision Processes*, 38, 7–27.

Green, Stephen G., & Liden, Robert C. (1980). Contextual and Attributional Influences on Control Decisions. *Journal of Applied Psychology*, 65, 453–458.

Green, Stephen G., & Mitchell, Terence R. (1979). Attributional Processes of Leaders in Leader-Member Interactions. *Organizational Behavior and Human Performance*, 23, 429–458.

Greenberg, Jerald (1996). "Forgive Me I'm New": Three Experimental Demonstrations of the Effects of Attempts to Excuse Poor Performance. *Organizational Behavior and Human Decision Proesses*, 66, 165–178.

Greenhaus, Jeffrey H., & Parasuraman, Saroj (1993). Job Performance Attributions and Career Advancement Prospects: An Examination of Gender and Race Effects. *Organizational Behavior and Human Decision Processes*, 55, 273–297.

Harvey, John H., & Weary, Gifford (1984). Current Issues in Attribution Theory and Research. *Annual Review of Psychology*, 35, 427–459.

Heerwagen, Judith H.; Beach, Lee R.; & Mitchell, Terence R. (1985). Dealing with Poor Performance: Supervisor Attributions and the Cost of Responding. *Journal of Applied Social Psychology*, 15, 638–655.

Heider, Fritz (1958). *The Psychology of Interpersonal Relations*. New York: Wiley.

Heneman, Robert L.; Greenberger, David B.; & Anonyuo, Chigozie (1989). Attributions and Exchanges: The Effects of Interpersonal Factors on the Diagnosis of Employee Performance. *Academy of Management Journal*, 32, 466–476.

Ilgen, Daniel R.; Major, Debra A.; & Tower, Spencer L. (1994). The Cognitive Revolution in Organizational Behavior. In Jerald Greenberg (Ed.), *Organizational Behavior: The State of the Science* (pp. 1–22). Hillsdale, NJ: Lawrence Erlbaum Associates.

Ilgen, Daniel R.; Mitchell, Terence R.; & Fredrickson, James W. (1981). Poor Performers: Supervisors' and Subordinates' Responses. *Organizational Behavior and Human Performance*, 27, 386–410.

Jones, Edward E., & Davis, Keith E. (1965). From Acts to Dispositions: The Attribution Process in Person Perception. In Leonard Berkowitz (Ed.), *Advances in Experimental Social Psychology* (Vol. 2, pp. 219–266). New York: Academic Press.

Jones, Edward E., & Nisbett, Richard E. (1971). The Actor and the Observer: Divergent Perceptions of the Causes of Behavior. In Edward E. Jones, D. E. Kanouse, Harold H. Kelley, Richard E. Nisbett, S. Valins, & Bernard Weiner (Eds.), *Attribution: Perceiving the Causes of Behavior* (pp. 79–94). New York: General Learning Press.

Jones, Edward E., & Wortman, Camille B. (1973). *Ingratiation: An Attributional Approach*. Morristown, NJ: General Learning Press.

Judge, Timothy A., & Martocchio, Joseph J. (1995). The Role of Fairness Orientation and Supervisor Attributions in Absence Disciplinary Decisions. *Journal of Business and Psychology*, 10, 115–137.

Kanfer, Ruth (1990). Motivation Theory and Industrial and Organizational Psychology. In Marvin D. Dunnette & Leaetta M. Hough (Eds.), *Handbook of Industrial and Organizational Psychology* (Vol. 1, pp. 75–170). Palo Alto, CA: Consulting Psychologists Press.

Kanfer, Ruth (1992). Work Motivation: New Directions in Theory and Research. *International Review of Industrial and Organizational Psychology*, 7, 1–53.

Kelley, Harold H. (1967). Attribution Theory in Social Psychology. *Nebraska Symposium on Motivation*, 15, 192–238.

Kelley, Harold H. (1973). The Processes of Causal Attribution. *American Psychologist*, 28, 107–128.

Kipnis, David (1987). Psychology and Behavior Technology. *American Psychologist*, 42, 30–36.

Klaas, Brian S., & Wheeler, Hoyt N. (1990). Managerial Decision Making about Employee Discipline: A Policy-Capturing Approach. *Personnel Psychology*, 43, 117–134.

Knowlton, William A., & Mitchell, Terence R. (1980). Effects of Causal Attributions on a Supervisor's Evaluation of Subordinate Performance. *Journal of Applied Psychology*, 65, 459–466.

Larson, James P., & Callahan, Christine (1990). Performance Monitoring: How It Affects Work Productivity. *Journal of Applied Psychology*, 75, 530–538.

Liden, Robert C., & Mitchell, Terence R. (1985). Reactions to Feedback: The Role of Attributions. *Academy of Management Journal*, 28, 291–308.

Liden, Robert C., & Mitchell, Terence R. (1988). Ingratiatory Behaviors in Organizational Settings. *Academy of Management Review*, 13, 572–587.

Liden, Robert C.; Mitchell, Terence R.; & Maslyn, John M. (1998). An Exploratory Investigation of Policy Use in the Management of Poor Performers. *Journal of Business and Psychology*, 13, 245–262.

Liden, Robert C.; Wayne, Sandy J.; Judge, Timothy A.; Sparrowe, Raymond T.; Kraimer, Maria L.; & Franz, Timothy M. (1999). Management of Poor Performance: A Comparison of Manager, Group Member, and Group Disciplinary Decisions. *Journal of Applied Psychology*, 84, 835–850.

Locke, Edwin A., & Latham, Gary P. (1990). *A Theory of Goal Setting and Task Performance*. Englewood Cliffs, NJ: Prentice Hall.

Lord, Robert G. (1995). An Alternative Perspective on Attributional Processes. In Mark J. Martinko (Ed.), *Attribution Theory: An Organizational Perspective* (pp. 333–350). Delray Beach, FL: St. Lucie Press.

Lord, Robert G., & Smith, Jonathan E. (1983). Theoretical, Information Processing, and Situational Factors Affecting Attribution Theory Models of Organizational Behavior. *Academy of Management Review*, 8, 50–60.

Martinko, Mark J. (1995). *Attribution Theory: An Organizational Perspective*. Delray Beach, FL: St. Lucie Press.

Martinko, Mark J., & Gardner, William L. (1987). The Leader/Member Attribution Process. *Academy of Management Review*, 12, 235–249.

Miner, John B. (1963). *The Management of Ineffective Performance*. New York: McGraw-Hill.

Miner, John B. (1991). Psychological Assessment in a Developmental Context. In Curtiss P. Hansen & Kelley A. Conrad (Eds.), *A Handbook of Psychological Assessment in Business* (pp. 225–236). New York: Quorum Books.

Miner, John B., & Brewer, J. Frank (1976). The Management of Ineffective Performance. In Marvin D. Dunnette (Ed.), *Handbook of Industrial and Organizational Psychology* (pp. 995–1030). Chicago: Rand, McNally.

Mitchell, Terence R. (1979). Organizational Behavior. *Annual Review of Psychology*, 30, 243–281.

Mitchell, Terence R. (1982). Attributions and Actions: A Note of Caution. *Journal of Management*, 8, 65–74.

Mitchell, Terence R. (1983). The Effects of Social, Task, and Situational Factors on Motivation, Performance, and Appraisal. In Frank Landy, Sheldon Zedeck, & Jeanette Cleveland (Eds.), *Performance Measurement and Theory* (pp. 39–59). Hillsdale, NJ: Lawrence Erlbaum Associates.

Mitchell, Terence R.; Green, Stephen G.; & Wood, Robert E. (1981). An Attributional Model of Leadership and the Poor Performing Subordinate: Devel-

opment and Validation. *Research in Organizational Behavior*, 3, 197–234.

Mitchell, Terence R., & Kalb, Laura S. (1982). Effects of Job Experience on Supervisor Attributions for a Subordinate's Poor Performance. *Journal of Applied Psychology*, 67, 181–188.

Mitchell, Terence R.; Larson, J.; & Green, Stephen G. (1977). Leader Behavior, Situational Moderators, and Group Performance: An Attributional Analysis. *Organizational Behavior and Human Performance*, 18, 254–268.

Mitchell, Terence R., & O'Reilly, Charles (1983). Managing Poor Performance and Productivity in Organization. *Research in Personnel and Human Resources Management*, 1, 201–234.

Mitchell, Terence R.; Smyser, Charles M.; & Weed, Stan E. (1975). Locus of Control: Supervision and Work Satisfaction. *Academy of Management Journal*, 18, 623–631.

Mitchell, Terence R., & Wood, Robert E. (1980). Supervisor's Responses to Subordinate Poor Performance: A Test of an Attributional Model. *Organizational Behavior and Human Performance*, 25, 123–138.

Naylor, James C., & Ilgen, Daniel R. (1984). Goal Setting: A Theoretical Analysis of a Motivational Technology. *Research in Organizational Behavior*, 6, 95–140.

Naylor, James C.; Pritchard, Robert D.; & Ilgen, Daniel R. (1980). *A Theory of Behavior in Organizations*. New York: Academic Press.

Pence, Earl C.; Pendleton, William C.; Dobbins, Greg H.; & Sgro, Joseph A. (1982). *Organizational Behavior and Human Performance*, 29, 227–240.

Pinder, Craig C. (1998). *Work Motivation in Organizational Behavior*. Upper Saddle River, NJ: Prentice Hall.

Pritchard, Robert D. (1990). Enhancing Work Motivation through Productivity Measurement and Feedback. In Uwe Kleinbeck, Hans-Henning Quast, Henk Thierry, & Hartmut Häcker (Eds.), *Work Motivation* (pp. 119–132). Hillsdale, NJ: Lawrence Erlbaum Associates.

Pritchard, Robert D.; Jones, Steven D.; Roth, Philip L.; Stuebing, Karla K.; & Ekeberg, Steven E. (1988). Effects of Group Feedback, Goal Setting, and Incentives on Organizational Productivity. *Journal of Applied Psychology Monograph*, 73, 337–358.

Rotter, Julian B. (1966). Generalized Expectancies for Internal versus External Control of Reinforcement. *Psychological Monograph*, 80, Whole No. 609.

Sankowsky, Daniel (1989). A Psychoanalytic Attributional Model for Subordinate Poor Performance. *Human Resource Management*, 28, 125–139.

Sawyer, John E. (1990). Effects of Risk and Ambiguity on Judgments of Contingency Relations and Behavioral Resource Allocation Decisions. *Organizational Behavior and Human Decision Processes*, 45, 85–110.

Sawyer, John E.; Latham, William R.; Pritchard, Robert D.; & Bennett, Winston R. (1999). Analysis of Work Group Productivity in an Applied Setting: Application of a Time Series Panel Design. *Personnel Psychology*, 52, 927–967.

Silver, William S.; Mitchell, Terence R.; & Gist, Marilyn E. (1995). Responses to Successful and Unsuccessful Performance: The Moderating Effect of Self-Efficacy on the Relationship between Performance and Attributions. *Organizational Behavior and Human Decision Processes*, 62, 286–299.

Smither, James W.; Skov, Richard B.; & Adler, Seymour (1986). Attributions for the Poorly Performing Blackjack Dealer: In the Cards or Inability? *Personnel Psychology*, 39, 123–139.

Sniezek, Janet A.; May, Douglas R.; & Sawyer, John E. (1990). Social Uncertainty and Interdependence: A Study of Resource Allocation Decisions in Groups. *Organizational Behavior and Human Decision Processes*, 46, 155–180.

Staw, Barry M. (1984). Organizational Behavior: A Review and Reformulation of the Field's Outcome Variables. *Annual Review of Psychology*, 35, 627–666.

Steinmetz, Lawrence L. (1969). *Managing the Marginal and Unsatisfactory Employee*. Reading, MA: Addison-Wesley.

Switzer, Fred S., & Sniezek, Janet A. (1991). Judgment Processes in Motivation: Anchoring and Adjustment Effects on Judgment and Behavior. *Organizational Behavior and Human Decision Processes*, 49, 208–229.

Tjosvold, Dean (1985). The Effects of Arbitration and Social Context on Superior's Influence and Interaction with Low Performing Subordinates. *Personnel Psychology*, 38, 361–376.

Weber, Elke U. (1998). From Performance to Decision Processes in 33 Years: A History of *Organizational Behavior and Human Decision Processes* under James C. Naylor. *Organizational Behavior and Human Decision Processes*, 76, 209–222.

Weiner, Bernard (1972). *Theories of Motivation: From Mechanism to Cognition*. Chicago: Markham.

Weiner, Bernard (1974). *Achievement Motivation and Attribution Theory*. Morristown, NJ: General Learning Press.

Weiner, Bernard, & Sierad, Jack (1975). Misattribution for Failure and Enhancement of Achievement Strivings. *Journal of Personality and Social Psychology*, 31, 415–421.

Wood, Robert E., & Mitchell, Terence R. (1981). Manager Behavior in a Social Context: The Impact of Impression Management on Attributions and Disciplinary Actions. *Organizational Behavior and Human Performance*, 28, 356–378.

Yukl, Gary (1998). *Leadership in Organizations*. Upper Saddle River, NJ: Prentice Hall.

Part VIII

Second-Generation Theories: Leadership

Chapter 24

Implicit Leadership Theories and Substitutes for Leadership

This chapter takes the matter of cognitive theorizing in organizational behavior one step further, and it places the subject squarely in the middle of the leadership domain. First, we consider the views of Robert Lord and his colleagues, some of which we have met in the preceding chapters. These views deal with the implicit theories held by others as they perceive leaders; this factor was also treated in connection with the discussion of consideration and initiating structure in chapter 10. They also relate to the attribution process as considered in chapter 23, and the cognitive mechanisms involved in that process. This line of theoretical development has its origins in psychology and in the thinking that has emerged from the study of computers as problem solvers.

The information processing approaches set forth by Lord and others tend to stand in opposition to the emphasis on leader behavior and leadership style that characterized many first-generation theories. Another theoretical thrust, which also disputes the pervasive significance of leadership style, is the theory of substitutes for leadership. This approach, which is the product of Steven Kerr, was influenced by the proposition from path-goal theory (see chapter 10 in this volume) that leader behaviors can be unnecessary and redundant under certain circumstances. It also was influenced by certain formulations developed by Joan Woodward (1970) and John Miner (1975) about the nature of control processes in organizations (Kerr,

1977; Kerr & Jermier, 1978). Thus substitutes for leadership theory, while also at variance with previous leadership approaches, departs from the cognitive views in that it is more fully rooted in prior thinking within the field of organizational behavior.

INFORMATION PROCESSING AND LEADERSHIP

Lord's views were developed over a period of roughly 15 years, during which he and his colleagues conducted a number of studies that culminated in several theoretical articles and later still in a book (Lord & Maher, 1991b). The version of the theory presented in this book is given primary attention here simply because it is more comprehensive than are the articles. However, the path followed in getting to *Leadership and Information Processing: Linking Perceptions and Performance* is outlined in order to provide insight into the sources of this more comprehensive presentation of the theory.

Background

Born in 1946, Lord received a Ph.D. in industrial/organizational psychology from Carnegie-Mellon University in 1975; his B.A. is in economics from the University of Michigan. At Carnegie he was strongly influenced by the thinking of Allen Newell and Herbert Simon (1972). Remember that Simon had fully migrated to the psychology department by 1970 (see chapter 22). At essentially the time of obtaining his doctorate, Lord accepted a faculty appointment in psychology at the University of Akron, where he has remained since.

In conducting his research and developing his publications, Lord has frequently been joined by various individuals who began as doctoral students in psychology at Akron. After these individuals moved on to their first professional positions at other universities, these collaborations continued in a number of instances. Karen Maher, Lord's co-author in writing up the comprehensive theory, and in several other scholarly endeavors as well, was one such individual. She took a position in the business school at the University of Missouri/St. Louis after completing her doctorate at Akron.

Developments before the 1990s

The initial impetus to Lord's research and theorizing on information processing and leadership came from laboratory investigations conducted at Carnegie in connection with his dissertation. This work dealt with relationships among task structure, leader behavior, and group performance; it extended to the matter of perceptions of leader behavior and the role of stereotypes in this process (Lord, 1976, 1977).

This work was followed by a series of studies that were intended to explain much of the variance in leader behavior questionnaires, with particular reference to consideration and initiating structure, in terms of implicit theories and biases of followers. The focus was on demonstrating that leader behavior as such could not explain the results obtained and that other factors of a primarily perceptual and cognitive nature within those providing the descriptions and ratings were heavily involved (Rush, Thomas, & Lord, 1977; Lord, Binning, Rush, & Thomas, 1978; Binning & Lord, 1980; Lord, Phillips, & Rush, 1980; Rush, Phillips, & Lord, 1981). A similar approach was applied to attribution theory findings, with the objective of demonstrating that causal attribution processes often stem from cognitive categorizations on the part of a perceiver. Some of this literature was discussed in chapter 23, but there were earlier studies as well (Phillips & Lord, 1981, 1982).

The studies noted to this point were all carried out with students in laboratory settings. A program of research involving perceptions of political leaders deviated somewhat from this model but still faced similar limitations (Foti, Fraser, & Lord, 1982). All of this research involved the testing of prestated hypotheses and in this sense involved theory, but the theory was not extensively developed and lacked integration. Beginning in 1982, however, Lord began to concentrate on the theoretical underpinnings of his research and to publish more extensively along theoretical lines (Lord, Foti, & Phillips, 1982). Research now became more theoretically based (Lord, Foti, & DeVader, 1984). This move from a primary concern with research controls and methodology to an emphasis on developing good theory continued up to and through the publication of the Lord and Maher (1991b) book. Examples include Lord (1985), Lord and Mary Kernan (1987), and David Day and Lord (1988).

Figure 24.1 provides a theoretical model developed in this period to indicate the steps involved in social perception. The following quote indicates what is involved:

> These steps were chosen because they represent the major points at which information is filtered or changed by social information processing. Information input involves a *selective attention/comprehension* step in which relevant information is selected from a complex social environment, in part through the process by which it is comprehended or recognized; a step in which noticed information is *encoded and simplified* into a form more easily stored in long-term memory; and a *storage and retention* step during which information is frequently altered through integration with subsequent information concerning the stimulus person. Information output involves two conceptually distinct but highly related steps: the *retrieval* of relevant information and the translation of information into required *judgments* such as causal attributions or

the selection of the appropriate response for each item on a questionnaire. (Lord, 1985, p. 89)

Figure 24.1 depicts these steps and shows that information processing is

highly dependent on heuristic or automatic processes associated with cognitive schema . . . which reduce information processing demand while still yielding reasonable, albeit suboptimal, social judgments. That is, perceivers simplify perceptions of complex social stimuli by classifying them into already existing, contextually meaningful categories such as leader/nonleader (A^*). Once these are classified, subsequent information processing can rely primarily on these well-learned schema (category prototypes) (A_1 to A_5) rather than on the observed stimulus characteristics (SA_1 to SA_3). Though cognitively economical, reliance on prototypes as an information processing aid can result in systematic distortions of stimulus descriptions (e.g., RA_4 and RA_5) or social judgments. In addi-

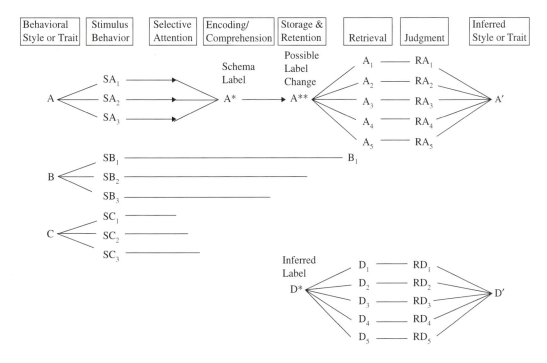

FIGURE 24.1 Model of information processing directed by cognitive schema. From Robert G. Lord (1985), An Information Processing Approach to Social Perceptions, Leadership and Behavioral Measurement in Organizations, *Research in Organizational Behavior*, 7, 90. Copyright 1985. Reprinted with permission from Elsevier Science.

tion, reliance on such automatic processes will reduce the relationship of "behavioral ratings" to the behaviors psychologists want to measure. Particularly troublesome is the possibility that "sensible" ratings (RD_1 and RD_5) can be produced for behaviors that were never seen. . . . Thus, clusters of "behavioral" items with high covariances may reflect rater effects rather than traits of the stimulus person being rated. (Lord, 1985, pp. 89–91)

Although there was a substantial development of theory during the 1980s, the intermixture of theory and research continued in this period (see, for example, Foti & Lord, 1987). This is not a theory that lacks for either research tests or inductive stimulation from empirical sources.

Linking Perceptions and Performance

From the preceding discussion it would seem that the theory developed deals only with perceptual processes and thus is more closely allied to the consideration of attribution processes in chapter 23 than to the leadership focus of part VIII. Certainly, perceptions of followers are given considerable attention. However, the theory also deals with how these perceptions influence the outcomes of the leadership process and more directly with leadership as a determinant of performance. The theory presented in Lord and Maher (1991b) is both one of leadership perception and of executive performance. Yet the authors define leadership as the process of being perceived by others as a leader. It involves "behaviors, traits, characteristics, and outcomes produced by leaders as these elements are interpreted by followers" (p. 11).

Human Information Processing

The theory uses the term *knowledge structure* to refer to cognitive schemas that also may be called scripts, plans, categories, implicit theories, prototypes, or heuristics. There is considerable variation in usage among these terms. Categorization processes serve to group nonidentical stimuli into sets that are treated as equivalent, even though they are not.

Four models of information processing are distinguished. The first is *rational* and is illustrated by the "naïve scientists" of attribution theory. It assumes an optimizing process as in the 1980 theory of James Naylor, Robert Pritchard, and Daniel Ilgen (see chap-

ter 23) that is often not possible. The second is of *limited capacity* and includes satisficing. The third is *expert* and, although limited capacity in nature, it relies on well-organized or highly developed knowledge structures as applied to a specific content domain (see chapter 22). The fourth is *cybernetic* and relies heavily on feedback from a task or social environment. Humans are flexible in their information processing and tend to move back and forth across these models, although the limited capacity form is the most frequent; leadership categorization theory is of this type. These four models are described elsewhere as well (Lord & Maher, 1990), and the distinctions involved are set forth in table 24.1.

Recognition-Based and Inferential Processes

Perceivers of leadership may use automatic processes, which operate outside awareness and are devoid of intent, without interfering with other cognitive tasks, and with minimal effort. In contrast are controlled processes, which have antithetical features—awareness, intent, interference, and effort. At the same time, leadership may be *recognized* from qualities and behaviors that are evidenced in the course of normal interactions, or it can be *inferred* from the outcomes of relevant events. Using these ideas, a two-by-two classification may be developed to describe alternative processes involved in leadership perceptions:

Automatic, recognition-based—prototype matching with face-to-face contact

Automatic, inferential—perceptually guided, involving simplified causal analyses

Controlled, recognition-based—prototype matching using socially communicated information

Controlled, inferential—logically based and comprehensive causal analyses

Category prototypes develop from experience and represent attributes that become associated with each other to form an abstract image in long-term memory; they are expected to vary across contexts. Because substantial experience is required to build prototypes, recognition-based perceptions involve expert information processing. Much recognition-based perception of leaders is automatic, but the same categories, along with prototype matching, can be used where the stim-

TABLE 24.1 Comparison and evaluation of information processing models

Features	Rational	Limited capacity	Expert	Cybernetic
Information requirements	Knowledge of expectancies and utilities for many alternatives	Knowledge of expectancies and utilities for a few salient alternatives	Highly selective use of schema-relevant information	Selective use of current information, along with recall and evaluation of past actions
Choice process	Optimization by maximizing expected utility; evaluating of all alternatives	Simplified by heuristic evaluation procedures; termination when satisfactory alternative is found	Very good alternative recognized by automatic match with information in long-term memory	Feedback-guided use of recognition or heuristic processes
Perceptual requirements	Accurate perception of environment based on surface features	Accurate perception of limited environment based on surface features	Accurate perception of limited environment based on meaning	Perception of limited environment and ability to shift perspectives over time
Short-term memory requirements	Extensive capacity	Moderate capacity	Low capacity	Very low capacity
Long-term memory requirements	Extensive information accessed and transferred to short-term memory	Moderate amount of information accessed and transferred to short-term memory	Extensive, highly organized, and accessible long-term memory; minimal information transferred to short-term memory	Varies depending on task familiarity: new task—same as limited capacity; familiar task—same as expert
Type of process emphasized	Controlled, serial, analytic	Controlled or automatic use of heuristics; serial	Automatic parallel	Learning; controlled or automatic; serial
Timing of processing	Prior to choice or behavior	Prior to choice or behavior	Prior or concurrent with choice or behavior	Intermixed with choice or behavior
Descriptive accuracy	Weak	Strong	Moderate	Strong
Prescriptive value	Strong	Weak	Strong	Strong

SOURCE: Adapted from Robert G. Lord & Karen J. Maher (1990), Alternative Information-Processing Models and Their Implications for Theory, Research, and Practice, *Academy of Management Review*, 15, 12, 17

ulus is socially communicated information, not face-to-face contact.

Inferential processes have an attributional aspect in that leadership is inferred from causal analyses that are related to successful task organizational performance in the past. While leadership at lower levels tends to be automatic and recognition-based, executive leadership may involve any of the other three processes (including both automatic and controlled inferential). Automatic inferential processing occurs when leadership is assumed because the person is salient for, or close to, favorable events. Controlled inferential processes reflect a more careful analysis of potential causal agents. Under conditions of information overload the automatic version tends to prevail.

Information Processing and Change

Person-based processing into memory results in classifying people as to traits and related behaviors. *Event-based processing* yields analogous schema called scripts, which are goal-based and help make sense of perceived events or generate actions to attain goals. Both person- and event-based processing may be updated and changed through cybernetic feedback, but there are differences between what happens when controlled processes and automatic processes are involved: change via controlled processing tends to be gradual and incremental, whereas automatic processing produces discontinuous change, as there may well be a shift to an entirely different category.

Changes of the latter type can be quite dramatic. Linear relationship models are not adequate to the task involved, and Lord and Maher (1991b) invoke graphs based on catastrophe theory to depict what occurs. Essentially, with automatic processing, an initial categorization serves as a source of cognitive inertia that must be overcome before a shift occurs. This resistance to change produces bias, but "exactly what processes produce the sudden shift to another category requires further research" (p. 84). A three-dimensional catastrophe theory graph with continuous change on the back surface and discontinuous change on the front is shown in figure 24.2. This graph combines the change mechanisms of both controlled and automatic processing. The former is considered to be by far the more accurate (free of distortion). Although catastrophe theory allows for mathematical statements of theory, only the graphical presentations are used by Lord and Maher (1991b) in their leadership theory.

This approach to the subject of changing cognitive structures is applied to perceptions of women in man-

agement in a separate chapter with an added coauthor (Baumgardner, Lord, & Maher, 1991). The essential idea is that female managers tend to be categorized as women, not as leaders, with a resulting bias that is a consequence of the limitations of information processing, not intentional discrimination. Included here is the resistance to recategorization from woman to leader when automatic processing is involved, even as increased leader performance information is received.

Sex-related stereotypes are hypothesized to operate differently at different hierarchic levels. Within lower management, gender-related categories are particularly easily accessed; because performance history is lacking, inferential processes tend to be weak. This is less true in middle management, and leadership categories are more readily accessed, so that women in these positions are more able to establish leadership perceptions. However, at the upper executive levels, a scarcity of women and the frequent resort to limited-capacity processes by external constituents can reverse this favorable trend.

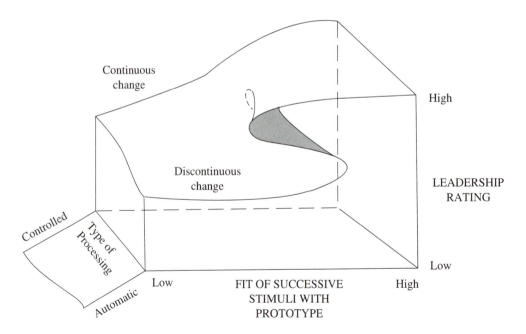

FIGURE 24.2 Catastrophe model of changing social perceptions. From Robert G. Lord & Karen J. Maher (1991), *Leadership and Information Processing: Linking Perceptions and Performance* (Boston: Unwin Hyman), 87. Copyright 1991. Reprinted by permission from Routledge.

Culture, Information Processing, and Leadership

The theory's handling of culture draws heavily on Edgar Schein's formulations (see chapter 21 in this volume). Culture perpetuation and change are a function of (1) values and beliefs, (2) schemas related to problem solving and behavior or to social perceptions and interactions (both equivalent to Schein's assumptions), and (3) a factor not considered by Schein—the type of information processing (rational, limited-capacity, expert, cybernetic). Although different facets of culture may be generated by different types of information processing, the limited-capacity type is the most frequent guiding process. Culture change is difficult simply because the rational processes that guide values do not operate often to generate cultural schemas.

Leaders can influence culture as Schein indicates, even if not easily. Change is most likely during periods of crisis, when leadership is defined so as to expand discretion (a type of perceptual credit-granting), and when the culture is weak. Cultures, especially strong cultures, constrain what leaders can do and thus the changes that are possible. The process of culture change may involve changing values, as many have proposed, but more frequently schemas must be changed (consistent with Schein), as when new leadership is installed or subcultures come to achieve dominance. One method of changing schemas is to shift from the limited-capacity or expert processing of an existing culture to cybernetic or rational modes, and then back to new schemas with automatic processing. In any event, changes in type of information processing are essential, along with schema changes, if substantially revised behavior is to be achieved.

Leadership Effects on Performance

To this point the theory has been concerned with the perception of leadership by others. However, there are also effects that leadership exerts on performance. Here the theory moves beyond the realm of perception. A distinction is made between direct and indirect means by which performance may be affected. In the *direct* case, influence is exerted on subordinates, decisions, or policies. At lower levels, this means that leader behavior shifts subordinate skills or motivation, thus affecting performance. At executive levels, changes are made in aspects of the organization—technology, size of workforce—that are closely related to organizational performance.

Indirect means, by contrast, involve influencing conditions that, in turn, affect subordinates, decisions, or policies. There is now an intervening mechanism in the linkage. At lower management levels, this can be the socialization process or the nature of dyadic exchange. At executive levels, it can be the organization's culture, as well as related cognitive schemas and the strategic thrust. Indirect leadership yields much slower feedback and has less effect on leadership perceptions than does direct leadership. In general, the leadership literature has been less concerned with indirect means, but they are important nevertheless.

Lord's theory advances a clear hypothesis that leadership can exert a causal impact on performance. The succession literature is reviewed and reanalyzed in this context (see chapter 10 in this volume). The conclusion, consistent with the dominant hypothesis, is that "if properly interpreted, these studies show that succession has a substantial impact on performance" (p. 190). Leadership effects are most likely to be in evidence when executive discretion is high and during periods of reorientation (rather than convergence).

Catastrophe theory is again brought to bear to explain how these change processes are expected to operate. The resulting graph is similar to figure 24.2, but the three variables are different. The nature of change (incremental to discontinuous) is substituted for the controlled-automatic variable in figure 24.2. This nature of organizational change variable and environmental fit (instead of prototype fit) are the two control variables:

> Discontinuous (catastrophic) change is represented on the front surface . . . continuous (linear) change is represented on the back face.
>
> Discontinuous change involves shifts in schemas that guide leaders' perceptions of the environment; continuous change reflects incremental shifts within an existing schema. The type of change affects organizational performance.
>
> The degree of fit with the environment is also a factor incorporated into this model. Thus, the degree of environmental fit and the nature of organizational change processes (convergence or reorientation) affect organizational performance. The model also accounts for the history of evolutionary processes within an organization. Organizations at the same level of environmental fit but approach-

ing it from different directions can have different levels of performance, based on their history.

The impact of leadership is also different, depending on the location of the organization on the performance surface. On the back face, lower- and middle-level managers can maintain the organization's performance. Similarly, symbolic activities on the part of top leaders also serve to keep the organization operating on the back surface. Organizations on the front, or discontinuous, face of the cusp model (the crisis region) may require substantive activities on the part of top leaders to yield considerable improvements in an organization's performance. (Lord & Maher, 1991b, pp. 208–209)

The theory then turns to the types of activities executives at the top level may adopt to affect organizational performance. These may be broadly classified as those targeted at the internal environment of the organization, at adapting to external environments, and at influencing external environments. The means proposed may be classified as direct or indirect, following the definitions noted previously. Table 24.2 provides examples of these influence processes.

Toward the end, the book presenting the theory focuses primarily on organizational level phenomena. Both groups and organizations are viewed as collective information processors, operating with much the same dynamics as individual processors. The concern here shifts sharply to issues that usually are considered to lie within the domain of strategic management, and thus outside the scope of the present volume. The theory and data of Raymond Miles and Charles Snow (1978) receive considerable attention, but a number of other theories dealing with strategic phenomena are introduced as well. This discussion is much more speculative, and the tie to the basic body of laboratory research is often lost. Yet the stress on leadership at the top is an effective antidote to the group dynamics emphasis that characterized most of the first-generation leadership literature.

Applied Value

Only in the last two paragraphs of their book do Lord and Maher (1991b) explicitly address the application issue. In this regard, it seems best to let them speak for themselves:

> Our bias has been to stress theoretical and conceptual development and to ground ideas in the extant scientific literature. We think, however, the

theory has applied value as well. Throughout this book, we discuss many practical issues, such as why females may not be perceived as leaders, how to expand discretion, and how context may limit leadership perceptions, to name just a few. We think that understanding such issues from a theoretical perspective is valuable. In addition, we have extended thinking about leadership by integrating it with theories of information processing and organizational evolution; such extensions are of practical value because they go beyond the experience and perspectives of most individual leaders or organizations.

> A widespread pragmatic issue is that real leaders address problems from a perspective that is too narrow. Our approach suggests ways of expanding leaders' perspectives by considering alternative types of information processing. . . . A key strategy for leaders to consider is first to diagnose the type of information processing they typically apply to problems and then to consider how the problems might be approached using alternative types of information processing. In doing so, leaders should focus both on processes related to social perceptions and on processes related to performance. (Lord & Maher, 1991b, p. 308)

Developments during the 1990s

Since the publication of the comprehensive theory in book form, the authors' major contribution has been an overview of cognitive theory generally, although with little specific reference to leadership processes (Lord & Maher, 1991a). In addition, Lord has provided several commentaries on information processing as related to aspects of leadership, but without particularly significant new theoretical input to the field (Lord & Hall, 1992; Lord, 1995).

However, later in the decade Lord began to develop ideas related to information processing at different levels of analysis, to affective considerations, and to self-identities, while writing with various coauthors, again primarily colleagues at Akron (Hall & Lord, 1995; Engle & Lord, 1997; Lord & Smith, 1999). As with the progression of publications leading up to the book with Maher (1991b), these statements ultimately culminated in a fully developed theoretical position (Lord, Brown, & Freiberg, 1999). This latter represents a significant extension of the basic theory, an extension which is in fact more theoretically elegant than its predecessor, since the ideas are stated in propositional form.

TABLE 24.2 Potential means that can be used by executives to influence organizational performance

| Target | Objective | Tactics | |
		Direct	Indirect
Adapting to and influencing internal environments			
Subsystem organization and management	Rationalization and integration	Define and specify function of roles	Shape top management's schemas; organizing; select those with similar schemas
	Coordination and appraisal	Design and implement management information systems	Use information as sign and symbol
Productivity	Increased organizational efficiency	Reduce capital or personnel costs	Strengthen productivity norms
Quality	Increased product quality	Increase quality control	Strengthen quality norms
Organizational climate and culture	Increased employee motivation and commitment	Determine or influence organizational politics	Enhance participative decision-making norms; symbolism of CEO
Adapting to external environments			
Choice of markets or environments	Increased stability and munificence	Improve strategic planning	Influence top management's schemas; select those with similar schemas
Management and production system	Fit with environment and strategy	Improve organizational design	Guide top management's labeling of environments
Influencing external environments			
Acquisition of resources and maintenance of boundaries	Increased stability and reduced competition	Integrate horizontally or vertically; promote entry barriers and noncompetitive pricing	Create favorable public opinion; enhance image of organization or product
Government policy (e.g., regulation, taxation, trade)	Policy change to reduce uncertainty or increase resources	Exercise direct political influence	Exercise political influence via other groups (e.g., unions, suppliers)

SOURCE: Adapted from David V. Day & Robert G. Lord (1988), Executive Leadership and Organizational Performance: Suggestions for a New Theory and Methodology, *Journal of Management*, 14, 461

Organization of the Self

The theory starts with the idea that follower self-concepts serve to influence follower behavior and that leaders can affect these self-concepts. The self is a system of self-schemas derived from experience, which have cognitive, affective, and behavioral consequences. At the core are highly stable schemas, but there are also more peripheral aspects whose accessibility depends on motivational and social contexts. An individual's self-identity is made up of *personal* and *social identities*; the former is a self-categorization based on perceptions of similarities and differences from others (the sense of uniqueness), while the latter is based on

how individuals define themselves in relation to the broader social world. There are two levels of social identities: *interpersonal* and *group* (or collective). It is assumed that followers are unable to focus on more than one of these three levels at the same time. Propositions which follow are:

Proposition 1. The importance of many leadership and social processes will vary with identity level.

1a. When the self is defined at the individual level, leader expectancy effects, effects of performance feedback, effects of contingent rewards, and procedures related to distributive justice will have greater effects on subordinate behavior and attitudes.

1b. When the self is defined at the relational level, perceived and actual leader-subordinate congruence in attitudes and values, leader affective behaviors, and interactional justice will have greater effects on subordinate behavior and attitudes.

1c. When the self is defined at the group (or organizational) level, structural aspects of procedural justice, organizational identities, and team-based leadership will have greater effects on subordinate behavior and attitudes.

Proposition 2. The effectiveness of leadership activities will depend on whether they are matched to appropriate identity levels. (Lord, Brown, & Freiberg, 1999, p. 175)

Also related to level considerations is a proposition that deals with theoretical matters which we will take up in the chapter which follows.

Proposition 3. Self-identity level will moderate the relation of (a) transactional and (b) transformational leadership to attitudinal and performance outcomes. Transactional leadership will be most effective when the subordinates' self is defined at an individual level, whereas transformation leadership will be most effective when the subordinate's self is defined at the group or collective level. (p. 176)

Next came a series of propositions related to the *working self-concept*, which is the portion of the potentially accessible aspects of the self that because of limited attention capacity is actually activated to guide information processing and behavior at a point in time. There are three components—self views, current goals, and possible selves (broader standards). Leaders' prophecies for their subordinates' performance influence self-views.

Proposition 4. The relationship between leaders' self-fulfilling prophecies and subordinates' expectancies is mediated by changes in subordinates' self-views. (p. 178)

Possible selves specify who the individual could be, and these images can be nourished by leaders.

Proposition 5. Self-views and possible selves will tend to have different underlying dynamics when defined at different levels such that: (a) social comparisons and differentiation from others will predominate when the self is defined at the individual level, (b) affect and reflected appraisals will predominate at the relational level, and (c) assimilation toward a group prototype will predominate at the collective level. (p. 180)

Proposition 6. Linking goals to self-views will accentuate self-enhancement motivations and affective reactions to task feedback, whereas linking goals to possible selves will promote self-verification motivation and cognitive reactions to task feedback.

Proposition 7a. The relation of current goal-performance discrepancies to task satisfaction will be highest when task goals are strongly linked to self-views.

Proposition 7b. The relation of rate of change in goal-performance discrepancies (i.e., velocity) to task satisfaction will be highest when task goals are strongly linked to possible selves.

Proposition 8. The resiliency of task motivation when discrepancies are encountered will be higher when task goals are strongly linked to possible selves and lower when task goals are linked to self-views. (p. 181)

Thus, leaders can exert a strong influence on follower self-identities.

Proposition 9. Leaders can (a) influence the level at which subordinates' self-identities are defined and (b) achieve their effects through the mediating mechanism of subordinates' self-identities.

Proposition 10. Leaders will have more enduring effects if they are able to create or alter chronic self-schemas than if they merely activate existing self-schemas. (p. 184)

Implication of the Self
for Leadership Theory

Individuals may compare their self-views to possible self-views either through using an *ideal standard* that they aspire to, or through using an *ought standard* that reflects their duty or obligation.

Proposition 11a. Leaders who emphasize negative outcomes will develop followers with ought orientations who avoid challenging tasks and who are normatively committed to work.

Proposition 11b. Leaders who emphasize positive outcomes will develop followers with ideal orientations who approach challenging tasks and are affectively committed to work. (p. 191)

When a self-descriptive trait is shared with a leader, conditions for a high-quality leader-member exchange (LMX) are established. Thus, the theory is tied rather closely to George Graen's formulations (see chapter 12 in this volume).

Proposition 12. Salient self-views and chronic self-schemas define the relevant domain for operationalizing actual leader-member similarity.

Proposition 13. Congruence between the identity level of the leader and of the follower (e.g., emphasis on individual, interpersonal, or collective identities) will predict liking and LMX.

Proposition 14. The greater the similarity between leaders and subordinates in their self-views and chronic self-schemas, the more positive will be followers' possible selves. (p. 192)

Taken as a whole, these propositions appear to have much in common with Fred Dansereau's (1995) views to the effect that the role of a leader is to support the follower's sense of self-worth and to participate in validating that self-worth (see chapter 12).

Evaluation and Impact

The amount of published research dealing with implicit leadership theories was much greater during the late 1970s and 1980s than during the 1990s. The earlier interest appears to have been sparked by the fact that a major research and theoretical thrust—the behavioral description of leadership styles—was in the process of being undermined. Yet research dealing with Lord's theorizing has continued to the present.

Research on the Perceptual Theory

The proposed four information processing models have not been considered in research that compares and contrasts them, but each model separately has been the subject of a substantial stream of research (Lord & Maher, 1990, 1991b). It is apparent that people do use rational, limited-capacity, expert, and cybernetic approaches, although there is no certainty that other approaches are not possible as well.

Of the four, Lord and his colleagues have been concerned in their research primarily with the limited-capacity approach. In this context they have developed considerable evidence in support of the roles of implicit theories and categorization processes in yielding biases inherent in the perceptions of raters. The methodology in much of this research has been to hold actual leader behavior constant via written descriptions or videotapes, and then to vary the labels applied to this behavior. Other studies show that the factor structures of actual (real) and contrived (imaginary) leader behavior patterns look much the same. The studies, whether conducted by Lord or without his participation (Larson, 1982; Phillips, 1984; Binning, Zaba, & Whattam, 1986) consistently indicates that implicit theories and categorization processes account for a sizable proportion, although certainly not all, of the variance in perceptions of leadership. Yet implicit theories do not appear to have variance in common with cognitive complexity (Weiss & Adler, 1981).

The theory is further supported by research which shows that leaders displaying more prototypical leader behaviors evoke stronger impressions of leadership, and that observers must both register and encode prototypical behaviors before classifying individuals as leaders (Palich & Hom, 1992). The automatic-controlled differentiation is clearly evident from the research, and automatic processes do occur more rapidly. Studies reported in Lord and Maher (1991b) demonstrate the validity of both recognition-based and inferential processes in leadership perceptions. Success enhances a perception of leadership, while failure removes it.

As noted in the previous chapter, Lord has been critical of attribution theory on the grounds that it overemphasizes rational, controlled processing at the expense of more automatic information approaches. Lord and Maher say: "We suggest that attribution processes of the kind described by Green and Mitchell (1979) are rarely used; rather, attributional processes are linked to more schema-driven processes" (1991b, p. 121). Certainly the evidence supports a role for automatic processes in attributions, but as we saw in chapter 23 this is less true when poor performance is involved. The comparative position of various approaches to information processing in attributions (and in other areas) does not appear to have been fully established by research as yet.

Also still to be established is the role that individual differences play in implicit theories. There is good evidence that they do have a role, but the extent of that role and exactly how they operate are uncertain (Hauenstein & Alexander, 1991; Keller, 1999). This uncertainty is confounded by the finding, reported by Lord and Maher (1991b), that the implicit theories of leadership held in the United States and in Japan are quite different; the two appear in fact to be totally uncorrelated, indicating that individual differences tied to cultures may be sizable.

Perceptual Changes

The ways in which perceptual changes operate vis-à-vis the theory are less well supported by research than are the information processing models and the fact of implicit theories. As Martin Chemers (1997) notes in his review, there is good evidence to indicate that once categorization occurs a significant inertia develops which holds back any shift to a new category. However, what triggers a change when it does occur remains unknown. Furthermore, there can be no certainty that controlled processing will inevitably result in incremental change; the possibility that reasoning can produce discontinuous changes must be entertained until clear evidence to the contrary is obtained.

The application of the perceptual change theory to the case of female managers makes sense in view of the literature. However, direct support from research is limited, especially for the view that hierarchic differences in perceptual biases, which operate most strongly at the bottom and top levels, serve to limit female managers at these levels in particular. We simply do not have the research to test the theory in this regard.

The theory as applied to culture and culture change appears to provide a useful extension of Schein's thinking as described here in chapter 21. However, like that theory, and theories about culture in general, Lord and Maher's (1991b) formulations lack research support. This is one place where the almost total absorption with laboratory research has hurt information processing theory. It is difficult to study organizational culture in the laboratory.

Research on Leadership and Performance

The distinction between direct and indirect influences on performance appears useful, and to be consistent with what is known in the area of socialization, culture, strategy formulation, and the like. The contention that the leadership field has not given sufficient attention to indirect means is certainly justified.

Although the perceptual theory indicates that actual leadership behavior explains only part of what is perceived, it says nothing that negates the view that such behavior directly or indirectly influences performance outcomes. However, certain interpretations of the succession research do come to the conclusion that the interjection of new leadership behaviors into a situation has no effect on performance and thus that leadership does not make any difference. Lord and Maher (1991b) go a long way toward reversing this conclusion with their reanalysis of certain studies and their introduction of other findings. At top levels, combinations of expert and cybernetic information processing seem to provide the key to organizational effectiveness. However, as noted in chapter 10, there has been further research to indicate that leadership, and succession, definitely can make a difference. According to the Lord theory, this occurs when leader discretion is high and during periods of reorientation and crisis. There is some evidence consistent with that view, but it would also seem that when leadership traits are appropriately aligned with existing needs, these traits may also be a contributing factor to effective performance. Personality factors are surely involved here (Pitcher, Chreim, & Kisfalvi, 2000).

Use of Catastrophe Theory

It is never entirely clear whether Lord and Maher (1991b) are using catastrophe theory as a vehicle for depicting their ideas or as a means of theory generation. Used in the former manner the three-dimensional graphs do appear to have some explanatory value, although the statements that this treatment is "hard work to get through" (Gioia, 1993) and "a somewhat difficult read" (Jago, 1994) do seem justified.

As a source of hypotheses, however, the catastrophe theory presentations fall short. On occasion they seem to lead to unintended conclusions, or at least counterintuitive ones, which are not well explained (Weick, 1993). More typically, the attempts at hypothesis generation resulting from the catastrophe theory presentations lack the crispness required to apply adequate research tests. Words such as "doubt," "may," "can," and the like serve to neutralize any specific commitment to hypotheses and leave the reader with a sense of equivocality. The authors simply do not seem to be convinced that catastrophe theory is a good source of leadership theory. The fact that it has not been mobilized to support more recent research or to contribute propositions for research testing adds to this impression.

Decline in Research Support

As one moves from the first two parts of *Leadership and Information Processing* to the last, there is a steady decline in the amount of research support adduced and a precipitous decline in relevant research conducted by Lord and those who worked with him. The work on perceptions of leadership and implicit theories is ingenious, significant, and grounded in solid research evidence. This work has been described as a productive synthesis (Chemers, 1997) and an important contribution (House & Aditya, 1997).

The theory developed later in the book is often equally ingenious, but it does not reflect quite the same level of relevant literature knowledge, nor is it grounded in research by the authors or those of a similar orientation. And the research needed to test these more macro theoretical formulations has not been forthcoming since, either. The difficulty appears to be that, like many of us, Lord has a particular type of research expertise—conducting tightly controlled laboratory studies to test very specific hypotheses using methods that exhibit a high degree of rigor. Lord is a very good scientist. But this approach is not applicable in the types of field situations that must be used to test his expanding theory. The same type of experimental control is rarely possible, and multiple studies are needed to compensate for this fact. In all likelihood Lord has not extended his research to the more macro aspects of his theory because his preferred research approach is less applicable there and he is not comfortable with those approaches that are applicable. Also, as I have noted previously, the research approach taken by a theory's author tends to establish a model for future researchers. Others may well have felt that they would be unable to uphold Lord's high standards in the field setting.

One possible way around the need for field studies here is to draw on evidence that laboratory and field studies produce very similar results. There is some evidence that appears to be of this kind (DeVader, Bateson, & Lord, 1986). A meta-analysis indicates strong support for attribution theory hypotheses across the fields of performance appraisal, motivation, and leadership. At the same time, the data indicated that this same conclusion could be generalized from laboratory to field studies. Many of the studies dealt with

matters that extend well outside the domain of attribution theory as it applies to poor performance, as discussed in chapter 23 of this volume, although a few studies within that domain were included. More significant for present purposes is the fact that there were only 14 studies dealing with leadership at all (roughly 20 percent of the total); the number of field leadership studies was well below what would normally be required for meta-analysis. Furthermore, the field studies that were used relate to attributions at lower organizational levels, not at the executive level with which the Lord theory is concerned. All in all, it does not seem appropriate to apply the findings of DeVader et al. (1986) to the later theory, and, in fact, Lord and Maher (1991b) do not attempt to do so.

To this point we have not considered the later theoretical formulations during the 1990s and the research on them. This work culminated in the 14 propositions set forth by Lord et al. (1999). In many respects the decline in research output associated with the successive chapters of the 1991 book has continued. The 1999 article contains no original research. The propositions often draw on other organizational behavior theories, a number of them theories considered in this book, and the research around them. As a result, a certain amount of general research support related to the propositions is gained, but this support is not focused on these specific formulations. Elaine Engle and Lord (1997) does contain research evidence that is consistent with the last three propositions that deal with LMX theory, although it is entirely possible that this research was an inductive source for these propositions rather than a test.

Certainly the trend has been for Lord to move away from empirical investigation to theoretical formulations, which are on occasion somewhat speculative. With regard to the 1999 theory on self-concepts, it is too early to know what the empirical future will be. We can only hope that Lord, and others, too, will make these propositions the basis for a renewed research outburst.

Individual and Cultural Differences

In the early period implicit theories of leadership were considered to be very similar, at least within a single culture. Thus, to a large extent, consideration and initiating structure ratings were seen as reflections of implicit theories and categorizations held in common by a large number of followers, and indeed other perceivers of leadership as well. This does not mean that the results of all studies employing leader behavior ratings are totally invalidated as Chemers (1997) points out. But it does mean that implicit theories shared by many have now come to encroach on the variance previously thought to be the province of leader behavior only.

A problem arises, however, with the finding that individual differences are related to the implicit theories held by followers. This suggests that implicit theories of leadership are, to some degree at least, an individual matter, rather than being held in common within a culture. At present it is not clear just how universal, versus individual, implicit theories of leadership are. That question can only be answered through research outside the laboratory, which remains to be done.

This problem is compounded by the finding that the cultures of the United States and Japan produce very different implicit theories of leadership. Theory proposes that these implicit theories are indeed culture bound, but what about the perceptual processes of Japanese-Americans? The point is that cultural differences can merge into group and individual differences, and may well produce substantial variations from universality. Robert House and Ram Aditya (1997) call for a much wider investigation of cultural differences in leadership perceptions; this seems essential if the universality problem is to be unraveled. We need to know just how much the categorization processes of different cultures, groups, and individuals have in common.

A related question has to do with the frequency with which different information processing approaches are used. Lord and his colleagues put substantial stress on the role of automatic processes at the expense of reasoning, especially in their treatment of attributions. Yet controlled processes are more pervasive than Lord indicates, as shown by evidence in chapter 23 of this volume. It is not surprising that a person who has identified a wholly new phenomenon in the leadership field (implicit theories) might overgeneralize the effect of that phenomenon, pushing the limits as far as they would go. Ultimately we need to know how people around the United States and around the world are predisposed to use one information processing approach or another. Knowledge of the demographics of information processing could prove immensely valuable.

These issues, including such matters as how expert processing comes into being, are understood to be important by the theory's authors (Lord & Maher, 1989). This is still a very new and rich field for investigation. I hope it will be pursued more vigorously, especially in field settings, than it has been in the past few years.

SUBSTITUTES FOR LEADERSHIP

Substitutes for leadership theory is best considered in the context of the existing leadership theory of the period in which it emerged. The dominant thrust at that time was to emphasize the leader behaviors and styles used by lower-level leaders in hierarchic organizational systems. Thus "substitutes" meant something other than the behaviors of these first-level supervisors, and, by implication, the theory clearly rejected the idea that an understanding of these behaviors is the key to unraveling the enigma of organizational functioning. There is much more to it than that, and the theory set out to establish what exactly that "more" is.

Background

Steven Kerr has had a career that has extended back and forth across the academic and corporate worlds several times. Educated at the Baruch School of the City University of New York, he began work on an MBA there while a programmer for Mobil Oil—part of some 8 years spent in industry in the New York City area. He was recruited into the doctoral program at CUNY by Robert House, and House remained his mentor throughout his doctoral studies (Frost, 1997). From there he moved to the business faculty at Ohio State University, where he remained for 7 years. Next came a lengthy period at the University of Southern California, where Kerr held a variety of administrative appointments within the business school. This association trailed off into several years on leave doing consulting, primarily with General Electric; this was in 1992–1993.

After a visiting appointment at the University of Michigan, which still permitted considerable consulting, Kerr ultimately moved to General Electric on a full-time basis and became vice president of corporate leadership development, with responsibility for the company's management development operation at Crotonville, New York. As of this writing he remains in that position.

The full theory with which we are concerned here was published early in the University of Southern

California years, after Kerr had left Ohio State which had been the primary source of the behavior description thrust in the leadership field (see chapter 10). However, much of the development work on the theory and some early formulations on the subject emanated from the Ohio State period. Kerr received his Ph.D. from CUNY in 1973, and the basic theory first appeared in print 4 years later. He was president of the Academy of Management in the late 1980s.

Approach to Theorizing

In considering Kerr's approach to theorizing, it is informative to note the similarities between his strategy and the one his early mentor House had adopted. Remember that House built path-goal theory of leadership on the structure of expectancy theory of motivation and on Evans's slightly earlier path-goal formulations (chapter 10). He also built many of his propositions regarding the implications of early organizational behavior research on the structure of classical management theory (see chapter 3; House & Miner, 1969). And, as we will see in the next chapter, he developed a theory of charismatic leadership based on Max Weber's earlier groundwork (see chapter 3).

Kerr often has used this same strategy of building on an existing theory that had already become widely recognized and well established. He joined House in preparing the second edition of the book grounded in classical theory (Filley, House, & Kerr, 1976). He wrote a very influential piece on the use of rewards to motivate behavior in organizations entitled "On the Folly of Rewarding A, While Hoping for B" (Kerr, 1975) which was grounded in Edward Thorndike's law of effect (circa 1900) and in earlier applications of that law to organizational practice (Haire, 1956). His substitutes for leadership theory was built on a structure of prior contributions of a related nature, as noted previously in this chapter, including House's own path-goal theory.

There is certainly nothing wrong with this strategic approach to theorizing; in fact, it has the value of adding directly to the current body of knowledge in a field and keeping promising theories at the center of scientific attention. The only proviso is that the new theory must indeed add something new and thus extend understanding in significant ways. There is no question that Kerr's theorizing, especially substitutes for leadership theory, has done this. So, too, have House's applications of this same strategic approach

to theory construction. Both have added many innovative ideas.

How the Substitutes Formulations Evolved

I have indicated that the basic substitutes for leadership theory was a product of the 1977–1978 time period. But Kerr had been using the terminology and providing examples of what he had in mind over several years before that. These early statements did not incorporate a truly systematic approach to theory development, however; they were typically appended to a treatment of some other leadership topic, and were brief in nature (Schriesheim, 1997).

Implications for Organizational Design

Characteristically Kerr (1977) presents the theory initially as if it were an adjunct to the topic of organizational design. It soon becomes apparent, however, that this time the real topic of concern is substitutes for leadership, whatever their nature. The latter are described as often serving to neutralize or substitute for a formal leader's ability to influence work group satisfaction and performance. Examples noted are as follows:

1. In the subordinate—ability, experience, training, knowledge, professional orientation, need for independence, and indifference to organizational rewards
2. In the task—repetitiveness and unambiguity, methodological invariance, intrinsic satisfaction, and task-provided feedback on accomplishments
3. In the organization—formalization, inflexibility, highly specified and active advisory or staff functions, closely knit and cohesive work groups, rewards outside the leader's control, and spatial distance between the leader and the subordinates (Kerr, 1977, p. 139)

The thrust of the presentation is evident from the following quote:

If the existence of substitutes for hierarchical leadership is ignored, then efforts at leadership training, organizational development, and task design may well result in ineffectiveness for the organization and frustration for its members, as they come to realize that inflexible policies, invariant work methodologies, or other barriers . . . are interfering with intended changes and preventing desired benefits. (Kerr, 1977, p. 139)

In this view substitutes are seen primarily as barriers to prevent such measures as human relations training and organization development from actually changing the organization, even though they may change the leader. Yet Kerr (1977) was also influenced by certain other work in which he was involved, dealing with professionals (Kerr, Von Glinow, & Schriesheim, 1977). Thus, he recognized that many aspects of professionals and their training (norms, standards, knowledge, independence, etc.) could serve to substitute for leader influence and at the same time create opportunities. Substitutes and their nature need to be given more attention. They need not only to be clearly identified but also, in certain instances, to be systematically created.

Meaning and Measurement

The next presentation of the theory (Kerr & Jermier, 1978) included considerable research, which we will consider shortly. The theoretical statement applied the substitutes considered previously to two leader behaviors—consideration and initiating structure— thus creating what amount to hypotheses on specific neutralization effects. Table 24.3 is the result. Feedback on performance may derive from the task itself or from other people—primary work group members, staff personnel, the client. If these types of instances prevail, the formal leader's role in performance feedback may be trivial.

A distinction is made between substitutes and neutralizers. Neutralizers make it impossible for the leader behaviors noted to make any difference. They are a type of moderator variable when they are uncorrelated with either predictor or criterion. They act as suppressor variables when correlated with predictors, but not the criterion. Substitutes make the leader behaviors not only impossible but unnecessary:

[They] may be correlated with both predictors and the criterion, but tend to improve the validity coefficient when included in the predictor set. . . . Substitutes do, but neutralizers do not, provide a "person or thing acting or used in place of" the formal leader's negated influence. The effect of neutralizers is therefore to create an "influence vacuum" from which a variety of dysfunctions may emerge. (Kerr & Jermier, 1978, p. 395)

Strictly speaking, the characteristics of table 24.3 are all neutralizers, but not all need be substitutes.

A further distinction is made between direct and indirect leader effects. A direct effect occurs when a subordinate is influenced by a leader behavior in and of itself. An indirect effect occurs when a subordinate is influenced by the implications of the leader behavior for some future consequence such as rewards. A factor can substitute for one type of effect without substituting for the other. The direct-indirect differentiation made here is not the same as the one used in Lord and Maher's (1991b) formulations.

The theory assumes, but does not specify, additional types of leader behaviors beyond consideration and initiating structure, each of which will have its own set of neutralizers and substitutes. Further extensions to the theory should also specify at what point a particular substitute becomes important (the threshold) and how substitutes combine to create a barrier to leader influence (interaction effects). The goal is to learn how things are accomplished in organizations, whether or not they are activated by hierarchical leadership.

Kerr's coauthor in this article, John Jermier, was a graduate student at Ohio State at the time. Jermier's primary interests were of a macro nature, and he identified more with sociology than with the prevailing psychological orientation of the Ohio State program. He saw the substitutes formulations as a means of dealing with the kinds of variables that held the greatest interest for him (Jermier & Kerr, 1997).

Controlling the Performance of People

Kerr's next coauthor, in contrast, was an established contributor to the organizational behavior field, John Slocum, who had been a visiting professor at Ohio State during Kerr's tenure there (Kerr & Slocum, 1981). Their article deals with the topic of control in organizations in a general sense but devotes considerable space to control via substitutes for leadership. Control by leaders is described as often time-consuming, detrimental to subordinate development, and weak. Thus, a case is made that control by substitutes can be the more effective mechanism.

The classification system used in this presentation to identify substitutes differs somewhat from that used previously. Substitutes for hierarchy used to obtain organizational control are specified as falling in four classes: task, professional orientation, work groups, and

TABLE 24.3 Neutralization effects of substitutes for leadership on two types of leader behavior

	Will tend to neutralize	
Characteristic	Relationship-oriented, supportive, people-centered leadership; consideration, support, and interaction facilitation	Task-oriented, instrumental, job-centered leadership; initiating structure, goal emphasis, and work facilitation
Of the subordinate		
Ability, experience, training, knowledge		X
Need for independence	X	X
"Professional" orientation	X	X
Indifference toward organizational rewards	X	X
Of the task		
Unambiguous and routine		X
Methodologically invariant		X
Provides its own feedback on accomplishment		X
Intrinsically satisfying	X	
Of the organization		
Formalization (explicit plans, goals, and areas of responsibility)		X
Inflexibility (rigid, unbending rules and procedures)		X
Highly specified and active advisory and staff functions		X
Closely knit, cohesive work groups	X	X
Organizational rewards not within the leader's control	X	X
Spatial distance between superior and subordinates	X	X

NOTE: X = a neutralizing effect occurs.

SOURCE: Steven Kerr & John M. Jermier (1978), Substitutes for Leadership: Their Meaning and Measurement, *Organizational Behavior and Human Performance*, 22, 378. Copyright 1978 by Academic Press. Reprinted with permission.

organizational development and training programs. Assuming that the development and training efforts may indeed be parceled out among hierarchic, task, professional, and group types, this classification system looks much like the one originally specified by Miner (1975) (see chapter 5 in this volume). This classification approach is then applied to the mechanistic-organic differentiation as set forth by Tom Burns and G. M. Stalker (see chapter 15). Table 24.4 presents the results. Note that the list of leader behaviors considered is now expanded well beyond the original two. These leader behaviors, of whatever type, are a primary source of control in mechanistic organizations; substitutes operate most strongly in organic organizations.

Moderator Variables

In an attempt to improve the original treatment of moderator variables within the theory, Kerr joined forces with two scholars at New Mexico State University, Jon Howell and Peter Dorfman, who had been conducting research on substitutes theory (Howell, Dorfman, & Kerr, 1986). Their presentation attempts to focus on the mechanisms by which moderators operate and establishes a typology of moderators as leadership neutralizers or enhancers, leadership substitutes or supplements, and leadership mediators.

Neutralizers interrupt the predictive relationship between the leader behavior and criteria; they remain much as previously defined. Enhancers serve to augment relationships between leader behaviors and criteria, but, like neutralizers, they have little if any influence on the criteria themselves. *Enhancers* represent a positive moderating influence, as opposed to neutralizers, which represent a negative moderating influence. This neutralizer/enhancers idea differs from the previous neutralizer concept as follows:

TABLE 24.4 Effects of various organizational characteristics on members' task-relevant information and motivation in mechanistic and organic organizations

	Sources of information or motivation in	
Characteristics	Mechanistic organizations	Organic organizations
Formal roles	Information, yes; functions, powers, methods, and responsibilities are explicit, though some ambiguity remains; motivation, no	No: position differentiation—based on expertise—exists, but the concept of responsibility as a limited field of rights and obligations does not exist
Leadership behaviors		
Role clarification	Yes: mechanistic systems are characterized by superior-subordinate role making, in the form of instructions and decisions	No: tasks are continually redefined through interactions with peers; however, role conflict and ambiguity are usually prevalent
Goal setting	Yes: goal setting by superiors is a source of task-relevant information, and of motivation under certain conditions	No: goals are set by each person in interaction with other people, possibly including, but certainly not primarily with, superiors
Leader initiation of structure	Yes: task-relevant knowledge is assumed to increase with hierarchical level, and the superior's job is to reconcile subordinates' performances. Motivation can also be increased under certain conditions	No: task-relevant knowledge is assumed to reside everywhere in the network
Feedback	Yes: formal leaders provide task-relevant information through feedback, and motivation under certain conditions	No: feedback stems primarily from peers
Consideration and stroking	Information, no; motivation sometimes: consideration by leaders is more necessary in mechanistic systems, since jobs tend to be routine and uninteresting	No
Participative leadership	No: although exceptions exist, participative leadership is uncharacteristic of mechanistic systems	Yes, under conditions such as those specified; participative leadership is one of the principal ways that formal leaders exert influence in organic systems
Charismatic leadership	Information, not usually; motivation, sometimes: charisma does not often exist, but is most likely to be attributed to leaders who are physically and hierarchically distant	No: day-to-day intimacy almost invariably destroys impressions of charisma
Administration of rewards and punishments	Information: no; motivation, yes, to the extent that rewards and punishments are linked to task-relevant behaviors	Information, no; motivation, yes, to the extent that rewards and punishments are linked to task-relevant behaviors
Substitutes for formal leadership behaviors		
Tasks	Information, yes, since tasks are likely to be highly predictable; motivation, no	Information, not usually, since tasks tend to be unstructured; however, tasks in organic systems tend to be closely related to organizational ends, so task-provided feedback is possible; motivation, yes, since tasks tend to be high in identity, significance, and other aspects characteristic of enriched jobs
Professional orientation	No, not in the sense of informal norms and values—if professional expertise is necessary, formal staff functions are usually created	Yes: autonomy, commitment to calling, and the other attributes of a professional orientation are highly valued in organic organizations

(continued)

TABLE 24.4 (continued)

| Characteristics | Sources of information or motivation in | |
	Mechanistic organizations	Organic organizations
Work group	Information, no; motivation, sometimes, when conditions such as those specified exist: differentiation of tasks, combined with emphasis on vertical channels of communication, often prevent group in mechanistic systems from contributing to members' motivation	Yes, particularly when conditions such as those specified exist
Organizational development and training	Yes: skills training is often emphasized	Yes: conceptual, interpersonal, and team-building methods are often emphasized

SOURCE: Steven Kerr & John W. Slocum (1981), Controlling the Performance of People in Organizations, In Paul C. Nystrom & William H. Starbuck (Eds.), *Handbook of Organizational Design* (New York: Oxford University Press), Vol. 2, p. 130. Copyright 1981 by Oxford University Press. Reprinted with permission.

1. It acknowledges the existence of partial neutralizers, removing the need to completely eliminate a leader behavior's impact in order to identify a neutralizer variable.
2. By adding the enhancer dimension it recognizes that some moderators . . . have the potential to augment as well as neutralize leader behavior-criterion relationships.
3. It recognizes the possibility that neutralizers/enhancers may have a main effect on the criterion as predictors in a multiple regression equation. (Howell, Dorfman, & Kerr, 1986, p. 91)

Substitutes also remain as previously defined. However, three criteria must be met for a variable to qualify as a substitute:

a. There must be a logical reason why the leader behavior and the potential substitute should provide the guidance and/or good feeling indicated by the criterion measure.
b. The potential substitute must be a neutralizer-moderator; at certain levels of the moderator it must weaken the leader behavior's effect on the criterion.
c. The potential substitute must have an important impact on the criterion; increasing levels of the substitute result in higher criterion levels. (Howell, Dorfman, & Kerr 1986, p. 92)

Supplements have the effect that they serve to supplement, rather than neutralize and replace, the leader's ability to influence a criterion. In contrast to substi-

tutes which produce low leader behavior impact and high criterion levels, supplements do not influence leader behavior yet they do result in higher criterion levels.

Mediators represent an intermediate step between leader behavior and a criterion, a step that operates as part of a causal chain; as such, mediators must be correlated with both the leader behavior and the criterion. This mediation process may be partial or complete, although the former is more typical.

The way in which these moderator concepts operate is depicted in figure 24.3. Suppressor variables are not included there, or in the theory, because they are viewed as statistical artifacts with high conceptual ambiguity, which in any event are rarely found in the organizational behavior field.

Alternatives to Ineffective Leadership

Up until the early 1990s Kerr limited his discussions of theoretical applications to urging companies to introduce and expand the use of substitutes. This changed with an article coauthored with a number of people who had been contributing research on the theory (Howell, Bowen, Dorfman, Kerr, & Podsakoff, 1990). The thrust of this article was that substitutes should be used as remedies for problems that had been created by ineffective and weak leadership. Special mention is made of the use of closely knit teams of highly trained individuals, of intrinsic satisfaction in the work, of computer technology especially as it provides immediate feedback, and of extensive professional education.

The treatment of what to do in dealing with specific problems is now quite detailed, as indicated by table 24.5. The suggested solutions are presented as examples of the many possibilities that can be invoked to deal with the various leadership problems noted. Also, a decision tree is implemented to show when substitutes might be most appropriate. These circumstances are as follows:

> Create substitutes when the traits and/or personality of the problem leader are inadequate *and* replacement of that leader is for some reason not feasible.

> Create substitutes when the traits and/or personality of the problem leader are adequate, the skills and/or knowledge of that leader are inadequate, *and* training the leader is not feasible.

> Eliminate neutralizers but create enhancers when the traits/personality are adequate *and* the skills/knowledge are adequate.

A listing of creative substitutes for an emphasis on leader behavior includes developing collegial systems of guidance (peer appraisals, quality circles), improving performance-oriented formalization (commission payment, group MBO), increasing administrative staff availability (training personnel, human relations troubleshooters), increasing the professionalism of subordinates (staffing with professionals, development planning), redesigning jobs to increase inherent performance feedback and ideological importance, and starting team-building activities to develop group self-management skills in solving work problems as well as resolving conflicts and providing support. A similar listing of creative enhancers includes increasing subordinate perception of leader influence and expertise, building organizational climate, increasing leader position power, and creating cohesive work groups with high performance norms.

Current Observations

The final additions to the theory derive from a retrospective which appears to have been written primarily by Jermier, the former graduate student at Ohio State with a macro perspective (Jermier & Kerr, 1997). This piece is significant more for its shift in emphasis than for its original contribution of content.

The emphasis on moderators of the leader behavior-criterion relationships that had been developing steadily over the years is now downplayed. In contrast, the main effects from substitutes to criteria or outcomes are stressed. This view is epitomized in the following:

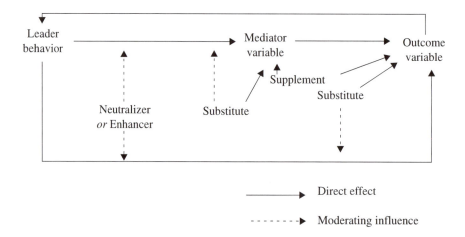

FIGURE 24.3 Causal model showing the roles of leader behaviors, moderators, and mediators. From Jon P. Howell, Peter W. Dorfman, & Steven Kerr (1986), Moderator Variables in Leadership Research, *Academy of Management Review*, 11, 97. Copyright 1986 by Academy of Management. Reproduced with permission.

TABLE 24.5 Effective coping strategies that might be used to deal with specific leadership problems

Leadership problems	Enhancer or neutralizer	Substitutes
Leader doesn't keep on top of details in the department; coordination among subordinates is difficult	Not useful	Develop self-managed work teams; encourage team members to interact within and across departments
Competent leadership is resisted through noncompliance or passive resistance	Enhancers: Increase employees' dependence on leader through greater leader control of rewards/resources; increase their perception of leader's influence outside of work group	Develop collegial systems of guidance for decision making
Leader doesn't provide support or recognition for jobs well done	Not useful	Develop a reward system that operates independently of the leader; enrich jobs to make them inherently satisfying
Leader doesn't set targets or goals, or clarify roles for employees	Not useful	Emphasize experience and ability in selecting subordinates; establish group goal setting; develop an organizational culture that stresses high performance expectations
Leader behaves inconsistently over time	Enhancers: Are dysfunctional Neutralizers: Remove rewards from leader's control	Develop group goal-setting and group rewards
Upper-level manager regularly bypasses a leader in dealing with employees, or countermands the leader's directions	Enhancers: Increase leader's control over rewards and resources; build leader's image via in-house champion or visible "important" responsibilities Neutralizer: Physically distance subordinates from upper-level manager	Increase the professionalization of employees
Unit is in disarray or out of control	Not useful	Develop highly formalized plans, goals, routines, and areas of responsibility
Leadership is brutal, autocratic	Enhancers: Are dysfunctional Neutralizers: Physically distance subordinates; remove rewards from leader's control	Establish group goal-setting and peer performance appraisal
There is inconsistency across different organizational units	Not useful	Increase formalization; set up a behaviorally focused reward system
Leadership is unstable over time; leaders are rotated and/or leave office frequently	Not useful	Establish competent advisory staff units; increase professionalism of employees
Incumbent management is poor; there's no heir apparent	Enhancers: Are dysfunctional Neutralizers: Assign nonleader duties to problem managers	Emphasize experience and ability in selecting employees; give employees more training

SOURCE: Jon P. Howell, David E. Bowen, Peter L. Dorfman, Steven Kerr, & Philip M. Podsakoff (1990), Substitutes for Leadership: Effective Alternatives to Ineffective Leadership, *Organizational Dynamics*, 19(1), 28, 29. Copyright 1990. Reprinted with permission from Elsevier Science.

It is not the study of interpersonal interactions between managerial leaders and subordinate followers that is the core of the substitutes for leadership framework, but the idea that managerial leadership works through technological, structural, and other impersonal processes in the organization to achieve its effects. That is, formal leaders do attempt to control the organization, but they do so by making decisions that minimize the need for the face-to-face exercise of power. (Jermier & Kerr, 1997, pp. 98–99)

In line with this position the essay argues that greater attention should be given to the study of the substitutes themselves: how they are created, how they influence outcomes, and how leadership interactions change as a result. The idea that substitutes for leadership theory is essentially a contingency theory is given a distinctly secondary role for the future. The ties between substitutes theory and classic group dynamics theory are downplayed in favor of a more macro, sociological emphasis.

Evaluation and Impact

From the beginning, substitutes theory has been closely tied to research. Measures were constructed at an early point, and Kerr and Jermier (1978) present research findings along with their statement of the theory. This set the stage for others, and indeed others have followed, most notably a group of researchers associated with Indiana University headed by Philip Podsakoff and Scott MacKenzie. The research is not as extensive as might be desired, but it is sufficient to answer a number of questions.

Research at the Inception

The first reported study was conducted using college students who completed a questionnaire that was intended to measure substitutes for leadership. The students were asked to assume the role of a popular television character who had been widely portrayed as a subordinate working for a particular boss; the characters were Mary Richards, Hawkeye Pierce, and Archie Bunker. Each student was asked to pick one character, or if unfamiliar with any character, to take the role of a low-level assembly line worker.

The measures were short, containing for most of the substitutes only three items, although a few measures had from six to nine items. Yet the Kuder-Richardson internal consistency reliabilities were good, ranging from .74 to .85 with a median of .80. Correlations among scales were as often positive as negative and tended to be low, with 60 percent under .20. High scores on the various scales were taken to indicate negation of leader influence and thus provided evidence for construct validity. The best evidence of this kind came from the ability-experience-training-knowledge scale, and thus focused on individual characteristics. However, some other substitutes appeared to operate as hypothesized also.

Also reported in Kerr and Jermier (1978) were two field studies conducted in police departments, which used the same questionnaire measure of various substitutes. Reliabilities calculated as before ranged from .53 to .85 with a median of .81 in one department and from .63 to .85 with a median of .77 in the other. Correlations among characteristics were again under .20 in the majority of instances. Once again, the mean scores for ability-experience-training-knowledge were highest, but spatial distance and several other factors also appeared to be strong substitutes.

In one of the police departments, data were also collected to determine how the various substitutes and leader behaviors (consideration and initiating structure) influence outcomes (organizational commitment and role ambiguity). These data indicate that leader behavior influences are minimal, when contrasted with the effects of substitutes such as intrinsically satisfying work and task-provided feedback. Yet aspects of initiating structure did appear to hold up against the onslaught of the various substitutes and remained independent predictors of outcomes. This aspect of the study is interpreted as supportive of the role of substitutes, but it also indicates that in any given context only certain substitutes will be operative and that leader behaviors may well not be eclipsed.

A study published only slightly later than the initial presentation of substitutes for leadership theory (Jermier & Berkes, 1979), although mentioning the theory, focuses primarily on other issues. It also uses police subjects, but substitutes from the theoretically specified set are considered only tangentially and the hypotheses tested derive from path-goal theory primarily, not substitutes theory. This does not appear to represent a true test of the theory in any comprehensive sense, and the findings vis-à-vis the stated hypotheses are mixed in any event.

Research continued during the early 1980s, but with inconclusive results. Two studies conducted in hospitals are typical, one of which used the Kerr and Jermier (1978) scales. This latter study (Howell & Dorfman, 1981) used a moderator design with organizational commitment and job satisfaction as criteria. The authors describe their findings as providing only mixed support for theory; only organizational formalization operated as hypothesized, although several other potential substitutes yielded evidence of weak or partial influence. The second study (Sheridan, Vredenburgh, & Abelson, 1984) operationalized the substitutes differently and both added to and deleted from the theoretically specified list. The results, using a performance criterion, provide some support for the theory, but with differential influences from the various substitutes appearing in different contexts. Given these inconsistent results and the extent to which this research test departed from theoretical specifications, it is inappropriate to view this study as providing conclusive evidence for or against the theory.

All in all, the field entered the middle 1980s with a positive disposition toward substitutes for leadership theory, but without adequate research findings to fully support that disposition. This is the point at which the Indiana University researchers began to exert an influence.

Psychometric Properties

One possible cause of the less than striking findings often reported in various studies is that, in spite of the Kerr and Jermier (1978) data, the reliabilities of their substitutes scales appear to be sufficiently low so as to limit the possibility of obtaining significant results. This problem was considered by Margaret Williams et al. (1988). They present internal consistency reliability data for six samples in which all, or in one instance most, of the substitutes were measured. These samples vary, but in no instance do they contain either students or police. The data are as follow:

1. Range .25–.86—median .53
2. Range .32–.84—median .59
3. Range .40–.80—median .60
4. Range .35–.81—median .59
5. Range .36–.70—median .52
6. Range .37–.83—median .59

Only one scale (organizational formalization) appears to have a reliability in the .80s, and two (closely knit, cohesive groups and spatial distance) are in the .70s. For the rest, the data seem to suggest that respondents do not have a clear picture of what is being asked. This raises questions about the findings, or lack of same, from studies that used the Kerr and Jermier (1978) measures. It also raises questions about why internal consistency coefficients across multiple samples would decline by over .20 on the average from the authors' original analyses to those reported by Williams et al. (1988). Time, subjects, perhaps methods of calculation may all be involved, but this is not the type of difference that one finds often in psycho-

metric research. One might think that findings like this would have triggered a resort to other types of reliability analysis beyond the internal consistency approach that has prevailed. Yet there are no reports of test-retest or parallel form analyses.

Correlations among the various substitutes measures remain low, as previously reported, and there is little evidence of social desirability effects. Analyses to establish the factor structure of the measures indicated that the items of certain measures loaded on a single factor, while in other instances this was not the case. Whether such factor purity is essential to the construct validity of a measure is still a matter of debate after many years. However, numerous indices in use do possess conceptual integrity without statistically loading on a single factor, and these indices have contributed substantially to both understanding and prediction in organizational behavior. On this evidence one would have to hold that although factor purity has its benefits, it is not essential.

In any event, the reliability data did indicate a need for new and better scales, if substitutes for leadership research was to progress. Accordingly, the Indiana researchers undertook the task of constructing such scales (Podsakoff & MacKenzie, 1994). Initially this effort involved writing many more items, although ultimately it proved possible to select an abbreviated set of items that accomplished much the same results.

The best estimates of internal consistency reliability for the longer and shorter measures created were as follows:

Longer: range .73–.92—median .82

Shorter: range .70–.91—median .77

Other evidence on the psychometric properties of these scales appeared to support their use. Factor loadings were on the hypothesized factors, and the different scales remained empirically distinct. Correlations with known, independent variables, which were hypothesized to be significant as evidence of construct validity, were indeed significant in over 25 comparisons. If previous research using the Kerr and Jermier (1978) scales had been damaged by the measures used, the scales now available should help correct this problem in subsequent research.

Moderator Analyses

A study carried out to test moderator relationships by Philip Podsakoff, William Todor, Richard Grover, and

Vandra Huber (1984) used the original Kerr and Jermier (1978) scales and found only 2 percent of the interactions to be significant at the .05 level. This lack of moderating effects might, of course, have been anticipated, given the unreliability of the scales. The leader behavior in this study involved leader administration of rewards and punishments, not consideration or initiating structure, but since this variable had been noted previously by Kerr and Slocum (1981)—see table 24.4—its use would not seem to be at variance with the theory.

Subsequent studies emanating from Indiana to be discussed here replaced the original substitutes measures with one of the new ones. The first of these dealt with both the traditional consideration and initiating structure leader behaviors and reward and punishment behavior. Eight different outcome criteria were measured, four of them based on ratings by supervisors (Podsakoff, Niehoff, MacKenzie, & Williams, 1993). Moderator effects were determined by using the substitutes as specified by Howell et al. (1986), and thus in accordance with the most recent directives from theory. Of the over 700 possible interactions, less than 3 percent were consistent with these theoretical criteria; the proportion of outcome variance thus accounted for was quite small. Overall, the identified moderator effects were minimal. However, the study does raise a question as to whether certain substitutes, such as group cohesiveness, might not have been produced by direct efforts from a leader. Are such substitutes really replacing leadership?

Another difficulty with the previous study is that the sample studied did not include professionals to any meaningful extent and thus may have failed to identify a major set of moderators. To remedy this difficulty, a sample with a substantial number of professionals was considered (Podsakoff, MacKenzie, & Fetter, 1993). In most respects this research followed the same procedures as its predecessor. Again, the amount of support for moderator effects as specified by the revised theory (Howell et al., 1986) is minimal. Furthermore, those effects identified in this new, more professional, sample are not at all consistent with the ones found previously. Whether this lack of consistency is at variance with theory is a matter of some disagreement; probably it is not in this instance, because of the wide variation in professional representation in the samples.

The next step by the Indiana researchers was an extensive literature review that focused on moderator effects, as specified both by path-goal theory and by substitutes for leadership theory (Podsakoff, MacKenzie, Ahearne, & Bommer, 1995). Focusing on the latter only, and insofar as possible holding to the dictates of the theory, something less than 9 percent of the moderator effects found proved to be significant. This is higher than chance expectancy but hardly overwhelming support for the theory; the authors interpret it as little support. Consistency in type of moderator effect across samples was low, suggesting a substantial chance component in the findings. Still, many studies used rather small samples, thus bringing power levels down to a point where significance would be hard to detect. Not all studies were so limited, however. The authors conclusions overall are worth noting:

> When we first began our research in this area, we firmly believed that there were a number of important situational factors that influenced a leader's effectiveness. . . . The findings summarized in this study have raised some serious doubts. Quite frankly, we find the lack of support for the moderating effects predicted by the path goal and substitutes for leadership models both shocking and disappointing. (Podsakoff et al., 1995, pp. 464–465)

One other study used much the same approach as that applied in previous Indiana studies but focused on transformational leader behaviors (Podsakoff, MacKenzie, & Bommer, 1996b). This is not a variable actually specified by the theory, but any such behavior is implicitly included and there is no basis for excluding it. The results of this study are of primary interest for the concerns of chapter 25, but it is important to note here that, once again, moderator findings consistent with the theory were minimal (some 2 percent). Also, support for the theory came only from self-report criteria where common method variance may have played a role. As in the other Indiana research, sample size was sufficiently large so that power considerations should not be a concern.

Main Effects

Although the research reviewed to this point has focused on moderator analyses, and has found the theory wanting in this area, these same studies have consistently found sizable main effects that extend from both substitutes and leader behaviors to criterion or outcome variables; both sets of factors tend to contribute to criterion variance. A study designed to look into these effects more fully was conducted by using measures calculated at both the within group or individual level and as averages for existing work groups (Podsakoff & MacKenzie, 1995). Controlling for the leader behaviors and substitutes for leadership at both levels of analysis using multiple regression, the study found the following:

1. The combination of leader behaviors and substitutes for leadership accounted for substantial amounts of variance in the subordinate's attitudes, role perceptions, and performance.
2. The leadership substitutes accounted for more variance in the subordinate criterion variables than did the leader behaviors.
3. Although the effects of within-group variation in leader behaviors and substitutes for leadership were substantially stronger than between-groups variation on subordinates' attitudes and role perceptions, both within-group and between-groups variation in the leader behaviors and leadership substitutes had important effects on . . . performance. (Podsakoff & MacKenzie, 1995, p. 289)

Consideration, initiating structure, and leader reward and punishment behaviors were studied along with 13 substitutes. Leader behaviors and substitutes were found to have quite a bit of variance in common, which suggests the need to include both in future research.

Subsequently, a meta-analysis of main effects from substitutes to criterion variables was carried out using 22 studies in which data were reported (Podsakoff et al., 1996a). The substitutes clearly accounted uniquely for more criterion variance than the leader behaviors, but, combined, the two had a much greater effect. Task feedback, task routinization, group cohesiveness, organizational formalization, and organizational inflexibility were the substitutes that had the most extensive ties to criteria. Although both common method variance and implicit theories of leadership may have influenced some of the findings, this is least likely in the case of the substitutes-performance relationships, which nevertheless were found to be strong. All in all, the evidence for the substitutes' main effects on criteria is quite convincing.

Elsewhere the Indiana researchers note that one might adopt the following argument:

The variables identified by Kerr and Jermier (1978) "substitute" for leadership in the sense that when these variables are added to the model, they eliminate the main effects of the leader behaviors. . . . Although this position is not consistent with the statistical criteria established by Howell, Dorfman, and Kerr (1986) . . . , it is somewhat consistent with the original statistical tests of the model by Kerr and Jermier (1978). (Podsakoff et al., 1993, p. 40)

Although the data for the overall effects of combined substitutes and combined leader behaviors do not support such a conclusion, it is true that the theory as originally formulated did give more attention to main effects than did subsequent versions.

Reactions within the Field

How has the field of organizational behavior reacted to the developing state of affairs? Schriesheim (1997) indicates a long-standing concern that substitutes theory is in fact no more than an elaboration of aspects of path-goal theory. He finds certain of the theoretical arguments less than compelling but recognizes the appeal the theory has had. At the present time, he feels the need is for better construct definitions and better conceptualization overall. A similar view is expressed by Gary Yukl (1998).

Henry Tosi and Scott Kiker (1997) call for a theory that is more fully developed and elaborated. They believe that the effects of particular substitutes as they operate in certain types of organizations needs specification, and, in fact, Tosi (1992) has provided hypotheses of this nature for the various managerial levels of mechanistic and organic organizations.

Howell (1997) stresses that substitute variables have been shown to play an important role in organizations. While recognizing the mixed nature of the research findings, he believes that statistical problems inherent in much of the research have produced a tendency to understate the prevalence of the various substitutes. Podsakoff and MacKenzie (1997), however, feel that the evidence on moderator effects is overwhelmingly negative. Yet they point to the main effects findings in endorsing continued study of the operation of substitutes for leadership variables.

Lord and Smith (1999) are particularly concerned that the theory does not incorporate the fact that so-called substitutes for leadership are in many cases indirect products of managerial action. They point to the similar main effects findings for substitutes and leader behaviors as evidence that leadership processes of a kind are involved in both instances. Yet professional characteristics, to cite an example, are influenced primarily by the profession, not by managers within a firm.

Another line of, at least intended, endorsement comes from those who claim substitute status for variables not included in the original list of substitutes. One such is Peter Gronn (1999), who nominates the leadership couple (or dyad) at the top of the hierarchy as a substitute for "the single-handed leader." Apparently, he has such phenomena as the office of the president and highly cohesive top management teams in mind as well. Yet these forms certainly include the leader and leader behavior. Thus there is a serious question as to whether they are substitutes for leadership in the same sense as the Kerr and Jermier (1978) factors.

Charles Manz and Henry Sims (1980) take a similar approach in nominating the capability of the follower for self-management as a substitute. Under self-management or self-control, individuals take responsibility for their own behaviors by setting their own standards, evaluating their performance against these standards, and administering consequences to themselves as appropriate. Yet, once again, the extent to which self-management in practice operates as a true substitute may be questioned. Manz and Sims (1987) discuss the important role played by external leaders for self-managing work teams. These external leaders, or coordinators, serve to encourage self-reinforcement and self-evaluation primarily, but this is stroking behavior of a kind and falls within the definition of leader behavior. The coordinators do occupy positions within the management hierarchy, and as Bernard Bass (1990) notes, self-management requires a considerable degree of delegation on the part of these external leaders.

As with most of the other reactions to substitutes theory, the endorsers of new substitutes present a mixed picture; they like the theory and want to include something they feel quite positively toward under its umbrella, but it is not at all clear that this "substitute" fits where they want to place it. Thus they may really be promoting something other than substitutes for leadership theory.

How then does Kerr feel about the theory, now? In an interview he reacted to a question regarding what he was proud of in his work as follows:

I like very much my work on "Substitutes for Leadership." But it never had solid empirical support, and I've never wavered in my conviction that it's right. . . . I've never wavered that there's something important there. And I could be flat out wrong, but I think there's probably something in there. So I like that a lot. (Frost, 1997, p. 346)

Yet Kerr is not saying that he believes first-line leadership in hierarchic organizations will be replaced completely by other factors. That has never been his position (Kerr, Hill, & Broedling, 1986). He simply holds that factors in addition to leadership play an important role in controlling and influencing subordinates. Chemers (1997) criticizes substitutes theory on the ground that it gives too little attention to the interpersonal and emotional aspects of the leader-follower relationship. But it is entirely possible that this is indeed what accounts for the leader behavior–produced criterion variance that remains after the substitutes are deleted. Nothing that Kerr has said or written appears to contradict this conclusion.

Repositioning the Theory

That the substitutes play an important role in performance and other outcomes is clearly evident from the main effects data. What is not evident is that the substitutes truly act as substitutes for leadership. In some instances they appear to be part of leadership, and technically at least they involve processes other than substituting—neutralizing, enhancing, and supplementing. However, the major problem is that substituting for leadership implies some type of moderation of the leader behavior-outcome relationship, and research fails to establish that the substitute characteristics operate in any way as moderators. The sum total of the evidence from research is that although the "substitutes" should be retained in the revised theory that the critics are calling for, the substitute aspect itself should not.

I believe that the answer required to reposition the theory lies in the classification system proposed by Kerr and Slocum (1981) and inherent in role motivation theory (see chapter 5 in this volume). Some of the substitute characteristics are bureaucratic in nature and extend beyond direct face-to-face leader behavior; they are hierarchic methods of control and influence, such as formalization, which achieve the same results as direct hierarchic leadership but in different ways.

Some of the characteristics are primarily associated with professional systems operating to achieve control and influence in this type of system along the lines indicated in table 24.4 for organic organizations. Some of the characteristics operate primarily within group systems; the cohesiveness of work groups achieves control and influence in this manner. Finally, some characteristics achieve control and influence within task or entrepreneurial systems through the impact of pushes and pulls that are inherent in the task itself—task-inherent feedback, for instance.

My point is that hierarchic leadership behavior has no special status that requires substituting for it. It is simply one among many mechanisms used in hierarchic systems to achieving control and influence. In this view it does not matter really whether a mechanism is classified as leader behavior (direct or indirect) or not. Hierarchic systems are managed systems, and all mechanisms for control and influence that are part of these systems derive from managerial behavior in some way.

Kerr's theory is a product of its times. The central role it gives to leadership was consistent with most thinking in the field at the time and probably remains so even now. It is doubtful that much attention would have been paid to the theory if it had not emphasized the salience of the leadership concept. Yet the research evidence that has accumulated over more than 20 years seems to be telling us that what is really needed is a theory of organizational control and influence processes that merely includes direct leader behavior as one factor among many.

CONCLUSIONS

The theories considered in this chapter represent reactions against the prevailing thinking in the leadership field that has given central billing to leader behavior description and leadership styles. Implicit theories and leadership substitutes accomplish this objective in quite different ways, but, taken together, they have served to expand the domain of leadership theory and research to a substantial degree.

References

Bass, Bernard M. (1990). *Bass & Stogdill's Handbook of Leadership*. New York: Free Press.

Baumgardner, Terri L.; Lord, Robert G.; & Maher, Karen J. (1991). Perceptions of Women in Management. In Robert G. Lord & Karen J. Maher, *Leadership and Information Processing: Linking Perceptions and Performance* (pp. 95–113). Boston: Unwin Hyman.

Binning, John F., & Lord, Robert G. (1980). Boundary Conditions for Performance Cue Effects on Group Process Ratings: Familiarity versus Type of Feedback. *Organizational Behavior and Human Performance*, 26, 115–130.

Binning, John F.; Zaba, Andrea J.; & Whattam, John C. (1986). Explaining the Biasing Effects of Performance Cues in Terms of Cognitive Categorization. *Academy of Management Journal*, 29, 521–535.

Chemers, Martin M. (1997). *An Integrative Theory of Leadership*. Mahwah, NJ: Lawrence Erlbaum.

Dansereau, Fred (1995). A Dyadic Approach to Leadership: Creating and Nurturing this Approach under Fire. *Leadership Quarterly*, 6, 479–490.

Day, David V., & Lord, Robert G. (1988). Executive Leadership and Organizational Performance: Suggestions for a New Theory and Methodology. *Journal of Management*, 14, 453–464.

DeVader, Christy L.; Bateson, Allan G.; & Lord, Robert G. (1986). Attribution Theory: A Meta-Analysis of Attributional Hypotheses. In Edwin A. Locke (Ed.), *Generalizing from Laboratory to Field Settings* (pp. 63–81). Lexington, MA: D. C. Heath.

Engle, Elaine M., & Lord, Robert G. (1997). Implicit Theories, Self-Schemas, and Leader-Member Exchange. *Academy of Management Journal*, 40, 988–1010.

Filley, Alan C.; House, Robert J.; & Kerr, Steven (1976). *Managerial Process and Organizational Behavior*. Glenview, IL: Scott, Foresman.

Foti, Roseanne J.; Fraser, Scott L.; & Lord, Robert G. (1982). Effects of Leadership Labels and Prototypes on Perceptions of Political Leaders. *Journal of Applied Psychology*, 67, 326–333.

Foti, Roseanne J., & Lord, Robert G. (1987). Prototypes and Scripts: The Effects of Alternative Methods of Processing Information on Rating Accuracy. *Organizational Behavior and Human Decision Processes*, 39, 318–340.

Frost, Peter J. (1997). Bridging Academia and Business: A Conversation with Steve Kerr. *Organization Science*, 8, 332–347.

Gioia, Dennis A. (1993). Review of *Leadership and Information Processing*. *Academy of Management Review*, 18, 153–156.

Green, Stephen G., & Mitchell, Terence R. (1979). Attributional Processes of Leaders in Leader-Member Interactions. *Organizational Behavior and Human Performance*, 23, 429–458.

Gronn, Peter (1999). Substituting for Leadership: The Neglected Role of the Leadership Couple. *Leadership Quarterly*, 10, 41–62.

Haire, Mason (1956). *Psychology in Management*. New York: McGraw-Hill.

Hall, Rosalie J., & Lord, Robert G. (1995). Multi-Level Information-Processing Explanations of Followers' Leadership Perceptions. *Leadership Quarterly*, 6, 265–287.

Hauenstein, Neil M. A., & Alexander, Ralph A. (1991). Rating Ability in Performance Judgments: The Joint Influence of Implicit Theories and Intelligence. *Organizational Behavior and Human Decision Processes*, 50, 300–323.

House, Robert J., & Aditya, Ram N. (1997). The Social Scientific Study of Leadership: Quo Vadis? *Journal of Management*, 23, 409–473.

House, Robert J., & Miner, John B. (1969). Merging Management and Behavioral Theory: The Interaction between Span of Control and Group Size. *Administrative Science Quarterly*, 14, 451–464.

Howell, Jon P. (1997). "Substitutes for Leadership: Their Meaning and Measurement"—An Historical Assessment. *Leadership Quarterly*, 8, 113–116.

Howell, Jon P.; Bowen, David E.; Dorfman, Peter W.; Kerr, Steven; & Podsakoff, Philip M. (1990). Substitutes for Leadership: Effective Alternatives to Ineffective Leadership. *Organizational Dynamics*, 19(1), 21–38.

Howell, Jon P., & Dorfman, Peter W. (1981). Substitutes for Leadership: Test of a Construct. *Academy of Management Journal*, 24, 714–728.

Howell, Jon P.; Dorfman, Peter W.; & Kerr, Steven (1986). Moderator Variables in Leadership Research. *Academy of Management Review*, 11, 88–102.

Jago, Arthur G. (1994). Review of *Leadership and Information Processing*. *Administrative Science Quarterly*, 39, 345–349.

Jermier, John M., & Berkes, Leslie J. (1979). Leader Behavior in a Police Command Bureaucracy: A Closer Look at the Quasi-Military Model. *Administrative Science Quarterly*, 24, 1–23.

Jermier, John M., & Kerr, Steven (1997). "Substitutes for Leadership: Their Meaning and Measurement"—Contextual Recollections and Current Observations. *Leadership Quarterly*, 8, 95–101.

Keller, Tiffany (1999). Images of the Familiar: Individual Differences and Implicit Leadership Theories. *Leadership Quarterly*, 10, 589–607.

Kerr, Steven (1975). On the Folly of Rewarding A, While Hoping for B. *Academy of Management Journal*, 18, 769–783.

Kerr, Steven (1977). Substitutes for Leadership: Some Implications for Organizational Design. *Organization and Administrative Sciences*, 8, 135–146.

Kerr, Steven; Hill, Kenneth D.; & Broedling, Laurie (1986). The First-Line Supervisor: Phasing Out or Here to Stay? *Academy of Management Review*, 11, 103–117.

Kerr, Steven, & Jermier, John M. (1978). Substitutes for Leadership: Their Meaning and Measurement. *Organizational Behavior and Human Performance*, 22, 375–403.

Kerr, Steven, & Slocum, John W. (1981). Controlling the Performances of People in Organizations. In Paul C. Nystrom & William H. Starbuck (Eds.), *Handbook of Organizational Design* (Vol. 2, pp. 116–134). New York: Oxford University Press.

Kerr, Steven; Von Glinow, Mary A.; & Schriesheim, Janet (1977). Issues in the Study of "Professionals" in Organizations: The Case of Scientists and Engineers. *Organizational Behavior and Human Performance*, 18, 329–345.

Larson, James R. (1982). Cognitive Mechanisms Mediating the Impact of Implicit Theories of Leader Behavior on Leader Behavior Ratings. *Organizational Behavior and Human Performance*, 29, 129–140.

Lord, Robert G. (1976). Group Performance as a Function of Leadership Behavior and Task Structure: Toward an Explanatory Theory. *Organizational Behavior and Human Performance*, 17, 76–96.

Lord, Robert G. (1977). Functional Leadership Behavior: Measurement and Relation to Social Power and Leadership Perceptions. *Administrative Science Quarterly*, 22, 114–133.

Lord, Robert G. (1985). An Information Processing Approach to Social Perceptions, Leadership and Behavioral Measurement in Organizations. *Research in Organizational Behavior*, 7, 87–128.

Lord, Robert G. (1995). An Alternative Perspective on Attributional Processes. In Mark J. Martinko (Ed.), *Attribution Theory: An Organizational Perspective* (pp. 333–350). Delray Beach, FL: St. Lucie Press.

Lord, Robert G.; Binning, John F.; Rush, Michael C.; & Thomas, Jay C. (1978). The Effect of Performance Cues and Leader Behavior on Questionnaire Ratings of Leadership Behavior. *Organizational Behavior and Human Performance*, 21, 27–39.

Lord, Robert G.; Brown, Douglas J.; & Freiberg, Steven J. (1999). Understanding the Dynamics of Leadership: The Role of Follower Self-Concepts in the Leader/Follower Relationship. *Organizational Behavior and Human Decision Processes*, 78, 167–203.

Lord, Robert G.; Foti, Roseanne J.; & DeVader, Christy L. (1984). A Test of Leadership Categorization Theory: Internal Structure, Information Processing, and Leadership Perceptions. *Organizational Behavior and Human Performance*, 34, 343–378.

Lord, Robert G.; Foti, Roseanne J.; & Phillips, James S. (1982). A Theory of Leadership Categorization. In James G. Hunt, Uma Sekaran, & Chester A. Schriesheim (Eds.), *Leadership—Beyond Establishment Views* (pp. 104–121). Carbondale: Southern Illinois University Press.

Lord, Robert G., & Hall, Rosalie J. (1992). Contemporary Views of Leadership and Individual Differences. *Leadership Quarterly*, 3, 137–157.

Lord, Robert G., & Kernan, Mary C. (1987). Scripts as Determinants of Purposeful Behavior in Organizations. *Academy of Management Review*, 12, 265–277.

Lord, Robert G., & Maher, Karen J. (1989). Cognitive Processes in Industrial and Organizational Psychology. *International Review of Industrial and Organizational Psychology*, 4, 49–91.

Lord, Robert G., & Maher, Karen J. (1990). Alternative Information-Processing Models and Their Implications for Theory, Research, and Practice. *Academy of Management Review*, 15, 9–28.

Lord, Robert G., & Maher, Karen J. (1991a). Cognitive Theory in Industrial and Organizational Psychology. In Marvin D. Dunnette & Leaette M. Hough (Eds.), *Handbook of Industrial and Organizational Psychology* (Vol. 2, pp. 1–62). Palo Alto, CA: Consulting Psychologists Press.

Lord, Robert G., & Maher, Karen J. (1991b). *Leadership and Information Processing: Linking Perceptions and Performance*. Boston: Unwin Hyman.

Lord, Robert G.; Phillips, James S.; & Rush, Michael C. (1980). Effects of Sex and Personality on Perceptions of Emergent Leadership, Influence, and Social Power. *Journal of Applied Psychology*, 65, 176–182.

Lord, Robert G., & Smith, Wendy G. (1999). Leadership and the Changing Nature of Performance. In Daniel R. Ilgen & Elaine D. Pulakos (Eds.), *The Changing Nature of Performance: Implications for Staffing, Motivation, and Development* (pp. 192–239). San Francisco: Jossey-Bass.

Manz, Charles C., & Sims, Henry P. (1980). Self-Management as a Substitute for Leadership: A Social Learning Theory Perspective. *Academy of Management Review*, 5, 361–367.

Manz, Charles C., & Sims, Henry P. (1987). Leading Workers to Lead Themselves: The External Leadership of Self-Managing Work Teams. *Administrative Science Quarterly*, 32, 106–129.

Miles, Raymond E., & Snow, Charles C. (1978). *Organizational Strategy, Structure, and Process*. New York: McGraw-Hill.

Miner, John B. (1975). The Uncertain Future of the Leadership Concept: An Overview. In James G. Hunt & Lars L. Larson (Eds.), *Leadership Frontiers* (pp. 197–208). Kent, OH: Kent State University Press.

Newell, Allen, & Simon, Herbert A. (1972). *Human Problem Solving*. Englewood Cliffs, NJ: Prentice Hall.

Palich, Leslie E., & Hom, Peter W. (1992). The Impact of Leader Power and Behavior on Leadership Perceptions: A LISREL Test of an Expanded Categorization Theory of Leadership Model. *Group and Organization Management*, 17, 279–296.

Phillips, James S. (1984). The Accuracy of Leadership Ratings: A Cognitive Categorization Perspective. *Organizational Behavior and Human Performance*, 33, 125–138.

Phillips, James S., & Lord, Robert G. (1981). Causal Attributions and Perceptions of Leadership. *Organizational Behavior and Human Performance*, 28, 143–163.

Phillips, James S., & Lord, Robert G. (1982). Schematic Information Processing and Perceptions of Leadership in Problem-Solving Groups. *Journal of Applied Psychology*, 67, 486–492.

Pitcher, Patricia; Chreim, Samia; & Kisfalvi, Veronika (2000). CEO Succession Research: Methodological Bridges over Troubled Waters. *Strategic Management Journal*, 21, 625–648.

Podsakoff, Philip M., & MacKenzie, Scott B. (1994). An Examination of the Psychometric Properties and Nomological Validity of Some Revised and Reduced Substitutes for Leadership Scales. *Journal of Applied Psychology*, 79, 702–713.

Podsakoff, Philip M., & MacKenzie, Scott B. (1995). An Examination of Substitutes for Leadership within a Levels-of-Analysis Framework. *Leadership Quarterly*, 6, 289–328.

Podsakoff, Philip M., & MacKenzie, Scott B. (1997). Kerr and Jermier's Substitutes for Leadership Model: Background, Empirical Assessment, and Suggestions for Future Research. *Leadership Quarterly*, 8, 117–125.

Podsakoff, Philip M.; MacKenzie, Scott B.; Ahearne, Mike; & Bommer, William H. (1995). Searching for a Needle in a Haystack: Trying to Identify the Illusive Moderators of Leadership Behaviors. *Journal of Management*, 21, 422–470.

Podsakoff, Philip M.; MacKenzie, Scott B.; & Bommer, William H. (1996a). Meta-Analysis of the Relationships between Kerr and Jermier's Substitutes for Leadership and Employee Job Attitudes, Role Perceptions, and Performance. *Journal of Applied Psychology*, 81, 380–399.

Podsakoff, Philip M.; MacKenzie, Scott B.; & Bommer, William H. (1996b). Transformational Leader Behaviors and Substitutes for Leadership as Determinants of Employee Satisfaction, Commitment, Trust, and Organizational Citizenship Behaviors. *Journal of Management*, 22, 259–298.

Podsakoff, Philip M.; MacKenzie, Scott, B.; & Fetter, Richard (1993). Substitutes for Leadership and the Management of Professionals. *Leadership Quarterly*, 4, 1–44.

Podsakoff, Philip M.; Niehoff, Brian P.; MacKenzie, Scott B.; & Williams, Margaret L. (1993). Do Substitutes for Leadership Really Substitute for Leadership? An Empirical Examination of Kerr and Jermier's Situational Leadership Model. *Organizational Behavior and Human Decision Processes*, 54, 1–44.

Podsakoff, Philip M.; Todor, William D.; Grover, Richard A.; & Huber, Vandra L. (1984). Situational Moderators of Leader Reward and Punishment Behaviors: Fact or Fiction. *Organizational Behavior and Human Performance*, 34, 21–63.

Rush, Michael C.; Phillips, James S.; & Lord, Robert G. (1981). Effects of a Temporal Delay in Rating on Leader Behavior Descriptions: A Laboratory Investigation. *Journal of Applied Psychology*, 66, 442–450.

Rush, Michael C.; Thomas, Jay C.; & Lord, Robert G. (1977). Implicit Leadership Theory: A Potential Threat to the Internal Validity of Leader Behavior Questionnaires. *Organizational Behavior and Human Performance*, 20, 93–110.

Schriesheim, Chester A. (1997). Substitutes for Leadership Theory: Development and Basic Concepts. *Leadership Quarterly*, 8, 103–108.

Sheridan, John E.; Vredenburgh, Donald J.; & Abelson, Michael A. (1984). Contextual Model of Leadership Influence in Hospital Units. *Academy of Management Journal*, 27, 57–78.

Tosi, Henry (1992). *The Environment/Organization/Person Contingency Model: A Meso Approach to the Study of Organizations*. Greenwich, CT: JAI Press.

Tosi, Henry L., & Kiker, Scott (1997). Commentary on "Substitutes for Leadership." *Leadership Quarterly*, 8, 109–112.

Weick, Karl E. (1993). Review of *Leadership and Information Processing. Leadership Quarterly*, 4,109–113.

Weiss, Howard M., & Adler, Seymour (1981). Cognitive Complexity and the Structure of Implicit Leadership Theories. *Journal of Applied Psychology*, 66, 69–78.

Williams, Margaret L.; Podsakoff, Philip M.; Todor, William D.; Huber, Vandra L.; Howell, Jon P.; & Dorfman, Peter W. (1988). A Preliminary Analysis of the Construct Validity of Kerr & Jermier's Substitutes for Leadership Scales. *Journal of Occupational Psychology*, 61, 307–333.

Woodward, Joan (1970). *Industrial Organization: Behavior and Control*. London: Oxford University Press.

Yukl, Gary (1998). *Leadership in Organizations*. Upper Saddle River, NJ: Prentice Hall.

Chapter 25

Charismatic and
Transformational Theories

The theories in this chapter have somewhat closer links to the leader behavior description constructs than those in the preceding chapter. The tension between prevailing theoretical approaches and alternative constructions has clearly been perpetuated into the second generation of leadership thinking. Here we put a few more pieces of this leadership puzzle into place.

There are a number of leadership theories of the second generation that emphasize such matters as the emotional attachment followers feel for the leader, the arousal of followers by the leader, enhancement of follower commitment to the mission set forth by the leader, follower trust and confidence in the leader, follower value orientations, and follower intrinsic motives. Leadership of this kind gives meaningfulness to follower activities by providing a sense of moral purpose and commitment. Leader behavior remains of concern, but it deals with symbolic acts, visionary messages, intellectual stimulation, displays of confidence in self and followers as well, expectations of personal sacrifice, and exhortations to performance beyond normal requirements (Shamir, House, & Arthur, 1993). Theories of this nature have their origins in the concept of charisma as articulated by Max Weber (see chapter 3 in this volume). They attempt to build on that construct, to fill in the blanks and iron out the inconsistencies, as well as to formulate propositions and hypotheses that are readily testable.

Two theories of this kind are detailed and evaluated in this chapter—Robert House's charismatic leadership theory and Bernard Bass's theory of transformational, as opposed to transactional, leadership. These formulations are the best known and most widely researched of the genre. They are not identical, nor are they the same as other theories on the same topic, but all of these theories have much in common, presumably because all are rooted in Weber's writings. We will consider House's charismatic leadership theory first, simply because it came into being first.

CHARISMATIC LEADERSHIP THEORY

House has been mentioned frequently in these pages, most notably in chapter 10, which was concerned with his path-goal theory. In 1996 he formulated an updated version of that theory as it related to work unit leadership (House, 1996). This statement lists 26 propositions that were categorized under the leader behaviors involved. One of the latter is labeled value-based behavior (articulate a vision, display passion for the vision, demonstrate confidence in vision attainment, arouse nonconscious relevant follower motives, take risks to attain the vision, communicate high expectations, use symbolic behaviors to emphasize vision values, exhibit positive evaluations of followers frequently). Three propositions dealing with value-based leadership are specified: numbers 23, 24, and 25.

All this sounds very much like charismatic leadership, and in fact it is. The charismatic theory had existed for almost 20 years at this point, and the three propositions of path-goal theory represent an attempt to bridge the two approaches. Yet in many respects path-goal theory is an effort to deal with the task of supervising work units within hierarchic organizations, while charismatic theory more often deals with leading organizations as a whole. In spite of the three propositions, the two theories tend to function in separate domains.

Background

House's background is described in chapter 10 and need not be repeated here. However, the background of his charismatic theory is of interest. The debt to Weber has already been noted. In addition, a major influence stemmed from the political science and sociological literature that built on Weber, including Amatai Etzioni's work (see chapter 19 in this volume). Into this background House integrated certain of the relevant research from psychology. He was particularly influenced by the thinking of David McClelland (see chapter 6 in this volume), which was interpreted for him by David Berlew, a former student of McClelland's. He says, "I learned a great deal from my conversations with Dave. He was a major influence on my thinking and the stimulus for the development of the 1976 theory" (House, 1993, p. 63).

I should note, to avoid confusion, that McClelland's theory also spawned a theoretical thrust that focused specifically on power in organizations and the role of power motivation (House, 1988). This thrust ultimately was extended to the nature of power relationships in organic and mechanistic organizations as considered here in chapter 15 (House, 1991, 1992). This work by House on power is closely related to the charismatic leadership theory, but it is an independent theory and is not treated directly here.

Diverse Array of Propositions

House's charismatic theory is stated in terms of various sets of propositions that extend from 1977 to 1999, and which may in fact not yet be ended. However, the key propositions of the theory appear, at least at this point, to have already been set in print.

Initial 1976 Theory

House (1977) defines charismatic leadership as referring to a leader who has charismatic effects on followers to an unusually high degree. These effects include devotion, trust, unquestioned obedience, loyalty, commitment, identification, confidence in the ability to achieve goals, and radical changes in beliefs and values. This definition is said to be free of tautology because the effects are operationally determined by independent observers.

The propositions follow:

1. Characteristics that differentiate leaders who have charismatic effects on subordinates from leaders who do not have such charismatic effects are dominance and self-confidence, need for influence, and a strong conviction in the moral righteousness of their beliefs. (In a footnote House indicates he would accept intellectual fortitude and integrity of character, as well as speech fluency or capacity for ready communication, as additional characteristics.)

2. The more favorable the perceptions of the potential follower toward a leader, the more the follower will model (a) the valences of the leader; (b) the expectations of the leader that effective performance will result in desired or undesired outcomes for the follower; (c) the emotional responses of the leader to work-related stimuli; and (d) the attitudes of the leader toward work and toward the organization. Here "favorable perceptions" is defined as the perceptions of the leader as attractive, nurturant, successful, or competent.

3. Leaders who have charismatic effects are more likely to engage in behaviors that are designed to create the impression of competence and success than are leaders who do not have such effects.

4. Leaders who have charismatic effects are more likely to articulate ideological goals than are leaders who do not have such effects.

5. Leaders who simultaneously communicate high expectations of and confidence in followers are more likely to have followers who accept the goals of the leader and believe that they can contribute to goal accomplishment and are more likely to have followers who strive to meet specific and challenging performance standards.

6. Leaders who have charismatic effects are more likely to engage in behaviors that arouse motives relevant to the accomplishment of the mission than are leaders who do not have charismatic effects. [In a footnote House indicates that the leader's ability to arouse subordinate motives is hypothesized to be a function of the extent to which subordinates hold favorable leader perceptions as specified in no. 2 above.]

7. Leaders are more likely to have charismatic effects in situations stressful for followers than in nonstressful situations. Further, it can be hypothesized that persons with the characteristics of dominance, self-confidence, need for influence, and strong convictions will be more likely to emerge as leaders under stressful conditions. Whether or not follower distress is a necessary condition for leaders to have charismatic effects or for persons with such characteristics to emerge as leaders is an empirical question that remains to be tested. [This paragraph is not stated as a numbered proposition, but it appears to be no. 7.]

8. A necessary condition for a leader to have charismatic effects is that the role of followers be definable in ideological terms that appeal to the follower. (House, 1977, pp. 194, 196–198, 201, 203–205)

Figure 25.1 is presented as a summary statement of the theory. Note that what would have been proposition no. 7, regarding situations stressful for followers, is not depicted in the figure. Also, a subsequent restatement of the theory (House & Baetz, 1979) fails to include the enigmatic proposition no. 7.

Personality and Charisma

There is roughly a 10-year gap in the published work on charisma theory at this point, although efforts in this area appear to have continued (House, 1993). What finally did emerge, however, on the theoretical front is a set of finely tuned hypotheses suitable (and indeed used) for empirical testing purposes. These hypotheses were a component of a research program in which documents related to the behavior and personality characteristics of U.S. presidents were analyzed. The research itself will be considered later, but what is important at this point is how these hypotheses tie into the theoretical perspective.

In the first instances the hypotheses are as follows:

1. The biographies of cabinet members reporting to charismatic U.S. presidents (will) include more incidents of positive affective relations with the presidents and more positive affective reactions to their positions than (will) noncharismatic United States presidents.

2. The biographies of cabinet members reporting to charismatic U.S. presidents (will) include more incidents of charismatic behaviors on the part of the presidents than (will) biographies of noncharismatic presidents. (House, Woycke, & Fodor, 1988)

In the second instance, hypotheses dealing with charisma are specified as follows:

1. Presidential behavioral charisma will be positively related to presidential need for power and presidential activity inhibition and negatively related to presidential needs for achievement and affiliation.

2. Presidential behavioral charisma will be positively related to presidential performance. This relationship will remain after control-

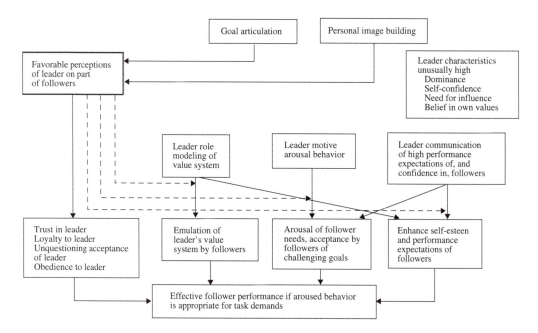

FIGURE 25.1 A model of charismatic leadership (Dashed line indicates a moderated relationship between leader and follower responses; leader characteristics are combined in a "possibly additive and possibly interactive" manner.) From Robert J. House (1977), A 1976 Theory of Charismatic Leadership, in James G. Hunt & Lars L. Larson (Eds.), *Leadership: The Cutting Edge* (Carbondale: Southern Illinois University Press), 206. Copyright 1977 by Southern Illinois University Press. Reprinted with permission.

ling for the effects of presidential motives on overall performance and on presidential behavioral charisma.

3. There will be positive relationships between presidential performance and need for power and activity inhibition, and there will be negative relationships between presidential performance and needs for achievement and affiliation, independent of any effects of motives on performance via behavioral charisma.

4. Crises are positively related to presidential behavioral charisma and presidential performance.

5. The institutional age of the presidency is positively related to presidential motives, level of crises within administrations, presidential behavioral charisma, and presidential performance. (House, Spangler, & Woycke, 1991, pp. 368–371)

These hypotheses derive from what is referred to as the integrated House-McClelland model. This model is developed further elsewhere (House & Howell, 1992) with the specification of the characteristics

of what are termed socialized and personalized charismatic leaders. The model does indeed draw on ideas advanced by McClelland about managers in hierarchic organizations, and it does appear to be aligned with House's (1977) earlier propositions on charismatic leaders. Yet it is well to recognize that McClelland's research was not dealing with charismatic leaders, only effective line managers.

Socialized charismatic leadership is defined to include (1) a basis for egalitarian behavior, (2) the services of collective interests rather than the leader's self-interest, and (3) the development and empowerment of others. Hypothesized characteristics of the socialized type are a high need for power, combined with high activity inhibition, a low level of Machiavellian behavior, nonauthoritarianism, internal beliefs, and high self-esteem.

Personalized charismatic leadership, by contrast, is defined as (1) being based on personal dominance and authoritarian behavior, (2) serving the self-interest of the leader and consequently self-aggrandizing, and (3) being exploitive of others. Such people are hypothesized to possess a high need for power in conjunction with low activity inhibition, high levels of Machiavellian behavior, high narcissism, high authoritarianism, external beliefs, and low self-esteem.

Motivational Effects of Charismatic Leadership

The next major extension of the theory involved an attempt to explain more fully the relationships between leader behaviors and their effects on followers (Shamir et al., 1993). These formulations begin with a set of assumptions about human motivation and the self-concept:

1. People are not only pragmatic and goal-oriented but also self-expressive.
2. People are motivated to maintain and enhance their self-esteem and self-worth.
3. People are motivated to retain and increase their sense of self-consistency.
4. Self-concepts are composed at least partially of identities that include values and links to society.
5. People may be motivated by faith, which is not the same as expectancies. (Shamir et al., 1993, p. 580)

Charismatic leaders achieve their effects by implicating followers' self-concepts. This, in turn, is accomplished by increasing the intrinsic valence of effort, increasing effort-accomplishment expectancies, increasing the intrinsic valence of goal accomplishment, instilling faith in a better future, and creating personal commitment. These motivational processes are activated by role modeling, whereby the leader assumes the role of a representative character, and by frame alignment, in accordance with which a set of follower values and beliefs become congruent and complementary with the leader's activities, goals, and ideology.

The theoretical propositions are then stated as follows:

1. In order to implicate the followers' self-concepts, compared to noncharismatic leaders, the deliberate and nondeliberate messages of charismatic leaders will contain:
   a. more references to values and moral justifications,
   b. more references to the collective and to collective identity,
   c. more references to history,
   d. more positive references to followers' worth and efficacy as individuals and as a collective,
   e. more expressions of high expectations from followers,
   f. more references to distal goals and less reference to proximal goals.
2. The more leaders exhibit the behavior specified above, the more their followers will have:
   a. a high salience of the collective identity in their self-concept,
   b. a sense of consistency between their self-concept and their actions on behalf of the leader and the collective.
   c. a high level of self-esteem and self-worth.
   d. a similarity between their self-concept and their perception of the leader.
   e. a high sense of collective efficacy.
3. The more leaders exhibit the behaviors specified in the theory the more followers will demonstrate:
   a. personal commitment to the leader and the mission,
   b. a willingness to make sacrifices for the collective mission,
   c. organizational citizenship behavior,
   d. meaningfulness in their work and lives.
4. A necessary condition for a leader's messages to have charismatic effects is that the message is congruent with the existing values and identities held by potential followers.
5. The more the potential followers have an expressive orientation toward work and life, the more susceptible they will be to the influence of charismatic leaders.
6. The more the potential followers have a principled orientation to social relations, the more susceptible they will be to the influence of charismatic leaders.
7. The emergence and effectiveness of charismatic leaders will be facilitated to the extent to which:
   a. There is an opportunity for substantial moral involvement on the part of the leader and the followers,
   b. Performance goals cannot be easily specified and measured,
   c. Extrinsic rewards cannot be made clearly contingent on individual performance,
   d. There are few situational cues, constraints and reinforcers to guide behavior and provide incentives for specific performance,
   e. Exceptional effort, behavior and sacrifices are required of both the leaders and follow-

ers. (Shamir, House, & Arthur, 1993, pp. 586–590)

In this context, the authors indicate that exceptional circumstances are not necessary for charismatic leadership to emerge; that exceptional conditions do not necessarily carry the implication of crisis, since opportunities may be involved as well; and that when crisis-handling and charisma occur together, the effects tend to be short-term. Here charismatic leadership and crises are clearly unbundled in seeming contradiction to the House (1977) position.

Integrating Charismatic Theory

House and Boas Shamir (1993) in a book chapter attempt an integration of the various theories with roots in Weber's charisma, focusing on the treatment of charismatic behaviors. They do this by again specifying a set of propositions that collectively are said to accomplish this integrative purpose. The first such proposition is in reality a version of proposition no. 2 given in the previous section. However, now a sixth consequence is added, apparently taken from proposition no. 3 of the same set: a higher sense of meaningfulness in their work and lives.

The following three propositions are closely aligned with those stated previously as well:

> 2. Leaders who have charismatic effects are more likely to engage in behaviors that arouse motives relevant to the accomplishment of the mission than are those who do not have charismatic effects.
> 3. Leaders who have charismatic effects are more likely to arouse motives in the context of references to the mission and the collective than are those who do not have charismatic effects.
> 4. Leaders who have charismatic effects are more likely to behave in a manner that provides a personal and vivid example of the values of the mission than are leaders who do not. (House & Shamir, 1993, pp. 90–91)

The last two propositions reflect an acceptance of ideas that were previously embodied in theories other than House's:

> 5. Leaders who have charismatic effects are more likely to challenge the assumptions, stereotypes, generalizations, and worldviews (weltanschauung) of followers than are leaders who do not have such effects.

> 6. Followers who are in charismatic relationships with their leaders are more likely to be intellectually stimulated by their leader's challenges to their assumptions, stereotypes, generalizations, and worldviews than are followers who are not in such a relationship. (House & Shamir, 1993, pp. 95, 100)

In spite of these latter formulations and the goal of producing an integrated theory, as well as the use of terminology from expectancy and path-goal approaches to theorizing as reflected in figure 25.2, there remain a number of differences among theories. Certain of these are noted by House and Shamir (1993); we will consider these differences in greater detail later in this chapter.

In another book chapter published at roughly the same time, House and Philip Podsakoff (1994) also argue for integration and apply the term *outstanding* (and outstanding leadership theory) to the various ideas dealing with charismatic, transformational, and visionary leadership phenomena; in this view, charismatic leadership is one form of the outstanding type, but all three constructs are closely related.

In this same publication the authors note certain behaviors that are "not associated with outstanding leadership" but which are advocated by other theorists. Among these are individualized consideration, environmental monitoring, leader adaptability, and intellectual stimulation. Yet in proposition no. 6 of House and Shamir (1993), intellectually stimulating behavior is accepted into charismatic leadership theory.

Rhetoric of Charisma

Based on prior theorizing, especially that dealing with motivational effects (Shamir et al., 1993), Shamir, Michael Arthur, and House (1994) set forth a set of propositions regarding the content of charismatic leaders' speeches, as opposed to the content of speeches by noncharismatic leaders. These propositions read as follows:

Charismatic speeches will contain

> 1. More references to collective history and to the continuity between the past and the present
> 2. More references to the collective and to collective identity, and fewer references to individual self-interest
> 3. More positive references to followers' worth and efficacy as individuals and as a collective

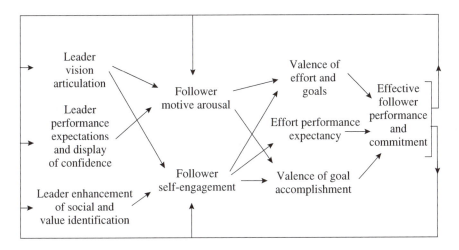

FIGURE 25.2 Model of the charismatic leadership process. From Robert J. House & Boas Shamir (1993), Toward the Integration of Transformational, Charismatic, and Visionary Theories, in Martin M. Chemers & Roya Ayman (Eds.), *Leadership Theory and Research: Perspectives and Directions* (San Diego: Academic Press), 88. Copyright 1993 by Academic Press. Reprinted with permission.

4. More references to the leader's similarity to followers and identification with followers

5. More references to values and moral justifications, and fewer references to tangible outcomes and instrumental justifications

6. More references to distal goals and the distant future, and fewer references to proximal goals and the near future

7. More references to hope and faith (Shamir et al., 1994, p. 29)

Homogeneity of Charisma among Followers

A set of propositions dealing with the homogeneity of charismatic reactions among followers is proposed by Katherine Klein and House (1995). The idea is that charisma may flow from the leader fairly evenly to the various group members, or it may settle in pockets within the group. These propositions regarding the diffusion of charismatic effects are as follows:

1. A leader may share charismatic relationships with (a) all of his or her followers (high group-level charisma), (b) some of his or her followers (variable, dyad-level charisma), or (c) none of his or her followers (low group-level charisma).

2. The more a leader treats all of his or her followers in a consistent fashion, the more homogeneous the level of charisma characterizing each follower's relationship with the leader.

3. The greater the homogeneity in the nature of subordinates' values and orientations to work and to social relations, the greater the homogeneity of the charisma shared by each subordinate and the leader.

4. Charisma among the followers of a leader with charismatic qualities is likely to be homogeneous when (a) followers have sought membership in the leader's following, (b) followers were selected by the leader, and (c) both the leader and the followers have opted to keep the followers within the group.

5. The greater the follower's task interdependence and interaction, the more homogeneous the charisma that characterizes each follower's relationship with their common leader.

6. The higher the average level of charisma *and* the greater the homogeneity of charismatic relations between a leader and his or her follower, the higher the morale and performance of the group.

7. The higher the average level of charisma *and* the greater the homogeneity of charismatic relations between a leader and his or her followers, the higher the risk of groupthink among the group.

8. Task interdependence and social interaction moderate the consequences of low homoge-

neity of charisma among the followers of a leader. When task interdependence and interaction are low, low homogeneity of charisma yields independent, dyadic relations with the leader. When task interdependence and interaction are high, high homogeneity of charisma yields intergroup conflict. (Klein & House, 1995, pp. 187, 189–190, 192–193)

In addition to the ideas about homogeneity that are inherent in these propositions, this article contains certain other significant statements. Both crises and a variety of environmental conditions that merely arouse uncertainty may give rise to charismatic leadership. The confluence of events that produce true, group-level charisma occurs only rarely; in this respect, charisma seems like Abraham Maslow's view of self-actualization (see chapter 6 in this volume). Thus, charismatic leadership training may well produce better subordinate relations, but it is unlikely to yield group-level charisma. The building of a group of subordinates who are open to charisma is a gradual process.

Reformulations for the Future

A chapter written by House (1995) covers much of the ground included in previous sets of propositions. However, there are some new ideas and some different ways of looking at old ones as well. The generic behaviors of outstanding leaders are described in a manner that appears to invoke "outstanding," as used in House and Podsakoff (1994). These behaviors are vision; passion and self-sacrifice; confidence, determination, and persistence; selective motive arousal; risk taking; expectations of and confidence in followers; developmental orientation; role modeling; and demonstration of integrity; frame alignment; and symbolic behavior. Some of these are more closely aligned with House's earlier positions than others, although he now appears to accept all.

Propositions dealing with charisma are sprinkled throughout the chapter:

1. The aforementioned leader behaviors will differentiate outstanding leaders from others in the twenty-first century.
2. When followers experience a high degree of stress or stressful uncertainty, the emergence and perceived effectiveness of leaders who engage in the aforementioned leadership behaviors will be enhanced.
3. Whenever the roles of followers can be authen-

tically described or defined as providing an opportunity for moral involvement, the potential leader can articulate ideological goals and values and have a strong influence on the motivational states of followers.
4. The emergence of outstanding leadership will be enhanced to the extent that
   a. performance goals cannot be easily specified and measured
   b. extrinsic rewards cannot be made clearly contingent on individual performance
   c. few situational cues, constraints, and reinforcers exist to guide behavior and provide incentives for specific performance
   d. exceptional effort, behavior, and sacrifices are required of both leaders and followers
   e. potential followers experience feelings of unfair treatment, persecution, and oppression from sources other than the leader.
5. Neocharismatic leadership causes followers to recognize values that are shared with the leader and among the members of the collective; arouses in followers powerful nonconscious motives, engages followers' strongly held self-concepts such as self-efficacy and self-worth, and brings about strong follower identification with the vision and the collective. (House, 1995, pp. 421–422, 424, 438)

Phases of Charismatic Change

The most recent set of propositions, as of this writing, uses the unfreezing-moving-refreezing model proposed by Kurt Lewin (see chapter 2 in this volume) to specify what happens at each phase of a charismatic transformation (Fiol, Harris, & House, 1999). These ideas are predicated on the finding from Spangler and House (1991) that the use of the word "not" in presidential writings and speeches may reflect a leader's motivation to break current frames through negation. This interpretation differs from McClelland's position that the use of "not" provides a measure of activity inhibition. The propositions advanced are as follows:

1. Charismatic leaders will use the word "not" more often than non-charismatic leaders.
2. A. During a transformation, charismatic leaders will use the word "not" frequently during the initial phase, more frequently during the middle phase, and infrequently during later phases.
   B. The use of "nots" by non-charismatic

leaders will not follow the curvilinear pattern of charismatic leaders.

3. Charismatic leaders will use more inclusive language than non-charismatic leaders.

4. Charismatic leaders will communicate at higher levels of abstraction than non-charismatic leaders.

5. All effective leaders will use more inclusive language with higher levels of abstraction.

6. A. During a transformation, charismatic leaders will use higher levels of inclusion and abstraction during the middle phase than in earlier or later phases.

B. The use of inclusion and abstraction by non-charismatic leaders will not follow the curvilinear pattern of charismatic leaders. (Fiol et al., 1999, pp. 462–463)

Although this is the end of his theorizing for present purposes, House (1999) does take the occasion of a response to criticism to clarify certain theoretical points. One such clarification is to emphasize that charisma in any form is in his view a rare phenomenon. Another points to the relationship of crisis and follower stress to charismatic leadership. The position stated is that some form of severe threat or stress experienced by followers operates to facilitate charismatic leadership, both as to its emergence and as to its effectiveness.

Evaluation and Impact

There is a chicken and egg problem in relating research to theory in the domain of charismatic leadership. Undoubtedly, the 1976 theory did precede the research to be considered, and thus that research, to the extent it is relevant, can be treated as theory testing. But as the theoretical propositions have evolved since, from 1988 to 1999, it becomes very difficult to disentangle research that prompted theory from research that evaluates it. This problem of theoretical source is compounded as House and his colleagues have moved from the basic charismatic theory to more integrated positions dealing with outstanding or neocharismatic leadership; these integrated considerations attempt, not always successfully, to bring together the theories of House and Bernard Bass, as well as other related formulations.

U.S. Presidents Research Program

A series of studies were undertaken by House and others working with him to look into the charismatic leadership process using U.S. presidents and documents relating to them. This research program appears to provide some direct tests of stated theory.

The initial study tested the hypotheses stated by House et al. (1988), which, in turn, relate closely to the 1976 theory (House 1977). The biographies of cabinet members of presidents determined by historians to be charismatic leaders were content analyzed and compared with similar data on noncharismatic leaders. Although sample sizes are small, significance was obtained. There was evidence that charismatic presidents had more charismatic effects on their cabinet members in terms of the frequency of affective responses aroused. Also these same presidents were found to exhibit more charismatic behaviors—display of self-confidence, high performance expectations, confidence in follower abilities, strong ideological goals, and individualized consideration for followers. The hypotheses were confirmed.

The next study used the cabinet member biographies plus a host of other sources to derive measures of presidential motivation (power, achievement, affiliation), activity inhibition (the use of "not"), crises faced, charisma, and performance (House et al., 1991). The results provide considerable support for the five hypotheses, particularly those that involve power motivation. Personality factors in a president do appear to make a difference in both charisma and performance. The data are least strong for the hypothesized negative relationships involving affiliation motivation. Consistent with hypothesis 4, crises faced were positively related to both charisma and performance. Thus both leader personality and contextual variables appear to be operating when charisma is engaged.

A less compelling study used content analysis of a speech given by Jesse Jackson to the Democratic National Convention to exemplify the seven propositions advanced by Shamir et al. (1994). The data are consistent with the propositions, but the findings are not presented in quantitative terms, and they include one speech by one former presidential candidate who was widely considered to be a charismatic leader.

Fiol et al. (1999) return to the data on past presidents, specifically to the use of negation in presidential speeches. The findings consistently support the propositions. Charismatic leaders do exhibit patterns of rhetoric involving not only the use of negation, but also inclusive language and high levels of abstraction. The phase variations anticipated based on Lewin's concept of change are clearly in evidence.

Recently House has taken the study of charisma global, working with a large number of colleagues in countries around the world. Only preliminary results on this program are available, but data from managers in over 50 countries indicate considerable agreement on the attributes and behaviors perceived to enhance charismatic leadership. The results indicate that charismatic leaders are universally seen as positive, encouraging, foresightful, planning ahead, motive arousers, confidence builders, dynamic, and motivational (Den-Hartog, House, Hanges, Ruiz-Quintanilla, & Dorfman, 1999). Thus considerable cross-cultural consistency exists in the way charisma is defined. Furthermore, this consistency appears around factors that are often the same as those earlier hypothesized by House.

Authors' Compendium of Support

In presenting many of their theoretical statements, the theory's authors open with a quick overview of existing studies said to support charismatic leadership theory in some form. These treatments refer to "at least twenty empirical investigations" (House et al., 1991), "at least 35 empirical investigations" (Shamir et al., 1993), "numerous studies" (House & Shamir, 1993), "over 30 studies" (House & Podsakoff, 1994), and the like. In most instances there is little discussion of the content of these studies, only the statement that they contain supporting evidence. The uncritical reader might well jump to the conclusion that this is proven theory.

These are reports of research in some form, a number of them qualitative studies, dating from the 1980s and early 1990s. A large number have not been formally published (dissertations, working papers, speeches, etc.) and thus are not readily available for review. Several relate primarily to Bass's transformational theory and will be considered later in this chapter. In other instances the studies appear to bear on charismatic leadership theory, but they were not undertaken specifically for the purpose of testing it. The authors cast a wide net and sometimes find research of a very tangential nature. There is nothing wrong with attempting to put a positive spin on one's theory, but the uncritical reader does need to be forewarned—things are not quite as positive as they are made out to be.

An example of a study cited to support charismatic theory, but clearly not conducted to test that theory is Gary Yukl and David Van Fleet (1982). Yet there are tests in this period, and good ones. This point is best illustrated with reference to two laboratory studies, not exactly the kind of research one would anticipate in the charismatic leadership domain.

In the first of these studies charismatic leadership as portrayed by professional actresses was compared with the more traditional initiating structure and consideration (Howell & Frost, 1989). Individuals working under charismatic leaders had higher task performance on various indices, higher satisfaction, and less role conflict than those working under consideration behavior. In comparison to initiating structure, charisma produced much the same effects as with consideration, but overall the differences were somewhat less pronounced. The findings are interpreted as consistent with House's 1976 theory.

The other study, also conducted with students, dealt with the effects of a crisis related to course grades. The reported results are as follow:

> Conditions of crisis facilitate the emergence of leaders who are perceived to be charismatic. Furthermore, such leaders are also perceived as more effective and more satisfying to followers than their less charismatic counterparts. . . . The increased charismatic appeal of leaders under conditions of crisis is particularly noteworthy in the absence of any evidence of the impact of crisis on ratings of transactional leadership. (Pillai & Meindl, 1991, p. 238)

To the extent charismatic theory anticipates such crisis effects, the theory is supported. But there has been some uncertainty in this regard.

Before turning to the more recent research, mention should be made of a study from the early period which has not been cited by House and his colleagues. This study involved the creation of an instrument directly from the charismatic effects specified in House (1977). An argument is then developed indicating that these effects may be reduced to the more mundane constructs of expert power, referent power, and job involvement (Halpert, 1990). Correlational analyses were then carried out, which indicate that, indeed, the reduction appears justified. The equating of charisma with power is certainly consistent with theory, but the findings also seem to remove any heroic quality from charismatic leadership. This is a finding that clearly calls for further research.

Recent Research on Personality

The second half of the 1990s saw a substantial number of research publications that advanced understanding of charismatic leadership considerably. Among these studies was one bearing on Jane Halpert's (1990) assertions. Jeffrey Kudisch, Mark Poteet, Gregory Dobbins, Michael Rush, and Joyce Russell (1995) found that leader charisma added to the prediction of subordinate attitudes above and beyond the variance accounted for by expert and referent power; thus charisma is distinguishable from these two types of power. However, the study did not consider job involvement and measured charisma quite broadly. Furthermore, the findings do replicate Halpert's (1990) results as to the important role played by expert and referent power in charismatic leadership.

Other studies add to the understanding of personality factors in charismatic leadership. In one such instance, historical figures who were categorized from biographical documents as exhibiting either socialized or personalized charismatic leadership were compared to establish the distinguishing characteristics of personalized charisma. Personalized leaders were viewed as more harmful to others, more aggressive, and less moral, and they generated more negative comments from biographers. In terms of personality, they exhibited an uninhibited need for power, a view of others as instruments to be used for one's own purposes, a destructive image of the world, a belief that personal goals would not be achieved because of prevailing uncertainties, narcissism (selfishness and a propensity to overvalue one's own achievements), and a fear that promoted strong self-protective tendencies. However, self-regulation and self-monitoring did not distinguish the two groups (O'Connor, Mumford, Clifton, Gessner, & Connelly, 1995). The theoretical distinction between socialized and personalized charismatic leadership receives considerable support.

Another biographical study focused on U.S. presidents and found that narcissism was associated not only with charisma but also with a variety of indices of performance effectiveness (Deluga, 1997). Unfortunately, this research did not deal directly with the socialized versus personalized distinction. Yet a subsequent effort utilized the same database to focus on the role of proactivity, which was defined as a disposition to influence the environment (Deluga, 1998). This characteristic deals with such behaviors as influencing followers, seizing opportunities for change, demonstrating initiative, and persevering in actions. Again, the personality variable emerges as playing an important role in both charismatic leadership and presidential effectiveness. This role appears to extend beyond any such roles played by the needs for power, achievement, or affiliation.

Recent Research on Crises

The role of crises in promoting charismatic leadership has continued to be a topic of research interest. In a retrospective analysis Rajnandini Pillai and James Meindl (1998) found that crises and stress were associated with lower, or reduced, perceptions of leader charisma, apparently because after the crisis ends there is a fall-off in the attribution of charisma by followers. This, however, does not controvert the previous conclusion that crises facilitate the *emergence* of charismatic leadership. This study is also significant in indicating that situational factors other than crises, namely organic structures and work group collective values, are related to charismatic leadership; both organicism and values are important to the nurturance of charisma.

A longitudinal study by James Hunt, Kimberly Boal, and George Dodge (1999) provides considerable support for the previous findings. These researchers identified two kinds of charismatic leadership: a visionary type and a crisis-responsive type. Over time, the effects of crisis-responsive charismatic leadership tend to decay, while this decline does not appear with the visionary type. However, this study did not find the same consistent positive effects of charisma on performance that others have observed. Overall, it appears that House's initial uncertainty regarding the effects of crises was justified. The relationships involved are complex, but crises are clearly more strongly related to charisma emergence and the early phases than to continued manifestation and termination.

Recent Research on Behavior

An aspect of charismatic behavior that has received recent attention is some type of self-sacrificing activity where there is either abandonment or postponement of personal interests or welfare (Choi & Mai-Dalton, 1999); this is part of the House theory. As hypothesized, self-sacrificing behavior is found to exhibit positive effects on charisma in both student and industrial samples. In a laboratory study Stefani Yorges, Howard Weiss, and Oriel Strickland (1999) obtained much the same result. Sacrifice led to charismatic ascriptions and thus greater influence over followers. In contrast, apparent personal benefit tended to deprive a leader of charisma, and this effect was particularly striking. Perhaps this is why charisma is less common in the business context (with its widely publicized high levels of compensation, stock options, and perquisites) than in politics and religion.

Another laboratory study looked specifically into the effects of communicating a vision, implementing the vision through task cues, and demonstrating a charismatic communication style—all core components of charismatic leadership theory (Kirkpatrick & Locke, 1996). The results were mixed. Vision affected follower attitudes but influenced performance primarily in an indirect manner. Task cues to implement the vision had the most pronounced direct effect on performance. Charismatic communication demonstrated few effects of any kind, suggesting that substance or content may be more important than style and rhetoric, at least for the influence of charismatic behavior on close, face-to-face followers.

Yet a study by Raed Awamleh and William Gardner (1999)—which considered the effects of vision content, vision delivery (communication), and organizational level performance on perceived leader charisma and effectiveness—found that all three independent variables played an important role. Charismatic communication clearly did have an impact here, as it has in certain other studies, but the results from Shelley Kirkpatrick and Edwin Locke (1996) suggest that this effect cannot be assumed in all instances. Organizational performance proved to be a strong predictor, mirroring a result that was previously obtained by Sheila Puffer (1990).

Further evidence in support of charismatic leadership theory comes from a study by Christine Shea and Jane Howell (1999), which found that charismatic behaviors produced high levels of task performance, whether or not feedback on performance was provided. Yet research conducted within the Israeli armed forces to test certain aspects of the self-concept extensions to charismatic leadership theory (Shamir et al., 1993) did not yield the expected results. Certain follower effects were found for leader behaviors that reflect an emphasis on the group's collective identity, but other leader behaviors did not operate in accordance with the theory at all. The authors say that "in general the self-concept-based theory did not receive much support in our study" (Shamir, Zakay, Breinin, & Popper, 1998, p. 404). The particular military context may have been a factor, but still some correc-

tion to the prevailing optimism regarding charismatic theory seems warranted.

Role of Close and Distant Leaders

A theoretical distinction that might have been made, but has not, is between charismatic behaviors addressed to and assessed by close, face-to-face followers and such behaviors as they are experienced at a distance, often through the medium of intervening processes. An example would be the close charismatic leadership of a U.S. president experienced by cabinet members versus the distant leadership experienced by members of the voting public. Charismatic leadership theory does not make such a distinction, but, in fact, almost all of its tests have been close in nature. However, Shamir (1995) has raised the possibility that perceptions at a distance are more idealized, more susceptible to image building, more prototypical, and based more on leader visions; they depend less on observable behavior and are influenced greatly by rhetoric. In this view, close and distant charisma are far from being the same thing.

Shamir (1995) also presents data bearing on this matter. Students were asked to identify charismatic leaders with whom they had and had not had direct relationships, and they were interviewed for details on each. As it turned out, over 80 percent of the distant leaders were political, while the close leaders were much more varied. Leader traits, behaviors, and effects (consequences) as perceived by the followers were identified and compared for close and distant relationships. In over 65 percent of these comparisons, differences of a significant nature were observed. In general, these differences followed a pattern very similar to that hypothesized.

A second attempt to look into this issue, also conducted in Israel, is described by Dana Yagil (1998). The followers were in the military and were asked to provide information about their attributions of charisma to their platoon leaders (close) and their battalion commanders (distant). The study was limited to a circumscribed set of characteristics, some of which proved to differentiate close and distant charisma and some of which did not. The data continue to suggest that the two types of charisma are not the same, but a clear picture of exactly what is involved in each instance requires further study. This is an issue that seems to be allied with the direct and indirect leadership distinction as developed by Robert Lord (see chapter 24 in this volume). Leadership theory has not given enough attention to such matters, and it should (see Waldman & Yammarino, 1999).

Research in Review

In closing an extensive review of charisma and leadership theory and research, Alan Bryman (1992) notes that he has been rather critical but adds that developments in this area are at an early stage and that he does not wish to "nip in the bud" what the future may hold. Given the outburst of activity in the latter 1990s, it is no longer possible to consider this an undernourished field, and Bryman appears to have been right in anticipating this state of affairs. The research base is rapidly becoming the equal of that available for numerous other organizational behavior theories. Furthermore, this research is often of an experimental nature, where charisma and variables with a theoretical relationship to it are manipulated in the laboratory. This is not exactly what would have been expected, but it has been a felicitous development and appears to have contributed both to an understanding of causality and to the generalizability of findings (Brown & Lord, 1999; Wofford, 1999).

A comparison of House's many propositions against this research base clearly leaves many propositions unaccounted for insofar as available studies are concerned. This is particularly true of some of the more recent propositions, although since the recent theorizing has often incorporated ideas from other related theories, particularly Bass's, there are additional studies that need to be brought to bear; we will get to these shortly. It can be said now, however, that these attempts at integration have both expanded the horizons of charismatic leadership theory and added a measure of ambiguity to it. There are some inconsistencies, on such matters as the role of crises and the scope of charisma for instance.

Overall, the research appears to provide considerable support for the basic theory, if not for each specific formulation, at least for the major thrusts. Something like charisma does appear to be a meaningful and important leadership construct, and personality, as well as follower (or group), variables do seem to play an important role in that construct.

As has been indicated, "the self-concept version of the theory needs a fuller description of the way each type of charismatic leader influences self-concepts, self-worth, internalized values, motive arousal, individual and collective self-efficacy, and identification with the leader and organization" (Yukl, 1993, p. 371). The theory as stated emphasizes a leader who empowers followers, rather than placing them in a dependent role. Perhaps this is one reason the self-concept views have not found support in a military setting (Shamir et al., 1998). In any event, charismatic leadership theory in its self-concept version exhibits considerable convergence with Lord's views on the subject (see chapter 24 in this volume). The parallels and divergences between the two approaches need to be spelled out, but even more important is the need for research in this area. Before the field moves further down the self-concept path, there needs to be some determination as to whether that path leads anywhere. To date the issue is clouded, at least within charismatic theory.

A problem that charismatic leadership theory faces is that charisma clearly can be a source of negative outcomes—people rise to the top who do not have the capability to produce positive outcomes once they get there (Hogan, Raskin, & Fazzini, 1990). Yet charismatic leadership needs to exist in an environment of positive outcomes to thrive; that is what the research says. Under failure conditions, followers will turn away. Theory has not really dealt effectively with this particular dark side of charisma. Three types of flawed charismatics have been described: the high likeability floater, the resentful person, and the narcissist. The narcissist, in particular, is a problem, especially since Deluga (1997) has found narcissism to be a common characteristic of charismatic leaders. Clearly we need a theory that will handle the role of narcissism in charismatic relationships. Is it tied in some way to self-efficacy? As we accumulate more significant research findings, we also get more problems for theory to deal with.

One of the charismatic behaviors that House describes is personal image building, and on the evidence this is important. The implication is that charismatic leaders are exceptionally expressive people whose use of rhetoric and drama comes naturally; they are actors and actresses, always on stage and at the center of attention. Their personalities are those of dramaturgy. This type of formulation has indeed been made the centerpiece of a theory of the charismatic relationship (Gardner & Avolio, 1998). It may be why professional actors and actresses appear to be so easily trained for performances in the laboratory experiments.

The difficulty, however, is that this same desire to be at the center of attention, to stand out from the group and act out a role, often has been found to characterize successful managers in general (see the discussion of hierarchic role motivation theory in chapter 5). In this regard, as in certain others, charismatic theory needs to make a clear distinction between characteristics and behaviors that typify charismatic managers and other kinds of effective managers. The research often raises questions in this area.

Back to Weber

One of the major sources of criticism that charismatic leadership theory has faced comes from certain more sociologically oriented scholars who feel that in his writings House has not been true to the Weberian origins (Nur, 1998). Is this type of criticism justified? For several reasons I do not believe it is, but that conclusion requires amplification.

The biggest difference is that Weber was concerned with a quality that had strong religious overtones. Charismatics were treated as endowed with supernatural, superhuman powers with divine origins. This belief was the source of their power over followers. Congruent with this power, charismatic leaders were sources of change who operated to mobilize efforts to subvert the status quo and existing routines within bureaucracy. They were rare because the attribution of divine powers is no everyday affair. They tended to thrive on crises.

House's propositions do not deal with divine attributions, however, and thus they serve to tame charisma: they focus on different sources of power; they do not necessarily concern themselves with revolutionary change; they are inconsistent in their consideration of the role of crises; and they seem on occasion to imply a wide dispersion of charisma, even though House often says charisma is rare. Furthermore, his research uses measures that seem far removed from Weber's concept of charisma. The operationalizations developed by Jay Conger and Rabindra Kanungo (1998), for instance, came much closer to the constructs proposed by Weber.

Yet, in spite of his debt to Weber, House was proposing his own theory, one he hoped would spark the leadership research that Weber's had not. He has succeeded in that objective, and the research has given

his ideas considerable, although not universal, support. He certainly has every right to propose any theory he wishes; that is how science advances. His formulations were not intended to be a mere reinterpretation of Weber, and they are not.

Furthermore, as we have seen, departures from Weber are to be found among those with a sociological approach to the field also. Etzioni placed charisma in many organizational contexts that Weber, with his emphasis on rarity, did not (see chapter 19). Bryman is critical of Etzioni's approach, stating that "in redefining charisma so that it has a broad application across a wide span of organizations, the resulting definition is so inclusive that it lacks a specific referent" (1992, p. 92). Bryman feels that this is the reason that Etzioni's views on charisma in his opinion have lacked impact. However, an alternative view is that the lack of operationalization has undermined the conduct of research. House's approach has been operationalized, however, and its expanded scope has made for a much more potentially significant and useful theory insofar as dealing with the topic of leadership is concerned.

A final point on which Weber and House differ is the extent to which the routinization of charisma—the processes through which charismatically introduced changes are institutionalized and carried on into the future—is a major theoretical focus. This was a primary concern for Weber; it is given little attention by House. Harrison Trice and Janice Beyer (1986), among others, have argued that a complete theory of charismatic leadership must deal with the routinization issue. I am inclined to agree. Routinization requires that matters of succession be considered and that positive outcomes be maintained long enough so that charisma can be retained to be institutionalized. These are important matters for charismatic leadership theory; they need to be addressed.

The preceding discussion must be considered just a partial evaluation of House's theory, simply because there is relevant research that has been an outgrowth of Bass's theory. After considering that theory, and the research on it, I will attempt a more complete evaluation of both theories.

TRANSFORMATIONAL LEADERSHIP THEORY

Transformational theory was developed by Bass relatively late in his professional career. While he himself was a product of organizational behavior's first generation, his major theory did not appear until the second generation. Unlike House, he was not primarily a theorist in his earlier years, having been much more concerned with research. Yet the two theorists do have in common that both came out of Ohio State during the period when the behavioral study of leadership was in its heyday there. That both should develop parallel theories, which at least in their Weberian origins go beyond the behavioral, seems a strange coincidence. Yet Ohio State had a very pervasive influence on leadership theorizing and research in that period.

Background

Bass was born (in 1925) and grew up in New York City, attending the College of the City of New York for several years before a stint in the Air Force. Subsequently he went to Ohio State University, where he received all his degrees in industrial psychology. He obtained the Ph.D. in 1949 at age 24. He was educated in the context of the Ohio State leadership program and did his dissertation on leaderless group discussion, which was really concerned with emergent leadership.

After Ohio State he joined the faculty in psychology at Louisiana State University. Subsequent to a visiting year in the psychology department at the University of California at Berkeley, in 1962, he moved to the business school at the University of Pittsburgh. He has continued his association with business schools throughout his career, although at different universities. The next of these was the University of Rochester and later the State University of New York at Binghamton. He is now emeritus from the latter, although he continues to work and publish from there (Hooijberg & Choi, 2000).

In moving from leaderless group discussions to transformational leadership Bass followed a highly differentiated scholarly route, albeit a route filled with many significant contributions, not only to leadership study but also to numerous other topic areas within organizational behavior. Figure 25.3 outlines the subjects of his endeavor over this period, up to the early 1980s, when he turned to the study of transformational leadership and developed his theory of the processes involved therein (Bass, 1981a).

Theoretical Statements

Bass does not appear to have been influenced primarily by House's earlier formulations on charismatic leadership, at least initially. The main source for his early ideas, in addition to Weber, was James Burns and his book on political leadership entitled *Leadership* (1968).

This book stimulated Bass's work on transformational leadership; he saw this work as providing a way to bridge the gap between group dynamics and the leadership demonstrated by the world's movers and shakers (Bass, 1992b). Not long after reading the Burns book he began to develop what amounted to an agenda for studying the application of transformational leadership at the mass level to the small group situation (Bass, 1981b). Before long, he had characteristically initiated a pilot study on the subject, using South African executives to describe transformational leaders they had known (Bass, 1982). However, the first formal theoretical presentation was his book *Leadership and Performance beyond Expectations* (1985b).

Leadership and Performance beyond Expectations

This book was preceded by a brief digest in article form (Bass, 1985a). I will draw on both publications in what follows, but primarily on the book.

The baseline against which transformational leadership is compared is set by transactional leadership. A leader of the transactional kind

1. Recognizes what it is we want to get from our work and tries to see that we get what we want if our performance warrants it
2. Exchanges rewards and promises of reward for our effort
3. Is responsive to our immediate self-interests if they can be met by our getting the work done (Bass, 1985b, p. 11)

A leader of the transformational kind, however, motivates people to do more than they had previously expected to do. This is accomplished

1. By raising our level of awareness, our level of consciousness about the importance and value of designated outcomes, and ways of reaching them
2. By getting us to transcend our own self-interest for the sake of the team, organization, or larger polity
3. By altering our need level on Maslow's (or Alderfer's) hierarchy or expanding our portfolio of needs and wants (Bass, 1985b, p. 20)

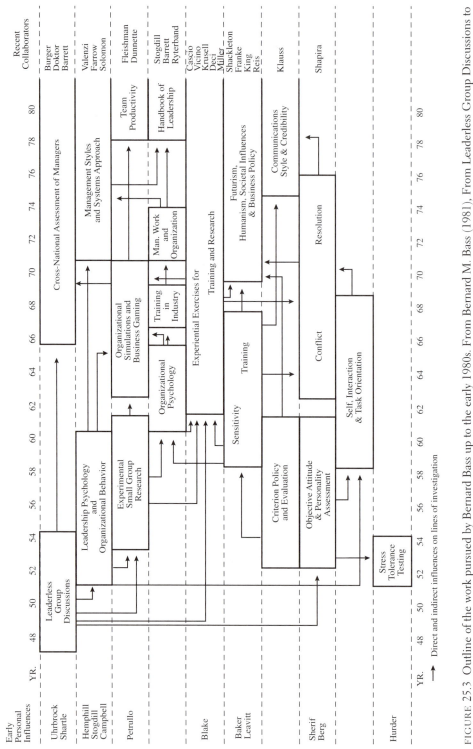

FIGURE 25.3 Outline of the work pursued by Bernard M. Bass up to the early 1980s. From Leaderless Group Discussions to the Cross-National Assessment of Managers, *Journal of Management*, 7(2), 65. Copyright 1981 by Journal of Management. Reprinted with permission.

Thus, the theory accepts and incorporates Maslow's hierarchy of needs and the prepotency concept, as well as the idea of self-actualization (see chapter 6), although other processes may be engaged by transformational leaders. Most leaders behave in both transactional and transformational ways in different intensities and amounts; this is not an entirely either-or differentiation. Figure 25.4 outlines the processes involved in both types of leadership.

Charismatic and transformational processes are closely related, but a person can be charismatic without being transformational in the influence exerted, as is the case with many celebrities. Thus charisma

is necessary for transformational leadership, although in and of itself it is not sufficient for the process to evolve. This suggests the operation of other factors within the context of transformational leadership. In addition to (1) *charisma*, which includes inspirational leadership, these are (2) *individualized consideration* and (3) *intellectual stimulation*. There are two transactional factors—(4) *contingent reward* and (5) *management-by-exception*. These five factors were identified through and emerged from factor-analytic studies. Yet it is important to remember that what comes out of factor analysis is a function of what goes in. Some theory, implicit or explicit, must have guided the writ-

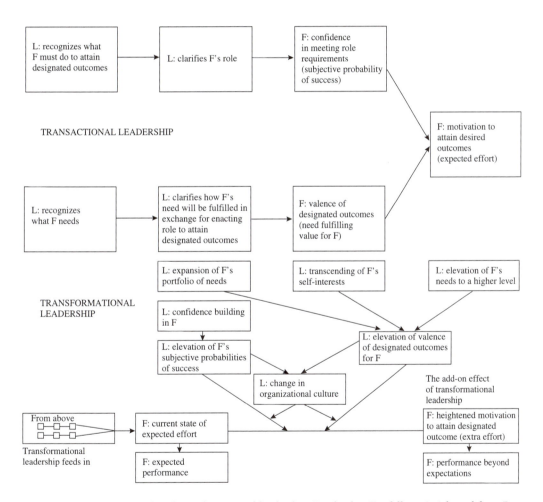

FIGURE 25.4 Transactional and transformational leadership (L = leader, F = follower). Adapted from Bernard M. Bass (1985), Leadership: Good, Better, Best, *Organizational Dynamics*, 13(3), 30, 32; Bruce J. Avolio & Bernard M. Bass (1988), Transformational Leadership, Charisma, and Beyond, in James G. Hunt, B. Rajaram Baliga, H. Peter Dachler, & Chester A. Schriesheim (Eds.), *Emerging Leadership Vistas* (Lexington, MA: D. C. Heath), 31.

ing and selection of potential items in the first place.

In discussing the charisma components of his theory, Bass (1985b) draws heavily on House (1977). In fact, he accepts the propositions and incorporates them in his own theory, describing them as "seven propositions about the more overt aspects of charismatic leadership in complex organizations that fit with social and organizational psychology" (Bass, 1985b, p. 53). He does not incorporate the hypothesis with regard to stress at this point, but he does include figure 25.1.

Then he goes on to propose an additional set of propositions on the same subject, designed to capture the more emotional aspects of charisma (the luster, the excitement) that he believes House (1977), with his emphasis on the observable and rational, fails to incorporate in the first seven:

8. The charismatic leader reduces resistance to attitude change in followers and disinhibitions of behavioral responses by arousing emotional responses toward the leader and a sense of excitement and adventure which may produce restricted judgments and reduced inhibitions.

9. The larger-than-life status of charismatic leaders makes them useful targets of their followers' projections and catalysts for rationalization, repression, regression, and disassociation.

10. Shared norms and group fantasies among followers facilitate the emergence and success of the charismatic leader.

11. The charismatic leader may make extensive use of successful argumentation in influencing others and justifying his position. The charismatic leader may display superior debating skills, technical expertise, and ability to appropriately muster persuasive appeals.

12. Analogous to thesis and antithesis, the very behaviors and qualities that transport supporters into extremes of love, veneration, and admiration of the charismatic personality send opponents into extremes of hatred, animosity, and detestation.

13. Charismatic leaders vary greatly in their pragmatism, flexibility, and opportunism.

14. Charismatic leadership is more likely to be seen when groups, organizations, cultures, and societies are in a state of stress and transition. (Bass, 1985b, pp. 56–59)

The last of these propositions appears designed to fill in the gap created by the failure to consider House's hypothesis dealing with stress effects.

Inspirational leadership is said to be a subfactor within charisma. As such, it can be self-generated and can occur outside the charismatic context. Within charisma, it involves providing models for followers; using emotional appeals to competitiveness, power, affiliation, altruism, and the like; and adopting persuasive words, symbols, and images.

Individualized consideration is transformational but not charismatic. Its essence is a developmental orientation. One aspect is mentoring, which includes, on the one hand, an enhanced self-image, security, integration of needs, and visibility and, on the other, fulfillment of follower desires for information and fate control. The second aspect is individualization, which means for the leader the fostering of one-on-one contact and two-way communications (a dyadic relationship), attention to individual differences in needs, and delegation of responsibilities. For the follower, individuation involves the fulfillment of unique needs, as well as a sense of ownership, personal responsibility, and fate control.

Intellectual stimulation can also serve to evoke heightened efforts on the part of followers. This means for the leader an orientation that is rational, empirical, existential, and idealistic; it also means competence in the form of intelligence, creativity, and experience. As a result, the leader is alert to threats, challenges, and opportunities; possesses diagnostic skills; and is capable of solution generation. In turn, followers experience easier comprehension, enhanced role clarity, the capturing of their attention, and enhanced role acceptance.

Transformational leaders will display some combination of the three factors—charisma, individualized consideration, and intellectual stimulation. They are likely to be high on all three.

Transactional Leaders

The theory is equally specific regarding transactional leaders, who are most likely to be found at the lower levels of hierarchic organizations. The key factors involved here are contingent reward and management by exception (to include negative feedback and contingent aversive reinforcement).

Contingent reward is said to be supported by a goodly body of research of the kind discussed in chapter 8. It may well incorporate the advantages of goal setting (see chapter 9) as well. Pay for performance operates in this manner.

Management-by-exception is described as involving a situation where the leader intervenes only when something goes wrong. This is not the exception principle as described by Frederick Taylor (see chapter 3) since in that instance both negative deviations in the form of ineffective performance *and* positive deviations in the form of outstanding performance were to be given special attention.

Figure 25.5 represents an attempt by Bass to show some of the most important linkages between contingent positive and aversive reinforcement and how these relate to follower efforts. This is the basis for transactional leadership.

Role of Personality

Bass (1985b) discusses both the role of the organizational environment and of personality factors as ante-

cedents of transformational leadership. In the former instance, he deals with such considerations as the association between transformational leadership and organic systems, the role of stress and rapid change (proposition 14), and the tendency for transformational leadership to blossom at higher organizational levels. However, the treatment of personality is the more specific.

Certainly Bass recognizes that personality factors play a role at both the follower and leader levels. Equalitarian, self-confident, highly educated, and high-status followers among others, are likely to be resistant to charismatic leadership. Inflexible followers will not respond well to individualized consideration and intellectual stimulation. Those who are more predisposed to extrinsic motivation will be particularly receptive to transactional leadership. The point is that follower personality makes a difference; dependent

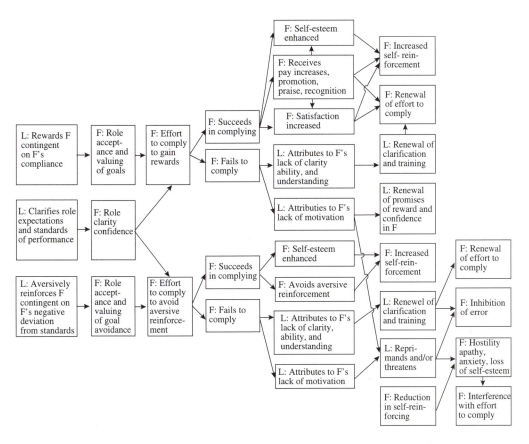

FIGURE 25.5 Contingent reinforcement in transactional leadership (L = leader, F = follower). From Bernard M. Bass (1985), *Leadership and Performance Beyond Expectations* (New York: Free Press), 148. Copyright 1985. Reprinted with permission of The Free Press, a Division of Simon & Schuster, Inc.

people should be attracted to transformational leaders and should exhibit more compliance as a result.

Leader personality also is important. Social boldness, introspection, thoughtfulness, and activity level (but not sociability, cooperativeness, and friendliness) should be at a high level among the transformationals; probably authoritarianism, assertiveness, need for achievement, maturity, integrity, creativity, and originality as well. Transactionals should be high on conformity, sense of equity, and a preference for social as opposed to political approaches. Thus power needs should predominate in transformational leaders and affiliation needs in transactional. Overall, personality factors would be expected to play a more significant role in transformational leadership.

Reemphases and Extrapolations

The theory as a whole has remained remarkably stable over time. However, Bass has tended to place his emphases in different places and to extend the theory's coverage in various respects. In most cases these alterations reflect a response to new research data, but on occasion the changes represent an attempt to deal with input from other theoretical positions as well.

At an early point Bass took steps to emphasize that transformational leadership is a widespread phenomenon, in contrast to Weber's charisma. Consonant with this view, he also emphasized that such leadership can be learned and that training to accomplish this should be instituted (Bass, 1990).

He also has given increased theoretical attention to the matter of stress as it relates to transformational and transactional leadership (Bass, 1992a). The position is that transformational leadership will act to reduce feelings of burnout and symptoms of stress. It does this by helping followers transcend their self-interest, increase their awareness, and shift their goals away from personal safety to achievement and self-actualization. Charisma acts to satisfy frustrated identity needs and any lack of social support. Individualized consideration helps convert crises to developmental challenges. Intellectual stimulation promotes thoughtful and creative solutions to stressful problems. Thus transformational leadership adds to what transactional leaders can accomplish in the face of crisis.

A particularly interesting essay deals with certain changes in the factors of leadership and with certain critiques that have been advanced against the theory—attempting to eliminate the "strawmen" thus created

(Bass & Avolio, 1993). The factors now specified and a typical item measuring each are as follows:

Transformational leadership

1. Charisma (idealized influence)—has my trust in his or her ability to overcome any obstacle
2. Inspirational motivation—uses symbols and images to focus our efforts
3. Intellectual stimulation—enables me to think about old problems in new ways
4. Individualized consideration—coaches me if I need it

Transactional leadership

5. Contingent reward—makes sure that there is close agreement between what he or she expects me to do and what I can get from him or her for my effort
6. Management-by-exception—takes action only when a mistake has occurred

Nonleadership

7. Laissez-faire—doesn't tell me where he or she stands on issues (Bass & Avolio, 1993, pp. 51–53)

The last of these (no. 7) extends the variance in leader behaviors considered; it harks back to the days of Lewin (see chapter 2) and thus is not original with this theory. There is also reference to two higher-order factors of an active and passive nature, but without much by way of detail on these factors.

The critiques are dealt with through 10 position statements, or arguments as they are called. Some of these represent theoretical statements and some are empirical generalizations from research, but in the interest of completeness of coverage all are noted here:

1. Questionnaires/surveys are being used appropriately.
2. Some attributions and effects on followers are being measured, but much is description of leadership behavior (the prototypical leader has many attributes and behaviors that have been linked to transformational leadership).
3. The factor structure underlying the MLQ is empirically supportable [MLQ = Bass's multifactor leadership questionnaire].
4. Charisma and transformational leadership are not synonymous (the three additional

transformational factors . . . are conceptually distinct from charisma).

5. Individualized consideration is not a reincarnation of the consideration scale of the Leader Behavior Description Questionnaire (LBDQ) (although . . . there is overlap between the two).

6. Initiation of structure and consideration cannot conceptually and empirically account for transformational and transactional leadership.

7. Transformational leadership can be either directive or participative, as well as democratic or authoritarian, elitist or leveling.

8. Transformational leadership is not necessarily synonymous with effective leadership; nor is transactional leadership (especially MBE) synonymous with ineffective leadership.

9. The best of leaders are both transformational and transactional; the worst are neither; the worst avoid displaying leadership.

10. Leaders can be taught and motivated to be more transformational with consequential effects on the organization's programs and policies for improving itself. (Bass & Avolio, 1993, pp. 55–73)

In a book published a year later (Bass & Avolio, 1994a), certain trends noted previously are solidified. Charisma is renamed "idealized influence"—thus creating the four I's of transformational leadership (idealized, inspirational, intellectual, individualized). Management-by-exception is divided into active (proactive monitoring) and passive (waiting for deviances) types. A factor hierarchy is established, extending from laissez-faire to passive management-by-exceptions, to active management-by-exception, to contingent reinforcement, to the four I's. This hierarchy is expected to be positively related to both the ineffective-effective dimension and the passive-active (which are distinct from each other). This book is primarily concerned with various ways in which the full-range model may be applied to specific problem areas; it is not intended to be a source of new theory, and it is not.

Bass (1997) provides an overview of previous theory and research on it. This article also contains three corollaries for the theory, which although not new, do serve to emphasize important theoretical points:

1. There is a hierarchy of correlations among the various leadership styles and outcomes in effectiveness, effort, and satisfaction (this runs from laissez-faire to transformational).

2. There is a one-way augmentation effect (transformational leadership adds explained variances in outcomes to that explained by transactional leadership).

3. In whatever the country, when people think about leadership, their prototypes and ideas are transformational. (Bass, 1997, pp. 134–135)

Levels of Analysis and the Pseudotransformational

Two theoretical extensions appeared in the latter 1990s, which indeed do move onto new ground. Let us take up the multiple levels matter first. Individualized consideration is the focus of this treatment, and the contention is that this construct may be considered and operationalized at three levels: as a characteristic of the leader's behavior (individual), as representing a group's behavior toward individuals (group), and as a characteristic of the organization's culture (organizational) (Avolio & Bass, 1995). The individualized consideration construct is the linchpin between transactional models of leadership and the transformational, in that, to a degree, it has a foot in both camps. In some organizations at least, individualized consideration emerges initially at the organizational level in top management, then diffuses down through the hierarchy to group leadership, and finally characterizes the work group itself and its members. In such cases, the construct becomes part of the culture, but it needs to be measured in a different way at each level. The theoretical proposition involved is this:

1. Individualized consideration needs to be operationally defined, measured, and interpreted relative to the level and context in which it is embedded. The context, accrued over time, sets a threshold on how such behavior is interpreted.

   Example items for measures of each level are:

   Organization—individuals are considered an essential building block for organizational development

   Group—members provide useful advice for each other's development
   Individual—the leader diagnoses each follower's needs

2. A behavior exhibited by a leader that is reinforced by the leader over time and within the context (which includes the people) can

emerge at subsequently higher levels of analysis representing a group norm or characteristic of the culture. This, in part, represents the core of what is transformed by a leader at multiple levels of analysis. (Avolio & Bass, 1995, pp. 210–211, 214)

Measures of the type needed to study a construct at multiple levels as indicated by these propositions have in fact been created (Bass, 1998). Previously the theory operated only at the individual leader level.

The second change in the theory introduces the concept of pseudotransformational leadership to deal with the personalized power factor (see House & Howell, 1992). What happened in this instance is described as follows:

Originally, the dynamics of transformational leadership were expected to be the same whether beneficial or harmful to followers (Bass, 1985[b]), although Burns (1978) believed that to be transforming, leaders had to be morally uplifting. I have come to agree with Burns. Personalized transformational leaders are *pseudotransformational*. They may exhibit many transforming displays but cater, in the long run, to their own self-interests. Self-concerned, self-aggrandizing, exploitative, and power-oriented, pseudotransformational leaders believe in distorted utilitarian and warped moral principles. This is in contrast to the truly transformational leaders who transcend their own self-interests. (Bass, 1998, p. 15)

Bass goes on to describe this type, which in fact had not truly been included previously within the theory, as narcissistic, impetuous, and impulsively aggressive. These people bring about compliance, but the commitment of followers is not internalized and is of a public nature only. They tend to manufacture crises. They can well be charismatic, inspirational, intellectually stimulating, and individually considerate, but this is all in the service of their own self-interest.

In contrast to the immorality of the pseudotransformational, true, socialized transformationals have followers who identify with them and their aspirations, wishing to actually emulate their leaders. Here the discussion closely follows Shamir et al. (1993). Authentic transformational leaders expand the effective freedom available to their followers, as well the scope for altruistic intention. Their actions are noble and moral; "they should be applauded, not chastised"

(Bass & Steidlmeier, 1999). In contrast, Bass really does not like the pseudotransformationals, among whom Adolf Hitler appears to represent the essential prototype in his mind.

Evaluation and Impact

The availability of an array of theory-related measuring instruments has served to foster a great deal of research on transformational theory. Bass and his colleagues at SUNY/Binghamton have been at the forefront of this research, and in the early years they produced almost all of what was done. Interest has diffused, however, to the point where in recent years the research has been widely dispersed. Yet Bass and those working with him continue to do significant work. This is an instance, like Fiedler's theories (see chapter 12), where the interplay between theory and research has been continual.

Research in the 1980s

In the early pre-theory period, a number of hypotheses did not fit the data, and other blind alleys often involved attempts to make factor analyses fit with constructs in ways that they stubbornly refused to accommodate (Bass, 1995). Much of this research involved aspects of consideration and initiating structure.

Finally, with the construction of a completely new item pool, meaningful factors began to emerge. At first there were five factors: charismatic leadership, contingent reward, individualized consideration, management-by-exception, intellectual stimulation. The charisma factor accounted for 65 percent of the total variance of consequence; no other factor accounted for as much as 10 percent. There was also some evidence to support a scale for extra effort, a scale for inspirational leadership, an active-proactive factor, and a passive-reactive factor (Bass, 1985b). Reliability of measurement was good. Preliminary support for validity against satisfaction and effectiveness, and an add-on effect from transformational leadership, was obtained, although problems with common method variance confounded these findings. This research produced the first version of the Multifactor Leadership Questionnaire (MLQ).

A study followed in which construct validity was investigated by using ratings of world-class leaders that were based on biographical data (Bass, Avolio, & Goodheim, 1987). Another study used the MLQ in a government agency in New Zealand and established that the degree of transformational leadership found at one managerial level tended to be evident at the next lower level as well (Bass, Waldman, Avolio, & Bebb, 1987). Another study compared MLQ results with measures of satisfaction and rated performance from a management-by-objectives program in a manufacturing firm (Waldman, Bass, & Einstein, 1987). The correlations were low for performance, although charisma and individualized consideration did achieve significance; add-on effects were mixed overall. Another study used the MLQ in the context of a management game where financial results were available; it found significant relationships for all MLQ factors but management-by-exception (Avolio, Waldman, & Einstein, 1988). However, only individualized consideration, and to a lesser degree charisma, contributed unique variance to the financial performance criterion.

In a study conducted at Federal Express (Hater & Bass, 1988) top performing managers, when rated by subordinates on the MLQ and on effectiveness, clearly produced superior results; the augmentation or add-on hypothesis was supported, they had higher transformational scores (except on intellectual stimulation), and even the transactional scores produced significant positive, although low, correlations (except for management-by-exception). Yet when performance ratings by the manager's superiors were used as criteria, only weak support for theory of any kind was obtained.

These studies, and certain others not mentioned, gave transformational theory a good start, especially the John Hater and Bass (1988) research, which is widely cited. Certain problem areas remained, however.

Subsequent Research from Binghamton

The Multifactor Leadership Questionnaire is almost invariably used in research on transformational theory. Yet as Bass (1998, p. 165) notes, there are problems here, in spite of the fact that numerous versions of this measure have been devised over the years in an attempt to provide an improved instrument. One such problem is multiple co-linearity between factors, specifically those of a transformational nature. The correlations are high, and efforts to eliminate them have consistently failed. In particular, inspirational motivation is so highly correlated with charisma that the two are not statistically differentiable. The rationale for

the inspirational factor lies not in factor analysis, but in the existence of a separate literature.

Although the internal consistency reliabilities of the scales have generally been good, that has not always been the case for active management-by-exception, when an active-passive distinction is made. It appears to be difficult to write items that clearly identify this factor, and as a result ambiguity intrudes into the factor.

Finally, Bass notes problems with the universality of the factor structure. Different studies with different samples, measured at different times, with somewhat different instruments have not always produced the same results. This has been a continuing source of difficulty because the basic theory is predicated to a large extent on factor-analytic findings. Recently, Bruce Avolio, Bass, and Dong Jung (1999) attempted to cope with this issue by extracting an optimal structure from 14 samples where the same MLQ version was used in all instances. The best fit involved six primary factors: charisma, intellectual stimulation, individualized consideration, contingent reward, management-by-exception-active, and passive-avoidant. The first four of these are highly and positively intercorrelated; the last two are positively correlated with each other and negatively correlated with the first four. In addition, three higher-order factors emerge—transformational, developmental exchange, and corrective avoidant. The former loads highest on charisma and the second on contingent reward, but both are correlated with each other; corrective avoidant loads highest on passive-avoidant and is negatively correlated with transformational.

This pattern is not entirely consistent with earlier theory, and to the extent it bundles the transformational factors with contingent reward it appears to depart from theoretical expectations. Either the theory needs to be changed, or the measure, or the theory needs to explicitly divorce itself from the results of factor analysis. The authors do none of these; they simply call for further study.

The three problems that Bass (1998) noted clearly remain.

Outcome Relationships Viewed from Binghamton

Next we need to consider the data presented by Bass and his colleagues as they relate to the three corollaries (Bass, 1997) and to the matter of outcome relationships generally. With regard to the hierarchy of relationships between MLQ variables and effectiveness, effort, and/or satisfaction (also measured in the MLQ), Bass and Avolio (1993) present evidence that strongly supports the theory. Correlations in the .60 to .80 range are reported for the transformational factors, with charisma producing the highest; in the 40 to .60 range for contingent reward; in the −.30 to .30 range for management-by-exception; and in the −.30 to −.60 range for laissez-faire leadership. Actual median correlations from 17 studies are .71 for charisma, .65 for inspirational motivation, .54 for intellectual stimulation, .55 for individualized consideration; then moving to transactional factors, .35 for contingent reward, .07 for management-by-exception, and −.41 for laissez-faire.

These results appear striking, but they are confounded to an uncertain degree by common method variance. Bass (1997) says the results are similar when independent outcome criteria are used, although the differentiation is less. Yet the early studies produced mixed results in this regard. A study in which criterion data were separated from MLQ scores by having different subordinates provide each, produced validities in the .22 to .34 range for charisma and from .18 to .35 for individualized consideration. Intellectual stimulation did not yield significant correlations (Seltzer & Bass, 1990). In another instance (Howell & Avolio, 1993), management-by-objectives performance was used as a criterion, with the result that common method bias was minimized, and the transformational factors produced validities in the .26 to .36 range. This study is unusual in that predictive validity (over a 1-year period) was involved.

These studies in the 1990s provide evidence for the add-on or augmentation effect, thus supporting corollary 2, but not with all criteria. A problem here is that when independent criteria are used, the transactional correlations with criteria may decrease, so that they are not significantly different from zero, or may even be negative. As a result, the "augmentation" is at best merely a consequence of the significant transformational findings; there is no positive transactional result to add on to.

Corollary 3 says that the positive results indicated for corollary 1 and 2 may be generalized internationally. Considerable data to support this conclusion are provided (Bass, 1997), but they are based primarily on studies that do not use a separate outcome measure. Some differences between cultures on MLQ factors are noted as well. However, a recent study in which U.S. and Asian university students were compared suggests caution; the authors conclude that "the effects of transformational and transactional leadership may not always generalize across Caucasian and Asian followers" (Jung & Avolio, 1999, p. 217).

Bass (1997) notes certain other findings that depart from theoretical expectations. Organic and mechanistic organizations have not always been found to differ in the proportion of leaders of different types within them. Inspirational motivation and satisfaction are usually highly correlated, but in one professional organization this figure was actually negative in direction. The tendency for intellectual stimulation to operate in unexpected ways, which has been noted previously, was compounded in a study of stress relationships: when other factors were held constant, stress and burnout increased under this type of leadership; charisma and individualistic consideration yielded the expected decrease in stress (Bass, 1998). There is some suggestion in these findings that professional and intellectual leadership may not operate in a manner entirely consistent with transformational theory.

A final study from Binghamton that bears mentioning dealt with the theory as it relates to multiple levels of analysis (Yammarino, Spangler, & Dubinsky, 1998). The data for the sales personnel studied did not support theoretical expectations well. Transformational leadership was unrelated to actual sales figures, although it did relate to affective outcome and rated performance variables. Analyses, which considered data for the group level and below, but not for the organizational level, indicated that the relationships held only at the individual level and were unaffected by dyad and group membership. Furthermore, transformational and contingent reward leadership operated similarly, thus suggesting that the two may not be as different as the theory presupposes. These data appear to be free of same source biases.

Meta-Analyses

The major meta-analytic study evaluating transformational theory used a large number of unpublished sources, as well as those we have been considering (Lowe, Kroeck, & Sivasubramaniam, 1996). Intercorrelations among the three transformational measures ranged from .68 to .85, and the management-by-exception measure correlated from .05 to .10 with these three, but contingent reward was much more highly correlated with the transformational measures (.63 to

.70) than with management-by-exception (.21). Internal consistency reliability was entirely adequate for all measures except management-by-exception (.65).

The major findings are given in table 25.1. These involve effectiveness outcomes only, but note the huge differences in validity coefficients when common method variance is removed. Yet charisma and individualized consideration remain significant even so; the other scales are not significant, including intellectual stimulation. The organizational measure values for transformational leadership are generally in line with the validities typically obtained in studies of predictors of managerial performance. There is no evidence of an extraordinary effect here. Also, contrary to the original hypothesis, transformational leadership is neither more prevalent nor more effective in higher management.

Bass (1998) refers to additional unpublished meta-analytic results, but the reporting is incomplete. It appears that these analyses are of an earlier vintage and include fewer relationships. Nevertheless, it is important to note that while validity coefficients using objective performance indices with the transformational measures ranged from .26 to .29 for civilian samples, these same values were in the .46 to .57 range for military samples. Bass (1998) also reports a failure to find transformational leadership more significant at the upper levels of hierarchy.

Research from beyond Binghamton

Although the great majority of the research on transformational theory has been conducted by Bass and his colleagues at SUNY-Binghamton, significant research has been conducted elsewhere as well; on occasion, however, these more distant studies do exhibit certain ties to the Binghamton group.

A particularly important finding derives from the study by Podsakoff, Scott MacKenzie, and William Bommer (1996) of transformational leadership and substitutes for leadership, as discussed in chapter 24. In this regard the authors say:

> The results of the aggregate analysis indicate that because of the large proportion of the shared variance between the transformational leader behaviors and substitutes for leadership, it is essential to include the substitutes variables in any test of the effects of transformational leadership. (pp. 289–290)

> Three reasons why the substitutes variables might be correlated with leader behaviors. First, . . . the relationships between the substitutes and leader behaviors might . . . be caused by other unrecognized factors. Second, . . . the substitutes may influence or constrain a leader's behavior in some way. A final possibility . . . is that leaders can influence the substitutes variables. (p. 295)

Thus it seems entirely possible that the failure to find a greater effect of transformational behaviors at higher levels is a consequence of the failure to incorporate substitutes for leadership in the research. Certainly top management has the greater influence over these variables. In any event, including contextual factors and substitutes in transformational leadership research has been a rather rare phenomenon.

TABLE 25.1 Mean corrected correlations between Multifactor Leadership Questionnaire (MLQ) scales and effectiveness criteria with (subordinate ratings) and without (organizational measures) common method bias

Scale	Subordinate ratings	Organizational measures	Correlations differ
Charisma	.81*	.35*	Yes
Individualized consideration	.69*	.28*	Yes
Intellectual stimulation	.68*	.26	Yes
Contingent reward	.56*	.08	Yes
Management-by-exception	.10	−.04	Yes

*Correlation is significantly different from 0 at p < .05 or better.

SOURCE: Adapted from Kevin B. Lowe, K. Galen Kroeck, & Nagaraj Sivasubramaniam (1996), Effectiveness Correlates of Tranformational and Transactional Leadership: A Meta-Analytic Review of the MLQ Literature, *Leadership Quarterly*, 7, 410

The uncertainty over the factor structure of the MLQ has not been limited to the Binghamton group. A study in the Netherlands, for instance, found various departures from theoretical expectations, including a failure to differentiate within the transformational domain (DenHartog, Van Muijen, & Koopman, 1997). These results raise questions about the statistical basis for the theory, as well as about its cross-cultural generalizability. Other problems arise out of other research. Peter Bycio, Rick Hackett, and Joyce Allen (1995) studied hospital nurses and found that the transactional contingent reward component was closely aligned with the transformational components. Thus in this professional context the transformation-transactional differentiation did not appear to be fully justified.

The question of the role of follower trust in transformational leadership has been a concern for some time, but it now is apparent that trust plays a positive mediating role between transformational leadership and organizational citizenship behaviors, which involve performances that go beyond expectations and role requirements (Podsakoff, MacKenzie, Moorman, & Fetter, 1990; Pillai, Schriesheim, & Williams, 1999). Transactional leadership does not relate to trust in this same way. Interestingly, however, in a predominantly professional context, intellectual stimulation related negatively to trust, but this effect was overridden by the positive impact of charisma and individualized consideration. These findings on trust offer the possibility of bridging the void between personalized and socialized charismatics. Quite possibly, in spite of the wide differences between the two types, the capacity to inspire trust in followers characterizes both and provides them with common ground.

The uncertainties that often seem to arise when transformational leadership is studied in a professional context are at least partially illuminated by a longitudinal analysis that deals with the effectiveness of research projects and developmental projects in an R&D setting (Keller, 1992). Transformational leadership, including intellectual stimulation, was a better predictor of outcomes for the research projects. These results appear to be independent of any same-source bias. Another similar finding is that charisma, inspirational motivation, and intellectual stimulation, but not individualized consideration, served to differentiate emergent informal leaders who took the role of product champions of technological innovations from those who did not take this role (Howell & Higgins, 1990).

What is clearly evident in these types of studies is that transformational leadership is closely allied to intellectual leadership in situational contexts where innovation is important.

Transformational Training

The most significant application of transformational theory that has appeared to date involves the training of leaders to become more transformational. Bass (1998) describes certain efforts along these lines.

One such approach involves individual counseling by organizational development practitioners or others, who feed back MLQ profile results, interpret them, and aid the target person in developing a set of priorities, plans, and goals. The counselor is consistently supportive in encouraging movement to a more active, transformational style. Limited evaluation data are reported, but the available evidence indicates that such a program can improve MLQ scores beyond any changes occurring in a control group.

Planning and goal setting of this kind may also be embedded in a formal training program. Such a program involves some simulations and exercises but focuses mostly on action learning to deal with on-the-job issues. The training emphasizes, in order of coverage; increasing awareness of the leadership paradigm; learning about alternatives that are conducive to improving oneself as well as one's followers; and adapting, adopting, and internalizing the new ways of thinking and acting (Bass, 1998, p. 103). The 14 modules are spread over several days of both basic and advanced training, with an interval of 3 months between to practice key skills.

Significant training effects on MLQ and outcome variables are reported from two studies that were conducted to evaluate this type of training. The most striking change was a substantial reduction in management-by-exception behavior. Increases in inspirational motivation and intellectual stimulation were also evident, thus supporting the transformational objective. In general, transformational variables that were the specific focus of a participant's leadership development plan were the ones most likely to rise from pretest to posttest.

In addition to the evaluation research reported in Bass (1998), several other studies bear mention. These used variants of the standard training but appear to be sufficiently similar to justify attention here. Gretchen Spreitzer and Robert Quinn (1996) report an extensive application within the Ford Motor Company that was successful in stimulating meaningful transformational change efforts on the part of slightly less than half of the participants. These change behaviors, though self-reported, do not appear to have been a function of social desirability factors and are described as being dramatic. Yet no ties between training effects and promotion rates subsequently could be established.

A second study involved a more abbreviated training effort but did use a control group (Barling, Weber, & Kelloway, 1996). The results indicated substantial improvements in transformational leadership, especially in intellectual stimulation, which was the major focus of the training. There was also evidence of an effect on financial outcomes. Common source bias does not appear to have operated anywhere within this study.

Overall, the research appears to have been sufficient in quantity and scientific controls to justify a conclusion that transformational leadership training can achieve the intended results; the changes appear to be based on actual increases in leader uses of transformational behaviors.

Strengths and Weaknesses

In discussing transformational theory, Bryman (1996) notes the impressive set of research findings and the very substantial impact on the study of leadership. Undoubtedly, the theory has done a great deal to revive the leadership area after consideration and initiating structure declined. Yet Bryman, and others, have bemoaned the limited attention to situational or contextual factors within the theory. There is some concern with the effects of crises, uncertainty, follower stress, and the like, largely because Weber indicated similar concerns, but beyond that there is much more in the research findings than in the theoretical formulations.

The issue can be epitomized by considering the finding that female managers are more transformational, on all dimensions, than men are, particularly on individualized consideration but to almost the same degree on the charismatic component as well (Bass & Avolio, 1994b). Yet studies of world leaders consistently identify more males, and more male charismatics. For instance, in the Bass, Avolio, and Goodheim (1987) study of "movers and shakers," 87 percent of the nominees were men. When one narrows the data down to focus on those who score high (3.0 or more) on charisma, individualized consideration, and

intellectual stimulation, the percentage of males is 82, 79, and 86, respectively. Most people would attribute this differential to opportunity differences or, put differently, to lack of opportunity for females. But that is exactly the point: both theory and research dealing with opportunity and its effects are totally lacking. What type of context nurtures transformational and charismatic leadership, and how does one get into that context?

The need to theorize about context has in fact been recognized, and, indeed, propositions about transformational leadership-maximizing conditions have been advanced. The following are examples for consideration:

1. Organizations will be more receptive to transformational leadership during adaptation orientation than during efficiency orientation.
2. Organizations with dominant boundary-spanning units will be more receptive to transformational leadership than will be organizations with dominant technical cores.
3. Both simple structure and "adhocracy" forms will be more receptive to transformational leadership than will the machine bureaucracy, professional bureaucracy, and divisional structure forms.
4. Organizations with a clan mode of governance will be more receptive to transformational leadership than will organizations with either market or bureaucratic modes of governance. (Pawar & Eastman, 1997, pp. 92, 94–95, 97)

I am not advocating these particular propositions, only the need for some such formulations. However, if one accepts Weber's view that charisma represents a means of changing bureaucracies, these propositions do have a certain cogency.

House and Ram Aditya (1997) note several other problems that transformational theory needs to handle. One is the reliance on Maslow's theory to deal with the linkage between leader behaviors and affective states of followers; this formulation is weak, given what is known about the validity of need hierarchy theory (see chapter 6). There has been no research on the ideas involved here, and little mention of them after Bass's 1985 book. Research and theory have simply gone off in different directions; this is unfortunate.

Given its name, transformational theory must be concerned with transforming or changing something. Yet there is little evidence that transformational leaders do, in fact, bring about stable, long-term changes in either followers or their organizations. Do transformationals account for more such change than nontransformationals? This would seem to be a simple test of theory. Yet predictive or longitudinal studies of any kind are very few in number.

Other weaknesses noted by House and Aditya (1997) include the failure to deal with routinization and the loss of charisma, as well as the remaining uncertainties about crises and stress. These are problems faced by charismatic theory also.

Yukl (1999) has presented an excellent critique of the theories considered in this chapter. He is particularly concerned, as I am, about basing the theory on a factor-analytically derived structure that can change as a function of many considerations, including the particular item input to a given factor analysis. This situation means that the constructs and the relations among them can change also, and theoretical constructs are not supposed to change except in some predetermined manner as specified by a theory. Thus there are definite construct validity problems. This is particularly true of the transactional factors, which do not appear to possess a common rationale. As a result, under certain research conditions, contingent reward tends to drift into the domain of transformational leadership and the relationship indicated by the key augmentation hypothesis loses any clear meaning.

There are numerous aspects of the theory that simply have not been tested, including the propositions Bass added to House's initial theory of charisma. Also, although the theory is strong on the positive aspects of transformational leadership, it is weak on the detrimental or negative aspects. Socially acceptable behaviors are emphasized, and manipulative behaviors such as intimidation are ignored. Bass has recognized this problem recently and has introduced the concept of pseudotransformational leadership, although Yukl (1999) apparently was unaware of this shift in position.

This shift, however, carries with it its own set of problems. Chief among these is the fact that existing measures do not deal with pseudotransformational behaviors, and operationalizations of the construct do not exist. Thus, what has been one of the major strengths of transformational theory is lost in this particular instance. The kinds of behaviors that would appear to need measuring are the following:

Manipulative behaviors that increase follower perceptions of leader expertise and dependence on the leader; . . . misinterpreting events or inciting incidents to create the appearance of a crisis; exaggerating the leader's positive achievements and taking unwarranted credit for achievements; creating the appearance of miracles; using staged events with music and symbols to arouse emotions and build enthusiasm; covering up mistakes and failures; blaming others for the leader's mistakes; limiting member access to information about operations and performance; limiting the scope of subordinate work roles; limiting communication of criticism or dissent; indoctrinating new members; using deference rituals and status symbols; and creating barriers to isolate members from contacts with outsiders. (Yukl, 1999, p. 296)

Bass (1998) says that pseudotransformationals can be charismatic, inspirational, intellectually stimulating, and individually considerate much like authentic transformationals but that they use these behaviors in their own self-interest, not for the benefit of others. That seems to compound the measurement problem. Yet measures of personalized and socialized power do exist, and these may provide entrée to the problem.

Conceptually, however, there is the issue of whether self-interest is sufficient to differentiate the two types. Overdetermination may well operate so that a transformational leader acts out of multiple motives, some of which are self-oriented and some of which are not. People can serve their own interests and still produce products that benefit the common good (as in the case of capitalism). My point is that hinging the pseudoauthentic differentiation on self-interest alone seems unlikely to work. Yet it is important to understand the dark side of transformational leadership. That Bass has raised this issue, even if he has not solved it, is a significant contribution.

How Transformational Leadership Works

Bass (1998) indicates that little research has been done to explicate exactly how transformational leadership works. He does note, however, the research on trust by Podsakoff et al. (1990) and the theoretical contributions of Shamir et al. (1993) dealing with follower self-concepts, as well as Howell and Frost's (1989) finding that charismatic leaders are able to maintain productivity in the face of sizable obstacles. In a prior article Bass (1995) lists these same publications as offering promising insights, but in that instance he does make some reference to the Maslow hierarchy that he initially (Bass, 1985b) invoked to explain how transformational leadership works.

House and Aditya (1997) echo Bass's call for greater understanding of the linkage to follower dynamics; others have done the same. Perhaps this area will indeed attract the research attention it requires. However, the findings of Shamir et al. (1998) give pause to pursuing the self-concept interpretations that were proposed by Shamir et al. (1993).

A view of how transformational leadership works, which departs sharply from the ideas considered to this point in this chapter, is the following:

Transformational leadership clearly represents a combination of the recognition-based and inferential modes of leadership perception discussed earlier. Many researchers describe transformational leaders as conforming to the notions of followers—recognition-based processes. It is also clear that transformational leadership involves the perception by followers that leaders have an agenda for producing favorable performance outcomes—inferential processes. Critical evaluation of the construct should ask whether transformational leadership is anything more than categorizing someone as an effective leader. . . . We would caution researchers interested in the topic to keep in mind the lessons learned from prior research on questionnaires and leadership perception. Like other "behavioral" measures, transformational leadership scales may tell us as much about how leaders are integrated with subordinates' implicit theories as they do about the actual behaviors of transformational leaders. (Lord & Maher, 1991, p. 290)

Yet Lord, Douglas Brown, and Steven Freiberg do accord a role to transformational behaviors in their proposition 3, which concerns follower self-concepts as well:

Self-identity level will moderate the relation of (a) transactional and (b) transformational leadership to attitudinal and performance outcomes. Transactional leadership will be most effective when the subordinates' self is defined at an individual level, whereas transformation leadership will be most effective when the subordinate's self is defined at the group or collective level. (1999, p. 176)

This suggests that the behaviors involved differ between transactional and transformational leadership and that different kinds of followers, or followers in different states, are responsive to each. Clearly this proposition needs research; it deals with relationships, as do charismatic and transformational theory.

A position much like that of Lord and Maher (1991) is advocated by Meindl (1990, 1995) under the label "romance of leadership." This view holds that people, including followers, often attribute more to leadership-as–cause than is warranted. When organizations are transformed, people tend to search for and to find a great leader to explain what has happened. Leadership is emphasized more when productivity changes occur, and there is a disproportionate tendency to explain extreme and unexpected changes as the effects of leadership. Biases of this kind are most likely in the emotion-laden situations that appear to provoke charismatic or transformational leadership. Romanticizing the leader in this way can be so extreme that charismatic leadership becomes nothing more than a set of follower attributions.

These views have received support from research (see Ehrlich, Meindl, & Viellieu, 1990, and Chen & Meindl, 1991, for some of the more significant findings). Furthermore, these findings are clearly antithetical to both of the theories considered in this chapter. If charismatic leadership is a mirage, it needs to be studied at the level of follower perceptions; much of current theory and research thus would seem to miss the point. From the evidence, the romance of leadership is a real enough phenomenon on occasion. However, we do not know how often it occurs, and when it does how much variance it accounts for. There is good evidence that leadership effects do occur (see chapter 24) and that the romance of leadership may not always operate (Awamleh & Gardner, 1999). Probably certain followers in certain states are more susceptible to the effects of the romance of leadership. Meindl has indeed unearthed an important factor for the study of leadership, but not, on the current evidence, one that totally explains away the charismatic phenomenon; quite the contrary.

CONCLUSIONS

Both charismatic and transformational theory have considerable research support, even though both have sizable untested gaps and some instances where aspects of the theories have not been confirmed by the research. To some degree the confirmatory studies apply to both theories, although investigations are typically initiated to focus on one theory or the other. This implies overlap between the theories. Such overlap has clearly existed from the beginning, and both House and Bass have made efforts to integrate the theories further.

Such attempts to achieve integration have not been successful; nor do either charismatic theory or transformational theory match up very well with Weber— both lack the emphasis on divine attributions and the definition of charisma as rare in scope, for instance, although House appears closer to Weber as regards the latter than Bass. As currently specified, the theories are obviously different, even though each has responded to the research evidence by moving closer to the other.

The question that remains is whether these two somewhat different theories are nevertheless wrestling with the same constructs. Yukl (1999) believes they are not. He raises a question as to whether charismatic and transformational leadership can occur at the same time in the same person and, furthermore, if so, whether this is common or unusual and whether it is stable or unstable. He believes that any such simultaneous occurrence will inevitably be uncommon and unstable.

Unfortunately, the data to answer Yukl's question are not presently available. It seems unlikely that research of this kind can be conducted effectively until the theories deal more completely with the various aspects of the dark side of charisma, and measure them too, and until the routinization phenomenon is mapped into the theories. In any event, whether the constructs involved are the same, or partially overlapping, or completely separate is not answerable on either theoretical or data-based grounds right now. This is part of an agenda for the future.

Finally, there is a need to scale down the rhetoric regarding these theories. They are not supertheories, with superexplanatory powers, modeled after their charismatic subject matter. The correlations and dependent variable relationships are commendable, but after biases are removed, much the same as those reported for other good theories in this volume. There is no evidence so far that would warrant a claim for extraordinary accomplishments for either theory.

References

Avolio, Bruce J., & Bass, Bernard M. (1988). Transformational Leadership, Charisma, and Beyond. In James G. Hunt, R. Rajaram Baliga, H. Peter Dachler, & Chester A. Schriesheim (Eds.), *Emerging Leadership Vistas* (pp. 29–49). Lexington, MA: D. C. Heath.

Avolio, Bruce J., & Bass, Bernard M. (1995). Individual Consideration Viewed as Multiple Levels of Analysis: A Multi-Level Framework for Examining the Diffusion of Transformational Leadership. *Leadership Quarterly*, 6, 199–218.

Avolio, Bruce J.; Bass, Bernard M.; & Jung, Dong I. (1999). Re-examining the Components of Transformational and Transactional Leadership Using the Multifactor Leadership Questionnaire. *Journal of Occupational and Organizational Psychology*, 72, 441–462.

Avolio, Bruce J.; Waldman, David A.; & Einstein, Walter O. (1988). Transformational Leadership in a Management Game Simulation: Impacting the Bottom Line. *Group and Organization Studies*, 13, 59–80.

Awamleh, Raed, & Gardner, William L. (1999). Perceptions of Leader Charisma and Effectiveness: The Effects of Vision Content, Delivery, and Organizational Performance. *Leadership Quarterly*, 10, 345–373.

Barling, Julian; Weber, Tom; & Kelloway, E. Kevin (1996). Effects of Transformational Leadership Training on Attitudinal and Financial Outcomes: A Field Experiment. *Journal of Applied Psychology*, 81, 827–832.

Bass, Bernard M. (1981a). From Leaderless Group Discussions to the Cross-National Assessment of Managers. *Journal of Management*, 7(2), 63–76.

Bass, Bernard M. (1981b). *Stogdill's Handbook of Leadership: A Survey of Theory and Research*. New York: Free Press.

Bass, Bernard M. (1982). Intensity of Relation, Dyadic-Group Considerations, Cognitive Categorization, and Transformational Leadership. In James G. Hunt, Uma Sekaran, & Chester A. Schriesheim (Eds.), *Leadership: Beyond Establishment Views* (pp. 142–150). Carbondale: Southern Illinois University Press.

Bass, Bernard M. (1985a). Leadership: Good, Better, Best. *Organizational Dynamics*, 13(3), 26–40.

Bass, Bernard M. (1985b). *Leadership and Performance beyond Expectations*. New York: Free Press.

Bass, Bernard M. (1990). From Transactional to Transformational Leadership: Learning to Share the Vision. *Organizational Dynamcis*, 18(3),19–31.

Bass, Bernard M. (1992a). Stress and Leadership. In Frank Heller (Ed.), *Decision-Making and Leadership* (pp. 133–155). Cambridge: Cambridge University Press.

Bass, Bernard M. (1992b). A Transformational Journey. In Arthur G. Bedeian (Ed.), *Management Laureates:*

A Collection of Autobiographical Essays (Vol. 1, pp. 65–105). Greenwich, CT: JAI Press.

Bass, Bernard M. (1995). Theory of Transformational Leadership Redux. *Leadership Quarterly*, 6, 463–478.

Bass, Bernard M. (1997). Does the Transactional-Transformational Leadership Paradigm Transcend Organizational and National Boundaries? *American Psychologist*, 52, 130–139.

Bass, Bernard M. (1998). *Transformational Leadership: Industrial, Military, and Educational Impact*. Mahwah, NJ: Lawrence Erlbaum.

Bass, Bernard M., & Avolio, Bruce J. (1993). Transformational Leadership: A Response to Critiques. In Martin M. Chemers & Roya Ayman (Eds.), *Leadership Theory and Research: Perspectives and Directions* (pp. 49–79). San Diego: Academic Press.

Bass, Bernard M., & Avolio, Bruce J. (1994a). *Improving Organizational Effectiveness through Transformational Leadership*. Thousand Oaks, CA: Sage.

Bass, Bernard M., & Avolio, Bruce J. (1994b). Shatter the Glass Ceiling: Women May Make Better Managers. *Human Resource Management*, 33, 549–560.

Bass, Bernard M.; Avolio, Bruce J.; & Goodheim, Laurie (1987). Biography and the Assessment of Transformational Leadership at the World-Class Level. *Journal of Management*, 13, 7–19.

Bass, Bernard M., & Steidlmeier, Paul (1999). Ethics, Character, and Authentic Transformational Leadership Behavior. *Leadership Quarterly*, 10, 181–217.

Bass, Bernard M.; Waldman, David A.; Avolio, Bruce J.; & Bebb, Michael (1987). Transformational Leadership and the Falling Dominoes Effect. *Group and Organization Studies*, 12, 73–87.

Brown, Douglas J., & Lord, Robert G. (1999). The Utility of Experimental Research in the Study of Transformational/Charismatic Leadership. *Leadership Quarterly*, 10, 531–539.

Bryman, Alan (1992). *Charisma and Leadership in Organizations*. London: Sage:

Bryman, Alan (1996). Leadership in Organizations. In Stewart R. Clegg, Cynthia Hardy, & Walter R. Nord (Eds.), *Handbook of Organization Studies* (pp. 276–292). London: Sage.

Burns, James M. (1978). *Leadership*. New York: Harper & Row.

Bycio, Peter; Hackett, Rick D.; & Allen, Joyce S. (1995). Further Assessments of Bass's (1985) Conceptualization of Transactional and Transformational Leadership. *Journal of Applied Psychology*, 80, 468–478.

Chen, Chao C., & Meindl, James R. (1991). The Construction of Leadership Images in the Popular Press: The Case of Donald Burr and People Express. *Administrative Science Quarterly*, 36, 521–551.

Choi, Yeon, & Mai-Dalton, Renate R. (1999). The Model of Followers' Responses to Self-Sacrificial Leadership: An Empirical Test. *Leadership Quarterly*, 10, 397–421.

Conger, Jay A., & Kanungo, Rabindra N. (1998). *Charismatic Leadership in Organizations*. Thousand Oaks, CA: Sage.

Deluga, Ronald J. (1997). Relationship among American Presidential Charismatic Leadership, Narcissism, and Rated Performance. *Leadership Quarterly*, 8, 49–65.

Deluga, Ronald J. (1998). American Presidential Proactivity, Charismatic Leadership, and Rated Performance. *Leadership Quarterly*, 9, 265–291.

DenHartog, Deanne N.; House, Robert J.; Hanges, Paul J.; Ruiz-Quintanilla, S. Antonio; & Dorfman, Peter W. (1999). Culture Specific and Cross Culturally Generalizable Implicit Leadership Theories: Are Attributes of Charismatic/Transformational Leadership Universally Endorsed? *Leadership Quarterly*, 10, 219–256.

DenHartog, Deanne N.; Van Muijen, Jaap J.; & Koopman, Paul L. (1997). Transactional versus Transformational Leadership: An Analysis of the MLQ. *Journal of Occupational and Organizational Psychology*, 70, 19–34.

Ehrlich, Sanford B.; Meindl, James R.; & Viellieu, Ben (1990). The Charismatic Appeal of a Transformational Leader: An Empirical Case Study of a Small, High-Technology Contractor. *Leadership Quarterly*, 1, 229–248.

Fiol, C. Marlene; Harris, Drew; & House, Robert J. (1999). Charismatic Leadership: Strategies for Effecting Social Change. *Leadership Quarterly*, 10, 449–482.

Gardner, William L., & Avolio, Bruce J. (1998). The Charismatic Relationship: A Dramaturgical Perspective. *Academy of Management Review*, 23, 32–58.

Halpert, Jane A. (1990). The Dimensionality of Charisma. *Journal of Business and Psychology*, 4, 399–410.

Hater, John J., & Bass, Bernard M. (1988). Superiors' Evaluations and Subordinates' Perceptions of Transformational and Transactional Leadership. *Journal of Applied Psychology*, 73, 695–702.

Hogan, Robert; Raskin, Robert; & Fazzini, Don (1990). The Dark Side of Charisma. In Kenneth E. Clark & Miriam B. Clark (Eds.), *Measures of Leadership* (pp. 343–354). West Orange, NJ: Leadership Library of America.

Hooijberg, Robert, & Choi, Jaepil (2000). From Selling Peanuts and Beer in Yankee Stadium to Creating a Theory of Transformational Leadership: An Interview with Bernie Bass. *Leadership Quarterly*, 11, 291–306.

House, Robert J. (1977). A 1976 Theory of Charismatic Leadership. In James G. Hunt & Lars L. Larson (Eds.), *Leadership: The Cutting Edge* (pp. 189–207). Carbondale: Southern Illinois University Press.

House, Robert J. (1988). Power and Personality in Complex Organizations. *Research in Organizational Behavior*, 10, 305–357.

House, Robert J. (1991). The Distribution and Exercise of Power in Complex Organizations: A Meso Theory. *Leadership Quarterly*, 2, 23–58.

House, Robert J. (1992). The Nature of Power in Complex Organizations. In Henry Tosi (Ed.), *The Environment/Organization/Person Contingency Model: A Meso Approach to the Study of Organizations* (pp. 119–144). Greenwich, CT: JAI Press.

House, Robert J. (1993). Slow Learner and Late Bloomer. In Arthur G. Bedeian (Ed.), *Management Laureates: A Collection of Autobiographical Essays* (Vol. 2, pp. 39–78). Greenwich, CT: JAI Press.

House, Robert J. (1995). Leadership in the Twenty-First Century: A speculative Inquiry. In Ann Howard (Ed.), *The Changing Nature of Work* (pp. 411–450). San Francisco: Jossey-Bass.

House, Robert J. (1996). Path-Goal Theory of Leadership: Lessons, Legacy and a Reformulated Theory. *Leadership Quarterly*, 7, 323–352.

House, Robert J. (1999). Weber and the Neo-charismatic Leadership Paradigm: A Response to Beyer. *Leadership Quarterly*, 10, 563–574.

House, Robert J., & Aditya, Ram N. (1997). The Social Scientific Study of Leadership: Quo Vadis? *Journal of Management*, 23, 409–473.

House, Robert J., & Baetz, Mary L. (1979). Leadership: Some Empirical Generalizations and New Research Directions. *Research in Organizational Behavior*, 1, 341–423.

House, Robert J., & Howell, Jane M. (1992). Personality and Charismatic Leadership. *Leadership Quarterly*, 3, 81–108.

House, Robert J., & Podsakoff, Philip M. (1994). Leadership Effectiveness: Past Perspectives and Future Directions for Research. In Jerald Greenberg (Ed.), *Organizational Behavior: The State of the Science* (pp. 45–82). Hillsdale, NJ: Lawrence Erlbaum.

House, Robert J., & Shamir, Boas (1993). Toward the Integration of Transformational, Charismatic, and Visionary Theories. In Martin M. Chemers & Roya Ayman (Eds.), *Leadership Theory and Research: Perspectives and Directions* (pp. 81–107). San Diego, CA: Academic Press.

House, Robert J.; Spangler, William D.; & Woycke, James (1991). Personality and Charisma in the U.S. Presidency: A Psychological Theory of Leader Effectiveness. *Administrative Science Quarterly*, 36, 364–396.

House, Robert J.; Woycke, James; & Fodor, Eugene M. (1988). Charismatic and Noncharismatic Leaders: Differences in Behavior and Effectiveness. In Jay A. Conger & Rabindra N. Kanungo (Eds.), *Charismatic Leadership: The Elusive Factor in Organizational Effectiveness* (pp. 98–121). San Francisco: Jossey-Bass.

Howell, Jane M., & Avolio, Bruce J. (1993). Transformational Leadership, Transactional Leadership, Locus of Control, and Support for Innovation: Key Predictors of Consolidated-Business-Unit Performance. *Journal of Applied Psychology*, 78, 891–902.

Howell, Jane M., & Frost, Peter J. (1989). A Laboratory Study of Charismatic Leadership. *Organizational Behavior and Human Decision Processes*, 43, 243–269.

Howell, Jane M., & Higgins, Christopher A. (1990). Champions of Technological Innovations. *Administrative Science Quarterly*, 35, 317–341.

Hunt, James G.; Boal, Kimberly, B.; & Dodge, George E. (1999). The Effects of Visionary and Crisis-Responsive Charisma on Followers: An Experimental Examination of Two Kinds of Charismatic Leadership. *Leadership Quarterly*, 10, 423–448.

Jung, Dong I., & Avolio, Bruce J. (1999). Effects of Leadership Style and Followers' Cultural Orientation on Performance in Group and Individual Task Conditions. *Academy of Management Journal*, 42, 208–218.

Keller, Robert T. (1992). Transformational Leadership and the Performance of Research and Development Project Groups. *Journal of Management*, 18, 489–501.

Kirkpatrick, Shelley A., & Locke, Edwin A. (1996). Direct and Indirect Effects of Three Charismatic Leadership Components on Performance and Attitudes. *Journal of Applied Psychology*, 81, 36–51.

Klein, Katherine J., & House, Robert J. (1995). On Fire: Charismatic Leadership and Levels of Analysis. *Leadership Quarterly*, 6, 183–198.

Kudisch, Jeffrey D.; Poteet, Mark L.; Dobbins, Gregory H.; Rush, Michael C.; & Russell, Joyce E. A. (1995). Expert Power, Referent Power, and Charisma: Toward the Resolution of a Theoretical Debate. *Journal of Business and Psychology*, 10, 177–195.

Lord, Robert G.; Brown, Douglas J.; & Freiberg, Steven J. (1999). Understanding the Dynamics of Leadership: The Role of Follower Self-Concepts in the Leader/

Follower Relationship. *Organizational Behavior and Human Decision Processes*, 78, 167–203.

Lord, Robert G., & Maher, Karen J. (1991). *Leadership and Information Processing: Linking Perceptions and Performance*. Boston: Unwin Hyman.

Lowe, Kevin B.; Kroeck, K. Galen; & Sivasubramaniam, Nagaraj (1996). Effective Correlates of Transformational and Transactional Leadership: A Meta-Analytic Review of the MLQ Literature. *Leadership Quarterly*, 7, 385–425.

Meindl, James R. (1990). On Leadership: An Alternative to the Conventional Wisdom. *Research in Organizational Behavior*, 12, 159–203.

Meindl, James R. (1995). The Romance of Leadership as a Follower-Centric Theory: A Social Constructionist Approach. *Leadership Quarterly*, 6, 329–341.

Nur, Yusuf A. (1998). Charisma and Managerial Leadership: The Gift That Never Was. *Business Horizons*, 41(4). 19–26.

O'Connor, Jennifer; Mumford, Michael D.; Clifton, Timothy C.; Gessner, Theodore L.; & Connelly, Mary S. (1995). Charismatic Leaders and Destructiveness: An Historiometric Study. *Leadership Quarterly*, 6, 529–555.

Pawar, Badrinarayan S., & Eastman, Kenneth K. (1997). The Nature and Implications of Contextual Influences on Transformational Leadership: A Conceptual Examination. *Academy of Management Review*, 22, 80–109.

Pillai, Rajnandini, & Meindl, James R. (1991). The Effect of a Crisis on the Emergence of Charismatic Leadership: A Laboratory Study. *Academy of Management Proceedings*, 51, 235–239.

Pillai, Rajnandini, & Meindl, James R. (1998). Context and Charisma: A Meso Level Examination of the Relationship of Organic Structure, Collectivism, and Crisis to Charismatic Leadership. *Journal of Management*, 24, 643–671.

Pillai, Rajnandini; Schriesheim, Chester A.; & Williams, Eric S. (1999). Fairness Perceptions and Trust as Mediators for Transformational and Transactional Leadership: A Two-Sample Study. *Journal of Management*, 25, 897–933.

Podsakoff, Philip M.; MacKenzie, Scott B.; & Bommer, William H. (1996). Transformational Leader Behaviors and Substitutes for Leadership as Determinants of Employee Satisfaction, Commitment, Trust, and Organizational Citizenship Behaviors. *Journal of Management*, 22, 259–298.

Podsakoff, Philip M.; MacKenzie, Scott B.; Moorman, Robert H.; & Fetter, Richard (1990). Transformational Leader Behaviors and Their Effects on Followers' Trust in Leader, Satisfaction, and Organiza-

tional Citizenship Behaviors. *Leadership Quarterly*, 1, 107–142.

Puffer, Sheila M. (1990). Attributions of Charismatic Leadership: The Impact of Decision Style, Outcome, and Observer Characteristics. *Leadership Quarterly*, 1, 177–192.

Seltzer, Joseph, & Bass, Bernard M. (1990). Transformational Leadership: Beyond Initiation and Consideration. *Journal of Management*, 16, 693–703.

Shamir, Boas (1995). Social Distance and Charisma: Theoretical Notes and an Exploratory Study. *Leadership Quarterly*, 6, 19–47.

Shamir, Boas; Arthur, Michael B.; & House, Robert J. (1994). The Rhetoric of Charismatic Leadership: A Theoretical Extension, A Case Study, and Implications for Research. *Leadership Quarterly*, 5, 25–42.

Shamir, Boas; House, Robert J.; & Arthur, Michael B. (1993). The Motivational Effects of Charismatic Leadership: A Self-Concept Based Theory. *Organization Science*, 4, 577–594.

Shamir, Boas; Zakay, Eliav; Breinin, Esther; & Popper, Micha (1998). Correlates of Charismatic Leader Behavior in Military Units: Subordinates' Attitudes, Unit Characteristics, and Superiors' Appraisals of Leader Performance. *Academy of Management Journal*, 41, 387–409.

Shea, Christine M., & Howell, Jane M. (1999). Charismatic Leadership and Task Feedback: A Laboratory Study of Their Effects on Self-Efficacy and Task Performance. *Leadership Quarterly*, 10, 375–396.

Spangler, William D., & House, Robert J. (1991). Presidential Effectiveness and the Leadership Motive Profile. *Journal of Personality and Social Psychology*, 60, 439–455.

Spreitzer, Gretchen M., & Quinn, Robert E. (1996). Empowering Middle Managers to Be Transformational Leaders. *Journal of Applied Behavioral Science*, 32, 237–261.

Trice, Harrison M., & Beyer, Janice M. (1986). Charisma and Its Routinization in Two Social Movement Organizations. *Research in Organizational Behavior*, 8, 113–164.

Waldman, David A.; Bass, Bernard M.; & Einstein, Walter O. (1987). Leadership and Outcomes of Performance Appraisal Processes. *Journal of Occupational Psychology*, 60, 177–186.

Waldman, David A., & Yammarino, Francis J. (1999). CEO Charismatic Leadership: Levels-of-Management and Levels-of-Analysis Effects. *Academy of Management Review*, 24, 266–285.

Wofford, Jerry C. (1999). Laboratory Research on Charismatic Leadership: Fruitful or Futile? *Leadership Quarterly*, 10, 523–529.

Yagil, Dana (1998). Charismatic Leadership and Organizational Hierarchy: Attribution of Charisma to Close and Distant Leaders. *Leadership Quarterly,* 9, 161–176.

Yammarino, Francis J.; Spangler, William D.; & Dubinsky, Alan J. (1998). Transformational and Contingent Reward Leadership: Individual, Dyad, and Group Levels of Analysis. *Leadership Quarterly,* 9, 27–54.

Yorges, Stefani L.; Weiss, Howard M.; & Strickland, Oriel J. (1999). The Effect of Leader Outcomes on Influence, Attributions, and Perceptions of Charisma. *Journal of Applied Psychology,* 84, 428–436.

Yukl, Gary (1993). A Retrospective on Robert House's "1976 Theory of Charismatic Leadership" and Recent Revisions. *Leadership Quarterly,* 4, 367–373.

Yukl, Gary (1999). An Evaluation of Conceptual Weaknesses in Transformational and Charismatic Leadership Theories. *Leadership Quarterly,* 10, 285–305.

Yukl, Gary A., & Van Fleet, David D. (1982). Cross-Situational, Multimethod Research on Military Leader Effectiveness. *Organizational Behavior and Human Performance,* 30, 87–108.

Part IX

Second-Generation Theories: Concepts of Organization

Chapter 26

Resource Dependence, Organizational Ecology, and Neoinstitutional Theories

This is the second-generation equivalent of parts IV (Systems Concepts of Organization) and V (Bureaucracy-Related Concepts) from the first generation of theories. New ideas came to the fore primarily during the late 1970s, and during the 1980s also, then rose to dominate large segments of macro organizational behavior. Systems theory began to take on an even more open demeanor, and the Weberian formulations became somewhat less evident. These new theories were (1) Jeffrey Pfeffer and Gerald Salancik's resource dependence theory; (2) a social ecology of organizational populations originally set forth by Michael Hannan and John Freeman, and then adopted in some form by a circle of others with a similar sociological orientation; and (3) what has come to be called neoinstitutionalism, or the new institutionalism in organizational analysis, which arose at roughly the same time from a number of sources. The most fully developed theoretical position among these is that of John Meyer and Richard Scott, but the views of Lynne Zucker and also of Walter Powell and Paul DiMaggio require attention as well.

These three theories, particularly the last two, have come to take on a role not unlike that which characterized the various schools of organizational behavior in its early years (see chapter 5). They are clearly group phenomena with adherents and various degrees of commitment to the "gospel." Yet they deal with testable theories, not philosophical positions, and the adherents are by and large sincere devotees of empirical research, not of philosophical speculation and advocacy. A considerable amount of research has evolved. Accordingly, I do not believe these theories represent a reversion to the schools of the past in organizational behavior. However, there are those who believe differently on this score, and it is appropriate to be aware of this fact.

EXTERNAL CONTROL OF ORGANIZATIONS: RESOURCE DEPENDENCE PERSPECTIVE

Pfeffer's work on resource dependence theory does not appear to have had major roots in prior writings. He labels his autobiography "Taking the Road Less Traveled" (Pfeffer, 1996) and describes a process of theory development that represents a break with existing positions. Presumably as a result of this iconoclastic bent, he had difficulty initially getting his theoretical ideas accepted for publication, although his empirical work had much better success. As a result, although the first statements of the theory were contained in his 1971 dissertation, it was not until 7 years later that a full and formal published version appeared (Pfeffer & Salancik, 1978). This presentation, which now included a collaboration with Gerald Salancik, represents a considerable refinement of the earlier views.

Background

Pfeffer, although a westerner by birth and upbringing, received his undergraduate and master's degrees at the same time in industrial administration from Carnegie Mellon University in Pittsburgh. That was in 1968. Subsequently he returned to the West Coast and entered the doctoral program in business at Stanford University, from which he obtained the Ph.D. in 1971. Next came another sojourn eastward to the business school at the University of Illinois, where he joined forces with Salancik who arrived there at the same time. This stint together, in fact, lasted only 2 years, before Pfeffer moved back west to the University of California at Berkeley. From there, in 1979, he shifted

back to his alma mater, Stanford, where he has remained since. His entire career has been in business schools and in organizational behavior.

Salancik came to resource dependence theory after considerable theoretical and empirical work had been completed on the subject, but at a point when the theory itself was going nowhere; in fact, its author had largely given up on attempting to publish the theory (Pfeffer, 1996). Salancik brought to this endeavor a master's degree in journalism from Northwestern University, a doctorate in social psychology from Yale University (in 1970), skills as an effective writer and editor, and a questioning mind, which paid little deference to the status quo (Leblebici & Porac, 1997). Salancik remained at the University of Illinois for a number of years after Pfeffer left, but ultimately moved on to the School of Industrial Administration at Carnegie Mellon. He died in 1996 at the age of 53.

Pfeffer-Salancik Theory

Resource dependence theory is one among several outgrowths of a somewhat more fundamental perspective. This position is set forth by Pfeffer (1990), in an essay that was originally presented on the occasion of the fiftieth anniversary of the publication of Chester Barnard's *The Functions of the Executive*. This basic perspective operates under the assumptions that (1) organizations and their people are interdependent with other organizations and people, and (2) consequent to this interdependence and the social relationships involved, understanding is much better served by investigating the effects and the constraints that emanate from the social contexts; this is true of both individual and organizational behavior. We have already seen some of the outgrowths of this perspective in chapter 1 of this book, specifically Pfeffer's views on the dispositions versus situations controversy and his treatment of consensus in science.

In the discussion that follows I focus directly on Pfeffer's resource dependence formulations and do not follow other outgrowths of his more fundamental perspective. The major source here is the book with Salancik (1978). However, there were earlier abbreviated theoretical statements, including Howard Aldrich and Pfeffer (1976) and Pfeffer (1978).

External Perspective

The Pfeffer approach to theorizing is essentially that of open systems in that the focus is on external social constraints on organizational action. In addition, the discussion draws heavily on the ideas of other organizational behavior theorists, many of them treated in prior chapters of this book. Among these are Katz and Kahn's social psychology of organizations (chapter 14), Trist and Emery's sociotechnical systems approach (chapter 14), Thompson's sociological open systems theory (chapter 15), Perrow's comparative framework (chapter 16), Blau's theory of differentiation (chapter 18), the contributions of Simon, Cyert, and March on organizational decision making (chapter 22), and Weick's views on organizing and sensemaking (chapter 22). Furthermore, the strategic contingencies theory of intra-organizational power (Hickson, Hinings, Lee, Schneck, & Pennings, 1971), which had close ties to the Aston studies (chapter 18), is used extensively. These reference points provide some indication of the domain within which the Pfeffer and Salancik theory operates.

The theory is largely concerned with how managers attempt to ensure organizational survival:

> Organizations survive to the extent that they are effective. Their effectiveness derives from the management of demands, particularly the demands of interest groups upon which the organizations depend for resources and support. . . . The key to organizational survival is the ability to acquire and maintain resources. . . . Organizations must transact with other elements in their environment to acquire needed resources. (Pfeffer & Salancik, 1978, p. 2)

Environments can change and resources can become scarce; environmental demands and constraints are constantly shifting. *Effectiveness* is the ability to create outcomes and actions that meet the external standards determining how well the organization meets the demands of environmental interests concerned with its activities. *Environments* are important to know about and understand because that is where judgments about organizational effectiveness reside. *Constraints* operate whenever one response to a situation, rather than being random, is more probable than other responses. Because behavior is widely if not exclusively constrained, individuals actually account for relatively little variation in organizational behavior. A major function of managers is to serve as symbols, thus enhancing feelings of predictability and control; in addition, there are many important possibilities

for managerial action, and these are often aimed at adjusting to and altering the social context.

If they are to survive, organizations must operate as parts of coalitions that contribute resources and support. Coalition participants that contribute more needed or valued inputs tend to have greater influence and control, and thus these factors become part of the exchange. Participants may institute inconsistent criteria and conflicting demands, any one of which will contribute only a proportion of its behavior. The boundary of an organization is established by the point at which the discretion to control an activity is less than the discretion of some other entity. In contrast to effectiveness, which is an external judgment, *efficiency* is the extent to which an organization accomplishes objectives, given the resources used. The managerial task is to manage the coalition to ensure continued support and survival of the organization.

Interdependence

Whenever one actor does not fully control all conditions for achieving an action or obtaining the desired outcome, *interdependence* exists. This interdependence varies with the scarcity of resources, characterizes transactions within the same environment, and is a consequence of the open-systems nature of organizations; it is virtually inevitable. A variety of conditions affect the extent to which an organization is subject to control under these circumstances:

1. The focal organization is aware of the demands.
2. The focal organization obtains some resources from the social actor making the demands.
3. The resource is a critical or important part of the focal organization's operation.
4. The social actor controls the allocation, access, or use of the resource; alternative sources for the resource are not available to the focal organization.
5. The focal organization does not control the allocation, access, or use of other resources critical to the social actor's operation and survival.
6. The actions or inputs of the focal organization are visible and can be assessed by the social actor to judge whether the actions comply with its demands.
7. The focal organization's satisfaction of the social actor's requests are not in conflict

with the satisfaction of demands from other components of the environment with which it is interdependent.

8. The focal organization does not control the determination, formulation, or expression of the social actor's demands.

9. The focal organization is capable of developing actions or outcomes that will satisfy the external demands.

10. The organization desires to survive. (Pfeffer & Salancik, 1978, p. 44)

External control becomes increasingly likely as more of these conditions exist. Vulnerability in this regard depends on the importance of the resource exchange (both the relative magnitude and the criticality) and on the degree of discretion over the allocation of the resource existing in some other social actor. Bases for control over a resource include possession, actual use, and the ability to regulate resource possession and use.

Dependence is the product of the importance of an input or output to an organization and the degree to which it is controlled by a few organizations. For dependence to operate, there must be asymmetry of exchange so that some net power exists in the hands of the less-dependent participant.

Knowing the Environment

Three levels of environment may be distinguished: the entire system created by an organization's transactions, those features among these with which the organization directly interacts, and the organization's enacted environment that has been created by its processes of perception and attention.

Figure 26.1 sets forth the strategic dimensions of organizational environments and the relationships among them. *Concentration* is the extent to which power is concentrated or dispersed in the environment. *Munificence* is the availability or scarcity of critical resources. *Interconnectedness* is the number and pattern of linkages among relevant organizations. If the interconnectedness is high, the environment of the focal organization tends to be more uncertain; if the system is loosely coupled, disturbances have a chance to be absorbed and certainty increases. Because of government actions, organizations are now experiencing greater interconnectedness.

Since environments are enacted as organizations respond to them, organizations tend to be in a lag position, reacting to what has been important in the past. Organizations may also misread interdependence, either by underestimating their dependence in certain respects or by failing to perceive the complex relationships that exist with other elements of their environments. A problem also exists when an organization is recognized as a potent influence, but the demands or criterion involved are misinterpreted. Then there is the matter of balancing competing demands. A procedure for determining the effectiveness of actions in the face of these problems in environmental enactment is outlined in figure 26.2.

Managing the Organization's Environment

Managers cope with environmental constraints and demands in various ways—compliance, adaptation, avoidance, and so on. An organization that permits itself to be subjected to long-term, successful influence attempts may well find its survival threatened. Thus some method of managing the dependence becomes necessary. Perhaps most effective for this purpose is to find some way to avoid those conditions that demand compliance. This may well require a resort to secrecy or the restriction of information.

Merger and growth are related ways of restructuring and increasing influence within environmental relationships. Organizations would be expected to merge into industries that create their greatest problems. Diversification is similarly motivated by a desire to avoid interdependence. Attempts to reduce sales in certain areas, or of particular product lines, can also serve to remove dependencies. Alternatively, growth can provide greater power over environmental factors and can enhance an organization's prospects for survival.

Coordination with external organizations serves to manage interdependence. Included here are cooptation, trade associations, cartels, reciprocal agreements, coordinating councils, advisory boards, interlocking boards of directors, joint ventures, and social norms that govern interdependent parties. The latter are particularly common among professionals. Boards of directors are commonly used to coopt external organizations with which important interdependencies exist. All of these approaches attempt to border on collusion without invoking legal actions.

Finally, another class of strategies may be used to manage interdependence:

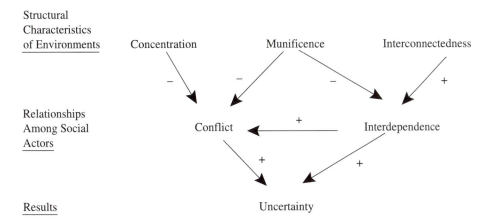

FIGURE 26.1 Relationships among the dimensions of organizational environments (+ = a positive influence, − = a negative influence). From Jeffrey Pfeffer & Gerald R. Salancik (1978), *The External Control of Organizations: A Resource Dependence Perspective* (New York: Harper & Row), 68. Copyright 1978. Reprinted by permission of Pearson Education, Inc.

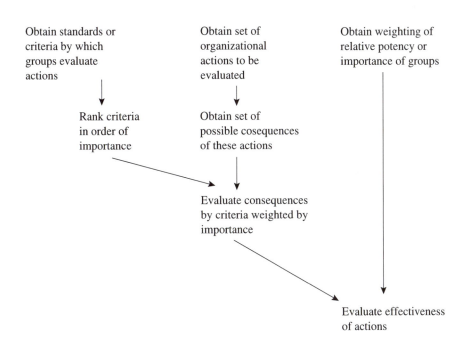

FIGURE 26.2 A methodology for evaluating the effectiveness of actions. From Jeffrey Pfeffer & Gerald R. Salancik (1978), *The External Control of Organizations: A Resource Dependence Perspective* (New York: Harper & Row), 87. Copyright 1978. Reprinted by permission of Pearson Education, Inc.

When dependence is not capable of being managed by negotiating stable structures of interorganizational action, . . . organizations seek to use the greater power of . . . government to eliminate the difficulties or provide for their needs. The organization . . . may seek direct cash subsidies, market protection, or may seek to reduce competitive uncertainty by charging competitors with antitrust violations. . . . The courts and the government are increasingly replacing the market in determining which organizations will survive and prosper. (Pfeffer & Salancik, 1978, p. 189)

Executive Succession

The basic proposition with regard to succession is that environmental contingencies influence the selection and replacement of top managers in such a way as to place the organization in greater alignment with environmental requirements. One possible model of adaptation along these lines is given in figure 26.3, which shows that organizational actions are a result of political processes within organizations, not a direct consequence of environmental requirements; the coupling is loose, with power as an intervening variable.

Power is conceptualized according to the strategic contingencies theory (Hickson et al., 1971) which involves the following:

1. The ability of a subunit to cope with organizational uncertainties or contingencies
2. The substitutability of the subunit's capabilities—these capabilities must be relatively unique

3. The pervasiveness or importance of the contingency and uncertainty to the organization.

Such power may become institutionalized, and subunit power serves to resolve political contests over administrative succession.

Top executives tend to be recruited from competitors if interfirm coordination appears to be an appropriate strategy. Turnover at the top is most likely when the contingencies faced are ones that present managers cannot handle. Thus, the theory is not one of direct environmental determinism.

Three managerial roles are posited: symbolic, responsive, and discretionary. The symbolic role has already been noted, and administrative succession may be invoked to change appearances in this manner. But it is typically the responsive and discretionary roles that contribute to whatever variance in outcomes does stem from managerial activity. In the responsive role a manager assesses the organizational context, determines how to cope with it, and implements that process; these are adaptive processes. In the discretionary role a manager goes beyond adaptation in taking action to modify the environment and to alter the existing system of constraints and dependencies.

The implications of the theory for organizational design relate to the design of environmental scanning systems, designs intended to loosen dependencies, designs for managing conflicting demands, and designs to modify chief executive positions. Clearly, knowing the environment well and creating mechanisms to

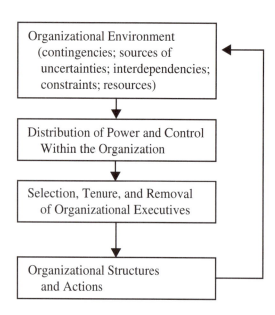

FIGURE 26.3 A model of organizational adaptation to environmental constraints via succession. Adapted from Jeffrey Pfeffer & Gerald R. Salancik (1978), *The External Control of Organizations: A Resource Dependence Perspective* (New York: Harper & Row), 229; Jeffrey Pfeffer (1982), *Organizations and Organization Theory* (Marshfield, MA: Pitman), 203.

accomplish this are a central focus of the resource dependence perspective. Loosening dependencies is best achieved through diversification, as by a resort to many small suppliers. Structural differentiation is introduced in this view, not as a direct means to cope with size but as a method of coping with conflicting demands, bringing them together in order to concentrate a specific structure on them. Finally, having multiple chief executives (rather than one) to cope with varied demands is recommended:

> This scenario does not suggest an increase in decentralized, participative management structures as a result of turbulent organizational environments. Rather, we would suggest that uncertainty will result in greater efforts at coordination, which require the concentration of power and decision discretion. . . . If turbulence and uncertainty is perceived as stress or pressure, then centralization is a more correct prediction than decentralization. (Pfeffer & Salancik, 1978, pp. 285–286)

Further on Power

Several recapitualizations of resource dependence theory have appeared since the basic statement in 1978. These are short, intended to place the theory in the context of organizational behavior theory as a whole, and add little if anything that is new. Pfeffer (1982) describes the theory as operating at the level of the total organization and taking a perspective on action that is externally constrained and controlled. In these respects the theory is grouped with population ecology theory. In Pfeffer (1997) the theory is described as a social model of behavior and is related to network models of organizations, which are said to have in a sense arisen out of the resource dependence perspective.

The primary subsequent enhancements to the theory came in the area of power, however, with most of them presented in Pfeffer (1981). That book contains an extensive treatment of the literature on power as a nonpsychological construct, and only limited attention is given to power in the context of resource dependence theory.

The theory as stated in Pfeffer (1981) emphasizes social power of a kind that derives from the ability to provide resources on which the organization depends. Accordingly, power may be organized around a large set of resources, including money, prestige, legitimacy, rewards and sanctions, expertise, and the ability

to deal with uncertainty. The latter had been considered in previous treatments under the rubric of strategic contingencies theory. The other resources operate in a manner similar to the way strategic contingencies formulations handle the ability to deal with uncertainty. Within resource dependence theory, uncertainty coping capability is defined as a crucial resource for an organization.

Although the ability to bring in crucial resources or to cope with critical uncertainties is important to power attainment, this is not the whole story. Power also accrues from a person's ability to affect some part of the decision process. The capacity to affect the decision premises or underlying values is particularly important; so, too, is control over the decision alternatives considered and over information about the alternatives. Clearly a person's position in the communication network has a great deal to do with individual power.

With regard to the symbolic role of managers, Pfeffer (1981) holds that the task of symbolic activity (and political language) is to rationalize and to justify decisions that have been reached on the basis of power, so as to make these results more acceptable and legitimate. Thus the exercise of power is facilitated. The theoretical position is that power derived from resource-based considerations is employed partly in the definition of social realities and justifications for behaviors that are consistent with the basic positions held by those with power.

Early on, Pfeffer says very little about "individual differences in ability, political skill, and the willingness to use those skills and abilities in contests within the organization" (1981, p. 131). The literature on these psychological matters is skimmed over lightly, and power motivation is not considered at all. Subsequently, in Pfeffer (1992), which was written primarily as a text on power, this coverage of psychological factors is expanded somewhat but is still incomplete. What treatment there is is couched in terms of criticism, largely on the grounds that research in the area does not give sufficient attention to contextual factors surrounding and preceding the manifestation of power motivation.

Evaluation and Impact

Almost all of the research bearing on resource dependence theory in the 1970s and 1980s was produced by the theory's authors. There was, in fact, a considerable amount of this research published, particularly in the period during the 1970s before the emergence of Pfeffer and Salancik's primary work (1978). The impact of this research on the field of organizational behavior was sizable. Its ties to the published theory are subject to some debate in that these research results clearly did influence specific formulations on occasion. Nevertheless, it is apparent that much of the theory preceded the research, and certainly the fundamental perspective regarding the role of interdependence and context did; thus it is appropriate to view the early research by the authors in a general sense as providing tests of theory.

Research by the Theory's Authors in the 1970s

As indicated, the body of research in this category is sizable, with over 25 studies reported. Among these I will focus on some of the more significant, in an attempt to show the diversity of findings marshaled behind the theory. These publications began to appear immediately after Pfeffer completed his doctorate and initially were based on his dissertation.

Pfeffer (1972c) dealt with the use of cooptation as a tactic for managing interdependence; like so many of the other studies, it used public data for purposes of analysis. The research was concerned with the composition and size of corporate boards and demonstrated that these factors are systematically related to the organization's need to deal with important environmental components: the percentage of board members from financial institutions is related to the firm's need for external capital, for instance. Eight out of nine such hypotheses are confirmed.

Pfeffer (1972a) used interview data collected from managers in Israel by a non-author. It showed how the companies involved were influenced by their dependence on government particularly, but on banks as well. Managers' attitudes, time allocations, and advancements were all related to these external contingencies, although the correlations obtained were generally rather low.

Next Pfeffer (1972b) turned to merger activity. A strong association between mergers and patterns of resource exchange was found, accounting for about one half of the variance in merger behavior. Merger was found to consistently reduce interdependence by acquiring competitors, suppliers, and customers or by diversifying into new areas so that reliance on an existing set of organizations is reduced.

Research on hospitals provided further evidence of environmental interdependence. Boards of directors were influenced by such factors as the need to raise money, the relationship to government, the importance of influence in the community, political connections, and the like (Pfeffer, 1973). The size of the board was influenced by the need for cooptation, thus supporting prior conclusions. An analysis that focused on the tenure and characteristics of hospital administrators indicated that here, too, variables descriptive of the external context played an important role (Pfeffer & Salancik, 1977).

Pfeffer and Huseyin Leblebici (1973) studied how such environmental factors as the number of organizations in the industry, growth in industry sales, technological change, and average firm size relate to the movement of executives between firms. A number of associations between the environmental context and executive recruitment were established, in particular those involving the promotion from within of the chief executive.

Other studies were conducted relating power indices to resource considerations in a university context, specifically at the University of Illinois. In the first of these a department's power was found to be positively related to the proportion of the university budget received; workload and student demand had little influence (Pfeffer & Salancik, 1974). Later it was found that departmental power was most highly correlated with the ability to bring in funds through grants and contracts, and somewhat less with indicators of national prestige (Salancik & Pfeffer, 1974). In one way or another, power was a function of the ability to provide needed resources.

In an investigation using Federal Trade Commission data Pfeffer and Phillip Nowak (1976) document that joint venture activity is consistently supportive of a number of hypotheses tying joint ventures to the process of managing interdependencies. However, the findings are not strong and account for only a small proportion of the variance in joint venture formation.

Finally, an analysis of United Fund distributions to member agencies indicated that the amount so designated was greater if the agency could raise more money outside the fund, and thus had greater ability to withdraw from United Fund participation (Pfeffer & Leong, 1977). If the fund was more dependent on the particular agency for visibility and fund-raising credibility, the relationship between outside support and fund allocation was particularly strong. Again, resource dependence was key.

Author Research in the 1980s

Research by the authors on resource dependence propositions generally tailed off in the 1980s, and appears nonexistent after that. Among the more significant studies from this period are several that deal with a university context other than the University of Illinois (Pfeffer & Moore, 1980a, 1980b). Average tenure of department heads (and thus little succession) was positively related to the level of paradigm consensus in the field and negatively related to department size. Both of these effects were more pronounced when resource scarcity in a monetary sense was greater. Paradigm consensus is assumed to reflect both shared beliefs internally and an external constraint system. This research also found support for the previous University of Illinois findings regarding departmental power, budget allocations, and contract funding. However, paradigm consensus as a characteristic of the field was now added to this mix, contributing to both budget allocations, and grants and contracts. It appears that paradigm considerations contribute to power, which, in turn, facilitates resource advocacy.

A study of the development of internal labor markets, defined as promotion from within and a limited number of ports of entry into the organization, tested the hypothesis that greater labor scarcity (recruitment difficulties) will create more internalized markets. This was the only one of 10 research hypotheses that was based on resource dependence formulations. It was not supported by the data (Pfeffer & Cohen, 1984).

Pfeffer and Alison Davis-Blake (1987) report on a test of resource dependence and power that compared the salaries paid to certain position incumbents in public and private universities. In public universities, community services, student placement, and athletics were found to be more prevalent and thus presumably more important; in private universities, the more important functions were development, admissions, and alumni affairs. The relative salaries of the directors of these various functions in the two sectors were determined and were generally found (with a few exceptions) to be higher in the context where the activities involved were viewed as more important, again supporting the Pfeffer and Salancik (1978) theory.

Replications and Expansions

Although the bulk of the research on resource dependence theory has been done by the authors, and a considerable body of research of a tangential nature has been invoked in its support, there have been a few studies by others that bear directly on the theory and require discussion.

One of the earliest of these studies involved a replication of the Pfeffer and Leong (1977) work on power relationships in United Fund activities (Provan, Beyer, & Kruytbosch, 1980). The results generally supported those found previously and thus resource dependency theory. There was some departure in the interpretation of these findings, however, which may or may not have represented a significant consideration; without further data, this cannot be determined. In any event it is clear that units that obtain more resources externally also are in a position to extract more internally. The study did not obtain this same result using alternative power measures, but did yield replication when the Pfeffer and Leong (1977) measure was used. The problem appears to be a lack of construct validity among the various power indices, none of which dealt with power motivation and individual difference measures. Had the latter been included, they may well have helped to explain the disparities.

Research by Sydney Finkelstein (1997) provided a replication of the Pfeffer (1972b) analysis of corporate merger activity, but with a more precise methodology. Again the results were consistent with the prior findings. Although significant results were found, however, the magnitudes of association and of explained variance were considerably less than previous research would have indicated, suggesting that resource dependence theory may have rather limited explanatory power. Clearly, other factors have a lot to do with merger activity, especially mergers across industries.

Amy Hillman, Albert Cannella, and Ramona Paetzold (2000) conducted a study that was intended to determine how boards of directors change with a drastic shift in the environmental context. The research focused on the airline industry in the United States, before and after deregulation. As hypothesized, board composition did change: during regulation, appointments were more frequently insiders and support specialists; after deregulation, the emphasis shifted to business experts and, in particular, community influentials. These findings are interpreted as supporting resource dependence expectations.

In three different areas these studies provide results that are entirely consistent with predictions from the Pfeffer-Salancik theory and from the authors' earlier investigations.

Looking at the Research

Overall, the evidence in support of research dependence theory appears to be varied and quite convincing. Some of the findings do not appear to explain a great deal of variance in dependent variables, but nevertheless the phenomenon is robust enough to cross-validate in new samples and contexts. The major criticisms seem to involve a call for research in areas of the theory not considered to date, rather than attacks on existing research or a serious deficiency in research overall. Pfeffer, and Salancik later on, have done an exemplary job of providing examples of what research on the theory and its variables should look like. In the process they have confirmed the theory in many of its aspects as well.

Pfeffer's own specifications regarding needed research relate to the succession process:

> New people are brought in and a new perspective on the organization and its issues comes to occupy more and more positions in the organization—perhaps until that power becomes institutionalized, the organization fails to adapt, and the process begins anew. (1989, p. 387)

Later he says:

> None of these assertions tying operation of power to succession and adjustment to environmental contingencies has, in fact, been adequately tested. So there is the question of to what extent succession actually reflects considerations of power and . . . the consequences of this for the organization. (p. 392)

The study of board succession by Hillman et al. (2000) deals with this issue in part, but much more longitudinal study along these lines is clearly needed, as Pfeffer indicates.

Another perspective on gaps in the research argues for more studies on the role of groups such as cartels, trade associations, oligopolies, coalitions of consumer organizations, and the like within the resource dependence perspective (Galaskiewicz, 1985). Similarly, there is a call for research on variations in the resource environment—rich or lean, stable or unstable, homogeneous or heterogeneous, concentrated or dispersed—as these influence managing interdependencies. The point is that major parts of the theory have not been studied at all. This appears to reflect

the fact that these areas have not been the subject of research by the authors and, consequently, lack the specific delineation that such research can provide.

Looking at the Theory

A major criticism that has been directed specifically at the Pfeffer-Salancik theory is that it intentionally uses linguistic ambiguity to increase the range of phenomena covered. Thus what is really a rather narrow-gauge theory comes to be extended to a much broader framework, so that studies that are very tangential become applicable. In support of this view, the three central concepts of the theory—power, resource dependence, and organizational coalitions—are accused of being so general and ambiguous in meaning that they are virtually incapable of refutation (Astley & Zammuto, 1992).

This critique has some validity in that the theory does appear to be relatively narrow in its application, given the limited amount of variance often accounted for in research and the failure to deal with internal organizational dynamics. Furthermore, the level of ambiguity of the theoretical statements is sufficient to accommodate citations to a literature that on other grounds would not seem appropriate. But the key consideration is that when variables are operationalized and when research is actually conducted, things become much less ambiguous. Thus in a sense the authors' research keeps the theory honest. Without the research, the theory might be considered to manifest excessive generality, although not to the point of being viewed as irrefutable; with the research, a large number of the theory's aspects achieve considerable precision.

An example of how this process works may be derived from the theory plus the research testing it conducted by Pfeffer and Davis-Blake (1987). David Balkin and Brendan Bannister (1993) developed a set of propositions based on this background to predict the use of special pay forms (executive incentives, commissions, team bonuses) for certain types of positions. Thus strategic employee groups and political considerations in pay decisions are encompassed. In this instance the theory, when adequately amplified by author research, proved sufficiently precise to serve as a building block for an applied theoretical extension. Adding precision to theory through research design is not the recommended approach to theory construction, but it appears to have worked well in this instance.

A different type of theoretical concern relates to the open systems nature of the formulations on resource dependence and the consequent stress on *survival* in the face of environmental constraints as the essential intended result of organizational efforts (Hall, 1987). In endorsing this perspective, Pfeffer and Salancik (1978) bypass any view of organizational goals as factors in decision processes. Yet simply endorsing internal goals as additional types of constraints (see chapter 22) to be considered in the mix with external environmental constraints when managerial decisions are under consideration would make the theory much more powerful, and closer to reality. To ignore profit considerations, for example, seems shortsighted.

This type of resort to blinders on the theory seems to represent an unnecessary limitation. There are other examples of this same type of problem, which seems to result from a doctrinaire commitment to avoiding any mention of the internal processes that guide organizational actors (see Jongbloed & Frost, 1985; Campling & Michelson, 1998). If the theory could be opened up in this manner, what is now a useful but constrained theory could become much more broadly valuable.

An example of this point can be provided with reference to Pfeffer's handling of the power variable. Pfeffer (1992) argues that treatments of power motivation and related individual differences are deficient because they do not consider external contextual factors and that for this reason such micro variables should not be incorporated in his theory. Thus he is left with a structural approach that amounts to an extended version of strategic contingencies theory. Yet Robert House (1988) has set forth a set of propositions that clearly do exactly what Pfeffer says individual differences theory does not do, thus bringing together micro and macro theories in the area. Elsewhere House says this of resource dependence theory:

> There are several reasons why the theory is likely to make rather weak predictions. That is, there are several reasons why correlations between the variables are likely to be substantially less than unity. First, the theory appears to apply more to organic than mechanistic organizations. Second, the theory appears to be more relevant to the long term than the short term. Third, the theory appears to apply to non-institutionalized organizations and organizations not embedded in a larger institution-

alized network of organizational relationships. Fourth, theoretical predictions of the theory are substantially weakened when the chief operating officer or the dominant coalition has a high degree of power relative to the board of directors, owners, or external agencies intended to exercise stewardship over the organization. (1991, p. 44)

In fact, the predictions often are weak, and the theory would seem to be in a position to benefit from incorporating additional types of individualized power constructs. Yet Pfeffer does not do this because these constructs are viewed as impure; thus he makes exactly the same type of error that micro organizational behaviorists are accused of making. The theory would benefit from a more open approach that lets individual differences in and thus explained more variance.

ORGANIZATIONAL ECOLOGY

In its early years organizational behavior gave little attention to biological perspectives on its organizational subject matter. The one visible exception was a paper by Mason Haire (1959), then at the University of California at Berkeley, which failed to spark either research or theoretical developments subsequently, in spite of its use of both mathematical models and biological analogies to growth. In contrast, the later development of a similar approach, based on an established underpinning in sociology, by two theorists also in the Bay area—Michael Hannan (Stanford) and John Freeman (Berkeley)—provoked a major impact and an outpouring of research. The major difference appears to be that the psychologist Haire had little institutional support to build on; Hannan and Freeman had an established, although still not substantial, framework within sociology on which to construct their ideas. The role of timing and the zeitgeist seem important here, but so does the power of the ideas themselves.

Background

Both Hannan and Freeman received their doctorates in sociology from the University of North Carolina. Both moved on to California in sociology; Hannan at Stanford University and Freeman at the University of California at Riverside; Freeman subsequently transferred to the business school at Berkeley. Both spent a considerable period at Cornell University,

Hannan in the sociology department from 1984 to 1991 and Freeman in the business school, where Freeman served as editor of the *Administrative Science Quarterly* from 1985 to 1993. Both ultimately returned to their former positions in California, although Hannan just recently has taken a major appointment in the business school at the age of 56.

At North Carolina both authors were strongly influenced by the ideas of Amos Hawley (1968), who was a long-term contributor to the sociological work on human ecology. Another major contributor to their thinking and to the development of the theory was Arthur Stinchcombe (1965). Although statements of the theory draw on numerous sources, mostly within sociology and biology, these two people appear to have exerted the most influence as the theory evolved.

Hannan-Freeman Theory

Organizational ecology theory was first published, although in a less than finished form, in the latter 1970s as a journal article and as a chapter in a book to which many of the theorists considered in this chapter contributed (Hannan & Freeman, 1977, 1978). During the 1980s there were a number of articles in the sociological literature, mostly jointly authored; these were brought together and supplemented to produce a book (Hannan & Freeman, 1989), which remains the major statement of the theory and is the primary source for the discussion here. In addition, I have used two book chapters that contain abbreviated and somewhat simplified versions of this same theory: Hannan and John Freeman, 1988, and Hannan and Glenn Carroll, 1995a. Although both authors contributed to the ecological literature during the 1990s, their collaboration was no longer in evidence. Hannan has been the major contributor in this more recent period. Also, along with a former student at Stanford, who is now on the Berkeley faculty, he has proposed a consequential theoretical refinement (Hannan & Carroll, 1992).

Theoretical Context

The theory seeks to answer the question—Why are there so many (or so few) kinds of organizations? This requires indicating both the sources of increasing diversity (such as new forms) and the sources of decreasing diversity (such as competitive exclusion). The theory thus attempts to achieve an understanding of the

rates of new organization and new form founding, the rates of organizational change, and the rates at which organizations and their forms die. Having only a few forms presents society with major problems when environments change. Also diversity provides more work opportunities for individuals with varied skills and characteristics.

A basic assumption is that organizational variation is a function primarily of the creation of new organizations and forms and the demise of others; actual change within organizations is rare, slow moving, and occurs early in their histories if at all. Environments change, but inertia prevails within organizations. Examination of such matters involves three levels of complexity:

1. The *demography of organizations*—founding rates, merger rates, disbanding rates
2. The *population ecology of organizations*—how the existence and density of other populations of organizations affect a focal population
3. The *community ecology of organizations*—a set of interacting populations, as for example firms, their labor unions, and relevant regulatory agencies (Hannan & Freeman, 1989, pp. 14–15)

The current diversity of organizational forms is a consequence of a long history of variation and selection (founding, mortality, and merger processes). Selection processes have general properties that hold across long historical periods. Yet the theory is only partial in its evolutionary treatment of organizational change; it focuses primarily on selection within organizational populations. The theory assumes the following:

[Change] is more Darwinian than Lamarckian. It argues that inertial pressures prevent most organizations from radically changing strategies and structures. Only the most concrete features of technique can be easily copied and inserted into ongoing organizations. Moreover, there are density-dependent constraints on adaptation by individual organizations: although it may be in the interests of the leaders of many organizations to adopt a certain strategy, the carrying capacity for organizations with that strategy is often quite limited. Only a few can succeed in exploiting such a strategy, and those in the vanguard . . . have decided advantages.

Even when actors strive to cope with their environments, action may be random with respect to adaptation, as long as the environments are highly uncertain or the connections between means and ends are not well understood. It is the *match* between action and environmental outcomes that must be random on the average for selection models to apply. In a world of high uncertainty, adaptive efforts by individuals may turn out to be essentially random with respect to future value. (Hannan & Freeman, 1989, p. 22)

This is a quite different approach from that of the Pfeffer-Salancik theory. Here selection is based on the importance of randomness to success; selection processes do not necessarily favor efficiency; in fact, they treat managerial action in distinctly antiheroic ways—as romanticized myth.

Four factors are posited that limit managerial potential to create change:

1. The organizations form, which is not easily changed
2. The scarcity of resources, which provides little slack to devote to change
3. The competitive pressures, which magnify the effects of other factors
4. The limitations on rationality, which have been emphasized by decision theorists (Hannan & Freeman, 1989, p. 41)

Boundaries of Forms and Populations

Organizational ecology theory assumes with regard to populations of organizations that they can be defined in ways that involve very similar environmental dependencies and that, consequently, there exist sizable discontinuities within the world of organizations. Furthermore, these populations can be identified a priori from information on organizational structures and social boundaries. However, the theory does not draw on anything approaching an organizational genetics approach to this problem of classification.

Organizational forms are defined by technological factors, differences in transaction costs, closure of social networks, successful collective action, and institutional processes. These segregating processes serve to establish boundaries, which also are subject to blending processes that serve to break down their influences; thus boundaries across organizational forms do change.

In spite of considerable discussion of the factors that might be used to build a theoretical typology of organizational forms, and their recognition that fur-

ther theoretical work in this area will be needed, the authors finally settle on the "conventional wisdom" of participants and observers to define forms. These "native" classifications appear to have had particular appeal because the data needed for research tend to come bundled in this manner. Thus, at least operationally, the theory is rather unsophisticated in its handling of the types of organizational forms and the boundaries among them. Because the conventional wisdom can change and even be a matter of some dispute, a degree of ambiguity is built into an otherwise quite sophisticated theory at this point.

Structural Inertia

As previously noted, a substantial inertia in structure and in other characteristics that define membership in an organizational population is assumed. Selection processes tend to favor organizations that exhibit this inertia in their core structures; thus inertia can be explained as a consequence of evolutionary processes and as a result of certain constraints on structural change. Among these are investments in assets not easily shifted to other uses, the limitations on information held by decision makers, internal political forces that act to thwart change, and the effects of normative agreements built into organizational histories. As well, there are external constraints to change such as legal and financial barriers, environmental restraints on the availability of information, and legitimacy claims on the part of important stakeholders.

The authors recognize that this emphasis on a limited potential for structural change (a change in form) is at variance with the mainstream position. Inertia does not mean that organizations never change, however, only that they respond rather slowly. The faster the speed with which organizations may be founded, the greater the inertia of the established structure. Selection favors organizations that can demonstrate *reliability* and *accountability*. Structures of roles and communications need to be reproducible, and this becomes achievable by creating processes of institutionalization and standardized routines—and thus resistance to change. Structural inertia increases directly with age, and organizational mortality rates decrease with age. Thus, there is a liability of newness, as Stinchcombe (1965) had proposed. Attempting reorganization serves to decrease reliability and increases mortality rates; it sets the liability of newness back toward zero, with all the risks thus entailed.

Once a *complex organization* begins change, the process will be longer lasting; thus complexity contributes to a greater mortality risk. The ability to react quickly to new opportunities conflicts with the ability to perform with reliability and accountability here. Inertia is not always a plus for selection. The theory, although it states a number of specific hypotheses related to inertia and similar matters as noted above, has a tendency to respond with statements such as "it is not clear," "it is indeterminate in our theory," and "it is an open question" at other points. The authors' willingness to admit the limits of their theoretical capabilities is admirable, but logical consistency tends to be lost and ambiguity often prevails.

Competition and the Niche

The theory as applied to niches focuses on interactions within and between populations of organizations. The argument starts with Hawley's principle of isomorphism:

> Units subjected to the same environmental conditions, or to environmental conditions as mediated through a given key unit, acquire a similar form of organization. They must submit to standard terms of communication and to standard procedures in consequence of which they develop similar internal arrangements within limits imposed by their respective sizes. (1968)

Thus organizational diversity results from the diversity of agents who control resources. Hawley's principle does not apply when a large number of resources are involved, however, as is typically the case. Accordingly, the theory turns to niche theory and the processes of competition and legitimation in search of a solution.

The niche of an organization form consists of the social arrangements through which a population can grow. To this the theory adds the process of *interaction* among populations, a process that occurs when one population affects the growth rate of others. At this point the discussion moves to a series of mathematical equations derived from bio-ecology. These deal with the carrying capacity of the environment for a given population, the intrinsic growth rate (the speed with which a population grows when there are no resource constraints), and competition coefficients that indicate how the carrying capacity for each population declines with the density of a competitor. The equa-

tions involved do not have a known solution, however, although competition coefficients can be estimated from data; the number of coexisting populations is constrained by the number of resources and constraints that are operating.

A related approach is to obtain estimates of competition from the overlap of niches and from niche width, which is the variance of the niche's resource utilization. Specialist organizations have less slack and thus less excess capacity than generalists, but they also are more vulnerable to uncertainty and changing environments. Thus stable environments favor populations of specialists, but under many conditions variable environments favor generalists. Talking about selection on the basis of niche width has the advantage that it takes into account the degree of specialization.

Dynamics of Organizational Populations

Population growth rates may be broken down into intrinsic speed of expansion, general environmental limits on growth or carrying capacities, and specific competition within and between populations (Hannan & Freeman, 1989, p. 117).

Speed of expansion varies markedly across organizational forms. Life history strategies may vary from opportunistic with many foundings and resources spread thinly, to the opposite with few foundings and heavy resource investments in each. Life chances vary accordingly, but even so, environments with rapid changes and high uncertainty favor the opportunistic approach. Populations with forms that foster high founding rates tend to continue to exist even though individual organizations do not survive long.

Both speed of founding and carrying capacities, which are set by time-varying social and material processes, are joined by density dependence in determining vital rates. Density serves as a surrogate for features of the social and material environment. Legitimacy, which increases as a particular form becomes more prevalent, produces a positive relationship between founding rates and density, while competition produces a negative relationship. Dense environments are characterized by limited resources and packed markets. Legitimacy processes dominate when the sample size is small and competition processes dominate when the sample size is large, so that the function as a whole is not monotonic. Formulas to show this are developed. Disbanding rates fall with increasing density up to the limits set by carrying capacity, after which they begin to rise. Merger processes, however, are more complicated and are beyond the capabilities of the theory to explain.

1992 Restatement

In many respects organizational ecology as treated by Hannan and Freeman is not so much an integrated theory as an exercise in applying a rich variety of formal models to the subject matter. One such area for formal modeling is the dynamics of organizational populations as discussed in the preceding section. This area has been reworked and restated several times; the Hannan and Carroll (1992) restatement is of particular interest because it is more precisely developed. The propositions set forth are as shown in table 26.1.

Evaluation and Impact

The preferred approach to conducting research on organizational ecology theory is to collect information on the life histories of organizational populations, in particular, on the occurrence of certain theory-relevant events of the type discussed previously; this is a kind of event-history procedure (Hannan & Tuma, 1979). This retrospective approach differs from the modal methodology in organizational behavior by emphasizing populations rather than focal organizations and longitudinal analyses that extend over long time periods. It has been at the core of research on the Hannan-Freeman theory from the beginning, although there are both major benefits and some drawbacks associated with it.

The benefits are that using archival data, events in the life histories of organizations of a given form and in a particular niche can be reconstructed. The only readily apparent alternatives are to start at the founding of the first organization and collect data forward until the last such organization dies (not a very parsimonious or perhaps even tenable procedure, although some truncation at the extremes might prove feasible) and to develop and run simulations of the processes involved (not the kind of approach one would want to rely on exclusively for evidence regarding a subject). Thus the event-history procedure clearly lends itself to testing this type of theory.

The problem is that events and theoretical constructs do not always match perfectly. For instance, archival data may differ in the way organizational foundings are defined, thus resulting in construct in-

validity (Hannan & Freeman, 1989). Other features of organizations may be used in different ways in different studies because the available information differs. Published histories and data sources may vary in the precision used to define events. Certain types of information may be unavailable for periods of time or even may be completely lacking for a particular population.

These difficulties in conducting research with archival, retrospective data sources constructed for purposes completely different from the theory they are used to test are problem enough. However, there is an even greater threat in that a theory constructed to be tested in this way might be driven in both its definition of variables and its specification of relationships by a knowledge of the available research data sets. That Hannan and Freeman (1989) often note their inability to formulate theory on a particular subject suggests that they are not forcing theory in this way and gives reason for optimism on this score. However, the real test is to look into studies conducted at a time and by researchers far removed from the original theorists. But first we need to consider the research that has involved participation by Hannan and Freeman themselves.

Initial Studies by Theory Authors

The book *Organizational Ecology* (Hannan & Freeman, 1989) draws on three primary organizational populations to test its theory. These are all populations that had been used and discussed to some extent in previous publications from the 1980s. They are as follows:

1. 479 U.S. labor unions founded in the period 1836–1985; foundings/year were close to 0 until the Civil War (see also Hannan & Freeman, 1987).
2. 1,197 entries into the semiconductor manufacturing industry between 1946 and 1984; a number were new entries who had a prior organizational existence (see also Brittain & Freeman, 1980).
3. 2,170 newspapers founded in the San Francisco Bay area in the 1840–1975 period; this is part of a wider study of seven urban newspaper populations in the United States (see Carroll, 1987).

For all three populations, founding rates were related to density, usually rising with increasing density to a point and then declining with further increases in

TABLE 26.1 Hannan and Carroll propositions in the 1992 restatement

Proposition no.	Description
1	The founding rate of an organizational population at time t, $\lambda(t)$, is inversely proportional to the intensity of competition within the population at that time, C_t. That is, $\lambda(t) \alpha C_t^{-1}$.
2	The mortality rate of organizations in a population at time t, $\mu(t)$, is directly proportional to the intensity of competition within the population at the time (contemporaneous competition). That is, $\mu(t) \alpha C_t$.
3	The mortality rate at time t of organizations founded at time f, $\mu(t,f)$, is directly proportional (at any age) to the intensity of competition at the time of founding, C_f. That is, $\mu(t,f) \alpha C_f$.
4	The founding rate in an organizational population at time t is directly proportional to the legitimation of its organizational form at that time, L_t. That is, $\lambda(t) \alpha L_t$.
5	The mortality rate in an organizational population at time t is inversely proportional to the legitimation of its organizational form at that time. That is, $\mu(t) \alpha L_t^{-1}$.
6	The intensity of contemporaneous competition, C_t, increases with density, N_t, at an increasing rate. That is, $C_t = \varphi(N_t)$; and $\varphi' > 0$ and $\varphi'' > 0$.
7	The intensity of competition at the time of founding, C_f, increases at an increasing rate with density at the time of founding, N_f. That is, $C_f = \psi(N_f)$, with $\psi' > 0$ and $\psi'' > 0$.
8	Legitimation increases with density at a decreasing rate. That is, $L_t = \vartheta(N_t)$; and $\vartheta' > 0$, and $\vartheta'' < 0$.
9	The relationship between density and legitimation is positive with a point of inflection ($\bar{N}_\lambda$) such that legitimation increases at an increasing rate with density to some point (the inflection point) beyond which legitimation grows with density at a decreasing rate. That is, $L_t = \upsilon(N_t)$; and $\upsilon' > 0$, and υ'' is $\begin{cases} > 0 & \text{if } N_t < \bar{N}_\lambda \\ < 0 & \text{if } N_t > \bar{N}_\lambda \end{cases}$
10	Legitimation is stronger than competition at very low densities. In particular, $\vartheta(N_t) > \varphi(N_t)$, and $\upsilon(N_t) > \varphi(N_t)$, when $N_t < 2$.

From propositions 1, 4, 6, 8, and 10:

Theorem 1. Density dependence in founding rates is nonmonotonic,

$$\lambda(t) \propto \frac{L_t}{C_t} = \frac{\varphi(N_t)}{\vartheta(N_t)}$$

and

$$\lambda(t)' \equiv \frac{d\lambda(t)}{dN_t} \text{ is } \begin{cases} > 0, & \text{if } N_t < N_\lambda^* \\ < 0, & \text{if } N_t > N_\lambda^* \end{cases}$$

where N_λ^* denotes the turning point in the relationship.

From propositions 1, 4, 6, 9, and 10:

Theorem 2. Density dependence in founding rates is nonmonotonic,

$$\lambda(t) \propto \frac{L_t}{C_t} = \frac{\upsilon(N_t)}{\vartheta(N_t)}$$

and

$$\lambda(t)' \equiv \frac{d\lambda(t)}{dN_t} \text{ is } \begin{cases} > 0, & \text{if } N_t < N_\lambda^* \\ < 0, & \text{if } N_t > N_\lambda^* \end{cases}$$

From propositions 2, 5, 6, 8, and 10:

Theorem 3. Contemporaneous density dependence in mortality rates is nonmonotonic,

$$\mu(t) \propto \frac{C_t}{L_t} = \frac{\vartheta(N_t)}{\varphi(N_t)}$$

and

$$\mu(t)' \equiv \frac{d\mu(t)}{dN_t} \begin{cases} < 0, & \text{if } N_t < N_\mu^* \\ > 0, & \text{if } N_t > N_\mu^* \end{cases}$$

From propositions 3, 5, and 7:

Theorem 4. Density at founding permanently increases mortality rates. That is, the mortality rate at time t of organizations founded at time f is proportional to the density at that time

$$\mu(t, f) \propto C_f = \psi(N_f)$$

and

$$\mu(t, f)' \equiv \frac{d\mu(t, f)}{dN_f} > 0; \quad \mu(t, f)'' > 0$$

density. This theoretically specified, non-monotonic pattern was characteristic of all but the independent foundings in the semiconductor industry; the latter do not appear to have encountered a carrying capacity in the same way as the other organizations did. As predicted, failure rates were consistently a monotonic function of age, the liability of newness phenomenon (see also Freeman, Carroll, & Hannan, 1983). Mortality rates were also a function of density, with rates falling with increasing density to a point and then rising. This consistency across populations was not maintained for the effects of competition on mortality rates; competitive pressures were particularly pronounced for the unions. Overall, across three very different populations, the theory received extensive, but not universal support.

Subsequent Hannan Research

Hannan has continued research and publishing with a variety of coauthors as he focuses on a multipopulation approach similar to that used in the initial studies. One such analysis used three populations of newspapers: the San Francisco Bay population noted previously, an Irish population for the 1800–1975 period, and an Argentinean population from 1800 to 1900, as well as the U.S. labor union data and a population of brewing firms in the United States from 1633 to 1988 (Carroll & Hannan, 1989). The question to be resolved was whether density at founding affects mortality rates. The conclusion was that it does in all five instances. However, whether this is a function primarily of resource scarcity or niche packing remains unresolved; the problem requires size-related data for its solution.

A later study by James Ranger-Moore, Jane Banaszak-Holl, and Hannan (1991) extended the density dependence research to Manhattan banks (1791–1980) and American life insurance companies (1759–1937). The non-monotonic function involving legitimacy and competition that was previously noted was again attained, thus confirming the theory in both instances. Furthermore, these data indicate that the theory is not merely applicable to small firms that are relatively free of regulation.

All of the populations discussed to this point, except the semiconductor firms, which did not match the theory as to entry, were used in the Hannan and Carroll (1992) analysis. That the results reported tended to support the theory is as expected, but it is also worth noting that certain computer simulations were attempted, and they also produced results consistent with theoretical expectations.

More recently Hannan and his colleagues have become involved in event-history studies of the automobile industry, particularly for the period from 1886 to 1981 in Europe (Hannan, Carroll, Dundon, & Torres, 1995). Again the predictions of the theory hold, and for all five countries studied, insofar as density dependence is concerned. In addition, there is evidence that the legitimation process is driven by density in Europe as a whole, while competition is a function of specific country densities. The generality of this apparently industry-specific finding is unclear.

One failure in this long list of research successes, other than what has been noted previously, involves the role of organizational size. This has been an area of considerable theoretical uncertainty, and attempts to deal with it, using the bank and insurance company data, have proved to be only partially effective (Hannan, Ranger-Moore, & Banaszak-Holl, 1990).

Subsequent Freeman Research

Among Freeman's contributions during the 1990s has been a study of rural cooperative banks in Italy over the period since 1948 when the banks were legalized (Freeman & Lomi, 1994). The data show a positive linear density effect on foundings. The competition effects usually associated with carrying capacity were not in evidence. There are reasons to believe, however, that this particular situation may not be typical and may not be the most appropriate for testing theory. This study, as others, also raises the question of the effects of population definition on the results obtained; regional analyses, for instance, produce certain findings that differ significantly from those at the national level. The theory needs to be specific in providing a priori guidance in this regard.

Findings That Give Reason for Pause

The research involving the authors provides considerable positive evidence in support of the theory. There are points at which exceptions appear, but these are commonly attributed to imperfections in the research data. Numerous studies by others yield an equally positive picture. Carroll's (1987) analysis of various newspaper populations, a particularly propitious setting for the conduct of event-histories, provides a good example of this positive set of findings.

Yet there are findings that introduce problems for organizational ecology theory. A study of voluntary social service organizations in Toronto from 1970 to 1982 obtained information on organizational changes from interviews (Singh, House, & Tucker, 1986). The data indicated that changes did not necessarily result in an increase in organizational death rates. Ecological theory best described core changes, but peripheral changes were best described by an adaptation perspective; thus a truly comprehensive theory of change would require the incorporation of both selection and adaptation processes. A subsequent study of the same population focused on specialist and generalist organizations and found substantial differences between the two forms (Tucker, Singh, & Meinhard, 1990). Both ecological dynamics and institutional changes appeared to influence specialists more than generalists.

An analysis of organizational failures in the California wine industry between 1940 and 1985 fails to support the Hannan-Freeman theory (Delacroix, Swaminathan, & Solt, 1989). That theory, as it applies to the density dependence of mortality, consistently overstates the negative effects of a lack of legitimacy. In a number of instances, overcrowding was avoided by migrating to a new niche or by enlarging the initial niche. A follow-up analysis of information from the wine industry indicated that both businesses founded in the table wine niche and those that diversified into it had lower failure rates (Swaminathan & Delacroix, 1991). Organizations appear to be more flexible in a strategic sense, and environments are less rigid than the density dependence concept of organizational demise would indicate.

An event-history analysis of newspapers in Finland over the period from 1771 to 1963 indicated that certain factors reduced failures, increased organizational transformations, and changed the chances of failure subsequent to transformation (Miner, Amburgey, & Stearns, 1990). These factors operated in conjunction with interorganizational linkages that served to buffer against failure, influence the likelihood of organizational transformation, and change the effects of transformation on failure. Thus, interorganizational linkages introduced a degree of flexibility in avoiding failures that was not otherwise available.

Trond Petersen and Kenneth Koput (1991) provide evidence that the decreasing mortality rate in the early part of a population's history is not necessarily a func-

tion of increasing legitimacy but can be explained as a result of unresolved heterogeneity. Thus there appears no need to invoke the process of legitimation. If legitimacy is to be invoked, however, direct measures are needed to support it, rather than the inferential procedures of the Hannan-Freeman theory. These findings are based on various simulations, but they do underscore the need for hard measures of legitimacy rather than proxies that are more readily derivable from archival data.

Taken as a whole, the research emphasizes greater adaptability and flexibility on the part of organizations than the Hannan-Freeman theory seems to permit. It also raises some serious questions as to whether the event-history approach to research alone is adequate to the task of validating the theory.

Critiques from Other Disciplines

Organizational ecology theory overlaps with several other disciplines and has as a result elicited comments from representatives of these fields. One such instance comes from mathematics and computer science and has contributed a formal logical analysis of the theory (Péli, Bruggeman, Masuch, & Ó Nualláin, 1994). The conclusion is that the theory is logically consistent, except that a clear distinction needs to be made between organizations under reorganization and those free of such conditions. Certain reductions in the domain of the theory to make it less general are recommended as well, and a number of instances of ambiguity in statement, some of which I have noted previously, are pointed out. All in all, however, the theory fares well at the hands of this analysis by formal logic.

Such is not the case at the hands of a biologist and a mathematician (Low & Simon, 1995). Their comment on reading the edited volume by Joel Baum and Jitendra Singh is that the terms from biology are used incorrectly; that "contradictory usages are rife and coherence is absent"; and that the evolutionary analogy "adds little, is frequently pushed too far, and in fact contributes confusion" (1994, pp. 738–740). These judgments would seem to apply to the approach taken by organizational ecology in general, since the book contains some 28 selections that range over a wide subject matter within the field. Certainly Hannan and Freeman have every right to develop their theory as they see fit, borrowing from biology as they go, but it would appear from this reaction that the resort to biological analogy has not contributed to the legitimacy of their ideas, at least within the biological community. Perhaps the theory would benefit from a major change in terminology that would completely remove it from the biological context. This might serve to eliminate ambiguities and to open up new domains for consideration as well. On this point it might be noted that other organizational writers in the evolutionary-ecology vein have had terminological problems as well (see Aldrich, 1999).

Critiques from Within

Most critiques have not come from other disciplines, or even from within organizational behavior as a whole, but from macro theorists and researchers, often with an organizational ecology orientation. One of the latter derives from a review symposium, again dealing with the Baum and Singh (1994) volume. Here both authors, Gerald Davis and Anand Swaminathan (1996), come down hard on the theory for failing to deal effectively with the concept of organizational form, which is basic to all that follows. The problem is that, by virtue of its research methodology, the Hannan-Freeman theory is forced to use groupings of organizations that exist in its archival data sources. These groupings then become the forms of which populations are composed. The forms and their populations are thus made up anew for each study, depending on the requirements of those who created the data, not the theorists. There is no overarching typology; the theory simply accepts what is given in whatever grouping is available. Accordingly, there is not, and cannot be, an unambiguous statement of what constitutes a form; nor is there any basis for determining when an organization changes its form and enters another population. The idea that organizations of considerable size might contain within them multiple forms is simply not entertained. This is not an issue that has been given much attention since Hannan and Freeman (1989). It needs to be.

Pfeffer (1997) notes that the liability of newness, and of size as well, is no longer much in dispute. However, Joel Baum (1996) raises certain issues in this regard. If one controls for organizational size, failure rates do not decline with age. Thus, the question becomes a matter of establishing whether such a correction is appropriate. One could argue that either way.

The concept of structural inertia depicts organizations as generally inert; adaptive changes are not only difficult and infrequent, but dangerous as well. This view has been the subject of considerable debate and more importantly of research. Baum's (1996) review of this research indicates that the findings offer only mixed support for theory. Organizations by no means face certain failure as a consequence of change efforts, but improvements in survival chances do not necessarily occur, either. The research does not appear to support organizational ecology's view of structural inertia with a great deal of consistency. Rather, the findings indicate a much more complex relationship involving both adaptive response and selection.

Pfeffer notes that organizational ecology in its denial of substantial effects to managerial choice and strategic action "is in its present versions reasonably far from a theory that permits knowledge to be translated into action" (1997, p. 169). There is little that can actually be put to use by a practitioner simply because the theory deals primarily with causal processes that are beyond the control of those who occupy positions in organizations. Consequently, this places a damper on the attractiveness of the theory for those seeking information on how to manage better. Again, since adaptive response does retain credibility based on the research, this inflexibility seems to operate to unnecessarily restrict the value of the theory. If, as Lex Donaldson (1995) indicates, the theory is viewed as anti-management, that would serve to restrict it even further.

Role of Density Dependence

To this point I have not considered issues related to density dependence. Yet this is the area where criticism has been most intense and the research most extensive. A number of the early attacks on the theory, in the 1980s when it first began to attract attention, were with regard to this aspect, among others. These early arguments have been in a number of cases discredited; a few have survived into the present. I will concentrate the present discussion on positions that are currently viable. It should be recognized, however, that when organizational ecology came on the scene it was a major innovation and drew a considerable amount of heat, some warranted but certainly a great deal that was not.

But to the matter of density dependence. In a review of Hannan and Carroll's (1992) *Dynamics of Organizational Populations*, Anne Miner says:

I believe the book provides convincing evidence that the negative effect of founding density on mortality is quite robust, and that predicted non-monotonic effects of contemporaneous density on foundings and failures are common if not universal. But the reader must make demanding leaps of inferential faith to conclude that this is strong evidence for the specific processes of legitimation and competition proposed to generate these results. (1993, p. 365)

One cannot rule out the authors' theory . . . but one also cannot rule out several other very plausible theories nor point to substantial collaborative evidence for the authors' theories. (p. 363)

In particular, the legitimacy interpretation, as to both individual organizations and forms, has been the subject of continuing controversy (see Amburgey & Rao, 1996). The problem is that even if the density dependence curve is valid, there is no measured evidence that legitimacy is part of the process; the concept of legitimacy appears to have been imposed "ex post facto and without direct measurement on empiricist findings that would otherwise remain unexplained" (Delacroix & Rao, 1994, p. 258). Furthermore, the evidence most frequently cited in support of the Hannan-Freeman theory and its interpretation comes from organizations (labor unions, newspapers, breweries) that are particularly subject to legitimacy problems. Other organizations may well not exhibit the same type of effect.

These questions require analyses of the research literature for an answer, of course. Baum and Walter Powell (1995), as part of a substantial challenge to the legitimacy interpretation, start to bring evidence to bear in this regard. They cite a large number of studies published since 1990 to the effect that founding studies support the theory's predictions 74 percent of the time and failure studies 55 percent of the time. Hannan and Carroll (1995b) challenge these data on several grounds and otherwise provide a rebuttal to the Baum and Powell (1995) thesis.

Yet, as we have seen, there are a number of studies extending back into the 1980s that do serve to question the density dependence formulations. Even if we accept the legitimacy and competition labeling, the density curve itself does not always take the expected form. Not all of these departures from theory can be attributed to the effects of truncation, or censoring as it is called in event-history analysis, on the left or right

sides of the distribution, although some of the studies do appear to be rather short term in nature for the purposes intended. Baum (1996) continues to provide substantial evidence that although a majority of the research is aligned with theoretical expectations, much is not. He also provides evidence that size needs to be factored into the competition part of the distribution.

What appears to be happening is that as new findings emerge, more and more researchers are adding new hypotheses and propositions onto the basic Hannan-Freeman package. The theory's authors have often tended to resist this process, but it is happening nevertheless. Accordingly, we are reaching a point where the weight of the theory, as amended to cover newly apparent exigencies, is becoming excessive. Again, I come to the conclusion that it is time to start over—perhaps by integrating the various theories considered in this chapter. Certainly the one best way in organizational ecology research, as represented by its use of the event-history approach, needs to be expanded. There should be a greater methodological diversification, including simulations, with more varied measures and probably the use of prospective designs. Archival data would seem to have been pushed as far as they will go at this point, and their close hold on the constructs of the theory needs to be relaxed.

NEOINSTITUTIONAL THEORY

As it originally emerged, neoinstitutional theory was a fragmented array of positions with some common ground but some that was not as well (Scott, 1987). By far the most fully developed of these positions and apparently the first also was that of John Meyer and Richard Scott, who were both at Stanford University. A second position in a somewhat similar vein was that of Lynne Zucker at the University of California at Los Angeles; it appeared at roughly the same time as Meyer and Scott's. Somewhat later came a position developed jointly by Paul DiMaggio and Walter Powell then at Yale University. I will focus primarily on the Meyer-Scott approach, but devote some attention to the other two, to provide a feel for the diversity. These three are generally considered to be the major current neoinstitutional theories, although there are other versions as well.

It is worth noting that the major theorists of this chapter—Pfeffer, Hannan and Freeman, Meyer and

Scott—were all located for most of their careers in the San Francisco Bay area of California. The reason for this is not clear, but all were aware of each other's work at an early point, and there appears to have been a certain amount of mutual stimulation. Why these pockets of theoretical innovation, such as Boston in an earlier era (see chapter 3), emerge would make a fascinating subject for more detailed analyses. In the process, one might also ask whether other locales have a depressing effect on theory development.

Background

Meyer received his Ph.D. in sociology from Columbia University. He has been on the sociology faculty at Stanford for many years and was at one point chairman of that department. In addition, he has held appointments in the School of Education where he has been engaged in research on various educational subjects throughout much of his career. This educational research preceded and was closely intertwined with the development of neoinstitutional theory.

Scott also has spent his career in the sociology department at Stanford and served a stint as its chairman. He was born in 1932. His Ph.D. in sociology from the University of Chicago in 1961 followed undergraduate work at the University of Kansas. He too has been active in the field of educational research and has held an appointment in Stanford's School of Education, but his organizational orientation has been somewhat broader, extending to medicine and business, areas in which he has held joint appointments as well. He has recently become emeritus from Stanford. Before beginning to develop neoinstitutional theory he was concerned with the nature of professional work, with authority systems, and with issues related to organizational effectiveness. Scott and Meyer developed their ideas on institutional processes together, publishing jointly on occasion but independently as well.

Zucker was a graduate student at Stanford with Meyer, but has spent most of her career beginning in 1974 at the University of California at Los Angeles in sociology, with joint appointments in education and industrial relations. She was born in 1945. DiMaggio and Powell started out together in the School of Organization and Management at Yale University, where they began their collaboration on neoinstitutional theory; Powell is now in the sociology department at the University of Arizona and DiMaggio holds a similar appointment at Princeton University.

Meyer-Scott Theory

Neoinstitutional implies that there was some type of preceding institutional emphasis, and indeed there was. This "old institutionalism" spread across many of the social sciences in a rather loose form, but within the study of organizations it is best manifested in the writings of the sociologist Philip Selznick (1949, 1957). That this old version is not entirely dead or displaced is evident from a recent attack on the new upstarts, saying they are "impoverished," by Arthur Stinchcombe, who was a student of Selznick's at Berkeley. His views will provide a useful backdrop against which to present the theoretical ideas to follow:

> The trouble with the new institutionalism is that it does not have the guts of institutions in it. The guts of institutions is that somebody somewhere cares to hold an organization to the standards and is often paid to do that. Sometimes that somebody is inside the organization, maintaining its competence. Sometimes it is an accrediting body. . . . Sometimes that somebody . . . is lacking, in which case the center cannot hold, and mere anarchy is loosed upon the world. (Stinchcombe, 1997, pp. 17–18)

Institutionalized Organizations: Formal Structures as Myth and Ceremony

Neoinstitutional theory began with an article by Meyer and Brian Rowan (1977) which had the above title. This article was reprinted in a book (Meyer & Scott, 1983) that contained a number of chapters—some previously published articles by the authors and a number newly written pieces as well. I refer to this 1983 volume in the following discussion.

Organizational structures are said to develop in highly institutionalized contexts. Thus, they are influenced to take on the practices and procedures that are defined by prevailing rationalized ideas about organizational work held in society. When they do this they increase their legitimacy and their chances of survival. However, these societal expectations are really myths and may well conflict with criteria of efficiency. Formal structures and the rules that govern them are in fact reflections of the institutional environment. These institutional effects are quite apart from the effects produced by networks of social behavior and relationships within and around a particular organization. Examples of institutionalized processes are professional rules, business functions, and established technologies. Following these approaches is viewed as appropriate, displays responsibility, and avoids charges of negligence.

These ideas are followed by a series of propositions interspersed with commentary:

1. As rationalized institutional rules arise in given domains of work activity, formal organizations form and expand by incorporating these rules as structural elements.
   1a. As institutionalized myths define new domains of rationalized activity, formal organizations emerge in these domains.
   1b. As rationalized institutional myths arise in existing domains of activity, extant organizations expand their formal structures so as to become isomorphic with these new myths.
2. The more modernized the society, the more extended the rationalized institutional structure in given domains and the greater the number of domains containing rationalized institutions.
   2a. Formal organizations are more likely to emerge in more modernized societies, even with the complexity of immediate relational networks held constant.
   2b. Formal organizations in a given domain of activity are likely to have more elaborated structures in more modernized societies, even with the complexity of immediate relational networks held constant.

Isomorphism with environmental institutions has some crucial consequences: (a) they incorporate elements that are legitimated externally, rather than in terms of efficiency; (b) they employ external or ceremonial assessment criteria to define the value of structural elements; and (c) dependence on externally fixed institutions reduces turbulence and maintains stability.

3. Organizations that incorporate societally legitimated rationalized elements in their formal structures maximize their legitimacy and increase their resources and survival capabilities.

Organizations may be ordered on a continuum from . . . production organizations under strong output controls . . . to institutionalized organizations whose success depends on the confidence and stability achieved by isomorphism with institutional rules.

Two problems face organizations of the latter type: (a) technical activities and demands for efficiency create conflicts and inconsistencies in an institutionalized organization's efforts to conform to the ceremonial rules of production; and (b) because these ceremonial rules are transmitted by myths that may arise from different parts of the environment, the rules may conflict with one another.

4. Because attempts to control and coordinate activities in institutionalized organizations lead to conflicts and loss of legitimacy, elements of structure are decoupled from activities and from each other.
5. The more an organization's structure is derived from institutionalized myths, the more it maintains elaborate displays of confidence, satisfaction, and good faith, internally and externally.
6. Institutionalized organizations seek to minimize inspection and evaluation by both internal managers and external constituents.

These propositions and arguments lead to three theses for research attention:

1. Environments and environmental domains that have institutionalized a greater number of rational myths generate more formal organization.
2. Organizations that incorporate institutionalized myths are more legitimate, successful, and likely to survive.
3. Organizational control efforts, especially in highly institutionalized contexts, are devoted to ritual conformity, both internally and externally. (Meyer & Scott, 1983, pp. 26–44)

Further to Organizational Environments

Organizational structures are expected to be generated as technologies and environmental interactions foster the development of bureaucratic systems (this is the technological side); they are also generated in that institutional structures operate to define roles and programs as being rational and legitimate (this is the institutional side).

The following propositions deal with what is involved:

1. Organizations evolving in environments with complex technologies create structures that coordinate and control technical work.
2. Organizations with complex technologies buffer their technical activities from the environment.

3. Organizations with efficient production and coordination structures tend to succeed in environments with complex technologies.
4. Organizations evolving in environments with elaborated institutional rules create structures that conform to those rules.
5. Organizations in institutional environments buffer their organizational structures from their technical activities.
6. Organizations with structures that conform to institutional rules tend to succeed in environments with elaborated institutional structures. (Meyer & Scott, 1983, pp. 47–48)

These propositions are straightforward enough as long as technology and institutions remain separate, but, as the authors say, ambiguity enters into the theory when, for instance, technologies become institutionalized—as medical technologies do in hospitals. The ambiguities involved here are not resolved.

Societal sectors are said to include all organizations that supply a particular type of product or service together with the suppliers, financial sources, regulators, and the like within the organizational set. The theory then attempts to develop hypotheses as to the effects of sector characteristics on organizational forms.

1. Organizations in technical sectors will attempt to control and coordinate their production activities, buffering them from environmental influences.
2. Organizations in technical sectors will succeed to the extent that they develop efficient production activities and effective coordination structures.
3. Organizations in institutional sectors will not attempt to closely control or coordinate their production activities, but will seek to buffer or decouple these activities from organizational structures.
4. Organizations in institutional sectors will succeed to the extent that they are able to acquire types of personnel and to develop structural arrangements and production processes that conform to the specifications of that sector.
5. Organizations functioning in sectors that are highly developed both institutionally and technically will develop more complex and elaborate administrative systems and will experience higher levels of internal conflict.
6. Organizations functioning in sectors that

are not highly developed technically or institutionally are expected to be relatively small in size and weak in terms of their capacity for survival.
7. Organizations located in more complex and uncertain environments develop more complex internal structures (holding constant the complexity of work processes).
8. Within public sectors in the United States, funding decisions are more highly centralized than are programmatic decisions and programmatic decisions are more highly centralized than are instrumental decisions.
9. The more highly professionalized a sector, the more likely that instrumental and programmatic decisions will be decentralized.
10. The centralization of decision making concerning funding, in the absence of centralized programmatic or instrumental decision making, is associated with the development of vertical interlevel controls exercised through accounting mechanisms.
11. Liberal political regimes that encourage a pluralistic approach to decision-making and that emphasize the separation of powers within nation state structures are likely to exhibit higher levels of fragmentation of decision making within sectors, as well as between sectors.
12. Organizations operating in sectors characterized by centralized, unified and concentrated programmatic decision making are expected to be tightly coupled across levels and to exhibit relatively small administrative components at each level.
13. Organizations operating in sectors characterized by fragmented or federalized programmatic decision making are expected to exhibit complex linkages across levels and elaborated and enlarged administrative components at each level.
14. The more centralized, unified, and concentrated is the programmatic decision making within a sector, the greater is the extent to which organizations within that sector will be limited and specific in the types of functional activities they perform.
15. The more centralized, unified, and concentrated is the decision making within a sector, the smaller is the number of different organization forms within the sector and the greater is the variance between them.
16. Organizations functioning in sectors that are highly developed technically but not

institutionally will be subjected primarily to interlevel controls emphasizing outcomes.

17. Organizations functioning in sectors that are highly developed institutionally but not technically will be subjected primarily to interlevel controls emphasizing structural measures.

18. Organizations functioning in sectors in which decision making is centralized but fragmented or federalized are likely to be subjected primarily to interlevel controls emphasizing processes.

19. The exercise of structural controls is more compatible with the loose coupling of administrative to production tasks than is the exercise of process controls, and the exercise of process controls is more so than the exercise of outcome controls. (Meyer & Scott, 1983, pp. 141–149)

Elsewhere Scott (1990) has reemphasized that in sectors where both technical and institutional environments are not well developed the organizations tend to be small and weak.

Institutional Environments and Organizations

The preceding theoretical statements wrap up what the authors refer to as the first wave. The second wave is reflected in a book with the same title as this section, which again contained a balance of previously published articles (1986–1993) and original papers (Scott & Meyer, 1994).

Here institutions are defined as cultural rules that give collective meaning (in terms of the collective purposes of progress and justice) and value to particular entities and activities, integrating them into the larger schemes. Institutionalization, accordingly, is the process through which a given set of units and a pattern of activities come to be normatively and cognitively held in place, so that they are taken for granted to be lawful (either as a result of formal law, custom, or knowledge). In this view, action is not a matter of individual choice but of broad social scripts; individualism loses out in large part to "the massive institutional features of the social system." In turn, these features are part of the culture.

The term *rationalization* is used to refer to the purposive or instrumental processes that structure everyday life within impersonal rules that constitute so-cial organization and lead to collective purpose. Institutions embody universalized claims tied closely to moral purpose and the rules of nature; consequently, specific institutional claims and definitions tend to be much the same throughout most of the world. The essential themes here are the following:

1. Rationalization . . . leads to the formation of an extraordinary array of legitimated actors reified as purposive and rational—individuals, associations, classes, organizations, ethnic groups, nation-states.

2. Collective actors command greater legitimacy and authority if they are founded on a theory of individual membership and activity, such as the nation-state or the rationalized firm.

3. Organizational entities that are tied into the theories of justice and progress gain special standing above all others.

4. Because they derive from universalistic cultural ideology, dominant organizational forms, including the structure and boundaries of collective action, are relatively standardized across societies. (Scott & Meyer, 1994, pp. 26–27)

Subsequently a general institutional model is set forth as follows:

1. Macro sociological processes—origins of environmental rationalization
↓
2. Dimensions of the rationalized environment—boundaries not clearly delineated
↓
3. Institutionalized elements in the environment—mechanisms influencing organizations
↓
4. The extant set of organizations—identities, structures, and activity patterns

Of these four, the first two are less developed in either a theoretical or research sense; 3 and 4 are the primary sources of attention. Figure 26.4 focuses on this interaction. The processes through which behavior is shaped noted there may be specified as follows:

1. Representational rules that involve shared logics or modes of reasoning that help to create shared understandings of reality that are "taken for granted"

2. Constitutive rules that create social actors—that is, identities linked to specified behaviors and action routines

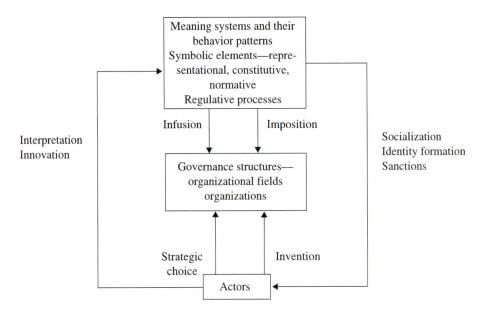

FIGURE 26.4 A layered model of institutional process. Adapted from W. Richard Scott & John W. Meyer (1994), *Institutional Environments and Organizations: Structural Complexity and Individualism* (Thousand Oaks, CA: Sage), 57.

3. Normative rules that stipulate expectations for behavior that are both internalized by actors and reinforced by the beliefs and actions of those with whom they interact

4. Enforcement mechanisms, both formal and informal, involving surveillance, assessment, and the application of sanctions rewarding conformity and punishing deviance (Scott & Meyer, 1994, p. 67)

Working from this perspective, *institutions* are now defined as symbolic and behavioral systems containing representational, constitutive, and normative rules together with regulatory mechanisms that define a common meaning system and give rise to distinctive actors and action routines. To this is added somewhat later: Institutions operate at a variety of levels, and their elements can be embodied in and carried by cultures, regimes, and formal organizations.

Interpreting Neoinstitutionalism

Scott (1987, 1995, 2nd edition 2001) has been not only a contributor to neoinstitutional theory but also a purveyor of its history and an interpreter of its development. Much of this is not relevant for present pur-

poses except to show the diversity of approaches. However, a discussion of the role of cognitive, normative, and regulative structures and activities in influencing social behavior provides an addition to what was said previously on this score. This discussion is summarized in table 26.2.

Alternative Theoretical Versions

Now we turn to two other ways of considering institutional processes in this new period, ways that differ considerably from those just considered and from one another.

Zucker Perspective

The primary statement of the neoinstitutional perspective set forth by Zucker (1977) is in fact an introduction to three experiments conducted to test that perspective. Institutionalization is defined as both a process, through which actors transmit what is socially considered to be real, and a property existing at any point in the process, where the meaning of an act can be said to be a taken-for-granted part of the social reality. Such institutionalized acts must be perceived as *ob-*

TABLE 26.2 The roles and workings of cognitive, normative, and regulative processes

| Variables | Structure and activities | | |
	Cognitive	Normative	Regulative
Characteristics			
Basis of compliance	Taken for granted	Social obligation	Expedience
Mechanisms	Imitation	Normative	Coercive
Logic	Orthodoxy	Appropriateness	Instrumentality
Indicators	Prevalence, isomorphism	Certification, accreditation	Rules, laws, sanctions
Basis of legitimacy	Culturally supported, conceptually correct	Morally governed	Legally sanctioned
Carriers			
Cultures	Categories, typifications	Values	Rules
		Expectations	Laws
Social structures	Isomorphism, identities	Regimes	Government systems
		Authority systems	Power systems
Routines	Performance programs, scripts	Conformity	Protocols
		Performance of duty	Standard procedures

SOURCE: Adapted from W. Richard Scott (1995). *Institutions and Organizations* (Thousand Oaks, CA: Sage), 35, 52

jective (potentially repeatable) and *exterior*, in that they are viewed as part of the world external to the individual.

Objectification and exteriority vary together, so that increasing one causes an increase in the other; thus institutionalization can vary from low to high, and acts can possess different degrees of institutionalization. Acts that have ready-made accounts are institutionalized acts. These accounts are socially created and function as objective rules in the absence of direct social control. In fact, invoking incentives or sanctions may serve to deinstitutionalize the acts involved. Acts performed by occupants of an organizational office tend to be seen as highly objective and exterior, thus institutionalized.

Institutionalization affects three aspects of cultural persistence: transmission, maintenance, and resistance to change. *Transmission* is the process by which cultural understandings are communicated to a succession of actors. The more the objectification and exteriority, the greater the transmission; continuity of the transmission process fosters institutionalization.

The basic assumption is that the fact of transmission of acts that are highly institutionalized will be sufficient to cause the *maintenance* of these acts. The institutionalization process serves to define a social reality that will be transmitted, and then maintained, as fact.

Acts high on institutionalization will exhibit *resistance to change*, and attempts to change them through

personal influence will face resistance simply because they are viewed as external facts. Failures of influence efforts in such circumstances may well extend to redefining the actor rather than the act.

The higher the level of institutionalization, the higher the transmission, maintenance, and resistance to change of cultural understanding hypothesized. This expectation, which is essentially one of cultural persistence, was tested in the research that we will take up shortly.

Zucker's (1977) theoretical statement is essentially presented at the micro level. Later she began to move toward a theory of organizations as institutions in which organizational power is based not on the control of resources, but on control of institutional structure and process (Zucker, 1983). This effort, however, resulted only in the presentation of "the basic outlines which such a theory might take" (p. 37). The objective was to stimulate others to work on a general theory of institutionalization.

In another later approach to macro level theorizing, Zucker (1988) set forth a view in which the starting principles are that social entropy threatens organizational stability, the organization of the social system is characterized by coherence and interconnectedness, the primary change agents are the formally organized collectivity and the power of organizations, institution building is a continual process to foster maintenance, and the key problem is maintaining a degree of stability. The net effect of this effort is the set of relationships indicated in figure 26.5 in which coherence is critical to the stability of the social system but is continually threatened by systemic entropy, as well as other factors. This approach also is considered to be "not yet either well developed or tightly interconnected" (p. 45) and is offered in the hope of stimulating the theoretical work of others.

DiMaggio-Powell Perspective

The seminal publication on this perspective, like Meyer and Rowan (1977) and Zucker (1977) previously, is DiMaggio and Powell (1983). Its primary concern is with the mechanisms of institutional isomorphic change, said to be *coercive* isomorphism (stemming from political influence and the problem of legitimacy), *mimetic* isomorphism (resulting from standard, imitative responses to uncertainty), and *normative* isomorphism (associated with professionalization).

A series of hypotheses is then presented dealing with the predictors of isomorphic change, first those operating at the organizational level and then those operating at the field level.

Organizational:

1. The greater the dependence of an organization on another organization the more similar it will become to that organization in structure, climate, and behavioral focus.
2. The greater the centralization of organization A's resource supply, the greater the extent to which organization A will change isomorphically to resemble the organization on which it depends for resources.
3. The more uncertain the relationship between means and ends the greater the extent to which an organization will model itself after organizations it perceives to be successful.

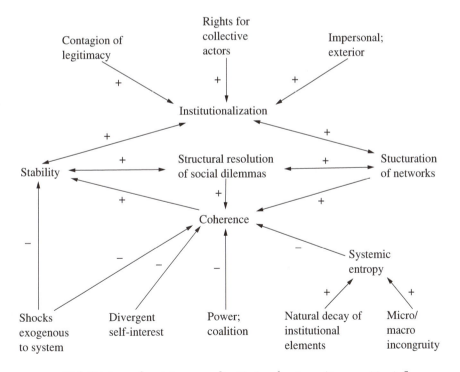

FIGURE 26.5 Origins and maintenance of institutional patterns (+ = a positive influence, − = a negative influence). From Lynne G. Zucker (1988), Where Do Institutional Patterns Come From? Organizations As Actors in Social Systems, in Lynne G. Zucker (Ed.), *Institutional Patterns and Organizations: Culture and Environment* (Cambridge, MA: Ballinger), 45. Copyright 1988 by Lynne G. Zucker. Reprinted with permission.

4. The more ambiguous the goals of an organization, the greater the extent to which the organization will model itself after organizations it perceives to be successful.

5. The greater the reliance on academic credentials in choosing managerial and staff personnel, the greater the extent to which an organization will become like other organizations in its field.

6. The greater the participation of organizational managers in trade and professional associations, the more likely the organization will be, or will become, like other organizations in the field.

Field:

7. The greater the extent to which an organizational field is dependent upon a single (or several similar) source of support for vital resources, the higher the level of the isomorphism.

8. The greater the extent to which the organizations in a field transact with agencies of the state, the greater the extent of isomorphism in the field as a whole.

9. The fewer the number of visible alternative organizational models in a field, the faster the rate of isomorphism in that field.

10. The greater the extent to which technologies are uncertain or goals are ambiguous within a field, the greater the rate of isomorphic change.

11. The greater the extent of professionalization in a field, the greater the amount of institutional isomorphic change.

12. The greater the extent of structuration in a field, the greater the degree of isomorphics. (DiMaggio & Powell, 1983, pp. 154–156)

The authors note that they have not attempted to develop measures of the variables they propose.

Subsequently DiMaggio (1988) attempted to deal theoretically with what he viewed as the failure of institutional theory to handle the matter of self-interest. His central thesis to this end is that

Institutionalization is a product of the political efforts of actors to accomplish their ends and the success of an institutionalization project and the form that the institution takes depend on the relative power of the actors who support, oppose, or otherwise strive to influence it. . . . The success of an institutionalization process creates new sets of legitimated actors who, in the course of pursuing

distinct interests, tend to delegitimate and deinstitutionalize aspects of the institutional forms to which they owe their own autonomy and legitimacy . . . Institutionalization as an *outcome* places organizational structures and practices beyond the reach of interest and politics. By contrast, institutionalization as a *process* is profoundly political. (DiMaggio, 1988, p. 13)

Beyond the writings already noted, both Powell and DiMaggio have contributed in various ways to the literature on institutionalism, but not in the form of concerted theoretical formulations. Rather, the tendency has been to argue for further development and broadening of the institutional perspective in various ways (see, for example, Powell & DiMaggio, 1991).

Evaluation and Impact

Research on neoinstitutional theory presents a number of difficulties for those searching for tests of the theory. First, much of it is oriented to the "old" institutionalism, not the new, and consequently may or may not be relevant in any given instance. Second, there is extensive use of qualitative studies to adduce support for theory, a practice that relies much more on the writer's particular interpretation and version of the story than on science. Third, although numerous reviews of the theories have been written, most tend to deal primarily with matters of logical consistency and speculative concerns, rather than with a comprehensive, objective coverage of the research evidence per se. Fourth, much of the research tends to use institutional measures that could be interpreted as reflecting the operation of some other theoretical perspective; the support for institutional theory is often not as specifically focused on institutional variables as one might wish.

Research Involving the Authors of the Meyer-Scott Theory

The Meyer-Scott theory arose out of studies of educational administration, and this is the context that receives primary attention here. In Meyer and Scott (1983), data from surveys that had been conducted within schools in the San Francisco Bay area are presented as typical of what has been found elsewhere as well. As expected, there was a high level of agreement across organizations on matters of policy, and school location accounted for only a small part of the variance. This homogeneity is viewed as evidence of institutional effects. Also the high level of satisfaction found among various stakeholders is interpreted as consistent with maintaining institutional rules. A second set of findings relate to loose coupling. The professional system, consisting primarily of teachers, was found to be decoupled from the administrative system, thus permitting the two types of institutional processes to operate together.

Meyer and Scott, working with others, also report relevant data in Zucker (1988). One such study dealt with the institutionalization of grievance procedures and affirmative action in organizations. These processes appear to be fostered by public visibility and linkages to government, as well as by size and the more modern period. Another study, again dealing with education, also obtained indices over time (40 years). A rapid expansion in bureaucratization was apparent, thus reflecting the dominance of a national educational culture. This move to a particular organizational structure is attributed to a complex institutional system rather than to the rise of a dominating organizational center.

The book by Scott and Meyer (1994) contains several other studies that the authors conducted. One compared data on private and public school systems and found substantial differences, with the public schools exhibiting much more elaborate organizational structures commensurate with their more complex environmental demands. Other studies suggest that the complex and fragmented environments of public schools, and not centralization in the hands of the federal government, result in greatly expanded administrative activities. Further data are also reported on the increasing bureaucratization of the educational system, and this is attributed to a national institutional structure, not to control by the central bureaucratic state. In another arena, internal labor markets within organizations are explained in terms of institutional processes in the environment rather than firm self-interest. All of these studies use data of some kind, mostly archival, to substantiate, but not in fact to prove, their theses.

A recent example of this approach involved an analysis of the antecedents and effects of legitimacy (as reflected in accreditation procedures) in San Francisco hospitals. Legitimacy clearly increases survival chances (Ruef & Scott, 1998). Evidence is presented to the effect that the logic of the surrounding institutional environment plays an important role. This work on healthcare organizations has been set forth in ex-

panded form very recently in a new book on the subject by Scott, Ruef, Mendel, and Caronna (2000).

It is important to note that none of this research is directly coupled with the specific theoretical propositions and hypotheses noted previously; in no instance is there said to be a direct test of a given hypothesis from the prior theory. The research is only loosely coupled with the theory.

Research by the Authors of Alternative Theories

As indicated previously, Zucker's (1977) theorizing introduced a set of research investigations. These were laboratory studies that used the autokinetic effect; the degree of institutionalization was manipulated by introducing various organizational conditions. The effects on the perceived movement of the light were obtained for transmission, maintenance, and resistance to change conditions. Institutionalization clearly had the anticipated impact under all three conditions; the hypothesized relationships between degree of institutionalization and cultural persistence were supported.

Subsequently Zucker (1983) reported several other investigations that provide evidence for the effects of institutional environments on organizations. An analysis of the spread of civil service reform over a 55-year period showed a gradual institutionalizing process. Although city characteristics were good predictors in the early years, these correlations disappeared later and adoption came to be expected even if not functional for a specific city. An analysis of the establishment of evaluation units in school systems showed a similar development as a function of state regulation and funding. An analysis of city responses to statewide budget cuts in California indicated that institutional forces established parameters for local responses.

In a particularly interesting study, Zucker and Ita Kreft (1994) used archival data to study the effects of strike activity on founding rates of union locals. They conclude that institutions (unions) form in response to demand and social conflict (strikes). Thus institutional development does *not* appear always to be a consequence of institutional isomorphism as prior theories had proposed; variance may be added, at least initially, and homogeneity may decrease. The data also suggest that institutional structures do not just happen. They evolve over a period of time as a consequence of human agency and demand and are maintained as resources to keep them going become available.

Finally, Zucker was involved in analyses of organizations that were inefficient but survived for long periods on the basis of their institutional status. Of this work she says: "The notion that organizations could survive despite very low objective performance implied the possibility of permanently failing organizations (Meyer & Zucker, 1989), that is organizations that survive despite evident inefficiencies that logically should cause them to fail" (Tolbert & Zucker, 1996, p. 178).

The Powell-DiMaggio perspective has not been the subject of significant quantitative research by its authors. There have been qualitative studies, referred to by the authors as case studies, that deal with institutional process as they relate to book publishing, public television, art museums, and the like (see, for example, their articles in Zucker, 1988, and Powell & DiMaggio, 1991), but these cannot be considered tests of either their or any other institutional theory. This situation exists in spite of the fact that both Powell and DiMaggio have conducted quantitative research in other areas.

Significant Outside Research in the Early Period

Much of the early research, during the late 1970s and the 1980s was conducted by either Meyer and Scott or Zucker. Yet there were studies conducted outside this nexus as well in this period. Some of the more significant of these require discussion.

One such study looked at institutionalization (in terms of industry norms and traditions) as it relates to sales compensation practices (Eisenhardt, 1988). The findings indicated that although institutional theory did contribute to an understanding of these practices, this effect was only partial; the theory operated most strongly in relation to founding conditions and industry traditions. Agency theory from economics was shown to operate jointly with institutional theory to provide the most complete understanding. Another similar study used variables from institutional and ecological theory to analyze relationships among vital measures by using an event history approach with voluntary organizations in Toronto (Singh, Tucker, & Meinhard, 1991). Both theoretical orientations proved to have a significant, complementary effect on foundings, deaths, and organizational changes. This latter conjoint operation of these two theories has been doc-

umented in studies since as well. That institutional theory provides only a partial explanation of dependent variables seems now to be well established.

Tolbert (1988) studied institutional factors in the operation of large U.S. law firms, specifically as regards the establishment of structures to ensure the socialization of new members. The results clearly established that professional organizations are affected by institutional processes, as various theorists had indicated previously.

Another area of institutional interest has been the diversification of large firms. Neil Fligstein (1991) studied this process among the hundred largest companies over the 1919 to 1979 period. He found that diversification put companies in the top 100, and failure to diversify led to more rapid exit. In the early period diversification appeared to follow from chief executive characteristics, but this correlation disappeared in the later years. The best index then was the proportion of firms already diversified. The data lend good support to institutional theory and its imitative processes.

Embellishments on the Imitative Theme

The process among those of neoinstitutional theory that received by far the most research attention from 1985 to 1995, and probably beyond, is that labeled as imitative, or mimetic, following on the DiMaggio and Powell (1983) nomenclature (Mizruchi & Fein, 1999). One such study looked into the diversification strategy that Fligstein had analyzed previously for the period up to 1979 (Davis, Diekmann, & Tinsley, 1994). The data, extended over the period up to 1990, showed a marked deinstitutionalization, with many firms merging and having their diversified components sold off and many others shunning the conglomerate growth pattern. Evidence is presented that this change occurred abruptly, was influenced by pressure from Wall Street, and appeared to reflect an underlying institutional shift. How these changes can be better understood and predicted remains a challenge to theory, but apparently market forces do interject themselves, at least in the business world.

Other studies in the business context (and apart from the prevailing educational context) raise similar problems. For example, in studying acquisitions and investment banker decisions, Pamela Haunschild and Anne Miner (1997) found three different imitation modes operating. Furthermore, these three may affect different components of a firm in different ways, producing variety at the level of the company overall, not homogeneity. Thus the usually predicted effects of imitative processes may well not occur in the manner theory anticipates. How often this sort of thing may occur is an open question.

An analysis of the adoption of total quality management programs by hospitals found that early adopters tended to customize the approach to meet their particular efficiency needs, while later adopters accepted the programs in standard form to gain legitimacy (Westphal, Gulati, & Shortell, 1997). Thus mimicking the normative model seems to be a late-stage process; before that, efficiency concerns may well exert considerable impact, producing variability not homogeneity. Another study, also in the hospital setting, dealt with the decision to undertake cesarean births, studied as a hospital-level phenomenon (Goodrick & Salancik, 1996). It was found that institutional forces set boundaries on the use of discretion in decisions. When risk was intermediate, and thus uncertainty the greatest, the characteristics of individual hospitals exerted the most influence on cesarean rates and thus hospital-level discretion was exercised. When risks were either high or low, institutionalized practices tended to prevail. Thus institutionalized actions do not emerge as direct mandates, but as frameworks within which technical forces may operate, setting the limits as it were and establishing bounds.

In a study undertaken to establish the domain limitations on neoinstitutional theory, Matthew Kraatz and Edward Zajac (1996) considered longitudinal data on a large number of private liberal arts colleges from 1971 to 1986. They found a substantial and pervasive move to professional and vocational curricula, a loss of homogeneity, and a failure to imitate the more prestigious institutions of this type. All this appears to have occurred in response to market conditions, and with positive consequences for enrollments and survival. In 1986, some 38 percent of all degrees granted were professional in nature, as contrasted with a comparable figure of 11 percent in 1971, but note that the majority still remains of a liberal arts nature. This study is interpreted as indicating a failure of neoinstitutional theory in a context that should be highly institutionalized; it also reflects the conjoint operation of factors that are probably best described in terms of resource dependence.

An interpretation of these results within institutional theory is also possible, however:

> *if* we consider that the institutional field consists not just of product or service providers (liberal arts colleges) but also of regulators, suppliers, and consumers;
>
> *if* we consider that legitimacy processes take place internal to the organizational field, but in an inter-related dynamic both internal and external to a product or service providing population of organizations;
>
> *if* we consider that legitimacy processes can be as much instrumental as cognitive and normative;
>
> *if* we consider that the joint operation of cognitive and instrumental legitimacy processes intensifies delegitimation for consumers of private liberal arts college educations and for individuals and groups inside the colleges whose interests are hindered by the "liberal arts" model of service provision but benefited by the "professionalized" model. (Stryker, 2000, pp. 219–220)

All of these more recent findings with regard to the imitative aspects of the theory appear to invoke corrections to and modifications of previously existing statements. Obviously there is room for much more refined theorizing, perhaps through the incorporation of aspects of other theoretical positions.

Critiques

As indicated previously, it is difficult to find good critiques of neoinstitutional theory that do not deviate considerably from the dictates of objectivity. There are the devotees of the "old" institutionalism (see, for example, Stinchcombe, 1997), the adherents of some version of the "new" theory (see, for example, Scott, 1995, 2001), and the advocates of alternative positions altogether (see, for example, Donaldson, 1995). All have something to say, but what they say does not always represent a balanced position. Yet there does appear to be a certain consensus that "institutional theory is clearly the leading perspective among organizational sociologists in the United States" (Mizruchi & Fein, 1999, p. 678).

In this context it may be helpful to explore some critiques in more depth to see what they do say. Tolbert and Zucker (1996) are critical of the Meyer and Rowan (1977) views on the grounds that there is an inherent ambiguity in their definition of institutionalization, as opposed to the idea that institutionalized structures are often decoupled from behavior. They feel that this leads to a confounding of institutional and resource dependence theory; it is this combination for which Zucker (1989) has previously indicated considerable reservations. It is evident from the Tolbert and Zucker (1996) review that a certain amount of controversy does exist not only vis-à-vis other types of macro theories, but within the neoinstitutional camp as well.

Another point made in this review is that more direct measures of institutionalization are needed to document when institutionalized structures are and are not present. Such measures could derive from survey research and from content analysis of written materials. This is a point well taken. It becomes particularly important where conflicting institutional streams may be operative, as in the case of the liberal arts colleges (Kraatz & Zajac, 1996). The use of such measures would also facilitate separating different alternative theoretical explanations of the same phenomena from one another. More often than not, the research simply assumes the operation of institutional processes under certain circumstances; more definitive evidence in the form of clear operationalizations of constructs is needed.

A final point is that institutional theory offers good reasons why and how bounded rationality and satisficing occur (see chapter 22 in this volume). Understanding in this regard, and the scope of both theories, would benefit from further theoretical development.

A quite different theoretical and research review, and by far the most negative that I have seen, is that of Donaldson (1995). This is part of his basic advocacy of structural contingency theory (see chapter 18) and the attempt to vitiate the influence of competing theories (see the section "Criticism of Other Positions" in chapter 18). It concludes that only the coercive isomorphism aspect of institutional theory can lay claim to unequivocal support from research. Numerous criticisms are offered, both of theory (usually as lacking logical consistency) and of early research (as inappropriately conceived and conducted). There are some good points made, and some clear errors as well, plus a considerable amount of emotionality and what many would consider overkill in the author's zeal to negate institutional formulations. Overall, the net effect is no more detrimental to neoinstitutional theory than are the similar attacks on population ecology theory and resource dependence theory for those approaches. However, useful questions are raised about the conduct and interpretation of certain specific research studies, particularly the early ones.

My own view is that the theory has a great deal of promise. It needs to deal more effectively with what appear to be changes away from institutionalization, as in the studies by Davis et al. (1994) and Kraatz and Zajac (1996), but it is not true that such changes are not considered by the theory. DiMaggio (1988) develops the role of political process in both institutionalization and deinstitutionalization at length. The theory needs to attain greater precision in this area, and to do so it probably will need to move to a treatment of dynamic processes within individual organizations, and even within individual personalities including the sources of their interests. The importance of developing measures of theoretical variables that Zucker (1996) stresses would seem to put emphasis on a crucial consideration for the conduct of research that will move the theory beyond its present bounds.

CONCLUSIONS

All three theories discussed have some evidence of validity, and several have quite a good deal. It is not surprising that there would be consideration of combining some of these theories, if only because they represent some of macro organizational behavior's best. Also these theories tend to emerge as partial in their coverage of the domain, especially neoinstitutional theory, and that also argues for some type of merger.

The merger that one hears about most, although not necessarily the one that involves the most compelling logic, is between the organizational ecology view and some version of neoinstitutionalism. Such a convergence has been given considerable attention with various degrees of approximation to a full theoretical statement (Carroll, Delacroix, & Goodstein, 1988; Singh & Lumsden, 1990). The common ground, of course, is the role of legitimacy as an overlapping construct, although that construct plays somewhat different roles in the two theories. Legitimacy could bring resource dependence theory in under the same large tent, but there it is not a key concept, being handled as only one among many organizational resources (Stryker, 2000). Legitimacy would have to be given an enlarged role in resource dependence formulations to serve as a bridge into the other theories. Certainly the common origins of the three theories and their overlapping constituencies suggest that some type of merger may be in the offing, however.

Yet another possibility suggests itself. All three theories seem to exhibit key lacunae of much the same kind—a space into which some type of formulation from micro organizational behavior might be placed to mutual advantage. Examples would be power motivation in resource dependence theory, group decision making and leadership in organizational ecology, and various motivational constructs in neoinstitutional theory. I am sure that many would demur at this point on the ground that this would require leaving the discipline of sociology and entering the domain of psychology. Realistically, for a sociologist this might represent a problem, both in terms of values and knowledge constraints. There are rational reasons for compartmentalizing knowledge to foster specialization and permit definitive identification of disciplinary participants. But the important consideration here is that for organizational behavior, with its professional school locus and its penchant for following problems wherever they may lead, such a disciplinary convergence presents no difficulties at all; meso theorizing and research of this kind are at the heart of our discipline.

Some idea of how institutional theory and micro constructs may come together can be found in a study that examines the interaction between institutional processes and turnover intentions in accounting firms (Robson, Wholey, & Barefield, 1996). Another example is suggested by the following quote: "The concept of taken-for-granteds in institutional theory is similar in logic to that of unconscious motives in Freudian theory; both are incapable of empirical test and are therefore unscientific" (Donaldson, 1995, p. 114). Given that unconscious motives of the type found in psychoanalytic theory are capable of scientific study (see chapter 6), there may be something in this analogy that could provide assistance to institutional theory. That was not exactly what Donaldson had in mind, but his error provides an opportunity to show how convergence across levels of theorizing might prove useful. But that will require breaking down some barriers.

References

Aldrich, Howard E. (1999). *Organizations Evolving*. London: Sage.

Aldrich, Howard E., & Pfeffer, Jeffrey (1976). Environments of Organizations. *Annual Review of Sociology*, 2, 79–105.

Amburgey, Terry L., & Rao, Hayagreeva (1996). Organizational Ecology: Past, Present, and Future Directions. *Academy of Management Journal*, 39, 1265–1286.

Astley, W. Graham, & Zammuto, Raymond F. (1992). Organizational Science, Managers, and Language Games. *Organization Science*, 3, 443–460.

Balkin, David B., & Bannister, Brendan D. (1993). Explaining Pay Forms for Strategic Employee Groups in Organizations: A Resource Dependence Perspective. *Journal of Occupational and Organizational Psychology*, 66, 139–151.

Baum, Joel A. C. (1996). Organizational Ecology. In Stewart R. Clegg, Cynthia Hardy, & Walter R. Nord (Eds.), *Handbook of Organization Studies* (pp. 77–114). London: Sage.

Baum, Joel A. C., & Powell, Walter W. (1995). Cultivating an Institutional Ecology of Organizations: Comment on Hannan, Carroll, Dundon, and Torres. *American Sociological Review*, 60, 529–538.

Baum, Joel A. C., & Singh, Jitendra V. (1994). *Evolutionary Dynamics of Organizations*. New York: Oxford University Press.

Brittain, Jack W., & Freeman, John H. (1980). Organizational Proliferation and Density Dependent Selection. In John R. Kimberly & Robert H. Miles (Eds.), *The Organizational Life Cycle: Issues in the Creation, Transformation, and Decline of Organizations* (pp. 291–338). San Francisco: Jossey-Bass.

Campling, John T., & Michelson, Grant (1998). A Strategic Choice-Resource Dependence Analysis of Union Mergers in the British and Australian Broadcasting and Film Industries. *Journal of Management Studies*, 35, 579–600.

Carroll, Glenn R. (1987). *Publish and Perish: The Organizational Ecology of Newspaper Industries*. Greenwich, CT: JAI Press.

Carroll, Glenn R.; Delacroix, Jacques; & Goodstein, Jerry (1988). The Political Environments of Organizations: An Ecological View. *Research in Organizational Behavior*, 10, 359–392.

Carroll, Glenn R., & Hannan, Michael T. (1989). Density Delay in the Evolution of Organizational Populations: A Model and Five Empirical Tests. *Administrataive Science Quarterly*, 34, 411–430.

Davis, Gerald F.; Diekmann, Kristina A.; & Tinsley, Catherine H. (1994). The Decline and Fall of the Conglomerate Firm in the 1980s: The Deinstitutionalization of an Organizational Form. *American Sociological Review*, 59, 547–570.

Davis, Gerald F., & Swaminathan, Anand (1996). Review Symposium—*Evolutionary Dynamics of Organizations. Administrative Science Quarterly*, 41, 538–550.

Delacroix, Jacques, & Rao, Hayagreeva (1994). Externalities and Ecological Theory: Unbundling Density Dependence. In Joel A. C. Baum & Jitendra V. Singh (Eds.), *Evolutionary Dynamics of Organizations* (pp. 255–268). New York: Oxford University Press.

Delacroix, Jacques; Swaminathan, Anand; & Solt, Michael E. (1989). Density Dependence versus Population Dynamics: An Ecological Study of Failings in the California Wine Industry. *American Sociological Review*, 54, 245–262.

DiMaggio, Paul J. (1988). Interest and Agency in Institutional Theory. In Lynne G. Zucker (Ed.), *Institutional Patterns and Organizations: Culture and Environment* (pp. 3–21). Cambridge, MA: Ballinger.

DiMaggio, Paul J., & Powell, Walter W. (1983). The Iron Cage Revisited: Institutional Isomorphism and Collective Rationality in Organizational Fields. *American Sociological Review*, 48, 147–160.

Donaldson, Lex (1995). *American Anti-management Theories of Organization: A Critique of Paradigm Proliferation*. Cambridge: Cambridge University Press.

Eisenhardt, Kathleen M. (1988). Agency- and Institutional-Theory Explanations: The Case of Retail Sales Compensation. *Academy of Management Journal*, 31, 488–511.

Finkelstein, Sydney (1997). Interindustry Merger Patterns and Resource Dependence: A Replication and Extension of Pfeffer (1972). *Strategic Management Journal*, 18, 787–810.

Fligstein, Neil (1991). The Structural Transformation of American Industry: An Institutional Account of the Causes of Diversification in the Largest Firms: 1919–1979. In Walter W. Powell & Paul J. DiMaggio (Eds.), *The New Institutionalism in Organizational Analysis* (pp. 311–336). Chicago: University of Chicago Press.

Freeman, John; Carroll, Glenn R.; & Hannan, Michael T. (1983). The Liability of Newness: Age Dependence in Organizational Death Rates. *American Sociological Review*, 48, 692–710.

Freeman, John, & Lomi, Alessandro (1994). Resource Partitioning and Foundings of Banking Cooperatives in Italy. In Joel A. C. Baum & Jitendra V. Singh (Eds.), *Evolutionary Dynamics of Organizations* (pp. 269–293). New York: Oxford University Press.

Galaskiewicz, Joseph (1985). Interorganizational Relations. *Annual Review of Sociology*, 11, 281–304.

Goodrick, Elizabeth, & Salancik, Gerald R. (1996). Organizational Discretion in Responding to Institutional Practices: Hospitals and Cesarean Births. *Administrative Science Quarterly*, 41, 1–28.

Haire, Mason (1959). Biological Models and Empirical Histories of the Growth of Organizations. In Mason Haire (Ed.), *Modern Organization Theory* (pp. 272–306). New York: Wiley.

Hall, Richard H. (1987). Organizational Behavior: A Sociological Perspective. In Jay W. Lorsch (Ed.), *Handbook of Organizational Behavior* (pp. 84–95). Englewood Cliffs, NJ: Prentice Hall.

Hannan, Michael T., & Carroll, Glenn R. (1992). *Dynamics of Organizational Populations: Density, Legitimation, and Competition*. New York: Oxford University Press.

Hannan, Michael T., & Carroll, Glenn R. (1995a). An Introduction to Organizational Ecology. In Glenn R. Carroll & Michael T. Hannan (Eds.), *Organizations in Industry: Strategy, Structure, and Selection* (pp. 17–31). New York: Oxford University Press.

Hannan, Michael T., & Carroll, Glenn R. (1995b). Theory Building and Cheap Talk about Legitimation: Reply to Baum and Powell. *American Sociological Review*, 60, 539–544.

Hannan, Michael T.; Carroll, Glenn R.; Dundon, Elizabeth A.; & Torres, John C. (1995). Organizational Evolution in a Multinational Context: Entries of Automobile Manufacturers in Belgium, Britain, France, Germany, and Italy. *American Sociological Review*, 60, 509–528.

Hannan, Michael T., & Freeman, John H. (1977). The Population Ecology of Organizations. *American Journal of Sociology*, 82, 929–964. [Also (1978) in Marshall W. Meyer & Associates (Eds.), *Environments and Organizations* (pp. 131–171). San Francisco: Jossey-Bass.]

Hannan, Michael T., & Freeman, John (1987). The Ecology of Organizational Founding: American Labor Unions, 1836–1985. *American Journal of Sociology*, 92, 910–943.

Hannan, Michael T., & Freeman, John (1988). Density Dependence in the Growth of Organizational Populations. In Glenn R. Carroll (Ed.), *Ecological Models of Organizations* (pp. 7–31). Cambridge, MA: Ballinger.

Hannan, Michael T., & Freeman, John (1989). *Organizational Ecology*. Cambridge: Harvard University Press.

Hannan, Michael T.; Ranger-Moore, James; & Banaszak-Holl, Jane (1990). Competition and the Evolution of Organizational Size Distributions. In Jitendra V. Singh (Ed.), *Organizational Evolution: New Directions* (pp. 246–268). Newbury Park, CA: Sage.

Hannan, Michael T., & Tuma, Nancy B. (1979). Methods for Temporal Analysis. *Annual Review of Sociology*, 5, 303–328.

Haunschild, Pamela R., & Miner, Anne S. (1997). Modes of Interorganizational Imitation: The Effects of Outcome Salience and Uncertainty. *Administrative Science Quarterly*, 42, 472–500.

Hawley, Amos (1968). Human Ecology. In David Sills (Ed.), *International Encyclopedia of the Social Sciences* (Vol 4, pp. 328–337). New York: Free Press.

Hickson, David J.; Hinings, C. Robert; Lee, C. A.; Schneck, R. H.; & Pennings, Johannes M. (1971). A Strategic Contingencies' Theory of Intraorganizational Power. *Administrative Science Quarterly*, 16, 216–229.

Hillman, Amy J.; Cannella, Albert A.; & Paetzold, Ramona L. (2000). The Resource Dependence Role of Corporate Directors: Strategic Adaptation of Board Composition in Response to Environmental Change. *Journal of Management Studies*, 37, 235–255.

House, Robert J. (1988). Power and Personality in Complex Organizations. *Research in Organizational Behavior*, 10, 305–357.

House, Robert J. (1991). The Distribution and Exercise of Power in Complex Organizations: A Meso Theory. *Leadership Quarterly*, 2, 23–58.

Jongbloed, Lyn, & Frost, Peter J. (1985). Pfeffer's Model of Management: An Expansion and Modification. *Journal of Management*, 11, 97–110.

Kraatz, Matthew S., & Zajac, Edward J. (1996). Exploring the Limits of the New Institutionalism: The Causes and Consequences of Illegitimate Organizational Change. *American Sociological Review*, 61, 812–836.

Leblebici, Huseyin, & Porac, Joseph (1997). Memorial for Gerald R. Salancik: 1.29.1943–7.24.1996. *Journal of Management Inquiry*, 6, 256–261.

Low, Bobbi S., & Simon, Carl P. (1995). Review of *The Evolutionary Dynamics of Organizations*. *Academy of Management Review*, 20, 735–741.

Meyer, John W., & Rowan, Brian (1977). Institutionalized Organizations: Formal Structure as Myth and Ceremony. *American Journal of Sociology*, 83, 340–363.

Meyer, John W., & Scott, W. Richard (1983). *Organizational Environments: Ritual and Rationality*. Beverly Hills, CA: Sage.

Meyer, Marshall W., & Zucker, Lynne G. (1989). *Permanently Failing Organizations*. Newbury Park, CA: Sage.

Miner, Anne S. (1993). Review of *Dynamics of Organizational Populations*. *Academy of Management Review*, 18, 355–367.

Miner, Anne S.; Amburgey, Terry L.; & Stearns, Timothy M. (1990). Interorganizational Linkages and Population Dynamics: Buffering and Transformational Shields. *Administrative Science Quarterly*, 35, 689–713.

Mizruchi, Mark S., & Fein, Lisa C. (1999). The Social Construction of Organizational Knowledge: A Study of the Uses of Coercive, Mimetic, and Normative Isomorphism. *Administrative Science Quarterly*, 44, 653–683.

Péli, Gábor; Bruggeman, Jeroen; Masuch, Michael; & Ó Nualláin, Breanndán (1994). A Logical Approach to Formalizing Organizational Ecology. *American Sociological Review*, 59, 571–593.

Petersen, Trond, & Koput, Kenneth W. (1991). Density Dependence in Organizational Mortality: Legitimacy or Unobserved Heterogeneity? *American Sociological Review*, 56, 399–409.

Pfeffer, Jeffrey (1972a). Interorganizational Influence and Managerial Attitudes. *Academy of Management Journal*, 15, 317–330.

Pfeffer, Jeffrey (1972b). Merger as a Response to Organizational Interdependence. *Administrative Science Quarterly*, 17, 382–394.

Pfeffer, Jeffrey (1972c). Size and Composition of Corporate Boards of Directors: The Organization and Its Environment. *Administrative Science Quarterly*, 17, 218–228.

Pfeffer, Jeffrey (1973). Size, Composition, and Function of Hospital Boards of Directors: A Study of Organization-Environment Linkage. *Administrative Science Quarterly*, 18, 349–364.

Pfeffer, Jeffrey (1978). *Organizational Design*. Arlington Heights, IL: AHM Publishing.

Pfeffer, Jeffrey (1981). *Power in Organizations*. Marshfield, MA: Pitman..

Pfeffer, Jeffrey (1982). *Organizations and Organization Theory*. Marshfield, MA: Pitman.

Pfeffer, Jeffrey (1989). A Political Perspective on Careers: Interests, Networks, and Environments. In Michael B. Arthur, Douglas T. Hall, & Barbara S. Lawrence (Eds.), *Handbook of Career Theory* (pp. 380–396). Cambridge: Cambridge University Press.

Pfeffer, Jeffrey (1990). Incentives in Organizations: The Importance of Social Relations. In Oliver E. Williamson (Ed.), *Organization Theory: From Chester Barnard to the Present and Beyond* (pp. 72–97). New York: Oxford University Press.

Pfeffer, Jeffrey (1992). *Managing with Power: Politics and Influence in Organizations*. Boston: Harvard Business School Press.

Pfeffer, Jeffrey (1996). Taking the Road Less Traveled: Serendipity and the Influence of Others in a Career. In Arthur G. Bedeian (Ed.), *Management Laureates: A Collection of Autobiographical Essays* (Vol. 4, pp. 201–233). Greenwood, CT: JAI Press.

Pfeffer, Jeffrey (1997). *New Directions for Organization Theory: Problems and Prospects.* New York: Oxford University Press.

Pfeffer, Jeffrey, & Cohen, Yinon (1984). Determinants of Internal Labor Markets in Organizations. *Administrative Science Quarterly,* 29, 550–572.

Pfeffer, Jeffrey, & Davis-Blake, Alison (1987). Understanding Organizational Wage Structures: A Resource Dependence Approach. *Academy of Management Journal,* 30, 437–455.

Pfeffer, Jeffrey, & Leblebici, Huseyin (1973). Executive Recruitment and the Development of Interfirm Organizations. *Administrative Science Quarterly,* 18, 449–461.

Pfeffer, Jeffrey, & Leong, A. (1977). Resource Allocation in United Funds: An Examination of Power and Dependence. *Social Forces,* 55, 775–790.

Pfeffer, Jeffrey, & Moore, William L. (1980a). Average Tenure of Academic Department Heads: The Effects of Paradigm, Size, and Departmental Demography. *Administrative Science Quarterly,* 25, 387–406.

Pfeffer, Jeffrey, & Moore, William L. (1980b). Power in University Budgeting: A Replication and Extension. *Administrative Science Quarterly,* 25, 637–653.

Pfeffer, Jeffrey, & Nowak, Phillip (1976). Joint Ventures and Interorganizational Interdependence. *Administrative Science Quarterly,* 21, 398–418.

Pfeffer, Jeffrey, & Salancik, Gerald R. (1974). Organizational Decision Making as a Political Process: The Case of a University Budget. *Administrative Science Quarterly,* 19, 135–151.

Pfeffer, Jeffrey, & Salancik, Gerald R. (1977). Organizational Context and the Characteristics and Tenure of Hospital Administrators. *Academy of Management Journal,* 20, 74–88.

Pfeffer, Jeffrey, & Salancik, Gerald R. (1978). *The External Control of Organizations: A Resource Dependence Perspective.* New York: Harper & Row.

Powell, Walter W., & DiMaggio, Paul J. (1991). *The New Institutionalism in Organizational Analysis.* Chicago: University of Chicago Press.

Provan, Keith G.; Beyer, Janice M.; & Kruytbosch, Carlos (1980). Environmental Linkages and Power in Resource-Dependence Relations between Organizations. *Administrative Science Quarterly,* 25, 200–225.

Ranger-Moore, James; Banaszak-Holl, Jane; & Hannan, Michael T. (1991). Density-Dependent Dynamics in Regulated Industries: Founding Rates of Banks and Life Insurance Companies. *Administrative Science Quarterly,* 36, 36–65.

Robson, Gary S.; Wholey, Douglas R.; & Barefield, Russell M. (1996). Institutional Determinants of Individual Mobility: Bringing the Professions Back In. *Academy of Management Journal,* 39, 397–420.

Ruef, Martin, & Scott, W. Richard (1998). A Multidimensional Model of Organizational Legitimacy: Hospital Survival in Changing Institutional Environments. *Administrative Science Quarterly,* 43, 877–904.

Salancik, Gerald R., & Pfeffer, Jeffrey (1974). The Bases and Uses of Power in Organizational Decision Making: The Case of a University. *Administrative Science Quarterly,* 19, 453–473.

Scott, W. Richard (1987). The Adolescence of Institutional Theory. *Administrative Science Quarterly,* 32, 493–511.

Scott, W. Richard (1990). Symbols and Organizations: From Barnard to the Institutionalists. In Oliver E. Williamson (Ed.), *Organization Theory: From Chester Barnard to the Present and Beyond* (pp. 38–55). New York: Oxford University Press.

Scott, W. Richard (1995, 2001). *Institutions and Organizations.* 1st ed., 2d ed. Thousand Oaks, CA: Sage.

Scott, W. Richard, & Meyer, John W. (1994). *Institutional Environments and Organizations: Structural Complexity and Individualism.* Thousand Oaks, CA: Sage.

Scott, W. Richard; Ruef, Martin; Mendel, Peter J.; & Caronna, Carol A. (2000). *Institutional Change and Healthcare Organizations: From Professional Dominance to Managed Care.* Chicago: University of Chicago Press.

Selznick, Philip (1949). *TVA and the Grass Roots.* Berkeley: University of California Press.

Selznick, Philip (1957). *Leadership in Administration: A Sociological Interpretation.* Berkeley: University of California Press.

Singh, Jitendra V.; House, Robert J.; & Tucker, David J. (1986). Organizational Change and Organizational Mortality. *Administrative Science Quarterly,* 31, 587–611.

Singh, Jitendra V., & Lumsden, Charles J. (1990). Theory and Research in Organizational Ecology. *Annual Review of Sociology,* 16, 161–195.

Singh, Jitendra V.; Tucker, David J.; & Meinhard, Agnes G. (1991). Institutional Change and Ecological Dynamics. In Walter W. Powell & Paul J. DiMaggio (Eds.), *The New Institutionalism in Organizational Analysis* (pp. 390–422). Chicago: University of Chicago Press.

Stinchcombe, Arthur L. (1965). Social Structure and Organizations. In James G. March (Ed.), *Handbook of Organizations* (pp. 153–193). Chicago: Rand McNally.

Stinchcombe, Arthur L. (1997). On the Virtues of the Old Institutionalism. *Annual Review of Sociology,* 23, 1–18.

Stryker, Robin (2000). Legitimacy Processes as Institutional Politics: Implications for Theory and Research in the Sociology of Organizations. *Research in the Sociology of Organizations*, 17, 179–223.

Swaminathan, Anand, & Delacroix, Jacques (1991). Differentiation within an Organizational Population: Additional Evidence from the Wine Industry. *Academy of Management Journal*, 34, 679–692.

Tolbert, Pamela S. (1988) Institutional Sources of Organizational Culture in Major Law Firms. In Lynne G. Zucker (Ed.), *Institutional Patterns and Organizations: Culture and Environment* (pp. 101–113). Cambridge, MA: Ballinger.

Tolbert, Pamela S., & Zucker, Lynne G. (1996). The Institutionalization of Institutional Theory. In Stewart R. Clegg, Cynthia Hardy, & Walter R. Nord (Eds.), *Handbook of Organization Studies* (pp. 175–190). London: Sage.

Tucker, David J.; Singh, Jitendra V.; & Meinhard, Agnes G. (1990). Organizational Form, Population Dynamics, and Institutional Change: The Founding Patterns of Voluntary Organizations. *Academy of Management Journal*, 33, 151–178.

Westphal, James D.; Gulati, Ranjay; & Shortell, Stephen M. (1997). Customization or Conformity? An Institutional and Network Perspective on the Content and Consequences of TQM Adoption. *Administrative Science Quarterly*, 42, 366–394.

Zucker, Lynne G. (1977). The Role of Institutionalization in Cultural Persistence. *American Sociological Review*, 42, 726–743.

Zucker, Lynne G. (1983). Organizations as Institutions. *Research in the Sociology of Organizations*, 2, 1–47.

Zucker, Lynne G. (1988). *Institutional Patterns and Organizations: Culture and Environment.* Cambridge, MA: Ballinger.

Zucker, Lynne G. (1989). Combining Institutional Theory and Population Ecology: No Legitimacy, No History. *American Sociological Review*, 54, 542–545.

Zucker, Lynne G., & Kreft, Ita G. G. (1994). The Evolution of Socially Contingent Rational Action: Effects of Labor Strikes on Change in Union Founding in the 1880s. In Joel A. C. Baum & Jitendra V. Singh (Eds.), *Evolutionary Dynamics of Organizations* (pp. 294–313). New York: Oxford University Press.

Part X

Second-Generation Theories: Organizational Decision Making

Chapter 27

Image Theory

Image theory emerged initially as an attempt to develop further the ideas of George Miller, E. Galanter, and K. H. Pribram (1960). It is directly in the tradition of behavioral decision theory (see chapter 23) and represents an approach to applying this type of theory first to individual decision processes and then to decisions at the organizational level. In doing this it moves to quite advanced conceptualizations in this area, of a kind that break considerably with the classical versions of decision theory and with those most frequently associated with economics.

Background

Image theory was created at the University of Washington by Lee Roy Beach in conjunction with a num-

ber of students and colleagues, including initially and most notably Terence Mitchell, whom we met in chapter 23 of this volume. Beach, however, has been by far the most consistent contributor to the theory's development and is an author of many articles on the topic, as well as of five books that he either wrote himself or edited.

He was born in 1936, did his undergraduate work at the University of Indiana, and obtained his doctorate from the psychology department at the University of Colorado in 1961. Thus, he is another who turned to major theorizing only later in his career and, in fact, only shortly before accepting a business school appointment. After obtaining his degree, Beach served in research positions of various kinds—as an aviation psychologist and a human factors scientist, as well as in a postdoctoral appointment in psychology at the University of Michigan. He joined the psychology faculty at the University of Washington in 1966 and ultimately became department chair. In 1989 he moved to the University of Arizona with a position in the business school, and it is there that the majority of his work on image theory occurred. He remains in this position.

Beach has been publishing research on decision processes since 1961. However, it was only in the latter 1980s that he began publishing on what he named image theory. The theory was developed in response to a felt need to correct earlier work on what was called the strategy selection model (Beach & Mitchell, 1978). The result was a rather large number of journal articles and essays, setting forth the theory in various forms (Mitchell, Rediker, & Beach, 1986; Beach & Mitchell, 1987; Beach, Smith, Lundell, & Mitchell, 1988; Beach & Frederickson, 1989; Beach & Strom, 1989). By the time he reached Arizona, however, Beach (1990) was ready to publish a comprehensive theory of individual decision making, and thus the major statement of image theory as applied to the individual level. This book is the primary source for what follows, although a parallel journal publication is used as well (Mitchell & Beach, 1990).

Individual Theory

The first book on image theory was originally intended to be a joint product with Terence Mitchell, but Mitchell had to withdraw because of time demands (Beach, 1990).

Essential Framework

Images are the cognitive structures that summarize a decision maker's knowledge of what is to be accomplished, why, how, and the results of action. The *value image* (elsewhere called the self-image) represents the decision maker's values, standards, ideals, precepts, beliefs, morals, and ethics (taken together these are called *principles*); these principles serve to establish whether a decision is right or wrong. The *trajectory image* represents an agenda for the future, consisting of goals. Concrete surrogate events serve as *markers* to indicate goal achievement. The *strategic image* contains the *plans* to achieve *goals*, the behavioral *tactics* to implement plans, and *forecasts* of the future anticipated if a plan is adopted and/or implemented. On occasion, strategic images are broken down into action images (plans and tactics) and projected images (forecasts).

These images, along with other elements of the

theory, are set forth in figure 27.1. This figure in somewhat varied forms is contained in a large number of Beach's publications of the early period.

Two kinds of decisions are noted. *Adoption decisions* are concerned with the adoption or rejection of candidates for inclusion in the images noted above. *Progress decisions* are concerned with whether a given plan on the strategic image is working to produce progress to the goal.

Framing occurs as the decision maker uses recognition or identification of the current context to define a subset of the constituents of images as having particular relevance for a decision to be made. Meaning comes from the image constituents so activated. Either some successful action from the past is mobilized in the form of a *policy* or appropriate goals and plans are created.

Two tests are applied in the process of making adoption and progress decisions:

> The *compatibility test* assesses whether the features of a candidate for adoption "violate" (are incompatible with) the relevant (framed) constituents of the various images, and whether the forecasts based on the constituents of the strategic image "violate" the relevant constituents of the trajectory image. The *profitability test*, which applies only to adoption decisions, assesses the relative ability of competing candidates to further the implementation of ongoing plans, attain existing goals, and comply with the decision maker's principles. The object of the compatibility test is to screen out the unacceptable. The object of the profitability test is to seek the best. (Beach, 1990, p. 9)

Candidates that pass the compatibility test are adopted if there is only one such candidate. In the case of progress decisions, there must be compatibility between the trajectory image (goals) and strategic image (forecasts). These processes are diagrammed in figure 27.1. The compatibility test is a screening process, while the profitability test is used to choose the best among multiple alternative candidates.

Organizational decisions are addressed only briefly; they develop from overlapping images among people, become shared as a result of similar experiences, or are simply a function of organization-wide images. Organizations exert influence on decisions by dividing up tasks, introducing standard practices, communicating objectives widely, and establishing communica-

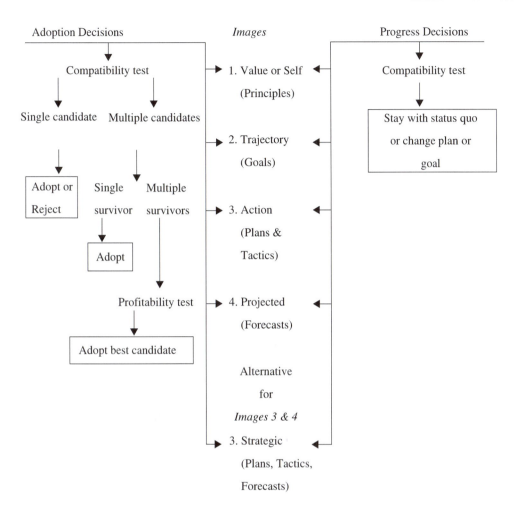

FIGURE 27.1 The elements and diagrams of image theory. Adapted from Terence R. Mitchell & Lee Roy Beach (1990), " . . . Do I love Thee? Let Me Count . . ." Toward an Understanding of Intuitive and Automatic Decision Making, *Organizational Behavior and Human Decision Processes*, 47, 11; Lee Roy Beach & Terence R. Mitchell (1990), Image Theory: A Behavioral Theory of Decision Making in Organizations, *Research in Organizational Behavior*, 12, 13.

tion channels; they also provide extensive training and socialization. Decisions must conform to these constraints and be congruent with decisions emanating from elsewhere. Top management, like everyone else, has its decisions constrained and is influenced by organizational principles. However, image theory assumes that decisions occur only as properties of individuals, and social processes merely inform, or restrict, these individual processes. Group decisions thus represent a transform of the individual's decisions; that transform is outside the domain of image theory.

Types of Images

The various types of images are cognitive processes, as are framing and the two tests. The images may be visual, mental (pictorial), or cognitive (a combination of pictorial, semantic, and emotional content). These images are in fact schemata for decision making. They are called frames in the instance where they consist of knowledge that gives meaning to contexts; often this occurs in the form of stories that are domain specific.

Value images, along with principles, serve to motivate the whole decision process. Principles are primarily products of culture. Trajectory images are the set of goals a person has decided to adopt and seek. In terms of a goal hierarchy, the value image is at the top, the trajectory image is intermediate, and the strategic image is at the lowest level of the list; these positions correspond to alternative courses of action.

The plans in the strategic image are for the purpose of achieving goals derived from the trajectory image. Planning is not necessarily all good, however. One can plan too much when forecasting is not feasible. Policies represent preformulated plans that can be activated when the framed context is seen to be one that has arisen previously. Forecasting involves the ability to devise possible futures, to establish the outcome of implementing a plan. Goals are a function of imperatives generated by principles, or of the need to introduce some type of goal to complement already existing goals; they may also stem from perceived external necessity or suggestion. Goals may be packaged alone without an accompanying plan, may be unstated but inherent in a plan, or may be explicitly stated with a goal and its plan operating together.

Framing and Deliberation

Framing acts to establish what a decision is about and defines the issues that may prove relevant. The context provides certain cues that the decision maker uses for purposes of framing. A frame is the portion of a person's knowledge base that is brought to bear on a particular context to endow it with meaning. As contexts evolve, frames must be changed. Failure of action can signal the need for such a change—the old frame is no longer effective. This kind of reframing is one way to deal with context-frame incongruity; another way is to act on the context to force it back into line with the frame. Different people, of course, may have quite different frames for the same context.

Decision deliberation is what happens as the decision maker thinks about making the decision and implementing it. Included are the compatibility and profitability tests, but the major function is to identify and clarify issues, which happens during framing. Also deliberation serves to generate new candidate principles, goals, and plans; to allow the decision maker to use the experiences considered to make forecasts; to permit confidence building and risk assessment; and

to deliberate over how the adopted candidate might be presented to others.

Compatibility Test

The function of the compatibility test is that it serves "to screen out adoption candidates that do not conform to the principles, or that adversely affect the goals and plans that make up the frame of the context within which adoption is being considered. . . . It also serves to detect the possible failure of ongoing plans when the forecasted results of their implementation do not include their goals" (Beach, 1990, p. 71). This test involves as its major variables violations, a rejection threshold, and the decision rule. The latter is that if the negative weighted sum of violations exceeds the negative rejection threshold, the candidate decision is rejected; if not, it is accepted.

Expressed in mathematical terms this may be summarized as follows:

$$C = \sum_{t=1}^{n} \sum_{c=1}^{m} W_c V_{tc}; \; V_{tc} = -1 \text{ or } 0, \; 0.00 \le W \le 1.00$$

where the compatibility C is zero when a candidate has no violations and decreases (i.e., is more and more negative) as the number of violations increases; t is a relevant attribute of the candidate; c is a relevant image constituent; V is a violation of image constituent c by attribute t of the candidate; and W is the importance weight for each of the relevant image constituents—W is between and including 0.00 and 1.00 (Beach, 1990, p. 73). Thus, violations of image constituents may be weighted differently (W_c).

Information about nonviolations is used in part to help define what a candidate is and in part to establish a stopping rule to limit search and deliberation. In addition, the profitability test is invoked only when there are multiple surviving candidates (see figure 27.1).

The compatibility test operates as a means to make intuitive decisions, and as such it may well not be part of conscious experience. Since image theory is not a normative theory, but rather entirely descriptive, the author notes that generally when intuition conflicts with rational analysis, intuition tends to win out.

Profitability Test

The profitability test involves a number of different strategies. The strategy selection process is influenced by aspects of the decision problem, of the environment, and of the decision maker. Depending on these factors, the person attempts to select the strategy that involves the least investment for a correct decision. The task is to balance perceived utilities against both probabilities and costs for each available strategy; thus to select a strategy that seems to offer the best hope of success with the least resource investment.

Most important decisions turn out to be compatibility ones, involving a single alternative weighed against the status quo. Thus the much more complex profitability process is not required very often. As evidence of the potential for applied usefulness of image theory, Beach (1990) presents descriptions of its use in auditing, in making decisions about childbearing, and as applied to government decision making (specifically with regard to the Cuban missile crisis).

Subsequent Theorizing

Since 1990 there have been a number of statements of the individual theory in some form. A chapter by Beach, Mitchell, Thaddeus Paluchowski, and Emily van Zee (1992) explores extensions in decision framing and deliberation, but the material is essentially the same as that presented previously. Beach (1993a) presents a historical analysis of the development of behavioral decision theory, contending that at each stage there has been a shift away from economic formulations and toward the psychological. The major theoretical contribution here is an emphasis on the role played by preformulated policies. Most behavior is guided by past experience in this way; only rarely does choice come into the picture with multiple surviving candidates and the invoking of a profitability test. Beach 1996 is basically devoted to applications and contains little by way of new individual theory by the author. We will return to these applications later. Beach 1997 is an overview of the psychology of decision making in general, which includes a limited statement of the individual theory. Beach 1998 is intended to draw together image theory research and extensions to theory. The latter, however, are not basic in nature and, in fact, are rarely a product of the theory's author at all (this is an edited volume with a third of the chapters entirely written by someone other than Beach).

The point is that over some 10 years individual image theory has been quite stable. It is not a theory that has continually evolved over the years like many

considered previously in this book, although it certainly may evolve further at some later point.

Organizational Theory

The organizational theory is closely tied to the individual version. It, too, had its early origins in the 1980s (Mitchell et al., 1986). However, I will focus on the more fully developed statements in the 1990s.

Decision Making in Organizations

The first of these statements is billed as a current update to the theory's organizational version (Beach & Mitchell, 1990). There are four images:

> The *organizational self-image* consists of the organizational decision makers' perceptions of the beliefs, values, morals, ethics, and norms that combine to form its principles and which serve as imperatives for the organization. This self-image is analogous to the organization's culture, gives rise to the organization as a collective, and transcends the characteristics of individual members.
>
> The *organizational trajectory image* is the organization's agenda for the future and may be articulated only in the minds of top managers or diffused more widely in the organization.
>
> The *organizational action image* consists of plans and tactics which, in turn, guide subunits.
>
> The *organizational projected image* refers to anticipated events and states that are forecasted if a plan were to be adopted or in process. (pp. 6–7)

From there the organizational theory moves to much the same ground as the individual theory (see figure 27.1). Choices are made between retaining the status quo and introducing change. Change is resisted by organizations because it violates images by expending energy that could be devoted to existing goal attainment. Yet nonoptional changes may emerge from the environment, and then top management's function is to provide for smooth transitions.

With regard to frames and policies, decisions are said to follow the processes depicted in figure 27.2. Policies are made up of goals and their associated plans when they are tied to a specific frame. The process set forth here remains more individual than organizational; there is no organizational memory, or

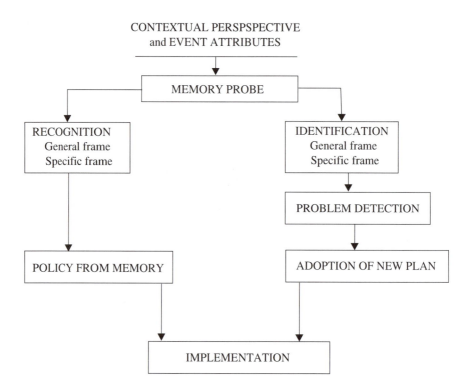

FIGURE 27.2 Elements of the framing process. From Lee Roy Beach & Terence R. Mitchell (1990), Image Theory: A Behavioral Theory of Decision Making in Organizations, *Research in Organizational Behavior*, 12, 14. Copyright 1990. Reprinted with permission from Elsevier Science.

learning, construct. However, group decision making is considered.

Joint decisions of this kind are fostered when a decision extends beyond the authority of a single person. With regard to a theory for such a situation the authors say:

> This is not the place to elaborate on small group interaction, the vagaries of intra-organizational communication, or the complexities of organizational politics, coalitions, bargaining, power-plays, etc. Instead, to avoid straying from the central issue of Image Theory, we will take an idyllic, if unrealistic, view of how groups work. (Beach & Mitchell, 1990, p. 18)

In the process they assume away most differences in images and frames. Only very specific frames are expected to differ to some extent and thus can serve as a source of conflict.

In such an idyllic social setting, discussion and persuasion are used to influence the decision process toward consensus. If this fails to produce image similarity, stalemates and postponement are likely—or perhaps voting. Thus individuals remain individuals: "The group's decision is not the result of it acting as some sort of single decision making organism that has a single will" (p. 19). One comes away at this point with the feeling that moving beyond the individual level leaves the author somewhat uncomfortable and takes him into territory that is not of great interest.

Further to Organizational Culture Factors

Yet Beach (1993b) develops the organizational culture construct in much more detail in a book that was intended primarily for business students, not as a theoretical statement. Theory certainly is embedded here, but it is handled tangentially, and references to image theory per se are minimized for some reason.

Decision responsibility rests within organizations. Understanding these organizations requires knowledge of their culture (the basic beliefs), their vision (the agenda of goals), and their activities (what is being done to achieve these goals and the plans that guide them). These three understandings provide mental images to a decision maker (the value, trajectory, and action images of figure 27.1). In turn, the images provide guidelines that enter into the making of right decisions—those that are compatible with, promote, and enhance the organization's culture, vision, and activities. In this context, *leadership* is defined as the art of understanding an organization so well that one can help it accomplish its goals without compromising its identity (culture is the core of that identity).

Culture serves in the role of principles where it does the following:

1. Specifies what is of primary importance to the organization, the standards against which its successes and failures should be measured
2. Dictates how the organization's resources are to be used, and to what ends
3. Establishes what the organization and its members can expect from each other
4. Makes some methods of controlling behavior within the organization legitimate and makes others illegitimate—that is, it defines where power lies within the organization and how it is to be used
5. Selects the behaviors in which members should or should not engage and prescribes how these are to be rewarded and punished
6. Sets the tone for how members should treat each other and how they should treat nonmembers: competitively, collaboratively, honestly, distantly, or hostilely
7. Instructs members about how to deal with the external environment: aggressively, exploitatively, responsibly, or proactively (Beach, 1993b, p. 12)

Changing culture requires changing activities initially and then permitting culture to adapt. The shift in activities may be imposed, or members may be convinced on the basis of crisis, or, ideally, a gradual evolution may be instituted. An Organizational Culture Inventory is developed, and presented, to measure beliefs about how employees should be treated and the opportunities afforded them, beliefs about professionalism and support of efforts to do a good job, and beliefs about how the organization interfaces with the environment and strives to accomplish its mission.

The vision provides direction, the agenda the organization perceives itself to be pursuing; it is rather imprecise, and establishes the general shape of plans. It is important that it be characterized by thrust and scope, as well as that it serve to build consensus within the organization. Culture and vision interact to influence decision making, which, in turn, leads to activities. Decision making is defined as the mechanism by which the need to abandon the status quo is evaluated and, if change is needed, the means by which a new direction is selected.

Organizational Decision Making

At this point the treatment moves to decision making, which is handled much as it was previously in theoretical discussions, but with some different terminology. The results are given in figure 27.3. The previous terminology is given at the end of arrows around the outside of the diagrams. There does not appear to be a great deal that is new here. Goals are tactical, operational, and strategic. Tests are carried out to determine if a forecast fits with the vision. Testing for quality (the compatibility test) to screen candidates for adoption requires that the organization do the following:

1. Only consider one candidate at a time.
2. Do not make comparisons between candidates.
3. Only take the candidate's violations into account.
4. Do not attempt to balance nonviolations against violations; meeting some standards does not compensate for failing to meet other standards.
5. Weight the seriousness of each violation by the importance of the violated standard.
6. Reject the candidate if its violations are too important or too many for you to feel comfortable with.
7. Assign all survivors to a choice set.
8. If, after all candidates have been screened, the choice set contains only one survivor, adopt it.
9. If the choice set ends up containing two or more survivors, choose the best of them

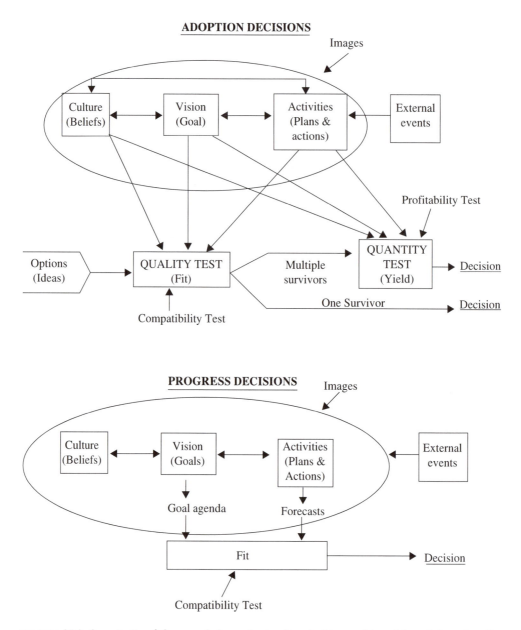

FIGURE 27.3 Organizational framework for understanding decision making. Adapted from Lee Roy Beach (1993), *Making the Right Decision: Organizational Culture, Vision, and Planning* (Englewood Cliffs, NJ: Prentice Hall), 94.

based on relative qualities of potential outcomes. (Beach, 1993b, p. 102)

Group decisions continue to be derived from the private decisions of group members. The decision that emerges from a group is negotiated based on these individual decisions. Negotiation strategies are yielding, compromise, contending, and problem-solving.

Elsewhere the essence of organizational decision making is set forth as follows:

The theoretical mechanism of primary interest involves assessment of the compatibility of a decision option with the organization's culture—where an option is defined as a possible course of action in the case of a member who is making a decision, or a proposed course of action in the case of a decision that has been made by leaders. Image theory predicts that when compatibility is low, the option will be rejected. This means that when an acculturated member is making decisions for the organization, he or she will tend not to make decisions that are incompatible with its culture; when leaders make culturally incompatible decisions, the organization's members will tend not to endorse the decision. (Weatherly & Beach, 1998, p. 212)

From this, hypotheses may be derived as follows:

1. Different groups will have different degrees of cultural fragmentation, and this can be measured.
2. The more compatible a decision option is with the culture, the more likely it will be chosen.
3. Members will be more likely to accept the decision of leaders if the goal or plan fits the culture.
4. When a culture differs from what members think it should be, these members will be less committed, less satisfied, and more inclined to turnover.

Evaluation and Impact

In a presentation of image theory research, Beach (1998) notes that the coverage is concerned with studies of the compatibility test and of the profitability test. Oddly missing is research dealing with the images themselves, an omission that Beach himself notes. He attributes this to difficulties in determining how to study images in a scientifically satisfying way. The problem is, however, that almost all of the studies are of a laboratory nature using student subjects, and a very high proportion of this extant research has involved Beach's participation. For this reason I do not report on findings on the images of the theory—there are none—and also will deal with all of the research at once. So much involves Beach that it would be pointless to separate his work out. In fact, almost all of it involves the author or his students.

Adoption Research on the Compatibility Test

Compatibility decisions are the aspect of the theory that have attracted the greatest amount of research historically, and they continue to do so. Adoption decisions have been studied most here. A common

concern has been to determine whether violation decisions dominate the decision process and, if so, what kind of a threshold emerges. One such study used a student looking for a job as the standardized role and a set of preestablished jobs to be considered. The use of violations to reject jobs was characteristic, with nonviolations playing practically no role (Beach & Strom, 1998). After four violations the candidate tended to be rejected, which reflects a reasonably stable threshold. All this is quite consistent with theory.

The next step is to determine whether differential weighting of violations during screening (as illustrated in the equation for the compatibility test) does occur. A study to determine this involved a decision to purchase a toaster with various descriptors entered into the process on a standardized basis (Beach, Puto, Heckler, Naylor, & Marble, 1998). The data clearly supported the hypothesis that weighting of violations is evident. Under time constraints, it was found that the compatibility test is retained, and no change in threshold appears, either. The subjects simply speed up or, depending on the conditions, perform more poorly. This research also used a job search scenario (Benson & Beach, 1998). The point is that time pressure does not result in a change in decision strategy.

A different research thrust looked into the question as to whether screening (the compatibility test) and choice (the profitability test) do in fact use different processes and information sources. The problem faced by the students was to choose a room to rent for a friend from out of town. Screening was done first to establish a short list, and then additional information was provided, followed by a specific choice (van Zee, Paluchowski, & Beach, 1998). Information used to carry out screening was not used in the subsequent choice process, only the additional information exerted an influence at this point. It appeared that screening and choice were viewed as completely different tasks with quite varied information requirements. A subsequent study confirmed this interpretation with a somewhat different decision task and also showed that, while screening for violations did not use probability information, choice decisions clearly did incorporate probability considerations (Potter & Beach, 1998). These results provide strong support for the compatibility-profitability differentiation, while at the same time demonstrating that the compatibility test is essentially conservative in nature.

The implication of these findings is that screening plays a very important role in decision making and that the two-step process hypothesized by image theory is entirely defensible. There are other data that lead to similar conclusions. Stephen Asare and W. Knechel (1995), for example, used auditors as subjects, and decisions were made with regard to audit clients. Decision making based on violations and the existence of thresholds were clearly apparent. In Germany, Christian Seidl and Stefan Traub (1998) found substantial support for the compatibility test by using a laboratory approach with students, a decision on screening candidates for a position, and a revised approach to analysis. Lisa Ordóñez, Lehman Benson, and Beach (1999) studied the effects of a manipulation that made the student subjects more accountable for the results of their decisions. This increased realism had no effect on the tendency to follow image theory by screening out bad options rather than screening in good ones, but it did serve to create greater stringency in screening by lowering threshold values.

An early study of adoption decisions deserves particular attention because it was not of a laboratory nature (Beach et al., 1988). It was conducted using managers from three firms who were interviewed about their firm's principles and decision making processes. The degree of agreement on principles was found to be closely associated with firm turnover. It was also related to agreement in evaluations of alternative plans considered to achieve a specific goal. Evaluated compatibility of any one of these alternative plans was a function of the extent to which company principles were violated by that plan. Thus both principles and violations operated in the manner image theory would anticipate. The compatibility equation received support as well.

Progress Research on the Compatibility Test

A major contributor to the research on progress decisions has been Kenneth Dunegon. In one such research program, he carried out various laboratory studies in which students made decisions in the context of project team scenarios. The data indicated that when goals and forecasts were compatible, subjects were more likely to continue a project and to commit additional resources to it (Dunegon, 1998). In further extensions of this program it became apparent that when progress toward goals is satisfactory, subjects devote little deep thinking to the project and invest more resources almost automatically. Only when

progress is unacceptable does real deliberation occur (Dunegon, Duchon, & Ashmos, 1998).

Dunegon (1993) also conducted studies on the framing of decisions; in one instance this involved engineering team personnel in a field setting. When the same information is framed both positively and negatively, the decision-making processes invoked tend to differ. Again, positive framing produces more automatic processes, while negative framing brings more controlled and thorough processes into play. Thus although compatibility remains in evidence, negative framing acts to reduce the fit between current and trajectory images. Accordingly, organizations may be best served by framing information negatively in order to induce deliberation; it pays to depict the glass as half empty rather than as half full.

Donald Schepers and Beach (1998) followed up on Dunegon's work by studying the amount of overtime subjects were willing to work, depending on the way a decision is framed. When the framing serves to produce low compatibility, motivation to improve progress toward the goal—and thus to work more overtime—is increased. Apparently in the case of progress decisions, violations and unsatisfactory progress do not necessarily mean that the person stops implementing the plan and looks for another plan. Rather, the incompatibility acts as feedback to elicit attempts to improve on the plan and, as appropriate, to work harder. This distinction between adoption and progress compatibility was not inherent in the original theory and appears to suggest much more complex processes in the latter instance than had been envisioned previously.

Research conducted in two government departments used questionnaire data to determine compatibility between perceived supervisory behavior and the ideal image for a supervisor. This discrepancy measure was related to measured satisfaction with supervision. As compatibility decreased, and violations increased, satisfaction levels decreased slowly up to 10 or 12 violations and then dropped sharply. The rejection threshold appeared to be roughly 10 violations (Bissell & Beach, 1996). This finding was replicated in another study of fast food restaurant employees. In this latter research, hope for improvement in the situation was also determined and was proven effective in adding to satisfaction levels above and beyond the effects of compatibility levels alone (Richmond, Bissell, & Beach, 1998). These studies represent the major efforts to study progress decisions outside the laboratory.

Research on the Profitability Test

Studies of the profitability test, and how decisions to select a strategy for making that test are made, are generally of a 1970s vintage and thus antedate image theory. The key studies were carried out in a laboratory setting and indicated that the costs and benefits of alternative strategies are taken into account by using a mechanism that is congruent with that of the subjective expected utility model. Yet strategy selection and then a decision using the strategy that appears most attractive does occur. All this does not prove that the subjective expected utility (SEU) model is actually used, but the results match up with such an approach (Christensen-Szalanski, 1998).

With regard to this situation, and presumably at the same time providing an explanation of why profitability research has not progressed further, Beach has the following to say:

> Neither Mitchell nor I have ever been completely comfortable with the SEU mechanism. On the other hand, the data seem to support the model, and we have not had a better idea about how to formulate the selection mechanism, so we are stuck with the SEU formulation until something better comes along. (1998, p. 140)

In the late 1970s also, McAllister, Mitchell, and Beach (1998) did a study in the laboratory in which significance, irreversibility, and accountability were varied. When all three were high, the strategy for choice selected was the most highly analytic available; when all three were low, the least analytic strategy was utilized. Again, it is important to note that this research preceded image theory, and influenced it as well. It appears that people do carry out the profitability test using a wide repertoire of approaches, but it is not entirely clear how this fact interfaces with and integrates into image theory.

Research on Organizational Theory

Research on the organizational theory, as opposed to the individual, is hard to find. There is one research effort, however, that builds on the idea that an organization's culture provides a value image for its members. The central concept is that, in view of their shared understandings of a common culture, vision, and set of plans, managers will tend to favor certain decision options and avoid others. The Organizational Culture Survey was used to test the hypothesis that different organizations are characterized by varying degrees of cultural fragmentation (Weatherly & Beach, 1996, 1998).

The initial study compared a financial services organization (successful) with a utility (on the verge of bankruptcy) on some 15 different cultural values. The profiles of different levels within the financial services firm were remarkably similar, suggesting a unified culture. In the utility, two different views of the culture appeared—one at the top and one at the lower levels. Score variances were consistently greater in the utility.

Additional studies moved to more specific hypotheses of image theory. A group of utility managers was used to determine whether a decision option that is more compatible with an organization's culture will be chosen or endorsed more than one that is not as compatible by members; this proved to be the case. Subjects from both companies were used to establish whether members were more likely to support a top management decision when the features of this option were compatible with the features of their organization's culture than when they were not compatible; this proved to be the case. Utility employees were involved in a study designed to test the hypothesis that the greater the difference between member perceptions of the existing culture and how they felt that culture should be (ideal), the less committed they would be, the less satisfied, and the more inclined to turnover; all three of these expectations proved to be correct.

These findings have much in common with those of Byron Bissell and Beach (1998). More data on the degree of fragmentation issue are presented elsewhere as well (Beach, 1993b), adding information on several government agencies (unified cultures) and on various professional school groups (fragmented cultures). Clearly, variations in fragmentation levels do occur. It would appear that they have consequences for organizational decision making as well.

Nevertheless, the lack of research on image theory's organizational aspects represents a problem. Certainly what research there is is supportive in the sense that the hypotheses tested were developed from image theory, and they were confirmed. Yet other theories may be supported by these same results. The findings would appear to be quite consistent with most theorizing in the area of organizational culture; they are not specific to image theory.

Normative Applications
of Descriptive Theory

Image theory is descriptive in nature and is aimed at achieving understanding, not at providing guidelines for practice. Thus Beach says, "Image theory is not sufficiently well-developed to justify giving managers advice about how to go about their work" (1998, p. 131). Yet after this disclaimer, he does move a few tentative steps in the direction of application, and this happens rather often throughout his writings. The edited volume *Decision Making in the Workplace* (Beach, 1996) contains a number of essays by Beach, his students, and others, who touch on various applications of image theory. Some examples follow.

The work with Cynthia Stevens carries implications for job and career decision making and for management's role as a source of information on positions. Byron Bissell's research on supervision is interpreted in terms of its implications for management. Thomas Lee provides what he calls an unfolding model of voluntary turnover in organizations and discusses possible applications. Both James Frederickson and Stephen Asare treat aspects of the auditing process and consider how image theory might be used in this context. The research involving Kristopher Weatherly discussed previously contains some quite specific recommendations for the management of culture, as does an essay by Kenneth Walsh.

There are a number of pieces in this book that carry implications for planning processes. Helmut Jungermann and Eric DeBruyn are concerned with the pluses and minuses of forecasting and policy use in planning under varied circumstances. Christopher Puto and Susan Heckler focus on the consumer's decision processes in developing ideas for designing marketing plans and communication strategies. This same consumer emphasis is evident in Kim Nelson's discussion of social responsibility dimensions, which deals with image theory's use in this context. We have already considered Kenneth Dunegon's research on framing and its implications for managerial decision making and planning.

All of these applications are presented more in the nature of suggestions for use than as specific guidelines. There is little by way of testing of fully developed application programs to see if they work in the real world of organizations. Yet a concern with normative applications is clearly evident, to a rather surprising degree for a descriptive theory. Furthermore, these implications for practice range over a wide panorama of topic areas.

Looking to the Future

Image theory represents a major departure from traditional decision theory (see Connolly, 1996). It has amassed a significant amount of research in support of several of its central constructs. For a quite recent theory, its accomplishments are indeed impressive, and as Connolly notes there are numerous avenues for research waiting to be opened (see also Connolly & Beach, 1998).

In some ways it is surprising that image theory has provoked so little research outside the boundaries of the Universities of Washington and Arizona where it has had its homes. Mention should be made of a study on decision risk conducted at Michigan State University, which although somewhat tangential does provide some support for image theory's views on choice (Hollenbeck, Ilgen, Phillips, & Hedlund, 1994). Also, the work on formulating a model of employee turnover by Thomas Lee mentioned previously has undergone considerable development on two fronts, both theoretical (Lee & Mitchell, 1994) and empirical (Lee, Mitchell, Wise, & Fireman, 1996). This model draws on contributions from image theory and demonstrates some of the more comprehensive uses to which the theory may be put; yet it remains a product of the University of Washington. Perhaps it is just too early in image theory's trajectory to anticipate a major outpouring of interest and research beyond its home grounds just yet.

In any event, for lack of such an outpouring, we are largely left with Beach's own views regarding the future of his theory. He lists a number of major tasks:

1. Images—research is lacking; the greatest need is for a measurement method so that the research can be conducted; perhaps a cognitive psychologist will take up this problem and develop a solution.
2. Compatibility and screening—the laboratory research remains somewhat stilted and artificial; in particular an approach which deals effectively with continuous variables is needed.
3. Compatibility and progress—there has been some movement to casting the theory in mathematical terms, but not enough; theory development that would result in mathematical formalization is needed.

4. Profitability and choice—this is the biggest flaw in image theory; the reliance on subjective expected utility theory is unacceptable; a whole new theory appears needed here, one which would not require the notion of different strategies or the idea of a repertoire of strategies.

5. Extensions—the most important idea here, as part of the organization theory, is that culture provides the value image that decision makers for organizations use; thus individuals have their own value image and one for the organization as well, but these two need not be very different; all this has profound implications for leadership and for dealing with organizational change. (Beach, 1998, pp. 263–268)

Beach ends with the following statement: "The image theory description of organizational decisions affords the opportunity to conduct theory-driven applied research" (1998, p. 268). At this point, then, normative applications of the descriptive theory are specifically envisaged. For this goal to be achieved a great deal more research on and in the organizational context will be required, and I suspect some more fully developed theorizing as well.

CONCLUSIONS

Image theory is in the tradition of behavioral decision theory, as is the theory of behavior in organizations (see chapter 23), but it takes a very different slant on the nature of decision-making processes, accepting the view that human beings will rarely if ever go through the lengthy weighting of alternatives that traditional theory requires. Thus, image theory comes out much closer to the view of bounded rationality discussed by Herbert Simon and James March (see chapter 22). It also seems to have the potential for integration with approaches such as Robert Lord's ideas about implicit leadership theories (see chapter 24). However, the constructs of Lord's and Beach's theories differ, and it will take considerable research to bring them together. To what extent Beach himself is now motivated to attempt this sort of thing, and extend his theory more fully into the domain of organizational behavior, is an open question. His presence in a business school bodes well on this score, but we will have to wait and see.

References

Asare, Stephen K., & Knechel, W. R. (1995). Termination of Information Evaluation in Auditing. *Journal of Behavioral Decision Making*, 8, 21–31.

Beach, Lee Roy (1990). *Image Theory: Decision Making in Personal and Organizational Contexts.* Chichester, UK: John Wiley.

Beach, Lee Roy (1993a). Four Revolutions in Behavioral Decision Theory. In Martin M. Chemers & Roya Ayman (Eds.), *Leadership Theory and Research: Perspectives and Directions* (pp. 271–292). San Diego: Academic Press.

Beach, Lee Roy (1993b). *Making the Right Decision: Organizational Culture, Vision, and Planning.* Englewood Cliffs, NJ: Prentice Hall.

Beach, Lee Roy (1996). *Decision Making in the Workplace: A Unified Perspective.* Mahwah, NJ: Lawrence Erlbaum.

Beach, Lee Roy (1997). *The Psychology of Decision Making: People in Organizations.* Thousand Oaks, CA: Sage.

Beach, Lee Roy (1998). *Image Theory: Theoretical and Empirical Foundations.* Mahwah, NJ: Lawrence Erlbaum.

Beach, Lee Roy, & Frederickson, James R. (1989). Image Theory: An Alternative Description of Audit Decisions. *Accounting, Organizations and Society*, 14, 101–112.

Beach, Lee Roy, & Mitchell, Terence R. (1978). A Contingency Model for the Selection of Decision Strategies. *Academy of Management Review*, 3, 439–449.

Beach, Lee Roy, & Mitchell, Terence R. (1987). Image Theory: Principles, Goals, and Plans in Decision Making. *Acta Psychologica*, 66, 201–220.

Beach, Lee Roy, & Mitchell, Terence R. (1990). Image Theory: A Behavioral Theory of Decision Making in Organizations. *Research in Organizational Behavior*, 12, 1–41.

Beach, Lee Roy; Mitchell, Terence R.; Paluchowski, Thaddeus F.; & van Zee, Emily H. (1992). Image Theory: Decision Framing and Decision Deliberation. In Frank Heller (Ed.), *Decision-Making and Leadership* (pp. 172–188). Cambridge: Cambridge University Press.

Beach, Lee Roy; Puto, Christopher P. ; Heckler, Susan E.; Naylor, Gillian; & Marble, Todd A. (1998). Differential versus Unit Weighting of Violations, Framing, and the Role of Probability in Image Theory's Compatibility Test. In Lee Roy Beach (Ed.), *Image Theory: Theoretical and Empirical Foundations* (pp. 41–49). Mahwah, NJ: Lawrence Erlbaum.

Beach, Lee Roy; Smith, B.; Lundell, J.; & Mitchell, Terence R. (1988). Image Theory: Descriptive Sufficiency of a Simple Rule for the Compatibility Test. *Journal of Behavioral Decision Making*, 1, 17–28.

Beach, Lee Roy, & Strom, Eric (1989). A Toadstool among the Mushrooms: Screening Decisions and Image Theory's Compatibility Test. *Acta Psychologica*, 72, 1–12.

Beach, Lee Roy, & Strom, Eric (1998). A Toadstool Among the Mushrooms: Screening Decisions and Image Theory's Compatibility Test. In Lee Roy Beach (Ed.), *Image Theory: Theoretical and Empirical Foundations* (pp. 31–40). Mahwah, NJ: Lawrence Erlbaum.

Benson, Lehman, & Beach, Lee Roy (1998). The Effects of Time Constraints on the Prechoice Screening of Decision Options. In Lee Roy Beach (Ed.), *Image Theory: Theoretical and Empirical Foundations* (pp. 51–60). Mahwah, NJ: Lawrence Erlbaum.

Bissell, Byron L., & Beach, Lee Roy (1996). Supervision and Job Satisfaction. In Lee Roy Beach (Ed.), *Decision Making in the Workplace: A Unified Perspective* (pp. 63–72). Mahwah, NJ: Lawrence Erlbaum.

Christensen-Szalanski, Jay J. J. (1998). Problem Solving Strategies: A Selection Mechanism, Some Implications, and Some Data. In Lee Roy Beach (Ed.), *Image Theory: Theoretical and Empirical Foundations* (pp. 159–175). Mahwah, NJ: Lawrence Erlbaum.

Connolly, Terry (1996). Image Theory and Workplace Decisions: Challenges. In Lee Roy Beach (Ed.), *Decision Making in the Workplace: A Unified Perspective* (pp. 197–208). Mahwah, NJ: Lawrence Erlbaum.

Connolly, Terry, & Beach, Lee Roy (1998). The Theory of Image Theory: An Examination of the Central Conceptual Structure. In Lee Roy Beach (Ed.), *Image Theory: Theoretical and Empirical Foundations* (pp. 249–259). Mahwah, NJ: Lawrence Erlbaum.

Dunegon, Kenneth J. (1993). Framing, Cognitive Modes, and Image Theory: Toward an Understanding of a Glass Half Full. *Journal of Applied Psychology*, 78, 491–503.

Dunegon, Kenneth J. (1998). Image Theory: Testing the Role of Image Compatibility in Progress Decisions. In Lee Roy Beach (Ed.), *Image Theory: Theoretical and Empirical Foundations* (pp. 101–112). Mahwah, NJ: Lawrence Erlbaum.

Dunegon, Kenneth J.; Duchon, Dennis; & Ashmos, Donde (1998). Image Compatibility and the Use of Problem Space Information in Resource Allocation Decisions: Testing a Moderating Effects Model. In Lee Roy Beach (Ed.), *Image Theory: Theoretical and Empirical Foundations* (pp. 113–124). Mahwah, NJ: Lawrence Erlbaum.

Hollenbeck, John R.; Ilgen, Daniel R.; Phillips, Jean M.; & Hedlund, Jennifer (1994). Decision Risk in Dynamic Two Stage Contexts: Beyond the Status Quo. *Journal of Applied Psychology*, 79, 592–598.

Lee, Thomas W., & Mitchell, Terence R. (1994). An Alternative Approach: The Unfolding Model of Employee Turnover. *Academy of Management Review*, 19, 51–89.

Lee, Thomas W.; Mitchell, Terence R.; Wise, Lowell; & Fireman, Steven (1996). An Unfolding Model of Voluntary Employee Turnover. *Academy of Management Journal*, 39, 5–36.

McAllister, Daniel W.; Mitchell, Terence R.; & Beach, Lee Roy (1998). The Contingency Model for the Selection of Decision Strategies: An Empirical Test of the Effects of Significance, Accountability, and Reversibility. In Lee Roy Beach (Ed.), *Image Theory: Theoretical and Empirical Foundations* (pp. 177–192). Mahwah, NJ: Lawrence Erlbaum.

Miller, George A.; Galanter, E.; & Pribram, K. H. (1960). *Plans and the Structure of Behavior*. New York: Holt, Rinehart, & Winston.

Mitchell, Terence R., & Beach, Lee Roy (1990). " . . . Do I Love Thee? Let Me Count . . . " Toward an Understanding of Intuitive and Automatic Decision Making. *Organizational Behavior and Human Decision Processes*, 47, 1–20.

Mitchell, Terence R.; Rediker, Kenneth J.; & Beach, Lee Roy (1986). Image Theory and Its Implications for Organizational Decision Making. In Henry P. Sims & Dennis A. Gioia (Eds.), *The Thinking Organization* (pp. 293–316). San Francisco: Jossey-Bass.

Ordóñez, Lisa D.; Benson, Lehman; & Beach, Lee Roy (1999). Testing the Compatibility Test: How Instructions, Accountability, and Anticipated Regret Affect Prechoice Screening of Options. *Organizational Behavior and Human Decision Processes*, 78, 63–80.

Potter, Richard E., & Beach, Lee Roy (1998). Imperfect Information in Prechoice Screening of Options. In Lee Roy Beach (Ed.), *Image Theory: Theoretical and Empirical Foundations* (pp. 73–86). Mahwah, NJ: Lawrence Erlbaum.

Richmond, Sandra M.; Bissell, Byron L.; & Beach, Lee Roy (1998). Image Theory's Compatibility Test and Evaluations of the Status Quo. *Organizational Behavior and Human Decision Processes*, 73, 39–53.

Schepers, Donald H., & Beach, Lee Roy (1998). An Image Theory View of Worker Motivation. In Lee Roy Beach (Ed.), *Image Theory: Theoretical and Empirical Foundations* (pp. 125–131). Mahwah, NJ: Lawrence Erlbaum.

Seidl, Christian, & Traub, Stefan (1998). A New Test of Image Theory. *Organizational Behavior and Human Decision Processes*, 75, 93–116.

Weatherly, Kristopher A., & Beach, Lee Roy (1996). Organizational Culture and Decision Making. In Lee Roy Beach (Ed.), *Decision Making in the Workplace: A Unified Perspective* (pp. 117–132). Mahwah, NJ: Lawrence Erlbaum.

Weatherly, Kristopher A., & Beach, Lee Roy (1998). Organizational Culture and Decision Making. In Lee Roy Beach (Ed.), *Image Theory: Theoretical and Empirical Foundations* (pp. 211–225). Mahwah, NJ: Lawrence Erlbaum.

van Zee, Emily H.; Paluchowski, Thaddeus F.; & Beach, Lee Roy (1998). The Effects of Screening and Task Partitioning Upon Evaluations of Decision Options. In Lee Roy Beach (Ed.), *Image Theory: Theoretical and Empirical Foundations* (pp. 61–72). Mahwah, NJ: Lawrence Erlbaum.

Part XI

From Generation to Generation

Chapter 28

Institutional Culture of Organizational Behavior and a Vision

This ends the presentation of theories—both first- and second-generation—amounting to a total of 70 or perhaps more, depending on where one sets the boundaries, and including both main and subsidiary versions; the theorists themselves number 85. In this part, and its single chapter, I return to the subject matter of Part I, but not from a historical perspective; rather this chapter represents an attempt to extend the time horizon out into the future and thus complete the contextual package. In doing this I hope to provide a more comprehensive picture of the framework within which organizational behavior's theorizing occurs.

The scientific foundations and historical origins of organizational behavior have been of concern to a number of authors. To provide a general overview of what others have written on this score, extending back over several decades, I include here a brief discussion of the writings on this subject.

Larry Greiner (1979) provided a chapter for an edited volume, which deals primarily with the intellectual history of the field, often from an organization development perspective. There is some discussion of the short-term future of the field.

Wendell French (1982) wrote a short article, adapted from his book on organization development, that presents the history of the latter field but in the process extends well beyond organization development into much of organizational behavior as a whole. The emphasis is on the intellectual leaders of the period up to 1960. Future developments are not considered.

Paul Lawrence (1987) included a chapter in the *Handbook of Organizational Behavior* providing a wide-ranging coverage of organizational behavior's emergence, development, methodology, and theory, as well as certain defining characteristics. This chapter contains a particularly good coverage of the Harvard contributions in the early period. Little is said regarding the future of the field.

Karlene Roberts et al. (1990) base a journal article on interviews conducted with major contributors to the field. These interviews covered origins and evolution, definitions, characteristics of the field, influences on the interviewees, sources of ideas, contributions, and public image. They reflect a wide variation in opinion. Minimal attention is given to the future of the field.

George Strauss (1993) provides an autobiographical essay that contains a substantial amount of material presented from the perspective of an observer of organizational behavior over the years of its history. The future of the field is not a major issue considered.

Milton Blood (1994) contributed a chapter to an edited volume, providing a brief history and focusing on the multidisciplinary origins of the field. The problems and challenges facing the field in the future are a subject for considerable discussion.

Paul Goodman and David Whetten (1998) wrote a chapter for an edited volume which utilizes interviews and analyses of journal articles from the 1950s to the 1990s to develop historical information. The chapter discusses the future of the field in terms of issues and choices.

Looking at these sources yields some interesting conclusions. Concern with the scientific foundations is minimal, presumably because all this is taken for granted. No real effort is made to assess the theories of the field in terms of the extent to which they have proved valid and made useful contributions, thus having the potential to guide us effectively into the future. Although challenges, issues, and choices facing the field in the future are considered by a few of the authors, especially in recent years, no comprehensive agenda for dealing with the future is attempted, and no strategic plan or vision is stated, either. The diversity of organizational behavior as a discipline is both lauded

and bemoaned, but little is offered as to how this diversity might be handled, whether reduced or perhaps used to advantage. What becomes apparent is that the field appears to be stuck dead center in an identity crisis, a crisis that might benefit from looking more closely at what our historical origins have to say about the subject; we need to learn who we are.

In this final chapter I seek to deal with these matters. Since they have received only limited attention elsewhere, this inevitably means breaking some new ground. As organizational behavior moves away from its first generation, with many of that generation's members either dead or no longer active in the field, and into a new century, assessing where and what we have been with a view to contributing to the understanding, prediction, and control of the future seems entirely appropriate. Even more, given the pessimism about the field evidenced by some of the more recent writings on the previous list, it seems desperately needed.

HISTORICAL CORE AND INHERENT IDENTITY

Organizational behavior is a profession with all the accoutrements of that status, and, accordingly, it is institutionalized. Consistent with most definitions of institutionalization, it has the potential to possess a professional culture, and I believe it does indeed possess such a culture, of a nature that we will need to consider.

It also has a history, as the chapters of this book testify and the publications just listed serve to document as well. Certain aspects of this history are more salient, constituting a core and serving to frame our decisions about the identity of organizational behavior.

Identity is one of those words in and about our field that I would prefer not to use, because of its ambiguity, and the variety of ways in which it is invoked. Yet it has a tradition in our science, and I know of no other effective means to express what I intend. It is important to have

> an internalized cognitive structure of what the organization stands for and where it intends to go—in short a clear sense of the organization's identity. A sense of identity serves as a rudder for navigating

difficult waters. . . . Because identity is problem-atic—and yet so critical to how and what one val-ues, thinks, feels, and does in all social domains, including organizations . . . the dynamics of iden-tity need to be . . . understood. . . . Identity and identification explain one means by which individ-uals act on behalf of the group or the organization. (Albert, Ashforth, & Dutton, 2000, pp. 13–14)

The usual definition of identity includes an indica-tion that it involves what is core or central, distinctive, and enduring about the character of an organization. This is the taken-for-granted position. However, an alternative view argues that *dynamic* should replace *enduring* in this trilogy (Goia, Schultz, & Corley, 2000). Whatever the merits of this latter position may be for other purposes, the usage here will assume that iden-tity is indeed an enduring property. This does not mean that changes cannot occur on occasion. Also, I accept the view that identity represents a self-categorization (Hogg & Terry, 2000) and is thus an image in the mind of the member.

Organizational behavior's history is short, and for that reason there has been limited time to develop traditions and entrenched characteristics. Yet there is much to be learned about the nature of the field and its potential for the future from this short history. Certain core characteristics do exist. What I propose in this chapter is to look at this historical core to establish distinguishing features, and then to use this knowledge to develop a strategic plan—or, probably better, a vision—through which organizational behav-ior might cope with the threats and opportunities it faces. In this process I attempt to provide a picture of organizational behavior's basic nature and then to show how this inherent identity provides a source of strength for coping with the future, and thus "a rud-der for navigating difficult waters" (Albert et al., 2000, p. 13).

In approaching the problem of defining the basic nature of organizational behavior, it seems appropriate to break down the characteristics of the field by us-ing the framework we have been following through-out this book, particularly in part I. Thus, I consider first what can be learned from the scientific founda-tions of the field, second what the multidisciplinary origins contribute, third what emerges from a consid-eration of the field in the context of its historical background, and fourth what role existing theory has and can play.

Contributions from Scientific Foundations

The idea inherent in the development of organiza-tional behavior from the very beginning was to intro-duce science into an area of business school operations that had previously lacked any scientific credentials whatsoever. Thus, that a close tie exists with sci-ence and the scientific method has been at the core of organizational behavior from the time the field emerged in the 1950s. This tie was much less in evidence in the preemergence period, as reflected in the thinking and approaches of the people considered in chapters 2 and 3.

Commitment to Science

Inherent in the commitment to science is the idea that theories are important, not only in their own right but because they nurture practice. As Law-rence notes "the strong bond between theory and practice is a crucial feature of organizational behav-ior. Theory has guided practice, and practice has provided crucial insights to research. Progress has been greatest when the two sides of the field move together" (1987, p. 9). Certainly organizational be-havior's theories have often suffered from ambigu-ity, but in many instances this ambiguity has eventu-ally been reduced by painstaking research that has served to narrow the definitions of both variables and domains.

This emphasis on research has certainly been im-portant for organizational behavior from the begin-ning. We have used it to test our theories, and in many instances to refine them, as well as to test hypoth-eses that have very limited theoretical underpinnings. Organizational behavior as a field is very adept, even ingenious, at conducting research studies, in part at least because it has been able to draw on so many different research strands. This is particularly evident in the creation of measures to operationalize the multi-tude of variables the field has unearthed in its pursuit of understanding the functioning of organizations, and functioning within them. Organizations were a new and uncharted domain as organizational behavior came on the scene, and few measures applicable to them existed; research since has found many ways to reduce the size of this void.

Philosophic Undercurrents

The scientific foundations of organizational behavior, although often taken for granted, have actually been the driving force in generating theories, research, measures, and applications—in short, the knowledge base of the field—and this has been true from the beginning. At the same time, numerous nonscientific, even antiscientific, forces have operated from an early period as well. These include strong values, such as humanism and those tied to disciplinary backgrounds in psychology and sociology, as well as various philosophic persuasions. These undercurrents have varied in content and source over the years, but they have always been there in one form or another. Much of this activity was closely allied with the schools phenomenon.

These specific undercurrents, coming and going as they do, have never become part of the core nature of the field. The schools approach has faded, at least in the United States. Now, however, a variety of antiscience philosophic positions that have much in common with the schools have emerged out of other parts of the world. It may well be that these movements reflect the fact that Europe, in particular, did not go through a schools phase in the 1960s and 1970s, as the United States did. Perhaps what is happening is that the schools phase has broken out in other parts of the world, that never went through it before, and this process in turn is now reinfecting the United States. Given its relatively recent experience with schools and with the activism of the 1960s and early 1970s, U.S. organizational behavior could well be vulnerable to such reinfection. If this is what is happening, and I strongly suspect it is, we can expect an episodic outburst that will gradually fade as schools tend to do in the face of scientific advance. In any event, postmodernism and its siblings are not part of the long-standing core characteristics of the field; they are a relatively recent transplant.

In chapter 1 the matter of the field's inability to compare competing theories was considered. This view holds that one cannot decide objectively between competing theories that use different languages, different assumptions, and different constructs, all of which reflect totally disparate value systems—theories that are in essence on completely different planes. Proponents of this position hold that this is the situation that organizational behavior faces at present and that, accordingly, the field is one in which theory pluralism

prevails and science becomes useless; there can be no consensus on the knowledge base of the field. The extended discussion in chapter 1 provides ample evidence that this type of theory pluralism is not characteristic of organizational behavior, and thus is not part of the field's core. However, the point to be made for present purposes is that theoretical anarchy exists only in the minds of those within organizational behavior who are by nature anarchistic; it is in fact a myth.

This is an idea on which I believe my experience in writing this book gives me some legitimacy as a basis for making comments. As one reads about a theorist, and his or her ideas, and the research of that theorist, as well as of others who have become interested in that theory, it is as if you get inside the theoretical context. An empathy and feeling develop that leave one living that theory for a period of time; you actually begin to think about the world around you in terms of the constructs of the particular theory on which you are working. I believe this is the same experience doctoral students often describe as they immerse themselves in one theory after another. Some theories seem more compatible in this manner than others, but I have experienced the same phenomenon to some degree in writing about every theory in this book. Having had this experience so often, it is very difficult for me to believe that the scientists among us are incapable of combating this "incommensurability" phenomenon in organizational behavior.

Speaking, then, to the philosophy-based positions that have attempted to infiltrate and sometimes actually permeated organizational behavior. If there is a core feature in these positions, it is that a nonscientific (ranging to contrascientific) undercurrent of some kind has existed in the field from a very early point. Its nature and proponents have varied and so have the apparent functions served, but the fact of some such continuing undercurrent cannot be denied. It may well simply be a part of the diversity of our field, like the multidisciplinary origins. It may even offer some positive benefits in terms of the stimulation of creative contributions, although on most days I find that very difficult to acknowledge.

Contributions from Multidisciplinary Origins

Goodman and Whetten have this to say: "We view OB as a field of inquiry characterized by tremendous diversity. Diversity comes in the form of many disciplinary perspectives (e.g., psychology, sociology, economics, political science) aimed at understanding organizations. The diversity comes in the form of different theories and methods" (1998, p. 46). Lawrence says that "characteristic of organizational behavior is its sustained capacity to bridge allied areas of study. . . . By drawing in ideas and methods from so many diverse allied areas, OB has kept alive the multidisciplinary tradition of its founders" (1987, pp. 8–9). He notes influences from psychology, sociology, business policy, economics, labor relations, human resource management, political science, and anthropology. There is some disagreement as to whether this disciplinary diversity has worked to the disadvantage or benefit of the field, but that it exists is unquestioned.

Probably this diversity of origins is greater within organizational behavior than in any other field. Often new fields arise at the border between two disciplines, as, for instance, between two sciences. But if we look back at the preemergence contributors considered in chapter 1, only one was a social scientist. The fields represented are medicine, philosophy, psychology, economics, social work, political science, sociology, law, history, management, and engineering. Of these, medicine and engineering are sciences but not social sciences. Philosophy, history, law, and the management of the times were not sciences of any kind. Thus in this very early period the social science base of the field was heavily diluted. It was only as organizational behavior actually emerged in the business schools that it achieved the posture of a multidisciplinary social science, Nevertheless, there seems to be no question that multidisciplinarity is at the very core of organizational behavior, distinguishing the field, in the extent of the diversity involved, from all other disciplines.

Contributions from Historical Development

The matters discussed in chapters 4 and 5 are greater in number than those considered in the earlier chapters of part I, and, accordingly, the contributions to organizational behavior's inherent identity are more extensive. In general, these contributions fall under four headings: rapid growth, lack of constraint, orientation to practice, and fuzzy boundaries.

Rapid Growth

Organizational behavior has experienced rapid growth on multiple dimensions from the beginning, to the point where it is appropriate to consider this a characteristic of the field (Lawrence, 1987). Given the lack of a true professional organization, it is hard to document growth in size precisely, but in the early 1960s something like 300 members appear to have existed. By the mid-1980s this figure was up to about 1,800 by Lawrence's estimate, and by the mid-1990s it was 3,200 using the same criterion. This growth is associated almost entirely with the expansion in the number of business schools and the size of their faculties. Whether organizational behavior grew because it was in the business schools or the business schools grew because organizational behavior was within them is almost impossible to disentangle; probably both factors were operative. Anyway the field got bigger very quickly.

A major factor in this growth has been the existence of doctoral programs that taught research and science from the beginning. These doctoral programs, especially at the major schools, have been a real source of strength. They have filled empty positions in the field and have driven membership growth in a variety of ways. Yet the field continues to attract faculty members from the outside as well, particularly psychologists and sociologists. Many of us who had thought our doctoral graduates would quickly come to monopolize the discipline have been surprised by this continuing openness to entry.

Along with the growth in members have come growth in status, power, reputation, and the like. This is well documented in the report by Lyman Porter and Lawrence McKibbin (1988). This process took a while to establish itself amid the internal wars that plagued organizational behavior in the early years, but by the 1970s the change in status had been achieved at most business schools.

Yet this diverse array of sources of continuing growth has not been joined by rapid curricular expansion in recent years. The sizable support for such expansion from the business community has had little impact on the business school administrators and faculties that make these decisions. Intransigence of this kind is in fact characteristic of the business school setting (Oviatt & Miller, 1989). Thus, growth, although pervasive in the history of organizational behavior, cannot be assumed on all dimensions. Success often spawns a certain amount of resentment and jealousy; I believe something of that kind is operating in the business schools now, and perhaps it contributes to the self-questioning and identity concerns that organizational behavior currently is experiencing. When a field has been the wunderkind among its peers for so long, it is somewhat disconcerting to return to the reality of normal development.

Lack of Constraint

Organizational behavior has long been an area characterized by a lack of constraint on what its members do. Much of this represents a freedom from disciplinary limitations, but there is more involved than that. Lawrence notes that "a characteristic of the field has been its responsiveness to important issues of the day. . . . Although some deplore this intimate involvement with contemporary values, I applaud it" (1987, p. 9). Elsewhere Lawrence (in Lawrence & Lawrence, 1993) lauds the problem-solving orientation of the field in other respects as well. All this is about being free to pursue problems wherever they may lead and whatever their nature without having to worry about disciplinary strictures and "political correctness."

As noted previously, such freedom and lack of constraining structures can lead to uncertainty, and organizational behavior has experienced its share of that throughout its history. Perhaps, over time, this uncertainty has been reduced somewhat as certain constraints have been introduced; this process may well continue. But as long as a problem-oriented focus remains, with its potential for leading to entirely new methodologies and solutions, uncertainty will remain.

Part of this syndrome, as well, is the potential for new and innovative theoretical ideas. In pursuing problems wherever they may lead, concepts, approaches, even values that had not been in close proximity before are often thrown together, thus yielding the potential for creative solutions. This triumvirate—problem orientation, high uncertainty, innovative theorizing—has been at the heart of organizational behavior ever since the long period of unfreezing began. It tends to attract certain kinds of people who are comfortable with the ambiguity of the field—and to drive others away.

Orientation to Practice

Closely tied to this freedom to follow problems to their source, and the uncertainty and conceptual innovativeness thus aroused, is a proclivity for valuing practice and the world of application. Certainly the fact that organizational behavior came into being in the business schools reflects this proclivity. The fact that the theories of the field are typically evaluated (in part, at least) in terms of their relevance for practice reflects it also.

For most people in the field of organizational behavior, practice is directly experienced in the role of part-time consultant, if it is experienced at all. Only a few have served in managerial capacities in business organizations. This is consistent with the finding that the strong motives of people in the field are those of professionals, not managers (Miner, 1980). Consulting permits the satisfaction of those motives, as would full-time business employment in a professional capacity as well. However, the latter is something of a rarity at present.

The long-standing orientation to practice of the field has had difficulties finding an appropriate outlet, to the point where some have contended it does not really exist. Yet the very frustration that many of us feel on this score is evidence that the orientation continues to operate. Janice Beyer suggests that "more of the results of organizational research would cross the gap between science and practice if the linking roles available to assist this transfer were restructured. It is unrealistic to expect organizational research to cross the gap between science and practice unless there are structures and roles dedicated specifically to making that transfer happen" (1992, p. 472). Full-time consultants specializing in organizational behavior would meet this need, as would practicing organizational behavior specialists who are employed by individual companies. Anne Huff (2000) made suggestions along these lines in her presidential address to the Academy of Management. In fact, something of this kind has indeed happened in the organization development field, but the somewhat tangential status of organizational development to organizational behavior as a whole at present, and the ups and downs of sensitivity training and the quality of work life movement, make this only a partial solution at best right now.

An opportunity, as yet not fully explored, seems to exist in the fact that organizational behavior's stakeholders in position of power in the business world are positively disposed toward the field and would like to see its role expanded within the business schools (Porter & McKibbin, 1988). Because of faculty intransigence, this opportunity may not be recognized in the business school setting itself, but it could lead to many new developments in the business world. We will return to this matter of orientation to practice shortly. However, the point to be made here is that the orientation has longstanding status in organizational behavior, and that, in spite of the frustrations experienced, it still exists.

Fuzzy Boundaries

Finally, associated with its multidisciplinary origins, organizational behavior has always had rather fuzzy boundaries (Blood, 1994). In the early period the overlap with organizational psychology was pronounced, and there were even moves to fully incorporate industrial/organizational psychology programs into business schools. This did not happen, but a certain amount of cooptation has occurred. More recently, the major overlap with organizational sociology has become manifest.

That this fuzzy boundary phenomenon remains a strong characteristic of the field may well be associated with the value of freedom from constraint and the openness to new entrants that has been apparent since the business schools unlocked their doors to a small group of social scientists who previously had been without an acceptable home. Over time, this openness has become evident in the opportunities extended to women and to organizational behaviorists from outside the United States. There has been a continuing porousness, in the best sense of that word, that goes back to the very beginnings of the field. In turn, this porousness has generated new research, new ways of teaching courses, new theories, and new practical applications. On balance it has been a real asset to organizational behavior, contributing among other things to its rapid growth.

Yet the lack of barriers to entry, on a disciplinary basis and in other respects, too, has created its share of problems. The problems inherent in this diversity are discussed at length by Goodman and Whetten (1998) and by Roberts et al. (1990). The consequence appears to be a major contributing factor to the identity crisis noted previously. Among all this diversity, who are we really?

One answer is that we are what our history and traditions say we are, but that is a somewhat fragmented picture. Nowhere is this more evident than on the professional association front. Some years ago Larry Cummings (1978) advocated bringing together

the divisions of organizational behavior, organization and management theory, personnel and human resources, organizational development, and organizational communication within the Academy of Management to create a true professional organization for organizational behavior. This has not yet happened, and now, with the addition of new divisions, the scope of the new federation would likely be greater. Yet it remains true that if organizational behavior is to fully resolve its identity crisis, it must have its own unified professional organization, either as a subsidiary of an organization such as the Academy of Management or as a stand-alone entity. This, too, is an issue I will return to later in this chapter, but at this point we need to recognize that organizational behavior's continuing tendency to keep its boundary lines somewhat muddied over the years has proven to be an asset, as well as on occasion a detriment. We have always had many members who possess other professional identities as well. That need not be a problem, but it becomes such, if at a given point in time a person does not know which hat to wear and thus lacks any true professional organizational identity at all.

Contributions from the Theories Themselves

We do not just have a commitment to theory development as part of our scientific foundations, we have a body of theory that constitutes a large part of the knowledge of the field. Much of this content is reviewed in the preceding chapters. What role do these theories play in the field of organizational behavior? Do we have from this source a stable underpinning for our teaching, consulting, and other practice activities, writing, research, and in fact practically everything we do in a professional role?

Theory Validity

At a much earlier point I reviewed 32 theories, most of them considered in this volume, and developed an index of validity for each (Miner, 1984). Providing this same type of detailed analysis now for the theories of this book is beyond my intentions for present purposes, although I do intend to do much more along those lines in a subsequent publication. Here all that is needed is a general overview of the extent to which organizational behavior possesses valid theories at the core of its knowledge base.

Now, with this book, we have well over twice as many theories given either primary or subsidiary attention to consider. About two-thirds of the theories appear to have some degree of validity in the sense that one can rely on the theory to provide correct knowledge in some area or under appropriate conditions; in over half of these instances the level of validity over all appears to be really high. These figures compare with 66 percent and 34 percent in the earlier sample of 32 theories. In short, the current data look at least as good as those obtained previously, and with many more theories available.

An obvious next question is how the two generations compare with one another. On that score there is a problem of sample selection. The earlier group was based in part (24 of the 32) on nominations from other scholars. Thus, the first-generation sample is heavily weighted with nominees provided by others, while the second-generation sample is all my doing (although with guidance from published sources). Any differences could be attributed to the way in which theories were selected. There clearly is a time difference as well. The early period produced many more theories in the first 20 years or so of organizational behavior's history than did the later period in over 25 years. Yet assuming that it takes at least 10 years to generate the research and activity to bring a theory to attention, this difference may not be as large as it seems. Nevertheless, there are many more first-generation theories, consistent with the view that this was a period of high creative output. But it simply may be that I went deeper into the theoretical pot in picking the first-generation representatives.

In short, I have no way of knowing whether the theories representing the two generations are comparable, and the second generation is not over yet in any event. With all this in mind, the data indicate that the second-generation theories discussed in parts VII–X are considerably more valid; in fact, none of them are basically invalid, and the majority are of high validity. This superiority does not hold, however, for the "bridging theories" noted at the beginning of chapter 23, which are second generation but with strong ties to others of an earlier vintage. Overall it looks very much as if our theories have gotten a good deal better over time, a trajectory that we can only hope will continue. Note, too, that many of the earlier theories, earlier in terms of their founding dates, continue to be active up to the present and most of these are the more valid theories. Few of the less valid formulations remain active today in a research sense. Thus the body of theoretical knowledge we have in hand right now from both generations is quite impressive in terms of its tested validity and potential to stimulate ideas.

Theory Usefulness

The introduction of usefulness as a criterion for judging theories has its detractors (Brief & Dukerich, 1991), but also its advocates (Weick, 1987). There has indeed been some ambiguity in the way the term is applied. Yet, it seems to me that we need some index of how well we are doing not just in making our customers happy but in providing them with applications that have the backing of scientific method. This latter is what usefulness is taken to mean here.

Of the theories considered, just over one half (53 percent) yields some evidence of usefulness for application, but few (26 percent) of these appear to warrant a high rating in this regard. This compares with figures of 59 percent and 22 percent for the earlier sample of 32 theories (Miner, 1984). The data from the two sources in fact are quite similar.

With the disclaimer as to comparability, it is also possible to look at rated usefulness from generation one to generation two within the sample of theories considered in this volume. In this regard the prior findings on validity are not in evidence. There is some drop in usefulness in the second generation, to the point where almost half of the theories give little or no meaningful attention to usefulness at all. Organizational behavior's theories appear to be suffering from a limited but clearly evident decline in this area. The field's theories do not seem to be generating solid prescriptions for practice at nearly the same positive rate that they are generating valid understanding of organizational processes. This decrease holds for all second generation theories (whether bridging or not).

However, Weick has pointed to the following consideration:

> A theory can also serve as a catalyst that sets action in motion. But once action is set in motion, the theory can be set aside in favor of trial and error and close scrutiny of tight feedback loops that are sensitive to local conditions. . . . This possibility extends dramatically the number of theories that now become useful and valid. (1987, p. 108)

In short, not very good theories can activate applications that achieve an identity of their own in the world of practice; even theories that pay little attention to practice can have such an effect on occasion, as consultants, for instance, rephrase them for their own purposes. Thus, our theoretical effect on the business world and on other types of organizations may be much greater than we either intended or thought was the case.

Strength of Organizational Behavior's Identity

Quite evidently, a number of contributions from various sources are candidates for consideration as aspects of organizational behavior's identity. The extent to which these can operate effectively, however, is a function of the consensus, the degree of cultural cohesiveness, that impinges on them. I do not know how much consensus of this kind exists at present. The multidisciplinary nature of organizational behavior's origins, and thus the multiple identities of its members, combined with the short time span since those origins, would seem to argue against consensus and for a rather fragmented culture. There may simply have been insufficient time to date to coalesce behind the identity that exists.

Yet the core characteristics of organizational behavior add up to more of a body of tradition and knowledge than many might have suspected. In particular, there appears to be some agreement on the values of science and the value of our theories. There is reason to believe that at least during the 1970s humanist values operated to confound the evaluation process, serving to reduce the amount of consensus around the theories (Miner, 1990). This influence appears to have waned more recently, although other philosophic undercurrents still are at work. Furthermore, with time has come a certain amount of institutionalization, which probably causes many to eulogize certain early theories that turned out not to be very good (valid), but which nevertheless hang on in people's minds and confound the evaluation process to a degree.

Overall, though, it is clear that organizational behavior has a core body of theoretical knowledge that goes back to the very early years of its development, and most knowledgeable scholars can agree on this body of knowledge, given that they accept that the relevant criteria derive from scientific research evidence. The theoretical strength of the field is of sufficient magnitude so as to be the envy of other disciplines that have had difficulty generating such a theoretical core.

I conclude, then, that the materials to build a clear and strong identity exist, with particularly strong potential residing in our theoretical base. The extent to which these materials have had the support of consensus has apparently been rather cyclical, but the potential is there to be brought together and used.

VISION FOR THE FUTURE

My original thought, at this point, was to propose a strategic plan for organizational behavior. That, however, involves making accurate forecasts and acting to implement the plan once established, neither of which I am in a position to do. Thus, I settle for simply setting forth my vision for the field, in the hope that to the extent it includes goals, it will serve to stimulate action along the lines I envisage. My intention in any event is to complete the package of organizational behavior's context extending from the past, through the present, to the future of an unknown duration.

Here I set forth my view of what organizational behavior should become in the future as it moves into a new century, not certainly in my lifetime but at some point. My intention is not to predict the future, but to help form it. This is of course a personal statement, but it is informed by my experience across the entire history of organizational behavior, by extensive study of the field's literature, and by practical work experience in many of the field's domains. Many probably would consider it a wisdom piece.

Developing Mechanisms for Professional Opportunities

Professional role motivation theory (see chapter 5) posits that five motive patterns are strong among successful professionals and that these motives match the role requirements of the work professionals do. Based on a search of the literature, which is primarily sociological, I consider these role specifications and their allied motive patterns to provide an indication of what professions need to do to keep their members, or more correctly their successful members, satisfied and committed. This theory has strong support from research extending across the professions, including organizational behavior (Miner, 1980). Let us look at organizational behavior from this perspective. What should, and does, the field, as a profession, provide?

Opportunities to Learn

It is apparent that a knowledge base does exist in the field, as indicated by our analyses of first- and second-generation theories and the research on them, as well as their applications. The field knows a lot, and this knowledge can be transmitted. Furthermore, a mechanism for supplementing existing knowledge exists in the form of theory building and research. Organizational behavior is a science, and it was so from the beginning. As long as this remains true, there will be plenty of opportunities to learn. The field's multidisciplinary nature is a plus here because it expands the size of the knowledge pool and the number of possible theoretical interconnections. The long-standing freedom from constraints and the problem orientation that characterizes the field should also facilitate new learning.

What is needed in the future is to continue building on these existing strengths, to use our historical identity to the utmost, and certainly not to deny its existence. There is nowhere where this is more important than in the conduct of doctoral programs in organizational behavior. These must remain strong and produce a sizable output of qualified professionals if the rapid growth that has been typical in the past is to be maintained. This is where the most concentrated opportunities to learn occur. Everything possible should be done to prevent diversion of resources to other programs; in fact, quite the opposite: doctoral education should come first.

Opportunities to Be Independent

Academic freedom is part of this desire for independence; the freedom to act based on one's professional knowledge without the need to acquiesce to political and other pressures is also involved. Organizational behavior's historical freedom from constraint provides a basis for providing this type of opportunity. Scientific freedom, which organizational behavior values, is an allied force for independence. The innovative theorizing that typified the first generation, and now the second, was an outgrowth of the opportunity to be independent and at the same time provides a basis for continuing to protect our freedoms.

In this instance, as with the opportunity to learn, organizational behavior seems to have within its historical core identity the means to provide the needed opportunities to its members. However, providing opportunities for independent action is going to be much easier in a growth situation where the field is moving forward, expanding into new areas, and reducing barriers on the scope of its activities.

Opportunities to Achieve Status

Status is important to professionals because it often is what attracts those who use the services provided (students and clients in the present instance). Anything a field can do to increase the status of the profession as a whole, and of its individual members, serves to provide the needed opportunities for members. Historically, organizational behavior has achieved considerable status within the university setting, and some members have done the same in the business world. There is room for more opportunities here, however. Science, discovery, solving problems, innovative theorizing are all means to this end. There is much in the core identity of the field that should contribute to the creation of opportunities for status.

An important consideration is that a field must possess sufficient critical mass to be recognized by possible publics and stakeholders. Organizational behavior appears to have achieved a size sufficient for recognition by its immediate publics in the academic community and in many sectors of the business world. Yet there are large numbers of people who have little idea what the field is, let alone sufficient knowledge to accord it status. To overcome this type of barrier, growth is absolutely essential. Also, professional associations can do a great deal to help build the status and recognition of a profession and its members. It is important to be sure that existing professional associations are configured to fill this need.

Opportunities to Help Clients (Including Students)

Organizational behavior is a helping profession; in fact, all professions are helping professions—in some manner, for some purpose, with some people. Thus, providing opportunities for members of the profession to teach, to consult, to use their knowledge in the service of others is essential for organizational behavior. Obviously, the tradition of valuing practice and the application of knowledge is important in this regard. So, too, are the field's growth status (because that increases the number of clients), the field's multidisciplinary origins (because that increases the scope of applications), and the field's fuzzy boundaries (because that increases the range of situations and clients where the field may find a useful niche). These considerations are probably less true of teaching at present than of service in other professional roles, but one still finds professional courses that are very much out of the mainstream, taught by someone with unusual skills to a non–business school audience. Multidisciplinarity and fuzzy boundaries can represent real assets when it comes to innovative helping. But their presence carries with it the perennial high uncertainty levels that have characterized the field in the past.

Creating new opportunities for helping by building on organizational behavior's core characteristics not only mobilizes uncertainty, it is best achieved once again through growth. A growing profession pushes out the boundaries and finds new ways to use its potpourri of skills. This is just as true of university teaching as of service to business and other similar organizations. However, there may well be differences between areas of service in their openness to new applications. Certainly organizational behavior already has a wide range of potential applications available, many of them a direct outgrowth of the field's theories, but with growth new vistas can open up as well.

Opportunities to Develop Professional Commitment

Professional commitment is what keeps members within a profession, working at its tasks, contributing to its welfare, and abiding by its norms. To the extent psychologists or sociologists, for instance, enter organizational behavior only to leave again and return to the disciplines from which they came, this would be reflective of a lack of commitment to organizational behavior. Certainly this has happened, sometimes in highly visible ways, although not widely. However, the key point is that a mature, stable, growing profession needs to take steps to create commitment. Within the historical origins of organizational behavior the dedication to science, the growth in status, the freedom from constraint, the orientation to following problems, and the value placed on practice all seem to serve in some way with some people to foster commitment. There are mechanisms in place to foster this end.

However, the identity crisis the field seems to be experiencing suggests this is not enough. The major source for developing commitment in a profession is the professional association the individual uses as a membership and a reference group. Organizational behavior has had some problems on this score, thus contributing to questions of the "Who are we?" type. My intent in writing this book has been to provide some answers to that question. But beyond that, we need professional structures that will provide opportunities to develop commitment, and we need strategies for getting to those structures. This is not a matter that is necessarily facilitated by growth; in fact, the problem may be compounded by growth, and by diversity too. Good doctoral training can help foster commitment, and organizational behavior has that as a strength. More, however, seems to be needed. We will return to the issues involved shortly.

Perpetuating Growth

Much of what is needed to create the opportunities required to perpetuate organizational behavior as a field is inherent in the core characteristics that were previously identified. In turn, these characteristics stem from the scientific foundations, the multidisciplinary origins, the conditions of historical development, and the existing theoretical knowledge base of organizational behavior. The message is to listen to the past and keep on doing what got us to this point. In particular, we cannot back away from characteristics such as multidisciplinarity, fuzzy boundaries, and high uncertainty that may seem on the surface to be detrimental. There are advantages hidden in these facets of the field's identity that may be put to very good use in the future, just as they were during the early years.

One facet of this identity has come up repeatedly and requires further elaboration. This is rapid growth. Historically, growth for organizational behavior has occurred hand in hand with growth in the number and size of business schools. There is reason to believe that this type of growth is stalling in the United States (Starbuck, 1999), and before long it may very well do the same elsewhere in the world. Thus the method of growth that has propelled us in the past looks to be running out of gas.

Scenarios of Growth

One possibility for future growth is to attempt to expand organizational behavior's contribution within the business schools—more courses, more research appointments, more students, more faculty, more programs, more administrators. There is nothing wrong with this approach, but the degree of power required to bring about a redistribution of resources along these lines is rarely present today in the organizational behavior components of existing business schools. We have noted the intransigence that characterizes many business school faculties. Without bringing a sizable store of new resources to the table, organizational behavior is unlikely to expand its domain very much within the business schools, and at present new resources on this scale simply do not appear to be in the offing (Rynes & Trank, 1999). Over time, windows of opportunity may open up for organizational behavior's growth within specific business schools, but capitalizing on these opportunities is not likely to bring about anything that could be characterized as representing rapid growth overall for the field.

An alternative scenario is to attempt to open up shop in other locations on the university campus. Some of this has been going on for years, primarily in other professional schools besides business, but not on a large scale. Opportunities may exist in areas such as education, public administration, dentistry, medicine, agriculture, engineering, journalism, and the like. This approach represents a departure from the historic ties to the business schools, but not necessarily from the value placed on practice that was so much a part of the business school experience. There is also some possibility of expansion into liberal arts departments such as psychology and sociology, not as prodigal sons and daughters returning to the fold but as organizational behaviorists finding new locations to practice their profession.

I believe a systematic effort to expand along these lines, going beyond the mere opportunism that has characterized such efforts in the past, could be of major benefit to other disciplines, as well as to organizational behavior. Fuzzy boundaries make this type of expansion relatively easy. The new positions could be staffed from doctoral programs in organizational behavior, as well as from doctoral programs in other fields, particularly industrial/organizational psychology and organizational sociology, thus maintaining the interdisciplinarity that is indigenous to the field.

Another scenario involves full-scale expansion into the world of practice and the world of organizations beyond academe. A growth strategy of this kind involves some break with the past in that the close identification with business schools is broken and the characteristic tendency for organizational behavior's members to possess little by way of practical business experience is jeopardized. However, other values and features of the field would be fostered, including valuing practice, multidisciplinarity, rapid growth, problem orientation, high uncertainty, fuzzy boundaries, and under certain circumstances the values of science. All this requires a considerable amount of explaining.

Practice of Organizational Behavior

Let us start with the specification that at present organizational behavior's core membership consists of the membership of the five divisions of the Academy of Management that Cummings (1978) noted, thus encompassing the academic aspects of organizational behavior, organization and management theory, human resources, organization development and change, and organizational communication. To this list might now be added at least a sizable component of careers, conflict management, gender and diversity in organizations, health care management, management education and development, managerial and organizational cognition, managerial consultation, and the public and nonprofit sector. My point in listing all of these is to emphasize that organizational behavior remains highly diverse. Yet this diversity, if applied to the world of practice, which it has not been, permits a wide range of applications.

At present organizational behavior is largely an academic discipline within the business schools, playing so to speak on its home field with few if any away games. What I am advocating is the addition of many more games on unfriendly turf to our schedule, playing perhaps before hostile crowds on occasion but with a set of plays that provide a good chance of winning. To equip our players with what it takes to win in the world of practice we need to teach them not just theories and research methods, but the applications the field has developed (yet at present says little about). This would require a somewhat expanded doctoral education process, one that would permit going out and winning on the alien fields of application. Many of organizational behavior's doctoral students start with this type of orientation but lose it under the impact of a constant bombardment with the academic values of their teachers. Instead, we should help equip them with the skills to do what many of them wanted to do in the first place.

I do not envisage a practitioner model that is devoid of research capabilities and theoretical knowledge. You need to know the underlying theories to use their applications effectively. Research has been a part of industrial psychology practice (personnel research) from the beginning, and it has served that field well. Research is part of following problems to a solution, and that is what organizational behavior does.

One approach would be to join forces with organization development, which is coming off its humanistic high and is currently using a broad range of techniques that make practical contributions without regard to their value orientation (Church, Burke, & Van Eynde, 1994; Bazigos & Burke, 1997). Given that organization development started within organizational behavior and is in fact its greatest practical extension to date, this makes considerable sense. However, I am also suggesting that organizational behavior take on consulting roles, applied scientist roles, and internal professional roles in conjunction with a wide range of other disciplines and groups that are already on the firing line, such as human resource management, economics, public administration, educational administration, industrial/organizational psychology, industrial engineering, labor relations, entrepreneurship, and many more.

This process of joining forces (engaging in cooptation, networking, forming partnerships) with practitioner groups who are already at the interface contains some risk of further loss of identity, but fuzzy boundaries make it easier, too. It entails high uncertainty, but that has been with organizational behavior from the beginning. It can be quite financially rewarding, and that is why the world of practice is so heavily populated in the first place. Yet organizational behavior has many techniques and approaches that provide added value beyond what currently exists; they just need to be sold.

Gaining Access to the World of Practice

How might an organizational behaviorist from academe gain access and acceptance within the various disciplines and groups that populate the world of practice? Again, it may be helpful to look back at the past. Abraham Maslow moved from comparative psychol-

ogy to clinical psychology by writing and doing research in his new area. Frederick Herzberg moved from the clinical field to industrial psychology in the same manner. David McClelland started in experimental psychology and wrcte his way into personality theory and then organizational behavior. There are many instances of this in the *Management Laureates* autobiographies. I myself have done this several times, moving from personality theory to industrial psychology, to organizational behavior, and even for periods of time into policy/strategy and entrepreneurship (Miner, 1993), simply by writing or researching my way in. The point is that by making contributions to the literature of a field one can become recognized in that field, and thus be accepted to perform other functions as well. This is the preferred route to joining a new field for academics with doctoral degrees, prefaced on the assumption that the doctorate prepares you to be able to teach yourself.

Following the expansion into practice scenario as I have suggested is a very proactive process. There are those who believe this is not characteristic of organizational behavior. Goodman and Whetten describe the field as typified by "a reactive versus a proactive orientation" and by "strong external and institutional forces that shape much of what we do, and that create both opportunities and stabilities" (1998, p. 47). But they also note the tremendous diversity of the field and an emphasis on application. Both of the latter should facilitate an effective entry into the world of practice. What Goodman and Whetten do not note is that in its origins organizational behavior was extremely proactive as its members streamed into business schools, which was facilitated by the foundations, true, but in a manner and from disciplines and in numbers that the foundations did not anticipate. There is no reason that this proactive bent cannot continue to manifest itself through a major expansion into practice. We have seen in the business world in recent years that downsizing, concentrating on core businesses, becoming lean and mean, and the like often carry with them many problems; growth strategies create more opportunities and more freedom, and they are a lot more fun to experience. It is hoped that the field of organizational behavior will learn from this. We need to get out and play more of our games away from home.

Something of what I have in mind was expressed in Huff's (2000) presidential address to the Academy of Management, although it is not clear to me that she envisages quite the degree of movement into the practitioner world that I do. Another related opportunity at present is represented by the widespread use of MBAs by the major consulting firms. Many of these firms would be happy to fill these positions with people who possess doctoral degrees, as they often do in Europe, if sufficient talent were made available. The starting salaries should be at least as attractive as those offered in the academic world. All that is needed is for organizational behavior to produce the doctorally trained talent.

The type of proactive onslaught on the world outside academe I envisage has much in common with the entrepreneurial push that emanated from industrial psychology during the early 1900s (Van De Water, 1997). In that instance industrial psychology joined forces with engineering to market itself to the business community, and with a great deal of success, thus creating the practice of industrial psychology and a number of consulting firms as well.

An opportunity of much the same kind appears to exist at present with the rapid increase in the number and scope of corporate universities operated by business firms themselves. Although the numbers here get rather fuzzy in their own right, the best data I know of indicate a rise from 400 in 1988 to 1,000 in 1998 with about 40 percent granting or interested in granting an accredited degree (Meister, 1998). This phenomenon is often presented as a major threat to the business schools, but there is no reason that it should not represent a golden opportunity to organizational behavior, if we create the talent to grasp it.

These are only examples. There probably are many more such opportunities waiting to be developed. But, yes, one does have to be proactive and perhaps a bit entrepreneurial. The kind of vision I describe, however, is certainly not without precedent in other fields. Education schools have been preparing doctoral specialists in many areas such as educational administration and counseling for many years. The physical sciences have sent their doctorates out into research labs for an equally long time. Other examples could be cited. This is an image for the future that is clearly attainable, and which would be of benefit to all involved.

Structuring for Growth

Setting forth growth scenarios, as I have done, almost inevitably raises a question about which structure is most appropriate for this purpose. Furthermore, the existence of a type of identity crisis in the field and the need to provide opportunities to develop professional commitment also have implications for structure. Structure in this instance means the structure of the profession, of its professional association or associations.

The history in this regard is straightforward. After a minimal effort to establish a discipline-based association of a strictly psychological nature, which obviously did not fit the multidisciplinary nature of the emerging field, organizational behavior found a home in the existing Academy of Management. In fact, from the late 1970s to the beginning of the 1990s, it almost became synonymous with the Academy of Management—but not quite. During this period organizational behavior dominated the governance structure of the academy and provided a great majority of the articles published in academy journals (Mowday, 1997a). Yet throughout most of this period the association was organized as a federation of divisions, some of which fell under the organizational behavior umbrella, and some of which did not.

This did not matter much as long as the governance of the Academy was in the hands of organizational behavior people. There was a superordinate group bringing together the diverse strands of organizational behavior. However, beginning in the 1990s the power structure of the Academy began to change. The key factor was the growth of strategic management in size and in influence. As a result there was no longer a stable superordinate body above the divisions coalescing the various forces within organizational behavior, and looking out for the interests of the whole. It seems unlikely that the Academy will ever provide this function for organizational behavior in the same way again; strategic management is a growing and vibrant field that has developed a solid research base and a body of theory as well. It has a very different relationship to economics than organizational behavior, and appropriately so in view of its content. It also has a completely different history and cultural identity (see Hoskisson, Hitt, Wan, & Yiu, 1999).

Yet, organizational behavior needs more than a set of structurally unrelated divisions, if it is to achieve substantial growth—and, in fact, if it is to do anything more than survive. The emergence of this structure, without a stable superordinate entity, was strangely congruent with the emergence in the field of what I have referred to as an identity crisis. There has to be some causal link here. How, then, to structure organizational behavior to provide a truly comprehensive professional association for the field that will maintain a solid base for growth many years into the future?

Restructuring within the Academy of Management

One approach to the structuring for growth problem would be to redesign the Academy of Management in such a way as to create an umbrella structure for organizational behavior as a whole and placing the relevant divisions, or some realignment of them, under a governing body for organizational behavior alone. This body would need to be much more autonomous within the overall academy than has been any such structure in the past, and certainly more autonomous than any division. Perhaps it would be matched by a similar body for strategic management.

However, I believe that following such a within-academy option requires something more. The name *Academy of Management* carries with it meanings that are inconsistent with the growth concept proposed on several counts. Academy means "academe" to most people, a group of professors gathered to do whatever professors do in a university setting. That does not portray a profession seeking to grow by expanding into the business world and elsewhere. Moreover, "management" has taken on so many meanings that it means nothing. For some, indeed, it may mean an identification with the long defunct principles of management school. I am reminded also of a colleague, a labor arbitrator, who was told by one of the unions he served to drop his membership in the academy because remaining a member put him clearly in the management camp. Caught between his job and his professional association membership, he chose the former. My point is that "Academy of Management" conveys no single meaningful message at the present time and certainly little that suggests organizational behavior.

There is another concern with regard to the Academy of Management as it is currently functioning. Over the past decade, several presidents of the organization have expressed opinions to the effect that the academy is somewhat ineffectual, especially in its dealings with its environments (see, for instance, Mowday, 1997b; Hambrick, 1994). Since my vision for growth requires nothing if not dealing with environments,

this becomes a matter that may well require attention. All in all, one has to wonder whether the Academy of Management is the right vehicle for organizational behavior's future.

Going Outside the Academy of Management

This raises the issue of establishing an institutional identity for organizational behavior outside the existing academy. Actually, strategic management already has such an organization, and there have been several limited-purpose professional associations within organizational behavior for a long time. Perhaps one of the latter could be reconstituted on a much larger scale to serve the purposes I have in mind. Or a new Association for Organizational Behavior, or some such, might be created. Such free-standing organizations have been emerging quite frequently in the social sciences, and creating one more would not represent a major problem, except perhaps for those directly involved. Such an association must provide its own publications, as the need arises. Most important, it must coordinate and implement the strategies of the profession, and have the resources to do so.

The question of how this association relates to the Academy of Management must remain indeterminate. If it can emerge and be effective within the academy (with a new name), that would save much time and effort. The academy has been very flexible in the past, and the need for a clear institutional identity for organizational behavior somewhere should be widely apparent. If restructuring within the existing system should not prove feasible, then the new association will have much to do itself without devoting its energies to trying to shape the academy. I see no reason, however, why most members of the organizational behavior discipline would not wish to remain active in the academy as well, as long as the academy continues to embrace activities that have relevance for our field.

CONCLUSIONS

I have set forth a vision—a set of scenarios and the structural implications inherent in them—for organizational behavior. Others almost certainly have very different choices for the future that they wish to see implemented. If my proposals do no more than initiate dialogue about the future of the field, something will have been accomplished, but my hope is that there will be more than that. Whatever develops, the field is clearly at a turning point. It has an identity rooted in its history, and this identity has the potential to provide a solid foundation for future building. The need is to be proactive about what is built, not merely to be reactive and build what someone outside the field wishes, or not to build at all, living only in the foundation. In any event, it seems to me, and I believe to many others, that organizational behavior is at a crossroads in its history. Something needs to be done, if only to maintain the investment in knowledge about organizations that has been made over the past 50 years.

References

Albert, Stuart; Ashforth, Blake E.; & Dutton, Jane E. (2000). Organizational Identity and Identification: Charting New Waters and Building New Bridges. *Academy of Management Review*, 25, 13–17.

Bazigos, Michael N., & Burke, W. Warner (1997). Theory Orientation of Organization Development (OD) Practitioners. *Group and Organization Management*, 22, 384–408.

Beyer, Janice M. (1992). Metaphors, Misunderstandings, and Mischief: A Commentary. *Organization Science*, 3, 467–474.

Blood, Milton R. (1994). The Role of Organizational Behavior in the Business School Curriculum. In Jerald Greenberg (Ed.), *Organizational Behavior: The State of the Science* (pp. 207–220). Hillsdale, NJ: Lawrence Erlbaum.

Brief, Arthur P., & Dukerich, Janet M. (1991). Theory in Organizational Behavior: Can It Be Useful? *Research in Organizational Behavior*, 13, 327–352.

Church, Allan H.; Burke, W. Warner; & Van Eynde, Donald F. (1994). Values, Motives, and Interventions of Organization Development Practitioners. *Group and Organization Management*, 19, 5–50.

Cummings, Larry L. (1978). Toward Organization Behavior. *Academy of Management Review*, 3, 90–98.

French, Wendell L. (1982). The Emergence and Early History of Organization Development: With Reference to Influences on and Interaction among Some of the Key Actors. *Group and Organization Studies*, 7, 261–278.

Gioia, Dennis A.; Schultz, Majken; & Corley, Kevin G. (2000). Organizational Identity, Image, and Adaptive Instability. *Academy of Management Review*, 25, 63–81.

Goodman, Paul S., & Whetten, David A. (1998). Fifty Years of Organizational Behavior from Multiple Perspectives. In Maurice F. Neufeld & Jean T. McKelvey (Eds.), *Industrial Relations at the Dawn of the New Millenium* (pp. 33–53). Ithaca: New York State School of Industrial and Labor Relations, Cornell University.

Greiner, Larry E. (1979). A Recent History of Organizational Behavior. In Steven Kerr (Ed.), *Organizational Behavior* (pp. 3–14). Columbus, OH: Grid.

Hambrick, Donald C. (1994). What if the Academy Actually Mattered? *Academy of Management Review*, 19, 11–16.

Hogg, Michael A., & Terry, Deborah J. (2000). Social Identity and Self-Categorization Processes in Organizational Contexts. *Academy of Management Review*, 25, 121–140.

Hoskisson, Robert E.; Hitt, Michael A.; Wan, William P.; & Yiu, Daphne (1999). Theory and Research in Strategic Management: Swings of a Pendulum. *Journal of Management*, 25, 417–456.

Huff, Anne S. (2000). Changes in Organizational Knowledge Production. *Academy of Management Review*, 25, 288–293.

Lawrence, Paul R. (1987). Historical Development of Organizational Behavior. In Jay W. Lorsch (Ed.), *Handbook of Organizational Behavior* (pp. 1–9). Englewood Cliffs, NJ: Prentice Hall.

Lawrence, Paul R., & Lawrence, Anne T. (1993). Doing Problem-Oriented Research: A Daughter's Interview. In Arthur G. Bedeian (Ed.), *Management Laureates: A Collection of Autobiographical Essays* (Vol. 2, pp. 111–148). Greenwich, CT: JAI Press.

Meister, Jeanne C. (1998). *Corporate Universities: Lessons in Building a World-Class Work Force.* New York: McGraw-Hill.

Miner, John B. (1980). The Role of Managerial and Professional Motivation in the Career Success of Management Professors. *Academy of Management Journal*, 23, 487–508.

Miner, John B. (1984). The Validity and Usefulness of Theories in an Emerging Organizational Science. *Academy of Management Review*, 9, 296–306.

Miner, John B. (1990). The Role of Values in Defining the "Goodness" of Theories in Organizational Science. *Organization Studies*, 11, 161–178.

Miner, John B. (1993). Pursuing Diversity in an Increasingly Specialized Organizational Science. In Arthur G. Bedeian (Ed.), *Management Laureates: A Collection of Autobiographical Essays* (Vol. 2, pp. 283–319). Greenwich, CT: JAI Press.

Mowday, Richard T. (1997a). Celebrating 40 Years of the Academy of Management Journal. *Academy of Management Journal*, 6, 1400–1413.

Mowday, Richard T. (1997b). Reaffirming Our Scholarly Values. *Academy of Management Review,* 22, 335–345.

Oviatt, Benjamin M., & Miller, Warren D. (1989). Irrelevance, Intransigence, and Business Professors. *Academy of Management Executive,* 3, 304–312.

Porter, Lyman W., & McKibbin, Lawrence E. (1988). *Management Education and Development: Drift or Thrust into the 21st Century?* New York: McGraw-Hill.

Roberts, Karlene H.; Weissenberg, Peter; Whetten, David; Pearce, Jone; Glick, William; Bedeian, Arthur; Miller, Howard; & Klimoski, Richard (1990). Reflections on the Field of Organizational Behavior. *Journal of Management Systems,* 2(1), 25–38.

Rynes, Sara L., & Trank, Christine Q. (1999). Behavioral Science in the Business School Curriculum: Teaching in a Changing Institutional Environment. *Academy of Management Review,* 24, 808–824.

Starbuck, William H. (1999). Our Shrinking Earth. *Academy of Management Review,* 24, 187–190.

Strauss, George (1993). Present at the Beginning: Some Personal Notes on OB's Early Days and Later. In Arthur G. Bedeian (Ed.), *Management Laureates: A Collection of Autobiographical Essays* (Vol. 3, pp. 147–190). Greenwich, CT: JAI Press.

Van De Water, Thomas J. (1997). Psychology's Entrepreneurs and the Marketing of Industrial Psychology. *Journal of Applied Psychology,* 82, 486–499.

Weick, Karl E. (1987). Theorizing about Organizational Communication. In Frederic M. Jablin, Linda L. Putnam, Karlene H. Roberts, & Lyman W. Porter (Eds.), *Handbook of Organizational Communication: An Interdisciplinary Perspective* (pp. 97–122). Newbury Park, CA: Sage.

Name Index

Subject Index

Page numbers followed by an italic *t* or *f* refer to tables or figures on those pages, respectively.